Battle for Belorussia

MODERN WAR STUDIES

Theodore A. Wilson
General Editor

Raymond Callahan
Jacob W. Kipp
Allan R. Millett
Carol Reardon
Dennis Showalter
David R. Stone
James H. Willbanks
Series Editors

Battle for Belorussia

The Red Army's Forgotten Campaign of October 1943–April 1944

David M. Glantz
with
Mary Elizabeth Glantz

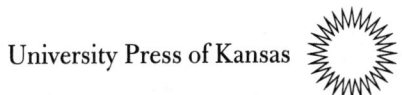
University Press of Kansas

© 2016 by the University Press of Kansas
All rights reserved

Published by the University Press of Kansas (Lawrence, Kansas 66045), which was organized by the Kansas Board of Regents and is operated and funded by Emporia State University, Fort Hays State University, Kansas State University, Pittsburg State University, the University of Kansas, and Wichita State University

Library of Congress Cataloging-in-Publication Data
Names: Glantz, David M., author. | Glantz, Mary E., author.
Title: Battle for Belorussia : the Red Army's forgotten campaign of October 1943–April 1944 / David M. Glantz with Mary Elizabeth Glantz.
Description: Lawrence, Kansas : University Press of Kansas, 2016. | Series: Modern war studies | Includes bibliographical references and index.
Identifiers: LCCN 2016028701 | ISBN 9780700623297 (cloth : alk. paper)
Subjects: LCSH: World War, 1939–1945—Campaigns—Belarus. | Soviet Union. Raboche-Krestīanskaia Krasnaia Armiia—History—World War, 1939–1945. | Belarus—History—German occupation, 1941–1944.
Classification: LCC D802.B38 G55 2016 | DDC 940.54/2178—dc23
LC record available at https://lccn.loc.gov/2016028701.
British Library Cataloguing-in-Publication Data is available.

Printed in the United States of America

10 9 8 7 6 5 4 3 2 1

The paper used in this publication is recycled and contains 30 percent postconsumer waste. It is acid free and meets the minimum requirements of the American National Standard for Permanence of Paper for Printed Library Materials Z39.48-1992.

*To Army General Makhmut Akhmetovich Gareev,
soldier, scholar, military leader, and accomplished military theorist,
who first revealed this forgotten campaign to memorialize the
many soldiers who served and suffered in it.*

Contents

List of Maps, Tables, and Illustrations   ix

Preface   xix

A Note on Maps and Tables   xxv

PART I: THE STRUGGLE FOR BELORUSSIA, OCTOBER–DECEMBER 1943

1. Context: The Summer–Fall Campaign (1 July–23 December)   3
2. The Kalinin and Baltic Fronts' Vitebsk and Nevel' Offensives (3–30 October)   18
3. The Western Front's Orsha Offensives (3–28 October)   60
4. The Central Front's Gomel'-Rechitsa Offensive (30 September–30 October)   90
5. The 1st and 2nd Baltic Fronts' Polotsk-Vitebsk and Pustoshka-Idritsa Offensives (2–21 November)   125
6. The Western Front's Orsha Offensives (14 November–5 December)   156
7. The Belorussian Front's Gomel'-Rechitsa and Novyi Bykhov–Propoisk Offensives (10–30 November)   172
8. The 1st Baltic and Western Fronts' Vitebsk (Gorodok) Offensive (13–23 December) and 2nd Baltic Front's Idritsa-Opochka Offensive (16–25 December)   209
9. The Belorussian Front's Kalinkovichi (Bobruisk) Offensive (8–12 December) and the German Counterstroke (20–27 December)   241

PART II: THE STRUGGLE FOR BELORUSSIA, DECEMBER 1943–APRIL 1944

10. Context: The Winter Campaign (24 December 1943–April 1944)   265
11. The 1st Baltic and Western Fronts' Vitebsk Offensive (24 December 1943–5 January 1944) and 2nd Baltic Front's Novosokol'niki Pursuit (30 December 1943–15 January 1944)   279

viii   Contents

12	The 1st Baltic and Western Fronts' Vitebsk-Bogushevsk Offensive (6–24 January)	307
13	The 1st Baltic and Western Fronts' Vitebsk Offensive (3–16 February)	332
14	The Western Front's Babinovichi and Vitebsk Offensives (22 February–5 March)	362
15	The Western Front's Orsha and Bogushevsk Offensives (5–29 March)	381
16	The Belorussian Front's Situation on 1 January 1944 and Preliminary Operations	402
17	The Belorussian Front's Kalinkovichi-Mozyr' Offensive (8–14 January)	417
18	The Belorussian Front's Ozarichi-Ptich' Offensive (16–30 January)	453
19	The Belorussian Front's Parichi-Bobruisk (Marmovichi-Dubrova) Offensive (16 January–23 February)	480
20	The Belorussian Front's Rogachev-Zhlobin and Mormal'-Parichi Offensives (21–29 February)	506
21	The Liquidation of German Bridgeheads on the Dnepr River's Eastern Bank (25–31 March)	526
22	Investigations, Recriminations, and Sokolovsky's Relief	540
23	Conclusions	572

Appendices

A–Q. Documents: Directives, Orders, and Reports	585
R. German Command Cadre in Eastern Belorussia	663
S. Selected Abbreviations	668

Notes	671
Selected Bibliography	703
Index of Appendix Documents	711
Index	717

Maps, Tables, and Illustrations

Maps

1.1	The Summer–Fall Campaign, 1943	2
2.1	The Situation on the Soviet-German Front, 6 October 1943	19
2.2	Red Army Operations in Belorussia, 23 August–31 December 1943	25
2.3	The Kalinin Front's Dukhovshchina Offensive Operation, 20 September–2 October 1943	32
2.4	The Kalinin Front's Nevel' Offensive Operation, 6–10 October 1943	40
2.5	Third Panzer Army's Situation, 1 October 1943	44
2.6	Third Panzer Army's Situation, 4 October 1943	46
2.7	Third Panzer Army's Situation, 8 October 1943	47
2.8	Third Panzer Army's Situation, 12 October 1943	49
2.9	The Baltic Front's Idritsa Offensive, 18–30 October 1943	55
2.10	Third Panzer Army's Situation, 17 October 1943	57
2.11	Third Panzer Army's Situation North of Vitebsk, 27 October 1943	58
2.12	Third Panzer Army's Situation East and Southeast of Vitebsk, 27 October 1943	59
3.1	The Western Front's Smolensk Offensive, 7 August–2 October 1943	63
3.2	Fourth Army's Situation in the Orsha Sector, 12 October 1943	64
3.3	Fourth Army's Situation in the Gorki Sector, 12 October 1943	65
3.4	Fourth Army's Situation in the Orsha Sector, 18 October 1943	76
3.5	Fourth Army's Situation in the Gorki Sector, 18 October 1943	77
3.6	Fourth Army's Situation, 20 October 1943	80
3.7	Fourth Army's Situation in the Orsha Sector, 28 October 1943	88
3.8	Fourth Army's Situation in the Gorki Sector, 28 October 1943	89
4.1	The Briansk Front's Briansk Offensive Operation, 17 August–3 October 1943	92
4.2	The Central Front's Chernigov-Pripiat' Offensive Operation, 26 August–30 September 1943	93
4.3	Second Army's Situation in the Gomel'-Loev Sector, 1 October 1943	98

4.4	Second Army's Situation in the Radul'-Liubech' Sector, 1 October 1943	100
4.5	65th Army's Operations to Cross the Sozh and Dnepr Rivers, 28 September–19 October 1943	102
4.6	The Central Front's Regrouping, 8–14 October 1943	107
4.7	The Central Front's Dispositions, 14 October 1943	108
4.8	Second Army's Situation, 11 October 1943	109
4.9	65th Army's Forced Crossing of the Dnepr River at Loev, 7–17 October 1943	111
4.10	Second Army's Situation in the Loev Sector, 20 October 1943	112
4.11	61st Army's Expansion of the Liubech' Bridgehead, 29 September–23 October 1943	113
4.12	Second Army's Situation in the Radul'-Liubech' Sector, 20 October 1943	113
4.13	Second Army's Situation in the Loev Sector, 21 October 1943	118
4.14	Second Army's Situation in the Loev Sector, 25 October 1943	119
4.15	Second Army's Situation in the Loev Sector, 30 October 1943	119
4.16	German Assessment of Red Army Operations in Belorussia, 3–31 October 1943	123
5.1	Third Panzer Army's Appreciation of Red Army Operations West of Nevel', 1–21 November 1943	127
5.2	Third Panzer Army's Intelligence Assessment, 20 November 1943	131
5.3	Third Panzer Army's Assessment of Red Army Operations North of Vitebsk, 3–21 November 1943	136
5.4	Third Panzer Army's Assessment of Red Army Operations East of Vitebsk, 3–21 November 1943	137
5.5	Third Panzer Army's Situation East of Vitebsk, 8 November 1943	143
5.6	Third Panzer Army's Situation East of Vitebsk, 17 November 1943	144
5.7	Third Panzer Army's Intelligence Assessment, 20 November 1943	145
5.8	Sixteenth Army's (Army Group North) Situation, 30 November 1943	155
6.1	Fourth Army's Situation in the Orsha Sector, 14 November 1943	163
6.2	Fourth Army's Situation in the Orsha Sector, 19 November 1943	165
6.3	Fourth Army's Situation in the Orsha Sector, 30 November 1943	167
6.4	Fourth Army's Situation in the Orsha Sector, 8 December 1943	169

Maps, Tables, and Illustrations   xi

7.1	The Belorussian Front's Plan for the Gomel'-Rechitsa Offensive Operation, November 1943	175
7.2	The Belorussian Front's Regrouping of Forces for the Gomel'-Rechitsa Offensive Operation, 27 October–9 November 1943	178
7.3	The Belorussian Front's Gomel'-Rechitsa Offensive Operation, 10–30 November 1943	183
7.4	Second Army's Situation on the Rechitsa Axis, 10 November 1943	184
7.5	Second Army's Situation on the Rechitsa Axis, 13 November 1943	184
7.6	Second Army's Situation on the Rechitsa Axis, 16 November 1943	185
7.7	Second Army's Situation, 16 November 1943	189
7.8	11th Army's Plan for the Liberation of Gomel', 12 November 1943	193
7.9	Second Army's Situation, 22 November 1943	194
7.10	Second Army's Situation along the Parichi-Bobruisk Axis, 28 November 1943	195
7.11	Second Army's Situation along the Kalinkovichi Axis, 28 November 1943	195
7.12	Second Army's Situation along the Parichi-Bobruisk Axis, 30 November 1943	199
7.13	Second Army's Situation along the Kalinkovichi and Mozyr' Axes, 30 November 1943	199
7.14	3rd Army's Novyi Bykhov–Propoisk Offensive Operation, 22–30 November 1943	201
7.15	German Assessment of Red Army Operations in Belorussia, 1–20 November 1943	207
8.1	The *Stavka*'s Plan for the Vitebsk (Gorodok) Offensive Operation, November 1943	211
8.2	The 1st Baltic Front's Plan for the Vitebsk (Gorodok) Offensive Operation, 23 November 1943	213
8.3	11th Guards Army's Plan for the Gorodok Offensive Operation, December 1943	215
8.4	The Gorodok Offensive Operation, 13–31 December 1943	221
8.5	11th Guards Army's Operations, 13–21 December 1943	222
8.6	The 1st Baltic Front's Gorodok Offensive Operation, 13–18 December 1943	224
8.7	Third Panzer Army's Appreciation of the Situation at Vitebsk, 15 December 1943	227
8.8	Third Panzer Army's Appreciation of the Situation at Vitebsk, 18 December 1943	228

xii Maps, Tables, and Illustrations

8.9	Third Panzer Army's Appreciation of the Situation at Vitebsk, 19–21 December 1943	232
8.10	Third Panzer Army's Intelligence Assessment of Operations East of Vitebsk, 18–21 December 1943	233
8.11	Third Panzer Army's Situation North and East of Vitebsk, 19 December 1943	235
8.12	Third Panzer Army's Situation North and East of Vitebsk, 21 December 1943	236
9.1	Second Army's Situation, 1 December 1943	244
9.2	Second Army's Situation, 8 December 1943	248
9.3	Second Army's Situation, 11 December 1943	249
9.4	Second Army's Situation, 20 December 1943	256
9.5	Second Army's Situation, 21 December 1943	257
9.6	Second Army's Situation, 27 December 1943	259
9.7	German Assessment of Red Army Operations in Belorussia, 22 November 1943–4 January 1944	262
10.1	The Winter Campaign of 1943–1944	271
11.1	Third Panzer Army's Appreciation of the Situation at Vitebsk, 23–24 December 1943	280
11.2	11th Guards Army's Operations, 22–31 December 1943	282
11.3	Third Panzer Army's Situation West of Vitebsk, 24 December 1943	286
11.4	Third Panzer Army's Situation West of Vitebsk, 26 December 1943	287
11.5	Third Panzer Army's Situation West of Vitebsk, 28 December 1943	288
11.6	Third Panzer Army's Situation West of Vitebsk, 31 December 1943	289
11.7	Third Panzer Army's Situation West of Vitebsk, 6 January 1944	290
11.8	Third Panzer Army's Situation East of Vitebsk, 23 December 1943	294
11.9	Third Panzer Army's Situation East of Vitebsk, 25 December 1943	295
11.10	Third Panzer Army's Situation East of Vitebsk, 28 December 1943	296
11.11	Third Panzer Army's Appreciation of the Situation at Vitebsk, 31 December 1943	298
11.12	The Situation at Vitebsk, 1–3 January 1944	299
11.13	The Situation at Vitebsk, 4–6 January 1944	301
11.14	Third Panzer Army's Appreciation of the Situation at Vitebsk, 6 January 1944	302
11.15	The Situation at Vitebsk, 7 January 1944	303

11.16	Army Group North's Situation, 29 December 1943–15 January 1944	305
12.1	The Situation at Vitebsk, 11 January 1944	311
12.2	Third Panzer Army's Situation West of Vitebsk, 8 January 1944	313
12.3	Third Panzer Army's Situation West of Vitebsk, 11 January 1944	316
12.4	The Situation at Vitebsk, 20 January 1944	317
12.5	Third Panzer Army's Situation East of Vitebsk, 8 January 1944	322
12.6	Third Panzer Army's Situation East of Vitebsk, 9 January 1944	323
12.7	Third Panzer Army's Situation East of Vitebsk, 16 January 1944	325
12.8	The Situation at Vitebsk, 11–16 January 1944	326
12.9	The Situation at Vitebsk, 17–20 January 1944	328
12.10	The Situation at Vitebsk, 21–24 January 1944	329
13.1	The Situation at Vitebsk, 2 February 1944	337
13.2	Third Panzer Army's Appreciation of the Situation at Vitebsk, 3 February 1944	341
13.3	Third Panzer Army's Situation West of Vitebsk, 3 February 1944	342
13.4	Third Panzer Army's Situation West of Vitebsk, 8 February 1944	345
13.5	Third Panzer Army's Situation West of Vitebsk, 9–13 February 1944	346
13.6	The Situation at Vitebsk, 10–13 February 1944	347
13.7	The Situation at Vitebsk, 14–16 February 1944	348
13.8	Third Panzer Army's Situation East of Vitebsk, 3 February 1944	354
13.9	Third Panzer Army's Situation East of Vitebsk, 8 February 1944	356
13.10	Third Panzer Army's Situation East of Vitebsk, 13 February 1944	358
13.11	Third Panzer Army's Situation East of Vitebsk, 16 February 1944	359
13.12	Third Panzer Army's Appreciation of the Situation at Vitebsk, 16–17 February 1944	360
14.1	The Situation at Vitebsk, 17–21 February 1944	363
14.2	The Situation at Vitebsk, 22–27 February 1944	366
14.3	The Situation at Vitebsk, 28 February 1944	374
14.4	The Situation at Vitebsk, 29 February–6 March 1944	378
14.5	The Situation at Vitebsk, 7–9 March 1944	379
15.1	Fourth Army's Situation at Babinovichi and East of Orsha, 19–29 February 1944	382
15.2	The Situation East of Orsha, 5–9 March 1944	384
15.3	The Situation at Vitebsk and East of Orsha, 10–18 March 1944	386
15.4	The Situation at Vitebsk, 19–20 March 1944	390
15.5	The Situation at Vitebsk, 21–29 March 1944	397
15.6	The Situation at Vitebsk, 29–31 March 1944	400
16.1	Ninth Army's Intelligence Assessment, 29 December 1943	406
16.2	50th Army's Situation East of Bykhov, 3–7 January 1944	410

16.3	10th Army's Situation in the Chausy Sector, 7 January 1944	411
17.1	65th and 61st Armies' Assault on Kalinkovichi, 8–14 January 1944	422
17.2	The Situation at Kalinkovichi, 6 January 1944	425
17.3	Ninth Army's Intelligence Assessment in the Zhlobin-Kalinkovichi Sector, 9 January 1944	428
17.4	The Situation at Kalinkovichi, 9 January 1944	429
17.5	The Situation at Kalinkovichi, 10 January 1944	433
17.6	The Situation at Kalinkovichi, 11 January 1944	435
17.7	The Situation at Kalinkovichi, 12 January 1944	437
17.8	The Situation at Kalinkovichi, 13 January 1944	445
17.9	The Situation at Kalinkovichi, 14 January 1944	447
18.1	The Situation in the Ozarichi-Ptich' Sector, 15–16 January 1944	457
18.2	The Situation in the Ozarichi-Ptich' Sector, 17 January 1944	463
18.3	The Situation in the Ozarichi-Ptich' Sector, 19 January 1944	465
18.4	The Situation in the Ozarichi-Ptich' Sector, 20 January 1944	467
18.5	The Situation in the Ozarichi-Ptich' Sector, 22 January 1944	469
18.6	The Situation in the Ozarichi-Ptich' Sector, 27 January 1944	472
18.7	The Situation in the Ozarichi-Ptich' Sector, 29 January 1944	475
19.1	48th Army's Situation along the Parichi Axis, 1–11 January 1944	482
19.2	Ninth Army's Intelligence Appreciation of 48th Army's Regrouping, 14–15 January 1944	487
19.3	48th Army's Situation along the Parichi Axis, 16–31 January 1944	488
19.4	48th Army's Situation along the Parichi Axis, 2–8 February 1944	497
19.5	48th Army's Situation along the Parichi Axis, 14–23 February 1944	503
20.1	3rd Army's Offensive along the Rogachev Axis, 21–26 February 1944	511
20.2	The Situation at Rogachev, 0600 hours, 21 February 1944	513
20.3	The Situation at Rogachev, 0600 hours, 22 February 1944	514
20.4	The Situation at Rogachev, 0600 hours, 23 February 1944	515
20.5	The Situation at Rogachev, 0600 hours, 25–26 February 1944	516
20.6	48th Army's Situation along the Parichi Axis, 24–26 February 1944	519
20.7	Ninth Army's Intelligence Appreciation along the Parichi Axis, 28–29 February 1944	522
21.1	Ninth Army's Situation in the Chausy-Bykhov Sector, 18–24 March 1944	527
21.2	50th and 10th Armies' Offensives in the Chausy-Bykhov Sector, 24–31 March 1944	531
21.3	65th Army's Seizure of State Farm Slobodka No. 1, 14–15 February 1944	536

Maps, Tables, and Illustrations   xv

21.4	Ninth Army's Intelligence Appreciation, 31 March 1944 (65th Army's Advance to the Tremlia River, 16–17 March)	537
23.1	German Assessment of Red Army Operations, 5 January–17 February 1944	574
23.2	German Assessment of Red Army Operations, 18 February–24 March 1944	575
23.3	Red Army Operations in Belorussia, October 1943–April 1944	576
23.4	The Red Army's Belorussian Offensives Compared	581

Notes on Maps
German Second Army's situation maps are as of 0600 hours daily
German Third Panzer Army's situation maps are as of 1500 hours daily
German Fourth Army's situation maps are as of 2200 hours daily

TABLES

1.1	Stages of the Red Army's Summer–Fall Campaign	8
1.2	Red Army Operations during the First Stage of the Summer–Fall Campaign	9
1.3	Red Army Operations during the Second Stage of the Summer–Fall Campaign	12
1.4	Red Army Operations during the Third Stage of the Summer–Fall Campaign	14
2.1	The Redesignation of Red Army *Fronts*, 10–20 October 1943	20
2.2	General View of Opposing German and Soviet Forces in Eastern Belorussia on 1 October 1943	26
2.3	Opposing Forces in Army Group Center's Sector on 14 October 1943	29
2.4	Weaponry of Army Group Center's Panzer Divisions on 1 October 1943	30
4.1	The Combat Formations of the Belorussian Front's 65th and 61st Armies and Opposing German Forces on 20 October 1943	117
6.1	The Western Front's Operational Formation for the 14 November 1943 Orsha Offensive and Opposing German Forces	158
8.1	The 11th Guards Army's Order of Battle on 13 December 1943	214
8.2	The 4th Shock Army's Order of Battle on 13 December 1943	217
8.3	The 43rd Army's Order of Battle on 13 December 1943	218
8.4	The 39th Army's Order of Battle on 13 December 1943	219
8.5a, 8.5b	The Correlation of Opposing Forces in the Vitebsk Offensive Operation	220
10.1	Red Army Operations during the Winter Campaign: The Traditional View	270

10.2	"Forgotten Battles" of the Winter Campaign	272
11.1	The Estimated Correlation of Opposing Forces in the Vitebsk Offensive, 24 December 1943–6 January 1944	281
11.2	The 1st Baltic and Western Fronts' Orders of Battle in the Vitebsk Offensive, 1 January 1944	283
11.3	The Combat Formations of the 1st Baltic Front's 39th Army and the Western Front's 33rd Army and Opposing German Forces on 23 December 1943	293
12.1	The Estimated Correlation of Opposing Forces in the Vitebsk-Bogushevsk Offensive, 8–24 January 1944	310
12.2	The Probable Combat Formations of 43rd, 39th, 33rd, and 5th Armies and Opposing German Forces on 8 January 1944	319
13.1	The 1st Baltic and Western Fronts' Orders of Battle in the Vitebsk Offensive, 1 February 1944	335
13.2	The Estimated Correlation of Opposing Forces in the Vitebsk Offensive, 2–16 February 1944	340
13.3	The Probable Combat Formations of 39th, 33rd, and 5th Armies and Opposing German Forces on 3 February 1944	350
14.1	The Estimated Correlation of Opposing Forces in the Babinovichi Offensive, 22–25 February 1944	364
14.2	The Western Front's Order of Battle in the Vitebsk Offensive, 1 March 1944	370
14.3	The Probable Combat Formations of 39th, 33rd, and 5th Armies and Opposing German Forces on 29 February 1944	373
14.4	The Estimated Correlation of Opposing Forces in the Vitebsk Offensive, 29 February–5 March 1944	376
15.1	The Probable Combat Formations of 31st and 49th Armies and Opposing German Forces on 5 March 1944	383
15.2	The Estimated Correlation of Opposing Forces in the Orsha Offensive, 5–9 March 1944	385
15.3	The Western Front's Order of Battle on 1 April 1944	389
15.4	The Estimated Correlation of Opposing Forces in the Bogushevsk Offensive, 21–29 March 1944	392
15.5	The Probable Combat Formations of 39th, 33rd, and 5th Armies and Opposing German Forces on 21 March 1944	394
16.1	The Estimated Correlation of Opposing Forces in the Bykhov-Chausy Offensive, 4–8 January 1944	412
17.1	The Belorussian Front's Order of Battle on 1 January 1944	420
17.2	The Estimated Correlation of Opposing Forces in the Kalinkovichi-Mozyr' Offensive, 8–14 January 1944	427
18.1.	The Tentative Combat Formations of 65th and 61st Armies and Opposing German Forces Late on 15 January 1944	456

18.2	The Estimated Correlation of Opposing Forces in the Ozarichi-Ptich' Offensive, 16–30 January 1944	462
19.1	The Postulated Combat Formations of 48th Army and 65th Army's Right Wing and Opposing German Forces Late on 15 January 1944	484
19.2	The Estimated Correlation of Opposing Forces in the Parichi-Bobruisk Offensive, 16–27 January 1944	485
19.3	The Belorussian Front's Order of Battle on 1 February 1944	495
19.4	The Probable Combat Formations of 48th Army and 65th Army's Right Wing and Opposing German Forces Late on 1 February 1944	498
20.1	The Estimated Correlation of Opposing Forces in the Rogachev-Zhlobin Offensive, 21–26 February 1944	512
20.2	The Probable Combat Formations of 48th Army and Opposing German Forces on 24 February 1944	518
20.3	The 1st Belorussian Front's Order of Battle on 1 March 1944	523
21.1	The Probable General Combat Formations of 10th and 50th Armies and Opposing German Forces Late on 23 March 1944	530
21.2	The Estimated Correlation of Opposing Forces in the Dnepr Bridgehead Offensive, 25–31 March 1944	530
21.3	The 1st Belorussian Front's Order of Battle on 1 April 1944	538
23.1	The Belorussian (1st Belorussian) Front's Offensive Operations, January–March 1944	577

ILLUSTRATIONS

Opposite page 17:
Marshal of Aviation N. N. Voronov
L. Z. Mekhlis, Stalin's representative and henchman

Following page 34:
Army General A. I. Eremenko, commander in chief, Kalinin (1st Baltic) Front
Army General I. Kh. Bagramian, commander in chief, 1st Baltic Front
Lieutenant General K. N. Galitsky, commander, 3rd Shock Army
Colonel General N. E. Chibisov, commander, 3rd Shock Army
Lieutenant General Shvetsov, commander, 4th Shock Army
Lieutenant General P. F. Malyshev, commander, 4th Shock Army
Lieutenant General K. D. Golubev, commander, 43rd Army
Lieutenant General N. E. Berzarin, commander, 39th Army
Lieutenant General of Tank Forces V. V. Butkov, commander, 1st Tank Corps

xviii   Maps, Tables, and Illustrations

Major General of Tank Forces M. G. Sakhno, commander, 5th Tank Corps
Lieutenant General N. S. Oslikovsky, commander, 3rd Guards Cavalry Corps

Following page 74:
Army General V. D. Sokolovsky, commander in chief, Western Front
Lieutenant General N. I. Krylov, commander, 21st Army
Lieutenant General V. A. Gluzdovsky, commander, 31st Army
Lieutenant General E. P. Zhuravlev, commander, 68th Army
Lieutenant General A. V. Sukhomlin, commander
Colonel General V. N. Gordov, commander, 33rd Army
Colonel General I. E. Petrov, commander, 33rd Army
Lieutenant General I. T. Grishin, commander, 49th Army
Lieutenant General V. S. Popov, commander, 10th Army
Major General of Tank Forces A. S. Burdeinyi, commander, 2nd Guards Tank Corps

Following page 196:
Army General K. K. Rokossovsky, commander in chief, Central
Lieutenant General I. V. Boldin, commander, 50th Army
Lieutenant General A. V. Gorbatov, commander, 3rd Army
Lieutenant General V. Ia. Kolpakchi, commander, 63rd Army
Lieutenant General P. L. Romanenko, commander, 48th Army
Lieutenant General P. I. Batov, commander, 65th Army
Lieutenant General P. A. Belov, commander, 61st Army
Major General of Tank Forces M. F. Panov, commander, 1st Guards Tank Corps
Major General of Tank Forces B. S. Bakharov, commander, 9th Tank Corps
Lieutenant General V. V. Kriukov, commander, 2nd Guards Cavalry Corps
Major General M. P. Konstantinov, commander, 7th Guards Cavalry Corps

Preface

History has recorded that, during the Soviet-German War (1941–1945), Stalin's Red Army liberated the Soviet Union's Belorussian Republic in the summer of 1944. It did so in dramatic fashion on 23 June 1944 by launching a massive offensive code-named Operation Bagration against three defending armies subordinate to German Army Group Center. During the ensuing offensive, three Red Army *fronts* (army groups) conducted simultaneous and successive envelopment operations that encircled and essentially destroyed Army Group Center's Third Panzer, Ninth, and Fourth Armies. Since that fateful summer, Operation Bagration has stood as a virtual monument to the Red Army's military prowess as it marched on to victory at Berlin in May 1945.

What history has not recorded is the fact that Operation Bagration was not the Red Army's first attempt to recapture Belorussia; rather, it was its second. Eight months before, in early October 1943, Stalin and his *Stavka* (Soviet High Command) had already ordered the three Red Army *fronts* operating along the western axis to liberate Belorussia and capture its capital city, Minsk. Acting in concert, the Red Army's Kalinin, Western, and Central Fronts complied by conducting multiple simultaneous and successive offensive operations along a roughly 600-kilometer-wide front extending from the Nevel' region in the north southward to the Pripiat' Marshes. This campaign, which involved more than five months of bitter and costly fighting and cost the Red Army in excess of 700,000 casualties (including 150,000 dead), ended in late March 1944 with much of Belorussia still in German hands. Because this five-month campaign failed to achieve its objectives and also resulted in the relief of one of the three participating Red Army *front* commanders, Army General V. D. Sokolovsky, who nonetheless ultimately reached the august position of chief of the Soviet Army General Staff from 1952 to 1960, Soviet and Russian historians have since studiously erased much of the campaign's conduct from the historical record. Interestingly enough, however, the expunging of this campaign from Soviet military history also rendered "forgotten" the exploits of another participating Red Army *front* commander, Army General K. K. Rokossovsky, whose efforts in the campaign were far more skillful and successful. This, perhaps, was done to avoid tarnishing the record of a truly "Russian" general when compared with the achievements of another general many considered merely a "Pole."

This study corrects the historical record by recounting in detail the course and outcome of the many "forgotten battles" fought during this prolonged and frustrating "ignored campaign." It does so by exploiting a wealth of German and recently released Soviet archival materials, along with formerly classified Soviet General Staff studies and bits and pieces of information about the campaign gleaned from Soviet and Russian open-source histories. What results is a grand mosaic of battles fought, won, or lost over that five-month period whose consequences and lessons learned ultimately paved the way for the Red Army to mount its far more dramatic and victorious liberation of Belorussia, code-named Operation Bagration, in the summer of 1944.

In early September 1943, six weeks after the Germans were defeated in the battle for Kursk, and the Red Army began a strategic counteroffensive ultimately encompassing the entire region from Velikie Luki southward to the Black Sea, Hitler ordered his battle-worn armies to fall back westward to the Dnepr River. There, the dictator hoped to stabilize the Eastern Front in the Panther Defense Line, known popularly as Germany's Eastern Wall. Reluctantly, Hitler gave this order because, during the previous six weeks, the Red Army had conducted four major offensives with the forces of eight full *fronts*. These offensives, which ultimately recaptured the cities of Smolensk, Roslavl', Orel, Briansk, Khar'kov, Chernigov, and Poltava, savaged Army Groups Center and South, leaving their forces severely shaken and presumably subject to even greater defeat. The ensuing German withdrawal and Soviet pursuit, now termed the "Race to the Dnepr River," propelled Red Army forces westward and southwestward to the Dnepr River, where in late September they seized a number of small bridgeheads on the river's western bank.

Anticipating even greater victories if not outright German collapse, in early October 1943, Stalin ordered the Red Army's *fronts* to pierce Germany's defenses along the Dnepr River and begin liberating Belorussia and the Ukraine from Army Groups Center and South. Accordingly, the Red Army planned and conducted twin strategic offensives aimed at defeating both German army groups and occupying at least half of those two former Soviet republics. In the first of these offensives, General A. I. Eremenko's Kalinin Front, General V. D. Sokolovsky's Western Front, and General K. K. Rokossovsky's Central Front were to attack westward to capture the cities of Nevel', Vitebsk, Orsha, Mogilev, and Bobruisk. Thereafter, they were to seize Belorussia's capital city of Minsk in a massive envelopment operation. In the second offensive, the Red Army's Voronezh, Steppe, and Southwestern Fronts were to pierce the German Panther Defense Line along the Dnepr River; capture the cities of Kiev, Kremenchug, and Krivoi Rog; ultimately seize the city of Vinnitsa, the site of Hitler's forward headquarters; and liberate all of central Ukraine. Terrain and weather considerations prompted the *Stavka* to spearhead its offensive into the Ukraine with its hastily refitted 3rd

Guards and 5th Guards Tank Armies and its advance into Belorussia with a handful of smaller tank, mechanized, and cavalry corps.

These two offensives, launched during the first week of October 1943, experienced markedly differing fates. Despite the Kalinin Front's initial success in the Nevel' region north of Vitebsk and the Central Front's artful crossing of the Dnepr River south of Gomel', the offensive into Belorussia languished by late October primarily because the Western Front's multiple attacks in the Orel and Gorki regions of eastern Belorussia ended as spectacularly bloody failures. Similarly, in November, despite the 1st Baltic (former Kalinin) Front's modest advance against Army Group Center's Third Panzer Army around Vitebsk and the Belorussian (former Central) Front's more dramatic seizure of the Rechitsa region in southern Belorussia from the German Second Army, the Western Front's assaults in eastern Belorussia scarcely dented the defenses of Army Group Center's Fourth Army. Frustrated over the offensive's limited gains, in December the *Stavka* shifted the focus of the Western Front's attacks northward to the Vitebsk region. Nevertheless, in spite of desperate fighting around Vitebsk, the combined efforts of the 1st Baltic and Western Fronts still fell short of encircling and destroying the Third Panzer Army's forces defending the city. In southern Belorussia, however, Rokossovsky's Belorussian Front overcame stiffening German resistance to make slow but steady progress toward the cities of Bobruisk, Kalinkovichi, and Mozyr'.

As was the case in Belorussia, the Red Army's offensive in the Ukraine also began haltingly in October when the three attacking Red Army *fronts* failed to penetrate the Panther Defense Line and seize Kiev and Krivoi Rog. However, this stalemate ended in November when the 1st Ukrainian (former Voronezh) Front finally broke out of its bridgeheads across the Dnepr and captured Kiev, Zhitomir, and Korosten'. Heartened by this success and after parrying strong German counterstrokes in late November and December, the three Ukrainian *fronts* (the former Voronezh, Steppe, and Southwestern Fronts, respectively) enlarged their bridgeheads on the Dnepr's southern bank, and, on Christmas Day, began a fresh offensive that ultimately propelled Red Army forces into the Vinnitsa region.

Based on these successes, in early January 1944, the *Stavka* decided to shift the focus of its main offensive efforts to the Ukraine and, in late January, to the Leningrad region as well. Accordingly, it dispatched its recently refitted 1st Tank Army to the Ukraine, where, together with 3rd and 5th Guards Tank Armies, it was to spearhead fresh offensives ever deeper into the region. Although Stalin still hoped to conquer as much of Belorussia as possible, he now truncated his aims in the region to seizing the cities of Vitebsk, Rogachev, and Bobruisk so as to facilitate a future strategic offensive in the region. Finally, in late January the *Stavka* further weakened its efforts in Belorussia by transferring the 1st Baltic Front's powerful 11th Guards

Army northward to help the Leningrad, Volkhov, and 2nd Baltic Fronts defeat Army Group North's forces in and south of the Leningrad region.

In the wake of these decisions, the 1st Baltic, Western, and Belorussian Fronts continued offensive operations in Belorussia from January through March 1944. In spite of heavy and often desperate fighting, the forces of General Sokolovsky's Western Front fell short of encircling German Third Panzer Army's forces in Vitebsk by a mere 26 kilometers before the attackers collapsed in utter exhaustion. To the south, by skillful maneuver and adroit economy-of-force operations, Rokossovsky's Belorussian Front succeeded in capturing the cities of Kalinkovichi, Mozyr', and Rogachev on the Dnepr River and advancing to within 20 kilometers of Parichi before prudence dictated that the offensive be halted.

In retrospect, when Soviet military historians began producing histories of the war in the 1950s and 1960s, they dismissed these operations in Belorussia as little more than a sideshow in the vast panoply of dramatic and successful offensives that unfolded in the Ukraine and the Leningrad regions during this period. In short, these and most subsequent histories maintain that Stalin and his *Stavka* consciously and deliberately chose the Ukraine and the Ukraine alone as the priority theater of military operations during the fall of 1943 and the winter of 1943 to 1944. However, the preponderance of existing documentary evidence, not the least the orders and directives the *Stavka* and Red Army General Staff issued during this period, sharply challenges this claim. Instead, based on this evidence, if not the amount of blood spilled, it is now clear that both Belorussia and the Ukraine were equally enticing targets in October 1943 and that the relative importance of Belorussia was likely reduced retrospectively based on what actually occurred in each region. In short, success in the Ukraine earned both its badge of strategic priority and its elevated historical importance.

The campaign in Belorussia became a "forgotten" (covered up) one for a variety of reasons: first and foremost because the results were disappointing and embarrassing for the Red Army and, in particular, for General Sokolovsky, whom the *Stavka* relieved from command for incompetence in April 1944. After Zhukov salvaged his career later in the war, Sokolovsky became a marshal of the Soviet Union in 1946, chief of the Soviet General Staff in 1952, and Minister of Defense of the Soviet Union from 1953 through 1960. This alone impelled erasing from Russian military history his record as a failed *front* commander in the Belorussian offensive. Second, but less important, historians "forgot" the Belorussian offensive because Rokossovsky's performance as a *front* commander clearly eclipsed that of Sokolovsky. This was intolerable to many because they considered Rokossovsky, who was born in Warsaw, a Pole; therefore, Russian history could not acknowledge the fact that a Polish *front* commander could outshine Sokolovsky, ostensibly a Russian Slav.[1]

This volume restores the first Belorussian offensive, with all of its many warts and blemishes, to the historical record of the Soviet-German War. While doing so, it also identifies the offensive's legacy, specifically the difficult and costly lessons learned in this six-month campaign that ultimately enabled the Red Army to conduct the far more famous, effective, and successful Operation Bagration, which began on 23 June 1944.[2] During Operation Bagration, the second Belorussian offensive, Soviet forces commanded in part by two veteran *front* commanders who had fought in the first Belorussian offensive, defeated and dismembered Army Group Center, in the process destroying the bulk of three German armies and killing, wounding, or capturing more than 350,000 German soldiers.

My heartfelt thanks in preparing this book go to my daughter, Mary Glantz, who carefully edited much of it, and to my wife, Mary Ann, who, as usual, proofed most of it. However, I alone am responsible for any and all errors the book contains.

Special thanks go to Army General Makhmut Gareev, in particular, and to the Russian Federation, in general, for their part in permitting these new truths to be revealed. Writing in the journal *New and Newest History (Novaia i noveishaia istorii)* in 1994, General Gareev was the first to "raise the veil" concealing the dismal performance of Sokolovsky's Western Front in this campaign, although he did so without mention of the campaign's far broader context. More recently, the Russian Federation has begun to release documents finally exposing the ambitious scope and high cost of the campaign.

Finally, as has been the case with my previous books on "forgotten battles," this study celebrates the suffering and silent sacrifices of the tens of thousands of Red Army and German soldiers who fought in, perhaps died in, or survived these battles only to be forgotten by history.

David M. Glantz
Carlisle, PA

A Note on Maps and Tables

Of necessity, this volume contains a large number of maps. This is so because Soviet and Russian military historians have described only bits and pieces of this campaign, specifically, the few relatively successful military operations the Red Army conducted during its course. These episodes include the Kalinin (1st Baltic) Front's Nevel' and Gorodok offensives in October and December 1943 and the Central (Belorussian) Front's seizure of crossing sites over the Dnepr River in October 1943 and its capture of Rechitsa in November 1943, Kalinkovichi in January 1944, and Rogachev in February 1944. Because these episodes constitute well under half of the operations conducted during this campaign, I have relied heavily on the operational and intelligence maps of participating German armies to depict the remaining operations—in essence, to prove they occurred.

Thus, the study contains three types of maps: (1) translated Russian maps pertaining to acknowledged operations during the campaign; (2) German maps showing the situation in specific army sectors where "forgotten battles" took place; and (3) composite maps showing the actual dispositions of opposing forces in these forgotten battles. Wherever necessary, I have corrected the translated Russian maps to show actual German opposing forces. Although the German situation maps illustrate the German perspective on what was taking place, overlays in bold italic print I have added to these maps show actual or postulated Red Army dispositions. Finally, the composite maps show the actual positions of opposing forces. Thus, a comparison of the German and composite maps illustrates the effectiveness of German intelligence strategically, operationally, and tactically.

Because archival documentation on many of these forgotten battles remains somewhat limited, I have deliberately titled many of the tables showing opposing forces and Red Army operational formations for combat "probable," "postulated," or "estimated." I have done this in the hope that the facts and events tentatively revealed by this study will be either substantiated or refuted by future Russian archival releases.

Part I
The Struggle for Belorussia, October–December 1943

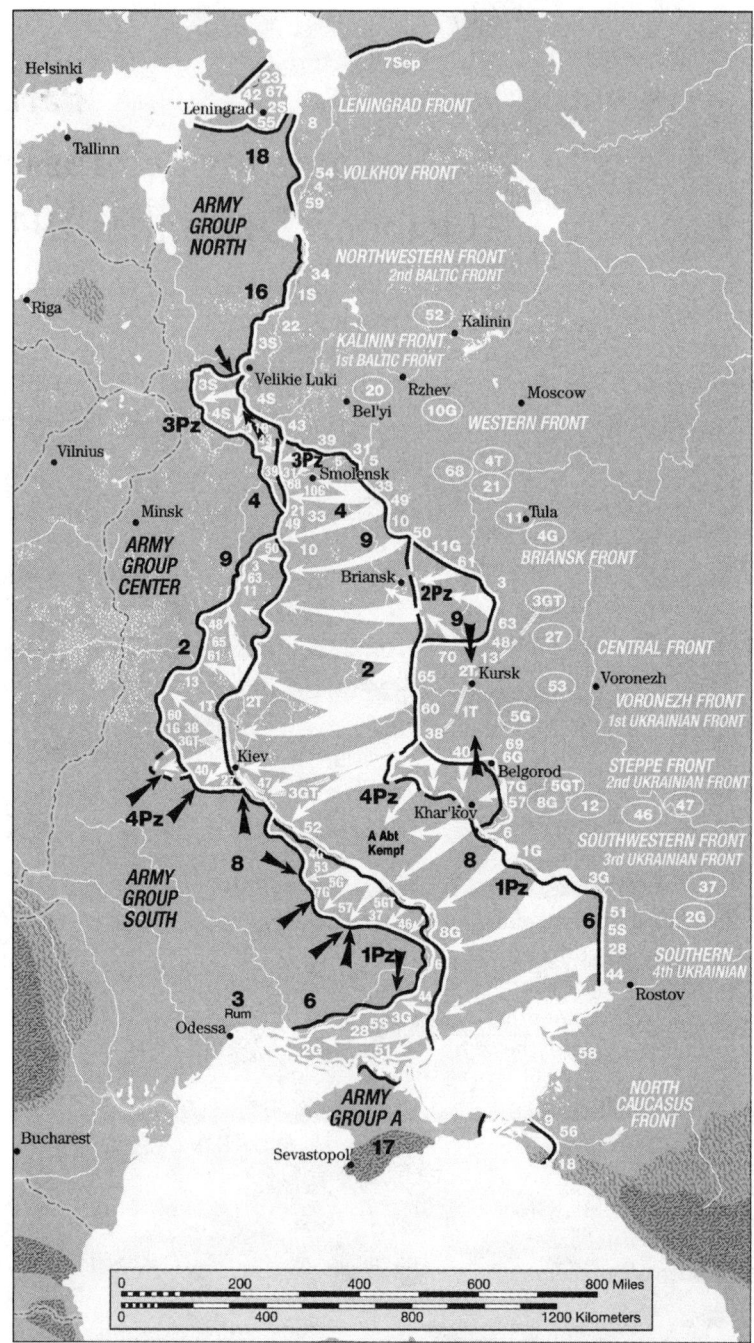

Map 1.1. The Summer–Fall Campaign, 1943

CHAPTER 1

Context: The Summer–Fall Campaign (1 July–23 December)

INTRODUCTION

The summer of 1943 was a pivotal period for both the Wehrmacht and the Red Army. By this time, the war on Germany's Eastern Front had evolved into a clear pattern of alternating strategic success unsettling to both contending parties. The Germans proved their offensive prowess in two massive summer campaigns that propelled their forces deep into the Soviet strategic depths. Nevertheless, at the culminating point of these offensives, when German forces were just short of their premier strategic objectives—Leningrad and Moscow in 1941 and Stalingrad and the Caucasus in 1942—the German Army's offensives faltered. Try as it did, it simply could not complete its strategic tasks before the onset of winter. Unanticipated Red Army strength and tenacity, the rigors of Russian weather, and the deterioration of its own forces and logistical support thwarted German offensive ends.

The Soviets suffered similar strategic frustrations. The Red Army successfully halted both German summer–fall offensives short of their objectives and mounted effective counteroffensives in December 1941 at Moscow and in November 1942 at Stalingrad. The *Stavka* was then able to expand these counteroffensives into massive winter campaigns that stretched German strategic defenses to the breaking point. In both cases, however, the German defenses bent but did not break. Soviet offensive ambitions were ultimately frustrated by a combination of its own excessive optimism, unanticipated German tenacity, and vexing spring thaws.

By the early summer of 1943, two years of war experience indicated that the Germans "owned" the summers and the Soviets the winters. By this time, both sides realized that this strategic pattern was a prescription for stalemate, a situation that frustrated the strategic aspirations of both sides. German frustration was the greatest for good reason because by mid-1943 Germany was waging a world war in an increasing number of continental and oceanic theaters. Great Britain stood like a redoubtable aircraft carrier off the northwestern coast of the German-dominated European continent. Supported by the seemingly inexhaustible resources of the United States, British forces confounded Axis forces in Northern Africa and, along with the United States, threatened to open a second front along the shores of Western Europe. The German Navy, particularly its U-boats, was locked in a death struggle to sever logistical umbilicals sustaining and nurturing the British war effort. Across the globe, Germany's premier ally, Japan, was now on the defensive across the vast span of the Pacific Ocean.

On the continent, German frustration was justified. Not only was it bogged down in Russia but also it was forced to retain vital forces in North Africa, on the French coasts, and in Norway as insurance against the threat of a second front. Moreover, the growing Allied bomber offensive over Germany, coupled with German Luftwaffe losses suffered at Stalingrad and during the winter campaign in Russia, sapped the strength of the air arm of *Blitzkrieg*.

It was clear to Hitler and his strategic military planners that Germany's success in the war, if not its overall fate, rested on the course of the war in the East. It was equally clear that the German Army lacked the strength necessary to mount a general strategic offensive along the entire Eastern Front as it had in 1941 or even along a single strategic axis as it had in 1942. With total victory over the Soviet Union no longer within his grasp, by the summer of 1943 Hitler nevertheless realized that Germany required some sort of dramatic military victory. But the questions were, "Where?" "How?" and "To what end?" The dilemma facing Germany was daunting. Based on past experience, reality indicated that whatever victory Germany achieved was likely to be fleeting. Given this stark truth, Germany could only hope for Soviet exhaustion and the negotiation of a separate peace on whatever terms possible. The German decision to launch its third major strategic offensive of the war, this time in the more restricted sector at Kursk, was based on these premises.

Although in a far less precarious position, the Soviet strategic leadership (the *Stavka*) also faced serious challenges in the summer of 1943. Even though the Germans had halted the Red Army's ambitious winter juggernaut short of the *Stavka*'s intended objectives, the Red Army had inflicted unprecedented defeat on the Wehrmacht and its allies. German forces ultimately stabilized the front from Orel in the north to Khar'kov and Mariupol' in the south, but they did so at immense cost. During the winter campaign of 1942–1943, the Germans lost the Demiansk and Rzhev salients, their twin key launching pads for future operations against Moscow. Far more devastating to the German cause, German forces also lost footholds on the Volga River and in the Caucasus and, in addition, seven Axis armies, which the Red Army destroyed or severely damaged.

Despite these impressive victories, the *Stavka* faced the task of regaining the strategic initiative it had lost in March 1943. This was necessary if it was to continue the painful process of expelling German forces from Soviet soil. But to do so, the Red Army had to prove it could operate as effectively in the summer as it had in winter. In short, the Red Army had to prove that it could "own" the summer as well as the winter. Soviet strategic planners well understood that the Red Army had never before halted a German summer offensive short of the strategic depths, much less the tactical and operational depths. If the Red Army was to resume large-scale offensive actions and expel German forces from Soviet soil, it first had to deal with this reality. It planned to do so at Kursk.

Thus, in the summer of 1943 two totalitarian systems mobilized their military power to resolve equally vital but starkly contradictory strategic ends. The Germans sought to stave off further defeat by crippling the Red Army's offensive potential. The Soviets searched for a decisive summer victory that would permit them to expand their offensive westward toward and into the German heartland. The campaign that ensued resolved the issue of which side would prevail in the war, leaving unanswered only the question, "How long would the ultimate resolution take?"

CONVENTIONAL WISDOM

German and Soviet accounts of the war generally agree on the course and consequences of the 1943 summer–fall campaign. The campaign began with the titanic Battle of Kursk in July and August of 1943. After stifling his natural inclination to resume offensive operations in early summer, Stalin heeded the advice of other *Stavka* members and agreed to begin the Red Army's summer strategic offensive with a deliberate defense along the most likely German attack axis, specifically, against Soviet forces lodged in the Kursk salient. After it halted the German assault on Kursk, the Red Army was to launch a series of counteroffensives in the Kursk region and, subsequently, expand these to the flanks. The *Stavka*'s ultimate aim in the summer–fall campaign was to propel its forces forward to the Dnepr River and, if possible, secure strategic bridgeheads over that imposing water barrier.

Subsequently, the summer–fall campaign began in three distinct stages: the Battle of Kursk, the advance to the Dnepr River, and the struggle for possession of bridgeheads across the Dnepr. The Battle of Kursk, which took place from 5 July to 23 August by Soviet definition, consisted of the initial Soviet premeditated defense north and south of Kursk, followed successively by two major counteroffensives against German forces around Orel and Khar'kov. From 5 to 23 July, the Soviet Central and Voronezh Fronts, supported by elements of the Steppe Front, defeated the forces of German Army Groups Center and South, which were attacking the flanks of the Kursk salient (German Operation Citadel). The *Stavka* then conducted two major counteroffensives. In operation "Kutuzov" (the Orel operation from 12 July through 18 August), the Western, Briansk, and Central Fronts attacked and defeated Army Group Center's forces defending the Orel salient and seized the city of Orel. Meanwhile, in Operation Rumiantsev (the Belgorod-Khar'kov operation from 3 through 23 August), the Voronezh and

Steppe Fronts defeated Army Group South's forces south of the Kursk bulge and liberated Belgorod and Khar'kov.

When it became apparent that the two Kursk counteroffensives would be successful, the *Stavka* initiated two powerful offensives along the more distant flanks. In operation "Suvorov" (the Smolensk operation from 7 August through 2 October), the Kalinin and Western Fronts drove Army Group Center's forces westward and, in stages, liberated Spas-Demensk, El'nia, Roslavl', and Smolensk. Shortly thereafter, the Briansk Front defeated German forces in the Briansk region and liberated the city in the Briansk operation (from 17 through 26 August). Far to the south, the Southwestern and Southern Fronts conducted the Donbas operation (from 13 August through 22 September) against Army Group South's forces and advanced to the outskirts of Zaporozh'e and Melitopol'. In close association with the Southern Front's advance, by late September the North Caucasus Front's forces drove German troops from the North Caucasus, Novorossiisk, and the Taman' regions into the Crimea.

With success on the flanks secured, in late August the *Stavka* ordered its Central, Voronezh, and Steppe Fronts to capitalize on the seizure of Khar'kov by commencing a drive to the Dnepr River. The ensuing Chernigov-Poltava operation (from 26 August through 30 September), which consisted of three distinct *front* offensives, propelled Red Army forces to the banks of the Dnepr River from south of Gomel' in the north to the approaches to Dnepropetrovsk in the south. During the culminating stages of the advance to the Dnepr (in late September and up to mid-October), Soviet forces captured small but vital bridgeheads over the river, the most important of which were south of Gomel', near Chernobyl' and Liutezh, at Bukrin south of Kiev, and south of Kremenchug. Meanwhile, the Southern Front completed clearing German forces from the Donbas in its Donbas operation (from 13 August through 22 September).

During the second half of October, the Belorussian (formerly Central) Front and 1st Ukrainian (formerly Voronezh) Front consolidated their footholds over the Dnepr River. During the same period, the 2nd and 3rd Ukrainian (formerly Steppe and Southwestern) Fronts cleared Army Group South's forces from the eastern bank of the Dnepr, seized the cities of Dnepropetrovsk and Zaporozh'e, and established bridgeheads on the river's western bank. Meanwhile, the 4th Ukrainian (formerly Southern) Front seized Melitopol' and the territory between the Dnepr River and the approaches to the Crimea.[1]

According to most accounts, the third stage of the Soviet summer–fall strategic offensive commenced in early November when the 1st, 2nd, and 3rd Ukrainian Fronts attacked from their tactical bridgeheads across the Dnepr. The 1st Ukrainian Front struck from the Liutezh bridgehead north of Kiev on 3 November and, during the ensuing Kiev strategic offensive (from 3 through 13 November), seized the cities of Fastov and Zhitomir and a strategic-scale bridgehead west of the Ukrainian capital. Thereafter, during the Kiev defensive operation (from 13 November through 22 December), it defended this bridgehead against fierce German counterstrokes orchestrated by Field Marshal Erich von Manstein, the commander of Army Group South. At the same time, the 2nd and 3rd Ukrainian Fronts drove across the Dnepr south of Kremenchug and Dnepropetrovsk in a drive that faltered by the end of October on the approaches to Krivoi Rog. In November and December, the two *fronts* fought to expand their bridgehead, particularly toward Kirovograd in the west. Meanwhile, the armies of the 4th Ukrainian Front besieged a sizable portion of German First Panzer Army in the Nikopol' bridgehead on the Dnepr River's eastern bank. Finally, in late December the reinforced 1st Ukrainian Front launched an offensive toward Berdichev and Vinnitsa (the Zhitomir-Berdichev operation) that continued well into the new year.

Most Soviet accounts assert that the *Stavka* accorded strategic priority throughout the entire fall period to operations along the southwestern axis, specifically to operations by the 1st, 2nd, and 3rd Ukrainian Fronts across the Dnepr and toward Vinnitsa, Kirovograd, and Krivoi Rog deep into the Ukraine. Accordingly, they argue, unlike previous campaigns, the *Stavka* concentrated its efforts along a single strategic axis rather than dissipating its strength in numerous offensives along several strategic axes. Operations conducted along other axes were thus clearly secondary and supporting in nature. These included:

- 1st Baltic (Kalinin) Front's attack at Nevel', at the junction of Army Groups North and Center, and the Central Front's advance south of Gomel' in October
- 1st Baltic Front's expansion of its Nevel' penetration and the Belorussian (Central) Front's advance into the Rechitsa region west of Gomel' in November
- 1st Baltic Front's advance to Gorodok (north of Vitebsk) and the Belorussian Front's advance on Kalinkovichi (west of Rechitsa) in December

Traditional Soviet accounts properly trumpet Red Army successes in the summer–fall campaign. During this period it repelled the last major German wartime strategic offensive (at Kursk), drove German forces back to the Dnepr River line, and established strategic bridgeheads across the Dnepr River necessary for the Red Army to continue its strategic offensive into the Ukraine during the winter campaign. At the same time, the Red Army seized footholds in eastern Belorussia from which it could commence a major strategic offensive in the summer of 1944.

THE EMERGING TRUTH

As accurate as most of these Soviet claims are, they fall short of telling the complete story. As had been the case in earlier wartime campaigns, in mid- and late 1943, the *Stavka* remained overly ambitious and continued to assign its *fronts* operational missions that they could not fully achieve. In fairness, the *Stavka's* excessive ambition reflected the entirely valid principle of attempting to exploit every strategic success to the greatest extent possible. However, contrary to its consistent postwar claims that the Red Army focused its efforts on a single strategic axis, the *Stavka* still insisted on conducting strategic offensives along multiple strategic axes during each and every stage of the campaign. Thus, during every stage, the Red Army conducted major offensive efforts along the western, southwestern, and southern axes and operations of lesser importance along other axes (the northwestern and the Caucasus).

A brief review of all Red Army operations during all stages of the summer–fall campaign illustrates these facts (see Table 1.1).

The First Stage

Dominated as it was by the titanic Battle of Kursk, the course and outcome of the first stage of the summer–fall campaign was and remains fairly transparent. German and Soviet definitions of the Battle of Kursk differ, but the general chronology of operations during the first stage of the summer–fall campaign is quite clear (see Table 1.2).

The initial stage of the campaign consisted of the Battle of Kursk as defined by the Soviets and lesser operations along the northwestern and Cauca-

Table 1.1. Stages of the Red Army's Summer–Fall Campaign

STAGE	BATTLE OR OPERATION	STRATEGIC AXIS	OPERATING FRONTS
1st Stage	The Battle of Kursk (5 July–23 August)	Western, Southwestern, Southern	Kalinin, Western, Briansk, Central, Voronezh, Steppe, Southwestern, Southern
2nd Stage	The Advance to the Dnepr River (7 August–2 October)	Western, Southwestern, Southern	Kalinin, Western, Briansk, Central, Voronezh, Steppe, Southwestern, Southern
3rd Stage	Battles for Belorussia and Dnepr River Bridgeheads (3 October–31 December)	Western, Southwestern, Southern	Kalinin (1st Baltic), Western, Central (Belorussian), Voronezh (1st Ukrainian), Steppe (2nd Ukrainian), Southwestern (3rd Ukrainian), Southern (4th Ukrainian)

Table 1.2. Red Army Operations during the First Stage of the Summer–Fall Campaign

NAME AND DATE	PARTICIPATING FRONTS
FIRST STAGE	
I. The Battle of Kursk: Operations along the Western, Southwestern, and Southern Axes, 5 July–23 August 1943	
Kursk strategic defense (5 July–23 July 1943)	Central, Voronezh, and Steppe *including:*
Defense along the Orel-Kursk axis (5–11 July)	Central (13A, 70A, 16AA)
Defense along the Belgorod-Kursk axis (5–23 July)	Voronezh and Steppe (6GA, 7GA, 40A 69A, 5GA, 1 TA, 5GTA, 2AA)
Donbas offensive (17 July–2 August 1943)	Southwestern, Southern *including:*
Izium-Barvenkovo offensive (17–27 July)	Southwestern (1GA, 3GA, 8GA, 17AA)
Mius offensive (17 July–2 August)	Southern (2GA, 5SA, 28A, 51A, 8AA)
Orel strategic offensive ("Kutuzov") (12 July–18 August 1943)	Briansk, Central, and Western *including:*
Bolkhov-Orel offensive (12 July–18 August)	Briansk (61A, 3A, 63A, 3GTA, 15AA)
Kromy-Orel offensive (15 July–18 August)	Western (50A, 11GA, 11A, 4TA, 1AA) Central (13A, 70A, 48A, 2TA, 16AA)
Belgorod-Khar'kov strategic offensive ("Rumiantsev") (3–23 August 1943)	Voronezh, Steppe, and Southwestern *including:*
Belgorod-Bogodukhov offensive (3–23 August)	Voronezh (38A, 40A, 6GA, 5GA, 1TA, 1TA, 5GTA, 27A, 47A, 4GA, 2AA)
Belgorod-Khar'kov offensive (3–23 August)	Steppe (53A, 69A, 7GA, 57A, 5AA)
Zmiev offensive (12–23 August)	Southwestern (57A, 1GA, 17AA)
II. The Battle for Leningrad: Operations along the Northwestern Axis, July–August 1943	
Mga offensive (22 July–22 August)	Leningrad (67A, 13AA) Volkhov (8A, 14AA)
III. The Battle for the Caucasus	
Taman' offensive (4 April–10 May and 26 May–22 August)	North Caucasus (9A, 56A, 18A, 4AA)

sus axes. According to the Soviets, the Battle of Kursk entailed the premeditated Soviet strategic defense followed by two powerful strategic offensives launched north and south of Kursk (along the western and southwestern axes), along with a supporting offensive along the southern axis against German forces in the Donbas. The *Stavka's* intent in this prolonged struggle was to establish conditions necessary to accomplish the missions it had failed to achieve during the final stage of its winter campaign in February and March of 1943. It intended to halt and defeat the German summer offensive and create a situation conducive to conducting subsequent operations aimed at driving the defeated German forces back to the line of the Dnepr and Sozh Rivers and seizing bridgeheads across those mighty river obstacles. Historians have described the Kursk, Orel, Belgorod-Khar'kov, and Mga operations in adequate detail, but they have largely forgotten (concealed) the Donbas and Taman' operations.

Action during the campaign began on 5 July when massed German forces assaulted the northern and southern flanks of Red Army positions in the Kursk bulge. The Soviet defensive battle lasted until 23 July, by which time the Red Army had either repulsed the German assault (in the north) or forced the Germans to suspend operations and withdraw to their starting positions (in the south). The Germans consider what the Soviets view as the defensive phase to constitute the entire Battle of Kursk. The Soviets, however, viewed and continue to view the Battle of Kursk in a far broader perspective. They consider the defense phase and the ensuing counteroffensives to have been a single entity, primarily because the *Stavka* planned both phases at the same time and well in advance of the German assault.

The initial Red Army counteroffensive targeted Army Group Center's forces defending the Orel salient north of Kursk. It began on 12 July, as soon as it became apparent that the German Ninth Army's offensive against the northern flank of the Kursk bulge had failed. The Western and Briansk Fronts initiated the counteroffensive along the western axis by attacking German positions north and east of Orel. Five days later the Central Front joined the attack, assaulting Orel from the south. Although significant in its own right, the Soviet Orel offensive, code-named "Operation Kutuzov," was only a prelude to the main Soviet attack along the southwestern (Khar'kov-Poltava) axis.

The second and more important Soviet counteroffensive, the Belgorod-Khar'kov offensive, code-named "Operation Rumiantsev," began on 3 August 1943. It involved an assault by the Voronezh and Steppe Fronts' forces against Army Group South's forces defending Khar'kov and the southern flank of the Kursk bulge. The *Stavka* understood that its chances for success in the Belgorod-Khar'kov operation would improve drastically if German panzer reserves were tied down in action elsewhere along the front. Therefore, it ordered the Southwestern and Southern Fronts to initiate offensive operations in the Donbas region two weeks before the Belgorod-Khar'kov operation was to begin. The Donbas offensive, which lasted from 17 July to 2 August (the day before the Belgorod-Khar'kov offensive began), did indeed draw German panzer reserves away from the threatened Khar'kov sector. However, the offensive also failed miserably, prompting most Soviet historians to dismiss the operation as largely a simple feint.

Finally, the *Stavka* planned and conducted two lesser operations during the first stage of the summer–fall campaign. The first, the Mga offensive in the Leningrad region, was designed to widen the corridor connecting the besieged city of Leningrad with the main Soviet front. Many Soviet sources provide details about this operation. The second and less significant offensive occurred in southern Russia, where the North Caucasus Front's forces attacked German defenses on the Taman' Peninsula and around the port of Novorossiisk. Soviet historians have "forgotten" this operation because it failed dramatically.

By the end of the summer–fall campaign's first stage, Red Army forces had sapped German offensive strength, collapsed German defenses in the critical sector from Orel to Khar'kov, and created the prerequisites for a subsequent advance along a broad front to and perhaps beyond the Dnepr River.

The Second Stage

The second stage of the summer–fall campaign involved a wholesale expansion of the Red Army's Kursk strategic offensive to encompass all *fronts* attacking along virtually every strategic axis. The *Stavka*'s intent was to drive German forces from all regions east of the Dnepr River, reach and cross the river, and secure strategic bridgeheads on the western (far) banks of the river. See Table 1.3 for the operations conducted in the second stage of the summer–fall campaign.

The *Stavka* initiated the second stage of its summer–fall offensive on 7 August 1943 with a massive offensive along the western strategic axis by the forces of the Kalinin and Western Fronts. Code-named "Operation Suvorov," the Smolensk strategic offensive sought to smash Army Group Center's defenses in the Dukhovshchina and Spas-Demensk sector, capture Smolensk, and reach and cross the Dnepr River along the eastern borders of Belorussia. In reality, the offensive developed slowly against strong and skillful German resistance. After several offensive impulses, Soviet forces liberated Smolensk and approached the Vitebsk and Orsha regions by early October. To the south the Briansk Front attacked on 17 August, liberated Briansk, and drove German forces westward toward Gomel'.

With German defenses in the Smolensk sector under heavy assault, on 13 August the *Stavka* launched a strategic offensive into the Donbas region with the Southwestern and Southern Fronts' forces, and on 26 August the Central, Voronezh, and Steppe Fronts began the massive Chernigov-Poltava strategic offensive. The latter soon turned into a race for the Dnepr River, with Soviet forces attempting to outrun their German foes and reach the Dnepr before the Germans could erect a coherent defense along that formidable water barrier.

By late September, advancing Soviet forces had reached or were approaching the Dnepr River across a broad front from Gomel' in the north to Zaporozh'e in the south and had secured small bridgeheads across the river north and south of Kiev (at Chernobyl', Gornostaipol', Liutezh, and Bukrin) and south of Kremenchug. Battle was also raging in German-held

Table 1.3. Red Army Operations during the Second Stage of the Summer–Fall Campaign

NAME AND DATE	PARTICIPATING FRONTS
SECOND STAGE	
I. The Advance to the Dnepr River: Operations along the Western Axis, 7 August–2 October 1943	
Smolensk strategic offensive ("Suvorov") (7 August–2 October 1943)	Kalinin and Western
including:	
Spas-Demensk offensive (7–20 August)	Western (10GA, 33A, 49A, 5A, 10A, 21A, 68A, 1AA)
Dukhovshchina-Demidov (14 September–2 October)	Kalinin (39A, 43A, 3AA)
Smolensk-Roslavl' (15 September–2 October)	Western (31A, 5A, 68A, 10GA, 21A, 33A, 49A, 10A, 1AA)
associated:	
Briansk offensive (17–26 August) (1 September–3 October)	Briansk (50A, 11A, 11GA, 3A, 63A, 4TA, 15AA)
II. The Advance to the Dnepr River: Operations along the Southwestern and Southern Axes, 13 August–30 September 1943	
Chernigov-Poltava strategic offensive (26 August–30 September 1943)	Central, Voronezh, and Steppe
including:	
Chernigov-Pripiat' offensive (26 August–30 September)	Central (13A, 48A, 70A, 65A, 61A, 60A, 2TA, 16AA)
Sumy-Priluki offensive (24 August–30 September)	Voronezh (38A, 40A, 47A, 4GA, 27A, 6GA, 5GA, 52A, 1TA, 3GTA, 2AA)
Poltava offensive (24 August–30 September)	Steppe (69A, 53A, 7GA, 57A, 37A, 5GTA, 5AA)
Donbas strategic offensive (13 August–22 September 1943)	Southwestern and Southern
including:	
Barvenkovo-Pavlograd offensive (13 August–22 September)	Southwestern (46A, 1GA, 6A, 8GA, 12A, 3GA, 17AA)
Mius-Mariupol' offensive (18 August–22 September)	Southern (51A, 5SA, 2GA, 28A, 44A, 8AA)
III. The Battle for Leningrad: Operations along the Northwestern Axis, September 1943	
The Mga offensive (15–18 September)	Leningrad and Volkhov Fronts (67A, 2SA, 13AA)
IV. The Battle for the Caucasus	
Novorossiisk-Taman' offensive (9 September–9 October)	North Caucasus (9A, 56A, 18A, 4AA)

bridgeheads on the river's eastern bank (at Dnepropetrovsk and Zaporozh'e) while the Southern Front's offensive stalled on the approaches to Melitopol'.

On the northern and southern flanks of the Soviet-German front, during the second stage of the summer–fall campaign, Soviet forces continued their attempts to widen the Leningrad corridor (the Siniavino operation) and finally compelled German forces to abandon their defenses on the Taman'

Peninsula. All of these operations save the Siniavino offensive at Leningrad have been well documented in both Soviet- and German-based accounts.

The Third Stage

The third and final stage of the summer–fall campaign commenced in late September and early October as Soviet forces attempted to breech the Dnepr River line and expand their bridgeheads on the river's western bank to strategic proportions. During the ensuing three months, the *Stavka* mounted major drives along all four strategic axes, into Belorussia, the Ukraine, and the northern entrance to the Crimean Peninsula. It also launched supporting attacks near Leningrad and from the Taman' Peninsula to Kerch' in the Crimea (see Table 1.4).

Although Soviet historians have claimed that the *Stavka* placed strategic priority on the southwestern and southern axes during this stage of the campaign, this is far from the truth. In reality, the *Stavka* also mounted a strategic effort along the western axis in an attempt to liberate Minsk and the eastern half of Belorussia. Red Army operations along these strategic axes developed in distinct phases, either because operations in the previous phase failed or because the *Stavka* sought to exploit earlier successes (see Map 1.1).

The Red Army began offensive operations along the southern axis in late September. The Steppe Front seized a bridgehead across the Dnepr River south of Kremenchug, the Southwestern Front completed its Donbas operation along the eastern approaches to Zaporozh'e, and the Southern Front completed its portion of the Donbas offensive and commenced its Melitopol' offensive. The Voronezh Front and the Central Front's left wing attempted to launch offensives along the southwestern axis against Kiev from their bridgeheads across the Dnepr River at Chernobyl', Liutezh, and Bukrin, but failed spectacularly. To the north along the western axis, the Kalinin, Western, and Central Fronts lunged into Belorussia through Nevel' and Orsha and from bridgeheads south of Gomel', but, after achieving notable initial successes, their operations ground to a halt.

In mid- and late October, the *Stavka* renewed its thrusts along all three strategic axes. Along the western axis, the Western Front repeatedly pounded the German Fourth Army's positions north and south of Orsha, while the Central Front conducted local operations to improve its positions south of Gomel'. Meanwhile, the Voronezh Front struck repeatedly at the German Fourth Panzer and Eighth Armies' positions north and south of Kiev but without appreciable success. Further to the south, the Steppe Front, with the Southwestern Front on its left, continued its prolonged and painful battles to expand its bridgehead south of the Dnepr toward Piatikhatki, while the Southern Front closed up to the Dnepr River from south of Zaporozh'e.

Table 1.4. Red Army Operations during the Third Stage of the Summer–Fall Campaign

NAME AND DATE	PARTICIPATING FRONTS
THIRD STAGE	
I. The Battle for Belorussia: Operations along the Western Axis, 3 October–31 December 1943	
The Belorussian strategic offensive (3 October–31 December 1943)	Kalinin (1st Baltic), 2nd Baltic, Western, and Central (Belorussian)
including:	
Vitebsk (and Nevel') offensives (3–12 October)	Kalinin (43A, 39A, 3SA, 4SA, 3AA)
Vitebsk (Riga), Idritsa, and Pskov Offensives (18–30 October)	Kalinin, Baltic, and Northwestern
Orsha offensive (3–11 October)	Western (10GA, 68A, 5A, 31A, 33A, 1AA)
Orsha offensive (12–18 October)	Western (10GA, 21A, 31A, 33A, 1AA)
Orsha offensive (21–26 October)	Western (10GA, 5A, 31A, 68A, 1AA)
Gomel'-Rechitsa offensive (30 September–30 October)	Central (3A, 48A, 50A, 63A, 61A, 65A, 16AA)
Polotsk-Vitebsk offensive (2–21 November)	1st Baltic (4SA, 43A, 39A, 3AA)
Pustoshka-Idritsa offensive (2–21 November 1943)	2nd Baltic (6G, 3SA, 11GA, 15AA)
Orsha offensive (14–19 November)	Western (10GA, 5A, 31A, 33A, 1AA)
Orsha offensive (20 November–5 December)	Western (10GA, 5A, 31A, 33A, 1AA)
Gomel'-Rechitsa offensive (10–30 November)	Belorussian (61A, 65A, 48A, 11A, 16AA)
Novyi Bykhov–Propoisk offensive (22–30 November)	Belorussian (63A, 3A, 50A, 16AA)
Vitebsk (Gorodok) offensive (13–31 December 1943)	1st Baltic (4SA, 11GA, 43A, 39A, 3AA) Western (33A, 1AA)
Idritsa-Opochka offensive (Novosokol'niki pursuit) (16–25 December 1943) (30 December–15 January 1944)	2nd Baltic (3SA, 6GA, 22A, 15AA)
Kalinkovichi (Bobruisk) offensive (8–11 December)	Belorussian (48A, 65A, 61A, 16AA)
The German Kalinkovichi counterstroke (20–27 December)	Belorussian (48A, 65A, 61A, 16AA)
II. The Battle for the Dnepr River: Operations along the Southwestern Axis, 1 October–31 December 1943	
Lower Dnepr strategic offensive (26 September–31 December 1943)	Steppe (2nd Ukrainian), Southwestern (3rd Ukrainian), Southern (4th Ukrainian)
including:	
Chernobyl'-Radomysl' offensive (1–4 October)	Central (13A, 60A, 16AA)
The German Chernobyl' and Gornostaipol' counterstrokes (3–8 October)	Central (13A, 60A, 16AA)
Liutezh offensive (11–24 October)	Voronezh (38A, 3AA)
Bukrin offensives (12–15 October) (21–24 October)	Voronezh Front (27A, 40A, 47A, 3GTA, 2AA)
The Kiev strategic offensive (3–13 November 1943)	1st Ukrainian (13A, 60A, 38A, 40A, 27A, 3GTA, 2AA)
The Kiev strategic defense (13 November–22 December)	1st Ukrainian (13A, 60A, 38A, 40A, 27A, 3GTA, 2AA)
The Zhitomir-Berdichev offensive (24 December 1943–14 January 1944)	1st Ukrainian (13A, 60A, 1GA, 18A, 38A, 40A, 27A, 1TA, 3GTA, 2AA)

Table 1.4. *continued*

NAME AND DATE	PARTICIPATING FRONTS
III. The Battle for the Dnepr River: Operations along the Southern Axis (Lower Dnepr), 26 September–31 December 1943	
Lower Dnepr strategic offensive (26 September–31 December 1943)	Steppe (2nd Ukrainian), Southwestern (3rd Ukrainian), Southern (4th Ukrainian) *including:*
Kremenchug offensive (26 September–10 October)	Steppe (2nd Ukrainian) (4GA, 5GA, 53A, 69A, 37A, 5AA)
Zaporozh'e offensive (10–14 October 1943)	Southwestern (12A, 8GA, 3GA, 17AA)
Kremenchug-Piatikhatki (Krivoi Rog) offensive (15 October–3 November)	Steppe (2nd Ukrainian) (5GA, 7GA, 37A, 46A, 53A, 57A, 4GA, 52A, 5GTA, 5AA)
Dnepropetrovsk offensive (23 October–23 December)	3rd Ukrainian (46A, 8GA, 12A, 6A, 17AA)
Melitopol' offensive (26 September–5 November)	Southern (4th Ukrainian) (51A, 5SA, 2GA, 28A, 44A, CMG, 8AA)
Krivoi Rog offensive (14–21 November)	2nd Ukrainian Front (37A, 53A, 7GA, 57A, 5GTA, 5AA)
Aleksandriia-Znamenka offensive (22 November–9 December)	2nd Ukrainian Front (53A, 5GA, 7GA, 5GTA, 5AA)
Krivoi Rog offensive (10–19 December)	2nd Ukrainian Front (7GA, 57A, 37A, 5GTA, 5AA)
Apostolovo offensive (14 November–23 December)	3rd Ukrainian Front (46A, 8GA, 6A, 17AA)
Nikopol' offensives (14 November–31 December)	4th Ukrainian (28A, 3GA, 5SA, 8AA)
IV. The Battle for the Caucasus	
Kerch'-El'tigen amphibious (31 October–11 December)	North Caucasus (56A, 18A, 4AA)

On 20 October the *Stavka* renamed the Kalinin, Central, Voronezh, Southwestern, and Southern Fronts the 1st Baltic, Belorussian, and 1st, 2nd, 3rd, and 4th Ukrainian Fronts, respectively. This seemingly unimportant process subtly revealed the focus of these *fronts'* efforts. By month's end, the 4th Ukrainian Front faced Army Group South's defenses along the Dnepr, at the entrance to the Crimea, and in bridgeheads on the river's eastern bank opposite Kherson and Nikopol'.

In early and mid-November, the *Stavka* ordered a new round of offensives along the same three axes. Along the western axis, the *Stavka* began a double envelopment of Army Group Center's forces in Belorussia by launching twin offensives northwestward from the Gomel' region and southwestward from Nevel', both of which were to converge on Minsk. Attacking from the north, the 1st Baltic Front hammered unmercifully on the German Third Panzer Army's defenses at Vitebsk, while the Belorussian Front cleaved deep into the German Second Army's defenses south of Bobruisk. All the while, the Western Front repeatedly attacked the German Fourth Army's positions around Orsha and east of Vitebsk. The Germans' strategic defense lines

Marshal of Aviation N. N. Voronov, *Stavka* coordinator

L. Z. Mekhlis, Stalin's representative and henchman and member of the Military Council (commissar), 2nd Baltic Front

sagged but held, and by year's end a persistent *Stavka* was forced to temporarily halt its offensive with relatively meager gains.

In the north, the newly formed 2nd Baltic Front attempted to expand its offensive north from the Nevel' salient in an attempt to sever communications between Army Groups North and Center and to threaten the former's defenses south of Leningrad.

In the south, in early November the 1st Ukrainian Front ended the month-long stalemate along the Dnepr by bursting from its bridgeheads north of Kiev, enveloping and capturing the city, and creating a strategic bridgehead on the Dnepr River's western bank. By midmonth the *front's* forces faced and parried intensified German counterattacks aimed at retaking the Ukrainian capital. Further south along the Dnepr, the 2nd and 3rd Ukrainian Fronts painfully widened their combined bridgehead across the Dnepr as they tried in vain to reach Krivoi Rog. Their intent was to link up with the 4th Ukrainian Front's forces, which were attacking across the Dnepr from the south, to cut off Army Group South's forces in the Dnepr River bend. However, the 4th Ukrainian Front was similarly frustrated as its forces repeatedly tried but failed to collapse the German bridgehead at Nikopol'. Finally, in support of operations along more critical axes, the *Stavka* ordered the North Caucasus Front to conduct an amphibious operation against Kerch' at the eastern extremity of the Crimean Peninsula.

Most of these operations are now a part of the historical record to a greater or lesser extent; however, a surprising number of them are not. The most important of these "forgotten" battles were the Belorussian strategic offensive, which endured throughout the entire fall, and the failed Kiev strategic offensive of October 1943. The former is now known only by virtue of its "rump" constituent operations at Nevel', Gorodok, Gomel', Rechitsa, Kalinkovichi, and Rogachev, which, in reality, were but pale reflections of what the *Stavka* really hoped to achieve. Soviet historians were able to conceal the October Kiev offensive only because it was "lost in the noise" of its brilliantly successful November counterpart. Many lesser operations also disappeared from the historical record either because they failed without a trace or because the action played out during the midst of more momentous Red Army operational successes. As a result, the complete history of the Battle for Belorussia, October–December 1943, has yet to be told.

CHAPTER 2

The Kalinin and Baltic Fronts' Vitebsk and Nevel' Offensives (3–30 October)

STRATEGIC SITUATION

The third stage of the Red Army's summer–fall campaign commenced in late September after Red Army forces reached the line extending from Velikie Luki and Rudnia in the north southward along the Pronia, Sozh, and Dnepr Rivers to Zaporozh'e and then southward through Melitopol' to the northern shores of the Sea of Azov (see Map 2.1). By the end of September, German forces were clinging to a bridgehead on the eastern bank of the Dnepr River around Gomel'. Further south, however, Red Army forces managed to seize small bridgeheads on the Dnepr's west bank near Loev, south of Gomel', at Chernobyl' and Liutezh north of Kiev, at Bukrin south of Kiev, and between Kremenchug and Dnepropetrovsk. At this juncture the *Stavka* had to decide precisely where its strategic priorities lay in its employment of the Red Army during the fall period. Ultimately, it decided to conduct strategic offensive operations along three of the most vital strategic axes—western, southwestern, and southern—to exploit what it perceived as fatal German weakness.

Accordingly, the *Stavka* ordered the Kalinin, Western, and Briansk Fronts, along with the northern half of the Central Front, to conduct deep operations along the western (Moscow-Smolensk-Minsk-Warsaw) strategic axis. The primary aim was to capture Minsk, occupy the eastern half of Belorussia, and, if successful, exploit to seize Pskov and Riga as well. To the south, the *Stavka* ordered the powerful Voronezh Front and the southern half of the Central Front to envelop Kiev, exploit along the Kiev-Vinnitsa-L'vov axis to establish a strategic-scale bridgehead across the Dnepr River, and liberate the central portion of the Ukraine. Finally, the *Stavka* required the Steppe, Southwestern, and Southern Fronts to seize strategic bridgeheads across the Dnepr River, defeat German forces defending in the great bend in the Dnepr River, liberate the eastern Ukraine, and isolate and destroy German forces defending in the Crimea.

As the campaign developed, the *Stavka* reorganized and renamed its *fronts* in customary fashion so that their names would correspond with their actual strategic missions. Accordingly, on 10 October it abolished the Briansk Front, assigned most of its armies to the Central Front, and transferred its headquarters to the north, where it became the Baltic (and later, 2nd Baltic)

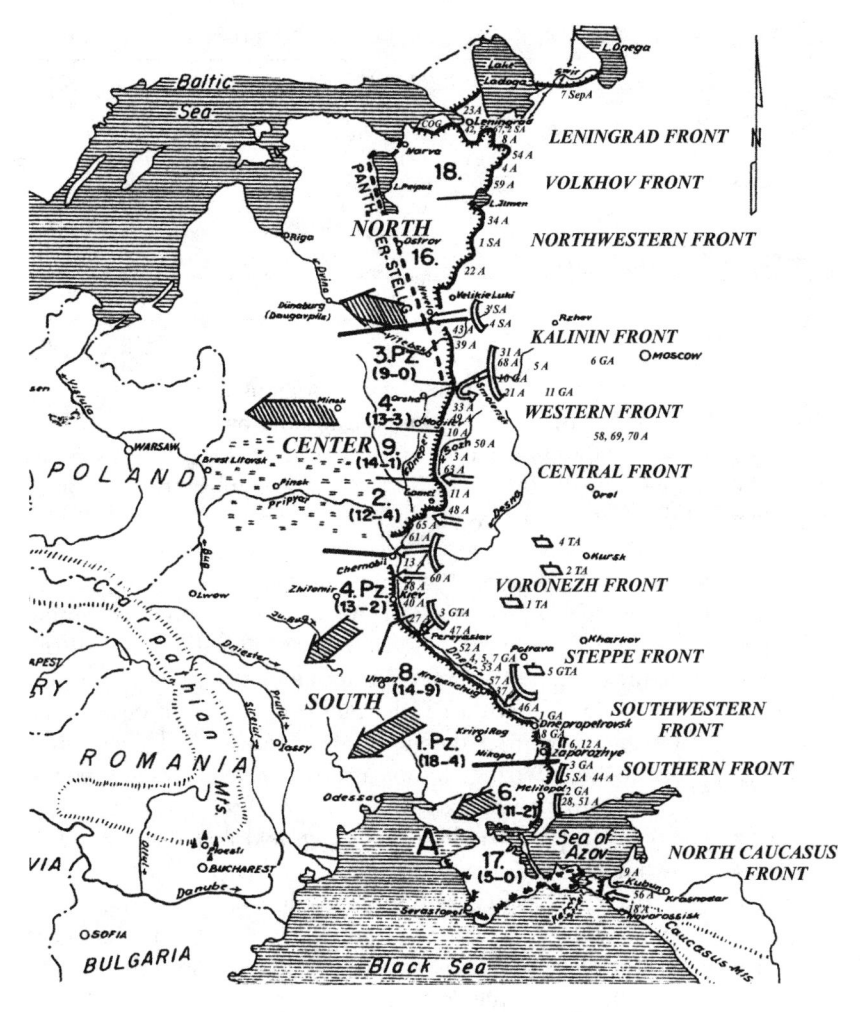

Map 2.1. The Situation on the Soviet-German Front, 6 October 1943

Front. The new Baltic Front's mission was to assist the Kalinin Front's offensive by operating toward Pskov. Ten days later, on 20 October 1943, the *Stavka* completed the reorganization and renaming process (see Table 2.1).

Histories based primarily on German sources have tended to describe Red Army operations along the western axis during the fall of 1943 in fragmented fashion by viewing each sector independently, as befits an axis perceived to be of secondary strategic importance. Thus, according to Earl Ziemke, "Even though it could be safely assumed that the *Stavka* would keep its main effort against Army Group South (best evidence was the combining of the *Briansk* and *Central Fronts* under a single command, since

Table 2.1. The Redesignation of Red Army *Fronts*, 10–20 October 1943

FORMER NAME	NEW NAME
Briansk	Baltic (10 October)
Baltic	2nd Baltic
Kalinin	1st Baltic
Western	Western
Central	Belorussian
Voronezh	1st Ukrainian
Steppe	2nd Ukrainian
Southwestern	3rd Ukrainian
Southern	4th Ukrainian

the Russians never undertook anything really ambitious with one *front* in so broad a sector), Army Group Center was concerned over its south flank."[1]

Likewise, as the official Soviet history of the war published in 1978 describes *Stavka* objectives in the fall of 1943, they too emphasize the premier importance of the southwestern axis:

> In developing its plan for the 1943 summer–fall offensive, the *Stavka* assigned its forces new missions at the end of September and beginning of October. The *fronts* along the northwestern axis were to defeat the opposing enemy grouping and prevent it from withdrawing to Dvinsk and Riga. Along the western axis, [the *Stavka*] planned to destroy the enemy central grouping, reach the Vil'no, Minsk, Slutsk, and Sluch' River line, and liberate the Baltic region and eastern Belorussia. It required the *fronts* along the southwestern axis to liquidate the Hitlerites' bridgeheads on the Dnepr, defeat the southern grouping, and reach the Mogilev-Podol'skii, Rybnitsa, and Kherson line.
>
> The main axis was Kiev, where the Voronezh Front was assigned the primary role. In cooperation with the Central Front's left wing, its forces had to liquidate the Fascist grouping in the Kiev region, liberate the capital of the Ukraine, and then develop the offensive toward Berdichev, Zhmerinka, and Mogilev-Podol'skii. . . .
>
> The subsequent course of events demonstrated that the *fronts* did not manage to accomplish all of their assigned missions in 1943. The penetration of the enemy's defensive front required considerable forces and weaponry, which the *fronts* were already missing in the concluding operations of 1943. . . .
>
> In accordance with the overall concept, the *Stavka* VGK continued to concentrate its main forces along the southwestern strategic axis, first and foremost, in the Central, Voronezh, and Steppe Fronts' sectors, whose overall expanse encompassed 15 percent of the entire Soviet-German front. In these [sectors] were 129 (29 percent) of the rifle, cavalry, and airborne divisions, 26 (37 percent) of the artillery, guards-mortars, and

antiaircraft artillery, 11 (more than 50 percent) of the tank and mechanized corps, and a considerable force of aircraft. Large Soviet forces were deployed along the western strategic axis (the Kalinin, Western, and Briansk Fronts).[2]

Soviet and Russian accounts of operations along the western axis during the fall, however, have also been candid enough to describe the *Stavka's* overall strategic aims accurately, but they routinely downplay the significance of operations along the western axis. For example, official histories acknowledge the importance of Belorussia but only as it related to the more important southwestern axis:

> By October 1943 Soviet forces in the central sector of the Soviet-German front had forced a series of large water obstacles, including the Desna, Sozh, and Dnepr, seized bridgeheads, and fought for the liberation of the eastern regions of Belorussia. . . .
>
> Belorussia occupied an important place in the strategic plans of the Wehrmacht. . . . Belorussia protected the path to the Baltic region, eastern Prussia, and Poland. In favorable conditions, the aggressor counted on launching attacks from the north against the flank of Soviet forces operating in the Ukraine with the large groupings that were concentrated in Belorussia.
>
> The German-Fascist command tried at all cost to hold off the Soviet Army's offensive along the western strategic axis. The enemy created a series of defensive lines by employing the forested-swampy terrain and water obstacles. Many populated points were prepared for all-round defense. Goebbels's propaganda claimed that the Russians would advance no further than Smolensk. The German forces received orders to defend their positions strongly and fight to the last soldier. On 1 October, Kluge, the commander of Army Group Center ordered, "Henceforth, put an end to any withdrawals."
>
> The German-Fascist command had a large grouping of more than seventy divisions of Army Group "Center" in the central sector of the front. They placed considerable hope in the fall *rasputitsa* [period of flooded roads] and the lack of trafficable roads, presuming that the Soviet Armed Forces conducted offensives only after an extended interval.[3]

This view is disingenuous in several respects. First, the Germans had neither the intention nor capability to conduct any sort of offensive of their own from Belorussia. Second, German Army Group Center's strength on 1 October 1943 was forty-two infantry divisions, eight panzer and panzer grenadier divisions, and four Luftwaffe (Air Force) field divisions, backed up by several security divisions. Furthermore, of this number, twelve infantry and four panzer divisions were *kampfgruppen* (KGr., or combat groups), that is, shrunken regimental-size remnants of full divisions worn down in previous combat.[4] Thus, effective German strength in Belorussia amounted to about forty-six division equivalents.

Despite its inaccuracies, this history correctly noted the *Stavka*'s fall objectives in Belorussia:

> In order to liberate Soviet Belorussia, the *Stavka* of the Supreme High Command planned to conduct a penetration of the enemy's defense, exploit the offensive, and deny him the opportunity to dig in at intermediate positions along the western axis. The newly created Baltic Front, under the command of General M. M. Popov, was deployed in the Velikie Luki region on the Kalinin Front's right. Its forces received the mission to attack along the Nevel', Idritsa, and Valga axis and, with part of its forces, along the Opochka, Ostrov, and Pskov axis.
>
> The Kalinin Front had to attack along the Vitebsk axis and, after capturing the Vitebsk region, its main forces were to aim a blow at Polotsk, Dvinsk, and Riga. The Western Front was to attack toward Orsha and Mogilev and, after liberating these regions, it was to continue its offensive along the Borisov, Molodechno, and Vil'no axis. After capturing the Kiev region together with the Voronezh Front, the Central Front was to develop the offensive along the Zhlobin, Bobruisk, and Minsk axis with its main forces. Thus, the *Stavka* of the Supreme High Command envisioned delivery of attacks on Army Group "Center's" flanks along the Vitebsk and Gomel'-Bobruisk axes and against its center—along the Orsha and Mogilev axes.
>
> The Leningrad, Volkhov, and Northwestern Fronts received orders to strengthen all types of reconnaissance, increase their vigilance and combat readiness, and, in the event of a withdrawal by Army Group "North," begin an energetic pursuit of the enemy.
>
> According to their combat and numerical strength, the Kalinin, Western, and Central Fronts did not have any sizable superiority over the enemy. The correlation of forces of the opposing groupings amounted to 1.2 to 1 in personnel, 1 to 1 in tanks, 3 to 1 in guns and mortars, and 2 to 1 in aircraft in favor of the Soviet forces. Therefore, the *front* and army commands paid special attention to creating superiority along the main attack axes. At that time, Soviet aviation soundly maintained air superiority along the western axis. The absence of tank armies in the *front* made it necessary to employ aircraft extensively to support and protect the ground forces during the penetration of the tactical defenses.[5]

Although candid in regard to the *Stavka*'s strategic objectives, this passage too contains errors, the most significant of which is the assessed correlation of opposing forces. For example, on 14 October 1943, Army Group Center numbered 914,500 men, 594 tanks (216 operable), and 2,577 guns and mortars. German intelligence assessed Red Army strength in the same sector at 1,664,000 personnel (162,500 of which were in reserve), supported by 3,060 tanks (1,740 in reserve), and 6,720 guns and mortars (350 in reserve).[6] Soviet documents assert that the Red Army's personnel strength in the same sector in March 1944 stood at 1,725,000 soldiers.[7] Considering losses suffered and replacements received during the intervening period, Soviet strength in this sector was likely between 1.6 and 1.7 million, that is, very close to the German estimate. Given these figures, Soviet superiority along the western axis was 1.8 to 1 in infantry, 5 to 1 in tanks, and almost 3 to 1 in artillery. This superiority only strengthened the *Stavka*'s confidence and resolve that the Red Army could indeed achieve success along the western axis in the fall.

Subsequently, this official history devoted only five pages to the ensuing offensive action along the western axis, whereas it spent almost twenty pages detailing the more spectacular and successful Red Army operations in the Ukraine. Likewise, the Russian four-volume history of the war published in 1999 devotes a mere paragraph to operations along the western strategic axis in the fall of 1943, whereas it spends an entire chapter detailing the course of operations around Kiev alone.[8]

Other Soviet military histories, operational studies, memoirs, and unit histories provide some details about operations conducted along the western axis but only when these operations achieved marked local successes. For example, these include descriptions of the Kalinin Front's operations at Nevel' in October 1943 and its operations (as the 1st Baltic Front) in the Gorodok region during November and December 1943. However, Soviet and Russian authors have written little or nothing about the same *front*'s savage battles on the eastern approaches to Vitebsk from early October to the end of December 1943. Similarly, these histories describe the Central (Belorussian) Front's Gomel' operation in late October and its Gomel'-Rechitsa offensive in November 1943 extensively. On the contrary, they pay little attention to the less dramatic attacks that characterized this period or the counterattacks the Germans conducted in December that restored the integrity of their defensive front.

Thus, Soviet and Russian historians have paid considerable attention to the Kalinin and Central Fronts' battles along the northern and southern flanks of the western axis, but until very recently have studiously ignored the events that took place in the center. There, over a period of three months, the Western Front conducted at least five offensives that ended in bloody failures, which prompted these historians to expunge these operations from the historical record almost en toto.[9] This chapter will restore the historical record and also fill in many of the gaps that exist in the record of operations in other sectors of the western axis.

24 The Struggle for Belorussia, October–December 1943

In late September 1943, at a time when the Kalinin, Western, and Briansk Fronts were completing their Smolensk and Briansk operations and the Central Front was driving westward from Kursk toward Chernigov and the Dnepr River, the *Stavka* had begun to widen its strategic horizons. In a clear exercise of foresight, it envisioned further offensive operations after the *fronts* participating in the summer strategic offensive had fulfilled their missions (see Map 2.2). Quite naturally, the *Stavka*'s gaze turned to the territory beyond the Dnepr, Sozh, and Pronia Rivers, specifically Belorussia and its capital city of Minsk. Beginning in mid-September, the *Stavka* began issuing a series of fresh directives to its *fronts* operating along the western axis. Collectively, these directives provided shape, form, and intent to what became the Belorussian strategic offensive operation, the capstone of the summer–fall campaign.

Like many major operations earlier in the war, the new offensive wave developed while most of the participating forces were literally still on the march westward. As the *Stavka* well knew, it was taking some strategic risks. Most of these advancing armies had been in continuous combat for almost two months, and the incessant and often heavy fighting had taken an inexorable toll on their combat capability. For example, the tank forces that had participated in and often spearheaded Soviet forces during the Smolensk, Briansk, and Chernigov-Pripiat' operations were worn out and required rest and refitting. The 3rd Guards Tank Army was diverted southward toward Kiev, and the 2nd and 4th Tank Armies, along with the 1st and 5th Guards Tank Armies, were refitting in the *Stavka*'s Reserves. Soviet rifle forces, that is, rifle divisions and rifle brigades, were weakened by months of combat, and, by October 1943, those in most sectors numbered 3,000 to 6,000 men each.

Despite the weakened state of its forces, the *Stavka* acted on the presumption that the defending Germans had also suffered and, given their inferior numbers, were unlikely to be able to withstand yet another major onslaught. Moreover, in fall 1943 the Germans would have to face two major onslaughts, one into the Ukraine and the second into Belorussia. Somewhere—perhaps everywhere—the *Stavka* reasoned, German defenses were bound to collapse under the unrelenting pressure of Red Army offensive actions.

German defenses in Belorussia were weak indeed, largely because of the losses Army Group Center suffered from July through September while trying in vain to halt the Soviet's Smolensk offensive (Operation Suvorov) and subsequent Briansk offensive.

As Table 2.2 indicates, the combined strengths of the three attacking Soviet *fronts* were markedly superior to Army Group Center simply in terms of the numbers of their subordinate forces. The comparison is even more pronounced when expressed in terms of soldiers, tanks, and artillery. For example, a periodic report that the German Army High Command's

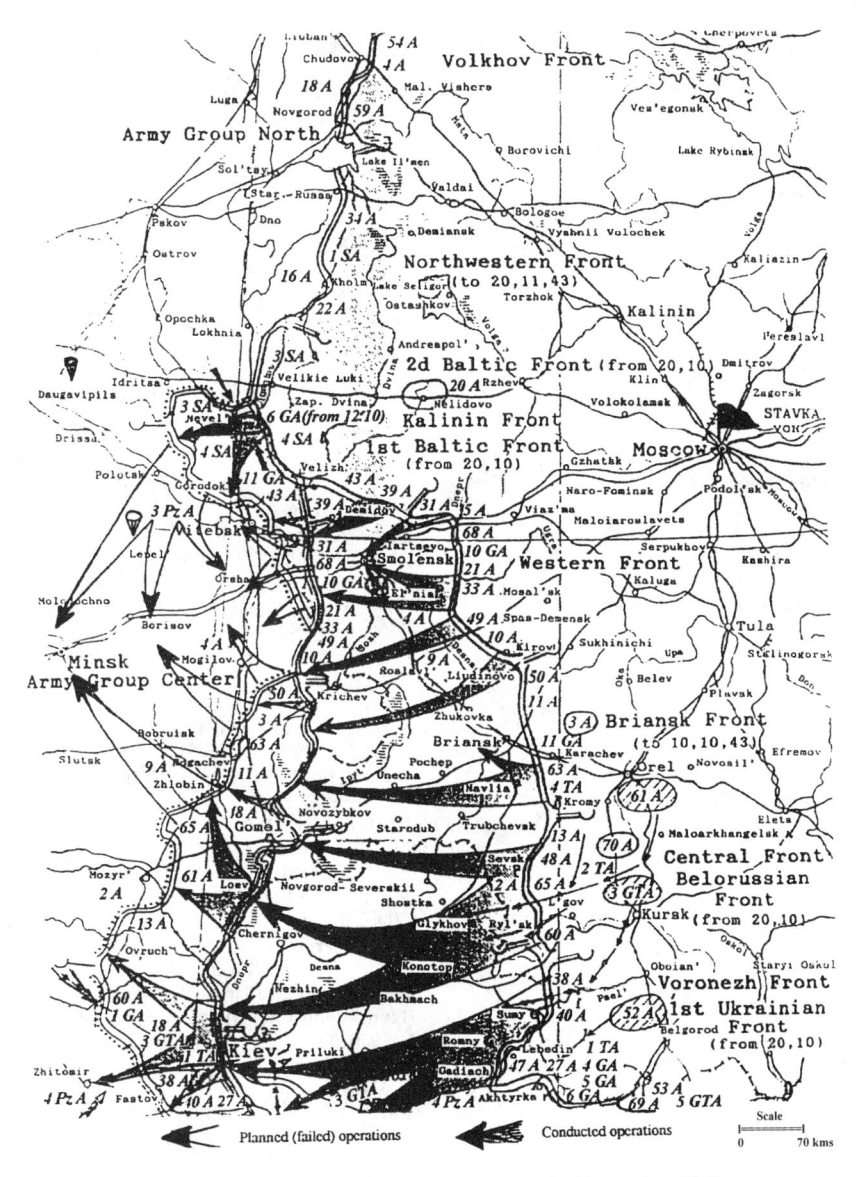

Map 2.2. Red Army Operations in Belorussia, 23 August–31 December 1943

(*Oberkommando des Heeres,* or OKH) intelligence organ, Foreign Armies East (*Fremde Heere Ost,* or FHO), issued on 17 October assessed the following balance of opposing forces in Army Group Center's sector (see Table 2.3).

In reality, the Soviet personnel strength figures shown in the FHO's report turned out to be underestimates of actual Red Army strength. For example,

Table 2.2. General View of Opposing German and Soviet Forces in Eastern Belorussia (the sector from Idritsa southward to the Pripiat' River) on 1 October 1943

GERMAN	SOVIET
Army Group North	
Sixteenth Army	**Northwestern Front**
II Army Corps	**22nd Army**
218th ID	8th G, 33rd RDs
93rd ID	54th RB
12th ID	44th RC (119th GRD, 11th, 15th GNRBs, 32nd, 46th RBs)
331st ID	**Kalinin Front**
XXXXIII Army Corps	**3rd Shock Army**
205th ID	21st, 46th G, 28th, 178th, 185th, 357th RDs
83rd ID	23rd, 31st, 100th RBs
263rd ID	5th, 118th FRs
	78th TB
Army Group Center	
Third Panzer Army	
II Luftwaffe Field Corps	**4th Shock Army**
2nd LFD	2nd GRC (16th, 117th, 360th RDs)
6th LFD	83rd RC (47th, 234th, 235th, 381st RDs)
3rd LFD	92nd RC (332nd, 358th RDs, 101stRB)
4th LFD	334th RD, 145th RB
	155th FR
	171st TBn
VI Army Corps	**43rd Army**
87th ID	1st RC (145th, 204th, 262nd RDs)
14th ID (Mot)	91st RC (179th, 270th, 306th RDs)
206th ID	114th RB
256th ID	28th GTB, 46th, 47th MBs, 105th TR
KGr., 246th ID	1820th SPR
	39th Army
	5th GRC (9th, 17th, 19th G, 97th RDs)
	84th RC (134th, 158th, 184th, 219th RDs)
	91st G, 32nd RDs, 124th RB
	60th TB, 27th TR, 1818th SPR
	Front Reserves
	8th RC (7th, 249th RDs)
	60th RC (119th, 154th RDs)
	146th, 236th TBs, 11th G, 203rd, 221st, 226th TRs
	Western Front
	5th Army
	207th, 312th RDs—208th RD (7 Oct.)
Fourth Army (Colonel General Gotthard Heinrici)	**31st Army**
XXVII Army Corps	36th RC (215th, 274th, 359th RDs)
KGr., 52nd ID	71st RC (82nd, 133rd, 331st RDs)
197th ID	42nd GTB, 2nd GMtcR
18th PzGrD	**68th Army**
18th PzD (remnants)	45th RC (88th, 251st RDs)
	72nd RC (192nd, 199th RDs)
	81st RC (Hq only)
	159th, 220th RDs
	1435th, 1445th SPRs

Table 2.2. *continued*

GERMAN	SOVIET
XXXIX Panzer Corps	
25th PzGrD	**10th Guards Army**
	7th GRC (29th G, 208th RDs)
	15th GRC (30th, 85th GRDs)
	19th GRC (22nd, 56th, 65th GRDs)
	153rd TB, 119th TR
337th ID	**21st Army**
KGr. 113th ID	61st RC (62nd, 95th, 157th RDs)
	69th RC (76th, 153rd, 174th RDs)
	63rd RD
	2nd GTC (4th, 25th, 26th GTBs, 4th GMRB, 1812th, 1813th SPRs)
	23rd GTB, 64th G, 248th TRs, 1494th, 1830th SPRs
95th ID	**33rd Army**
IX Army Corps	65th RC (58th, 144th RDs)
78th AssltD	70th RC (338th, 371st RDs)
252nd ID	42nd, 164th, 173rd, 222nd, 290th RDs
	43rd G, 256th TBs, 56th GTR, 1495th, 1537th SPRs, 520th TBn
342nd ID	**49th Army**
KGr. 330th ID	62nd RC (70th, 160th RDs)
35th ID	277th, 344th, 352nd RDs, 36th RB
	106th TB
XII Army Corps	**10th Army**
26th ID	38th RC (64th, 330th, 385th RDs)
KGr., 56th ID	49th, 139th, 212th, 247th RDs
	***Front* Reserves**
	1st ID (Polish)
	152nd, 154th FRs
	3rd GCC (5th, 6th G, 32nd CDs, 1814th SPR)
	6th GCC (8th, 13th G, 8th CDs)
	5th MC (2nd, 9th, 45th MBs, 233rd TB, 1827th SPR)
	2nd G, 94th, 120th, 213th TBs, 58th, 63rd G, 161st, 187th TRs, 12th, 41st AerosanyBns
Ninth Army (Field Marshal Walther Model)	***Central Front***
XXXXI Panzer Corps	**50th Army** (from the Briansk Front)
131st ID	46th RC (238th, 369th, 413th RDs)
260th ID	108th, 110th, 324th, 380th RDs
267th ID	8th G, 233rd TRs
LV Army Corps	**3rd Army** (from the Briansk Front)
Rest., 36th ID	41st RC (120th G, 186th, 283rd RDs)
211st ID	80th RC (121st G, 17th, 362nd RDs)
110th ID	269th RD
	13th G, 36th, 225th TRs, 1538th SPR
XXIII Army Corps	**63rd Army**
383th ID	35th RC (5th, 250th, 397th RDs)
296th ID	40th RC (129th, 287th, 348th RDs)
253rd ID	41st, 169th RDs
	26th GTR, 1901st SPR

Table 2.2. continued

GERMAN	SOVIET
Second Army (Colonel General Walter Weiss)	
XXXV Army Corps	**48th Army**
299th ID	42nd RC (73rd, 307th, 399th RDs)
216th ID	102nd, 137th, 170th, 175th, 194th RDs
292nd ID	193rd TR
45th ID	
XX Army Corps	**65th Army**
KGr., 6th ID	19th RC (37th G, 140th, 162nd, 354th RDs)
KGr., 31st ID	27th RC (149th, 193rd RDs, 115th RB)
KGr., 102nd ID	18th RC (60th, 69th, 246th RDs)
XXXXVI Panzer Corps	106th RD
Rest, 7th ID	45th, 255th TRs
KGr., 137th ID	**61st Army**
KGr., 251st ID	29th RC (15th, 55th, 81st RDs)
LVI Panzer Corps	89th RC (336th, 356th, 415th RDs)
KGr., 86th ID	9th GRC (12th, 76th, 77th GRDs)
	7th GCC (14th, 15th, 16th GCDs, 1897th SPR)
	68th TB
KGr., 4th PzD	**13th Army**
KGr., 12th PzD	28th RC (181st, 211th RDs)
2nd PzD	15th RC (8th, 74th, 148th RDs)
5th PzD	17th GRC (6th, 70th G, 322nd RDs)
	129th TB, 29th GTR
	Front Reserves
	115th, 119th, 161st FRs
	9th TC (23rd, 95th, 108th TBs, 8th MRB, 1455th SPR)
	2nd GCC (from Briansk Front) (3rd, 4th, 17th GCDs, 1812th SPR)
	251st TR
Army Group Reserves	
VIII Army Corps (Hungarian) (1st, 5th, 9th, 12th, 18th, 23rd IDs	
201st, 203rd, 286th SecDs	
2nd Slovak ID	
OKH Reserves	
KGr., 20th PzD	
129th ID	
134th ID	
707th ID	

Sources: "Kriegsgliederung der Heeresgruppe Mitte (Stand: Anfang Oktober 1943)," BA-MA, Studie ZA 1/2053; KTB OKW, Bd 3/2, S. 1157; and *Boevoi sostav Sovetskoi Armii, chast' III (Ianvar'–dekabr' 1943 g.)* [The combat composition of the Soviet Army, pt. 3 (January–December 1943) (Moscow: Voenizdat, 1972), 244–250.

although the FHO estimated that the Red Army numbered 5,510,000 troops on 1 October, Soviet records indicate that the strength of the Red Army's operating armies was about 6,500,000 troops, backed up by about 500,000 troops in the RVGK. If this underestimation of roughly 20 percent is applied to the central portion of Germany's Eastern Front, then Army Group Center likely faced slightly more than 2 million Red Army troops, that is, a twofold

Table 2.3. Opposing Forces in Army Group Center's Sector on 14 October 1943

Category	ARMY GROUP CENTER at the Front	in Reserve	Total	SOVIET FORCES at the Front	in Reserve	Total
Infantry divisions	46	0	46	161	11	172
Panzer divisions	7	1	8	45	56	101
Troops	914,500	10,500	925,000	1,501,500	162,500	1,664,000
Tanks and self-propelled (SP) guns	594 (216)	0	594 (216)	1,320	1,740	3,060
Artillery and Mortars	2,577	0	2,577	6,370	350	6,720

Notes:
1. Subordinate forces are as of 14 October, personnel and panzer (tank) figures are as of 1 October, and artillery and mortar numbers are as of 1 September.
2. Figures in parenthesis ( ) denote combat ready tanks and SP guns.
3. For Soviet figures, 2 rifle brigades = 1 rifle division, 2 cavalry divisions = 1 rifle division, 1 tank brigade = 1 tank unit, 6 tank regiments = 5 tank units, and 3 tank battalions = 2 tank units.

Source: "Kräftegegenüberstellung Stand: 14.10.43," *Anlage 4 c zu Abt. Fr. H. Ost (I) Nr. 80/43 g.Kdos vom 17.10.43.* This is a copy of the original.

Soviet superiority.[10] Mitigating this clear superiority was the fact that most of the Red Army's divisions and brigades were operating at or below 50 percent of their required strength, that is, within a range of 5,000 to 6,000 troops per division and 3,000 to 4,000 per brigade. Although German units were also woefully understrength, with many divisions operating in *kampfgruppe* configuration, the Soviet shortage of full-strength divisions and brigades seriously damaged the cohesion and combat effectiveness of Red Army armies and corps, especially while on the offense.

The discrepancy between German and Soviet forces in terms of armor was even more pronounced in the Red Army's favor. For example, Table 2.4 shows the strength of the five panzer divisions subordinate to Army Group Center on 1 October in terms of tanks, armored personnel carriers (APCs), self-propelled (SP) *Paks* (antitank guns), and artillery pieces, some of which were self-propelled.

Thus, the six panzer divisions subordinate to Army Group Center fielded 126 tanks (including 66 in short-term repair), 50 SP *Paks* (antitank guns; including 15 in short-term repair), and 140 artillery pieces (including 20 in short-term repair), some of which were self-propelled, on 1 October 1943. In addition, the remainder of the 216 operable tanks, assault guns, and SP *Paks* in the army group were situated in *Abteilungen* (detachments) attached to the army group and to its subordinate corps and divisions, especially panzer grenadier divisions.

According to German assessments, the three Red Army *fronts* operating against Army Group Center fielded an estimated 1,320 tanks and SP guns, backed up by another 1,700 in the *Stavka*'s Reserve, meaning that the Soviets enjoyed a superiority of more than 6 to 1 in armor. The Russians

Table 2.4. Weaponry of Army Group Center's Panzer Divisions on 1 October 1943

- **2nd Panzer Division**—15 tanks (4 Pz. III and 4 Pz. IV operable) (7 in short-term repair), 222 (39) APCs, 11 (5) SP *Paks*, and 18 (1) artillery pieces, including 9 (1) SP;
- **4th Panzer Division**—9 operable Pz. IV tanks, 132 (8) APCs, 11 SP *Paks*, and 24 (2) artillery pieces;
- **5th Panzer Division**—21 tanks (1 Pz. III and 1 Pz. IV operable) (19 in short-term repair), 180 (35) APCs, 12 (3) SP *Paks*, and 38 (7) artillery pieces;
- **12th Panzer Division**—31 tanks (2 Pz. III and 15 Pz. IV operable) (14 in short-term repair), 26 (11) APCs, 8 (4) SP *Paks*, and 32 (4) artillery pieces, including 4 (2) SP;
- **18th Panzer Division**—26 tanks (6 Pz. III and 6 Pz. IV operable) (14 in short-term repair); and
- **20th Panzer Division**—24 tanks (3 Pz. III and 9 Pz. IV operable) (12 in short-term repair), 31 (8) APCs, 8 (3) SP *Paks*, and 28 (6) artillery pieces.

Notes: 1. The numbers in parenthesis denote equipment in short-term repair.
2. The 18th Panzer Division was disbanded, with its personnel and equipment turned over to XXVII Army Corps and the corps' 18th Panzer Grenadier Division.
Source: Kamen Nevenkin, *Fire Brigades: The Panzer Divisions, 1943–1945* (Winnipeg, Canada: J. J. Fedorowicz, 2008), 112–113, 160–161, 182–183, 326–327, 438, and 475–476.

have not released enough data to verify the precise armored strength of the Kalinin, Western, and Central Fronts and their subordinate armored forces on 1 October. However, based on their initial combined strength of 1,883 tanks in late August and their documented loss of 863 tanks during the Smolensk offensive, on 1 October the Kalinin and Western Fronts fielded at least 1,020 tanks and SP guns. Similarly, based on its strength of 610 tanks and SP guns in early September, its loss of about 250 tanks and SP guns during the Chernigov-Pripiat' offensive, and the tanks and SP guns it received from the disbanded Briansk Front, the Central Front probably fielded upward of 500 tanks on 1 October.[11] Therefore, even discounting replacement armor received, the armored strength of the three Red Army *fronts* was likely more than 1,500 machines, roughly 200 more than the FHO's estimate for Soviet forces at the front.

In regard to the FHO's estimate of more than 1,700 tanks and SP guns from the *Stavka*'s Reserve in Army Group Center's sector, it is likely too high. The fact is that most of the armored vehicles the Soviets produced in August and September 1943 were used to make up for losses suffered during July and August. For example, during late August and September the *Stavka* withdrew the Red Army's 1st, 2nd, and 4th Tank Armies and 5th Guards Tank Army, along with 5 tank and 3 mechanized corps, 8 tank brigades, and 12 tank regiments into its Reserve for rest and refitting.[12] This process required equipping each tank army with 400 to 650 tanks, tank corps with 202 tanks, mechanized corps with 229 tanks, brigades with 53 tanks, and regiments with 39 tanks, for a total of between 4,389 and 4,989 tanks and SP guns.[13] Given this requirement, the *Stavka* had precious few tanks and SP guns it could allocate to its *fronts* operating in eastern Belorussia. As a result, during the fall offensive, it dispatched 1st and 5th Tank Corps, the former part of 11th Guards Army, to reinforce the Kalinin (1st Baltic) Front and 1st Guards Tank Corps to reinforce the Central (Belorussian) Front. This amounted to a total of about 650 tanks and SP guns. The 1st Baltic and Belorussian Fronts employed all three of these corps as mobile groups designated to conduct deep operations. In addition, when the *Stavka* finally committed its five refitted tank armies to combat at the front during the late fall, it did so in the Ukraine because it believed terrain and weather conditions in that region were more conducive to their effective employment.

Finally, the largest tank formations facing Army Group Center were the Western Front's 2nd Guards Tank Corps and 5th Mechanized Corps and Central Front's 9th Tank Corps, all of which were understrength from previous fighting and likely fielded no more than 100 tanks each. None of these corps was strong enough to conduct exploitation operations. In addition, the three *fronts* included 18 tank brigades, 25 separate tank and 12 separate self-propelled artillery regiments, and 2 separate tank battalions, which, if at full strength, should have counted 2,001 tanks and 252 self-propelled guns. The *fronts* employed these forces primarily for infantry support. For the sake of comparison, by 1 January 1944, the same three *fronts* fielded 17 tank brigades, 16 separate tank and 13 separate self-propelled artillery regiments, and 1 separate tank battalion. Although these armored forces may have been stronger than those present on 1 October, the quantity of infantry support armor available to the three *fronts* clearly did not increase significantly during the fall.

THE KALININ FRONT'S VITEBSK AND NEVEL' OFFENSIVES (3–12 OCTOBER 1943)

The first stage of the Belorussian strategic offensive operation began in early October when all three Soviet *fronts* launched major assaults in the entire sector stretching from Vitebsk in the north to the mouth of the Pripiat' River in the south. Their objective was to dismember and defeat Army Group Center, the Red Army's principal nemesis, whose commander was Field Marshal Gunter von Kluge. The northernmost of these *fronts* was Army General A. I. Eremenko's Kalinin Front, which in late September was in the process of completing its participation in the Dukhovshchina-Demidov offensive alongside the Western Front, whose forces were assaulting German defenses at Smolensk (see Map 2.3). Most histories have detailed the Kalinin Front's dramatic offensive against Nevel', but few have even mentioned its operations against the *front*'s principal target, the city of Vitebsk.

The 1976 Russian official history of the war provides the accepted view of the course and outcome of the Vitebsk operation but covers only the successful portion, specifically, the capture of Nevel':

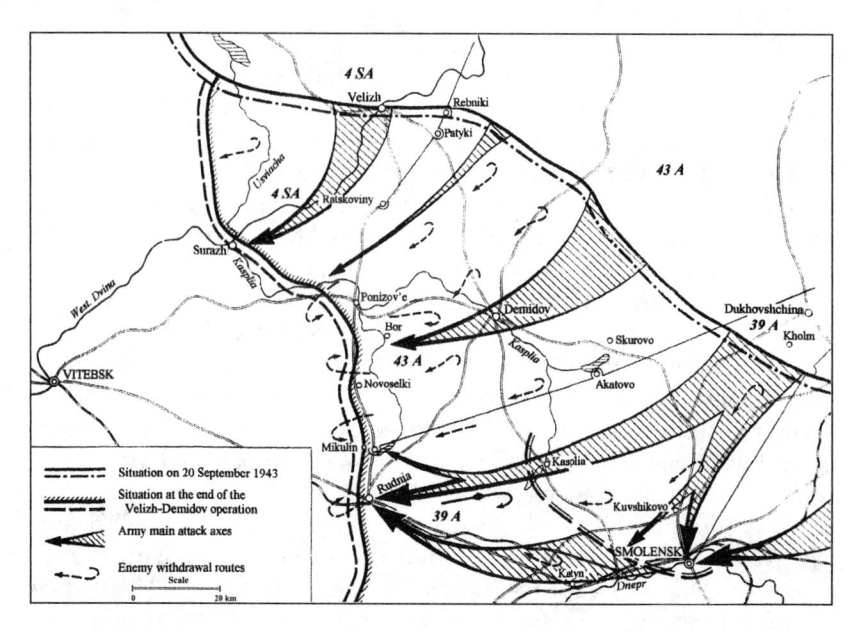

Map 2.3. The Kalinin Front's Dukhovshchina Offensive Operation, 20 September–2 October 1943

The offensive along the western axis began on 6 October along a 550-kilometer front from Nevel' to the mouth of the Pripiat' River. The forces on the right wing of the Kalinin Front launched an offensive along the Nevel' axis. The attack occurred against the 3rd Panzer Army, which was defending the junction between Army Groups "North" and "Center." Nevel' was located in a region abounding in forests, lakes, and swamps that were difficult to traverse. The Fascists had strongly fortified the city and the adjacent heights and mined the roads on the approaches to them. Therefore, the battles of the 3rd and 4th Shock Armies under the command of Generals K. N. Galitsky and V. I. Shvetsov became sustained and bitter from the very first day. On Goering's order, a considerable part of 6th Air Fleet's aircraft was transferred to the Nevel' region to support the defending formations.

General N. F. Papivin's 3rd Air Army took part in the struggle against the enemy aircraft. The strength of the Soviet attack increased. Destroying the strong points on the approaches to Nevel' one after another, they penetrated into the city on the night of 7 October and liberated it in the morning. The 3rd and 4th Shock Armies had advanced 25–30 kilometers by 10 October.

The liberation of Nevel' had great importance. The Hitlerites' defense, anchored on the triangle formed by Novosokol'niki, Velikie Luki, and

Nevel', was smashed. The main Dno-Novosokol'niki, Nevel' railroad line, which connected Army Groups "North" and "Center," was cut, and a 20-kilometer gap was formed between them. . . .

The Kalinin Front opened the roads to Polotsk and Vitebsk. Considering Vitebsk to be the gate to the Baltic region, the German command decided to hold on to Vitebsk at all cost. They also strove to prevent Soviet forces from approaching the Polotsk region, where the extensive Polotsk-Lepel' partisan region existed. The loss of these cities would threaten the rear area of Army Groups "North" and "Center."

Hoping to localize the penetration and prevent a subsequent advance by the attacking forces, the enemy transferred two infantry divisions from Leningrad and five infantry and panzer divisions from the southern group of Army Group "Center" into the Gorodok region, which was located between Nevel' and Vitebsk, and reinforced his aviation. However, his urgent attempts to liquidate the penetrating Soviet forces and drive them back from Nevel' turned out to be unsuccessful.[14]

Eremenko, the commander of the Kalinin Front, recalled the origins of the Vitebsk operation more fully in his memoirs. As he did, he reflected on the hasty planning for the operation, which began before the previous Dukhovshchina operation was complete:

An attack on Velizh and Demidov was planned long before the beginning of the Dukhovshchina operation as the first step of the Polotsk-Vitebsk operation. Then the situation changed, and it was decided to carry out the Dukhovshchina operation first. As soon as Dukhovshchina was captured, the Velizh-Demidov operation was to begin in turn in order to strengthen the blow. By doing so we had in mind that the heavy fighting at Dukhovshchina would force the enemy to weaken his forces along the Velizh-Demidov axis. . . .

The *front* staff prepared a plan for the Velizh-Demidov operation and dispatched the document with its views to the General Staff as early as 15 September.[15]

Quoting from his proposal to the *Stavka*, Eremenko added:

I think that it is time to open the Smolensk "gate" with a strong blow along the Velizh-Demidov axis by the Kalinin Front's forces to reach the Liozno and Rudnia regions, break up the left wing of enemy Army Group Center's front, and carry operations into Belorussia. Our forces' victorious offensive has created all of the prerequisites to do so.

I propose to conduct the operation in three stages.

The first stage—the destruction of the units of the enemy's 6th Army Corps, the capture of the towns of Velizh, Surazh-Vitebsk, and Demidov, and the forces' arrival at the Kasplia River line. To do so, it is necessary to penetrate the enemy's defense in the Velizh–Lake Baklanovskoe sector along a 30-kilometer front to a depth of 30–35 kilometers. The duration of this stage will be limited to 4–5 days.

The second stage—the final destruction of the Velizh-Demidov grouping, arrival in the Vitebsk, Krynki Station, and Liozno region, and the capture of Vitebsk. To do so, it is necessary to force the Kasplia River along a 6–10 kilometer front and advance to a depth of 45–50 kilometers in 8–10 days.

The third stage involves the development of the offensive along the Polotsk and Lepel' axes up to the arrival of the *front's* forces on the Gorodok, Beshenkovichi, and Senno front, that is, 40–50 kilometers deep in 5–6 days.

Thus, the entire operation to a depth of 115–130 kilometers can be carried out in the course of 14–17 days.[16]

Although the *Stavka* could not provide Eremenko any reinforcements, the fighting around Dukhovshchina drew German reserves to that region and facilitated Eremenko's newly planned operation. Accordingly, on 19 September he ordered 4th Shock and 43rd Armies to advance on Velizh and Demidov, respectively, while 39th Army assaulted Dukhovshchina. Velizh fell to 4th Shock Army at day's end on 20 September, and 43rd Army seized Demidov the following day.

Given the Kalinin Front's success, the *Stavka* issued a new directive to the *front* on 20 September (see Appendix A-1). The directive required Eremenko's main forces to advance to the Ponizov'e, Punitsy, Kasplia, and Tishino line by 26–27 September and to capture Vitebsk no later than 9–10 October. The *front* commander was to present his completed plan to the *Stavka* for approval by day's end on 22 September. Eremenko immediately ordered 43rd and 39th Armies to advance southwestward and westward toward Vitebsk in tandem with 5th Army on the Western Front's right flank. On 43rd Army's right flank, 4th Shock Army wheeled southwestward from the Velizh region toward Surazh. Finally, 3rd Shock Army anchored the *front's* right flank by manning defenses east of Nevel'. The 39th Army led its advance with 5th Guards Rifle Corps and a mobile group headed by Colonel I. F. Dremov, which consisted of 46th and 47th Mechanized, 28th Guards Tank, and 4th Antitank (Tank Destroyer) Artillery Brigades.[17]

As this advance developed, Eremenko and the *Stavka* exchanged proposals and counterproposals regarding the Kalinin Front's future actions. Collectively, these negotiations gave shape to his *front's* role in the forthcoming Belorussian strategic offensive. Eremenko led off on 22 September, when he presented a new set of proposals to the *Stavka* (see Appendix A-2):

Army General A. I. Eremenko, commander in chief, Kalinin (1st Baltic) Front, April–November 1943

Army General I. Kh. Bagramian, commander in chief, 1st Baltic Front, November 1943–February 1945

Lieutenant General K. N. Galitsky, commander, 3rd Shock Army, October and November 1943, and 11th Guards Army, November 1943–May 1945

Colonel General N. E. Chibisov, commander, 3rd Shock Army, November 1943–April 1944

Lieutenant General Shvetsov, commander, 4th Shock Army, May–December 1943

Lieutenant General P. F. Malyshev, commander, 4th Shock Army, December 1943–May 1945

Lieutenant General K. D. Golubev, commander, 43rd Army, October 1943– May 1944

Lieutenant General N. E. Berzarin, commander, 39th Army, September 1943– May 1944

Lieutenant General of Tank Forces
V. V. Butkov, commander, 1st Tank Corps,
September 1942–May 1945

Major General of Tank Forces
M. G. Sakhno, commander, 5th Tank
Corps, January 1943–October 1944

Lieutenant General N. S. Oslikovsky,
commander, 3rd Guards Cavalry Corps,
December 1942–May 1945

1. To make the main attack with 4th Shock, 43rd, and 39th Armies in the general direction of Vitebsk. To that end:
   (a) I will reinforce 4th Shock Army with four rifle divisions (the 234th, 235th, 117th, and 16th Lithuanian Rifle Divisions), 155th Fortified Region, 17th Antitank Brigade, 106th RVGK Artillery Regiment, and 20th Guards-Mortar Brigade;
   (b) I will form two force groupings on 4th Shock Army's front: the Velizh group, consisting of six rifle divisions, two rifle brigades, and one antitank artillery brigade, for an attack towards Vitebsk along both banks of the Western Dvina River; and the Usviaty group, consisting of three rifle divisions, for an attack in the direction of Mezha and Gorodok and, farther, on Shumilino';
   (c) I will reinforce 43rd Army with 1st Rifle Corps, consisting of two rifle divisions, the intermediate grouping of Dremov, consisting of one tank brigade, two mechanized brigades, and an antitank artillery brigade, and a howitzer brigade. While attacking in the general direction of Vitebsk, their mission is to Rudnia to assist 39th Army's offensive and cut the Vitebsk-Smolensk road and railroad line; and
   (d) The 39th Army, consisting of 10 rifle divisions and 1 rifle brigade, will attack along the Verkhov'ia-Volokovaia axis with the mission to assist the Western Front's forces in the capture of Smolensk. Subsequently, it will attack toward Rudnia and Liozno.
2. During the present stage of the operation, the *front's* forces have been ordered to defeat the Germans' Vitebsk-Demidov grouping and reach the Surazh-Vitebsk, Ponizov'e, Sel'tso, Kasplia, and Arkhipovka line by the end of 25–26 September 1943. . . .
3. The *front's* forces will reach the Kurino, Kosov, Lake Vymno, Polenovka, Ushivka, Rudnia, and Eliseevka line during the period from 26 through 29 September 1943.
4. The Kalinin Front's forces will capture Vitebsk and reach the Beguny (16 kilometers southwest of Gorodok), Ustiianova, Shchemilovka, Teliazh, and Babinovichi line along the Luchesa River during the period from 30 September through 6 October 1943.
5. The *front's* forces will reach the Sirotino, Gnezdilovichi, Tepliaki, Bogushchevsk, and Babinovichi line by the end of 9 October 1943. The 4th Shock Army's Usviaty grouping will launch its attack from the Klenidovka and Tarasovo front towards Mezha and Gorodok on 27 September 1943.
6. In order to guarantee the plan is fulfilled, I request:
   (a) Permit 8th Estonian Corps to relieve two rifle divisions on 3rd Shock Army's front for participation in the offensive.[18]

Two days later, the *Stavka* approved Eremenko's plan but required him to make several amendments to it (see Appendix A-3):

1. Shvetsov's 4th Shock Army will consist of no fewer than 13 rifle divisions with reinforcing equipment and 3 corps headquarters. Employ seven of that army's rifle divisions to attack from the Usviaty region toward Gorodok and roll up the enemy's defense with part of the force by operations toward Usviaty and Nevel'. Use no fewer than six rifle divisions for an attack on Vitebsk along the Western Dvina River.
2. Golubev's 43rd Army will consist of six-seven divisions, and Berzarin's 39th Army of no fewer than five rifle divisions. Reinforce 4th Shock Army at the expense of these two armies and three divisions being sent to you by the *Stavka*. To hasten the regrouping, carry it out by means of transferring divisions from one neighboring army to another neighboring army.
3. Leave the Estonian Corps in *front* reserve. Henceforth, do not weaken 3rd Shock Army.[19]

In late September, while Eremenko was finalizing his plans for the advance on Vitebsk, he also planned a supporting operation toward Nevel' by 3rd Shock Army on the *front*'s right wing. Eremenko later described the genesis of the Nevel' operation:

> With the completion of the Dukhovshchina-Smolensk and Velizh-Demidov operations, the Kalinin Front's forces developed the offensive against Vitebsk. The Nevel' operation was next in turn. We also planned the Nevel' operation in advance. In doing so we had in mind that, as soon as Smolensk fell, the Kalinin Front's main forces would turn to the west—against Vitebsk, thus creating conditions for the conduct of the Nevel' operation. The written directive concerning the preparation of this operation was not handed out so that we could preserve secrecy. However, 3rd and 4th Shock Armies' commanders were assigned missions to prepare this operation.
>
> They prepared the Nevel' operation over the course of one month. Given the fact that both shock armies' forces were rather limited (many had been taken from them and become worn down in previous operations), the main operational aim was to penetrate the enemy's front in a narrow sector and seize Nevel'. The town of Nevel', which was a heavily fortified strong point, was a very important railroad and road center and a large supply base. In addition, the capture of Nevel' would place the Kalinin Front's forces on the flank of the Hitlerites' Vitebsk grouping.[20]

Eremenko therefore candidly admitted that the operation against Nevel' was clearly designed to support the *front's* main effort toward Vitebsk. Other Soviet accounts written during the late 1960s confirm Eremenko's intent.

For example, two survey articles of the Nevel' operation written during this period supported Eremenko's claim that Soviet intent in the Nevel' operation was to support the main attack on Vitebsk. For example:

> [The Nevel' operation] was a local operation of the Kalinin Front. The attack on Nevel' should have riveted enemy reserves there and facilitated the offensive by the *front's* main forces against Vitebsk. In addition, the capture of Nevel'—an important railroad and road center—would seriously disrupt the German-Fascist forces' entire communications system along that axis and hamper their capability to maneuver [forces] from the Baltic to Belorussia and the Ukraine.[21]

According to yet another article:

> The planned operation had limited aims and was a part of the Kalinin Front's offensive along the Vitebsk axis. The forces of our army [3rd Shock] were to capture the road center and city of Nevel' and then, while holding to it firmly, protect the offensive by the *front's* main forces on Vitebsk from the north. Simultaneously, 3rd Shock Army's operations should have created conditions for the development of the offensive along the Gorodok and Novosokol'niki axes.[22]

While the Kalinin Front's 4th Shock, 43rd, and 39th Armies continued pressing German forces westward from Demidov and Smolensk toward Rudnia and Vitebsk, between 25 September and 3 October, Eremenko made final refinements to his plan for the Vitebsk offensive. As he did so, however, the *front* commander also added provisions for an attack on Nevel' to his grander offensive plan. This required forming a new shock group on the *front's* right wing for use in the attack on Nevel' and the concentration of forces for the assault on Vitebsk proper from the east. Eremenko formed his Nevel' shock group from the forces of his 3rd and 4th Shock Armies. He assigned 2nd Guards and 83rd Rifle Corps and 21st Artillery Division, previously controlled by 39th Army, to 4th Shock Army on 25 September. The two corps' seven rifle divisions were to join 3rd Shock Army for the assault on Nevel'. He then assigned the *front's* mobile group, consisting of 46th and 47th Mechanized and 28th Guards Tank Brigades and commanded by Colonel Dremov, to spearhead 39th Army's advance along the Smolensk-Vitebsk road. Finally, with the *Stavka's* approval, Eremenko created 60th Rifle Corps, assigning to it 119th, 154th, and 156th Rifle Divisions, for use in exploiting whatever success either of the *front's* shock groups achieved. Eremenko himself remained with 39th and 43rd Armies on the *front's* left flank to control the key operation.[23]

At the time the Nevel' operation began, Galitsky's 3rd Shock Army consisted of five rifle divisions; three rifle brigades; one tank brigade; seven gun, howitzer, mortar, tank destroyer, and antiaircraft regiments; and two field fortified regions. The rifle divisions averaged 5,000–6,000 men each, and the rifle brigades 3,000–4,000 men each. Galitsky concentrated these forces in a 4-kilometer-wide penetration sector, supported by all 54 of the army's tanks and 814 of its 886 artillery pieces and mortars. He defended the remainder of his 105-kilometer-wide sector with two fortified regions, the army's reserve regiment, four blocking detachments, and two weak understrength rifle divisions. Galitsky's operational formation consisted of a first echelon (28th and 357th Rifle Divisions), an echelon to develop success (78th Tank Brigade, with 54 tanks, 21st Guards Rifle Division, with one regiment mounted on trucks, and three artillery regiments), and a reserve (46th Guards Rifle Division and 31st and 100th Rifle Brigades). The army commander planned to precede his main attack with a reconnaissance in force beginning at 0500 hours on 6 October.[24]

On 1 October 1943, the Kalinin Front's forces faced the right wing of Army Group North's Sixteenth Army and all of Army Group Center's Third Panzer Army. The former was commanded by Field Marshal Ernst Busch, who would rise to command Army Group Center at the end of October, and the latter by Colonel General Georg Hans Reinhardt, who had commanded Third Panzer for almost two years. In fact, the boundary line separating the two army groups extended from east to west roughly 12 kilometers south of Nevel', directly opposite the focal point of Eremenko's planned offensive. North of this boundary, 263rd Infantry Division of General of Infantry Karl von Oven's XXXXIII Army Corps defended the roughly 24-kilometer-wide sector east and northeast of Nevel'. It was flanked on the left by the corps' 83rd and 205th Infantry Divisions, whose defenses stretched northward east of Novosokol'niki for about 26 kilometers. South of the boundary, 2nd Luftwaffe Field Division of General of Airborne Troops Alfred Schlemm's II Luftwaffe Field Corps defended the 14-kilometer-wide sector extending southeastward from Army Group Center's northern boundary to the northern extremity of Lake Sennitsa. It was flanked on the right by the Luftwaffe corps' 6th, 3rd, and 4th Field Divisions, whose defenses formed a 50-kilometer-long arc from northwest to southeast centered just west of the town of Usviaty, 70 kilometers northeast of Vitebsk.

While General Schlemm's four Luftwaffe divisions secured the northeastern approaches to Vitebsk, the eastern approaches to the city were protected by Third Panzer Army's VI Army Corps, commanded by Lieutenant General Hans Jordan. The VI Corps' 87th, 14th, 206th, 246th, and 256th Infantry Divisions occupied defenses in a 73-kilometer-wide sector extending from the village of Sherkovo, almost 60 kilometers northeast of Vitebsk, southward to about 10 kilometers south of the town of Rudnia, situated on the Vitebsk-Smolensk highway and railroad line, 70 kilometers southeast of Vitebsk. Although II Luftwaffe Corps' sector was relatively quiet, VI Army Corps' divisions were contending with incessant Soviet attacks. The strongest of these were in the region between the Western Dvina River and the railroad line running southeastward from Vitebsk. In particular, VI Corp's 246th and 256th Infantry Divisions, the former already reduced to *kampfgruppe* size, were struggling to contain intensifying Soviet attacks along and on both sides of the railroad west of Rudnia.

Because both II Luftwaffe and VI Army Corps were already defending in single echelon formations, with tactical reserves available only at the regimental level, both corps required assistance from Third Panzer Army should their defenses falter.

As is the case with all subsequent memoirs about these operations, Eremenko devoted most of his account of the ensuing fighting to the successful operations along the Nevel' axis, dropping only occasional hints about what actually occurred along the Vitebsk axis. Thus we know that the *front* concentrated 459 guns along the Nevel' axis (9 per kilometer of front) and 548 guns and mortars along the Vitebsk axis (12 per kilometer of front). According to Eremenko, Soviet forces outnumbered the opposing German by factors of 1.45 to 1 in infantry and 2 to 1 in artillery.

Eremenko did add a few remarks about the action along the Vitebsk axis, writing:

> While planning the Nevel' operation, we anticipated supporting the general *front* operation along the Vitebsk axis and also creating conditions conducive for developing success southward toward Gorodok and also northward and northwestward to seize the Novosokol'niki center of resistance. Thus, in the event of success in the successive and closely coordinated operations, we intended to protect the flank of the main army grouping conducting the attack on Vitebsk by an attack on Gorodok or, in favorable circumstances, capture Novosokol'niki by a surprise attack. Furthermore, the attack on Nevel' diverted considerable German forces, and its success would disrupt the entire enemy communications system, since it [Nevel'] was the Novosokol'niki-Gorodok, Pustoshka-Opochka-Pskov-Polotsk-Idritsa-Sebezh, and Nevel'-Velizh road center. This would prevent the enemy from maneuvering from the north to support his Vitebsk grouping.[25]

Numerous detailed Soviet and German accounts exist of the fighting around Nevel' (see Map 2.4). There, Eremenko's forces commenced their assault at 1000 hours after conducting a reconnaissance in force at 0500 hours and a ninety-minute artillery preparation at 0840 hours, followed by bombing strikes by several groups of six to eight aircraft from 21st Assault Aviation Regiment.[26] Lieutenant General K. N. Galitsky's 3rd Shock Army began its attack in the Zhigary-Shliapy sector, precisely at the boundary between Army Groups North and Center. The 28th Rifle Division spearheaded the

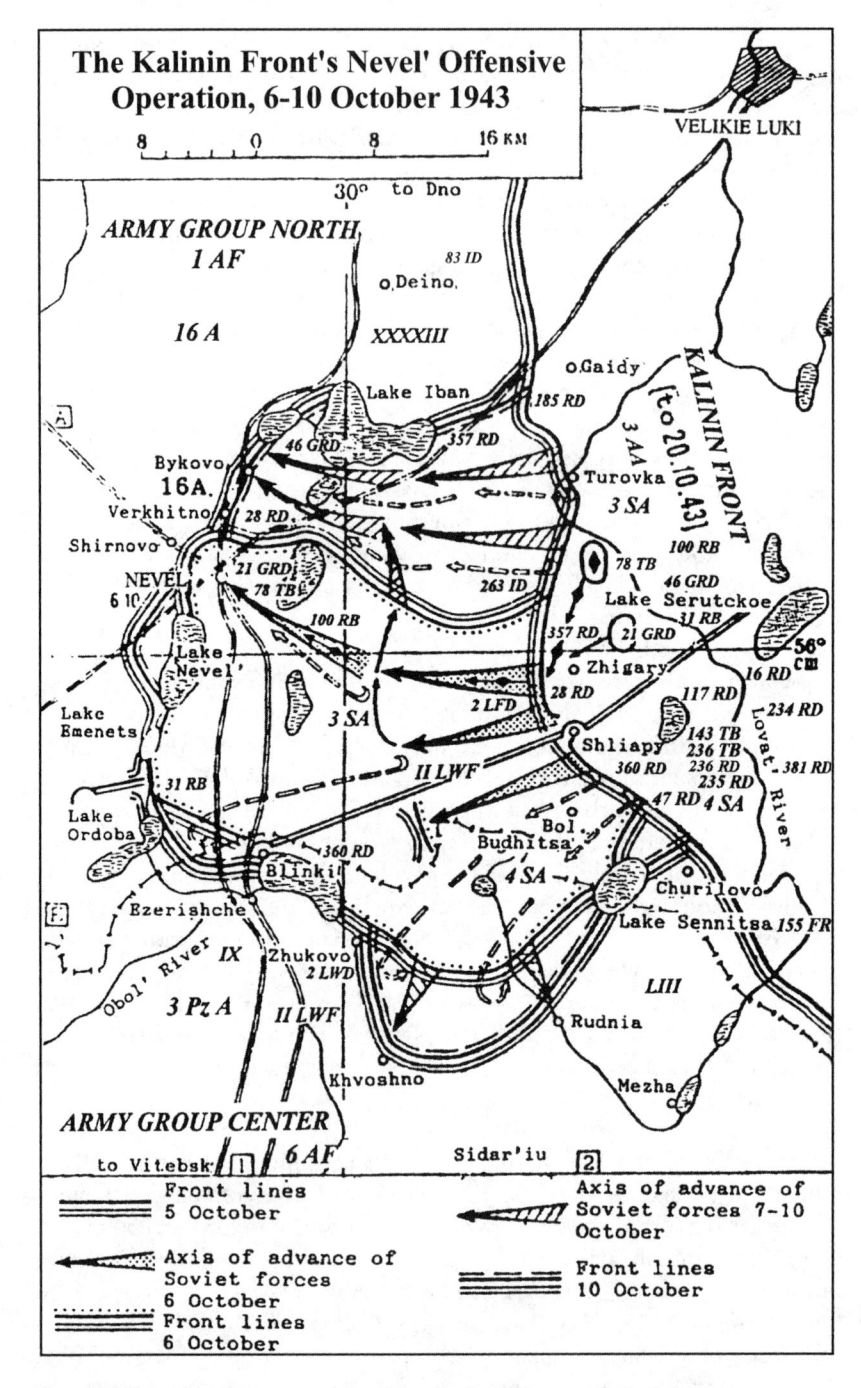

Map 2.4. The Kalinin Front's Nevel' Offensive Operation, 6–10 October 1943

assault in the first echelon, followed closely by an echelon to exploit success consisting of 21st Guards Rifle Division and 78th Tank Brigade, the latter with a force of fifty-four tanks. The assaulting force struck and demolished 2nd Luftwaffe Field Division (II Luftwaffe Corps) of Army Group Center's Third Panzer Army and smashed the right flank of 263rd Infantry Division (XXXXIII Army Corps) of Army Group North's Sixteenth Army. Although the Germans were able to contain 357th Division's attack, 28th Rifle Division penetrated the Germans' first defensive position by 1200 hours on 6 October, and the follow-on 78th Tank Brigade and mounted regiment of 21st Guards Rifle Division tore deep into the German defenses, seizing Nevel' in a coup de main by day's end. Galitsky's other forces, including 357th Rifle and 46th Guards Rifle Divisions and 100th and 31st Rifle Brigades, joined the assault and by 10 October had seized the city of Nevel' along with a 25-kilometer-deep salient in the former German defense anchored on the city.

General Galitsky's message to *front* headquarters that evening announced:

> By day's end on 6.10.43, after the penetration of the enemy's defenses by 28th Rifle Division, the echelon to develop success of the army's shock group, consisting of 78th Tank Brigade, 21st Guards Rifle Division, and 163rd Antitank and 827th Howitzer Artillery Regiments, captured the city of Nevel' by a decisive advance, and, while destroying separate enemy garrisons en route, occupied a defense north and northwest of the city. In the city of Nevel', the enemy garrison was destroyed, and many warehouses, vehicles, and other equipment were seized. There are prisoners. The quantity of trophies is being calculated.[27]

Simultaneously, Major General V. I. Shvetsov's 4th Shock Army, deployed on 3rd Shock Army's left, also launched an attack toward Gorodok. General Shvetsov conducted his attack with a shock group formed from two rifle corps, each advancing abreast in three echelons. On the right, 2nd Guards Rifle Corps' 360th Rifle Division led the assault, followed by 117th Rifle and 16th Lithuanian Rifle Divisions and 236th and 143rd Tank Brigade. On the shock group's left wing, 83rd Rifle Corps attacked with 47th Rifle Division, supported by 234th, 235th, and 381st Rifle Divisions and 236th and 143rd Tank Brigades. Shvetsov's attack penetrated German defenses to a depth of about 20 kilometers but ultimately faltered in the face of increasing German resistance just short of the Nevel'-Gorodok-Vitebsk railroad and highway.

Despite the spectacular initial success the Kalinin Front achieved in the Nevel' operation, by 10 October hastily assembled German reserves (Sixteenth Army's 58th and 122nd Infantry Divisions and elements of 281st Security Division) contained the attacking force around Nevel'. Although German forces were unable to recapture the critical communication hub, they thwarted any subsequent Soviet advance on Vitebsk. Soviet histories have lauded the spectacular Soviet accomplishments in the operation. On the contrary, although they admit the seriousness of the loss of Nevel', Western histories underscore the opportunities the attacking Soviets missed. According to Earl Ziemke:

> But in warfare combatants can occasionally have more good luck than convenient to handle, and apparently something of that sort befell *Kalinin Front* in the attack on Nevel'. For a highly skilled, flexible leadership such an occurrence could be a pleasant challenge; for a Soviet *front* command, even in late 1943, it raised many distressing uncertainties. On 9 October, the day Kuechler [the commander of Army Group North] postponed the counterattack, Yeremenko suddenly reined in on the offensive. During the several days' pause that followed, Army Groups North and Center threw a line around the western limits of the breakthrough, and each moved in a corps headquarters to command the battle area. To take further advantage of the respite the two army groups planned a counterattack by three divisions, two from Army Group North and one from Center, timed for mid-month; but at the last minute, on 14 October, Hitler forbade it because he believed the force was not strong enough.[28]

Although Soviet sources state that the Nevel' operation ended on 10 October, fighting continued through 18 October as Soviet forces attempted to improve their tactical positions and prepare for a new offensive effort.

The cost of victory at Nevel' was relatively light for Galitsky's 3rd Shock Army. The 3rd Shock's personnel losses included roughly 2,000 soldiers, 500 of whom were killed or missing in action. The 78th Tank Brigade lost only 7 of its 54 tanks. For the Germans, however, the Soviet offensive was far more costly. The surprise Soviet attacks decimated 263rd Infantry and 2nd Luftwaffe Field Division. The personnel strength of the infantry companies in the two divisions decreased from 90 to 100 men each to 27 to 30 each, and Sixteenth Army's total losses exceeded 7,000 men killed and wounded. Soviet trophies amounted to roughly 400 prisoners, 150 guns and mortars, more than 200 machine guns, 40 warehouses of various types captured in the Nevel' region, and a host of other equipment. In the wake of the fighting, Army Group Center reported, "The enemy surprise attack, supported by tanks, at the boundary of the army group led to a deep penetration and forced the withdrawal of the northern flank of II Luftwaffe Corps and the southern flank of XXXXIII Corps. Thus, there is a gap of around 20 kilometers with Army Group 'North.'"[29]

At least in part, Eremenko's failure to exploit his opportunities around Nevel' was because of his preoccupation with the progress (or lack thereof) of the *front's* main attack along the Vitebsk axis. Eremenko provides very little information in his memoirs about his conduct of operations along this axis in October and November, other than the terse comment, "However, the forces of 43rd and 39th Armies on the left flank advanced forward only 10–15 kilometers."[30] A *Stavka* directive issued on 16 October reflected this judgment by stating, "The forces of the Kalinin Front did not fulfill their assigned mission—to capture Vitebsk by 10 October."[31] As true as these statements are, they provide precious little information about the fate of the Kalinin Front's main assault on Vitebsk. Nor have other Soviet sources provided much additional information.

The only available Soviet source on the fighting east of Vitebsk is a brief combat history of 39th Army written by Lieutenant General V. R. Boiko, the "member" (commissar) of the army's Military Council. In it Boiko devoted four pages to the army's assault on German positions east of Vitebsk but provided precious little detail on what has become of one of the most elusive of many Soviet "forgotten battles."[32] Fortunately, with existing German archival materials, we can now determine the basic form and nature of this elusive operation.

Eremenko's force attacking along the Vitebsk axis consisted of 92nd Rifle Corps on 4th Shock Army's right wing and the concentrated forces of 43rd and 39th Armies (see Map 2.5). The 4th Shock Army's 92nd Rifle Corps consisted of 332nd and 358th Rifle Divisions, 101st Rifle Brigade, 171st Separate Tank Battalion, and at least four penal companies (the 39th, 40th, 43rd, and 46th). Eremenko also deployed the *front's* 334th Rifle Division and 145th Rifle Brigade on 92nd Rifle Corps' right and left wings with orders to support the corps' assault, which was to take place along the Velizh-Surazh-Vitebsk axis. On Eremenko's orders, General Shvetsov deployed 155th Fortified Region in the extended gap between his corps attacking along the Gorodok and Vitebsk axes. The reinforced 92nd Rifle Corps faced the defending German VI Army Corps' 87th Infantry Division.

Lieutenant General K. D. Golubev's 43rd Army consisted of 1st Rifle Corps (145th, 204th, and 262nd Rifle Divisions), 91st Rifle Corps (179th, 270th, and 306th Rifle Divisions), 114th Rifle Brigade, and 105th Separate Tank Regiment. Golubev deployed his two rifle corps abreast with orders to attack westward through the town of Kolyshki toward Vitebsk. His force focused its attack at the boundary between the German VI Army Corps' 14th and 206th Infantry Divisions.

Finally, 5th Guards and 84th Rifle Corps of Lieutenant General N. E. Berzarin's 39th Army, supported by Colonel Dremov's small mobile group, were to conduct the *front's* main attack through Rudnia and Liozno toward Vitebsk. Berzarin decided to conduct his main attack along the Smolensk-Vitebsk road on the army's left wing. There, he deployed 9th, 17th, and 19th Guards and 97th Rifle Divisions of Major General V. G. Pozniak's 5th Guards Rifle Corps, supported by 47th Mechanized and 28th Guards Tank Brigades,

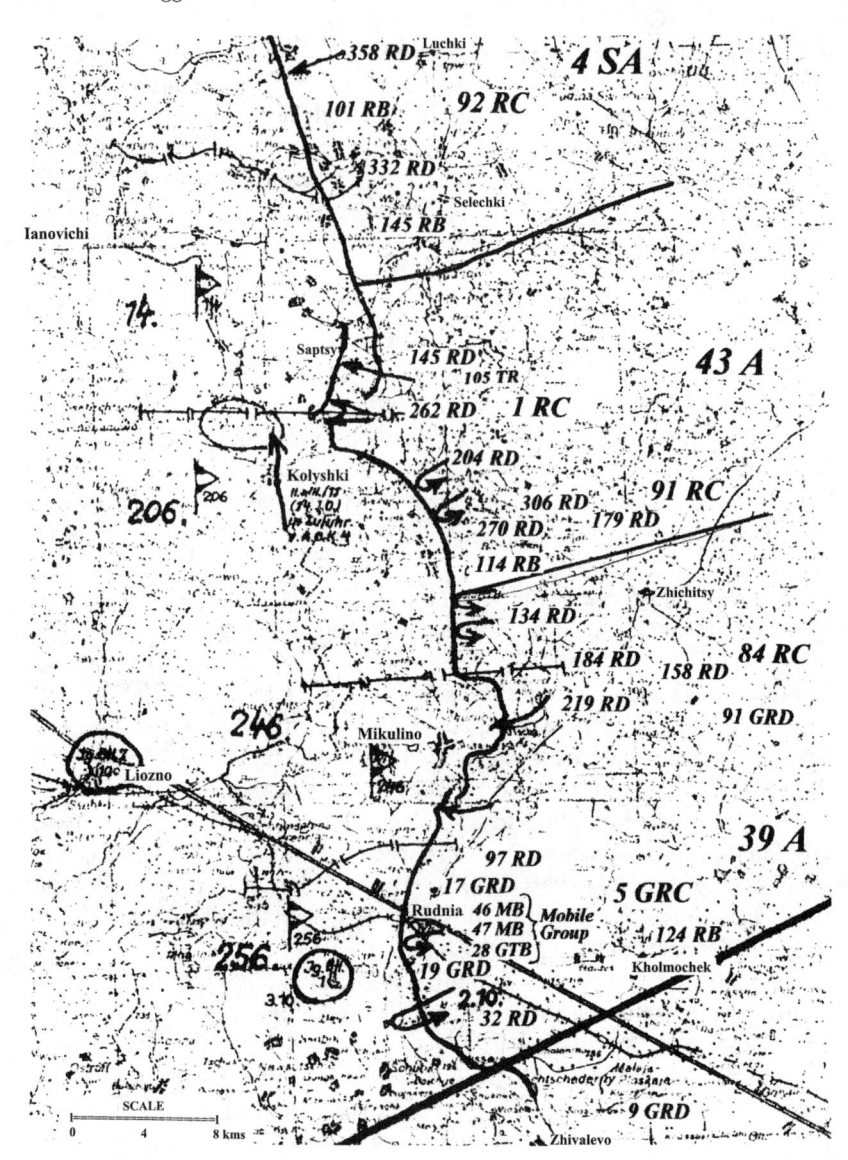

44   The Struggle for Belorussia, October–December 1943

Map 2.5. Third Panzer Army's Situation, 1 October 1943

and 1820th Antitank Regiment of Dremov's mobile group. Berzarin deployed 84th Rifle Corps' 134th, 158th, 184th, and 219th Rifle Divisions, supported by 46th Mechanized Brigade of Dremov's group, on 5th Guards Rifle Corps' right. The 4th Antitank Brigade supported the army's attack, and 91st Guards and 32nd Rifle Divisions and 124th Rifle Brigade were in the army's reserve with orders to exploit success wherever it occurred. The 39th Army faced German VI Army Corps' 246th and 256th Infantry Divisions, defending the sector from east of Mikulino to south of Rudnia.[33]

Despite Eremenko's claims to the contrary, the combined forces of 4th Shock Army's 92nd Rifle Corps and the 43rd and 39th Armies clearly outnumbered the opposing German defenders. The Kalinin Front's shock force deployed along the Vitebsk axis numbered nineteen rifle divisions, three rifle corps, two mechanized brigades, and two tank brigades, plus supporting artillery. These forces faced five German infantry divisions (the 87th, 14th, 206th, 246th, and 256th), which had virtually no tactical or operational reserves. Moreover, during the later stages of the Soviet offensive (on about 12 October) the Germans redeployed 87th Infantry Division to counter the Soviet thrust north of Gorodok. The resulting correlation of forces favored the Soviets by a factor of roughly 2 to 1 in infantry and more than 3 to 1 in artillery and armor.

During their defensive operations, the Germans concentrated their efforts on holding on to heavily fortified towns such as Liozno and Kolyshki and lesser village strong points. When these points became untenable, German forces conducted fighting withdrawals to new defensive lines prepared in advance to the rear. This tactic caused the advancing Soviet forces to deploy and regroup repeatedly throughout the operation. This, in turn, delayed the advance and caused additional Soviet casualties by forcing the attackers to conduct repeated penetration operations.

The Soviets began their attack along the Vitebsk axis almost without a halt, beginning with the assault on Rudnia in late September. Spearheaded by 1st Assault (Penal) Battalion and supported by Dremov's mobile group and 4th Antitank Artillery Brigade, 5th Guards Rifle Corps' 17th and 19th Guards and 97th Rifle Divisions captured the town on 29 September. The defending German 246th and 256th Infantry Divisions immediately withdrew to new defensive positions just west of Rudnia that covered the approaches to the next strongpoint at Liozno.[34]

While heavy fighting raged along the Kalinin Front's entire front but with only minimal Soviet gains, on 3 October 262nd Rifle Division and 105th Tank Regiment of 43rd Army's 1st Rifle Corps finally penetrated the Germans' defenses northeast of Kolyshki and advanced to the northern outskirts of the town the next day (see Map 2.6). Further south, 39th Army's 134th and 184th Rifle Divisions (of 84th Rifle Corps) breached German defenses northeast of Mikulino, and the same army's 5th Guards Rifle Corps did likewise south of Rudnia. Faced with the looming collapse of its defenses, on 6 October German forces began a fighting withdrawal to new defensive positions extending north and south of Liozno.

The pursuing Soviet forces maintained pressure on the defending Germans across the entire front but concentrated their efforts on seizing the

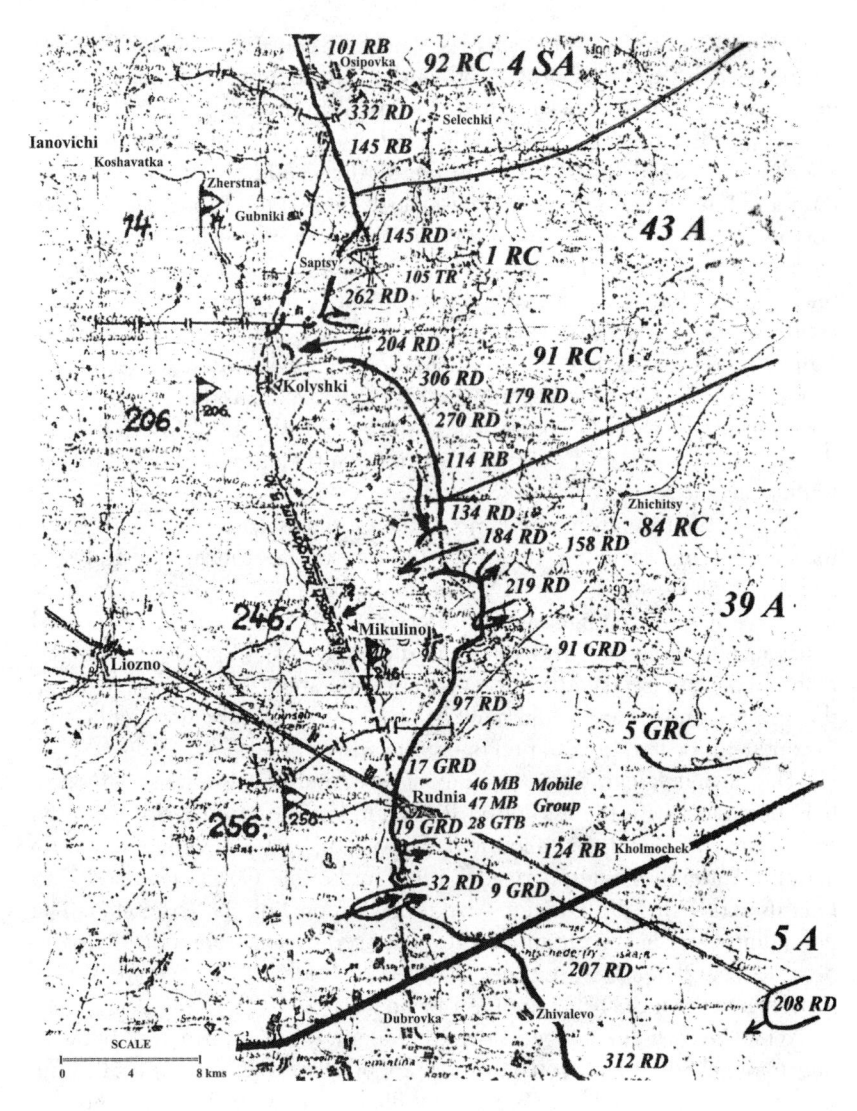

46   The Struggle for Belorussia, October–December 1943

Map 2.6. Third Panzer Army's Situation, 4 October 1943

strong-point towns of Surazh, Ianovichi, and Liozno. After closing up on the new German defense line, on 8 October 4th Shock Army's 92nd Rifle Corps launched strong attacks against the defensive positions of German 87th and 14th Infantry Divisions east of Surazh and Ianovichi (see Map 2.7). At the same time, 43rd Army's 204th Rifle Division (of 1st Rifle Corps), supported by 46th Mechanized Brigade, tore a small hole through the German 206th Infantry Division's defenses west of Kolyshki. The heaviest fighting, however,

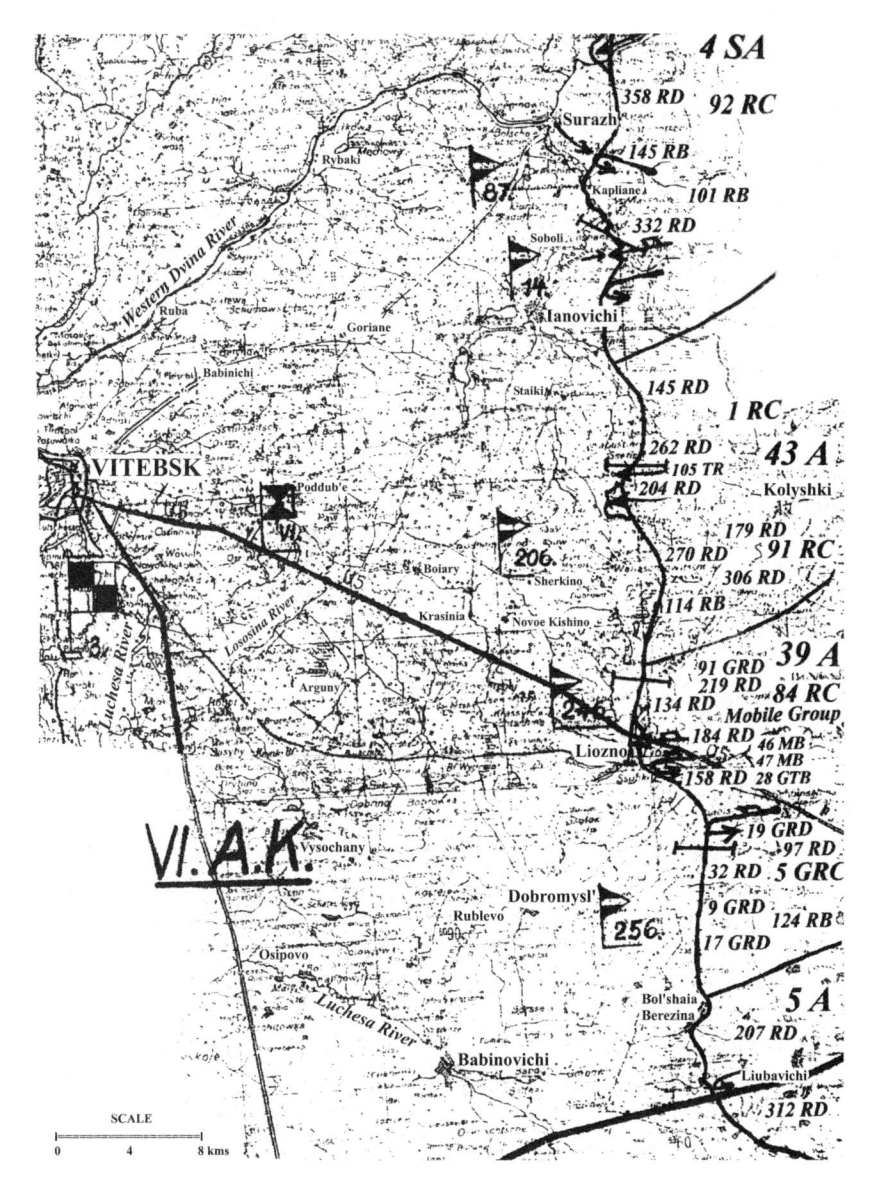

Map 2.7. Third Panzer Army's Situation, 8 October 1943

took place at Liozno, where 39th Army's 84th Rifle Corps and its mobile group conducted strong assaults against the defending German 246th Infantry Division. The 84th Corps' 134th and 158th Rifle Divisions, supported by 28th Guards Tank, 47th Mechanized, and 4th Antitank Brigades, and 1820th Self-propelled Artillery Regiment, fought for two days to clear the German defenders from the town.[35] Unable to withstand the pressure, the German defenders finally began withdrawing to new defense lines 10 kilometers to the west late on 9 October.

The German decision to withdraw was prompted both by the heavy Soviet pressure against their defenses at Surazh, Ianovichi, and Liozno and also by fresh attacks conducted by the Western Front's smaller 5th Army, operating toward and south of the town of Dobromysl' on 39th Army's left flank. The 5th Army's 207th, 208th, and 312th Rifle Divisions had added their weight to the Soviet assault by 9 October, striking the German 256th Infantry Division's right flank south of Liozno.

Although the Kalinin Front's forces pursued the withdrawing Germans vigorously, on 12 October the advancing forces encountered yet another German defensive line extending from west of Surazh southward west of Ianovichi to Babinovichi (see Map 2.8). German Third Panzer Army's decision to withdraw II Luftwaffe Corps to new positions northeast of Vitebsk in response to the fighting at Nevel' permitted the army to shorten its defensive lines and regroup its 87th Infantry Division to the Gorodok region, which was also threatened by the Soviet advance. Given the attrition caused by the nine days of heavy combat, Eremenko permitted his 43rd and 39th Armies and 4th Shock Army's 92nd Rifle Corps to pause to regroup and prepare yet another assault on Vitebsk from the east.[36]

Precious little Soviet commentary exists on this stage of the Vitebsk operation. In his account, General Boiko of 39th Army simply rationalized the Kalinin Front's failure to capture Vitebsk from the march:

> The army's forces continued active combat operations [after the fall of Liozno]. They were struck by persistent and, at times, fierce counterattacks by an enemy who was striving unsuccessfully to push us back from the positions we had seized. But, as a result of the offensive battles conducted east of Vitebsk, our units advanced a modest depth—only 25–30 kilometers east of Vitebsk—which later led some Comrades to term the actions of our army at that time unsuccessful. However, I think that such a judgment ought to be considered as extreme, which always occurs as a result of insufficiently full and objective assessment of the facts.
>
> As I already stated, the combat composition of our units and formations had been weakened considerably, especially in the guards regiments which were constantly deployed on the main axis. Furthermore, the army's forces did not concede the initiative to the enemy and did not give him the opportunity to amass forces and recover his breath in its sector of the "Belorussian balcony" (as the Germans called the salient in its defense formed to the east).
>
> In summary of the active operations on the approaches to Vitebsk, we achieved results of no small importance. First, a considerable por-

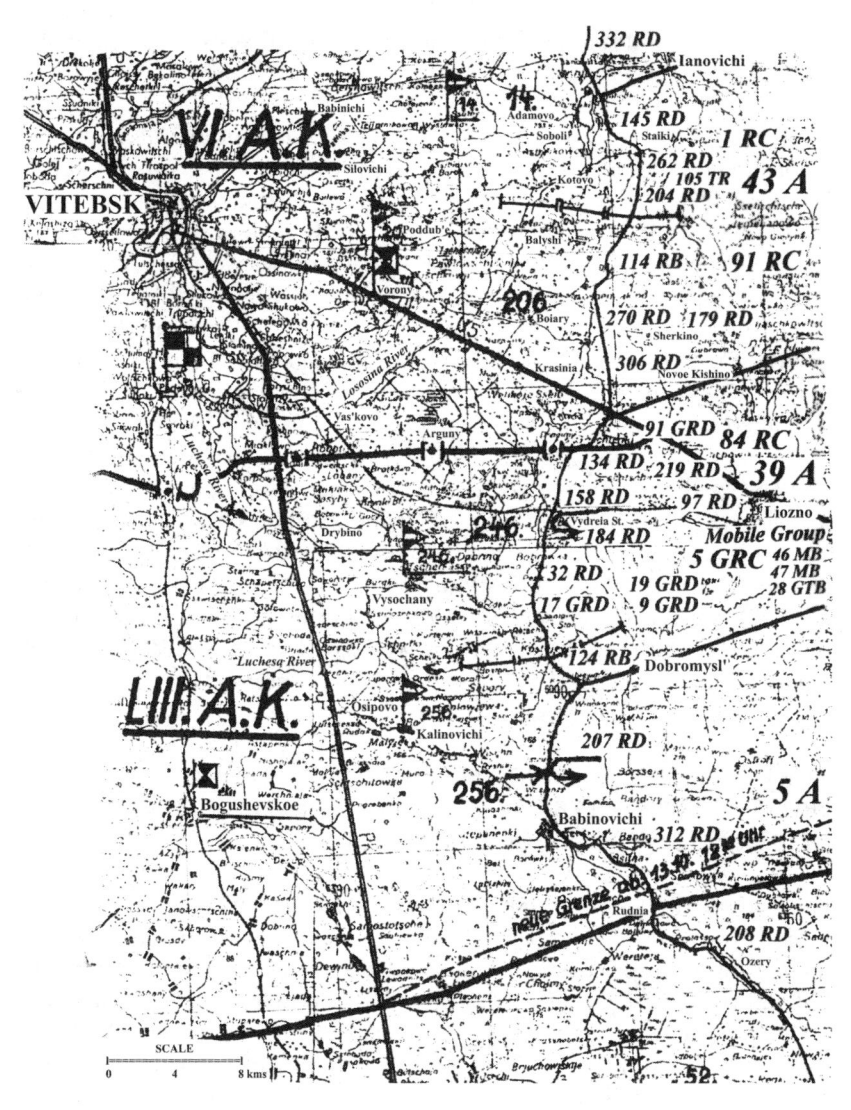

Map 2.8. Third Panzer Army's Situation, 12 October 1943

tion of enemy Army Group "Center" was tied down, which prevented his command from withdrawing any units at all from the region to assist German-Fascist forces which were at that time suffering severe defeats on the Right Bank of the Ukraine and at Leningrad. Second, we captured almost all of the commanding heights in the Vitebsk highlands and seized a sizable bridgehead on the left (western) bank of the Luchesa River. By doing so, we created the most favorable conditions for operations by our army's forces during the Belorussian strategic offensive in the summer of 1944.[37]

As the paucity of Soviet accounts of this operation indicates, this was pure rationalization on Boiko's part. In fact, the Kalinin Front's offensive on Vitebsk failed and failed badly. The *Stavka*'s 16 October directive explains why this occurred: "One of the reasons for this [failure] is the disorganized offensive. . . . It is being conducted without all of the *front*'s forces, more or less simultaneously but with separate armies in separate sectors . . . which gives the enemy an opportunity to maneuver his forces and create fists for resistance."

Attesting to the scale of this failure, although the Kalinin Front lost roughly 7,000 men at Nevel', its casualties during the October battles amounted to 56,474 men killed, wounded, and missing.[38] As a result, Soviet and Russian historians have since focused only on the more dramatic seizure of Nevel' and have largely ignored the far more bitter fighting on the approaches to Vitebsk. Furthermore, as future operations would indicate, the Kalinin Front was far from through with its attempts to achieve success east of Vitebsk. In fact, the *Stavka* still harbored grand designs for a vastly expanded offensive. These plans included an offensive to capture Riga on the Baltic Sea, the hitherto elusive objective of Pskov with its implications for the relief of Leningrad, and, at the very least, to seize Vitebsk.

THE KALININ FRONT'S VITEBSK (RIGA) OFFENSIVE, THE BALTIC FRONT'S IDRITSA OFFENSIVE, AND THE NORTHWESTERN FRONT'S PSKOV OFFENSIVE (18–30 OCTOBER 1943)

Even before the Kalinin Front began its Vitebsk operation and its advance toward Nevel', the *Stavka* began taking measures to assemble forces along the northwestern axis that it deemed capable of exploiting the successes its Kalinin, Western, and Central Fronts achieved in Belorussia. Previous combat experience had vividly evidenced the inability of the Leningrad, Volkhov, and Northwestern Fronts to engage Army Group North's forces effectively. Time and time again, and, specifically, in the winter of 1942–1943 and in February and March of 1943, these *fronts* had failed to make any appreciable progress against the defending Germans. Clearly, thought the *Stavka*, sizable additional forces were required in the region to defeat Army Group North. In the *Stavka*'s judgment, no less than a full additional *front* was required to achieve success. Furthermore, there was no better launching pad for that new *front*'s operations than the territory it expected the Kalinin Front to seize in the Belorussian operation.

Accordingly, on 1 October 1943, the *Stavka* moved boldly to create and deploy that new *front* to the critical region north of Vitebsk. That day the

Stavka issued a directive creating a new Baltic Front, which consisted of forces rendered surplus by virtue of the Red Army's victories in the Smolensk, Briansk, and Chernigov-Pripiat' operations:

2. Transfer the Briansk Front's headquarters, *front* units, and rear service facilities, 11th Guards Army with nine rifle divisions, 11th Army with seven rifle divisions, 15th Air Army, 1st Tank Corps, and 2nd Artillery Corps by rail to the Ostashkov, Toropets, and Selizharovo region. The *front* headquarters will be in the Toropets region by 15 October. Complete the movement of the *front's* forces by 15 November.
3. By 20 October the *front* will receive 22nd Army with two rifle divisions and five rifle brigades from the Northwestern Front, 3rd Shock Army with five rifle divisions and three rifle brigades and 8th Estonian Rifle Corps with two rifle divisions from the Kalinin Front, and 6th Guards Army with seven rifle divisions and 20th Army with six rifle divisions from the *Stavka's* Reserve.
4. This new *front*, which will consist of 3rd Shock, 11th, 22nd, 20th, 6th Guards, 11th Guards, and 15th Air Armies and 8th Estonian Corps, will be named the Baltic Front, effective 20 October.
5. Confirm the receipt of this directive. Submit a *front* operational plan by 15 October.
    The *Stavka* of the Supreme High Command
    I. Stalin
    A. Antonov[39]

A week later, after the Nevel' and Vitebsk operations were well under way, on 8 October the *Stavka* issued the first in a series of directives that detailed its ambitious offensive plans for both the newly forming Baltic Front and the existing Kalinin Front. The directive instructed the Baltic Front to "launch an offensive no later than 15 October, with the mission to defeat the enemy's northern grouping and prevent it from withdrawing to Dvinsk and Riga." The *Stavka* ordered the *front* to deliver its main attack in "the general direction of Riga, Idritsa, Ludza, Gulbene, and Valga" and "subsequently, reach the Pskov, Vygua, Valga, and Valmiera line." At the same time, the *Stavka* ordered the Kalinin Front to "attack along both banks of the Western Dvina River in the general direction of Vitebsk, Polotsk, Daugavpils (Dvinsk) and Riga" (see Appendix A-4).[40]

This directive gave the new Baltic Front control of all forces operating in the 140-kilometer-wide sector extending from Nevel' northward to Kholm. Specifically, this meant 3rd Shock Army in the Nevel' salient, 6th Guards and 20th Armies deploying forward from *Stavka's* Reserve, 22nd Army from the Northwestern Front, 11th Guards Army en route from the Briansk Front, and 15th Air Army. The *Stavka* later countermanded its orders to transfer 11th Army northward from the Central Front. After this regrouping was complete, in addition to the Northwestern Front's 1st Shock and 34th Armies, the Baltic Front would have five armies with which to engage the southern wing of Army Group North's Sixteenth Army. In the *Stavka's* judgment, the Volkhov Front's four armies (4th, 8th, 54th, and 59th) and the Leningrad Front's five armies (2nd Shock, 23rd, 42nd, 55th, and 67th, plus its Coastal Operational Group) would possess more than enough strength to defeat Army Group North's Eighteenth Army.

Success in this entire venture to clear the Baltic and Leningrad regions of German forces, however, depended directly on the Kalinin Front's ability to exploit the success it achieved at Nevel' and seize Vitebsk. On the same day, the *Stavka* issued a directive to the Kalinin Front, which defined its role in the forthcoming operation (see Appendix A-5):

> After capturing the Vitebsk region, continue the offensive, delivering your main attack along both banks of the Western Dvina River in the direction of Polotsk, Dvinsk, and Riga while reliably protecting the operations of the main force from the Vil'nius axis. The immediate mission is to reach the Osveia, Drissa, Disna, and Plisa line. Subsequently, attack in the general direction of Dvinsk, with your final aim being the capture of Riga, the capital of Latvia.[41]

Two days later another *Stavka* directive defined the Northwestern Front's role in the operation by ordering Eremenko's Kalinin Front, along with the Baltic Front, to "destroy the enemy's Porkhov grouping by an offensive in the general direction of Dno and Pskov and reach the Shelon' River, Dno, and Chikhachevo Station front." The *Stavka* instructed the Northwestern Front to subsequently "attack in the general direction of Pskov" (see Appendix A-6).[42] Another directive the same day ordered the Kalinin Front to transfer 3rd Shock Army and the Northwestern Front to transfer 22nd Army to the newly formed Baltic Front, directing that the transfer take place by 2400 hours on 12 October (see Appendix A-7).[43]

After the fall of Nevel' to the Kalinin Front, General Eremenko reported to the *Stavka* why his forces were not able to exploit their success as rapidly as the *Stavka* expected (see Appendix A-8):

> By exploiting the temporary calm on other fronts, the enemy has concentrated considerable aircraft against the Kalinin Front's forces and, by doing so, has achieved temporary air superiority along this axis. Enemy aviation in groups of 50–60 aircraft are continuously attacking and bombing the combat formations of the attacking forces of the 3rd and 4th Shock Armies, driving them to the ground, retarding their advance, and weakening the offensive impulse.

Eremenko ended his message by requesting, "In order to accelerate the tempo of our offensive, I request that one fighter aviation corps and, if only as many as 150 tanks, half of them T-34s, be allocated and assigned to me."[44] The *Stavka* responded promptly, ordering Eremenko to "prepare an operation for the destruction of enemy aviation in the Vitebsk, Orsha, and Ulla regions" (see Appendix A-9).[45]

In accordance with the *Stavka's* previous directive, the next day Army General M. M. Popov, the newly appointed commander of the Baltic Front, submitted his proposal for the new offensive to the *Stavka*. Popov said that the offensive's missions were (see Appendix A-10) "the widening of the Nevel' penetration, the clearing out of the Novosokol'niki sector of the enemy's defense, and reaching the Navsa, Lake Bol'shoe Ostrie, Pustoshka, Zarech'e, and Lake Usvecha line. The depth is 60–70 kilometers. The time required is 8–10 days."[46]

Popov's plan required 3rd Shock Army to "conduct local battles to widen the penetration in the vicinity of Nevel' until 16 October in order to attract enemy forces and attention to his army's sector." Meanwhile, the 3rd Shock was to concentrate its reinforcing 93rd Rifle Corps to the region east of Lake Malyi Ivan on 15 October and attack on 16 October to reach the Borshchanka, Okin, Rechki, Borovichi, and Tochino front by day's end on 17 October. When further reinforced by 79th Rifle Corps on the 17th, 3rd Shock was to broaden its attack on the 18th and reach the Novosokol'niki, Tumashi, Teplukhina, and Nevel' line by day's end on 19 October.

Further, after concentrating three divisions of 22nd Army west of Velikie Luki on 19 October, the 22nd was to join the attack early on 20 October and reach the Lake Bol'shoe Ostrie, Pustoshka, Zarech'e, and Lake Usvecha line by 24–25 October. This would conclude the first stage of the offensive. Thereafter, 3rd and 22nd Armies would be reinforced with one rifle corps each from 6th Guards and 11th Armies in the region between Velikie Luki and Toropets and, soon after, by 11th Guards Army. The combined force would then resume its offensive on or about 25 October. The *Stavka* quickly approved General Popov's plan in a directive issued at 0100 hours on 15 October (see Appendix A-11).[47]

Significantly, this exchange of messages confirmed that both the Baltic and Kalinin Fronts would undertake offensive action on or about 18 October. The former was to attack toward Idritsa and Pustoshka with the forces of 3rd Shock Army, and the latter toward Vitebsk from the northeast and east with 4th Shock, 43rd, and 39th Armies. In a virtual footnote to ongoing operations and a confirmation of the strategic focus of the *fronts* operating along the northwestern and western axis, on 16 October the *Stavka* issued an order renaming many of its operating *fronts* (see Appendix A-12): "Establish the following new names for the *fronts* effective 20 October: name the Central

Front the Belorussian Front; name the Kalinin Front the 1st Baltic Front; [and] name the Baltic Front the 2nd Baltic Front."[48]

The operational pause that ensued, which followed the initial stage of Eremenko's Nevel' operation, lasted from 9 through 14 October. During this period Army Groups North and Center assembled three divisions, two from the former (the 58th and 122nd), and one from the latter (20th Panzer), with which to conduct counterattacks against the flanks of the Soviet Nevel' salient. However, Hitler refused to authorize the counterattacks because he felt the force was not yet strong enough to achieve its mission.

Beginning on 15 October, 3rd Shock Army on the northern flank of the Nevel' salient attacked the villages of Moseevo and Izocha on the northeastern flank of the salient near Lake Bol'shyi Ivan' with 100th Rifle Brigade and one regiment of 28th Rifle Division (see Map 2.9). The remainder of 28th Division soon joined the battle, supported on the right by the newly arrived 93rd Rifle Corps' 165th and 379th Rifle Divisions. Although the Germans contained the Soviet assaults, they recognized that a significant Soviet buildup was taking place in this sector and the sector of 22nd Army, operating further to the north opposite the Germans' defenses protecting the critical railroad junction at Novosokol'niki. In fact, 100th Rifle Brigade's assault was designed to capture more favorable jumping-off positions for the fresh 6th Guards Army, slated to deploy to the region by month's end.[49]

Still farther to the north, the forces of the Northwestern Front's 1st Shock Army and those of the new Baltic Front's 22nd Army attacked to gain more favorable offensive positions near Novosokol'niki. An account by Lieutenant General L. M. Sandalov, the chief of staff of the Baltic (soon 2nd) Front, described these actions:

> Our *front* set about conducting local offensive operations at the end of October. The 1st Shock Army, under the command of the young and energetic Lieutenant General G. P. Korotkov, organized an attack by several divisions on Staraia Russa, striving to envelop that city from the southwest. The 22nd Army of the very experienced Lieutenant General V. A. Iushkevich, whom I knew from the Civil War, conducted an operation north of the town of Novosokol'niki.
>
> Units from three of that army's divisions tried to destroy the garrison of Novosokol'niki and capture that town and the large railroad junction. [178th Rifle Division and 8th Estonian Rifle Corps' 7th and 249th Rifle Divisions conducted this assault.]
>
> The 1st Shock and 22nd Armies' forces were not able to fulfill their missions completely. The German-Fascist command transferred five divisions to this axis from other front sectors. The enemy resistance, which was based on a previously prepared defense system, increased sharply. By 5 November our force's advance had been brought to a complete halt.[50]

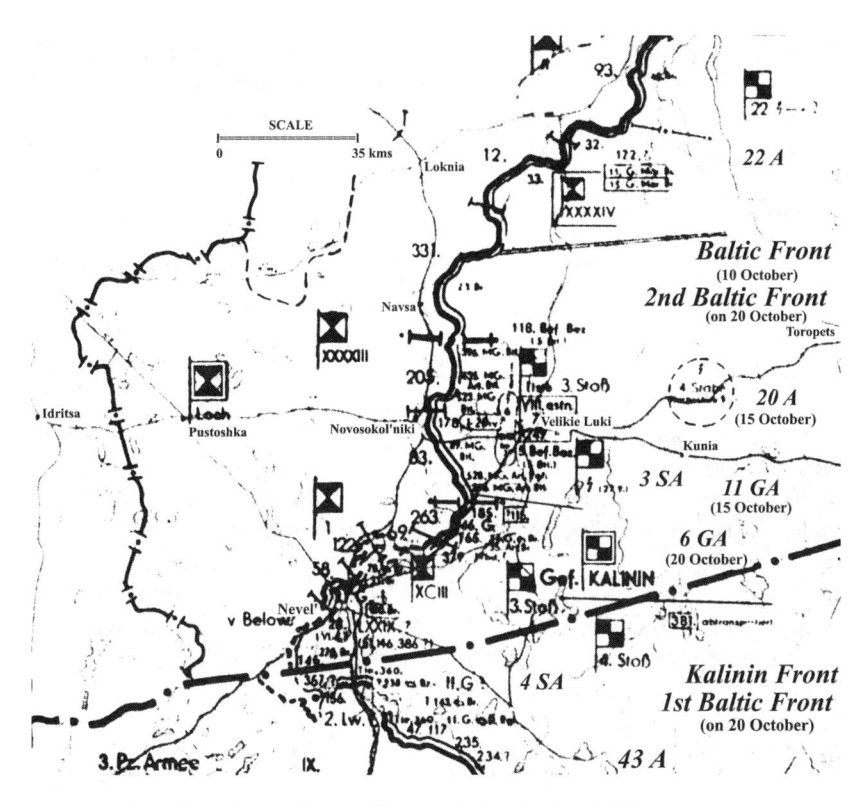

Map 2.9. The Baltic Front's Idritsa Offensive, 18–30 October 1943

While these local actions were taking place, Lieutenant General I. M. Chistiakov's 6th Guards Army moved into assembly areas northeast of Nevel' in between 3rd Shock and 22nd Armies' sectors. The stage was finally set for the 2nd Baltic Front to resume major offensive operations in early November.

After mid-October, the Kalinin Front's 4th Shock Army, still operating against Vitebsk from the southern half of the Nevel' salient, conducted nearly constant operations either to improve its positions or defend against German counterattacks. Although local actions took place daily in the sector flanking Lake Ezerishche north of Gorodok, the Kalinin Front's only offensive gains took place in the sector northeast of Vitebsk. Admittedly, these gains resulted more from the necessity for the Germans to shorten their defense line rather than Soviet offensive action.

As was the case in the Nevel' sector, the Kalinin Front's 43rd and 39th Armies resumed their attacks on 15 October, but the first few of these were only of a local nature. In 43rd Army's sector, 92nd Rifle Corps' 358th and 322nd Rifle Divisions, 145th Rifle Brigade, and 105th Separate Tank Regiment struck on 15 October at the boundary between German 87th and 14th

Infantry Divisions in the Surazh and Ianovichi sectors. On the same day, 39th Army's 158th, 32nd, and 184th Rifle Divisions attacked the defenses of Third Panzer Army's 246th Infantry Division's (LIII Army Corps) positions west of Liozno. Although the Germans repelled these assaults with ease, stronger assaults on 17 October by 4th Shock Army against Third Panzer Army's 129th Infantry Division (IX Army Corps) and the flank and rear of the II Luftwaffe Field Corps threatened to collapse German defenses north of Vitebsk (see Map 2.10). The attack was conducted by 4th Shock Army's 83rd Rifle Corps' (47th, 234th, and 235th Rifle Divisions) and 2nd Guards Rifle Corps' 117th and 360th Rifle Divisions, supported by 146th and 236th Tank Brigades.

In response to this attack, Third Panzer Army ordered 20th Panzer Division, which had arrived in the region on 11–12 October, to launch a counterattack to blunt the Soviet advance. Despite being severely understrength and with a force of less than 20 tanks, the 20th Panzer was able to contain the attacking force after two days of heavy fighting. However, the intense fight on its left flank forced II Luftwaffe Field Corps to withdraw its three divisions (6th, 3rd, and 4th Luftwaffe Field Divisions) back to new defensive positions to the rear, as did VI Army Corps' left flank 87th Infantry Division. The 39th Army's 5th Guards Rifle and 84th Rifle Corps then resumed their attacks on 18 October in the sector west of Dobromysl' and westward along the Liozno road. However, after two days of fighting, these attacks also died out without achieving any notable success, and, by the end of October, the front stabilized north and east of Vitebsk (see Maps 2.11 and 2.12).[51]

Try as he might, General Eremenko simply could not crack German defenses around Vitebsk. To his credit, the 1st Baltic Front was able to establish a vital bridgehead at Nevel' from which its forces and those of 2nd Baltic Front could launch subsequent offensives in three directions (north, east, and south). However, he failed to exploit the Nevel' operation to the extent that the *Stavka* believed it was capable. Nor did his armies on the eastern approaches to Vitebsk achieve their missions. Eremenko explained why in a telegram he dispatched to the *Stavka* (see Appendix A-13), which stated, "The Kalinin Front's formations and units have been significantly exhausted during the course of over two or more months of uninterrupted combat. The rifle divisions have 3,500 to 4,500 men each. Such a situation has had a telling effect on the nature and results of the recent combat." After acknowledging that "my carefully organized and personally prepared operation by 43rd and 39th Armies east of Vitebsk have had no success," Eremenko requested that the *Stavka* permit his *front's* forces to pause for ten to twelve days and that two rifle corps and one tank or mechanized corps be dispatched to reinforce the *front* so that it could fulfill its assigned missions.[52]

The *Stavka*'s response is still unknown. Regardless of what might have been, Eremenko's failures did not dampen its offensive ardor. The Kalinin (1st Baltic) Front had driven a wedge between Army Groups North and Cen-

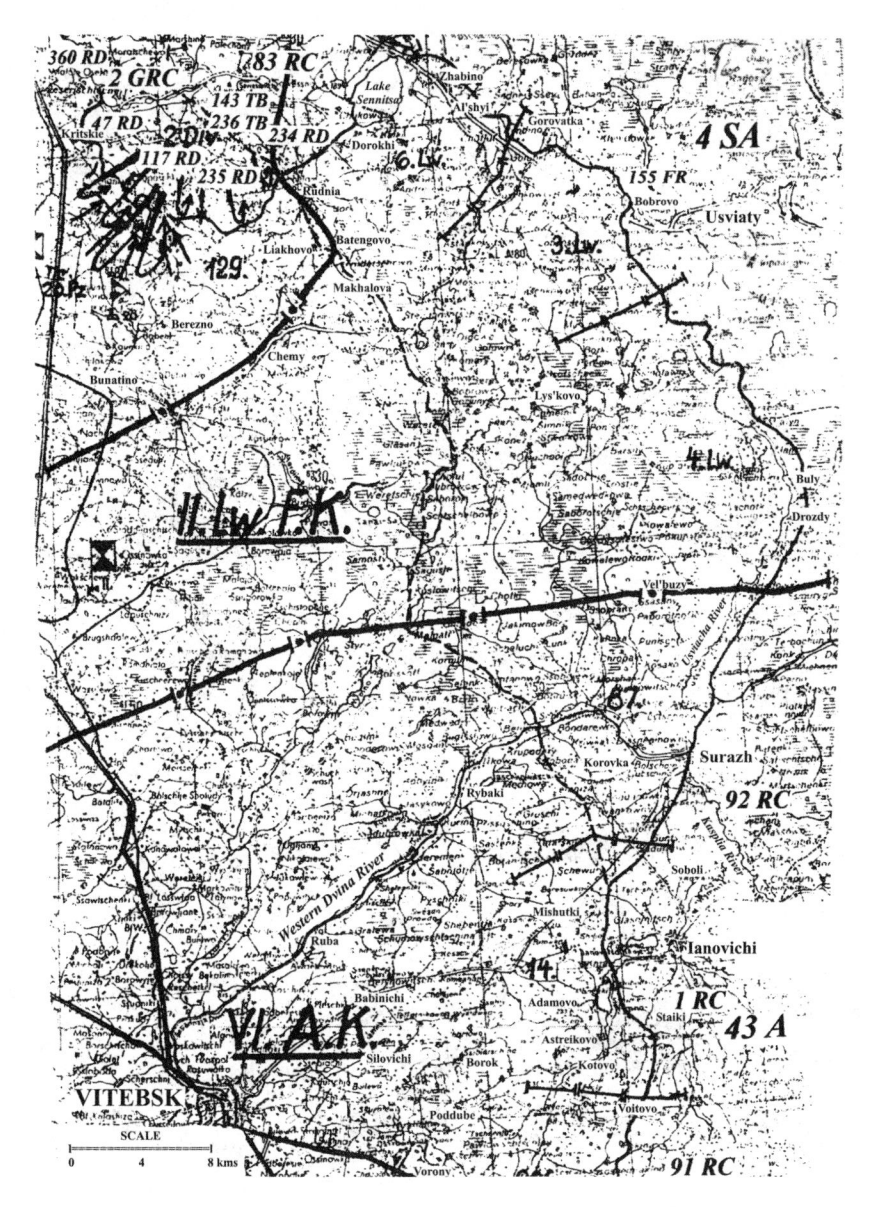

Map 2.10. Third Panzer Army's Situation, 17 October 1943

ter, and it was apparent to all that this breach was irreparable. In the *Stavka*'s view, the Nevel' salient was an admirable launching pad for future offensive operations. The *Stavka* would exploit the *front*'s enviable position and, while doing so, once again attempt to crack the German defenses at Vitebsk.

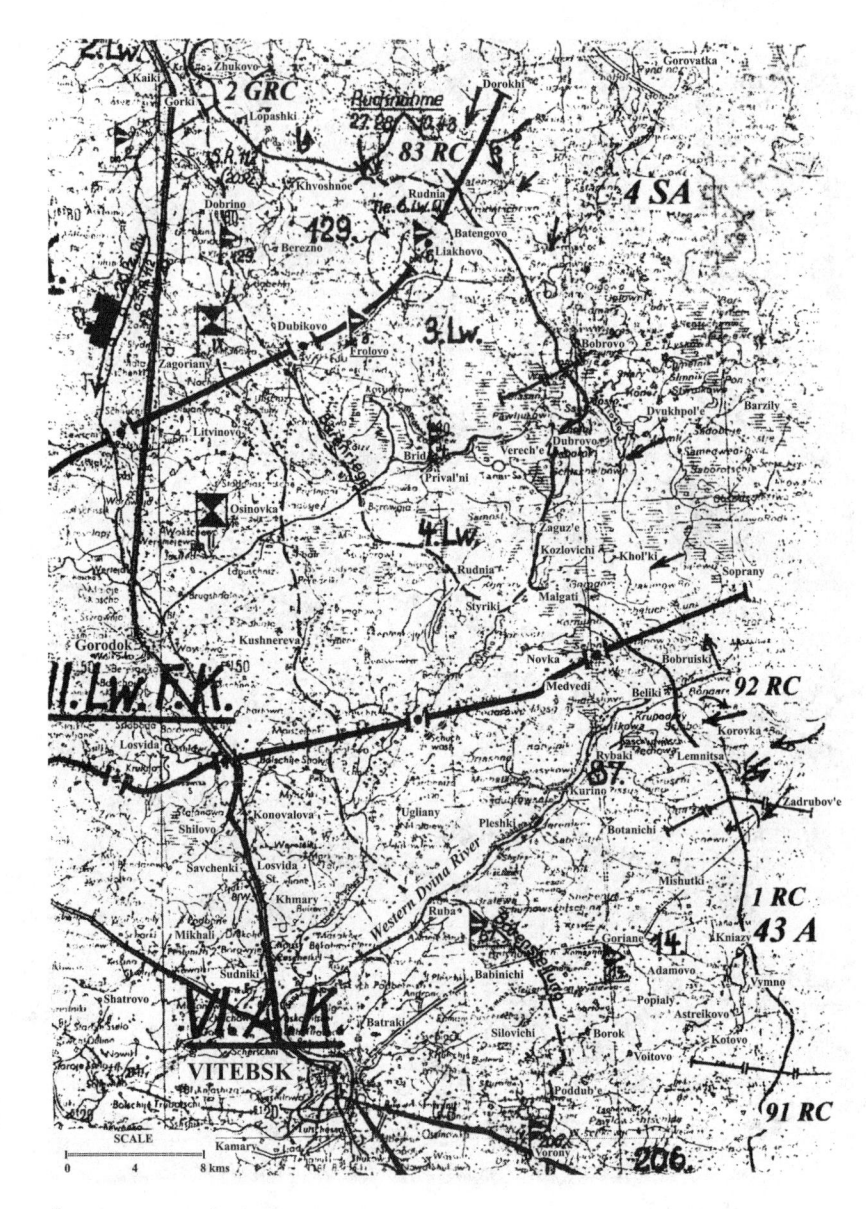

Map 2.11. Third Panzer Army's Situation North of Vitebsk, 27 October 1943

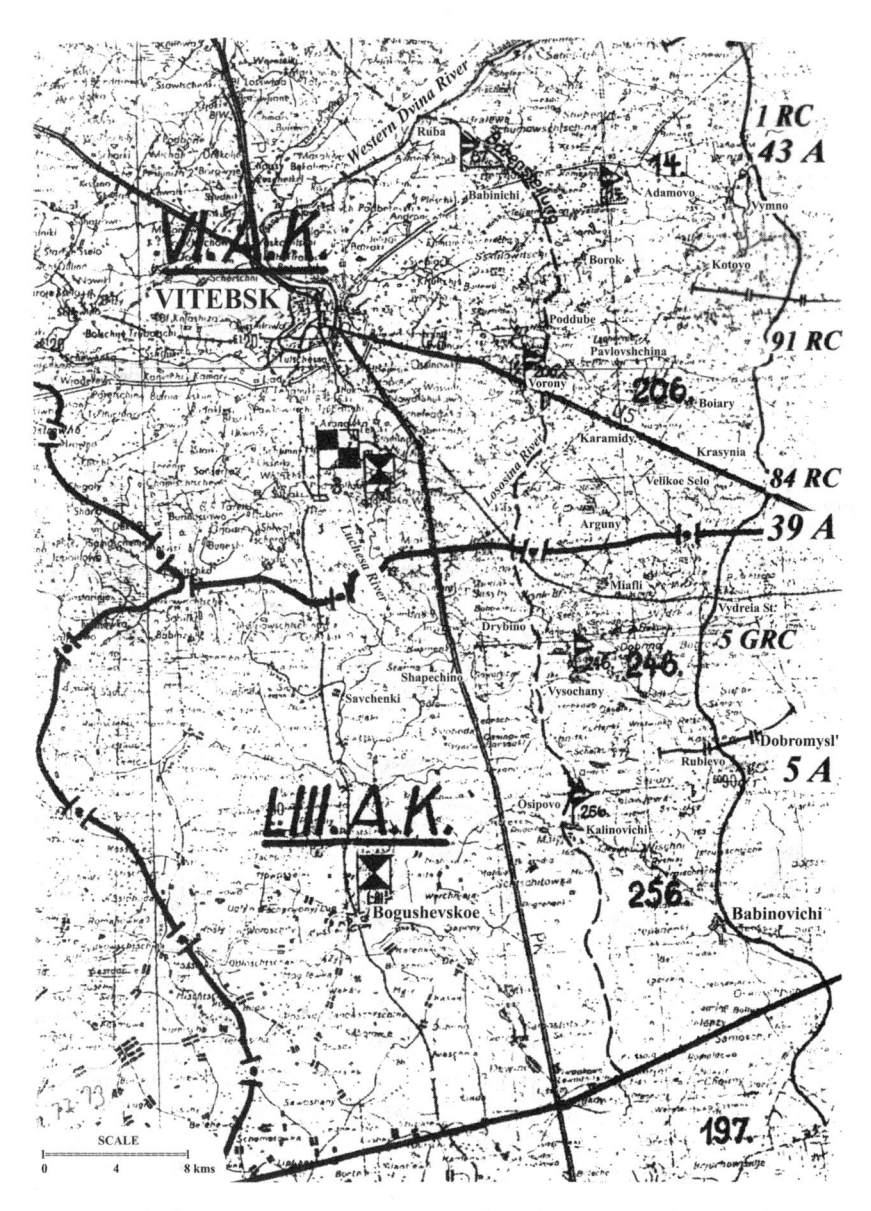

Map 2.12. Third Panzer Army's Situation East and Southeast of Vitebsk, 27 October 1943

CHAPTER 3

The Western Front's Orsha Offensives (3–28 October)

THE FIRST ORSHA OFFENSIVE (3–11 OCTOBER 1943)

While the Kalinin Front's forces were conducting their first futile attacks against German positions at Vitebsk, the Western Front too began its march westward from Smolensk toward the Belorussian cities of Orsha and Mogilev. The Soviet official history provides only a brief but incomplete overview of the Western Front's initial assault in early October, stating:

> At the same time that combat was continuing along the Vitebsk axis, the Western Front's main forces developed an offensive on Orsha and Mogilev. They were to penetrate the enemy defense along the Mereia and Pronia River lines, reach the Dnepr, and smash the sector of the Eastern Wall [German Panther defense line] protecting the routes to the central region of Belorussia.
>
> The Western Front's Military Council reported its decision concerning the conduct of subsequent operations to the *Stavka* of the Supreme High Command as early as 30 September. In particular, it underscored that the enemy had implemented every measure to halt the *front's* forces in previously prepared positions along the western banks of the Mereia and Pronia and intensive defensive work by the Hitlerites on the right bank of the Dnepr. The Military Council intended to penetrate the defenses along the Mereia and Pronia by day's end on 1 October and force the Dnepr during the first half of October. In this regard, it asked the *Stavka* to reinforce the *front* with personnel and tanks and allocate ammunition and fuel. The *Stavka* approved the Military Council's request but to an insufficient degree, since an extensive offensive was developing to the southwest at that time, to which the main material reserves and personnel reserves were being directed.
>
> The *front's* main grouping, consisting of 10th Guards, 21st, and 33rd Armies, resumed their offensive in the direction of Orsha on 3 October after a short artillery and air preparation. The battle became extremely intense. In order to halt the Soviet forces, the German-Fascist command hurriedly transferred infantry and panzer formations from other sectors of the Eastern Front. The offensive brought the Western Front only tactical success.[1]

Very few Soviet or Russian sources document the progress of the Western Front's offensive during the fall of 1943. Fragmentary accounts exist in the combat histories of 5th, 31st, and 33rd Armies and in some Red Army divisional histories as well. However, prior to 1994, utter silence enveloped the Western Front's operations during this period and well into the winter of 1944. For example, if it exists at all, no comprehensive account of Western Front operations in the extensive series of operational studies the Red Army General Staff published during and after the war has yet been released by the Russian archives administration. Nor has any comprehensive account of the operations appeared in Soviet open-source literature. In 1994, however, two journal articles appeared that lifted the veil of secrecy cloaking the Western Front's operations. Written by the preeminent military historian and theorist, Army General Makhmut Gareev, who served as a junior officer in 5th Army during this period, these articles expose the scope and futility of the military operations the Western Front conducted during the fall of 1943 and the winter of 1944.[2] Collectively, these two articles set a new standard for candor in Russian military-historical literature. Despite this fact, their limited scope and length prevented full exposure of what actually occurred during these important "forgotten operations." However, with the help of German records and recently released Soviet archival materials, we can now reconstruct the course of those operations as well as the *Stavka's* intent in ordering their conduct.

These new Russian archival materials, especially *Stavka* and Red Army General Staff directives and orders, provide necessary context for what subsequently transpired along the Orsha and Mogilev axes into Belorussia. The first of these documents is a directive the *Stavka* issued on 20 September 1943 that established the parameters of the Western Front's forthcoming Belorussian offensive (see Appendix B-1). In this directive, the *Stavka* ordered the *front* to capture Smolensk on 26–27 September, while continuing its offensive to destroy the Germans' Smolensk grouping. After capturing Smolensk, the *Stavka* instructed the *front* to attack in the general direction of Orsha with its main grouping, "occupy the Pochinok and Roslavl' line" with its left wing, "reach the Sozh River, Khislavichi, and Shumiachi line by this time," and seize the Orsha and Mogilev regions on 10–12 October. The *front* was to provide the *Stavka* with its offensive plan by 22 September.[3]

Army General Vasilii Danilovich Sokolovsky, the commander of the Western Front since replacing General Zhukov in February of 1943, implemented the *Stavka's* 20 September directive after the fall of Smolensk to Red Army forces on 25 September. On the same day, the *Stavka* broadened Sokolovsky's mission by stating, "After capturing the Orsha and Mogilev regions, continue a general offensive in the general direction of Borisov and Moledochno and reach the Dokshinsty, Dolginovo, and Radoshkovichi front. Subsequently, have the aim of capturing the capital of Lithuania—Vil'no

[Vil'nius]."[4] This expanded his objectives to the Dokshinsty, Dolginovo, and Radoshkovichi line, a depth of 170–200 kilometers, and to Vil'nius, at a depth of 300 kilometers. Furthermore, his *front* was to accomplish these missions from the march and without any pause, in its present grouping and without any significant reinforcements, and at a time when his logistical umbilicals were overstretched and ammunition was already in short supply. Nonetheless, Sokolovsky responded promptly by ordering his 31st, 68th, 10th Guards, 21st, 33rd, 49th, and 50th Armies to continue their offensive westward toward Orsha and Mogilev (see Map 3.1).

From the German perspective, however, it seemed unlikely that the Red Army would press matters further in Belorussia during the fall. Taking into account the costly fighting in late summer, German intelligence organs formulated a more optimistic appraisal of likely Soviet actions in the central portion of the Eastern Front. Accordingly, the OKH's *Fremde Heeres Ost* (Foreign Armies East [OKH's intelligence service]) assessed, "The enemy, apparently, will now already be striving to create an operational pause during the period of the *rasputitsa* so as to replenish his forces. It is possible that, up to the onset of that pause, he will try to occupy as favorable jumping-off positions as possible for a supposed winter offensive."[5] Based on this assessment, Army Group Center maintained its existing defensive formation, leaving its front defended largely by infantry and panzer grenadier divisions, many organized in *kampfgruppe* (KGr., or combat group) configuration, but all severely weakened by the summer fighting. These were backed up by a handful of equally weakened panzer divisions.

After clearing Smolensk proper of Germans, 5th Army followed along the Smolensk-Orsha road in the wake of 31st Army, with the mission to fill in the gap between the Kalinin Front's 39th Army and the Western Front's 33rd Army. Advancing on a broad front, the Western Front's forces fought their way across the Sozh River, liberated the towns of Krasnyi, Mstislavl', and Krichev, and reached positions extending from Eliseevka through Liady, Lenino, and Dribin and southward along the Pronia River to Petukhovka by 2 October (see Map 3.1). The 10th Army, deployed on the Western Front's extreme left wing, cooperated closely with the Briansk Front's forces. On 2 October, the Briansk Front's 50th Army, then completing its mission in the Briansk offensive operation, closed up to the Pronia River south of Petukhovka.

At this juncture, an optimistic *Stavka* sent a directive to Sokolovsky ordering him to accelerate his *front's* offensive deep into Belorussia, advance through Borisov and Molodechno, and capture the city of Vil'nius in Lithuania (see Appendix B-2). Supporting Sokolovsky's advance, on the Western Front's right, the Kalinin Front was to attack in the general direction of Vitebsk, Polotsk, and Daugavpils (Dvinsk) to capture Riga, the capital of Latvia; on his left, the Central Front would attack toward Zhlobin and Bo-

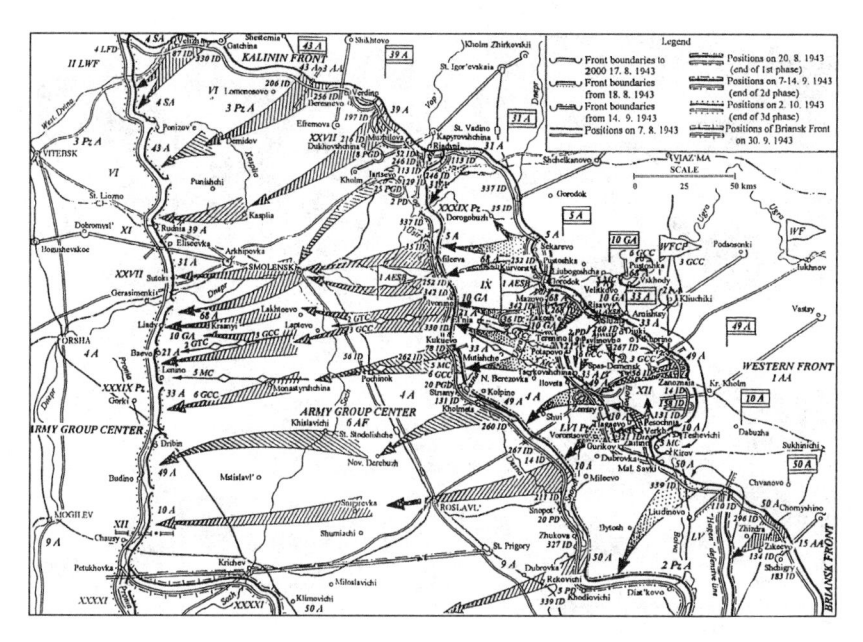

Map 3.1. The Western Front's Smolensk Offensive, 7 August–2 October 1943

bruisk to capture the city of Minsk, the capital of Belorussia.[6] Accordingly, Sokolovsky ordered his armies "to penetrate enemy defenses along the line of the Mereia and Pronia Rivers by day's end on 1 October and force the Dnepr River during the first half of the month" (see Appendix B-3 for the Western Front's situation report on 1 October 1943).[7]

As was the case in the Kalinin Front's offensive sector, the Western Front's renewed offensive developed along multiple axes across a broad front (see Maps 3.2 and 3.3). Sokolovsky's forces literally attacked from the march and achieved only limited success. On the *front's* right wing north of the Dnepr River and the Orsha-Smolensk road, Lieutenant General V. A. Gluzdovsky's 31st Army mounted its attack frontally against German Fourth Army's defenses north of the Dnepr River and the Smolensk-Orsha highway. At the same time, the newly arriving divisions of Lieutenant General V. S. Polenov's 5th Army struck German defenses in between the 31st Army and the Kalinin Front's 39th Army, which was then attacking Rudnia along the Smolensk-Vitebsk highway to the north.

Polenov conducted his assault initially with 207th and 312th Rifle Divisions, whereas the army's 208th Rifle Division and 152nd Fortified Region followed several days to the rear. Crossing the Malaia Berezina River between Danki and Privol'e, the two lead rifle divisions struck defenses occupied by troops from 52nd and 197th Infantry Divisions of German Fourth Army's XXVII Army Corps, the former of which had been reduced in earlier fighting

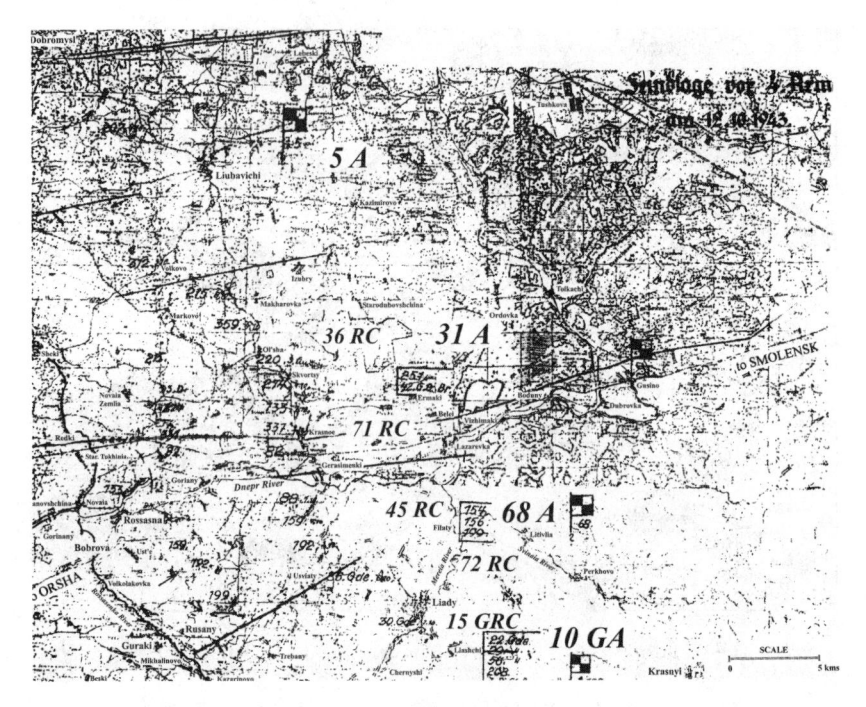

Map 3.2. Fourth Army's Situation in the Orsha Sector, 12 October 1943

to *kampfgruppe* configuration. By the evening of 3 October, the two divisions had crossed the river, captured the villages of Lukavo and Morosovka, and driven a wedge into 52nd Infantry Division's defensive front. The 5th Army's history claimed, "The surprise attack demoralized the Hitlerites, and by morning they began to withdraw in disorder."[8]

Whether this was true, Fourth Army's daily operational map indicates that, by the evening of 4 October, 5th Army's two rifle divisions had indeed torn a gap 10 kilometers wide and 6 kilometers deep into the Germans' defenses west of the Malaia Berezina River, rendering German defenses along that river untenable. Three days later, on 8 October 208th Rifle Division arrived at the front and reinforced the bridgehead. By this time, 5th Army's success and pressure by 39th Army at Rudnia farther to the north forced the Germans to pull their defense lines back several kilometers to the west. The three Soviet divisions followed, occupying the strong point and key road junction at Liubavichi and reaching the Bol'shaia Berezina River between Shalkovo and Izubry, forcing yet another German withdrawal.

The 207th and 312th Rifle Divisions pursued the German rear guards and reached the Chernitsa River along its entire length from Dobromysl' to Vospintsy Station by midday on 11 October. The 207th Rifle Division's 397th

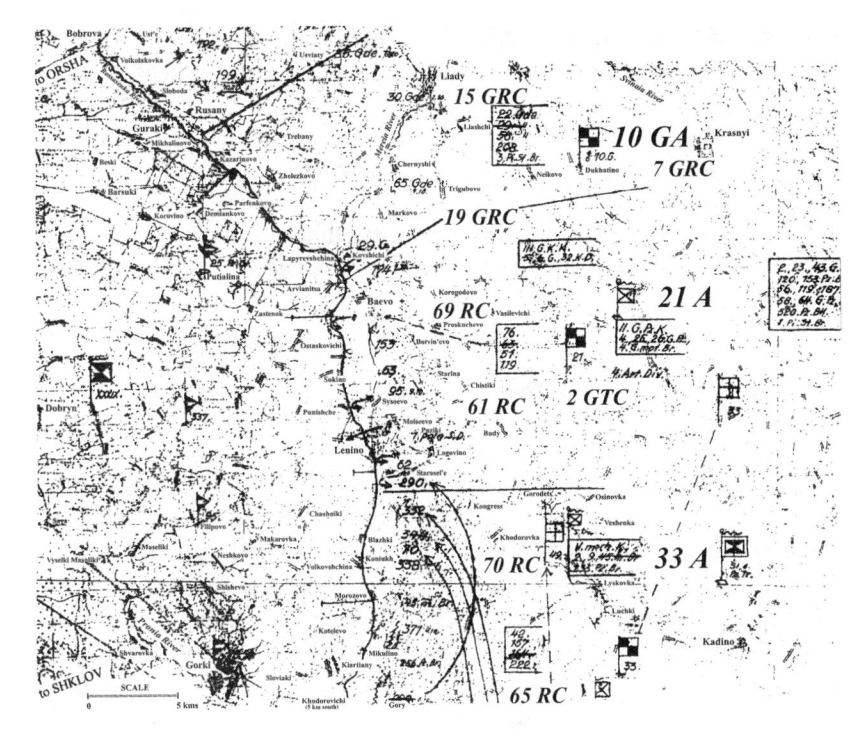

Map 3.3. Fourth Army's Situation in the Gorki Sector, 12 October 1943

Regiment then captured Dobromysl' and seized a small bridgehead on the Chernitsa River's western bank. The next day 208th Rifle Division advanced to the river's bank on the 207th's left and reached the Verkhita River line from Lake Sitna to Zhukovka. Finally, 152nd Fortified Region occupied forward positions extending from Zhukovka to Sheki, several kilometers north of the Smolensk-Orsha highway, on 31st Army's right flank. Here, however, 5th Army's advance ground to a halt.

Despite the fact that it consisted of only three rifle divisions and a fortified region, 5th Army's advance proved more spectacular than that of any of the Western Front's other armies. This was so both because it struck a weak spot in the German defenses and because the Germans were preoccupied with the threat posed by the stronger 31st Army, attacking westward along the Smolensk-Orsha road.

General Gluzdovsky's 31st Army also began its attack on the morning of 3 October. The army commander deployed his 36th and 71st Rifle Corps north of and astride the Smolensk-Orsha road and advanced directly against the Germans' defenses in the center of 197th Infantry Division of German Fourth Army's XXVII Army Corps. In 36th Rifle Corps' first echelon, 359th and 215th Rifle Divisions assaulted westward in the sector between Ordovka and Ermaki north of the highway, backed up by 274th Rifle Division in second echelon. The 71st Rifle Corps' 331st, 133rd, and 82nd Rifle Divisions, deployed side by side in the corps' first echelon, attacked westward astride the Smolensk-Orsha highway and the railroad line north of the Dnepr River. The 42nd Guards Tank Brigade supported 71st Rifle Corps' attack. During the ensuing three days of heavy fighting, 71st Rifle Corps' assault stalled in front of the strong German defenses, which Fourth Army had reinforced with elements of 18th Panzer Grenadier Division. By this time, Fourth Army's XXVII Army Corps defended the sector from east of Liubavichi southward to just south of Liady with a *kampfgruppe* organized from the remnants of 52nd Infantry Division, flanked to the south by 197th Infantry and 18th Panzer Grenadier Divisions.

However, in tandem with 5th Army's attack to the north, 31st Army's 36th Rifle Corps, which by now had been reinforced by 220th Rifle Division from 68th Army's 45th Rifle Corps, unhinged the German defenses north of the highway and drove the defending Germans westward through the village of Ermaki. The intense pressure applied to the Germans' defenses, coupled with the nearly incessant Soviet attacks over the next few days, forced German 197th Infantry Division to withdraw on 9 October to new defensive positions astride the highway running from Krasnoe to Gerasimenki. The German withdrawal, together with 31st Army's pursuit, continued until late on 11 October, when the Germans occupied yet another defense line extending from Shcheki on the Verkhita River southward across the Smolensk-Orsha highway at Red'ki to the Dnepr River at Novaia. Here, General Gluzdovsky received new orders to halt the attacks briefly in preparation for a renewed assault on 12 October.

The modest advance by 31st Army along the Smolensk-Orsha highway was facilitated by intense pressure south of the Dnepr River by the advancing Soviet 68th Army. By 3 October Lieutenant General E. P. Zhuravlev's 68th Army had reached a front extending from the southern bank of the Dnepr River south of Vizhimaki southward along the Mereia River to Liady. As his army's 45th Rifle Corps raced to close up to the front, its 159th Rifle Division, the 192nd and 199th Rifle Divisions (of 72nd Rifle Corps), and 6th Guards Cavalry Division of supporting 3rd Guards Cavalry Corps attacked German defensive positions at Filaty on the Mereia River. Fourth Army's 18th Panzer Grenadier Division, just ordered to defend in XXVII Army Corps' sector from the Dnepr River through Liady to Kiseli, was severely overextended and hard-pressed. When 45th Rifle Corps' forces arrived forward late on 8 October, its 88th Rifle Division reinforced 159th Rifle Division's assault across the Mereia River, forcing the 18th Panzer Grenadier to withdraw westward. Pursued by forward detachments from 68th Army's lead divisions, the 18th Panzer Grenadier wheeled its front back toward the east and, on 11 October, occupied new defensive positions along the Rossasenka River from Volkolakovka southeastward to Parfenkovo. The 68th Army pursued, while preparing to resume its assaults on the 12th. By this time, Zhuravlev's army had already transferred its 220th Rifle Division to 31st Army's control to reinforce the latter's attack westward along the Smolensk-Orsha highway. The 45th Rifle Corps' 88th and 251st Rifle Divisions also reverted to 31st Army's control soon after, leaving 68th Army with only three rifle divisions (72nd Rifle Corps' 192nd and 199th Division and 159th Rifle Division).

South of 68th Army's attack sector, the lead elements of Lieutenant General A. V. Sukhomlin's 10th Guards Army reached positions extending from Liady southward along the Mereia River to the town of Baevo late on 2 October. In anticipation of the 3 October attack, he deployed his army's 15th and 19th Guards Rifle Corps from right to left (north to south) in first echelon and retained 7th Guards Rifle Corps in reserve. The 15th Guards Corps' 30th Guards Division was to assault German defensive positions at Liady, backed up by 85th Guards Division and 153rd Tank Brigade. Meanwhile, 19th Guards Corps' 22nd and 65th Guards Divisions, supported by 56th Guards Division and 3rd Guards Cavalry Corps' 5th Guards Cavalry Division, prepared to assault German positions across the Mereia River between Kiseli and Kovshichi. The 7th Guards Corps' 29th Guards and 208th Rifle Divisions were in reserve. Shortly after the operation began, however, *front* commander Sokolovsky ordered General Sukhomlin to transfer his 208th Rifle Division to 5th Army so that it could reinforce the latter's attack north of the Smolensk-Orsha highway. The 10th Guards Army's main attack sector was at the boundary between XXVII Army Corps' 18th Panzer Grenadier Division and XXXIX Panzer Corps' 25th Panzer Grenadier Divisions. This meant that the shock group of Sukhomlin's army faced roughly half of each German division; however, in addition, by this time 25th Panzer Grenadier was soon to be reinforced by infantrymen from 1st SS Infantry Brigade. Finally, German Fourth Army also had at its disposal the remnants of 18th Panzer Division. However, because this division had been severely depleted during the fighting since July and was assessed as not combat worthy, by 1 October, it consisted of a weak *kampfgruppe* equipped with only twelve tanks (six Pz. III and six Pz. IV models).[9]

The 10th Guards Army began its assault early on 3 October, with the fiercest fighting taking place in the Liady region on the army's left wing and for possession of crossing sites over the Mereia River near Kiseli and Rudashkov. The 15th Guards Rifle Corps' 30th Guards Rifle Division, reinforced by 662nd and 188th Artillery, 317th Mortar, and 132nd Antitank Artillery Regiments, spent four days assaulting the strong German defenses at Liady before overcoming them on the night of 8 October.[10] On General Sukhomlin's orders, 15th Guards Corps then committed from reserve its

85th Guards Division, which soon thrust across the river north of Liady. This maneuver, coupled with 31st and 68th Armies' advance to the north, forced the two German panzer grenadier divisions to begin a fighting withdrawal to the west. At the same time, after days of fruitless struggle to overcome German defenses along the Mereia River, 19th Guards Rifle Corps' 22nd and 65th Guards Rifle Divisions finally crossed the river and joined in the pursuit. The ensuing pursuit brought the lead elements of 10th Guards Army to the eastern approaches to the town of Dubrovno (15 kilometers east of Orsha) by day's end on 11 October. At this time, 85th and 30th Guards Rifle Divisions of the army's 15th Guards Corps' reached the Rossasenka River between the villages of Rusany and Kazarinovo. By this time, the guards corps was flanked on the left by 19th Guards Corps' 22nd and 65th Guards Divisions, whose troops closed into positions between Kazarinovo and the Mereia River west of Kovshichi. Meanwhile, the infantry of 29th Guards Division pounded 25th Panzer Grenadier Division's defenses on the Mereia River near Baevo, albeit in vain.

The Western Front's 21st Army, commanded by Lieutenant General N. I. Krylov, advanced westward on 10th Guards Army's left flank. The lead elements of the army's 61st and 69th Rifle Corps reached positions along the Mereia River from Baevo southward to Lenino by late on 2 October. They were supported by Major General of Tank Forces A. S. Burdeinyi's 2nd Guards Tank Corps, which was essentially worn out from previous fighting, 23rd Separate Guards Tank Brigade, and 64th Guards and 248th Separate Tank and 1494th and 1830th Self-propelled Artillery Regiments. Although imposing on paper, Burdeinyi's tank corps, which had lost more than 40 percent of its roughly 150 tanks in the Smolensk offensive, probably fielded no more than 50 tanks on any given day in the Belorussian offensive. The 3rd Guards Cavalry Corps' 32nd Cavalry Division, which had led the pursuit from Roslavl', was in army reserve. Krylov's forces faced the right flank of 25th Panzer Grenadier Division defending opposite Baevo and the full 337th Infantry Division defending the river sector at Lenino, both subordinate to Fourth Army's XXXIX Panzer Corps.

Krylov conducted his 3 October assault with 153rd and 174th Rifle Divisions of his army's 69th Rifle Corps, which tried to force its way across the Mereia River south of Baevo, and with 95th and 62nd Rifle Divisions of 61st Rifle Corps, which launched their assaults at and north of Lenino. The strong attacks were, however, in vain, as the German's river defenses held firm. Despite committing a tank group from 2nd Guards Tank Corps to support the attack at Lenino, Krylov's forces could not budge the German defenses. The fighting abated in this sector after 8 October, as Krylov regrouped his forces for a new attempt to force the river on 12 October.

On 21st Army's left, Colonel General V. N. Gordov's 33rd Army was to cross the Mereia River, seize the town of Gorki, and then advance to the eastern bank of the Dnepr River midway between the cities of Shklov and Orsha. Gordov deployed for the 3 October attack with 70th Rifle Corps' 338th and 371st Rifle Divisions on the army's right wing between Lenino and Mikulino, a town north of the Gorki-Gory road; 290th and 173rd Rifle Divisions, which were directly subordinate to the army, in the army's center; and 65th Rifle Corps' 58th and 144th Rifle Divisions, which deployed on the army's left wing along the Remistrianka River between Nikol'skoe on the railroad line running southeast of Gorki northward to Khodorovichi. Major General S. V. Sokolov's 6th Guards Cavalry Corps, which had led the pursuit westward, and Major General M. V. Volkov's 5th Mechanized Corps, whose forces had been seriously depleted during the pursuit, supported the army by attaching small tank units to the attacking rifle divisions. The 43rd Guards and 256th Tank Brigades, 56th Guards Separate Tank Regiment, and 1495th and 1537th Self-propelled Artillery Regiments also provide a degree of support to Gordov's army. The army retained 42nd, 164th, and 222nd Rifle Divisions in reserve.

The Germans defended against 33rd Army's attacks with XXXIX Panzer Corps' 95th Infantry Division in the sector from south of Lenino to Mikulino and XX Army Corps' 78th Assault, 252nd, and 342nd Infantry Divisions deployed between Mikulino and Remistrianka River opposite Dribin. Thus, Gordov's army faced stronger German defenses than its neighboring armies to the north.

Beginning on 3 October, Krylov's forces launched their heaviest assaults from the villages of Mikulino and Gory along the Gorki road. Supported by 256th Tank Brigade and a small tank group from 5th Mechanized Corps, 290th and 173rd Rifle Divisions struck German defenses repeatedly but failed to make any progress. Thereafter, 33rd Army's assaults expired by 9 October without achieving any success.

Meanwhile, the Western Front's 49th and 10th Armies plowed forward on the Western Front's extended left wing, attempting to keep pace with the *front's* armies operating along the main axis of advance farther to the north. The forward elements of Colonel General I. T. Grishin's 49th Army reached the Pronia River from just north of Dribin southward to Budino by late on 2 October. It led its advance with 62nd Rifle Corps' 70th and 160th Rifle Divisions in the sector north of Dribin and 352nd, 277th, and 344th Rifle Divisions, whose positions stretched out to the south along the eastern bank of the Pronia River. Following in their wake were 36th Rifle and 106th Tank Brigades. The strong German defenses in this region, manned by IX Army Corps' 342nd and 35th Infantry Divisions, along with his army's relative weakness, convinced Grishin that any further offensive action would be futile.

On the Western Front's extreme right wing, Lieutenant General V. S. Popov's 10th Army confronted a different problem than that of its neighbors to the north. As it advanced westward in late September, it had to coordinate its operations with those of the Briansk Front's 50th Army, operating on its left. Because the Briansk Front's offensive progress lagged behind that of the Western Front, 10th Army had to watch its left flank carefully as it advanced. Although 50th Army did not close up to the Pronia River until late on 2 October, 10th Army timed its advance to reach its assigned sector at the same time. When it did so, its forces were arrayed along the river from Budino southward to Petukhovka. By this time, Popov arrayed his army with 247th and 139th Rifle Divisions, backed up by 49th Rifle Division, deployed in the sector south of Budino, and 38th Rifle Corps' 64th, 330th, and 385th Rifle Divisions deployed into forward positions in the bend of the Pronia River southeast of Chausy. Finally, Popov left 212th Rifle Division to protect the army's left flank near the village of Petukhovka. At this stage of the Belorussian operation, the relatively small size of Grishin's 49th and Popov's 10th Armies, along with the major offensive being conducted by the armies of General Rokossovsky's Central Front farther toward the south, relegated both armies to a passive, secondary role in the Western Front's Belorussian offensive.

Thus, by day's end on 11 October, Sokolovsky's initial assaults had achieved limited but still promising success in his *front's* right wing. The combined attacks by 5th, 31st, 68th, and 10th Guards Armies succeeded in pressing German Fourth Army's forces back to defensive positions roughly 20 kilometers east of Orsha. However, the Germans conducted their withdrawal in orderly fashion and, after they completed it, occupied formidable defensive positions protecting the approaches to all vital Soviet objectives in eastern Belorussia. None of Sokolovsky's attacking Soviet armies had achieved a "clean" penetration, and, worse still for the *front* commander, his main attack force, specifically, 10th Guards and 21st Armies, had failed to penetrate or even damage the German Fourth Army's defenses in the vital sector on the Mereia River west of Baevo. As a result, although the Soviet assaults forced German forces to pivot westward north of Baevo, the main German defense line along the Pronia River remained intact and held firm. Therefore, and logically, the strong German defenses west and northwest of Baevo became Sokolovsky's next target.

Sokolovsky's report to the *Stavka*, which he submitted in the wake of his attacks on 3 and 4 October, stated that his offensive was "hampered in connection with over-extended lines of communication (up to 200 kilometers), by poor roads, and by inadequate auto-transport for supply of types of goods, especially ammunition."[11] Further, he asserted, because his forces' ammunition stocks had decreased to 0.1–0.2 combat loads, and it would take up to eight days to replenish them to requisite levels, his front would have "to cease offensive operation until approximately 12 October."[12] No doubt, the Germans took good advantage of the brief respite.

THE SECOND ORSHA OFFENSIVE (12-18 OCTOBER 1943)

Encouraged by his modest successes north of Baevo and along the Smolensk-Orsha road, after conducting local regroupings to strengthen his *front's* new shock groups and replenish their ammunition stocks, General Sokolovsky ordered his forces to resume operations early on 12 October. This time, however, the offensive was to be conducted by shock groups formed by the *front's* 31st, 10th Guards, 21st, 33rd, and 49th Armies, supported by whatever armor 2nd Guards Tank and 5th Mechanized Corps could muster and by the horsemen and mobile artillery of 3rd and 6th Guards Cavalry Corps. North of the Dnepr River, General Gluzdovsky's heavily reinforced 31st Army was to advance along the Smolensk-Orsha road toward Orsha, while south of the river, Sukhomlin's 10th Guards, Krylov's 21st, Gordov's 33rd, and Grishin's 49th Armies were to advance westward from the region north and south of Baevo toward Orsha in a 15-kilometer-wide penetration sector. To do so, 21st and 33rd Armies had to regroup and then concentrate their forces in the critical Baevo-Lenino sector.

In preparation for the new assault, Sokolovsky shifted his forces across the front to reinforce the armies designated to conduct his *front's* main efforts. General Gluzdovsky concentrated his 31st Army astride the Smolensk-Orsha highway, with 36th Rifle Corps' 215th, 274th, and 359th Rifle Divisions deployed north of the main highway and 71st Rifle Corps' 82nd, 133rd, and 331st Rifle Divisions in attack positions between the highway and the Dnepr River. The 45th Rifle Corps' 88th and 251st Rifle Divisions, and 220th Rifle Division, transferred to the corps from 68th Army, constituted Gluzdovsky's second echelon and reserve. To further strengthen its assault, the army designated 42nd Guards Tank Brigade to support 71st Rifle Corps' attack. Finally, Sokolovsky tasked the far smaller 5th Army's 207th, 208th, and 312th Rifle Divisions with the mission of protecting 31st Army's right flank and 68th Army's 159th, 192nd, and 199th Rifle Divisions with defending 31st Army's left flank south of the Dnepr River. This left the remainder of 68th Army with the task of simply defending the sector immediately south of the Dnepr River, essentially in the gap between the *front's* attacking shock groups.

To augment 31st Army's northern thrust, Sokolovsky ordered General Krylov's 21st and General Gordov's 33rd Armies to conduct the *front's* southern thrust, supported and protected on the right by 10th Guards Army and on the left by 49th Army. To strengthen this blow, Sokolovsky ordered 33rd Army to regroup all of its forces northward into a new, more concentrated sector in 21st Army's former sector north and south of Lenino. For its part, 21st Army was to castle and concentrate its forces into new attack positions south of Baevo. In turn, 49th Army transferred forces from its left to its right wing and took control of 33rd Army's former sector south of Starosel'e (5 kilometers south of Lenino). Accordingly, 21st Army concentrated 69th Rifle

Corps' 76th, 153rd, and 174th Rifle Divisions, reinforced by the army's 63rd Rifle Division, on its right wing south of Baevo and 61st Rifle Corps' 62nd, 95th, and 157th Rifle Divisions on its left wing midway between Baevo and Lenino. Finally, a tank group from Burdeinyi's 2nd Guards Tank Corps, 23rd Guards Tank Brigade, and the army's two tank and two self-propelled artillery regiments were to support 21st Army's assaulting infantry with a force of eighty-five tanks and SP guns.[13]

General Gordov regrouped his 33rd Army into the sector vacated by 21st Army north and south of Lenino. As he recalled, his army's mission was

> to deliver the main attack along the Polzukhi, Staryi Diatel, and Shklov axis, penetrate the enemy defense in the Ponizov'e and Lenino sector (a penetration of 5 kilometers width), destroy the units of the [enemy's] 337th Infantry Division [Fourth Army's XXXIX Panzer Corps], and capture positions along the western bank of the Pnevka River. Then, while widening the offensive sector, the intention was to commit the army's mobile group (the 5th Mechanized and 6th Guards Cavalry Corps) into combat, and, while strengthening the attack, reach the Dnepr River line.[14]

When 33rd Army formed up for its attack, its first-echelon 42nd Rifle, the Polish 1st Infantry, and 290th Rifle Divisions, supported by 164th and 222nd Rifle Divisions in the army's second echelon, were to assault German defenses across the Mereia River just north of Lenino. As soon as they arrived, 247th and 139th Rifle Divisions, transferred by road march from 10th Army to Gordov's army, were to reinforce the army's second echelon. To support and sustain his assaults, Gordov's army employed a small mobile group formed from Volkov's 5th Mechanized and Sokolov's 6th Guards Cavalry Corps, along with 65th and 70th Rifle Corps' 58th, 144th, and 371st Rifle Divisions. Assigned to 33rd Army's second echelon and reserve, these forces were earmarked to exploit the offensive whenever and wherever it succeeded.

To provide protection for 33rd Army's left flank, 49th Army shifted its forces to the right into 33rd Army's former positions. The 338th Rifle Division of 33rd Army's 70th Rifle Corps, which remained behind in 49th Army's newly assigned sector for several days, concealed and protected this movement. Meanwhile, 49th Army also regrouped its forces to the right from 12 through 14 October, when its 344th and 352nd Rifle Divisions moved from the Dribin region on the army's left wing northward into 33rd Army's vacated positions. Finally, 10th Army also dispatched 139th and 247th Rifle Divisions northward to reinforce and support 33rd Army's assault.[15] Once concentrated for the attack, Gordov's 33rd Army was markedly superior to the defending Germans, with a 4-or-5-to-1 advantage in infantry, 7.3 to 1 in artillery, and a breathtaking 17 to 1 superiority in artillery and mortars.[16]

The Western Front's Orsha Offensives   73

Finally, on 21st Army's right, General Sukhomlin deployed his 10th Guards Army with two rifle corps abreast, backed up by his third rifle corps. The 15th Guards Rifle Corps' was deployed on the army's right wing, with 85th Guards Division in first echelon and 30th in second. On the army's left wing, 19th Guards Rifle Corps deployed 22nd Guards Division in first echelon and the 56th and 65th in second. Completing 10th Guards Army's attack formation, 29th Guards Division deployed opposite the sharp angle jutting eastward in the German defenses northwest of Baevo.

After this complex regrouping process was complete, the nucleus of Sokolovsky's attacking force consisted of 19 rifle divisions (8 in first echelon and 11 in second), supported by an armored group of 85 tanks and SP guns from 2nd Guards Tank Corps, 3rd Guards Cavalry Corps, 3 separate tank brigades, 6 tank and self-propelled artillery regiments, 12 artillery brigades, 20 RGK artillery regiments, and small elements of 5th Mechanized Corps. Overall, the force fielded 134 tanks and self-propelled guns and achieved an artillery density of 150–200 tubes per kilometer of front.[17]

Initially, the opposing German forces included XXVII Army Corps' 197th and 337th Infantry Divisions and three to five artillery regiments. However, as the operation developed, Fourth Army reinforced these forces with 252nd Infantry and 18th and 25th Panzer Grenadier Divisions and three to four artillery regiments. The resulting correlation of opposing forces favored the attacking Soviets by a factor of better than 5 to 1 initially, and 3 to 1 subsequently in infantry and more than 2 to 1 in tanks and self-propelled guns.

Sokolovsky's armies began their assault early on 12 October across the entire front after firing an artillery preparation that lasted for eighty-five minutes (see Map 3.3 for regrouping Soviet forces). Although heavy fighting raged on for two days in each and every Soviet attack sector, the German defenses proved effective and deadly to the attacking Red Army soldiers. Soviet critiques of the offensive credit this failure to the strength of the German defenses, the inability of the attackers to maneuver because of the paucity of tanks, and failures to integrate infantry, tanks, and artillery fires effectively. As a result, the attacks by 31st Army and 10th Guards Army immediately stalled without recording any appreciable gains. Furthermore, 21st Army's gains west of Baevo were limited to no more than several hundred meters at an immense cost in terms of casualties it suffered.

A recent Russian source explained why the offensive faltered almost immediately after it began:

However, [the artillery preparation] did not surprise the enemy. Therefore, the subunits of his first echelon were withdrawn in timely fashion to the second trenches and occupied covered positions. Only observers and on-duty firing means remained along the forward edge. Because of poor reconnaissance and the absence of corrective fire, army and divisional artillery delivered area strikes and not against concrete targets. The effectiveness of such actions [fire] was low and, as a result, did not succeed in suppressing the infantry in strong points and destroy the firing systems of German forces. From the beginning of the attacks, our direct fire weapons could not conduct fire on the enemy because of the fear of striking their own rifle subunits that were moving across the battlefield in dense ranks.

The offensive immediately took on the form of a slow "gnawing away" at the enemy's defense. The *front's* forces were drawn into prolonged and bloody combat for populated points and heights. The German infantry subunits, with small groups of tanks supported by artillery and mortar fire, delivered many counterattacks. Enemy aircraft dominated the skies and inflicted tangible casualties on the attacking unit. Their attacks in the sector of Lieutenant General N. I. Krylov's 5th Army prevented any sort of positive results.[18]

Sokolovsky's armies resumed their assaults on 13 October after firing a short ten-to-fifteen-minute artillery fire raid. Although all of the attacking armies reinforced their shock groups with rifle divisions allocated from their second echelons, the results were no better than what little was achieved the day before. One account records that when the rifle subunits encountered artillery and mortar fire, "they immediately went to ground," adding candidly, "Attempts by the commanders of squads, platoons, and companies to raise them into the attack were not crowned with success."[19]

The only attacking army that achieved any measurable success was Gordov's 33rd, which mounted its assaults in the Lenino sector. There, Polish 1st Infantry Division, along with a small armored combat group from 5th Mechanized Corps, supported on the left by 42nd Rifle Division and on the right by 290th Rifle Division, managed to carve a shallow 1-to-3-kilometer-deep wedge into the defenses of German 337th Infantry Division west of Lenino by day's end on 14 October. However, this was not easy because "they were under constant attack by German aircraft, which carried out 1,500 combat sorties during the day." [20] Meanwhile, the assaults by Sukhomlin's 10th Guards and Grishin's 49th Armies achieved no progress whatsoever against German forces defending the villages of Lapyrevshchina and Arvianitsa, several kilometers northwest of Baevo.

Nor did the intense German air activity abate. For example, on 14 October, the Germans supposedly unleashed up to 1,300 air sorties, while the pilots of Lieutenant General of Aviation M. M. Gromov's 1st Air Army managed to conduct only 237 sorties. This almost negated the limited gains recorded the day before:

> Enemy bombers inflicted immense casualties in personnel and equipment and disorganized the command and control of forces. For example,

Army General V. D. Sokolovsky, commander in chief, Western Front, February 1943–April 1944

Lieutenant General N. I. Krylov, commander, 21st Army, July–October 1943, and 5th Army, October 1943–October 1944 and December–September 1945

Lieutenant General V. A. Gluzdovsky, commander, 31st Army, February 1943–May 1944

Lieutenant General E. P. Zhuravlev, commander, 68th Army, March–October 1943, and 21st Army, October 1943–February 1944

Lieutenant General A. V. Sukhomlin, commander, 10th Guards Army, September 1943–January 1944

Colonel General V. N. Gordov, commander, 33rd Army, October 1942–March 1944

Colonel General I. E. Petrov, commander, 33rd Army, March–April 1944

Lieutenant General I. T. Grishin, commander, 49th Army, June 1943–May 1945

Lieutenant General V. S. Popov, commander, 10th Army, February 1942–April 1944

Major General of Tank Forces A. S. Burdeinyi, commander, 2nd Guards Tank Corps, June 1943–May 1945

the Polish 1st Infantry Division, which operated successfully on 12 October, was subsequently subjected to air strikes and enemy counterattacks from the flanks. As a result, the headquarters of the division and its regiments lost command and control, and its subunits became mixed up on the battlefield. Some of them were scattered and taken captive. It should be noted that instances of surrender had occurred in this formation even before combat operations began, when, on the night before the offensive, 25 Polish soldiers fled to the German side. Overall during the two days of battle, the division lost more than 500 killed and more than 1,680 men wounded, and 661 men became missing-in-action. On 15 October, in accordance with decision of the *front's* military council, it [the division] was withdrawn into 33rd Army's reserve to restore its combat readiness.[21]

As the fighting raged on from 15 through 18 October, 21st and 33rd Armies succeeded in expanding their bridgehead across the Mereia River between Baevo and Lenino by a depth of 1 to 2 kilometers (see Maps 3.4 and 3.5). But in order to do so, they were forced to commit forces from their second echelon into the bridgehead fight. Initially, these included 139th and 222nd Rifle Divisions and, ultimately, 139th and 247th Rifle Divisions in the Lenino sector. However, the cost in losses, especially human lives, was staggering and in no way commensurate with the meager gains. Thus, in two days of fighting, by day's end on 16 October, 33rd Army had lost more than thirty of its eighty-five tanks.[22] In fact the heavy fighting was as futile as it was costly. Although 33rd Army's forces reached and secured the low ridgeline east of the Mereia River, by 18 October the Germans committed 252nd Infantry Division into combat between 25th Panzer Grenadier and 337th Infantry Divisions. These and other reserves successfully sealed the shallow Soviet breach.

Measured against meager gains of no more than 1 to 1.5 kilometers over the course of the offensive, the immense casualties suffered by the Western Front staggered even the normally callous *Stavka*. Specifically, during the seven days from 12 through 18 October, the Western Front lost 5,858 men killed and 17,478 wounded, for a total of 23,336 soldiers.[23] In 33rd Army's attack sector alone, Polish 1st Infantry Division lost 502 men killed and the army's other attacking divisions more than 1,700 men.[24]

Sokolovsky's report to the *Stavka* acknowledged the failure but emphasized its causes:

> The organized offensive along the Orsha axis on 12 October did not achieve the required development for the following reasons. The enemy, through deserters, knew about the penetration being prepared and took countermeasures (prepared large groups of aircraft, strengthened the axis with tanks and self-propelled guns, and covered [protected] personnel and weapons during the period of our artillery and aerial preparation). And all of this opposed our forces during the time of our attack. . . .

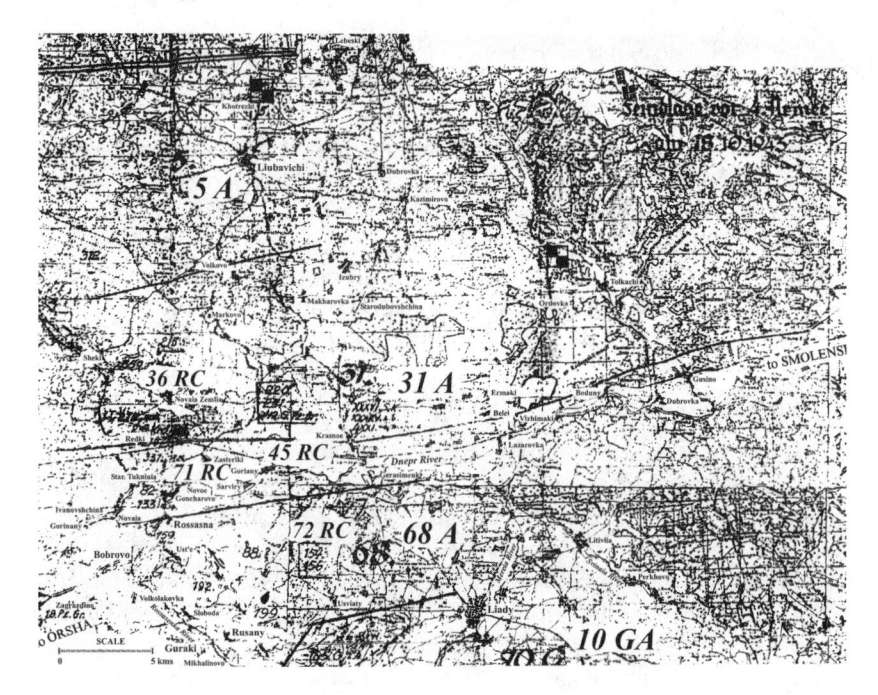

76 The Struggle for Belorussia, October–December 1943

Map 3.4. Fourth Army's Situation in the Orsha Sector, 18 October 1943

The *front* continued to experience great difficulties with the supply of automobile fuel, ammunition, foodstuffs, and aviation gas to the forces. The railroad still worked very weakly up to Smolensk and provided 6–7 trains per day. The road supply routes were very long and required considerable time and excessive fuel for round trips [to the front].

The combat was conducted by artillery, mortars, and understrength infantry; the tanks for operating with infantry were very few, and they frequently were disabled. Failing to achieve the required success in this operation, the forces . . . were forced to cease offensive operations."[25]

Despite Sokolovsky's excuses for failure, something else was clearly wrong, and the *Stavka* thought it knew why. It believed that Sokolovsky had failed to concentrate his forces properly and to choose the proper location to conduct his main attack. Specifically, the *Stavka* believed that selecting a main attack sector in the very center of the *front*'s offensive sector was incorrect, if not sheer folly. Given this decision, it believed that, when the *front*'s shock group reached the Dnepr River, it could not overcome it in a short period, making any subsequent exploitation highly unlikely. Conversely, organizing the main attack on the *front*'s right wing would permit Sokolovsky's forces to envelop German Fourth Army's defenses from its left

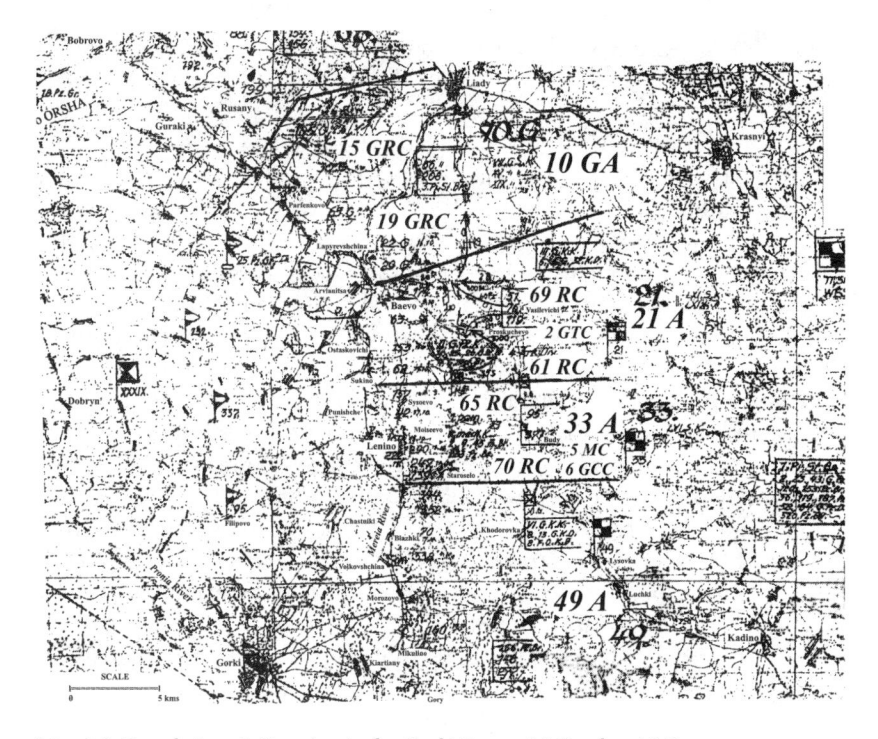

Map 3.5. Fourth Army's Situation in the Gorki Sector, 18 October 1943

flank, reach its rear, and clear German forces from the western bank of the Dnepr without having to organize a complicated and costly forced crossing of the river.[26]

Nonetheless, because the *Stavka* believed that, at the very least, the Western Front's superiority over the Germans along the Smolensk-Minsk axis was sufficient to achieve an operational penetration, it gave no thought to halting or delaying the offensive. Instead, it urged Sokolovsky on, convinced that he would be able to replicate the success the forces of Eremenko's Kalinin Front had achieved at Nevel'. Accordingly, the *Stavka* issued new directives designed to remedy the situation. In retrospect, it is now clear that the *Stavka* itself was overly optimistic, largely because it woefully underestimated German strength, defensive skills, and resolve.

THE THIRD ORSHA OFFENSIVE (21–26 OCTOBER 1943)

Faced with the Western Front's failure to penetrate German defenses in the central sector of the western strategic axis during the first half of October, the *Stavka* took immediate corrective action. The Soviet official history of the war recorded the *Stavka*'s new orders and the Western Front's subsequent actions:

> The *Stavka* called the *front* command's attention to inadmissible errors. It demanded, in particular, that the *front* form a shock group on its right flank rather than in its center. The *Stavka* noted that, in the event of "[the shock group's] successful advance [in the center of the *front*], this grouping will stew [sweat] its way to the Dnepr River and, as a result, further development of the offensive will be limited. At the same time, the *front's* right wing can attack without having to force the Dnepr River and is capable of clearing the Dnepr by means of an attack against the flank and rear of the enemy defending along the Dnepr." The *Stavka* ordered the Western Front commander to regroup his forces rapidly so as to reinforce his right wing. Accordingly, it resubordinated 5th Army's three divisions to 31st Army, and it withdrew 5th Army's headquarters into the *front's* reserve. The 68th and 10th Guards Armies transferred part of their forces to 21st and 33rd Armies.
>
> The formations of the 1st Polish Division . . . participated with Soviet forces in the Western Front's offensive. . . .
>
> The 1st Polish Division began its attack on 12 October. It operated in the Lenino region of Mogilev *oblast'*.
>
> The Western Front's active operations along the Orsha and Mogilev axes continued until year's end. Their forces tied down considerable enemy forces and prevented him from transferring divisions to the southwestern strategic axis. Furthermore, the Wehrmacht command had to reinforce Army Group "Center's" 3rd Panzer and 4th Armies, which were opposing the Western Front, continuously. Six divisions, including panzer [divisions], were transferred to 3rd Panzer and 4th Armies from 9th and 16th Armies and Army Group Center's reserves in October and 10 divisions, including a motorized [division], in November and December.[27]

Thanks to *Stavka* documents, fragmentary Soviet accounts, a recent account published in Belarus, and German archival records, we can now reconstruct a fairly detailed account of the Western Front's futile efforts to penetrate Army Group Center's defenses at Orsha in late October and reach and capture Minsk. Three days after Sokolovsky's initial assaults during his second offensive against German defenses failed, on 15 October 1943, the *Stavka* sent a directive to the *front* commander detailing his mistakes, ordering corrective actions, and mandating the conduct of a new offensive (see Appendix B-4). As noted in the official history, the *Stavka* complained that the offensive had failed "because of the incorrect grouping of the *front*'s forces. The main grouping . . . has been created in the *front*'s center sector. . . . In the event this grouping advances successfully, it will stew [sweat] its way to the Dnepr River" and the offensive would bog down. In addition, the *Stavka* complained, "The 5th and 68th Armies, which have only three rifle divisions each, are extremely weak and are operating with a very cumbersome army command and control apparatus and rear service structure."[28] As a result, the *Stavka* directed Sokolovsky to:

- Transfer all three of 5th Army's divisions to 31st Army and subsequently combine them into a corps and withdraw 5th Army's headquarters into the *front's* reserve.
- Reinforce 68th and 10th Guards Armies at the expense of 21st and 33rd Armies, increasing the number of divisions in each of these armies up to nine (three corps in each army).
- Leave one army with eight rifle divisions on the front previously occupied by 21st and 33rd Armies so that it does not cease active operations, and withdraw one army headquarters' armies into the *front's* reserve.
- Complete regrouping forces no later than 21 October.
- Allocate the bulk of reinforcing weapons and equipment to 31st, 68th, and 10th Guards Armies.
- Conduct 31st Army's offensive, planned for 17 October, depending on the regrouping of forces.
- Replace Zhuravlev with another commander from an army being withdrawn into the *front's* reserve if he believes he is not capable of coping with an army as large as the 68th.
- Submit an operational plan for the *front's* new grouping by 19 October 1943.[29]

In accordance with the *Stavka's* instructions, General Sokolovsky conducted a major regrouping of forces from 16 through 20 October in order to create a new shock group of requisite size in the sector along the Smolensk-Orsha road (see Map 3.6). However, because this regrouping was incomplete by 21 October and, in fact, continued to month's end, while active operations were under way along the Smolensk-Orsha road, it is virtually impossible to track changes in the Western Front's order of battle in late October. Making things more difficult, the few existing sources telescope the ensuing regroupings and attacks conducted by the Western Front's armies in late October and early November. For example, 10th Guards Army's history states:

> By order of the Western Front's commander, 10th Guards Army was withdrawn from the forward edge [of the front] on 20 October 1943.
> With the *Stavka's* approval, the *front* commander decided to punch a hole in the enemy's defenses somewhat farther to the north, in the sector adjacent to the Minsk highway. Here, the enemy defenses were more solid, but the presence of such a fine road as the Minsk highway and

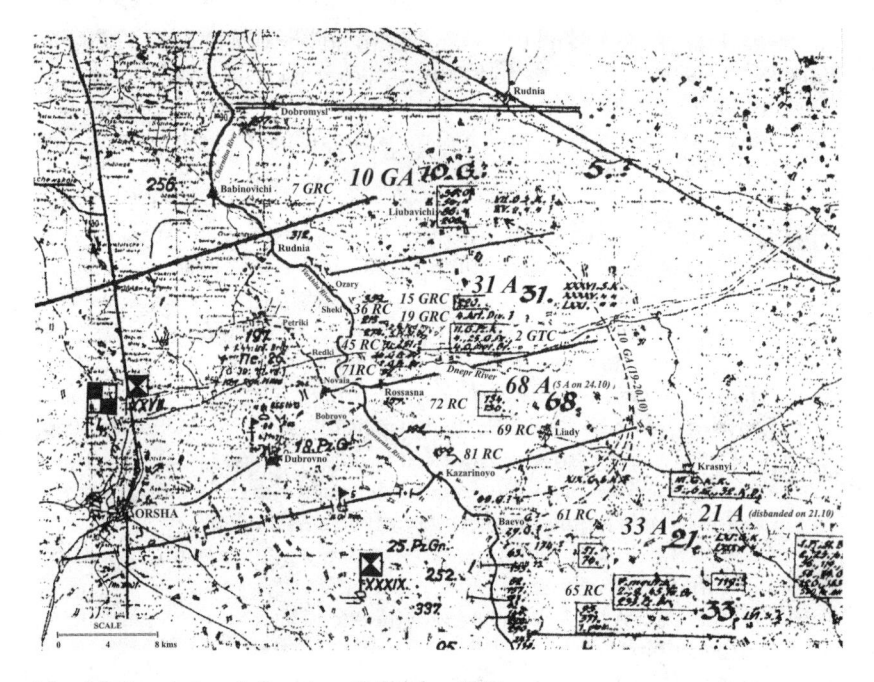

80   The Struggle for Belorussia, October–December 1943

Map 3.6. Fourth Army's Situation, 20 October 1943

the Smolensk-Shukhovtsy railroad provided more favorable conditions for resupply.

The shock group was to consist of 10th Guards Army, which had deployed north of the railroad and highway and had relieved the forces of 5th Army, and 31st Army, which had relieved 68th Army's formations south of the road.

After giving up its former sector, the army's forces began regrouping to the new region. The 15th and 19th Guards [Rifle] Corps, each with three rifle divisions, entered the new region in full complement. Having turned its 208th Rifle Division over to 5th Army, 7th Guards Rifle Corps' headquarters entered the Liubavichi region, where it took over 207th and 312th Rifle Divisions and 152nd Fortified Region, which were operating in that sector. The regrouping took place during a period of intensifying *rasputitsa* [period of flooded roads].[30]

The history of 22nd Guards Rifle Division history seconded this account:

> After turning its defensive sector over to 29th Guards Rifle Division, the division marched from Zverovichi through Krasnyi to Varechki on the night of 20 October, and concentrated west of Iur'evka.

At that time, our forces began an offensive along the Orsha axis. Our division was deployed in the corps' second echelon during the initial days of the offensive, but on 5 November it replaced units of 65th Guards Rifle Division and fought to penetrate the enemy's heavily fortified defensive belt along the approaches to Orsha.[31]

Finally, the history of 65th Guards Rifle Division provides further clues in regard to 10th Guards Army's regrouping: "The division turned its sector over to 62nd and 63rd Rifle Divisions on the night of 20 October and, after marching along the route from Liady through Klimenki, Krasnyi, Skvortsy, and Blashkino, arrived in the Sharino region on the following day. The division relieved units of 359th Rifle Division during the night of 23 October and occupied jumping-off positions for an offensive along the Sheki, Skulaty and Tkhorino front."[32]

In contrast, the history of 5th Army only muddies our understanding of what actually occurred:

Lieutenant General N. I. Krylov was assigned to command 5th Army on 24 October. . . . Major General N. Ia. Prikhid'ko, who had previously headed 68th Army staff, replaced the Chief of Staff, Colonel F. E. Pochem, several days later. . . .

During this period, the greater part of 68th Army's forces were transferred to 5th Army, which was completely reconstituted. It [the 5th Army] consisted of two rifle corps by the end of 1943. One of them, the 72nd, commanded by Major General Iu. M. Prokof'ev, consisted of 159th, 174th, and 192nd Rifle Divisions. The other, the 81st, commanded by Colonel A. K. Ivanov, consisted of 95th and 199th Rifle Divisions.

At that time [from 21 to 26 October], 5th Army's [former] forces continued to fight along the line of the Chernitsa, Verkhita, and Rososianka [Rossasenka] Rivers. The units of 72nd Rifle Corps attacked along the Dnepr in the direction of Dubrovno.[33]

However, a more recent brief history of operations in Belorussia helps resolve these matters:

Consequently, in accordance with the *Stavka* VGK's decision, it was planned to conduct the main attack along the Minsk highway. The offensive on a new axis avoided arriving at a serious water obstacle—the Dnepr—but at the same time would be conducted in the difficult conditions of forested swampy terrain. In light of this, the German command, considering the possibility of a blow being delivered here by the Soviets, prepared three echeloned defensive lines ahead of time: the first, along the Lake Afanas'evskoe, Staraia Tukhinia, and Novaia Tukhinia line; the second, the Ostrov Iur'ev, Kireevo, and Gorinany line, 12–15 kilometers from the first; and the third, 6–8 kilometers northeast of Orsha.

When preparing the operation, 10th Guards Army accepted 5th Army's formations, together with its reinforcements and the sectors it occupied, into its composition. Simultaneously, 21st Army gave all of its forces to 33rd Army. The *front*'s headquarters conducted a mobilization in the liberated territories to replenish its personnel. This permitted increasing the strength of rifle divisions up to 4,000–4,500 men in a short time. However, the majority of the new replacements lacked necessary military training. Their morale and psychological state after two years living under occupation left much to be desired. It should be added that the movement about of the force did not remain unnoticed by German intelligence.[34]

Given this confusing picture, periodic and often daily situation and intelligence reports produced by German *Fremde Heeres Ost* and German Fourth Army help sort out this complex situation and identify major changes in the Western Front's order of battle fairly precisely. These reports, coupled with the new account published in Belarus and older fragmentary Soviet descriptions, produce the following picture:

- The headquarters of General Polenov's 5th Army withdrew temporarily to reorganize, rest, and refit, while turning its sector and its three rifle divisions (the 207th, 208th, and 312th) over to 10th Guards Army's 7th Guards Rifle Corps. This corps, with its three new divisions, was assigned responsibility for 5th Army's former sector along the Chernitsa and Verkhita River from Dobromysl' through Babinovichi to Ozery north of the Smolensk-Orsha road. However, 5th Army was reactivated on 24 October under General Krylov's command and assumed control over 68th Army's forces on 5 November.
- General Sukhomlin's 10th Guards Army transferred its former sector, which extended from Kazarinovo to west of Baevo, to 33rd Army. It then moved 15th Guards Rifle Corps' 30th and 8th Guards Divisions and 19th Guards Rifle Corps' 22nd, 56th, and 65th Guards Divisions northward to occupy the Ozery-Sheki [Shcheki] sector along the Verkhita River north of the Smolensk-Orsha road on 31st Army's right. The army's two guards rifle corps then deployed in two echelons to spearhead the new offensive, with one division from each of its two corps in first echelon and the remainder in reserve.
- General Gluzdovsky's 31st Army concentrated its forces in the narrow sector along the Smolensk-Orsha highway and between the highway and the Dnepr River on 10th Guards Army's left. It now consisted of 36th Rifle Corps' 215th, 274th, and 359th Rifle Divisions, 45th Rifle Corps' 88th, 220th, and 251st Rifle Divisions, and 71st Rifle Corps'

82nd, 133rd, and 381st Rifle Divisions. The 58th Rifle Division from 33rd Army also reinforced the army. Gluzdovsky deployed his army for the 21 October assault with 71st Rifle Corps on its left wing, just north of the Dnepr River, 45th Rifle Corps in its center, astride the highway and railroad line, and 36th Rifle Corps on its right wing north of the highway. Each corps attacked with two rifle divisions in first echelon and one in second. The army then formed a tank or motorized rifle group around the nucleus of 2nd Guards Tank Corps' brigades, and employed its organic 42nd Guards Tank, 26th Guards Tank, and 4th Guards Motorized Rifle Brigades, respectively, to provide infantry support for its three rifle corps. In addition, Sokolovsky supported 31st Army's assault with 3rd and 4th Guards Artillery Penetration Divisions, provided by the *Stavka* and the Western Front.

- South of the Dnepr River, General Zhuravlev's 68th Army temporarily assumed control over 72nd Rifle Corps' 159th, 174th, and 192nd Rifle Divisions and 81st Rifle Corps' 95th and 199th Rifle Divisions. The 95th had been transferred to the army from 33rd Army and the 174th from 21st Army. The 69th Rifle Corps also joined General Krylov's army during its assault in late October. Its corps headquarters and 76th and 157th Rifle Divisions came from 21st Army, and the 290th had been transferred from 33rd Army. At the same time, 173rd Rifle Division was transferred from 33rd Army to 81st Rifle Corps. The 68th Army controlled the three rifle corps during the initial stages of the 21 October offensive. However, shortly after General Krylov was appointed as 5th Army's commander on 24 October, his headquarters assumed control over 68th Army's forces, supposedly on 5 November.[35] Before this occurred, the army's 159th Rifle Division participated in the 21 October attack and was supported later by 69th Rifle Corps' 174th Rifle Division. The remaining divisions of the army's 72nd Rifle Corps defended on the army's right wing and 81st Rifle Corps defended on its left wing.
- General Krylov's 21st Army turned all of its tactical combat forces and its combat sector over to 33rd Army and transferred its 69th Rifle Corps to 68th Army on 21 October. Its headquarters and supporting units and facilities reverted to the *Stavka's* Reserve on 28 October, after General Krylov took command of 5th Army on the 24th.
- General Gordov's 33rd Army assumed responsibility for 21st Army's sector and transferred 58th Rifle Division to 31st Army and 95th, 173rd, and 290th Rifle Divisions to 68th Army on 21 October. As of 1 November, however, the army consisted of 61st Rifle Corps' 62nd and 63rd Rifle Divisions, 65th Rifle Corps' 144th, 153rd, and 222nd Rifle Divisions, and 42nd and 164th Rifle Divisions. The 256th Tank Brigade, 63rd Guards, 64th Guards, and 248th Separate Tank Regiments,

and 1495th Self-propelled Artillery Regiment provided the army with armor support. To conduct the 21 October assault, Gordov deployed 61st Rifle Corps on his army's right wing, in 10th Guards Army's former sector and south of Baevo. It was flanked on the left by 65th Rifle Corps and two separate divisions near Lenino.

- 49th and 10th Armies occupied defenses along the *front's* extended left wing, basically in their former configuration.
- Because of their dilapidated and weakened condition, the *Stavka* withdrew 5th Mechanized and 6th Guards Cavalry Corps into its reserve on 21 October.[36]

By virtue of this extensive regrouping, by day's end on 20 October Sokolovsky's Western Front had formed a powerful offensive shock group along the Smolensk-Orsha highway and to its north and south, whose forces were poised to strike westward. However, the resubordination of so many units into unfamiliar sectors certainly increased confusion in Soviet ranks and had a debilitating effect on command and control. No doubt all of this contributed to the failure of the Western Front's subsequent offensives.

Summarizing these changes based on recent accounts and subsequent analysis of the fighting, the nucleus of Sokolovsky's shock group consisted of 31st Army' three rifle corps in first echelon, followed by two guards rifle corps from 10th Guards Army (one dedicated to reinforce on the shock group's right flank) in second echelon, and one division from 68th Army. The 2nd Guards Tank Corps and two artillery penetration divisions provided armor and artillery support to the first echelon. The shock group deployed 11 rifle divisions for the initial assault, 8 in first echelon and 3 in second. One tank corps, 2 tank brigades, 3 tank and self-propelled artillery regiments, 13 artillery brigades and 19 RGK artillery regiments, which fielded a force of 172 tanks and created an artillery density of 115 to 260 tubes per kilometer of front, supported the shock group. In addition, south of the Dnepr River, 68th Army committed its 69th Rifle Corps' 174th Rifle Division to combat on 24 October to assist in developing the penetration. After 31st Army's reinforced shock group completed the first stage of the offensive, 10th Guards Army, supported by 3rd Guards Cavalry Corps, would be committed into first echelon to commence the second-stage advance on the city of Orsha.

Initially, Sokolovsky's attacking forces faced 197th Infantry Division and a single battalion deployed on the right wing of 18th Panzer Grenadier Division, both subordinate to German Fourth Army's XXVII Army Corps. During the ensuing fighting, Fourth Army reinforced its defending forces with 26th Infantry Division, 1st SS Infantry Brigade, a battalion *kampfgruppe* from 78th Assault Division, and Army Group Center's separate motorized regiment. Once reinforced, the German defenders fielded as many as sixty tanks and six to seven artillery regiments, although the defenders' antitank guns (*Paks*) did most of the damage to the attacking Soviet tanks. Therefore, Sokolovsky's shock group possessed an initial numerical superiority over the German defenders of more than 5 to 1 in infantry and an absolute superiority in armor and artillery. However, that Soviet superiority decreased quickly to about 3 to 1 during the course of the fighting.

Sokolovsky's shock group commenced its assault early on 21 October after firing a two-hour-and-ten-minute artillery preparation. Striking the 197th Infantry Division's first defensive line shortly after dawn, the lead divisions of Gluzdovsky's punched through the German defenses and the next day were reinforced on the right by the lead division of 10th Guards Army, 19th Guards Rifle Corps' 65th Guards Division. The 65th's history confirmed its role, stating:

> The division relieved the units of 359th Rifle Division during the night of 22–23 October and occupied jumping-off positions for the offensive along the Shcheki, Skulaty, and Tkhorino front.
>
> The 332nd and 181st Infantry Regiments of German 198th [*sic*] Infantry Division were defending positions in front of 65th Guards Rifle Division. The first positions in the enemy's defensive belt consisted of three dense trenches with communications trenches, pillboxes, antitank and antipersonnel minefields, and two to three lines of barbed wire entanglements. The Siberians had to assault such a strong defensive position.
>
> The guardsmen launched their attack at 1400 hours on 23 October, delivering their main attack on the left flank toward height marker 148.8, Petriki, and Zapol'e. Fierce combat raged along the entire front. Overcoming the enemy resistance and having repelled four counterattacks, the division's units had thrown the subunits of 181st Infantry Regiment back from their occupied positions by 25 October and forced them to withdraw to the previously prepared positions along the Shera, Novoe Selo, Pushchai, and Kireeva line. However, further attempts by the division to develop offensive success failed, and, by order of the corps commander, it temporarily went over to the defense. The division turned its combat sector over to units of 22nd Guards Rifle Division on the night of 5 November and was withdrawn into the corps' second echelon.[37]

German situation maps and fragmentary Soviet accounts indicate that 31st Army's assault was comparable to that of 65th Guards Rifle Division. After the intense artillery preparation, the first echelon divisions of the army's 36th, 45th, and 71st Rifle Corps conducted a frontal assault with densely massed infantry supported by tanks scattered throughout the army's assault formation. From north to south, the attacking divisions included 274th, 215th, 88th, 251st, 82nd, and 133rd Rifle Divisions backed up by 359th, 220th, and 331st Rifle Divisions in second echelon. Despite suffering staggering casualties, this massive force smashed the defenses of German 197th Infantry Division between the village of Red'ki, situated 1 kilometer north of the main highway, and that of Novaia, on the northern bank of the Dnepr River. By early evening, the lead elements of the assaulting force had penetrated 4 kilometers deep on a 1-kilometer-wide front toward the village of Kireevo, situated on the main railroad line to Orsha, and to the village of Ivanovshchina, on the northern bank of the Dnepr River. With Sokolovsky's approval, at about midday Gluzdovsky unleashed two tank brigades of General Burdeiny's 2nd Guards Tank Corps into the penetration. However, according to one account, "Soon they were halted, since the German command moved reserves to the threatened axis and concentrated on it the fires of more than 40 artillery and mortar batteries."[38]

Meanwhile, on 31st Army's left, 68th Army's 159th Rifle Division forced its way across the Rossasenka River and advanced .5 kilometer to the approaches to Height Marker (Hill) 180.8, where heavy German fire brought its advance to an abrupt halt. Thereafter, no reinforcements were available to assist the 159th's assault because intense German artillery fire from the vicinity of the height marker prevented any additional Soviet forces from crossing the Rossasenka River. In fact, on the first day of the offensive, because of rapid German reactions, the forward divisions of 10th Guards and 68th Armies were not able to advance more than 200–300 meters into the Germans' defenses.[39]

Although inspired by its gains on 21 October, 31st Army was unable to match these on 22 October, when its attacking divisions managed to advance an average of 1 kilometer. Nor did the commitment of the two tank brigades of 2nd Guards Tank Corps improve the situation, for "having lost 41 tanks and, in effect, their combat capabilities, they failed to produce a turning point in the course of the fighting."[40] As a result, Sokolovsky decided to withdraw General Burdeiny's tank corps into his reserve, signaling an end to his hopes of quickly achieving a decisive penetration.

German Fourth Army and its XXVII Army Corps reacted quickly and effectively to the dangerous Soviet attack. On German Fourth Army's orders, two regiments of 26th Infantry Division, elements of 1st SS Infantry Brigade, several battalions of 52nd Infantry Division (then in *kampfgruppe* configuration), and a separate motorized regiment from Army Group Center's reserve moved forward into the fray. Counterattacks conducted by these forces on 22 and 23 October contained the main Soviet thrust short of the town of Kireeva and forced 68th Army to withdraw its 159th Rifle Division back to its bridgehead over the Rossasenka River (see Map 11.12). This left General Gluzdovsky with no other option but to commit the second echelon divisions of his corps into combat.

Fighting intensified further on 24 October, when 31st Army's second-echelon rifle divisions joined the fray in what turned out to be one final attempt to pierce the German defenses (see Map 3.6). Once again, withering German artillery and mortar, to which Soviet artillery was unable to respond because of ammunition shortages, cut down the advancing ranks of untrained infantry unmercifully before they achieved anything whatsoever. On 31st Army's right, 10th Guards Army's forces, now reinforced by 56th Guards Division, managed to clear the German defenders from the bogs south of the Verkhita River by nightfall on 26 October but were finally halted well short of the rail station at Osintori and the region just south of Petriki. By now reinforced by 58th Rifle Division, 31st Army's forces had reached Kireeva on the Orsha-Smolensk railroad line, but they were abruptly halted there by the stiffening resistance from the remainder of German 26th Infantry Division.

Meanwhile, along the Dnepr River, newly redesignated 5th Army (formerly the 68th) committed 72nd Rifle Corps' 174th Rifle Division to combat in support of the 159th Rifle Division, still pinned down in its bridgehead across the Rossasenka River. The 174th Rifle Division advanced along the northern bank of the Dnepr under the cover of darkness on the night of 24–25 October. Then, under cover of 72nd Corps' artillery, it crossed the Dnepr in small boats, attacked, and captured the German strongpoint on Height Marker 180.8 by day's end on the 26th. Despite repelling what its history termed as eleven strong enemy counterattacks, somehow the 174th was able to cling successfully to its prize.[41]

Frustrated over his forces' repeated inability to achieve a clean and deep penetration through the German defenses, Sokolovsky ordered the assaults to halt at nightfall on 26 October. By this time, 10th Guards and 31st Armies' forces had managed to advance 4 to 6 kilometers westward in five days of heavy fighting (see Maps 3.7 and 3.8). Reportedly, they did so only at a cost of 19,102 casualties, including 4,787 killed and 14,315 wounded. As one recent account correctly recorded:

> By the end of the day on 26 October, the offensive capabilities of the forces were completely exhausted, and they set about digging into the position they had reached. The maximum depth of their penetration into the enemy's defense amounted to 4–6 kilometers. While doing so, the Western Front lost more than 4,700 men killed and more than 14,200 wounded. The next report by Army General V. D. Sokolovsky to the *Stavka* VGK pointed out that the command of German 4th Army had paid special attention to fortifying its defenses north of the Dnepr River and along the Orsha axis. Here, it concentrated up to six infantry divisions and the SS brigade, whose average strength (6–7,000 men) exceeded the strength of the rifle divisions by 35–50 percent. The depth of the first defensive line reached 6 kilometers. Anti-infantry and antitank obstacles were located in front of the forward edge of the defense and in its depths. The enemy

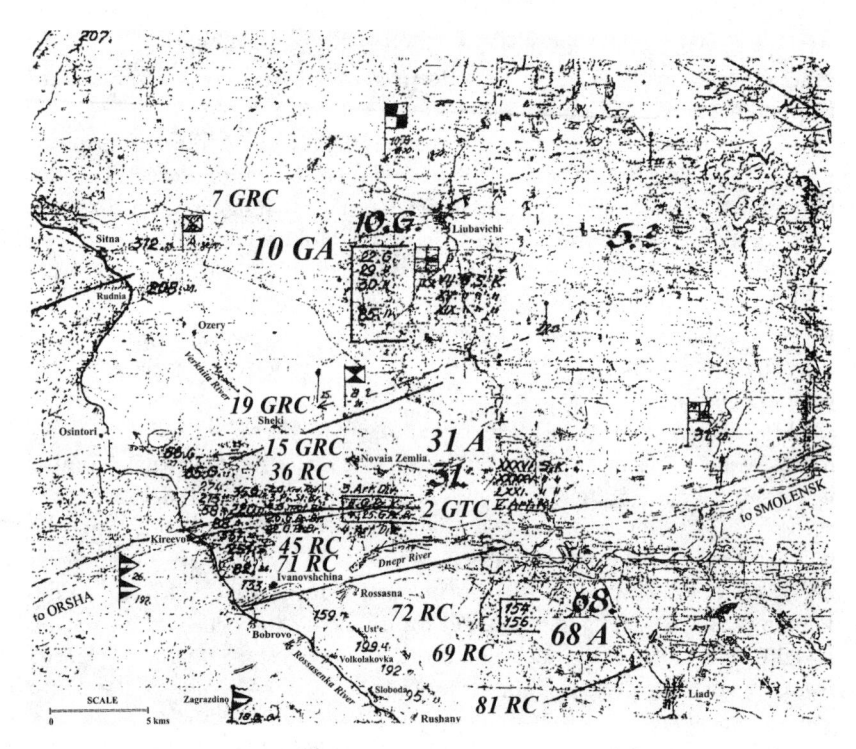

Map 3.7. Fourth Army's Situation in the Orsha Sector, 28 October 1943

had prepared an intermediate position along the line of the Lake Orekhi and the Basia River and a rear line—from Bogushevsk through Orsha to the western bank of the Dnepr River. Throughout the course of the combat operations, the enemy infantry was actively supported by the fires of six-barreled mortars [*Werfers*]. Worse still, all types of weapons were supported by great quantities of ammunition.[42]

This report and others also provided detailed explanations as to why the Western Front's forces performed so poorly in this and previous offensives in eastern Belorussia:

> At the same time, the combat capabilities of Soviet rifle divisions in the *front*'s shock group had decreased significantly as a result of the prolonged offensive. The quantity of replacements, the tempo of their arrival, and the quality of the arriving personnel did not permit the timely restoration of the forces' combat effectiveness. Sharp shortages of ammunition, which amounted to from 0.5 up to 0.75 combat loads for all types of weapons and calibers, were also experienced. Therefore, the at-

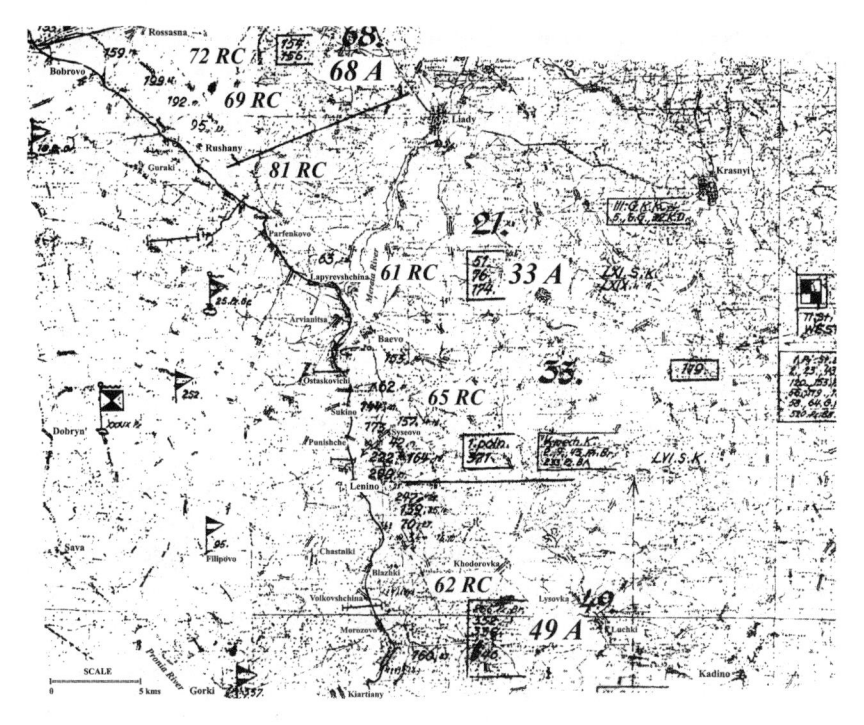

Map 3.8. Fourth Army's Situation in the Gorki Sector, 28 October 1943

tempt to resume the offensive and penetrate the second defensive lines with the forces of 10th Guards and 31st Army had no success.[43]

In the wake of the failed offensive, the fighting along the Orsha axis went on well into early November as the Soviets conducted local attacks and the Germans counterattacked to improve their tactical positions. Although it was clear to Sokolovsky that his offensive had failed, as had been the case in February and March of 1943, an overly ambitious *Stavka* refused to recognize reality and planned to pursue the offensive with unrequited resolve.

CHAPTER 4

The Central Front's Gomel'-Rechitsa Offensive (30 September–30 October)

PRELUDE

As the forces of the Kalinin and Western Fronts were pounding the left wing of German Army Group Center's defenses in the sector from Nevel' southward through Vitebsk to the Dnepr River east of Mogilev, Army General K. K. Rokossovsky's Central Front commenced equally ambitious offensive operations to penetrate the defenses on the army group's right wing along the Sozh, Pronia, and Dnepr Rivers. By 3 October, the *Stavka* had transferred most of the former Briansk Front's forces, together with its offensive sector, to Rokossovsky's control. This meant that Rokossovsky's *front* now consisted of nine armies deployed along a broad front extending from just north of Propoisk on the Sozh River southward east of a German bridgehead on the eastern bank of the Sozh River at Gomel' to the mouth of the Pripiat' River. The *front's* immense size and the vast expanse of its offensive sector required Rokossovsky to conduct multiple operations along several operational and tactical axes.

As was the case with the Kalinin and Western Fronts' operations, Soviet and recent Russian official histories provide only a fragmentary account of the Central Front's actions in October:

> Simultaneously with the operations along the Vitebsk, Orsha, and Mogilev axes, the Central Front developed an offensive along the Gomel'-Bobruisk axis, exploiting the bridgeheads it had seized on the Sozh and Dnepr Rivers.
>
> An offensive directly against Gomel' could have led to great losses. Therefore, the *Stavka* VGK gave orders to attack north and south of Gomel', penetrate enemy defenses along the Sozh and Dnepr Rivers, envelop Army Group "Center" from the south by advancing into the Bobruisk region, and separate Army Groups "Center" and "South" by seizing the city of Bobruisk. The right wing armies of the Voronezh Front, which were advancing on Kiev, were to protect the Central Front's left flank.
>
> General P. A. Belov's 61st Army and [General] P. I. Batov's 65th Army, on the Central Front's left wing, began an offensive along the Gomel' axis on 15 October. It developed in the general direction of Rechitsa and Zhlobin on the Dnepr, in the rear area of the enemy's Gomel' grouping. The forces forced the Dnepr at the mouth of the Sozh River, captured

Loev, and advanced up the Dnepr toward Rechitsa, carrying out a deep envelopment of Gomel' from the southwest.

The bridgehead formed in the Loev region considerably worsened the position of the German 2nd Army. The importance of the Sozh River as a water obstacle on the approaches to Gomel' was reduced to virtually nothing. Attempting to save their position and fearing for their rear area, the Wehrmacht command reinforced their operating grouping with formations transferred from other sectors of the eastern front.[1]

Although correct in the main, this brief description avoids telling the full story. As was the case with its other operating *fronts*, the *Stavka* began defining the parameters of the Belorussian strategic offensive even before the Briansk and Central Fronts completed their August and September of 1943 operations (the Briansk and Chernigov-Pripiat' offensive operations, respectively). For example, in the midst of the Briansk Front's operations, in response to a *Stavka* directive, Colonel General M. M. Popov, the commander of the Briansk Front, submitted a plan to the *Stavka* for subsequent operations by his *front* to and across the Dnepr River into Belorussia. Popov's proposal, which he prepared on 19 September just as his *front's* forces were crossing the Iput' River on a broad front, reported, "Protected by rear guards, the enemy is withdrawing his main forces to the west while organizing his defense along intermediate lines." He added that his *front's* forces were "organizing a pursuit of the withdrawing enemy with the missions to disrupt the organized enemy withdrawal and cut his forces up into separate groups, which can then be defeated in detail by means of throwing a cavalry-mechanized group forward and by maneuvering the armies' forces." As a result, Popov proposed that the Briansk Front "deliver the main attack in the central sector between the Kletnia forests and the Pochep and Klintsy line, a width of 40–50 kilometers, in the direction of Mglin, Surazh, Checkersk, and Zhlobin." Popov's timetable called for the conduct of a two-stage offensive, whose first stage was aimed at "reaching the Krichev, Surazh, and Novozybkov line" and would be completed by 27–29 September" (see Appendix C-1).[2] The offensive was to be spearheaded by a cavalry-mechanized group formed around the nucleus of 2nd Guards Cavalry Corps, 1st Tank Corps, and 30th Motorized Rifle Brigade. The next day the *Stavka* approved Popov's proposal (see Appendix C-2).

Popov's forces (50th, 3rd, 11th, and 63rd Armies) fulfilled the first part of their assigned mission by closing into positions along the Pronia and Sozh Rivers between 1 and 3 October (see Map 4.1). Although the Briansk Front's offensive was successful, the *front* faced a vexing problem at month's end, specifically, a bridgehead German forces retained at the city of Gomel', east of the Dnepr and Sozh Rivers, which separated Popov's forces from the advancing armies of Rokossovsky's Central Front.

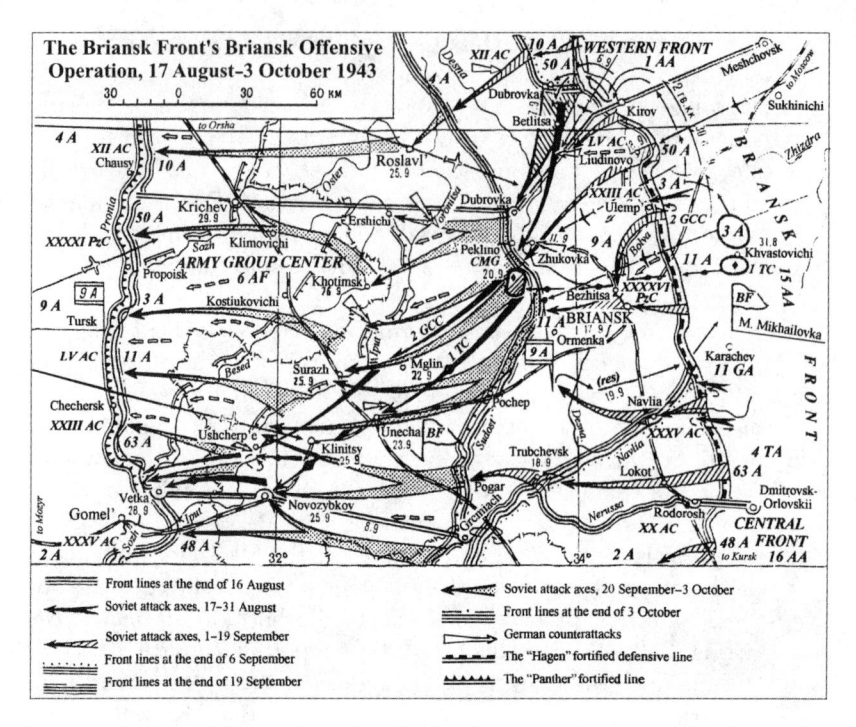

92   The Struggle for Belorussia, October–December 1943

Map 4.1. The Briansk Front's Briansk Offensive Operation, 17 August–3 October 1943

Attacking on Popov's left, the armies of Rokossovsky's Central Front recorded even more spectacular progress than the Briansk Front during late September. In fact, by the 30th, Rokossovsky's five armies (the 48th, 65th, 61st, 13th, and 60th) reached the Sozh and Dnepr Rivers from south of Gomel' to north of Kiev (see Map 4.2). By this time, 65th and 61st Armies on his *front's* right wing had seized small bridgeheads across the Sozh River south of Gomel' and across the Dnepr River west of the town of Liubech'. On his left wing, 13th and 60th Armies had secured even larger bridgeheads on the river's western bank near the junction of the Pripiat' and Dnepr Rivers. By posing a serious threat to the southern flank of Army Group Center's Second Army and the northern flank of Army Group South's Fourth Panzer Army, if exploited, advancing Soviet forces could sever communications between the two army groups. Making matters worse, Army Group South's Fourth Panzer and Eighth Armies were already contending with bridgeheads under Red Army control at Liutezh, north of Kiev, and at Velikii Bukrin, south of the Ukraine's capital city.

All of this convinced the *Stavka* by 1 October that the time was right to conduct a concerted, sustained, and rapid advance into southern Belorussia. The only problem the *Stavka* faced was determining precisely where and

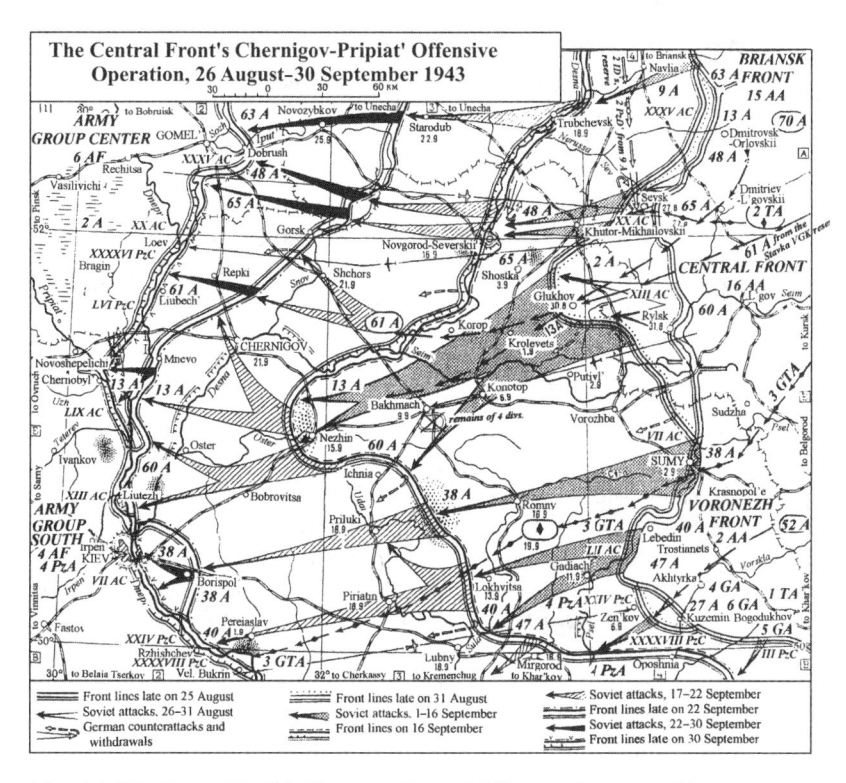

The Central Front's Gomel'-Rechitsa Offensive   93

Map 4.2. The Central Front's Chernigov-Pripiat' Offensive Operation, 26 August–30 September 1943

how to exploit the Central Front's successes, because the forward progress of Rokossovsky's armies seemed to offer enticing prospects for victory along both the Belorussian and Kiev axes.

Accordingly, on 1 October the *Stavka* dispatched a directive to Rokossovsky that ordered him to transfer 13th and 60th Armies, together with their offensive sectors, to the Voronezh Front (see Appendix C-3). It also assigned him the task of defeating the enemy's Zhlobin-Bobruisk grouping and capturing Minsk, the capital of Belorussia, by "delivering its main attack in the general direction of Zhlobin, Bobruisk, and Minsk." In a broader context, this offensive would be in conjunction with a thrust by the Western Front "in the general direction of Orsha, Borisov, and Molodechno."[3] In addition, Rokossovsky was to create a separate group of forces "for an offensive along the northern bank of the Pripiat' River toward Kalinkovichi and Zhitkovichi." Thus, by virtue of this directive, the *Stavka* was mandating simultaneous offensives aimed at securing both Minsk and Kiev. Once again, however, a woefully overly optimistic *Stavka* was underestimating German capabilities while seriously overestimating its own.

This directive, which Rokossovsky implemented on 6 October, focused the Central Front's attentions on southern Belorussia. However, by virtue of its secondary drive on Zhitkovichi, it also facilitated the Voronezh Front's offensive toward Kiev and even deeper into central Ukraine. The *Stavka* presumed (incorrectly, as it turned out) that the Central Front's 13th and 60th Armies would be able to seize Kiev in conjunction with the adjacent armies of the Voronezh Front. However, in acknowledging the Central Front's focus on Belorussia, it also recognized that it would have to reinforce Rokossovsky's *front* significantly before it could perform that critical mission. Based on this recognition, thirty minutes later the *Stavka* ordered the Briansk Front to disband and turn the bulk of its forces over to the Central Front no later than 10 October (see Appendix C-4). These forces included 50th Army with seven rifle divisions, 3rd Army with seven rifle divisions, 63rd Army with eight rifle divisions, and 2nd Guards Cavalry Corps. Rokossovsky was to submit a draft operational plan to the *Stavka* no later than 15 October.

The directive also recognized the strategic importance of employing an additional *front* (the Baltic) along the northwestern strategic axis. The new Baltic Front was to consist of 22nd Army with two rifle divisions and five rifle brigades from the Northwestern Front, 3rd Shock Army with five rifle divisions, three rifle brigades, and 8th Estonian Rifle Corps with two rifle divisions from the Kalinin Front, along with 6th Guards Army with seven rifle divisions and 20th Army with six rifle divisions from the *Stavka*'s Reserve. When fully formed by 20 October, the *front* included these armies and corps, reinforced by refurbished 11th Guards and 11th Armies, and 15th Air Army.[4]

The Briansk Front disbanded in accordance with the *Stavka's* instructions, and its 11th Guards and 11th Armies, the former already in the *front's* reserve, concentrated in assembly areas to rest and refit before being transferred northward to join the Baltic Front. Later, however, largely because of the failure of the Soviet offensive against Gomel', the *Stavka* changed its mind and on 23 October ordered 11th Army to rejoin the Belorussian (former Central) Front.[5] The 11th Army rejoined the Belorussian Front in early November, just in time to participate in its new offensive to seize Gomel'.

Once reorganized, Rokossovsky's Central Front conducted several offensive operations simultaneously across its entire front during early and mid-October 1943. The first of these operations, conducted by 48th, 65th, and 61st Armies, sought to expel German forces from their defenses along the Sozh River east of Gomel', force them to fall back to the Dnepr River, and capture Rechitsa, Zhlobin, and Rogachev. At the time, the Sozh bridgehead was defended by four infantry divisions from XXXV Army Corps of Army Group Center's Second Army, flanked on the left by the army's XXIII Army Corps and on the right by the army's XX Army Corps, which defended the Loev region. In terms of available panzer reserves, Second Army supported the bridgehead sector with a *kampfgruppe* (combat group) from XXXXVI

Panzer Corps' 4th Panzer Division, equipped with a meager force of just nine Pz. IV tanks.[6] The remainder of the panzer corps defended the sector on XX Corps' right opposite the Central Front's 61st Army.

The *Stavka* considered this operation essential in order to align all of the Central Front's armies along the line of the Dnepr River. Only then, it reasoned, could the Central Front begin its concerted thrust toward Bobruisk and Minsk. At the same time, Rokossovsky ordered the armies on his *front's* right wing (the 50th and 3rd) to attack across the Pronia River to keep pace with the Western Front's advance. Finally, before their transfer to the Voronezh Front on 6 October, Rokossovsky ordered his *front's* 13th and 60th Armies to expand their bridgeheads westward across the Dnepr River toward Chernobyl' and then southward toward Kiev to assist the Voronezh Front's advance on that city. Secondarily, 13th Army was to press Army Group Center's right wing southeast of Mozyr' to help 65th and 61st Armies consolidate and expand their bridgeheads across the Dnepr River south of Gomel'.

THE OFFENSIVE

Soviet and Russian historians have covered certain aspects of the Gomel'-Rechitsa operation in considerable detail. They have described Rokossovsky's initial operational plan and have detailed many of the divisional- and corps-scale operations conducted to secure a bridgehead across the Dnepr River. However, the operation they have covered in the greatest detail is 65th Army's complex operation to cross the Dnepr River and establish tactical and operational bridgeheads at and around the town of Loev, which is situated roughly 60 kilometers south of Gomel'. While doing so, they have generally ignored the *front's* major assault on Gomel' itself and 61st Army's failure to establish a sizable bridgehead over the Dnepr in its sector during early October, from which it was to participate in the Gomel'-Rechitsa operation.

The Central Front, redesignated as the Belorussian Front on 20 October, conducted its Gomel'-Rechitsa operation in several stages, each of which was closely coordinated with the offensives being conducted by the Western and Kalinin Fronts to the north. During the first stage, which began at the end of September, Lieutenant General P. I. Batov's 65th Army and its neighbors to the north (Lieutenant General A. V. Gorbatov's 3rd, Lieutenant General V. Ia. Kolpakchi's 63rd, and Lieutenant General P. L. Romanenko's 48th Armies) and south (Lieutenant General P. A. Belov's 61st Army) fought to seize and expand multiple bridgeheads over the Pronia, Sozh, and Dnepr Rivers north and south of Gomel'. These assaults, which coincided with Western Front attacks toward Orsha, Gorki, and Mogilev, faltered by late on 10 October. Then, between 8 and 14 October, Generals Romanenko, Batov, and Belov regrouped their armies and prepared for a fresh offensive.

The second stage of the offensive began on 15 October, when 65th and 61st Armies launched fresh attacks toward Rechitsa in an attempt to outflank German forces defending Gomel' from the southwest. This offensive once again struck the defenses of Second Army's XXXV, XX, and XXXXVI Panzer Corps in the same sector as before. However, by this time virtually all of Second Army's panzer forces (2nd, 4th, 5th, and 12th Panzer Divisions) were fighting in the Chernobyl' region farther to the south under the control of Second Army's LVI Panzer Corps, which was operating to defend the army's right wing. This meant that the defenders had to rely primarily on their *Paks* and other antitank systems to contend with Rokossovsky's armor.

The assaults by 65th and 61st Armies on 15 October were accompanied by strong diversionary attacks launched by forces of 3rd, 63rd, and 48th Armies against German defensive positions north and east of Gomel' and by 48th Army and the rifle corps on 65th Army's extreme left wing south of Gomel' from 9 through 12 October. This stage coincided closely with the Western Front's heavy assaults along the Orsha and Gorki axes from 12 through 18 October.

This stage of the operation supposedly ended on 19 or 20 October, after German forces had abandoned most of their Gomel' bridgehead and after 65th and 61st Armies' had carved sizable bridgeheads on the Dnepr River's west bank. However, German records indicate that 65th and 61st Armies actually continued their intense offensive operations until the end of October. At the same time, General Gorbatov's 3rd Army delivered attacks on German defenses north of Gomel' on 24–25 October in an attempt to revive its offensive toward Novyi Bykhov on the Dnepr River and to distract the Germans' attention from pending Red Army assaults further to the south. These Central Front operations coincided with the offensive the Western Front conducted from 21 through 26 October 1943. Even though Batov's and Belov's armies succeeded in establishing stable operational-scale bridgeheads on the Dnepr River's western bank by month's end; because of the skillful German defense in the often marshy terrain, the paucity of Soviet armor, and the vulnerability of what tanks they did have to antitank fire, the Red Army troops proved unable to penetrate the Germans' defenses completely and fully accomplish the missions the *Stavka* assigned to them. This failure necessitated yet another major regrouping and a new (third) stage of the operation, which began on 10 November.

In brief, the first stage of the Gomel'-Rechitsa operation developed as a natural outgrowth of both the ongoing fighting for possession of crossings and bridgeheads over the Sozh and Dnepr Rivers and Rokossovsky's planned exploitation operation toward Rechitsa, Bobruisk, and Minsk. The lead elements of the Briansk Front's 50th, 3rd, 11th, and 63rd Armies fought their way toward the Sozh River north of Gomel' in late September and reached the river, establishing some small bridgeheads on the river's western bank between 1 and 3 October. At roughly the same time, the Central Front's 48th Army reached the eastern outskirts of the defenses of Second Army's XXXV Army Corps east of Gomel', and the *front's* 65th and 61st Armies reached the Dnepr in the almost 70-kilometer-wide sector stretching from just south of Gomel' southward to west of Dubrovka. At this juncture, on 1 October the *Stavka* ordered the Briansk Front to disband and transfer its 50th, 3rd, and 63rd Armies and 2nd Guards Cavalry Corps to the Central Front. The *Stavka* also ordered the Briansk Front to transfer its 11th Army to the new Baltic Front, an order that it countermanded later in the month.

The *Stavka's* 1 October order required Rokossovsky to regroup the Central Front's armies operating north of Gomel'.[7] Ultimately, this reduced the strength and slowed the momentum of his offensive in this sector. Within a single week, Colonel General I. V. Boldin's 50th and Colonel General A. V. Gorbatov's 3rd Armies lengthened their fronts and took over much of the offensive sector of Lieutenant General I. I. Fediuninsky's 11th Army. This regrouping left 50th Army operating along the eastern bank of the Pronia River in the 30-kilometer-wide sector extending southward from Chausy to Propoisk (now Slavgorod), 3rd Army in roughly the same size sector from Propoisk southward to Zagor'e, and several divisions of 63rd Army in a like sector stretching from Zagor'e southward to Sherstin, a town immediately north of Vetka and Gomel'.[8] These forces closed into their forward positions along the Pronia and Sozh River between 1 and 6 October.

Meanwhile, just north of Gomel', 5th and 250th Rifle Divisions of 35th Rifle Corps of Lieutenant General V. Ia. Kolpakchi's 63rd Army captured Vetka and a small bridgehead across the Sozh River from 253rd Infantry Division of Ninth Army's XXIII Army Corps on 30 September. While his forces tried in vain to expand the Vetka bridgehead, Kolpakchi reinforced them with 40th Rifle Corps' 287th and 348th Rifle Divisions (see Map 4.3). These forces, all now concentrated against XXIII Army Corps' 253rd Infantry Division, received the mission to break out of the Vetka bridgehead and attack the forces of German XXXV Army Corps defending the Gomel' bridgehead from the north.[9]

On 63rd Army's left, General Romanenko's 48th Army closed up to the German defenses at Gomel' from the east and south on 29 and 30 September. Romanenko's 42nd Rifle Corps (399th and 73rd Rifle Divisions, supported by 193rd Separate Tank Regiment) faced the German XXXV Army Corps' defenses in the 28-kilometer-wide sector extending from Vetka southeastward to the town of Dobrush, 30 kilometers east of the city. Romanenko arrayed his army's remaining rifle divisions (the 137th, 170th, 175th, 194th, and 102nd) in an arc extending from Dobrush southwestward 25 kilometers along the Iput' River to its confluence with the Sozh River south of the city.[10] On the army's extreme left wing, 102nd Rifle Division linked up with 65th Army's 19th Rifle Corps (37th Guards, 140th, 162nd, and 354th Rifle Divi-

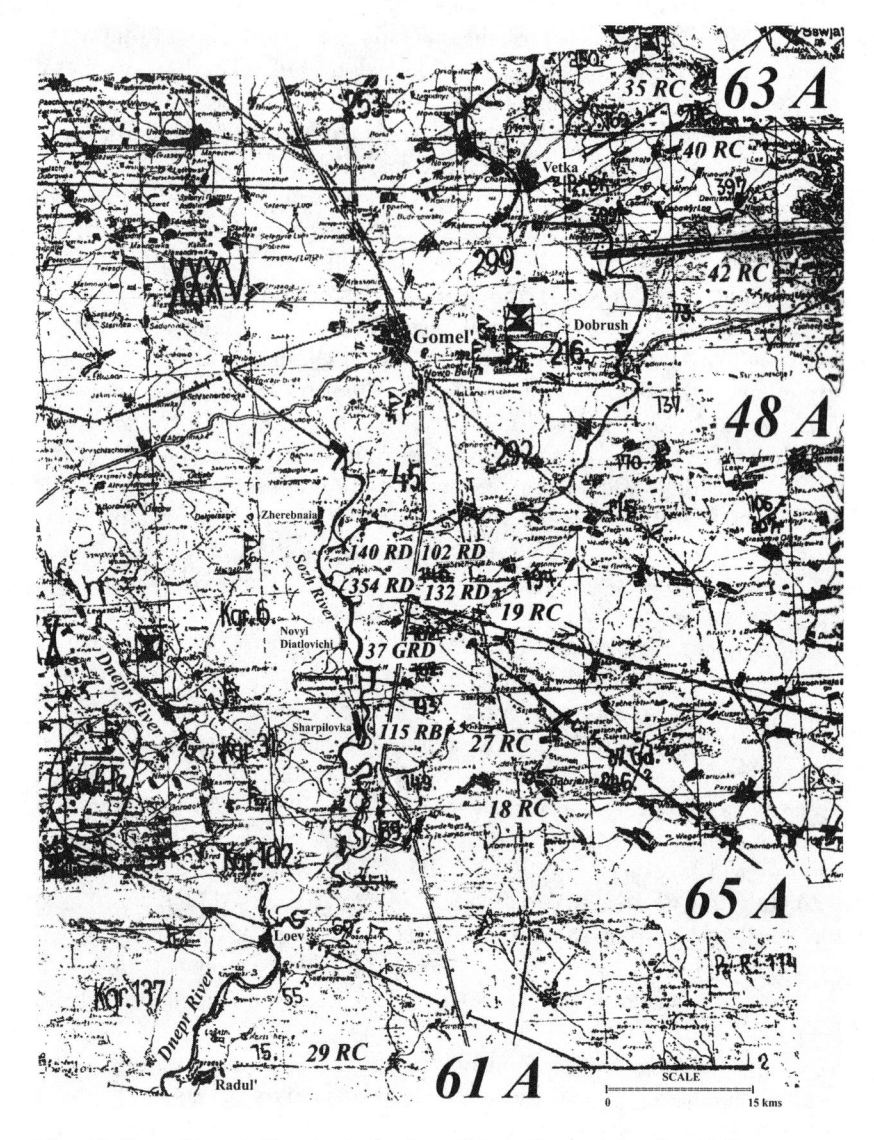

98 The Struggle for Belorussia, October–December 1943

Map 4.3. Second Army's Situation in the Gomel'-Loev Sector, 1 October 1943

sions) as it prepared to complete its crossing of the Sozh River. Opposing 48th Army's forces, German Second Army's XXXV Army Corps manned strong defenses around the perimeter of the Gomel' bridgehead with its 299th, 216th, 292nd, and 45th Infantry Divisions. South of the Gomel' bridgehead, 6th Infantry Division of Second Army's XX Army Corps, now organized into a smaller *kampfgruppe* because of its losses in previous fighting, defended southward along the Sozh River opposite the left wing of 48th Army's 102nd Rifle Division and the bulk of 65th Army's newly arrived 19th Rifle Corps.

South of Gomel', General Batov's entire 65th Army had reached the Sozh River between the mouth of the Iput' River and Loev, where it had seized several small bridgeheads on the river's western bank by 29 September. Batov's army was arrayed with three corps abreast. The 19th Rifle Corps' 140th, 162nd, 354th Rifle, and 37th Guards Rifle Divisions were deployed on the army's right flank south of the Iput' River. The 354th Division had already seized a small bridgehead across the Sozh River from German 6th Infantry Division. That day Batov reinforced the 354th Rifle with a handful of tanks from the army's 255th Tank Regiment. On 19th Corps' left, 27th Rifle Corps' 193rd and 149th Rifle Divisions, along with 115th Rifle Brigade, occupied positions in the army's center, and 18th Rifle Corps' 60th, 69th, and 246th Rifle Divisions occupied positions on the army's left wing north of Loev. Although Batov's armies succeeded in capturing multiple bridgeheads on the western bank of the Sozh, all of these were too small to contain a force large enough to mount a legitimate breakout. Therefore, Batov had no choice but to orchestrate a full-scale attack to enlarge these bridgeheads and force the Germans to abandon Gomel'.

Batov planned to conduct his main attack from the bridgehead that 354th Rifle Division had seized, with the forces of Major General D. I. Samarsky's 19th Rifle Corps.[11] Simultaneously, Major General F. M. Cherokmanov's 27th and Major General I. I. Ivanov's 18th Rifle Corps were to conduct supporting attacks from their bridgeheads farther to the south. Together, the entire force was to clear German forces from the territory between the Sozh and Dnepr Rivers and envelop the four German divisions defending Gomel' from the south and west. From north to south, Batov's forces faced the defenses of German Second Army's XX Army Corps, whose 6th, 31st, and 102nd Infantry Divisions, supported by a *kampfgruppe* from 4th Panzer Division, occupied defenses in the 48-kilometer-wide sector from the village of Zherebnia, 18 kilometers south of Gomel', to the town of Radul', situated on the western bank of the Sozh 15 kilometers south of Loev.

On 65th Army's left wing, the three rifle corps of General Belov's 61st Army reached the Dnepr River on a broad front extending from Loev to south of Liubech' in late September (see Map 4.4). The 55th and 15th Rifle Divisions of Major General A. N. Slyshkin's 29th Rifle Corps were able to capture several small bridgeheads between Loev and Radul' by 30 September. However, 336th, 356th, and 415th Rifle Divisions of Major General G. A. Khaliuzin's 89th Rifle Corps, which reached the Dnepr River south of Radul', were unable to secure any foothold on the river's western bank because of strong German resistance and well-organized artillery and mortar fire. Farther to the south, 12th Guards Rifle Division of Major General A. A. Boreiko's 9th Guards Rifle Corps seized a small bridgehead on the Dnepr's

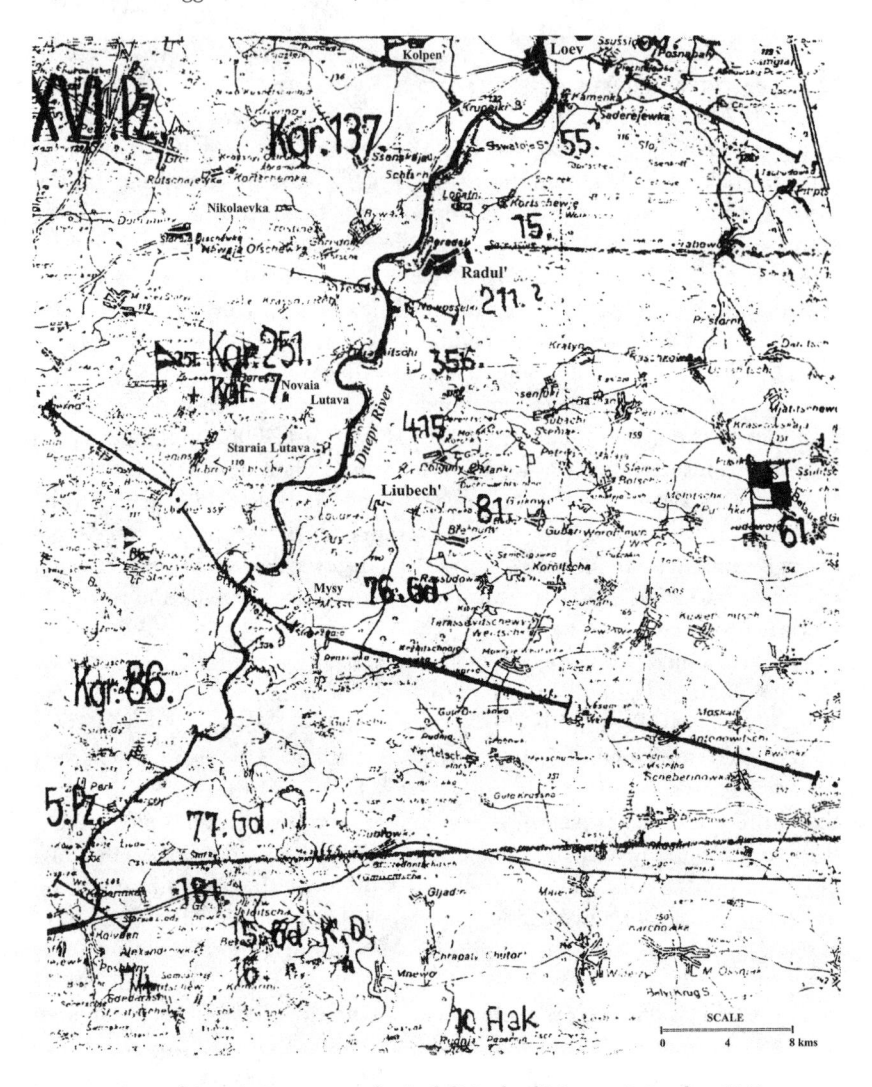

100   The Struggle for Belorussia, October–December 1943

Map 4.4. Second Army's Situation in the Radul'-Liubech' Sector, 1 October 1943

western bank south of the town of Liubech', 28 kilometers south of Loev; however, stronger German defenses to the south contained 76th Guards Rifle Division's advance on the Dnepr River's eastern bank. Still farther south, 9th Guards Corps' 77th Guards Division, cooperating with 181st Rifle Division of 13th Army's 28th Rifle Corps and forward detachments from Major General M. F. Maleev's 7th Guards Cavalry Corps, were operating along an extended front. The 181st Rifle Division had exploited 13th Army's successes by crossing to the western bank of the Dnepr River west of Dubrovka and advancing toward Koporenka, 20 kilometers north of Chernobyl'. However, German LVI Panzer Corps' 2nd, 12th, and 5th Panzer Divisions halted this entire Soviet force, along with 13th Army's lead elements, cold in its tracks.[12] From north to south, Belov's forces faced the German Second Army's XXXXVI Panzer Corps' (137th, 251st, and 7th Infantry Divisions) and elements of LVI Panzer Corps (86th Infantry and 5th Panzer Divisions).

Batov's army commenced its assault on 1 October with its 19th Rifle Corps, the night after 140th and 37th Guards Rifle Divisions reinforced 354th Rifle Division's bridgehead (see Map 4.3).[13] Fanning out on the river's western bank, the 37th Guards on the right, the 354th in the center, and the 140th on the right captured the villages of Noyve and Starye Diatlovichi in heavy fighting with 6th Infantry Division of German Second Army's XX Army Corps. By late on 2 October, the attacking Soviets had expanded the bridgehead to a depth of 4 kilometers on the river's western bank (see Map 4.5). Heavy fighting raged in the bridgehead during the next several days as German Second Army reinforced this sector with elements of 216th Infantry Division. However, even though Batov committed 162nd Rifle Division from 19th Rifle Corps' reserve into combat west of the river, the combined force was not able to break out of its bridgehead and seize the key town of Zherebnaia, which controlled the southwestern approaches into the city. This was so because the swampy terrain south of Gomel' inhibited operations and because Second Army shifted 216th Infantry Division and a combat group of 45th Infantry Division from Gomel' to the threatened sector. Nor was 63rd Army successful in breaching the strong defenses of XXIII Army Corps' 253rd Infantry Division at Vetka or XXXV Corps' defenses east of Gomel', even though Second Army directed XXXV Corps to pull 216th Infantry Division out of its defensive lines. Now, only three instead of four German divisions were defending Gomel'.

From Rokossovsky's perspective, the situation on 65th Army's left wing to the south was little better. There, the five rifle divisions and one rifle brigade from 27th and 18th Rifle Corps (193rd, 149th, 246th, 69th, and 60th Rifle Divisions and 115th Rifle Brigade) assaulted across the Sozh River and seized several shallow bridgeheads in the 19-kilometer-wide sector extending from the village of Sharpilovka, 35 kilometers south of Gomel', to the village of Karpovka, roughly 10 kilometers north of Loev. However, German XX Corps' 31st and 102nd Infantry Divisions reacted quickly to halt the Soviet advance with their tactical reserves and sealed off the bridgeheads after only minimal Soviet gains.

Still farther to the south, General Belov's 61st Army was also unable to make any forward progress from its numerous but miniscule bridgeheads west of the Dnepr River. Here, as was the case along virtually the entire course of the Dnepr River, the heights on the river's western bank dominated its eastern bank and the relatively narrow flood plain on its western bank.

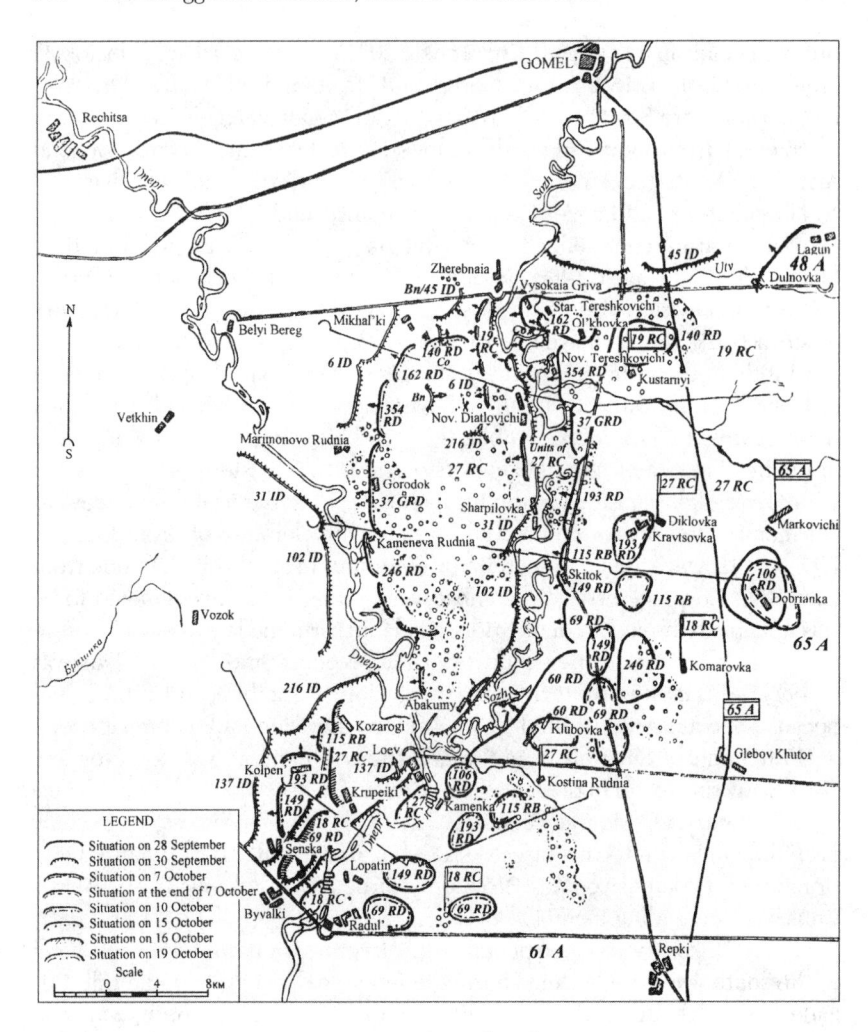

102   The Struggle for Belorussia, October–December 1943

Map 4.5. 65th Army's Operations to Cross the Sozh and Dnepr Rivers, 28 September–19 October 1943

First, on 28 September, and later, on 2 October, Belov attempted to break through German defenses along the Dnepr in the 12-kilometer-wide sector from Liubech' southward to the village of Red'kovka. The 61st Army did so by employing a shock group consisting of 12th, 76th, and 77th Guards Divisions of General Boreiko's 9th Guards Rifle Corps, supported by elements of 7th Guards Cavalry Corps. Here too, however, stout resistance by XXXXVI Panzer Corps' 251st Infantry Division and LVI Panzer Corps' 86th Infantry Division halted Belov's attacks. Attacking in the shock group's left and center from a narrow bridgehead in the floodplain on the Dnepr's western bank west of the village of Mysy, 12th Guards Division, supported by elements of 76th Guards, succeeded in expanding its bridgehead 2–3 kilometers to the west before being halted by strong enemy artillery and machine gun fire from the dominating heights west of the river. This strong German resistance confounded Belov's mission to exploit toward Rechitsa with 7th Guards Cavalry Corps and roll up German Second Army's defenses facing 61st and 65th Armies.

Thwarted in his first attempt to seize Gomel' and reach Rechitsa, Rokossovsky searched for a way to resolve his dilemma. Clearly, there was no sense in attempting once again to crack German defenses in the narrow belt between the Sozh and Dnepr Rivers. Neither the poor terrain nor the strong German defenses in this sector offered any prospects for further success. However, Soviet intelligence reported that the 14-kilometer-wide sector extending along the Dnepr River from Loev southward to Radul', then defended by forces from 15th and 55th Rifle Divisions of 61st Army's 29th Rifle Corps, might be a more suitable site at which to conduct a forced crossing of the river. German defenses in this sector were relatively weaker than elsewhere, and the river's western bank in this region seemed more conducive for mounting a successful amphibious crossing. Furthermore, once across the Dnepr, Rokossovsky's forces could outflank German XXXV Corps' defenses at Gomel' from the south by attacking northward along the Dnepr River's western bank. Rokossovsky submitted his plan for the new offensive to the *Stavka* on 7 October. The *Stavka* immediately approved the *front* commander's plan.

The second stage of the Central Front's Gomel'-Rechitsa operation began with a major regrouping by the forces of its 48th, 65th, and 61st Armies. While this regrouping proceeded, pursuant to Rokossovsky's orders, 50th and 3rd Armies conducted strong diversionary assaults against German defenses in the Vetka region north of Gomel', and 63rd and 48th Armies did the same against German defenses at Gomel' proper. An excerpt from the Belorussian (former Central) Front's combat journal explains the concept and intent of the second stage of the Gomel'-Rechitsa offensive operation:

> Based on a *Stavka* VGK directive and a decision of the *front* command, a plan was developed for an offensive operation which envisioned the delivery of the main attack in the general direction of Zhlobin, Bobruisk, and Minsk, the successive destruction of enemy's Gomel' and Zhlobin-Bobruisk groupings, and the arrival of the *front's* forces at the Ostroshitsky, Gorodok, Minsk, Slutsk, and Sluch' River line by 11 November 1943.
> The operational plan was divided into two stages:
> (a) The destruction of the enemy Gomel' and Zhlobin-Rogachev groupings and the arrival of the *front's* main forces along the Drut' River, Rogachev, Zhlobin, Shatsilki, and Kalinkovichi line; and

(b) The destruction of the enemy's Bobruisk grouping, the seizure of the Minsk region, and the arrival of the *front's* main forces at the Ostroshitskii, Gorodok, Minsk, Slutsk, and Sluch' River line.

The operational plan envisioned a preparatory period up to 9 October for the regrouping of 3rd, 50th, and 63rd Armies and for shifting the bases of aviation and rear services. The offensive was to begin on 10 October 1943.[14]

Lieutenant General K. F. Telegin, the Central Front's member (commissar) of the Military Council, described the front's mission in his memoirs:

The concept of the operation involved the conduct of attacks against the flanks of the enemy's Gomel' grouping to encircle and destroy it. The main attack was intended from the bridgehead at Loev in the general direction of Rechitsa to arrive subsequently in the enemy rear. An attack was planned from the region north of Gomel' along the Zhlobin axis on the fourth day of the operation, with the mission of enveloping the Hitlerites from the northwest and, in cooperation with the main forces, liquidating the Gomel' grouping. The forces on the *front's* right wing were to reach the Dnepr north and south of Novyi Bykhov.

Rokossovsky's plan called for the formation of three shock groups on the Central Front's right wing, which at that time included 48th, 65th, and 61st Armies, 1st Guards and 9th Tank Corps, 2nd and 7th Guards Cavalry Corps, and 4th Artillery Penetration Corps. Operating along an extended front south of Gomel', these shock groups were to attack toward Bobruisk and Minsk near dawn on 15 October. Rokossovsky designated 61st Army's assault as the *front's* main attack. Meanwhile, 50th, 3rd, and 63rd Armies, along with the right wing of 48th Army, which were situated on the *front's* right wing north and south of Gomel', were to initiate local operations prior to 15 October to prevent the Germans from shifting their forces into the sector where Rokossovsky planned to conduct his main attack.

The first of Rokossovsky's three attacking shock groups included seven rifle divisions from 48th Army and four rifle divisions of 65th Army's 19th Rifle Corps. This group was to attack the southern flank of German XXXV Corps' defenses at Gomel' and also westward from the Soviet bridgeheads south of the city. The 65th Army's 19th Rifle Corps was to begin this attack on 7 October. Thereafter, 48th Army's 102nd, 307th, and 194th Rifle Divisions, along with its other divisions, would join the attack as soon as they completed their regrouping.

The Central Front's second shock group, which consisted of six rifle divisions and one rifle brigade from 65th Army's 18th and 27th Rifle Corps, was to assault across the Dnepr River in the 20-kilometer-wide sector between

Loev and Radul' on 15 October and then advance northward along the western bank of the Dnepr River through Kolpen' toward Rechitsa. As soon as the two rifle corps completed penetrating the defenses of German Second Army's XX Army Corps, Major General of Tank Forces M. F. Panov's 1st Guards Tank and Major General V. V. Kriukov's 2nd Guards Cavalry Corps were supposed to exploit deeply toward Bobruisk in the rear of both German Second and Ninth Armies. In an attempt to guarantee the second shock group's success, 65th Army formed a strong artillery group whose mission was to suppress German artillery and mortars on the river's western bank reliably enough to facilitate the seizure of bridgeheads by the attacking rifle division's advance battalions. However, as one recent account admits:

> The supply of shells and mines [mortar rounds] was insufficient. The guns of divisional and regimental artillery (76mm), as well as the army artillery group, had only one combat load each in their firing positions. Therefore, 50–60 percent of all guns on hand in the corps and all of the regimental and a considerable part of the divisional artillery were employed for conducting direct fire. Thus, 78 guns in 27th Corps and 187 guns in 18th Corps were used for this.[15]

Rokossovsky's third shock group included the three guards' rifle divisions of 61st Army's 9th Guard Rifle Corps and at least one rifle division each from the army's 29th and 89th Rifle Corps. This force was to concentrate in the vicinity of Liubech' on the army's left wing and conduct the *front's* main attack northwestward toward Bragin and Mozyr' on 15 October. Major General of Tank Forces B. S. Bakharov's 9th Tank and Major General M. P. Konstantinov's 7th Guards Cavalry Corps were to exploit 61st Army's offensive toward Mozyr'. Konstantinov had replaced General Maleev as the commander of the cavalry corps on 7 October, although we know not why.

In early October Panov's 1st Guards Tank Corps was the strongest armored force earmarked for service in the Central Front during operations in the fall of 1943. After it completed an extended period of rest and refitting in the wake of the summer fighting in the Orel and Briansk regions, the corps received new weaponry and was assigned to Rokossovsky's *front* on 12 October. By this time it was equipped with 218 T-34 tanks (65 in each of its three tank brigades) armed with 85mm guns and 51 self-propelled guns. It included 1001st Self-propelled Artillery Regiment armed with 76mm self-propelled guns (SU-76s), 1541st Self-propelled Artillery Regiment with 12 SU-152 self-propelled guns, and 43rd Separate Guards-Mortar Battalion equipped with *Katiusha* multiple-rocket launchers.[16] After spending twelve to fifteen days en route to Rokossovsky's *front* by rail and road, Pavlov's corps completed its concentration in the wooded region east of Loev on 2 November, too late to participate in the initial stage of the Gomel'-Rechitsa offensive.

The absence of 1st Guards Tank Corps during October largely explains why the initial stages of the offensive developed so slowly. Until the tank corps arrived, Rokossovsky's forces had to rely on the far weaker 9th Tank Corps to support 61st Army's operations and separate tank brigades and regiments, all severely understrength, to support 65th and 48th Armies. This meant that the attacking armies possessed enough tanks to provide support for the infantry but not enough with which to conduct and sustain an operational exploitation.

In preparation for the offensive, the staff of Rokossovsky's army conducted a massive regrouping of forces between 8 and 14 October (see Maps 4.6 and 4.7). This included:

- Transferring 65th Army's 18th Rifle Corps (149th and 169th Rifle Divisions) and 27th Rifle Corps (106th and 193rd Rifle Divisions and 115th Rifle Brigade) from the Sozh River front to the Dnepr River between Loev and Radul';
- Transferring 48th Army's 102nd, 194th, and 307th Rifle Divisions into the Sozh River bridgehead south of Gomel' and transferring 137th, 170th, and 175th Rifle Divisions into the former sectors of these divisions south of Gomel';
- Concentrating 61st Army's 9th Guards Rifle Corps (12th, 76th, and 77th Guards Rifle Divisions) into the bridgehead west of Liubech', moving 29th Rifle Corps (55th, 15th, and 81st Rifle Divisions) into positions between Radul' and Liubech', and concentrating 89th Rifle Corps (336th, 356th, and 415th Rifle Divisions) into new positions south of Liubech'.
- Regrouping 1st Guards Tank Corps from the Orel to the Loev region and 9th Tank, 2nd and 7th Guards Cavalries, and 4th Artillery Penetration Corps into their newly assigned assembly areas.

With the notable exception of 1st Guards Tank Corps, the Central Front completed this entire regrouping by 14 October, largely undetected by German intelligence, and launched 61st Army's main attack on 15 October as planned.[17] However, a week before the main attack was to begin and while this regrouping was still in progress, on 7 October 65th Army's 19th Rifle Corps and 48th Army's three rifle divisions attacked from their bridgeheads on the western bank of the Sozh River south of Gomel' (see Map 4.8). This assault struck German Second Army's defenses precisely at the boundary between XXXV Army Corps' 216th Infantry Division and XX Army Corps' 6th Infantry Division, and within hours, also engaged XXXV Corps' 45th Infantry Division, which was defending the southern approaches to Gomel'. Although the shock group's assault slowed somewhat by 9 October, German Second Army was left no choice but to order XXXV Army Corps to slide 45th

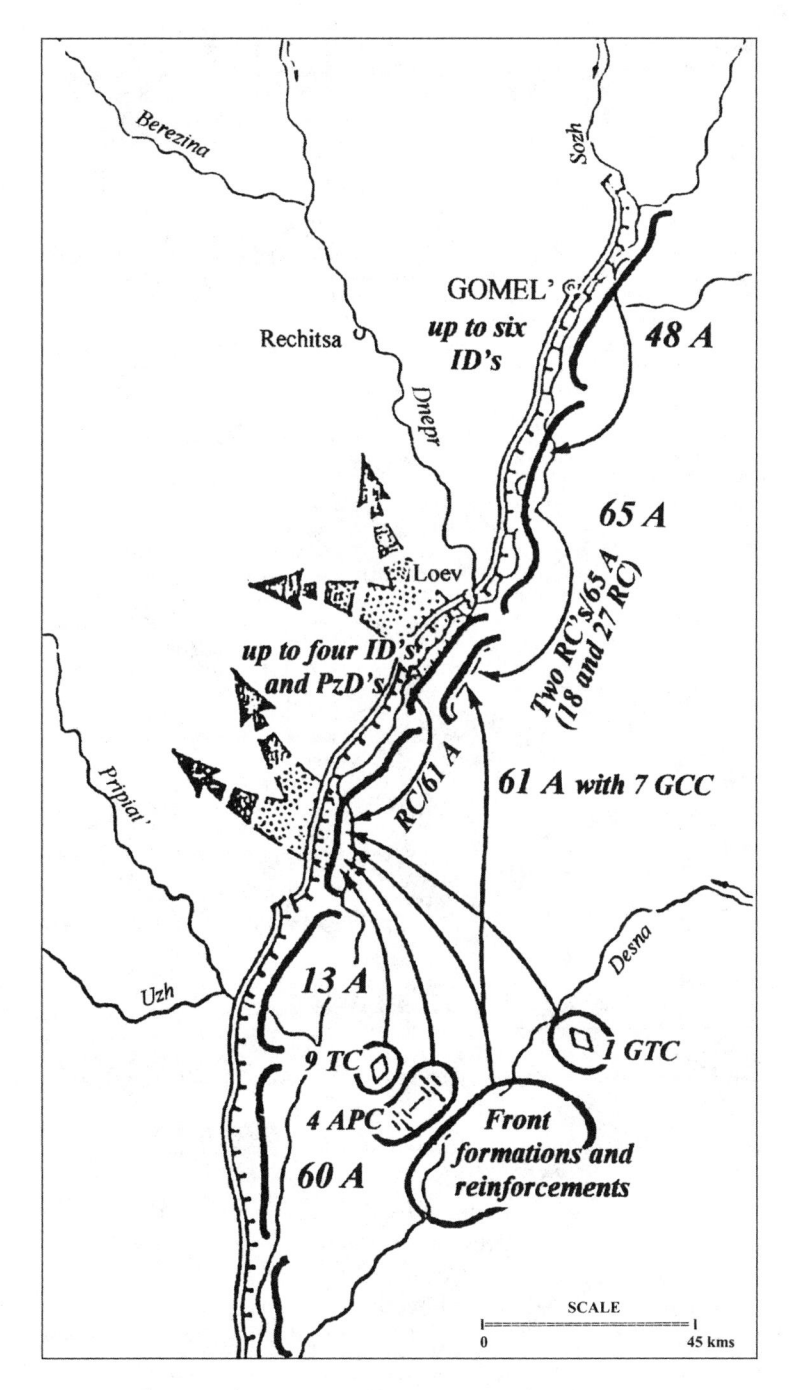

Map 4.6. The Central Front's Regrouping, 8–14 October 1943

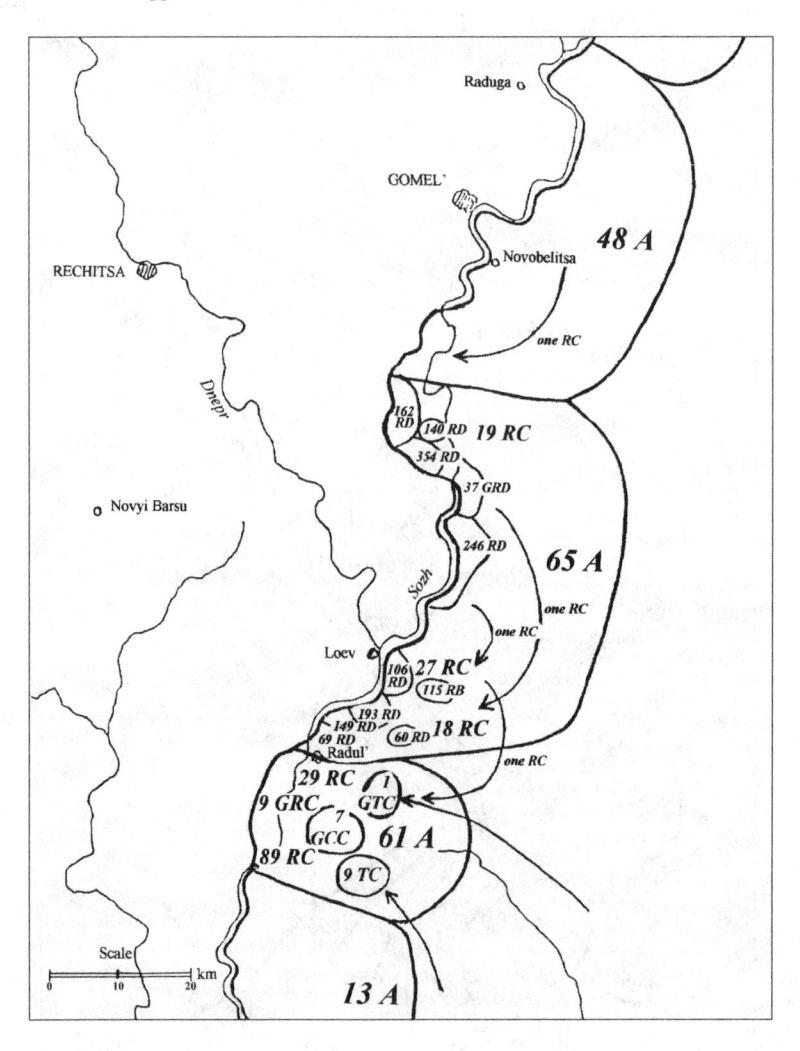

108   The Struggle for Belorussia, October–December 1943

Map 4.7. The Central Front's Dispositions, 14 October 1943

Infantry Division to the right to assist the beleaguered 216th Division to withdraw its 299th and 292nd Infantry Divisions from their defenses east of Gomel' and insert them into defenses along the Sozh River's western bank south of the city to contain the Soviet offensive. As this took place on the night of 9–10 October, XXXV Corps had no choice but to reduce the size of its Gomel' bridgehead by well over 50 percent and leave its defense to 134th Infantry Division and roughly half of 299th Division. Therefore, by the morning of 11 October XXXV Corps' defenses around Gomel' proper were in the immediate outskirts of the city on its southern and eastern sides. Thus,

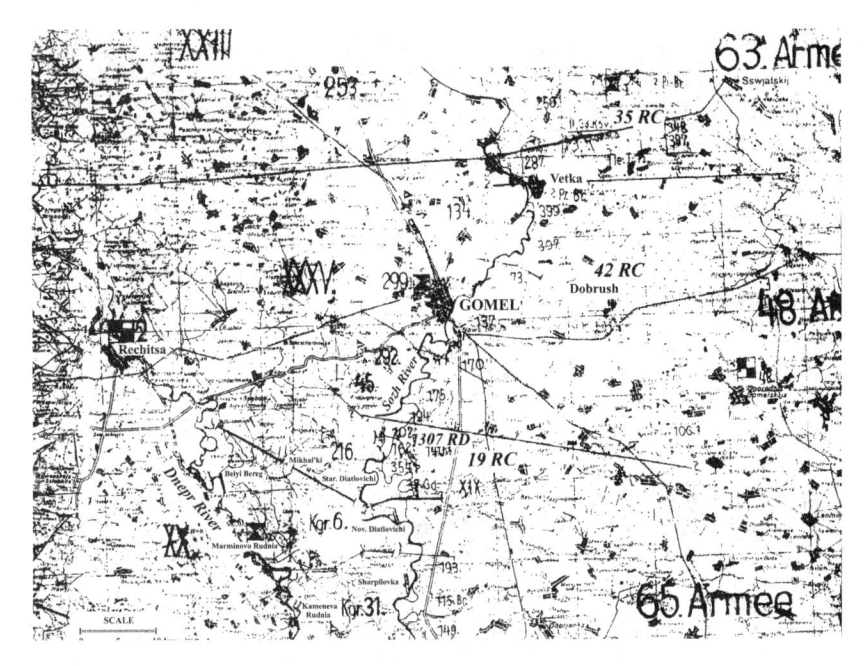

The Central Front's Gomel'-Rechitsa Offensive   109

Map 4.8. Second Army's Situation, 11 October 1943

by nightfall on 12 October, 65th Army's 19th Rifle Corps, along with the forces of 48th Army, had established a sizable contiguous bridgehead on the western bank of the Sozh River south of Gomel' and were on the outskirts of the city on its southern and eastern sides. However, by virtue of skillful force regroupings and considerable exertion, XXXV Corps' 134th, 299th, 292nd, 45th, and 216th Infantry Divisions had largely contained the Soviet advance.

No sooner had German Second Army's crisis abated than a new one loomed for German Ninth Army farther to the north. At the time General Walter Model's Ninth Army had occupied defenses along the Sozh River to block any Soviet advance toward Dovsk and Rogachev on the Dnepr River. Rokossovsky tasked Lieutenant General A. V. Gorbatov's 3rd Army with seizing a bridgehead over the Sozh to divert German attentions and reserves from the fighting in the Gomel' region. Accordingly, at dawn on 12 October, 3rd Army's 120th Guards, 269th, and 121st Guards Rifle Division attacked across the Sozh and succeeded in capturing small bridgeheads 1–2 kilometers deep at Kostiukovka, Salabuty, and Studenets, all south of the city of Propoisk. Although strong German counterattacks over the next several days prevented the attackers from enlarging their bridgeheads, Gorbatov's assaults did indeed prevent Ninth Army from sending reinforcements to Second Army.[18] The 50th Army also conducted local attacks across the Pronia River with similar lack of success. These assaults, together with Rokossovsky's north of

110   The Struggle for Belorussia, October–December 1943

Gomel', however, totally blinded the Germans to what was about to occur in the Loev and Radul' sector.

Rokossovsky's main attacks began early on 15 October on 61st and 65th Army's fronts; however, they achieved only limited success. The 65th Army's 18th and 27th Rifle Corps successfully fought their way across the Dnepr River between Loev and Radul' and, by the night of 20 October, had carved a bridgehead 18 kilometers wide and 13 kilometers deep in the Loev sector (see Maps 4.9 and 4.10).[19] However, the forces' forward progress was not great enough to warrant the commitment into the penetration of 2nd Guards Cavalry Corps, and 1st Guards Tank Corps had yet to reach the region. Surprised by the sudden Soviet thrust south of Loev, the Germans had no choice but to withdraw their defense lines along the Sozh River north of its confluence with the Dnepr westward to its western bank. This they did on the night of 17–18 October, with 65th Army's 19th Rifle Corps in close pursuit. This German withdrawal left Batov's army in control of a sizable bridgehead south of Gomel' along both banks of the Dnepr.

After completing its regrouping, General Belov's 61st Army also began its assault on 15 October from positions in and adjacent to the Liubech' bridgehead, supported by a heavy artillery barrage by 4th Artillery Penetration Corps (see Map 4.11). The 9th Guards Rifle Corps' 12th Guards Rifle Division then assaulted and broke through the defensive positions of XXXXVI Panzer Corps' 251st Infantry Division and seized Hill 114.0, a vital position that dominated the Soviet enclave, by day's end. The corps' 76th and 77th Guards Rifle Divisions expanded the bridgehead on 12th Guards Division's left and right flanks, respectively, and 29th Rifle Corps' 81st Rifle Division managed to cross the Dnepr on 77th Guards Division's right.[20] As a result, by day's end on 18 October, 61st Army's five assaulting divisions succeeded in carving out a 4–5-kilometer-deep and 20-kilometer-wide bridgehead on the Dnepr's western bank west of Liubech'. However, Belov was unable to commit his mobile forces (7th Guards Cavalry and 9th Tank Corps) into the penetration because of the bridgehead's limited size and irregular configuration. Worse still for his offensive, a combat group from German Second Army's 2nd Panzer Division, regrouped into this sector from the Chernobyl' region, began counterattacking against Belov's now exhausted forces early on 18 October (see 4.12). Although 2nd Panzer fielded fewer than ten tanks, these, plus its panzer grenadiers and armored personnel carriers, managed to contain the Soviet attack.[21] Rokossovsky, faced with what amounted to a stalemate in 61st Army's sector, ordered Belov to cease his attacks in the Liubech' sector until further notice. During this action, on 16 October the *Stavka* redesignated the Central Front as the Belorussian Front effective on 20 October.

Although Belov's offensive had faltered, and with it the Belorussian Front's main attack, the success of Batov's army at Loev discouraged the German command and encouraged Rokossovsky. The *front* commander sum-

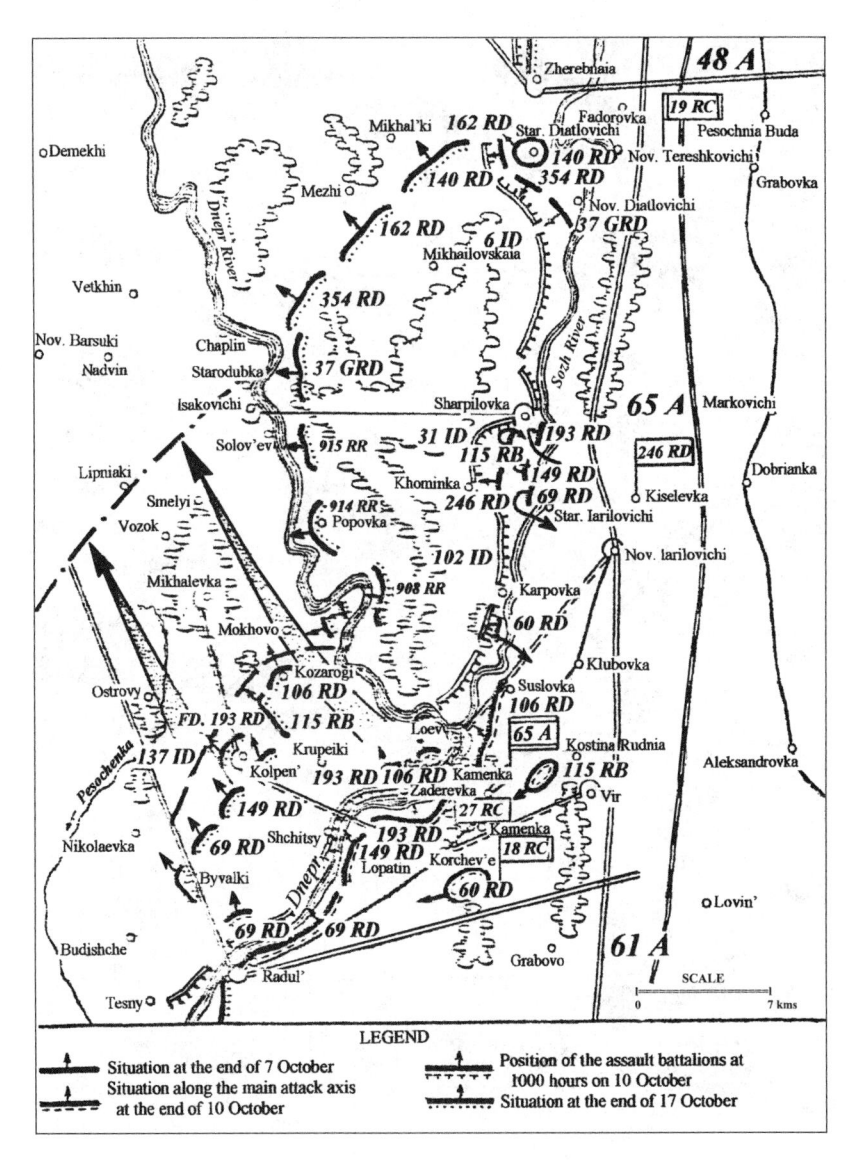

The Central Front's Gomel'-Rechitsa Offensive   111

Map 4.9. 65th Army's Forced Crossing of the Dnepr River at Loev, 7–17 October 1943

marized his achievements and the problems his forces experienced in the Belorussian Front's combat journal:

> As a result of the offensive, the armies penetrated the forward edge of the enemy's defenses and secured bridgeheads on the western banks of

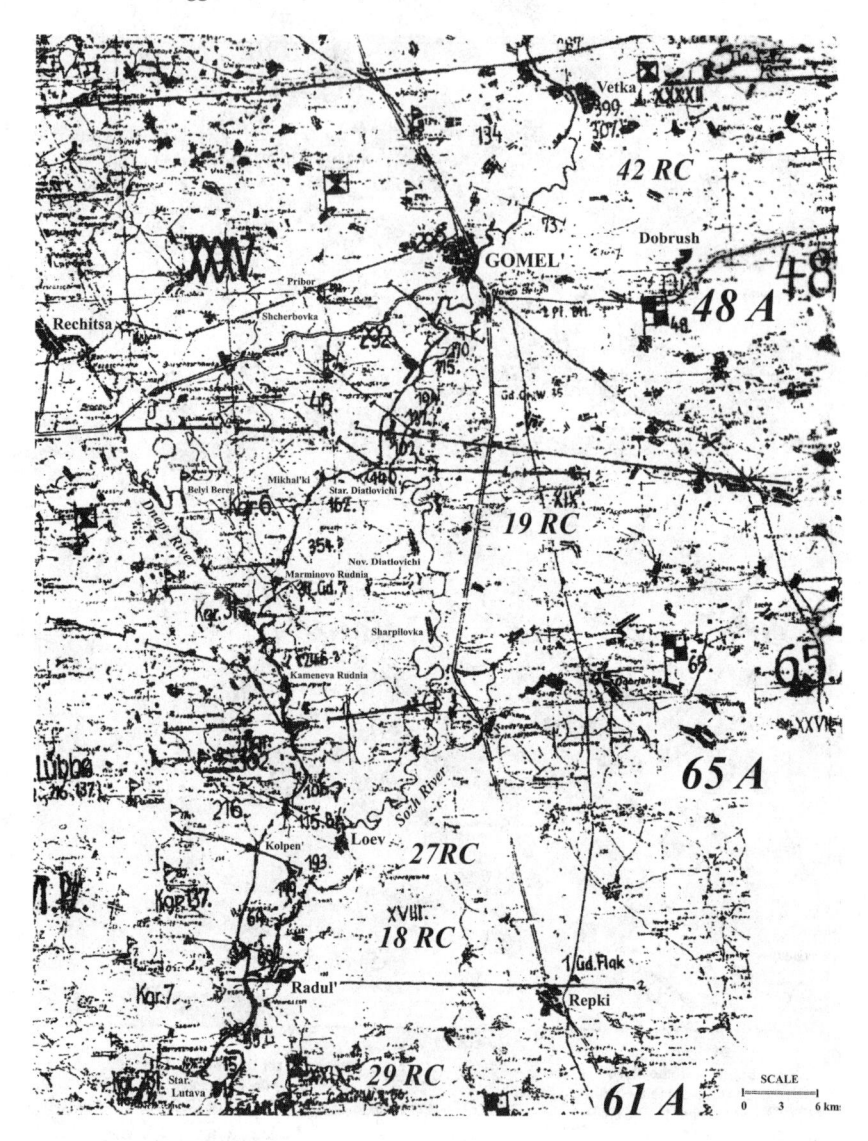

112   The Struggle for Belorussia, October–December 1943

Map 4.10. Second Army's Situation in the Loev Sector, 20 October 1943

the Sozh, Pronia, and Dnepr Rivers; however, they could not develop the offensive and reach the tactical depths of his defenses for the following reasons: . . .

In the planning itself of the operation, where the main attack by the *front*'s forces was determined—on the Pronia River or on the Sozh River and in the Gomel' region or in the Dnepr region?—was not conveyed.

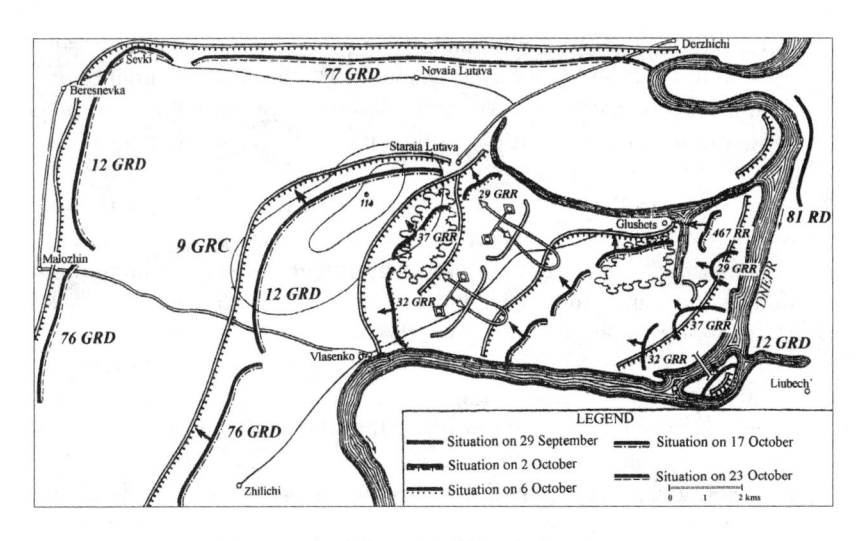

Map 4.11. 61st Army's Expansion of the Liubech' Bridgehead, 29 September–23 October 1943

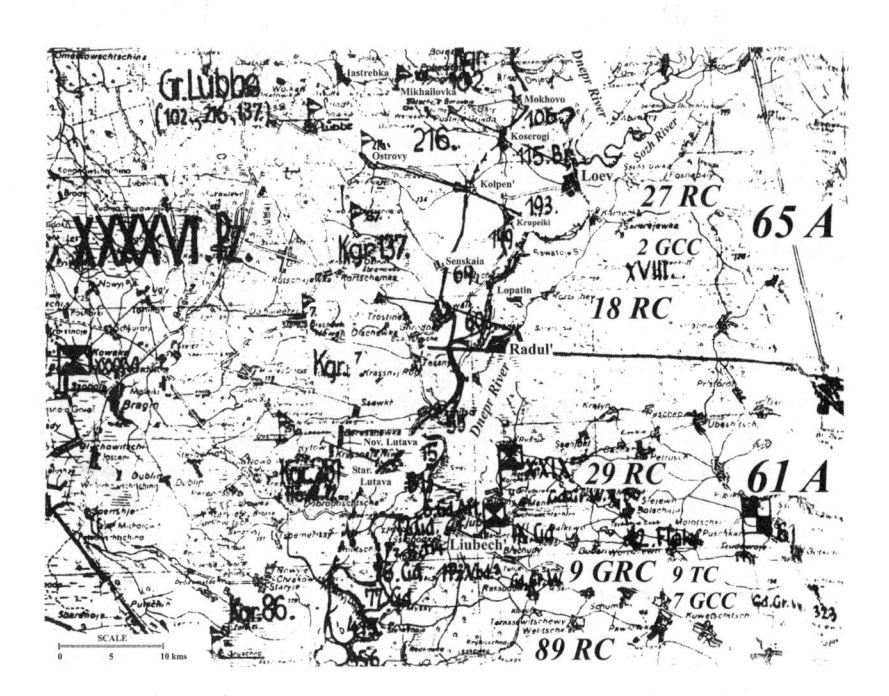

Map 4.12. Second Army's Situation in the Radul'-Liubech' Sector, 20 October 1943

It turned out to be a spread-out striking force, which wanted to seize everything, but the force was not enough. The plan was at variance with realities in terms of time, space, and, chiefly, the forces and means [weapons], and material support of the operation—the acute shortage of ammunition . . .

The poor artillery preparation of the forward edge of the defense . . . as a result of deficiencies in artillery fire, which was enough for conducting an artillery preparation of only 5–10 minutes and a maximum of 30 minutes, and ammunition was not sufficient for accompanying tanks and infantry, and, especially for striking the depths of the defenses. . . .

The enemy studied our shortcomings and the locations of our penetrations well and, ahead of time, created a very dense system of strong points there and succeeded in protecting them with his fires. . . . The varied times our offensive began and the dispersal of forces and means of penetration . . . dissipated the force of our blow, and, in addition, the enemy was able to parry our weak blows successfully with small counterattacking forces.[22]

Even though Rokossovsky's forces fell well short of their goal, Earl Ziemke described the dilemma the limited Soviet success posed to the German defenders:

By that time [9 October] the trouble was brewing further south. While Second Army was occupied with its flanks, Rokossovsky built a strong concentration south of Loev. . . . There a thrust across the Dnepr toward Rechitsa could outflank both the Panther position and the Dnepr switch position and confront Second Army with the unhappy task of trying to create a front in the partisan-infested woods and swamps west of the Dnepr.

On 15 October the attack began on a 20-mile-wide front south of Loyev. It gained ground fast, partly because Kluge, still worried more about keeping contact with Army Group South [west of Kiev], hesitated for two days before letting one of the panzer divisions be taken off the Second Army right flank. By the 20th the Russians had carved out a bridgehead sixty miles wide and ten miles deep on both sides of the Dnepr. Then, for two days, they attempted to thrust northeast toward Rechitsa on the railroad west of Gomel.[23]

Although the initial stage of Batov's attacks ended on 20 October, Rokossovsky soon decided to resume his attacks along both banks of the Dnepr to exploit 65th Army's limited successes. However, Soviet sources have all but ignored this stage of the operation. For example, in his memoirs, Rokossovsky failed to mention any action after 20 October, simply stating, "I decided to halt the offensive temporarily, and the date for a new 'D-day' was tentatively set for November 10, by which time the operation was to be thoroughly prepared."[24] Nor did General Batov provide any information about the continued fighting. Rokossovsky's commissar, Lieutenant General K. F. Telegin, repeated their omission:

> The *front's* Military Council reached a decision on 20 October to halt the offensive temporarily, to dig in along achieved positions, and to prepare the already mentioned operation with the long-term aim of capturing Rechitsa and reaching the rear of the enemy's Gomel' grouping.
> The pause, which the Military Council mandated until 10 November, provided the opportunity in these complex conditions to regroup the forces to the desired degree, bring the supply bases forward, and supply the forward units with all the necessities for developing active offensive operations.[25]

Demonstrating clearly that the accounts provided by Rokossovsky, Telegin, Batov, and those contained in Red Army divisional histories were incomplete, German records prove that heavy fighting in the Loev and Radul' sectors continued virtually unabated through the end of October as Rokossovsky resolutely strove to fulfill his assigned mission. Earl Ziemke noted some, but not all of this ensuing action:

> On 22 October Kluge called Zeitzler for reinforcements. Second Army, he said, was exhausted and could not stand up against the continuing attack. The army group could give no guarantees with respect to future developments, and unless help was given it might become necessary to pull the whole front back. On the same day, having failed to achieve a breakout, Rokossovsky stopped his offensive in the Loev bridgehead.
> In the last week of the month Rokossovsky shifted his attack to the Ninth Army's flanks, denting the Panther position in several places and posing the threat of multiple breakthroughs. On 27 October Kluge and Model discussed taking Ninth Army and Second Army back to the Dnepr below Mogilev. The next day Rokossovsky added to their concern by resuming the offensive in the Loyev bridgehead; but at the end of the month, satisfied for the time being with local gains, he called another halt.[26]

Contradicting most Soviet accounts of the Gomel' operation, on 20 October Rokossovsky ordered Belov and Batov to regroup their armies, resume their attacks on 22 October, and exploit to capture Rechitsa, Kalinkovichi, and Mozyr'. This time Batov's 65th Army was to conduct the *front's* main attack toward Rechitsa.[27] Accordingly, 61st Army shifted its 9th Guards Rifle

Corps northward from its bridgehead west of Liubech' into 29th Rifle Corps' smaller bridgehead opposite Novaia and Staraia Lutava, situated 4–7 kilometers north of Liubech' and precisely at the boundary between the defending 7th and 251st Infantry Divisions of Second Army's XXXXVI Panzer Corps. The 29th Rifle Corps then concentrated its three divisions in a smaller bridgehead south of Radul', on 9th Guards Corps' right flank. The mission Rokossovsky assigned to General Belov's army was to expand its bridgehead, link it up to 65th Army's farther north and, along with 65th Army, penetrate German defenses around the bridgehead and exploit northwestward toward Kalinkovichi and Mozyr'. The 2nd Guards Cavalry Corps' history confirms this mission by stating that its mission was "to cross the Dnepr in the Loev region, seize the regional center at Poles'e Vasilevichi, and then occupy the Mozyr'-Kalinkovichi region by enveloping it from the north."[28]

For his part, General Batov was to reinforce his forces in the Loev bridgehead with two rifle divisions (the 354th and 246th) from 19th Rifle Corps' forces in the Sozh bridgehead and attack from the Loev bridgehead with 18th and 27th Rifle Corps. In addition to its organic 2nd Guards Cavalry Corps, Rokossovsky reinforced Batov's army with 9th Tank, 7th Guards Cavalry, and 4th Artillery Penetration Corps, thus providing it roughly fifty tanks. After this regrouping was complete, Batov and Belov's forces were arrayed from north to south as shown in Table 4.1.

When 65th and 61st Armies completed their regrouping, the bulk of their forces (twelve rifle divisions, one rifle brigade, and one tank and two cavalry corps) were concentrated in the 45-kilometer-wide sector between the village of Mokhovo, 9 kilometers north of Loev, southward through Novaia and Staraia Lutava to Mysy, 7 kilometers south of Liubech'. These forces faced five German infantry divisions—from north to south, XX Army Corps' 102nd, 216th, 137th Infantry Divisions, organized temporarily in Group Lubbe, facing 65th Army, and XXXXVI Panzer Corps' 7th and 251st Infantry Divisions, backed up by a small combat group from 2nd Panzer Division, facing 61st Army. All of the German divisions were severely worn down by previous fighting and organized into combat group *kampfgruppe* configuration of the size of no more than two regiments. The 2nd Panzer's *kampfgruppe* had only a handful of tanks, with more numerous armored personnel carriers. Hence, Rokossovsky's force enjoyed superiority in infantry of at least 3 to 1 and an absolute superiority in armor.

General Batov's 18th and 27th Rifle Corps, supported by about fifty tanks from 9th Tank Corps and infantry from the tank corps' motorized rifle brigade, began their assault on 20 October, even before their regrouping had been completed (see Map 4.13). These assaults overran the German defenses, forcing the defenders back about 2 kilometers between the Dnepr River and Radul' on the first day of the attack. Two days later, 61st Army's two corps launched their assaults, and 2nd and 7th Guards Cavalry Corps

Table 4.1. The Combat Formations of the Belorussian Front's 65th and 61st Armies and Opposing German Forces on 20 October 1943

FORCE (Sector)			OPPOSING GERMAN FORCE
1st/2nd Echelons (Mobile group)			**SECOND ARMY**
			XXXV AC
BELORUSSIAN FRONT			292nd ID
65th Army (Novyi Diatlovichi-Radul')			45th ID
19th RC (Novyi Diatlovichi-Dnepr River)			XX AC
140th RD			KGr., 6th ID
162nd RD			
37th GRD			KGr., 31st ID
27th RC (Dnepr River-Kolpen')	(2nd GCC)	(9th TC)	XXXXVI PzC
106th RD	3rd GCD	23rd TB	Gp. Lubbe
115th RB/354th RD	4th GCD	95th TB	KGr., 102nd ID
246th RD	17th GCD	108th TB	KGr., 216th ID
		8th MRB	
18th RC (Kolpen'-Radul')	(7th GCC)		KGr., 137th ID
149th RD	14th GCD		
69th RD/193rd RD	15th GCD		
60th RD	16th GCD		KGr., 7th ID
61st Army (Radul'-Liubech')			
29th RC (Radul'-Novaia Lutava)			
55th RD			
15th RD			KGr., 251st ID
81st RD			KGr., 2nd PzD
9th GRC (Novaia Lutava-Staraia Lutava)			
77th GRD			
12th GRD			
76th GRD			
89th RC (Staraia Lutava-Liubech')			
356th RD			KGr., 86th ID
415th RD			
336th RD			

Sources: *Boevoi sostav Sovetskoi Armii, chast' III (Ianvar'–dekabr' 1943 g.)* [The combat composition of the Soviet Army, pt. 3 (January–December 1943) (Moscow: Voenizdat, 1972), 249; and "Anlage, Bd. 102, A.O.K 2, Ia, Oct–Nov 1943," *AOK 2, 41181/102 file*, in NAM Series T-312, Roll 1266.

advanced to help expand and exploit 65th Army's penetration. Heavy fighting raged for more than a week as the attacking Soviet forces prompted German Second Army to order Group Lubbe's forces to begin a phased withdrawal to new positions in the rear. By the evening of 28 October, Batov's two rifle corps had advanced another 15–20 kilometers, reaching positions extending from Isakovichi on the Dnepr, 23 kilometers northwest of Loev, southwestward through Smelyi to Vozok, and then southward to the vicinity of Nikolaevka, 12 kilometers west of Radul', where their left flank linked up with the right flank of the advancing forces of 61st Army.

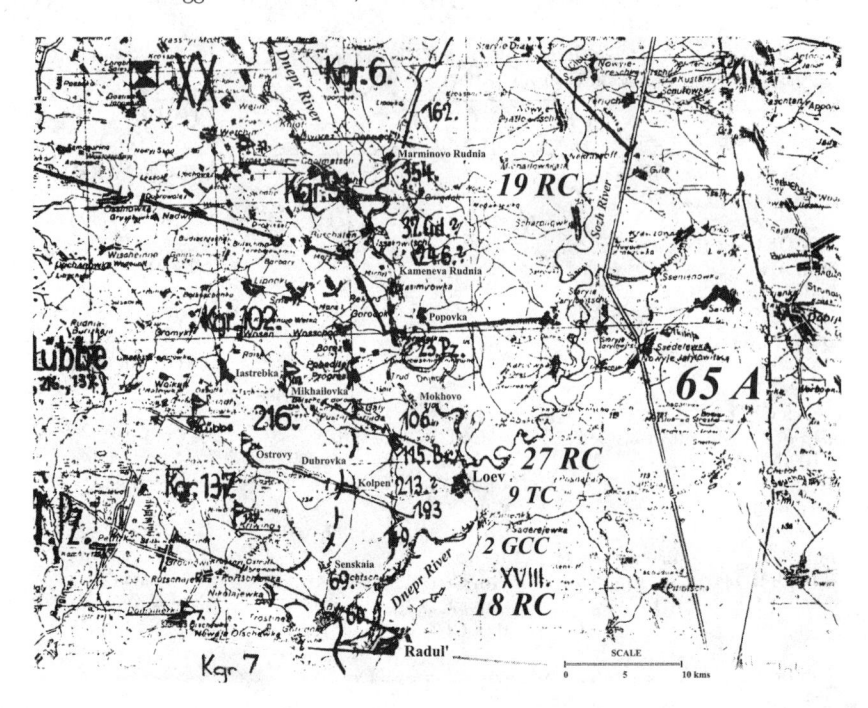

Map 4.13. Second Army's Situation in the Loev Sector, 21 October 1943

During this fighting, the attacking divisions of 65th Army's 27th Rifle Corps punched a 5-kilometer-wide breach in German 102nd Infantry Division's defenses south of Lipniaki on 24 October, into which Batov committed General Kriukov's 2nd Guards Cavalry Corps. Only the timely arrival of the combat group from 2nd Panzer Division contained the dangerous penetration (see Map 4.14). Thereafter, Batov transferred 37th Guards Rifle Division from the Sozh River bridgehead into the Lipniaki sector on the 27th. Along with 246th and 193rd Rifle Divisions, the 2nd and 7th Guards Cavalry Corps, and about twenty tanks from 9th Tank Corps, 37th Guards Rifle Division then carved yet another breach in German defenses west of Lipniaki on 29 October. Reacting quickly, German Second Army dispatched a newly arrived *kampfgruppe* from 12th Panzer Division against the northern flank of the Soviet penetration. This quick reaction, together with stout resistance by the remnants of 102nd Rifle Division and 216th Infantry Division, both still reinforced by 2nd Panzer Division's now-split-up combat group, contained the penetration, but only barely (see Map 4.15). The key to German success here was the roughly fifteen tanks in 12th Panzer Division's *kampfgruppe*.

One of the few existing Soviet accounts of this operation is found in the history of 7th Guards Cavalry Corps, whose account of the fighting is unique, accurate, and candid:

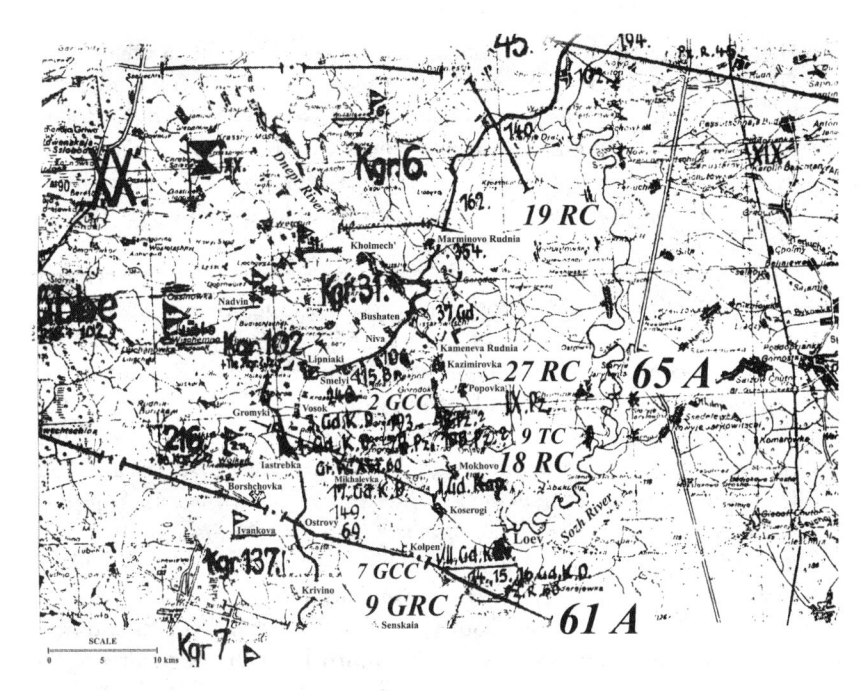

Map 4.14. Second Army's Situation in the Loev Sector, 25 October 1943

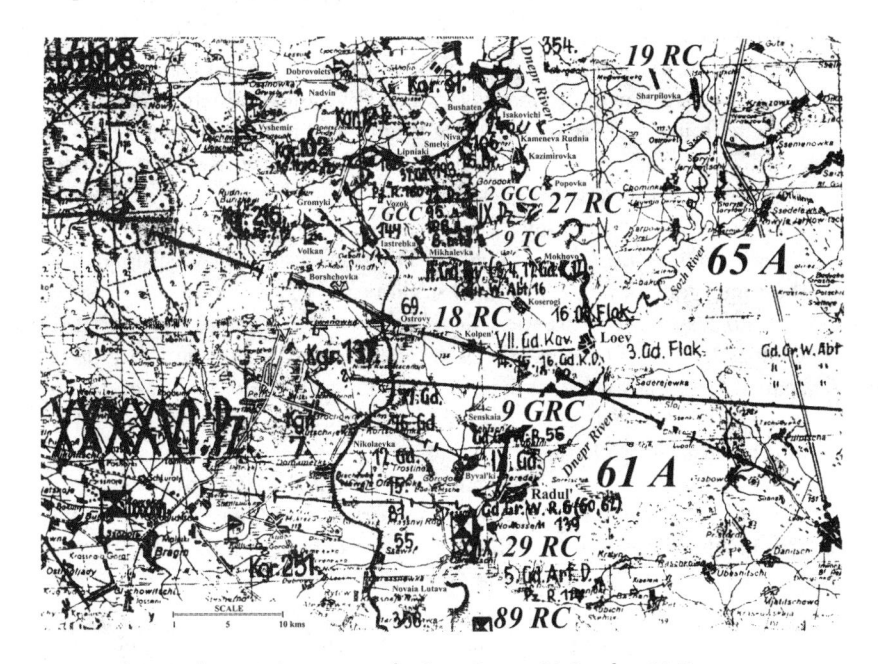

Map 4.15. Second Army's Situation in the Loev Sector, 30 October 1943

Having evaluated the situation on the 61st Army's operational sector, Guards Major General M. P. Konstantinov, the corps commander . . . asked permission from the *front* commander, Army General K. K. Rokossovsky to castle 7th Guards Cavalry Corps into the sector of 65th Army, which, at that time, had seized a sizable bridgehead on the Dnepr River's right bank that was suitable for the commitment of the corps into the penetration.

The *front* commander agreed with corps commander's decision and ordered that the cavalry corps be placed under the operational subordination of Lieutenant General P. I. Batov, 65th Army's commander.

Having completed a 35-kilometer march, 7th Guards Cavalry Corps crossed the Dnepr River south of Loev on 22 October and launched an attack with two of its cavalry divisions. The 14th Guards Cavalry Division [attacked] along the Smelyi, Lipniaki, and Grushevka axis and 15th Guards Cavalry Division along the Smelyi and Dubrovka axis. However, from the very beginning of the offensive, the corps' units and formations encountered heavy resistance from the enemy's 31st and 137th Infantry Divisions [*sic*], supported by aviation and artillery.

At a cost of great effort, 15th Guards Rifle Division's 55th and 53rd Guards Cavalry Regiments captured Dubrovka at the beginning of the attack but were then forced to withdraw from this village by the onslaught of superior enemy forces. The units repelled the counterattacks and inflicted considerable losses on the enemy. As a result, he was forced to withdraw to his jumping-off positions from Niva to Lipniaki.

On 24 October 15th Guards Cavalry Division conducted surprise attacks with its 53rd Guards Cavalry Regiment on Dubrovka and its 55th and 57th Guards Cavalry Regiments on Smelyi, which were crowned with success and captured these villages.

In response, the enemy, supported by tanks and artillery, counterattacked against 15th Guards Cavalry Division's units but was repelled by their energetic defense, losing 80 soldiers and officers killed.

A no less serious situation developed in the combat sector of 14th Guards Cavalry Division, which was also forced to go on the defense against large enemy forces supported by tanks, artillery, and aircraft. The division withstood 5 enemy bombing attacks by groups of from 12–18 aircraft just on 23 October.

On order of the corps' commander, 14th and 15th Guards Cavalry Divisions relinquished their defensive sectors to 37th Guards Rifle Division and 115th Rifle Brigade on 25 October and concentrated in the forests in the Voskhod region. There they prepared to exploit the success of 65th Army forces in the direction of Lipniaki.

After a strong artillery preparation, the rifle formations launched an attack along that axis on 28 October.

Before the attack began, Guards Colonel K. V. Fiksel', 14th Guards Cavalry Division commander, was situated with 37th Guards Rifle Division with an operational group from his division's staff. He personally directed his units' operations so that he could provide a timely signal for the commitment of his division into the penetration.

The headquarters of 37th Guards Rifle Division, which was located in the forests southeast of Lipniaki, was fired on by the enemy at 1000 hours. Guards Colonel Fiksel' and several of his staff officers perished during the artillery raid. . . .

Soon after, Guards Colonel G. P. Koblov was assigned to command 14th Guards Cavalry Division.[29]

This short account, one of the few to describe the action after 20 October 1943 in some detail, dovetails perfectly with German archival records and confirms the heavy fighting that took place in the Loev bridgehead between 20 and 30 October.

Meanwhile, in heavy fighting to the south, 9th Guards Rifle Corps' 77th, 12th, and 76th Guards Rifle Divisions of Belov's 61st Army seized Staraia and Novaia Lutava from the German 137th and 7th Infantry Divisions on 23 October. Joined by 29th Rifle Corps' divisions attacking on their right, these forces pushed the defending Germans back, advanced more than 10 kilometers westward from Radul', and linked up with the forces on 65th Army's right flank near the village of Nikolaevka. However, Batov's and Belov's forces had "shot their bolt" by 30 October. Despite several local penetrations, they had been unable to achieve a clean operational breach, largely because of the desperate but skillful actions of German tactical reserves. However, the heavy fighting took a terrible toll on the defending Germans, who were barely able to hold on to their shaky defenses.

To support the heavy assaults south of Loev, Rokossovsky ordered General Gorbatov's 3rd Army to attack across the Pronia River north and south of Krasnaia Sloboda against the German Ninth Army's defenses. Gorbatov's mission was to distract German attention from Rokossovsky's main attack sector further south and, if possible, exploit to Novyi Bykhov on the Dnepr River. The latter was unrealistic, however, because Gorbatov's army was experiencing severe ammunition shortages as the Red Army logistical organs directed the bulk of critical supplies to Batov's and Belov's forces. As noted by Ziemke, Gorbatov's forces attacked at dawn on 25 October with the 41st Rifle Corps' 120th Guards, 186th, and 269th Rifle Divisions in the lead, backed up by the corps' 17th Rifle Division. In two days of ever-intensifying fighting, Gorbatov's force carved a bridgehead 1 kilometer deep and 5 kilometers wide in the defenses of the German 267th Infantry Division but could accomplish nothing more. Having suffered heavy losses, Gorbatov halted his attacks late on 26 October.[30]

On 1 November the fatigue of Soviet forces left Rokossovsky with no choice but to order his forces to halt their assaults. However, the respite for the beleaguered Germans would be brief. Although Rokossovsky had failed to fulfill the missions assigned to him by the *Stavka*, he had come close to doing so. On the plus side, he had employed deception and maneuver skillfully to seize an operational-scale bridgehead over the Dnepr from which his forces could conduct future offensives. Had he possessed a full tank army or cavalry-mechanized group, or had Panov's 1st Guards Tank Corps reached his region as was hoped, it is likely that his offensive would have progressed far deeper than it did. As it was, he used his existing forces to his greatest advantage. While doing so, he so damaged the defending German forces that their capability for resisting another determined Soviet offensive simply vanished. This would become evident on 10 November, when Rokossovsky's forces commenced the third and final stage of their Gomel'-Rechitsa offensive.

In the interim, at Rokossovsky's request, the *Stavka* decided to reinforce his *front* so that his third attempt to reach Rechitsa, Bobruisk, and Minsk would have greater chances of being successful. As the fighting raged on west of Loev, early on 23 October the *Stavka* issued a directive assigning the 2nd Baltic Front's 11th Army to Rokossovsky's control. Commanded by Lieutenant General I. I. Fediuninsky, the 11th's seven rifle divisions and supporting units and facilities were to move southward by rail and deploy westward by truck and foot into 48th Army's sector adjacent to Gomel' so that the 48th could be regrouped to reinforce the Rechitsa axis. While 11th Army was en route, Rokossovsky was to begin regrouping 48th Army to its new sector, leaving two or three rifle divisions behind and, if necessary, reinforcing them with forces from 63rd Army (see Appendix C-5).[31]

A short period of calm set in across the combat front in eastern Belorussia on 1 November, produced in part by the onset of the fall *rasputitsa* (period of flooded roads), in part by the exhaustion of Red Army forces operating along the western strategic axis, and in part by the necessity of moving 11th Army southward to reinforce Rokossovsky's *front* (see Appendix C-6). Although the *Stavka* had achieved some notable successes during the first stage of its Belorussian strategic offensive, it had also experienced bitter failures (see Map 4.16).

On the offensive's right wing north of Vitebsk, General Eremenko's Kalinin (1st Baltic) Front had seized Nevel' and driven a shallow wedge between Army Group Center's Third Panzer Army and Army Group North's Sixteenth Army. Eremenko's *front* was now admirably positioned to advance northward in concert with the forces of General Popov's 2nd Baltic Front to turn the right wing of Army Group North's Sixteenth Army in the Kholm and Staraia Russa regions; to strike out westward along the Western Dvina River toward Daugavpils in Latvia, thus broadening the wedge separating Army

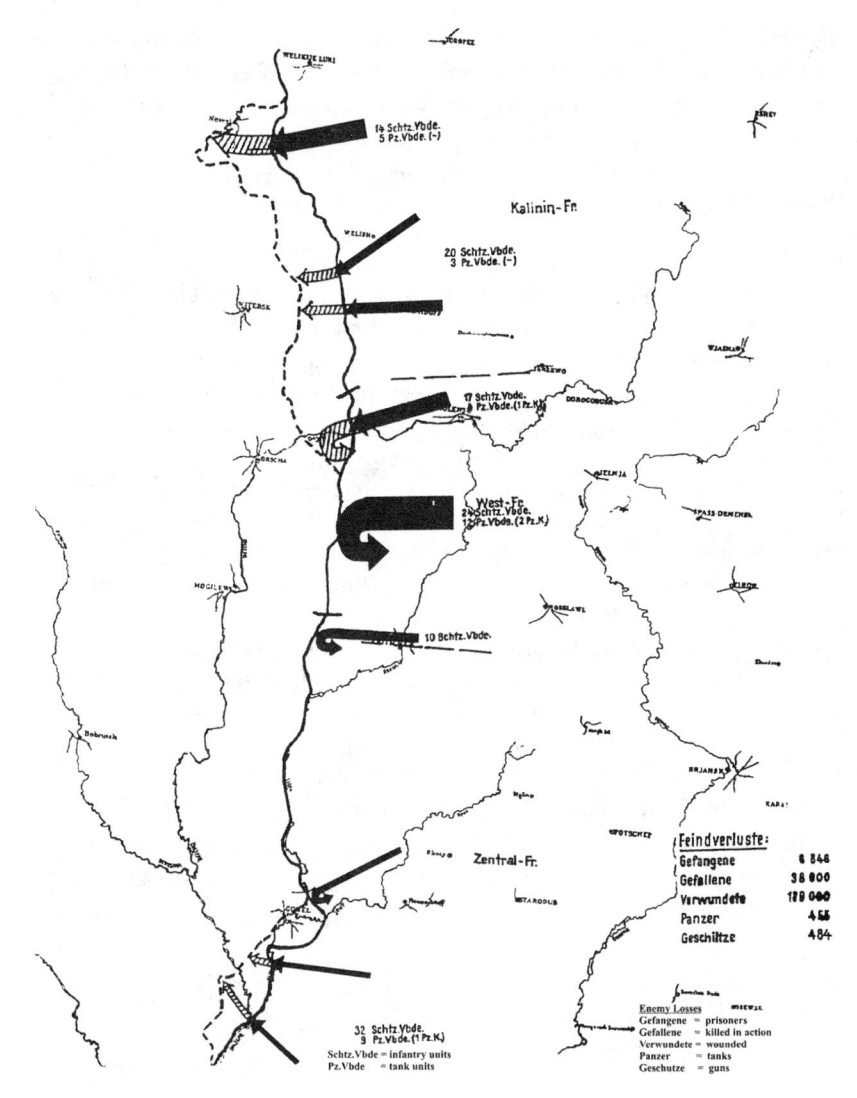

Map 4.16. German Assessment of Red Army Operations in Belorussia, 3–31 October 1943

Group North from German Army Group Center; or to move southward against Army Group Center's Third Panzer Army at Vitebsk in cooperation with the armies of Sokolovsky's Western Front.

On the offensive's left wing in southern Belorussia, Rokossovsky's Central (Belorussian) Front had seized an operational-size bridgehead across the Dnepr River south of Gomel' and, along with General Vatutin's Voronezh (1st Ukrainian) Front, which had seized a similar bridgehead in the Chernobyl' region north of Kiev, it threatened to advance westward and separate the forces of Army Groups Center and South. On 6 October the *Stavka* transferred 13th and 60th Armies on the Central Front's right wing to the Voronezh Front so that they could reinforce Vatutin's advance on Chernobyl'. This, in turn, enabled Rokossovsky to concentrate his attentions and forces to his ongoing offensive along the Rechitsa, Bobruisk, and Minsk axis.

However, in the central sector of the Belorussian offensive, the armies of General Sokolovsky's Western Front experienced repeated, frustrating defeats as they tried in vain to penetrate the defenses of Army Group Center's Fourth Army in eastern Belorussia. All Sokolovsky had to show for his *front's* efforts were staggeringly heavy losses and only meager gains. However, he did take solace in the knowledge that the three major assaults his *front* conducted during the month riveted German forces to the region, produced substantial German casualties, and prevented Army Group Center from transferring forces from this axis to other threatened sectors. Furthermore, by month's end, the bulk of the Western Front's forces were finally concentrated on one key axis—the Orsha-Minsk axis.

From the *Stavka's* perspective, despite limited gains and many frustrations, by the end of October it had every reason to believe that the forces of 1st Baltic, Western, and Belorussian Fronts would be able to defeat and destroy Army Group Center's forces in Belorussia before the spring of 1944. It was equally convinced that, with the assistance of the new 2nd Baltic Front, the Leningrad and Volkhov Fronts could perform the same feat against Army Group North's two armies in the Leningrad region and to the south. Thus, beginning on 2 November, the *Stavka* ordered its operating *fronts* to set about doing so.

CHAPTER 5

The 1st and 2nd Baltic Fronts' Polotsk-Vitebsk and Pustoshka-Idritsa Offensives (2-21 November)

PRELUDE

The second stage of the Belorussian strategic offensive began in early November when the *Stavka* ordered the 1st Baltic, Western, and Belorussian Fronts to resume offensive operations against German Army Group Center and capture Minsk and eastern Belorussia. This time, 2nd Baltic Front was to join the fray by attacking the defenses of Army Group North's Sixteenth Army and rolling up the army group's right wing south of Leningrad. The official Soviet history described the action in the north, in and around the Nevel' salient, and in the vicinity of Vitebsk sector:

> The fierce fighting north and south of Nevel' and east of Vitebsk did not die down in November and December 1943. The 2nd Baltic Front's 6th Guards and 3rd Shock Armies attacked along the Pustoshka-Idritsa and Polotsk axes, and 1st Baltic Front's 4th Shock, 11th Guards, and 43rd Armies fought intense battles north and east of Vitebsk. An especially severe battle developed for Gorodok.
>
> The German-Fascist command attached great significance to that point on the approaches to Vitebsk and strongly fortified it. The enemy created four defense lines. Three of these were located one behind the other on the approaches to the city, and the fourth girdled its outskirts. Broken terrain, isolated by dominant heights, lakes, and streams, was used in the erection of the powerful defense.
>
> However, the German-Fascist forces were driven back from Gorodok on 24 December as a result of the heavy combat. Soviet forces severed the Vitebsk-Polotsk railroad line. Active operations by partisan detachments, which helped to seize and hold crossings and important lines, assisted their offensive.
>
> During the Soviet's offensive north and south of Nevel', Army Group North's command intended to attack the advancing Soviet divisions. However, the operations of the Leningrad, Volkhov, and Northwestern Fronts' forces tied down the enemy forces.
>
> By the end of the year, the Soviet Army had advanced 90 kilometers along the Polotsk axis, liberated more than 500 villages, and reached

125

positions extending from south of Pustoshka through Dretun' and southeastward along the Western Dvina River to east of Vitebsk.[1]

Desultory but often bitter fighting of a local nature persisted north and south of Nevel' and east of Vitebsk throughout the second half of October as the 1st Baltic Front's armies fought to improve their tactical dispositions, while regrouping, replenishing, and resting their forces. At the same time, the 2nd Baltic Front assembled its forces north of Nevel'. All the while, the *front* commands and *Stavka* exchanged views concerning where and how the offensive was to be resumed. A directive prepared on 25 October by the 1st Baltic Front provided keen insights regarding the *front's* offensive intent, noting, "The forces of 1st Baltic Front have been assigned the mission to destroy the enemy's Vitebsk-Gorodok grouping and capture the city of Vitebsk." They were to do so "by concentric attacks by 4th Shock Army in the general direction of Gorodok and Sirotino and by 43rd and 39th Armies on Vitebsk" (see Appendix D-1).[2]

Urged on by the *Stavka*, the 1st and 2nd Baltic Fronts completed their planning for the upcoming offensive by 29 October 1943. According to these plans, the 2nd Baltic Front's 3rd Shock Army, commanded by Lieutenant General K. N. Galitsky, was to begin the offensive by advancing westward from the Nevel' region on 2 November, with the mission of severing the Nevel'-Polotsk railroad line, penetrating deeply, and enveloping German Sixteenth Army's forces defending west of Nevel' from the south and west (see Map 5.1). Specifically, together with Lieutenant General V. I. Shvetsov's 4th Shock Army, 3rd Shock Army was "to launch an offensive . . . in the direction of Ust'-Dolyssy" with the mission "to destroy the opposing enemy, who consisted of two infantry and two security divisions, and secure a bridgehead for a subsequent offensive in the direction of Pustoshka."[3] At the same time, Shvetsov's 4th Shock Army was to penetrate westward and then southwestward along the railroad line through Dretun' toward Polotsk on the Western Dvina River and capture the town of Gorodok. In addition, on 8 November the *front's* 43rd and 39th Armies, commanded by General Golubev and Lieutenant General N. E. Berzarin, respectively, were to punch through German defenses east of Vitebsk, capture the city, and advance on Minsk from the northeast. Thus, when the operational plan came to fruition in early November, it took the form of two distinct operations. The first of these was 1st Baltic Front's Polotsk-Vitebsk offensive operation, conducted by the *front's* 4th Shock and 43rd and 39th Armies. The second was 2nd Baltic Front's Pustoshka-Idritsa offensive operation, conducted by the 2nd Baltic Front's 3rd Shock and 6th and 11th Guards Armies.

In conjunction with the 1st Baltic Front's offensive, the *Stavka* also ordered the *front* to plan and conduct an airborne operation in cooperation with attacks by local partisan formations to facilitate the *front's* advance. The

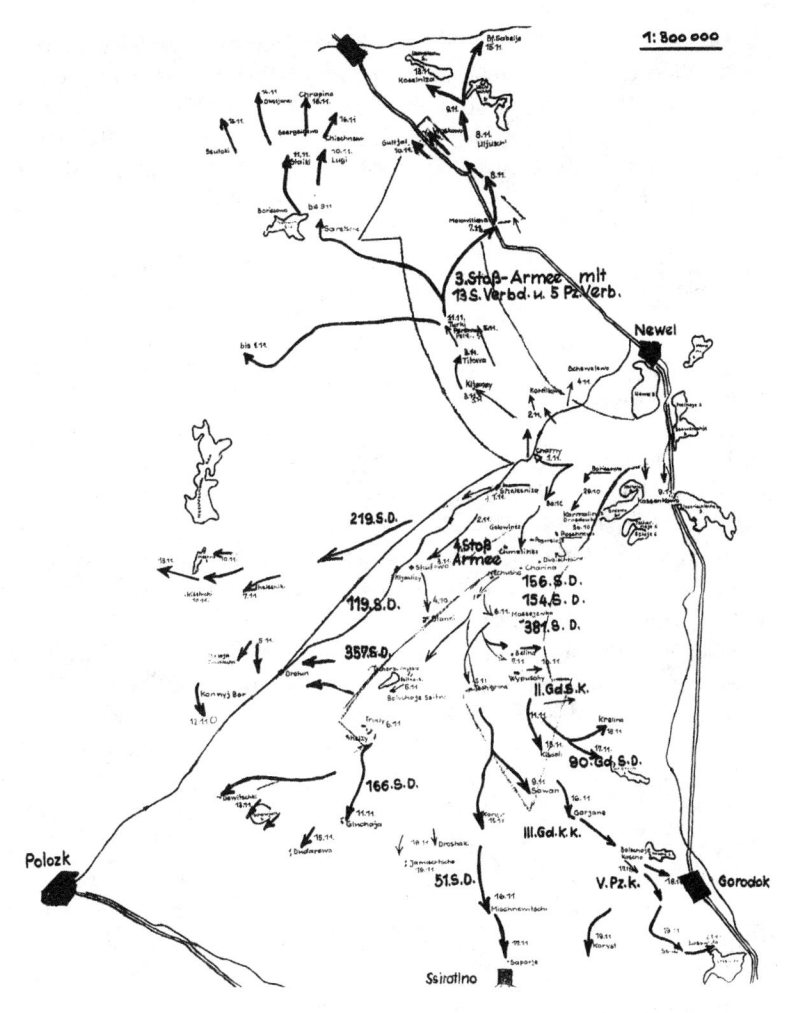

Map 5.1. Third Panzer Army's Appreciation of Red Army Operations West of Nevel', 1–21 November 1943

joint operations between the airborne troops and partisan detachments force sought to disrupt communications and command and control in the Germans' rear area at and behind the boundary between Army Groups North and Center. The 1st Baltic Front dispatched a report to the *Stavka* on 1 November, describing the airborne operation's form and intent (see Appendix D-2.):

> I will conduct an airborne operation effective on 8 November in accordance with your orders. [The operation will be] aimed at inserting

a *desant* [airborne assault] in the Seliavshchina [35 kilometers north of Polotsk] region, destroying the enemy in the Polotsk region by means of joint operations of the *front*'s forces with partisan brigades, and capturing the city. . . . The air assault and the partisan brigades will be ready for combat operations on 12 November 1943. The operation will begin according to a special order.[4]

The *front*'s report indicated that Major General Zatevakhin, the deputy commander of the Red Army's Airborne Forces, would control participating airborne forces, and the Central Headquarters of the Partisan Movement, whose representative was situated at the 1st Baltic Front's command post, was to control the combat operations of the partisan brigades. The forces allocated to the airborne assault included 1st, 2nd, and 11th Guards Airborne Brigades; 1714th Antiaircraft Artillery Regiment; 120–150 transport aircraft provided by Long-range Aviation; 300 fighters and 100 Il-2 aircraft from 3rd and 15th Air Armies; 10 TB-3 and 10 SB and Il-4 aircraft; 50 gliders; 4 antiaircraft artillery regiments from 1st and 2nd Baltic Fronts; and 2 automobile battalions from 1st and 2nd Baltic Fronts, all supported by 5 airfield support battalions from 15th Air Army.[5]

However, at the last minute, the 1st Baltic Front revised its plans for the airborne operation because the Germans began a major antipartisan operation in the very location of the planned Soviet assault, perhaps because it knew about Soviet plans. Earl Ziemke describes the nature and intent of the German antipartisan operation:

> In October the larger part of Army Group North's antipartisan force, twelve battalions of Osttruppen (former Russian prisoners of war, mostly Cossacks, who had volunteered to fight on the German side) were transferred to Germany and France at Kuechler's request. They had become unreliable, and whole units were deserting to the partisans with their weapons and equipment. On 14 October Hitler ordered SS-Obergruppenfueher (Lt. Gen.) Erich von dem Bach-Zelewski, who was responsible for antipartisan warfare in the area of Belorussia under civil administration, to stage an operation against the Rossono partisans. During the next two weeks von dem Bach moved in nineteen mixed battalions of police, Latvian volunteers, and security troops, and on 1 November he launched Operation HEINRICH, employing two approximately division-sized units in a converging attack toward Rossono from the north and south.[6]

Because of Operation Heinrich, whose area of operations included the Seliavshchina region, where the Soviet command intended to conduct its airborne drop, the Soviet command changed its plans. It postponed the airborne operation and instead planned to conduct it with the same forces, only now in the region south of Polotsk.⁷ In any case, deteriorating weather in mid-November forced 1st Baltic Front, with the *Stavka*'s approval, to call off the airborne assault.

THE 1ST BALTIC FRONT'S POLOTSK-VITEBSK OFFENSIVE (2–21 NOVEMBER 1943)

The 1st Baltic Front's 4th Shock Army began its offensive on 2 November as planned, and achieved immediate success. Earl Ziemke describes the subsequent action in the sector north of Vitebsk from the German point of view and the dilemmas it produced for the German command:

> In an early morning fog on 2 November the *Third and Fourth Shock Armies* penetrated the Third Panzer Army left flank southwest of Nevel'. They had paved the way during the five previous days with heavy attacks that drove a deep dent in the Third Panzer Army line. After the breakthrough, which opened a 10-mile wide gap, *Third Shock Army* turned north behind Sixteenth Army's flank and *Fourth Shock Army* turned southwest behind Third Panzer Army.
> Army Group Center shifted a panzer division [20th] north from Ninth Army. With that division it was able to strengthen the Third Panzer Army flank below the breakthrough and deflect *Fourth Shock Army* southwestward away from the panzer army's rear. Army Group North was less fortunate. *Third Shock Army's* more aggressive mode of operating indicated that it had been assigned the main effort in the renewed offensive. . . .
> At the end of the first week of November the Germans were still holding fast on the flanks of the breakthrough, but *Fourth Shock Army* had sent parts of two divisions probing as far west as Dretun', thirty miles behind the Third Panzer Army flank. To place at least token limits on the Russians' westward advance, the Germans stopped Operation Heinrich before it was completed and turned von dem Bach's antipartisan units east to form a screening line behind the army groups' flanks. . . .
> After mid-November, following several weeks of below-freezing weather, the temperature began to rise, an unusual phenomenon for that time of the year in northern Russia and a disastrous one for the German [counterattack] plans. Since the temperature hovered just above freezing, the ground began to thaw. At the beginning of the last week in the month the roads were stretches of mud two feet deep. Supplies could only be moved to the front on tracked vehicles, and in some places Army Group North had to resort to airdrops.
> The counterattack set for 24 November could not begin until 1 December, and then in rain and mud.⁸

Lieutenant General A. P. Beloborodov, the commander of 4th Shock Army's 2nd Guards Rifle Corps, later described the army's assault:

> The offensive began during the first few days of November. Cooperating closely, the 3rd (it was now part of the newly formed 2nd Baltic Front) and 4th Shock Armies delivered a strong attack south of Nevel', penetrated through the defile between the lakes, and advanced rapidly to the northwest, west, and southwest. Since the depth of the penetration expanded but the mouth of the penetration remained narrow as before, a huge sack formed in the enemy defense. The 4th Shock Army's formations, which were situated in its southern part, menacingly hung over the Fascists' Gorodok grouping. In turn, while holding firm to the so-called Ezerishche salient, this grouping, whose apex dug its heels in at the mouth of the penetration, also represented a great danger for us. The enemy command could (and as we shall see, did attempt to) cut off the mouth of the sack and encircle the 3rd and 4th Shock Armies' forces with an attack northward from the Ezerishche salient.
>
> Thus, the complex configuration of the front created for us and for the enemy the opportunity to operate with decisive aims of encirclement and destruction. These circumstances predetermined the ferocity of the battles, which, with a few interruptions, endured here for almost two months.[9]

Several Soviet sources cover the fighting that occurred between Nevel' and Gorodok during November in considerable detail (see Map 5.2). General Shvetsov's 4th Shock Army initially attacked the defenses of Army Group Center's Third Panzer Army, west of Nevel'. Specifically, the shock army's 60th Rifle Corps (119th, 154th, 156th, and 357th Rifle Divisions), backed up by 143rd Tank Brigade, struck the defenses of IX Army Corps' 87th Infantry (Group von Below) and 2nd Luftwaffe Field Divisions in a 10-kilometer-wide sector centered 16 kilometers south of Nevel'. The army's 83rd Rifle Corps (235th, 234th, and 360th Rifle Divisions) launched local attacks and defended on 60th Corps' left, and 47th and 381st Rifle Divisions of Beloborodov's 2nd Guards Rifle Corps in the shock army's second echelon followed the 60th Corps' advance. After the 60th Rifle Corps' troops had penetrated the German defenses to a depth of roughly 10 kilometers, on 6 November Shvetsov committed 2nd Guards Rifle Corps to combat, at the same time giving it control of 47th, 154th, 156th, and 381st Rifle Divisions and 236th Tank Brigade. The corps commander, General Beloborodov, had to regroup his forces quickly and effectively because some of his forces were already engaged in heavy combat at the front, while others were still traversing the mouth of the penetration. His aim was to generate sufficient forces to maintain the momentum of his offensive while protecting his ever-lengthening and increasingly vulnerable right flank.

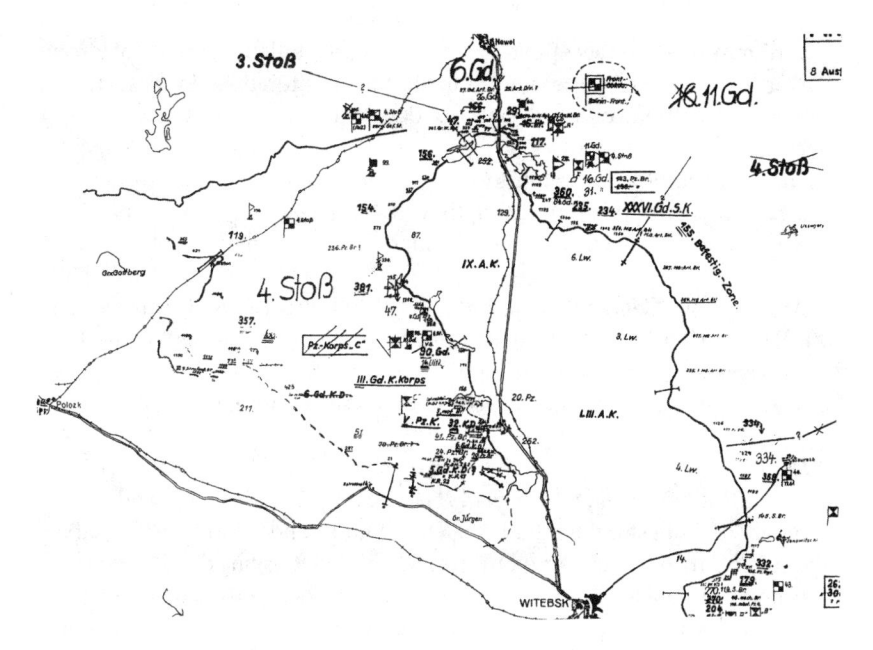

Map 5.2. Third Panzer Army's Intelligence Assessment, 20 November 1943

Shvetsov had assigned Beloborodov's corps with the mission "to widen the mouth to the south and destroy the defending enemy."[10] At the time, 2nd Guards Corps' 154th and 156th Divisions were already attacking southward along the Ezerishche-Gorodok-Vitebsk road. The mission of its newly assigned 381st and 47th Rifle Divisions was to "advance along the right shoulder [of the penetration], attack the Gorodok grouping from the west (from the sack), and, in cooperation with other 4th Shock Army formations that were attacking from the east, slam shut the encirclement of the enemy."[11] Although Beloborodov neglected to say so, 1st Baltic Front's 43rd and 39th Armies were also attacking Vitebsk from the east, along the Smolensk-Vitebsk road.

However, as Earl Ziemke later recorded, the Germans were strongly contesting the Soviet advance:

> On 8 November two Third Panzer Army divisions, one infantry and one panzer, attacked north into the breakthrough area. Before the end of the day, they gained nearly five miles. Army Group North was scheduled to attack from its side on the morning of the 9th, but Kuechler protested that all of his units were tied down. Army Group Center accused Army Group North of refusing to attack simply "because it did not want to." Hitler, apparently irked by Kuechler's lukewarmness at the conference four days

earlier, refused to "accept any further excuses" and ordered Army Group North "as a matter of honor" to begin the counterattack in its sector no later than 10 November. The next day, while the Army Group Center force waited for Army Group North to make the next move, Kuechler hastily assembled a scratch force of seven battalions. When these units attacked as ordered on the 10th, they ran into heavy artillery fire and then were thrown back to their line of departure by a counterattack.[12]

Army Group Center's counterattacking force was the 87th Infantry and 20th Panzer Divisions of Third Panzer Army's IX Army Corps. At the time 20th Panzer was a relatively strong division with 32 tanks (29 Pz. IVs and 3 Pz. Vs).[13] General Beloborodov recorded the impact of their assault:

> On the morning of 8 November, we received an alarming report from 156th Rifle Division, which read, "The enemy are advancing and attacking 417th Rifle Regiment with up to 50 tanks and infantry." The subsequent hours passed, marked by ever increasing tension. The Fascists succeeded in penetrating the regiment's sector between Lakes Ezerishche and Ordovo. The enemy's tanks were moving along the road to the north toward Nevel'. By 1500 hours they had captured Blinki, Borok, and a number of other villages. I was forced to change 47th Rifle Division's combat mission. Its regiments counterattacked against the penetrating enemy directly from the march.
> I phoned General Shvetsov.
> "What is happening to you?" he asked.
> I reported the situation: "Enemy tanks are penetrating in a narrow sector. Chernov's division is being committed against them."
> "And where is the 381st Division?" he asked.
> "On the march and fulfilling its previously assigned mission."
> "It looks like you are extremely calm," noted the commander.
> The army commander approved the plan of action that I presented for the second half of the day and the next morning.
> To be accurate I must say that this plan was only a variant of the corps' previous offensive plan. The attack by the fascist tank group on the mouth of the Nevel' sack forced us to change only the details of the concept. The essence remained as before, an extensive maneuver by the right flank formation, an attack on the enemy from the west, and the arrival in his rear.[14]

Shvetsov's and Beloborodov's plans unfolded on the night of 9 November. While the latter's rifle divisions contained German 20th Panzer Division's *kampfgruppe* along the Gorodok-Nevel' road, 4th Shock Army regrouped and dispatched two forces into the deep rear area of the Germans. The 357th and 119th Rifle Divisions drove southwestward toward Polotsk, and Beloborodov's 381st and 154th Rifle Divisions, supported by 236th Tank Brigade, wheeled southward to assault German defenses at Gorodok from the west. After crossing the Obol'ia River west of Gorodok, on 11 November the attacking force was only 22 kilometers west of the key German stronghold. Hastily, Third Panzer Army's IX Army Corps moved 113th Infantry Division into positions to block the Soviet advance on Gorodok, while smaller German combat groups protected the approaches to Polotsk. After a combination of deteriorating weather conditions and desperate German resistance finally halted the Soviet advance temporarily, Third Panzer Army had no choice but to abandon 20th Panzer Division's drive toward Nevel'.

Undeterred by this temporary halt in the action, shortly after midnight on 12 November, the *Stavka* ordered General Shvetsov to commit fresh mobile forces to "break the German grip on Gorodok and Vitebsk" and provided additional forces to shore up the 1st Baltic Front's defenses at the mouth of the Nevel' sack (against German 20th Panzer Division) (see Appendix D-3):

1. Concentrate 5th Tank Corps, two rifle divisions, and the tank brigade, which have arrived from the 2nd Baltic Front, in the Lake Svino region. You will attack [from this region] in the general direction of Bychikha Station on the morning of 15 November with 2nd Guards Rifle Corps, reinforced by the arrived divisions, with the mission of defeating the enemy grouping south of Ezerishche.
2. The 5th Tank Corps will attack in the direction of Gorodok and Vitebsk, defeat the enemy's Vitebsk grouping in cooperation with 43rd and 39th Armies, and capture the Gorodok and Vitebsk regions.
3. Employ 3rd Guards Cavalry Corps to strengthen the attack on Gorodok and Vitebsk.
4. Combine the rifle divisions, which are attacking from the north to the isthmus between Lakes Melkoe and Ezerishche, into a corps, and employ the corps' headquarters arriving from 2nd Baltic Front for that purpose. Support that corps' attack with the artillery division assigned from 2nd Baltic Front.
5. Continue 43rd and 39th Armies' attacks along the Vitebsk axis.
6. Report on all orders given.[15]

This order began two trends that would endure through December. First, it required 4th Shock Army to commit ever-increasing forces in attacks against Gorodok from the west, and second, it transferred growing numbers of forces from 2nd Baltic Front to 1st Baltic Front. The first of these transferred forces was 11th Guards Army's 8th Guards Rifle Corps (5th, 26th, and 83rd Guards Divisions and 29th Rifle Division). This corps, along with 4th Shock Army's newly formed 22nd Guards Rifle Corps (117th, 154th, and 156th Rifle Divisions), was given the mission of defending the southern flank of the Nevel' sack's mouth against any counterattacking German force. Within days, however, all of 11th Guards Army would join 1st Baltic Front's offensive to seize Polotsk and Vitebsk.

Shortly after providing him with reinforcements and ordering him to attack Gorodok from the west, at 1400 hours on 12 November, the *Stavka* also upbraided General Eremenko, the 1st Baltic Front's commander, for apparently losing his composure over the German counterattacks (see Appendix D-4):

> The racket, which you kicked up about the attack of large enemy forces, supposedly up to two tank divisions from Ezerishche to Studenets, turned out to be a totally baseless and panicky report. This means that you personally and your staff accept in faith and do not verify all reports coming in from below.
>
> I am calling your attention to the necessity for a critical attitude toward all incoming reports and demanding you carefully verify them, especially information about the enemy.
>
> Henceforth do not permit the presentation to the *Stavka* and General Staff of reports containing unverified and ill-considered panicky conclusions about the enemy.[16]

This message foreshadowed by a few days the relief of Eremenko from his duties as *front* commander.

In the meantime, the *front* and Shvetsov's 4th Shock Army saluted smartly and began implementing the *Stavka*'s instructions. Within hours, 6th Guards Army began shifting its forces to protect the *front*'s central sector south of Nevel', and Eremenko committed the *front*'s new and stronger mobile forces into battle. The 5th Tank Corps, commanded by Major General of Tank Forces M. G. Sakhno and equipped with 205 tanks and 38 SP guns, entered the fray on the morning of 16 November.[17] However, the rigors of a two-day, 50-kilometer march through forested and swampy terrain took a heavy toll on Sakhno's corps. For example, by the morning of 15 November, only the lead tanks of 24th and 41st Tank Brigades and the infantry of 5th Motorized Rifle Brigade, the latter marching on foot, had reached their jumping off position. As a result, Shvetsov postponed the attack to 16 November, and, when it did kick off, only about half of the corps' armored vehicles were available to participate. Sakhno's tanks and SP guns were followed into battle by the cavalrymen of Lieutenant General N. S. Oslikovsky's 3rd Guards Cavalry Corps.

Despite the terrible weather conditions, the two mobile corps, supported by follow-on rifle formations, tore through the defenses of Third Panzer Army's 113th Infantry Division on 16 November and by 18 November reached within 5 kilometers of the main road between Gorodok and Nevel' (see Maps

5.1 and 5.2).[18] At 2300 hours that evening, three tanks and mounted infantry from 5th Tank Corps' 5th Motorized Rifle Brigade penetrated into Gorodok from the southwest, supposedly destroying twenty-five German vehicles and two tanks. However, quick reaction by the Germans and the inability of the tank corps to reinforce its advanced party permitted a small tank force from 20th Panzer Division to reach the town and totally destroy the small Soviet force within it by 0300 on 19 November.[19]

Subsequently, fierce combat raged for more than a week in the narrow sector just west of Gorodok and the Gorodok-Nevel' road as 5th Tank and 3rd Guards Cavalry Corps repeatedly maneuvered and attacked to capture the town and sever the key road. In response, the Germans withdrew the remainder of 20th Panzer and part of 129th Infantry Division from their counterattack positions south of Nevel' and threw them, together with whatever other units Third Panzer Army could assemble, into a desperate fight to defend the road and town.[20]

A Russian account summarizes the ensuing action:

> Then, the Soviet command resolved to cut communications between Gorodok and Nevel' and Gorodok and Vitebsk and to capture Gorodok with concentrated blows from the north and south.
>
> On 19–20 November fierce fighting developed anew. The 24th and 70th Tank Brigades, after capturing the villages of Silki, Slobodka, Bvozdy, Duborezy, and Kovali successively, were not able to advance further because of the resolute enemy resistance, and, subjected to constant enemy counterattacks from the Berezovka, Volkovo, and Gorodok regions, went over to the defense. The Red Army's situation was even worse in the other offensive sectors of 5th Tank Corps' forces. Therefore, in accordance with a decision by the corps commander, Soviet forces went over to a defense in that sector of the front with the aim of maintaining the bridgeheads they had seized. The corps fulfilled this mission up to 5 December 1943, when, in accordance with a decision of the commander of 4th Shock Army, it was withdrawn into the army's reserve in the Selishche region. By this time, the corps had 55 operational tanks and SP guns. The 5th Tank Corps' losses in the operation amounted to 148 tanks and 17 SP guns.[21]

By the end of the month, the defending Germans contained the Soviet assaults but only barely, largely because of the appalling weather conditions that inhibited rapid movement of the Soviet forces (see Maps 5.3 and 5.4). Earl Ziemke records the German perspective on these intense operations:

> The warm weather had also imposed a drag on the Russians' movements. In the third week of November *Fourth Shock Army*, which until then had been working its way south and west without giving any clear indica-

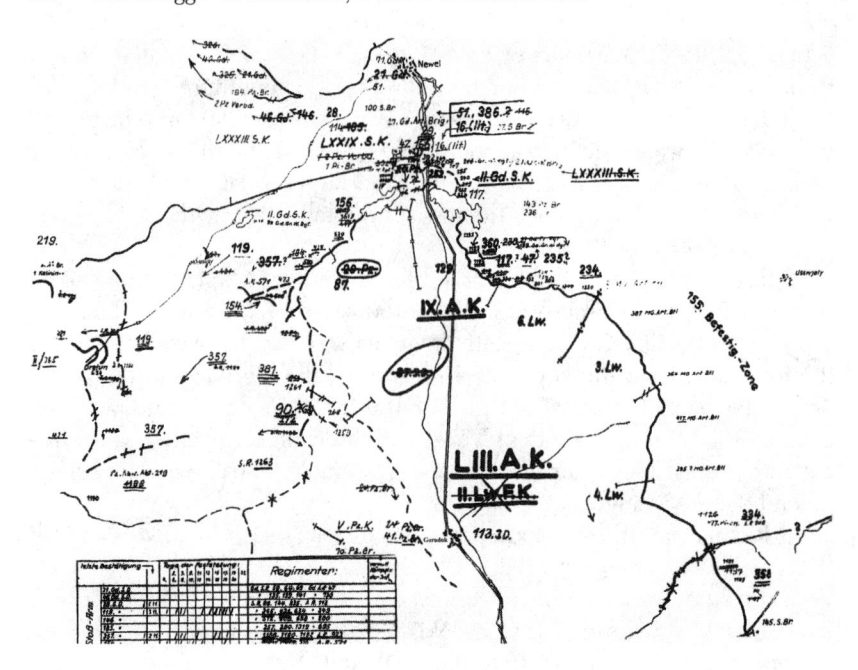

136   The Struggle for Belorussia, October–December 1943

Map 5.3. Third Panzer Army's Assessment of Red Army Operations North of Vitebsk, 3–21 November 1943

tion of its actual objective, had turned east behind Third Panzer Army toward Gorodok and Vitebsk. By 23 November it had pushed to within three miles of Gorodok, the road and rail center controlling the communications lines to the Third Panzer Army north flank, and had tank and cavalry spearheads standing ten miles northwest of Vitebsk. That confronted Third Panzer Army with a choice of either pulling back its flank, in which case it would be able to defend Vitebsk handily, or running the risk of having the flank smashed and losing Vitebsk as well. The Commanding General, Third Panzer Army, Reinhardt, urged taking back the flank, but Busch [the Army Group Center commander] refused, citing two of Hitler's favorite tactical principles, which, valid as they were under the proper circumstances, had lately produced more than one disaster or near disaster: shortening the front freed up more Soviet than German troops, and flank insensitivity on the German side reduced the force of Soviet offensives. During the thaw *Fourth Shock Army* failed to carry its advance any farther toward Gorodok and was forced to draw back slightly northwest of Vitebsk.[22]

During the final stages of the 1st Baltic Front's November drive to capture Gorodok and Vitebsk, the *Stavka* undertook drastic measures to help

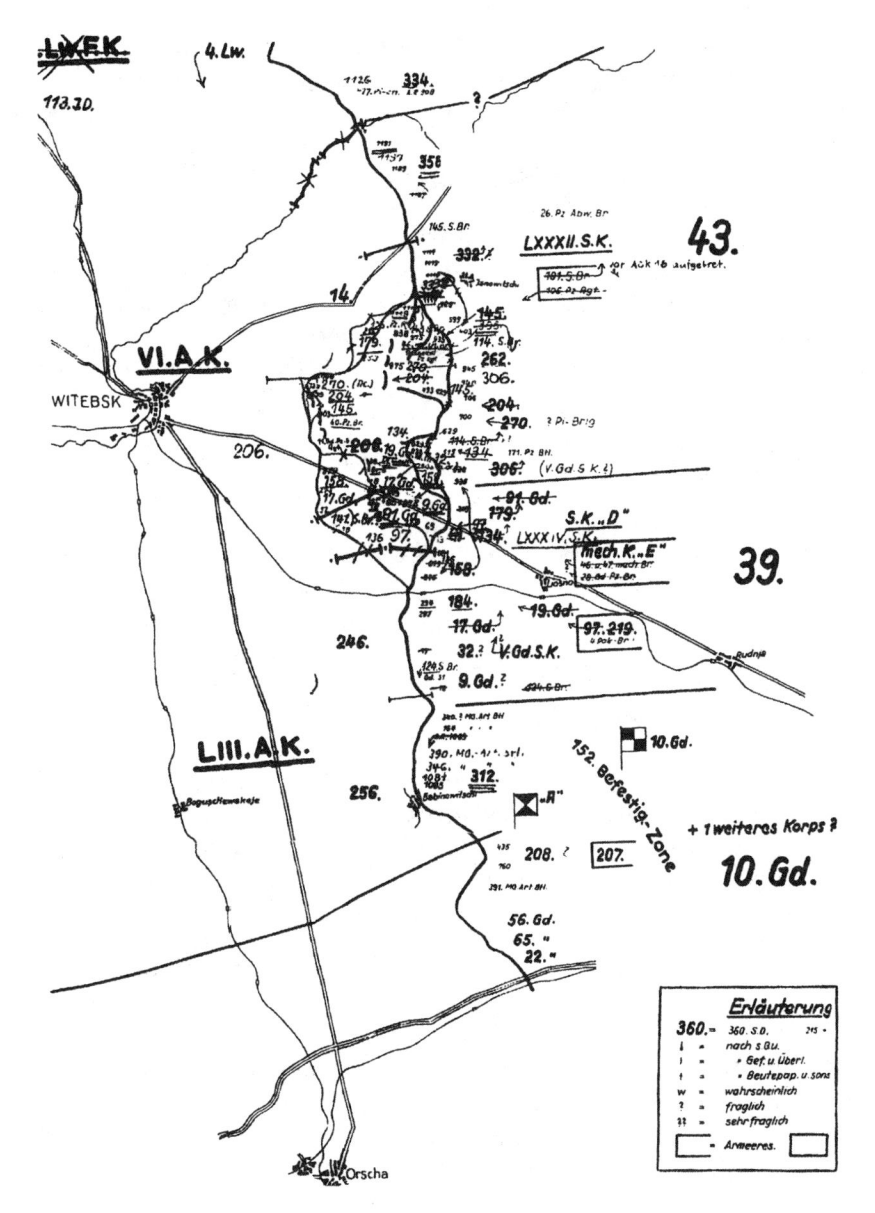

Map 5.4. Third Panzer Army's Assessment of Red Army Operations East of Vitebsk, 3–21 November 1943

ensure success. First, exasperated by what it perceived as the *front* commander's inability to control operations effectively, on 17 November it relieved Eremenko of his post and replaced him with I. Kh. Bagramian, formerly the commander of 11th Guards Army, who also received a promotion from Colonel General to Army General when he assumed his new post. In the same directive, the *Stavka* appointed Lieutenant General Galitsky, the commander of 3rd Shock Army, as the new commander of 11th Guards Army (see Appendix D-5).[23] Shortly thereafter, the *Stavka* reinforced the 1st Baltic Front with what it thought were the forces necessary to complete the offensive successfully. Then, early on 18 November, it directed the new *front* commander, Bagramian, to commit those forces to combat immediately (see Appendix D-6):

1. ... deploy 11th Guards Army along the Zhukovo and Rudnia front for an offensive toward Kuz'mino and Sirotino on 23 November.
2. Protect the operation from the west and cut the Polotsk-Vitebsk road and railroad line.
3. Develop an energetic offensive on 43rd and 39th Armies' fronts simultaneously with the beginning of 11th Guards Army's offensive.[24]

At the same time, the *Stavka* dispatched a similar directive to the 2nd Baltic Front mandating the *front* transfer (see Appendix D-7):

The commander-in-chief of the 2nd Baltic Front will transfer the complete 11th Guards Army, including 18th Guards Rifle Corps, 10th Guards Tank Brigade, 1st Tank Corps, 2nd Guards Tank Penetration Regiment, three guards-mortar brigades, four guards-mortar regiments, 10th Assault Engineer Brigade, and 17th Antiaircraft Artillery Division, to the 1st Baltic Front effective 1200 hours on 18 November 1943. ... Leave 15th Artillery Division, which is temporarily subordinate to 1st Baltic Front, in that *front*.[25]

The 11th Guards Army's history recorded what transpired:

The 11th Guards Army completed concentrating its forces southwest of Velikie Luki in the beginning of November. It consisted of three guards rifle corps [the 8th, 16th, and 36th], with nine rifle divisions and a number of formations and units subordinate to the army.

Having assessed the complex situation in the Nevel' region, the *front* commander decided to conduct a new operation in which 11th Guards Army would participate. He planned to attack along the Gorodok-Vitebsk axis to destroy the enemy Gorodok grouping, liquidate the southern salient, and capture Vitebsk.

Five divisions and a considerable part of the reinforcing weaponry were concentrated in an 8-kilometer sector. The intention was to cut off the northwestern part of the Gorodok salient and encircle and destroy the group of enemy forces in the lake region southwest of Ezerishche, in cooperation with 4th Shock Army. Thereafter, while developing the main effort of the offensive along the Mekhovoe-Gorodok axis, [the force was to] liquidate the northeastern portion of the Gorodok salient and encircle and destroy the enemy grouping defending that region. Subsequently, while exploiting the success to the south in the direction of Shumilino, [we intended] to cut off the fascists' withdrawal routes to the west, and part of the force would capture Vitebsk in cooperation with 43rd Army.

The 16th and 36th Guards Rifle Corps would deliver the main attack toward Mekhovoe and Gorodok with their adjoining flanks. Considering the terrain, the enemy's defense, and other conditions, 36th Corps' combat formation was single echelon, with all three divisions in first echelon. The 16th Guards Rifle Corps formed its combat formation in two echelons, with two divisions in the first and one in the second.

In order to fulfil its assigned mission, it regrouped its forces by their flanks from the Velikie Luki region to the region southeast of Nevel' during the period from 13 through 25 November.

Colonel General I. Kh. Bagramian, the army commander, was appointed to command the 1st Baltic Front on 1 November.... Major General A. S. Ksenofontov temporarily took over command of the army....

Lieutenant General K. N. Galitsky, who formerly commanded 3rd Shock Army, was assigned to command the army on 26 November.[26]

Two days after ordering reinforcements be transferred to the 1st Baltic Front, the *Stavka* underscored its growing frustrations once again by ordering Bagramian to resume the offensive immediately and to "finish with Gorodok on 20 November" (see Appendix D-8).[27]

Late the next day, the *Stavka* sent Bagramian two directives that contained detailed guidance as to how he was to conduct his offensive and altered the boundary line between his *front* and the 2nd Baltic Front (see Appendix D-9). The *Stavka* delayed the beginning of 11th Guards Army's offensive from 23 to 26 November and temporarily halted 4th Shock Army's offensive on Gorodok in order to "arrange the supply of that army's forces and repair the roads" (see Appendix D-10).[28] After the supply and road repairs, the *Stavka* directed Bagramian to "resume the offensive [with 4th Shock Army] against Gorodok simultaneously with that of 11th Guards Army and, in favorable conditions, even earlier" (see Appendix D-11).[29]

Dutifully complying, Bagramian issued new orders to his troops: "The *front's* immediate mission is to destroy the Germans' Vitebsk-Gorodok grouping, which consists of 9th and 6th Army Corps, and capture the cities of

Gorodok and Vitebsk. Subsequently, decisively develop the offensive in the general direction of Lepel' and capture the cities of Polotsk and Lepel', having smashed the enemy's Polotsk grouping with 4th Shock Army's forces."[30] However, despite the *Stavka's* desires and Bagramian's attempts to satisfy his masters in Moscow, poor weather and an unexpected late fall thaw frustrated the Soviet's offensive plans.[31] By the end of November, virtual stalemate had set in west and north of Vitebsk, and there was nothing either side could do about it. Later, after relating the appalling terrain conditions and the ensuing logistical chaos, General Galitsky recorded his conversation with Bagramian regarding the fate of the planned 26 November offensive:

> Therefore, I confess with a heavy heart, I reported to the *front* commander by enciphered telephone that my units had occupied their jumping-off positions for the attack. But I did not fail to mention the unfavorable weather forecast.
>
> "Urgently continue the preparations for the operation," answered I. Kh. Bagramian. But after a short pause he unexpectedly added, "Phone me again in the evening."
>
> It was not difficult to ascertain that the *front's* Military Council was also concerned about the existing conditions. However, any delay in the operation did not depend on [the conditions]; Stalin would resolve that question. It goes without saying that, at that very time, the corps commanders and the branch chiefs' headquarters were duplicating the *front* commander's orders. But in my soul I believed that the *Stavka* would not demand that the offensive begin in such unfavorable circumstances.
>
> Two hours passed. Little time remained until nightfall. Suddenly, the secure phone rang. I heard the *front* commander's voice. [He said,] "Comrade Stalin has decided to postpone the beginning of the offensive until early December. He orders that combat operations be begun no earlier than when good winter weather has set in, when we can employ aviation and all types of forces, particularly tanks. Accordingly, take all measures to ensure that the enemy cannot penetrate our defenses along the Nevel' axis and cut off 4th Shock Army. Form the appropriate force combat formation over the next two nights."[32]

Thus, the month of November ended with German forces clinging desperately to Gorodok and their deep salient that extended northward from Vitebsk along the Gorodok-Nevel' road and with Soviet forces wedged deeply along the German's Vitebsk-Gorodok grouping's right flank. Fortunately for the Germans, the bad weather also brought the Soviet advance toward Polotsk to a muddy halt. There, barely 26 kilometers short of their objective, 4th Shock Army's 119th, 357th, and 166th Rifle Divisions (60th Rifle Corps) faced Combat Group von Gottberg (several composite battalions) and 211th Infantry Division.

Soviet and Russian accounts of the Polotsk-Vitebsk offensive operation describe 4th Shock Army's assaults from the Nevel' salient and the army's dramatic but unsuccessful advance on Gorodok from the west in fairly detailed fashion. However, lost in all of these accounts is any mention whatsoever of the heavy fighting that took place east of Vitebsk throughout the bulk of November. While declassified documents mention these operations, Russian open sources have neglected them. This is a significant omission because the threat to Vitebsk from the east made the situation far more perilous for the Germans, and their successful defense in this sector added significant luster to the feat they accomplished in the defense of Vitebsk.

The only account of any substance of the action east of Vitebsk is contained in the memoirs of Major General V. P. Boiko, 39th Army's military commissar. However, his account simply subsumes all information about the army's November offensive into simplified generalities about the October assault. Fortunately, however, we can now fill in this "blank page of history" by exploiting German records.

In early November General Eremenko ordered 43rd and 39th Armies to concentrate their forces north of the Smolensk-Vitebsk railroad and highway opposite defenses occupied by German 206th and 14th Infantry Divisions of Third Panzer Army's VI Army Corps. These two armies were to conduct a concerted assault toward Vitebsk on the morning of 8 November, link up with the 4th Shock Army's forces advancing toward the city via Gorodok in the northwest, and, ultimately, capture the city. As of 1 November, General Berzarin's 39th Army consisted of 5th Guards Rifle Corps (9th, 17th, and 19th Guards Rifle Divisions), 84th Rifle Corps (91st Guards and 97th, 134th, and 158th Rifle Divisions), 32nd and 184th Rifle Divisions, 124th Rifle, 28th Guards Tank, and 46th and 47th Mechanized Brigades, and 11th Separate Guards Tank Regiment. The 39th Army was to attack westward along and north of the Smolensk-Vitebsk road with both of its rifle corps abreast, supported by a composite mobile corps made up of three mechanized and tank brigades, commanded once again by Colonel Dremov. The 184th and 32nd Rifle Divisions and 124th Rifle Brigade protected the attacking forces' left wing.

At the same time, General Golubev's 43rd Army consisted of 1st Rifle Corps (145th, 204th, and 262nd Rifle Divisions), 91st Rifle Corps (179th, 270th, and 306th Rifle Divisions and 114th Rifle Brigade), 92nd Rifle Corps (332nd and 368th Rifle Divisions and 145th Rifle Brigade), 26th Separate Destroyer and 60th Tank Brigades, and 105th Separate Tank Regiment. Golubev's army was to attack westward toward Vitebsk on 39th Army's right flank with 1st Rifle Corps on the left and 91st Rifle Corps on the right. The 92nd Rifle Corps' forces were to protect the army's right flank to the boundary with adjacent 4th Shock Army.

So configured, 43rd and 39th Armies had fivefold superiority over their opponents in infantry and absolute superiority in artillery and armor, despite the fact that their forces had eroded to about half their required strength. There was every reason for Eremenko to count on success.

The 39th and 43rd Armies began their assault early on 8 November (see Maps 5.4 and 5.5). The 43rd Army's forces launched a heavy assault against German Third Panzer Army's defenses south of Ianovichi and tore a gaping hole through these defenses at the junction of VI Army Corps' 14th and 206th Infantry Divisions. Simultaneously, 39th Army's 184th Rifle Division and 124th Rifle Brigade struck the defensive positions of the German LIII Army Corps' 246th Infantry Division between Dobromysl' and the Smolensk-Vitebsk railroad line but were repulsed. During the day, the 206th Infantry sped forces northward in an attempt to contain the penetration. The next morning, however, it became clear that the latter was only a diversion, as 39th Army's main body attacked and ripped through the German 206th Infantry Division's defenses just north of the Smolensk-Vitebsk road.

The 9 November combined assault by the forces of both Soviet armies breached the Germans' defenses across a 10-kilometer front, and, by evening, the lead elements of the attacking force reached Poddub'e just 10 kilometers east of the defense lines around Vitebsk proper. The German 206th Infantry Division's defensive front was a shambles by nightfall, and the 14th Infantry Division's right flank was both turned and wide open.

Although the German defenders contained 43rd Army's assaults at Poddub'e on 11 November, 39th Army's shock group managed to advance 5 kilometers along the highway to Karamidy and the banks of the Lososina River (10 kilometers east of Vitebsk). Then General Berzarin committed his mobile group into combat. A swirling battle ensued into which the Germans committed a small combat group from the already disbanded 18th Panzer Division formed around the remnants of its 101st Panzer Grenadier Regiment.[33] The fresh German forces counterattacked and, along with other hastily formed combat groups from 246th and 206th Infantry Divisions, partially encircled and severely damaged the forces of Dremov's mobile group. By 17 November the Germans were able to restore a fairly continuous front west of Poddub'e, Karamidy, and Argun, and the Soviet assault expired in exhaustion (see Maps 5.6 and 5.7) In almost ten days of fighting, 39th and 43rd Armies had advanced 10 kilometers closer to Vitebsk along a 20-kilometer front. However, although complicating the German defense further north, they had achieved little more. In late November, 43rd Army transferred its 1st Rifle Corps, together with its sector and the corps' 145th and 204th Rifle Divisions, to 43rd Army. Having placed all of its shock forces along the Smolensk-Vitebsk road under unified command, the *Stavka* waited for yet another opportunity to strike against Vitebsk from the east. That opportunity would come on 13 December, when the entire 1st Baltic Front would resume its offensive.

Soviet (Russian) historians have published no casualty figures on the November Polotsk-Vitebsk operation. Instead, they have lumped the operation

1st and 2nd Baltic Fronts' Polotsk-Vitebsk and Pustoshka-Idritsa Offensives   143

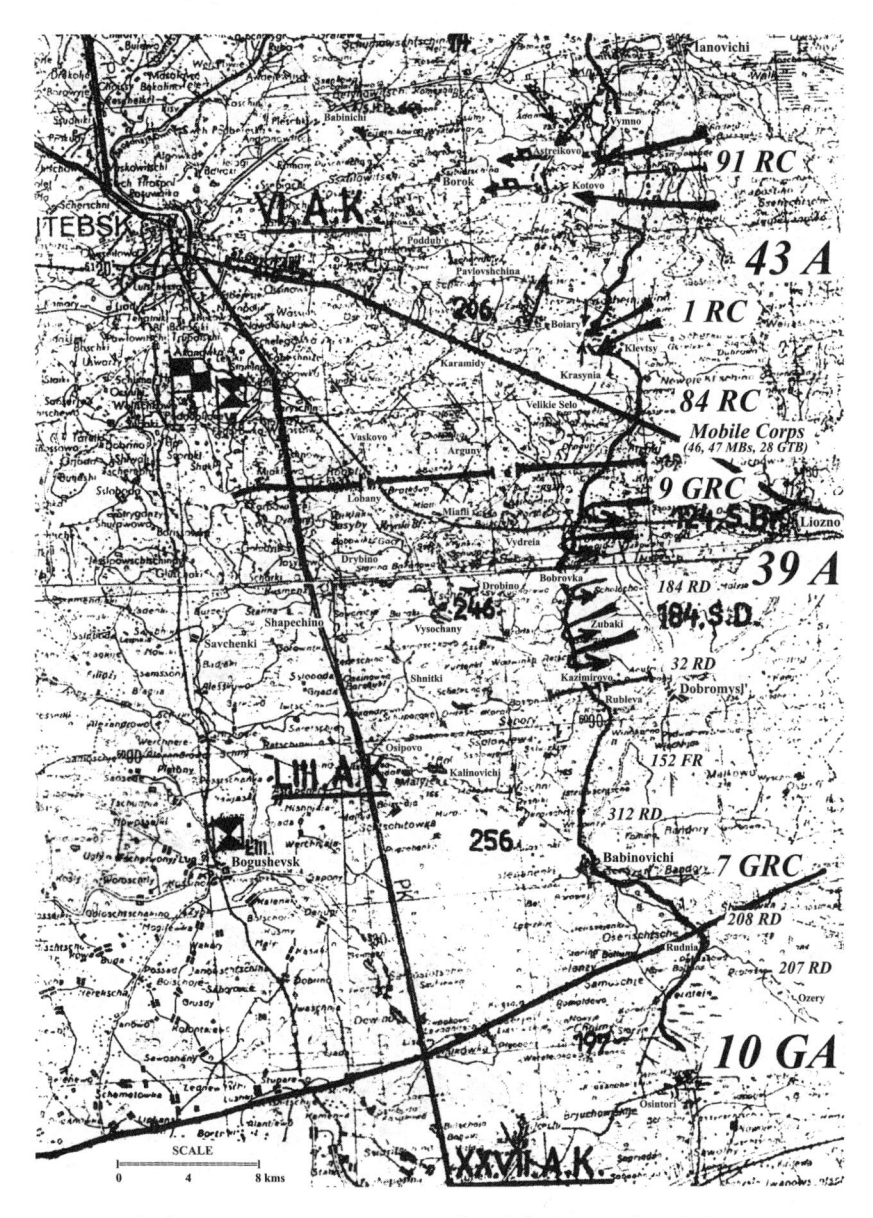

Map 5.5. Third Panzer Army's Situation East of Vitebsk, 8 November 1943

into the catchall category of the so-called "Nevel'-Gorodok offensive operation," which they now date from 6 October to 31 December. Although this categorization better matches reality, it does not clarify the *Stavka*'s overall offensive aim, that is, the capture of Vitebsk and the liberation of northern

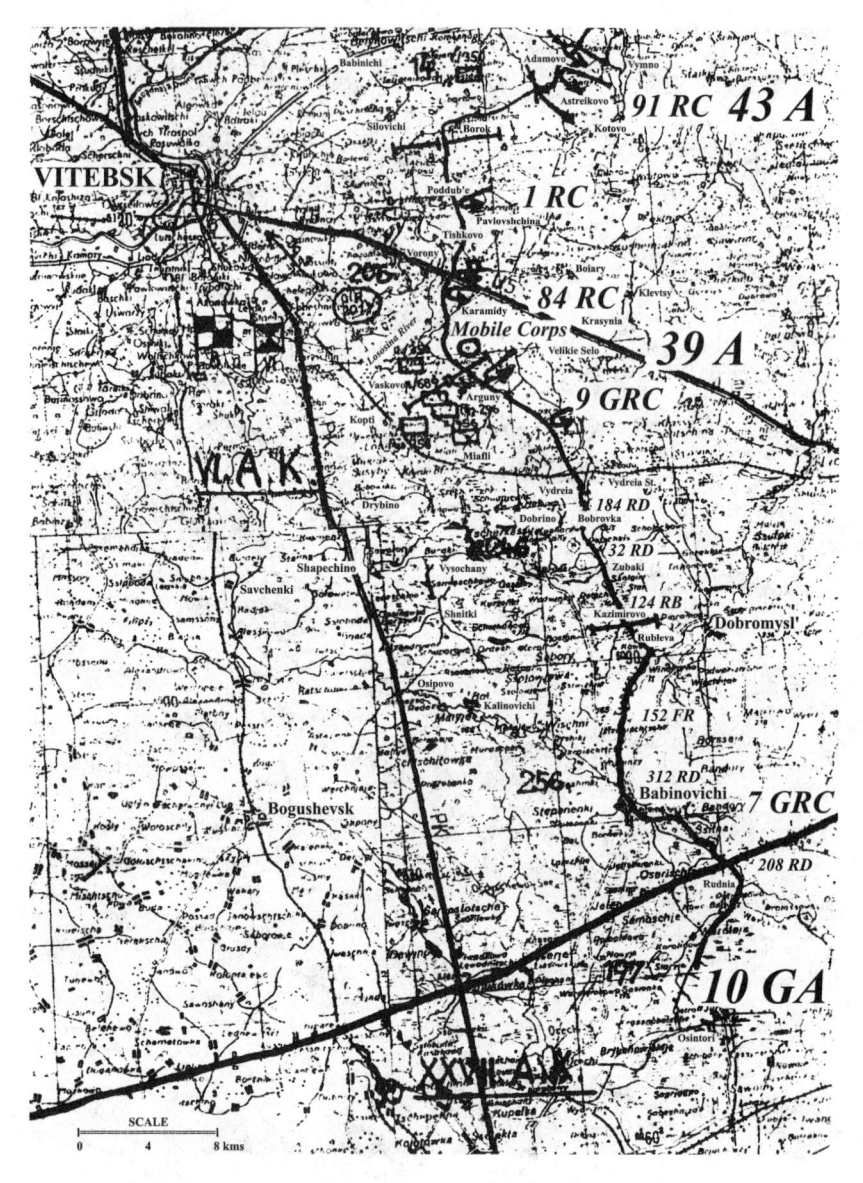

144 The Struggle for Belorussia, October–December 1943

Map 5.6. Third Panzer Army's Situation East of Vitebsk, 17 November 1943

Belorussia. Nor does this categorization even include 39th Army in its calculations. It is clear that significant new archival releases are necessary before we can develop a more detailed understanding of how this operation unfolded.

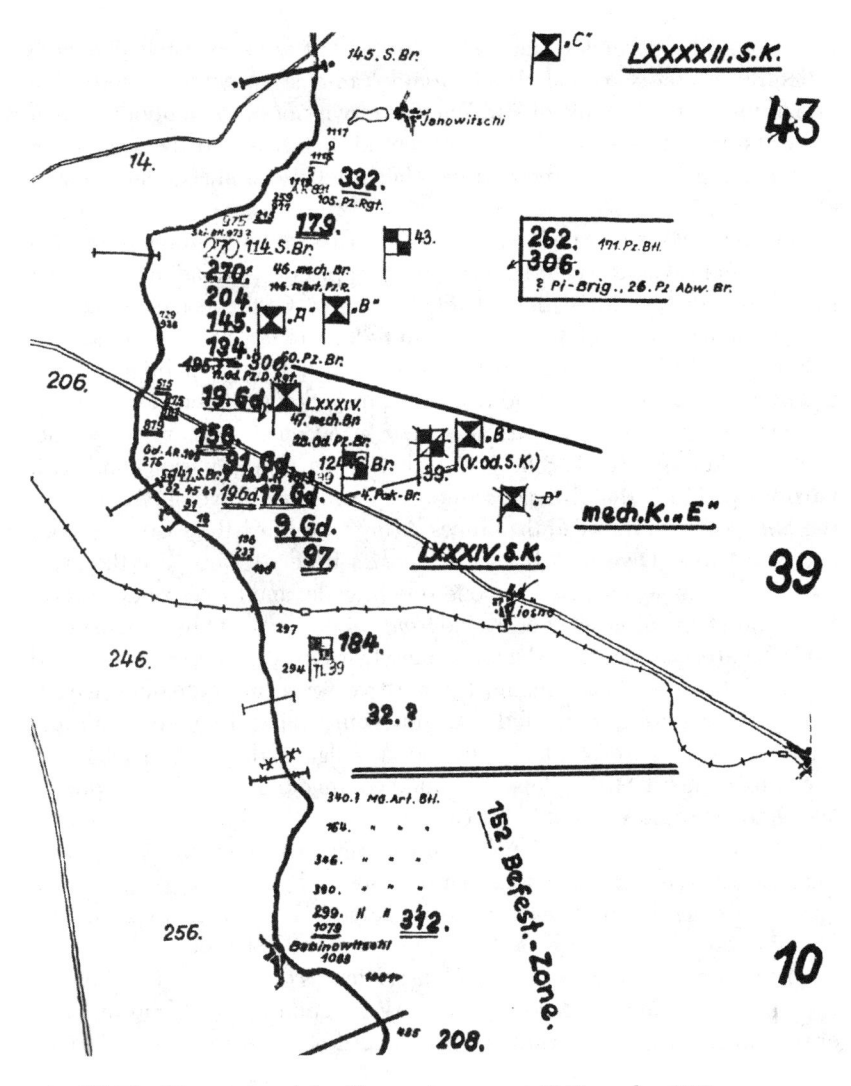

Map 5.7. Third Panzer Army's Intelligence Assessment, 20 November 1943

THE 2ND BALTIC FRONT'S PUSTOSHKA-IDRITSA OFFENSIVE (2–21 NOVEMBER 1943)

The northern half of the Soviet's November offensive from the Nevel' bridgehead suffers from the same historical neglect as operations conducted south of Nevel'. Although many unit histories, including those of 3rd Shock and 6th Guards Armies, cover the operation in considerable detail, the operation has yet to be accorded a finite name. Instead, it is lumped together with action during the so-called Nevel'-Gorodok offensive operation, and, even under this rubric, the role of 6th Guards Army is not even mentioned. Nevertheless, with the help of German archival materials and the few Soviet accounts, it is possible to reconstruct a fairly detailed and accurate account of the operation.

In preparation for the assault, General Eremenko thoroughly reorganized General Galitsky's 3rd Shock Army, replacing formations worn out by the Nevel' operation with relatively fresh ones. Of the army's original six rifle divisions (21st and 46th Guards and 28th, 178th, 185th, and 357th), only 21st and 46th Guards and 28th remained. Of the four brigades (the 23rd, 31st, and 100th Rifle and the 78th Tank), the army retained only the 100th Rifle and 78th Tank Brigades. The army received as replacements 115th, 146th, and 326th Rifle and 18th Guards Rifle Divisions and 34th Guards and 118th Tank Brigades. Shortly before the 2 November offensive, the *Stavka* also reinforced 3rd Shock Army with 93rd Rifle Corps (165th and 379th Rifle Divisions) from the *Stavka*'s Reserve. This gave the army a strength of nine rifle divisions, one rifle brigade, and three tank brigades. Shortly after the offensive began, the *front* reinforced 3rd Shock Army with 119th Guards and 219th and 245th Rifle Divisions, the first two from 22nd Army and the latter from 4th Shock Army. In essence, after the offensive developed successfully, Popov fed a seemingly unending stream of reinforcements into the ever-expanding penetration bridgehead.

Army General M. M. Popov assumed command of 2nd Baltic Front in late October 1943. The *Stavka* allocated his *front* 6th, 10th, and 11th Guards Armies, each with nine to ten well-equipped rifle divisions with which he was to eventually reinforce his November offensive.

As approved by the *Stavka,* Popov's operational plan called for "the defeat of enemy forces along the line of the Nevel'-Polotsk railroad . . . , the deep envelopment of the grouping of fascist forces defending west of Nevel' from the south and southwest, and the destruction of the group in cooperation with 6th Guards Army."[34] Galitsky's 3rd Shock Army struck German defenses west of Nevel' at dawn on 2 November (see Map 2.9).[35] The army's 21st and 46th Guards Rifle Divisions led the assault, supported by 100th Rifle and 118th Tank Brigades. The 79th Rifle Corps 146th and 326th Rifle Divisions, with 78th Tank Brigade in support, were echeloned to the rear of the shock group's left wing, and 28th Rifle Division was echeloned to the right, north of Nevel'. The assault force smashed through the defenses of German Sixteenth Army's Group von Below almost immediately and then turned the right flank of German I Army Corps' 58th Infantry Division. The entire force then pivoted to the right (northward) and headed deep into the German rear area toward their objective, the town of Pustoshka on the Velikie Luki–Riga railroad line. As they advanced ever deeper, Galitsky committed 115th, 146th, and 245th Rifle Divisions into the penetration on the shock group's right flank (soon reorganized as 100th Rifle Corps) and 219th Rifle Division on the left flank to maintain communications with 4th Shock Army. Subsequently, the lead elements of 3rd Shock Army penetrated more than 30 kilometers deep along a 40-kilometer front by 7 November, although German forces still clung to positions along the flank of the 15–20-kilometer-wide corridor through which the Soviet force had attacked.

As mid-November approached, 115th and 146th Rifle Divisions and 78th Tank Brigade formed the northwestern portion of 3rd Shock Army's growing salient on the southwestern approaches to Pustoshka. At the same time, the shock army's 119th Guards Rifle Division and 118th Tank Brigade, flanked on the left by 146th Rifle Division, captured Podberez'e and directly threatened to sever the Novosokol'niki-Pustoshka railroad line. As one Soviet observer noted, "It seemed as if yet another effort—the mission assigned to us by the *front* commander—had been fulfilled. The army's forces had created a bridgehead for a deep flank attack on the Idritsa-Novosokol'niki enemy grouping from the south in the direction of Idritsa and Sebezh, which would allow us to sever the withdrawal routes of a considerable force of Hitlerites."[36]

Galitsky later described the situation roughly ten days after the offensive began:

> The operation began in early November. By this time warm and dry weather had set in. The forest roads had dried out and become firm. This facilitated the offensive, which was initially quite successful. The army's forces advanced far to the west of Nevel' and reached the approaches to the small city of Pustoshka. Up to that time there were no heavy battles. The immense forested and swampy region through which the army's forces advanced was, in fact, controlled by partisan detachments. The enemy occupied only scattered villages in the region. Our attacking forces destroyed them there.
>
> The Hitlerites offered heavy resistance on the approaches to Pustoshka. The same thing happened to those who were attacking in the offensive sector to our left and entering the partisan region of 4th Shock Army. Having approached Polotsk, they met sharply increasing resistance from the enemy just as we were at Pustoshka.
>
> The fact was that the arrival of 3rd and 4th Shock Armies' units in the Pustoshka and Dretin' regions and their linkup with the partisan detachments seriously worried the German-Fascist command.
>
> It is understandable that the enemy command would immediately commit large forces against us.[37]

Earl Ziemke later described the dangerous situation confronting Army Group North from its perspective shortly after 3rd Shock Army advanced west and northwest of Nevel' in the wake of its 2 November assault:

Kuechler [the Army Group North commander] transferred six infantry battalions from Eighteenth Army, and with these Sixteenth Army managed to bend its right flank around to the northwest. Both the army group and army expected the Russians to continue pressing around that flank.

On 4 November Hitler called Kuechler and Busch [the Army Group Center commander] to Fuehrer headquarters. After characterizing the October Nevel' battle as a *Schweinerei* (filthy mess) and blaming the subsequent failure to recoup the loss on the chief of staff of Army Group North's right flank corps, an officer whom he described as a defeatist to whom everything was impossible, Hitler declared that he intended to eliminate the gap at once. Busch, whose headquarters had already proposed a joint counterattack by the two army groups, agreed. Kuechler objected. He did not want to risk a counterattack while his flank was exposed, and, as he revealed indirectly, he did not fully share Hitler's and Busch's feeling of urgency about the army groups' flanks. He was more worried by signs of a buildup for an attempt to liberate Leningrad, and he warned Hitler that since the temperature there had been well below freezing for the past several days, that offensive could come at any time. For those reasons Kuechler was reluctant to weaken the north by taking out troops for the flanks. To try to gain troops by shortening the front, he maintained, would be particularly dangerous since it might set off a chain reaction. Brushing aside Kuechler's doubts, Hitler at the close of the conference ordered the two army groups to be ready on 8 November to counterattack from the north and south, close the gap, and cut off the two shock armies.

At the end of the first week in November the Germans were still holding fast on the flanks of the breakthrough....

Kuechler ordered four infantry divisions, two from the Eighteenth Army and two from the Sixteenth Army, to his right flank, but they had to be taken out of static positions and, in some instances, moved several hundred miles by truck and rail, which took time. On 7 November *Third Shock Army* gained more ground behind Army Group North. Yeremenko was pouring troops of the Sixth and Eleventh Guards Armies through the gap and by a process of rapid erosion carving out a pocket, elongated on its north-south axis, behind both army groups. He appeared still to be concentrating on the northern rim of the pocket. So far he had not shown much interest in directing his weight west, which was fortunate for the Germans since the army group commands had observed that the SS generals were conducting operations in their sector "in broad impressionistic strokes."[38]

The situation Army Group North faced worsened sharply on 10 November, when Colonel General I. M. Chistiakov's veteran 6th Guards Army went into action in the lake region northeast of Nevel'. Chistiakov's army had begun its movement northward to the Toropets region in mid-October. After assembling in the Toropets region on 17 October under the *Stavka's* control, on 28 October Chistiakov ordered the army to move to Nevel', where it occupied defensive positions northwest of the city between 3rd Shock and 22nd Armies. The army consisted of the following forces on 1 November:

- 22nd Guards Rifle Corps (67th, 71st, and 90th Guards Rifle Divisions)
- 23rd Guards Rifle Corps (51st and 52nd Guards Rifle and 29th Rifle Divisions)
- 166th Rifle Division

However, during the offensive, the army's composition altered significantly to match the complex situation. Thus, the army's structure was as follows by the end of the month:

- 23rd Rifle Corps (51st and 52nd Guards Rifle Divisions and 31st and 100th Rifle Brigades)
- 90th Rifle Corps (282nd and 370th Rifle Divisions)
- 96th Rifle Corps (67th and 71st Guards Rifle Divisions)
- 97th Rifle Corps (165th, 185th, and 379th Rifle Divisions)

In addition, the army was assigned 29th and 34th Guards Tank Brigades from 3rd Shock Army at various times during the offensive.

After fully assembling the 6th Guards, General Popov ordered the army over to the attack in the narrow sector between Lakes Bol'shoi Ivan' and Nevel' against German defenses at Karataia, manned by 56th and 69th Infantry Divisions of German Sixteenth Army's I Army Corps. According to General Chistiakov, his army's mission was "to penetrate the enemy's defenses northeast of Nevel', destroy the forces of the 43rd Army Corps defending the Novosokol'niki-Nevel' salient, and then link up with General K. N. Galitsky's 3rd Shock Army, which was to attack from the Nevel' region in a generally northeast direction. The final aim of the army operation was the widening of the neck of the 'bottle.'"[39]

Popov ordered Chistiakov to locate his command post north of Nevel', a decision Chistiakov later criticized:

The *front* commander's directive indicated that 6th Guards Army's command post must be north of Nevel'. This meant that we were ordered to enter that very same "bottle." Such a decision seemed incorrect to me, and I tried to report to M. M. Popov that the army commander should not enter the "bottle," since the army's main forces remained outside of it. With me located inside, it would be difficult to control the forces.

However, Markian Mikhailovich did not agree with me, and I was sent through the neck of the "bottle" with an operational group.[40]

Chistiakov's army went into action on the morning of 10 November with 23rd Guards Rifle Corps' on the left wing and 22nd Guards Rifle Corps on the right, supported by 29th and 34th Guards Tank Brigades. The 71st and 90th Guards Rifle Divisions attacked in 22nd Guards Corps' first echelon, and 23rd Guards Corps led its attack with 51st and 52nd Guards Divisions. The 97th Rifle Corps' 379th, 165th, and 185th Rifle Divisions, assigned to his army from 22nd Army, protected Chistiakov's right flank. The forward progress, however, was painfully slow as indicated by an account in 71st Guards Rifle Division's history:

> The division's first echelon regiments advanced 600–700 meters on the first day of combat and approached right up to the forward edge of the enemy's defense. However, on this and on the following day, the division achieved no success.
>
> Occupying dominating heights, the enemy had created powerful and well-camouflaged defensive positions.
>
> The division artillery was not able to destroy or even suppress the enemy's firing systems. The terrain, which was broken up by ravines and swamps, did not permit the full use of tanks in the attack, and the foul weather hindered the employment of aircraft.
>
> The attack by the division and the other formations of 6th Guards Army did not produce the expected results at that time.[41]

General Galitsky recorded the action from the perspective of 3rd Shock Army, noting the reasons for the failure:

> As a result [of the German concentration of forces against us], our two armies, understandably, themselves ended up in a difficult situation. We had penetrated the Germans' defense on a very narrow front and, while driving to the west, had occupied a very extensive region. But the neck of the penetration remained very narrow. In width, it did not exceed 8–9 kilometers, and, furthermore, the majority of our units had to pass between Lakes Nevel', Emenets, and Ordovo. A single road went through this neck along which the Hitlerites directed mortar and, in some sectors, even machine gun fire. Worse still, the weather, which had been so favorable during the first days of the month, deteriorated beginning on 15 November—torrential rains began, and the *rasputitsa* (period of flooded roads) set in. Transport of supplies, and first and foremost ammunition, practically ceased. One could not pass through the neck, even at night. . . .
>
> The situation also worsened with regards to what turned out to be the unsuccessful offensive by neighboring 6th Guards Army on the right. It

was begun on 10 November with the aim of destroying the enemy grouping northwest of Nevel' and cutting off the salient it occupied 4–5 kilometers from the city. The enemy managed to repel 6th Guards Army's attack, and it went over to the defense on 15 November.[42]

At the 2nd Baltic Front's headquarters, the *front's* chief of staff, General Sandalov, provided the *front's* perspective of the action, the problems encountered, and the diminished chances for success:

> The flank attacks of our *front* and the 1st Baltic Front's shock armies had advanced more than 50 kilometers by 10 November and extended the penetration up to 60 kilometers into the depth of the enemy's defense. However, while placing the enemy in a serious situation, our forces turned out to be stretched out along a 60-kilometer bulge, and, moreover, gaps had formed between our units in several sectors.
>
> The fact was that the neck that had formed at the mouth of our forces' penetration, which at first reached 10 kilometers, narrowed by one half as a result of several enemy counterattacks from the north and south by fresh divisions that had been thrown in there. The supply of ammunition, fuel, and foodstuffs for both armies went along that cramped mouth that was subject to methodical enemy artillery fire. The transport thread was very thin, and the forces experienced shortages of everything. Reserves and replacements that were arriving in the armies managed to overcome the mouth only during the night by moving in columns through the mud along both sides of the road, along which the transport moved continuously. It was the period of the fall *rasputitsa*. Light, freezing rain fell steadily, sometimes with wet snow. The great number of rivers and streams flowing across the region, the countless lakes and ponds, and the numerous swampy regions covered with light forests and brush severely hampered not only combat operations and supply but also the movement of units and subunits. We traveled to the forces in cross-country vehicles and often on the hoods. The twilight came early, especially on foul days.[43]

While the Soviets' expanding offensive was struggling with bad weather and appallingly difficult terrain conditions, the Germans were trying to implement countermeasures to compound the Soviet's discomfiture. Describing the Third Panzer Army's attack on the Nevel' corridor on 8 November, Ziemke stated:

> Army Group North was scheduled to attack from its side on the morning of the 9th, but Kuechler protested that all of his units were tied down. Army Group Center accused Army Group North of refusing to attack simply "because it did not want to." Hitler, apparently irked by Kuechler's lukewarmness at the conference four days earlier, refused to "accept any

further excuses" and ordered Army Group North "as a matter of honor" to begin the counterattack in its sector no later than 10 November. The next day, while the Army Group Center force waited for Army Group North to make the next move, Kuechler hastily assembled a scratch force of seven battalions. When these units attacked as ordered on the 10th, they ran into heavy artillery fire and then were thrown back to their line of departure by a counterattack [6th Guards Army's assault].

In the meantime, the Russians had continued on the move behind the flanks of the army groups, extending the pocket to a length of fifty miles. In the south they were at the level of Polotsk and Gorodok, and in the north, south of Pustoshka, less than ten miles from the railroad running west out of Novosokol'niki. Once again, this time with greater strength than before, they began turning east against the right flank corps of Army Group North.

For a week Hitler and Kuechler debated the next move. Hitler demanded a counterattack and instructed Kuechler to strip Eighteenth Army if he had to. Kuechler insisted on getting rid of the threat to his flank first. Finally, on 18 November, after a trip to Fuehrer headquarters, Kuechler secured an order giving the army group the missions of first eliminating the bulge behind its flank and then mounting an attack into the gap south of Nevel'. The next day Kuechler transferred another division from Eighteenth Army. On 21 November, the weight of nearly the whole *Eleventh Guards Army* forced Army Group Center to take the two divisions which had advanced into the gap back to their line of departure. How greatly that reduced the chances of closing the front was demonstrated by the increase in the number of Soviet units moving into the pocket; but Hitler insisted that Army Group North go ahead with both of its assigned missions.

After mid-November, following several weeks of below-freezing weather, the temperature began to rise, an unusual phenomenon for that time of the year in northern Russia and a disastrous one for the German plans.[44]

What Ziemke neglected to say was that the thaw was as disastrous for Soviet plans as it was for the Germans. Not only did 1st Baltic Front's advance on Gorodok and Vitebsk flounder in the mud but also so did 6th Guards Army's ambitious offensive north of Nevel'.

The *Stavka* was already displaying doubts about the ability of the two *fronts* to accomplish their missions as early as 10 November. As a result, it began to shift forces from the 2nd Baltic Front to the 1st Baltic Front in an attempt to revive what it considered the more critical offensive drive. For example, on 10 November it ordered the transfer of several divisions to help overcome the stiff German resistance north of Gorodok. At the same time, the directive ordered the 1st Baltic Front "to clear the enemy from the isthmus between Lakes Melkoe and Ezerishche with 29th, 166th, 47th, 16th Lithuanian, and 117th Rifle Divisions and 83rd Rifle Corps and capture the Lake Beloe, Ezerishche, and Zhukovo line, where it will dig in and firmly protect the Nevel' axis from the south" (see Appendix D-12). In addition, 4th Shock Army was to transfer 83rd Rifle Corps and 155th Fortified Region to 43rd Army "to ease its command and control," and the latter was to employ 83rd Corps to cut the railroad line between Zhukovo and Ezerishche.[45]

Two days later, the *Stavka* issued a directive to the 2nd Baltic Front ordering it to cease all but local offensive operations and to "firmly dig in along occupied lines," while enjoining the front to "Protect Nevel' especially reliably." The same directive transferred more forces from the 2nd to 1st Baltic Fronts, including the powerful 5th Tank Corps (see Appendix D-13).[46]

General Sandalov, the 2nd Baltic Front's chief of staff, recalled how, why, and when the *Stavka* reached this decision:

At this time, I. V. Stalin was very interested in the situation in our *front* and phoned General M. M. Popov several times by *VCh* [secure] telephone. In particular, he was worried and said, "You do not think that the enemy will plug up the neck, and our forces west of Nevel' will find themselves in an encirclement?" The *front* commander assured the Supreme Commander that he and the 1st Baltic Front's commander were strengthening the forces defending the neck with artillery and engineer means that would prevent the enemy from cutting through the neck. And as soon as I. Kh. Bagramian's army arrived, he would commit it and Lieutenant General I. M. Chistiakov's 6th Guards Army with two tank corps for the development of a penetration to Idritsa.

According to Popov, I. V. Stalin agreed with him.

A. I. Antonov telephoned M. M. Popov by *VCh* telephone on 16 November. He informed him, "The Supreme Commander orders you and the 1st Baltic Front to go over to the defense in the Nevel' salient temporarily." He added, "Continue local offensive operations in the sectors of other armies of your *front*. You will receive a directive confirming this. Bear in mind, that 1st Baltic Front will begin an offensive operation in the direction of Gorodok in the near future. The liberation of that town will offer our forces favorable opportunities to envelop Vitebsk and the entire left wing of Army Group 'Center' from the north. This attack on Gorodok will liquidate the southern half of the Nevel' salient and eliminate the danger of the enemy closing it."

"And what sort of mission will be assigned to our *front* to assist our neighbor in this operation?," General Popov asked.

"We will not present you with an offensive mission," answered Antonov. "But you should not grieve; at the time of that operation your *front* will 'dispossess the Kulaks' somewhat. Ivan Khristoforovich Bagramian is being assigned to command 1st Baltic Front in place of Eremenko. He is being awarded the rank of army general. You will transfer one of 6th Guards Army's rifle corps to Bagramian. General Galitsky will leave you to command 11th Guards Army, and Colonel General Chibisov will command your 3rd Shock Army in his place. A new army of equal value to that being transferred to Bagramian will be sent to you before the multi-*front* offensive operation to de-blockage Leningrad. A cavalry corps will be sent to your *front* in the near future in place of the tank corps. You will find it of better use than the tank corps in the conditions in which you are operating. In addition, you will be provided with reinforcements of personnel, tanks, ammunition, and fuel."[47]

Thus, having failed to achieve its objectives in this stage of the Pustoshka-Idritsa offensive, the *Stavka* began undertaking measures to guarantee success in December. One of the first measures it took was to issue a directive on 15 November abolishing the Northwestern Front and assigning most of its forces to the 2nd Baltic Front but withdrawing its 34th Army into its reserves. The directive assigned Lieutenant General P. A. Kurochkin as Army General M. M. Popov's deputy and appointed the distinguished and highly skilled General Staff officer Lieutenant General F. E. Bokov as the member of the *front's* military council alongside Stalin's infamous crony, Lieutenant General L. Z. Mekhlis. By virtue of this directive, by 20 November, the reconfigured 2nd Baltic Front was to consist of 1st and 3rd Shock, 6th Guards, and 22nd Armies, supported by 15th Air Army (see Appendix D-14).[48]

This measure rid the Red Army force structure of a formation that had been trying in vain for two years to crush German defenses at Staraia Russa. Henceforth, the focus of Soviet offensive operations in the region would permanently shift from Staraia Russa to the new, no-less-bloody battleground east of Idritsa.

Local fighting continued in 2nd Baltic Front's sector until 21 November, when Popov finally ordered his forces to go over to the defense. Just prior to this date, 3rd Shock Army made several final futile attempts to break through the German defenses east of Pustoshka but achieved only minimal gains. By month's end, a stalemate ensued in the *front's* operational sector that neither side would attempt to break until early December (see Map 5.8).

Although 2nd Baltic Front recorded spectacular initial progress in the Pustoshka-Idritsa operation, a combination of stiff and skillful German resistance, deteriorating weather, and difficult terrain on which to move and maneuver halted the offensive long before it achieved the *Stavka's* strategic ends. The operation did, however, unhinge German strategic defenses along

1st and 2nd Baltic Fronts' Polotsk-Vitebsk and Pustoshka-Idritsa Offensives   155

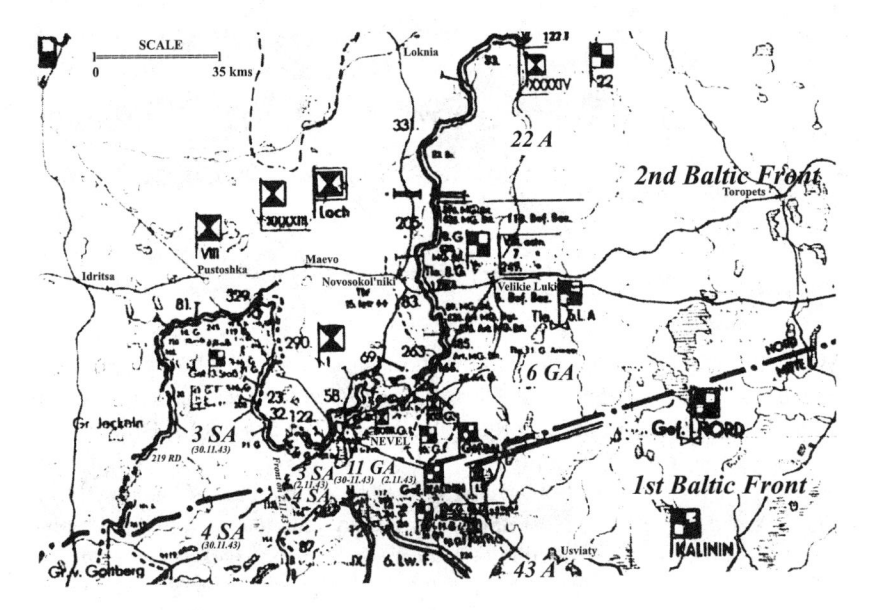

Map 5.8. Sixteenth Army's (Army Group North) Situation, 30 November 1943

the northwestern strategic axis by forming a breach between Army Groups North and Center that neither army group was able to repair. Even worse for the Germans, the offensive forced Army Group North to transfer six divisions from the Leningrad and Staraia Russa regions southward in order to stem the Soviet onslaught. This seriously weakened German Eighteenth Army's defenses around Leningrad and, ultimately, contributed to the disaster that would befall this army in that region after the turn of the year. Nor was the German agony in this sector over. Within a matter of weeks, Army Group North would once again face a major Soviet offensive toward Idritsa.

CHAPTER 6

The Western Front's Orsha Offensives (14 November–5 December)

PLANNING

While the 1st Baltic Front expanded its bridgehead west of Nevel' and advanced against the defenses of Third Panzer Army on German Army Group Center's left wing and flank in the Polotsk and Vitebsk regions, General Sokolovsky's Western Front continued its unrelenting pressure on the defenses of Army Group Center's Fourth Army east of Orsha. In accordance with the *Stavka*'s orders, in early November Sokolovsky's *front* regrouped and reinforced its armies operating along the Smolensk-Orsha road to make yet another attempt to seize Orsha, a city whose possession the *Stavka* now considered vital to the occupation of eastern Belorussia (see Map 3.7 and Appendix E-1). This time the Red Army's Main Artillery Directorate assured the *front* commander it could supply his forces the requisite ammunition during the first ten days of November.[1]

Replicating his October offensives, Sokolovsky once again relied on 10th Guards, 31st, 33rd, and 5th Armies, although the latter was the former 68th, whose forces were turned over to General Krylov's 5th Army on 5 November after the 68th was disbanded. Likewise, all of these armies remained concentrated along and on both sides of the Smolensk-Orsha highway to carry out the operation. As was the case with the October operations, until very recently, the ensuing offensives have languished in almost total obscurity for more than sixty years. Typical of Soviet and Russian treatment of these operations is the account in 31st Army's history, which simply states, "The 31st and 10th Guards Armies undertook yet another attempt to penetrate the enemy's defenses along this axis on 14 November, but unsuccessfully."[2]

Sokolovsky assembled his forces for the new offensive during early November. After being assured that his forces would be supplied necessary ammunition stocks, the *front* commander dispatched his projected operational plan to the *Stavka* on 9 November. The overall objective differed little from his previous offensive plans. This time, he intended to penetrate German Fourth Army's defenses with two shock groups formed from the forces of four armies, with each shock group conducting its attack in 12-kilometer-wide sectors north and south of the Dnepr River. This relatively narrow sector of about 25 kilometers extended from the village of Osintori, north of the Smolensk-Orsha highway, southward across the Dnepr River to Rusany, a

156

small village on the eastern bank of the Rossasenka River 2 kilometers south of the Liady-Dubrovno-Orsha road.

The first shock group, which consisted of General Sukhomlin's 10th Guards and General Gluzdovsky's 31st Armies, was to mount its assault along and on both sides of the Minsk highway north of the Dnepr River. General Burdeinyi's 2nd Guards Tank Corps, which constituted this shock group's mobile group, was designated to exploit the penetration with the mission of penetrating the Germans' second defensive line from the march and reaching the western bank of the Orshitsa River north of Orsha. The second shock group, made up of Generals Krylov's and Gordov's 5th and 33rd Armies, was to deliver a supporting attack south of the Dnepr River toward Dubrovna and Orsha. Both shock groups were to deploy their forces in triple-echelon formation in order to increase the strength of the attack, and Sokolovsky reinforced them with virtually all of the *front's* armor and artillery. The attack was to commence early on 14 November, after the *front's* and armies' artillery conducted a three-and-one-half hour artillery and air preparation.

When fully concentrated, the four armies deployed as shown in Table 6.1.

This formation created a massive concentration of forces along the entire 25-kilometer-wide front. When fully assembled, the force included 32 rifle divisions, 18 of which were in first echelon and 14 in second. The average strength of the *front's* rifle divisions at this time was 4,500 men.[3] These rifle forces were supported by 1 tank corps, 4 tank brigades, 7 tank and self-propelled artillery regiments, 16 artillery brigades, and 23 RVGK artillery regiments (allocated from the *Stavka's* Reserve). The attacking force possessed 410 tanks, and its artillery densities ranged from 120 to 260 guns and mortars per kilometer of front.[4]

During the course of the brief operation, the attacking Soviet force faced elements of two infantry and two panzer grenadier divisions subordinate to German Fourth Army's XXVII Army Corps, subsequently reinforced by 1st SS Infantry Brigade and several smaller combat groups dispatched by Fourth Army from other sectors. On XXVII Corps' left, 197th Infantry Division defended the sector north of Osintori, just north of the Western Front's main attack sector. On the 297th's right, 78th Assault Division and 25th and 18th Panzer Grenadier Divisions, the latter reinforced by 260th Infantry Regiment, defended the sector extending from Osintori southward to Kosiany, 2 kilometers northwest of Rusany, and, further south, 26th Infantry Division's reconnaissance battalion and a sapper company defended the sector from Kosiany to Rusany. Although recent Russian sources credit the Germans with a force of roughly seventy tanks and self-propelled guns, these figures were far fewer. As a result, the defenders had to rely on the ubiquitous *Paks* and self-propelled artillery as their primary antitank weapons. Given these forces, the Soviet force superiority along the Smolensk-Orsha axis was better than 8 to 1 in infantry, almost 6 to 1 in armor, and almost 10 to 1 in artillery.

Table 6.1. The Western Front's Operational Formation for the 14 November 1943 Orsha Offensive and Opposing German Forces

FORCE (Sector)	OPPOSING GERMAN FORCE
1st/2nd/3rd Echelons/Reserve	
WESTERN FRONT	**FOURTH ARMY**
	LII AC
10th Guards Army (Dobromysl'-Orsha highway)	256th ID
7th GRC (Dobromysl'-Osintori)	XXVII AC
312th RD	197th ID
152nd FR	321st IR
207th RD	347th IR
208th RD	931st IR
19th GRC (Osintori-Sudilovichi)	332nd IR
56th GRD/22nd GRD/65th GRD	78th AssltD
15th GRC (Sudilovichi-Orsha highway)	195th IR
85th GRD/29th GRD	
30th GRD	215th IR
Support	
153rd TB	
119th TR	
1445th SPR	
31st Army (Orsha highway-Dnepr at Gorinany)	
70th RC (Orsha highway-Kireevo)	14th IR
338th RD/371th RD/58th RD	
36th RC (Kireevo)	25th PzGrD
359th RD/215th RD/274th RD	119th PzGrR
45th RC (Kireevo south)	
251st RD/88th RD	
220th RD	
71st RC (Kireevo south-Gorinany)	
331st RD/82nd RD	35th PzGrR
133rd RD	
Support	
2nd GTC	
42nd GTB	
1435th SPR	
1830th SPR	
5th Army (Dnepr River–Volkolakovka)	
72nd RC (Dnepr-Hill 180.8)	1st SS IB
174th RD/159th RD, 192nd RD	
81st RC (Hill 180.8-Bobrova)	18th PzGrD
173rd RD/199th RD	260th IR
95th RD	
69th RC (Bobrovo-Volkolakovka)	
76th RD/290th RD	51st PzGrR
157th RD	30th PzGrR
Support	
23rd GTB	
1537th SPR	
33rd Army (Volkolakovka-Baevo)	
65th RC (Volkolakovka-Rusany)	
222nd RD/153rd RD, 144th RD	
42nd RD/164th RD	
61st RC (Rusany-Baevo)	26th ID
62nd RD	39th IR
63rd RD	77th IR

Table 6.1. continued

FORCE (Sector)	OPPOSING GERMAN FORCE
Support 256th TB 63rd GTR 64th GTR 248th TR 1495th SPR	78th IR

Sources: Boevoi sostav Sovetskoi Armii, chast' III (Ianvar'–dekabr' 1943 g.) [The combat composition of the Soviet Army, pt. 3 (January–December 1943) (Moscow: Voenizdat, 1972), 275–276; and "Ia, Kartenband zum KTB Nr. 21, Nov–Dec 1943," *AOK 4, 49111/55* in NAM T-312, Roll 226 and "Ic, Taetigkeitsbericht, Nov–Dec 1943," *AOK 4, 48448/5* in NAM T-312, Roll 1362.

Because Soviet and Russian accounts of this operation are so rare, it is worth quoting the few accounts that exist. The first of these described 10th Guards Army's offensive:

> The 56th, 85th, and 30th Guards Rifle Divisions attacked the enemy after an artillery and aviation preparation. They captured the first trenches by an audacious dash, but an antitank ditch up to 6 meters wide and 4 meters deep obstructed the attackers' subsequent advance route. It was so well concealed that even one close to it could not discover it. During the summer the ditch had become overgrown with grass. It was a distinctive trap not only for tanks but also for infantry. The obstacle was ranged in by enemy artillery firing from concealed positions in timely fashion.
>
> Our units managed to overcome that obstacle and capture the second trenches only by 1500 hours. When the infantry had cleaned it out, conditions were created for the operations of the infantry support tanks.
>
> Mobile detachments had been created in the divisions to exploit success. The detachment formed in 30th Guards Rifle Division consisted of 10 tanks, 4 self-propelled artillery guns, and an infantry battalion from 98th Guards Rifle Regiment. The detachment went into combat at 1600 hours and advanced 3–4 kilometers. During this action, a tank company under the command of Senior Lieutenant G. Briskin, after overcoming the antitank ditch, courageously advanced forward protecting the riflemen's advance during the seizure of the important strong point south of Osintori. The enemy launched a counterattack at the junction between 30th Guards Rifle Division and its neighbor to the left, 31st Army's 338th Rifle Division. During its repulse, the crew of Junior Lieutenant N. Mitrofanov destroyed a German tank, and Tank Sergeant I. Gubanov destroyed an enemy self-propelled gun. The enemy's counterattack was repelled.
>
> The enemy launched seven counterattacks in 85th Guards Rifle Division's sector during the day on 15 November. During the last of these, the attack struck a battalion of 253rd Guards Rifle Regiment commanded

by Captain I. N. Nosov. The battalion commander decided to let the counterattacking Germans pass into the depth of his positions and then to destroy them. He informed the regimental commander and the commander of the neighboring battalion from 249th Guards Rifle Regiment about his decision. The plan was successfully implemented, and the encircled enemy soldiers were destroyed to the last man. Senior Lieutenant P. K. Batalin, the assistant battalion commander, displayed special bravery in the battle. Having hidden in the enemy rear, he and three other soldiers cut off [the enemy's] withdrawal route and provided the opportunity for the full destruction of the penetrating enemy. The fires of that group destroyed more than 20 Hitlerites.

The prolonged battles continued during the second half of November and in the beginning of December 1943. Overall, our forces advanced from 6 up to 8 kilometers from 14 November through 5 December. In light of the obvious hopelessness of any further attempts to smash enemy resistance on the approaches to Orsha, on 5 December the Western Front commander decided to cease offensive operations and withdraw 10th Guards Army into reserve. The army received the mission to regroup its forces to the Velikie Luki region.[5]

The official history of Latvian rifle divisions in the Red Army adds some details about 10th Guards Army's operations:

The 85th Guards Rifle Division

The division conducted so-called "battles of local importance" along the Orsha axis during October and November, which at times were quite severe. For example, combat raged for Novoe Selo, an enemy strongpoint on the Minsk road, from 14 through 18 November. We used the procedure of employing rolling barrage fire to accompany the infantry for the first time during that offensive. The division seized Novoe Selo, but sometimes the enemy's resistance was as stubborn as it had ever been, since that penetration smashed his main defense line. A battalion under the command of Major Dzhunusov, whose personnel consisted of replacement recruits from the Central Asian republics, particularly distinguished itself. After an artillery rolling barrage, Dzhunusov's battalion advanced forward rapidly at 0900 hours on 14 November. Crushing German resistance, the battalion penetrated into Novoe Selo. The enemy first withdrew in panic but then launched a counterattack. The battles lasted until late in the evening. The Germans conducted six counterattacks; however, all of them faltered. [The battalion] held on to Novoe Selo. All of the battalion's personnel displayed high offensive spirit, persistence, and massive heroism.

On 18 November the division was ordered to turn its sector over to 207th Rifle Division.[6]

The 22nd Guards Rifle Division

At that time [late October], our forces began an offensive along the Orsha axis. Our division was situated in the second echelon during the initial days of the offensive, but on 5 November it replaced 65th Guards Rifle Division and fought to penetrate the strongly fortified enemy defensive belt on the approaches to Orsha. These battles, which lasted for almost the entire month of November, were very intense. Here the Soviet forces immediately approached the enemy's main defense line, which the Germans called "The Eastern Wall." They threw all of their reserves into combat, while trying at all costs to prevent a penetration of their defensive line. The Hitlerites launched 20 counterattacks against the division's units during just the three days from 14 through 16 November. The strongest counterattack struck 65th Regiment. Three ranks of up to 2,000 Hitlerites attacked the positions of the regiment, whose rifle companies at that time numbered 35 men each. At the critical moment, Guards Lieutenant Colonel M. A. Anikin, the regimental commander, made a singularly correct decision: to cover the enemy ranks with machine gun fire and then conduct a counterattack. Inspired by their commander and Guards Major Moskvin, his assistant for political affairs, the regiment rushed at the enemy, and the Germans, not able to withstand the hand-to-hand combat, ran back to their foxholes. The soldiers of 65th Regiment penetrated to the enemy foxholes on the heels of the panicked Hitlerites and captured them along with 35 prisoners.

However, the division and all of the other 10th Guards Army formations did not succeed in fully penetrating the enemy defense at Orsha. Significant losses in personnel, ammunition shortages, and also the bad fall weather prevented us from converting the notable tactical successes we achieved in smashing the enemy defense into an operational penetration. Digging into their achieved positions, the division repelled enemy counterattacks and conducted reconnaissance at the end of November and the beginning of December.[7]

The 65th Guards Rifle Division

After heavy and bloody combat during the next two weeks [after 4 November], the guardsmen rested. The units of 207th Rifle and 56th Guards Rifle Divisions replaced them on the night of 20 November and occupied jumping-off positions for an attack.[8]

THE FOURTH ORSHA OFFENSIVE (14–19 NOVEMBER 1943)

Despite the dearth of information from Soviet sources regarding the Western Front's 14–18 November assault, we can now reconstruct the action with a fair degree of accuracy. After conducting the lengthy artillery preparation, all four Soviet armies made minimal gains against the Germans' first defense position on the first day of the attack (see Map 6.1). With penal and assault battalions in the lead, 10th Guards Army's 56th, 85th, and 30th Guards Rifle Divisions advanced up to 2.5 kilometers despite the heavy fog that shrouded the battlefield and managed to seize the eastern edge of Novoe Selo before being struck and halted by German counterattacks. The 31st Army's 338th Rifle Division kept pace, advancing up to 1.5 kilometers; however, the army's remaining divisions bogged down in the German forward security belt in front of the forward defenses because of withering German machine gun fire. To the south, forces along the adjoining flanks of 5th and 33rd Armies managed to force their way across the Rossasenka River between Bobrova and Rusany and captured a lodgment 50 meters to 1 kilometer deep on the river's western bank. Specifically, 174th and 173rd Rifle Divisions of 5th Army's 72nd and 81st Rifle Corps fought successfully until their assault faltered on the northern approaches to Bobrova. Further south, 76th and 157th Rifle Divisions of 5th Army's 69th Rifle Corps, supported by tanks from 23rd Guards Tank Brigade, managed to capture the villages of Zagrazdino and Volkolakovka, although at a cost of more than twenty tanks.[9] Meanwhile, 33rd Army's 222nd and 42nd Rifle Divisions pushed westward and reached the eastern outskirts of Guraki. The attacks by the remainder of the armies' first-echelon divisions faltered in the face of strong German defenses and withering artillery and machine gun fire.

On 15 November, General Sukhomlin, 10th Guards Army's commander, ordered 19th and 15th Guards Rifle Corps to commit their second echelons to combat (see Map 6.1). This occurred because 19th Guards Corps' lead division, the 56th, had been forced to abandon several villages because of a German counterattack by a battalion of infantry and a handful of tanks. The 22nd and 65th Guards Rifle Divisions then reinforced 56th Guards Division and also supported 85th Guards Division's fight to secure the village of Novoe Selo. However, at this point, the counterattacking Germans struck the flank of 10th Guards Army's shallow penetration, drove the 22nd and 56th Guards Divisions back, and, in turn, threatened the northern flank of 85th and 65th Guards Divisions' forces fighting for Novoe Selo. Meanwhile, on 10th Guards left, 31st Army's divisions recorded no progress whatsoever against the defenses of 78th Assault and 25th Panzer Grenadier Divisions along the Orsha highway. Consequently, General Gluzdovsky too ordered the second-echelon divisions of 70th and 36th Rifle Corps into combat. Thus, instead of beginning the exploitation as planned and hoped, 31st Army's second echelon had no choice but to contend with German counterattacks.

Further south, along the Rossasenka River, as on the previous day, General Krylov's 5th Army fought for but failed to seize Bobrova and the heights west of the Rossasenka River (Hill 201.8) largely because of determined

The Western Front's Orsha Offensives 163

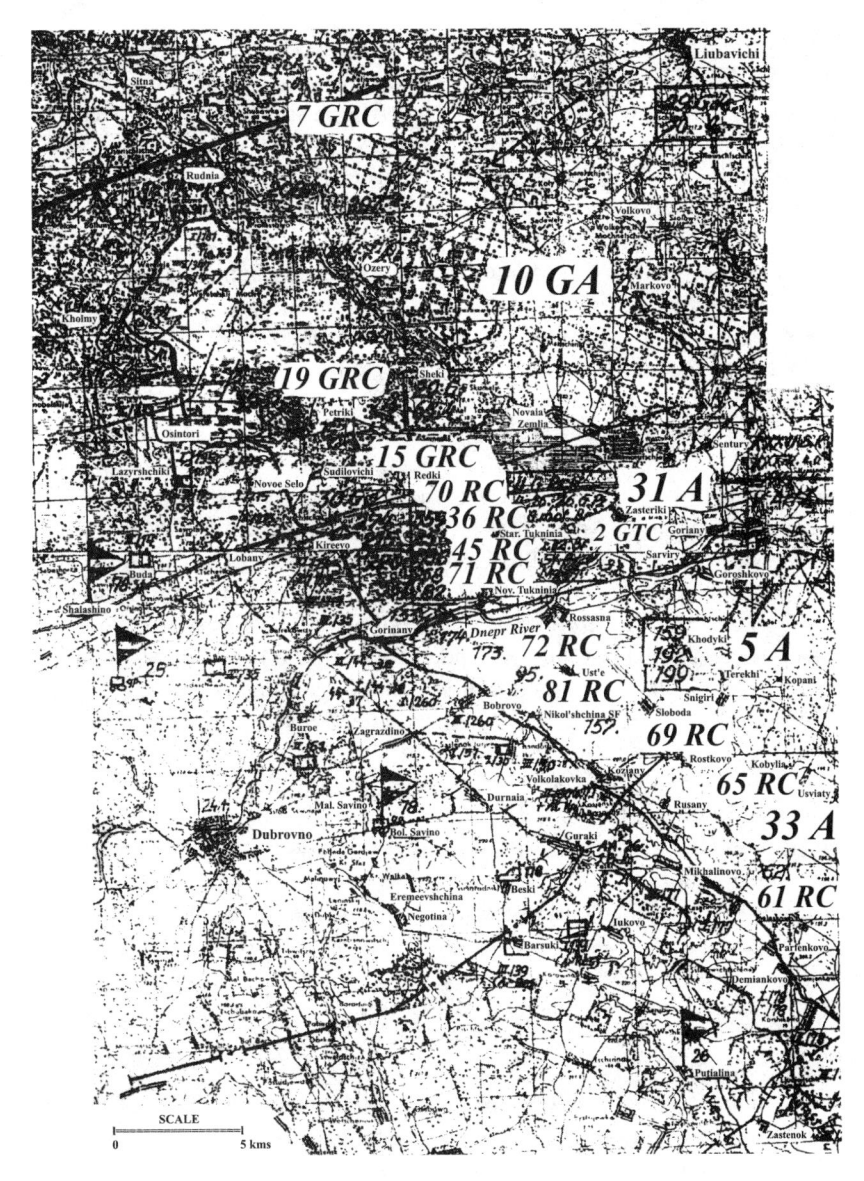

Map 6.1. Fourth Army's Situation in the Orsha Sector, 14 November 1943

German counterattacks in battalion strength. On 5th Army's left, General Gordov, the commander of 33rd Army, committed his second-echelon 153rd and 164th Rifle Divisions in repeated attacks against 18th Panzer Grenadier Division's defenses at the village of Guraki, but nonetheless failed to break the Germans' iron grip on the village.

By committing virtually all of his reserves to combat, over the next few days, Sukhomlin's 10th Guards Army finally succeeded in capturing Novoe Selo and pushing forward to just short of the Osintori-Lobany line. The attack on 17 November, conducted jointly by the divisions of 10th Guards Army's 15th Guards Rifle Corps and 31st Army's 70th Rifle Corps, was spearheaded by 4th and 25th Guards Tank Brigades of Burdeinyi's 2nd Guards Tank Corps. This final thrust struck the boundary between German 78th Assault and 25th Panzer Grenadier Divisions' defenses along and north of the Orsha highway. However, this attack too faltered on the approaches to the German strongpoint Zavoloki (Sawolnyi on German maps).

Thus, in five days of intense combat, Sokolovsky's 10th Guards and 31st Armies managed to advance a mere 4 to 5 kilometers westward from their original jumping-off positions. The 5th and 33rd Armies, too, were unable to achieve penetrations of any significance in the face of stiffening German resistance. Only by committing a fresh division (the 144th) to combat, they finally managed to secure a 10-kilometer-wide and 3–4-kilometer-deep bridgehead on the western bank of the Rossasenka River by day's end on 18 November (see Map 6.2). By then, however, their offensive expired from utter exhaustion.

Overall, from 14 through 18 November, the Western Front's shock groups managed an advance of from 400 meters up to 4 kilometers in five days of brutally heavy fighting. But they did so at an appalling cost in dead and wounded. In addition to causing genuine embarrassment, the failed attacks cost the Western Front's four armies 38,756 casualties, including 9,167 killed and 29,589 wounded.[10] Nonetheless, despite this high death toll and only meager offensive gains, the *Stavka* insisted that the Western Front continue the assaults. Saluting smartly, Sokolovsky's *front* did so ten days later after yet another regrouping.

Reflecting on Sokolovsky's failure to rupture German Fourth Army's defenses, a recent account published in Belarus asserted that ammunition was in short supply, and, when conducted at all, the artillery offensives were stereotypical and wholly inadequate. Worse still:

> As before, there were many shortcomings in the combat training of personnel. The main mass of replacements arrived in the period from 10 through 14 November, just before the beginning of the offensive. Their training was conducted formally, in unprepared field exercises. The subunit commanders primarily devoted attention to the matter of the simultaneous rising up in the attack and the unceasing forward movement of the ranks of riflemen. Because of economizing on ammunition, training in the conduct of fire from rifle weapons in place and even more while moving was not worked out. Weapons, including automatics (machine pistols and submachine guns), were issued without consideration of individual responsibilities and the level of the soldiers' training. In 5th Army,

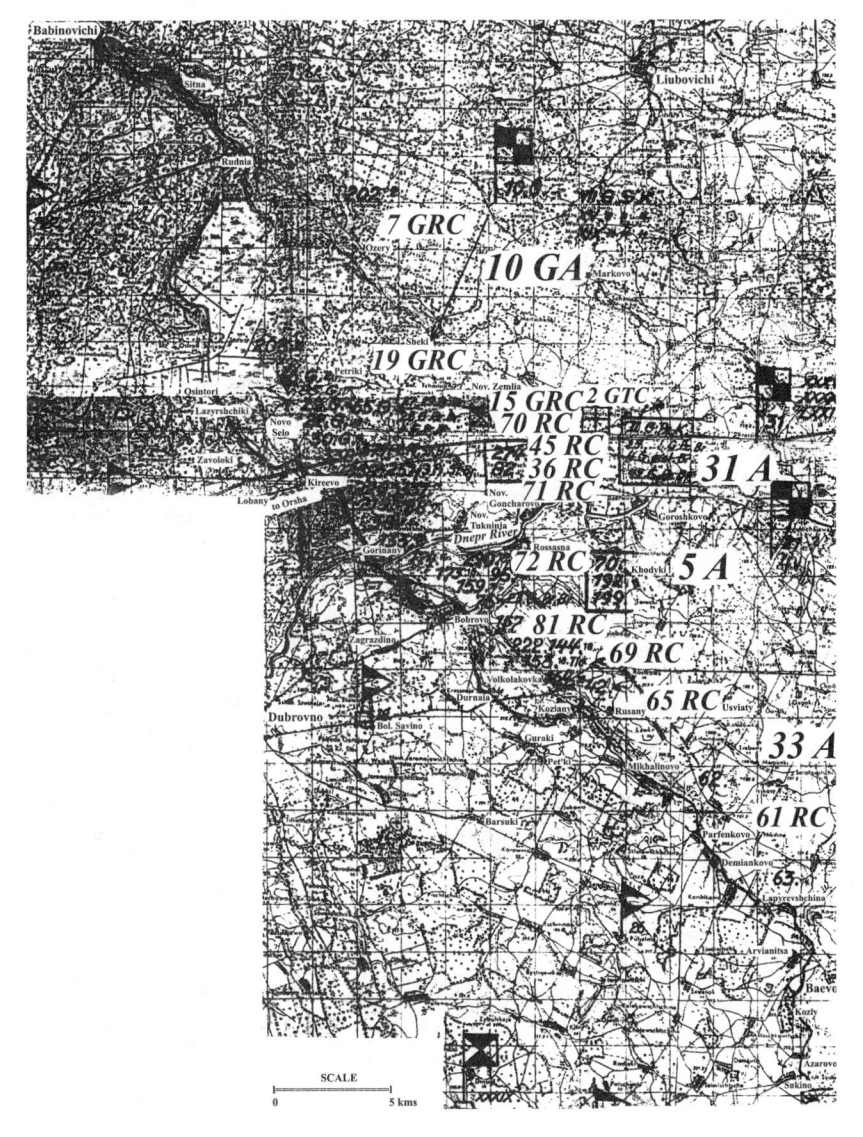

Map 6.2. Fourth Army's Situation in the Orsha Sector, 19 November 1943

on the whole, exercises were not conducted with the arriving march replacements. In 31st Army, artillery and tanks were absent in exercises. In essence, the subunits had to enter combat untrained.[11]

With deficiencies such as these, the results of attacks against well-prepared German defenses were utterly predictable.

THE FIFTH ORSHA OFFENSIVE (30 NOVEMBER–5 DECEMBER 1943)

If the Western Front's mid-November offensive languished in obscurity, the operation that began on 30 November has received even less attention from Soviet historians. In fact, until very recently, a thorough search of all Soviet materials revealed only three short accounts of the fighting. In the first, quoted above, 10th Guards Army's history admits that heavy fighting occurred until 5 December, after which the *Stavka* transferred the army to another sector.

A second account is found in 5th Army's history:

> The offensive combat here [in the sector south of the Dnepr River] continued until 5 December. Wet snow arrived during this period, and the roads were converted into a complete jumble. However, this did not hinder 174th Rifle Division's units, together with 76th Rifle Division from the neighboring army, from attacking the fortified point of Bobrova, which was situated 2 kilometers south of Hill 180.8, on 1 December. The enemy's motorized and infantry units had been driven back from Bobrova by the night of 2 December. Thus, our forces once again improved their positions.
>
> The German command threw large reserves along this axis in an attempt to impede our advance. The 5th Army's attacking forces were too weak to continue the advance. For example, the divisions' personnel strength varied from 3,088 up to 4,095 soldiers and officers by the end of November. As a result, the enemy succeeded in halting 5th Army's offensive.[12]

The third brief reference to this operation appears in the history of 10th Guards Army's 65th Guards Rifle Division:

> They [the division's units] relieved 207th and 56th Guards Rifle Divisions on the night of 20 November and occupied jumping-off positions for an attack. By this time German 197th Infantry and 78th Assault Divisions were defending along the Ostrov, Iur'ev, Osintori, and Slepni line (25–30 kilometers northeast of Orsha) opposite the division's front. The enemy's second defense line ran along the line from the cemetery 3 kilometers west of Vydritsa through Viritsa to Gausin Bor and further to Hill 183.7.
>
> The division's seven days of offensive combat did not produce the expected results. It did not succeed in penetrating the enemy's defenses along the distant approaches to Orsha.
>
> The division's units gave their defensive sector to 220th Rifle Division's 653rd Rifle Regiment on 8 December and concentrated in the forest a kilometer east of Skumaty.[13]

The Western Front's Orsha Offensives 167

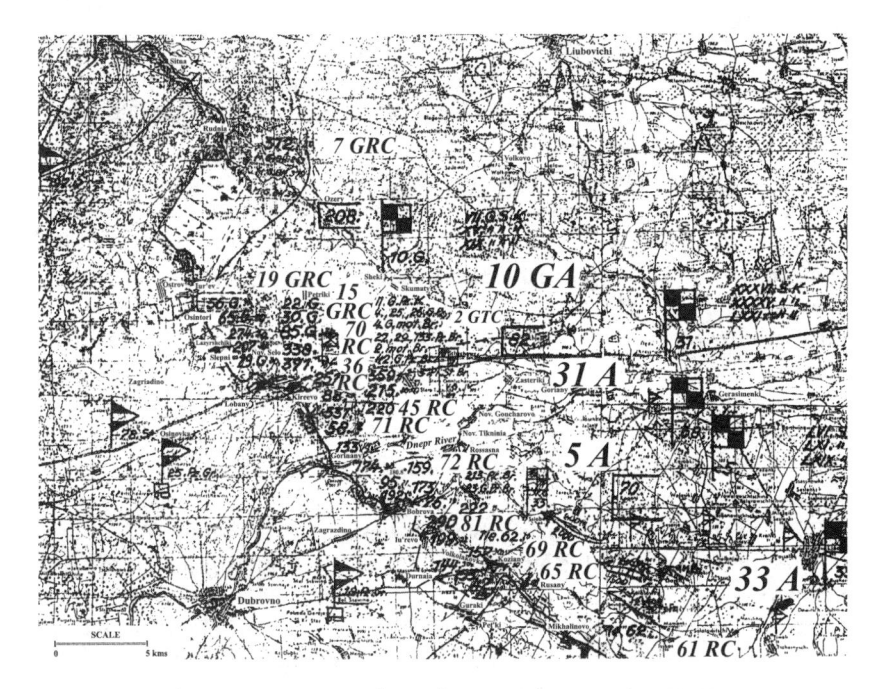

Map 6.3. Fourth Army's Situation in the Orsha Sector, 30 November 1943

General Sokolovsky once again regrouped his forces in preparation for the 30 November offensive, this time further narrowing his offensive sector (see Map 6.3). The *front*'s new main attack sector extended from the village of Osintori southward across the Dnepr River at Gorinany to the eastern edge of Bobrova and then along the bridgehead west of the Rossasenka River to just east of Guraki. Sokolovsky concentrated the forces of Sukhomlin's 10th Guards and Gluzdovsky's 31st Armies in the 12-kilometer-wide sector between Osintori and the Dnepr River and those of Krylov's 5th Army in the 4-kilometer-wide sector from the Dnepr to Bobrova. Gordov's 33rd Army shifted additional forces into the Rossasenka River bridgehead on the army's right wing and took over the portion of 5th Army's sector south of Bobrova, together with 5th Army's 76th Rifle Division. Once its forces regrouped, 33rd Army's sector decreased in width to roughly 10 kilometers.

Sokolovsky assigned 10th Guards Army the mission of penetrating German defenses in the 3-kilometer-wide sector from Osintori to Novoe Selo (Lazyrshchinki), capturing the Zagriadino and Osinovka Station line and, subsequently, advancing to the Vydritsa line, 4 kilometers west of Goliashei. All of this required an advance of 10 kilometers. Accordingly, General Sukhomlin positioned five divisions in his shock group's first echelon and three in its second. The 10th Guards Army's mobile group, once again General

Burdeiny's 2nd Guards Tank Corps, was to exploit westward to cut the Vitebsk-Orsha road, secure crossings over the Orshitsa River in the vicinity of Vysokoe State Farm and the railroad bridge east of Barsuki, and then attack southward toward Orsha.

Attacking on 10th Guards Army's left, 31st Army was to conduct its main attack in a 3-kilometer-wide sector and advance 10 kilometers westward to keep pace with Sukhomlin's army. General Gluzdovsky allocated four divisions to his shock group's first echelon and five to its second. South of the Dnepr River, 5th Army was to attack westward from its sector to capture Hill 201.7 (202.0 on current maps) and Zagrazdino and then exploit the attack toward the city of Dubrovno, 12 kilometers distant. General Krylov placed seven divisions in his first echelon and two in his second.

Overall, the Western Front's three attacking armies consisted of thirty-four rifle divisions, twenty-four in first echelon and ten in second. These rifle forces were supported by four tank brigades, ten tank and self-propelled artillery regiments, thirteen artillery brigades, and twenty-four RVGK artillery regiments. As such the attacking force fielded 284 tanks, and its artillery densities ranged from 120 to 170 guns and mortars per kilometer of front.[14]

This attacking force faced essentially the same forces Sokolovsky had attacked on 14 November, specifically, two infantry and two panzer grenadier divisions subordinate to Fourth Army's XXVII Army Corps. On the corps' left wing, 197th Infantry Division defended north of Osintori, just outside the Soviet main attack sector but during the operation shifted two of its regiments to the south into the Soviet main attack sector. On the 197th's right, 78th Assault and 25th and 18th Panzer Grenadier Divisions defended the sector from Osintori southward to Guraki. The 26th Infantry Division provided some protection on 18th Panzer Grenadier's right flank. According to Soviet count, the Germans fielded roughly 200 tanks and self-propelled guns, but this count seems too high in that the defenders lacked any supporting panzer division. Given these forces, the Soviet force superiority along the Orsha axis was better than 8 to 1 in infantry, almost 2 to 1 in armor, and almost 10 to 1 in artillery.

When the offensive began early on 30 November, after a one-hour artillery preparation, the attacking Soviet shock groups achieved only minimal success, essentially limited to gains only in the Bobrova-Guraki sector (see Map 6.3). The 10th Guards and 31st Armies gained virtually no ground along and north of the Orsha highway, even after they committed their second echelons and reserves into combat. Symptomatic of their difficulties, the 274th Rifle Division, attacking in the first echelon of 31st Army, suffered significant casualties when it was struck by its own aircraft and artillery. However, the combined forces of 5th and 33rd Armies achieved greater success south of the Dnepr River. Here, 174th and 76th Rifle Divisions finally captured the German strongpoint at Bobrova during the first several days of fighting.

The Western Front's Orsha Offensives 169

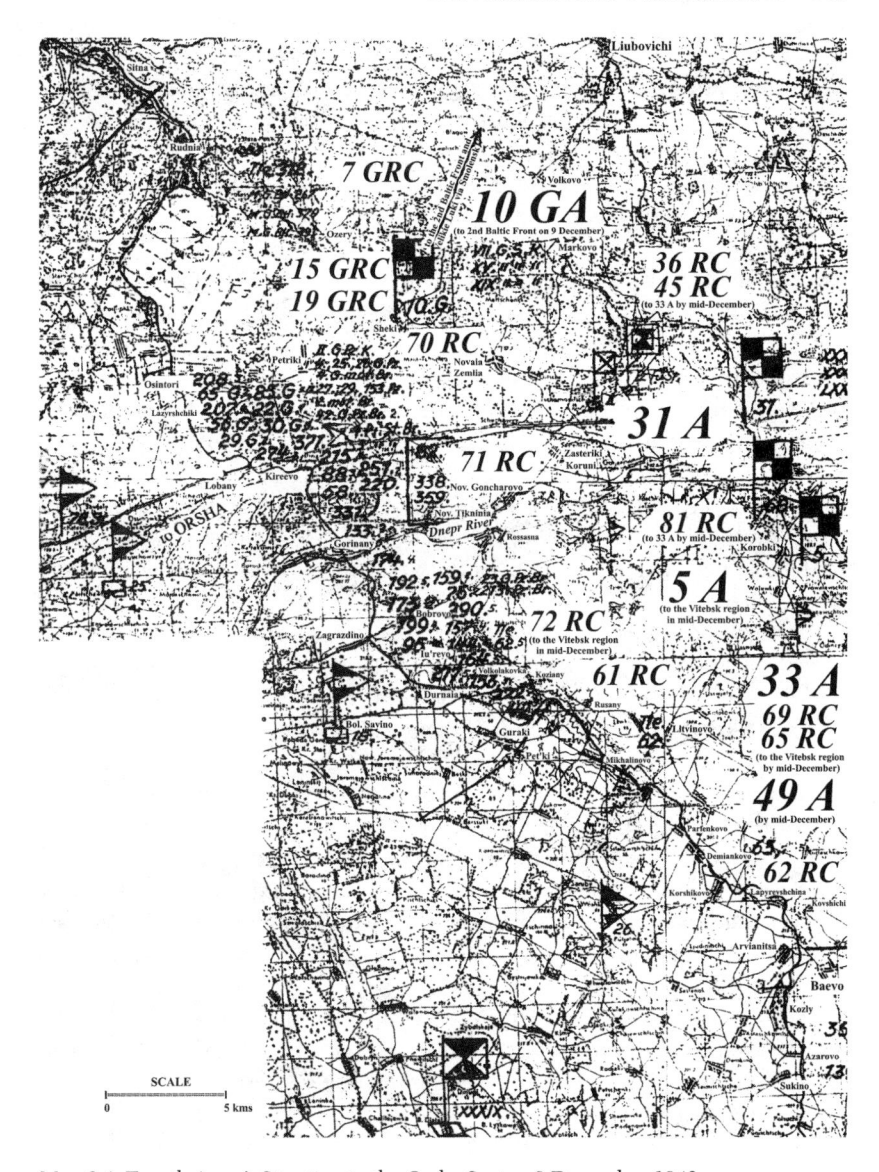

Map 6.4. Fourth Army's Situation in the Orsha Sector, 8 December 1943

This forced the German defenders to withdraw to new defensive positions extending along a line from just east of Zagrazdino southeastward through Durnaia to east of Guraki, roughly 4 kilometers to the west of their original positions. There the front lines stabilized on 4 December, and, despite subsequent heavy Soviet attacks, the German defenses held (see Map 6.4). By late on 5 December it was apparent to all concerned that, like the previous

Soviet offensives, this one too had faltered. Accordingly, that same day Sokolovsky ordered his *front's* armies go over to the defense and withdrew 10th Guards Army into its reserve. Three days later, at 0215 hours on the 8th, the *Stavka* transferred 10th Guards Army from the Western to the 2nd Baltic Front, with loading on railroad cars for the trip from Smolensk to the Velikie Luki region slated to begin on 9 December.

Recent Russian sources indicate that, in return for what they claim was a 1–2 kilometer advance, the Western Front's armies suffered 22,870 casualties, including 5,611 dead and 17,259 wounded.[15] The combat journal of 33th Army for 1–3 December underscores this hideously high price paid in terms of casualties for the army's meager gains (see Appendix E-2). This bloodletting along the Orsha axis proved to be the last. Admitting his inability to smash or even dent German defenses in this sector, Sokolovsky soon ordered his forces to regroup to the north, where, by midmonth, they would join 1st Baltic Front in a fresh effort to seize Vitebsk. Soon the forces of 5th and 33rd Armies would begin a march northward to what they hoped would be a more hospitable new attack axis south of the Smolensk-Vitebsk road. They would be mistaken.

In retrospect, the Western Front's 30 November offensive failed because of many of the same problems Sokolovsky's forces experienced earlier in the month. For example, a General Staff officer whom the *Stavka* assigned to the Western Front summarized these difficulties:

> Any sort of surprise was absent. The enemy knew about the preparations for the operation, and that we would attack on the morning of 30.11.43. . . . We did not succeed in stunning the enemy, paralyzing his will, and depriving him of the opportunity of rendering organized resistance to our attacking forces. . . . The infantry rose to the attack in spite of the fact that his firing systems, especially the enemy artillery and mortars, had not been suppressed. It [the infantry] began to suffer great losses from artillery and mortar fire. Thus, for example, on the first day of battle our infantry lost 70 percent of the total number of wounded on that day to exploding shells and mines. . . . The infantry, as a result of poor training, in general, and in the conduct of offensive combat, in particular, attacked in dense groups. The groups, having fallen under enemy artillery and mortar fire, did not disperse but instead laid down densely, by doing so presenting enemy artillery and mortars with very favorable targets.[16]

Surprisingly enough, despite the General Staff's acute knowledge of what had gone wrong and why, the *Stavka* remained determined to achieve victory in Belorussia, apparently regardless of the cost.

The cost of the Western Front's persistent but stereotypical offensives east of Orsha was high and in no way commensurate with the *front's* meager gains. In almost two full months of fighting, the *front's* forces advanced 6–12 kilometers and failed to accomplish the missions the *Stavka* assigned to Sokolovsky. The cost to the *front* in terms of personnel losses was staggering because it suffered roughly 94,200 casualties, including about 25,500 men killed and 78,700 men wounded, which amounted to about 30 percent of the *front's* overall strength. At the same time, the *front* also lost 177 tanks and SP guns and more than 130 combat aircraft.[17]

In the wake of the Western Front's frustrating defeats in November, the *Stavka* apparently gave up on its hopes of smashing Army Group Center by means of hammer blows delivered against the latter's center, specifically, the defenses of its Fourth Army in the Orsha and Mogilev regions. Given the successes 1st Baltic Front's forces recorded in the Gorodok region on Third Panzer Army's left wing and the gains the Belorussian Front made against Second Army's defenses in the Gomel' region, an opportunity arose to envelop Army Group Center and its four subordinate armies by conducting strengthened offensives against both of its wings. To that end, in early December the *Stavka* decided to shift the full weight of the Western Front's strength northward so that it could join the advance of General Bagramian's 1st Baltic Front on Vitebsk. In the meantime, it ordered General Rokossovsky's Belorussian Front to expand its offensive from the Gomel' region toward Rechitsa and provided him the forces necessary to do so. Therefore, a concerted effort to envelop and destroy Army Group Center was in the offing.

CHAPTER 7

The Belorussian Front's Gomel'-Rechitsa and Novyi Bykhov–Propoisk Offensives (10–30 November)

PLANNING

After seizing an operational bridgehead across the Dnepr River west of Loev and Radul' during the first two stages of its Gomel'-Rechitsa operation in October 1943, the Belorussian Front prepared to resume its general offensive toward Rechitsa, Bobruisk, and Minsk in November. As recorded by the Soviet official history:

> The Belorussian Front was replenished with personnel and received ammunition and fuel at the end of October and the beginning of November. Its forces numbered 719,000 men, 7,560 guns and mortars, 247 tanks and self-propelled guns, and 526 combat aircraft by 10 November. The enemy had 660,000 men, 3,600 guns and mortars, up to 300 tanks and assault guns, and around 400 combat aircraft. Thus, the Soviet forces outnumbered the enemy by 1.1:1 in personnel, 2:1 in guns and mortars, and 3:1 in combat aircraft. The quantity of tanks and self-propelled (assault) guns was roughly equal.
>
> The *front* commander concentrated his main grouping in the Loev bridgehead from which he delivered his main attack and achieved [here] considerable superiority over the enemy in forces and weaponry. "The initiative is in our hands," wrote Marshal of the Soviet Union K. K. Rokossovsky. "We can take the risk and demonstrate a concentration of forces in one sector of the front, while, at the same time, preparing an attack along an entirely different axis. We did so. I. I. Fediuninsky's 11th Army, together with the forces of V. Ia. Kolpakchi [63rd Army], repeatedly attacked the enemy north of Gomel', riveting his attention on that sector. And we were already preparing the main attack from the Loev bridgehead."
>
> The *front*'s main grouping, which consisted of 61st and 65th Armies, began its offensive south of Gomel' on 10 November after a powerful artillery and air preparation. The enemy offered stubborn resistance by relying on well-prepared defenses. However, our rifle formations wedged into his defenses on the first day of battle. We committed the tank and cavalry corps into combat on the second day in order to develop the success. The *front*'s forces cut the Gomel'-Kalinkovichi road by a decisive

attack into the enemy's rear and captured Rechitsa on 18 November. At this time, the Belorussian partisans increased their activities in the German rear area, cooperating with the advancing Soviet Army units.

The Wehrmacht command tried to hold on to Gomel' at all costs. Divisions withdrawn from the Rechitsa region with tanks and artillery reinforced the city's garrison. However, we crushed the enemy's resistance as a result of the shock grouping's arrival in the enemy's rear area, the successful offensive on the *front's* right flank and center, and also the attacks directly on the city. Soviet forces liberated the important road and rail center of Gomel' on the morning of 26 November after a fierce night battle. . . .

The Belorussian Front's forces had inflicted a serious defeat on the enemy, driven him back 130 kilometers, and liberated a number of regions in eastern Belorussia by the end of November.[1]

This account is essentially correct. Furthermore, because Rokossovsky's operation was moderately successful, particularly in comparison with the other failures that occurred during the Belorussian strategic offensive, numerous Soviet sources have covered it in considerable detail under the rubric of the "Gomel'-Rechitsa operation." As we have seen, however, the assertion that this was the one and only "Gomel'-Rechitsa operation" is incorrect. In essence, it represented Rokossovsky's third attempt to fulfill the *Stavka*'s orders to liberate Gomel', Rechitsa, Bobruisk, and Minsk. Even though his forces failed to achieve the ultimate objectives the *Stavka* assigned to them, this operation turned out to be the most successful of all three. Although Soviet and Russian military historians have covered this stage of the operation in literally hundreds of books, including numerous survey histories, memoirs, and unit histories, they have prepared no comprehensive study of the offensive. Therefore, the limited Russian sources make it quite difficult to reconstruct precisely who did what to whom and at what time throughout the course of the offensive. This is particularly vexing because the operation's initial successes created genuine dilemmas for the beleaguered opposing German commands. This was, after all, the most successful *front* offensive conducted during the Belorussian strategic offensive operation. Therefore, one must assume that the Soviets and Russians neglected this operation and downplayed its significance either because it ultimately failed or because they wished to protect the reputation of the general officers who conducted it. For these reasons, this chapter will provide a more complete picture of this fascinating operation than a normal "forgotten battle" would warrant.

In accordance with the *Stavka*'s guidance, General Rokossovsky, the commander of the Belorussian Front, planned an operation whose overall objectives were virtually identical to those the *Stavka* assigned to him in late September. Specifically, his *front* was to penetrate German Second Army's defenses west of the Dnepr River, initially exploit to capture Rechitsa, envelop and destroy the Germans' so-called Gomel'-Rechitsa grouping, and, subsequently, advance on Bobruisk and Minsk to envelop the right wing of Army Group Center. As encapsulated in the new Russian military encyclopedia, the operation was to develop as follows:

> The concept of the operation envisioned the delivery of blows against the flanks of the enemy Gomel'-Rechitsa grouping to envelop and destroy it. The forces of 48th Army (Lieutenant General P. L. Romanenko), 65th Army (Lieutenant General P. I. Batov), 61st Army (Lieutenant General P. A. Belov), and two tank and two cavalry corps attached to 65th Army were to deliver the main attack from the Loev bridgehead on the *front*'s left wing in the general direction of Rechitsa. On the fourth day of the operation, the forces of 63rd Army (Lieutenant General V. Ia. Kolpakchi) and 11th Army (Lieutenant General I. I. Fediuninsky) were to deliver the other blow from the region north of Gomel' toward Zhlobin to envelop the German-fascist grouping from the northwest and, together with the main forces, destroy it. The forces on the *front*'s right wing—50th Army (Lieutenant General I. V. Boldin) and 3rd Army (Lieutenant General A. V. Gorbatov)—were to reach the Dnepr River in the region north and south of Novyi Bykhov. The massing of forces and weaponry in 65th and 61st Armies' sectors permitted the creation of superiority over the enemy of 1.5–2 to 1 in personnel, 3–4 to 1 in guns and mortars, and 2 to 1 in tanks and self-propelled artillery.[2]

According to Rokossovsky's original offensive plan, his forces were to seize Rechitsa and the Bragin, Nasavichi, Zhlobin, and Propoisk line by 16 November and Kalinkovichi, Bobruisk, Klichev, and Dashkovka by 5 December in concert with the Western Front's advance on Orsha (see Map 7.1). If both *fronts* achieved their missions, Mogilev and Army Group Center's entire defensive line along the Dnepr River would become untenable.

Recently released Russian correlation-of-forces figures for the operation are somewhat disingenuous. In actuality, based on a strength report issued by the Belorussia Front, its strength in terms of combat personnel and weapons as of 15 November was as follows:

> On 15 November 1943, the Belorussian Front has 485,293 personnel, including 58,991 officers, 104,107 sergeants, and 322,195 enlisted personnel.
> The armies' personnel strengths are:
> 3rd Army—42,072
> 11th Army—63,167
> 48th Army—60,335
> 50th Army—39,394

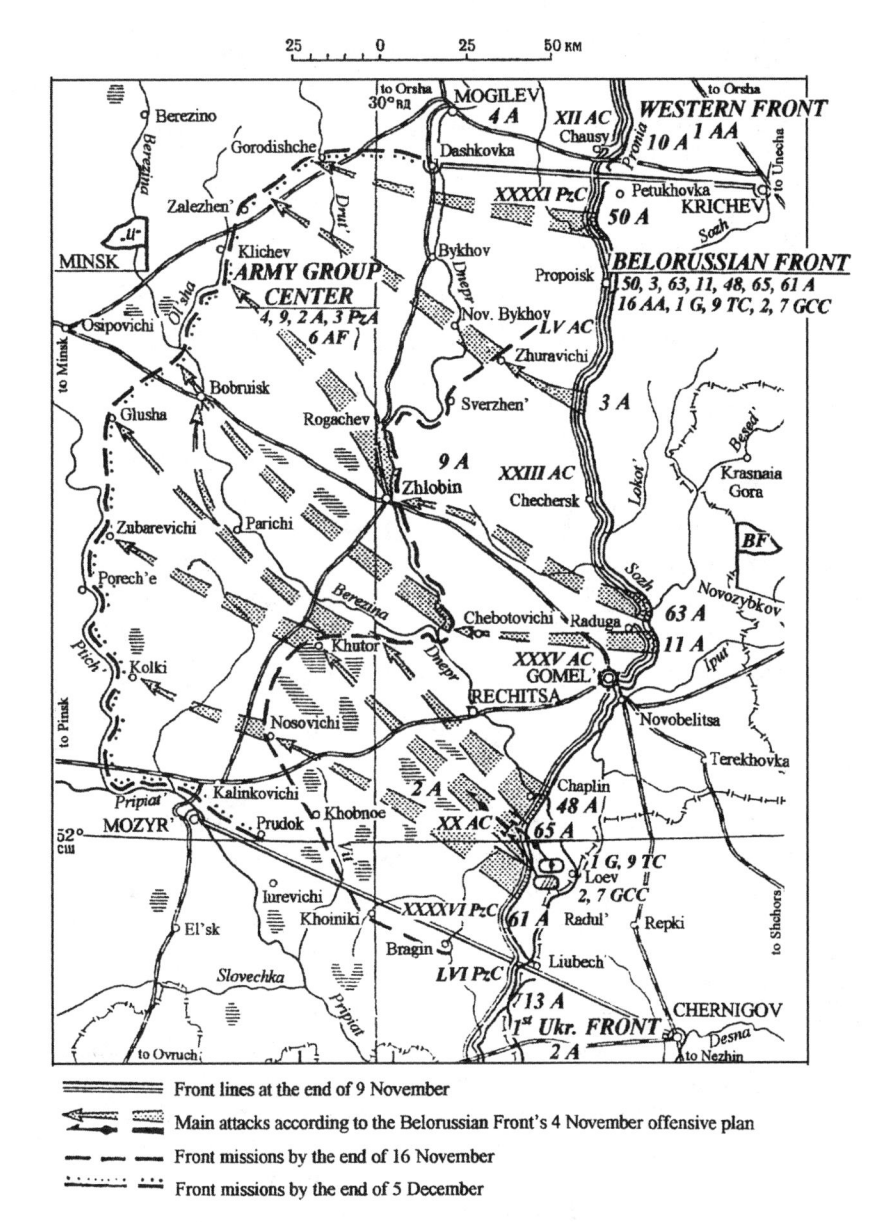

Map 7.1. The Belorussian Front's Plan for the Gomel'-Rechitsa Offensive Operation, November 1943

61st Army—50,049
63rd Army—60,587
65th Army—142,201
Front reserve units—27,488
The *front* has:
Horses—80,203
Rifles—258,127
PPSh, PPD—100,404
Light machine guns—14,271
Heavy machine guns—3,925
Antiaircraft machine guns—863
120mm mortars—1,590
82mm mortars—3,178
50mm mortars—1,146
122mm guns—31
122mm howitzers—814
57mm guns—106
76mm guns—2,658
45mm guns—1,917
Antitank rifles—10,111
Vehicles—17,558
Tanks—493
Armored cars—123[3]

Based on Army Group Center's strength reports, on 10 October 1943, the army group numbered 914,500 men, with 594 tanks, of which 216 were operational.[4] These figures included Third Panzer and Fourth, Ninth, and Second Armies. Of this number, about one-third (or 300,000) faced the Belorussian Front's more than 485,000 men. When fully concentrated, 11th, 63rd, 48th, 61st, and 65th Armies included more than 380,000 soldiers, which faced roughly 200,000 German troops, whereas 61st and 65th Armies' more than 195,000 soldiers faced about 50,000 German troops. Therefore, in terms of personnel, the Belorussian Front was superior to opposing German forces by a factor of slightly more than 2 to 1. Through concentration, this allowed Rokossovsky to achieve superiorities over opposing enemy forces in main attack sectors approaching 4 to 1 in manpower and even greater in armor (tanks and self-propelled guns) and artillery. In fact, the Belorussian Front's tank and self-propelled gun strength on 15 November (493) was more than double the number of tanks and assault guns operational in Army Group Center at the same time (185). The more than 300 tanks and self-propelled guns in Rokossovsky's main attack sectors were almost four times as many tanks and assault guns as were available to the *kampfgruppen* of 12th and 2nd Panzer Divisions (88 tanks and assault guns), defending at and west of Loev.[5]

Rokossovsky's offensive plan required the *front* to conduct a major regrouping of forces into the Dnepr River bridgehead west of Loev and Radul' and to concentrate a large assault force around Gomel' proper (see Map 7.2). In brief, this involved deploying General Fediuninsky's 11th Army into attack positions east of Gomel', moving one of 48th Army's rifle corps and several rifle division into the *front's* bridgehead south of Loev, and concentrating the *front's* four mobile corps in 65th Army's sector.

When the regrouping was complete, Rokossovsky had concentrated several powerful shock groups deployed from north of Gomel' southward to Radul' on the Dnepr River. On the *front's* extended left wing along the Sozh and Pronia Rivers, General Boldin's 50th Army occupied defensive positions in the 30-kilometer-wide sector along the Pronia River between Petukhovka and Propoisk. The 50th opposed XXXXI Panzer Corps, situated on German Ninth Army's left wing.[6] Boldin's mission was to defend until 22 November and then attack westward toward Bykhov on the Dnepr River. South of 50th Army, General Gorbatov concentrated his 3rd Army in the 45-kilometer-wide sector along the Sozh River between Propoisk and Zagor'e.[7] His army was to defend initially and then attack across the Sozh River on 22 November and advance to seize the Dnepr River line between Rogachev and Bykhov. The 3rd Army faced elements of German Ninth Army's LV Army Corps. South of 3rd Army, General Kolpakchi's 63rd Army turned its sector over to the newly arrived 11th Army and occupied positions in the 50-kilometer-wide sector along the Sozh River between Zagor'e and Raduga north of Gomel'.[8] Kolpakchi's army was to assault across the Sozh River north of Gomel' after 3rd Army's attacking forces reached the Dnepr River between Rogachev and Zhlobin. The 63rd Army faced elements of German Ninth Army's XXIII Army Corps.

East of Gomel' proper, General Fediuninsky's 11th Army was tasked with conducting the assault against Gomel' proper. Fediuninsky deployed his army with two rifle corps abreast in the 25-kilometer sector extending from the village of Raduga, north of Gomel', to the railroad junction at Novo-Belitsa, southeast of the city. The army's 53rd Rifle Corps was to deliver the army's main attack in the sector north and south of Vetka with 260th, 96th, and 323rd Rifle Divisions deployed from south to north (left to right) in first echelon, backed up by 273rd, 217th, and 197th Rifle Divisions in the army's second echelon. As this force was enveloping Gomel' from the north and northeast, 25th Rifle Corps' 4th and 273rd Rifle Divisions, with 96th Rifle Division in the corps' reserve, were to clear the German defenders from Gomel'. After capturing Gomel', 11th Army was to advance to Zhlobin on the Dnepr River. Fediuninsky's forces faced 134th and 299th Infantry Divisions of German Second Army's XXXV Army Corps.

General Romanenko's 48th Army had the twin missions of holding firmly to the Soviet bridgehead extending from Bobrovichi on the western bank of the Sozh River south of Gomel' to Chaplin on the Dnepr River and also

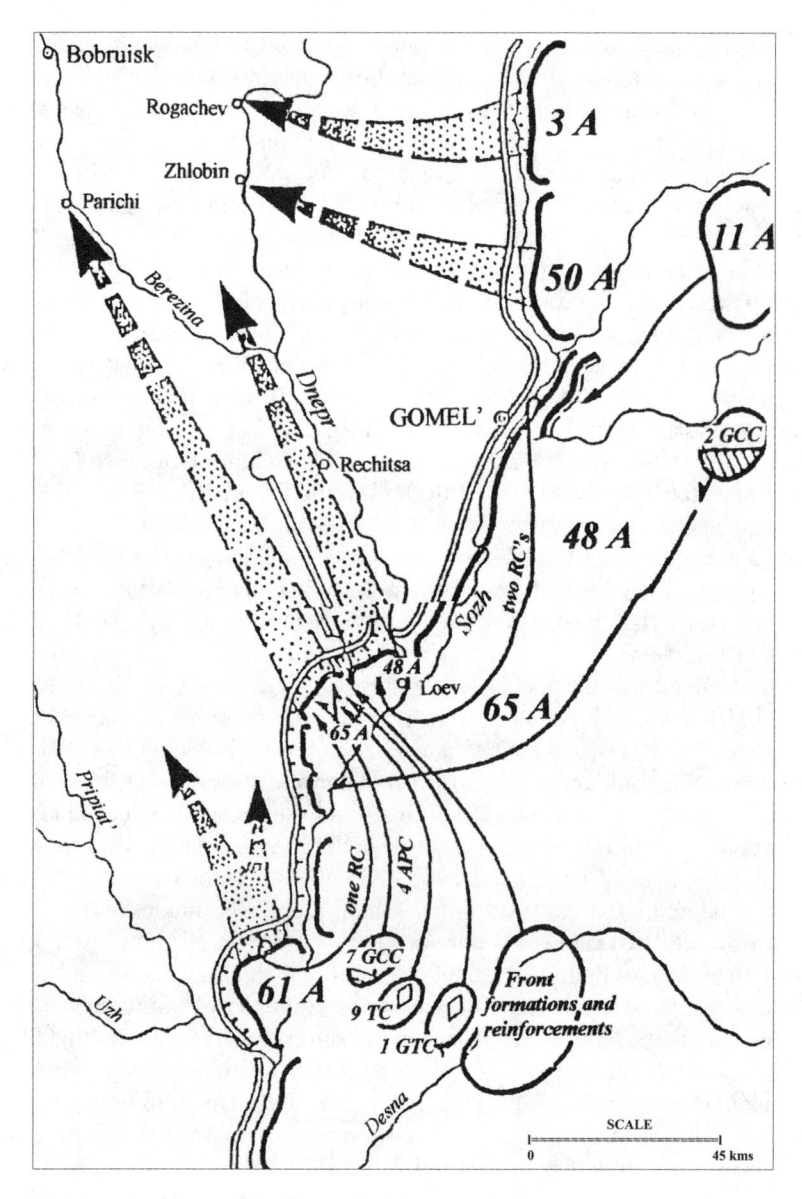

Map 7.2. The Belorussian Front's Regrouping of Forces for the Gomel'-Rechitsa Offensive Operation, 27 October–9 November 1943

reinforcing Rokossovsky's main attack out of the Loev bridgehead with two rifle corps. Romanenko deployed 102nd, 73rd, and 175th Rifle Divisions in the bridgehead between the Sozh and Dnepr Rivers and moved the remainder of his army southward into the Loev bridgehead. The 42nd Rifle Corps' 307th, 399th and 194th Rifle Divisions deployed in first-echelon assault positions in the 5-kilometer-wide sector between the village of Bushatin and the Dnepr River and were backed up by 170th and 137th Rifle Divisions in the corps' second echelon. Romanenko's three rifle divisions in the Sozh River bridgehead faced (and were outnumbered by) 292nd and 45th Infantry Divisions and KGr., 6th Infantry Division of Ninth Army's XXXV Army Corps. Soon Rokossovsky placed these rifle divisions under the control of 29th Rifle Corps headquarters, which he transferred from 61st Army. The 48th Army's 42nd Rifle Corps deployed opposite the left wing of KGr., 31st Infantry Division of Second Army's XX Army Corps.

General Batov's 65th Army occupied the place of honor in the center of the *front's* main attack sector. Batov deployed his army in single-echelon formation of rifle corps in the 13-kilometer-wide sector from Uborok to Bushatin, with 18th, 19th, and 27th Rifle Corps deployed from south to north (left to right). General Ivanov's 18th Rifle Corps deployed its shock group, consisting of 149th and 69th Rifle Divisions, supported by two tank brigades of General Bakharov's 9th Tank Corps (including the 23rd) in the Uborok and Lipniaki sector (5 kilometers), with orders to capture the German strongpoint at Volkoshanka and reach the Gancharov Podel-Nadvin road (5–6 kilometers deep).[9] The 193rd Rifle Division, the remainder of 9th Tank Corps, and General Kriukov's 2nd Guards Cavalry Corps were in second echelon with orders to exploit success. This mobile group, one of two in 65th Army's sector, which consisted of 9th Tank and 2nd Guards Cavalry Corps, was to exploit through the penetration, advance 50 kilometers west-northwestward to capture the regional center of Vasilevichi (50 kilometers to the west), and then swing southwest to envelop the cities of Mozyr' and Kalinkovichi from the north and west.[10] To protect 65th Army's left, 60th Rifle Division was deployed in the sector from Uborok to Borshchovka on the corps' left wing at the junction with 61st Army. Ivanov's rifle corps was opposed by 216th and 102nd Infantry Divisions (both now *kampfgruppen*) of German Second Army's XX Army Corps, which defended the Borshchovka and Uborok sector and *kampfgruppen* from 12th and 2nd Panzer Divisions, reinforcing and backing up German infantry in the Uborok and Lipniaki sector.

In 65th Army's center, Major General D. I. Samarsky's 19th Rifle Corps deployed in the sector from Lipniaki to just west of Bushatin (5 kilometers) on 18th Rifle Corps' right. The corps deployed its 162nd Rifle and 37th Guards Rifle Divisions from left to right in first echelon, backed up by 140th Rifle Division. The corps' immediate mission was to penetrate German defenses between Gancharov Podel and Budishche (5 kilometers deep) and facilitate the commitment of the mobile groups on the corps' left and right flanks. The 19th Rifle Corps attacked at the junction of German XX Army Corps' Kgr., 2nd Panzer Division's left wing and KGr., 31st Infantry Divisions' right wing.

Major General F. M. Cherokmanov's 27th Rifle Corps deployed for combat on 65th Army's right wing, with the corps' 354th Rifle Division and 115th Rifle Brigade in first echelon and 106th and 246th Rifle Divisions in second echelon. The corps' mission was

> to penetrate the enemy defense in the Bushatin region (a sector of 4 kilometers), destroy the opposing enemy in their strongpoints, and capture Hill 131.6 and the village of Prokisel' (at a depth of 6 kilometers). Subsequently, it was to attack in the direction of Demekhi Station on 65th Army's right wing, while protecting it [the flank] in cooperation with 48th Army, which was developing the attack along the western bank of the Dnepr River toward Rechitsa. The 37th Guards Rifle Division was attacking on the left.[11]

Rokossovsky's plan required his *front's* second mobile group, which consisted of Major General Panov's 1st Guards Tank Corps and Major General Konstantinov's 7th Guards Cavalry Corps, to begin their exploitation through 27th Rifle Corps' sector. The 7th Guards Cavalry Corps' history described its deployment and mission:

> Once again, 14th and 15th Guards Cavalry Divisions received an order on 9 November to deploy to the forested region south of Smelyi Farm and the forest west of the village of Voskhod and be prepared for operations toward Lipniaki and Volkoshanka.
>   The 7th Guards Cavalry Corps was to enter the penetration in 65th Army's sector following 1st Guards Tank Corps. Its mission was to attack along the Gancharov Podel, Budishche, and Korovatichi axis, cut the Korosten'-Rechitsa and Rechitsa-Kalinkovichi roads, and prevent the approach of enemy reserves from the south and southwest.[12]

Meanwhile, 1st Guards Tank Corps was to exploit northward to sever German communications routes into Rechitsa from the west and, subsequently, lead the army's advance toward Parichi and Bobruisk along with 7th Guards Cavalry Corps.

Batov later described the formation he employed for the commitment of the mobile forces:

> Two tank brigades from each tank corps entered the penetration in a wedge. The base of the wedge expanded as the force advanced. The divisions of the cavalry corps penetrated through the region cleared by the

tanks. The tank corps' third brigade entered the penetration following them [the cavalry], forming the rear section of the diamond-shape combat formation. The combat missions of the tank and cavalry were strictly limited. The *tankists* destroyed enemy combat weaponry, and the cavalry pursued the infantry. After the tanks and cavalry reached the operational depths, the rifle corps' divisions deployed in columns and engaged in combat only with the remains of the badly beaten enemy forces. They achieved a high offensive tempo. The tank corps advanced resolutely without fearing for their immediate and deep rear area.[13]

The second element of Rokossovsky's main shock group was General Belov's 61st Army, deployed in the 34-kilometer-wide sector extending from Borshchovka in the Loev bridgehead southward to Liubech' on the Dnepr River. Belov planned to launch his main attack with General Boreiko's 9th Guards Rifle Corps on the army's right wing, supported by General Khaliuzin's 89th Rifle Corps attacking on its left. When regrouped, 9th Guards Rifle Corps occupied the Borshchovka and Kuchaevka sector (10 kilometers) with 12th and 77th Guards Rifle Divisions and 68th Tank Brigade in first echelon and 76th Guards Rifle Division in second. Further south 89th Rifle Corps deployed in the Kuchaevka-Domamerki sector (6 kilometers) with its 15th and 55th Rifle Divisions in first echelon and 81st Rifle Division in second. The 356th Rifle Division defended 61st Army's extended left flank from Domamerki to Liubech'. In accordance with the *Stavka's* orders, Belov transferred 89th Rifle Corps' former 336th and 415th Rifle Divisions, along with their sectors south of Liubech', to the adjacent 13th Army (of 1st Ukrainian Front). Coincidentally, the *front* transferred the headquarters of 61st Army's 29th Rifle Corps northward to take control of 48th Army's three rifle divisions operating between the Sozh and Dnepr Rivers.

The main shock group of General Belov's 61st Army faced 137th and 7th Infantry Divisions of German Second Army's XXXXVI Panzer Corps. Further south, the army's 356th Rifle Division faced 251st Division Group of the same German corps' composite Corps Detachment E. Although Rokossovsky's forces were markedly numerically superior to their foes along the entire front, largely because of terrain considerations the *front* commander chose to deliver his main attack in the strongest German sector, defended by elements of three German infantry divisions, albeit organized into combat groups, as well as *kampfgruppen* from 12th and 2nd Panzer Divisions.

THE GOMEL'-RECHITSA OFFENSIVE (10–30 NOVEMBER 1943)

Rokossovsky's forces struck from the Loev bridgehead early on 10 November across a broad front of 38 kilometers extending from the village of Domamerki northward to the Dnepr River at Chaplin (see Maps 7.3 and 7.4). Within three days, the attacking forces had torn a 15-kilometer-wide and 8–12-kilometer-deep gap in the German defenses from west of Uborok northward to the Dnepr River north of Velin and were almost half of the way to Rechitsa. The 65th Army's 27th and 19th Rifle Corps, supported by lead brigades of 1st Guards Tank and 7th Guards Cavalry Corps, carved out the penetration on 10 and 11 November, and the two mobile corps lunged into the German's operational rear late on 12 November (see Map 7.5). The 1st Guards Tank Corps smashed through 12th Panzer Division's defenses and raced northward toward Rechitsa, while 7th Guards Cavalry Corps widened the breach to the west. The cavalry corps' 14th and 15th Cavalry Divisions captured the villages of Berezovka and Avrora just south of the Rechitsa-Khoiniki road, as well as Perevoloka south of the Rechitsa-Kalinkovichi road, all 20 kilometers south of Rechitsa, late on 12 November. At the same time, 16th Guards Cavalry Division, protecting the cavalry corps' right flank, encountered and defeated a small German infantry and armor force along the Rechitsa-Khoiniki road near Malodusha. After driving German forces from both roads, 16th Guards Cavalry Division seized Tishkovka, 15 kilometers west of Rechitsa, at midday on 15 November, and 14th and 15th Guards Divisions attacked and captured Korovatichi and Babichi, 15 kilometers northeast and east of Vasilevichi, thus severing all German communications between Rechitsa and Kalinkovichi once and for all (see Map 7.6). By this time, 7th Guards Cavalry Corps' three divisions had advanced up to 40 kilometers in five days and were nearing their first major objective, the key road junction at Vasilevichi.

After regrouping, the cavalry corps continued to advance westward the following day, capturing a bridgehead over the Vedrech' River against increasing resistance from the newly arrived German 4th Panzer Division. The 4th Panzer, which had been fighting to defend the Chernobyl' region under the control of Second Army's LVI Panzer Corps, had raced forward to help contain Soviet forces advancing on Rechitsa and Kalinkovichi. At the time, 4th Panzer fielded 14 tanks and 14 assault guns operational or in short-term repair and 144 APCs and would receive another six self-propelled infantry guns during the ensuing month.[14] On the evening of 16 November, the cavalry corps received an order "to capture Vasilevichi by the morning of 17 November and, simultaneously, be prepared to repel counterattacks from the direction of Novinki [6 kilometers north of Vasilovichi] and along the highway to Kalinkovichi."[15] The corps advanced westward late on 16 November but once again encountered 4th Panzer Division's forces manning defensive positions near Griady Farm (in the vicinity of Korovatichi, 17 kilometers east of Vasilevich). Together, 14th and 15th Guards Cavalry Divisions captured the farm and drove into the outskirts of Vasilevichi, where they ran into heavily fortified German defensive positions. The 7th Guards Cavalry Corps' history described the ensuing battle:

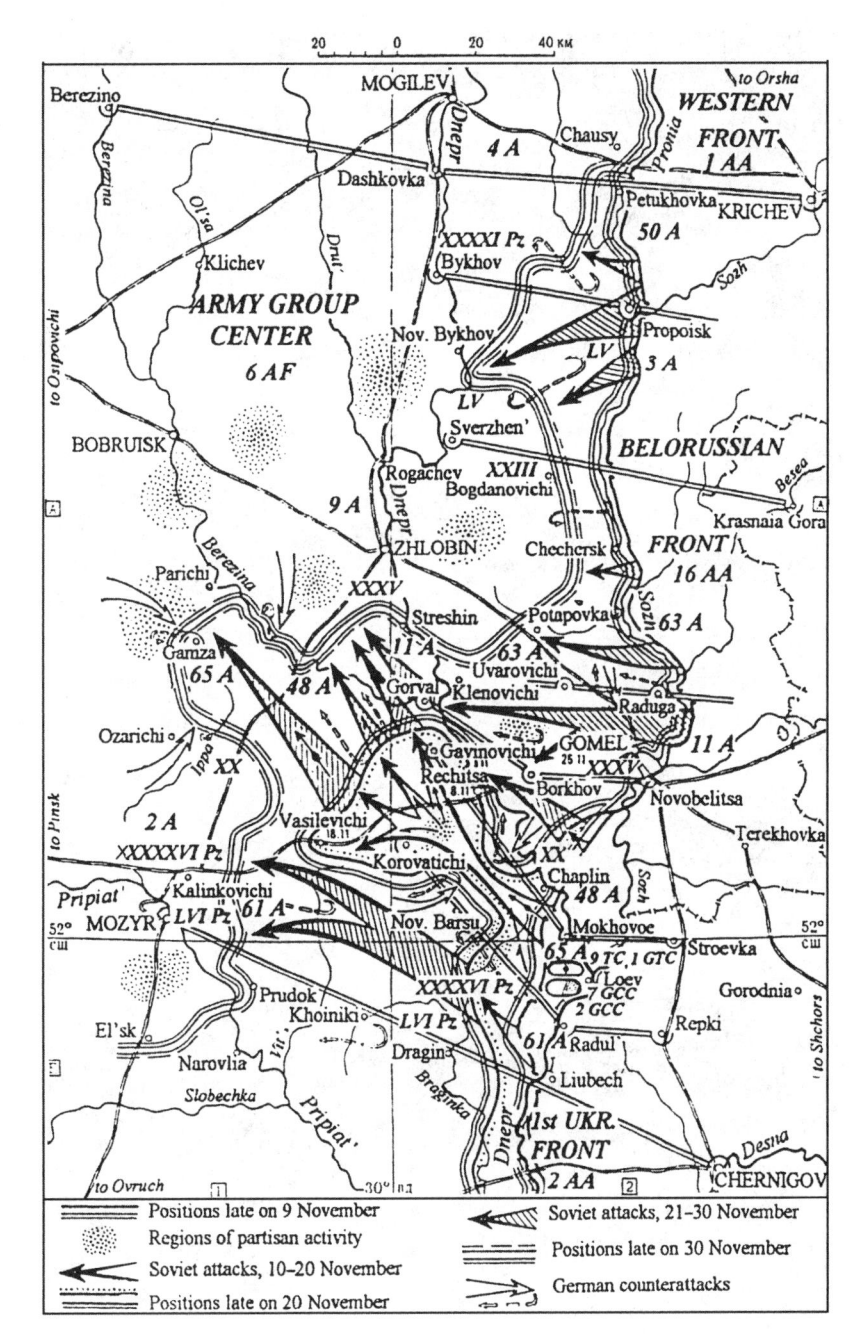

Map 7.3. The Belorussian Front's Gomel'-Rechitsa Offensive Operation, 10–30 November 1943

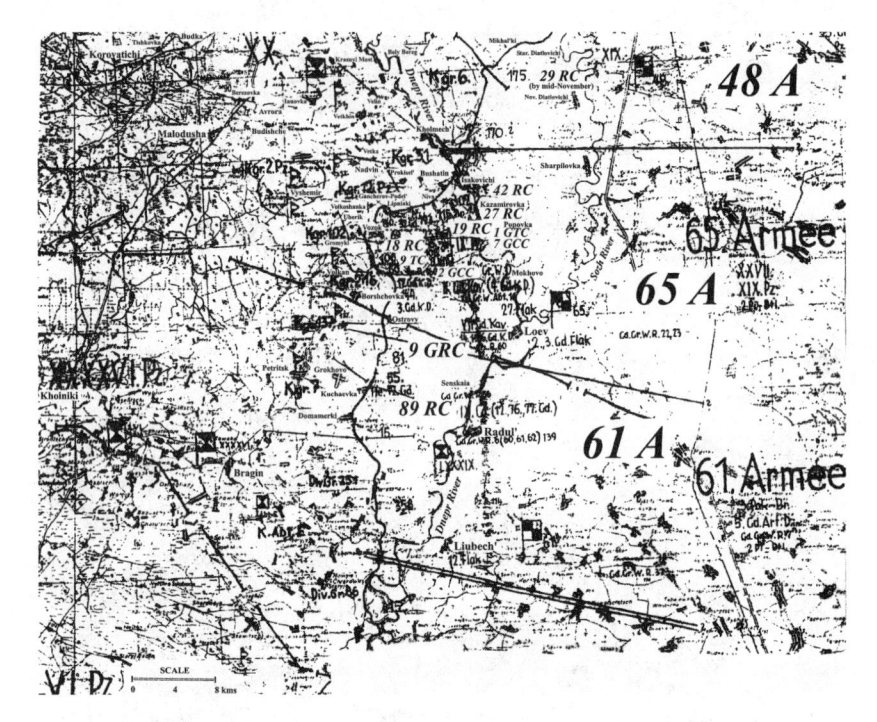

Map 7.4. Second Army's Situation on the Rechitsa Axis, 10 November 1943

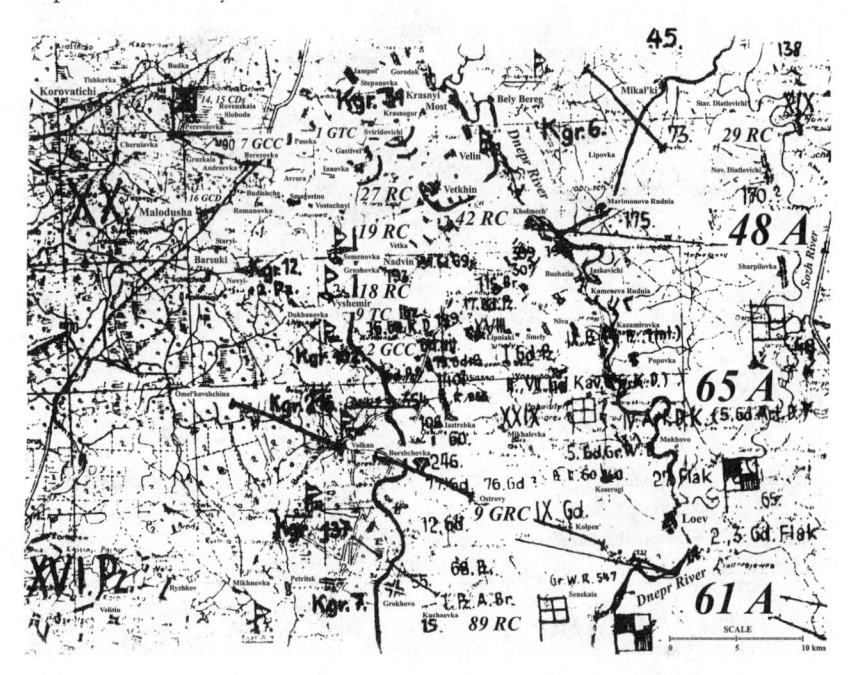

Map 7.5. Second Army's Situation on the Rechitsa Axis, 13 November 1943

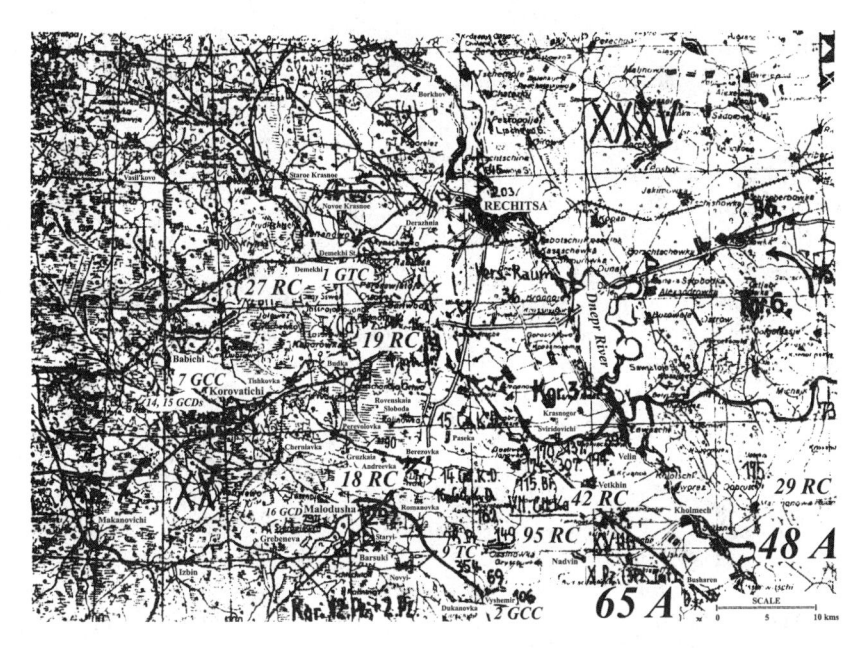

Gomel'-Rechitsa and Novyi Bykhov–Propoisk Offensives 185

Map 7.6. Second Army's Situation on the Rechitsa Axis, 16 November 1943

Combat raged for possession of Vasilevichi on 17 and 18 November. The units of 15th Guards Cavalry Division, overcoming the resistance of 389th Security Battalion and 4th Panzer Division's 47th Panzer Grenadier Regiment, who were supported by fire from artillery and an armored train, were able to capture this town only by morning on 19 November. [Thus], they inflicted a defeat on the enemy and forced him to withdraw toward Nakhov.

The 15th Guards Cavalry Division's units seized several warehouses, a great quantity of equipment and ammunition, and destroyed up to 300 enemy soldiers and officers during the capture of Vasilevichi. . . .

Having captured the Korovatichi and Vasilevichi regions, 7th Guards Cavalry Corps' formations cut the Rechitsa-Kalinkovichi communication route, depriving the enemy of the shortest route for transferring reserves from Gomel' and, by doing so, assisted 48th and 65th Armies in the liberation of Rechitsa.[16]

The 16th Guards Cavalry Division and 15th Guards Division's 55th Guards Cavalry Regiment widened the scope of their operations on 19 November by striking southward and capturing the village of Kobylevo, 16 kilometers southeast of Vasilevichi. Joined by the remainder of 15th Guards, the two divisions seized Zashcheb'e, 8 kilometers south of Vasilevichi and just 37 kilometers east of Kalinkovichi. There, it commenced a two-day battle with 4th Panzer Division, which was again trying to block their path.

Meanwhile, two brigades of 1st Guards Tank Corps, with 19th Rifle Corps' 37th Guards, 162nd, and 140th Rifle Divisions in their wake, raced northward toward Rechitsa. Beginning on 14 November, they attacked the city from the northwest and on the following day began heavy street fighting in the city's western outskirts. The day before, General Panov's remaining tank brigades and 27th Rifle Corps captured Demekhi, 12 kilometers west of Rechitsa, severing German rail communications with the city from the west. The 354th Rifle Division and the corps' other formations wheeled northwestward in an attempt to reach the Dnepr River south of Parichi, thereby enveloping Rechitsa from the north. As 1st Guards Tank Corps sped forward, German Second Army's XXXV Army Corps withdrew its forces northward along the banks of the Dnepr River toward Rechitsa, pursued by the divisions of 48th Army's 29th and 42nd Rifle Corps. The Germans reinforced their defenses at Rechitsa, held by a portion of 203rd Security Division, with elements of 45th and 36th Infantry Divisions, which they had withdrawn from forward defensive positions at and north of Gomel'.

Without halting, 19th and 27th Rifle Corps continued their march northward past Rechitsa toward Parichi, on the western bank of the Berezina River, 80 kilometers to the north. The 19th Rifle Corps' 37th Guards Rifle Division reached the Berezina River near Gorval', 20 kilometers north of Rechitsa, flanked by 140th and 162nd Rifle Divisions, early on 20 November. By nightfall, 37th Guards had seized a small bridgehead on the river's eastern bank. At the same time, 27th Rifle Corps' 354th Rifle Division was approaching Vasil'kov, 25 kilometers northwest of the city, with 106th and 246th Rifle Divisions and 115th Rifle Brigade on its flanks and in its wake. Shortly before, Batov had withdrawn Bakharov's 9th Tank Corps from combat for rest and refitting and halted 1st Guards Tank Corps for regrouping.[17] However, within days, 9th Tank Corps was prepared to resume its attacks, this time in support of 61st Army, fighting to the south. Meanwhile, to the east, 48th Army's 42nd Rifle Corps closed in on German defenses west and southwest of Rechitsa between 15 and 20 November and, in heavy fighting, drove the defending 31st and 45th Infantry Divisions of Second Army's XXXV Army Corps back into the city. The Germans withdrew most of their forces from Rechitsa to the eastern banks of the Dnepr River on 20 November, pressured by 42nd Rifle Corps and 1st Guards Tank Corps' forces, operating north of the city.

The Soviet capture of Rechitsa and the bridgehead over the Berezina River at Gorval' imperiled the flanks and rear of the German XXXV Army Corps' forces, still defending Gomel', as well as the Ninth Army's forces, still defending northward along the Sozh River. It appeared, in fact, that Rokossovsky's bold thrust had unhinged all of Army Group Center's defenses in southern Belorussia. In truth, it had. The two outstanding questions were, "How deep could Rokossovsky's forces advance before the German stopped them?" and "Could Ninth and Second Armies muster sufficient forces to halt or cut off the attacking Soviet forces?"

To the west, after smashing halfway through the Germans' tactical defenses on 10 November, the divisions of 65th Army's 18th Rifle Corps completed their penetration and began their pursuit on the 11th, spearheaded by 9th Tank and 2nd Guards Cavalry Corps. The 69th and 149th Rifle Divisions captured their initial objectives, Volkoshanka and Prokhod, by day's end on 10 November, and, after repelling several German counterattacks, completed penetrating 12th Panzer Divisions tactical defenses the next day. After battling against stiff enemy resistance for almost two days on the outskirts of Nadvin, 6 kilometers deep into the German defenses, during which one of the division's regimental commanders was killed, 69th Rifle Division bypassed the village to the west. Joined by 193rd Rifle Division committed from second echelon and advancing abreast, 149th, 69th, and 193rd Rifle Divisions swept northward in the wake of 7th Guards Cavalry Corps, capturing Romanovka, Andreevka, Gruzkaia, and Perevoloka north and south of the Rechitsa-Khoiniki road and 20–23 kilometers south of Rechitsa by the evening of 14 November from elements of XX Army Corps' 292nd Infantry Division, hastily regrouped westward from XXXV Army Corps in an attempt to maintain a continuous defense line in the region southwest of Rechitsa. Wheeling northwestward, 193rd Rifle Division continued pursuing the Germans, capturing Tishkovka and Vasilevichi, halfway between Rechitsa and Kalinkovichi and deep in the rear of the Second Army's now wide-open left flank. At the same time, 69th and 149th Rifle Divisions began a five-day pitched battle against stubbornly resisting German forces from 292nd Infantry and 12th Panzer Divisions, dug in around the town of Malodusha, 25 kilometers south-southwest of Rechitsa.

The German strongpoint at Malodusha marked the extreme left flank of German Second Army's beleaguered XXXXVI Panzer Corps and, in fact, of the Second Army as a whole. Northward beyond that flank and all the way to German defenses west of Rechitsa was nothing but a yawning 20-kilometer-wide gap filled with exploiting Soviet forces. In a premature and futile attempt to close this gap, the day before, General Weiss, the commander of Second Army, had ordered 4th Panzer Division, just returned from fighting in the Chernobyl' region, to advance eastward along the Kalinkovichi-Rechitsa road. The forward elements of that division encountered the lead elements of General Konstantinov's 7th Guards Cavalry Corps west of Korovatichi and Babichi late on 15 November, but the Red Army cavalry brought 4th Panzer Division's advance to a dead halt. At the time, 193rd Rifle Division of General Ivanov's 18th Rifle Corps and all of 7th Guards Cavalry Corps had already bypassed 4th Panzer Division's left flank to the north.

Sensing that the momentum of his advance might be ebbing and anxious to sustain his exploitation, late on 15 November, General Batov ordered newly arrived 95th Rifle Corps (44th Guards and 172nd Rifle Divisions), commanded by Major General V. A. Belonogov, forward to relieve 18th Rifle Corps. His intention was to employ 18th Rifle Corps to envelop the German Second Army's left flank by an attack on Kalinkovichi from the north via Korovatichi, Babichi, and Vasilevichi, that is, along the path carved by 193rd Rifle Division. In the meantime, however, 18th Rifle Corps' three remaining divisions (69th, 149th, and 60th) struggled with the German defenders of Malodusha until 22 November. While the fighting for Malodusha continued, the lead elements of 95th Rifle Corps' 172nd Rifle Division lunged into combat east of Korovatichi on 17 November. Together with troopers of 7th Guards Cavalry Corps, it recaptured the town on 19 November (the town had fallen to a counterattack by 4th and 5th Panzer Divisions the day before).[18] The 5th Panzer, also just transferred northward from the Chernobyl' region, went into action at Malodusha on 18 November with its 13th and 14th Panzer Grenadier Regiments, equipped with roughly 15–20 tanks, 12 assault guns, and about 160 APCs.[19]

While Batov's shock groups and 48th Army's 42nd Rifle Corps were recording spectacular progress in their drive toward Rechitsa and Parichi, Batov's left wing division and the two attacking corps of Belov's 61st Army were encountering stiffer German resistance. The 60th Rifle Division on 18th Rifle Corps' left wing and the divisions of 61st Army's 9th Guards and 89th Rifle Corps attacked German defenses north and south of Borshchovka on 10 November. They were supported by elements of 9th Tank and 2nd Cavalry Corps. Extremely heavy fighting raged for three days as the German defenses held off repeated Soviet infantry and tank assaults. The entire front from Zaskor'e southward through Volkan to Gorodok blazed as German 216th, 137th and 7th Infantry Divisions fought for their very lives. Finally, on 13 November 9th Guards Rifle Corps' 12th, 76th, and 77th Guards Rifle Divisions forced the defenders to withdraw to new defensive lines deep in the Bragin swamps, roughly 20 kilometers to the west (see Map 7.7). By 20 November, German XX Army and XXXXVI Panzer Corps' 292nd, 2nd and 12th Panzer, 102nd, 137th, and 7th Infantry Divisions, now reinforced by one regiment of 216th Infantry at the junction of the two corps, were defending along a line extending southward from Malodusha through Plav'e to Novyi Put'. However, the German defenses were sagging dangerously under the constant pressure of 61st Army's 9th Guards and 89th Rifle Corps.

The German defense lines had been irreparably breached along the Rechitsa axis, Soviet forces had advanced up to 70 kilometers deep into the German rear, and the German defenses were in jeopardy of total collapse. Earl Ziemke recorded the results of the first ten days of fighting from the German perspective:

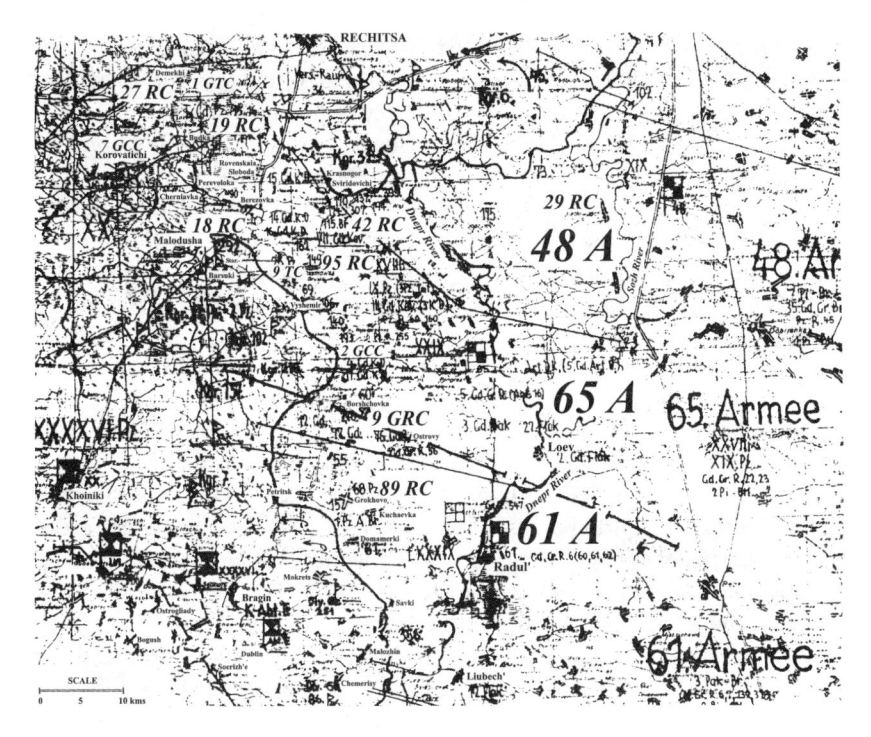

Map 7.7. Second Army's Situation, 16 November 1943

On the 10th Rokossovskiy tried for the third time to break out of the Loev bridgehead. The German line held the first day but broke on the second... On 12 November Weiss [Second Army] asked permission to take troops off his south flank to meet the greater danger in the center, but the OKH again ordered him to hold Chernobyl' [along the Pripiat' River to the south]. The next day, when *Belorussian Front's* thrust carried to the west of Rechitsa, he proposed giving up Gomel' and taking the army north flank back to the Dnepr to gain troops. This Hitler forbade. By the 14th Rokossovsky had spearheads turning east toward the Dnepr from northwest of Rechitsa.

After the gap in the Second Army center had opened to eight miles, Hitler told Model [Ninth Army] to supply one division and Weiss another for a counterattack to close it. Adding a third division [the 4th Panzer], one of the two panzer divisions from his south flank, Weiss opened the counterattack on 18 November, but when the division failed to make headway in two days, the attack had to be cancelled. Vatutin's forces [1st Ukrainian Front] in the meantime had taken Chernobyl', and Rokossovskiy's had turned west behind Rechitsa toward Kalinkovichi, the railroad junction controlling all of the Second Army supply lines.

On 20 November Weiss shifted two of the divisions that had taken part in the counterattack west, to screen Kalinkovichi, and transferred control of his sector north of the Berezina River and east of the Dnepr, including Gomel', to Ninth Army. Thereafter, Second Army's paramount concern was to establish a defensible front forward of the Pripiat' Marshes.... On the night of the 19th [Hitler] commanded Weiss to keep the part of his front that had not been broken through where it was until further orders. That left the army in the peculiar, though by then no longer unusual, position of having its main force tied down forty miles forward of the crucial zone of the battle.

The next morning, with Busch's permission, Weiss called Zeitzler [at Fuehrer headquarters]. Soviet tanks and cavalry with strong infantry support, he reported, were within nineteen miles of Kalinkovichi. If they took the town, the army would be out of motor fuel in two days and out of ammunition in four. Accordingly, he added, the same effect could be accomplished by cutting the two railroads. That could be done with cavalry alone, which in the wooded and swampy terrain was far more maneuverable than the defending German armor. Even if the two panzer divisions managed to stop the advance on Kalinkovichi, it would only be a matter of time until the Russians, bypassing the town to the north, forced them to extend until the whole line was hopelessly weakened. Therefore, the entire front had to be taken back, and the decision had to come soon because if the withdrawal was executed in haste most of the heavy vehicles would be left stuck in the swamps. Zeitzler replied that he had tried the night before to talk Hitler into giving Second Army freedom of movement and failed. He would try again but at the moment could promise nothing. Shortly before midnight the OKH operations chief called the Army Group Center headquarters to report that Hitler had again refused to permit any withdrawal.[20]

The date, 22 November, was decisive both for the German Second and Ninth Armies and for Rokossovsky's offensive. That day, while Batov's forces continued to expand their operations toward Kalinkovichi and Parichi in the deep German rear, Rokossovsky's forces struck three fresh blows. The first, delivered by General Fediuninsky's 11th Army, had actually begun on 12 November in coordination with Rokossovsky's main attack from the Loev bridgehead. After days of near constant but desultory combat, on 22 November 11th Army finally began its decisive assault on the city's defenses. Second, and at the same time, General Gorbatov's 3rd Army struck across the Sozh River to the north. Third, General Belov's 61st Army launched its 9th Guards Rifle Corps on an attack that shattered the German defensive front south of Malodusha. Once again Ziemke described the nature and effects of the three assaults:

The next day [22 November] the Russians tore through Second Army north of Udalevka [at Malodusha] and started a sweep to the southwest that threatened to envelop the army's right flank. On the afternoon of 22 November Hitler finally accepted the inevitable and allowed Weiss to take his front back—but no farther than a line he had plotted in detail running east of Kalinkovichi and the railroad north of the town. The army diary noted that had the order been given a week earlier it could have been executed smoothly and would have prevented sizable losses. That night Weiss reported to Army Group that the line Hitler had laid out would be difficult "to reach, occupy, or hold." It traversed a swampy forest with thick undergrowth, an old and established partisan haunt. He asked for freedom within the limits of his mission—to establish a front east of the Pripiat' Marshes—to operate without reference to a specific line.

In the meantime, Rokossovsky had readied an unpleasant surprise. Early on 22 November, after a quick regrouping, he launched a thrust into the Ninth Army center south of Propoysk. It dealt Ninth Army a sudden, staggering blow. The next day he pushed a strong spearhead into the gap between the Second and Ninth Armies south of the Beresina and cut the railroad line that ran north from Kalinkovichi.

The Ninth Army front around Gomel' had by then become a great, sagging, tactically useless bulge. As a railhead the city had lost its value ten days before when the Russians cut the railroad west of Rechitsa. On 23 November Hitler allowed Model to begin taking out the troops, but he hesitated another twenty-four hours before signing the evacuation order because he was worried about the "echo" the loss of Gomel' would create. Reluctant as he was to give ground under any circumstances, he had lately become even more reluctant when the loss of territory also involved the loss of a city large enough to be noticed in the world press and set off a celebration in Moscow.

Nikolaus

On 25 November Busch ordered Ninth Army to seal off the bridgehead at Propoysk and the Ninth and Second Armies to counterattack into the gap between their flanks, close it, and regain control of the railroad. The first order could not be executed for the lack of troops. The Russians had already torn open a 50-mile stretch of the PANTHER position and gone twenty miles west. The most Ninth Army could do was try to exert a slight braking action. The armies intended to execute the second order on 30 November, but in the next few days the Russians advanced to the northwest so rapidly and in such strength that neither army could spare troops for the counterattack. The OKH promised the 16th Panzer Division from Italy, and, since that one division would not be enough, Busch proposed taking the Ninth Army center back to the Dnepr to gain two more divisions. Hitler resisted until the 30th. By then, Rokossovsky's troops were on the Dnepr west of Propoysk and had smashed the last remnants of the PANTHER position farther south.

At the end of the month Second Army had set up a new front east of Kalinkovichi, albeit some miles west of the line Hitler had demanded.[21]

We can now flesh out Ziemke's skeletal account of the critical action that took place between 20 and 30 November by using both German archival materials and fragmentary Soviet open-source materials. Because Soviet historians have covered 3rd and 50th Armies' operations in considerable detail, this chapter will only briefly summarize the operation.

Rokossovsky's plan for the Gomel'-Rechitsa operation required General Fediuninsky's 11th Army to defeat German forces defending Gomel' and advance to the Dnepr River. A history of the army's 197th Rifle Division, a formation manned primarily by Tartars, spelled out the army's mission, stating:

> By decision of the army's military council, the army was to make its main attack on its right flank. It entrusted 53rd Rifle Corps with that mission. The corps' forces were to smash the defending enemy in their strongpoints, reach the Gomel'-Zhlobin highway and railroad line, and, by doing so, cut the enemy withdrawal routes to the northwest. Then, linking up with 25th Rifle Corps, [it was to] encircle the city and destroy the enemy's Gomel' grouping.[22]

On 12 November General Fediuninsky's 11th Army struck German defenses around Gomel', manned by XXXV Army Corps' 134th and 299th Infantry Divisions (see Map 7.8). The 323rd, 96th, and 260th Rifle Divisions attacked German strongpoints between Raduga and Kirpichni Factories but encountered extremely stiff resistance from well-dug-in German troops. Especially heavy fighting took place in the center of the army's main attack sector, where 96th Rifle Division attacked the strongpoints at Khal'ch and Hill 141.1 from a small bridgehead on the western bank of the Sozh River.

While the guns of 22nd Artillery Division pounded German defenses, the division's lead regiments gained a small lodgment in Khal'ch and on the slopes of the hill in the face of repeated German counterattacks. Heavy fighting went on for three days, but the division was unable to dent the German defenses. Khal'ch finally fell late on 15 November after 217th Rifle Division forced its way across the river on 96th Division's left flank. The capture of Khal'ch eased the task of the army's remaining divisions, and Fediuninsky ordered a general assault along the entire front.

The new assault began on 16 November after a ten-minute artillery raid, but it too encountered fierce resistance. The 96th Rifle Division finally fought its way to the outskirts of Raduga, but the neighboring 323rd and 260th Divisions failed to keep pace. By 17 November both 96th and 323rd

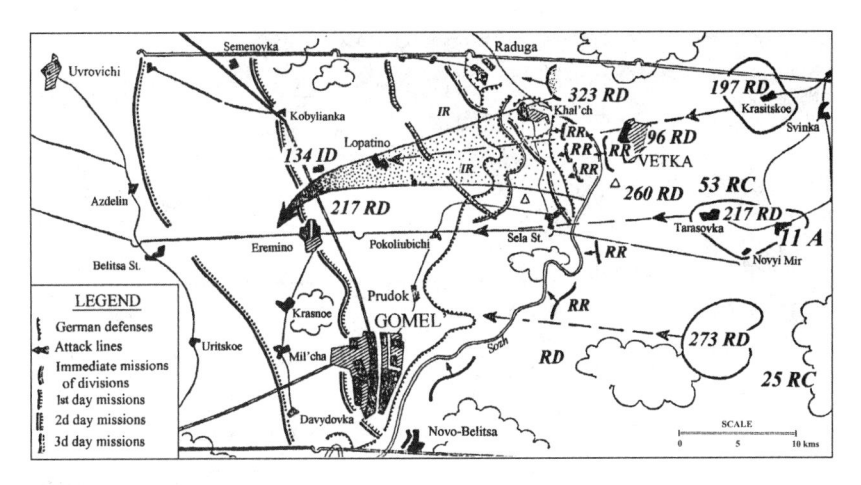

Map 7.8. 11th Army's Plan for the Liberation of Gomel', 12 November 1943

Divisions concentrated on seizing Raduga, while the 217th headed straight for the eastern defenses of Gomel'. The ensuing sustained fight lasted until 22 November as the divisions painfully inched their way forward against unrelenting and effective resistance. As the 96th and 323rd Rifle Divisions closed in on Gomel' from the north, 217th Division captured Pokoliubichi, 8 kilometers northeast of the city's center. However, German resistance finally began flagging on 23 and 24 November, primarily because of the Soviet successes to the north and south. Threatened by the fall of Rechitsa to Batov's forces and a new advance by 3rd Army across the Sozh River, on 24 November German Ninth Army decided to withdraw its forces from the city and begin a retrograde operation back to the Dnepr River.

Although merely a sideshow to the more dramatic fighting to the north and south, the assault by Fediuninsky's 11th Army on Gomel' was a bloody and often frustrating interlude. Gomel' fell but almost in spite of the army's efforts.

In terms of the German Second Army's fate, the attack by Belov's 61st Army on 22 November had a far more telling effect than the fighting around Gomel'. Early that day 61st Army's 9th Guards Rifle Corps attacked westward from Rudnaia Buritskaia with its 77th, 12th, and 76th Guards Rifle Divisions formed in dense formation, supported by 68th Tank Brigade and 9th Tank and 2nd Cavalry Corps (see Map 7.9). The assault unhinged the defenses of the German XXXXVI Panzer Corps' 216th and 102nd Infantry Divisions and opened an immense gap in the German defenses. Lead elements of the Soviet force reached Dubrovitsa on the Rechitsa-Khoiniki road by day's end, splitting the defending German force into two segments. At the same time, 65th Army's 18th Rifle Corps (69th, 149th, and 60th Rifle Divisions) smashed

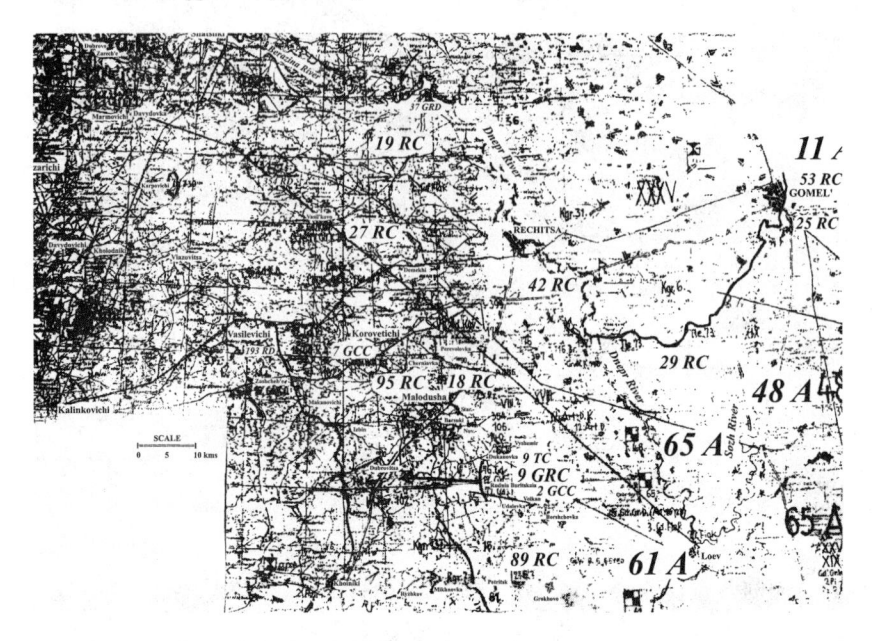

Map 7.9. Second Army's Situation, 22 November 1943

German defenses around Malodusha, almost encircling the German 292nd and 2nd Panzer Divisions and a single supporting regiment of 216th Infantry Division. To the north, on 7th Guards Cavalry Corps' left flank, 18th Rifle Corps' 193rd Rifle Division raced southwestward toward Vasilevichi, while the newly arrived 95th Rifle Corps' 172nd and 44th Guards Rifle Divisions swept into the rear of the Germans defending Malodusha.

The shock of the Soviet attack literally shattered the defenses of XX Army and XXXXVI Panzer Corps east of Kalinkovichi, leaving German Second Army with no choice but to order its shattered forces to withdraw westward to more defensible lines. The ensuing withdrawal lasted six days and involved repeated assaults by Soviet forces against the withdrawing Germans (see Maps 7.10 and 7.11). The 61st Army's 9th Guards and 89th Rifle Corps and the supporting 9th Tank and 2nd Guards Cavalry Corps made the most spectacular progress during that period. Early in the drive, Rokossovsky also transferred 7th Guards Cavalry Corps from the Vasilevichi region to participate in 61st Army's assault. The 9th Guards Rifle Corps' 76th, 12th, and 77th Guards Rifle Divisions and 7th and 2nd Guards Cavalry Corps swung southward and then westward through the inhospitable terrain of the Sholb Swamp, bypassing Vasilevichi to the south and capturing Dubrovitsa, Velikii Bor, and Rudenka, the latter two villages only 45 kilometers east of Mozyr'. By doing so, the force drove a broad wedge between German 292nd Infantry and the combat groups of 2nd and 12th Panzer Divisions to the north and

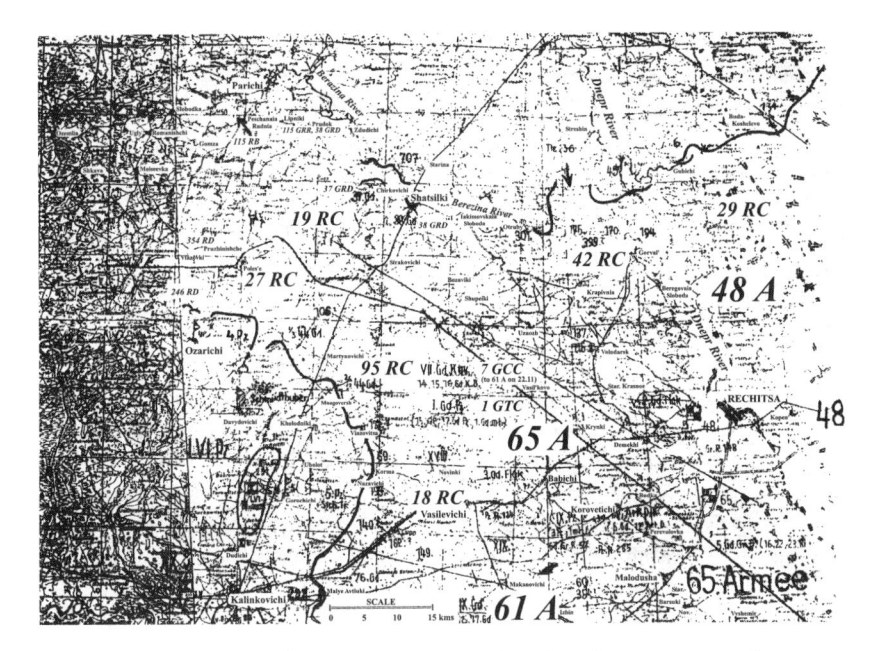

Map 7.10. Second Army's Situation along the Parichi-Bobruisk Axis, 28 November 1943

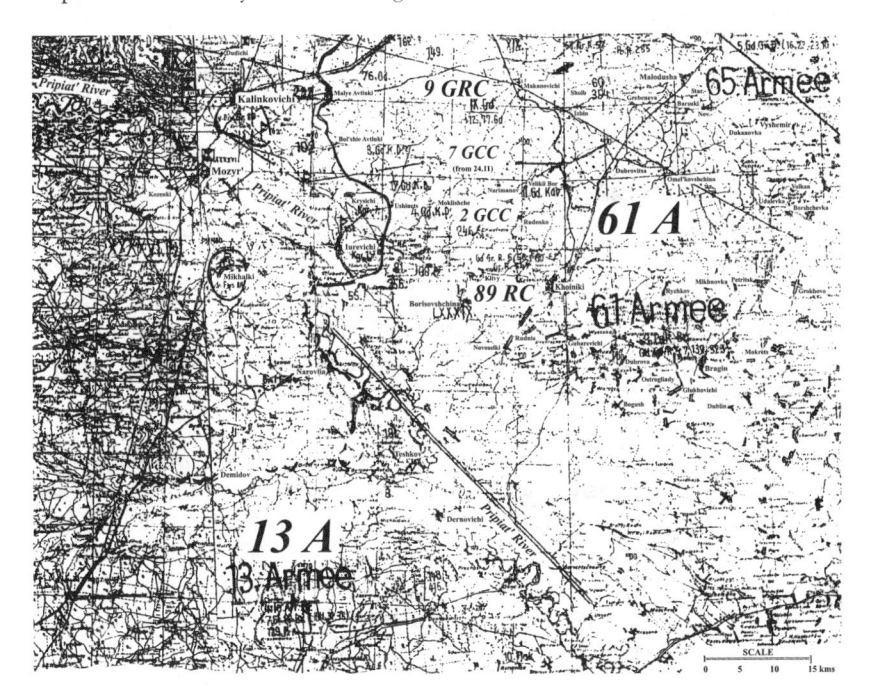

Map 7.11. Second Army's Situation along the Kalinkovichi Axis, 28 November 1943

102nd, 137th , and 7th Infantry Divisions to the south. The commander of German Second Army responded by ordering the grenadier regiments and few supporting tanks of 5th Panzer Division and the small combat group from 4th Panzer Division to shore up its defenses east of Kalinkovichi. These forces arrived just in time to save the defense from total collapse.

The 9th Guards Rifle and 2nd and 7th Guards Cavalry Corps' advance posed the most serious threat to the coherence of the Germans' defenses. The 2nd Guards Cavalry's history recorded its role in Rokossovsky's dramatic drive on Kalinkovichi:

> The corps commander [General Kriukov] ordered 17th Guards Cavalry Division to reach the Iurevichi region [on the northern bank of the Pripiat' River 20 kilometers southeast of Mozyr'] and cut the enemy withdrawal routes by marching through the forested mass in the general direction of Velikii Bor, Moklishche, and Uzhinets. The 3rd Guards Cavalry Division's regiments advanced on the right, and 4th Guards Cavalry Division, cooperating with 61st Army's forces, captured Khoiniki [50 kilometers southeast of Mozyr'] and developed the offensive on Iurevichi from the east.
>
> Dug in to heavily wooded defiles in the forested swamps, the enemy tried to halt the Soviet offensive at the important railroad center of Kalinkovichi.
>
> The division's advanced guard approached Moklishche [33 kilometers east of Mozyr'] on the evening of 23 November. Here the forest road exited from the swamp and the high road to the crossings over the Pripiat' River began.
>
> Units of German 7th Infantry Division occupied Uzhinets, Moklishche, Narimanov, and Korenevka, blocking the cavalry's exit from the forest.
>
> The first unit to reach the high road was 59th Guards Cavalry Regiment's fourth squadron [which attacked the German defenses]. . . .
>
> Fierce fighting raged for possession of Moklishche. . . . However, soon after, enemy reinforcements began arriving from nearby villages. The enemy went over to the attack, supported by the fires of three artillery and mortar batteries.
>
> Suffering losses, 61st Guards Cavalry Regiment withdrew from Moklishche and dug into a grove northeast of the village. Having repelled two attacks, the regiment launched an attack together with 59th Guards Cavalry Regiment at 1630 hours, but the attack faltered in the face of heavy enemy fire. A second attack also failed. Only under the pressure of a third attack by all three regiments did the enemy withdraw to a new defensive position. . . .
>
> The division advanced forward, but [again] encountered heavy enemy resistance along the Iurevichi-Bol'shie Avtiuki line.[23]

Army General K. K. Rokossovsky, commander in chief, Central (Belorussian and 1st Belorussian) Front, October 1943–February 1944

Lieutenant General I. V. Boldin, commander, 50th Army, November 1941–February 1945

Lieutenant General A. V. Gorbatov, commander, 3rd Army, June 1943– May 1945

Lieutenant General V. Ia. Kolpakchi, commander, 63rd Army, May 1943– February 1944

Lieutenant General P. L. Romanenko, commander, 48th Army, February 1943– December 1944

Lieutenant General P. I. Batov, commander, 65th Army, October 1942–May 1945

Lieutenant General P. A. Belov, commander, 61st Army, June 1942–May 1945

Major General of Tank Forces M. F. Panov, commander, 1st Guards Tank Corps, April 1943–May 1945

Major General of Tank Forces
B. S. Bakharov, commander, 9th Tank
Corps, September 1943–July 1944

Lieutenant General V. V. Kriukov,
commander, 2nd Guards Cavalry Corps,
March 1942–May 1945—purged and
imprisoned in 1952 but rehabilitated
in 1953

Major General M. P. Konstantinov,
commander, 7th Guards Cavalry Corps,
October 1943–May 1945

Despite spotty German resistance, the combined forces of 9th Guards Rifle Corps' 76th, 12th, and 77th Guards Rifle Division's and 7th Guards Cavalry Corps finally reached the villages of Malye Avtiuki and Bol'shie Avtiuki, only 12 kilometers east of Kalinkovichi, on 28 November. Here, their offensive halted in front of defensive positions manned by XX Army Corps' 292nd and 102nd Infantry Divisions and XXXXVI Panzer Corps' 7th, and 137th Infantry Divisions, backed up by a division group from 86th Infantry Division. To the south, 61st Army's 89th Rifle Corps (15th, 55th, and 81st Rifle Divisions and 68th Tank Brigade), supported by 2nd Guards Cavalry Corps, managed to drive another wedge into German defenses on the approaches to Iurevichi on the Pripiat' River but was unable to exploit its success. By 30 November, after withdrawing from Iurichi, XX Army and XXXXVI Panzer Corps occupied relatively contiguous defenses east of Kalinkovichi with its right flank anchored on the banks of the Pripiat'.

Meanwhile to the north, 65th Army's 18th and 95th Rifle Corps, now supported by elements of 1st Guards and 9th Tank Corps, attempted to turn German Second Army's left flank north of Kalinkovichi. After its relief by 95th Rifle Corps, 18th Corps' 69th, 140th, and 60th Rifle Divisions, now reinforced by 106th Rifle Division from 27th Rifle Corps, marched 50 kilometers to the Novinki and Vasilevichi region, where they relieved units of 7th Guards Cavalry Corps. The cavalry corps then regrouped to the southwest to support 61st Army's advance on Kalinkovichi.

The 18th and 95th Rifle Corps attacked early on 23 November across a broad front east, west, and south of Novinki. The 95th Corps' 44th Guards Rifle Division encountered strong resistance as it reached the outskirts of the villages of Mnogoversh and Viazovitsa, 30 kilometers north of Kalinkovichi, and 172nd Rifle Division's advance ground to a halt just south of those villages. Further south, 27th Rifle Corps' 69th and 193rd Rifle Divisions, backed up by 149th Rifle Division, encountered German 5th Panzer Division's 13th Panzer Grenadier Regiment near Liady and Korma, 30 kilometers northeast of Kalinkovichi, and despite repeated heavy assaults, could not break through the German defenses. In fact, 5th Panzer Division's timely arrival at last restored some stability to the German defenses north and northeast of Kalinkovichi, which on 25 November came under the control of LVI Panzer Corps. The German Second Army's front finally stabilized by month's end, along a defensive line occupied by LVI Panzer Corps' 4th and 5th Panzer Divisions, reinforced by elements of the shattered 251st and 86th Infantry Divisions, and Corps Detachment E, which extended from Ozarichi, 38 kilometers north of Kalinkovichi southeastward through Mnogoversh to just west of Korma and then southward through Nasavichi to Malyi Avtiuki, on the Vasilevichi-Kalinkovichi road 15 kilometers east of Kalinkovichi.

As the Belorussian Front's offensive developed, Rokossovsky and Batov regrouped their forces from 23 through 30 November by moving 27th Rifle

Corps' 106th Rifle Division and 19th Rifle Corps' 140th and 162nd Rifle Divisions northward to reinforce 18th Rifle Corps north of Kalinkovichi. Meanwhile, the remainder of Batov's 27th and 19th Rifle Corps continued their advance northward along the Berezina River toward Parichi and across the Berezina north of Rechitsa. The 27th Rifle Corps' 354th Rifle Division reached the Viazovki, Mikul', Gorodok, and Pruzhinishche region 25 kilometers south of Parichi on 29 November.[24] It was flanked by 106th Rifle Division on its left and 115th Rifle Brigade on its right and opposed by virtually no German forces. The corps' lead elements established close contacts with local partisan brigades, forming the so-called Rudobel'skie Gates, through which a steady supply of arms, ammunition, and personnel flowed to and from the partisans. Shortly before the end of the month, Batov ordered the bulk of 27th Rifle Corps to wheel southward to increase the pressure on German defenses north of Kalinkovichi. At this point he transferred 115th Rifle Brigade to 19th Rifle Corps, which now formed his army's extreme right wing.

During the same period, Batov reinforced 19th Rifle Corps with the newly arrived 38th Guards Rifle Division. This division, originally part of 95th Rifle Corps, joined 19th Rifle Corps on 22 November. The mission Batov assigned to the division late on 22 November was "to attack the enemy from the Boroviki and Elany line on the morning of 24 November and, together with its neighbor to the right—115th Separate Rifle Brigade and on the left—37th Guards Rifle Division, capture the large town of Strakovichi and the town and railroad station at Shatsilki [today Svetlogorsk]."[25]

The 19th Rifle Corps resumed its northward advance early the next day. While 37th and 38th Guards Rifle Divisions, supported by 86th Artillery Brigade, advanced on Shatsilki, 115th Rifle Brigade bypassed the town to the west. The assault struck German 707th Security Division, the only force available to the Germans to defend south of the Berezina River. The Soviet force had captured Strakovichi by late on 25 November but encountered heavy resistance from German forces dug in on the outskirts of Shatsilki. In two days of heavy fighting, 38th Guards Division encircled and destroyed the German garrison in Iakimovskaia Sloboda, 7 kilometers east of Shatsilki, while the remainder of the division enveloped the city from the northwest. The two guards divisions finally drove the last German defenders from the city at 1600 hours on 27 November. However, the Germans were able to cling to a small bridgehead on the southwestern bank of the Berezina River until 10 December (see Appendix F-1 for 65th Army's situation on 1 December). Meanwhile, 38th Guards Rifle Division's 115th Regiment, with 115th Rifle Brigade on its left, advanced northward toward Prudok, 7 kilometers south of Parichi, and reached the Lipniki and Gomza line at month's end.[26] This marked the northernmost point reached by Batov's forces during the Gomel'-Rechitsa operation (see Maps 7.12 and 7.13).

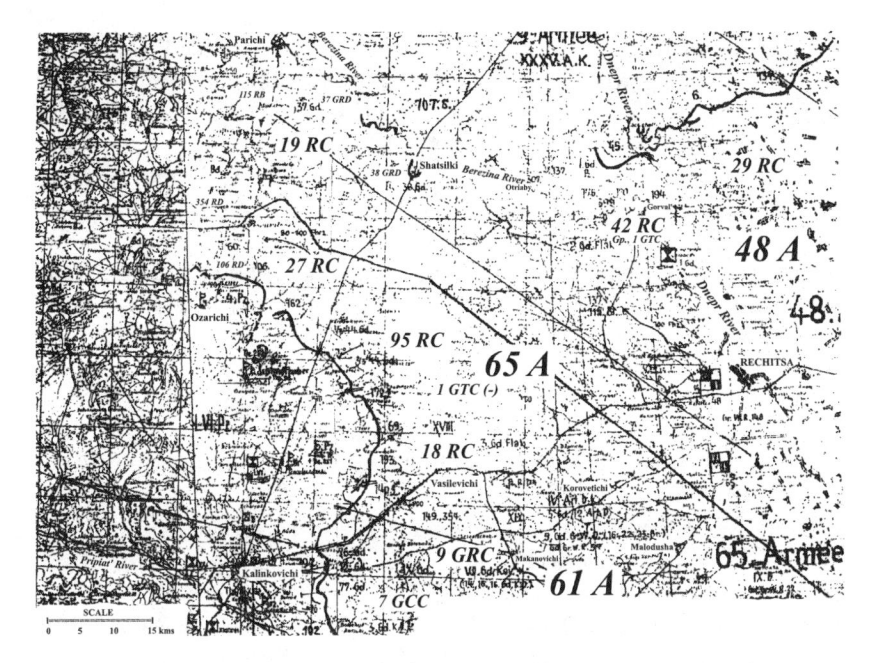

Map 7.12. Second Army's Situation along the Parichi-Bobruisk Axis, 30 November 1943

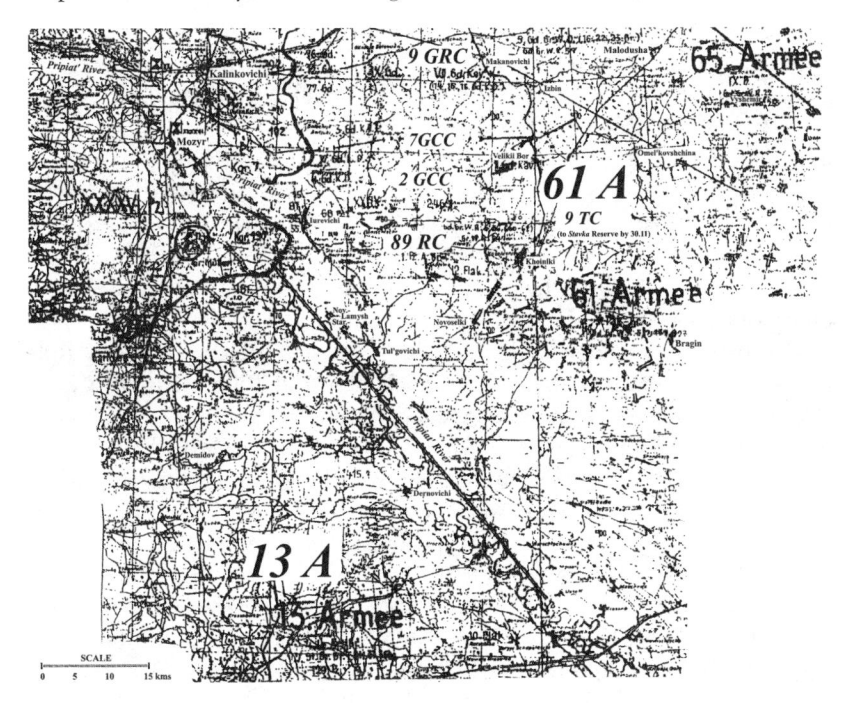

Map 7.13. Second Army's Situation along the Kalinkovichi and Mozyr' Axes, 30 November 1943

Further south, after capturing Rechitsa, 48th Army's 42nd Rifle Corps crossed the Dnepr River and linked up with the remainder of the army. Along with a small tank group from 1st Guards Tank Corps, 48th Army joined the advance of 11th and 63rd Armies, who were pursuing the forces of the German Ninth Army's XXXV Army Corps as they withdrew westward from Gomel'. By 30 November the combined forces of 48th, 11th, and 63rd Armies had pushed the forces of Ninth Army's corps westward and northwestward to the Klenovichi and Potapovka line, 25 kilometers southeast of Zhlobin. The precipitous but orderly withdrawal by German Ninth Army was largely a product of 3rd and 50th Armies' successful penetration of Ninth Army's defenses along the Sozh River on 22 November.

THE NOVYI BYKHOV–PROPOISK OFFENSIVE (22–30 NOVEMBER 1943)

Although often treated as a separate operation, 3rd and 50th Armies' Novyi Bykhov–Propoisk offensive (22–30 November 1943) formed an integral part of Rokossovsky's Gomel'-Rechitsa offensive operation. According to Rokossovsky's original directive, the two armies were to attack across the Sozh River in time-staggered sequence (see Map 7.14). The 3rd Army was to attack across the Sozh River on 22 November, and 50th Army, on 3rd Army's right, was to join the assault on 24 November. Finally, on 3rd Army's left, 63rd Army was to join the assault on 26 November, by which time the entire front from Petukhovka through Propoisk to Gomel' would be ablaze. In fact, 63rd Army's assault formed the essential link between 3rd and 50th Armies' attacks in the north and 11th Army's assault on Gomel' proper.

General Gorbatov's 3rd Army played the key role in this operation. According to Gorbatov, his army's mission was "to attack from the southern bridgehead [over the Sozh] with the mission to reach the Dnepr, seize the crossroads at Dovsk, and, by doing so, cut the withdrawal routes of the enemy Gomel' grouping."[27]

Gorbatov planned to conduct his army's main attack with 80th Rifle Corps' 121st Guards and 17th, 283rd, and 362nd Rifle Divisions in the 5-kilometer-wide sector between Studenets and Kostiukovka. The 17th and 283rd Rifle Divisions were to make a frontal assault toward Khlebno (also spelled Glebno), Rekta, and Zhuravichi, while the other two divisions advanced along the flanks to tie down German forces and prevent them from launching counterattacks against the army's main attack. Accordingly, 121st Guards Rifle Division was to attack toward Korma and 362nd Division toward Propoisk. The three remaining divisions in the army's 41st Rifle Corps (120th Guards, 186th, and 269th) remained in second echelon with the mission of "strengthening the blow and developing the offensive to the southwest and west."[28] After the assault began, 63rd Army reinforced 3rd Army

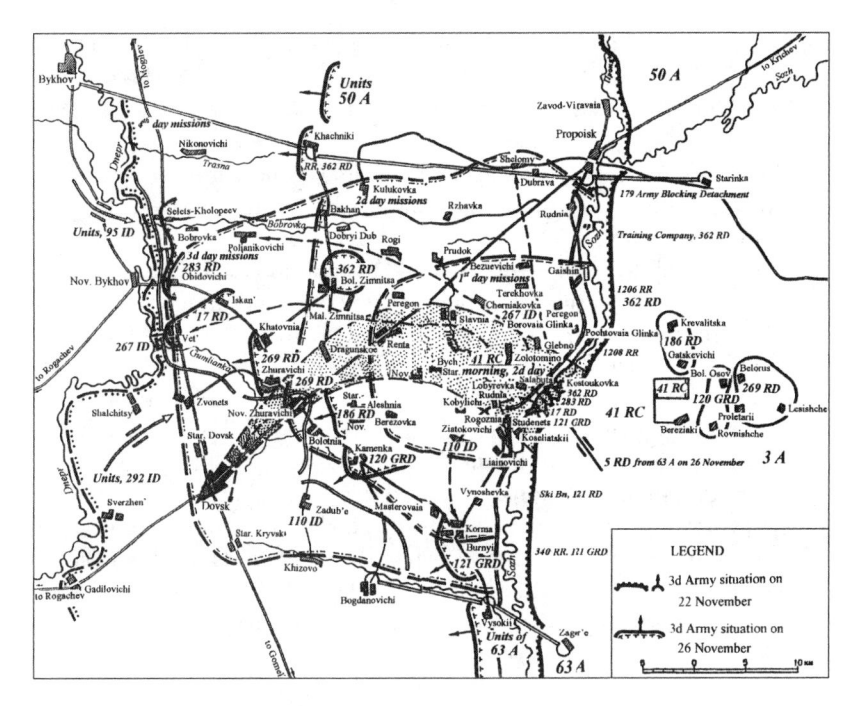

Map 7.14. 3rd Army's Novyi Bykhov–Propoisk Offensive Operation, 22–30 November 1943

with its 5th Rifle Division on 26 November. Gorbatov defended his extended left and right flanks with single regiments from 121st Guards and 362nd Rifle Divisions. Finally, 36th Separate Tank and 1538th Self-propelled Artillery Regiments provided armor support. Gorbatov's force faced German Ninth Army's 267th and 110th Infantry Divisions.

Gorbatov's shock group struck at 0900 hours on 22 November after a ten-minute artillery preparation. The assaulting forces quickly overcame the Germans' tactical defenses and expanded the bridgehead to a depth of 8–10 kilometers across a front of up to 20 kilometers by day's end. The 41st Rifle Corps' 186th and 120th Guards Rifle Divisions, which followed and reinforced the assault force, cleared the remaining German forces from the forests around Lobyrevka at 2000 hours, while 269th Rifle Division assembled in reserve in the Khlebno region. Most of the army's artillery crossed the Sozh River that night. Soviet sources reported capturing 200 prisoners, 41 guns, and 50 mortars.

Providing the shaken German defenders little respite, Gorbatov committed the two divisions of 41st Rifle Corps to combat on 23 November and 269th Rifle Division the next day in order to "strengthen" the attack and also fill in the gaps in the expanding penetration front. The ensuing attack continued day and night. On the army's right wing, 362nd Rifle Division enveloped and seized Propoisk, even though that city was in the sector of adjacent 50th Army. Gorbatov later explained:

> Having captured Rudnia and Shelomy, its [362nd Rifle Division] units enveloped the city of Propoisk from the east, south, and west. Propoisk was in the sector of 50th Army, which had not yet attacked. The right wing units of 3rd Army were not able to continue the offensive without settling with the German grouping in Propoisk, which hung over its flank. While reporting to the army commander about his attack, Major General V. N. Dalmatov, the division commander, declared that the division's units could capture the city. However, the soldiers and officers asked that the army commander not petition for the award of the tiresome honorific name "Propoisk" to the division and regiments, which liberated the city of Propoisk. Having been assured that such a petition would not be made, 362nd Rifle Division's units attacked and liberated the city and, soon after, occupied Rzhavka. Despite the fact that its neighbors lagged behind, 283rd Rifle Division captured Selets-Kholopeev by evening, and its reconnaissance elements reached the Dnepr River.[29]

Shortly after 3rd Army's attack began, General Model, the commander of Ninth Army, requested permission from Hitler to abandon the territory between the Sozh and Dnepr Rivers. After demurring for several days, Hitler permitted only a partial withdrawal. That withdrawal however, accelerated after 3rd Army began its race eastward toward the Dnepr and became total when 50th Army joined the assault.

Colonel General I. V. Boldin's 50th Army occupied positions along the Pronia River from Petukhovka south to Propoisk opposite the defenses of (from north to south) 131st, 260th, 95th, and part of 267th Infantry Divisions of the German Ninth Army's XXXXI Panzer Corps. According to 50th Army's history:

> The army's 46th Rifle Corps (369th, 380th, and 238th Rifle Divisions) was defending on the right wing, and 413th and 110th Rifle Divisions attacked in the Uzgorsk and Krasnaia Sloboda sector just north of Propoisk on 24 November after a 10-minute artillery raid. The 108th Rifle Division was in second echelon. The army's forces penetrated the enemy defense and, while overcoming strong resistance and repelling repeated counterattacks in *rasputitsa* conditions and the near total absence of roads, developed the offensive in the general direction of Zhelezinka and Bykhov.
> The units of German 131st, 260th, 95th, and 267th Infantry Divisions, a combat group of 589th Assault Battalion, and 417th Construction Battalion, supported by five artillery regiments and 4th Special Designation Panzer Brigade, withdrew along the army's front.

The army crushed the opposing enemy's resistance and penetrated into the depths from 16 to 30 kilometers along a 37-kilometer front in 15 days of battle. [It] liberated 137 towns and villages and, while inflicting heavy personnel and equipment losses on the enemy, it approached the Dnepr River in the region of Novyi Bykhov and reached a line 10–35 kilometers west of Chausy. However, it was stopped in a bridgehead line, where, in accordance with a *front* directive, it went over to the defense, with 369th, 238th, 413th, 110th, and 324th Rifle Divisions in first echelon and 380th and 108th Rifle Divisions in the second echelon.[30]

Although essentially correct, this brief account of 50th Army's operations neglects to mention several key points. First, shortly after the army launched its main attack on 25 November, the Western Front's 10th Army also attacked across the Pronia River just north of Petukhovka on its boundary with 50th Army. Specifically, 10th Army's 38th Rifle Corps, consisting of 64th, 212th, and 385th Rifle Divisions, attacked at the boundary between German 131st and 260th Infantry Divisions' defenses south of Chausy. It did so in conjunction with attacks by 50th Army's 369th Rifle Division south of Petukhovka. The 10th Army attacked across the river on 28 November with 385th and 64th Rifle Divisions deployed from left to right in first echelon and the 212th in second echelon. Within two days, the two lead divisions had penetrated German defenses at Vysokoe, wheeled northward, and attacked German defenses at Chausy, a city that anchored the Ninth Army's right flank. Boldin then committed his 212th Rifle Division, which advanced as far as Shaparovo, 5 kilometers south of Chausy, before being halted by strong German defenses. Meanwhile, 64th and 385th Rifle Divisions seized Lepeny and other villages southwest of Chausy.

The 50th Army's 368th Rifle Division attacked across the Pronia River just south of Petukhovka, penetrated German defenses, and turned 260th Infantry Division's left flank, capturing the villages of Kuzminichi and Khomenki, 3–5 kilometers deep in the German rear area. Coming as it did during 50th Army's successful attack to the south, the defending Germans had no choice but to abandon their river defenses and withdraw westward. This they did on 28 November, with 50th Army's 369th and 380th Rifle Divisions in hot pursuit.

The 50th Army's history also fails to mention that its initial offensive progress remained slow until General Model, the Ninth Army commander, issued orders for his forces to withdraw to new defenses. Thereafter, Soviet forces essentially pursued the withdrawing Germans without fighting any pitched battles. Boldin's pursuing forces closed up to the new German defense lines, which extended from just south of Chausy diagonally to the Dnepr River at Novyi Bykhov, by late on 30 November.

The forces of General Kolpakchi's 63rd Army did not join 3rd Army's attack until 26 November. Up to this date, 63rd Army's mission was "to attract the enemy's attention away from the [*front*] main attack axis" and subsequently "attack toward Zhlobin to envelop the enemy Gomel'-Rechitsa grouping from the northwest."[31] Having fulfilled this mission, 63rd Army exploited 3rd Army's success by attacking across the Sozh River on 26 November with the mission of seizing the sector of the Dnepr River between Rogachev and Zhlobin. Spearheaded by 40th Rifle Corps' 41st, 129th, and 169th Rifle Divisions, the army soon joined 3rd Army's pursuit of German Ninth Army's withdrawing XXXV Army Corps. By month's end, 3rd and 63rd Armies' forces closed up on new German defense lines west and northeast of Potapovka, where the front stabilized.

General Gorbatov later summed up the results of the Novyi Bykhov–Propoisk operation:

> The threat of reaching the rear of the German Gomel' grouping from the north was real. The enemy, while desperately attempting to halt our offensive, hurriedly began to withdraw his forces from the Gomel' region back across the Dnepr. On 26 November the country knew that the Belorussian Front's forces had captured Gomel'—a large regional industrial center of Belorussia, an important railroad junction, and a powerful strongpoint in the enemy defense along the Poles'e axis.
>
> The 3rd Army reached the Dnepr River from Selets-Kholopeev to Gadilovichi in the beginning of December and went over to the defense in the positions it had seized. Having advanced 35 kilometers on its left wing, 50th Army was situated 15 kilometers from the Dnepr. The 63rd Army advanced 50 kilometers along its entire front and reached the defenses of the enemy, who were holding on to a bridgehead 45 kilometers wide and 6 to 12 kilometers deep on the eastern bank of the Dnepr east of Rogachev and Zhlobin.[32]

What Gorbatov failed to note was that his offensive had failed to achieve all of its objectives. That is, 11th, 63rd, 3rd, and 50th Armies failed to reach the Dnepr River between Novyi Bykhov and Zhlobin. This was so because the Germans formed a sizable bridgehead on the river's eastern bank and successfully defended these defenses until Rokossovsky had no choice but to call off further attacks. This failure would set the stage for subsequent heavy fighting in December when the Belorussian Front once again tried to seize Zhlobin and Rogachev.

According to the official Soviet definition, the Gomel'-Rechitsa offensive ended on 30 November. By this time, Rokossovsky's main attack force, Romanenko's 48th, Batov's 65th, and Belov's 61st Armies, had driven a deep wedge between German Ninth and Second Armies. The 65th Army's 19th Rifle Corps, whose divisions had reached Gomza and the outskirts of Parichi, just 35 kilometers south of Bobruisk, formed the westernmost point of this wedge. On the wedge's right wing, 48th Army's forces were north of the Berezina River on the Dnepr River's western bank and only 20 kilometers south of Zhlobin. On the wedge's left wing, 65th Army's 18th and 95th Rifle Corps hung menacingly over German Second Army's open left flank north of Kalinkovichi. To the south, 9th Guards and 89th Rifle Corps of Belov's 61st Army, deployed on a broad front stretching from Vasilevichi to the northern bank of the Pripiat' River, threatened German defenses at Kalinkovichi from the east. Overall, the Gomel'-Rechitsa offensive cost Rokossovsky's *front* 66,556 men, 21,650 of which were irrevocable (killed, missing, or captured).[33]

From the perspective of the German Second Army commander, his three corps (LVI Panzer, XX Army, and XXXXVI Panzer) now faced serious threats against both their left flank and their front. Worse still, while Rokossovsky's forces were closing in on Kalinkovichi, the forces of 1st Ukrainian Front's 13th Army were oozing their way through the Pripiat' Marshes against the Second Army's right flank, anchored on the city of Mozyr'.

German Ninth Army's position was scarcely more favorable. Although its left wing was still secure, the offensive by the Belorussian Front's 11th, 63rd, and 3rd Armies had pushed its center back to a bridgehead on the eastern bank of the Dnepr east of Rogachev and Zhlobin. Making matters worse, the *front*'s 48th Army and one rifle corps of 65th Army had turned the Ninth Army's right flank south and west of Zhlobin, and that flank remained "up in the air." It seemed to the Germans as if the road to Bobruisk and Minsk was wide open to the Red Army on 30 November. Hitler and the OKH could not cope with this reality.

Thus, the two defending German armies faced three stark challenges. First, they had to hold firmly to their defenses on the approaches to Rogachev, Zhlobin, Kalinkovichi, and Mozyr'. Second, they had to close the yawning gap between Ninth and Second Armies. Third, they had to do so quickly before Rokossovsky's forces advanced further and rendered the gap irreparable. All of these challenges dictated the Germans' future actions. Within days they would mount a serious effort to close the perilous gaps and, by doing so, seal off the Soviet penetration.

While victorious, Rokossovsky too was faced with major challenges. First, his forces had not completely fulfilled their missions. They had not reached the Dnepr River in the Rogachev and Zhlobin regions. Although they had torn an immense hole in the Germans' strategic defenses, their forces were still well short of Bobruisk. Finally, the Germans' defensive salient at Kalinkovichi tied down the bulk of the *front*'s forces and prevented them from mounting a concerted advance northward toward Bobruisk and Minsk. As December arrived, Rokossovsky's challenge was to revive his offensive toward Bobruisk and Minsk. To do so, however, he first had to capture Kalinkovichi and keep open the penetration toward Bobruisk.

Both the Germans and the Soviets would seek to master these challenges in December 1943 in a contest that degenerated into a complex and bloody slugfest both on the flanks of the road to Bobruisk and along the approaches to Kalinkovichi and Rogachev.

At the end of November 1943, the Red Army's *fronts* operating along the western strategic axis were far from achieving the ambitious tasks the *Stavka* had assigned to them in late September (see Map 7.15). They had failed to fulfill their missions for a variety of reasons. As in previous years, the Germans resisted skillfully and tenaciously, regardless of their dwindling resources. By fall 1943, however, this resistance was also driven by frustration and increasing desperation. The weather, too, proved as serious an adversary as the Germans. Although the Soviet *front* recorded several spectacular gains, particularly around Nevel' in the north and west of Loev in the south, deteriorating weather in mid-November prevented them from exploiting these successes. Sheer exhaustion also worked as a brake on the Soviet realization of their anticipated victories. By November most Soviet rifle divisions had dwindled in strength to between 3,500 and 4,500 men each, and the stream of replacements decreased to a trickle as a result of the competing requirements of Red Army forces attempting to conduct operations along both the western and southwestern axes. Worse still, the armored spearheads upon which the Red Army depended to exploit success along any axes (the tank armies and tank, mechanized, and cavalry corps) also eroded in strength. Finally, the Red Army's critical logistical umbilicals through which flowed the ammunition and fuel necessary to sustain operations became overextended and choked because of bad road conditions and unreconstructed and overburdened railroad lines.

If a variety of physical conditions inhibited the Red Army's success in November, so also did instances of timidity, poor leadership, or combat ineptitude on the part of some Red Army *front* and army commanders. Whereas *front* commanders such as General Rokossovsky doggedly and skillfully overcame the bad weather and the troops' exhaustion, other *front* commanders did less well. After his brilliant coup de main at Nevel' in October, General Eremenko failed to exploit the operation adequately. His successor, Bagramian, did somewhat better but found himself foiled by bad weather and determined German resistance at Gorodok and Vitebsk. In the center General Sokolovsky and some of his army commanders repeatedly displayed their ineptitude as they flailed away at Army Group Center's defenses in eastern Belorussia in vain.

Despite the clearly limited progress and the numerous failures, the *Stavka* was still hopeful that, sooner or later, Army Group Center's defenses would collapse, if not in December, then in the dead of winter. The *Stavka* catalogued the impressive offensive gains of November and had every reason to be optimistic. The forces of the 2nd and 1st Baltic Fronts were firmly lodged in the gap between Army Groups North and South, poised to strike at the open flanks of both German Army Groups. Vitebsk was ripe for capture,

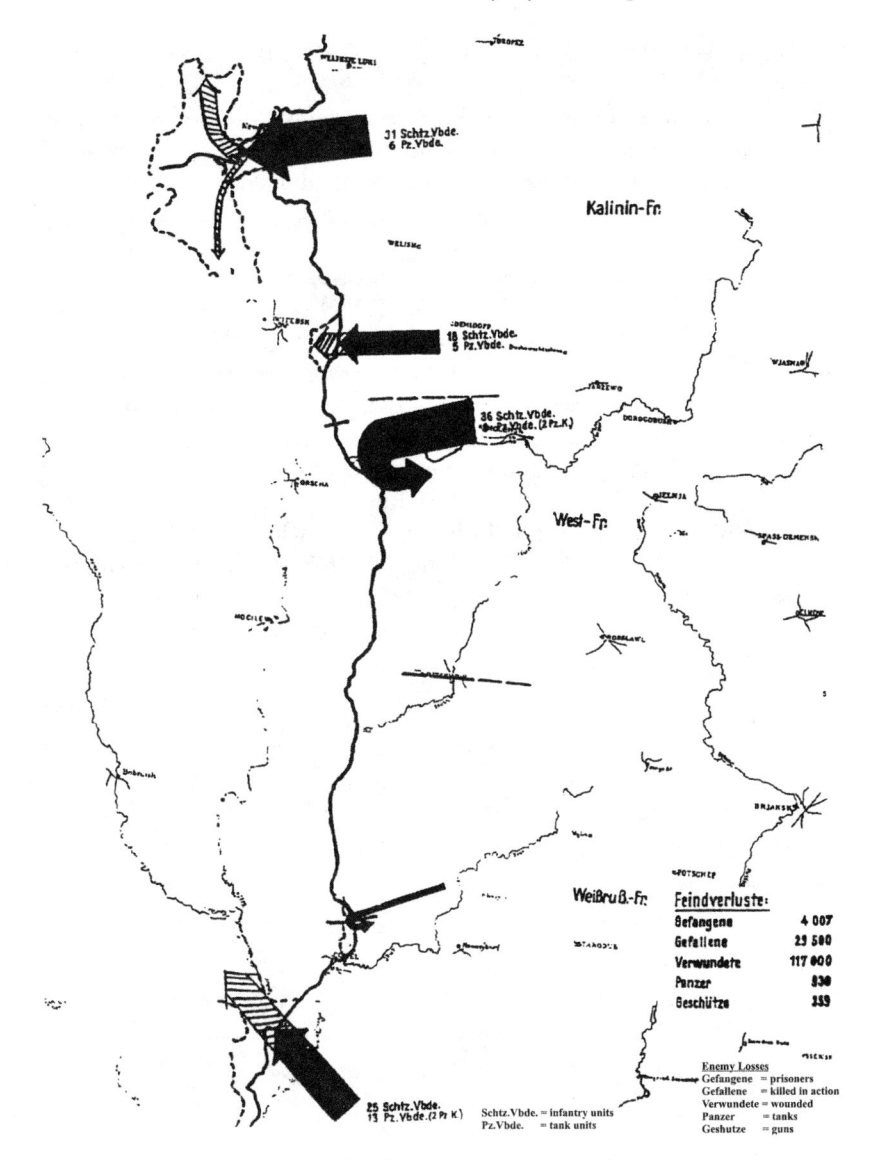

Map 7.15. German Assessment of Red Army Operations in Belorussia, 1–20 November 1943

and, with it, Third Panzer Army and the entire left wing of Army Group Center was vulnerable to envelopment. In the south, the Belorussian Front had split the German Ninth and Second Armies apart, and the breach seemed irreparable. After Kalinkovichi fell, it seemed as if nothing could stop the collapse of Army Group Center's right wing. In short, with Army Group Center threatened with defeat on both flanks, what occurred in its central sector seemed almost irrelevant.

Therefore, in early December the *Stavka* ordered the Red Army to resume its offensives in northern and southern Belorussia. Specifically, General Bagramian's 1st Baltic Front, soon to be reinforced by roughly half of General Sokolovsky's Western Front, was to destroy German Third Panzer Army's forces in the Gorodok and Vitebsk regions. General Rokossovsky's Belorussian Front was to destroy German Second Army's forces in the Kalinkovichi region and then wheel northward to seize Bobruisk, roll up Army Group Center's right wing, and then sever the army group's jugular by capturing Minsk. To ensure victory, the *Stavka* ordered the Western Front to cease its futile attacks toward Orsha and instead regroup its forces to its right wing and assist 1st Baltic Front's operations against Third Panzer Army's defenses at Vitebsk. At the same time, the *Stavka* ordered the Western Front to dispatch its 10th Guards Army to reinforce the 2nd Baltic Front. With this powerful new army, the *Stavka* believed 2nd Baltic Front's forces could overcome the resistance offered by Army Group North's Sixteenth Army at Pustoshka and Novosokol'niki and begin liberating the Baltic and Leningrad regions.

CHAPTER 8

The 1st Baltic and Western Fronts' Vitebsk (Gorodok) Offensive (13–23 December) and 2nd Baltic Front's Idritsa-Opochka Offensive (16–25 December)

PLANNING

The intense fighting that characterized the 1st Baltic Front's struggle in the Gorodok and Vitebsk regions during November 1943 died out in early December. It did so because, as the *Stavka* directed, on 8 December Bagramian's *front* ordered its armies to go over to the defense and regroup and refit so that they could mount yet another attempt to crack German defenses around Vitebsk (see Appendix G-1). This respite was essential because the 1st Baltic Front's forces had been in nearly constant combat since early October and were beginning to show clear evidence of the severe wear and tear. During the ensuing interval of roughly two weeks, the *front* did what was required to prepare a fresh offensive, this time in conjunction with an attack by the Western Front along the Vitebsk axis. Jointly, the 1st Baltic and Western Fronts were to conduct what the *Stavka* believed would be the culminating effort to seize Vitebsk. Traditionally, Soviet historians treated the ensuing offensive as one conducted by the 1st Baltic Front's 11th Guards and 4th Shock Armies with only limited aims, specifically, capturing the elusive objective of Gorodok and then advancing on Vitebsk from the north and northwest. For example, the 1976 *Soviet Military Encyclopedia* describes the operation's intent:

> The concept of the operation required the 1st Baltic Front's (commanded by Army General I. Kh. Bagramian) 11th Guards and 4th Shock Armies to penetrate the enemy's defenses on the flanks of the Gorodok salient, encircle and destroy his grouping by concentric attacks in the direction of Bychikha Station, and then develop the attack to the south to capture Gorodok and advance on Vitebsk. The 11th Guards Army, in whose penetration sector we created a threefold superiority over the enemy in manpower and fourfold in artillery, was assigned the main role in the operation.[1]

However, the most recent Russian Military Encyclopedia, published in 1994, subtly alters its description of the operational concept:

> According to the concept, they [11th Guards and 4th Shock Armies, with 1st and 5th Tank and 3rd Guards Cavalry Corps] were to penetrate the enemy's defenses on the flanks of the Gorodok salient, encircle and destroy his grouping by concentric attacks in the direction of Bychikha Station, and then capture Gorodok and Vitebsk, while developing the attack to the south. The 43rd Army (Lieutenant General K. D. Golubev) and 39th Army (Lieutenant General N. I. Berzarin) were supposed to tie down the opposing enemy by active operations and assist in the encirclement of his Gorodok grouping.[2]

Although more accurate than the previous description, this expanded concept statement still failed to capture the full dimensions of the Vitebsk (Gorodok) operation. In fact, the operation was a full-fledged attempt to capture Vitebsk involving not only all four of the 1st Baltic Front's armies but also one army provided by the Western Front. We can now reconstruct the operation in detail from existing Russian open-source materials, recently released Russian archival documents, and German archival materials.

The Vitebsk operation as a whole evolved in three distinct operational phases (see Map 8.1). The first phase involved an offensive by 11th Guards and 4th Shock Armies on the right wing of Bagramian's *front* against Third Panzer Army's forces defending the key town of Gorodok, which dominated the northern approaches to both Vitebsk and Polotsk. This operation commenced on 13 December 1943 and ended with the fall of the town to Red Army troops on 24 December. The second phase, which took place while the assault on Gorodok was under way, involved assaults by 43rd and 39th Armies on the 1st Baltic Front's left wing against Third Panzer Army's defenses east of Vitebsk. This phase lasted from 19 through 24 December and constituted what the recent Russian military encyclopedia article termed "covering attacks." The third and final phase of the Vitebsk offensive has gone virtually unreported. This was an offensive conducted jointly by the 1st Baltic Front's 39th Army and the Western Front's 33rd Army (reinforced) against German defenses southeast of Vitebsk in conjunction with an offensive west of Vitebsk by the 1st Baltic Front's 4th Shock and 11th Guards Armies. The latter two armies joined the attack after they captured Gorodok. Taken together, the offensive represented a two-pronged assault aimed at encircling and destroying Third Panzer Army's forces in the Vitebsk region. The 39th and 33rd Armies began their attacks on 23 December, and 4th Shock and 11th Guards Armies' began theirs on 25 December. This phase lasted well into the new year.

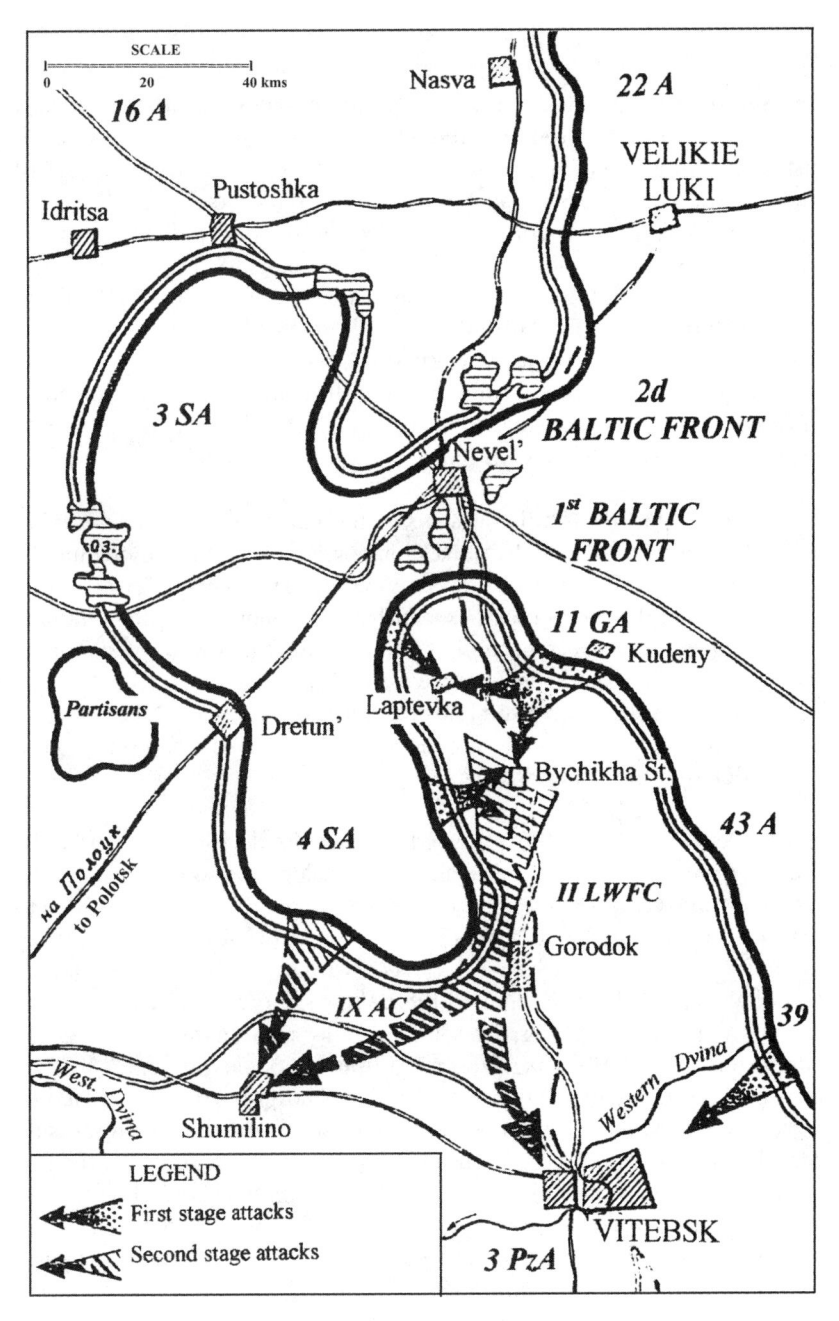

Map 8.1. The *Stavka*'s Plan for the Vitebsk (Gorodok) Offensive Operation, November 1943

GORODOK (13-23 DECEMBER 1943)

The *Stavka* issued a series of directives to the 1st Baltic and Western Fronts in early December that required them to shift and regroup their forces, adjust their mutual boundary lines, and resume offensive operations toward Vitebsk. The first of these, dispatched to both *fronts* and the *Stavka* representative, General N. N Voronov, on 3 December, directed the 1st Baltic Front to transfer three rifle divisions and their sectors to the Western Front and both *fronts* to shift the boundary line between them further to the north (see Appendix G-2).[3] The second, issued the same day, ordered the commander of the Western Front, General Sokolovsky, to "cease the offensive on the *front's* right wing" immediately and shift the center of gravity of his front to its right wing, while leaving sufficient forces on its left wing to cooperate with the Belorussian Front's advance on Mogilev (see Appendix G-3):

2. Leave up to 10–12 rifle divisions on the Dobromysl' and Baevo front. Regroup 18–20 rifle divisions, along with their main reinforcements, to the Velikoe Selo, Dobromysl', and Liozno regions by 15 December. Conduct the regrouping in secret from the enemy. Continue intensified reconnaissance in the Dobromysl' and Baevo sector and employ dummy tanks and guns extensively.
3. Reinforce 10th Army with four-five rifle divisions by 10 December and continue the offensive along the Mogilev axis in cooperation with the Belorussian Front's right wing.[4]

Collectively, these orders reflected the *Stavka*'s decision to abandon its futile attempts to penetrate German defenses along the western axis by direct blows into central Belorussia via Orsha or Mogilev. Instead, it decided to regroup the Western Front's forces so that they could participate jointly with the 1st Baltic Front's forces in an all-out offensive to smash German defenses east of Vitebsk at the same time as the Belorussian Front savaged German Army Group Center's defenses in southern Belorussia. In the *Stavka*'s grand design for operations during December, the 1st Baltic Front was to concentrate its 11th Guards and 4th Shock Armies northwest of Vitebsk and its 43rd and 39th Armies east of the city, where they would deploy side by side with the Western Front's 33rd Army. After forming, shock groups of the two *fronts* would attack Vitebsk concentrically, with the northern shock group advancing via Gorodok and the southern via the Smolensk-Vitebsk road (see Map 8.2). Although the *Stavka* envisioned conducting one continuous operation to capture Vitebsk, circumstances ultimately dictated that the two *fronts* conduct this offensive in three distinct phases.

The 1st Baltic Front's shock group designated to conduct the Gorodok phase of the Vitebsk offensive operation consisted of General Galitsky's 11th

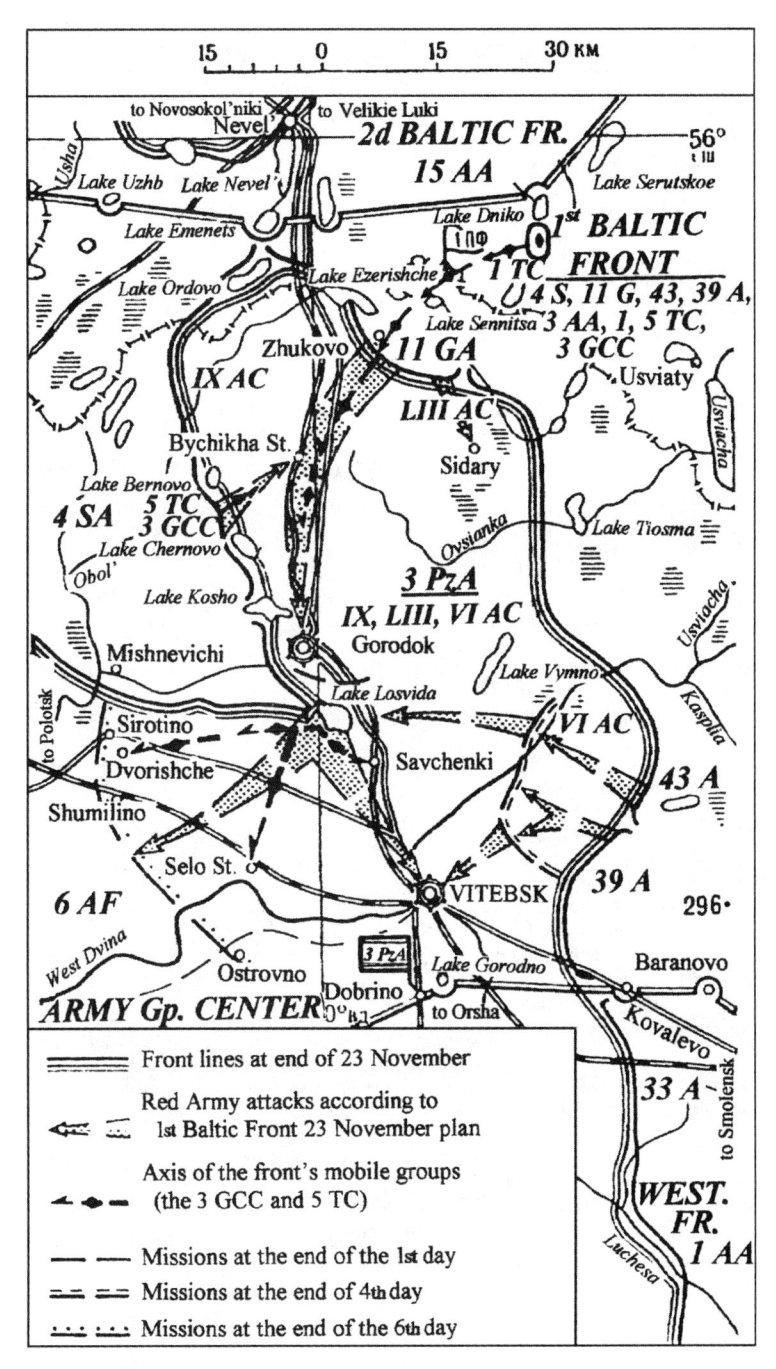

Map 8.2. The 1st Baltic Front's Plan for the Vitebsk (Gorodok) Offensive Operation, 23 November 1943

Table 8.1. The 11th Guards Army's Order of Battle on 13 December 1943

8th Guards Rifle Corps—Major General P. F. Malyshev
   5th Guards Rifle Division
   26th Guards Rifle Division
   83rd Guards Rifle Division
   29th Rifle Division
16th Guards Rifle Corps—Major General I. F. Fediun'kin
   1st Guards Rifle Division
   11th Guards Rifle Division
   31st Guards Rifle Division
36th Guards Rifle Corps—Major General P. G. Shafranov
   16th Guards Rifle Division
   84th Guards Rifle Division
   360th Rifle Division
83rd Rifle Corps—Major General A. A. D'iakonov
   234th Rifle Division
   235th Rifle Division
1st Tank Corps—Lieutenant General of Tank Forces V. V. Butkov
   89th Tank Brigade
   117th Tank Brigade
   159th Tank Brigade
   44th Motorized Rifle Brigade
10th Guards Separate Tank Brigade
2nd Guards Separate Heavy Tank Regiment
15th Artillery Penetration Division
21st Artillery Penetration Division
17th Antiaircraft Artillery Division
46th Antiaircraft Artillery Division
3rd Guards Mortar Brigade
17th Guards Mortar Brigade
26th Guards Mortar Brigade
22nd Guards-mortar Regiment
24th Guards-mortar Regiment
34th Guards-mortar Regiment
85th Guards-mortar Regiment
93rd Guards-mortar Regiment
10th Assault Engineer-Sapper Brigade
6th Guards Separate Engineer Battalion
226th Separate Engineer Battalion
243rd Separate Engineer Battalion

Source: Boevoi sostav Sovetskoi Armii, chast' III (Ianvar'–dekabr' 1943 g.) [The combat composition of the Soviet Army, pt. 3 (January–December 1943)] (Moscow: Voenizdat, 1972), 302; and *Boevoi sostav Sovetskoi Armii, chast' IV (Ianvar'–dekabr' 1944 g.)* [The combat composition of the Soviet Army, pt. 4 (January–December 1944)] (Moscow: Voenizdat, 1988), 12.

Guards Army and General Shvetsov's 4th Shock Army, supported on the left by a portion of General Golubev's 43rd and General Berzarin's 39th Armies. Galitsky's army, which was to conduct the *front's* main attack, consisted of four rifle corps; twelve rifle divisions; one tank corps; one tank brigade; one heavy tank regiment; two artillery penetration divisions; two antiaircraft artillery divisions; three M-31 guards-mortar brigades; five M-13 guards-mortar regiments; four gun, howitzer, and mortar regiments; one engineer brigade; and three separate engineer battalions (see Table 8.1).

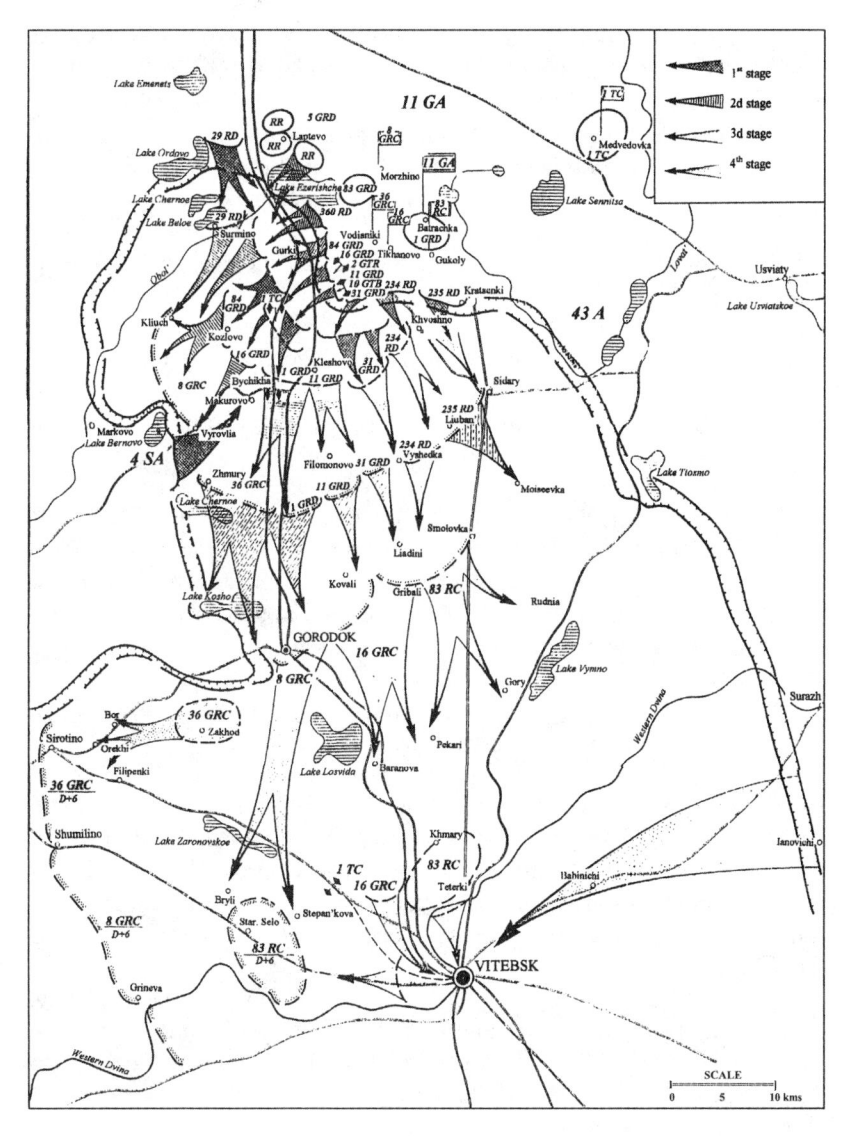

Map 8.3. 11th Guards Army's Plan for the Gorodok Offensive Operation, December 1943

So configured, 11th Guards Army fielded 160 serviceable tanks and self-propelled guns, including 97 in 1st Tank Corps, 46 in 10th Separate Guards Tank Brigade, and 17 in 2nd Separate Guards Heavy Tank Regiment.[5] In addition, 11th Guards Army was to be supported by 2 assault aviation divisions and protected by the fighter aviation subordinate to the *front*.

The army's history accurately describes the army's mission (see Map 8.3):

The plan was to deliver the main attack along the Gorodok-Vitebsk axis to destroy the Fascists' Gorodok grouping, liquidate the southern salient, and capture Vitebsk.

Five divisions with a considerable portion of the weaponry were concentrated in an 8-kilometer sector. The intention was to cut off the northwestern portion of the Gorodok salient and, in cooperation with 4th Shock Army, encircle and destroy the grouping of enemy forces in the lake region southwest of Lake Ezerishche. Subsequently, while developing the attack in the direction of Mekhovoe and Gorodok with the main forces, it was to liquidate the northeastern part of the Gorodok salient and encircle and destroy the enemy grouping defending that region. Further, while exploiting success southward toward Shumilino, it was to cut off the enemy's withdrawal routes to the west and capture Vitebsk with part of 11th Guards Army's forces in cooperation with 43rd Army.

The adjoining flanks of 16th and 36th Guards Rifle Corps were to conduct the main attack toward Mekhovoe [6 kilometers north of Bychikha] and Gorodok. Considering the terrain, the enemy defense, and other factors, 36th Corps formed for combat in single echelon, with all three divisions in first echelon. The 16th Corps formed in two echelons, with two divisions in the first echelon and one in the second.[6]

The 4th Shock Army, which concentrated on the 1st Baltic Front's right wing, was to launch the *front's* secondary attack on Gorodok from the west. This army consisted of three rifle corps, twelve rifle divisions, one rifle brigade, one tank corps, one cavalry corps, and one tank regiment (see Table 8.2).

The 4th Shock Army fielded more than 150 tanks and self-propelled guns, including 91 in 5th Tank Corps, 24 in 34th Guards Tank Brigade, and the remainder in the separate heavy tank regiment and the cavalry corps' tank regiment.[7] Weakened in previous fighting, the cavalry corps fielded only about 12,000 sabers.[8]

Because 4th Shock Army was operating across a broad front, it planned to deliver its main attack with 2nd Guards Rifle Corps' five divisions, supported by 60th Rifle Corps' 166th Rifle Division, 5th Tank and 3rd Guards Cavalry Corps, and 34th Guards Tank Brigade. This force was to attack eastward through the narrow 6-kilometer-wide sector between Lakes Bernovo and Chernovo and advance northeastward to link up with the spearheads of 11th Guards Army at Bychikha Station, 18 kilometers north of Gorodok.

General Golubev's 43rd Army was deployed across a broad front extending from 11th Guards Army's left flank at the village of Krasenki, 35 kilometers north-northeast of Gorodok, southward to the village of Borok, 18 kilometers due east of Vitebsk. Golubev's army consisted of two rifle corps with seven rifle divisions, two rifle brigades, a fortified region, one tank and one mechanized brigade, and a separate tank regiment (see Table 8.3).

The 1st Baltic and Western Fronts' Vitebsk (Gorodok) Offensive 217

Table 8.2. The 4th Shock Army's Order of Battle on 13 December 1943

2nd Guards Rifle Corps—Major General A. P. Beloborodov
  90th Guards Rifle Division
  16th Rifle Division
  47th Rifle Division
  381st Rifle Division
22nd Guards Rifle Corps—Major General N. B. Ibiansky
  117th Rifle Division
  154th Rifle Division
  156th Rifle Division
60th Rifle Corps—Major General A. N. Ermakov
  119th Rifle Division
  166th Rifle Division
  357th Rifle Division
  101st Rifle Brigade
51st Rifle Division
3rd Guards Cavalry Corps—Lieutenant General N. S. Oslikovsky
  5th Guards Cavalry Division
  6th Guards Cavalry Division
  32nd Cavalry Division
5th Tank Corps—Major General of Tank Forces M. G. Sakhno
  24th Tank Brigade
  41st Tank Brigade
  70th Tank Brigade
  5th Motorized Rifle Brigade
  161st Self-propelled Artillery Regiment
  1515th Self-propelled Artillery Regiment
  1546th Self-propelled Artillery Regiment
34th Guards Tank Brigade (attached from the *front*)
203rd Separate Heavy Tank Regiment

Source: *Boevoi sostav Sovetskoi Armii, chast' III (Ianvar'–dekabr' 1943 g.)* [The combat composition of the Soviet Army, pt. 3 (January–December 1943)] (Moscow: Voenizdat, 1972), 301; and *Boevoi sostav Sovetskoi Armii, chast' IV (Ianvar'–dekabr' 1944 g.)* [The combat composition of the Soviet Army, pt. 4 (January–December 1944)] (Moscow: Voenizdat, 1988), 11.

Golubev deployed his army with the artillery-machine gun battalions of 152nd Fortified Region covering the broad front northeast of Vitebsk and 92nd Rifle Corps defending the sector west of Surazh and Ianovichi. He concentrated 91st Rifle Corps, 114th and 145th Rifle Brigades, 60th Tank and 47th Mechanized Brigades, and 105th Tank Regiment on his left wing with orders to attack German defenses in the sector between Goriane and Kasenki (20 and 32 kilometers northeast of Vitebsk, respectively) on 19 December in support of the *front's* main attack on Gorodok. Golubev's army fielded about sixty tanks, which he employed primarily in an infantry support role.

General Berzarin's 39th Army was deployed on the 1st Baltic Front's left wing astride and north of the Smolensk-Vitebsk road. Berzarin's army consisted of three rifle corps, eleven rifle divisions, one rifle brigade, two tank brigades, one mechanized brigade, and a separate tank regiment (see Table 8.4).

Initially Berzarin concentrated his 5th Guards and 1st Rifle Corps, reinforced by 84th Rifle Corps' 91st Guards Rifle Division and 124th Rifle, 28th

Table 8.3. The 43rd Army's Order of Battle on 13 December 1943

91st Rifle Corps—Major General F. A. Volkov
   179th Rifle Division
   262rd Rifle Division
   270th Rifle Division
   306th Rifle Division
92nd Rifle Corps—Major General I. S. Iudintsev
   332nd Rifle Division
   334th Rifle Division
   358th Rifle Division
114th Rifle Brigade
145th Rifle Brigade
155th Fortified Region
60th Tank Brigade
46th Mechanized Brigade
105th Separate Tank Regiment

Source: Boevoi sostav Sovetskoi Armii, chast' III (Ianvar'–dekabr' 1943 g.) [The combat composition of the Soviet Army, pt. 3 (January–December 1943)] (Moscow: Voenizdat, 1972), 302; and *Boevoi sostav Sovetskoi Armii, chast' IV (Ianvar'–dekabr' 1944 g.)* [The combat composition of the Soviet Army, pt. 4 (January–December 1944)] (Moscow: Voenizdat, 1988), 12.

and 39th Guards Tank and 47th Mechanized Brigades in the 7-kilometer-wide sector between Borok and Goriane (18 kilometers east and 20 kilometers northeast of Vitebsk, respectively) on 43rd Army's left wing. This force, along with 43rd Army's 92nd Rifle Corps, was to attack German positions east of Vitebsk on 19 December. He left the rest of his forces in defensive positions across the remainder of his front. Berzarin's army fielded at least 100 tanks, the bulk assigned to a mobile group consisting of the two tank and one mechanized brigades.

Army Group Center's Third Panzer Army defended the salient north of Vitebsk and Gorodok with four infantry divisions and one panzer division assigned to its IX Army Corps. The corps' 252nd Infantry, 20th Panzer, and 87th Infantry Divisions defended the western flank of the salient from the village of Berzovka, 17 kilometers southwest of Gorodok, northward past Gorodok to the vicinity of Lake Beloe, 32 kilometers north of Gorodok. These forces faced those of 4th Shock Army. On the northern and northeastern "nose" of the German salient north of Gorodok, IX Army Corps' 129th Infantry and 6th Luftwaffe Field Divisions defended positions west and southeast of Lake Ezerishche opposite the forces of 11th Guards Army. On the salient's northeastern face, LIII Army Corps' 3rd and 4th Luftwaffe Field Divisions defended the roughly 40-kilometer-wide sector stretching from Liakhovo to Malgati (60 kilometers north and 35 kilometers north-northeast of Vitebsk, respectively), opposite the forces of 43rd Army. On the salient's eastern flank, 14th, 206th, and 246th Infantry Divisions of Third Panzer Army's VI Army Corps deployed from left to right, defended the 50-kilometer-wide sector north of, astride, and south of the Smolensk-Liozno-Vitebsk highway and railroad line. The VI Corps' three divisions faced 43rd Army's 92nd Rifle

Table 8.4. The 39th Army's Order of Battle on 13 December 1943

5th Guards Rifle Corps—Major General V. G. Pozniak
9th Guards Rifle Division
17th Guards Rifle Division
19th Guards Rifle Division
97th Rifle Division
1st Rifle Corps—Major General V. P. Kotel'nikov
145th Rifle Division
204th Rifle Division
84th Rifle Corps—Major General E. V. Dobrovol'sky
91st Guards Rifle Division
134th Rifle Division
158th Rifle Division
32nd Rifle Division
184th Rifle Division
124th Rifle Brigade
28th Guards Tank Brigade
39th Guards Tank Brigade
47th Mechanized Brigade
11th Separate Guards Tank Regiment

Source: Boevoi sostav Sovetskoi Armii, chast' III (Ianvar'–dekabr' 1943 g.) [The combat composition of the Soviet Army, pt. 3 (January–December 1943)] (Moscow: Voenizdat, 1972), 302; and *Boevoi sostav Sovetskoi Armii, chast' IV (Ianvar'–dekabr' 1944 g.)* [The combat composition of the Soviet Army, pt. 4 (January–December 1944)] (Moscow: Voenizdat, 1988), 12.

Corps as well as 39th Army's 5th Guards and 1st Rifle Corps. On 13 December, Third Panzer Army's only panzer division, the 20th, fielded thirty-one tanks operable and in short-term repair, plus six assault guns and thirty-two armored self-propelled howitzers.[9]

Soviet accounts of the ensuing operation claim that the attacking forces possessed two- to threefold superiority over their foes (see Table 8.5a).

However, these figures include only 11th Guards and 4th Shock Armies and overestimate German strength in terms of divisions committed. When adjusted to reflect reality (by including 43rd and 39th Armies), the correlation tips further in the Soviets' favor (see Table 8.5b).

In addition, these figures do not include the reinforcements each side received during the operation, including the Western Front's 33rd Army on the Soviet side, which joined the attack east of Vitebsk on 23 December. However, considering the reduced strength of Soviet divisions, the actual infantry correlation did not exceed 5 to 1 even after 33rd Army joined the offensive.

Earl Ziemke has summarized the fate of the Third Panzer Army in the Gorodok operation:

> On 13 December *Eleventh Guards Army* attacked the northern tip of the Third Panzer Army flank from the northeast, northwest, and southwest. In two days it cut in deeply and was clearly on the way toward forming two encirclements and trapping a German division in each. A request to take his front back brought Reinhardt [the commander of Third Panzer

Table 8.5a. The Correlation of Opposing Forces in the Vitebsk Offensive Operation

SOVIET (11th GA, 4th SA)	FORCES AND WEAPONS	GERMAN	CORRELATION
20	Divisions (including cavalry)	10	2:1
275	Tanks and self-propelled guns	120	2.3:1
2,150	Artillery and mortars	800	2.7:1

Table 8.5b. The Correlation of Opposing Forces in the Vitebsk Offensive Operation

SOVIET	FORCES AND WEAPONS	GERMAN	CORRELATION
49	Divisions (including cavalry)	10	5:1
470	Tanks and self-propelled guns	120	4:1
over 3,500	Artillery and mortars	800	4.4:1

Note: These figures count one tank corps and two rifle brigades as equivalent to one rifle division and cavalry divisions as if they were rifle divisions.

Army] a blunt refusal from Busch and a further admonition from the OKH that Hitler wanted the flank held under all circumstances because he was determined to close the gap from the north. In another day Reinhardt's northernmost division [the 87th Infantry] was encircled and the division southwest of it [the 129th Infantry] cut off from the road and railroad. Reinhardt then had no choice but to order the encircled division to break out, which it did on 16 December at a cost of 2,000 of its 7,000 troops and all of its artillery, heavy weapons, and vehicles.

On the 16th Hitler at last conceded that to close the Nevel' gap was no longer possible. But, as always, reluctant to permit any changes in the front, he told the army groups to deny the enemy any further successes. Between 17 and 23 December Reinhardt, harassed all the way by reminders from Hitler that withdrawals were not permitted except under overwhelming pressure, took his army's flank back to an irregular arc twenty miles north of Vitebsk.

The still unanswered question was what the Russians would do next. On the chance that they might turn west, Reinhardt strengthened his line on the west, and the OKH transferred two divisions [*Feldherrnhalle* and 5th Jäger] from Army Group North to the Army Group Center left flank east of Polotsk.[10]

Although generally correct, Ziemke fails to identify completely the Soviet force that attacked on 13 December, which, in addition to 11th Guards Army, also consisted of 4th Shock, and later, 43rd and 39th Armies.

The 11th Guards and 4th Shock Armies began their offensive early on 13 December, after artillery preparations that lasted two and one-and-one-half hours respectively but were without air support because of poor flying weather (see Maps 8.4 and 8.5). Only 84th Guards Rifle Division of 11th

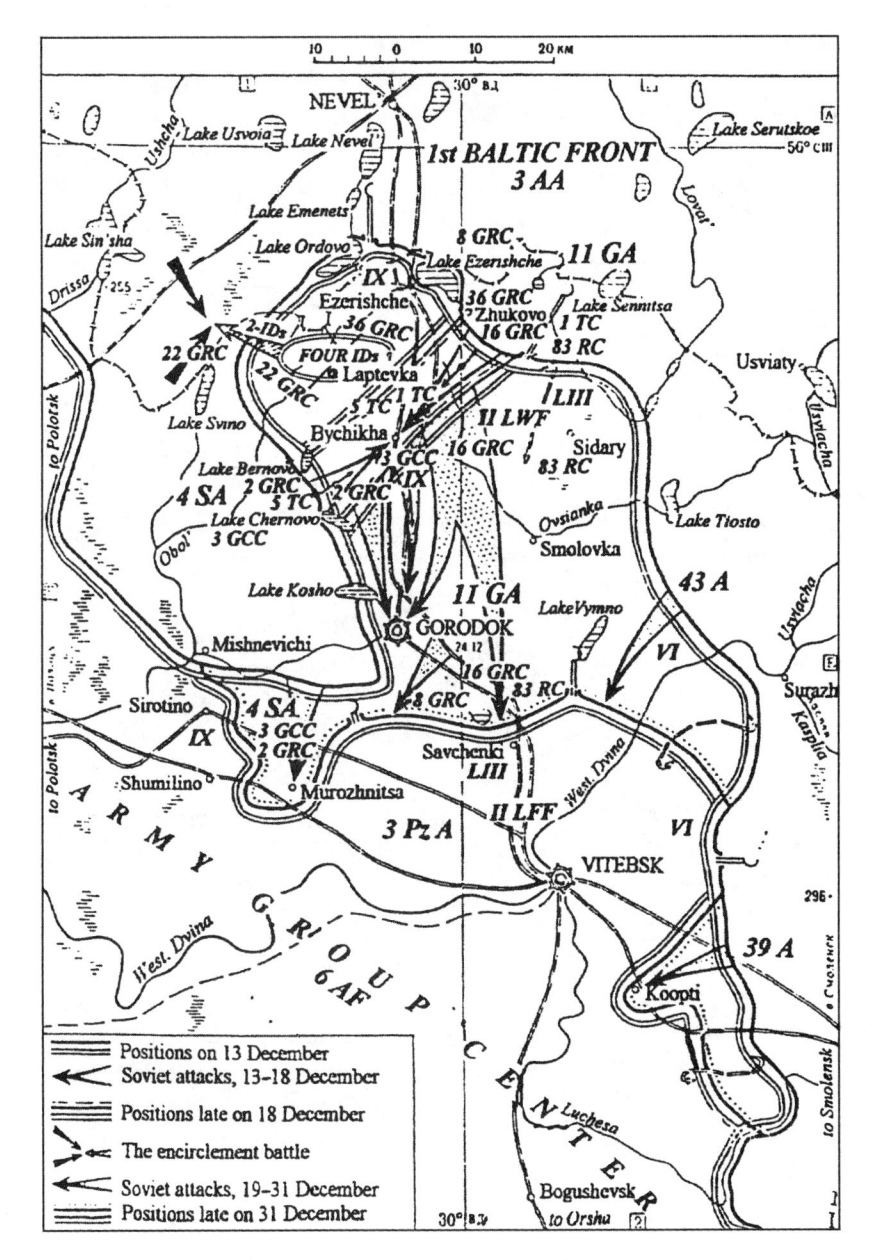

Map 8.4. The Gorodok Offensive Operation, 13–31 December 1943

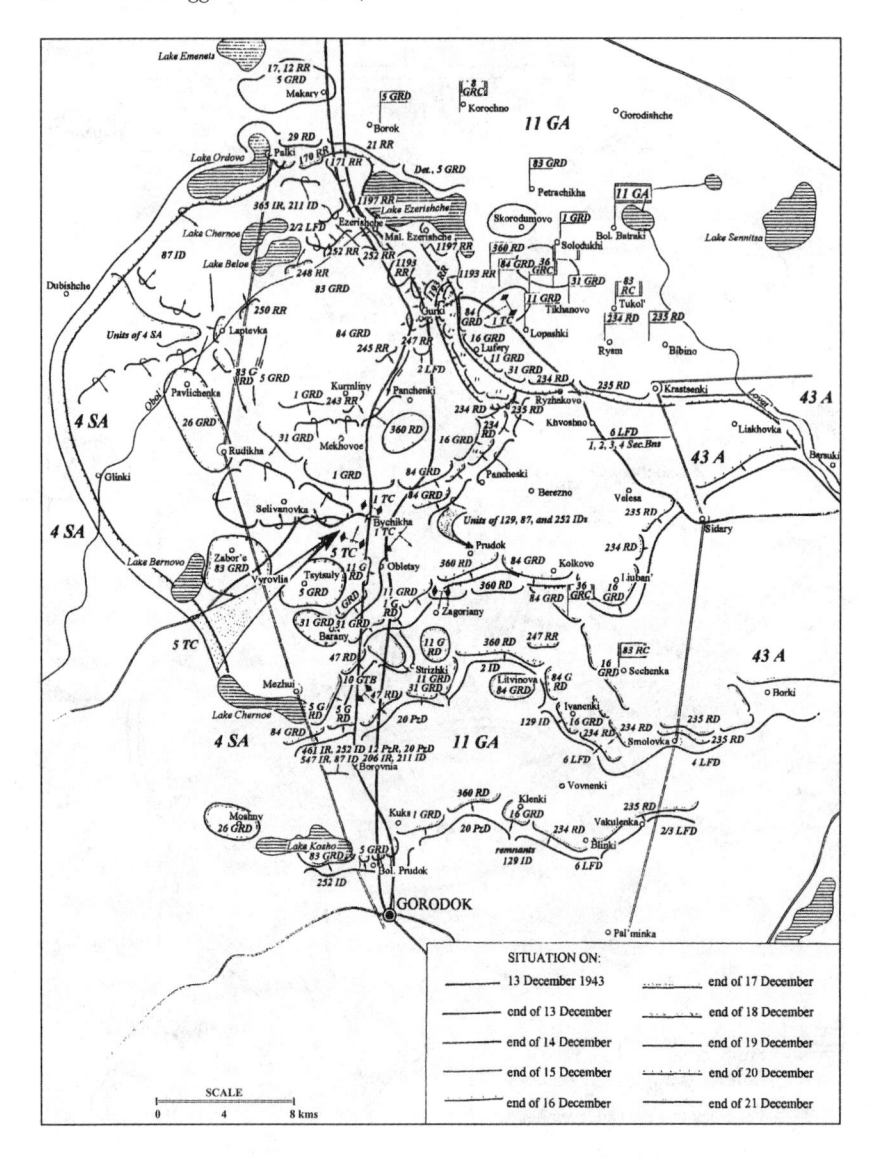

222 The Struggle for Belorussia, October–December 1943

Map 8.5. 11th Guards Army's Operations, 13–21 December 1943

Guards Army's 36th Guards Rifle Corps was able to penetrate the Germans' first defensive positions on the first day of the assault.[11] After advancing about 2 kilometers on a front of 1.5 kilometers, the reserves of IX Army Corps' 129th Infantry Division halted the Soviet advance by conducting a skillful counterattack. Alarmed over the failure to smash German defenses on the first day of the offensive, Galitsky decided to shift his army's main attack into

36th Guards Rifle Corps' sector. To that end, he ordered Lieutenant General V. V. Butkov's 1st Tank Corps and 83rd Guards Rifle Division to regroup and attack through 84th Guards Rifle Division's sector on the morning of 14 December "to complete the penetration and reach Bychikha Station."[12] After regrouping overnight, 84th Guards Rifle Division and 1st Tank Corps' 159th Tank Brigade attacked early on 14 December after yet another artillery preparation. This time the attack succeeded in smashing through 129th Infantry Division's forward defenses. Late in the morning, Butkov committed his tank corps' 117th Tank and 44th Motorized Rifle Brigades, and the entire force tore through German defenses and cut the Nevel'-Gorodok road 4 kilometers to IX Corps' rear. On the flanks of the penetration, 16th and 83rd Guards Rifle Divisions exploited the German collapse and expanded the penetration toward Laptevka and Surmino (35 kilometers north of Gorodok) in the rear of the German 87th Infantry Division, which was already being pressed eastward by assaults conducted by 4th Shock Army's 22nd Guards Rifle Corps.

In 4th Shock Army's sector on the morning of 13 December, 47th Rifle Division of General Beloborodov's 2nd Guards Rifle Corps, supported by 24th Tank Brigade of General Sakhno's 5th Tank Corps, penetrated a depth of 5 kilometers through 20th Panzer Division's defenses between Lakes Bernovo and Chernovo, 14–20 kilometers north of Gorodok (see Map 8.6). On 2nd Guards Corps' right, 90th Guards Rifle Division, cooperating with 5th Tank Corps' 70th Tank Brigade, nearly kept pace by pushing 3 kilometers deep into 20th Panzer's second defensive position. However, the attack by 381st Rifle Division on 2nd Guards Corps' left wing faltered after only minimal gains. Therefore, Shvetsov ordered Sakhno to commit his tank corps' 41st Tank Brigade into 90th Guards Rifle Division's sector as well as two cavalry divisions from General Oslikovsky's 3rd Guards Cavalry Corps into 47th Rifle Division's sector early on 14 October. As a result, by day's end on 14 December, 47th Rifle Division and 5th Guards Cavalry Division reached and cut the Nevel'-Gorodok railroad line near Rosliaki Station, only 12 kilometers north of Gorodok. On their left, 90th Guards and 381st Rifle Division, supported by 5th Tank Corps' 70th Tank Brigade, succeeded in encircling a modest number of German troops in the village of Vyrovlia, 20 kilometers north of Gorodok, and dispatched its forward elements 1.5–2 kilometers to the north to link up with the advancing forward detachments of 11th Guards Army.

Major General Otto Heidkämper, the chief of staff of Third Panzer Army, later recounted 4th Shock Army's success:

> On 13 December the Soviets began a great offensive with the aim of encircling the northern wing of our panzer army. The winter battle of Vitebsk . . . had begun. Four Soviet rifle divisions and approximately 45 tanks struck 129th Infantry Division south of Lake Ezerishche from the northeast. Simultaneously, two rifle divisions and up to 50 tanks attacked

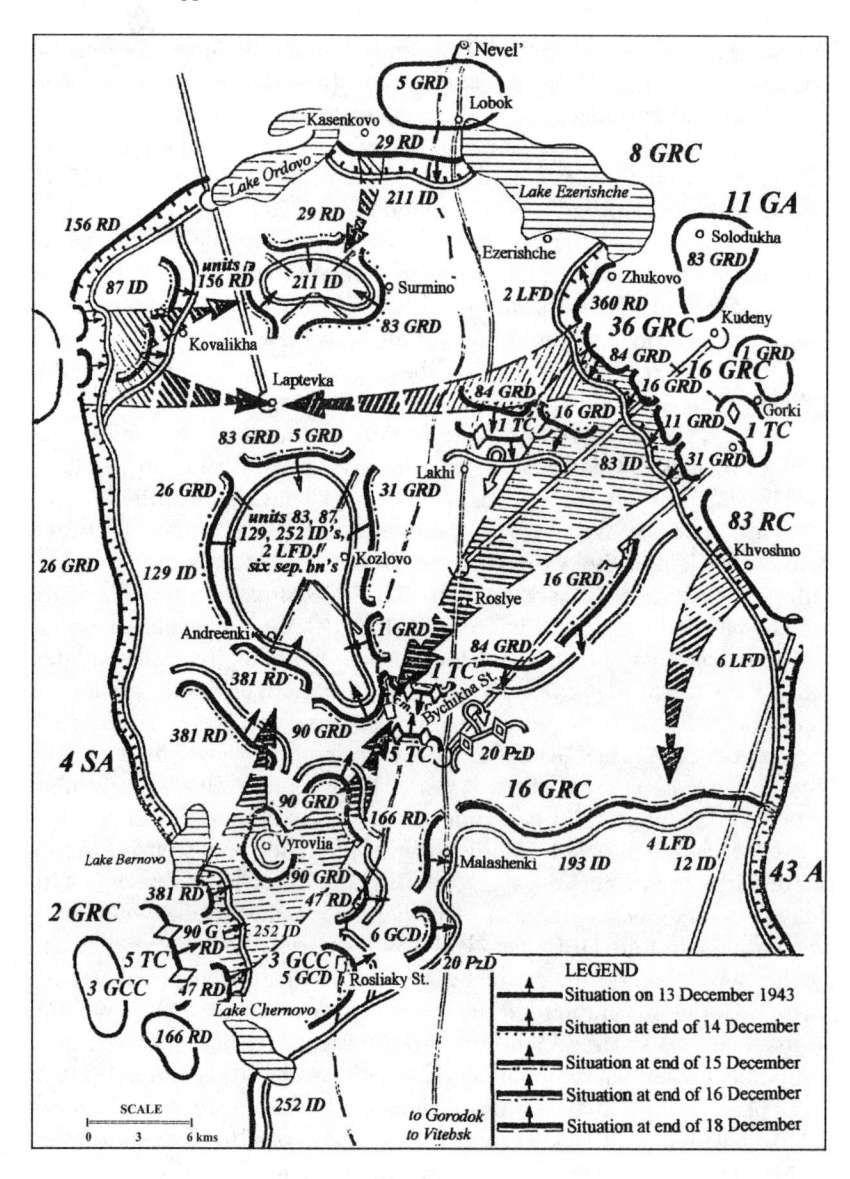

224   The Struggle for Belorussia, October–December 1943

Map 8.6. The 1st Baltic Front's Gorodok Offensive Operation, 13–18 December 1943

20th Panzer Division along the Lake Bernovo and Lake Chernovo line from the southwest. The right flank of 129th Infantry Division was driven back 4 kilometers. The enemy reached the Nevel'-Gorodok road by the evening, and the army command, trying to restore the position, committed its last reserves. At the positions of 20th Panzer Division, the Russians succeeded in penetrating up to a depth of 3 kilometers on a broader front, but his further advance was halted as a result of our counterattacks.

At the request of the army commander for permission to conduct a rapid withdrawal of the forces on the army's northern flank, General Fieldmarshal E. Busch [the commander of Army Group Center] in a telegram received in the army headquarters on the evening of 13 December, once again underscored that such requests will be categorically denied. He said, "The order of the Fuhrer that the final aim of Third Panzer Army's operations is the destruction of the enemy who has penetrated west of Nevel' requires of the army the unconditional holding of its present positions."[13]

In addition, on 14 December, 4th Shock Army's 22nd Guards Rifle Corps began heavy assaults against IX Army Corps' 87th Infantry Division's front along the western flank of the salient. By day's end its divisions had advanced up to 1.5 kilometers through heavily forested and swampy terrain to the village of Skarinino, 10 kilometers west of Laptevka. If 11th Guards Army could reach Laptevka, 4th Shock Army's lead elements now threatened 87th Infantry Division with encirclement.

Despite the obvious successful beginning of the offensive, later on 14 December, an obviously impatient General Bagramian, who believed that 4th Shock Army's offensive had "died," sent a caustic message to its temporary commander, Lieutenant General M. N. Gerasimov, who had replaced Shvetsov when the latter fell ill. His missive read, "Develop the offensive resolutely day and night.... Today, on 14 December, cut the Nevel'-Vitebsk railroad in the Barkhi and Maleshenki sector at all costs" (see Appendix G-4).[14]

This message clearly belied the success both of Bagramian's attacking armies were now achieving. Moreover, the weather improved on 14 December; therefore, both sides began enjoying air support. In fact, by early on 15 December, despite counterattacks conducted by 20th Panzer Division with a force of seven to fifteen tanks, the forward elements of 4th Shock and 11th Guards Armies had completely encircled German 87th Infantry Division and part of 129th Infantry Division in the northern half of the Gorodok salient. First, shortly after dawn on 15 December, 4th Shock Army's commander committed his reserve 166th Rifle Division, supported by 5th Tank Corps' 41st Tank Brigade, into combat on 3rd Guards Cavalry Corps' left flank. This fresh force penetrated 20th Panzer Division's already shattered defenses and reached the railroad line at Maleshenki by day's end. On 166th Rifle's left, 90th Guards Division and 70th Tank Brigade pushed on toward Bychikha Station, splitting IX Army Corps' 87th Infantry and 20th Panzer Divisions from each other.

Further north, 156th Rifle Division of 4th Shock Army's 22nd Guards Rifle Corps linked up near Laptevka with the forward elements of 11th Guards

Army's 83rd Guards and 29th Rifle Divisions, thereby encircling all of 87th Infantry Division west of Surmino. The remnants of the encircled German division struggled over the next twenty-four hours to escape the trap to the southwest. Some did, but many did not.

General Butkov's 1st Tank Corps and the forward detachment of 1st Guards Rifle Division (of 11th Guards Army's 36th Guards Rifle Corps) linked up at Bychikha Station with 4th Shock Army's 5th Tank Corps and 90th Guards Rifle Division on the morning of 16 December. Soon after, the forward elements of 11th Guards Army's 16th Guards Rifle Corps approached the region from the northeast and 90th Guards Rifle Division from the northwest. At this moment, the trap slammed shut around the remnants of German IX Army Corps. Caught in the blazing caldron were 129th Infantry Division; elements of 87th Infantry, 20th Panzer, and 2nd Luftwaffe Field Divisions; and a variety of German security and police units.

With the northern portion of the Gorodok salient crushed, the two victorious armies simultaneously set about reducing the encircled German forces and reorienting their attack southward toward Gorodok. Elements of 11th Guards Army's 8th and 16th Guards Rifle Corps and 4th Shock Army's 2nd Guards Rifle Corps undertook the first task. Concentric attacks by 16th Guards Rifle Corps' 31st and 1st Guards Rifle Divisions from the east, 8th Guards Rifle Corps' 83rd and 5th Guards Rifle Divisions from the north, 8th Guards Rifle Division from the west, and 2nd Guards Rifle Corps' 29th, 90th Guards, and 381st Rifle Divisions from the southwest crushed the encircled German forces in two days of heavy fighting. Soviet sources claim that up to 20,000 Germans fell victim during the cauldron fighting, whereas German sources admit to just over 2,000 losses.[15] In either case, the fighting decimated 87th Infantry Division, whose survivors were evacuated to the rear, and tore apart Third Panzer Army's defenses, precipitating further intense fighting and the withdrawal of IX Army Corps to more defensible lines around Vitebsk (see Map 8.7).

During the following two days (17 and 18 December), the remainder of the two Soviet armies' forces advanced 6–8 kilometers to the south toward Gorodok against hastily erected defenses occupied by German 252nd Infantry, 20th Panzer, 129th Infantry, and 6th Luftwaffe Field Divisions. The Germans exploited the brief respite afforded to them by the complex Soviet regrouping to withdraw forces from their northernmost defensive positions in the shrinking salient to more defensible lines to the south. While 20th Panzer Division dug in grimly along the road north of Gorodok, 129th Infantry and 6th and 3rd Luftwaffe Field Divisions completed a relatively orderly withdrawal 20 kilometers to the rear by day's end on 19 December (see Map 8.8). Frantically, Army Group Center dispatched 197th Infantry Division northward from the sector of Fourth Army's XXVII Army Corps to assist Third Panzer Army's beleaguered IX Army Corps.

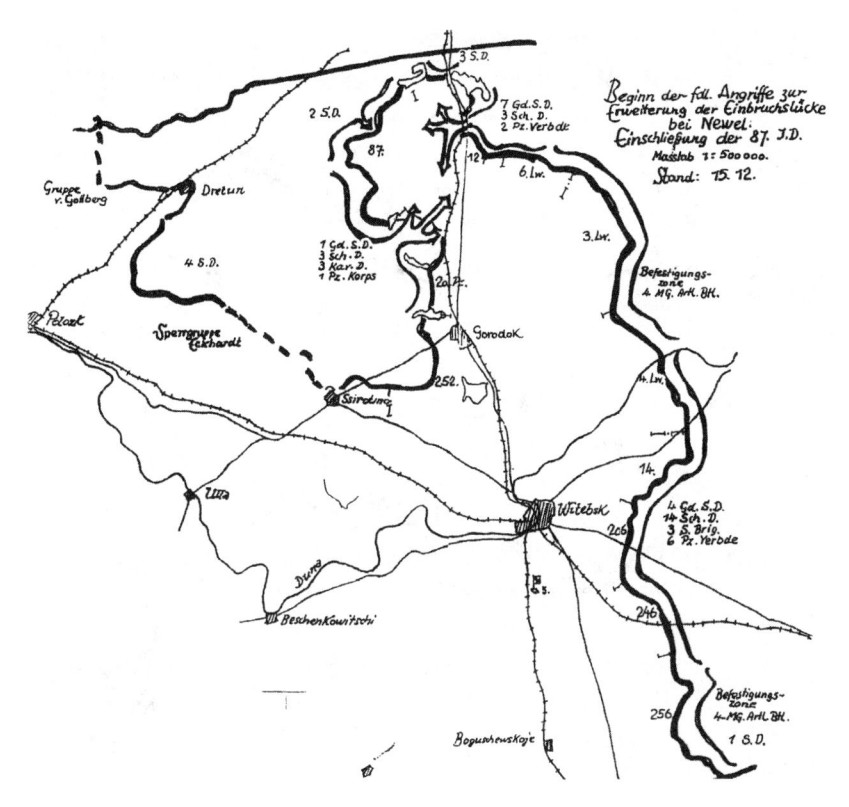

Map 8.7. Third Panzer Army's Appreciation of the Situation at Vitebsk, 15 December 1943

At this point most Soviet sources lapse into silence about subsequent events that took place between 19 and 23 December and, instead, describe the ensuing battle for Gorodok proper briefly and incorrectly:

> The 11th [Guards] Army's 8th Guards Rifle Corps captured Gorodok during the second stage of the operation, which began on 23 December, by delivering the main attack by an enveloping blow with two divisions from the west. The formations of 4th Shock Army's 2nd Guards Rifle and 3rd Guards Cavalry Corps developed an offensive in the direction of Shumilino. They advanced forward 15–16 kilometers in five days of heavy fighting and cut the Vitebsk-Polotsk highway and railroad line east of Shumilino. By this time the forces of 11th Guards Army had also advanced forward 18–20 kilometers and reached the immediate approaches to Vitebsk. But our forces were able to achieve no more since they encountered stubborn resistance of a sizable enemy force. With this, the 1st Baltic Front's Gorodok operation ended.[16]

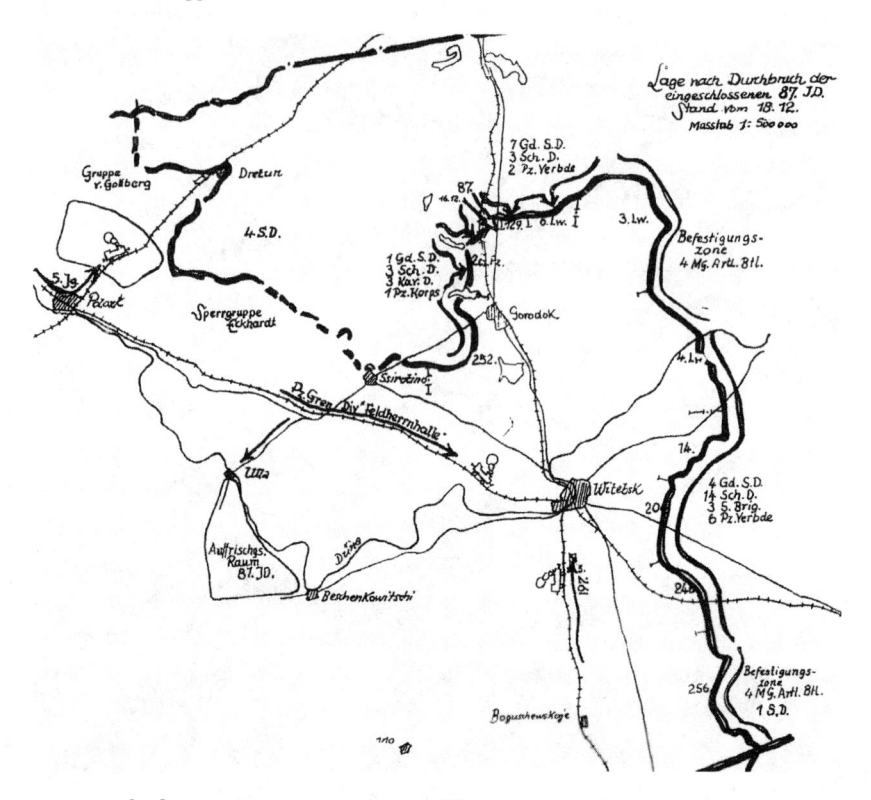

Map 8.8. Third Panzer Army's Appreciation of the Situation at Vitebsk, 18 December 1943

In fact, while the final Soviet assault on Gorodok was still under way, the 1st Baltic Front commenced a new offensive by its 43rd and 39th Armies east of Vitebsk.

VITEBSK EAST (19–24 DECEMBER 1943)

The second phase of the Vitebsk operation began on 19 December when the 1st Baltic Front's forces resumed their advance on Gorodok and, simultaneously, attacked Third Panzer Army's defenses east of Vitebsk. Soviet accounts of this phase of the operation are quite brief, and those few that do exist concentrate only on the battle for and capture of Gorodok. For example, in his memoirs, General Beloborodov simply states, "The 2nd Guards Rifle Corps [of 4th Shock Army] completed a march to a new concentration region—to the south of Lake Kosho (the villages of Sukhorukino, Star, Voikhana, and Beguny) on 18 December, in other words, castled to the right along the front line—to the west."[17]

The 1st Baltic and Western Fronts' Vitebsk (Gorodok) Offensive   229

General Bagramian, the commander of the 1st Baltic Front, devoted slightly more than two pages in his memoirs to the seizure of Gorodok:

> We were to continue the offensive without a pause. I issued the appropriate orders to the commanders of 11th Guards, 4th Shock, and 43rd Armies. The main burden of resolving the mission of capturing Gorodok was entrusted to 11th Guards. . . .
>
> The 11th Guards Army's shock group resumed its offensive on the morning of 20 December. The enemy, who was relying on prepared lines, offered fierce resistance.
>
> During two days of intensive fighting, General K. N. Galitsky's guardsmen advanced 35 kilometers on the left wing and in the center and, having penetrated two defensive lines, advanced 15 kilometers on the right wing. . . .
>
> Nevertheless, we did not achieve the full measure of expected success. Gorodok was not taken, and our concept for encircling the main enemy forces, which were defending its approaches, was threatened with disruption. The enemy maneuvered skillfully and resisted stubbornly. The necessity for withdrawing 1st Tank Corps from combat also complicated the situation. Unfortunately, deficiencies also appeared in command and control of the forces. I had to travel to General Galitsky's command post and provide him assistance on the spot.
>
> As a result of accelerating the repair of tanks and arranging for closer cooperation among the force branches—in particular, the improved employment of artillery, especially in direct fire—we managed to achieve a turning point in the course of operations on 22 December. . . .
>
> The artillery preparation began at 1100 hours on 23 December. . . . The 11th Guards and 43rd Armies' soldiers rushed into the attack after a one-hour artillery preparation against the enemy's defenses. Despite the Hitlerites' fierce resistance, General K. N. Galitsky's and K. D. Golubev's attacking units penetrated into the enemy's fortified third defensive belt in several key sectors and then everywhere. . . .
>
> The 11th Guards Army's commander was inclined to give his forces the opportunity to rest on the night of 24 December and continue the operation at first light. However, after a comprehensive discussion of that question, scrupulously weighing all of the pros and cons, we decided to carry out a night assault. . . .
>
> The night of 24 December proved to be decisive in the Gorodok operation. The attack signal was given to 83rd and 26th Guards Rifle Divisions, which were operating from the west, and the 11th Guards, which was attacking from the east, at 0200 hours. As we expected, after the initial shock generated by a surprise night attack by infantry and tanks, the enemy resisted fiercely along both axes, opening dense area fire and organizing counterattacks with tanks and assault guns.

Having waited for the moment when combat in both attack sectors reached a fever pitch, I ordered General N. K. Galitsky to throw Major General N. L. Soldatov's 5th Guards Division into the storm of the city....

The guardsmen's attack was savage and relentless. Overcoming the river channel on the ice, they penetrated into the northern part of the town. Moscow saluted the 1st Baltic Front's forces, which liberated Gorodok on the evening of 24 December.[18]

Although Bagramian mentions 43rd Army just in passing, nowhere does he describe the part either it or 39th Army played in the operation.

General Galitsky, the commander of 11th Guards Army, provides more details about the capture of Gorodok in his memoirs, stressing in particular the weakness and exhaustion of his forces and, coincidentally, addressing some of Bagramian's criticism. First, he described his army's mission, stating, "Our subsequent offensive was directed at cutting the Vyshedki-Gorodok road and severing the withdrawal routes of the enemy force defending at the junction of our [army] and 43rd Army by an attack from the northeast." Galitsky explained why the mission was more challenging than it seemed:

However, one ought not to forget that the enemy had already been encircled and defeated twice during the course of only five days during the previous operation. Therefore, it is not surprising that he observed the actions of our forces with special suspicion and attentiveness. Having discovered the threat of a new "cauldron," on the night of 18 December, he began withdrawing hurriedly his grouping that was opposing the left wing of 11th Guards Army's 83rd Rifle Corps and the right wing of 43rd Army. He covered the flanks of the withdrawal with 20th Panzer and 129th Infantry Divisions and also with the remnants of separate subunits and combat groups of 87th and 252nd Infantry Divisions, which had escaped from the encirclement in the previous days.

That night our forces prepared to deliver the aforementioned attack. We carried out the necessary unit regroupings and brought up ammunition, and the sappers cleared lanes for the passage of artillery. We detected the enemy withdrawal at 0200 hours, the very time it began. Having received the news of the withdrawal, I ordered 83rd Guards Rifle Corps, which was commanded by Major General A. A. D'iakonov, to begin the pursuit....

Unfortunately, 83rd Guards Rifle Corps . . . had been weakened during the previous combat, and, as a result, only two of its rifle divisions, the 234th and 235th, with limited reinforcements, were able to attack. The ranks of 36th Guards Rifle Corps, which was ordered to attack the withdrawing enemy with its left wing, were also basically thinned out. Finally, the enemy withdrew rather quickly, while . . . covering his flanks with groups of tanks and infantry.

As a result, he managed to separate his withdrawing main forces from ours [escaped].[19]

Galitsky went on to candidly describe the deteriorating condition of his forces:

> The army's offensive capabilities decreased. This was not just a consequence of its losses, although they were considerable. We suffered particularly heavy losses in tanks. In particular, in this regard, 10th Guards Tank Brigade and 2nd Tank Regiment had already been withdrawn from combat by 17 December to repair their damaged tanks. The quantity of combat machines remaining operable in 1st Tank Corps also decreased considerably. We also began to appreciate the fatigue of the forces, which had already been attacking day and night for six days, mainly through roadless forests and swamps.
>
> In addition, we once again began experiencing ever-more-serious shortages in ammunition. Despite the fact that the roads were improving, and we could employ not only motor transport but also sleigh transport, new complexities now arose. Once again, we were a far distance from our supply bases and, worse still, the *front* warehouses were just beginning to receive ammunition in significant quantities.
>
> This basically explained why we did not succeed in destroying the Fascist grouping that was defending at the junction of our [army] and 43rd Army and successfully withdrew from the threat of encirclement.[20]

Galitsky's subsequent detailed description of how his army finally seized Gorodok during the next five days matched that of Bagramian.

Although these accounts of 11th Guards Army's operations are essentially correct, they ignore fully two-thirds of what occurred north of Gorodok and east and west of Vitebsk from 19 through 24 December. The first event ignored, which also went unseen by German observers, was a major force regrouping conducted by 4th Shock Army. Rather than participate in the assault of Gorodok, on 18 December 4th Shock Army began regrouping all of its forces into positions south of Lake Kosho, 5–8 kilometers northwest of Gorodok and even further to the southwest, on its extreme right wing. Bagramian's new *front* plan called for completing 4th Shock Army's regrouping by day's end on 23 December. The next morning, 4th Shock was to launch a major offensive southward to sever the Vitebsk-Polotsk highway and railroad line, and isolate and destroy German forces in the Vitebsk region, in cooperation with powerful assaults by 43rd and 39th Armies from the east. The ensuing regrouping required three days to complete and went on while 11th Guards Army was advancing on and capturing Gorodok.

Meanwhile, east of Vitebsk, on 19 December the combined forces of 43rd and 39th Armies struck the defenses of 14th Infantry Division of Third Panzer Army's VI Army Corps (see Maps 8.9 and 8.10). German records indicate

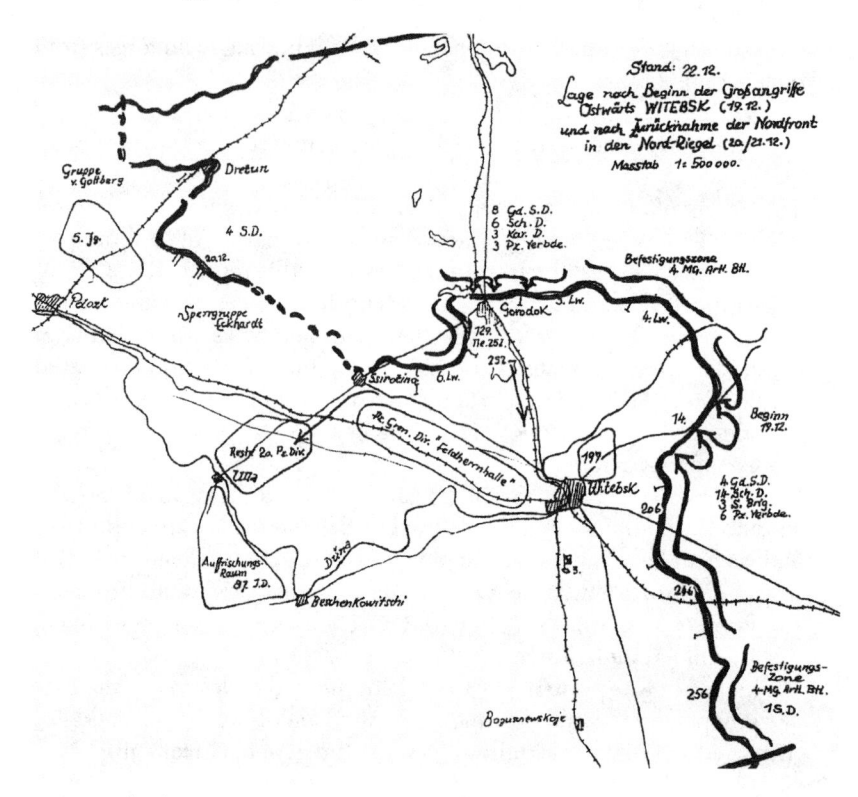

Map 8.9. Third Panzer Army's Appreciation of the Situation at Vitebsk, 19–21 December 1943

that eight rifle divisions, one rifle brigade, and two tank units participated in the initial assault in the 16-kilometer-wide sector from Borok northeastward to Kasenki, south of the Vitebsk-Surazh road. These were subsequently reinforced by several additional Soviet divisions before the attacks died out on 23 December. German intelligence assessments made during and after the attack, together with Third Panzer Army's daily situation maps, indicate that the assaulting Soviet force consisted of at least one reinforced rifle corps from General Golubev's 43rd Army and elements of two rifle corps from General Berzarin's 39th Army, specifically, 43rd Army's 91st Rifle Corps and 39th Army's 5th Guards and 1st Rifle Corps.

Analysis of this intelligence material indicates that General Golubev concentrated his 91st Rifle Corps, 114th and 145th Rifle Brigades, 60th Tank and 46th Mechanized Brigades, and 105th Tank Regiment in the Goriane-Kasenki sector on his army's left wing. Golubev's army fielded about sixty tanks, which he employed primarily in an infantry support role. Initially, Berzarin's force consisted of 5th Guards and 1st Rifle Corps, reinforced by 84th Rifle

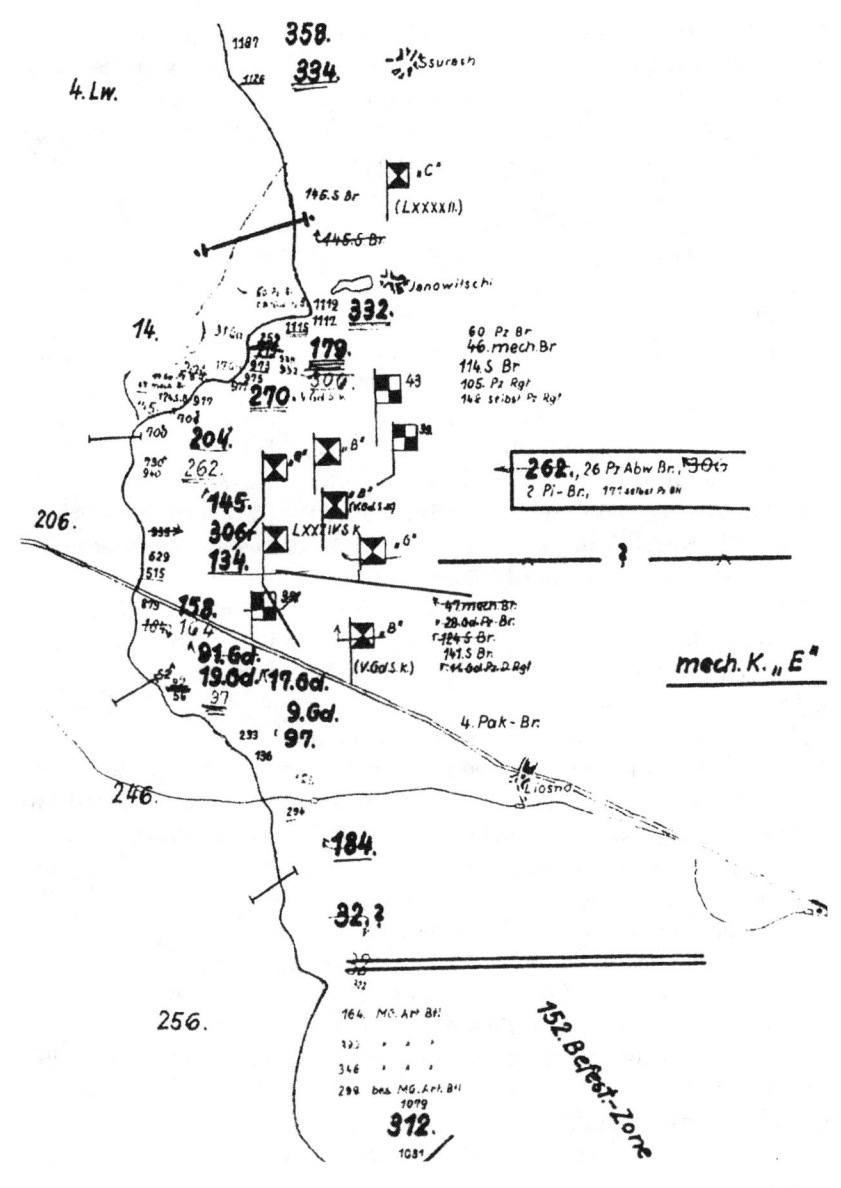

Map 8.10. Third Panzer Army's Intelligence Assessment of Operations East of Vitebsk, 18–21 December 1943

Corps' 91st Guards Rifle Division and 124th Rifle, 28th and 39th Guards Tank, and 47th Mechanized Brigades deployed in the Borok-Goriane sector on 39th Army's right wing. The combined force was to attack German positions east of Vitebsk on 19 December to envelop Third Panzer Army's LIII Army Corps, in conjunction with 11th Guards Army's assault on Gorodok. Berzarin's attacking force fielded at least 100 tanks, the bulk assigned to a mobile group consisting of the two tank brigades and one mechanized brigade.

The two armies began their attack early on 19 December with the first-echelon divisions of at least two rifle corps (see Map 8.11). These included (from left to right) 145th and 204th Rifle Divisions of 39th Army's 1st Rifle Corps, 17th and 91st Guards Rifle Divisions of the same army's 5th Guards Rifle Corps, and 179th and 270th Rifle Divisions of 43rd Army's 91st Rifle Corps. The 39th Army supported 1st Rifle Corps' attack with 39th Guards Tank and 47th Mechanized Brigades and 5th Guards Rifle Corps with 28th Guards Tank Brigade. The 43rd Army supported its assault with 60th Tank and 46th Mechanized Brigade. This force drove the German defenders back up to 3 kilometers along an 8-kilometer front by day's end on 19 December and almost reached the Surazh-Vitebsk road.

The next day the two armies committed their second-echelon divisions to develop the attack. These included at least 91st Rifle Corps' 306th Rifle Division and 5th Guards Rifle Corps' 17th Guards Rifle Division. In heavy fighting, the right wing of this attacking force advanced up to 2 kilometers and reached but was unable to cross the main road. The LIII Army Corps' 14th Infantry Division committed all of its tactical reserves to contain the Soviet advance and was reinforced by 197th Infantry Division's 332nd Fusilier Regiment, which had just been transferred from Fourth Army's Orsha sector. Intense combat raged on for two more days until 23 December, during which the attacking Soviet forces reached the Vitebsk-Surazh road in the 10-kilometer sector from Piatiletna to Kasenki, 21 to 31 kilometers northeast of Vitebsk (see Map 8.12). However, on 23 December this fierce but local battle was overshadowed by an even larger Soviet offensive to the south between the Vitebsk-Smolensk highway and railroad line. Moreover, late in the attack, and probably by 21 December, General Berzarin's 39th Army withdrew its 5th Guards Rifle Corps from combat and transferred it southward to the Smolensk-Vitebsk road.

Although the joint attack by 43rd and 39th Armies achieved only limited gains, it did succeed in drawing critical German reinforcements, especially 197th Infantry Division, away from the Gorodok sector. In doing so, it assisted in the Soviet capture of that town while weakening the shrinking German defensive salient north of Vitebsk. However, the cost to Soviet forces was high. During the entire operation from 13 through 23 December, the *front's* tank forces reportedly lost 156 tanks and 27 SP guns, of which 65 tanks and 17 SP guns were totally destroyed.[21]

Map 8.11. Third Panzer Army's Situation North and East of Vitebsk, 19 December 1943

THE 2ND BALTIC FRONT'S IDRITSA-OPOCHKA OFFENSIVE (16–25 DECEMBER 1943)

If major aspects of the Vitebsk (Gorodok) offensive operation remain shrouded in anonymity, so also do the actions of the 2nd Baltic Front during the same period. Few Soviet sources speak of the offensive operation the

236   The Struggle for Belorussia, October–December 1943

Map 8.12. Third Panzer Army's Situation North and East of Vitebsk, 21 December 1943

front conducted toward the town of Idritsa in late December 1943 and early January 1944, largely because, in January, Army Group North decided to abandon its Nevel'-Novosokol'niki salient, largely without a fight.

For example, the Soviet official history of World War II plays down operations north and south of the Nevel' salient from November and December:

Intense combat north and south of Nevel' and east of Vitebsk did not die down in November and December 1943. The 2nd Baltic Front's 6th Guards and 3rd Shock Armies attacked along the Pustoshka-Idritsa and Polotsk axes. The 1st Baltic Front's 4th Shock, 11th Guards, and 43rd Armies conducted sustained combat north and east of Vitebsk. An especially fierce battle developed for Gorodok.

The German-Fascist command attached great importance to that point on the approaches to Vitebsk and strongly fortified it. The enemy created four defense lines. Three of these were positioned one after another on the approaches to the city, and the fourth encircled its outskirts. They exploited the broken-up terrain, which abounded with dominating heights, lakes, and rivers, to form a powerful defense.

However, the German-Fascist forces were driven from Gorodok on 24 December as a result of sustained combat. Soviet units cut the Vitebsk-Polotsk railroad line. Active operations by partisan detachments, which helped to seize and hold crossings and important lines, assisted their offensive.

The Army Group "North" command intended to attack the advancing Soviet divisions during the Soviet forces' offensive north and south of Nevel'. However, the Leningrad, Volkhov, and Northwestern Fronts' formations tied the enemy forces down with their own actions.

By the end of the year, the Soviet Army had advanced 90 kilometers along the Polotsk axis, liberated more than 500 populated points, and reached the line from south of Pustoshka through Dretun' and further to the southwest along the Western Dvina River and east of Vitebsk.[22]

Nor does Earl Ziemke provide many details of the operation in his excellent survey of the war, which simply notes that the Soviet attack on Gorodok in November forced Army Group North to abandon its attempts to close the Soviets' Nevel' corridor via attacks from the north. Instead, it had to send the two divisions it had concentrated for that purpose southward to participate in the defense of Vitebsk. As a result:

After Third Panzer Army retreated to the Vitebsk perimeter, the flank of Army Group North projecting toward Nevel' became a useless appendage. Late on the night of 27 December Hitler decided to let Kuechler straighten his line and so gain enough troops to strengthen the west face of the Nevel' bulge, which was still manned only by miscellaneous SS and security troops. After 29 December Sixteenth Army in six days drew back to an almost straight line south of Novosokol'niki.[23]

Because of recent Russian archival releases and more careful evaluation of German records, we can now reconstruct the course of events north of

Nevel' in fair detail. In early December, 2nd Baltic Front's 3rd Shock and 6th Guards Armies defended the northern half of the Nevel' salient from the Pustoshka region eastward to Novosokol'niki (see Map 5.7). The 3rd Shock, now commanded by Colonel General N. E. Chibisov, who had replaced General Galitsky when the latter took command of 11th Guards Army in November, consisted of 79th, 93rd, and 100th Rifle Corps. Major General F. A. Zuev's 79th Rifle Corps defended the western flank of the salient from the boundary with the 1st Baltic Front to just south of Pustoshka with 219th and 171st Rifle Divisions in first echelon, backed up by 28th Rifle Division. Major General M. F. Bukshtynovich's 100th Rifle Corps defended the western half of the northern protrusion of the salient south of Pustoshka with 146th, 115th, 18th, and 46th Guards and 245th Rifle Divisions. Finally, Major General P. P. Bakhrameev's 93rd Rifle Corps defended the eastern half of the protrusion with 119th Guards and 326th Rifle Divisions and the eastern flank of the protrusion southward toward the Nevel' corridor with 21st Guards and 200th Rifle Divisions. The 3rd Shock Army was opposed by 81st and 329th Infantry Divisions of German Sixteenth Army's VIII Army Corps, defending along the railroad line east of Pustoshka, and by 23rd and 290th Infantry Divisions of the same army's I Army Corps, which were deployed from the railroad line southward to the Nevel' corridor.

Colonel General I. M. Chistiakov's 6th Guards Army consisted of 23rd Guards and 90th, 96th, and 97th Rifle Corps. The 71st and 67th Guards Rifle Divisions of Major General Ia. D. Chanysgev's 96th Rifle Corps and 282nd and 370th Rifle Divisions of Major General G. I. Sherstnev's 90th Rifle Corps occupied defensive positions north of the Nevel' corridor. The 6th Guards Armies defended to the east and the junction with Lieutenant General V. A. Iushkevich's 22nd Army with 52nd and 51st Guards Rifle Divisions and 31st and 100th Rifle Brigades of Major General N. T. Tavartkiladze's 23rd Guards Rifle Corps and 165th, 185th, and 379th Rifle Divisions of Lieutenant General Iu. V. Novosel'sky's 97th Rifle Corps. General Chistiakov's army faced 32nd, 122nd, and 58th Infantry Divisions of Sixteenth Army's I Army Corps, whose forces were deployed north of the Nevel' corridor, and the same corps' 69th and 263rd Infantry Divisions, defending the front stretching toward the northeast.

On several occasions during early December, the Germans tried to pressure 3rd Shock and 6th Guards Armies' forces defending the Nevel' corridor north of the city, and they also strove to improve the position of their forces defending Pustoshka. For example, a fierce local struggle began on 1 December, when 23rd Infantry Division of Sixteenth Army's I Army Corps attacked the overextended defenses of 200th Rifle Division of 3rd Shock Army's 93rd Rifle Corps. During the attack, 23rd Infantry Division's forces captured the village of Turki-Perevoz, advanced 3–4 kilometers, crossed the Ushcha River, and reached the outskirts of the village of Somino, where the

200th Rifle finally managed to contain the German advance. The attack was particularly dangerous because whoever controlled the heights near the village would then dominate the only road along which the Soviets supplied their forces south of Pustoshka. Therefore, control of that road threatened the entire Soviet force south of Pustoshka with encirclement.

In response to the German attack, on 1 December General Chibisov dispatched 18th Guards (from 100th Rifle Corps) and 379th Rifle Divisions to the threatened sector and placed them under the control of General Sherstnev's 90th Rifle Corps.[24] On 5 December Colonel General M. M. Popov, the commander of the 2nd Baltic Front, and L. Z. Mekhlis, the *front*'s military commissar, arrived at 3rd Shock Army's command post to supervise the operation. That day, the attacking Germans briefly seized Somino heights only to be driven back by a counterattack by the two newly arrived Soviet divisions and 28th Rifle Division attacking from the south. The situation in this sector stabilized by 10 December with the Somino heights still under 3rd Shock Army control. A Soviet source noted:

> On 15 December quiet set in for a short time in the most serious sector of combat operations—in the region of the village of Somino. Having given up hope of penetrating to Lake Iazno "to cut off and destroy Russian 3rd Shock Army," the German-Fascist forces went over to the defense. However, they could not sit on the fence, restore their spirits, and gather their strength. Soon the remnants of the enemy's 23rd and 32nd Infantry Divisions were thrown back even farther from Turki-Perevoz.[25]

Similar local actions took place elsewhere across the 2nd Baltic Front's sector in early December. For example, on 8 December I Army Corps' 122nd Infantry Division attacked 6th Guards Army's defenses northwest of Nevel' and punched a small penetration through the defenses of 95th Rifle Corps' 71st Guards Rifle Division.[26] The 3rd Shock expelled the German forces from the penetration by shifting 51st Guards Rifle Division from its right to its left wing for a counterattack and also by conducting diversionary operations with 23rd Guards Rifle Corps' forces south of Novosokol'niki to weaken German attacks elsewhere. All of these actions strengthened Soviet resolve to settle once and for all with the German force poised north of Nevel'.

While the 1st Baltic and Western Fronts were attempting to capture Vitebsk and Polotsk in December 1943, on 9 December the *Stavka* ordered the 2nd Baltic Front to pierce German defenses at Pustoshka, capture the town of Idritsa, and destroy the German forces occupying the salient between Nevel' and Novosokol'niki (see Appendix G-5). The directive ordered the *front* to "conduct an operation with 6th Guards and 3rd Shock Armies to destroy the enemy's Nevel' grouping," with the immediate mission "to capture the Lake Bol'shoi Ivan' and Ust'-Dolyssy line and, subsequently, attack toward Maevo and Novosokol'niki with a part of the forces to roll up the enemy defense along that axis."[27] The offensive was to begin 14 December.

Very few Soviet accounts exist of this attack because most simply subsume the mid-December operation within the context of the even larger operation the *front* mounted at month's end. It does appear that the attack finally kicked off on 16 December, but only in several sectors, and was handily repulsed by the defending German forces. One account of 6th Guards Army's conduct of this operation read, "On the morning of 16 December, Major General P. P. Bakhromeev's 93rd Rifle Corps attacked in the Ust'-Dolyssa region, north of Turki-Perevoz. It had the mission of penetrating the enemy defense, reaching the Demeshkino and Govorukha line, and destroying the enemy Ust'-Dolyssa grouping during the offensive."[28]

During the attack, which lasted for several days, 93rd Rifle Corps' 21st and 119th Guards Rifle Divisions and 20th and 326th Rifle Divisions, supported by 118th Tank Brigade, dented but were unable to penetrate the defenses of I Army Corps' 290th Infantry Division, which was defending the western side of the German salient north of Nevel'. However, the 290th, soon reinforced by elements of 122nd Infantry Division, halted the attacking force short of its objectives. The other Soviet attacks farther to the south and east also failed.

CHAPTER 9

The Belorussian Front's Kalinkovichi (Bobruisk) Offensive (8–12 December) and the German Counterstroke (20–27 December)

PLANNING

As the 1st and 2nd Baltic and Western Fronts were making one last futile attempt to capture Vitebsk in December 1943, Rokossovsky's Belorussian Front was striving to exploit its November successes in southern Belorussia. After the Belorussian Front's offensive momentum ebbed in late November, a bitter struggle ensued as the Soviets attempted to achieve their ultimate objectives, and the Germans sought desperately to repair the yawning breach in their strategic front.

The Soviet official history passes over this phase of the Belorussian Front's operation rather superficially:

> Combat along the Zhlobin-Bobruisk axis did not die down in December. Especially fierce fighting raged in 65th Army's sector. Its forces entered the rear area of the enemy's Zhlobin grouping. Exploiting the fact that the army's formations were overextended and formed a large salient in the Parichi region, the Hitlerites inflicted a strong counterattack on them from three directions. They concentrated three infantry and two panzer divisions, which they brought up from Bobruisk and other regions, against 65th Army's right wing. This attack struck General I. A. Kuzovkov's 95th Rifle Corps. Bloody combat occurred day and night. The Soviet soldiers fought heroically and held back the enemy's onslaught. The enemy was not able to reach Rechitsa again and drive the *front's* forces back to the Sozh River. Describing this battle, P. I. Batov wrote:
>
> "Such days and even months of encounters with the enemy, which by their significance were of equal value to the capture of large cities, were not uncommon in the war. Salutes in honor of victories did not resound, but the forces displayed no less and, sometimes, even more doggedness, courage, bravery, selflessness, and skill. Among such instances one cannot shy away from the December defense of Parichi. Having lost more than 7,000 killed and wounded and many tanks, the enemy had to give up his plan."

By the end of December [typo reads November], the Belorussian Front's formations reached positions extending from Chausy through Novyi Bykhov, east of Rogachev and Mozyr', to the Pripiat' River. Here the front stabilized until 1944.[1]

Earl Ziemke recalls this period from the German perspective in his study of the war, describing the situation after the German Second Army had established a new front east of Kalinkovichi:

> During the night of 4 December Ninth Army completed its withdrawal. Having improved their positions somewhat, the armies could prepare the counterattack to close the gap. On 6 December they issued orders for the counterattack, code-named NIKOLAUS, and, allowing time for the 16th Panzer Division to arrive, set 16 December as the start date. After the 8th, heavy attacks on the north flank of Second Army tied down all that army's reserves; and on the 14th a flare-up in the angle of the Berezina and the Dnepr forced Ninth Army to ask for a delay to 20 December.
> That the counterattack began on time on the 20th was something of a surprise, and its initial success surpassed all expectations. On the second day the Ninth Army and Second Army spearheads met at Kobyl'shchina. The army group ordered the divisions to regroup fast and turn east to clear the railroad. Until then neither the army group nor the army commands had expected to do more than close the gap, and they had not been very confident of accomplishing that.
> On the 22nd the attack continued, gaining ground to the east against stiffening resistance as the Russians poured in troops from the flanks. In three more days the Germans reached the railroad in the north, but in the south were stalled by a strong line on the Ipa River. On the 26th, Busch, worried about his northern flank, took out the 16th Panzer Division for transfer to Third Panzer Army and told Model and Weiss to stop the counterattack and find a favorable line.
> After nearly three months the Ninth and Second Armies once more held a continuous front.[2]

In early December General Rokossovsky still hoped to accomplish the mission assigned to him by the *Stavka*—to capture the city of Bobruisk. However, a variety of circumstances were conspiring against him. First and foremost, German forces had established a firm defense around Kalinkovichi and refused to budge. Rokossovsky well understood that eliminating the German Kalinkovichi grouping was an essential prerequisite for any further offensive success. He also realized that, if he did not revitalize his offensive, inevitably the *Stavka* would lose patience with him and shift his forces elsewhere— where they could be employed with greater effect. The most likely destination for these forces was General N. F. Vatutin's 1st Ukrainian Front because it had already captured Kiev and was defending a strategic bridgehead in that region against strong German counterattacks.

Rokossovsky's hunch was correct. On 9 December the *Stavka* ordered him to transfer six rifle divisions (initially, 140th, 149th, and 246th) and one rifle corps headquarters from his *front*'s 48th Army to the control of Vatutin's 1st Ukrainian Front. The transfer was to occur in two stages, with the first three divisions dispatched by 15 December and another three by 18–19 December.[3] Rokossovsky did not need this reminder, for he had already ordered a new assault on German positions at Kalinkovichi, this time on 8 December from the north and northeast.

Assembling forces strong enough to crush the German's Kalinkovichi defense was no mean task, primarily because, while doing so, Rokossovsky had to defend his November gains, in particular, the immense gap his forces weakly occupied between the German Ninth and Second Armies. Furthermore he had to do so with significantly reduced forces. For example, on 29 November, the *Stavka* had ordered General Bakharov's 9th Tank Corps to be withdrawn into its reserve no later than 3 December for rest and refitting in the Chernigov region, east of the Sozh River.[4] The next day the *Stavka* also removed General Kriukov's 2nd Guards Cavalry Corps from his control, although they replaced it with Major General S. V. Sokolov's 6th Guards Cavalry Corps, which was destined to reach his *front* later in the month.[5] Somewhat later, ostensibly to improve command and control within Rokossovsky's *front*, the *Stavka* ordered 11th Army (on 18 December) and 63rd Army (on 20 December) to disband and turn their forces over to adjacent armies.[6] The *Stavka* later countermanded its order and did not abolish 63rd Army until mid-February 1944.

Although Rokossovsky's forces had improved their positions somewhat by 1 December 1943, they still faced a number of serious problems associated with the *front*'s overextended geographical configuration (see Map 9.1). Specifically, east of the Dnepr River, General Kolpakchi's 63rd Army occupied positions opposite German Ninth Army's bridgehead on the Dnepr River's eastern bank from Proskurin (also spelled Proskurni; south of Zhlobin) to Gadilovichi (east of Rogachev). On 63rd Army's right, General Gorbatov's 3rd and General Boldin's 50th Armies faced German Ninth Army's defenses along the Dnepr from east of Rogachev northward to Novyi Bykhov and then eastward to just south of Chausy. West of the Dnepr, General Romanenko's 48th Army was continuing to confront the troops of German Ninth Army's XXXV Army Corps, who were trying to stem the Red tide between the Berezina and Dnepr Rivers from south of Zhlobin westward to Parichi. Completing the Belorussian Front's staggered array, General Batov's 65th Army and General Belov's 61st Army were facing German Second Army's forces trying to cling to their defenses north and east of Kalinkovichi and Mozyr'.

244   The Struggle for Belorussia, October–December 1943

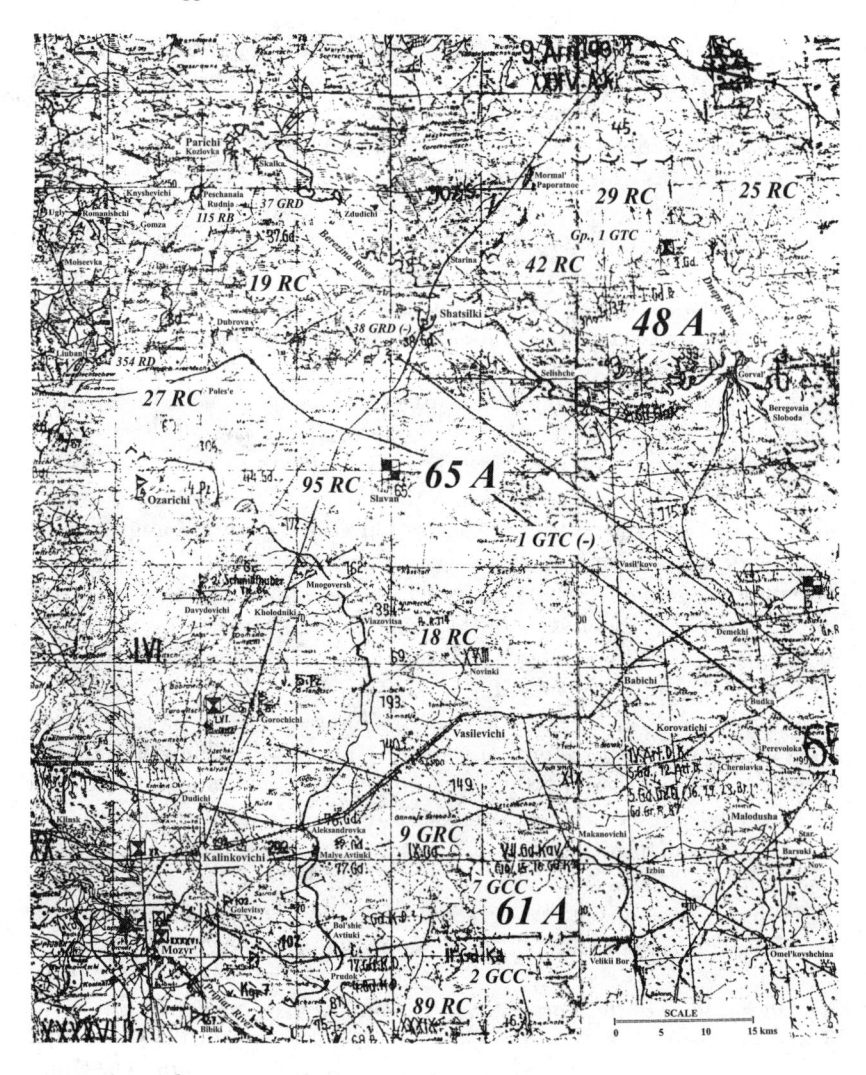

Map 9.1. Second Army's Situation, 1 December 1943

Most vexing to Rokossovsky, however, was the fact that the Germans held firmly to a bridgehead over the Berezina River at Shatsilki (today Svetlogorsk). This bridgehead, on German Ninth Army's extreme right flank and defended by the relatively weak 707th Security Division, sat at the junction between Romanenko's 48th and Batov's 65th Armies. As such, if significantly reinforced, it represented a dagger pointed at the northern flank of his immense penetration and a potential launching pad for a future German counterstroke. At the beginning of December, only 38th Guards Rifle Division of Rokossovsky's 19th Rifle Corps contained the pesky bridgehead but was unable to eliminate it.

Nor were Rokossovsky's forces in the so-called Rudobel'skie Gates very strong. The "gate" was the narrow belt of relatively dry ground midway between Parichi and Ozarichi that led to the vast swampy region south of Glutsk termed the Poles'e swamps. The "gates" themselves were along the dirt roads extending from Poles'e, 25 kilometers west of Shatsilki, westward through Liuban' to Karpilovka (now Oktiabr'skii) on the Ptich' River, about 60 kilometers west of Shatsilki. The village of Rudabelka, 3 kilometers east of Karpilovka, gave the "gates" their name.

The 19th and 27th Rifle Corps of General Batov's 65th Army defended the flanks of the "gates" while trying to expand the penetration through Parichi on the Berezina River to Bobruisk. However, both corps did so along overextended fronts. One mixed combat group from 19th Rifle Corps' 38th Guards Rifle Division was attempting to reduce the bridgehead on the southern bank of the Berezina River at Shatsilki, held by elements of German Army Group Center's 707th Security Division. The remainder of the 38th Guards, along with 37th Guards Rifle Division and 115th Rifle Brigade, were defending the Skalka and Peschanaia Rudnia regions, 5–6 kilometers southeast and south of Parichi, attempting to drive German security forces from that city. Within days, German 1st SS Infantry Brigade would establish even more durable defenses at Kozlovka, 1 kilometer south of Parichi, and hold the position until the German 134th Infantry Division arrived in Parichi on 7 December.

General Cherokmanov's 27th Rifle Corps of Batov's 65th Army defended the western flank of the Rudobel'skie Gates, with 354th Rifle Division positioned west of Ozarichi and 60th and 106th Rifle Divisions facing the defenses of LVI Panzer Corps' 4th Panzer Division at Ozarichi on the Second Army's open left flank. The western extremity of the Rudobel'skie Gates was occupied by several partisan brigades, which cooperated with the two Soviet rifle corps, threatened German defenses between Parichi and Bobruisk, and harassed and disrupted German Second Army's supply lines and rear area. The 4th Panzer Division's reconnaissance battalion was operating against these partisans west of Ozarichi during the first week of December. Further to the south, 44th Guards; 172nd, 162nd, 69th, and 193rd Rifle Divisions of 65th Army's 95th; and 18th Rifle Corps faced German LVI Panzer Corps' 5th Panzer and 292nd Infantry Divisions, which defended positions from the town of Mnogoversh southward west of Vasilevichi to the Rechitsa-Kalinkovichi road. By early December Rokossovsky had ordered General Panov's 1st Guards Tank Corps into the rear for rest and refitting.

General Belov's 61st Army faced 102nd and 7th Infantry Divisions of German Second Army's XXXXVI Panzer Corps, which were dug into an arc of strong defenses east of Kalinkovichi stretching from the Rechitsa road southward to the northern bank of the Pripiat' River. Belov's army deployed for action with 89th Rifle Corps' 15th, 55th, and 81st Rifle Divisions on the left and 9th Guards Rifle Corps' 12th, 76th, and 77th Guards Rifle Divisions on the right, supported by the much-depleted 2nd Guards Cavalry Corps.

Given the awkward configuration of his forces and their relatively depleted state as well as the ambitious missions assigned to him by the *Stavka*, the only consolation to Rokossovsky was that German forces were also exhausted after nearly two months of near incessant combat. Unless they were reinforced, he reasoned, his forces had every chance to achieve additional success. With that fact in mind, Rokossovsky orchestrated yet another offensive, this time against the northeastern flank of the Germans' Kalinkovichi grouping.

THE KALINKOVICHI OFFENSIVE (8–12 DECEMBER 1943)

In early December Rokossovsky ordered Batov to regroup his 65th Army so that, beginning on 8 December, it could conduct an offensive against German forces defending Kalinkovichi from the Novinki region, 35 kilometers northeast of the target city. Deliberately weakening his right wing, Rokossovsky left General Samarsky's 19th Rifle Corps to defend the Berezina River sector from Shatsilki to Parichi. However, he withdrew 354th Rifle Division from General Cherokmanov's 27th Rifle Corps, rested it briefly, and concentrated it at the village of Koreni, 12 kilometers east of Ozarichi. There, together with 27th Rifle Corps' 106th and 60th Rifle Divisions, it was to attack German 4th Panzer Division's defenses at Ozarichi.[7] Rokossovsky also reinforced General Kuzovkov's 95th Rifle Corps with 69th Rifle Division from General Ivanov's 18th Rifle Corps. Parenthetically, General Kuzovkov had replaced General Belonogov on 2 December, when the latter became deputy commander of 19th Rifle Corps. The *front* commander ordered 95th Rifle Corps' 44th Guards, 172nd, and 69th Rifle Division, as well as the adjacent 18th Rifle Corps' 162nd and 193rd Rifle Divisions, "to attack Kalinkovichi from the Novinki, Nakhov, and Vasilevichi region," rupture German defenses, and capture Kalinkovichi.[8] The attack, scheduled to commence on 8 December, would strike directly at the defenses of LVI Panzer Corps 5th Panzer Division.

Little appears in Soviet sources about Batov's 8 December assault. A notable exception is an account in 69th Rifle Division's history:

> Having turned over its occupied positions to 193rd Rifle Division, 69th Division completed a 25-kilometer march and concentrated in the Karpovichi region [40 kilometers north-northeast of Kalinkovichi].
> Major General I. I. Sankovsky, the new division commander, committed his units to the attack at 0900 hours on 8 December. With an of-

fensive gusto so characteristic of them, the subunits penetrated into the enemy's trenches, but the left-flank company of 237th Rifle Regiment was halted in them, and a decisive advance did not occur. The enemy immediately began to counterattack. The battle threatened to turn into a long and drawn-out one.

Attentively directing the battle, General Sankovsky decided to exploit the forested and swampy terrain and undertake an enveloping maneuver. As soon as the Hitlerites felt the threat of envelopment to their flanks, they immediately abandoned the forward edge and withdrew into the depth of the defense.

The division's units captured Ostrov Farm on the heels of the withdrawing enemy and halted 2 kilometers north of Davydovichi, having cut the Zhlobin-Kalinkovichi road. Attempts to develop success toward Ostrokorma were unsuccessful.[9]

As demonstrated by German Second Army's daily situation maps, this account is remarkably accurate. The 27th, 95th, and 18th Rifle Corps did indeed attack on the morning of 8 December (see Map 9.2). The attack by 27th Rifle Corps' 60th and 106th Rifle Divisions on 4th Panzer Division's defenses forward of Ozarichi faltered almost immediately. However, the corps' 354th Rifle Division overcame German defenses at Koreni, captured the heights to the south, advanced 4 kilometers, and split 4th Panzer Division from Group Schmidthuber (of 5th Panzer Division), which was defending the panzer division's right flank. At the same time, 18th Rifle Corps' 44th Guards, 69th, and 172nd Rifle Divisions and 18th Rifle Corps' 162nd Rifle Division, attacking Group Schmidthuber's front, pierced the German defenses and drove the defending Germans back 4 kilometers to the outskirts of the villages of Kholodniki and Buda.

The next day, reinforcements dispatched by 5th Panzer Division contained 95th Rifle Corps' attack in its existing positions, and 4th Panzer Division's defenses held firm at Ozarichi. South of the Zhlobin-Kalinkovichi road, 18th Rifle Corps' 162nd and 193rd Rifle Divisions carved another 5-kilometer salient out of 5th Panzer Division's defenses, capturing Buda and reaching the northern outskirts of Ubolot. Here, however, Rokossovsky's and Batov's offensive ground to an abrupt halt on 11 December (see Map 9.3). Although German records indicate that General Bakharov's 9th Tank Corps supported this offensive, exactly what Soviet armor participated in the attack remains unclear.

Rokossovsky's forces had shot their offensive bolt by 12 December. The principal question that remained was whether he could maintain the breach between the German Second and Ninth Armies long enough to mount yet another offensive, first toward Kalinkovichi and then to capture Bobruisk. Rokossovsky believed that he could, and, during the week following his

248　The Struggle for Belorussia, October–December 1943

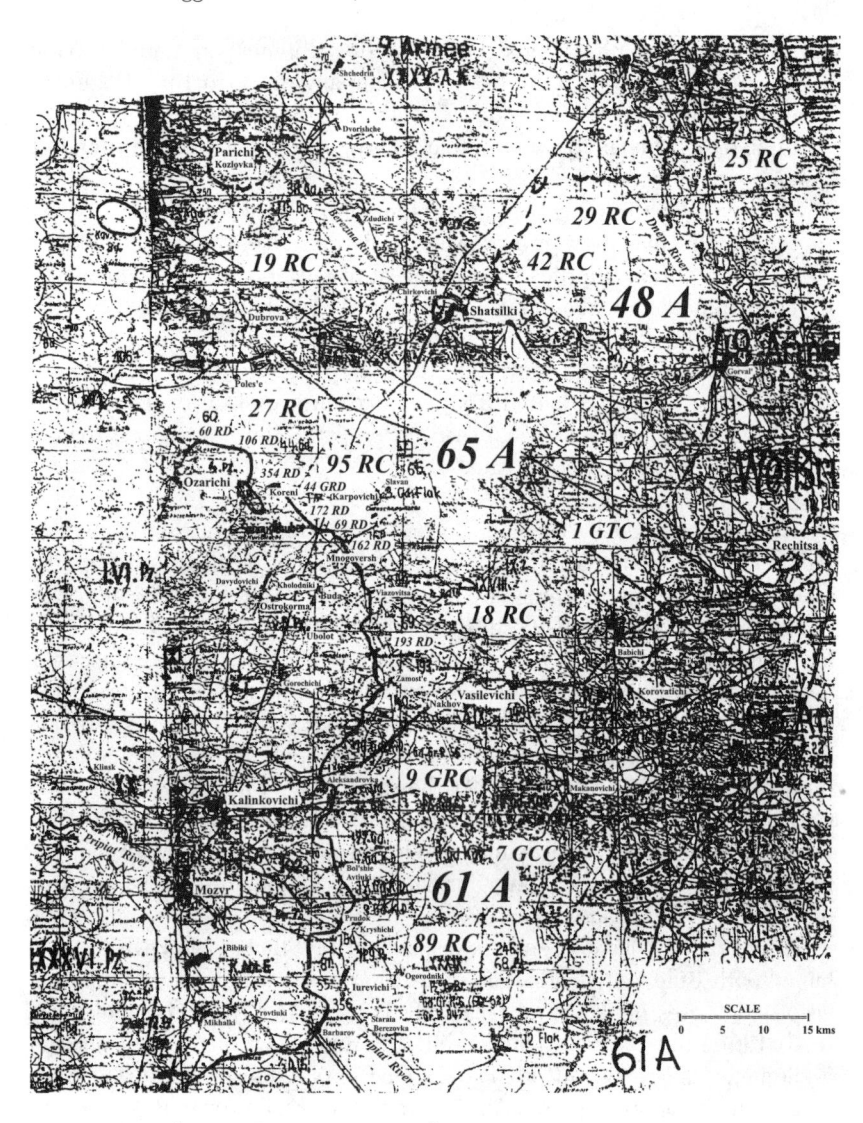

Map 9.2. Second Army's Situation, 8 December 1943

aborted 8 December offensive, he took some measures to help keep the Rudobel'skie Gates open. Although Soviet records are entirely silent about the matter, the German Second Army reported that, beginning on 11 December, the Belorussian Front conducted two airborne assaults in unknown strength in the western portion of the "gates." One brigade was dropped near the village of Khvoiniki, 5 kilometers northeast of Karpilovka on the railroad line running from Bobruisk southward to the Pripiat' River, and the

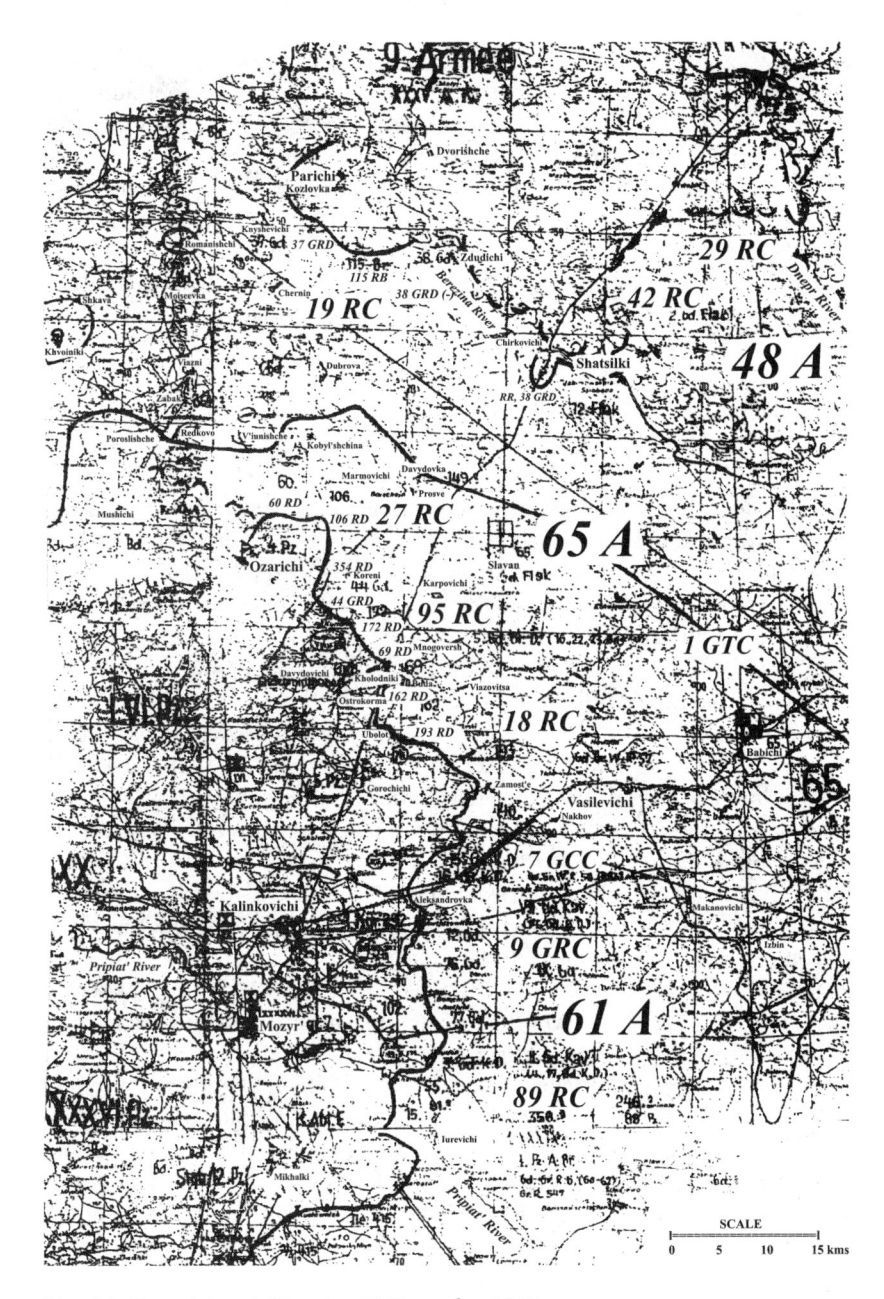

Map 9.3. Second Army's Situation, 11 December 1943

second was just east of Kholopenichi, 10 kilometers northwest of the first drop zone. These records indicate that the airborne activity continued until 16 December. Because subsequent German reports never identified any airborne unit designations, two possibilities exist. The first is that the Soviets indeed inserted two airborne forces of company or battalion size that were subsequently absorbed in the partisans' efforts. The more likely possibility is that the airborne drops simply provided reinforcements, arms, and supplies to the partisan brigades operating in the region. In either case, they did not contribute much, if anything, to the subsequent course of battle.

THE GERMAN COUNTERSTROKE (OPERATION NIKOLAUS) (20–27 DECEMBER 1943)

Meanwhile, before Rokossovsky and Batov could mount another offensive, Army Group Center undertook its own measures to deal with the menacing gap between its Second and Ninth Armies. First, it reinforced their forces adjacent to the gap and improved the tactical disposition of these forces. The Ninth Army ordered XXXV Army Corps to regroup its forces between 12 and 19 December and assigned it responsibility for defending the Berezina River crossing at Shatsilki. Similarly, on 15 December, the army's XXXXI Panzer Corps received the mission to defend the Bobruisk-Parichi sector. While XXXV Corps held firm to its bridgehead at Shatsilki, XXXXI Panzer Corps then enlarged its bridgehead at Parichi and seized other bridgeheads across the Berezina River further to the north. The panzer corps then concentrated 134th Infantry Division, 16th Panzer Division (newly arrived from France), and 1st SS Infantry Brigade in the Parichi bridgehead with orders to assault southward on 16 December to close the gap between Ninth and Second Armies. At the time, the refurbished 16th Panzer Division, the Germans' strongest armored force on the Eastern Front, fielded 113 tanks (15 Pz. III and 98 Pz. IV), 251 APCs, and 21 mobile assault guns and had a "combat worth" of I (the highest state of readiness).[10]

South of the gap, German Second Army assembled a combat group from 12th Panzer Division in 4th Panzer Division's rear area along the Rechitsa-Kalinkovichi road. Its orders were to relieve 4th Panzer so that it could attack northward on 16 December to link up with the XXXXI Panzer Corps' forces attacking southward from Parichi. At the time, 4th Panzer fielded roughly forty tanks operable or in short-term repair and 12th Panzer another forty-five Pz. III and Pz. IV tanks.[11] Although the Germans delayed the operation because of Rokossovsky's 8 December offensive, all German forces were ready to attack by the night of 19 December.

That night 37th and 38th Guards Rifle Divisions and 115th Rifle Brigade of Batov's 19th Rifle Corps were still containing German forces around

Parichi, although on the previous night German forces had cleared Soviet outposts from the western bank of the Berezina north of Parichi. Along the river to the south, 38th Guards Division still monitored the German bridgehead at Shatsilki with a mixed battalion group. West of the gap, partisan brigades and 60th and 106th Rifle Divisions of General Cherokmanov's 27th Rifle Corps screened the broad expanse of front extending from the depths of partisan country to 4th Panzer Division's defensive positions north of Ozarichi. It was a feeble force, certainly no match for a full-strength German panzer division.

After conducting "feeling-out attacks" the previous day, the German offensive hammer fell on the unsuspecting Soviet forces lodged in the gap early on 20 December. Almost immediately, the Soviet anvil shattered irrevocably. Rokossovsky, however, later dismissed the importance of the German counterstroke:

> On the Byelorussian Front, meanwhile, events continued to develop favorably. The 65th Army's left flank had advanced to Kalinkovichi; the 61st Army was on the approaches to Mozyr'. Taking into account our extremely lean supplies, this was, in the circumstances, a great achievement.
>
> To be sure there were setbacks as well. Batov, engrossed in his efforts on his left flank, had failed to notice that the enemy had pulled up large forces against his right flank, though we warned him to be on the lookout. He realized the danger only when the Nazis dealt a powerful blow, overran the weakened units of the right flank and began to pour into the rear of the Army's main forces. Resolute measures taken by the Army and Front Command eliminated the danger. However, the Army Commander's failure to organize adequate reconnaissance and the fact that he had ignored the Front's warning of the danger to his right flank cost us dearly, and we lost substantial territory on the very important Parichi direction.[12]

The Belorussian Front's military commissar, General Telegin, provided a bit more detail about the German counterattack:

> In the heat of the battle on the approaches to Kalinkovichi, the *front's* reconnaissance organs detected intense transfer by the enemy of his forces to the right, specifically the flank defended by a grouping of P. I. Batov. A situation developed here that was reminiscent of the well-known situation that occurred during the unsuccessful penetration of General V. V. Kriukov's corps during the first stage of the winter battles at Kursk [the February Central Front offensive].
>
> Having discovered a weak spot on P. I. Batov's right flank, the enemy intentionally weakened his resistance along his main attack axis. Quickly exploiting this circumstance, P. I. Batov exploited success and reinforced

his main attack axis, unfortunately, at the expense of the forces on his right flank.

Judging from everything, they expected exactly this. Exploiting the weakening of his right flank, the Hitlerite forces launched a strong counterstroke here, which surprised the army commander.

It stands to reason that the command simply did not take into consideration the information it had received from the *front* about the concentration of enemy forces. General P. I. Batov was informed about everything in timely fashion and warned about the danger hanging over his right flank. However, captivated by the prospects for capturing Kalinkovichi (which, in this instance, with the inescapable capture of Mozyr' by the forces of 61st Army, created an extraordinarily favorable situation for the development of subsequent operations), he had come to believe in the feasibility of forestalling the enemy and in the opportunity to present the enemy with the fact of a partial encirclement of a large group of his forces by bold maneuver.

However, everything developed contrary to the commander's calculations. When P. I. Batov, who was enthusiastic over his pursuit of the withdrawing enemy, crossed the Kalinkovichi-Zhlobin railroad, seized the town of Parichi, and even transferred his command post there, the enemy attacked the army's weakened right flank with forces he had brought up from the depths and pressed back somewhat the formations that had not expected such a strong attack.

The command post in Parichi was subjected to artillery fire about which General P. I. Batov reported to the *front's* Military Council, having added to the report a request to move his command post. Inasmuch as the abandonment of Parichi in these circumstances was extremely unfavorable for us, K. K. Rokossovsky quite reasonably refused to approve P. I. Batov's request.[13]

Telegin then stated that Rokossovsky dispatched him to Parichi, where he spent "five days" and, as a result of his visit, arranged for the beleaguered force to be reinforced by 4th Artillery Penetration Corps and several rifle and artillery regiments. Then, said Telegin, "the forces on the army's right wing, which were reinforced by *front* reserves, liquidated the penetration and quickly restored the situation in close coordination with partisan formations."[14] Telegin invented this account from "whole cloth," first because Batov's forces never captured Parichi and second because they never "restored the situation" in the Rudobel'skie Gates.

Finally, we have Batov's description of the action, a remarkably frank and accurate description of what actually occurred:

While I reinforced the right wing with two divisions from 95th Rifle Corps, we were too late. The corps possessed limited maneuverability, especially 172nd Rifle Division. It was jokingly referred to as "the oxen." It had been formed in the Ukraine, and someone managed to give it oxen to move all of its rear services and artillery. The division slowly hauled itself to its assigned line and did not manage to occupy a defense. The enemy delivered a strong counterattack from three directions on 20 December. The Hitlerites concentrated three infantry and two panzer divisions, which they had brought up from Bobruisk and other sectors, against 65th Army's right wing. As we later understood, in accordance with the *front's* orders, 48th Army's 73rd Rifle Division was advancing to positions south of Parichi to reinforce our army's right wing. However, it also did not succeed in occupying a firm defense. A meeting battle ensued between this division and the counterattacking enemy on the morning of 21 December.

The 37th Guards Rifle Division and 46th Artillery Brigade met the enemy courageously. Unable to resist the onslaught, they began to withdraw in heavy fighting. The enemy advanced rapidly on the first day. The 37th Division was partially encircled. Colonel L. M. Molchanov, the artillery commander, perished. Two batteries of 46th Artillery Brigade were cut off from our forces. Enemy tanks and motorized infantry rushed into the breach that had formed, and we almost lost the entire headquarters of 95th Rifle Corps. Here is how it happened.

While regrouping his corps to the army's right flank, I. A. Kuzovkov moved his forward command post to the village of Velikii Bor. At nightfall the penetrating enemy occupied Zarech'e and Velikii Bor [20–25 kilometers south of Parichi] and cut off the withdrawal route of the corps' command post. A single road remained through the swampy forests. . . . [95th Rifle Corps' headquarters ultimately made its way out of the trap but lost all of its equipment.]

The 95th Rifle Corps' forces absorbed the full force of the enemy counterstroke. The tempo of the enemy offensive decreased, but nevertheless his numerical superiority managed to drive our units from their occupied positions in several sectors. The situation in the Shatsilki region was the most serious. Here there was a very sensitive open flank, and the Germans managed to take us in the rear.

Only now can we properly assess the importance of the small fortification (*tet de pon*) left to the enemy on the left bank of the Berezina River at Shatsilki. No one attached significance to that sector during the period of the army's rapid advance to the west. However, the Hitlerites exploited it, expecting to link up there with its Kalinkovichi grouping.

Bloody battles raged night and day in that region. The enemy threw tanks into the assault. The *front* headquarters knew about the counterstroke based on our operational reports, but, in the spirit of self-criticism, one must say that we were not able to provide it with a completely objective assessment of the situation.

The enemy attacks not only affected the divisions. They also retreated, albeit slowly. They managed to halt the enemy along the Zherd' Station and Davydovka line and, further, along the Ipa River. Colonel N. V. Korkishko's 44th Guards Rifle Division fought stubbornly and resolutely during these battles. . . .

On the third day of combat, Nikolai Antonovich asked me, "Have you reported to Rokossovsky on the situation?" "No," [I said], "we will repel the counterstroke, restore the situation, and then report." "It would be more correct if you report on the situation now," [he responded]. Radetsky was correct, but the pill presented to us by the surprise counterstroke turned out to be too bitter. I wanted to deal with it with my own forces and not run for help to the higher commander.

It turned out that, in addition to me, the *front* commander knew about the true situation in the army. As first, he phoned not me but Radetsky. He asked, "Can you tell me the truth about what is happening on the army's right wing?" "The divisions are retreating," answered Radetsky, "They cannot halt the Germans." Nikolai Antonovich came to my observation post and told me about the conversation. After several minutes I phoned Rokossovsky. "Pavel Ivanovich," he said quietly, "how long do you intend to move backwards?" I admitted my mistake. "You should have reported about that earlier," he said.

It was an object lesson. I have remembered it my entire life. In conclusion, Rokossovsky said, "If you need to, move Ignatov's entire artillery corps to your right wing. Transfer other forces there. The situation must be restored. I am sending you one rifle division from the *front* reserve."

I had already moved almost two divisions of General N. V. Ignatov's artillery corps to that flank. The artillerymen were conducting direct fire, even from the large caliber guns. However, there were too few shells. Their resupply was very difficult. We mobilized all of the divisional, corps, and army transport. The vehicles were moving along the beaten-up roads of the swampy Poles'e region with great difficulty. Traffic jams had formed at the crossing sites over the numerous rivers and canals. Although enemy aircraft were not numerous, they were bombing the crossings.

The defensive battle continued for three days. The forces on the army's right wing withdrew 25–30 kilometers in some sectors. However, having suffered heavy losses, the enemy was weakened. The Hitlerites once again tried to penetrate 95th Rifle Corps' defenses along the railroad to Kalinkovichi on 25 December. By this time we had succeeded somewhat in replenishing the army's reserve of artillery shells. The Hitlerites were met by dense fire from Colonel A. I. Snegurov's artillery division, which consisted primarily of multiple rocket launchers. The strike was so heavy that the enemy halted during the first minutes of his attack. This day was the turning point. The force of the enemy counterstroke dried up. I must give proper credit to our neighbor on the right—the 48th Army—which assisted us while absorbing part of the enemy attack in its sector. It also conducted a heavy defensive battle on its left wing from 23 through 25 December and prevented the enemy forces from reaching 65th Army's deep rear. The repulse of the enemy counterstroke in the Parichi region was a great victory for the army's forces.[15]

We are now able to test these accounts of what occurred against German archival records and a superb description of the attack contained in the history of Soviet 38th Guards Rifle Division. General Samarsky's 19th Rifle Corps was defending the Parichi-Shatsilki sector with its 37th and 38th Guards Rifle Divisions, deployed west and south of German Ninth Army's Parichi bridgehead proper, and with 115th Rifle Brigade, defending along the southern bank of the Berezina River from Prudok to Chirkovichi, just north of Shatsilki. A battalion group from 38th Guards Rifle Division still contained the German bridgehead at Shatsilki. The opposing XXXXI Panzer Corps of German Ninth Army concentrated 253rd Infantry Division, 16th Panzer Division, and 134th Infantry Division's 439th Grenadier Regiment, deployed from left to right (east to west) in the Parichi bridgehead, with a portion of 1st SS Infantry Brigade (SS *Verbande* [Detachment] Wiedermann) protecting their right flank. At 1400 hours on 19 December, the day prior to their main attack, two German infantry regiments and twenty-six tanks attacked the defenses of 37th Guards Rifle Division's 109th Guards Regiment northwest of Parichi, forcing the regiment to withdraw several kilometers to the south.

The next day, having already unhinged Soviet defenses west of Parichi, the main German force attacked with overwhelming force (see Map 9.4).[16] After a forty-five-minute artillery preparation, at 0745 hours the massed German force attacked, spearheaded by the fresh 16th Panzer Division, whose strength the Soviets placed at 160 tanks and assault guns. The initial assault struck and shattered 37th and 38th Guards Rifle Divisions' entire defensive front. Lunging southward astride the Parichi-Ozarichi road, 16th Panzer Division's *kampfgruppen* advanced more than 5 kilometers on the first day, seizing the villages of Chernin and Selishche, 20–25 kilometers south of Parichi, and splitting the two Soviet guards rifle divisions' defenses. The 134th Infantry Division's regiment kept pace to the west and 253rd Infantry Division attacked southward along the western bank of the Berezina River, striking 115th Rifle Brigade's weak left wing. Further to the south, simultaneously with 16th Panzer's assault, LVI Panzer Corps' 4th Panzer Division struck northward from Ozarichi, smashing through the defenses of 27th Rifle Corps' 60th and 106th Rifle Divisions. Operating on 4th Panzer's left wing, its panzer reconnaissance battalion swept aside partisans and drove northward to link up with 134th Infantry Division's regiment advancing from the north.

256   The Struggle for Belorussia, October–December 1943

Map 9.4. Second Army's Situation, 20 December 1943

The 4th Panzer Division's reconnaissance battalion succeeded in linking up with forward elements of 134th Infantry Division's 439th Regiment near the village of Myslov Rog, 10 kilometers north of Ozarichi, late on 21 December (see Map 9.5). By this time, 16th Panzer Division's spearheads were approaching the village of Dubrova, midway between Parichi and Ozarichi

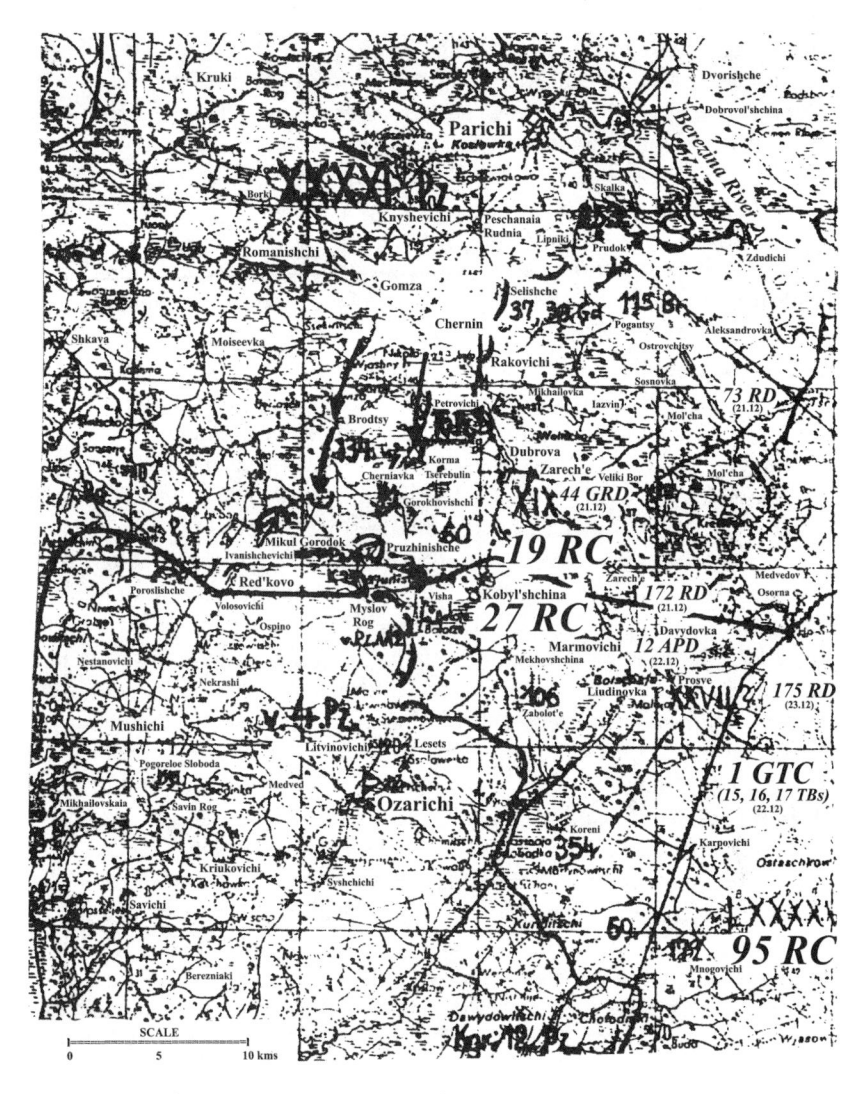

Map 9.5. Second Army's Situation, 21 December 1943

and due west of Shatsilki. Caught between LVI Panzer Corps' 4th Panzer Division moving up from the south and XXXXI Panzer Corps' 16th Panzer and 253rd Infantry Divisions advancing down the western bank of the Berezina River from the north, 37th and 38th Guards and 60th Rifle Divisions and 115th Rifle Brigade had to fight for their lives.

Batov did attempt to support his beleaguered forces. Although it is unclear exactly when he gave the order, by 21 December he ordered 95th Rifle Corps to pull its 44th Guards and 172nd Rifle Divisions from their defenses near Mnogovichi and move them northward to support 19th Rifle Corps' flagging defenses. General Kuzovkov's two divisions first occupied blocking positions facing northward between Zarech'e and Velikii Bor north of the railroad line running west from Shatsilki. However, the German advance gave them no time to dig in properly. Batov also ordered 12th Artillery Penetration Division to move its forces to support 95th Corps. The first to do so were 46th Light and 32nd Gun Artillery Brigades. In addition, General Romanenko of 48th Army sent, first, 73rd Rifle Division and, soon after, 175th Rifle Division from his 29th Rifle Corps across the Berezina River to help stem the German juggernaut. These divisions took up positions on 95th Rifle Corps' right flank northwest of Shatsilki. Finally, Batov alerted General Panov's 1st Guards Tank Corps, still refitting in the rear, and ordered it to commit its brigades to combat as soon as they became available.

The German shock group continued its assaults on 22 and 23 December, attempting to encircle and destroy the opposing Red Army forces. The 134th Infantry and 4th Panzer Divisions pushed eastward toward Marmovichi and Davydovka, 15–20 kilometers west of Shatsilki, driving 60th and 106th Rifle Divisions' remnants before them. Further east, along the western bank of the Berezina River, 16th Panzer Division, now reinforced with forces from 253rd Infantry Division and 1st SS Infantry Brigade, advanced southeast to Chirkovichi, 6 kilometers north of Shatsilki, driving the defending 115th Rifle Brigade southward. The remnants of 37th and 38th Guards Rifle Divisions, which now found themselves caught between the two German pincers, held their positions briefly. However, late on 22 December, General Batov ordered the entire 19th Rifle Corps to fall back to a new 5-kilometer-wide defensive line occupied by 29th Rifle Corps' 73rd Rifle Division, which extended from Rosov, 6 kilometers west of Shatsilki, southwestward through Kremen to Pechishche, 9 kilometers southwest of Shatsilki. West of the Parichi-Kalinkovichi railroad line, 95th Rifle Corps' 44th Guards and 172nd Rifle Divisions occupied positions in the 9-kilometer-wide sector extending from Pechishche to Davydovka. By this time, Panov's 1st Guards Tank Corps had dispatched a tank brigade each to reinforce 19th, 29th, and 95th Rifle Corps.

While Soviet forces were regrouping, on 24 December XXXXI Panzer Corps' 16th Panzer Division thrust southwestward from Chirkovichi through Medvedov to Davydovka, deep into 19th Rifle Corps' rear area. Its intent was to link up near Davydovka with LVI Panzer Corps' 134th and 4th Panzer Divisions' forces attacking from the west. The German pincers reached Davydovka by nightfall on 26 December, trapping elements of 65th Army's 37th and 38th Guards, 60th, and 172nd Rifle Divisions and 16th Guards Tank Brigade in an encirclement north of the village. Meanwhile, to the east, German 253rd Infantry Division expanded its small bridgehead west of Shatsilki.

During the ensuing three days, the Germans tried to destroy the encircled Soviet force; however, many of the latter's remnants succeeded in

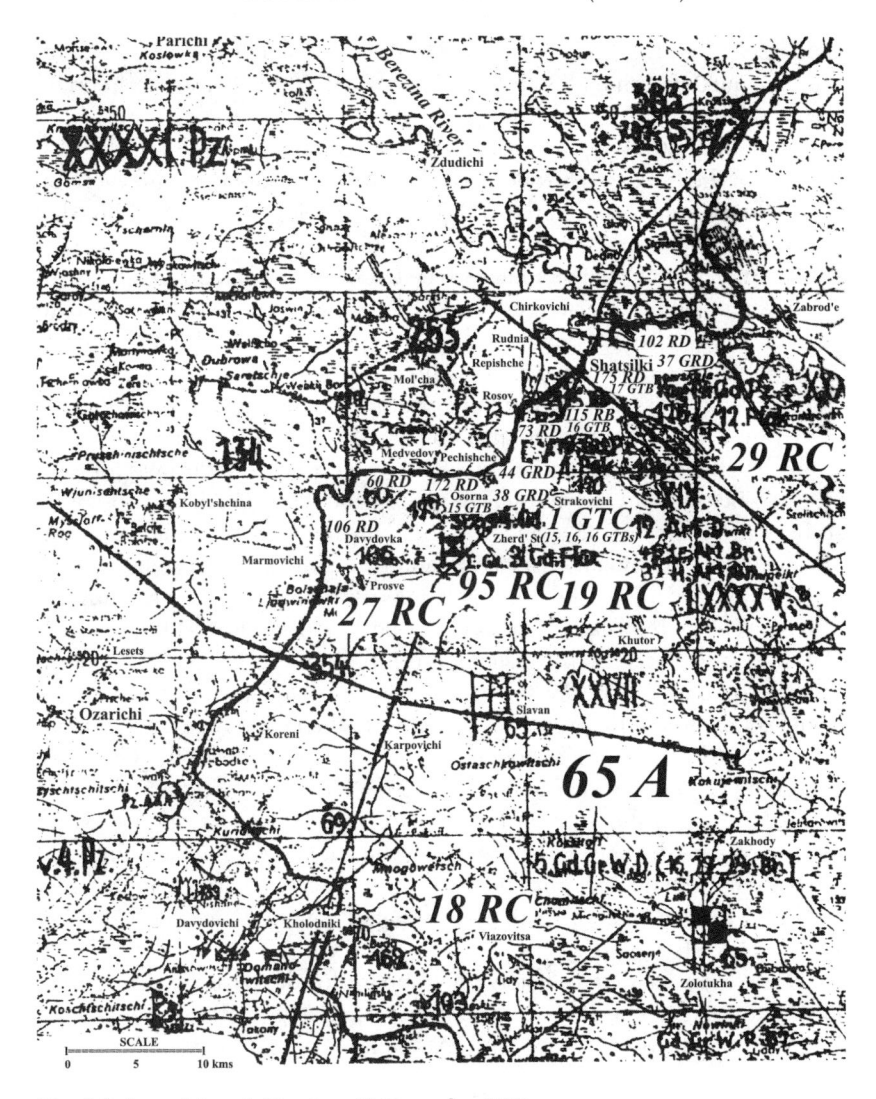

The Belorussian Front's Kalinkovichi (Bobruisk) Offensive   259

Map 9.6. Second Army's Situation, 27 December 1943

escaping to the south (see Map 9.6).[17] There they reinforced a new Soviet defense line, which extended from Davydovka eastward just north of the railroad line to Shatsilki and was manned at first by 44th Guards and 175th Rifle Divisions and, soon after, the remainder of Panov's 1st Guards Tank Corps. There the German counterstroke ended. Batov established a new defense line by 27 December occupied from west to east by 27th Rifle Corps' 106th and 60th Rifle Divisions, 95th Rifle Corps' 172nd and 44th Guards Rifle Divisions, 19th Rifle Corps' 115th Rifle Brigade, and 29th Rifle Corps' 175th and 102nd Rifle Divisions. Immediately after returning from encirclement, the remnants of 37th and 38th Guards and 73rd Rifle Divisions reinforced these defenses.

German Ninth Army had no choice but to call off further attacks both because of the increased Soviet resistance and because events elsewhere on the Eastern Front required the 16th Panzer's services. First, Field Marshal Busch, the commander of Army Center, withdrew the panzer division from Ninth Army on 26 December because he felt it was needed in the defense of Vitebsk. Ultimately, however, events in the Ukraine compelled the OKH to transfer 16th Panzer Division to Army Group South's Fourth Panzer Army, where it went into action in January. This transfer was necessary because, on Christmas day 1943, the 1st Ukrainian Front's armies launched a strong and successful offensive against Fourth Panzer Army's defenses in the Brusilov region, southwest of Kiev. The 16th Panzer's departure to deal with the far more serious crisis to the south finally tipped the scales in southern Belorussia back to the Soviets' favor and precluded further German offensive operations. However, by Rokossovsky's own admission, the German counterstroke had also severely damaged his hopes for continuing any offensive toward Kalinkovichi or Bobruisk. Not only had he lost the valuable Rudobel'skie Gates as well as his offensive momentum but also he had been forced to expend some of his precious armored reserves. Undeterred, Rokossovsky would soon attempt to resume his offensive in the new year. Although modestly successful, the Parichi counterstroke was also costly to the Germans. According to new German sources, "These attacks achieved limited results and *16. Pz. Div.* suffered heavy losses."[18] At the very least, as was the case in other sectors of the Soviet-German front, the outcome of the German counterstroke indicated that, unlike the case in previous years, Red Army infantry and artillery could contend with and ultimately contain a concerted German armored thrust.

Overall, Soviet sources reserve high praise for the performance of their forces during the fall stage of the Belorussia strategic offensive operation. For example, the Soviet official history noted:

> The offensive by Soviet forces along the western strategic axis from August through December was one of the most important events of 1943 and had immense military-political significance. During that period, the Soviet forces destroyed more than 40 of Army Group "Center's" divisions, including 7 panzer and motorized. Large water obstacles—the Desna, Sozh, Dnepr, Pripiat', and Berezina—were forced, Smolensk and part of Kalinin *oblast'*, as well as eastern regions of Belorussia, were liberated. The Soviet Army liberated hundreds of thousands of Soviet people from fascist slavery.

The offensive by Soviet forces along the western axis was a component part of the Battle for the Dnepr. Having forced the Sozh and Dnepr (from south of Zhlobin to Loev), they captured a more than 500-kilometer-wide sector of the Eastern Wall. The defeat of the large Hitlerite grouping changed the situation significantly. The Wehrmacht's plan to win time necessary for the restoration of its exhausted formations collapsed. Having captured the Smolensk gate and advanced along the Gomel' axis, Soviet forces posed a threat to Army Group "Center's" flanks. This secured favorable prerequisites for the conduct of an operation to liberate Belorussia.

The arrival of Soviet forces in the Poles'e region disrupted the continuity of the enemy's strategic front and hindered cooperation between Army Groups "Center" and "South." The attacks along the western axis disrupted the Wehrmacht command's plan to transfer his formations to the southwestern strategic axis. Moreover, during these battles, the German-Fascist command had to send up to 13 divisions from other sectors of the Soviet-German front and 7 divisions from Western Europe to the western axis.[19]

This assessment accords with the long-standing Soviet insistence that Red Army operations in eastern Belorussia in fall 1943 were secondary to those the Red Army conducted along the southwestern axis into the Ukraine. Even so, by focusing on the feats performed by Soviet arms at Nevel', at Loev on the Dnepr, and in the Belorussian Front's November advance to Rechitsa, this and other assessments overstate what the Red Army accomplished in what they term local operations. Seldom do these accounts measure Red Army achievements against the standard of the *Stavka's* intent to capture Kalinkovichi, Bobruisk, Vitebsk, Minsk, and all of eastern Belorussia (see Map 9.7). Measured against this standard, the first stage of the Belorussian strategic offensive was clearly a failure. Undeterred, the *Stavka* would renew its Belorussian offensive in the winter.

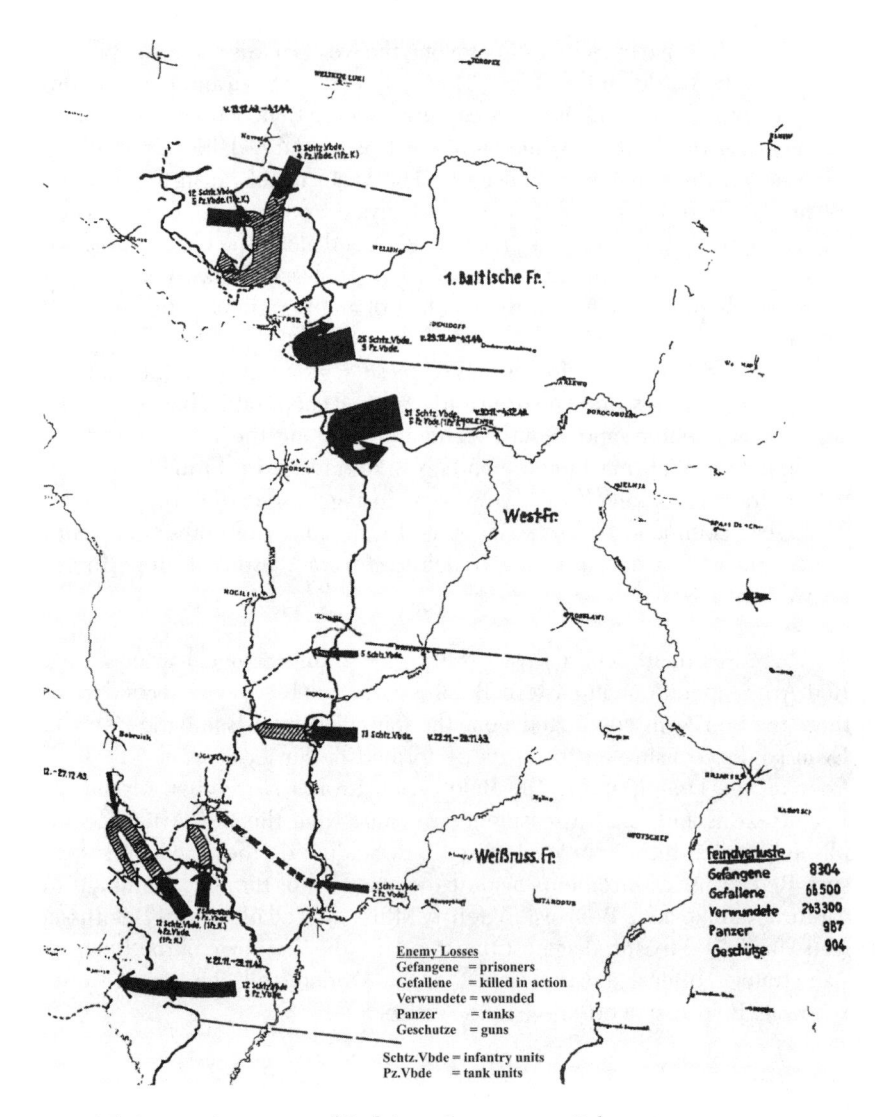

Map 9.7. German Assessment of Red Army Operations in Belorussia, 22 November 1943–4 January 1944

Part Two
The Struggle for Belorussia, December 1943–April 1944

CHAPTER 10

Context: The Winter Campaign (24 December 1943–April 1944)

INTRODUCTION

Most Soviet and Western histories that address this campaign focus exclusively on the Red Army's successful offensives in the Leningrad region during January and February 1944, in the Ukraine from late December through early April 1944, and in the Crimea during late March and April 1944. Therefore, histories of this campaign routinely emphasize two enduring theories; the first maintains that Stalin conducted a "narrow-front" strategy that facilitated Red Army victory during this period, and the second argues that Hitler adopted a "stand-fast" policy that had an adverse impact on Wehrmacht military operations. Although the first of these theories is mythical, the second does contain a grain of truth.

The first theory contends that, as he directed the campaign, Stalin adhered tenaciously to a "narrow-front" strategy throughout its duration by requiring the Red Army to focus its most important offensive operations along two principal axes, specifically, the northwestern axis in the Leningrad region and the southwestern axis in the Ukraine. Most historians argue that Stalin's military strategy required the Red Army to concentrate the bulk of its soldiers, weaponry, and material along these axes so that its operating *fronts* could achieve the missions the *Stavka* assigned to them. While doing so, the *Stavka* economized on the expenditure of vital Soviet human and material resources. All of these historians agree that the *Stavka* and Red Army concentrated most of their offensive efforts in the Ukraine. Newly released archival evidence, however, indicates that this assertion is only partially correct.

In reality, with the full agreement of his chief military advisers, Stalin ordered the Red Army to conduct major offensives along the entire Soviet-German front during the winter campaign. Furthermore, this strategy represented a continuation of a "broad-front" strategy Stalin had pursued since the beginning of the war and was in clear consonance with his long-standing rationale that, if the Red Army applied pressure everywhere, the Wehrmacht's defenses were likely to break somewhere. Therefore, in addition to ordering the Red Army to conduct offensive operations to expel Wehrmacht forces from the Leningrad region and the Ukraine, during the winter campaign Stalin also ordered the Red Army to launch major assaults against the German

Panther Defense Line in the Baltic region and across the entire expanse of eastern Belorussia.

It is also noteworthy, however, that, although Stalin and his *Stavka* indeed devoted special attention to organizing and pressing offensive operations in the Baltic region, they also ordered Red Army forces in the Ukraine to mount further ambitious offensive operations after their initial offensives in the Ukraine proved successful and their offensives in Belorussia bogged down. Specifically, when the Red Army's forces reached the Dnestr River in mid-April, Stalin ordered the 2nd and 3rd Ukrainian Fronts to continue offensive operations in order to project Soviet forces deeper into Romania and the Balkans region. This marked the beginning of Stalin's long-standing strategy to project Red Army forces into the Balkans to secure a more favorable postwar settlement and division of the spoils of war with his western Allies.

Historians have correctly asserted that Hitler's "stand-fast" strategy matured during the winter of 1943–1944 to such a degree that it seriously inhibited future Wehrmacht military operations. Indeed, during this campaign Hitler's strategy for the conduct of the war began its evolution from a "stand-fast" strategy to an outright *festung* (fortress) strategy, although with only mixed success. Even though Hitler's "stand-fast" orders failed to thwart the Red Army's Leningrad-Novgorod offensive, his *festung* strategy did halt the Red Army juggernaut in the north along the fortified defenses of the Panther Line. In Belorussia, Hitler's conversion of Vitebsk and other cities into virtual fortresses forestalled defeat in the winter of 1944 but fostered even more disastrous defeats in the summer of 1944 all along the periphery of the Belorussian "balcony." In southern Russia, Hitler's "stand-fast" strategy caused the Wehrmacht to lose the better part of two army corps in the Korsun' (Cherkassy) pocket, almost an entire panzer army at Kamenets-Podolsk, and sizable forces at Sevastopol' in the Crimea. Later, however, Hitler's "stand-fast" orders defeated a major Red Army thrust into northern Romania.

Thus, by focusing on these two theories, existing accounts of military operations during the winter campaign ignore failed Red Army offensives that took place after the successful offensives in the Leningrad region and the Ukraine ended and in Belorussia throughout this entire period.

CONVENTIONAL WISDOM

In early December 1943, the *Stavka* formulated strategic plans for conducting its third winter campaign that required the Red Army to drive German Army Group North's forces from the Leningrad region and Army Group South's forces from the Ukraine and the Crimea and to create favorable conditions for the subsequent destruction of Army Group Center's forces in Belorussia. The Red Army's 1st, 2nd, 3rd, and 4th Ukrainian Fronts were to conduct the main effort in the Ukraine, first by attacking successively and later simultaneously. This permitted the *Stavka* to switch key artillery and mechanized resources from *front* to *front*, while concealing the true scope and intent of the offensive.

The first phase of the Red Army's offensive in the Ukraine, which began in late December 1943 and lasted through late February 1944, consisted of five major offensive operations, each conducted by one or two *fronts* against the armies of Field Marshal Erich von Manstein's Army Group South. The first two operations, which the 1st and 2nd Ukrainian Fronts conducted, were continuations of the previous operations designed to expand the Red Army's bridgeheads across the Dnepr River. On 24 December 1943, Army General N. F. Vatutin's 1st Ukrainian Front attacked from its bridgehead at Kiev toward Zhitomir, Berdichev, and Vinnitsa in the Zhitomir-Berdichev offensive. Although Army Group South's Fourth Panzer and First Panzer Armies (the latter transferred to this region on 1 January) were hard-pressed to contain the offensive, a counterstroke by three of Manstein's panzer corps (the III, XXXXVI, and XXXXVIII) halted the *front's* two exploiting tank armies (1st and 3rd Guards) just short of their objective of Vinnitsa. Subsequently, from 5 to 16 January, Army General I. S. Konev's 2nd Ukrainian Front wheeled westward from its previous objective, Krivoi Rog, and its tank army (the 5th Guards) seized Kirovograd from Army Group South's Eighth Army. Ultimately, the twin Red Army offensives pinned two of Eighth Army's army corps into a large salient along the Dnepr River north of Korsun'-Shevchenkovskii.

After these initial offensive successes, from 24 January through 17 February the 1st and 2nd Ukrainian Fronts struck the flanks of Eighth Army's defenses at the base of the Korsun'-Shevchenkovskii salient, and two exploiting tank armies (the new 6th and existing 5th Guards) encircled the defending German corps. In several weeks of heavy fighting, Red Army troops claimed destroying as many as 30,000 Wehrmacht troops while fending off fierce German counterstrokes before Army Group South was able once again to stabilize its defenses.

While German attention was riveted on the fierce fighting at Korsun'-Shevchenkovskii, the *Stavka* ordered Red Army forces to strike both wings of Army Group South to capitalize on the fact that the bulk of the army group's panzer reserves were decisively engaged in the Korsun'-Shevchenkovskii region. Accordingly, on the 1st Ukrainian Front's right wing, from 27 January through 11 February, 13th and 60th Armies and 1st Guards and 6th Guards Cavalry Corps attacked Manstein's overextended left wing south of the Pripiat' Marshes, unhinged German defenses, and seized Rovno and Lutsk, creating favorable positions from which to conduct future operations far deeper into Army Group South's rear. Still farther to the south, from 30 January to 29 February, Army General R. Ia. Malinovsky's 3rd and Army General F. I. Tolbukhin's 4th Ukrainian Fronts launched concentric blows against the defenses of Army Group South's Sixth Army anchored in the "great bend" of the Dnepr River, collapsed German defenses in the Nikopol' bridgehead on the Dnepr's southern bank, seized the salient in the river's "great bend," and captured the key city of Krivoi Rog.

Consequently, by the end of February, Red Army forces had cleared German defenders from the entire Dnepr River line. Deprived of their river defenses, Manstein's forces were now vulnerable to complete defeat in detail in the vast interior plains of the Ukraine. In addition, during this same period, Army General L. A. Govorov's Leningrad Front and Army General K. A. Meretskov's Volkhov Front, soon joined by Army General M. M. Popov's 2nd Baltic Front, conducted the massive Leningrad-Novgorod offensive in the Leningrad region. This offensive, which began dramatically with rapid penetrations of German defenses south of Leningrad on 14 January, ultimately morphed into a painfully slow Soviet advance that endured through February and drove the forces of Army Group North's Eighteenth and Sixteenth Armies back to their Panther Line defenses. During the same period, the 1st Baltic, Western, and Belorussian Fronts conducted more limited operations against Army Group Center's forces in eastern Belorussia.

The offensive operations the Red Army conducted along the main strategic axis in the Ukraine continued virtually without a halt in early March, despite miserable terrain conditions created by the spring *rasputitsa* (period of flooded roads). During the second phase of this offensive, which began on 4 March and lasted through late April, five additional Red Army offensives involving all six of the Red Army's tank armies completed clearing Wehrmacht forces from the Ukraine and the Crimea. The *Stavka's* strategic objective in this instance was to separate Army Groups Center and South from each other and destroy the latter by pinning it against the Black Sea or Carpathian Mountains.

On 4 March the 1st Ukrainian Front, now personally commanded by Marshal of the Soviet Union G. K. Zhukov after Vatutin's death at the hands of Ukrainian partisans, attacked southwestward from the Shepetovka and Dubno regions toward Chernovtsy near the Romanian border. Initially, two of Zhukov's tank armies (the 3rd Guards and 4th) tore a gaping hole in the defenses of Army Group South's Fourth Panzer Army and by 7 March approached the city of Proskurov, where Manstein's panzer reserves (the III and XXXXVIII Panzer Corps) temporarily halted their advance. Soon after, however, 1st Tank Army joined the attacking Soviet forces, and on 21 March it and 4th Tank Army once again burst into Manstein's operational rear. Exploiting deep into Army Group South's rear, by 27 March the tank armies reached and crossed the Dnestr River, by doing so encircling virtually all of German First Panzer Army in the Kamenets-Podolsk region. By 17 April 1st Tank Army reached the Carpathian Mountains, effectively cutting off Manstein's army group (now renamed Army Group North Ukraine) from contact with Army Group South Ukraine, now operating to the south in northern Romania. Despite the panzer army's perilous predicament, by mounting a dramatic relief operation from southern Poland with an SS panzer corps, Manstein succeeded in extricating the beleaguered First Panzer Army to safety so that it could fight another day.

On 5 March, only a day after Zhukov's 1st Ukrainian Front commenced its offensive toward Proskurov, Konev's 2nd Ukrainian Front attacked toward Uman', spearheaded by three more tank armies (the 2nd, 5th Guards, and 6th). The *front's* exploiting tank armies captured Uman' and Vinnitsa on 10 March, and on 17 March 5th Guards Tank Army reached and crossed the Dnestr River, effectively separating Army Group North Ukraine's First Panzer Army from Army Group South Ukraine's Eighth Army to the south. While the six tank armies were setting the offensive pace for the 1st and 2nd Ukrainian Fronts, on 6 March Malinovsky's 3rd Ukrainian Front unleashed its own offensive (the Bereznegovatoe-Snigirevka operation) along the Black Sea coast against Army Group A, an army group that Hitler had formed in late 1943 to defend the southern Ukraine. By 18 March the 3rd Ukrainian Front had encircled but failed to destroy Army Group A's Sixth Army and created conditions conducive to a subsequent advance on Odessa. Simultaneously, Tolbukhin's 4th Ukrainian Front assaulted German Seventeenth Army's defenses in the Crimea on 8 April and bottled German forces up in Sevastopol' by 16 April, forcing the Germans to evacuate the city by 10 May.

As far as Soviet operations in Belorussia were concerned, Russian official histories acknowledge only two offensive operations conducted in the region. First, between 3 February and 13 March, Army General I. Kh. Bagramian's 1st Baltic Front and Army General V. D. Sokolovsky's Western Front pounded the defenses of Army Group Center's Third Panzer and Fourth Armies around Vitebsk but to no avail. Second, from 21 to 26 February, Army General K. K. Rokossovsky's Belorussian Front struck the defenses of Army Group Center's Ninth Army at Rogachev and Zhlobin, driving the Germans back but capturing only the former. Characteristically, these histories term both offensives only "diversionary" in nature.

Chronologically and by strategic axis, major military operations constituting the winter campaign of 1943–1944 traditionally include those shown in Table 10.1.

THE EMERGING TRUTH

Conventional accounts of Red Army offensive operations during the winter campaign of 1943–1944 focus almost exclusively on the successful offensives in the Leningrad region and in the Ukraine and the Crimea. They overlook two major categories of major Red Army offensives, specifically, those that

Table 10.1. Red Army Operations during the Winter Campaign: The Traditional View

The Northwestern Axis
- The Leningrad and Volkhov Front's Leningrad-Novgorod Offensive (14 January–1 March 1944)

The Western Axis
- The 1st Baltic and Western Fronts' Vitebsk Offensive (3 February–13 March 1944)
- The Belorussian Front's Kalinkovichi Raid (11–14 January 1944)
- The Belorussian Front's Rogachev-Zhlobin Offensive (21–26 February 1944)

The Southwestern Axis
- The 1st Ukrainian Front's Zhitomir-Berdichev Offensive (24 December 1943–14 January 1944)
- The 2nd Ukrainian Front's Kirovograd Offensive (5–16 January 1944)
- The 1st and 2nd Ukrainian Fronts' Korsun'-Shevchenkovskii Offensive (Cherkassy) (24 January–17 February 1944)
- The 1st Ukrainian Front's Rovno-Lutsk Offensive (27 January–11 February 1944)
- The 1st Ukrainian Front's Proskurov-Chernovtsy Offensive (Kamenets-Podolsk) (4 March–17 April 1944)
- The 2nd Ukrainian Front's Uman'-Botoshany Offensive (5 March–17 April 1944)
- The 3rd Ukrainian Front's Bereznegovatoe-Snigirevka Offensive (6–18 March 1944)
- The 3rd Ukrainian Front's Odessa Offensive (26 March–14 April 1944)
- The 4th Ukrainian Front's Crimean Offensive (8 April–12 May 1944)

took place at the end of the Red Army's strategic advance in the Leningrad region and the Ukraine and the vital Red Army offensive into Belorussia, a continuation of operations that had begun in October 1943 (see Map 10.1).

Although it is relatively easy to overlook these follow-on and continuation offensives because most of them failed, the *Stavka's* rationale for conducting these offensives in the first place is quite clear. Unfortunately, by their very nature, they have been easy to conceal. Based on its previous wartime experiences, by 1944 it was fairly routine practice for the *Stavka* to expand its strategic horizons while the Red Army was conducting major offensive operations and to assign its operating *fronts* new and more ambitious missions. In general, the *Stavka* justified this practice on the ground that one could not determine whether or when German collapse would occur, and, unless one pressed the offensive relentlessly, opportunities would be lost. Of course, when the *Stavka* ordered its overextended forces to perform these new missions, it always faced the risk that its attacking forces could fall victim to the sort of counterstrokes that Manstein had sprung on Red Army forces in the Donbas in early 1943. This, in fact, occurred on a smaller scale in the spring of 1944.

In fairness to Russian historians, the dramatic successes that the Red Army's strategic offensives achieved in 1944 and 1945 make it far more difficult to assess accurately whether additional military operations at the end of any major offensive thrust were attempts to exploit success or were simply designed to posture forces more advantageously for subsequent offensive action or to deceive the enemy regarding future offensive intentions.

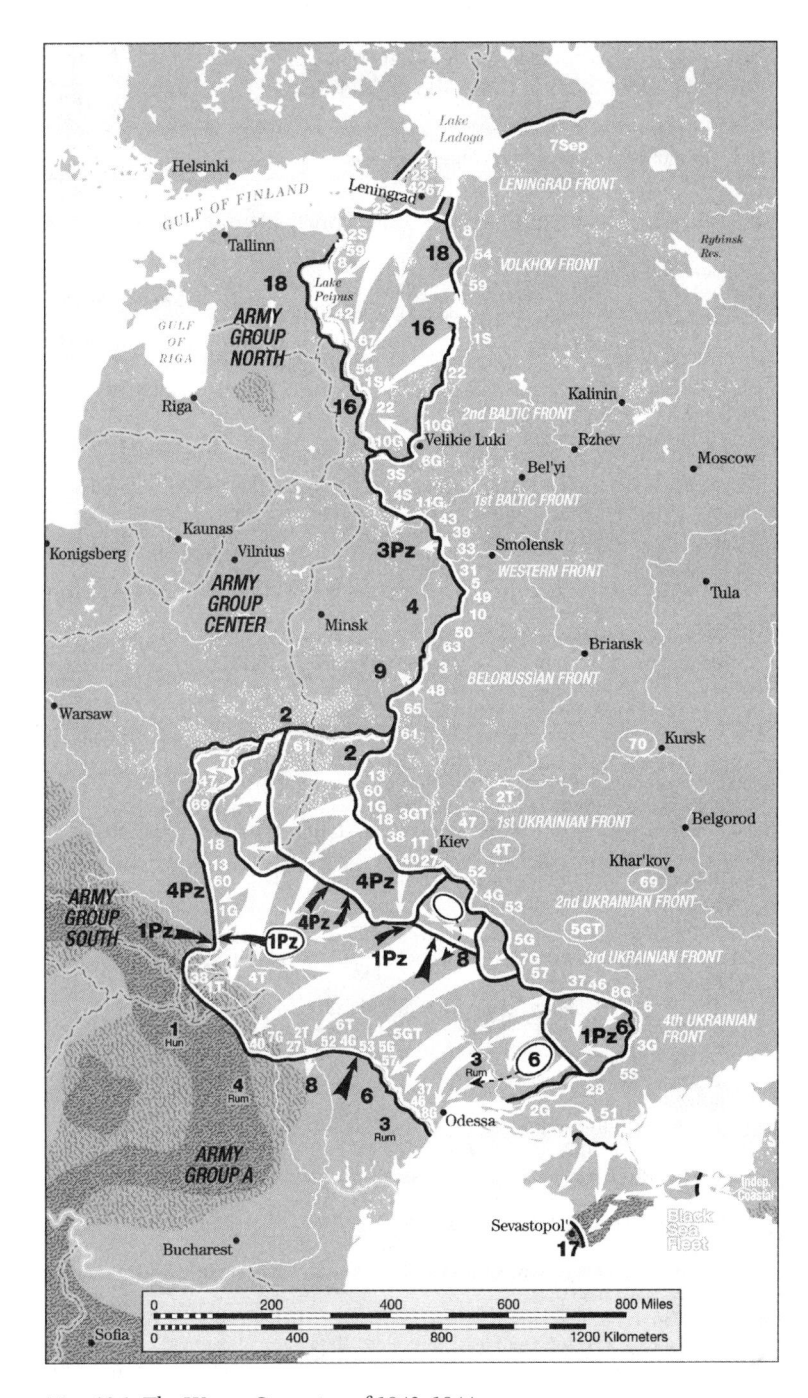

Map 10.1. The Winter Campaign of 1943–1944

The so-called "forgotten" battles that took place during the winter campaign of 1943–1944 include those shown in Table 10.2.

Table 10.2. "Forgotten Battles" of the Winter Campaign

The Northwestern Axis
- The Leningrad Front's (8th, 54th, and 2nd Shock Armies) Narva Offensives (2–28 February, 1–16 and 17–24 March 1944)
- German Army Group Narva's Counterstrokes (26 March–24 April 1944)
- The 2nd Baltic Front's (1st and 3rd Shock, 6th and 10th Guards, and 22nd Armies) Pustoshka-Idritsa Offensive (12–16 January 1944)
- The 2nd Baltic Front's (1st and 3rd Shock, 6th and 10th Guards, and 22nd Armies) Novosokol'niki-Idritsa Offensive (31 January–13 February 1944)
- The 2nd Baltic Front's Offensive Preparations and Pursuit to the Panther Line (17 February–1 March 1944)
- The Leningrad Front's (42nd and 67th Armies) Pskov-Ostrov Offensive: The Struggle for the Panther Line (2–17 March, 7–19 April 1944)
- The 1st Baltic Front's (4th Shock and 6th and 11th Guards Armies) and 2nd Baltic Front's (1st and 3rd Shock, 10th Guards, and 22nd Armies) Opochka and Sebezh Offensives (1–8 March, 10–26 March, and 7–18 April 1944)

The Western Axis
- The 1st Baltic and Western Fronts' Vitebsk Offensive (23 December 1943–6 January 1944)
- The 1st Baltic and Western Fronts' Vitebsk-Bogushevsk Offensive (8–24 January 1944)
- The 1st Baltic and Western Fronts' Vitebsk Offensive (3–16 February 1944)
- The Western Front's Babinovichi Offensive (22–25 February 1944)
- The Western Front's Vitebsk Offensive (29 February–5 March 1944)
- The Western Front's Orsha Offensive (5–9 March 1944)
- The Western Front's Bogushevsk Offensive (21–29 March 1944)
- The Belorussian Front's Kalinkovichi-Mozyr' Offensive (6–14 January 1944)
- The Belorussian Front's Ozarichi-Ptich' Offensive (14–30 January 1944)
- The Belorussian Front's Bobruisk (Marmovichi-Mormal') Offensive (29 January–9 March 1944)
- The Belorussian Front's Rogachev-Zhlobin Offensive) (21–26 February 1944)

The Southwestern Axis
- The 2nd Belorussian Front's Poles'e (Kovel') Offensive (15 March–5 April 1944)
    - The 2nd Belorussian Front's Penetration Battle, Exploitation, and Encirclement of Kovel' (14–29 March 1944)
    - The German Relief of Kovel' (29 March–5 April 1944)
- The 1st Ukrainian Front's Encirclement Battle at Brody (Proskurov-Chernovtsy Offensive) (20 March–17 April 1944)
    - The 13th Army's Penetration Battle, Exploitation, and Encirclement of Brody (15–26 March 1944)
    - The German Relief of Brody (27 March–7 April 1944)
    - The Aftermath (8–17 April 1944)
- The 2nd and 3rd Ukrainian Fronts' Iasi (Iassy)-Kishinev Offensive (Tirgu-Frumos and Dnestr River Bridgeheads) (8 April–6 June 1944)
    - The 2nd Ukrainian Front's Advance to Tirgu-Frumos, Iasi, and Dubossary (8–23 April 1944)
    - The 3rd Ukrainian Front's Advance to the Dnestr River and the Bridgehead Battles (11–25 April 1944)
    - The 2nd and 3rd Ukrainian Front's Iasi-Kishinev Offensive (25 April–8 May 1944)
    - German Sixth Army's Counterstrokes along the Dnestr River (8–30 May 1944)
    - Army Group Wöhler's Iasi Counterstroke (Operations "Sonja" and "Katja") (30 May–5 June 1944)

OVERVIEW

Throughout the entire winter campaign, the Red Army's 1st Baltic, Western, and Belorussian Fronts continued their efforts to smash Army Group Center's defenses in Belorussia. Pursuant to *Stavka* orders, the three *fronts* conducted repeated assaults on Wehrmacht defenses across the entire front in an attempt to collapse and defeat Army Group Center (see Map 2.2). The 1st Baltic Front, commanded by Army General I. Kh. Bagramian, struck German Third Panzer Army's defenses north and northeast of Vitebsk in near constant offensive operation from late December 1943 through January 1944, severed the communications between German forces in Vitebsk and Polotsk, and advanced into the western suburbs of Vitebsk city proper. At the same time, Army General Sokolovsky's Western Front pounded German defenses southeast and south of Vitebsk, trying to cut German communications lines extending southward from Vitebsk to Orsha and encircle the city from the south. Finally, Army General Rokossovsky's Belorussian Front captured Kalinkovichi and Rogachev in January and assaulted the southern flank of Army Group Center's Ninth Army along the Pripiat' River in late January and February in an attempt to sever the communications between Army Groups Center and South.

Between 29 December 1943 and 29 March 1944, the 1st Baltic, Western, and Belorussian Fronts launched at least seven separate and distinct offensive operations that cost the attackers more than 200,000 casualties. Try as they did, however, they were unable to make further significant advances into Belorussia. During the waning stages of the offensive, an angry *Stavka* relieved Sokolovsky from command of the Western Front. At least in part, the entire Belorussian offensive has languished in obscurity to protect the reputation of Sokolovsky, who, thanks to Zhukov's assistance, during the period from 1952–1960, survived the wartime embarrassment to become the chief of the Soviet Army General Staff and one of the Soviet Union's leading strategic theorists.

Even though all three of the Red Army's *fronts* operating along the western strategic axis participated actively in the Belorussian offensive, in effect, after mid-January 1944, these operations degenerated into two distinct Red Army offensives along two widely separate strategic-operational axes. The first of these efforts, which the 1st Baltic and Western Fronts conducted against Army Group Center's left wing, sought to collapse German defenses in the vicinity of the cities of Vitebsk and Polotsk. The second offensive, conducted by the Belorussian Front, sought to collapse German defenses in the Kalinkovichi, Ptich', and Pripiat' River regions on Army Group Center's right wing. Although the *Stavka* clung tenaciously to the concept of shattering German defenses in eastern Belorussia and capturing Minsk, any real hope for doing so had dissipated by mid-January. Therefore, for convenience's

274   The Struggle for Belorussia, December 1943–April 1944

sake, this study subdivides the Belorussian offensive into two distinct parts, the first dealing with operations in the Vitebsk region and the second with operations in southern Belorussia.

STRATEGIC SITUATION

As the new year approached, the combined forces of the Red Army's 1st Baltic and Western Fronts, both operating under the general supervision of *Stavka* representative Chief Marshal of Artillery N. N. Voronov, had already been pounding German defenses in the Vitebsk region for more than two months. This fighting represented a continuation of the Red Army's three-month Belorussian offensive, conducted during the fall of 1943, during which the two *fronts* attempted to collapse Army Group Center's left wing, capture Vitebsk, and develop the offensive deeper into Belorussia toward its capital city of Minsk. The culminating point of this offensive was the 1st Baltic Front's Gorodok offensive operation, which began on 13 December and ended with the capture of Gorodok on 24 December (see Map 8.4). During the first two phases of this offensive, the 1st Baltic Front's 11th Guards Army ruptured German Third Panzer Army's defenses north of Vitebsk, captured the town of Gorodok, and advanced southeastward toward Vitebsk, threatening the city's vital communication lines to the west and southwest. While 11th Guards Army was seizing Gorodok, the 1st Baltic Front's 39th Army and the Western Front's 33rd Army attacked Third Panzer Army's defenses southeast of Vitebsk in an attempt to reach and sever German communications routes between Vitebsk and Orsha, thus rendering the Germans' Vitebsk defenses untenable.

The third phase of the Red Army's Vitebsk offensive actually began on 23 December, the day before Gorodok fell to 11th Guards Army, and did not end until 6 January 1944. During this phase, on 23 December the 1st Baltic Front's 39th and 43rd Armies and the Western Front's 33rd Army commenced intense assaults against Third Panzer Army's defenses northeast, east, and southeast of Vitebsk city. Days later, the 1st Baltic Front's 4th Shock and 11th Guards Armies joined the offensive by launching equally heavy attacks on Third Panzer's positions west and northwest of the city. Although German accounts describe this, the most dangerous phase of the Vitebsk operation, in some detail, Soviet historians largely ignore these operations, probably because they failed.

For example, writing from the German perspective, Earl Ziemke notes the perilous situation facing German Third Panzer Army at the end of December:

On 23 December Yeremenko [the presumed commander of the 1st Baltic Front] gave the answer. *Fourth Shock, Eleventh Guards, Thirty-*

ninth, and *Forty-third Armies* attacked around the Vitebsk perimeter. In the first two days they pushed the German line back several miles. Northwest and southeast of the city tanks and infantry drove deep wedges into the Third Panzer Army front, cutting the Vitebsk-Polotsk rail line and threatening the Vitebsk-Orsha line. To prevent an encirclement Army Group Center moved in the two divisions recently received from Army Group North and on the 28th transferred a division each from the Ninth and Second Armies. Thereafter the front held even though Yeremenko kept punching away with rigid determination for another six weeks.[1]

Yet even Ziemke missed the full extent of the operation. In addition to misidentifying the 1st Baltic Front commander as Eremenko rather than its real commander, Bagramian, he also failed to note the participation of the Western Front's 33rd Army in the operation.

Soviet sources have maintained an even stonier silence about this offensive, which was supposed to have been the culminating assault on Vitebsk. For example, in his memoirs General A. P. Beloborodov, then the commander of 4th Shock Army's 2nd Guards Rifle Corps, simply stated:

> On 24 December 4th Shock Army continued its offensive along the Vitebsk axis in cooperation with 11th Guards Army. Once again, the enemy front was penetrated to a great depth. As a result of this penetration, after liberating Gorodok, 11th Guards Army approached right up to the Vitebsk fortified region from the northwest, and 4th Shock Army reached the Vitebsk-Polotsk railroad line on a broader front. The 1st Baltic Front's forces went over to the defense along that line—the summer–fall campaign of 1943 had ended.[2]

Beloborodov's brief account, however, was only partially correct. Although his description of the overall operation was accurate, what he failed to note was that the Western Front participated in the operation and that his army did, in fact, reach the railroad line connecting Vitebsk to Polotsk, but not until early January. Finally, the operation went on until 8 January 1944.

When he wrote his memoirs, General Bagramian, who was the 1st Baltic Front's commander at that time, made no mention whatsoever of the final stage of the Vitebsk operation. In contrast, although General Galitsky, the commander of 11th Guards Army, provided a more comprehensive account of his army's participation in these battles, he too failed to note the full extent of the operation:

> After the liberation of Gorodok, the army's forces continued to attack to the south in the direction of Vitebsk. Overcoming stubborn resistance, they fought their way forward only 4–5 kilometers by the end of 25 December. The further offensive was halted by powerful and carefully

organized artillery-mortar and machine gun fire and also by enemy counterattacks. We stood in front of an enemy fortified line that extended along a line from Belodedovo through Sloboda, Borovka, Zaluch'e Station, to Shpaki.

As became apparent later, this was the external defense belt around Vitebsk, which was located 25 kilometers from the city and had two-three full-profile trench lines, barbed wire, and minefields. A second line, 6–8 kilometers to the south, ran from Zaviaz'ia through Gorodishche to Lake Losvida. There was yet a third line located 5–8 kilometers from the city along the line of the Pestunitsa River, Mikhali, and Lake Sosna. These lines were tactically favorable both from the standpoint of their disposition on the terrain and from their [the Germans] capability for gradually shifting their forces to new positions in the depth.

The Hitlerites had transformed all of the populated points and the dominant heights between them into strongpoints. . . .

After 11th Guards Army's units liberated Gorodok, the enemy immediately strengthened the combat formations of his forces along the Vitebsk axis, bringing new formations forward to this region from other sectors of the front. By 26 December 3rd and 4th Luftwaffe Field, 256th and 197th, and 87th, 211th, and 129th Infantry Divisions, which had been defeated earlier but were now reinforced considerably, were operating against [our army] and 4th Shock Army, which was attacking on our right [flank]. [There were also] part of 12th Infantry Division, 505th Separate Tank Battalion [*Abteilung*], 190th Heavy Assault Gun Battalion, and 990th Artillery Battalion of the High Command reserve and a number of other separate units. . . .

Several days after [11th Guards Army] reached the above-mentioned line extending from Belodedovo through Sloboda, Borovka, and Zaluch'e Station to Shpaki, and after we finally developed a clearer idea of the [strength] of Fascist forces opposing us, the correlation of our forces and those of the enemy was 1.2 to 1 in infantry, 3 to 1 in guns and mortars (but based on the existing ammunition, 1 to 1), 1.6 to 1 in machine guns, and 0.9 to 1 in tanks.

Consequently, we were slightly superior to the enemy only in infantry but were inferior in quantity of tanks. In the presence of a powerful and deep enemy defense, such a correlation of forces meant that the mission assigned to 11th Guards Army, that is to capture Vitebsk by 30–31 December in cooperation with 4th Shock Army, was unrealistic. I presume that the *front* commander would not have assigned it to us if he had possessed reliable information regarding the enemy's forces and the nature of his defenses. Unfortunately, the *front* and army headquarters received such information much later while combat was already raging to penetrate the enemy defenses on the approaches to Vitebsk. . . .

The strength of 11th Guards Army [had also been] considerably weakened. The 83rd Rifle Corps had been dispatched into the *front's* reserve, and 1st Tank Corps had been withdrawn for refitting.

Therefore, the army became weaker, and its assigned mission became more difficult. This determined the course and outcome of our combat operations at Vitebsk, which we tried to capture not only while the enemy was really superior but also essentially without any preparation. As proof of the latter, it is sufficient to understand that we had to capture Vitebsk only 6–7 days after seizing Gorodok.

It would seem as if the army could not attack in such extremely unfavorable conditions.

Despite all of this, we went forward. Our formations advanced to southward slowly and with immense strain, on average overcoming no more than a single kilometer per day. We managed to achieve this [rate of advance] by attacking repeatedly on first one and then another axis. The divisions detected the weak links in the enemy's defense in some respect by [conducting] short duration combat reconnaissance and then managed to advance forward a bit by destroying this or that strongpoint. . . .

As a result, from 25–31 December, the army's forces advanced only 5–7 kilometers.

The three guards rifle divisions that were advancing on the right wing, specifically, 16th Guards Rifle Corps' 11th Guards Rifle Division and 8th Guards Rifle Corps' 31st and 26th Guards Rifle Divisions, operated with the greatest degree of success. After overcoming the enemy's first defensive line, they cleared his forces from west of Lake Losvida. The advance was somewhat less [successful] on the army's center and right wing.

The formations on the army's right wing approached the second lines, which lay to the southwest of this lake, by day's end on the final day of 1943, but here heavy enemy fire once again halted them. On the [army's] right wing, this [defensive] line passed along the shore of Lake Zaronovskoe. The 4th Shock Army's formations reached this point, where they were also forced to halt their offensive.[3]

To his credit, unlike all of the other memoir writers, Galitsky openly admits that his army's offensive actually continued well into January, and he provides some sketchy details of the subsequent operations. While doing so, however, he also woefully overstates the strength and number of opposing German forces. Actually, during late December, German Third Panzer Army initially committed IX Army Corps' 252nd Infantry Division and LIII Army Corps' 6th Luftwaffe Field and 129th Infantry Divisions and a portion of 3rd Luftwaffe Field Division to oppose 11th Guards and 4th Shock Armies' assault and reinforced their defenses in this sector with 5th Jäger Division by 31 December.

During the same period, the remainder of 3rd Luftwaffe Field Division and 4th Luftwaffe Field and 197th and 14th Infantry Divisions faced the 1st Baltic Front's 43rd Army northeast and east of Vitebsk. Finally, the Third Panzer Army held its 87th Infantry Division reforming in reserve to the rear and defended its long left wing opposite 4th Shock Army's equally long right wing with 12th Infantry Division. After the first day of the new year, however, the heavy Soviet assaults at Vitebsk forced Third Panzer Army to commit its 12th Infantry Division to combat against the Soviet shock group west of Vitebsk.

Therefore, throughout the entire third stage of the offensive, 11th Guards and 4th Shock Armies enjoyed a clear numerical superiority of as much as 3 to 1 over their opponents. In addition, Galitsky neglected to mention that the 1st Baltic Front's 43rd and 39th Armies and the Western Front's 33rd Army also took part in the offensive, albeit along another axis—toward Vitebsk from the east.

Based on German archival materials and newly released Soviet archival materials, we can now finally reconstruct this phase of the operation in significant detail. The most important circumstance affecting the outcome of these operations, not depicted on tactical and operational maps, is the challenging weather conditions. As is normally the case during winters in the Vitebsk region, the skies were normally cloudy or stormy, the temperatures were often well below freezing, and the near incessant snowfall severely hindered movement on, but especially off, the roads. Infantry could advance, albeit slowly, but tanks and other vehicles did so with extreme difficulty.

CHAPTER 11

The 1st Baltic and Western Fronts' Vitebsk Offensive (24 December 1943– 5 January 1944) and 2nd Baltic Front's Novosokol'niki Pursuit (30 December 1943–15 January 1944)

VITEBSK (24 DECEMBER 1943–5 JANUARY 1944)

The Plan

In brief, the *Stavka* ordered the shock groups of Bagramian's 1st Baltic and Sokolovsky's Western Fronts to smash German defenses west and southwest of Gorodok and north and south of the Vitebsk-Smolensk highway, commit their mobile groups, and advance to the Ostrovno and Diaglevo region, where they were to link up and encircle and destroy German forces in the Vitebsk region (see Map 11.1).

The *Stavka* also allocated enough forces to the 1st Baltic and Western Fronts to establish clear numerical superiorities over German forces in most categories of types of forces (see Table 11.1).

Vitebsk West

Prior to and during the initial stages of the 24 December attack, both 4th Shock and 11th Guards Armies conducted a major regrouping aimed at shifting the bulk of their forces west of the Gorodok-Vitebsk road. After it regrouped, the force was to wheel southeastward west of Lake Losvida, cut the Vitebsk-Polotsk road and railroad line east of Shumilino, and advance on Vitebsk from the northwest. During the regrouping, 4th Shock Army concentrated Major General A. A. D'iakonov's 83rd and General Beloborodov's 2nd Guards Rifle Corps on the army's left wing, deployed in attack positions stretching from east to west along the Sirotino-Gorodok road between Ostrovliane and Myl'nishche. The two corps were supported by General Sakhno's newly refitted and rested 5th Tank and General Oslikovsky's 3rd Guards Cavalry Corps, designated to serve as the army's mobile group to exploit the expected penetration. On the shock group's right, Major General N. B.

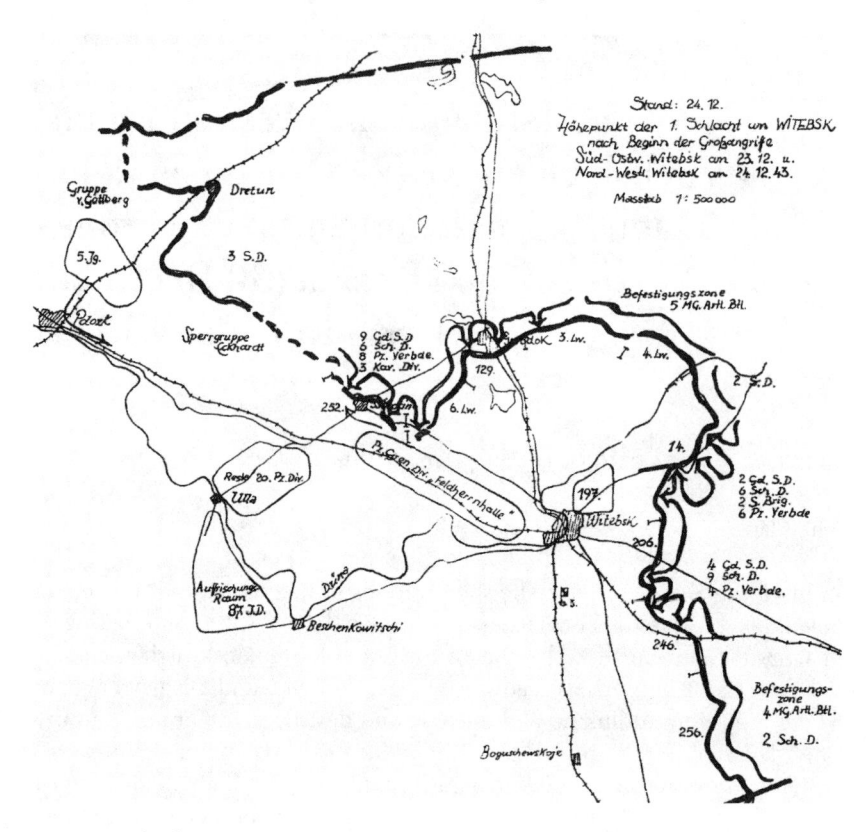

280 The Struggle for Belorussia, December 1943–April 1944

Map 11.1. Third Panzer Army's Appreciation of the Situation at Vitebsk, 23–24 December 1943

Ibiansky's 22nd Guards Rifle Corps deployed its 156th, 154th, and 51st Rifle Divisions in positions extending westward from Bandury. Finally, the 119th and 357th Rifle Divisions and 101st Rifle Brigade of Major General A. N. Ermakov's 60th Rifle Corps remained in defensive positions on the army's left wing along an extended front opposite the western extremity of the immense salient jutting westward from Nevel' and Gorodok.

The 11th Guards Army began its advance southwest of Gorodok with General Malyshev's 8th Guards Rifle Corps (26th, 83rd, and 5th Guards Rifle Divisions) (see Map 11.2). However, 235th Rifle Division relieved the divisions of Generals Fediun'kin's and Shafranov's 16th and 36th Guards Rifle Corps east of Gorodok, and the two corps castled their divisions to the west, where they occupied new assault positions on 8th Guards Rifle Corps' right flank. After the regrouping was complete, the army attacked southeastward south of Lake Losvida with 8th, 36th, and 16th Guards Rifle Corps advancing abreast (from left to right). General Galitsky supported the advance with

The 1st Baltic and Western Fronts' Vitebsk Offensive   281

Table 11.1. The Estimated Correlation of Opposing Forces in the Vitebsk Offensive, 24 December 1943–6 January 1944

OPPOSING FORCES	
Soviet	**German**
1st Baltic Front	
4th Shock Army	5th Jäger Division
11th Guards Army	12th Infantry Division
12 rifle divisions	6th Luftwaffe Field Division
2 tank corps	129th Infantry Division
1 cavalry corps	281st and 667th Assault Gun
3 tank brigades (200 tanks)	and 505th Panzer *Abteilung* (40 armored fighting vehicles—AFVs)
Western Front	
33rd Army	206th Infantry Division
5th Army	Panzer Grenadier Division
11 rifle divisions	*Feldherrnhalle*
1 tank corps	131st Infantry Division
4 tank brigades with 147 tanks	246th Infantry Division
	245th Assault Gun *Abteilung* (60 AFVs)
Strength: 436,180 men	200,000 men
640 tanks and SP guns (est.)	200 tanks and SP guns (est.)

Depth of Soviet advance: 8–12 kilometers
Casualties (Western Front): 35,596 men including 6,692 killed and 28,904 wounded

Sources: Makhmut Gareev, "O neudachnykh nasutatel'nykh operatsiiakh sovetskikh voisk v Velikoi Otechestvennoi voine. Po neopublikovannym dokumentam GKO" [About unsuccessful offensive operations of Soviet forces in the Great Patriotic War. According to unpublished GKO documents], *Novaia i noveishaia istoriia* [New and newest history] 1 (January 1994): 16; and H Gr Mitte/Ia, KTB: Lagenkarten, 1–31 January 1944, *H. Gr Mitte, 65002/60 file*, in NAM series T-311, Roll 224.

Butkov's 1st Tank Corps and retained 18th and 90th Guards Rifle Divisions in reserve.

Certainly the *Stavka* believed that the forces it assembled to conduct the decisive assault on Vitebsk were sufficient to accomplish their assigned tasks (see Table 11.2).

The *Stavka* issued its final directive to the 1st Baltic Front mandating the offensive late on 23 December, the day after its forces east of Vitebsk began their assault, stating, "The 1st Baltic Front will direct its main forces in the destruction of the enemy Vitebsk grouping and capture the city of Vitebsk no later than 1 January 1944. Subsequently, attack in the direction of Lepel' with the *front's* main forces and toward Polotsk with 4th Shock Army" (see Appendix H-1).[1] Bagramian confirmed receipt on 25 December in a message that detailed the tasks being assigned to 43rd and 39th Armies (see Appendix H-2): "While developing an offensive, 39th Army, in cooperation with the Western Front's units, will cut the Vitebsk-Orsha road and reach the Volkovo, Sokol'niki, Seliuty, and Baryshino front by day's end on 27 December. . . . Subsequent to the [39th Army's] offensive, 43rd Army will strike a decisive blow against the city of Vitebsk and occupy the southeastern portion of the city no later than 29 December."[2]

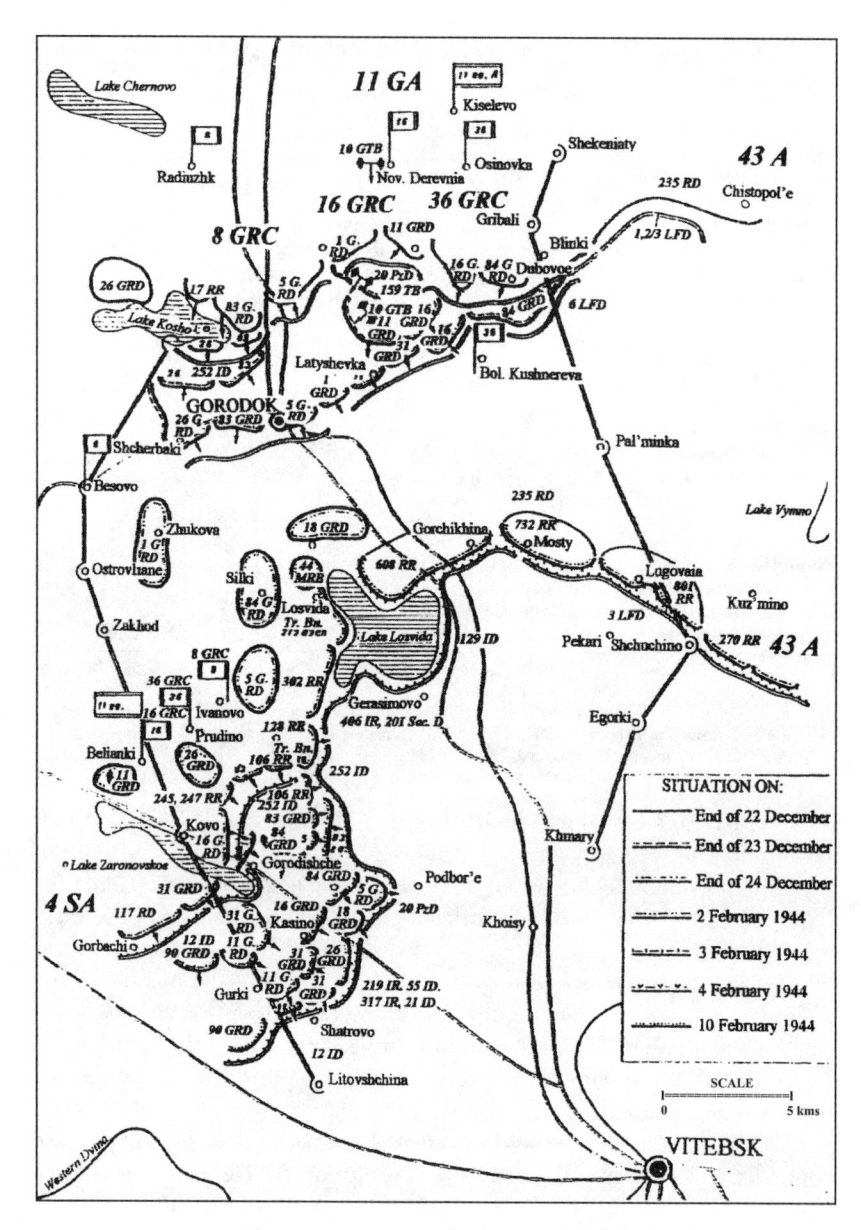

Map 11.2. 11th Guards Army's Operations, 22–31 December 1943

Table 11.2. The 1st Baltic and Western Fronts' Orders of Battle in the Vitebsk Offensive, 1 January 1944

1ST BALTIC FRONT: Army General I. Kh. Bagramian	WESTERN FRONT: Army General V. D. Sokolovsky
4th Shock Army: LTG P. F. Malyshev	5th Army: LTG N. I. Krylov
2nd Guards Rifle Corps: MG A. P. Beloborodov	72nd Rifle Corps: MG Iu. M. Prokof'ev
29th Rifle Division	153rd Rifle Division
166th Rifle Division	159th Rifle Division
381st Rifle Division	277th Rifle Division
22nd Guards Rifle Corps: MG N. B. Ibiansky	1537th Self-propelled Artillery Regiment
51st Rifle Division	
154th Rifle Division	33rd Army: Col. G V. N. Gordov
156th Rifle Division	36th Rifle Corps: MG N. N. Oleshev
60th Rifle Corps: MG A. N. Ermakov	199th Rifle Division
119th Rifle Division	215th Rifle Division
357th Rifle Division	274th Rifle Division
101st Rifle Brigade	36th Rifle Brigade
83rd Rifle Corps: MG A. A. D'iakonov	45th Rifle Corps: MG S. G. Poplavsky
117th Rifle Division	32nd Rifle Division
234th Rifle Division	97th Rifle Division
360th Rifle Division	184th Rifle Division
155th Fortified Region	65th Rifle Corps: MG V. A. Reviakhin
3rd Guards Cavalry Corps: LTG N. S. Oslikovsky	(2 Jan)
5th Guards Cavalry Division	42nd Rifle Division
6th Guards Cavalry Division	173rd Rifle Division
32nd Cavalry Division	222nd Rifle Division
1814th Self-propelled Artillery Regiment	69th Rifle Corps: MG N. N. Mul'tan
144th Guards Tank Destroyer Regiment	144th Rifle Division
3rd Guards-Mortar Regiment	164th Rifle Division
64th Guards Mortar Battalion	81st Rifle Corps: Col A. K. Ivanov
3rd Guards Separate Tank Destroyer Artillery Battalion	(Col. V. Ia. Poiarov on 11 Jan)
1731st Antiaircraft Artillery Battalion	95th Rifle Division
5th Tank Corps: MGTF M. G. Sakhno	157th Rifle Division
24th Tank Brigade	2nd Guards Tank Brigade
41st Tank Brigade	23rd Guards Tank Brigade
70th Tank Brigade	213th Tank Brigade
5th Motorized Rifle Brigade	256th Tank Brigade
161st Self-propelled Artillery Regiment	1445th Self-propelled Artillery
1515th Self-propelled Artillery Regiment	1494th Self-propelled Artillery Regiment
1546th Self-propelled Artillery Regiment	1830th Self-propelled Artillery Regiment
92nd Motorcycle Battalion	
277th Mortar Regiment	*Front* Reserves:
731st Separate Tank Destroyer Battalion	388th Rifle Division
47th Guards-Mortar Battalion	371st Rifle Division
1708th Antiaircraft Artillery Regiment	2nd Guards Tank Corps: Col. A. S. Burdeinyi
34th Guards Tank Brigade	4th Guards Tank Brigade
236th Tank Brigade	25th Guards Tank Brigade
171st Separate Tank Battalion	26th Guards Tank Brigade
	4th Guards Motorized Rifle Brigade
11th Guards Army: LTG K. N. Galitsky	1819th Self-propelled Artillery Regiment
8th Guards Rifle Corps: LTG A. S. Ksenofontov	1833rd Self-propelled Artillery Regiment
5th Guards Rifle Division	79th Motorcycle Battalion
26th Guards Rifle Division	
83rd Guards Rifle Division	
16th Guards Rifle Corps: MG I. F. Fediun'kin	19th Separate Armored Car Battalion

Table 11.2. *continued*

1ST BALTIC FRONT: Army General I. Kh. Bagramian	WESTERN FRONT: Army General V. D. Sokolovsky
1st Guards Rifle Division	1500th Tank Destroyer Regiment
11th Guards Rifle Division	755th Separate Tank Destroyer
31st Guards Rifle Division	Artillery Battalion
36th Guards Rifle Corps: MG P. G. Shafranov	273rd Mortar Regiment
16th Guards Rifle Division	28th Guards-Mortar Battalion
84th Guards Rifle Division	1695th Antiaircraft Artillery Regiment
235th Rifle Division	43rd Guards Tank Brigade
18th Guards Rifle Division	120th Tank Brigade
90th Guards Rifle Division	153rd Tank Brigade
1st Tank Corps: LGTF V. V. Butkov	56th Guards Separate Tank Regiment
89th Tank Brigade	63rd Guards Separate Tank Regiment
117th Tank Brigade	64th Guards Separate Tank Regiment
159th Tank Brigade	248th Separate Tank Regiment
44th Motorized Rifle Brigade	1495th Self-propelled Artillery Regiment
1437th Self-propelled Artillery Regiment	12th Separate Aerosleigh Battalion
86th Motorcycle Battalion	41st Separate Aerosleigh Battalion
1514th Tank Destroyer Regiment	145th Antiaircraft Armored Train
388th Separate Tank Destroyer Artillery Battalion	
108th Mortar Regiment	
10th Guards-Mortar Battalion	
1720th Antiaircraft Artillery Regiment	
10th Guards Tank Brigade	
2nd Guards Separate Tank Regiment	

43rd Army: LTG K. D. Golubev
  1st Rifle Corps: MG V. P. Kotel'nikov
    145th Rifle Division
    204th Rifle Division
  91st Rifle Corps: MG F. A. Volkov
    179th Rifle Division
    270th Rifle Division
    306th Rifle Division
  92nd Rifle Corps: MG I. S. Iudintsev
    332nd Rifle Division
    334th Rifle Division
    358th Rifle Division
  145th Rifle Brigade
  114th Rifle Brigade
  60th Tank Brigade
  143rd Tank Brigade
  46th Mechanized Brigade
  105th Separate Tank Regiment

39th Army: LTG N. E. Berzarin
  5th Guards Rifle Corps: MG V. G. Pozniak
    9th Guards Rifle Division
    17th Guards Rifle Division
    19th Guards Rifle Division
    91st Guards Rifle Division
  84th Rifle Corps: MG E. V. Dobrovol'sky
    134th Rifle Division
    158th Rifle Division
    262nd Rifle Division

Table 11.2. continued

1ST BALTIC FRONT: Army General I. Kh. Bagramian	WESTERN FRONT: Army General V. D. Sokolovsky
124th Rifle Brigade 28th Guards Tank Brigade 39th Guards Tank Brigade 47th Mechanized Brigade 11th Guards Separate Tank Regiment	

Front Reserves:
103rd Rifle Corps: MG D. F. Alekseev
  16th Latvian Rifle Division
  47th Rifle Division	

Source: Boevoi sostav Sovetskoi Armii, chast' IV (Ianvar'–dekabr' 1944) [The combat composition of the Soviet Army, pt. 4 (January–December 1944)] (Moscow: Voenizdat, 1988), 11–13.

The 11th Guards Army's forces, still in the process of regrouping, made only minimal gains in their attack south of Gorodok on 24 December. However, west of Vitebsk, 4th Shock Army's 83rd and 2nd Guards Rifle Corps smashed their way through the German defenses at the junction of LIII Army Corps' 6th Luftwaffe Field Division and IX Army Corps' 252nd Infantry Division (see Map 11.3). The assault, spearheaded by at least two tank brigades of 5th Tank Corps, penetrated up to 4 kilometers through the German defenses, and forward Soviet forces reached the Sirotino-Vitebsk road east and west of Grabnitsa (33 kilometers northwest of Vitebsk). The next day, 4th Shock Army expanded its penetration to the west, when 22nd Guards Rifle Corps' 154th and 156th Rifle Divisions reached the northern outskirts of 252nd Infantry Division's defenses at Sirotino. When 2nd Guards Rifle Corps tore a gaping hole in German defenses near Grabnitsa, Third Panzer Army dispatched 5th Jäger Division from its reserve to plug the gap. At the same time, Third Panzer Army ordered LIII Corps' 129th and 3rd and 4th Luftwaffe Field Divisions and VI Army Corps' 14th Infantry Division to withdraw to a new defense line closer to Vitebsk's outer defenses. This they did overnight on 24–25 December, to counter both 4th Shock Army's advance west of Vitebsk and the strong Soviet attacks against VI Corps' right wing southeast of the city.

On 26 December a fierce meeting engagement raged along and south of the Sirotino-Vitebsk road west of the city (see Map 11.4). The 4th Shock Army's 2nd Guards Rifle Corps, spearheaded by several brigades of 5th Tank Corps and 3rd Guards Cavalry Corps' divisions, pushed southward from Grabnitsa, momentarily cut the Vitebsk-Polotsk railroad line, and created a salient 8 kilometers deep and 6 kilometers wide south of the Vitebsk-Sirotino road. However, in late afternoon, 5th Jäger Division met them with strong battalion-scale counterattacks from the south and west. In two days of heavy

286 The Struggle for Belorussia, December 1943–April 1944

Map 11.3. Third Panzer Army's Situation West of Vitebsk, 24 December 1943

seesaw fighting, the 5th Jäger managed to clear Soviet forces from the railroad line and contained the threatening penetration (see Map 11.5).

To the north, the regrouped forces of 11th Guards Army added their weight to the assault on 27 December by attacking the defenses of LIII Army Corps' 6th Luftwaffe and 129th Infantry Divisions south of Gorodok. When these attacks intensified toward day's end, early on the 28th, Third Panzer Army ordered the two divisions to conduct a fighting withdrawal to new defense lines 6 kilometers to the rear so that they could align their de-

Map 11.4. Third Panzer Army's Situation West of Vitebsk, 26 December 1943

fenses with those of 5th Jäger Division south of the Sirotino-Vitebsk road. The 11th Guards Army's lead divisions pursued, only to be halted in front of the new defense line late on 29 December. Heavy fighting continued to the south as 5th Jäger and 6th Luftwaffe Field Divisions fought hard to eliminate or at least contain 4th Shock Army's penetration. By 31 December the two German divisions reconquered about half of the Soviet salient south of the Sirotino-Vitebsk road but were unable to eliminate it entirely (see Map

Map 11.5. Third Panzer Army's Situation West of Vitebsk, 28 December 1943

11.6). Nor was 11th Guards Army able to resume its offensive, even though it continued heavy assaults right up to month's end.

Driven on by the *Stavka,* Bagramian's forces persistently continued their attacks during the first few days in January 1944. Particularly intense fighting raged in a narrow salient extending southward west of Lake Zaronovskoe to the northern outskirts of the village of Gorbachi astride the Vitebsk-Polotsk railroad line. Within this salient, two rifle divisions of Beloborodov's 2nd Guards Rifle Corps, two rifle divisions of D'iakonov's 83rd Rifle Corps,

Map 11.6. Third Panzer Army's Situation West of Vitebsk, 31 December 1943

the bulk of Sakhno's 5th Tank Corps, and all three dismounted cavalry divisions from Oslikovsky's 3rd Guards Cavalry Corps tried repeatedly to break through the Germans' defenses around the strongpoint at Gorbachi but in vain (see Map 11.7).

All the while, the struggling Soviet shock groups had to contend with attempts by 5th Jäger Division to break through into their rear area, pin them against the lake's shore to the north, and encircle them. At the same time, the shock groups of Galitsky's 11th Guards Army continued pounding the Germans' defense northeast of Lake Zaronovskoe but also to no avail. By 5 January the fighting had tailed off as both attackers and defenders exhausted themselves in the desperate fighting.

Map 11.7. Third Panzer Army's Situation West of Vitebsk, 6 January 1944

Vitebsk East

German Third Panzer Army was indeed fortunate to have been able to contain 11th Guards and 4th Shock Armies' assaults west of Vitebsk because it did so at a time when its defenses east of Vitebsk were also imperiled by a renewed and even stronger Soviet offensive. The fresh Soviet shock groups east of Vitebsk now consisted of the regrouped forces of the 1st Baltic Front's

43rd and 39th Armies, now reinforced by the Western Front's regrouped 33rd Army.

During early December, while the Gorodok operation was still under way, the *Stavka* directed General Sokolovsky to regroup the forces of his Western Front so as to form a new shock group on the *front's* right wing.[3] It instructed Sokolovsky to employ this shock group to reinforce the 1st Baltic Front's left wing so that Bagramian's forces could seize Vitebsk by enveloping Third Panzer Army's defenses around the city from both west and southeast. Accordingly, Sokolovsky transferred General Gordov's 33rd Army to the *front's* right wing southeast of Vitebsk, while the *Stavka* shifted the boundary between the 1st Baltic and Western Fronts northward to a point midway between the Smolensk-Vitebsk highway and the railroad line 10 kilometers to the south. Gordov complied by moving his army's 65th and 69th Rifle Corps northward, leaving 61st Rifle Corps, along with its sector, behind under 49th Army's control. Sokolovsky also reinforced Gordov's army with Major General N. N. Oleshev's 36th and Major General S. G. Poplavsky's 45th Rifle Corps from 31st Army, Colonel A. K. Ivanov's 81st Rifle Corps from 5th Army, and General Burdeinyi's partially refurbished 2nd Guards Tank Corps from the *front's* reserve. Gordov's force was also supported by 2nd and 23rd Guards and 213th and 256th Tank Brigades and 1445th, 1494th, and 1830th Self-propelled Artillery Regiments.

When complete by day's end on 22 December, this regrouping provided Gordov a force of five rifle corps with thirteen rifle divisions, supported by one tank corps, four tank brigades, ten tank and self-propelled artillery regiments, ten artillery brigades, and four *Stavka* Reserve (RVGK) artillery regiments. So configured, 33rd Army fielded 147 tanks and was able to create an artillery density of 110 guns per kilometer of front. Gordov's force faced one German infantry division (roughly half of VI Army Corps' 206th and 246th Infantry Divisions), supported, according to Russian sources, by five artillery regiments and sixty tanks, although this figure is much too high. Thus the initial Soviet superiority in 33rd Army's sector was at least 5 to 1 in infantry and probably more than 5 to 1 in tanks and artillery.

If this force was not imposing enough, at the *Stavka's* direction, General Bagramian ordered General Berzarin, the commander of 39th Army, to concentrate General Pozniak's 5th Guards and General Dobrovol'sky's 84th Rifle Corps along and south of the Smolensk-Vitebsk highway on 33rd Army's right flank and support Gordov's assault. Berzarin responded by transferring General Kotel'nikov's 1st Rifle Corps (145th and 204th Rifle Divisions) to 43rd Army and concentrating 5th Guards and 84th Rifle Corps, supported by 28th and 39th Guards Tank and 47th Mechanized Brigades, in attack positions on his army's left wing. Admittedly, 5th Guards Rifle Corps' 9th, 17th, and 19th Guards Rifle Divisions and 84th Rifle Corps' 134th, 158th, and 262nd Rifle Divisions had been severely weakened in previous attacks, the last of which had just ended only two days before. However, these forces faced only a single regiment of German 206th Infantry Division. Their inclusion in the attack raised the overall Soviet strength along this axis to seven rifle corps and twenty rifle divisions and the Soviet superiority along this axis to better than 8 to 1 in infantry and more than 6 to 1 in armor.

In addition to ordering this major assault, the *Stavka* directed General Golubev, the commander of 43rd Army, to conduct yet another supporting attack against German 14th Infantry Division's defenses northeast of Vitebsk on 23 December. Golubev planned to make this attack in the Piatiletna (Goriane) and Kovali sector along and south of the Surazh-Vitebsk road (18–23 kilometers east-northeast of Vitebsk) with 179th, 270th, and 306th Rifle Divisions of General Volkov's 91st Rifle Corps, supported by the remaining tanks of 60th and 146th Tank Brigades and motorized infantry from 46th Mechanized Brigade.

It is abundantly clear that the *Stavka* believed that an attack by so large a force east of Vitebsk in conjunction with a heavy assault west of Vitebsk would finally result in a collapse of German defenses and the capture of the city. The fact that it did not largely explains why Soviet and Russian accounts have been so silent about the operation.

The *Stavka* also ensured that *front* commander Sokolovsky and army commander Gordov followed its instructions regarding the new offensive to a tee. It did so, first, by relieving the Western Front's deputy commander, General Khozin, and then by transferring Stalin's "crony," the feared and often hated L. Z. Mekhlis, from the 2nd Baltic Front to the Western Front as its member of the military council (commissar) (see Appendices H-3 and H-4).

The Soviet 39th and 33rd Armies began their assaults east and northeast of Vitebsk simultaneously early on 23 December. Initially, the defending German forces reported that two Red Army divisions struck in the north and as many as ten in the south. They were not far from the mark. Gordov's 33rd Army attacked with 81st and 36th Guards and 65th and 69th Rifle Corps deployed abreast from left to right, each organized into two or three echelons of rifle divisions. The 184th and 32nd Rifle Divisions of the army's 45th Rifle Corps protected the army's long right wing. Although the tremendous density of forces in 33rd Army's penetration sector defies absolutely accurate reconstruction, Table 11.3 shows the army's probable combat formation, along with that of adjacent 39th Army's 5th Guards and 84th Rifle Corps.

To the north, to conduct his supporting or diversionary attack, General Berzarin concentrated 306th and 270th Rifle Divisions as his shock group's first echelon in the sector extending from Kovali to Piatiletna (Goriane), backed up by 179th Rifle Division and his three mobile brigades. These faced the right wing of German LIII Army Corps' 14th Infantry Division. The 1st and 91st Rifle Corps defended 43rd Army's left and right wing op-

Table 11.3. The Combat Formations of the 1st Baltic Front's 39th Army and the Western Front's 33rd Army and Opposing German Forces on 23 December 1943

FORCE (Sector)	OPPOSING GERMAN FORCE
1st/2nd/3rd Echelons (Mobile group)	
1st BALTIC FRONT	**THIRD PANZER ARMY**
39th Army (Tishkova-Kovaleva)	VI AC
84th RC (Tishkova-Vitebsk highway)	206th ID
134th RD/262nd RD	
158th RD	
5th GRC (Vitebsk highway-Kovaleva)	
19th GRD/17th GRD	
9th GRD/91st GRD	
WESTERN FRONT	
33rd Army (Kovaleva-Dobromysl')	
69th RC (south of Kovaleva)	
144th RD	
164th RD	
Support	
2nd GTB	
65th RC (north of Khoteml'e)	246th ID
173rd RD/42nd RD/222nd RD	
Support	
23rd GTB	
36th RC (Khoteml'e-Arguny)	
215th RD/199th RD/274th RD	
Support	
256th TB	
81st RC (Arguny-Pogostishche)	
157th RD/95th RD	
Support	
213th TB	
45th RC (Pogostishche-Dobromysl')	
184th RD/97th RD (to 81st RC)	
32nd RD	256th ID
2nd GTC (mobile group)	
(4th, 25th, 26th GTBs, 4th GMRB)	

Sources: Boevoi sostav Sovetskoi Armii, chast' IV (Ianvar'–dekabr' 1944 g.) [The combat composition of the Soviet Army, pt. 4 (January–December 1944)] (Moscow: Voenizdat, 1988), 12–13; and "Anlagen zum Kriegstagebuch Nr. 7, Lagenkarten Band VII, Pz AOK 3, Ia, 1 Dec–31 Dec 1943," *Pz AOK 3, 49113/26 file*, in NAM Series T-313, Roll 296.

posite LIII Corps' 3rd and 4th Luftwaffe Divisions and roughly half of 14th Infantry Division.

Initially, on 23 December 33rd Army's shock groups pushed the defending Germans back about 1 kilometer between Kovaleva and Arguny at the junction between German 206th and 246th Infantry Divisions (see Map 11.8). The next day, however, 65th, 36th, and 81st Rifle Corps committed their second-echelon divisions and succeeded in enlarging the penetration to a depth of 2–3 kilometers, by doing so threatening to split the two German divisions. Late that evening VI Army Corps organized a counterattack by specially organized Group F for the next day against the penetration's southern

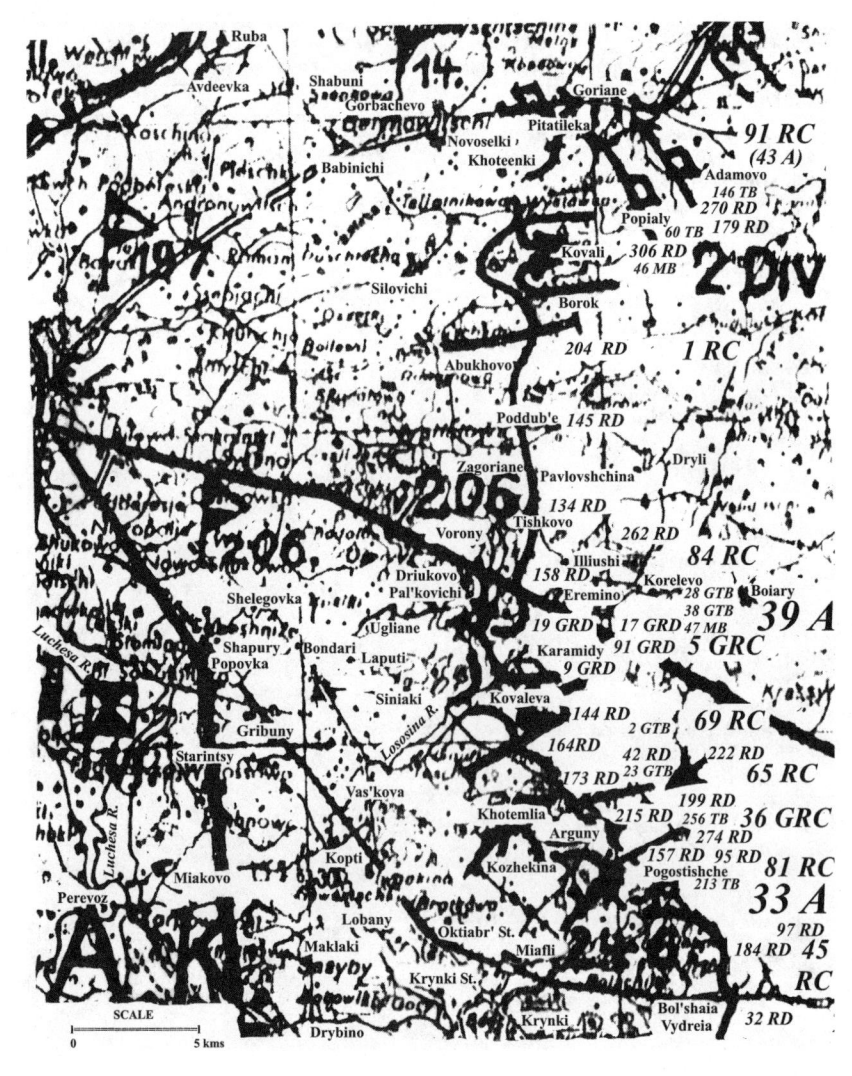

Map 11.8. Third Panzer Army's Situation East of Vitebsk, 23 December 1943

flank. Group F was a special *kampfgruppe* formed from Panzer-Grenadier Division *Feldherrnhalle,* which reached the Vitesbk region from southern France on 23 and 24 December.[4] The *kampfgruppe* consisted of the panzer grenadier division's panzer reconnaissance battalion (*Pz.Aufkl.Abt.* "FHH"), reinforced by the division's assault guns, engineers, and an artillery battalion (*Art.Abt.* "FHH"). The division fielded seventeen Pz. IV tanks and forty-two StuG assault guns in December, but it is unclear how many of these made it to the battlefield.[5] However, despite *Feldherrnhalle's* appearance on the

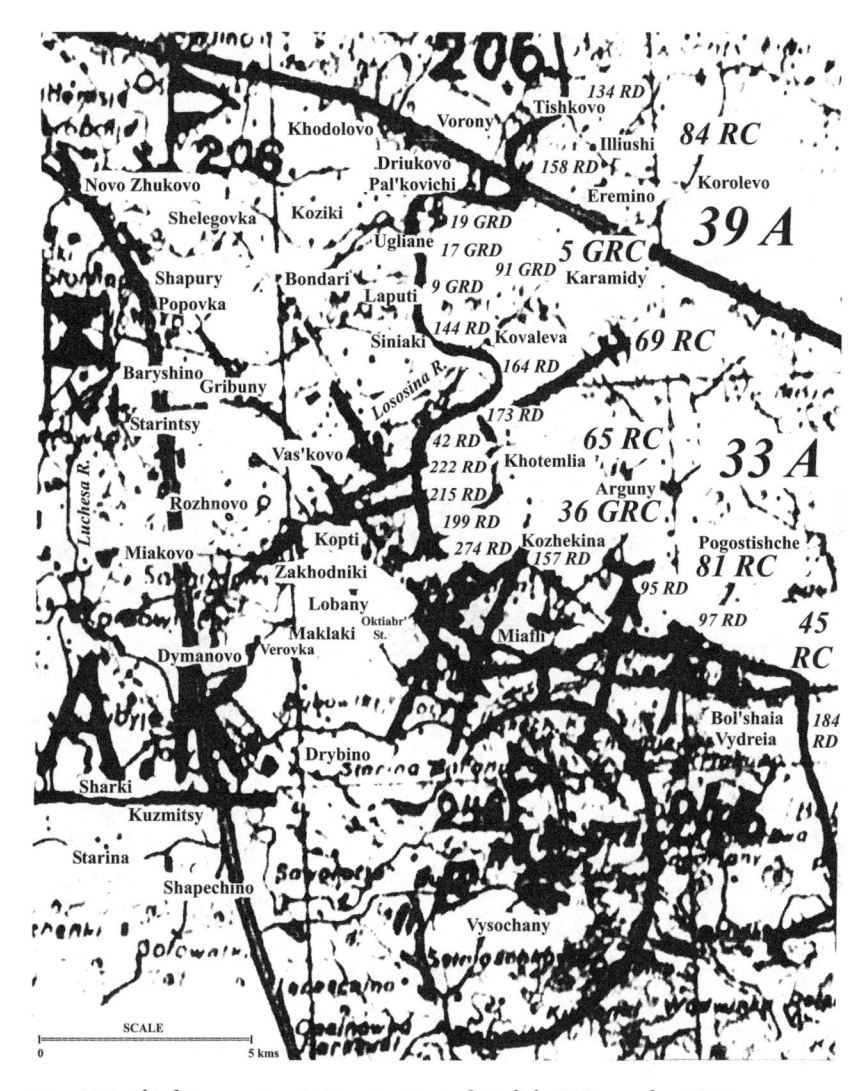

Map 11.9. Third Panzer Army's Situation East of Vitebsk, 25 December 1943

battlefield, on 25 December, the entire 33rd Army burst forward from 2–7 kilometers, disrupted the German counterattack, and reached and severed the Smolensk-Vitebsk railroad line at and south of Oktiabr' Station, 20 kilometers southeast of Vitebsk's central square (see Map 11.9).

The advance by the Western Front's 33rd Army continued on 26 December when elements of 36th Rifle Corps' 215th and 199th Rifle Divisions fought for the village of Zakhodniki, situated west of the railroad line, only 2 kilometers east of the Vitebsk-Orsha highway and 15 kilometers south of

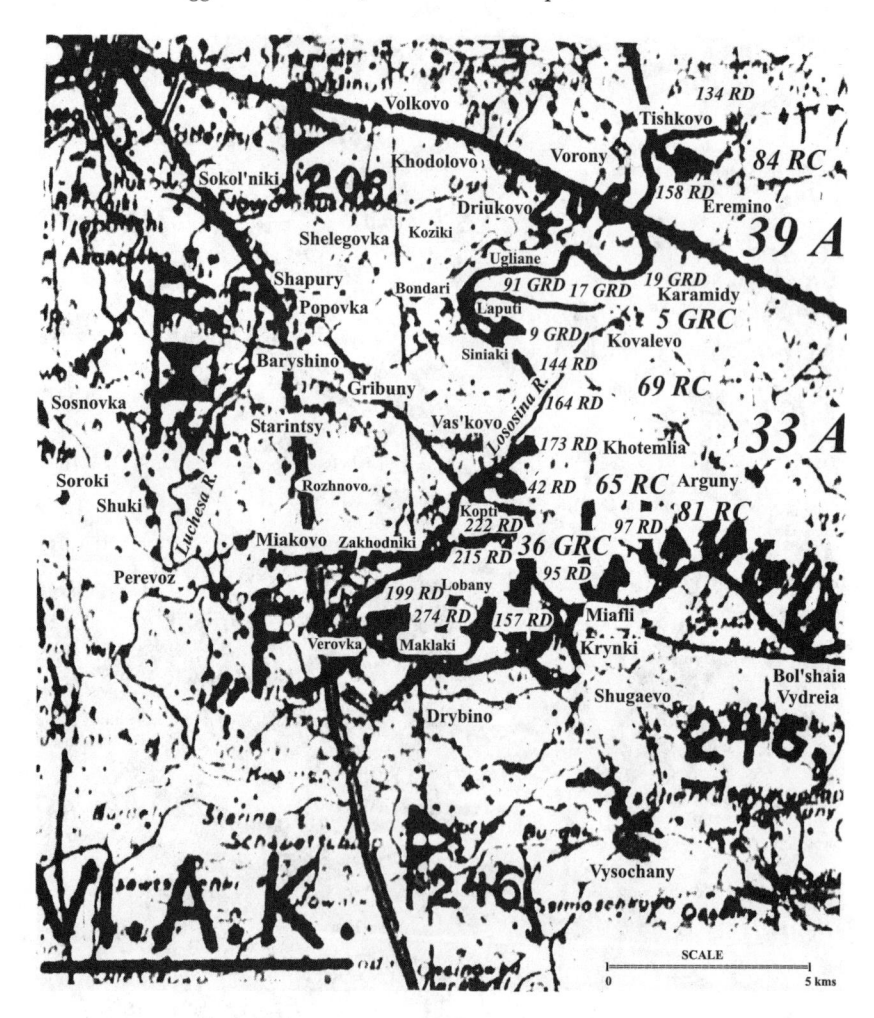

296   The Struggle for Belorussia, December 1943–April 1944

Map 11.10. Third Panzer Army's Situation East of Vitebsk, 28 December 1943

the city. Thereafter, intense fighting raged for two days in the Maklaki region, 3 kilometers south of Zakhodniki, as German *Kampfgruppe* F struggled mightily to prevent the attacking Soviet force from severing its critical supply artery (see Map 11.10).

Meanwhile, to the north, 43rd Army's attack on 23 December penetrated to within 2 kilometers south of the Surazh-Vitebsk road. The next day, the 358th and 334th Rifle Divisions of its 92nd Rifle Corps succeeded in biting a chunk out of German 14th Infantry Division's defenses further northwest along the same road. This pressure, along with 4th Shock Army's successes south of Gorodok, impelled the Germans to withdraw LIII Army Corps' divisions fighting in the region northwest of Vitebsk to new defenses even closer to the city.

The *Stavka* noted 33rd Army's progress with considerable satisfaction but was displeased with the performance of 39th Army's shock groups, which by 26 December had advanced westward a mere 2–3 kilometers. Hence, a peeved *Stavka* sent Bagramian a caustic telegram (see Appendix H-5): "The 33rd Army is advancing toward the Vitebsk-Orsha highway in heavy combat and is fighting along the Rozhnovo and Verovka line. At the same time, Berzarin's 39th Army has been idle for a second day. The People's Commissar of Defense has ORDERED: Demand that Berzarin's left wing launch a decisive offensive no later than the morning of 28 December 1943."[6] General Berzarin complied, but his two weakened corps managed to advance only 1–2 kilometers on 28 December before stalling entirely. By this time, 33rd Army's forces had captured Maklaki and were within sight of the Vitebsk-Orsha road. During the following two days, these forces swung northwest and, while searching for a more favorable route across the road, captured the village of Kopti, 15 kilometers south of Vitebsk. Try as they did, however, they were unable to locate a weak spot in German VI Army Corps' defenses. By 31 December the corps' *Kampfgruppe* F succeeded in thwarting the Soviet advance just short of the highway but only barely (see Map 11.11).

It is unclear from German records whether General Gordov was able to commit General Burdeinyi's 2nd Guards Tank Corps to combat. Apparently, he was not, either because of the corps' weakness, the failure by 33rd Army to seize requisite terrain through which it could commit the corps, or because of the rough terrain itself, especially in the Lososina River valley. In any event, by 31 December the Soviet forces were still well short of their objectives. They would not, however, halt their offensive. It would go on until 6 January in the new year.

Under unrelenting *Stavka* pressure, Gordov's 33rd Army continued its assaults on 1 January, although this time Berzarin's 39th Army, whose attacks along and south of the Vitebsk-Smolensk road had utterly stalled, could offer little or no assistance (see Map 11.12). At day's end on 1 January, Berzarin's army occupied positions stretching from Poddub'e north of the Vitebsk-Smolensk road to Ugliane west of the highway. By this time, Pronin's 65th Rifle Corps had withdrawn its 42nd and 222nd Rifle Divisions from combat for a short rest, leaving 173rd Rifle Division in first-echelon positions between Ugliane and Vaskova protecting the army shock group's right flank. Gordov formed a new shock group, this time consisting of Oleshev's 36th Rifle Corps, which was already located in the northern half of the *front's* penetration sector, reinforced by 95th Rifle Division from Ivanov's 81st Rifle Corps, which regrouped from the Drybino region.

In addition, Sokolovsky ordered Lieutenant General N. I. Krylov, the commander of 5th Army, to move Major General Iu. M. Prokof'ev's 72nd

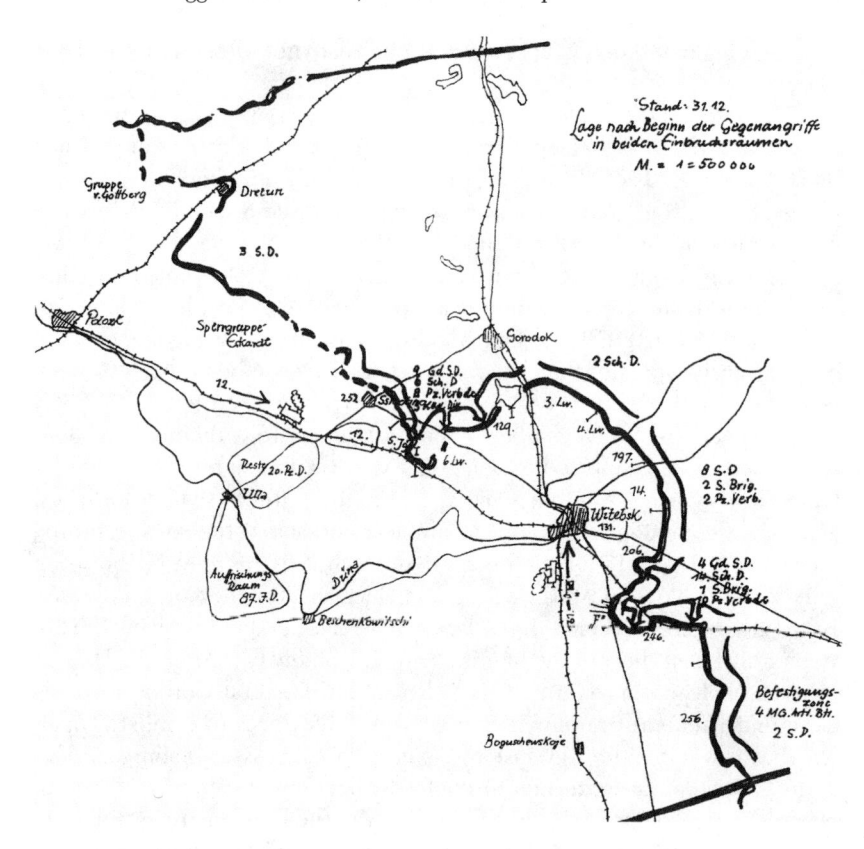

Map 11.11. Third Panzer Army's Appreciation of the Situation at Vitebsk, 31 December 1943

Rifle Corps from its former positions south of the penetration into new assault positions between the villages of Maklaki and Krynki in the southern half of the *front's* penetration sector. At the same time, he transferred 45th Rifle Corps, along with 157th Rifle Division of Ivanov's 81st Rifle Corps, from Gordov's 33rd to Krylov's 5th Army with orders to defend the southern flank of the penetration from Krynki to Bol'shaia Vydreia. Finally, Gordov withdrew the two rifle divisions of Mul'tan's 69th Rifle Corps into second echelon for rest and refitting.

After it was assembled, Gordov's new shock group consisted of Oleshev's 36th Rifle Corps, whose 199th and 274th Rifle Divisions were in first-echelon assault positions between Gribuny and Kopti and whose 215th Rifle Division was in second echelon, 95th Rifle Division of Ivanov's 81st Rifle Corps, situated between Kopti and Maklaki, and 371st Rifle Division, which Sokolovsky assigned to Oleshev's rifle corps on 2 January from his *front's* reserve. Gordov

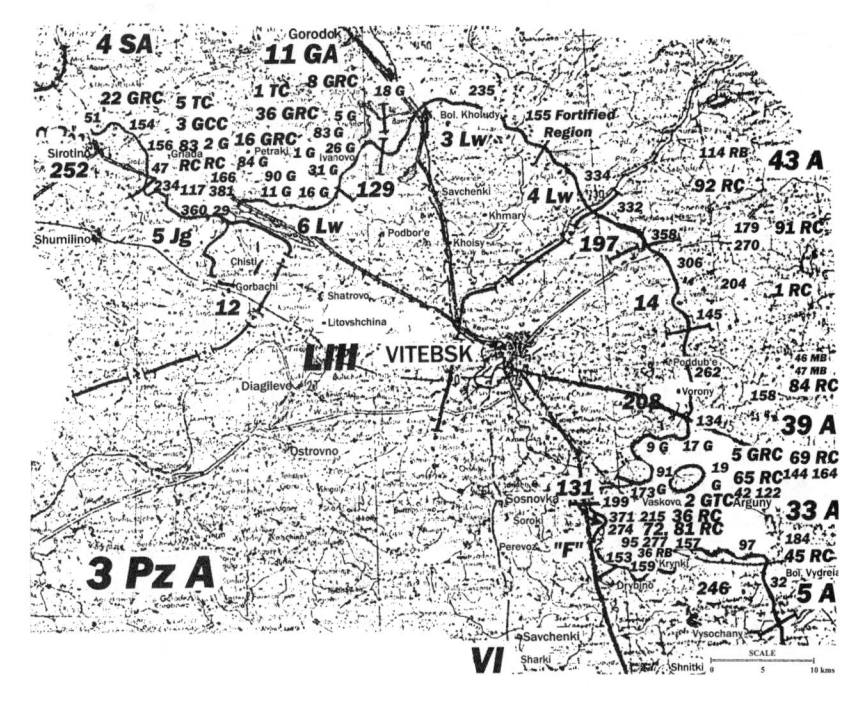

Map 11.12. The Situation at Vitebsk, 1–3 January 1944

planned to commit 371st Rifle Division at the junction of 199th and 274th Rifle Divisions to spearhead the advance on Sosnovka.

On Oleshev's left flank, Prokof'ev's 72nd Rifle Corps formed Gordov's second shock group, which consisted of 153rd and 159th Rifle Divisions in first echelon, backed up by 277th Rifle Division and 36th Rifle Brigade (newly assigned to 36th Rifle Corps) in second echelon. Prokof'ev's rifle corps was to advance southwestward, capture Drybino and Krynki, cut the Vitebsk-Orsha highway, and protect 33rd Army's left flank. As before, the armies' separate tank brigades and those of Burdeinyi's 2nd Guards Tank Corps were to provide necessary armor support for the assault.

The mission of Gordov's shock group was to penetrate German defenses in the sector from Gribuny to Maklaki along the Vitebsk-Orsha road, advance westward through Starintsy, Soroki, and Perevoz, cross the Luchesa River, cut the Vitebsk-Orsha railroad line, and advance along the Sosnovka, Ostrovno, and Diaglevo axis to link up with the 1st Baltic Front's forces in the Diaglevo region to encircle German Third Panzer Army's forces in Vitebsk. Krylov's shock group was to penetrate German defenses in the sector between Maklaki and Krynki, capture Drybino, and exploit westward toward Savchenki on the Vitebsk-Orsha railroad line to protect 33rd Army's right flank. In one of the few Soviet accounts of this offensive, Krylov recorded his recollections of the offensive in his memoirs:

> Five rifle divisions and three tank brigades participated in the offensive 5th Army undertook during the beginning of January 1944. They were supported by artillery from 81st and 72nd Rifle Corps. The sharpest fighting developed in the sectors of understrength 159th Rifle Division and 36th Rifle Brigade.
>
> Plentiful snow began falling on that morning, and soon after a blizzard began. All of the regiments went over to the attack and skillfully forced their way across the thick ice on the Lososina River [which blocked the advance on Drybino]. All of the routes were covered [with snow], and it was impossible for either the infantry or tanks to advance further. The attack advanced no further than a kilometer during the day.
>
> The army commander, who was situated all day at 72nd Rifle Corps' forward observation post, concluded that it was necessary to reinforce the axis along which 36th Rifle Brigade was operating since it was the weakest of the attacking formations. At a time when the blizzard abated and we could resume active operations, he replaced this brigade with 277th Rifle Division, which had just arrived in the army. This measure had a positive effect on the army's offensive.[7]

What Krylov failed to report was that the initial offensive in early January fell well short of accomplishing its aims, and, after it expired by 6 January, the *Stavka* ordered Gordov to organize a new offensive on 8 January. Nevertheless, Krylov's account does substantiate why Sokolovsky's renewed assaults east of Vitebsk in early January ultimately failed.

Gordov's and Krylov's shock groups struck at dawn on 1 January despite a heavy snowstorm that gripped the entire region (see Maps 11.13 and 11.14). In the ensuing five days of heavy fighting, Gordov's shock group expanded the penetration about 1 kilometer westward toward the Vitebsk-Orsha road, forcing Third Panzer Army to commit its reserve 131st Infantry Division to contain the assault just short of the road. During this fighting 199th and 371st Rifle Divisions of Oleshev's 36th Rifle Corps captured Gribuny, reaching within rifle shot distance of the road, while 274th Rifle Division actually captured a small portion of the road west of Kopti until halted by counterattacks launched by the *Feldherrnhalle* Division's *kampfgruppe*.

To the southeast, in the sector of Krylov's 5th Army, 159th Rifle Division and 36th Rifle Brigade of Prokof'ev's 72nd Rifle Corps forced their way across the Lososina River, reached the northern outskirts of Drybino, and captured the strongpoint at Krynki from German 246th Infantry Division, only to be halted by heavy tank fire from the newly arrived 245th Assault Gun *Abteilung* (detachment). By late on 6 January, however, it was clear that the bad weather and stout German resistance prevented any further ad-

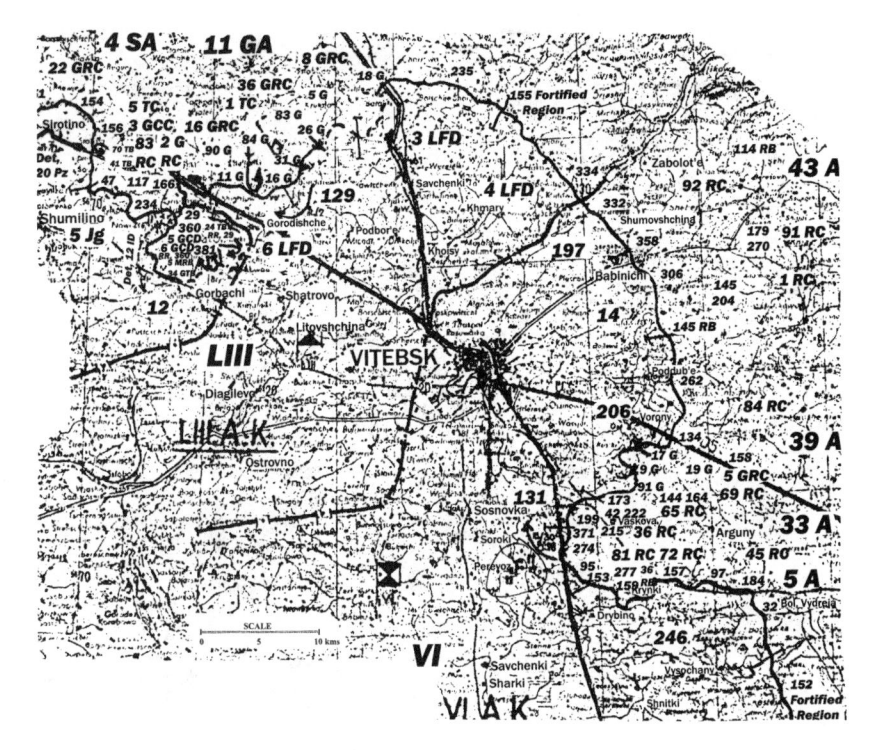

Map 11.13. The Situation at Vitebsk, 4–6 January 1944

vance. Reluctantly, the *Stavka* approved Sokolovsky's request to halt further offensive action but only temporarily (see Map 11.15).

Although few Soviet accounts provide any details about the 1st Baltic and Western Fronts' joint offensive against German forces defending Vitebsk during late December 1943 and early January 1944, some fragmentary Russian archival materials cast some light on what transpired. For example, the combat journal of 1st Baltic Front summed up its achievements as of 31 December stating: "The *front's* forces penetrated the enemy defense southwest of Gorodok on 24 December and captured this important communications point, by so doing liquidating the Gorodok salient in the enemy's front. Having overcome exceptionally strong resistance by enemy forces in conditions of difficult swampy terrain, the absence of roads, snowstorms, and fog, the *front's* forces liberated 1,220 populated points."[8] At the same time, a report prepared by the 1st Baltic Front's Political Section on the same day totally obfuscates any mention of the heavy fighting east of Vitebsk in late December:

> During one day of fighting at the beginning of October 1943, the Kalinin Front's forces penetrated a strongly fortified enemy defense southeast

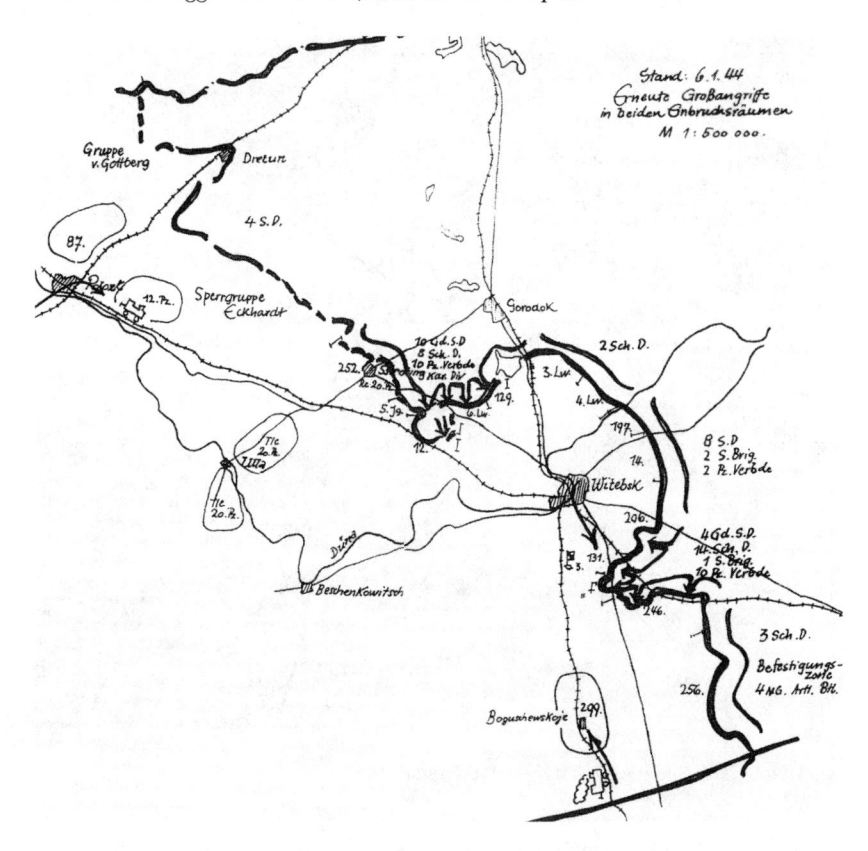

Map 11.14. Third Panzer Army's Appreciation of the Situation at Vitebsk, 6 January 1944

and north of the city of Nevel', advanced up to 40 kilometers, and captured Nevel' on 7 October.

While developing the offensive in November, [the *front*] wedged considerably into the enemy's defense along the Polotsk axis. In the beginning of November, the enemy made several attempts to cut off our penetrating units northeast of Polotsk and capture the city of Nevel'. Our forces wore down the enemy in sustained combat and made the transition to the offensive from the Nevel' region on 13 December.[9]

This innocuous and incomplete summary belies the complexity of the Vitebsk offensive operation and the frustration it caused to the expectant *Stavka* and the *fronts* that participated in it. And no one felt this frustration more than the Soviet soldiers who participated in the operation because they had no choice but to endure the three months of near constant combat in the most miserable of winter weather conditions. Despite the Kalinin (1st Baltic) Front's relatively spectacular achievements in Octo-

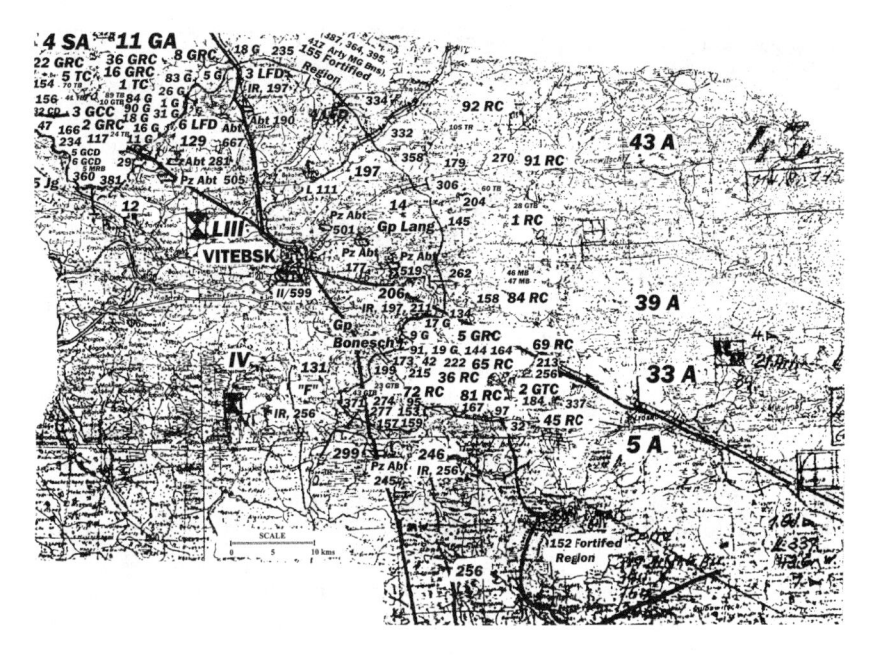

Map 11.15. The Situation at Vitebsk, 7 January 1944

ber, by 31 December the Vitebsk operation had turned into an agonizing slugfest and an obvious failure. Nevertheless, the *Stavka* continued to remain optimistic about its chances for strategic success in northern Belorussia and the Vitebsk region. Undeterred by defeat, it would order attack after attack on the German stronghold at Vitebsk throughout the winter of 1944.

The Russians have published precious few casualty figures associated with the Red Army's operations along the Vitebsk axis. They have published figures for what they term the "Nevel'-Gorodok offensive operation," which encompasses the entire period from 6 October through 31 December 1943. These indicate that, out of a total of 198,000 troops initially engaged in the operation, 168,902 became casualties, including 43,551 killed, captured, or missing, and 125,351 wounded or sick.[10] However, this figure includes only 3rd and 4th Shock, 11th Guards, 43rd, and 3rd Air Armies. It does not include 39th Army or 33rd Army in the December phase of the operation. One exception, however, is the recent study by Abaturov, which places 33rd Army's losses at 33,500 men killed, wounded, or missing and thirty-four mortars and sixty-seven guns lost.[11] Thus, when the Russians reveal actual casualty figures for the entire Vitebsk operation, it is likely that they will exceed 200,000 men.

THE 2ND BALTIC FRONT'S NOVOSOKOL'NIKI PURSUIT (30 DECEMBER 1943–15 JANUARY 1944)

Lieutenant General L. M. Sandalov, the chief of staff of the 2nd Baltic Front, flew back to Moscow midmonth, where he met with Army General A. I. Antonov, the chief of the Red Army's General Staff, to plan future operations. There, Antonov revealed the *Stavka*'s plans to conduct a massive operation in early January to raise the Leningrad siege and, if possible, to destroy German Army Group North's Eighteenth Army. The *Stavka* plans called for the Leningrad and Volkhov Fronts to attack the German Eighteenth Army from positions at Leningrad and Novgorod and drive it back into the Baltic region. Simultaneously, the 2nd Baltic Front was to attack to tie down the German Sixteenth Army, which served as the source for the Eighteenth Army's operational reserves. Thereafter, in Sandalov's words, "All three of our *fronts* were to attack in the direction of Narva, Pskov, and Idritsa, destroy 16th Army, and fully liberate the Leningrad region. The 2nd Baltic Front's offensive was planned first."[12]

Sandalov then explained the 2nd Baltic Front's role in the operation: "In accordance with the *Stavka* decision, we were ordered first to destroy the enemy forces in the region north of Nevel' and then strike toward Idritsa and to the north of Novosokol'niki in order to deprive the enemy of the opportunity to exploit the main railroad lines and to prevent him from transferring forces from the Sixteenth Army to Leningrad and Novgorod."[13] Weeks before, early on 8 December, the *Stavka* had already ordered the Western and 1st Baltic Fronts to transfer 10th Guards Army and 3rd Guards Cavalry Corps to the 2nd Baltic Front's control, effective the next day, so that they could spearhead the offensive (see Appendix H-6).[14] General Sandalov later provided details about the 2nd Baltic Front's operational plan for the Idritsa-Opochka offensive operation, stating: "We intended to deliver our main attack on the *front*'s left wing with two armies: 3rd Shock Army toward Pustoshka and Opochka and 10th Guards Army, which would arrive shortly, on Idritsa and Zilune. The armies on the *front*'s right wing, each with 2–3 rifle divisions, were to attack a day earlier than the armies on the left flank to tie down the opposing enemy forces."[15]

However, the well-planned Soviet offensive aborted for two reasons. First, 10th Guards Army's redeployment had to be delayed to replenish the army with personnel replacements and required equipment and supplies.[16] Consequently, the army was not prepared to attack on 10 January. Worse still from the standpoint of Soviet planners, on 29 December General Kuechler, the Army Group North commander, began an operation designed to withdraw his forces from the Nevel' salient (see Map 11.16). The withdrawal, which took place over a period of six days, began on 29 December, when the Sixteenth Army's I Army Corps withdrew its 32nd, 122nd, and 290th Infantry

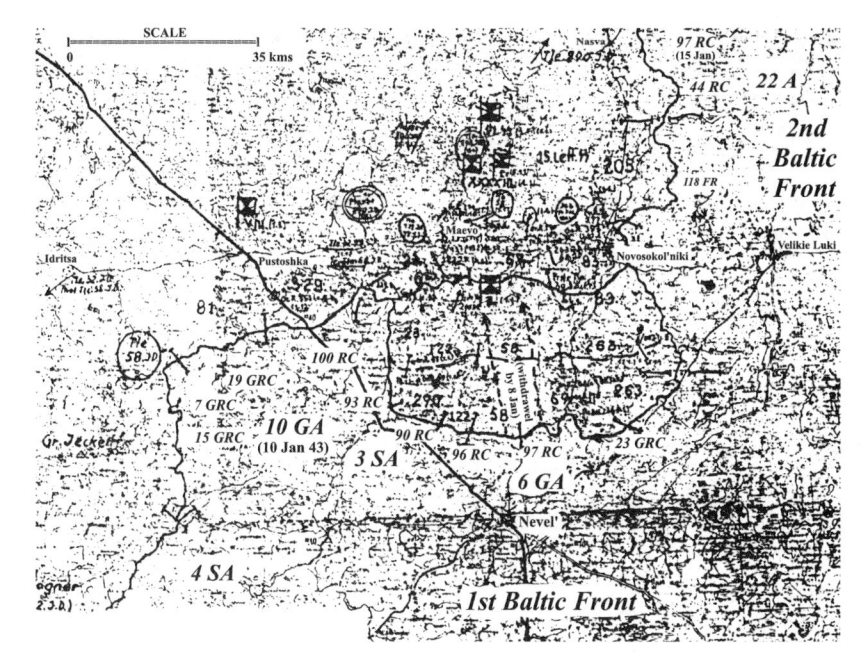

Map 11.16. Army Group North's Situation, 29 December 1943–15 January 1944

Divisions from the nose of the salient north of Nevel'. The withdrawal, which caught the Soviets by surprise, prompted a Soviet reaction resembling the way Soviet forces had dealt with the German withdrawals at Rzhev-Viaz'ma and Demiansk in early 1943. That is, the Soviets hastily ordered a pursuit that, ultimately, accomplished nothing more than to harass the retreating German forces.

Initially, after detecting the withdrawal, General Chistiakov's 6th Guards Army began the pursuit with its 97th and 23d Guards Rifle Corps. The 3rd Shock Army's 93rd and 100th Rifle Corps joined the pursuit by pressuring German forces in the salient from the west.[17] Soviet accounts, in particular those about 6th Guards Army's actions, explain how Soviet forces drove the Germans back in heavy fighting. However, it is abundantly clear from the German records and Soviet casualty figures that whatever fighting occurred did so episodically, and the only heavy fighting occurred when Soviet forces reached the new German defense line. By 6 January the new German defense line extended eastward from Idritsa south of Pustoshka to Novosokol'niki and northward to Lake Il'men. By withdrawing its forces and truncating its front line, the German Sixteenth Army was able to establish new and stronger defenses capable of fending off renewed Soviet offensive activity in the region but only for a brief time. Within a month, the Red

Army's January offensive at Leningrad and Novgorod forced the Sixteenth Army to wheel its defenses to the northwest back to the city of Pskov.

Soviet sources place 3rd Shock and 6th Guards Army's losses in this pursuit operation at 12,395 men out of 199,700 troops engaged in the operation. This included 2,574 killed, captured, or missing, and 9,821 wounded or sick.[18] The relative paucity of casualties offers ample testimony to the low intensity of the combat involved.

CHAPTER 12

The 1st Baltic and Western Fronts' Vitebsk-Bogushevsk Offensive (6-24 January)

THE PLAN

Very few Soviet sources even mention the offensive operations the 1st Baltic and Western Fronts conducted in the Vitebsk region during the first three months of 1944. For example, although he prepared detailed memoirs of his military career, Bagramian, the commander of the 1st Baltic Front, says absolutely nothing about his *front's* operations from January through June 1944. Sokolovsky, the commander of the Western Front, wrote no memoirs whatsoever. In fact, only two Russian sources pierce the nearly impenetrable veil of silence that still shrouds the 1st Baltic and Western Fronts' attempts to resume their offensive against Vitebsk during the first week of January 1944. The most complete account to escape the censors' scalpel is the postwar memoir written by General Galitsky, the commander of 11th Guards Army. Although this memoir provides precious little in the way of details about this operation, it does provide hints as to why the offensive failed to achieve its ends. First and foremost, Galitsky argues that his army, which had suffered severe attrition in both troops and material, urgently needed to rest and refit before resuming offensive operations:

> We had little time to spend on that inasmuch as we were supposed to resume offensive operations as early as 5 January. Therefore, we conducted the preparations far less thoroughly than we wished. In particular, as before, information about the enemy was insufficient. Due to the poor flying weather, air reconnaissance provided very little in that regard. Also, only to some degree were the forward units able to "feel out" the forward edge of the enemy's defense by means of fire, reconnaissance-in-force, and operations by reconnaissance subunits. As regards the quantity of ammunition, which the bases supplied, it turned out to be considerably less than we expected because of the heavy snowfall and the roads, which were basted by the snow.
>
> In a word, either in terms of its forces and weaponry or by virtue of its readiness, the army was in no condition to carry out a decisive offensive to great depths—we were still approximately 20 kilometers from Vitebsk—against a strong enemy who was relying on powerful defenses. But it was absolutely necessary to attack, even though with only limited aims.

This requirement was dictated by the overall situation; once again the mission assigned to our *front* and neighboring *fronts* to tie down the enemy's forces. Powerful offensives by Soviet forces were continuing in the south. Preparations were being completed for the Leningrad, Volkov, and 2nd Baltic Fronts' attacks against Army Group North. There could be no doubt but that the enemy would try to transfer his forces from close-by sectors, including the Vitebsk sector, to Leningrad.

By creating the greatest possible tension here to prevent this—such was the mission of our forces along the Vitebsk axis, including 11th Guards Army.

Thus we resumed the offensive. However, not on 5 January, since not only was aviation unable to operate due to the heavy snow but the artillery was also deprived of the opportunity to conduct aimed fire. The commencement of our offensive was postponed until the following day. The weather improved a little, but further delay was not possible, and the army received the order to attack the enemy.

I must note that, on that day, we could allocate only one fourth of a combat load of ammunition to the guns for the artillery preparation and the same amount for the subsequent conduct of fire. And this was during an offensive against strongly fortified enemy positions. Naturally, in such a situation the effectiveness of the artillery fire turned out to be inadequate.[1]

Other than Galitsky's brief account, General Krylov, the commander of the Western Front's 5th Army, was the only other army commander who served in the 1st Baltic and Western Fronts during this period to even mention the battles around Vitebsk. More recently, after the fall of the Soviet Union in 1991, Army General Makhmut A. Gareev, who served as a major in the Western Front during these battles in Belorussia and became a leading Soviet military theorist in the 1970s and 1980s, wrote two articles surveying the nature and causes of the Western Front's failed offensives in eastern Belorussia during the fall of 1943 and winter of 1944.

Gareev's articles, published with clear political sanction, identify all eleven of the failed offensives the Western Front conducted during this period, the dates they were conducted, the forces involved in each offensive, and a tally of the casualties the *front* suffered in each operation. In addition, Gareev includes verbatim *Stavka* critiques of these operations. For the purposes of this study, the most valuable information contained in these *Stavka* documents are summary tallies of the strength of the opposing forces in each of these eleven offensive operations and the casualties the Western Front's forces suffered in each. Along with the brief recollections of General Krylov, these summaries provide the only hard data available from the Soviet perspective that researchers can use to reconstruct the actual course of these operations. In regard to the so-called Bogushevsk offensive, these *Stavka* documents provide the following raw data:

The Bogushevsk Operation 8–24 January 1944
Our forces. The following forces were concentrated to conduct the operation: 16 rifle divisions, including 11 rifle divisions in first echelon and 5 rifle divisions and 1 rifle brigade in second echelon, 1 tank corps, 12 artillery brigades, 6 RVGK artillery regiments, 6 tank brigades, and 8 self-propelled artillery regiments, for a total of 295 tanks.
Enemy forces. 4 infantry divisions, parts of 2 motorized [panzer grenadier] divisions, up to 9 artillery regiments, and up to 130 tanks.
The offensive on the Bogushevsk axis, 8–14 January, penetrated to a depth of 2–4 kilometers. Our losses were 5,517 men killed and 19,672 men wounded, for a total of *25,128 men*.[2]

In addition to this summary, excerpts from the daily combat journals of 43rd and 39th Armies provide details of the situation in each of these armies on the eve of the offensive (see Appendix I-1 and Appendix I-2)

As had been the case during the previous stage of the Vitebsk offensive, in early January the *Stavka* ordered Bagramian's and Sokolovsky's 1st Baltic and Western Fronts to penetrate German Third Panzer Army's defenses west and southeast of Vitebsk, advance to link up in the Ostrovno and Diaglevo regions, and encircle and destroy German forces defending the city of Vitebsk (see Map 11.13). Bagramian was to commence his offensive on 6 January using General Malyshev's 4th Shock Army and General Galitsky's 11th Guards Army to deliver the *front's* main attack west of Vitebsk.

Specifically, the two armies were to conduct their attack in the broad sector extending southward from the southern shore of Lake Losvida past Lake Zaronovskoe to the German strongpoint Gorbachi and then westward from Gorbachi to the Vitebsk-Sirotino road east of Sirotino. The bulk of Malyshev's and Galitsky's forces was concentrated in a narrow salient bulging southward due south of Lake Zaronovskoe. After the two armies' shock groups penetrated the Germans' defenses, the mobile forces of General Butkov's 1st and General Sakhno's 5th Tank Corps, along with the cavalrymen of General Oslikovsky's 3rd Guards Cavalry Corps, were to lead the exploitation toward Vitebsk and Diaglevo to link up with the forward elements of Sokolovsky's shock groups, advancing from the east.

The *Stavka* ordered Sokolovsky to begin his offensive southeast of Vitebsk on 8 January. General Gordov's 33rd Army, serving as the Western Front's main shock group, was to advance westward from the salient west of Arguny, penetrate Third Panzer Army's defenses along the Smolensk-Orsha road, and cross the Luchesa River. After his rifle forces were safely across the Luchesa River, Gordov was to commit General Burdeinyi's 2nd Guards Tank

Table 12.1. The Estimated Correlation of Opposing Forces in the Vitebsk-Bogushevsk Offensive, 8–24 January 1944

OPPOSING FORCES	
Soviet	*German*
1st Baltic Front	
4th Shock Army	5th Jäger Division
11th Guards Army	12th Infantry Division
15 rifle divisions	6th Luftwaffe Field Division
1 tank corps	129th Infantry Division
1 tank brigade (120 tanks)	406th Grenadier Regiment
	Detachment, 12th Panzer Division
	281st and 245th Assault Gun, 21st Panzer, and 667th Panzer *Jagt Abteilung* (60 AFVs)
Western Front	
43rd Army	197th Infantry Division
	14th Infantry Division
39th Army	206th Infantry Division
33rd Army	131st Infantry Division
5th Army	299th Infantry Division
16 rifle divisions	246th Infantry Division
1 tank corps	Panzer Grenadier Division *Feldherrnhalle*
6 tank brigades	
8 self-propelled artillery regiments (295 tanks)	Detachments, 14th Infantry Division, 189th, 655th, and 190th Assault Gun, and 667th Panzer *Jagt Abteilung* (130 AFVs)
Depth of Soviet advance: 2–4 kilometers	
Casualties (Western Front): 25,189 men, including 5,517 killed and 19,672 wounded	

Sources: Makhmut Gareev, "O neudachnykh nastupatel'nykh operatsiiakh sovetskikh voisk v Velikoi Otechestvennoi voine. Po neopublikovannym dokumentam GKO" [Concerning unsuccessful offensive operations of Soviet forces in the Great Patriotic War. Based on unpublished GKO documents], *Novaia i noveishaia istoriia* [New and newest history] 1 (January 1994): 16; and H Gr Mitte/Ia, KTB: Lagenkarten, 1–31 January 1944, *H. Gr Mitte, 65002/60 file,* in NAM series T-311, Roll 224.

Corps to combat, with the task of exploiting to the Ostrovno region, where it was to link up with the forward elements of Bagramian's shock groups. While Gordov's shock group was penetrating the Germans' defenses, one rifle corps from Berzarin's 39th Army was to invest Vitebsk from the southeast, and one rifle corps from Krylov's 5th Army was to widen the penetration to the south and protect 33rd Army's left flank.

As evidenced in its after-action critiques, the *Stavka* believed that the forces it allocated to Bagramian's and Sokolovsky's *fronts* were more than adequate to accomplish their assigned missions (see Table 12.1).

VITEBSK WEST

In accordance with the *Stavka*'s orders, Bagramian ordered General Galitsky's 11th Guards Army and General Malyshev's 4th Shock Army to conduct the

The 1st Baltic and Western Fronts' Vitebsk-Bogushevsk Offensive 311

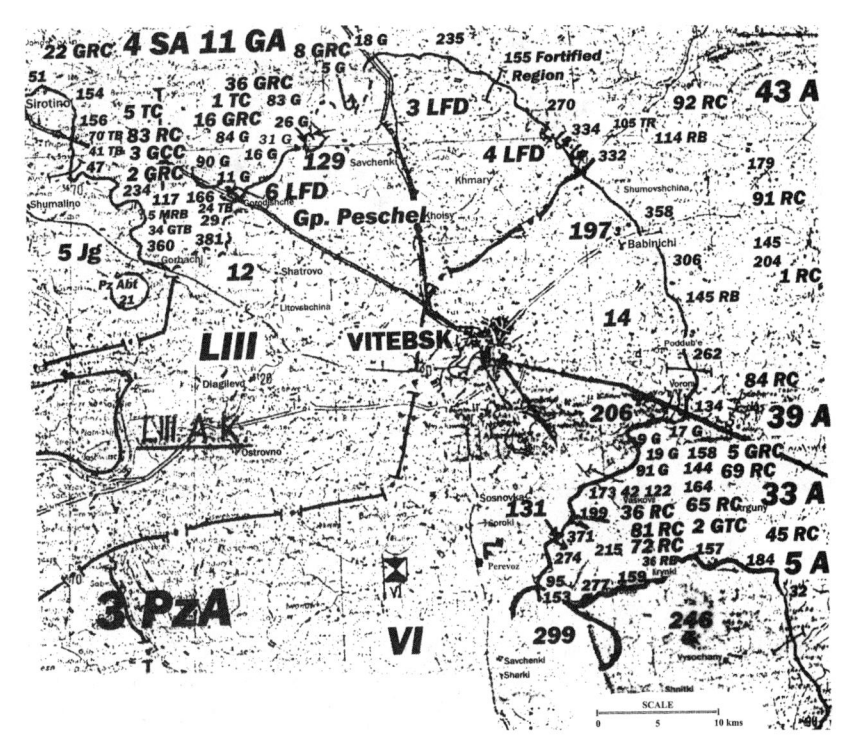

Map 12.1. The Situation at Vitebsk, 11 January 1944

front's main attack early on 6 January in the sector extending from Mashkina, located midway between Lake Losvida and the Vitebsk-Sirotino road, 20 kilometers northwest of Vitebsk, southwestward to Gorbachi on the Vitebsk-Shumilino road, and then northwestward south of Lake Zaronovskoe to Mazurino, a village situated 10 kilometers west of Lake Zaronovskoe and 35 kilometers northwest of Vitebsk. This sector formed a broad salient jutting southward into Third Panzer Army's defenses west-northwest of Vitebsk.

In turn, Galitsky designated General Shafranov's 36th and General Fediun'kin's 16th Guards Rifle Corps as the army's shock group and ordered them to conduct the army's main attack (see Map 12.1). Deployed from left to right in a two-echelon formation of divisions, Shafranov's and Fediun'kin's rifle corps were to penetrate defenses manned by the German LIII Army Corps' 6th Luftwaffe Field and 129th Infantry Divisions in the Mashkina and Lake Zaronovskoe sector and then advance directly toward Vitebsk along an axis extending southeastward north of the Sirotino-Vitebsk road. General Butkov's 1st Tank Corps, 10th Guards Tank Brigade, and 2nd Separate Guards Tank Regiments were to support Galitsky's shock group during the penetration and then lead the exploitation to Vitebsk. General Ksenofontov's 8th Guards Rifle Corps, deployed on the shock group's left wing, was to launch a supporting attack with 26th and 83rd Guards Rifle Divisions in the sector north of Mashkina.

In 4th Shock Army's sector south and west of Lake Zaronovskoe, Malyshev designated General D'iakonov's 83rd and Beloborodov's 2nd Guards Rifle Corps as his army's shock group and ordered them to conduct the army's main attack from the southern tip of the salient southwest of Lake Zaronovskoe. Beloborodov's rifle corps, which deployed on the shock group's left wing with 29th and 381st Rifle Divisions in first echelon and 166th Rifle Division in second echelon, was to assault the defenses of 12th Infantry Division of Third Panzer Army's LIII Army Corps in the sector extending from the southern shore of Lake Zaronovskoe to Gorbachi at the southern extremity of the salient. D'iakonov's rifle corps, which deployed on Beloborodov's right, with 234th and 360th Rifle Divisions in first echelon and 117th Rifle Division in second echelon, was to attack defenses of 5th Jäger Division in the sector extending from Gorbachi westward to Mazurino. The 5th Jäger was deployed on the right wing of Third Panzer Army's IX Army Corps, responsible for defending the panzer army's extended left wing.

Malyshev reinforced D'iakonov's rifle corps with 47th Rifle Division, which Bagramian had assigned to him from *front* reserve, to strengthen his assault and protect the shock group's right flank. Sakhno's 5th Tank Corps, Oslikovsky's 3rd Guards Cavalry Corps, and three tank brigades, most of whose forces were already located within the salient, were supposed to support the penetration operation and then exploit southward to Diaglevo, on the northern bank of the Western Dvina River 22 kilometers west of Vitebsk, where, if possible, they were to seize crossings over the river. The three rifle divisions of Ibiansky's 22nd Guard Rifle Corps, deployed in the Sirotino region echeloned to the north on the shock group's right wing, were to conduct local attacks against the defenses of IX Army Corps' 252nd Infantry Division around Sirotino to tie down these forces and prevent them from reinforcing their defenses in Malyshev's projected penetration sector.

Even though all of Galitsky's and Malyshev's rifle divisions, which averaged roughly 4,500–5,000 men each on 6 January, were considerably understrength, Bagramian was able to concentrate eight rifle divisions against the defenses of German 6th Luftwaffe Field and 129th Infantry Divisions and seven more against the defenses of 5th Jäger and 12th Infantry Divisions. Because each German division counted roughly 10,000 men, this meant that Bagramian's forces were roughly twice as strong as the defending Germans in terms of infantry.

In terms of armor, 1st and 5th Tank Corps fielded a force of about 300 tanks, plus another 100 in the supporting tank brigades. However, in addition to fielding a considerable force of antitank artillery (*Paks*), the Germans were able to stiffen their defenses west of Vitebsk with 505th Panzer and

Map 12.2. Third Panzer Army's Situation West of Vitebsk, 8 January 1944

21st and 281st Assault Gun, and 667th Panzer *Jagt* (antitank) *Abteilungen* (detachments). Along with the strong prepared defenses, these assault guns and tanks, in particular, the Tiger tanks assigned to the 505th, negated much of Bagramian's advantage in armor.

Galitsky's and Malyshev's shock groups began their assault early on 6 January after a short but intense artillery preparation (see Map 12.2). Almost immediately, however, the attacking forces encountered determined resistance. In 11th Guards Army's sector, the assaulting divisions of Shafranov's 36th Guards Rifle Corps and Fediun'kin's 16th Guards Rifle Corps, each supported by a tank brigade either from 1st Tank Corps or the army, made little progress against the well-dug-in Germans. Galitsky later described the assault:

> True, on 6 January our rifle formations, together with the brigades of 1st Tank Corps, which were once again committed to battle and were operating as infantry support tanks, gained ground in a number of sectors. On the following day, however, matters became worse. Operating on prepared defensive lines, the enemy inflicted serious losses on our attacking units, especially in tanks, by his heavy artillery fire and particularly his numerous antitank guns. Thus, over the first two days of combat, 89th Tank Brigade [from 1st Tank Corps] lost 43 of its 50 combat vehicles.
>
> Combat took on an even more sustained and fierce character than before. By maneuvering his firing systems, the enemy halted the attackers, drove them to the ground, and forced them to withdraw to their jumping-off positions.[3]

In particular, the devastating effects of the German tank and assault gun detachments, which constantly maneuvered around the battlefield and met every Soviet threat as it developed, impressed Galitsky:

> The separate tanks, assault guns, and heavy mortars and guns, configured to deliver direct fire, which the enemy employed extensively and which frequently changed their firing positions, especially hindered the offensive. In those sectors where our units achieved success and gained ground, the Hitlerites quickly organized counterattacks by forces in up to infantry battalion strength supported by 5–8 tanks and assault guns. The guardsmen burned the enemy "Tigers" and "Ferdinands" and destroyed the infantry but were unable to advance further because of the constant subsequent counterattacks by the German-Fascist forces.
>
> Again, new enemy units, which had not been previously noted in our army's sector, began to appear. This meant that the enemy command was continuing to strengthen his forces in the region north of Vitebsk, trying at all cost to hold us off. Nevertheless, we advanced forward. We did so by employing constantly changing tactical measures, in particular, night attacks, simultaneous actions along various axes with regimental-size forces supported by 8–10 tanks, and so forth.
>
> As a result, in persistent battles our forces here and there captured separate villages and either destroyed or drove back groups of enemy. However, as a whole, the combat lessons of these operations were, as before, not great, and our forward movement remained insignificant.[4]

As a microcosm of the fighting, Galitsky described in some detail the fierce struggle that took place for possession of the German strongpoint at the village of Kukhori, roughly 20 kilometers northwest of Vitebsk, situated just east of Lake Zaronovskoe in the sector of 36th Guards Rifle Corps' 16th Guards Rifle Division. This battle typified the heavy and usually frustrating fighting that characterized the penetration battle as a whole:

> This small village, which was located on the high ground, dominated the terrain. The enemy fitted out the stone houses that predominated here with pillboxes and prepared them for all-round defense. Full-profile trenches connected by communications trenches were dug out of the outskirts of the village. Blindages with 3–5 levels to protect the soldiers during our artillery fire were situated not far away from open machine gun positions. Three networks of barbed wire entanglements were stretched 30–40 meters in front of the trenches. Many layers of machine gun and automatic weapons fire crisscrossed any point on the approaches to the village.
>
> The garrison of Kukhori consisted of 2–3 companies, numbering 80–100 men, armed with 8–9 heavy machine guns, 10–12 light machine guns, several antitank rifles, 2 assault guns, and also a battery of mortars. In addition, the garrison was supported by fire from no fewer than three artillery and three mortar batteries firing from the depths.[5]

A full rifle regiment from 16th Guards Rifle Division assaulted the strongpoint twice during the period from 9 through 11 January, but even an assault by two complete battalions supported by a sapper company and heavy artillery fire failed to dislodge the German defenders. After these repeated failures, the division commander, Major General E. V. Ryzhikov, finally decided to employ a specially tailored assault detachment to capture the strongpoint in a night attack. After it was formed from a rifle battalion from Colonel A. P. Skrynik's 43rd Guards Regiment, supported by a reinforced reconnaissance company and sappers, the detachment was subdivided into several small assault groups, each required to assault its own specific objective. The assault groups attacked the village strongpoint at 0200 hours on the night of 13–14 January from two directions, the first group from the west along the road and the second from the northeast. Reconnaissance parties and sappers led both groups. The suddenness of the attack prevented the enemy from employing timely artillery fire, and, as a result, the assault forces captured the village at 0600 hours.

This successful attack, however, proved the exception rather than the rule. As Galitsky candidly noted:

> However, Kukhori was only one of many tens of strongpoints the enemy organized on the road to Vitebsk. They were integrated into his overall defense system and were situated in such a fashion as to subject not only

Map 12.3. Third Panzer Army's Situation West of Vitebsk, 11 January 1944

the close but also the distant approaches to Vitebsk to intense fire. Furthermore, many of these strongpoints were considerably more powerful than Kukhori, and it required much time and many forces to capture each of them.[6]

Galitsky's shock groups had advanced only 1–2 kilometers forward by 14 January but generated little or no offensive momentum (see Map 12.3). To the south, in the region north and west of Gorbachi, the shock group of Malyshev's 4th Shock Army experienced similar frustrations. Even though Beloborodov, the commander of 2nd Guards Rifle Corps, managed to commit his 166th Rifle Division to combat between his two first echelon rifle divisions, his forces advanced roughly 1 kilometer along the front north of

Map 12.4. The Situation at Vitebsk, 20 January 1944

Gorbachi but could accomplish little more. Further to the west, D'iakonov's forces fared little better, and, by 14 January, Malyshev's 4th Shock Army had also shot its bolt.

Despite this lack of offensive progress, the *Stavka* insisted Bagramian's two shock groups continue their assaults. Dutifully complying, Galitsky and Malyshev launched attack after unsuccessful attack before the *Stavka* finally permitted Bagramian to call a halt to his offensive on 24 January. Throughout this entire period, the commanders of Third Panzer and LIII Army Corps continually regrouped and reinforced their forces in the most threatened sectors (see Map 12.4).

For example, on 16 January the Third Panzer Army released a *kampfgruppe* from the newly arrived 12th Panzer Division for employment in the sector between Mashkina and Lake Losvida.[7] This *kampfgruppe*, along with a battalion-size *kampfgruppe* from 406th Grenadier Regiment, went into action from 17–20 January against 11th Guards Army's 8th and 36th Guards Rifle Corps. During the same period, the Germans reinforced their defenses in the same sector with 667th Panzer *Jagt* (Hunter) and 281st Assault Gun Detachments and the sector between Lake Zaronovskoe and Gorbachi with 245th Assault Gun, 21st Panzer, and 505th Panzer (Tiger) Detachments.

In addition, during the last four days of Bagramian's assaults, Third Panzer Army replaced 129th Infantry Division north of the Sirotino-Vitebsk road with the fresher 87th Infantry Division.

All of these regroupings and reinforcements had the net effect of confounding Bagramian's plans, bloodying Bagramian's forces, and bringing his offensive to a grinding halt after only minimal gains.

VITEBSK EAST

The dizzying complexity of Soviet forces wedged into the relatively small salient southeast of Vitebsk; the frequent regroupings of forces that Sokolovsky and his subordinate army commanders conducted, frequently on a daily basis; and the restricted size of the salient west of Arguny made it exceptionally difficult to reconstruct the operations in this region with any degree of exactitude. Existing German intelligence reports and the few extant Soviet accounts, however, now make it possible to reconstruct action in this sector with a fair degree of accuracy.

Pursuant to the *Stavka*'s orders, Sokolovsky ordered Gordov's 33rd Army and one corps each from Berzarin's 39th and Krylov's 5th Armies to conduct the *front's* main attack on 8 January in the sector extending from the Vitebsk-Smolensk highway southward around the western perimeter of the Arguny salient to Miafli (see Table 12.2 and Map 12.1).

Gordov designated Oleshev's 36th Rifle Corps as his army's shock group and ordered it to attack the defenses of 131st Infantry and *Feldherrnhalle* Panzer Grenadier Divisions (VI Army Corps) in the 6-kilometer-wide sector between Gribuny and Maklaki at the western extremity of the salient, 12–16 kilometers south-southeast of Vitebsk. Oleshev concentrated his 199th, 371st, 274th, and 95th Rifle Divisions in first echelon, backed up by 215th Rifle Division in second echelon. Gordov also allocated 2nd and 23rd Guards Tank Brigades, as well as the forward brigades of 2nd Guards Tank Corps, to support Oleshev's shock group.

After penetrating the Germans' forward defenses, Oleshev's force was to capture the villages of Starintsy and Miakovo; cross the Luchesa River at and north of Perevoz, 15 kilometers due south of Vitebsk; and support the passage of lines by the remainder of Burdeinyi's 2nd Guards Tank Corps, which was designated to lead the army's exploitation to Ostrovno, a town 25 kilometers to the west-northwest. Gordov retained 144th and 164th Rifle Divisions of Major General N. N. Mul'tan's 69th Rifle Corps in his army's second echelon, with orders to reinforce his first-echelon corps whenever and wherever it achieved success.

On Oleshev's right, Major General V. A. Reviakhin's 65th Rifle Corps was deployed with 173rd Rifle Division in first echelon, in a 6-kilometer-wide

Table 12.2. The Probable Combat Formations of 43rd, 39th, 33rd, and 5th Armies and Opposing German Forces on 8 January 1944 (as deployed from north to south)

FORCE (Sector)	OPPOSING GERMAN FORCES
1st/2nd/3rd Echelons (Mobile group)	
	THIRD PANZER ARMY
1st BALTIC FRONT	LIII Army Corps
43rd Army (Popovichi, Poddub'e)	
92nd Rifle Corps (Popovichi, Babinichi)	4th LFD
270th RD (Popovichi, Trigubtsy)	
334th RD/114th RB (Trigubtsy, Graleva)	
332nd RD (Graleva, Sen'kovo)	VI Army Corps
358th RD (Sen'kovo-Babinichi)	197th ID
91st RC (Babinichi, Poddub'e)	
306th RD/179th RD (Babinichi, Khoteenka)	
145th RB (Khoteenka, Poddub'e)	14th ID
1st RC (145th, 204th RD) (Ianovichi region)	
39th Army (Poddub'e, Vaskova)	
84th RC (Poddub'e, Vitebsk-Smolensk highway)	
262nd RD (Poddub'e, Tishkova)	
134th RD/158th RD (Tishkova, Vitebsk-Smolensk highway	206th ID
5th GRC (Vitebsk-Smolensk highway, Vaskova)	
9th GRD/17th GRD (Vitebsk-Smolensk highway, Eremino	
19th GRD (Eremino, Ugliane)	
91st GRD (Ugliane, Vaskova)	
33rd Army (Vaskova, Maklaki)	
65th RC (Vaskova, Gribuny)	
173rd RD/44th and 222nd RDs	131st ID
36th RC (Gribuny, Maklaki)	
199th RD (Gribuny, Starintsy)	PzGrD *Feldherrnhalle*
371st RD/215th RD (Starintsy, Kopti)	
274th RD (Kopti, Miaklovo)	
95th RD (Miaklovo, Maklaki)	
81st RC (HQ) (Khotemlia region)	
69th RC (144th, 164th RD) (Arguny region)	
2nd GTC (mobile group) (Kozhekina region)	
(4th, 25th, 26th GTBs, 4th GMRB)	
5th Army (Maklaki, Belyi Bor)	
72nd RC (Maklaki, Miafli)	299th ID (arrived 6–8 Jan.)
153rd RD (Maklaki, west of Drybino)	
159th RD/277th RD (west of Drybino, Krynki)	246th ID
36th RB (Krynki, Miafli)	
45th RC (Miafli, Belyi Bor)	
157th RD (Miafli, Chernyshi)	
184th RD/338th RD (Chernyshi, Leutino)	
32nd RD (to *front* reserve) (Leutino, Belyi Bor)	

Sources: Boevoi sostav Sovetskoi Armii, chast' IV (Ianvar'–dekabr' 1944 g.) [The combat composition of the Soviet Army, pt. 4 (January–December 1944)] (Moscow: Voenizdat, 1988), 12–13; and "Anlagen zum Kriegstagebuch Nr. 7, Lagenkarten Band VII, Pz AOK 3, Ia, 1 Dec–31 Dec 1943," *Pz AOK 3, 49113/26 file*, in NAM Series T-313, roll 296.

sector from Vaskova to Gribuny along the Vitebsk-Orsha road, and 44th and 222nd Rifle Divisions in second echelon. Because German defenses were strongest in this sector, Reviakhin's orders were to remain on the defense initially, but when Oleshev's assault succeeded, to commit his two second-echelon divisions to support 199th Rifle Division's advance and also protect its right flank as it crossed the Luchesa River. Thereafter, Reviakhin's corps was to envelop the city of Vitebsk from the south. Reviakhin's forces concentrated their efforts at the junction between VI Army Corps' 206th and 131st Infantry Divisions.

On 33rd Army's right, Berzarin ordered Major General V. G. Pozniak's 5th Guards Rifle Corps, whose three rifle divisions constituted 39th Army's shock group, to conduct its assault westward in the 6-kilometer-wide sector between the Vitebsk-Smolensk-road and Vaskova against the defenses of VI Army Corps' 206th Infantry Division. Arrayed from left to right in first echelon, 91st, 19th, and 9th Guards Rifle Divisions, supported by 120th Tank and 43rd Guards Tank Brigades, were to lead the assault, backed up by 17th Guards Rifle Division in second echelon.

Pozniak's mission was to penetrate German defenses near Ugliane, advance through Shelcgovka toward Vitebsk proper, and protect the right flank of Gordov's shock group in conjunction with 65th Rifle Corps. Finally, the three rifle divisions of Dobrovol'sky's 84th Rifle Corps, which defended the sector on 39th Army's right wing from Poddub'e southward to the Vitebsk-Smolensk road, received orders to tie down German forces with local probing attacks and join the general assault only if and when the *front*'s main shock groups successfully penetrated the Germans' defenses and forced German forces to either withdraw back into or abandon Vitebsk.

On 33rd Army's left, Krylov designated Prokof'ev's 72nd Rifle Corps as 5th Army's shock group and ordered it to conduct its assault in the 7-kilometer-wide sector from Maklaki eastward to Miafli along the southern face of the Arguny salient. Prokof'ev deployed his 153rd and 159th Rifle Divisions and 36th Rifle Brigade in first echelon, supported by 213th and 256th Tank Brigades, and the 277th Rifle Division in second echelon. Prokof'ev's rifle corps, which faced German VI Corps' 246th Infantry Division, was to capture the German strongpoints at Dymanovo, Drybino, and Krynki, 2 to 4 kilometers distant, and then exploit southwestward through Shapechino to Savchenki on the Vitebsk-Orsha road, 23 kilometers south of Vitebsk, to widen the penetration and protect Gordov's left flank. Finally, Krylov ordered Major General S. G. Poplavsky's 45th Rifle Corps, whose three rifle divisions were deployed on 5th Army's long left wing, to support the assault and advance to capture Vysochany should Third Panzer Army's defenses collapse.

As was the case in Bagramian's 1st Baltic Front, Sokolovsky's rifle divisions and separate tank brigades had been severely weakened in previous operations and were at less than 40 percent strength. Nevertheless, Sokolovsky managed to concentrate 16 rifle divisions, 295 tanks, and 8 self-propelled artillery regiments (with up to 100 self-propelled guns) against 3 German infantry divisions and 1 panzer grenadier division, creating a better than twofold superiority over the Germans in infantry and a better than threefold superiority in armor.[8] During the battle, however, the Germans were able to reinforce their defenses with the fresh 299th Infantry Division, which German Army Group Center transferred north from Second Army's XXXV Army Corps, and, at various times, with up to six panzer and assault gun detachments (the 245th, 177th, 301st, 190th, and 655th). These forces significantly reduced the Soviets' advantage in armor.

The shock groups of Sokolovsky's three rifle corps struck the Germans' defenses early on 8 January after an artillery preparation (see Map 12.5). On the right wing, Pozniak's 5th Guards Rifle Corps from Berzarin's 39th Army encountered fierce resistance by VI Army Corps' 206th Infantry Division south of the Vitebsk-Smolensk road, and its attack immediately floundered after advancing only about 1 kilometer.

However, the assault by Oleshev's 36th Rifle Corps from Gordov's 33rd Army achieved significant initial success. Although 199th Rifle Division, on the shock group's right wing, failed to capture either Gribuny or Starintsy, the corps' 371st, 274th, and 95th Rifle Divisions surged forward and penetrated *Feldherrnhalle* Division's defenses along a 6-kilometer front from Starintsy to Maklaki. In two days of heavy fighting, 371st Rifle Division crushed a small salient defended by 2nd Battalion of *Feldherrnhalle*'s Fusilier Regiment, advanced across the Vitebsk-Orsha road, and captured the eastern outskirts of the village of Miakovo, 2 kilometers deep into the Germans' defenses (see Map 12.6). During the same period, 274th and 95th Rifle Divisions, attacking on the 371st's left, advanced 3–4 kilometers, overcoming defenses occupied by several battalions of *Feldherrnhalle*'s Fusilier Regiment, and reaching the villages of Karpovichi and Makarovo, less than a kilometer from the Luchesa River and the key town of Perevoz, 15 kilometers south of Vitebsk.

In the sector of Krylov's 5th Army on Gordov's left, 153rd and 277th Rifle Divisions and 36th Rifle Brigade of Prokof'ev's 72nd Rifle Corps kept pace with Oleshev's riflemen. Prokof'ev conducted his offensive from his corps' bridgehead on the western bank of the Lososina River in the sector extending from Maklaki to Zyzyby with 153rd Rifle Division and 36th Rifle Brigade deployed in first echelon and 277th Rifle Division in second echelon. Krylov described the action in his memoirs, beginning with the arrival of 277th Rifle Division to reinforce Prokof'ev's shock group:

> Colonel S. T. Gladyshev, the commander of the newly arrived division, immediately settled down at 36th Rifle Brigade's command post and, on the night of 8 January, committed his two forward rifle regiments, the

322 The Struggle for Belorussia, December 1943–April 1944

Map 12.5. Third Panzer Army's Situation East of Vitebsk, 8 January 1944

850th and 854th, directly from the march. He left the third, the 852nd, in second echelon. A day later the division commander committed his regiments, together with 256th and 213th Tank Brigades, in an attack from the bridgehead southeast of Lobany westward toward Dymanovo.

By means of a concerted attack, they expelled the enemy from his pillboxes, trenches, and blindages and began to drive him through the deep snow to the Luchesa River.

The 850th Rifle Regiment distinguished itself in this combat, particularly its 4th Company under the command of Senior Lieutenant A. D.

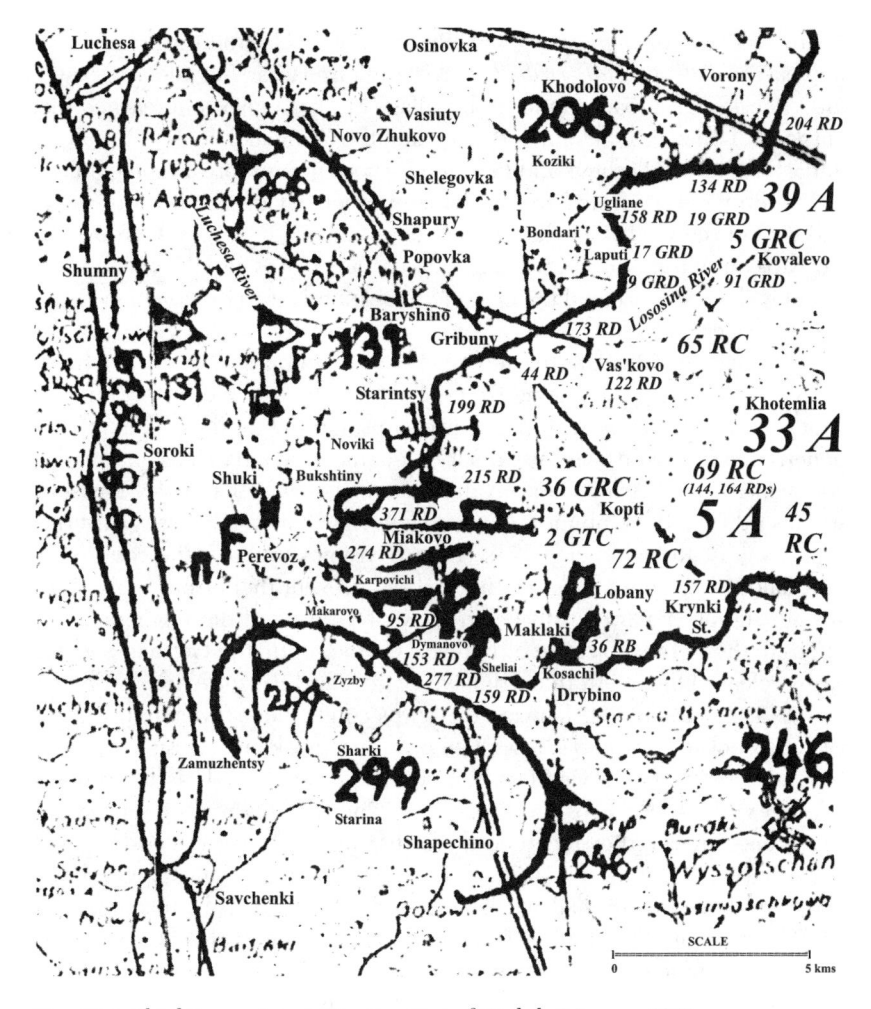

Map 12.6. Third Panzer Army's Situation East of Vitebsk, 9 January 1944

Starostenko. It was the first [company] to penetrate into Dymanovo, and it drove the enemy from the village and cut the Vitebsk-Orsha road, one of the Hitlerites' main communications lines. Soon the remainder of the regiment arrived there. Its [the regiment's] commander wanted to penetrate to the cutoff position in the Mozhentsy [Zamozhentsy]-Kosachi sector and seize a bridgehead over the Luchesa. However, he did not succeed in carrying out that intention since the commander of the enemy's Third Panzer Army moved 229th [should read 299th] Infantry Division to this region on trucks. It halted 277th Rifle Division's offensive by launching counterattacks against its penetrating regiments.[9]

In two days of intense fighting, Prokof'ev's shock group overcame defenses manned by *Feldherrnhalle* Division's Grenadier Regiment, crossed the Vitebsk-Orsha road, captured the village of Dymanovo, and reached the outskirts of Sheliai, 4.5 kilometers deep into the German defenses. Thus, the initial assaults by Oleshev's and Prokof'ev's shock groups tore a gaping hole 8 kilometers wide and from 2 to 4.5 kilometers deep in German defenses along and west of the Vitebsk-Orsha road. By day's end on 10 January, Gordov was close to committing Burdeinyi's 2nd Guards Tank Corps into the penetration but only if his forces could traverse the final kilometer to the Luchesa River and seize a crossing site.

However, the Germans reacted quickly and vigorously to thwart the fresh Soviet successes and, by doing so, denied the Russians the opportunity to conduct an exploitation with their tank corps. On the northern flank of the penetration sector, on 9 and 10 January, General of Infantry Hans Jordan, the commander of VI Army Corps, shifted elements of 131st Infantry Division southward from the Gribuny region and launched counterattacks against the right flank of the advancing 371st Rifle Division. Although the counterattack failed to drive the Russians back, it did prevent them from seizing the strongpoint at Miakovo, a village on the eastern bank of the Luchesa River opposite the 371st's objective of Perevoz. To the south, the German Second Army released the 299th Infantry Division to Third Panzer Army's VI Army Corps, and, on 9 and 10 January, the corps commander committed the division to bolster *Feldherrnhalle*'s defenses and block any Russian advance beyond Sheliai. These vigorous counteractions succeeded, and, although Oleshev's 36th Rifle Corps and Prokof'ev's 72nd Rifle Corps tried repeatedly to advance further, they recorded no further progress over the ensuing five days of combat (see Maps 12.7 and 12.8). By late on 14 January, Oleshev's and Prokof'ev's assaults had totally burned themselves out. By this time, the rifle divisions in 33rd and 5th Armies numbered from 2,500 to 3,500 men each, rifle regiments consisted of one or two battalions, battalions of one or two companies, and companies, eighteen to twenty-five men each.[10]

Faced with the standoff along the Vitebsk-Orsha road and on the shock group's right wing southeast of Vitebsk, Sokolovsky, Gordov, and Krylov searched for new opportunities to revive their offensive. As described by Krylov in his memoirs, they finally found that opportunity on the southern face of the now-expanded Arguny salient:

> Undoubtedly, the seizure of the Vitebsk-Orsha main road was a major success. At the same time, this situation created certain complications since the enemy continued to hold on to the region around the village of Krynki, situated 5 kilometers east of Dymanovo, which was occupied by our forces. By doing so, he [the enemy] threatened 5th Army's entire left wing with a penetration to the north in the direction of Eremino [on

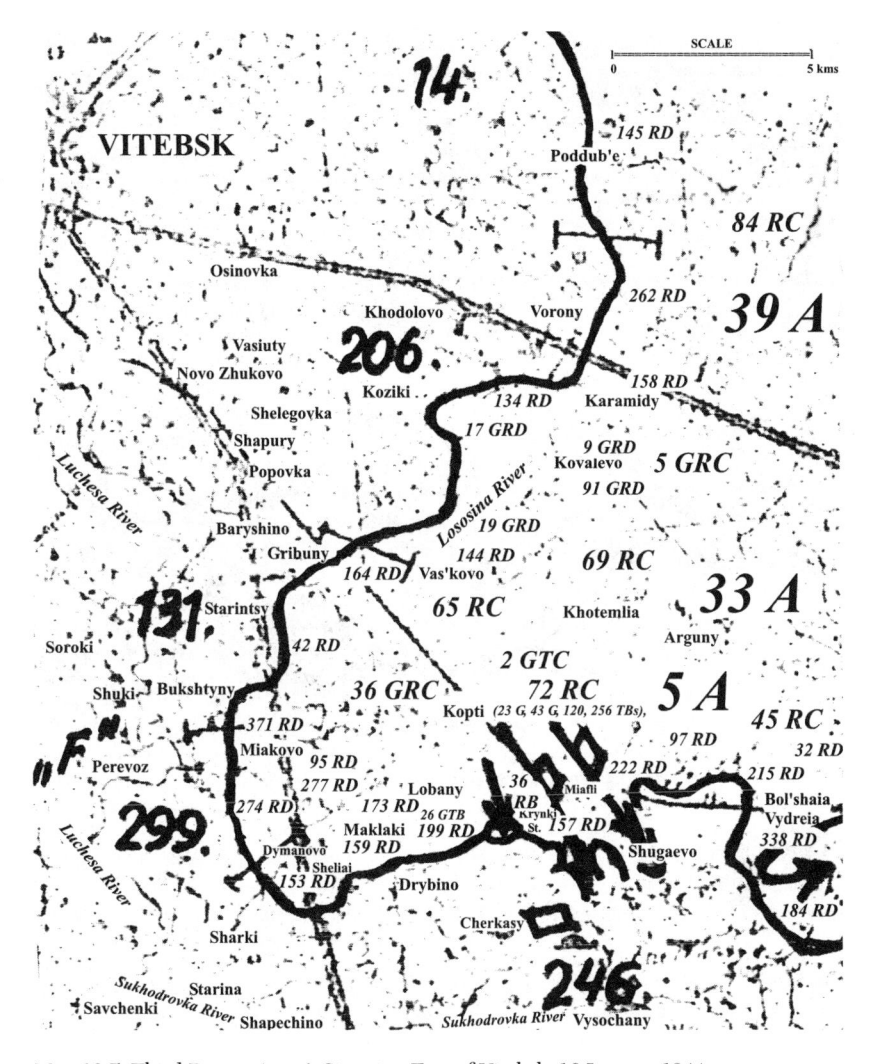

The 1st Baltic and Western Fronts' Vitebsk-Bogushevsk Offensive   325

Map 12.7. Third Panzer Army's Situation East of Vitebsk, 16 January 1944

the Vitebsk-Smolensk road 17 kilometers southeast of Vitebsk], which, if carried out, could force our forces to withdraw behind the line of the Vitebsk-Smolensk railroad.

Thus, the mission of improving its position now gained far greater importance for 5th Army since only by doing so could we prevent an enemy penetration to the north.[11]

With Sokolovsky's permission and support, Krylov organized a new offensive, to be conducted on 15 January, this time southward toward Krynki.

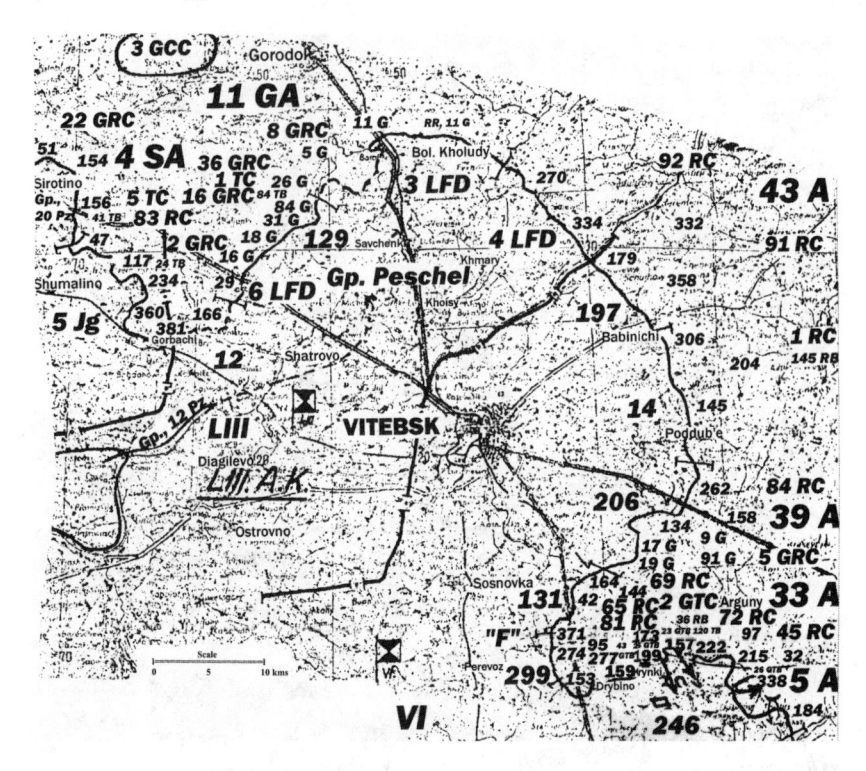

Map 12.8. The Situation at Vitebsk, 11–16 January 1944

In preparation for the offensive, Sokolovsky transferred 199th, 173rd, and 222nd Rifle Divisions, whose earlier attacks southeast of Vitebsk had immediately faltered, from Oleshev's 36th and Reviakhin's 65th Rifle Corps to Prokof'ev's 72nd Rifle Corps of Krylov's army. In addition, Sokolovsky also designated several tank brigades, including 23rd and 43rd Guards and 256th and 120th Separate Tank Brigades and 26th Guards Tank Brigade from Burdeinyi's 2nd Guards Tank Corps, to support Krylov's new offensive.

After it was concentrated for the attack in the 6-kilometer-wide sector from Zyzyby eastward to Miafli, Krylov's new shock group consisted of 159th, 199th, and 157th Rifle Divisions in first echelon and 173rd and 222nd Rifle Divisions and 36th Rifle Brigade in second echelon. Although command relationships remain obscure, 72nd Rifle Corps probably controlled 159th, 199th, and 173rd Rifle Divisions on the shock group's right wing, and 36th Rifle Corps' headquarters probably directed 157th and 222nd Rifle Divisions and 36th Rifle Brigade on the shock group's left wing (see Map 12.8).

Regardless of command relationships, Krylov's shock groups began their assault early on 15 January. Once again, Krylov accurately described the action, taking care to highlight the weather that impeded its conduct:

The army commander decided to [prevent an enemy attack along the Krynki-Vitebsk axis by attack[ing] the enemy. He proposed to throw the enemy back to the south beyond the Sukhodrovka River [which ran westward into Luchesa 5 kilometers south of Perevoz] with an attack by the forces of 159th and 199th Rifle Divisions and, by doing so, to protect the army's left wing. In the event of success, we also intended to capture Vysochany [28 kilometers south-southeast of Vitebsk], where the enemy had created a strongpoint that protected the bridge and dam on the Sukhodrovka.

The offensive began on the night of 15 January [14–15 January]. It turned bitterly cold, and a blizzard left heavy snow cover and prevented observation of the enemy's positions in the Krynki region. But neither the weather nor the enemy fire stopped the attacking units of 159th and 199th Rifle Divisions and 2nd Guards Tank Corps' 26th Tank Brigade.

This brigade had already contributed to the success of 5th Army's rifle divisions many times.... [The 159th Rifle Division and 26th Tank Brigade had conducted a successful night attack on Hill 189.6 and the village of Shvedy, which the Hitlerites had turned into a strongpoint after expelling its inhabitants.] Our subunits threw the enemy out of their first and second trenches but were able to advance no further. The 199th Rifle Division's 617th Rifle Regiment, which was reinforced with 4 tanks and was committed to combat at 0500 hours on the morning of 16 January, did not achieve success. Attacking along the Krynki-Cherkasy road, it drove back the counterattacking enemy. However, during its subsequent movement forward it came under destructive fire, which the Hitlerites were conducting from Hill 189.6 and was also forced to the ground....

[The 617th Rifle Regiment and several T-34 tanks assaulted the village after an artillery raid], and the enemy, who were not able to withstand the blow, quickly withdrew to the Sukhodrovka River.

In subsequent battles our units pressed the enemy back further and captured the village of Cherkasy, which had also been converted by them into a strongpoint. But we were not able to hold on to it at this time (it was liberated somewhat later), and, in the end, we dug in 400–500 meters north of Hill 189.6.[12]

As a result of several days of heavy fighting, Krylov's shock group captured Krynki and drove the German defenders back about 2 kilometers east of the fortified village, although the Germans still clung grimly to a segment of the Vitebsk-Smolensk railroad line east of Miafli (see Map 12.9).

After regrouping his forces one more time, on 20 January Krylov's 199th and 157th Rifle Divisions, this time supported by 274th Rifle Division, transferred from the 33rd Army and elements of 45th Rifle Corps, drove German forces away from the railroad sector from Miafli to Leutino (22–28 kilome-

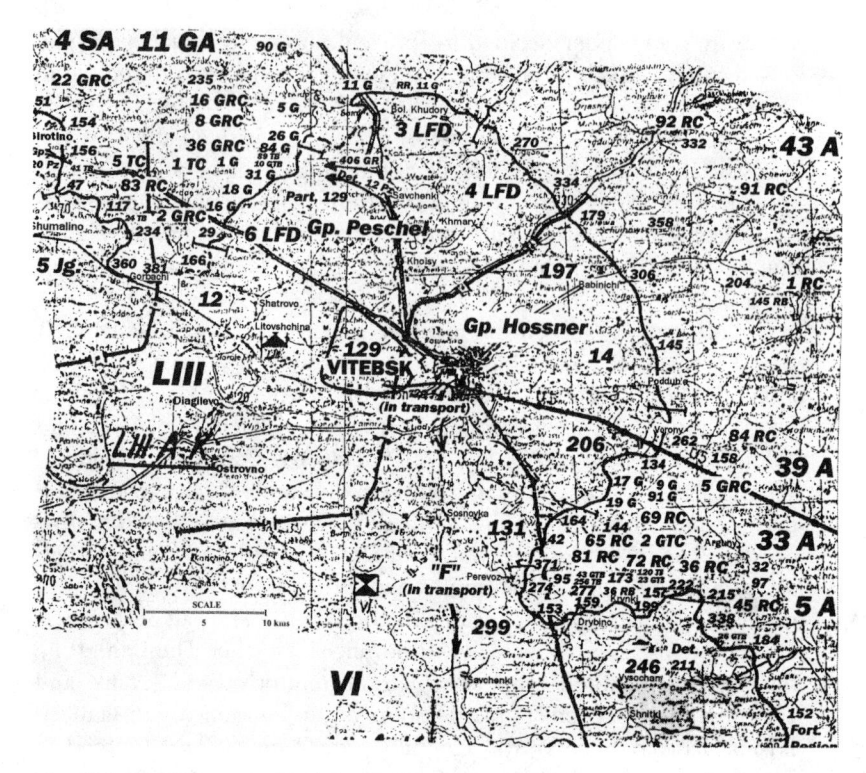

328 The Struggle for Belorussia, December 1943–April 1944

Map 12.9. The Situation at Vitebsk, 17–20 January 1944

ters southeast of Vitebsk) and advanced to the northern approaches of the villages of Shugaevo and Kriukovo. By this time all of the local supporting attacks launched by Gordov's forces west of the Vitebsk-Orsha road ended, and Sokolovsky's January offensive came to an end. As if signifying the Western Front's failure, between 21 and 24 January, Third Panzer Army withdrew the *Feldherrnhalle* Division and, at the OKH's direction, began transferring it to the south (see Map 12.10). However, as insurance, Army Group Center began transferring 211th Infantry Division northward from Ninth Army's IX Army Corps. This division, originally part of Ninth Army's LV Army Corps before being transferred to IX Corps in October, began closing into the region north of Bogushevskoe on 17 January. Thereafter, it remained in Third Panzer Army's reserve until 23–24 January, when its 317th Regiment reinforced VI Army Corps' 246th Infantry Division east of Vysochany, replacing 201st Security Division's 406th Regiment. The remainder of the 211th moved into the sector between 14th and 256th Infantry Divisions on 1 February.

At a cost of more than 25,000 casualties, including more than 5,500 dead, in sixteen days of combat, the shock groups of Sokolovsky's Western Front

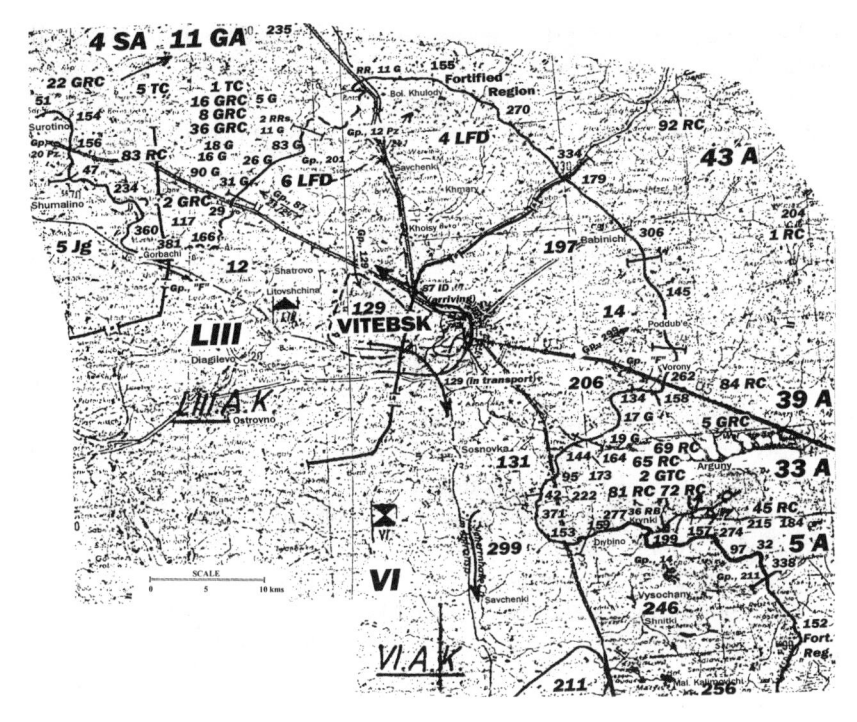

Map 12.10. The Situation at Vitebsk, 21–24 January 1944

advanced from 2–4 kilometers, severed the Vitebsk-Orsha road, and expelled German forces from the last segment of the Vitebsk-Smolensk railroad line under their control.[13] Despite these meager gains, as was the case with Bagramian's 1st Baltic Front, Sokolovsky's forces failed dismally in their primary mission of crossing the Luchesa River, reaching Ostrovno, and encircling the German Vitebsk grouping.

The Western Front cryptically recorded the results of its offensive in a report it submitted to the *Stavka* in early February 1944 (see Appendix I-3). Highlighting the context of the offensive, the report attributed the offensive's failure to stout German resistance; effective enemy artillery and antitank fire; timely German counterattacks; and, first and foremost, poor command and control practices in Sokolovsky's armies. In particular, it noted, "The commanders of the formations, regiments, and subunits are continuing to emphasize the command and control of forces in telephone conversations by spending up to 90 percent of their time on this. Everything 'hangs' on the telephones. On a daily basis, the corps commanders call the division commanders on telephones, the division commanders [call] the regimental commanders, and the regimental commanders [call] the battalion commanders." Therefore, the officer command cadre gather information about the situation in their units, while their staffs perform secondary tasks, and are employed primarily as special messengers.[14]

As for the *front's* losses during January 1944, yet another report detailed the gruesome cost of the unsuccessful offensive (see Appendix I-4.)

- Personnel (1–20 January)—4,738 men killed, 16,142 wounded, 4,012 sick, 15 frostbitten, and 184 missing in action.
- Personnel (21–31 January)—2,067 men killed, 6,213 wounded, 4,509 sick and evacuated to the hospital, 9 frostbitten, 197 missing in action, and 10 captured by the enemy.
- Weapons (1–10 January)—954 rifles and 78 antitank rifles.
- Weapons (10–20 January)—1,180 rifles, 120 submachine guns, 31 heavy machine guns, and 27 antitank rifles.
- Weapons (20–31 January)—4,165 rifles, 120 antitank rifles, and 140 76mm antitank guns, including 118 in 33rd Army and 18 in 5th Army.
- Horses (1–20 January)—780 killed, 84 wounded, 181 sick, and 5 missing in action.
- Horses (21–31 January)—271 killed.
- Trophies captured (28 December 1943–10 January 1944)—6 tanks, 3 trucks, 11 guns, 6 mortars, 104 machine guns, and others.[15]

The German Third Panzer Army's records confirm the 1st Baltic and Western Fronts' heavy losses, at the same time indicating that German intelligence had an accurate appreciation of the threat they faced. This was evident in a report on the battle prepared by Third Panzer Army in late February 1944, which summarized enemy strength and losses from 13 December 1943 through 18 January 1944, what it termed as the "1st Battle at Vitebsk" (see Appendix I-5).

- Confirmed enemy strength:
  - In the region southwest of Lake Jeserischtche—11th Guards Army, with 12 guards rifle and rifle divisions and 1st Tank Corps (4 tank units [brigades]).
  - In the Ordowo and Lake Tschernowo region—4th Shock Army with 14 rifle divisions and 5th Tank Corps (4 tank units [brigades]).
  - In the region northeast of Vitebsk—39th and 43rd Armies with 14 rifle divisions and 6 tank units [brigades].
  - In the region southeast of Vitebsk—33rd, 5th, and 39th Armies, with 24 rifle divisions, 1 rifle brigade, and 10 tank units [brigades].
  - Total: Third Panzer Army's 15 combat-ready divisions faced 6 armies, with 58 guards rifle and rifle divisions, 1 rifle brigade, and 24 panzer units, for a total of 83 units.

- Enemy personnel losses:
  - 190,000 men combat losses
  - 2,361 men captured
  - 248 deserters
- Enemy equipment losses (est.):
  - 1,124 tanks destroyed
  - 91 tanks captured
  - 159 guns
  - 194 antitank guns
  - 39 grenade launchers
  - 309 machine guns
  - 21 aircraft by antiaircraft or ground fire[16]

On or about 23 January, the *Stavka* reluctantly granted Bagramian and Sokolovsky permission to abandon their offensive efforts, albeit only temporarily.

CHAPTER 13

The 1st Baltic and Western Fronts' Vitebsk Offensive (3–16 February)

THE PLAN

With the single notable exception of General Gareev's brief description of the fighting, other Soviet open-source accounts remain utterly silent regarding the offensive the 1st Baltic and Western Fronts conducted in February 1944. In fact, with very few exceptions, these sources also ignore all of the subsequent offensives the Western Front launched in March 1944. Therefore, in order to reconstruct these offensives, one must rely solely on recently released *Stavka* orders, snippets of information from Soviet memoir literature, and Gareev's short descriptions, supplemented by information gleaned from German intelligence records.

All of these sources confirm that the final offensive effort conducted jointly by Bagramian's 1st Baltic and Sokolovsky's Western Fronts against German Third Panzer Army's defenses around Vitebsk took place between 3 and 16 February 1944. Further, this evidence indicates that the fighting was particularly heavy, and Soviet forces were almost successful in the effort, although at immense cost in lives.

Stavka critiques of this offensive provide us the following thumbnail sketch of the offensive:

The Vitebsk Operation 3–16 February 1944
Our forces. The following forces were concentrated to conduct the operation: 16 rifle divisions, including 9 rifle divisions in first echelon and 7 rifle divisions in second echelon, 1 tank corps, 15 artillery brigades, 9 RGK artillery regiments, 2 tank brigades, and 2 self-propelled artillery regiments, for a total of 129 tanks. The artillery density ranged from 115 to 140 tubes per kilometer of front.

Enemy forces. 5 infantry divisions, up to 9 artillery regiments, and around 140 tanks. Subsequently, [the Germans] committed about two infantry regiments [from reserve].

The offensive on the Vitebsk axis, 3–16 February, penetrated to a depth of 3–4 kilometers. Our losses were 9,651 men killed and 32,844 wounded, for a total of *42,495 men*.[1]

Despite its earlier operational failures, the *Stavka* remained adamant in its demands that Vitebsk be captured at all cost. This was evident from an order it issued to Bagramian and Sokolovsky on 18 January, during the waning stages of the January offensive (see Appendix J-1). Dispatched to the two *front* commanders and *Stavka* representative N. N. Voronov early on 18 January, this directive ordered them, categorically, to defeat the enemy's Vitebsk grouping once and for all and capture the city of Vitebsk. To do so, the 1st Baltic Front was to concentrate its forces on 4th Shock Army's left wing and on 11th Guards Army's right wing, while reinforcing both armies at the expense of 43rd Army. After they were reinforced, the shock groups of the two armies were to advance on Vitebsk from the northwest and capture the city in cooperation with an assault by shock groups on the Western Front's right wing. All the while, the *Stavka* enjoined the *front* to protect its attacking forces against German counterstrokes from the west (Polotsk and Beshenkovichi). Finally, to strengthen the Western Front's offensive, Bagramian was to transfer the 1st Baltic Front's entire 39th Army (six rifle divisions) to the Western Front by 2400 hours on 19 January.

As for the Western Front's role in this offensive, supported by Krylov's 5th Army, 33rd and 39th Armies of Sokolovsky's Western Front were to attack toward Vitebsk from the southwest to seize the city in cooperation with the 1st Baltic Front. To strengthen this blow, Sokolovsky was to reinforce 33rd Army with three to four rifle divisions from neighboring 5th Army. To allow Bagramian and Sokolovsky the time necessary to organize the offensive, they were to conduct it no later than the end of January.[2]

Days before the *Stavka* issued this directive, Bagramian, in a thoughtful exercise in foresight, had already submitted a new attack plan to Stalin (see Appendix J-2). Although still in the midst of the January offensive, on the 14th, Bagramian optimistically declared, "I have decided to employ 20 understrength rifle divisions, 2 tank corps, 3 tank brigades, and almost all of the *front's* artillery and aviation in a penetration operation."[3] His plan called for delivering "a well-prepared crippling blow" with twelve rifle divisions from 11th Guards and 4th Shock Army toward Vitebsk from the northwest and seven rifle divisions from 43rd Army from the southeast to defeat Third Panzer Army and capture the city.

Later on the 18th, in the *Stavka*'s name, the General Staff issued two more orders, the first transferring Oslikovsky's badly shopworn 3rd Guards Cavalry Corps from the 1st Baltic Front to its own reserves and the second transferring 39th Army from the 1st Baltic Front to the Western Front (see Appendices J-3 and J-4).[4] The General Staff issued the second order because the *Stavka* already assumed that one of the principal reasons the Western Front's most recent offensive failed was a lack of unified control over the attacking forces. This order remedied that problem by placing the two armies operating east and southeast of Vitebsk (33rd and 39th) under Sokolovsky's direct control. Otherwise, the order simply set the stage for yet another round of fierce but frustrating fighting on the approaches to the city of Vitebsk as the bloodletting continued unabated.

In accordance with the *Stavka*'s 18 January order, both Bagramian and Sokolovsky regrouped their forces to form two formidable shock groups with which to conduct the offensive (see Table 13.1 and Map 13.1). So extensive was this regrouping that both commanders requested and received *Stavka* permission to postpone the attack by several days. Instead of attacking no later than the end of January as the *Stavka* had directed, Bagramian's forces ultimately went into action on 2 February and Sokolovsky's a day later.

The *Stavka*'s directive required Bagramian to shift his *front*'s main effort somewhat to the south by transferring one rifle corps from Galitsky's 11th Guards Army into the Gorbachi salient south of Lake Zaronovskoe. There, it was to conduct its attack jointly with the shock group on the left wing of Malyshev's 4th Shock Army. In addition, prior to the offensive, Bagramian transferred General Volkov's 91st Rifle Corps, supposedly consisting of 332nd and 358th Rifle Divisions from 43rd Army and 117th Rifle Division from 4th Shock Army's 83rd Rifle Corps, to second-echelon assembly areas near Krasnopol'e in 4th Shock Army's deeper rear area. Ultimately, however, as German records and Galitsky's account indicate, the 117th Rifle Division remained with 4th Shock's 2nd Guards Rifle Corps to support its attack.

At the same time, Bagramian activated the headquarters of 103rd Rifle Corps in his *front*'s reserve, assigned General I. F. Fediun'kin, the former commander of 16th Guards Rifle Corps, as the corps' new commander, and assigned 11th Guards and 29th and 235th Rifle Divisions to Fediun'kin's new corps. The 103rd Rifle Corps then took over responsibility for the sector extending from Lake Losvida southward to Mashkina at the northern extremity of the Vitebsk salient on 11th Guards Army's left wing. This permitted Galitsky to shift 8th Guards Rifle Corps to the right (south) and castle his army's 16th Guards Rifle Corps farther southwestward into its new main attack sector south of Lake Zaronovskoe. Finally, Bagramian also reshuffled his corps and division commanders, assigning Major General Ia. S. Vorob'ev to replace Fediun'kin in command of 16th Guards Rifle Corps.

As mandated by the *Stavka*'s directive, Galitsky's 11th Guards and Malyshev's 4th Shock Armies, which constituted the shock group of Bagramian's *front*, were to attack Vitebsk from the northwest and capture the city in cooperation with the shock group of Sokolovsky's Western Front attacking from the southeast. At the same time, Bagramian was to ensure that his *front* shock group's right flank was well protected against German counterattacks from the Polotsk and Beshenkovichi regions.

Bagramian's offensive plan required Galitsky to form two shock groups, the first consisting of 8th and 36th Guards Rifle Corps north of Lake

Table 13.1. The 1st Baltic and Western Fronts' Orders of Battle in the Vitebsk Offensive, 1 February 1944

1ST BALTIC FRONT: Army General I. Kh. Bagramian	WESTERN FRONT: Army General V. D. Sokolovsky
4th Shock Army: LTG P. F. Malyshev	39th Army: LTG N. E. Berzarin
2nd Guards Rifle Corps: MG A. P. Beloborodov	5th Guards Rifle Corps: MG I. S. Bezuglyi
90th Guards Rifle Division	17th Guards Rifle Division
166th Rifle Division	19th Guards Rifle Division
381st Rifle Division	91st Guards Rifle Division
22nd Guards Rifle Corps: MG N. B. Ibiansky	84th Rifle Corps: MG E. V. Dobrovol'sky
51st Rifle Division	32nd Rifle Division
154th Rifle Division	134th Rifle Division
156th Rifle Division	158th Rifle Division
60th Rifle Corps: MG A. N. Ermakov	262nd Rifle Division
16th Rifle Division	28th Guards Tank Brigade
119th Rifle Division	47th Mechanized Brigade
357th Rifle Division	
101st Rifle Brigade	
83rd Rifle Corps: MG A. A. D'iakonov	5th Army: LTG N. I. Krylov
47th Rifle Division	45th Rifle Corps: MG S. G. Poplavsky
234th Rifle Division	157th Rifle Division
360th Rifle Division	184th Rifle Division
91st Rifle Corps: MG F. A. Volkov	338th Rifle Division
117th Rifle Division	72nd Rifle Corps: MG Iu. M. Prokof'ev
332nd Rifle Division	97th Rifle Division
358th Rifle Division	153rd Rifle Division
155th Fortified Region	159th Rifle Division
5th Tank Corps: MGTF M. G. Sakhno	277th Rifle Division
24th Tank Brigade	120th Tank Brigade
41st Tank Brigade	1537th Self-propelled Artillery Regiment
70th Tank Brigade	
5th Motorized Rifle Brigade	33rd Army: Col. G V. N. Gordov
161st Self-propelled Artillery Regiment	36th Rifle Corps: Col. M. K. Boiko
1515th Self-propelled Artillery Regiment	173rd Rifle Division
1546th Self-propelled Artillery Regiment	215th Rifle Division
92nd Motorcycle Battalion	371st Rifle Division
277th Mortar Regiment	65th Rifle Corps: MG V. A. Reviakhin
731st Separate Tank Destroyer Battalion	164th Rifle Division
47th Guards-Mortar Battalion	274th Rifle Division
1708th Antiaircraft Artillery Regiment	36th Rifle Brigade
10th Guards Tank Brigade	69th Rifle Corps: MG N. N. Mul'tan
34th Guards Tank Brigade	42nd Rifle Division
39th Guards Tank Brigade	144th Rifle Division
143rd Tank Brigade	222nd Rifle Division
105th Separate Tank Regiment	81st Rifle Corps: Col V. Ia. Poiarov
171st Separate Tank Battalion	95th Rifle Division
	199th Rifle Division
11th Guards Army: LTG K. N. Galitsky	23rd Guards Tank Brigade
8th Guards Rifle Corps: LTG A. S. Ksenofontov	43rd Guards Tank Brigade
5th Guards Rifle Division	213th Tank Brigade
83rd Guards Rifle Division	256th Tank Brigade
16th Guards Rifle Corps: MG Ia. S. Vorob'ev	722nd Self-propelled Artillery Regiment
1st Guards Rifle Division	1445th Self-propelled Artillery Regiment
18th Guards Rifle Division	1830th Self-propelled Artillery Regiment
31st Guards Rifle Division	

Table 13.1. *continued*

1ST BALTIC FRONT: Army General I. Kh. Bagramian	WESTERN FRONT: Army General V. D. Sokolovsky
36th Guards Rifle Corps: MG P. G. Shafranov	*Front* Reserves:
16th Guards Rifle Division	154th Fortified Region
26th Guards Rifle Division	2nd Guards Tank Corps: Col. A. S.
84th Guards Rifle Division	Burdeinyi
103rd Rifle Corps: MG I. F. Fediun'kin	4th Guards Tank Brigade
11th Guards Rifle Division	25th Guards Tank Brigade
29th Rifle Division	26th Guards Tank Brigade
235th Rifle Division	4th Guards Motorized Rifle Brigade
1st Tank Corps: LGTF V. V. Butkov	1819th Self-propelled Artillery
89th Tank Brigade	Regiment
117th Tank Brigade	1833rd Self-propelled Artillery
159th Tank Brigade	Regiment
44th Motorized Rifle Brigade	79th Motorcycle Battalion
2nd Guards Tank Regiment	1500th Tank Destroyer Regiment
1437th Self-propelled Artillery Regiment	755th Separate Tank Destroyer
86th Motorcycle Battalion	Artillery Battalion
1514th Tank Destroyer Regiment	273rd Mortar Regiment
388th Separate Tank Destroyer Artillery	28th Guards-Mortar Battalion
Battalion	1695th Antiaircraft Artillery Regiment
108th Mortar Regiment	2nd Guards Tank Brigade
10th Guards-Mortar Battalion	153rd Tank Brigade
1720th Antiaircraft Artillery Regiment	56th Guards Separate Tank Regiment
	63rd Guards Separate Tank Regiment
43rd Army: LTG K. D. Golubev	248th Separate Tank Regiment
1st Rifle Corps: MG V. P. Kotel'nikov	735th Self-propelled Artillery Regiment
145th Rifle Division	1494th Self-propelled Artillery Regiment
204th Rifle Division	12th Separate Aerosleigh Battalion
306th Rifle Division	41st Separate Aerosleigh Battalion
92nd Rifle Corps: MG I. S. Iudintsev	145th Antiaircraft Armored Train
179th Rifle Division	
270th Rifle Division	
334th Rifle Division	
46th Mechanized Brigade	
Front Reserves:	
9th Guards Rifle Division	
3rd Guards Cavalry Corps: LTG N. S. Oslikovsky	
5th Guards Cavalry Division	
6th Guards Cavalry Division	
32nd Cavalry Division	
1814th Self-propelled Artillery Regiment	
144th Guards Tank Destroyer Regiment	
3rd Guards-Mortar Regiment	
64th Guards-Mortar Battalion	
3rd Guards Separate Tank Destroyer Artillery	
Battalion	
1731st Antiaircraft Artillery Battalion	

Source: Boevoi sostav Sovetskoi Armii, chast' IV (Ianvar'–dekabr' 1944) [The combat composition of the Soviet Army, pt. 4 (January–December 1944)] (Moscow: Voenizdat, 1988), 39–41.

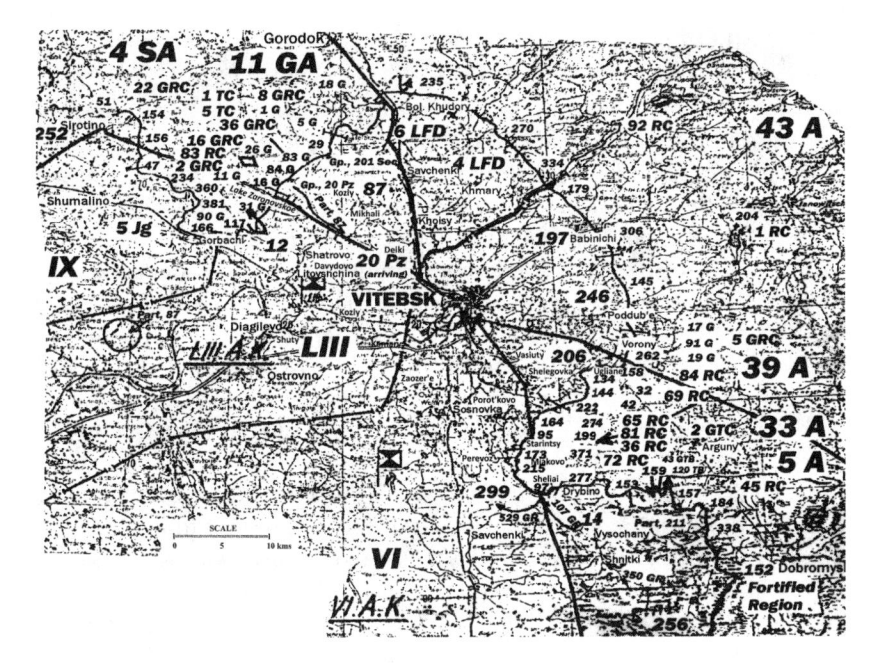

Map 13.1. The Situation at Vitebsk, 2 February 1944

Zaronovskoe and the second of 16th Guards Rifle Corps deployed south of the lake. The latter was to cooperate closely with the shock group of Malyshev's 4th Shock Army, which consisted of two rifle corps (2nd Guards and 83rd), whose forces were concentrated in the southern two-thirds of the Gorbachi salient south of Lake Zaronovskoe. Bagramian assigned Butkov's 1st Tank Corps the task of supporting Galitsky's attacks and Sakhno's 5th Tank Corps to spearhead Malyshev's attacks.

Attacking southeastward north of Lake Zaronovskoe, Ksenofontov's 8th and Shafranov's 36th Guards Corps of Galitsky's army were to advance toward Vitebsk along the Kozly, Mikhali, and Deiki axis north of the Vitebsk-Sirotino road directly into the city from the northwest. Operating south of Lake Zaronovskoe, Galitsky's third rifle corps (Vorob'ev's 16th) was to advance southeastward along the Shatrovo, Davydovo, and Kozly (another Kozly) axis in close cooperation with the left wing corps (2nd Guards Rifle) of 4th Shock Army, cut the Vitebsk-Polotsk road, and reach the northern bank of the Western Dvina River west of Vitebsk to link up with the forward elements of Sokolovsky's Western Front and isolate German forces in the city.

Deployed from left to right in the Gorbachi salient, Malyshev's two rifle corps, Beloborodov's 2nd Guards, and D'iakonov's 83rd Rifle were to assault southeastward and southward in tandem with Galitsky's rifle corps, cut the Vitebsk-Polotsk railroad line and road, and reach the Western Dvina River to link up with the forward elements of Sokolovsky's Western Front. Malyshev's two remaining first-echelon rifle corps, Ibiansky's 22nd Guards and Ermakov's 60th Rifle, deployed in the sector extending from the Sirotino region westward to the western flank of the Gorbachi salient, were to protect the shock groups' right flank by parrying any German counterattacks from the Polotsk and Beshenkovichi regions. Finally, when deployed forward from reserve in the Krasnopol'e region to the western extremity of 4th Shock Army's sector, Volkov's 91st Rifle Corps was to initiate operations southwestward toward Polotsk but only if the Vitebsk offensive proved successful.

East of Vitebsk city, the *Stavka* required Sokolovsky's Western Front to attack the city from the southeast with shock groups made up of all of 33rd Army and two rifle corps from 39th Army and capture the city in cooperation with the 1st Baltic Front. Krylov's 5th Army was to support the attack by the *front*'s shock group and protect its left flank against German counterattacks from the Vysochany and Bogushevsk (Bogushevskoe) regions. The *Stavka* transferred Berzarin's 39th Army from the 1st Baltic Front to the Western Front with instructions that Sokolovsky employ at least one of the army's corps to reinforce the shock group designated to attack Vitebsk from the southeast along the Vitebsk-Smolensk road. Berzarin's remaining corps was to either reinforce the main effort or conduct supporting or diversionary attacks to the north. In addition, the *Stavka* reinforced Gordov's 33rd Army with 173rd, 199th, 215th, and 222nd Rifle Divisions and 36th Rifle Brigade from Krylov's 5th Army. These forces had been transferred from 33rd Army to 5th Army in mid-January.

Sokolovsky formed two shock groups with which to conduct his offensive. The first, which consisted of 84th Rifle and 5th Guards Rifle Corps from Berzarin's 39th Army, was to assault and penetrate German defenses north and south of the Vitebsk-Smolensk road and advance northwestward astride the highway to enter the city from the southeast. The second, which consisted of 36th, 65th, 69th, and 81st Rifle Corps of Gordov's 33rd Army, was to attack and penetrate German defenses south of Vitebsk and east of the Luchesa River in the sector extending from Ugliane southward to Sheliai.

The two rifle corps on the right wing of Gordov's shock group, Reviakhin's 65th and Mul'tan's 69th, were to attack in the sector stretching from Ugliane southwestward to the Vitebsk-Orsha railroad line and then advance along the Shelegovka and Vasiuty axis in tandem with 39th Army to assault Vitebsk from the south. The two rifle corps on the left wing of Gordov's shock group, Poiarov's 81st and Boiko's 36th, were to attack westward in the sector extending from the Vitebsk-Orsha railroad to Sheliai; penetrate German defenses east of the Luchesa River; capture Starintsy, Makarovo, and Miakovo; and seize crossings over the Luchesa River between Porot'kovo and Perevoz. Subsequently, these corps were to push northwestward along the Sosnovka and Zaozer'e axis to capture Kamery and Shuty on the Western Dvina River,

10–16 kilometers west of Vitebsk, where they were to link up with the forward elements of the 1st Baltic Front's 11th Guards Army to encircle Third Panzer Army's forces defending in the vicinity of Vitebsk.

As for the use of the Western Front's armor, Burdeinyi's 2nd Guards Tank Corps was to support the penetration operation and, if possible, spearhead the exploitation to the Western Dvina River. As was the case in January, however, this was quite problematic given the heavy snow cover in the region. Finally, Sokolovsky also made some command changes, ostensibly to tighten up the *front*'s command and control. He appointed Major General I. S. Bezuglyi, a former airborne force commander, to replace Major General V. G. Pozniak as commander of 39th Army's 5th Guards Rifle Corps and replaced General Oleshev, the commander of 33rd Army's 36th Rifle Corps, wounded late in the January offensive, with Colonel M. K. Boiko.

Thus, the *Stavka*'s February plan differed fundamentally from previous Soviet offensives against Vitebsk. Instead of requiring the two *fronts* to conduct a broad envelopment of the city by a combined advance to the Diaglevo and Ostrovno regions, 20 kilometers west of Vitebsk, this time the two *fronts* were to conduct a far shallower envelopment of the city, coupled with a direct assault on the city from the east and west. The forces the *Stavka* allocated to this task should have been more than sufficient to achieve its objectives (see Table 13.2).

VITEBSK WEST

As the *Stavka* directed, Bagramian ordered Galitsky's 11th Guards Army and Malyshev's 4th Shock Army to deliver the *front*'s main attack at first light on 2 February in the 12-kilometer-wide sector extending from Mashkina southward past Lake Zaronovskoe to Gorbachi (see Map 13.2). Galitsky designated Ksenofontov's 8th and Shafranov's 36th Guards Rifle Corps as the army's main shock group and ordered them to conduct the army's main attack, supported by Butkov's 1st Tank Corps. Deployed from left to right in a two-echelon formation of rifle divisions, the two rifle corps' five rifle divisions were to penetrate defenses occupied by German LIII Army Corps' 87th Infantry Division and *kampfgruppen* from 20th Panzer and 201st Security Divisions in the sector extending from Mashkina southward to Lake Zaronovskoe and thereafter advance on Vitebsk along the Kozly, Mikhali, and Deiki axis north of the Vitebsk-Sirotino road to assault the city's inner defenses from the northwest. As of 1 February, 20th Panzer Division fielded a total of forty-six tanks and thirty-one assault guns and mobile *Paks*, with eight and six of these, respectively, requiring short-term repairs. In addition, the division had eleven so-called *Pz-H* armored self-propelled howitzers.[5] This gave the division a capability of dealing effectively with a full Soviet tank corps.

Table 13.2. The Estimated Correlation of Opposing Forces in the Vitebsk Offensive, 2–16 February 1944

OPPOSING FORCES	
Soviet	**German**
1st Baltic Front	
4th Shock Army	5th Jäger Division
11th Guards Army	12th Infantry Division
16 rifle divisions	95th Infantry Division
2 tank corps	20th Panzer Division (-)
4 tank brigades (250 tanks)	Detachments, 87th, 95th, 197th Infantry, 4th and 6th Luftwaffe Field, and 201st Security Divisions
	505th Panzer *Abteilung* (40 AFVs)
Western Front	
33rd Army	206th Infantry Division
5th Army	131st Infantry Division
16 rifle divisions	299th Infantry Division
1 tank corps	350th IR, 221th SecD
2 tank brigades	Detachments, 246th, 197th, 292nd, 14th, 95th Infantry Divisions
2 self-propelled artillery regiments (129 tanks)	14th Infantry Division
	211th InfantryDivision
	501st Panzer and 281st Assault Gun *Abteilungen* (80 AFVs)

Depth of Soviet advance: 3–4 kilometers
Casualties (Western Front): 49,495 men, including 9,651 killed and 32,844 wounded.

Sources: Makhmut Gareev, "O neudachnykh nastupatel'nykh operatsiiakh sovetskikh voisk v Velikoi Otechestvennoi voine. Po neopublikovannym dokumentam GKO" [About unsuccessful offensive operations of Soviet forces in the Great Patriotic War. According to unpublished GKO documents], in *Novaia i noveishaia istoriia* [New and newest history], 1 (January), 1994, 17; and H Gr Mitte/Ia, KTB: Lagenkarten, 1–28 February 1944, *H. Gr Mitte, 65002/61 file*, in NAM series T-311, Roll 224.

Galitsky concentrated his second shock group, the three rifle divisions of Vorob'ev's 16th Guards Rifle Corps, in the sector just south of Lake Zaronovskoe. Vorob'ev's rifle corps was to cooperate closely with the shock group from Malyshev's 4th Shock Army in a direct attack on Vitebsk from the west. Specifically, attacking in two-echelon formation and supported by an army tank brigade from 4th Shock Army, the three rifle divisions of Vorob'ev's corps were to penetrate the defenses of LIII Army Corps' 12th Infantry Division south of Lake Zaronovskoe and advance along the Shatrovo, Davydovo, and Sloboda axis south of the Vitebsk-Sirotino road; reach Slizhiki on the Western Dvina River, where it would link up with the forward elements of the Western Front; and assault Vitebsk's inner defenses from the west.

Malyshev designated Beloborodov's 2nd Guards and D'iakonov's 83rd Rifle Corps as his army's main shock group and ordered the two corps to conduct his army's main attack, supported by the armor of Sakhno's 5th Tank Corps and three army tank brigades. Attacking from left to right in a two- or three-echelon combat formation of rifle divisions, the two rifle corps' six rifle

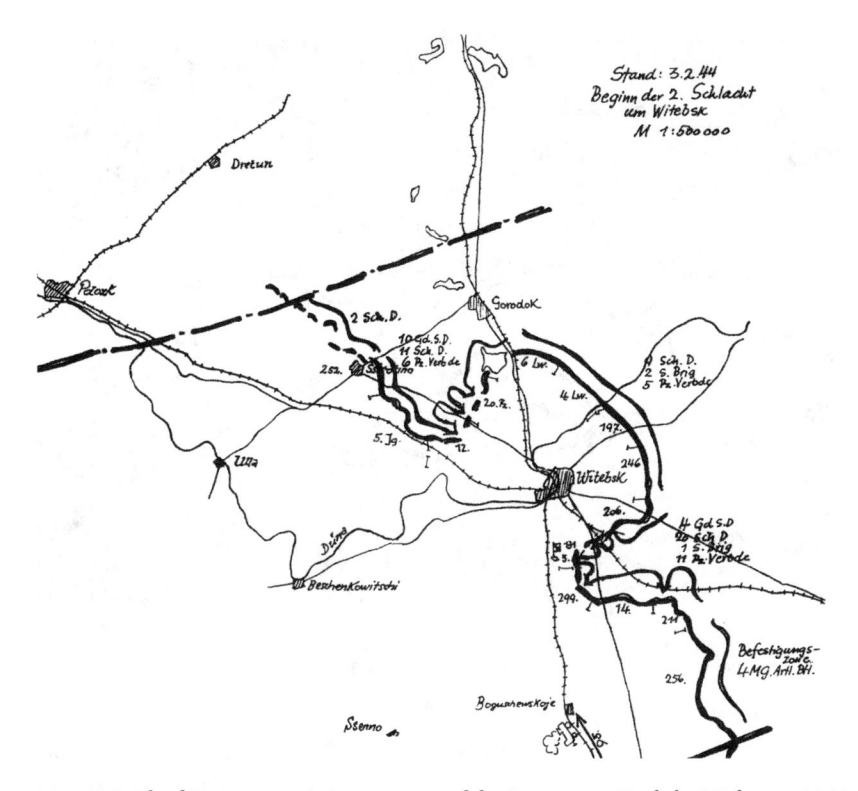

Map 13.2. Third Panzer Army's Appreciation of the Situation at Vitebsk, 3 February 1944

divisions were to penetrate the defenses of LIII Army Corps' 12th Infantry Division in the 5-kilometer-wide sector from west of Gorbachi to Osinniki and, in cooperation with 11th Guards Army's 16th Guards Rifle Corps, advance along two axes to the western outskirts of Vitebsk and the Western Dvina River.

Specifically, Beloborodov's 2nd Guards Rifle Corps was to advance along the Stepan'kova and Shevino axis and reach the Western Dvina River at Novoselki, where it was to link up with forward elements of the Western Front. Volkov's 91st Rifle Corps was to overcome German defenses at and west of Gorbachi and advance southward to Diagilevo on the Western Dvina River, where it too was to link up with the exploiting forces of the Western Front.

Farther to the west, the six rifle divisions of D'iakonov's 83rd and Ibiansky's 22nd Guards Rifle Corps were to pin down the IX Army Corps' 5th Jäger and 252nd Infantry Divisions in the sector extending from west of Gorbachi northwestward to Sirotino, join the assault when feasible, and protect 4th Shock Army's shock group against attack from the Polotsk and Beshenkovichi regions.

Map 13.3. Third Panzer Army's Situation West of Vitebsk, 3 February 1944

Thus, Bagramian was able to concentrate fourteen understrength rifle divisions, two tank corps, and four tank brigades, with a total armor strength of roughly 250 tanks against two German infantry divisions (the 12th and 87th) and combat groups from 20th Panzer and 201st Security Divisions, supported by 505th Panzer *Abteilung*. The opposing German fielded in excess of seventy armored vehicles, including many Tiger tanks. This accorded Bagramian an overall superiority of better than 3 to 1 in infantry and almost 4 to 1 in armor. Moreover, in the critical sector of the Gorbachi salient, Bagramian concentrated nine rifle divisions and about 150 tanks against German 12th Infantry Division, for a superiority of about 5 to 1 in infantry and an absolute superiority in armor. However, the congenitally cold and snowy weather and the strong German prepared defenses largely negated Bagramian's advantage.

After an extensive artillery preparation, Bagramian's two shock groups from 11th Guards and 4th Shock Armies began their offensive early on 2 February (see Map 13.3). The ferocious assaults quickly overcame the forward defenses of 87th and 12th Infantry Divisions north and south of Lake Zaronovskoe, and, in two days of heavy fighting, the assaulting forces advanced up to 3.5 kilometers deep along a 9-kilometer-wide front.

North of Lake Zaronovskoe, in the sector of Galitsky's 11th Guards Army, 83rd Guards Division of Ksenofontov's 8th Guards Rifle Corps captured the

German strongpoint at Mashkina from LIII Army Corps' 87th Infantry Division, and 84th and 16th Guards Divisions of Shafranov's 36th Guards Rifle Corps pushed forward up to 3 kilometers, reaching the western outskirts of Kisliaki and capturing the German strongpoint at Gorodishche on the northern shore of Lake Zaronovskoe near the boundary between 87th and 12th Infantry Division's. The LIII Army Corps responded to these Soviet successes by withdrawing the badly shaken 87th Infantry Division from its shattered defenses and relieving it with the fresher and far stronger Group Breidenbach, formed from 20th Panzer Division. South of the lake, 31st Guards Division of Vorob'ev's 16th Guards Rifle Corps smashed German 12th Infantry Division's defenses just south of the lake and advanced 3 kilometers, capturing the German strongpoint at Toporino and establishing direct contact with the remainder of Galitsky's army operating north of the lake.

In the sector of Malyshev's 4th Shock Army on Vorob'ev's left, 90th Guards Division, attacking in the first echelon of Beloborodov's 2nd Guards Rifle Corps, tore a gaping hole in 12th Infantry Division's defenses, captured the infantry division's strongpoints at Prudniki and Kozaki (Kosaki on German maps), and advanced 3.5 kilometers, producing a 1-kilometer-wide breach in 12th Infantry's defenses. Late on 3 February, Bagramian released Sakhno's 5th Tank Corps to Malyshev's control, and the tank corps' lead tank brigades conducted a passage of lines through 90th Guards Rifle Division to begin their exploitation toward Vitebsk. However, LIII Army Corps responded quickly by forming a special detachment made up of its *Jagt* (Hunter, or antitank) command and an infantry battalion and deployed it south of the breach to block the Soviet armored advance.

Farther west in the Gorbachi salient, 117th Rifle Division, the first-echelon division on the right wing of Beloborodov's 2nd Guards Rifle Corps, tried repeatedly to penetrate 12th Infantry Division's defenses between Gorbachi and Bryli only to fail when LIII Army Corps reinforced the 12th Infantry with 169th Grenadier Regiment.

By day's end on 3 February, Galitsky's and Malyshev's shock groups had made enough progress that Bagramian authorized their rifle corps to commit their second-echelon divisions into combat to widen and deepen the penetration and facilitate the exploitation by Butkov's and Sakhno's tank corps. The two tank corps went into action early on 4 February, Butkov's 1st Tank Corps in 36th Guards Rifle Corps' sector north of the lake and Sakhno's 5th Tank Corps in 2nd Guards Rifle Corps' sector south of the lake.

North of the lake, in the main attack sector of Galitsky's 11th Guards Army, Butkov's tank corps attacked along the Kozly and Mikhali axis at dawn on 4 February, supported by 84th and 16th Guards Divisions of Shafranov's 36th Guards Rifle Corps, the latter just committed from second echelon, and 5th Guards Division of 8th Guards Rifle Corps, which Ksenofontov had just committed from his second echelon to widen the penetration south of

Mashkina and Kozly. In two days of heavy fighting, Butkov's tanks and supporting riflemen advanced another 4 kilometers to the east and southeast to capture the strongpoints at Kozly and Novoselki from 20th Panzer Division's Group Breidenbach but were halted just short of Mikhali and Skviria late on 5 February by skillful counterattacks conducted by 20th Panzer's main body. This brought Butkov's *tankists* to within 15 kilometers northwest of downtown Vitebsk.

By this time, however, Third Panzer Army's LIII Army Corps had been able to reinforce its defenses from the southern shore of Lake Losvida to Mikhali with battalion-size *kampfgruppen* from 87th, 197th, and 6th Luftwaffe Field Divisions. Together with 20th Panzer Division, these groups managed to stabilize the panzer army's defenses north of the Vitebsk-Sirotino road and limit further Soviet progress in this sector.

South of the Vitebsk-Sirotino road, the armor of Sakhno's 5th Tank Corp went into action early on 4 February, supported by riflemen from Vorob'ev's 16th Guards Rifle Corps of Galitsky's 11th Guards Army and Beloborodov's 2nd Guards Rifle Corps of Malyshev's 4th Shock Army. Sakhno's tank corps managed to advance roughly 3 kilometers to the southeast in two days of heavy fighting before it became enmeshed in defenses erected by LIII Army Corps' blocking force, which included the corps' *Jagt* Command and elements of 87th Infantry Division. Frustrated in his eastward thrust, early on 6 February, Sakhno then began regrouping his corps, preparing to wheel it southward toward Shatrovo and Litovshchina. As Sakhno's armor advanced, Vorob'ev committed his corps' second-echelon rifle divisions to combat, and they advanced to the northern outskirts of Bol'shie Rubny, west of Skviria and 16 kilometers northwest of Vitebsk.

Meanwhile, on Vorob'ev's right, 90th Guards Rifle Division of Beloborodov's 2nd Guards Rifle Corps recorded only minimal forward progress south of Kozaki. Beloborodov then committed 166th and 381st Rifle Divisions from his second echelon into combat in the sector extending from Kozaki westward to Bryli on 90th Guards Division's left wing. These two divisions then assaulted German 12th Infantry Division's defenses in conjunction with 117th Rifle Division, whose main force was still assaulting 12th Infantry's defenses between Bryli and Gorbachi.

By day's end on 5 February, Bagramian's two shock groups had broken cleanly through the forward defenses of Third Panzer Army's LIII Army Corps between Mashkina and Bryli. By committing his two tank corps, his shock groups had advanced up to more than 6 kilometers deep along a front of almost 10 kilometers. However, by this time the Germans had firmed up their defenses along the left (eastern) flank of the penetration north of the Vitebsk-Sirotino road, and, by skillfully maneuvering numerous small *kampfgruppen,* had blocked the two tank corps' further advance toward Vitebsk. General Reinhardt, the commander of Third Panzer Army, noted the inten-

Map 13.4. Third Panzer Army's Situation West of Vitebsk, 8 February 1944

sity of the fighting, stating, "Today, a very intense day of combat, unfortunately, led to a considerable loss of territory."[6]

Faced with this dilemma, Bagramian decided to shift the axis of his advance slightly to the south to circumvent the German blocking forces. Specifically, he ordered Galitsky to alter the direction of attack of Shafranov's 36th and Vorob'ev's 16th Guards Rifle Corps toward the south. Shafranov's rifle corps was to assault southeastward astride and south of the Vitebsk-Sirotino road and Vorob'ev's corps southward toward Shatrovo, both supported by what was left of Butkov's 1st Tank Corps. To the south, in 4th Shock Army's sector, on Bagramian's instructions Malyshev also reoriented his shock group southward. Beloborodov's 2nd Guards Rifle Corps, supported by Sakhno's 5th Tank Corps, was to assault German defenses between Bryli and Kozaki and D'iakonov's 83rd Rifle Corps, German defenses between Gorbachi and Bryli.

Supported by their armies' tank brigades, Galitsky's and Malyshev's shock groups struck once again early on 7 February after a short period of regrouping. After twenty-four hours of fierce fighting, which stretched but did not break German 12th Infantry Division's new and reinforced defenses, by day's end on 8 February, 90th Guards Division of Beloborodov's 2nd Guards Rifle Corps drove a narrow 1-kilometer-wide wedge into 12th Infantry Division's defenses just west of Kozaki (see Map 13.4). Malyshev and Galitsky then committed their two tank corps into combat in tandem, along with renewed assaults by infantrymen from Vorob'ev's 16th Guards Rifle Corps.

346   The Struggle for Belorussia, December 1943–April 1944

Map 13.5. Third Panzer Army's Situation West of Vitebsk, 9–13 February 1944

Spearheaded by a force of almost 100 tanks, on 8 and 9 February, 90th Guards and 381st Rifle Divisions of Beloborodov's rifle corps and 11th and 31st Guards Rifle Divisions of Vorob'ev's rifle corps carved a penetration 5 kilometers wide and up to 3 kilometers deep into 12th Infantry Division's defenses, in the process capturing the German strongpoint at Bol'shie Rubny (see Map 13.5). This propelled Bagramian's forces to the northern outskirts of Shatrovo, slightly less than 3 kilometers short of the vital Vitebsk-Polotsk railroad line and 15 kilometers northwest of Vitebsk. Elsewhere along the front, however, the Germans halted all other Soviet attacks in their tracks. This in turn, permitted LIII Army Corps to reinforce its forces in the Shatrovo sector, which it did with *kampfgruppen* from 6th Luftwaffe Field and 95th Infantry Divisions.

Urged on by the *Stavka* and Bagramian, Galitsky and Malyshev repeatedly assaulted German defenses in the Shatrovo region from 10 through 13 February, and, although they advanced less than 2 kilometers, 11th Guards Rifle Division succeeded in capturing Shatrovo, and 90th Guards and 381st Rifle Divisions seized Stepan'kova, 1.5 kilometers to the south (see Map 13.6). During this period, LIII Army Corps once again reinforced its defenses in the threatened sector with additional *kampfgruppen* from 95th Infantry and 5th Jäger Divisions.

Still frustrated by his forces' inability to achieve a clean penetration, on 14 February Bagramian ordered Malyshev to mass all of D'iakonov's 83rd

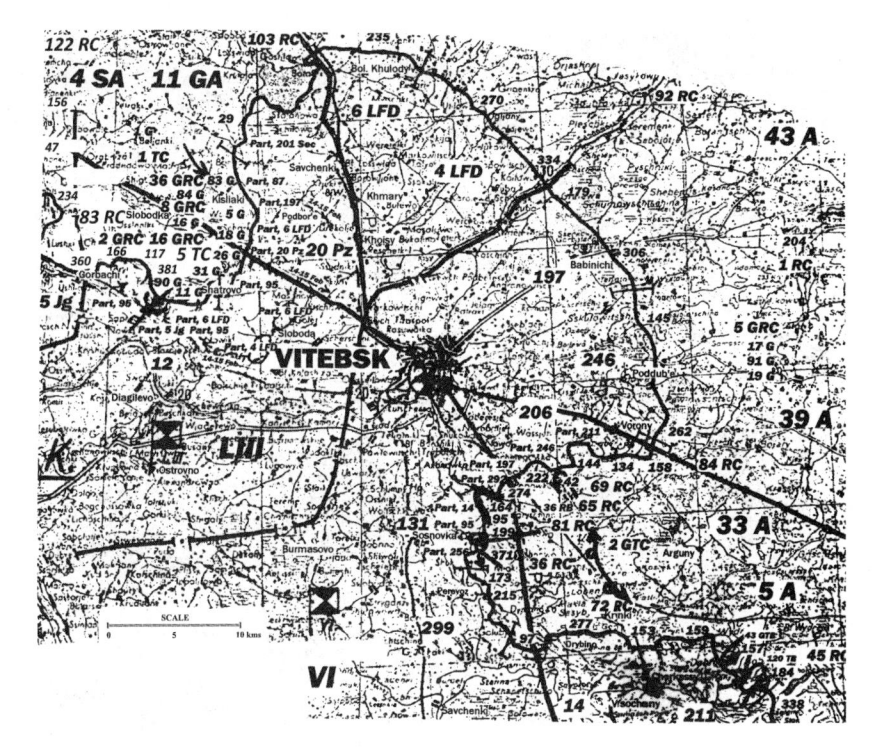

Map 13.6. The Situation at Vitebsk, 10–13 February 1944

Rifle Corps and Beloborodov's 2nd Guards Rifle Corps for one final massive assault on German defenses from Gorbachi eastward through Bryli to Stepan'kova in concert with a supporting assault by Vorob'ev's 16th Guards Rifle Corps. All of Butkov's and Sakhno's approximately fifty remaining tanks were to support the assault.

These concentrated forces struck early on 15 February, with the sheer weight of the assault collapsing German defenses at Gorbachi and Bryli. In two days of intense but confused fighting, the assault forced the defending Germans to withdraw 2 kilometers to new defenses along the Vitebsk-Polotsk railroad line (see Map 13.7). During this struggle, 360th and 166th Rifle Divisions of D'iakonov's 83rd Rifle Corps, supported by 117th Rifle Division on 2nd Guards Rifle Corps' right wing, captured the German strongpoints at Gorbachi and Bryli, 381st Rifle and 90th Guards Divisions from Beloborodov's 2nd Guards Rifle Corps penetrated from Kozaki to the railroad north of Lebedy and Staroe Selo, and 11th and 31st Guards Divisions from Vorob'ev's 16th Guards Rifle Corps reached the northern approaches to Litovshchina and filled in the front northeastward to Stepan'kova. However, this is as far as Bagramian's forces would advance in this short but violent offensive.

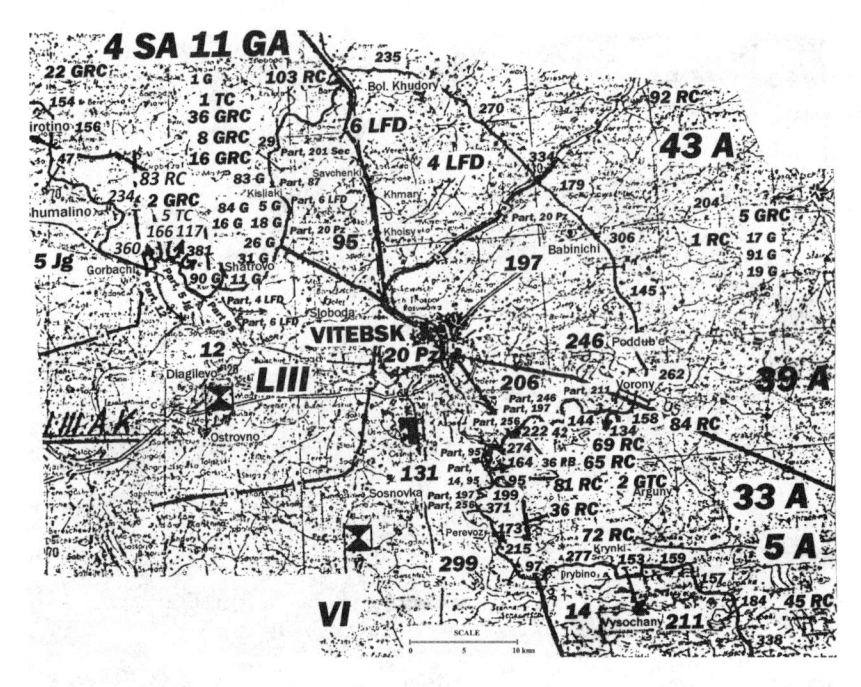

348 The Struggle for Belorussia, December 1943–April 1944

Map 13.7. The Situation at Vitebsk, 14–16 February 1944

German LIII Army Corps countered the threatening Soviet advance by maneuvering *kampfgruppen* to and fro across the snow-covered battlefield in response to each threat as it emerged. For example, a battalion group from 5th Jäger Division arrived just in time to forestall a disorderly German retreat from Gorbachi and Bryli and, by its swift action, managed to cling to a small salient north of the railroad line. To the southeast, other battalion groups from 5th Jäger and 95th Infantry Divisions managed to restore 12th Infantry Division's defenses along the railroad north of Staroe Selo, and one group each from 4th and 6th Luftwaffe Field Divisions did likewise further east near the villages of Litovshchina and Stepan'kova. However, it was a close thing indeed. After the fighting ended on the 16th, 12th Infantry Division was thoroughly worn out by the incessant assaults and, as a result, was withdrawn and replaced by the entire 5th Jäger Division within a matter of days. By this time, 20th Panzer Division, which had lost well over half of its armor, also withdrew, to be replaced by the relatively fresh 95th Infantry Division.

If attrition took a terrible toll on the defending Germans, it also wrought havoc in the ranks of the attacking Soviets. By day's end of 16 February, for example, both Sakhno's and Butkov's 1st and 5th Tank Corps numbered between them no more than ten to twenty serviceable tanks. Worse still, on average, the rifle divisions of Galitsky's and Malyshev's shock groups, most of which had been in nearly constant combat since mid-fall, numbered fewer than 3,000 men each, and both armies had used up most of their ammunition. Bagramian had followed the *Stavka*'s instructions to a tee; as a result, his 11th Guards and 4th Shock Army had advanced up to 8 kilometers along a front of 11 kilometers in almost two weeks of fighting in terrible winter weather conditions against an enemy occupying well-prepared defenses. It was no wonder that both Galitsky's and Malyshev's armies emerged from the fighting as mere shells of their former selves.

Late on 16 February, the *Stavka* finally recognized the realities of the situation and approved Bagramian's recommendation that the offensive be terminated. Besides, by this time the *Stavka* had bigger fish to fry. Far to the north, the collapse of German Army Group North in the face of the Leningrad, Volkhov, and 2nd Baltic Fronts' offensive provided dramatic new offensive opportunities along another axis. The next day the *Stavka* ordered Bagramian to withdraw Galitsky's 11th Guards Army from the Vitebsk region, rest and refit the army, and prepare to commit it against Army Group North's right wing along the Sebezh and Pustoshka axes to the northwest. At least in part, however, the *Stavka*'s decision to terminate the 1st Baltic Front's participation in offensive operations against Vitebsk was prompted by the meager results Sokolovsky's Western Front achieved by the February offensive against Vitebsk.

VITEBSK EAST

Because the *Stavka*'s orders to Sokolovsky required him to shift the axis of the Western Front's assault northward toward Vitebsk proper, Sokolovsky faced a daunting task of regrouping and concentrating his shock groups for the new offensive. Sokolovsky ordered his first shock group, which consisted of the two rifle corps of General Berzarin's 39th Army, to conduct its attack along and south of the Vitebsk-Smolensk highway in the sector defended by German VI Army Corps' 206th Infantry Division (see Table 13.3 and Map 13.1).

In turn, Berzarin configured his army in two echelons of rifle corps, with Dobrovol'sky's 84th Rifle Corps in first echelon and Bezuglyi's 5th Guards Rifle Corps in second echelon. While 262nd Rifle Division of Dobrovol'sky's 84th Rifle Corps continued defending the sector from the highway northward to Poddub'e, the new boundary between 39th and 43rd Armies and their parent *fronts*, 84th Corps' 134th and 158th Rifle Divisions, supported by 28th Guards Tank Brigade and backed up by 32nd Rifle Division in second echelon, were to attack westward in the sector from the highway southward to Ugliane, only 12 kilometers southeast of downtown Vitebsk. After

Table 13.3. The Probable Combat Formations of 39th, 33rd, and 5th Armies and Opposing German Forces on 3 February 1944 (as deployed from north to south)

FORCE (Sector)	OPPOSING GERMAN FORCES
1st/2nd/3rd Echelons (Mobile group)	
WESTERN FRONT	**THIRD PANZER ARMY**
39th Army (Poddub'e, Ugliane)	VI ArmyCorps
84th RC (Poddub'e, Ugliane)	246th ID
262nd RD (Poddub'e, Vitebsk-Smolensk Highway)	
158th RD/32nd RD (Vitebsk-Smolensk highway, Eremino)	206th ID
134th RD (Eremino, Ugliane)	
28th GTB	
5th GRC (17th, 19th, 91st GRD, 47th MB) (Korolevo, Boiary region)	
33rd Army (Ugliane, Sheliai)	
69th RC (Ugliane, Vaskova)	
144th RD (Ugliane, Skinderovka)	
222nd RD/42nd RD (Skinderovka, Vaskova)	
65th RC (Vaskova, Vitebsk-Orsha railroad)	131st ID
164th RD/274th RD/36th RB	
81st RC (Vitebsk-Orsha railroad, south of Gribuny)	
95th RD/199th RD	
36th RC (south of Gribuny, Sheliai)	
173rd RD/371st RD (south of Gribuny, Miakovo)	299th ID
215th RD (Miakovo, Sheliai)	350th IR
23rd GTB	
213th TB	
2nd GTC (mobile group) (Kopti region)	
(4th, 25th, 26th GTBs, 4th GMRB)	
5th Army (Sheliai, Mar'ianovo)	
72nd RC (Sheliai, Chernyshi)	
97th RD (Sheliai, west of Drybino)	14th ID
277th RD (west of Drybino, Krynki)	
153rd RD/159th RD (Krynki, Chernyshi)	211st ID
45th RC (Chernyshi, Mar'ianovo)	
157th RD (Chernyshi, Leutino)	
184th RD (Leutino, Belyi Bor)	
338th RD (Belyi Bor, Mar'ianovo)	256th ID
43rd GTB	
120th TB	

Sources: Boevoi sostav Sovetskoi Armii, chast' IV (Ianvar'–dekabr' 1944 g.) [The combat composition of the Soviet Army, pt. 4 (January–December 1944)] (Moscow: Voenizdat, 1988), 40; "Anlagen zum Kriegstagebuch Nr. 8, Lagenkarten Band VII, Pz AOK 3, Ia, 1 Jan–31 Jan 1943," *Pz AOK 3, 49113/26 file*, in NAM series T-313, roll 296; and H Gr Mitte/Ia, KTB: Lagenkarten, 1–28 February 1944, *H. Gr Mitte, 65002/61 file*, in NAM series T-311, roll 224.

penetrating the Germans' defenses and reaching their immediate objectives in the vicinity of Driukovo, roughly 4 kilometers to the west, the three guards divisions of Major General I. S. Bezuglyi's 5th Guards Rifle Corps, supported by 47th Mechanized Brigade, were to enter combat and exploit northwestward south of the railroad line to assault Vitebsk's inner defenses from the southeast.

Gordov's heavily reinforced 33rd Army constituted Sokolovsky's second and most important shock group. To increase the weight and shock power of his initial assault, Sokolovsky ordered Gordov to deploy his army in a single echelon of four rifle corps deployed across a 16-kilometer-wide front extending from Ugliane southward to Sheliai, with the two corps on the shock group's right wing attacking northward toward Vitebsk proper and the two corps on the shock group's left wing attacking westward across the Luchesa River to effect the shallow envelopment of Vitebsk from the southwest.

Gordov positioned Reviakhin's 65th and Mul'tan's 69th Rifle Corps, each formed in a two-echelon formation of rifle divisions, positioned from left to right on his shock group's right wing to sustain the assault into the German depths. Mul'tan's 69th Rifle Corps, which deployed on 39th Army's left with 222nd and 144th Rifle Divisions in first echelon and 42nd Rifle Division in second echelon, was to penetrate the defenses of German 206th Infantry Division in the 4-kilometer-wide sector from Ugliane to Vaskova and advance northwestward along the Shelegovka and Vasiuty axis to assault Vitebsk's inner defenses from the southeast in close coordination with 39th Army's 5th Guards Rifle Corps.

Reviakhin's 65th Rifle Corps, which deployed on Mul'tan's left with 164th Rifle Division in first echelon and 274th Rifle Division and 36th Rifle Brigade in second echelon, was to attack the Germans' defenses in the 3-kilometer-wide sector extending from the Vitebsk-Orsha railroad to Vaskova at the boundary of German VI Army Corps' 206th and 131st Infantry Divisions. After breaking through the Germans' forward defenses, the corps was to advance northward through Zabolotinka Station and Shapury to attack Vitebsk's inner defenses from the south.

Gordov designated 81st Rifle Corps, now commanded by Colonel V. Ia. Poiarov, and Boiko's 36th Rifle Corps to conduct the critical assault toward and across the Luchesa River on his shock group's left wing. Poiarov's rifle corps, deployed with 95th Rifle Division in first echelon and 199th Rifle Division in second echelon, was to attack westward in the 4-kilometer-wide sector from the Vitebsk-Orsha railroad to south of Gribuny against the defenses of VI Army Corps' 131st Infantry Division. Once through the Germans' forward defenses, the corps was to capture the German strongpoint at Starintsy, cross the Luchesa River and seize Porot'kovo, and advance northward along the western bank of the Luchesa River through Rogi and Novka to cut the Vitebsk-Minsk road and assault Vitebsk's inner defenses from the south.

On Poiarov's left, Boiko's 36th Rifle Corps, with 173rd and 215th Rifle Divisions in first echelon and 371st Rifle Division in second echelon, was to conduct its assault in the 5-kilometer-wide sector from south of Gribuny southward to Sheliai against the right wing of VI Corps' 131st Infantry Division and the left-flank battalion of 299th Infantry Division, which was reinforced on 4 February by 221st Security Division's 350th Infantry Regiment.

The corps' mission was to capture the German strongpoints at Miakovo, Bukshtyny, Karpovichi, and Makarovo; cross the Luchesa River; capture a bridgehead at Perevoz; cut the Vitebsk-Orsha railroad near Sosnovka; and advance northwestward through Zaozer'e to reach the Western Dvina River between Shuty and Kamery. There, it was to link up with the forward elements of Bagramian's 1st Baltic Front. Gordov supported his shock group with one army tank brigade and Burdeinyi's 2nd Guards Tank Corps, whose brigades were to support the penetration operations and, if the snow permitted, later lead the exploitation to the Western Dvina River.

Sokolovsky assigned the two rifle corps of Krylov's 5th Army the mission of supporting his main shock group's attack by protecting the shock group's left flank and conducting local operations to tie down German forces and prevent them from reinforcing their defenses on the approaches to Vitebsk. Specifically, on Krylov's right wing, the four rifle divisions of Prokof'ev's 72nd Rifle Corps were to defend the 12-kilometer-wide sector from Sheliai eastward to Chernyshi with 97th, 277th, and 153rd Rifle Divisions in first echelon and 159th Rifle Division in second echelon and with armor support provided by 43rd Guards and 120th Tank Brigades. On Krylov's left wing, Poplavsky's 45th Rifle Corps was to defend the 10-kilometer-wide sector from Chernyshi southward to Mar'ianovo with 157th, 184th, and 338th Rifle Divisions deployed in single-echelon formation.

Krylov's two rifle corps were to perform several other critical roles during the offensive. First, to deceive the Germans regarding the location of the *front*'s main attack, on 2 February, the day before the main attack was to begin, Prokof'ev was to assault German defenses around Shugaevo, 5 kilometers north of Vysochany, with 153rd and 159th Rifle Divisions and 43rd Guards and 120th Tank Brigades. Second, after Gordov's shock group successfully penetrated VI Army Corps' defenses, Prokof'ev's 97th and 277th Rifle Divisions were to join the assault, capture Shemetovo and Drybino, reach the Luchesa River's eastern bank, and protect the shock group's left flank against German counterattacks from the Bogushevsk region. Third, while the shock group's offensive was developing successfully, Poplavsky's 45th Rifle Corps was to assault German 14th and 211th Infantry Divisions' defenses northeast of Vysochany to distract the Germans and prevent them from shifting forces to the Vitebsk sector proper.

Ultimately, Sokolovsky's offensive plan concentrated sixteen rifle divisions, one tank corps, two army tank brigades, and two self-propelled artillery regiments equipped with 129 tanks and about thirty self-propelled guns against three German infantry divisions supported by about thirty armored vehicles, which included some Tiger tanks from 501st Panzer *Abteilung* (detachment). This accorded Sokolovsky an overall superiority of more than 3 to 1 in infantry and more than 5 to 1 in armor. However, the Germans committed other panzer and assault gun detachments to combat in this sector during the attack, thus negating some of the Russians' advantage in armor. The superiority of Sokolovsky's forces was also reduced by the strong German defenses and the fact that his main shock group had to fight in severe winter conditions and force its way across the formidable obstacle of the Luchesa River.

In addition, prior to Sokolovsky's new offensive, the Third Panzer Army's commander replaced 246th Infantry Division, defending south of the Arguny salient, with the more powerful 14th Infantry Division (Motorized). Although this division was capable of a more effective defense, from the Soviet perspective, it also posed a greater counterattack threat against the salient itself. Furthermore, prior to and after 2 February, German 211th Infantry Division, which Army Group Center transferred from Ninth to Third Panzer Army, took over a sector of VI Army Corp's defenses northeast of Vysochany on 14th Infantry Division's right. Thus, Sokolovsky had no choice but to retain seven rifle divisions in Krylov's 5th Army to defend the salient's southern flank.

Early on 2 February, just as the sounds of Bagramian's immense cannonade resounded from the northwest, 153rd and 159th Rifle Divisions of Krylov's 5th Army struck the defenses of the *kampfgruppe* of 211th Infantry Division defending Shugaevo (see Map 13.8). Because the attacking forces advanced less than 1 kilometer on 2 February, the operation failed to distract the Germans' attentions from their Luchesa River front. In fact, suspicious over Russian intentions, on 2 February Third Panzer Army's VI Army Corps began moving 299th Infantry Division's 529th Grenadier Regiment and 221st Security Division's 350th Grenadier Regiment from their defenses further south northward to reinforce the Luchesa front. Nor could these movements have been timelier, for, at dawn on 3 February, an intense artillery preparation announced the beginning of Sokolovsky's offensive to capture Vitebsk.

As soon as the tumult of the artillery preparation faded away, Sokolovsky's two shock groups launched massive attacks across the entire front from the Vitebsk-Smolensk highway southward to Sheliai. Unfortunately for the attackers, because of ammunition shortages, the artillery preparation did not effectively silence many of the German strongpoints and artillery and mortar positions.[7] Therefore, the assaults by Berzarin's shock group, which faced formidable defenses along and south of the Vitebsk-Smolensk road, encountered strong resistance and intense German artillery and antitank fire and faltered almost immediately. The 134th and 158th Rifle Divisions of Dobrovol'sky's 84th Corps scarcely dented 206th Infantry Division's defenses and fell back on their jumping-off positions after suffering heavy losses. With the *Stavka*'s permission, Sokolovsky called off further attacks in this sector and, instead, ordered Bezuglyi's 5th Guards Rifle Corps, in 39th Army's second echelon, to prepare to reinforce the shock group on the right wing of Gordov's 33rd Army should its assault on Vitebsk from the south succeed.

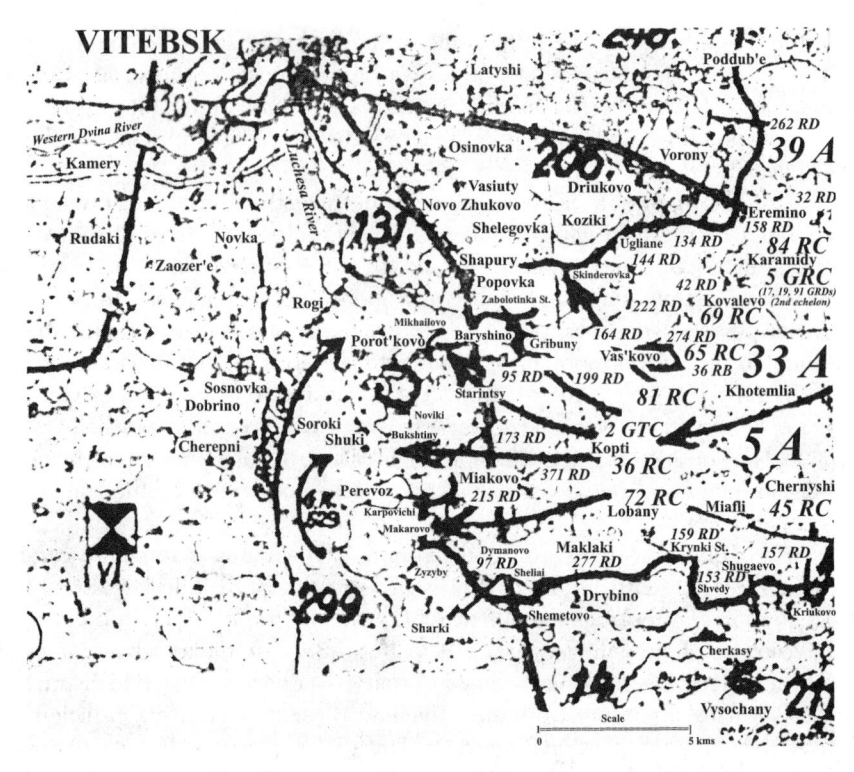

Map 13.8. Third Panzer Army's Situation East of Vitebsk, 3 February 1944

Gordov's shock group, however, achieved immediate success by breaking through the Germans' defenses and advancing up to 2 kilometers across its entire front on the first day of its assault. On the shock groups' right, 144th and 222nd Rifle Divisions of Mul'tan's 69th Rifle Corps overcame 206th Infantry Division's forward defenses between Ugliane and Skinderovka, penetrated 2 kilometers, and captured the German strongpoints at Novka, Bondari, and Laputi. On Mul'tan's left, 164th Rifle Division of Reviakhin's 65th Rifle Corps penetrated to a depth of 1.5 kilometers, capturing the German-held village strongpoints of Baryshino and Semenovka on the Vitebsk-Orsha railroad line, 10–11 kilometers south of Vitebsk.

The two rifle corps constituting the left wing of Gordov's shock group kept pace by making modest progress south of Vitebsk. Supported by a tank brigade from 2nd Guards Tank Corps, 95th Rifle Division of Poiarov's 81st Rifle Corps smashed the forward defenses of 131st Infantry Division in the Gribuny sector, fought its way across the Vitebsk-Orsha highway, and captured the German strongpoints at Dymanovo and Starintsy. After advancing almost 2.5 kilometers more, the division approached the eastern bank of the

Luchesa River east of Porot'kovo, also 10 kilometers south of Vitebsk. However, the Germans managed to cling desperately to a bridgehead at Noviki on the river's eastern bank, which threatened Poiarov's left flank and served as an ideal base from which to launch counterattacks.

On the left wing of Poiarov's rifle corps, 173rd and 215th Rifle Divisions of Boiko's 36th Rifle Corps, also supported by a tank brigade from 2nd Guards Tank Corps, tore a gaping hole in the defenses of 131st Infantry Division from south of Gribuny to just south of Miakovo, advanced 1–2 kilometers, captured the village strongpoints at Makarovo and Zaprudy, and approached the Luchesa River north and south of Perevoz. However, as was the case to the north, the Germans were able to retain a small bridgehead on the river's eastern bank at Karpovichi, a small village east of Perevoz, and quickly reinforced this bridgehead with the newly arrived 529th Grenadier Regiment.

Capitalizing on his initial success, at Sokolovsky's direction, Gordov ordered his corps commanders to begin committing their second-echelon rifle divisions to combat on 4 February to expand the penetration and, in particular, to seize crossings over the Luchesa River. Although partially frozen, the river was almost 50 meters wide, 1.5 to 4.5 meters deep, and had banks with 45–60 degrees of slope, which made it a formidable obstacle for tanks as well as infantry. The fresh assault was preceded by a ten-to-fifteen-minute artillery raid.[8] This signaled the beginning of a fierce three-day struggle for possession of the Luchesa River line during which the Germans juggled their defending units and committed fresh *kampfgruppen* to deny the Russians possession of the vital river crossing sites.

East of the Luchesa River and south of Vitebsk, the rifle divisions of Mul'tan's 69th and Reviakhin's 65th Rifle Corps recorded only meager gains in the ensuing three days of heavy fighting. The defending 206th Infantry Division, now reinforced by a *kampfgruppe* from 246th Infantry Division, held Mul'tan's 144th and 222nd Rifle Divisions at bay, while to the southwest, Reviakhin managed to advance another kilometer and capture the railroad station at Shapury and the adjacent German strongpoint at Pavliuki by committing his second-echelon 274th Rifle Division to combat. This success propelled Reviakhin's forces to positions less than 10 kilometers from Vitebsk's center. However, the forward progress in this sector was not yet deep enough to warrant the commitment of 5th Guards Rifle Corps. Therefore, Sokolovsky decided to retain it in reserve.

To the south, a seesaw battle raged for three days along the Luchesa River front as Gordov and his two corps commanders committed their second-echelon divisions into the battle for possession of the critical bridgeheads, and the Germans launched counterattack after counterattack to deny them their goals. Intense fighting ensued for the German village strongpoints at Pavliuchenki, Bodino-Moaino, Bukshtyny, and Miakovo.[9] Early on 4 February, Poiarov committed 199th Rifle Division from second echelon on 95th

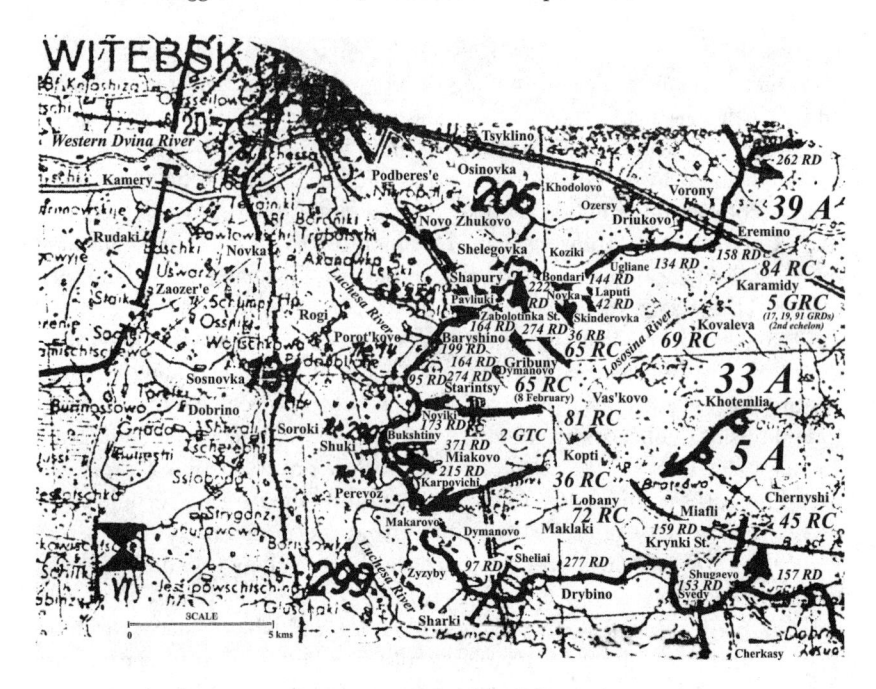

Map 13.9. Third Panzer Army's Situation East of Vitebsk, 8 February 1944

Rifle Division's right, with orders to drive across the river east of Porot'kovo. However, the 199th was not able to crush the German forces defending the bridgehead at Noviki nor was 95th Division able to cross the river east of Porot'kovo. Still further to the south, 173rd and 215th Rifle Divisions of Boiko's 36th Corps compressed the German bridgehead at Karpovichi east of Perevoz; however, their attacks faltered before they could eliminate it entirely. In short, Poiarov's and Boiko's advance was measured only in hundreds of meters as the frustrating battle continued unabated.

Despite intense fighting, a virtual stalemate continued to exist on 7 February (see Map 13.9). While both Poiarov's and Boiko's corps struggled in vain to breach the Luchesa River line, only Mul'tan's and Reviakhin's corps recorded any forward progress. By committing 42nd Rifle Division from its second echelon, Reviakhin's rifle corps was able to advance slightly northward along the railroad line north of Shapury but no further. The cost to the attackers of 39th and 33rd Armies during the fighting from 4 to 6 February was more than 3,600 men killed and wounded.[10]

Throughout the first five days of Sokolovsky's offensive, the Germans were able to absorb the shock of the Soviet assaults and bend but not break because of their skillful regrouping of forces along the front. For example, they were able to halt the Soviet attack short of the Luchesa River by committing 529th and 350th Infantry (Grenadier) Regiments to combat from 3 to 5 February. Later, VI Army Corps reinforced its river defenses with two *kampfgruppen* from 14th Infantry Division and its defenses south of Vitebsk with a *kampfgruppe* from 246th Infantry Division. In addition, it stiffened its defenses with Tiger tanks from 501st Panzer Detachment and assault guns from 281st Assault Gun Detachment. Most critical of all to the ultimate outcome of the battle were the small bridgeheads the Germans retained at Noviki and Karpovichi on the eastern bank of the Luchesa River.

After failing to break cleanly through the Germans' defenses during the first five days of combat, Sokolovsky and Gordov desperately sought a weak place in VI Army Corps' defenses that they could exploit. Together, they decided to focus all of their efforts on the Shapury sector east of the Vitebsk-Orsha railroad line, 9 kilometers south of Vitebsk, and on the vital sectors along the Luchesa River, where the Germans still retained bridgeheads, and regrouped their forces accordingly.

First, Gordov assigned Mul'tan's 69th Rifle Corps responsibility for the entire 4-kilometer-wide sector from Ugliane to the Vitebsk-Orsha railroad line and ordered him to concentrate his forces there for an attack northward toward Vitebsk. At the same time, he ordered Reviakhin's 65th Rifle Corps to turn its offensive sector over to Mul'tan's corps and move its 164th and 274th Rifle Divisions to new attack positions west of the Vitebsk-Orsha railroad, from which they were to attack northwestward toward and across the Luchesa River in tandem with Poiarov's 81st Rifle Corps as it employed its 95th and 199th Divisions to launch a concerted assault against the Germans' bridgehead at Noviki. Finally, Gordov ordered Boiko's 36th Rifle Corps to employ all three of its divisions to crush the Germans' bridgehead at Karpovichi east of Perevoz.

Five days more of heavy fighting began on 8 February as Gordov's corps attempted to fulfill their new missions (see Maps 13.6 and 13.10). First, on 8 February Mul'tan's 222nd and 42nd Rifle Divisions drove a small wedge into the defenses of 206th Infantry Division along the Vitebsk-Orsha railroad line northwest of Bondari only to be halted by the timely arrival of a *kampfgruppe* dispatched by 246th Infantry Division. At the same time, however, the assaults by Poiarov's 81st and Boiko's 36th Rifle Corps against 131st and 299th Infantry Divisions farther south proved utterly futile.

After shifting their attack axes eastward, Mul'tan's 144th and 42nd Rifle Divisions assaulted 206th Infantry Division's defenses once again on 9 February, this time with additional armor support. The intense assaults propelled Mul'tan's forces almost 2 kilometers through the Germans' forward defenses east of Kozaki before a *kampfgruppe* dispatched by 20th Panzer Division brought these attacks to an abrupt halt. Incapable of conducting further assaults in the face of such murderous fire, Mul'tan's exhausted forces then went over to the defense.

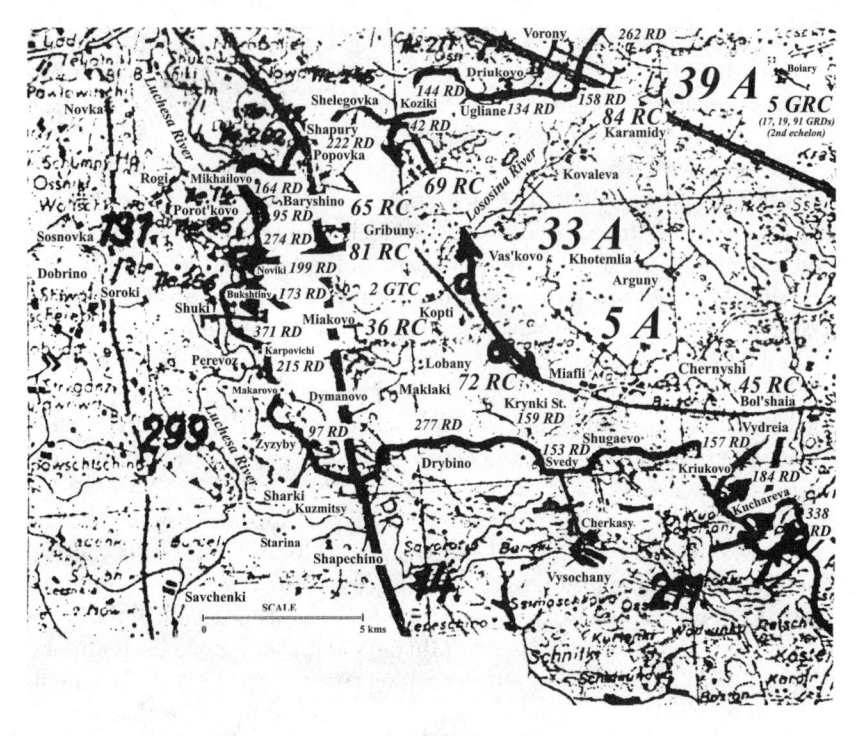

358   The Struggle for Belorussia, December 1943–April 1944

Map 13.10. Third Panzer Army's Situation East of Vitebsk, 13 February 1944

Farther south, however, the combined forces of Reviakhin's 65th and Poiarov's 81st Rifle Corps continued their attacks for three more days and on 11 February finally succeeded in crossing the Luchesa River northwest of Starintsy and seizing a lodgment at the village of Mikhailovo, situated on the river's western bank 10 kilometers south of Vitebsk. After repelling numerous counterattacks by *kampfgruppen* from 14th and 95th Infantry Divisions, Reviakhin's 164th Rifle Division and Poiarov's 95th Rifle Division managed to carve a 2-kilometer-deep bridgehead anchored on Mikhailovo on the river's western bank just east of Porot'kovo. To the south, Poiarov's 199th Rifle Division captured Noviki but left two smaller German bridgeheads intact on the river's eastern bank north and south of Bukshtyny. During the same period, Boiko's 36th Rifle Corps committed its 371st Rifle Division from second echelon and managed to compress, but not eliminate, 131st Infantry Division's bridgehead on the river's eastern bank at and north of Karpovichi.

Although Sokolovsky and Gordov insisted that Gordov's 33rd Army continue its assault for three more days, after 13 February all of these assaults proved utterly futile (see Maps 13.7 and 13.11). By this time, as exhausted and worn down by attrition as they were, it was clear that Gordov's forces were simply incapable of achieving anything more. Furthermore, because

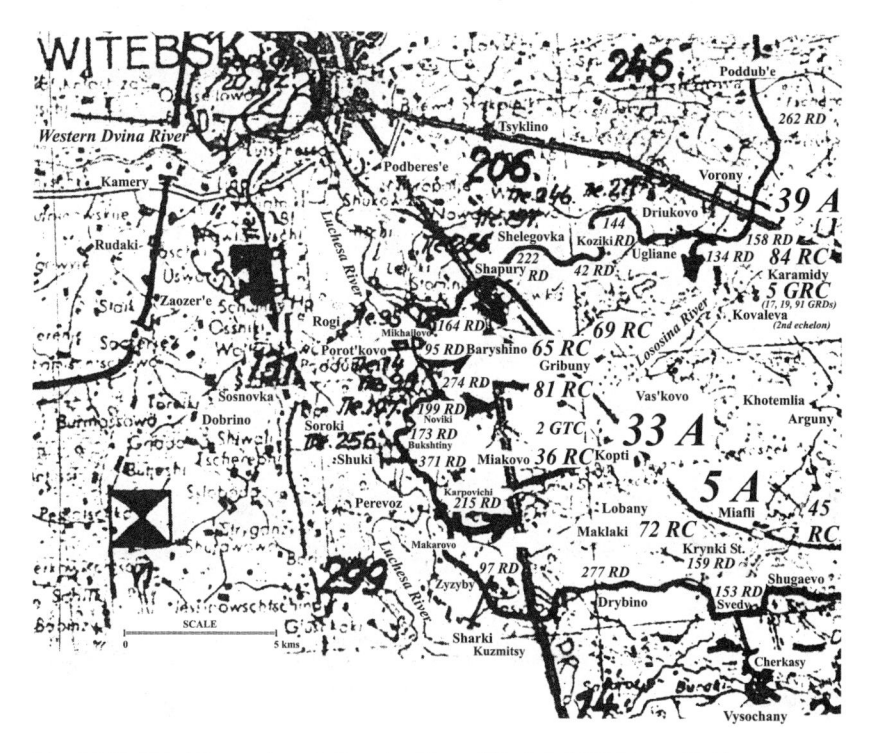

Map 13.11. Third Panzer Army's Situation East of Vitebsk, 16 February 1944

Bagramian's offensive northwest of Vitebsk had also faltered, even the *Stavka* saw reason in a halt to further bloodletting.

As a mere sideshow to the heavier fighting south of Vitebsk and along the Luchesa River, on 13 February Krylov's 5th Army attempted to take advantage of the Germans' apparent weakness northeast of Vysochany by conducting an assault against their defenses east of Dobrino. However, unbeknownst to Krylov, the Dobrino sector was now defended by the entire 211th Infantry Division. In this venture, 157th and 184th Rifle Divisions of Poplavsky's 45th Rifle Corps, supported by tanks from 43rd Guards and 120th Tank Brigades, struck the 211th Infantry's defenses between Chernyshi and Belyi Bor, capturing the village of Kuchareva and driving the German defenders back to new positions extending from the eastern outskirts of Kriukovo to Kuchareva. There, however, this local offensive also ground to a halt, signaling the utter frustration of Soviet hopes along the axis southeast of Vitebsk.

During two weeks of intense fighting in appalling winter conditions, Sokolovsky's forces managed an advance up to 6 kilometers along a front of more than 13 kilometers but at a high cost of 42,495 casualties, including 9,651 soldiers killed and 32,844 wounded.[11] This high price earned for

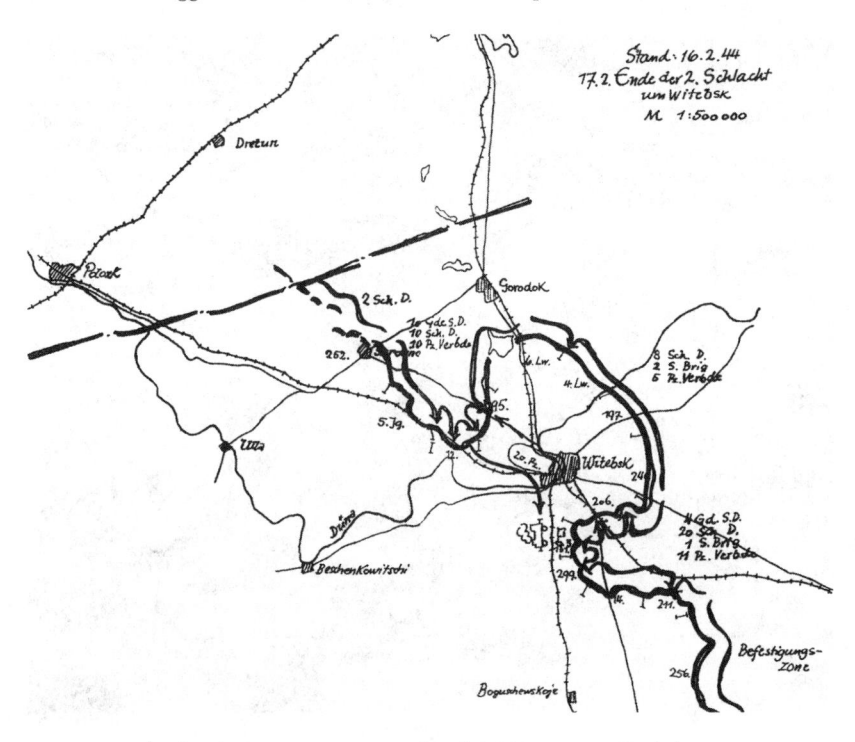

Map 13.12. Third Panzer Army's Appreciation of the Situation at Vitebsk, 16–17 February 1944

the Western Front a pitifully small bridgehead across the Luchesa River around Mikhailovo but failed to crack German defenses south of Vitebsk and along the remainder of the Luchesa River (see Map 13.12). By 16 February, Sokolovsky's armored force had dwindled to fewer than fifty tanks and self-propelled guns, and his rifle divisions, most of which had been in near constant combat as long as those in Bagramian's *front*, were in a similarly dilapidated state. Although their losses have not been revealed, it is likely that Bagramian's two armies lost as many as 40,000 soldiers in the operation. It was little wonder then that the *Stavka* decided to terminate its efforts to capture Vitebsk with the 1st Baltic and Western Fronts.

On the positive side of the ledger for the two Soviet *fronts*, their forces had reduced Third Panzer Army's salient around Vitebsk by well over one-half and failed to encircle the beleaguered panzer army by a mere 26 kilometers (16 miles). Furthermore, by the time the fighting was over, the defending German divisions were far weaker than before, and the struggle drew what little armor was left north of the Pripiat' Marshes to save the city of Vitebsk. In fact, by mid-February it is safe to say that Colonel General Reinhardt's panzer army was literally at the end of its tether, with disaster just around the corner. In the end, it was the perception by the *Stavka* that new opportunities were at hand that saved Reinhardt's army from further damage and likely destruction.

From the *Stavka*'s perspective, the gains made by its Leningrad, Volkhov, and 2nd Baltic Fronts to the north offered these enticing new opportunities, which, if successfully exploited, would eclipse its frustration over the failure to capture Vitebsk. By shifting the 1st Baltic Front's main effort to the northwest, and with it the *front*'s 11th Guards Army, the *Stavka* convinced itself that it could complete the destruction of Army Group North, penetrate the Germans' Panther Defense Line, and begin to liberate the Baltic region.

At the same time, however, it remained important to tie down German forces in Vitebsk to prevent them from reinforcing Army Group North. Therefore, the *Stavka* ordered Sokolovsky to continue offensive action, albeit at a lower level of intensity, against Army Group Center's defenses at and south of Vitebsk. In practical terms, the *Stavka*'s decision to continue active offensive operations by the Western Front meant that the bloodletting around and south of Vitebsk would continue unabated. It did so after a respite of only six days but this time in 31st Army's sector farther to the south.

CHAPTER 14

The Western Front's Babinovichi and Vitebsk Offensives (22 February–5 March)

THE BABINOVICHI OFFENSIVE (22–25 FEBRUARY 1944)

Within days after the Western Front's February offensive faltered, the *Stavka* ordered Sokolovsky to prepare a new offensive against Vitebsk to begin during the month of March. By that time, thought the *Stavka*, the matter of German Army Group North's defeat would be completely resolved. However, before this new offensive began, it directed the *front* commander to launch preliminary attacks southeast of the Arguny salient not only to weaken German defenses in that sector but also to distract the Germans' attention from the Luchesa River front to the north where Sokolovsky was to conduct his new offensive's main attack (see Map 14.1). Although Sokolovsky did not complete his detailed plan for the March offensive and submit it to the *Stavka* until 25 February, he received the *Stavka*'s permission to plan and begin the preliminary attack before submitting that final plan. Accordingly, following the *Stavka*'s guidance, Sokolovsky proposed conducting a preliminary attack southeast of the Arguny salient on 22 February, specifically, in the 15-kilometer-wide sector stretching from Mar'ianovo southward to Babinovichi, 27–45 kilometers south-southeast of Vitebsk.

Because this sector had been a quiet one before and was therefore defended by weak German forces, Sokolovsky assumed that attacking there would inevitably draw German forces southward from the Luchesa River front. Although correct in the main, Sokolovsky's assumption ultimately proved superfluous because General Reinhardt chose this moment to shorten his defensive lines around Vitebsk, by doing so freeing up forces to deal not only with Sokolovsky's diversion but also with his planned main attack.

Sokolovsky's plan required the left wing of Krylov's 5th Army to launch an assault south of Mar'ianovo and the right wing of Gluzdovsky's 31st Army to launch an attack north of Babinovichi. Krylov's shock group, which consisted of 45th Rifle Corps' 159th, 184th, and 338th Rifle Divisions, was to attack westward south of the Sukhodrovka River at Mar'ianovo to outflank German 211th Infantry Division's stronghold at Vysochany from the southeast. Simultaneously, Gluzdovsky's shock group, composed of 251st, 42nd, and 220th Rifle Divisions, was to advance northwestward along the northern bank of the Luchesa River from the Babinovichi region to smash the defenses of VI Army Corps' 256th Infantry Division and outflank the so-called German

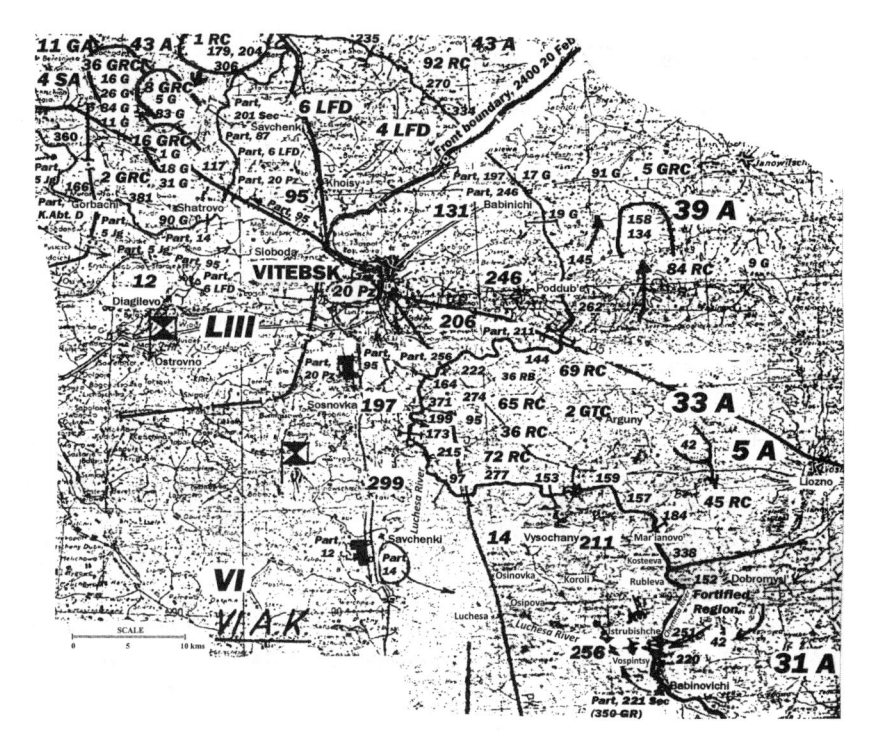

Map 14.1. The Situation at Vitebsk, 17–21 February 1944

Vysochany grouping (the 14th, 211th, and 256th Infantry Divisions) from the south. Sokolovsky ordered this attack to begin on 22 February, three days before he submitted his completed offensive plan to the *Stavka* for approval.

When choosing the Mar'ianovo and Babinovichi sector as his target, Sokolovsky made three basic assumptions. First, he assumed that the Germans had significantly weakened their defenses in this sector by dispatching forces to reinforce the Luchesa front. This assumption was correct, since German VI Army Corps had shifted a regiment from 256th Infantry Division and 221st Security Division's 350th Infantry Regiment northward in early February to reinforce its sagging defenses along the Luchesa River.

Second, Sokolovsky also assumed that, if successful, this attack would outflank German VI Army Corps and force it to withdraw its 14th, 211th, and 256th Infantry Divisions southwest to new defenses behind the Luchesa River. This would permit 5th Army to play an even larger role in the *front*'s main attack further north along the Luchesa River.

Third, in the event the preliminary attack failed, Sokolovsky assumed that the sector was distant enough from the Luchesa front to prevent whatever reinforcements it attracted from returning northward to counter his

Table 14.1. The Estimated Correlation of Opposing Forces in the Babinovichi Offensive, 22–25 February 1944

OPPOSING FORCES	
Soviet	*German*
Western Front	
5th Army	256th Infantry Division
31st Army	IR, 14th Infantry Division
6 rifle divisions	350th Grenadier Regiment,
1 tank brigade	221st Security Division
1 tank regiment (40 tanks)	281st Assault Gun *Abteilung*
	Co., 501st Panzer *Abteilung* (30 AFVs)

Depth of Soviet advance: 1–2 kilometers
Casualties: 5,767 men, including 1,288 killed and 4,479 wounded

Sources: Makhmut Gareev, "O neudachnykh nastupatel'nykh operatsiiakh sovetskikh voisk v Velikoi Otechestvennoi voine. Po neopublikovannym dokumentam GKO" [About unsuccessful offensive operations of Soviet forces in the Great Patriotic War. According to unpublished GKO documents], *Novaia i noveishaia istoriia* [New and newest history] 1 (January 1994): 17; H Gr Mitte/Ia, KTB: Lagenkarten, 1–28 February 1944, *H. Gr Mitte, 65002/61 file*: and H Gr Mitte/Ia, KTB: Lagenkarten, 1–30 March 1944, *H. Gr Mitte, 65002/62 file*, in NAM series T-311, roll 224 in NAM series T-311, roll 224.

main attack along the Luchesa River. This assumption was partially correct because by early March, VI Army Corps reinforced this sector with 406th Grenadier Regiment, 281st Assault Gun *Abteilung* (detachment), a company from 501st Panzer *Abteilung*, and, ultimately, elements of 6th Luftwaffe Field Division, all of which remained in the Mar'ianovo and Babinovichi regions through early March. However, Third Panzer Army partially negated this assumption by replacing the worn-out 131st Infantry Division along the Luchesa with the fresher 197th Infantry Division as it shortened its defensive line around Vitebsk.

Sokolovsky ordered Lieutenant General V. A. Gluzdovsky's 31st Army to conduct the preliminary assault in the sector north of Babinovichi with a force of no fewer than three rifle divisions and a tank brigade (see Table 14.1). His attacking forces were to penetrate German 256th Infantry Division's defenses in the 5-kilometer-wide sector extending from Istrubishche southward to Babinovichi, capture Vospintsy, and advance westward along the northern bank of the Luchesa River toward Osipova and the Vitebsk-Orsha road to outflank the German Vysochany grouping from the south. At the same time, Poplavsky's 45th Rifle Corps, deployed on the left wing of Krylov's 5th Army, was to conduct its supporting assault in the 3-kilometer-wide sector between Mar'ianovo and Rubleva, 10–15 kilometers north of Babinichi, penetrate the defenses on 256th Infantry Division's left wing, capture the strongpoints at Rubleva and Kazimirovo, and advance westward through Koroli to Osinovka and the Vitebsk-Orsha road in tandem with Gluzdovsky's shock group.

Gluzdovsky planned to conduct his attack along the Chernitsa River between Istrubishche and Malye Babinovichi with 220th and 251st Rifle Divisions arrayed from left to right, supported by 42nd Guards Tank Brigade, against VI Army Corps' 256th Infantry Division. After breaking through the Germans' forward defenses, Gluzdovsky planned to reinforce the assault with 42nd Rifle Division and 23rd Guards Tank Regiment, transferred from 33rd Army. Initially, at least, Gluzdovsky's total force of roughly 18,000 men and forty tanks faced no more than 3,000 defending Germans, organized into two to three battalion groups but with no tanks whatsoever. However, the Germans occupied well-prepared defenses equipped with sufficient antitank guns (*Paks*).

Krylov planned to conduct his main attack in the Kosteevo and Rubleva sector with 184th and 338th Rifle Divisions of Poplavsky's 45th Rifle Corps, supported by elements of the corps' 159th Rifle Division, deployed in the Mar'ianovo and Kosteevo sector on the corps right wing.[1] The attack focused on two battalions on 256th Infantry Division's left wing.

Gluzdovsky's two first-echelon rifle divisions began their assault early on 22 February, rather easily tearing a 5-kilometer-wide gap through 256th Division's forward defenses (see Map 14.1). By day's end, 220th Rifle Division penetrated to a depth of 1 kilometer and captured Vospintsy before its attack faltered on the eastern outskirts of the village of Ryzhiki and the Germans' second defensive position along the Vitebsk-Babinovichi road. To the north, on the 220th Rifle's left, 251st Rifle Division and its supporting armor advanced almost 2 kilometers, reached the eastern edge of Vishni, forming a narrow gap through the 256th Infantry's defenses that the division was unable to close. On 23 February, committed from second echelon, 42nd Rifle Division began expanding the northern portion of 31st Army's penetration roughly .5 kilometer to the north and west, capturing the southern half of the village of Sivitskie before its attack also faltered before strong German counterattacks.

The VI Army Corps reacted quickly to Gluzdovsky's assault. Just as 42nd Rifle Division was trying to expand the penetration, German reinforcements reached the region. Late on 22 February, a battalion-size *kampfgruppe* from 14th Infantry Division reached the region north of Sivitskie and counterattacked to bring 42nd Rifle Division's advance to an abrupt halt. The next day reinforcements from 221st Security Division's 350th Grenadier Regiment arrived to shore up German defenses along the southern flank of the penetration. Late on 23 February, the security regiment sent its 2nd Battalion to reinforce the defenses around Babinovichi and its 1st Battalion northward to reinforce German defenses at Vishni. Counterattacking along with 256th Infantry Division's 1st Battalion, 481st Infantry Regiment, the combined force managed to contain the penetration. The next day, 14th Infantry Division's *kampfgruppe* continued pressing 42nd Rifle Division's forces back to the southeast from Sivitskie.

The battle in Gluzdovsky's sector lasted well into March and was still under way when Sokolovsky ordered 31st Army to shift its attention and forces

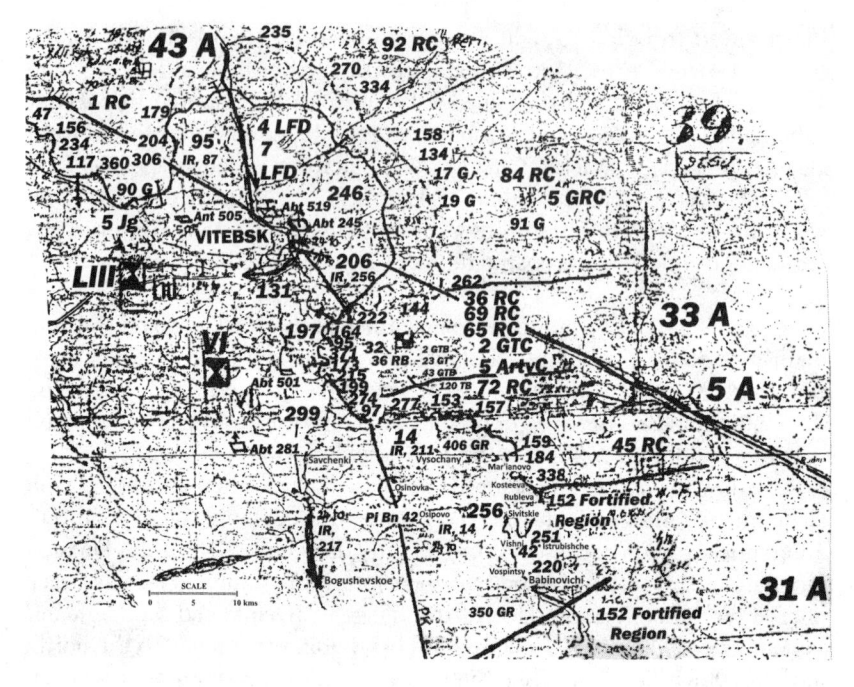

Map 14.2. The Situation at Vitebsk, 22–27 February 1944

southward to the region northeast of Orsha (see Map 14.2). At a cost of 5,767 casualties, including 1,288 dead and 4,479 wounded, Gluzdovsky had accomplished only a small portion of the mission assigned to him by Sokolovsky.[2]

Nor did Krylov's shock group achieve any greater success. Attacking on 22 February, 184th and 338th Rifle Divisions of Poplavsky's 45th Rifle Corps succeeded in penetrating German 211th Infantry Division's defenses between Kosteevo and Rubleva to a depth of about 1 kilometer before being halted on the eastern outskirts of Kazimirovo. Because 159th Rifle Division's assault south of Mar'ianovo failed outright, largely as a result of the timely arrival in the region of 406th Grenadier Regiment, Krylov's assault also failed.[3] This failure also doomed all of Sokolovsky's hopes for a successful preliminary offensive to assist his forces along the Luchesa River.

In the wake of 5th Army's defeat, Army Group Center exploited the occasion by directing Third Panzer Army to return 211th Infantry Division to its reserve for rest and refitting. Accordingly, leaving one of its regiments behind to stiffen 14th Infantry Division's defenses, the 211th departed for the rear 26–27 February. Ultimately, its sector reverted to 201st Security Division's 406th Regiment, backed up by part of 14th Infantry Division's 101st Regiment. Soon after, 221st Security Division's 350th Regiment took over the southern part of 211th Infantry Division's sector.

The only Russian archival documents released thus far concerning the Western Front's February offensives are a brief summary of the action and a grim count of the *front*'s losses for the month. "Report No. 15 on the Generalization of the Western Front's Combat Experiences for February 1944" simply states, "The *front*'s forces conducted offensive operations along the Vitebsk axis and defended along other axes. We did not observe new methods of operations by the enemy during the course of this period. His tactics were ordinary—numerous counterattacks in threatened sectors."[4]

As for the *front*'s losses in February 1944, a second report, "Documentation of the Western Front's Losses for 1944," starkly summarizes the cost of the unsuccessful offensives to Sokolovsky's *front* (see Appendix K-1).

- Personnel (1–10 February)—6,163 killed, 21,757 wounded, 4,840 sick, 10 frostbitten, 148 missing in action, 3 captured by the enemy, and 62 for other reasons, for a total of 32,983 men.
- Personnel (11–20 February)—4,594 killed and 13,950 wounded, for a total, including other categories, of 22,352 men.
- Personnel (21–29 February)—16,354 men.
- Weapons (10–20 February)—4,173 rifles, 224 submachine guns, 156 antitank rifles, 43 mortars, and others.
- Weapons (20 February–1 March)—2,753 rifles, 158 submachine guns, 69 heavy machine guns, 63 antitank rifles, 47 mortars, 65 guns, and 27 self-propelled guns.
- Horses (1–10 February)—779.
- Horses (11–20 February)—668.
- Horses (21–29 February)—530.
- Enemy losses (23 December 1943–10 February 1944):
  - Captured—44 prisoners, 51 tanks, 17 self-propelled guns, 122 guns, 79 mortars, 4 6-barreled mortars [*Nebelwerfer*], 254 machine guns, 472 automatic weapons, 1,465 rifles, 4,920 shells and mines, 5,345 grenades, 139,000 rounds of ammunition, and 61 trucks.
  - Destroyed—9 aircraft, 175 guns, 160 mortars, 375 machine guns, 950 rifles, and 96 vehicles.
  - Personnel (23 December 1943–10 February 1944)—33rd and 5th Armies lost 26,459 men killed, wounded, or missing and 123 tanks burned and 134 tanks destroyed, for a total of 257 tanks.[5]

This meant that the Western Front suffered a total of 71,689 casualties from all causes during February 1944, most of them in Gordov's and Krylov's hapless 33rd and 5th Armies.

The records of German Third Panzer Army provide estimated Soviet strength and casualty figures for the period from 3 February through 17 March, during which what it termed the "2nd Battle at Vitebsk" took place.

These confirm the more fragmentary Soviet figures, and, at the same time, demonstrate that German intelligence kept close and accurate track of the Soviet forces they faced (see Appendix K-2).

- Confirmed enemy strength:
  - In the region southeast of Vitebsk—33rd, 5th, and 39th Armies, with 23 guards rifle and rifle divisions, 1 rifle brigade, and 6 tank units [brigades]
  - In the region east and northeast of Vitebsk—43rd Army, with 8 rifle divisions and the 1 tank unit [brigade]
  - In the region northwest of Vitebsk—11th Guards and 4th Shock Armies, with 22 guards rifle and rifle divisions and 3 tank units
  - The presence of 3 remaining tank units [brigades] in the region southwest of Vitebsk is probable
  - Total: Third Panzer Army's 12 combat-ready divisions faced 6 armies, with 53 guards rifle and rifle divisions, 1 rifle brigade, and 10 panzer units [brigades], for a total of 64 units
- Enemy personnel losses:
  - 113,000 men combat losses
  - 832 men captured
  - 68 deserters
- Enemy equipment losses:
  - 332 tanks destroyed
  - 31 tanks captured
  - 24 guns
  - 51 antitank guns
  - 15 grenade launchers
  - 266 machine guns
  - 39 aircraft by antiaircraft or ground fire[6]

THE VITEBSK OFFENSIVE (29 FEBRUARY–5 MARCH 1944)

The Plan

All that remains of the published Soviet historical record regarding this stage of the Western Front's operations against Vitebsk is the short and cryptic summary from the *Stavka's* critique:

The Vitebsk Operation 29 February–5 March 1944
Our forces. The following forces were concentrated to conduct the operation: 15 rifle divisions, including 13 rifle divisions in first echelon and 2 rifle divisions and 1 rifle brigade in second echelon, 7 artillery brigades, 10 RGK artillery regiments, and 6 tank brigades, for a total of 87 tanks.

Enemy forces. 5 infantry divisions, 10 artillery regiments, and around 90 tanks.

The offensive on the Vitebsk axis, 29 February–5 March 1944, penetrated to a depth of 2–6 kilometers. Our losses were 2,650 men killed and 9,205 wounded, for a total of *11,855 men.*[7]

In addition to this short summary, we also know the definitive order of battle of the Western Front on 1 March 1944 (see Table 14.2).

Sokolovsky completed his draft plan for the proposed new offensive on 25 February, as required, and submitted it to the *Stavka* late that day (see Appendix K-3). It called for General Gordov's 33rd Army to conduct the *front's* main attack along the Vitebsk axis with a force of three rifle corps consisting of nine rifle divisions. Gordov was to launch this attack in the 6-kilometer-wide sector along the Luchesa River stretching from Pavliuchenko southward to Perevoz, that is, from 9 to 15 kilometers due south of Vitebsk. After Gordov's forces penetrated the Germans' tactical defenses, they were to advance westward along the Shuki, Pushkari, and Pesochna axis and subsequently turn northwestward to reach Ostrovno (20 kilometers west of Vitebsk) in the rear of the enemy's Vitebsk grouping.

The 33rd Army's immediate mission was to cross the Luchesa River, advance westward to cut the Vitebsk-Orsha railroad in the Sosnovka State Farm and Stupishche sector (10–13 kilometers south of Vitebsk), and subsequently reach the rear area of the enemy's Vitebsk grouping and capture Vitebsk by an attack from the southwest. Simultaneously with 33rd Army's turn toward Vitebsk from the southwest, General Berzarin's 39th Army was to attack westward from the Poddub'e region with three rifle divisions. As for the offensive's timing, 33rd Army was to be prepared to attack on 3 March and, after two days of reconnaissance-in-force, begin the offensive on 5 March.

Above and beyond the offensive on the Luchesa River front, Sokolovsky added two supporting attacks to his offensive plan. First, he confirmed that the preliminary supporting attack in the Rubleva and Babinovichi regions by the adjoining wings of 31st and 5th Armies was already under way. The plan revealed that this diversionary offensive was being supported by an army artillery group, one tank destroyer brigade, and one mortar brigade and was designed to draw German forces away from the Luchesa River front. Finally, if the diversionary offensive proved successful, he informed the *Stavka*, he hoped the two attacking armies could continue their offensive toward Bogushevsk to "turn" German Fourth Army's left flank.

Second, and more surprising still, Sokolovsky displayed his continued optimism over prospects for ultimate success in Belorussia by adding to his plan an ambitious supporting attack to the south. This part of the plan required Lieutenant General Grishin's 49th Army to launch an attack along the Orsha axis. This attack was to involve a force of five rifle divisions, supported by

Table 14.2. The Western Front's Order of Battle in the Vitebsk Offensive, 1 March 1944

WESTERN FRONT:
Army General V. D. Sokolovsky

39th Army: LTG N. E. Berzarin
  5th Guards Rifle Corps: MG I. P. Ivanov
    17th Guards Rifle Division
    19th Guards Rifle Division
    91st Guards Rifle Division
  84th Rifle Corps: MG E. V. Dobrovol'sky
    134th Rifle Division
    158th Rifle Division
    262nd Rifle Division
    28th Guards Tank Brigade
    134th Rifle Division
    158th Rifle Division
    262nd Rifle Division
    28th Guards Tank Brigade

33rd Army: Col. G V. N. Gordov (Col. G I. E. Petrov on 13 March)
  36th Rifle Corps: MG S. I. Iovlev
    173rd Rifle Division
    215th Rifle Division
    274th Rifle Division
  65th Rifle Corps: Col. V. M. Komarov
    199th Rifle Division
    371st Rifle Division
  69th Rifle Corps: MG N. N. Mul'tan
    144th Rifle Division
    222nd Rifle Division
    36th Rifle Brigade
    164th Rifle Division
  2nd Guards Tank Corps: Col. A. S. Burdeinyi
    4th Guards Tank Brigade
    25th Guards Tank Brigade
    26th Guards Tank Brigade
    4th Guards Motorized Rifle Brigade
  1500th Tank Destroyer Brigade
  1819th Self-propelled Artillery Regiment
  79th Motorcycle Battalion
  755th Separate Tank Destroyer Artillery Battalion
  273rd Mortar Regiment
  28th Guards-Mortar Battalion
  1695th Antiaircraft Artillery Regiment
  23rd Guards Tank Brigade
  43rd Guards Tank Brigade
  213th Tank Brigade
  256th Tank Brigade
  735th Self-propelled Artillery Regiment
  1830th Heavy Self-propelled Artillery Regiment

5th Army: LTG N. I. Krylov
  45th Rifle Corps: MG S. G. Poplavsky
    159th Rifle Division
    184th Rifle Division
    338th Rifle Division
  72nd Rifle Corps: MG Iu. M. Prokof'ev
    97th Rifle Division
    277th Rifle Division
    157th Rifle Division
  120th Tank Brigade

31st Army: LTG V. A. Gluzdovsky
  71st Rifle Corps: MG A. Ia. Vedenin
    88th Rifle Division
    331st Rifle Division
    42nd Rifle Division
    220th Rifle Division
    251st Rifle Division
    152nd Fortified Region
  42nd Guards Tank Brigade
  63rd Guards Separate Tank Regiment
  1435th Self-propelled Artillery Regiment
  2nd Guards Motorcycle Regiment
  52nd Separate Armored Train Battalion

49th Army: LTG I. T. Grishin
  61st Rifle Corps: MG A. M. Il'in
    62nd Rifle Division
    174th Rifle Division
    192nd Rifle Division
  62nd Rifle Corps: MG A. F. Naumov
    63rd Rifle Division
    247th Rifle Division
    352nd Rifle Division
  113th Rifle Corps: MG T. P. Krugliakov
    70th Rifle Division
    344th Rifle Division
  6th Separate Armored Train Battalion

Front Reserves:
  154th Fortified Region
  2nd Guards Tank Brigade
  153rd Tank Brigade
  722nd Self-propelled Artillery Regiment
  1445th Self-propelled Artillery Regiment
  12th Separate Aerosleigh Battalion
  41st Separate Aerosleigh Battalion
  145th Antiaircraft Armored Train

Source: Boevoi sostav Sovetskoi Armii chast' IV (Ianvar'–dekabr' 1944) [The combat composition of the Soviet Army, pt. 4 (January–December 1944) (Moscow: Voenizdat, 1988), 70.

one army artillery and one tank destroyer brigade, one RGK howitzer artillery regiment, and one M-13 regiment. This force was to attack westward in the 5-kilometer-wide sector extending from Parfenkovo southward to Lapyrevshchina (13 kilometers southwest of Liady and 38–42 kilometers east of Orsha). After breaking through the Germans' tactical defenses, Grishin's attacking force was to advance westward along the Demiankovo, Putialino, Dobryn', and Leonovka axis, and subsequently turn either northward along the railroad to Orsha or southward toward Shklov (see Maps 3.3, 3.5, and 3.8). In the event this operation succeeded, Sokolovsky intended to employ all of 49th Army's eight rifle divisions, along with two divisions on 31st Army's left wing, to advance along the highway toward Orsha from the east. Sokolovsky proposed that 49th Army begin its offensive on 3 March.[8]

Whereas Sokolovsky's previous offensive plans had involved employing no more than two shock groups, this venture called for employing three and possibly four shock groups, three of which would operate along entirely separate axes. Sokolovsky also planned to conduct his main attack across the Luchesa River along the very same axes where his main shock groups had previously operated with only limited success. Given these facts, together with Sokolovsky's less than stellar previous performance as a *front* commander, it was no wonder the *Stavka* ordered him to alter his plan. It did so sharply and cryptically in a directive it dispatched to Sokolovsky's headquarters early on 26 February (see Appendix K-4).

Advising Sokolovsky not "to disperse your forces and weaken the blow," the *Stavka* ordered him to attack on two rather than four axes. Thus, it authorized 33rd Army to attack to cut the Vitebsk-Orsha railroad and subsequently attack Vitebsk from the south, and it permitted 39th Army to join the offensive after 33rd Army reached the Vitebsk-Orsha railroad and turned north toward Vitebsk. However, Stalin categorically rejected the other two proposed attacks, demanding that Sokolovsky "cease the offensive at the junction of 5th and 31st Armies and go over to the defense in this region," and, using the imperial "we," adding, "We consider the offensive that you propose with 49th Army toward Dobryn' and Leonovka as pointless." Instead, Stalin directed Sokolovsky "to organize an offensive north of the Dnepr River toward Orsha by employing the forces you intended to use in 49th and 31st Armies' shock groups" and ordered him to submit a revised plan no later than 27 February.[9] As if to highlight the fact that the Western Front's planned offensive was now the "only show in town," at midnight the next day, the *Stavka* confirmed that Bagramian's 1st Baltic Front would no longer conduct any offensive operations against Vitebsk. It did so by ordering Bagramian's forces to begin pursuing Army Group North, which only days before had begun withdrawing its forces back to the Panther Defense Line.[10]

By demanding that Sokolovsky revise his offensive plan and attack along two axes rather than four, the *Stavka* demonstrated that it understood the limitations of both Sokolovsky and his forces. For example, the six rifle divisions subordinate to Krylov's 5th Army numbered fewer than 4,000 men each.[11] Nor is there any evidence that the *Stavka* provided Sokolovsky any of the reinforcements he requested.[12] The *Stavka*'s response also signaled that, regardless of cost, it had no intention of giving up its hopes of achieving offensive success at Vitebsk. In short, if Sokolovsky could not fulfill his assigned missions, the *Stavka* would replace him with someone who could. In the meantime, it left the Red Army's most feared and hated senior commissar and Stalin's premier henchman, L. Z. Mekhlis, to watch over Sokolovsky as he performed his job.[13] As Mekhlis's previous record indicated, he was nothing short of poison to their military careers.

As he planned his new offensive, Sokolovsky had to wrestle with several formidable problems, not the least of which was the severe attrition his forces had already suffered in both troops and weaponry. In addition, he had to plan and coordinate two separate offensives, one south of Vitebsk and the other east of Orsha, while bringing a third already under way between Mar'ianovo and Babinovichi to an immediate end. The winter weather only complicated matters further because alternating thaws and freezes limited his forces' mobility by ruining the few roads in the region.

Finally, the *Stavka* insisted that he begin the offensive by the end of February rather than in early March. These and other problems prevented Sokolovsky from coordinating the offensives effectively in regard to their timing. Ultimately, 33rd Army began its attack toward Vitebsk on 29 February, and 31st and 49th Armies commenced their assaults toward Orsha on 5 March. In the end, however, the poor timing probably had little or no effect on their outcome.

Sokolovsky's revised plan for the offensive across the Luchesa River designated Gordov's 33rd Army as the Western Front's main shock group, allocated Gordov's army three rifle corps with nine rifle divisions, and ordered it to penetrate the Germans' defenses along and east of the Luchesa River from Pavliuchenko (east of Porot'kovo), where 164th Rifle Division had already seized a bridgehead on the river's western bank, southward to Perevoz (see Table 14.3 and Map 14.3).

Initially, the assaulting shock group of the Western Front's 33rd Army was to liquidate the bridgeheads defended by VI Army Corps' 197th Infantry Division on the Luchesa River's eastern bank north and south of Bukshtyny as well as the small bridgehead at Karpovichi east of Perevoz. After eliminating these bridgeheads and crossing the river, the shock group was to advance westward along the Shuki, Pushkari, and Pesochna axis, sever the Vitebsk-Orsha railroad line, the sector from Poddubliany southward to Cherepin, exploit northwestward to capture Ostrovno, and then wheel northward to envelop German forces defending Vitebsk from the south.[14] As soon as the main shock group captured Ostrovno and wheeled northward, a second

Table 14.3. The Probable Combat Formations of 39th, 33rd, and 5th Armies and Opposing German Forces on 29 February 1944 (as deployed from north to south)

FORCE (Sector)	OPPOSING GERMAN FORCES
1st/2nd/3rd Echelons (Mobile group)	
	THIRD PANZER ARMY
WESTERN FRONT	VI Army Corps
	(LIII Army Corps at 1300 hours 3 March)
39th Army (Graleva, Vaskova)	
84th RC (Graleva, Vaskova)	
158th RD (Graleva, Babinichi)	246th ID
134th RD (Babinichi, Poddub'e)	
262nd RD (Poddub'e, Vaskova)	206th ID
5th GRC (17th, 19th, 91st GRDs)	
(Karamidy region)	
33rd Army (Vaskova, Dymanovo)	
95th RD (Vaskova, Shapury)	(VI Army Corps at
(to 20th A, *Stavka* Res. on 1 March)	1300 hours 3 March)
164th RD (Mikhailovo bridgehead)	197th ID
65th RC (Starintsy, Bukshtyny)	
371st RD (south of Starintsy)	299th ID
199th RD (north of Bukshtyny)	
69th RC (Bukshtyny, Miakovo)	
144th RD/222nd RD, 36th RB	
36th RC (Miakovo, Dymanovo)	
173rd RD/215th RD (Miakovo, Zaprudy)	
274th RD (Zaprudy, Dymanovo)	
5th Army (Dymanovo, Rubleva)	
72nd RC (Dymanovo, Miafli)	
97th RD (Dymanovo, west of Drybino)	14th ID
277th RD (west of Drybino, Miafli)	
153rd RD (Miafli, Leutino) (to 20th A, *Stavka* Res.)	
157th RD (Leutino, Belyi Bor)	406th IR, 201st SecD
45th RC (Belyi Bor, Rubleva)	
159th RD (Belyi Bor, Rechki)	
184th RD (Rechki, Mar'ianovo)	350th IR, 221st SecD
338th RD (Mar'ianovo, Rubleva)	
2nd GTC (Mobile group)	
(4th, 25th, and 26th GTBs, 4th GMRB)	

Source: Boevoi sostav Sovetskoi Armii, chast' IV (Ianvar'–dekabr' 1944 g.) [The combat composition of the Soviet Army, pt. 4 (January–December 1944)] (Moscow: Voenizdat, 1988), 70; and "Anlagen zum Kriegstagebuch Nr. 8, Lagenkarten Band VII, Pz AOK 3, Ia, 1 Jan–31 Jan 1943," *Pz AOK 3, 49113/26 file*, in NAM Series T-313, roll 296; and H Gr Mitte/Ia, KTB: Lagenkarten, 1–30 March 1944, *H. Gr Mitte, 65002/62 file*, in NAM series T-311, roll 224.

shock group formed from one rifle corps with three rifle divisions from 39th Army was to attack westward from the Poddub'e region north of the Vitebsk-Smolensk road to collapse the Germans' defenses east of Vitebsk.

The German VI Army Corps manned its defenses east of Vitebsk from Poddub'e to the Vitebsk-Orsha road with 206th Infantry Division and along the Luchesa River with 197th Infantry Division, which had replaced 131st Infantry Division on 18 and 19 February, and roughly half of 299th Infantry Division. Because the 197th Infantry defended the sector north of Shuki and

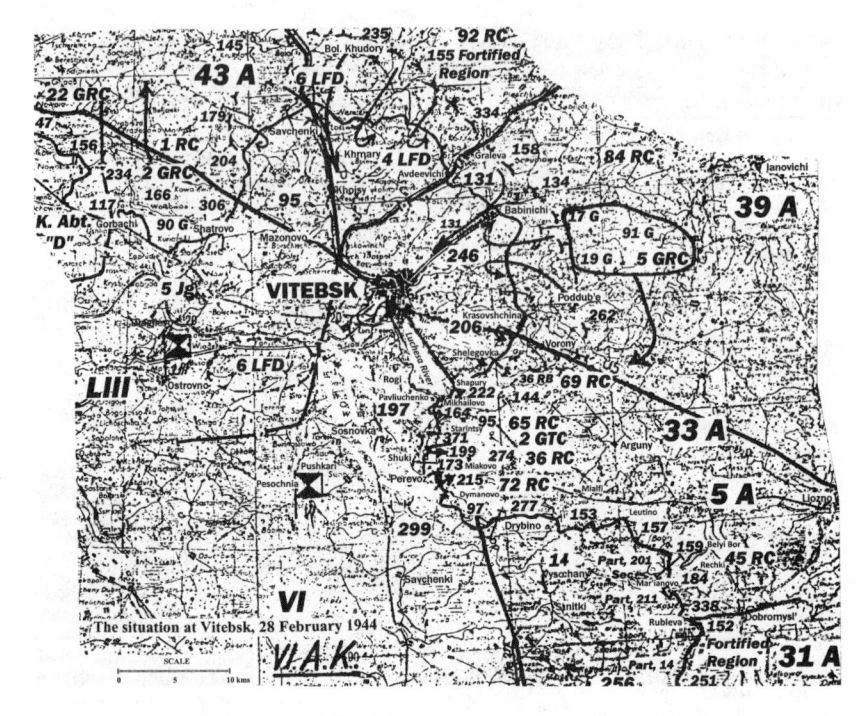

374   The Struggle for Belorussia, December 1943–April 1944

Map 14.3. The Situation at Vitebsk, 28 February 1944

the 299th Infantry the sector south of Shuki, Sokolovsky planned his main attack against the boundary line between the two German divisions.

After regrouping his forces for the attack, Gordov's shock group consisted of three rifle corps with nine rifle divisions and one rifle brigade. Gordov planned to conduct his main attack along the Luchesa River front with 36th, 69th, and 65th Rifle Corps arrayed from left to right. The 36th Rifle Corps, now commanded by Major General S. I. Iovlev and consisting of 173rd, 274th, and 215th Rifle Divisions, was to conduct its attack in the southern third of the penetration sector from Dymanovo northward to Perevoz with 173rd and 274th Rifle Divisions in first echelon and 215th Rifle Division in second echelon. The 215th's task was to seize the German bridgehead at Karpovichi east of Perevoz, force the Luchesa River, and protect the shock group's left flank as it advanced to Ostrovno.

On Iovlev's right, Mul'tan's 69th Rifle Corps, with 144th and 222nd Rifle Divisions and 36th Rifle Brigade formed in three-echelon configuration, was to assault German defenses from just north of Perevoz to Bukshtyny, liquidate the Germans' bridgehead at Bukshtyny, force the river, and spearhead the advance to Ostrovno. On Mul'tan's right, 65th Rifle Corps, now commanded by Colonel V. M. Komarov and consisting of 199th and 371st Rifle Divisions, was to assault and capture the Germans' bridgehead at Noviki north of Bukshtyny, cross the Luchesa River, capture Sosnovka, and support Mul'tan's exploitation toward Ostrovno.

Finally, on the shock group's right wing, as the main attack developed successfully, 164th Rifle Division, directly subordinate to 33rd Army, was to assault from its bridgehead on the western bank of the Luchesa River at Mikhailovo and, supported by 95th Rifle Division in second echelon, advance northwestward along the southern bank of the Luchesa River through Rogi toward Vitebsk to protect the shock group's right flank. During the initial stages of the shock group's operations, 95th Rifle Division was to man defenses on the salient's northern face in conjunction with forces from Berzarin's 39th Army. Gordov supported his shock group with four army tank brigades and two composite brigades formed from 2nd Guards Tank Corps' remaining armor, which amounted to only eighty-seven tanks.

Sokolovsky's second shock group consisted of three rifle divisions from Berzarin's 39th Army operating under 5th Guards Rifle Corps' control. Initially, 158th, 134th, and 262nd Rifle Divisions of Dobrovol'sky's 84th Rifle Corps occupied the army's broad defensive sector from Babinovichi southward to the Vitebsk-Smolensk road and westward to the Vaskova region, where it tied in with 95th Rifle Division's defenses. However, while Gordov's shock group was conducting its offensive across the Luchesa River, Major General I. P. Ivanov, who had replaced Bezuglyi as the commander of 5th Guards Rifle Corps, was to concentrate the corps' 19th, 91st, and 17th Guards Rifle Divisions in the Karamidy region and, on order, then attack westward astride the Vitebsk-Smolensk road.

Finally, the seven rifle divisions subordinate to 72nd and 45th Rifle Corps of Krylov's 5th Army were to remain on the defense in the 12-kilometer-wide sector from Dymanovo eastward to Leutino on the southern flank of the Arguny salient and then southward another 10 kilometers to Rubleva and its boundary with 31st Army.

After regrouping his forces, Sokolovsky concentrated nine rifle divisions from Gordov's 33rd Army, supported by six tank brigades with eighty-seven tanks, along the Luchesa River front. These forces faced the bulk of two infantry divisions subordinate to Third Panzer Army's VI Army Corps. Farther to the north, the six rifle divisions of Berzarin's 39th Army faced two German infantry divisions of VI Army Corps, with two of Berzarin's divisions (the 158th and 134th) defending against one German division (the 246th), while four (the 262nd and 19th, 91st, and 17th Guards) prepared to attack the second German division (the 206th). This enabled Sokolovsky to achieve up to a fourfold superiority over German forces in the Luchesa River sector and a twofold superiority over the Germans in his secondary attack sector (see Table 14.4). However, the armored forces available to both sides were roughly equal.

The day before Sokolovsky unleashed his new offensive, General Reinhardt, the commander of Third Panzer Army, threw a monkey wrench into Sokolovsky's plans by once again shortening his army's defensive line around

Table 14.4. The Estimated Correlation of Opposing Forces in the Vitebsk Offensive, 29 February–5 March 1944

OPPOSING FORCES	
Soviet	**German**
Western Front	
39th Army	246th Infantry Division
	206th Infantry Division
33rd Army	197th Infantry Division
15 rifle divisions	299th Infantry Division
6 tank brigades (87 tanks)	505th Panzer *Abteilung* (50 AFVs)

Depth of Soviet advance: 2–6 kilometers
Casualties: 11,855 men, including 2,650 killed and 9,205 wounded.

Source: Makhmut Gareev, "O neudachnykh nastupatel'nykh operatsiiakh sovetskikh voisk v Velikoi Otechestvennoi voine. Po neopublikovannym dokumentam GKO" [About unsuccessful offensive operations of Soviet forces in the Great Patriotic War. According to unpublished GKO documents], *Novaia i noveishaia istoriia* [New and newest history] 1 (January 1994: 17; and H Gr Mitte/Ia, KTB: Lagenkarten, 1–30 March 1944, *H. Gr Mitte, 65002/62 file*, in NAM series T-311, roll 224.

Vitebsk. To the point, just as Gordov's forces were conducting reconnaissance-in-force along the Luchesa River front, Reinhardt ordered LIII and VI Army Corps to withdraw their divisions defending northeast of Vitebsk back to shorter and more defensible lines. Accordingly, on 28 February LIII Army withdrew 95th Infantry and 6th and 4th Luftwaffe Field Divisions 6–10 kilometers back to new defensive lines extending from north of Savchenki eastward to the Western Dvina River at Avdeevichi. Simultaneously, VI Army Corps withdrew its 246th and 206th Rifle Divisions a slightly shorter distance to new defensive lines extending from Avdeevichi on the Western Dvina River, southeastward to Babinichi, southward to Krasovshchina, and southwestward across the Vitebsk-Smolensk road to Shelegovka. This maneuver permitted LIII Army Corps to withdraw 6th Luftwaffe Field Division into its reserve and VI Army Corps, which had already dispatched its 211st Infantry Division to Army Group Center's reserve, to also withdraw its 131st Infantry Division and send it into Army Group Center's reserve.

Later still, on 2 March, Reinhardt altered the subordination of its divisions to improve the panzer army's command and control. Effective 1300 hours on 3 March, he transferred 246th and 206th Infantry Divisions, along with their sectors east of Vitebsk, from General Jordan's VI Army Corps to General Gollwitzer's LIII Army Corps. This permitted Gollwitzer to concentrate his full attention on the Luchesa River front and the southern face of the Arguny salient protecting the approaches to the town of Vysochany. Soon, Reinhardt would reinforce Gollwitzer's corps with elements of 5th Jäger and 4th Luftwaffe Divisions, plus much of the army's armor and assault guns.

From Sokolovsky's perspective, the German withdrawal subverted his planned assault by 39th Army east of Vitebsk and freed up reserves the panzer army could use to reinforce its front along the Luchesa River. Worse still for Sokolovsky, no sooner did Gordov's shock group unleash its assault along the Luchesa than the *Stavka* began to badger him to commence a strong and resolute pursuit of the German forces withdrawing north and east of Vitebsk. The *Stavka* did so based on the mistaken assumption that, as had already been the case with Army Group North, Army Group Center, along with Third Panzer Army, was about to abandon Vitebsk and withdraw to new defense positions farther west in Belorussia.

As a result, after dispatching several preliminary verbal orders to Sokolovsky on 28 and 29 February, early on 1 March, the *Stavka* sent Sokolovsky and *Stavka* representative Marshal of the Soviet Union S. K. Timoshenko a formal directive ordering them to alter their planned assault, which was already under way, and to begin a vigorous pursuit east and southeast of Vitebsk (see Appendix K-5). Concluding that "the enemy has weakened his defense along the Vitebsk axis and is beginning to withdraw, apparently to assemble reserves with which to resist the operations of the 1st and 2nd Baltic Fronts," the *Stavka* ordered the Western Front "to immediately pursue the withdrawing enemy by employing for that purpose all of 39th Army's forces and the forces of 33rd Army that are prepared to attack. The main forces of 33rd Army will go over to the offensive against Vitebsk from the southeast no later than 2 March 1944." To sweeten the pot further, Stalin ordered Bagramian's 1st Baltic Front "to attack Vitebsk from the northwest with 43rd Army no later than 2 March 1944."[15]

Because Sokolovsky could do nothing whatsoever with the first-echelon forces of Gordov's shock group, which were already assaulting German defenses along the Luchesa River front, he simply stripped 36th and 65th Rifle Corps' of their second-echelon 215th and 222nd Rifle Divisions and dispatched those divisions northward to reinforce 39th Army's presumed westward pursuit along the Vitebsk-Smolensk road. At the same time, Sokolovsky ordered General Berzarin to begin his pursuit east of Vitebsk with 84th Rifle Corps' 262nd Rifle Division as well as the three guards divisions of General Ivanov's 5th Guards Rifle Corps. However, within hours it became apparent that, instead of withdrawing from Vitebsk, Third Panzer Army was simply shortening its defensive lines. When it did, Berzarin's pursuit soon degenerated into another bloody and ultimately unsuccessful frontal assault against the Germans' defenses east of the city.

The Attack

On the eve of all of this command confusion, the three rifle corps of Gordov's 33rd Army struck hard at the defenses of Third Panzer Army's VI Army Corps along and forward of the Luchesa River at dawn on 28 February, after an artillery preparation softened up the Germans' defenses (see Map 14.4). From the very outset, the battle proved both intense and futile for Sokolovsky. Although 164th Rifle Division was stymied in its efforts to expand its

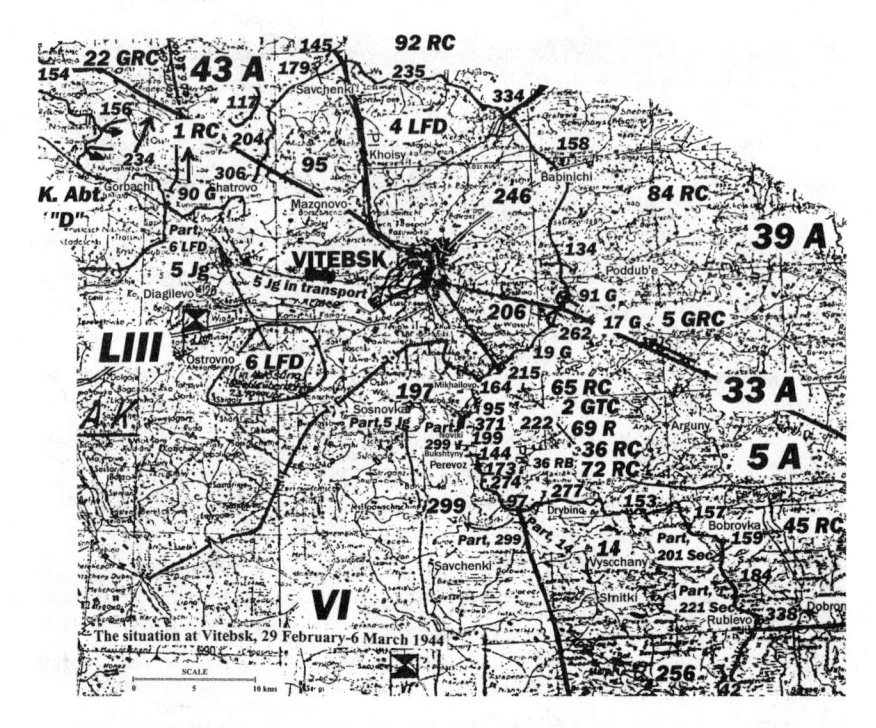

Map 14.4. The Situation at Vitebsk, 29 February–6 March 1944

bridgehead at Mikhailovo, in three days of heavy fighting, 371st Rifle Division of Komarov's 65th Rifle Corps managed to erase the Germans' bridgehead on the river's eastern bank west of Noviki defended by 197th Infantry Division's 2nd Battalion, 332nd Infantry Regiment.

At the same time, 199th Rifle Division of Komarov's corps, along with 144th Division of Mul'tan's 69th Rifle Corps, captured the Germans' bridgehead at Bukshtyny, which was defended by 197th Infantry Division's 1st Battalion, 332nd Infantry Regiment. Then, on 1 March, supported by a tank brigade, 199th and 144th Rifle Divisions jointly forced their way across the Luchesa River, seizing a small lodgment on the river's western bank on the approaches to the village of Shuki. Heavy fighting ensued as reserve battalion-size *kampfgruppen* from German 197th and 299th Infantry Divisions struggled to contain the penetration. Meanwhile, to the south, 173rd and 274th Rifle Divisions of Iovlev's 36th Rifle Corps likewise reduced the Germans' bridgehead at Karpovichi east of Perevoz, which was defended by two battalions of 299th Infantry Division but were unable to force the river successfully.

The heavy fighting raged on at Shuki from 3 through 5 March as Gordov concentrated all of his available forces in an attempt to enlarge the bridgehead. However, Third Panzer Army reinforced its defenses in the threat-

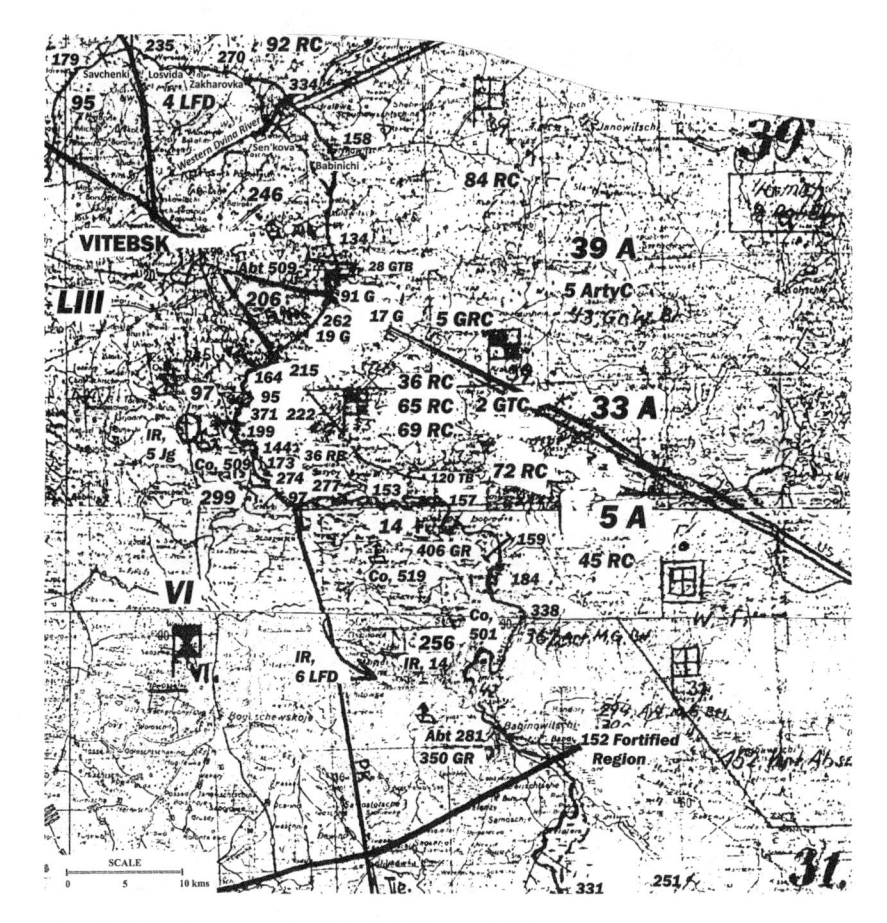

Map 14.5. The Situation at Vitebsk, 7–9 March 1944

ened sector with another *kampfgruppe* from 299th Infantry Division as well as several battalions from 5th Jäger Division, relieved days before from its positions west of Vitebsk by 6th Luftwaffe Field Division. These German reinforcements finally counterattacked and recaptured most, although not all, of the bridgehead. Lacking their second-echelon divisions, which they had sent northward toward Vitebsk on the *Stavka's* orders, Sokolovsky and Gordov could do nothing about the situation but look on in dismay. By day's end on 5 March, their offensive ground to a halt after recording only minimal gains.

While this dramatic fighting was raging along the Luchesa River, a confused but equally intense struggle was taking place around the Germans' defensive perimeter north and east of Vitebsk (see Map 14.5). Within two days after Third Panzer Army's VI Army Corps withdrew its divisions to shorter lines, Bagramian and Sokolovsky began what the *Stavka* termed "their pursuit." In the sector of Golubev's 43rd Army north of Vitebsk, 92nd Rifle Corps' 235th and 334th Divisions and 145th Rifle Division on their right launched probing attacks against 4th Luftwaffe Field Division's defenses in the vicinity of Losvida and Savchenki only to suffer a sharp rebuff. Two days later, Berzarin's 39th Army commenced its "pursuit" by conducting heavy assaults westward along the Vitebsk-Smolensk highway with its 262nd Rifle Division and 5th Guards Rifle Corps' 91st Guards Rifle Division. When these attacks encountered stiffer than expected resistance, the next day Berzarin ordered the remainder of his army to join the fray. Excerpts from 1st Baltic Front's daily combat journal captured the action on 1 and 2 March (see Appendix K-6).

Early on 5 March, 5th Guards Rifle Corps' 19th Guards Division went into action south of the highway in conjunction with attacks by 215th Rifle Division from Gordov's 33rd Army in the sector north of Vaskova. At the same time, 158th Rifle Division of Dobrovol'sky's 84th Rifle Corps, attacking in conjunction with 334th Rifle Division of the adjacent 43rd Army's 92nd Rifle Corps, struck the German 246th Infantry Division's defenses in the 6-kilometer-wide sector from the Western Dvina River southward to Babinichi. The defending Germans gave way before the assault, withdrawing to new defense lines in the sector from Zakharovka to Sen'kova, 2 kilometers west of Babinichi. Farther to the east, General Krylov's 5th Army protected 33rd Army's left flank and conducted operations to divert German attention away from the action under way to the northwest (see Appendix K-7).

By day's end on 5 March, however, Gordov's and Berzarin's forces had shot their bolt. With all of their divisions stymied by unrelenting German resistance and the once-frozen ground now turning into a quagmire, Sokolovsky requested and received the *Stavka*'s permission to halt his offensive in the Vitebsk sector.[16] Although General Gareev claims that the Western Front's forces penetrated up to 6 kilometers during the weeklong fight, in the end, most of these gains represented only voluntary German withdrawals north and east of Vitebsk. In Sokolovsky's vital main attack sector along the Luchesa River and the Vitebsk-Smolensk road, the Soviets measured their forward progress only in hundreds of meters and utterly failed to crack the Germans' defenses. The cost to the Western Front was 11,855 casualties, including 2,650 dead and 9,205 wounded, and most of its remaining tanks destroyed or otherwise put out of action. Adding insult to injury, the strong resistance indicated that the Germans were not yet willing to weaken their tight hold on their fortress at Vitebsk.[17]

Sokolovsky, however, had no time to lament his defeat because on 5 March his attention was also on the Orsha axis, where Generals Gluzdovsky's and Grishin's 31st and 49th Armies were still decisively engaged in heavy combat.

CHAPTER 15

The Western Front's Orsha and Bogushevsk Offensives (5–29 March)

THE ORSHA OFFENSIVE (5–9 MARCH 1944)

Other than the *Stavka* order that mandated its conduct, the only existing Soviet open source that mentions the offensive that the Western Front conducted in the Orsha region early March is the *Stavka's* brief critique of the operation, which describes only its overall dimensions:

> **The Orsha Operation 5–9 March 1944**
> *Our forces.* The following forces were concentrated to conduct the operation: 8 rifle divisions, including 3 rifle divisions in first echelon and 5 rifle divisions in second echelon, 3 artillery brigades, 6 RGK artillery regiments, 1 tank brigade, and 2 tank regiments, for a total of 80 tanks. The artillery density was 100 tubes per kilometer of front.
> *Enemy forces.* 1 infantry division and 3 artillery regiments, for up to 35 tanks.
> The offensive on the Orsha axis from 5–9 March 1944 had no success. Our losses were 1,898 men killed and 5,639 men wounded, for a total of 7,537 men.[1]

Planning

Gluzdovsky's 31st Army and Lieutenant General I. T. Grishin's 49th Army received orders from Sokolovsky to prepare their offensive east of Orsha on 27 February, only two days before the assault was to begin (see Map 15.1). This presented Gluzdovsky with several daunting problems that proved insurmountable to resolve in timely enough fashion to meet the timetable set by the *Stavka* and Sokolovsky. First and foremost, better than half of his army, including 42nd, 251st, and 220th Rifle Divisions, was still conducting offensive operations in the Babinovichi sector. This left only 331st and 88th Rifle Divisions of Major General A. Ia. Vedenin's 71st Rifle Corps, deployed astride the road and railroad line northeast of Orsha, with which to conduct the attack against Orsha. Because Sokolovsky ordered him to employ the bulk of his shock group at Babinovichi in the attack east of Orsha, Gluzdovsky had no choice but to disengage at least two rifle divisions from

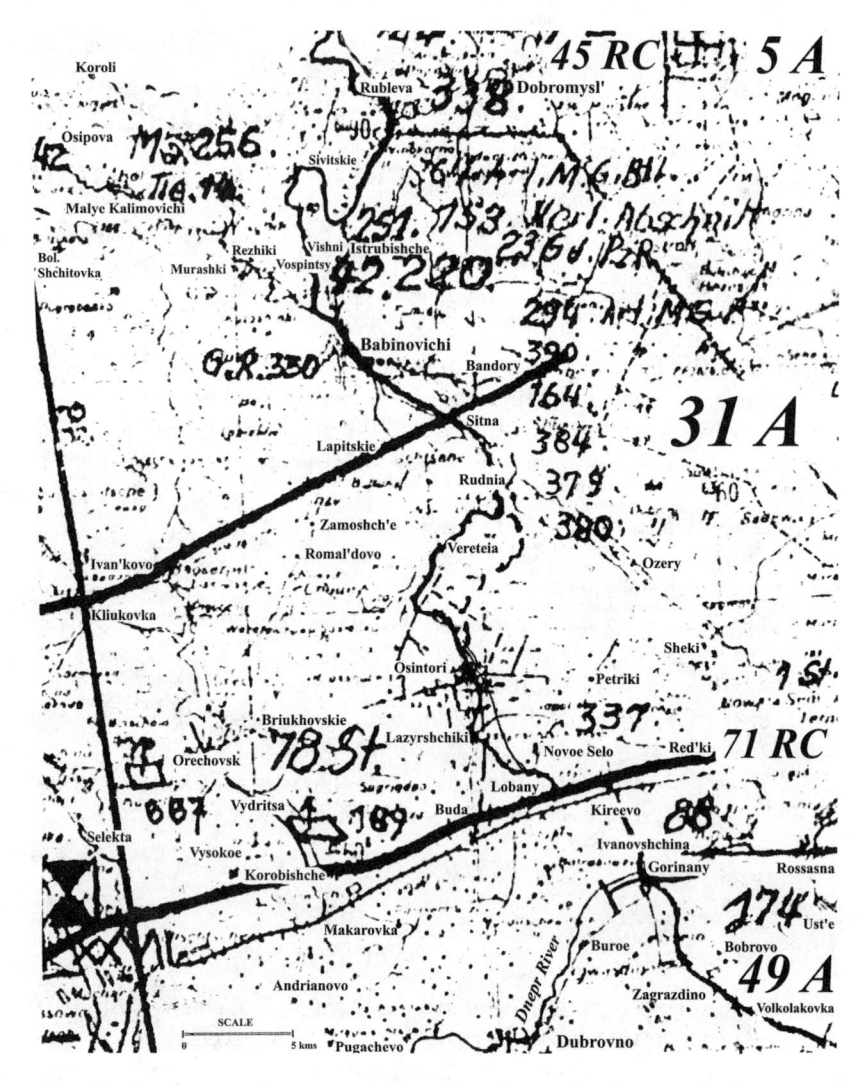

382　The Struggle for Belorussia, December 1943–April 1944

Map 15.1. Fourth Army's Situation at Babinovichi and East of Orsha, 19–29 February 1944

combat in that sector and move them southward across terrain rendered soggy by the spring *rasputitsa* (period of flooded roads) to participate in the new offensive. Making matters worse, to conceal the large-scale troop movement, the army commander had to conduct all of this movement at night.

Ultimately, Gluzdovsky decided to leave 331st and 88th Rifle Divisions in their existing positions north and south of the Orsha-Smolensk road, regroup 251st and 220th Rifle Divisions southward from the Babinovichi region into second-echelon assembly areas to the rear of the 331st Rifle, and place all

Table 15.1. The Probable Combat Formations of 31st and 49th Armies and Opposing German Forces on 5 March 1944 (as deployed from north to south)

FORCE (initial/subsequent sectors)	OPPOSING GERMAN FORCES
1st/2nd/3rd Echelons (Mobile group)	
	THIRD PANZER ARMY
	VI Army Corps
WESTERN FRONT	256thID
31st Army (Rubleva, Lobany)	Co., 501st Pz.*Abt*.
367th MG-Arty Bn (Rubleva, Istrubishche)	
42nd RD (Istrubishche, Babinovichi)	350th IR, 221st SecD
152nd Fortified Region (Babinovichi, Osintori)	**FOURTH ARMY**
71st RC (Osintori, Lobany)	XXVII Army Corps
331st RD/251st RD/220th RD (Osintori, Lobany)	78th AssltD
42nd GTB, 63rd GTR, 1435th SPR	
49th Army (Lobany, Ivanovshchina)	
61st RC (Lobany, Ivanovshchina)	
88th RD/192nd RD (Lobany, Gorinany)	25th PzGrD
174th RD (Gorinany, Kazarinovo)	
62nd RD (Kazarinovo, Ivanovshchina)	
Second Echelon	
62nd RC (Petriki, Sheki, Red'ki)	
247th RD/63rd RD/352nd RD	

Source: Boevoi sostav Sovetskoi Armii, chast' IV (Ianvar'–dekabr' 1944 g.) [The combat composition of the Soviet Army, pt. 4 (January–December 1944)] (Moscow: Voenizdat, 1988), 70; and "Anlagen zum Kriegstagebuch Nr. 8, Lagenkarten Band VII, Pz AOK 3, Ia, 1 Jan–31 Jan 1943," *Pz AOK 3, 49113/26 file*, in NAM Series T-313, roll 296; and H Gr Mitte/Ia, KTB: Lagenkarten, 1–30 March 1944, *H. Gr Mitte, 65002/62 file*, in NAM series T-311, roll 224.

three divisions north of the road under the control of Vedenin's 71st Rifle Corps (see Table 15.1). Prior to the attack, Gluzdovsky assigned 331st Rifle Division the tasked of covering and protecting the forward deployment of 49th Army's 62nd Rifle Corps into its jumping-off position north of the Orsha-Smolensk road. When it completed that mission, the 331st Rifle was to shift to the right into its assigned assault sector. When the offensive planning was completed, 31st Army's mission was "to deliver its main attack along the Minsk highway, penetrate the Germans' defenses in the Osinstroi [Osintori] and Pushchai sector, reach the Vydritsa, Korobishche, Andrianovo, Pugachevo, and Gat'kovshchina line, and subsequently capture Orsha."[2]

After it was fully concentrated, 331st Rifle Division was to conduct 71st Corps' initial assault in the sector extending from Osintori southward to Lazyrshchina against the center sector of German XXVII Army Corps' 78th Assault Division. The 251st and 220th Rifle Divisions of Vedenin's corps were to reinforce the assault when it became feasible to do so. Gluzdovsky left 71st Rifle Corps' 88th Rifle Division in its position south of the Orsha-Smolensk road, placed it under the operational control of 49th Army's 61st Rifle Corps, which was to conduct its attack in the sector south of the Orsha-Smolensk road, and ordered the division to cover and protect the corps' forward deployment.

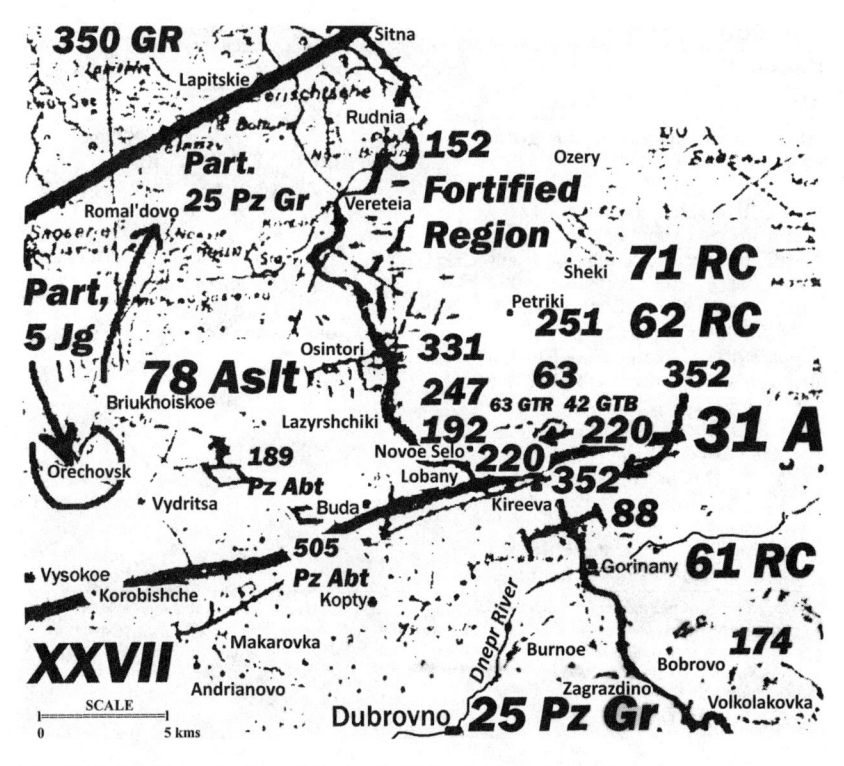

Map 15.2. The Situation East of Orsha, 5–9 March 1944

Grishin designated the three rifle divisions of Major General A. F. Naumov's 62nd Rifle Corps and the two rifle divisions of Major General A. M. Il'in's 61st Rifle Corps as his army's shock group and ordered the group to conduct its assault on 71st Rifle Corps' left (see Map 15.2). The 62nd Rifle Corps was to attack in the sector extending from Lazyrshchina southward to Lobany against 78th Assault Division's center sector, with its 247th Rifle Division in first echelon and 63rd and 352nd Rifle Divisions in second echelon. Il'in's 61st Rifle Corps, with 88th Rifle Division attached, was to conduct its attack in the sector extending from Lobany to the Dnepr River against 78th Assault Division's right wing, with its newly assigned 88th Rifle Division in first echelon and with 192nd Rifle Division in second echelon. The 174th Rifle Division of Il'in's corps, which remained on the defense south of the Dnepr River, was to join the assault only if and when it succeeded.

To the north, on 31st Army's right wing, 42nd Rifle Division and 23rd Guards Tank Brigade were to continue local operations in the region north of Babinovichi so as to pin down the opposing forces of German 256th Infantry Division and 221st Security Division's 350th Infantry Regiment and attract other German operational and tactical reserves to its sector.

Table 15.2. The Estimated Correlation of Opposing Forces in the Orsha Offensive, 5–9 March 1944

OPPOSING FORCES	
Soviet	**German**
Western Front	
31st Army	78th Assault Division
49th Army	*Kampfgruppen*, 5th Jäger
8 rifle divisions	and 25th Panzer
1 tank brigade	Grenadier Divisions
2 tank regiments (80 tanks)	189th Assault Gun and 505th
	Panzer *Abteilung* (35 AFVs)

Depth of Soviet advance: None
Casualties: 7,537 men, including 1,898 killed and 5,639 wounded

Source: Makhmut Gareev, "O neudachnykh nastupatel'nykh operatsiiakh sovetskikh voisk v Velikoi Otechestvennoi voine. Po neopublikovannym dokumentam GKO" [About unsuccessful offensive operations of Soviet forces in the Great Patriotic War. According to unpublished GKO documents], *Novaia i noveishaia istoriia* [New and newest history] 1 (January 1994): 17.

This plan concentrated eight rifle divisions, one tank brigade, and two tank regiments of Gluzdovsky's 31st and Grishin's 49th Armies, with a total of eighty tanks, in the main attack sector northeast of Orsha. These forces faced a single German division, the 78th Assault, backed up initially by 189th Assault Gun and 505th Panzer *Abteilungen* (detachments), which fielded roughly thirty-five tanks and assault guns. This accorded the Soviet shock group an overall superiority of better than 3 to 1 in infantry and a similar superiority in armor (see Table 15.2). However, the fact that the two armies conducted their initial assault with only three of their eight divisions largely negated this superiority. The defending German forces were able to resist the piecemeal assault successfully and ultimately halt it by employing redeployed reserves.

Because of problems they encountered in regrouping so large a force in timely fashion, Gluzdovsky and Grishin requested and received Sokolovsky's permission to delay the attack until 5 March. By this time, however, 33rd Army's offensive along the Luchesa River had failed, rendering the Orsha offensive largely irrelevant. Nevertheless, Sokolovsky insisted it take place.

The Battle

Gluzdovsky and Grishin commenced their assault north and south of the Orsha-Smolensk road at 0930 hours on 5 March after firing a fifty-minute artillery preparation (see Map 15.2). However, by themselves, the three assaulting first-echelon divisions made only minimal progress against the strong German defenses. The combined forces of 331st Rifle Division and the reinforcing 247th Rifle Division managed to advance up to 1 kilometer

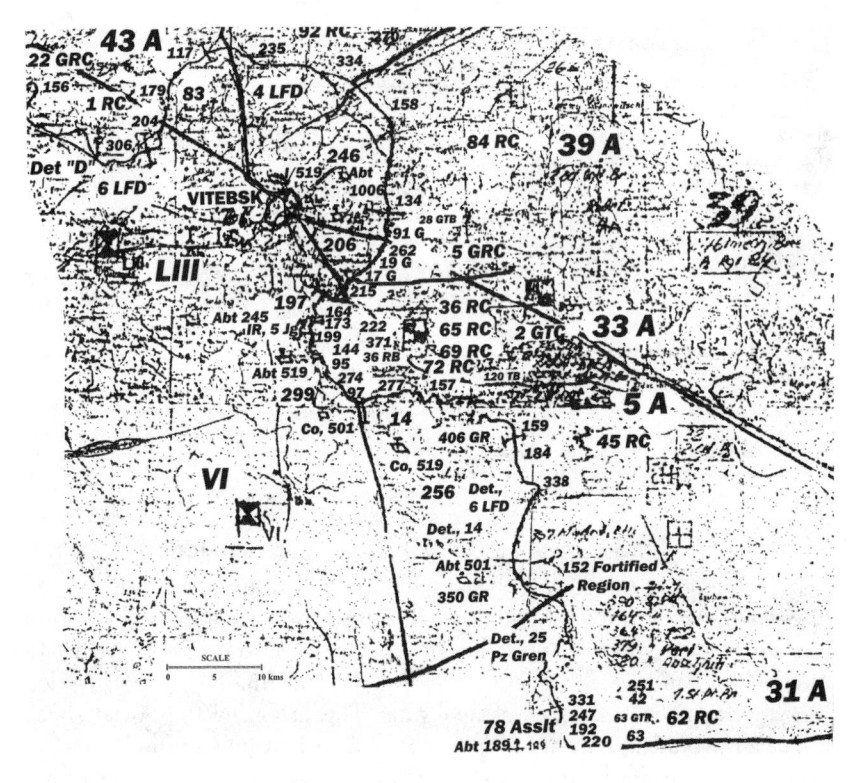

386   The Struggle for Belorussia, December 1943–April 1944

Map 15.3. The Situation at Vitebsk and East of Orsha, 10–18 March 1944

deep into the German defenses, capture the strongpoint at Lazyrshchiki, 3 kilometers south of Osintori, and record even more modest gains to the north in two days of heavy fighting. However, from the very start, the attack north and south of the Orsha-Smolensk road stalled in the face of withering German fire. Gluzdovsky and Grishin committed 220th and 192nd Rifle Divisions to combat along the road on 6 March, but neither force was able to make any progress, and the entire offensive collapsed in failure by 9 March.

During this short but violent offensive, German Fourth Army and XXVII Army Corps reinforced 78th Assault Division with a *kampfgruppe* from 25th Panzer Grenadier Division, which it committed on 4 March north of Osintori, and Tiger tanks from 505th Panzer *Abteilung*, which went into action along the Orsha-Smolensk road. In addition, as if to underscore the utter futility of Sokolovsky's poorly coordinated offensive, Third Panzer Army dispatched most of 5th Jäger Division from the Luchesa River front to the Orsha region by 9 March, by doing so ensuring the futility of any further Soviet attacks along the Orsha axis. Although desultory fighting continued in the region until mid-March, Sokolovsky would have to look elsewhere if he hoped to fulfill any of the missions assigned to him by the *Stavka* (see Map 15.3).

Sokolovsky's forces suffered another 7,537 casualties in the Orsha offensive, including 1,898 dead and 5,639 wounded, but with virtually nothing to show for it in terms of territorial gains. Nowhere did the attacking forces gain more than a single kilometer of ground. However, if Sokolovsky believed this would affect the *Stavka*'s ambitions for some offensive success in the region, he was sorely mistaken. Within days after his *front*'s assault at Vitebsk and Orsha failed, the *Stavka* ordered him to mount a fresh assault in the region, this time in an effort to expand the Arguny salient southward toward Bogushevsk.

THE WESTERN FRONT'S BOGUSHEVSK OFFENSIVE (21–29 MARCH 1944)

Planning

As was the case with previous stages of the fighting around Vitebsk, Soviet open-source literature describing the Western Front's final offensive in this region during its winter campaign is minimal at best. The *Stavka*'s critique contained in General Gareev's exposé provides only a skeletal description of this offensive, which it terms the "Bogushevsk Operation":

> **The Bogushevsk Operation 21–29 March 1944**
> *Our forces.* The following forces were concentrated to conduct the operation: 9 rifle divisions, including 6 rifle divisions in first echelon and 3 rifle divisions in second echelon, 10 artillery brigades, 6 RGK artillery regiments, 5 tank brigades, and 4 self-propelled artillery regiments, for a total of 73 tanks. The artillery density ranged from 100 to 150 tubes per kilometer of front.
> *Enemy forces.* 2 infantry divisions, up to 5 artillery regiments, and up to 40 tanks.
> The offensive on the Bogushevsk axis, 21–29 March 1944, penetrated to a depth of from 1 to 3.5 kilometers [.6 to 2.2 miles]. Our losses were 9,207 men killed and 30,828 men wounded for a total of *40,035 men*.[3]

General Krylov, the commander of 5th Army, who directed the operation, provides only brief remarks on its nature and conduct:

> Returning to the army's offensive operations during the first few months of 1944, one must note that they were aimed primarily at improving the position of our forces for the delivery of subsequent blows against the enemy. The nature of these battles, which took place, in particular, during the period from 21 through 23 March, is best exemplified, for example, by the operations by 277th Rifle Division to capture Hill 181.3 and the populated point of Starintsy, which was located nearby.

The enemy well understood that the loss of these important positions would mean opening the way to Vitebsk for our forces. This is why he created a strong defense here with trenches, coils of barbed wire, minefields, and pillboxes girdling the hill and the village. This immediately led to combat of a most fierce nature.[4]

As far as Soviet documents are concerned, as of yet, none have been released on the March 1944 stage of the Vitebsk operation. However, we do know that the *Stavka* replaced some of the Western Front's senior command cadre in March, probably because of its poor combat performance during January and February. For example, on 13 March the *Stavka* relieved General Gordov as commander of 33rd Army, replacing him with Colonel General I. E. Petrov.[5] During the same period, General Oleshev returned from convalescent leave to take command of 33rd Army's 36th Rifle Corps from General Iovlev, and the *Narodnyi komissariat oborony* (NKO, or Peoples Commissariat of Defense) assigned Major General G. N. Perekrestov to replace General Komarov as the commander of the army's 65th Rifle Corps.

As he prepared for a new offensive, Sokolovsky retained all of his other corps commanders, but the *Stavka* shuffled the *front's* task organization to suit the missions it ordered him to perform (see Table 15.3).

For example, the *Stavka* withdrew 81st and 61st Rifle Corps from 33rd and 49th Armies, assigning the former to the new 20th Army and the latter to 69th Army, both of which it retained in its reserve. The divisions subordinate to the two corps, however, remained with the Western Front. In addition, the *Stavka* transferred 62nd Rifle Corps and its three rifle divisions from 49th Army to 33rd Army and directed Sokolovsky to employ the corps in his new offensive.

Because Sokolovsky's forces had failed to destroy the so-called German Vysochany Grouping (VI Army Corps' 14th and 256th Infantry Divisions and 201st and 221st Security Divisions' 406th and 350th Grenadier Regiments) on the southern flank of the Arguny salient by employing an indirect approach, in mid-March the *Stavka* ordered him to do so by attacking it frontally. In response, Sokolovsky decided to conduct a massive assault against German defenses along the southern face of the Arguny salient with a shock group consisting of three full rifle corps, supported by a fourth rifle corps deployed on the shock group's left and a fifth rifle corps in reserve (see Map 15.4). He designated 69th and 36th Rifle Corps of General Petrov's 33rd Army, with a total of five rifle divisions and one rifle brigade, and 72nd Rifle Corps of General Krylov's 5th Army, with three rifle divisions, as the nucleus of his main shock group. Then he ordered the three rifle corps to assault the defenses of German 299th and 14th Infantry Divisions in the 12-kilometer-wide sector between Makarova, southeast of Perevoz, and Shugaevo.[6] The 33rd Army's shock group was to be supported by 23rd and 213th Tank Brigades.

Table 15.3. The Western Front's Order of Battle on 1 April 1944

WESTERN FRONT
Army General V. D. Sokolovsky (Colonel General I. D. Cherniakhovsky on 12 April)

39th Army: LTG N. E. Berzarin
  5th Guards Rifle Corps: MG I. P. Ivanov
    17th Guards Rifle Division
    19th Guards Rifle Division
    91st Guards Rifle Division
  84th Rifle Corps: MG E. V. Dobrovol'sky
    158th Rifle Division
    262nd Rifle Division
  28th Guards Tank Brigade

33rd Army: Col. G I. E. Petrov
  36th Rifle Corps: MG N. N. Oleshev
    199th Rifle Division
    215th Rifle Division
    371st Rifle Division
  62nd Rifle Corps: MG A. F. Naumov
    63rd Rifle Division
    251st Rifle Division
    352nd Rifle Division
  65th Rifle Corps: MG G. N. Perekrestov
    144th Rifle Division
    164th Rifle Division
  69th Rifle Corps: MG N. N. Mul'tan
    42nd Rifle Division
    222nd Rifle Division
  274th Rifle Division
  36th Rifle Brigade
  2nd Guards Tank Corps: Col. A. S. Burdeinyi
    4th Guards Tank Brigade
    25th Guards Tank Brigade
    26th Guards Tank Brigade
    4th Guards Motorized Rifle Brigade
  1500th Tank Destroyer Brigade
  79th Motorcycle Battalion
  755th Separate Tank Destroyer Artillery Battalion
  273rd Mortar Regiment
  28th Guards-Mortar Battalion
  1695th Antiaircraft Artillery Regiment
  23rd Guards Tank Brigade
  43rd Guards Tank Brigade
  213th Tank Brigade
  256th Tank Brigade
  735th Self-propelled Artillery Regiment
  1819th Self-propelled Artillery Regiment
  1830th Heavy Self-propelled Artillery Regiment

5th Army: LTG N. I. Krylov
  45th Rifle Corps: MG S. G. Poplavsky
    157th Rifle Division
    159th Rifle Division
    338th Rifle Division
  72nd Rifle Corps: MG Iu. M. Prokof'ev
    97th Rifle Division
    173rd Rifle Division
    184th Rifle Division
    277th Rifle Division
  120th Tank Brigade
  153rd Tank Brigade
  1435th Self-propelled Artillery Regiment

31st Army: LTG V. A. Gluzdovsky
  71st Rifle Corps: MG A. Ia. Vedenin
    192nd Rifle Division
    220th Rifle Division
    331st Rifle Division
  88th Rifle Division
  152nd Fortified Region
  42nd Guards Tank Brigade
  63rd Guards Separate Tank Regiment
  2nd Guards Motorcycle Regiment
  52nd Separate Armored Train Battalion

49th Army: LTG I. T. Grishin
  113th Rifle Corps: MG T. P. Krugliakov
    70th Rifle Division
    344th Rifle Division
    62nd Rifle Division
    174th Rifle Division
  6th Separate Armored Train Battalion

Front Reserves:
  154th Fortified Region
  2nd Guards Tank Brigade
  722nd Self-propelled Artillery Regiment
  1445th Self-propelled Artillery Regiment
  12th Separate Aerosleigh Battalion
  41st Separate Aerosleigh Battalion

Source: Boevoi sostav Sovetskoi Armii, chast' IV (Ianvar'–dekabr' 1944) [The combat composition of the Soviet Army, pt. 4 (January–December 1944)] (Moscow: Voenizdat, 1988), 100–101.

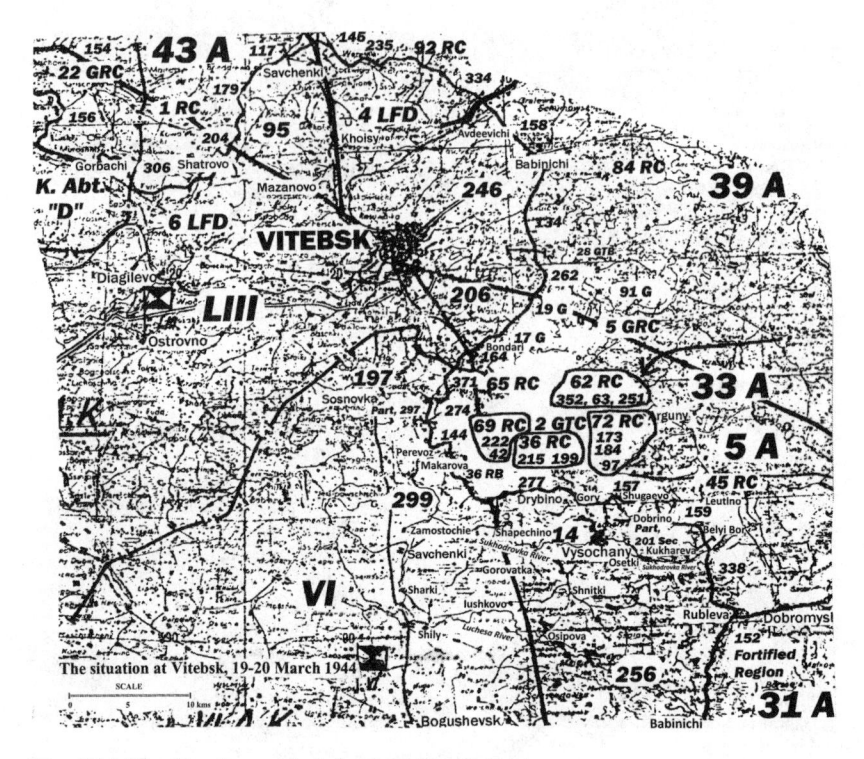

Map 15.4. The Situation at Vitebsk, 19–20 March 1944

The shock group's immediate mission was to penetrate German defenses in the sector indicated, capture the Germans' strongpoints at the towns of Drybino and Dobrino, and then advance southward 5 to 10 kilometers to the Sukhodrovka River line.[7] Subsequently, the shock group was to force the Sukhodrovka, capture the towns of Gorovatka and Vysochany, drive German forces back to the upper reaches of the Luchesa River from Sharki to Osipova, and seize bridgeheads across the river for use in future offensives. This required the shock group's forces to advance up to 15 kilometers into the Germans' defenses.

After the Western Front's shock group successfully penetrated the Germans' forward defenses, the three rifle divisions of 5th Army's 45th Rifle Corps were to join the offensive by conducting a supporting attack from the Leutino region on the shock group's left flank and advance southward in tandem with the main shock group to reach the Luchesa River between Osipova and Babinovichi. Finally, Sokolovsky retained the three divisions of 33rd Army's 62nd Rifle Corps in second echelon with orders to reinforce the shock group whenever necessary throughout its advance.

Meanwhile, on the shock group's right flank and the Western Front's right wing, 84th and 5th Guards Rifle Corps of Berzarin's 39th Army were to remain on the defense in the sector from Avdeevichi on the Western Dvina River, 13 kilometers northeast of Vitebsk, southward to Bondari, 10 kilometers southeast of Vitebsk, and 65th Rifle Corps of Petrov's 33rd Army was to defend the sector from Bondari to Perevoz along the Luchesa River front.

Prior to the offensive, Sokolovsky tried to conceal his offensive intent and preparations by retaining only a minimal force in his forward positions, particularly in the sectors from which he planned to launch his main and supporting attacks. As he did so, he attempted to regroup and assemble the rifle corps that constituted his massive main shock group secretly deep in the *front*'s rear area. For example, 36th Rifle Brigade served as the covering force for 69th Rifle Corps, and 277th and 157th Rifle Divisions performed the same function on the behalf of 36th and 72nd Rifle Corps. After the shock group's corps deployed forward into their jumping-off positions, most likely during the two nights preceding the attack, the covering divisions and brigade either reverted to second echelon or concentrated into narrower sectors to participate in the attack.

Unlike previous offensives, this time Sokolovsky provided 33rd Army a far greater density of supporting artillery, ultimately producing a density of 150 artillery and mortar tubes per kilometer of front. However, the excessive distance from the front to its ammunition warehouses still kept the combat loads of artillery well below what was required.[8]

After it was completed, Sokolovsky's plan pitted the shock group's eight rifle divisions, one rifle brigade, five tank brigades, and four self-propelled artillery regiments, with a total of seventy-three tanks, against an initial German force of two infantry divisions supported by roughly forty tanks and assault guns (see Table 15.4). This accorded Sokolovsky a fourfold superiority in infantry and a twofold superiority in armor during the penetration battle. Thereafter, Sokolovsky planned to reinforce his main effort with three more rifle divisions from 33rd Army's 62nd Rifle Corps. In addition, in his supporting attack, Sokolovsky planned to unleash two to three additional rifle divisions against a force of roughly two German infantry regiments. The principal unanswered question was, "How soon could the Germans reinforce their defenses and with how many forces could they do so?"

The Third Panzer Army's chief problem during the March phase of its defensive fighting was its near total lack of operational or even sizable tactical reserves. Coupled with the end of Soviet offensive action northwest of Vitebsk, the heavy fighting in other sectors of the front during February and March prompted the OKH to transfer, in succession, 12th, 211th, and 131st Infantry and 20th Panzer Divisions to other sectors of the front or to the rear for rest and refitting. Consequently, by 20 March the panzer army's LIII Army Corps was defending the northwestern, northern, northeastern, and eastern approaches to Vitebsk with 6th Luftwaffe Field, 95th Infantry, 4th Luftwaffe Field, and 246th and 206th Infantry Divisions. The latter two divisions, which defended the roughly 25-kilometer-long, arc-shaped sector

Table 15.4. The Estimated Correlation of Opposing Forces in the Bogushevsk Offensive, 21–29 March 1944

OPPOSING FORCES	
Soviet	**German**
Western Front	
33rd Army	299th Infantry Division
5th Army	14th Infantry Division (Mot)
14 rifle divisions (8 in the shock group)	Kampfgruppen, 95th, 256th Infantry
1 rifle brigade (shock group)	and 201st SecurityDivisions, and
5 tank brigades	K. Abt. D
4 self-propelled artillery regiments (73 tanks)	501st Panzer and 519th Panzer Jäger Abteilung (about 20 guns and 20 Hornet 88mm antitank guns)

Depth of Soviet advance: 1–3.5 kilometers
Casualties: 40,035 men, including 9,207 killed and 30,828 wounded

Source: Makhmut Gareev, "O neudachnykh nastupatel'nykh operatsiiakh sovetskikh voisk v Velikoi Otechestvennoi voine. Po neopublikovannym dokumentam GKO" [About unsuccessful offensive operations of Soviet forces in the Great Patriotic War. According to unpublished GKO documents], *Novaia i noveishaia istoriia* [New and newest history] 1 (January 1994): 17; H Gr Mitte/Ia, KTB: Lagenkarten, 1–30 March 1944, *H. Gr Mitte, 65002/62 file*, in NAM series T-311, Roll 224; and "Anlagen zum Kriegstagebuch Nr. 8, Lagenkarten, Pz AOK 3, Ia, 1 Mar–31 Mar 1944," *Pz AOK 3, 54349/39 file*, in NAM series T-313, roll 304.

extending from the Western Dvina River to the Luchesa River, faced six rifle divisions of the Western Front's 39th Army and one rifle division from 33rd Army. Thus, LIII Army Corps' five divisions defending Vitebsk faced seven rifle divisions of the 1st Baltic Front's 43rd Army and seven more divisions of the Western Front's 39th Army. West of Vitebsk was LIII Corps' *Korps Abteilung* D (Corps Detachment D), a composite force made up of the remnants of three infantry divisions now reduced to regimental size.

Southeast and south of Vitebsk, VI Army Corps' defended the roughly 9-kilometer-wide Luchesa River front with 197th Infantry Division and the more than 20-kilometer-wide sector south of the Arguny salient with 299th and 14th Infantry Divisions and 201st Security Division's 406th Regiment. Thus, the most perilous situation that Third Panzer Army faced was along the Luchesa River front and along the southern face of the Arguny salient, where German intelligence estimated that VI Army Corps' three divisions and one separate regiment faced at least thirteen and perhaps as many as sixteen rifle divisions, one tank corps, and one rifle brigade.

Complicating matters for Third Panzer Army, both LIII and VI Army Corps defended with the bulk of their divisions deployed forward, backed up by company- and battalion-size reserves to the rear of each defending regiment, and neither army corps possessed operational reserves or tactical reserves larger than a battalion. Therefore, the only way these corps could contain Soviet assaults was by maneuvering their battalion-size *kampfgruppen* to and fro around the battlefield or by withdrawing forces from one sector of the front for employment in another. Although the Germans had already proved they could do this with ease, to do so effectively required excellent intelligence, and, even so, it was extremely dangerous.

The only saving grace for the German defenders was the presence in or near the Vitebsk sector of several panzer and assault gun detachments belonging to German Army Group Center but assigned to Third Panzer Army to stiffen its defenses. These included 501st Panzer and 519th Panzer *Jäger Abteilungen,* which fielded deadly *Hornisse* (Hornet) 88mm antitank guns, and 189th, 245th, and 281st Assault Gun *Abteilungen,* which, in theory, were equipped with 34 Stug III 75mm assault guns but seldom fielded that quantity. Given the paucity of armor available to the Soviets, these detachments often either turned the tide of battle in the Germans' favor or at least forestalled major defeats.

The three rifle corps forming the forward element of Sokolovsky's main shock group deployed forward into their jumping-off positions on the nights of 19–20 and 20–21 March and prepared to commence their assault the following morning (see Map 15.4). On the shock group's right wing, 222nd and 42nd Rifle Divisions of 33rd Army's 69th Rifle Corps relieved 36th Rifle Brigade, and the latter withdrew into the corps' second echelon. In the shock group's center, 33rd Army's 36th Rifle Corps deployed its 215th Rifle Division forward into positions occupied by 5th Army's 277th Rifle Division, the 277th concentrated on 36th Corps' right wing and 199th Rifle Division deployed in second echelon. On the shock group's left wing, 5th Army's 72nd Rifle Corps deployed its 97th and 184th Rifle Divisions forward into positions occupied by 157th Rifle Division; the 157th then shifted to the left, and the corps retained its 173rd Rifle Division in second echelon.

The 5th Army's 45th Rifle Corps, earmarked to conduct the supporting attack after the main shock force successfully penetrated the Germans' forward defenses, left its 157th, 159th, and 338th Rifle Divisions in their existing forward positions, although 157th Division moved its forces to the left after 72nd Rifle Corps relieved the forces on its right. However, as soon as the main shock group launched its attack, the 157th and 159th Rifle Divisions were to concentrate their forces in the Belyi Bor region, where their flanks adjoined, and prepare to join the attack.

The shock group's missions and final combat formation reflected the simplicity and directness of Sokolovsky's offensive plan (see Table 15.5).

In the 3.5-kilometer-wide sector extending from Makarova eastward to the Vitebsk-Orsha road on the shock group's right wing, Mul'tan's 69th Rifle Corps deployed 42nd and 222nd Rifle Divisions from left to right in first echelon backed up by 36th Rifle Brigade in second echelon. The mission of Mul'tan's corps was to penetrate defenses manned by 1st and 2nd Battalions of German 299th Infantry Division's 530th Grenadier Regiment and the division's 299th Pioneer Battalion; capture the strongpoints at Sheliai,

Table 15.5. The Probable Combat Formations of 39th, 33rd, and 5th Armies and Opposing German Forces on 21 March 1944 (as deployed from north to south)

FORCE (sector)	OPPOSING GERMAN FORCES
1st/2nd/3rd Echelons (Mobile group)	
	THIRD PANZER ARMY
WESTERN FRONT	LIII Army Corps
39th Army (Avdeevichi, Bondari)	
84th RC (Avdeevichi, Krasovshchina)	246th ID
158th RD (Avdeevichi, Babinichi)	
134th RD (Babinichi, Pushkari)	
262nd RD (Pushkari, Krasovshchina)	
5th GRC (Krasovshchina, Bondari)	206th ID
19th GRD/91st GRD (Krasovshchina, Ugliane)	
17th GRD (Ugliane, Bondari)	
33rd Army (Bondari, west of Gory)	
65th RC (Bondari, Makarova)	
164th RD (Bondari, Luchesa River)	VI Army Corps
371st RD (Mikhailovo bridgehead)	197th ID
274th RD (Starintsy, Bukshtyny)	
144th RD (Bukshtyny, Makarova)	
MAIN SHOCK GROUP	
69th RC (Makarova, Vitebsk-Orsha road)	
222nd RD/36th Rifle Brigade (Makarova, Sheliai)	299th ID
42nd RD (Sheliai, Vitebsk-Orsha road)	
36th RC (Vitebsk-Orsha road, west of Gory)	
215th RD/199th RD (west of Gory, Zyzyby)	
277th RD (Zyzyby, west of Gory)	14th ID, part,
62nd RC (63rd, 251st, 352nd RDs)	299th ID
(Kopti region)	
5th Army (west of Gory, Rubleva)	
72nd RC (west of Gory, Shugaevo)	Kgr., Corps Abt. D
97th RD/173rd RD (west of Gory, D'iakovina)	
184th RD (D'iakovina, Shugaevo)	
SUPPORTING ATTACK GROUP	
45th RC (Shugaevo, Rubleva)	
157th RD (Shugaevo, Belyi Bor)	406th IR,
159th RD (Belyi Bor, Mar'ianovo)	201st SecD
338th RD (Mar'ianovo, Rubleva)	456th IR, 256th ID
2nd GTC (mobile group)	
(4th, 25th, and 26th GTBs and 4th GMRB)	

Source: *Boevoi sostav Sovetskoi Armii, chast' IV (Ianvar'–dekabr' 1944 g.)* [The combat composition of the Soviet Army, pt. 4 (January–December 1944)] (Moscow: Voenizdat, 1988), 70, 100; "Anlagen zum Kriegstagebuch Nr. 8, Lagenkarten Band VII, Pz AOK 3, Ia, 1 Jan–31 Jan 1943," *Pz AOK 3, 49113/26 file*, in NAM Series T-313, Roll 296; and "Anlagen zum Kriegstagebuch Nr. 8, Lagenkarten, Pz AOK 3, Ia, 1 Mar–31 Mar 1944," *Pz AOK 3, 54349/39 file*, in NAM series T-313, roll 304.

Luskinopol', Pushcha (Kuzmintsy), and Podgorno; seize a bridgehead over the Sukhodrovka River; advance southward along the Luchesa River's eastern bank to capture Zamostochie, Sharki, and Shily; establish defenses on the river's eastern bank; and protect the shock group's right flank.

On Mul'tan's left and in the shock group's center, Oleshev's 36th Rifle Corps was to attack in the 5-kilometer-wide sector from the Vitebsk-Orsha road eastward to just west of Gory, with 215th and 277th Rifle Divisions in first echelon and 199th Rifle Division in second echelon. Oleshev's forces were to penetrate defenses occupied by 2nd Battalion of 14th Infantry Division's 101st Grenadier Regiment and 1st Battalion of its 53rd Grenadier Regiment; capture the strongpoints at Kossetachi, Drybino, and Starina; secure a bridgehead over the Sukhodrovka River east of Shapechino; and continue their advance southward to occupy defenses along the Sukhodrovka River from Shily eastward to Iushkovo.

On the shock group's left wing, Prokof'ev's 72nd Rifle Corps was to attack in the 3.5-kilometer sector from west of Gory to Shugaevo, with 97th and 184th Rifle Divisions in first echelon and 173rd Rifle Division in second echelon. After penetrating defenses occupied by 2nd Battalion of 14th Infantry Division's 53rd Grenadier Regiment, the division's fusilier and engineer (pioneer) battalions, and a *kampfgruppe* from 201st Security Division's 406th Regiment, Prokof'ev's corps was to capture the German strongpoints at Cherkassy and Vysokoe, force the Sukhodrovka River and capture Buraki and Vysochany, and continue the attack southward to reach the Luchesa River from Iushkovo eastward to Osipova.

Although all three of the forward rifle corps in Sokolovsky's shock group occupied sectors 3.5–5 kilometers wide to increase the shock and penetrating power of the attack, each corps concentrated its assault in two 3-kilometer-wide main attack sectors. This meant that Sokolovsky's rifle divisions, still significantly understrength, attacked in sectors approximately 1 to 1.5 kilometers wide.

After the forward rifle corps of his shock group had fulfilled their immediate missions of seizing bridgeheads across the Sukhodrovka River, Sokolovsky planned to commit the three rifle divisions of Major General A. F. Naumov's 62nd Rifle Corps into action in the sector of 36th Rifle Corps, with the mission to lead the advance to the Luchesa River, the army's final objective. After Naumov's corps reached the river, it and the shock group's other rifle corps were to employ whatever means necessary to seize bridgeheads across the river for use in subsequent offensives.

On the shock group's left, Poplavsky's 45th Rifle Corps of Krylov's 5th Army was to conduct a supporting attack after the *front*'s main shock group finished penetrating German defenses farther to the west. Poplavsky was to conduct his assault with most of 157th and 159th Rifle Divisions, which were to concentrate their forces in the Belyi Bor sector, 2 kilometers east of Dobrino. Attacking in a 2-kilometer-wide sector defended by a battalion of 201st Security Division's 406th Regiment and 1st Battalion of 14th Infantry Division's 101st Regiment, the force was to capture the strongpoints at Zagorny and Kukhareva (Kuchareva), 2–3 kilometers east of Vysochany; seize a crossing over the Sukhodrovka River at Osetki, 4 kilometers southeast of Vysochany; and continue their advance southward in tandem with the *front*'s shock group to reach the Luchesa River in the sector from Osipova southeastward 15 kilometers to Babinichi.

If Sokolovsky's attack proved successful, the Western Front's forces would be ideally positioned to conduct a future major offensive effort to expel German forces from Vitebsk, Orsha, or both vital German defensive bastions.

The Battle

The three first-echelon rifle corps of Sokolovsky's shock group assaulted the Germans' forward defenses across the entire penetration front at dawn on 21 March after an intense artillery preparation (see Map 15.5). The immense force of the initial assault collapsed German defenses along the entire front from Makarova to D'iakovina, and the corps' first-echelon rifle divisions advanced 1 to 4 kilometers on the first day of the attack. On the shock group's right flank and in its center, 222nd Rifle Division of Mul'tan's 69th Rifle Corps captured the Germans' strongpoint at Sheliai, and 215th and 277th Rifle Divisions of Oleshev's 36th Rifle Corps seized the strongpoint at Kossetachi, reached the northern outskirts of Starina, and isolated the German defenders in the Drybino strongpoint from three sides. On the shock group's left, however, while 97th Rifle Division, situated on the left wing of Prokof'ev's 72nd Rifle Corps, was able to crush the Germans' salient south of Gory, the corps' 184th Rifle Division was stopped cold by the Germans' defenses at Shugaevo.

The fierce fighting continued on 22 March, when 215th and 277th Rifle Divisions of Oleshev's 36th Rifle Corps captured the Germans' strongpoints at Drybino and Starina and forced the defending German forces to withdraw roughly 1 kilometer southward to new defense lines north of the Sukhodrovka River. However, despite conducting repeated heavy assaults, neither Mul'tan's 69th Rifle Corps nor Prokof'ev's 72nd Rifle Corps recorded any additional gains on the second day of fighting.

In his memoirs, Krylov provides a brief description of the sharp fight for Starina, which seems to have characterized the fierce nature of the struggle across the entire front:

> Our subunits [from 277th Rifle Division] operated courageously and tenaciously [in their assaults on Hill 181.3 and Starina]. Private Andrei Kovalenko of 850th Rifle Regiment especially distinguished himself during the storming of the hill. At one of the decisive moments in the battle, he led a group of soldiers that penetrated to the heights of the hill and drove the Hitlerites from their bunkers with grenades. After forcing the enemy to turn and run, the group captured part of the bunker.

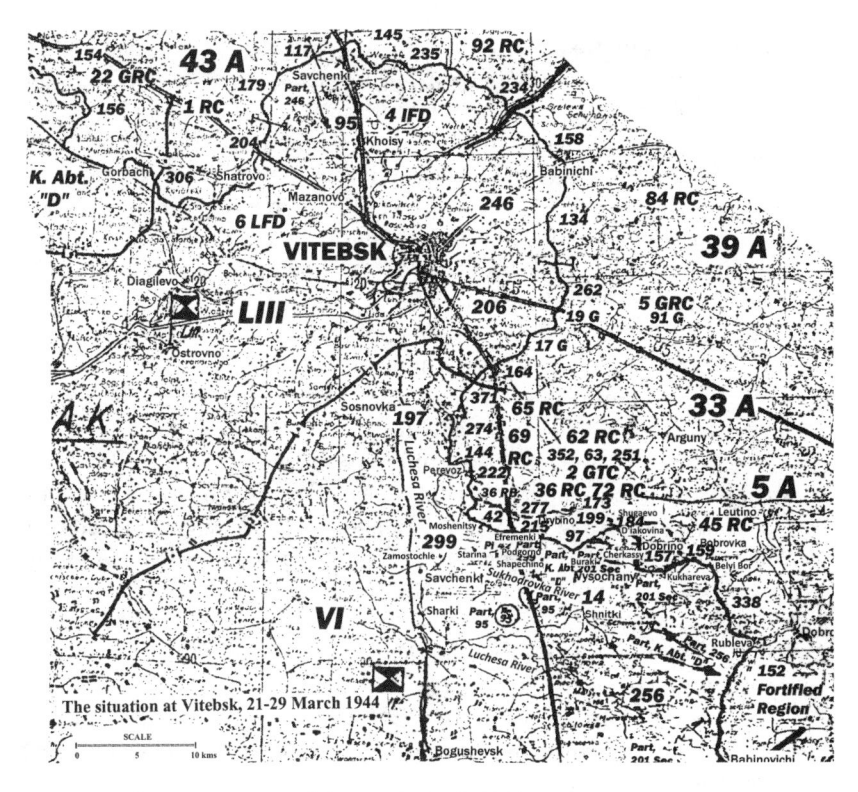

Map 15.5. The Situation at Vitebsk, 21–29 March 1944

After regaining their composure, the enemy tried to counterattack three times but was thrown back by automatic weapons fire and grenades. The handful of heroes held on to the hill until its battalion arrived.

Sergeant Makhmet Utarov's squad of 854th Rifle Regiment acted just as boldly in the battle for Starina. After fearlessly penetrating into the enemy's first trenches, the squad's soldiers blazed a path for themselves into the second with the bayonets and grenades. However, they fell under a hail of large-caliber machine gun fire and failed to reach it. The Hitlerites who were firing from it occupied very favorable positions—under burned-out tanks. They covered the entire space that Utarov's squad and the subunits following it advanced. It seemed as if the Fascists' machine guns themselves were invulnerable. However, Komsomol member Utarov was of a different mind over the matter.

Attentively examining the terrain, he crawled on all fours from hollow to hollow, beginning to move forward. The daredevil managed to approach right up to the machine gun unnoticed. He then destroyed the positions with an accurately thrown grenade. The machine gun fell silent.

The way forward was clear. The soldiers sprang up on the signal of their commander. One more impetuous rush, and they were not far from the village. The entire platoon was approaching it.

The Hitlerites then began to launch a counterattack. They were clearly trying to encircle the platoon. During this time the platoon's commander was severely wounded, and some confusion reigned among the soldiers. But it lasted only for a single moment. Utarov, who had also been wounded, found the strength to take command of the platoon. After this the soldiers repelled the counterattack. Soon after, the regiment's artillery began raining shells on the enemy, and Utarov's subunit penetrated into the village hard on the heels of the artillery fire.

All of this occurred so quickly that the battalions' approaching main forces succeeded in finally driving the Hitlerites from Starina.

The army's forces halted their offensive on 24 March. After this date, we undertook active operations only in local sectors. Finally, in mid-April the army went over to the defense for a long period, digging in along the Moshenitsy, Kosachi, Drybino, Cherkassy, and Rubleva line, where its forces began to prepare for a decisive offensive in the future.[9]

As brief and sparse as they as they are, Krylov' few remarks fit nicely into the battle as it was actually fought.

The German Third Panzer Army and VI Army Corps responded quickly, effectively, and resolutely to the looming threat. Immediately after the Soviet attack began, 299th Infantry Division deployed its reserve infantry battalion and engineer battalion forward, the former to reinforce its defenses at Starina and the latter its defenses at Podgorno. Shortly thereafter, Third Panzer Army moved a *kampfgruppe* from Corps Detachment D into defenses along the Vitebsk-Orsha road to reinforce its defenses at the boundary of 299th and 14th Infantry Divisions. In addition, it shifted a battalion from 201st Security Division's 406th Regiment from the Mar'ianovo sector to Starina, replacing it with a battalion from 256th Infantry Division.

Although these reinforcements helped contain 69th Rifle Corps assault west of the Vitebsk-Orsha road, they did not prevent the loss of Starina to 36th Rifle Corps' 277th Rifle Division the next day. Therefore, on 22 March the Third Panzer Army sent fresh reinforcements to the sounds of the guns. Then, it dispatched another battalion from 299th Infantry Division to the Drybino region as well as a *kampfgruppe* from Corps Detachment D to Starina, although the two forces did not arrive in time to prevent the town from falling to an assault by 36th Rifle Corps' 215th Rifle Division.

In addition, Third Panzer deployed two *kampfgruppen* from 95th Infantry Division to the Starobobyl'e region on the Vitebsk-Orsha road south of Shapechino, the first of which arrived late on 22 March and the second early on 23 March. While these forces blocked the Soviet advance southward along the road, another *kampfgruppe* from Corps Detachment D reached the same region early on 23 March.

Although these reinforcements helped ease the situation somewhat, a renewed assault by Sokolovsky's shock groups on 23 March again threatened the Germans with disaster. This time, Sokolovsky ordered his three rifle corps to commit their second-echelon divisions to action in an attempt to break through to and across the Sukhodrovka River. Although Mul'tan's 69th Rifle Corps made little progress west of the Vitebsk-Orsha road, in two days of heavy fighting, Oleshev's 36th and Prokof'ev's 72nd Rifle Corps succeeded in penetrating 14th Infantry Division's defenses and new defenses erected by reinforcing *kampfgruppen* from Corps Detachment D and 201st Security Division south of Starina; captured the German strongpoints at Sharki, Kuzmentsy, and Efremenki; and advanced up to 1 kilometer toward Buraki.

The VI Army Corps responded by committing one of 95th Infantry Division's *kampfgruppe* on the left flank of Corps Detachment D west of Cherkassy and a *kampfgruppe* from 256th Infantry Division to bolster 201st Security Division's defenses east of the village strongpoint. The combined efforts of these forces, plus the defending units of 14th Infantry Division, managed to contain the Soviet attack, if only barely, thus preventing Krylov's forces from breaking through to the Sukhodrovka River.

Early on 24 March, Sokolovsky ordered his main shock group's three rifle corps to redouble their efforts to break through German VI Army Corps' defenses. To that end, he began releasing the forces of Naumov's 62nd Rifle Corps to reinforce the shock group's assault. Although the timing of their commitment to combat and the precise sector in which each entered combat remains unclear, during the ensuing three days, he likely reinforced 69th Rifle Corps with 352nd Rifle Division, 36th Rifle Corps with 63rd Rifle Division, and 72nd Rifle Corps with 251st Rifle Division. Strengthened by these reinforcements, Prokof'ev's reinforced 72nd Rifle Corps, then captured the D'iakovina strongpoint, advanced up to 2 kilometers more, and reached the northwestern outskirts of Vysochany, where its advance once again ground to a halt.

Once again, VI Army Corps was able to halt or contain the Soviets' new offensive by reinforcing its defenses, particularly north of Vysochany, with an impressive array of *kampfgruppen* quickly redeployed from other sectors of the front. These included a second *kampfgruppe* from 95th Infantry Division, battalion-size *kampfgruppen* from 246th Infantry Division and Corps Detachment D, and several more battalions from 256th Infantry Division. Perhaps most important of all, it also committed Tiger tanks and assault guns from 501st and 519th Panzer Detachments and 187th Assault Gun *Abteilungen* into the fray to stiffen 14th Infantry Division's sagging forward defenses.

As Sokolovsky's main effort was unfolding north and northwest of Vysochany, 45th Rifle Corps of Krylov's 5th Army began its secondary effort in

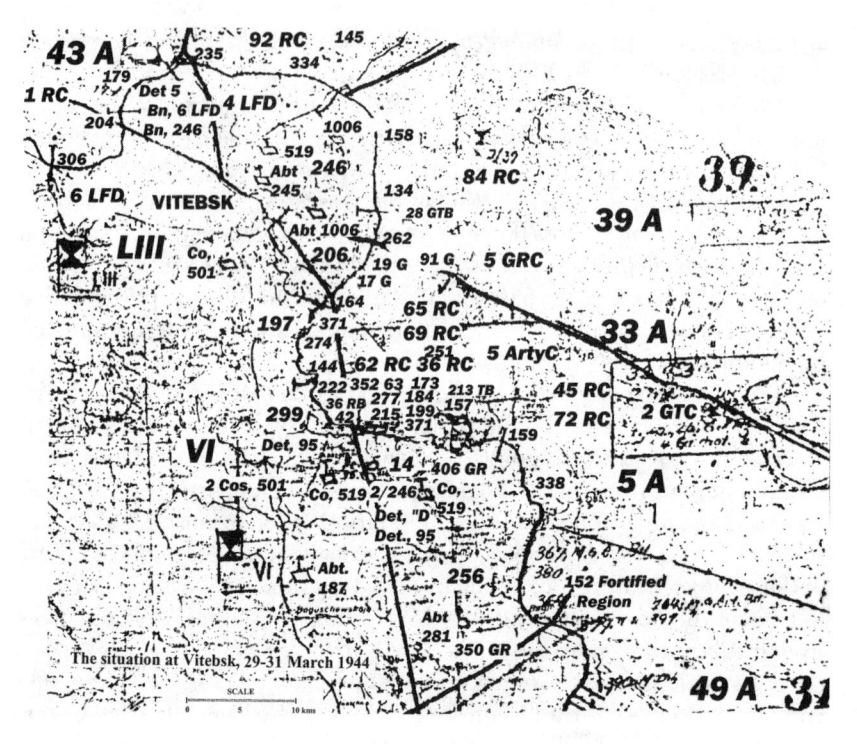

400   The Struggle for Belorussia, December 1943–April 1944

Map 15.6. The Situation at Vitebsk, 29–31 March 1944

the Belyi Bor region 6 kilometers to the east. On either 24 or 25 March, 157th and 159th Rifle Divisions of Poplavsky's corps struck the defenses of 201st Security Division's 406th Regiment southwest of Dobrino. Because the security division had already dispatched several battalions westward to assist in the defense against the Soviet main shock group, Poplavsky's two divisions penetrated to a depth of 2 kilometers and captured Kukhareva, threatening to outflank German defenses at Dobrino from the south. Once again, however, rapid reaction by VI Army Corps staved off defeat. On 26 March it reinforced 201st Security Division's beleaguered regiment with a battalion from 256th Infantry Division and, together, the defenders brought Poplavsky's assault to an abrupt halt short of both Dobrino and Vysochany.

Although fighting continued unabated through 29 March, after the 27th it was clear to Soviet and German alike that Sokolovsky's offensive had faltered. Furthermore, there was nothing he could do to reinvigorate it (see Map 15.6). In just over a week of heavy fighting, his shock group had advanced between 1 and 3.5 kilometers along a 14-kilometer front. Although his shock group managed to capture several German strongpoints in VI Army Corps' forward defenses, it not only failed to reach the Sukhodrovka

River, much less the Luchesa but also it proved unable to penetrate even the corps' first defensive belt. Worse still for Sokolovsky, his Western Front paid for its meager gains with another 40,035 casualties, including 9,207 dead and 30, 828 wounded.[10]

Once again, a Soviet archival document sums up the carnage the Western Front experienced in March 1944 (see Appendix L-1).

- Personnel (1–10 March)—27,258 men, with 33rd Army losing 12,261 men, including 2,146 killed and 8,849 wounded.
- Personnel (11–21 March)—9,973 men.
- Personnel (21–30 March)—20,630 men, including 4,029 killed and 12,855 wounded.[11]

This meant that the Western Front suffered another 57,861 casualties from all causes during March 1944, once again, most of them in Petrov's and Krylov's 33rd and 5th Armies.

After receiving reports of the fresh bloodletting in the Vitebsk region, the *Stavka* bowed to reality and permitted Sokolovsky to end his offensives and go over to the defense. It did not, however, forget his repeated failures, which in three months of fighting had cost the Red Army 235,832 casualties, including 39,055 dead and 186,777 wounded. This grim figure amounted to well over one-half of the force of 436,180 that the Western Front fielded on 3 January 1944.[12] No shrinking violet when it came to expending the Red Army's manpower in offensive operations, this toll was too high for even Stalin to endure. Within two weeks, Stalin would relieve the hapless Sokolovsky of his command.

CHAPTER 16

The Belorussian Front's Situation on 1 January 1944 and Preliminary Operations

PUNCH AND COUNTERPUNCH

As the Red Army's Kalinin (1st Baltic) and Western Fronts were pounding the defenses of German Army Group Center's Third Panzer Army in the Nevel', Gorodok, Vitebsk, and Orsha regions throughout the fall of 1943, at first registering notable gains but later only frustrating failures, Army General K. K. Rokossovsky's Central (Belorussian) Front recorded steady if not spectacular progress against the defenses of Army Group Center's Second and Ninth Armies in southern Belorussia (see Map 7.3). In October, Rokossovsky's forces pushed across the Sozh and Dnepr Rivers, seizing a sizable bridgehead at Loev on the Dnepr's western bank and pressing German forces on the river's eastern bank back into a bridgehead around the city of Gomel'. Skillfully exploiting his October gains, in early November, Rokossovsky's 65th and 61st Armies burst out westward from their bridgehead at Loev, captured Rechitsa on the Berezina River on 18 November and Gomel' on 25 November, and advanced to the eastern approaches to Parichi and Kalinkovichi by the time the offensive ended at month's end.

In early December, as the 1st and 2nd Baltic and Western Fronts were making yet another futile attempt to capture Vitebsk, Rokossovsky's Belorussian Front strove to exploit its November successes by fulfilling the mission assigned to him by the *Stavka,* that is, to capture Bobruisk and, if possible, Minsk. To do so, however, his *front* had to eliminate the formidable German center of resistance at Kalinkovichi, which, unless liquidated, posed a deadly threat to the left flank of any Red Army force advancing along the Parichi, Bobruisk, and Minsk axis.

Therefore, Rokossovsky directed General Batov to regroup his 65th Army and begin an offensive toward Kalinkovichi from the northeast on 8 December. Leaving his army's 19th Rifle Corps to defend the sector along the Berezina River from Shatsilki to south of Parichi, Batov ordered his 27th, 95th, and 18th Rifle Corps to attack the defenses of German Second Army's 4th Panzer Division at Ozarichi, north of Kalinkovichi, and 5th Panzer Division, northeast of Kalinkovichi. After they penetrated the Germans' defenses, the three corps were to capture Kalinkovichi and force Second Army to withdraw its forces from the Mozyr' region and all of southeastern Belorussia.[1]

Beginning their assault at dawn on 8 December, the three attacking corps recorded modest gains in three days of fighting, during which they drove a wedge between the two defending panzer divisions. Batov's offensive, however, faltered on 11 December with both Ozarichi and Kalinkovichi still in German hands. Nevertheless, although it failed, the limited successes 65th Army achieved caused a serious problem for Army Group Center and the OKH because Batov's forces succeeded in carving a sizable breach between the defenses of the army group's Second and Ninth Armies. This left Rokossovsky with the option of attacking westward toward Kalinkovichi or northwestward toward Bobruisk. Complicating matters further, Soviet possession of the so-called Rudobel'skie Gates, an undefended gap through the army group's defenses west of Parichi, offered Rokossovsky's forces unfettered access to Red partisan forces operating in the Germans' deep rear. Faced with this threat, the OKH had no choice but to order Army Group Center to close this menacing breach.

Field Marshal Busch's army group moved quickly to do so by ordering General Harpe's Ninth and General Weiss's Second Armies to mount counterstrokes against Batov's forces from the north and south. Catching both Batov and Rokossovsky by surprise, shock groups from Ninth Army's XXXXI Panzer Corps and Second Army's LVI Panzer Corps struck the right wing corps (the 19th) of Batov's 65th Army on 20 December. Spearheaded by fresh and the powerful 16th Panzer Division, XXXXI Panzer Corps attacked southward from Parichi, collapsing 65th Army's right wing. Simultaneously, Second Army's LVI Panzer Corps struck eastward from Ozarichi with its 12th Panzer Division. Several days later, the twin German panzer pincers encircled more than one-third of Batov's army. Thereafter, the two German panzer corps struggled mightily for three days to destroy Batov's encircled force, while Rokossovsky and Batov fought frantically to stave off further defeat.

In the end, however, this dramatic struggle ended with a whimper on 27 December, when a combination of stiffening Soviet resistance and the need to transfer 16th Panzer Division elsewhere left Ninth Army with no choice but to end its counterstroke. Despite the significant damage the counterstroke inflicted on Batov's army, by early January the offensive momentum in southern Belorussia inevitably swung back into Soviet hands. Although he acknowledged disappointment over his failure to reach Bobruisk or Kalinkovichi by the new year, Rokossovsky remained confident that his forces could at least seize Kalinkovichi and Mozyr' shortly after the year began.

Not only are there precious few Soviet open sources that describe the Belorussian Front's operations during the ensuing winter campaign but the Russians also have yet to release any formerly classified accounts of the action. Two articles about the Kalinkovichi offensive have appeared in Russian military journals as well as several more about the attack on Rogachev.

Otherwise, there are only fragmentary references to these operations in Russian memoir literature. Sadly, the memoirs of some of the most important Red Army military leaders, such as Batov, the commander of 65th Army, make no mention whatsoever of the winter fighting.

For example, the memoirs of Rokossovsky, the commander of the Belorussian Front, provide only a short but accurate description of his *front*'s role in the winter campaign:

> The so-called Zhitomir-Berdichev offensive operation by our neighbor to the left—the 1st Ukrainian Front, which continued until the first half of January 1944, began at the end of December. As a result, Soviet forces captured Novgorod-Volynskii, Zhitomir, Berdichev, and Belaia Tserkov and inflicted a serious defeat on the enemy.
>
> Everything led us to feel that the *Stavka* had shifted the center of gravity to the Ukraine and generally to the southern wing of the Soviet-German front. Formations from the *Stavka* Reserve—combined arms and tank armies, tank corps, artillery formations, tanks, guns, and aircraft were dispatched there.
>
> At the time, the Belorussian Front received nothing, even though our mission remained as before. We had to attack, but, as the *Stavka* perfectly well knew, our forces were ever decreasing.
>
> But we understood that it was impossible to do otherwise. Our mission was to attract as many enemy forces to us as possible by active operations and, by doing so, facilitate the offensive along the main axis. And we applied every effort to fulfill that mission. We did not count on major successes, but we did not stand in place.
>
> During the developing major offensives by the four Ukrainian *fronts*, while cooperating with the forces on the right wing of Vatutin's *front*, our units also achieved something: 61st Army captured Mozyr', the 65th—Kalinkovichi, the 48th improved its positions of the right bank of the Berezina [River], and, in exceptionally difficult conditions, 3rd Army forced the Dnepr River and captured Rogachev and a bridgehead on western bank, after forcing the enemy to clean out his bridgehead on the Dnepr River's eastern bank at Zhlobin. The 50th Army advanced a little on its left wing but was forced to deploy its front to the north since its neighbor—the Western Front's 10th Army—remained in place.
>
> The *front*'s forces conducted these operations with meager norms of ammunition.
>
> Only on 15 April was the Belorussian Front ordered to go on the defense by a *Stavka* directive.[2]

Characteristically, while understating his *front*'s achievements, the innately modest Rokossovsky shies away from any comparison between his *front*'s accomplishments and those of Sokolovsky's neighboring Western Front, leaving it to historians to restore his feats to the historical record.

Despite the paucity of source materials regarding the Belorussian Front's operations during the winter of 1944, German archival materials, supplemented by some newly released Russian archival materials, finally permit reconstruction of what actually took place in this hitherto obscure sector of the front. These materials prove that, although its main attention was indeed riveted to the south, the *Stavka* still harbored high expectations for what its *fronts* in eastern Belorussia could achieve. Furthermore, unlike Sokolovsky's Western Front to the north, Rokossovsky's Belorussian Front actually justified those high expectations.

As he focused on his most important objectives, specifically, the cities of Kalinkovichi, Mozyr', and Bobruisk, Rokossovsky devised an offensive plan designed to keep Army Group Center's Ninth and Second Armies perpetually off balance. In essence, his plan involved conducting a series of offensives in staggered fashion across the entire front to register gains wherever possible, to tie down German front-line forces and reserves, and to distract German attention and combat resources from what he considered the most vital operational sectors. This plan, which ultimately characterized Rokossovsky's operations throughout the entire winter campaign, required his armies, either singly or in combination, to conduct a series of successive operations. Although many of these operations were local (tactical) in nature, others were important operationally and, at least potentially, even strategically. Furthermore, while all of these offensive operations helped distract German attention and resources from the vital battles under way in the Ukraine, they also sought and often succeeded in attaining genuine objectives of their own.

Rokossovsky's offensive plan began unfolding in earnest along the eastern bank of the Dnepr River in the first few days of January 1944. For context, the daily combat journals of 48th and 63rd Armies provide an overview of the situation on 1 January 1944 (see Appendix M-1 and Appendix M-2).

THE BYKHOV OFFENSIVE AND 10TH ARMY'S SUPPORTING ATTACK AT CHAUSY (3–8 JANUARY 1944)

Planning

The first stage of Rokossovsky's winter offensive took the form of local attacks east of the Dnepr River aimed both at seizing more favorable positions along the river for future offensive actions and also distracting German attentions and reserves away from the Kalinkovichi and Mozyr' axes (see Map 16.1). While Rokossovsky was planning and regrouping his forces for the offensive against the two key southern Belorussian cities, he ordered

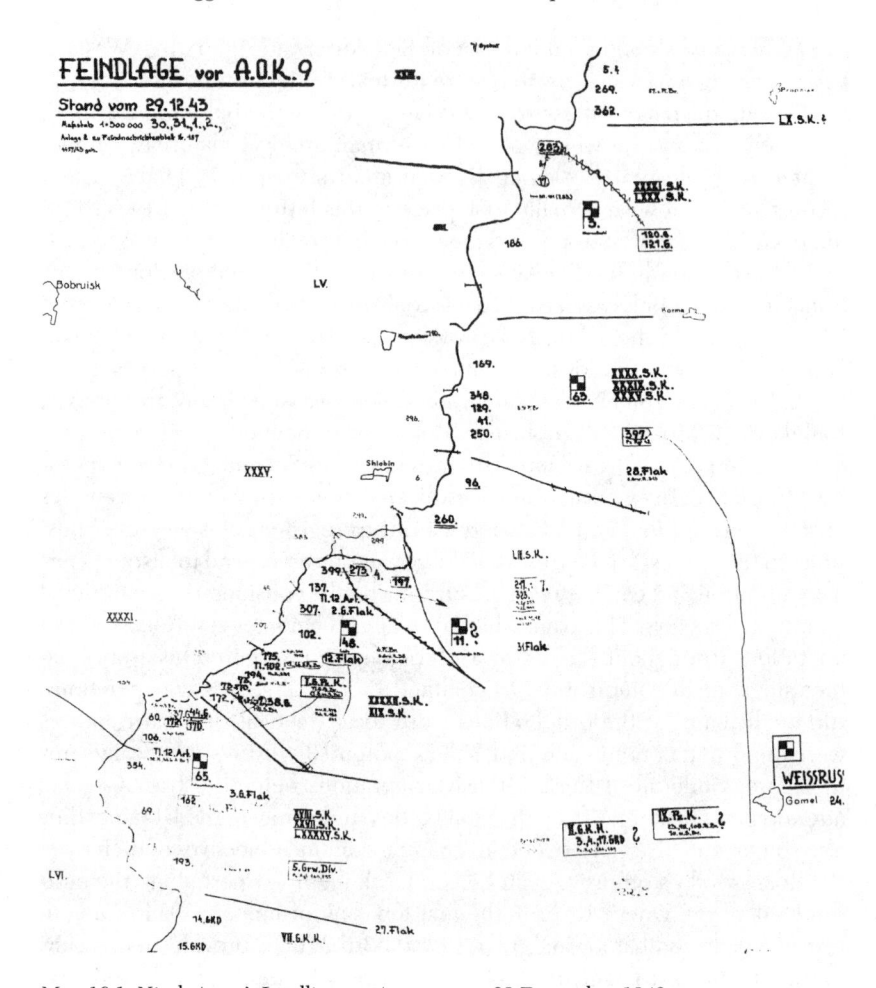

Map 16.1. Ninth Army's Intelligence Assessment, 29 December 1943

Lieutenant General A. V. Gorbatov's 3rd Army and Lieutenant General I. V. Boldin's 50th Army to mount an offensive east of the Dnepr. As evidence of its clear involvement in the offensive, the *Stavka* also ordered Sokolovsky's Western Front to support Rokossovsky's offensive with a local offensive by Lieutenant General V. S. Popov's 10th Army south of Chausy and along the Pronia River further to the north.

Only a few fragmentary sources reveal the scope and intent of this offensive. These include, for example, an excerpt from documents regarding 3rd Army's combat experiences. Prepared on 10 February 1944, "Short Summary No. 2 of the Generalized Combat Experience of the Belorussian Front's 3rd Army for January 1944" describes the army's actions in brief:

At the end of December 1943, units of 80th Rifle Corps, which were on the army's right wing, began preparing an offensive operation with the mission of destroying the enemy's 267th Infantry Division between the Ukhliast', Bobrovka, and Dnepr Rivers and reaching the Dnepr River along a front extending from Ur Kuty through Paseka and Pribor to Staraia Trasna. On 4 January the army's units penetrated the enemy's defense along a 24-kilometer-wide front and advanced 4–5 kilometers in the center and up to 7 kilometers on the flanks.

From a 12 January speech by Lieutenant General A. V. Gorbatov, the commander of 3rd Army, at a critique of the 4–5 January 1944 battle, at which the corps commanders, division commanders, their deputies, and the chiefs of the force branches and services were present, [Gorbatov stated], "Many trophies were seized and [according to prisoner reports] 267th Infantry Division was 50 percent destroyed, but we could have done more if we had operated more decisively. . . . Once again, all of this confirms that a well-prepared operation and systematic study and investigation of the enemy support the fulfillment of missions with fewer losses."

From a speech by Major General [I. P.] Konnov, the member of 3rd Army's military council, [Konnov said], "One of the most serious deficiencies . . . was the excessive losses in the past battles. During these [battles] the greatest losses were suffered by the replacements from the local regions, which reinforced the units before the operation. This is normal. There were great fluctuations in losses in different divisions and subunits. . . . We need more extensive training to reduce the losses. The 269th Rifle Division exploited the most active combat members and experienced soldiers very effectively during the preparatory period for the past operation. They taught the replacements how to conduct themselves in combat. . . . Each of them attached themselves to 2–3 young soldiers. This resulted in comparatively fewer losses. This very instructive experience of 269th Rifle Division must be widely disseminated to the army's units."[3]

The 50th Army's participation in the offensive is highlighted in an extract from a 12 February 1944 army's combat report, "Short Summary of the Generalized Combat Experience of the Belorussian Front's 50th Army for January 1944," which states, "During the beginning of January (4–8 January), the army conducted individual offensive operations of local significance, as a result of which the enemy was driven from his occupied defensive lines and dug in along new lines."[4]

Finally, in his memoirs, Gorbatov, the commander of 3rd Army, left a particularly vivid account of situation in early January and the general parameters of his army's offensive operation:

The 3rd Army reached the Dnepr River on 2 December along a front extending from the Bobrovka River [southward] to the village of Gadilovichi. Our neighbor [50th Army] had not yet reached the Dnepr. We could have halted along that line with a calm conscience until a general offensive began. However, as I recall it, the situation itself suggested that we had to seize a bridgehead over the Dnepr as soon as the ice strengthened. We had already selected a region at the village of Shapchitsy in the bend of the river [32 kilometers south of Bykhov], and we withdrew three divisions of our eight into second echelon to prepare them for the operation.

On our right wing, the Germans continued to hold on to the so-called Bykhov combat sector—a four-cornered area of about 140 square kilometers on the left bank [east] of the Dnepr, which was bordered from the west by the Dnepr River, from the south by the Bobrovka River, from the north by the Ukhliast' River, and from the east by the villages of Uzniki and Palki. This sector was very important for the enemy as well as for us. It protected the normal operations of the Germans' Zhlobin-Mogilev railroad, which ran along the right bank of the Dnepr River. It constantly threatened us with an attack by the enemy from the north along the road running along the left bank of the Dnepr through Dovsk to Gomel', and, as a result, we were forced to keep two divisions on the defense against that salient. This was the only place we had not reached the Dnepr, and, therefore, this salient was a thorn in our flesh. In order to capture a bridgehead over the Dnepr, we first had to liquidate the Bykhov combat sector, reach its bank, free up two more divisions for combat operations, and pull our neighbor on the right [50th Army] closer to the river.

Our concept for liquidating that sector matured during the first few days of January 1944. The operational plan was prepared, submitted to the *front* commander, and approved by him.

The main attack was delivered from east to west—from Uzniki toward Nikonovichi and Voronovo, and a secondary attack to the north along the road. In addition, a specially prepared ski detachment had to penetrate along the valley of the Dnepr into the enemy's rear area at night and, before first light on 4 January, the date our offensive was to begin, destroy the headquarters of 267th Infantry Division in the village of Pribor. We learned about the location of the German headquarters from prisoner interrogations, which were confirmed by a local inhabitant of Zagrishchev . . . who was arrested by the Germans but escaped and came to us through the front lines. He volunteered as a guide for the ski detachment, which was made up of 200 of the best volunteer skiers under the command of the experienced Captain Taivakainen. My deputy, General P. P. Sobennikov, supervised the preparation of the detachment. . . . The detachment had an assault group, a security group, and a reserve. . . . Major Levchenko, an exceptionally brave officer, was attached to the detachment for communications between the detachment and the army's operations department. . . .

Notified about the beginning of our operation, our neighbor to the right—50th Army—advanced to within 5–7 kilometers of the Dnepr by going over to the offensive immediately behind us.

Now we could leave three divisions on the defense (two of them received sectors of 20 kilometers each and the right flank division, 12 kilometers) and withdraw five divisions into second echelon so as to finish filling them out and prepare to force the Dnepr River.[5]

Based on these accounts and a variety of German archival sources, Rokossovsky's offensive plan required that Gorbatov's 3rd Army assault and destroy German Ninth Army's forces in the Bykhov salient, in conjunction with an attack by the left wing of General Boldin's 50th Army (see Map 16.2). At the same time, General Popov's 10th Army was to attack German defenses north and south of Chausy at the junction of the Sozh and Pronia Rivers. In addition to eliminating the pesky German salient south of Bykhov, at a minimum, Rokossovsky hoped to capture a bridgehead across the Pronia River north of Chausy and perhaps even evict German forces from Chausy as well. If more successful, the offensive had the potential of forcing German forces back to a new front line extending from the Pronia River north of Chausy southwestward through Volkovichi to Staraia Trasna on the Dnepr River or even to prompt them to withdraw their forces defending east of Shklov and Mogilev back to the Dnepr River line.

Gorbatov's 3rd and Boldin's 50th Armies were to launch Rokossovsky's main attack at dawn on 4 January against the defenses of 267th and 95th Infantry Divisions of German Ninth Army's XXIII Army Corps. These two divisions defended the 23-kilometer-wide sector extending from Palki on the Bobrovka River northward to Momachino on the Ukhliast' River. Supported by 36th Tank Regiment, 283rd, 362nd, and 5th Rifle Divisions of Major General I. L. Ragulia's 80th Rifle Corps, which were concentrated from left to right in the 7-kilometer-wide sector from Palki on the Bobrovka River northward to Uzniki, were to conduct 3rd Army's main attack, penetrate the center of 267th Infantry Division's defenses, and exploit westward to the Dnepr River along the Nikonovichi and Staraia Trasna axis.

Along the Bobrovka River on 80th Rifle Corps' left, during the night before the main attack, a 200-man special ski detachment was to infiltrate through the Germans' front lines just west of Selets Kholopeev (7 kilometers west of Palki) to conduct a raid against 267th Infantry Division's headquarters at Pribor, situated on the Dnepr's eastern bank 9 kilometers to the north. The following morning, 3rd Army's 17th Rifle Division was to assault

410   The Struggle for Belorussia, December 1943–April 1944

Map 16.2. 50th Army's Situation East of Bykhov, 3–7 January 1944

northward across the Bobrovka River toward Staraia Trasna to exploit the ski detachment's success. Gorbatov deployed 5th Rifle Division and 324th Rifle Division, temporarily detached from the neighboring 50th Army, along the Ukhliast' River on 80th Rifle Corps' right wing. As soon as 80th Rifle Corps' divisions had penetrated the Germans' forward defenses, these two rifle divi-

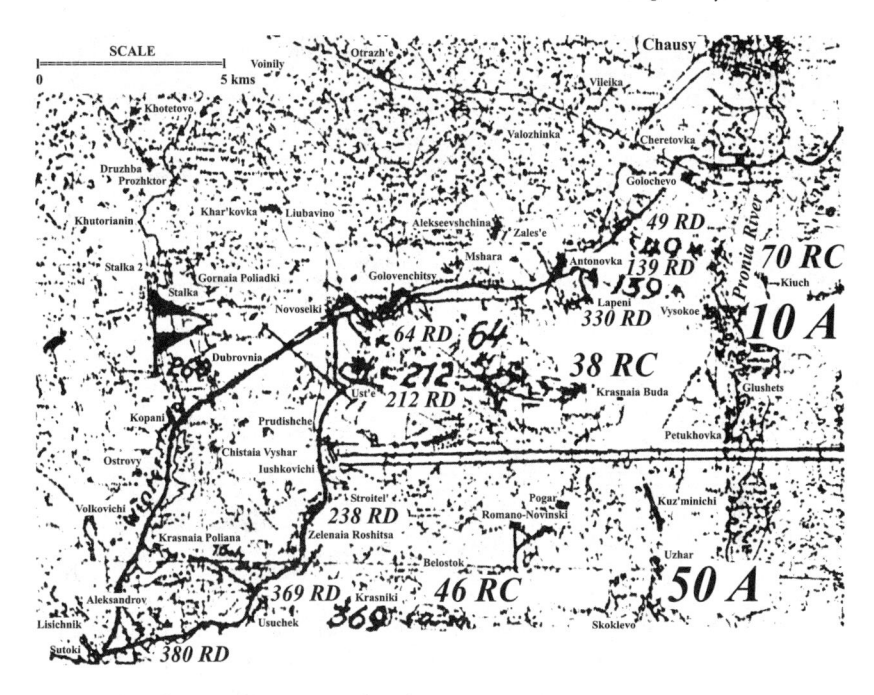

Map 16.3. 10th Army's Situation in the Chausy Sector, 7 January 1944

sions were to advance westward across the Ukhliast' River toward Vetrenka in support of 80th Rifle Corps' attack. Finally, Gorbatov retained 269th Rifle Division in his second echelon behind 80th Rifle Corps with orders to reinforce the rifle corps' attack when required.

On the right (northern) flank of Gorbatov's 3rd Army, 108th, 110th, and 413th Rifle Divisions of Boldin's 50th Army were to penetrate the defenses of German XXIII Army Corps' 95th Infantry Division west of the Ukhliast' River early on 4 January in the 7-kilometer-wide sector between Smolitsa and Krasnitsa, capture the German strongpoint at Krasnitsa, and exploit to the northwest in tandem with 3rd Army's advance. On the right wing of Boldin's 50th Army, 380th, 238th and 369th Rifle Divisions of Major General K. M. Erastov's 46th Rifle Corps were to remain on the defense opposite XXIII Army Corps' 260th Infantry Division. Their orders required them to join the offensive if it proved successful.

Finally, in conjunction with the assaults by Rokossovsky's 3rd and 50th Armies, the Western Front also ordered General Popov's 10th Army to conduct a two-pronged assault against the defenses of German Fourth Army's XII Army Corps north and south of Chausy. North of the city (not shown on Maps 16.2 and 16.3), 10th Army's 160th, 290th, 76th, and 385th Rifle Divisions were to force the Pronia River in the 8-kilometer-wide sector from Put'ki

Table 16.1. The Estimated Correlation of Opposing Forces in the Bykhov-Chausy Offensive, 4–8 January 1944

OPPOSING FORCES	
Soviet	*German*
Western Front	
10th Army	IR, 35th Infantry Division
9 rifle divisions	Corps Detachment D
Belorussian Front	
50th Army	260th Infantry Division
3rd Army	95th Infantry Division
12 rifle divisions	267th Infantry Division
1 tank regiment (20 tanks)	18th Panzer Grenadier Division
Strength: 110,000 men (est.)	50,000 men
20 tanks	Initially no tanks, but ultimately, about 20 tanks
Depth of Soviet advance: 2–15 kilometers	

Sources: A. V. Gorbatov, *Gody i voiny* [Years and wars] (Moscow: Voenizdat, 1980), 249–250; and "Feindlage vor A.O.K. 9 Stand vom 6.1.44," in Anlage 3 zum Tatigkeitsbericht de Abt. Ic/A.O. 1 Jan–10 Jul 1944, *AOK 9, 62717/4 file*, in NAM T-312, Roll 342.

northward to Skvarsk at the boundary between the defending 35th Infantry Division and Corps Detachment D and, if possible, attack southwestward to cut the communications routes into Chausy from the west. These three divisions were to launch their assault across the Pronia at dawn on 3 January to divert German attention from the main attack sectors further south. Then, early on 4 January, 10th Army's 70th Rifle Corps (49th, 139th, and 330th Rifle Divisions) and 38th Rifle Corps (64th and 212th Rifle Divisions) were to attack the defenses of Corps Detachment D in the 12-kilometer-wide sector from just south of Chausy to Golovenchitsy, penetrate the detachment's defenses, and advance to link up with other 10th Army forces advancing westward north of the city.

Although Rokossovsky's 3rd and 50th Armies and Popov's 10th Army outnumbered the opposing German forces at least fourfold in terms of divisions, all of these divisions were woefully understrength, numbering roughly 3,500 men each. This reduced the Soviet superiority to just more than 2 to 1, although concentration produced much greater superiorities locally (see Table 16.1). For example, the German 267th Infantry Division alone faced a Soviet force of six rifle divisions. However, the extensive prepared defenses German forces occupied negated much of this Soviet numerical superiority.

Realistically, because the *Stavka,* Sokolovsky, and Rokossovsky well understood that German Ninth Army's defenses along the Pronia River north of Chausy were particularly strong and deeply echeloned, they did not expected to register major gains in this region. They did, however, expect that 10th Army's local assaults would assist Rokossovsky's forces by diverting German attention away from the Bykhov combat sector.

The Battle

The 10th Army's 290th Rifle Division, supported by most of 160th and 76th Rifle Divisions, assaulted across the Pronia River between Put'ki and Skvarsk, 10–15 kilometers north of Chausy, at dawn on 3 January (see Map 16.3 for the fighting south of Chausy). In heavy fighting, the three rifle divisions seized bridgeheads north and south of the fortified village of Prilepovka, 2.5 kilometers north of Put'ki, but were not able to capture the village itself. After being reinforced overnight by elements of 385th Rifle Division, the next day the force captured the village of Baryshevka, 2 kilometers north of Prilepovka, and also the village of Put'ki, only to be halted on the eastern outskirts of Voskhod, 5 kilometers to the west, by counterattacking 35th Infantry Division's reserves. Although further attacks stalled, in two days of fighting, 10th Army's forces fighting north of Chausy captured a 1.5–2-kilometer-deep bridgehead on the Pronia River's western bank. Although this diversionary attack failed to attract sizable German forces away from other key sectors, it did distract the Germans' attention from what was about to occur to the south.

Just as planned, Gorbatov's ski detachment embarked on its daring raid during darkness on the night of 3–4 January. The army commander vividly described its attack in his memoirs:

> The detachment descended down the river valley on the night of 3 January. Undetected by the enemy, it entered his rear area along its planned route. The night was overcast, hazy, and slightly freezing. The detachment did not hurry. The security element with the guide who knew the march route and an officer who knew the necessary German words moved in front. Those in front marched with sharp mine probes in their hands and were roped together with those who followed. Several times, this foresight saved men when they broke through under the ice. The soaked people soon redressed themselves in reserve clothing and felt boots.
>
> Passing through more than 15 kilometers of virgin soil, the detachment crossed the river channel four times and its tributaries six times. After five hours, it observed the outline of buildings on the bank to the right. It was the village of Pribor. It was quiet in the village, and only crowing cocks could be heard. They encountered a barbed wire fence on the outskirts. As soon as the sappers prepared passages in the wire, the officers detailed the missions to the detachment's groups. The soldiers remembered that they were not to cut the discovered telephone lines before the first shots (so as not to warn the enemy). After resting, they placed "beacons" in the passages in the wire and moved into the village.
>
> The translator, Senior Sergeant Telesh, advanced in front of the group that was heading to the division headquarters. When the sentry

challenged him, he answered in German that he was his officer and he approached the German soldier, killing him on the spot with a dagger thrust. However, the post had a pair of sentries, and, in turn, the other sentry, who was standing to the side, wounded Telesh in the leg with automatic weapons fire. Telesh, in turn, killed him, and these first shots were the signal for the attack.

The German headquarters security was almost completely destroyed. The scouts showered the buildings with grenades and then burst into them, finishing off the remaining Hitlerites. Those Fascists who succeeded in jumping out into the streets were killed in ambushes on the road.

After 40 minutes, the signal "Withdraw" was given. As was agreed, they waited 15 minutes at the assembly area for those who had fallen behind, after which the detachment made its way to the south along the previously designated route. Eighteen men did not appear at the assembly area, but 12 of them later caught up with the detachment.

At 0530 hours a radiogram was received from Major Levchenko, which read, "Everything is all right. The mission has been fulfilled." At that time, we could see a great glow over the village of Pribor.

The daring sortie of the ski troops was crowned with great success: more than 30 Hitlerites were killed, including many officers, among them von Schlier, the chief of staff of the division, more than 50 different vehicles, a communications center, and warehouses with fuel and food were destroyed, and important documents were captured.

A bulletin of the *Sovinformburo,* dated 6 January 1944, reported about our ski detachment's raid.[6]

At dawn on 4 January, the remainder of Gorbatov's main shock group began its assault to exploit the ski detachment's success. Once again, Gorbatov described the action:

The ski detachment's operations facilitated the forces' mission. Even before first light, one of the regiments of Colonel Romanenko's division [17th Rifle Division] attacked between the road and the Dnepr to link up with the ski detachment, and, soon after a short artillery preparation, General Ragulia's main force [80th Rifle Corps] went on the offensive from the Uzniki region toward Nikonovichi.

During the initial hours our units advanced 4–5 kilometers. The garrison at the village of Palki was encircled and destroyed. The enemy tried to stop us along an intermediate line from Nikonovichi through Usokha to Luzhki, but, by delivering a new attack, we threw them back from this line.

The enemy's fortified sector was liquidated within two days. Our army reached the Dnepr in its entire sector and was able to conduct artillery fire against the railroad station at Bykhov.[7]

If the raid by the ski detachment caught the Germans unaware, the assault by Ragulia's 80th Rifle Corps only increased that surprise, in the process hastening the collapse of the entire German salient south of Bykhov. At dawn on 4 January, 17th Rifle Division advanced northward across the Bobrovka River along the Selets Kholopeev-Staraia Trasna road toward Usokha, crushing 267th Infantry Division's right wing. Simultaneously, 283rd and 362nd Rifle Divisions from Ragulia's corps quickly penetrated 267th Infantry Division's defenses south and north of Palki, encircling German forces in the strongpoint and driving northwest toward Nikonovichi. The next day, just as the Germans were trying to erect defenses along intermediate lines, Ragulia committed his 269th Rifle Division from second echelon. Supported by 5th Rifle Division on its right, the fresh force collapsed the new German defenses and prompted the XXIII Army Corps to order its forces to fall back to new defenses, the so-called *Winterstand* Line, situated along the northern bank of the Ukhliast' River.

Meanwhile, on Gorbatov's right wing, 324th Rifle Division penetrated 267th Infantry Division's defenses east of Smolitsa and captured the German strongpoint but was unable to cross the Ukhliast' River at Vetrenka, 5 kilometers to the west. Farther east, 110th and 413th Rifle Divisions and 233rd Tank Regiment, deployed on the left wing of Boldin's 50th Army; assaulted the Germans' defenses at the boundary between 267th and 95th Infantry Divisions; and captured the German strongpoint at Viliaga, 5 kilometers north of Smolitsa but were halted just short of the strongpoint at Krasnitsa, 4 kilometers north of Viliaga.

While Colonel P. S. Romanenko's 17th Rifle Division and the three rifle divisions of Ragulia's 80th Rifle Corps were closing up against the new German defense line along the Ukhliast' River late on 5 January, Boldin reinforced his shock group west of Viliaga with 108th Rifle Division, and the next day with 324th Rifle Division, which Gorbatov returned to his control. The two divisions joined 110th and 413th Rifle Divisions in renewed assaults on German defenses around Krasnitsa. Despite these reinforcements, however, Boldin's force failed to crack the German defenses. The Germans countered the heavy assaulted by transferring battalion-size *kampfgruppen* from 95th and 18th Panzer Grenadier Divisions to the Krasnitsa region, and, after they were committed to action, these forces brought Boldin's attacks to a standstill.

In reality, the remnants of the retreating 267th Infantry Division and the fresh German forces withdrew to a new defense line, the so-called *Winterstand* line, which German engineers had already erected along the Ukhliast' River to protect against the eventuality of a Red Army assault in this sector. The erection of this line in advance proved prudent indeed, as it successfully halted both Gorbatov's and Boldin's assaults.

While heavy fighting raged between the Bobrovka and Ukhliast' Rivers, Popov unleashed the five rifle divisions of 10th Army's 38th and 70th Rifle

Corps in heavy assaults on Corps Detachment D's defenses southwest of Chausy. Despite registering minor gains with attacks by 64th and 212th Rifle Divisions in the Golovenchitsy sector, 12 kilometers southwest of the city, within a matter of hours, Popov's assaults too collapsed in the face of the imposing German defenses. So successful was the German defense that XXIII Army Corps was able to postpone an anticipated withdrawal to the northern sector of the *Winterstand* Line, which extended from 1–6 kilometers to the rear between Golovenchitsy and Krasnitsa.

Late on 8 January, Rokossovsky authorized his forces to cease their offensive southeast of Bykhov. By this time, although 3rd, 50th, and 10th Armies' assaults had stalled along the remainder of the front, 80th Rifle Corps of Gorbatov's 3rd Army had severely damaged the German 267th Infantry Division and captured most of the Germans' Bykhov combat salient. Within a matter of days, XXIII Army Corps withdrew the remnants of its shattered 267th Division to new defenses west of the Dnepr River, shifted its 95th Infantry Division into the *Winterstand* Line defenses between Pribor and Vetrenka, and assigned 18th Panzer Grenadier Division responsibility for defense of the key Krasnitsa sector. Most important from Rokossovsky's perspective, his offensive southeast of Bykhov provided more than adequate cover for his new and more important offensive against Kalinkovichi, which commenced early on 8 January, even before the guns fell silent east of the Dnepr River.

CHAPTER 17

The Belorussian Front's Kalinkovichi-Mozyr' Offensive (8–14 January)

PLANNING

Soviet source materials on this offensive include brief accounts of the operation in a number of open-source general surveys and unit histories, two journal articles, and fragmentary reports from the archives of the Russian Federation's Ministry of Defense, most of which were prepared by the General Staff's Directorate for the Exploitation of War Experience. All of these sources cover only the capture of Kalinkovichi during the period from 8–14 January and ignore subsequent operations. For example, short selections of generalized war experience gleaned from reports prepared by 65th and 61st Armies provide summary sketches of both armies' operations.

The first, "Short Summary No. 1 of 65th Army's Generalized War Experience for January 1944," issued on 9 February 1944, states:

> The 65th Army's forces firmly defended their occupied positions and conducted reconnaissance of the enemy's forward defensive edge during the period from 1–7 January. . . . This period was used to intensify preparations for the Kalinkovichi operation. The army commander issued instructions to the corps commanders concerning the verification of readiness for the offensive, which addressed all of the main issues related to organizing and controlling battle. The army began the offensive on 8 January with the mission of penetrating the enemy's defense in the sector from Kazanskie Farm to Kholodniki Station, advancing in the direction of Koshchichi, Sukhovichi, and Gorbovichi, reaching the Iakimovichi, Klinsk (inclusive), Rudnia, and Gobachevskaia line, and, in cooperation with 61st Army, destroying the enemy's Kalinkovichi grouping. As a result of six days of offensive battle, the army's forces advanced forward 25–35 kilometers and captured 70 populated points, including the railroad station and city of Kalinkovichi.[1]

Likewise, a second report, "Short Summary No. 1 of 61st Army's Generalized War Experience for January 1944," prepared on 10 February 1944, reads:

> Having penetrated the enemy's defenses on the intermediate line of the Ipa River, after an insignificant pause, by the end of January the [61st]

army went over to the offensive, conducted heavy combat in forested and swampy terrain, and pushed the enemy back to the Ptich' River line [30 kilometers west of Kalinkovichi]. After forcing the Ptich' River and penetrating the enemy's previously prepared defensive positions on the western bank, the army seized several bridgeheads and fought to expand them. The left wing drove a wedge forward and repelled enemy counterattacks in the direction of Ivanov Sloboda. . . .

The enemy offered especially dogged resistance in the center (along the northeastern approaches to Kalinkovichi and Mozyr'). The enemy's stubbornness in the center of the front was conditioned by the necessity of evacuating weaponry and valuables and the withdrawal of his main forces. Only the threat of encirclement forced the enemy in the center to withdraw to the Kalinkovichi and Mozyr' line and then abandon these points. Together with doggedness, the enemy's defensive combat was characterized by great defensive energy [*aktivnost'*]. While resisting our offensive, the enemy undertook 84 counterattacks in from infantry platoon up to two-battalion strength supported by from 2–4 to 6–10 tanks and self-propelled guns. In addition, up to 10 times, he conducted reconnaissance-in-force in from platoon to company strength. The absence of reserves and the understrength nature of his infantry formations forced the enemy to commit a large quantity of separate specialized units into combat. Besides the 7 tattered infantry and 2 panzer divisions, 13 various separate battalions, 2 separate infantry regiments, 1 cavalry regiment, and a separate ski Jäger brigade were operating opposite our front.[2]

The *Stavka* set the stage for the Belorussian Front's offensive on 2 January by adjusting the *front*'s boundary line with the 1st Ukrainian Front on its left flank and by ordering Rokossovsky's *front* to capture both Kalinkovichi and Mozyr' with a concerted assault by 65th and 61st Armies. Issued at 1820 hours on 2 January and citing the successful offensive by Vatutin's *front* and the necessity for destroying the enemy's Mozyr' grouping, the directive established a new boundary between the *fronts* designed to facilitate Rokossovsky's operations. As of 2400 hours on 2 January, this boundary was "to Chernigov, as before, and, farther, to the mouth of the Slovechna River, Kuz'michi, Len'chitsy, and Stolin (all points, besides Len'chitsy and Stolin, are inclusive for the Belorussian Front)." In addition, it transferred 415th Rifle Division, operating on the extreme right wing of the 1st Ukrainian Front's 13th Army, to the Belorussian Front. Most important, it directed Rokossovsky's *front* to "begin an offensive with its left wing no later than 8 January, with the mission of defeating the enemy's Mozyr' grouping and capturing Kalinkovichi and Mozyr' by 12 January by enveloping them from the north and from the south." Subsequently, Rokossovsky's forces were "to attack with the *front*'s main forces in the general direction of Bobruisk and

Minsk," with part of its forces operating westward along the Pripiat' River toward Luninets.[3]

A recent Soviet account of the offensive provides a summary description of the missions the *Stavka* assigned to Rokossovsky's *front* on 2 January 1944 and a surprisingly accurate assessment of the German forces it opposed (see Appendix N-1 for the complete *Stavka* directive):

> Begin an offensive with the forces on the *front*'s left wing, defeat the enemy's Kalinkovichi-Mozyr' grouping, and subsequently attack toward Bobruisk and Minsk. The 65th and 61st Armies were responsible for its fulfillment. The 12th Panzer and 251st Infantry Divisions, and also units from the enemy's XX Army Corps, were operating against 65th Army. The forward edge of the enemy's defense extended from Kazansk through Terebnia and Kholodniki to Viazovitsa.[4]

During the first stage of this offensive, 65th and 61st Armies were to capture Kalinkovichi and Mozyr', drive German forces back to the Ipa River in the sector from east of Ozarichi in the north southward through Iakimovichi to the junction of the Ipa River with the Pripiat' River south of Klinsk (13 kilometers west of Kalinkovichi), and clear German forces from the southern bank of the Pripiat' River as far west as Balazhevichi, 35 kilometers west of Mozyr'. During the second stage of the offensive, which essentially amounted to a separate offensive operation, 65th and 61st Armies were to penetrate German defenses along the Ipa River northwest of Kalinkovichi, and, in conjunction with an offensive by 48th Army to the north, capture Ozarichi and Mikhnovichi; advance to secure bridgeheads across the Ptich' River; and, ultimately continue the offensive northwestward toward Bobruisk. During this stage, cavalry forces subordinate to 61st Army were to advance along the southern bank of the Pripiat' River to Luninets, 175 kilometers west of Mozyr', in order to sever communications between German Army Groups Center and South.

As was the case with the Western Front, the *Stavka* allocated Rokossovsky's *front* only those forces it felt were necessary for it to accomplish its initial missions. This included General Panov's 1st Guards Tank Corps, earmarked to spearhead 65th Army's advance, and Generals Kriukov's and Konstantinov's 2nd and 7th Guards Cavalry Corps, which were ideally suited to leading 61st Army's advance in the more restrictive terrain along the swampy banks of the Pripiat' River (see Table 17.1).

In accordance with the *Stavka's* guidance, Rokossovsky decided to conduct a double envelopment of German forces defending Kalinkovichi and Mozyr' by employing his mobile corps to spearhead his two pincers (see Map 17.1). By this time, the Kalinkovichi and Mozyr' regions were defended by LVI Panzer and XX Army Corps and Corps *Abteilung* (detachment) E of Army Group

Table 17.1. The Belorussian Front's Order of Battle on 1 January 1944

BELORUSSIAN FRONT:
Army General K. K. Rokossovsky

3rd Army: LTG A. V. Gorbatov
  41st Rifle Corps: MG V. K. Urbanovich
    120th Guards Rifle Division
    186th Rifle Division
  80th Rifle Corps: MG I. L. Ragulia
    5th Rifle Division
    283rd Rifle Division
    362nd Rifle Division
    17th Rifle Division
    269th Rifle Division
  36th Separate Tank Regiment
  31st Separate Armored Train Battalion
  55th Separate Armored Train Battalion

48th Army: LTG P. L. Romanenko
  25th Rifle Corps: MG A. B. Barinov
    4th Rifle Division
    197th Rifle Division
    273rd Rifle Division
  29th Rifle Corps: MG A. M. Andreev
    102nd Rifle Division
    137th Rifle Division
    307th Rifle Division
  42nd Rifle Corps: LTG K. S. Kolganov
    170th Rifle Division
    194th Rifle Division
    399th Rifle Division
  73rd Rifle Division
  175th Rifle Division
  217th Rifle Division
  42nd Separate Tank Regiment
  231st Separate Tank Regiment
  1897th Self-propelled Artillery Regiment

50th Army: LTG I. V. Boldin
  46th Rifle Corps: MG K. M. Erastov
    238th Rifle Division
    369th Rifle Division
    380th Rifle Division
  108th Rifle Division
  110th Rifle Division
  324th Rifle Division
  413th Rifle Division
  233rd Separate Tank Regiment
  21st Separate Armored Train Battalion
  43rd Separate Armored Train Battalion

63rd Army: LTG V. A. Kolpakchi
  35th Rifle Corps: MG V. G. Zholudev
    129th Rifle Division
    250th Rifle Division
    348th Rifle Division
  40th Rifle Corps: MG V. S. Kuznetsov

61st Army: LTG P. A. Belov
  9th Guards Rifle Corps: MG A. A. Boreiko
    12th Guards Rifle Division
    76th Guards Rifle Division
    77th Guards Rifle Division
  89th Rifle Corps: MG G. A. Khaliuzin
    15th Rifle Division
    55th Rifle Division
    81st Rifle Division
    356th Rifle Division
  2nd Guards Cavalry Corps: LTG V. V. Kriukov
    3rd Guards Cavalry Division
    4th Guards Cavalry Division
    17th Guards Cavalry Division
    149th Guards Tank Destroyer Regiment
    2nd Guards Separate Tank Destroyer Artillery Battalion
    10th Guards-Mortar Regiment
    60th Guards-Mortar Battalion
    1730th Antiaircraft Artillery Regiment
  7th Guards Cavalry Corps: MG M. P. Konstantinov
    14th Guards Cavalry Division
    15th Guards Cavalry Division
    16th Guards Cavalry Division
    145th Guards Tank Destroyer Regiment
    7th Guards Separate Tank Destroyer Artillery Battalion
    7th Guards-Mortar Regiment
    57th Guards-Mortar Battalion
    1733rd Antiaircraft Artillery Regiment
  68th Tank Brigade
  1459th Self-propelled Artillery Regiment

65th Army: LTC P. I. Batov
  18th Rifle Corps: MG I. I. Ivanov
    69th Rifle Division
    162nd Rifle Division
    193rd Rifle Division
    115th Rifle Brigade
  19th Rifle Corps: MG D. I. Samarsky
    38th Guards Rifle Division
    82nd Rifle Division
  27th Rifle Corps: MG F. M. Cherokmanov
    60th Rifle Division
    106th Rifle Division
    354th Rifle Division
  95th Rifle Corps: MG I. A. Kuzovkov
    37th Guards Rifle Division
    44th Guards Rifle Division
    172nd Rifle Division

Table 17.1. *continued*

41st Rifle Division	105th Rifle Corps: MG D. F. Alekseev
169th Rifle Division	75th Guards Rifle Division
53rd Rifle Corps: MG I. A. Gartsev	132nd Rifle Division
96th Rifle Division	253rd Rifle Division
260th Rifle Division	1st Guards Tank Corps: MGTF M. F.
323rd Rifle Division	Panov
26th Guards Separate Tank Regiment	15th Guards Tank Brigade
1901st Self-propelled Artillery Regiment	16th Guards Tank Brigade
	17th Guards Tank Brigade
Front Reserves:	1st Guards Motorized Rifle Brigade
121st Rifle Corps: MG D. I. Smirnov	237th Self-propelled Artillery Regiment
23rd Rifle Division	1001st Self-propelled Artillery Regiment
218th Rifle Division	1541st Self-propelled Artillery Regiment
115th Fortified Region	1st Guards Motorcycle Battalion
119th Fortified Region	65th Motorcycle Battalion
161st Fortified Region	732nd Tank Destroyer Artillery Regiment
6th Guards Cavalry Corps: LTG S. V.	455th Mortar Regiment
Sokolov	43rd Guards-Mortar Battalion
8th Guards Cavalry Division	80th Guards Antiaircraft Artillery
13th Guards Cavalry Division	Regiment
8th Cavalry Division	2nd Guards Tank Brigade
1813th Self-propelled Artillery Regiment	255th Separate Tank Regiment
142nd Guards Tank Destroyer Regiment	1816th Self-propelled Artillery Regiment
6th Guards Separate Tank Destroyer	1888th Self-propelled Artillery Regiment
Artillery Battalion	
11th Guards-Mortar Regiment	
47th Guards-Mortar Battalion	
1732nd Antiaircraft Artillery Regiment	
193rd Separate Tank Regiment	
251st Separate Tank Regiment	
253rd Separate Tank Regiment	
1444th Self-propelled Artillery Regiment	
1538th Self-propelled Artillery Regiment	
39th Separate Armored Train Battalion	
40th Separate Armored Train Battalion	
59th Separate Armored Train Battalion	

Source: Boevoi sostav Sovetskoi Armii, chast' IV (Ianvar'–dekabr' 1944) [The combat composition of the Soviet Army, pt. 4 (January–December 1944)] (Moscow: Voenizdat, 1988), 14–15.

Center's Second Army. The armored nucleus of General Weiss's Second Army was 4th, 5th, and 12th Panzer Divisions, all of which had been fighting in the region throughout the fall. However, during the first week of January, the OKH dispatched most of the 12th Panzer northward to support Army Group North's forces fighting in the Leningrad region. As a result, on 1 January 1944, 4th and 5th Panzer Divisions fielded a total of seventy-nine tanks, twenty-nine in short-term repair. These were supplemented by thirty-seven mobile assault guns and *Paks,* five sidelined for short-term repair.[5] Otherwise, virtually all of the infantry divisions subordinate to Second Army were configured as *kampfgruppen,* or division divisional groups, often in regimental size, because of the heavy losses they had sustained in the previous fighting.

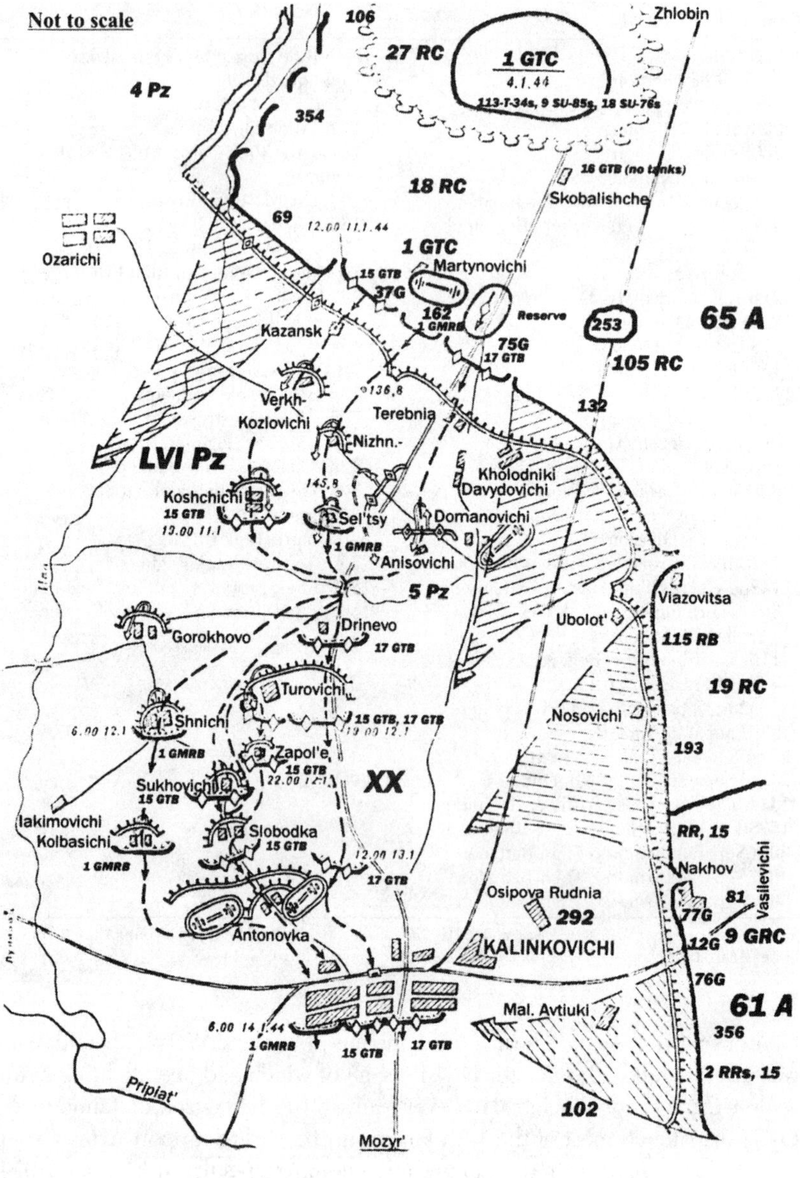

422 The Struggle for Belorussia, December 1943–April 1944

Map 17.1. 65th and 61st Armies' Assault on Kalinkovichi, 8–14 January 1944

Operating as the mobile group of General Batov's 65th Army, General Panov's 1st Guards Tank Corps was to exploit 65th Army's penetration north of Kalinkovichi and envelop the city from the north and northwest. Farther to the south, Generals Kriukov's and Konstantinov's 2nd and 7th Guards Cavalry Corps, which served as the mobile groups of General Belov's 61st

Army, were tasked with exploiting westward south of the Pripiat' River to envelop Mozyr' from the southwest. Thereafter, Panov's tank corps was to support 65th Army's advance westward to the Ptich' River, and the two cavalry corps were to spearhead 61st Army's advance westward along the Pripiat' River toward Luninets.

Rokossovsky ordered Batov's 65th Army to conduct its main attack in the roughly 15-kilometer-wide sector extending from the Ipa River north of Kalinkovichi to Viazovitsa northeast of the city with two rifle corps and a supporting attack in the 15-kilometer-wide sector centered on Nosovichi northeast of the city with one rifle corps. Batov designated General Ivanov's 18th and General Alekseev's 105th Rifle Corps to conduct his main attack in the Kazansk and Kholodniki sector against defenses manned by LVI Panzer Corps' 4th and 5th Panzer Divisions. The former was defending the sector from the Ipa River southward to Kholodniki and the latter the sector from Kholodniki southward to almost due east of Kalinkovichi.

Ivanov's and Alekseev's rifle corps were to penetrate the Germans' first defensive belt on 8 and 9 January and then support the commitment of Panov's 1st Guards Tank Corps into combat. Ivanov deployed his corps' 162nd and 69th Rifle Divisions from left to right in first echelon, with orders to assault and capture the German strongpoints at Nizhne-Kozlovichi and Verkhne-Kozlovichi, respectively, and retained his 37th Guards Rifle Division in second echelon. Likewise, Alekseev deployed his corps' 132nd and 75th Guards Rifle Divisions in first echelon, with orders to capture Davydovichi, Kholodniki, and Domanovichi, and held his 253rd Rifle Division in second echelon. The 255th Tank Regiment, 2nd Guards Tank Brigade, and 1816th and 1888th Self-propelled Artillery Regiments provided the two rifle corps with direct armor and self-propelled artillery support.

Panov's tank corps, concentrated in assembly areas around Skobalishche (38 kilometers north of Kalinkovichi) before its attack, fielded 113 T-34 tanks, 9 SU-85 self-propelled guns, and 18 SU-76 self-propelled guns. Because the tank corps was severely understrength, Panov assigned all of his armor and self-propelled guns to his 15th and 17th Guards Tank Brigades and left his 16th Guards Tank Brigade and 1001st and 1541st Self-propelled Artillery Regiments in reserve without any tanks or self-propelled guns. To compensate for this weakness in armor, Batov assigned the 1888th Self-propelled Artillery Regiment, 20th Tank Destroyer Artillery Battalion, and 7th Engineer Obstacle Battalion to Panov's corps during the course of the offensive.

After the two rifle corps completed the first stage of their penetration operation Panov's tank corps was to begin its exploitation in the broad sector from Kazansk past Hill 136.8 to the village of Davydovichi, tentatively at day's end on the second day of combat. Thereafter, Panov's forces were to advance along the Davydovichi, Turovichi, and Slobodka axis to envelop the city of Kalinkovichi from the northwest. Panov later described his tank corps' initial plan as follows:

According to the first operational plan, 15th [Guards] Tank Brigade, reinforced by two batteries of 1888th Self-propelled Artillery Regiment, a company from 7th Engineer Obstacle Battalion, and a company from 121st Sapper Battalion, was to attack in the general direction of Nizhne-Kozlovichi, Koshchichi, Sukhovichi, Antonovka, and the northwestern outskirts of Kalinkovichi.

The 1st [Guards] Motorized Rifle Brigade, with 455th Mortar Regiment and 732nd and 20th Tank Destroyer Artillery Battalions, was to attack in the general direction of Terebnia, Anisovichi, Turovichi, and Kalinkovichi.

The 17th [Guards] Tank Brigade, with two batteries of 1888th Self-propelled Artillery Regiment, a company of 121st Sapper Battalion, and a company from 7th Engineer Obstacle Battalion, constituted the second echelon, and the remaining units were in the corps' reserve.[6]

However, as is so often the case, the original plan did not survive the first day of combat.

Batov ordered General Samarsky's 19th Rifle Corps to conduct the army's supporting attack northeast of Kalinkovichi, with its 193rd Rifle Division and 115th Rifle Brigade arrayed from left to right in a sector formerly occupied by 2nd and 7th Guards Cavalry Corps. After relieving the two cavalry corps, Samarsky's corps was to penetrate 5th Panzer Division's defenses in the Nosovichi region and advance on Kalinkovichi from the northeast in tandem with the right wing of 61st Army. However, overnight on 5–6 January, 5th Panzer Division withdrew 10 kilometers from its forward defenses in the swampy region around Nosovichi to new defenses extending from just east of Gorochichi southward to east of Buda. This forced Alekseev's corps to advance its lines and regroup its forces before launching its assault (see Map 17.2).

Rokossovsky ordered Belov's 61st Army to conduct its main attack with the three guards rifle divisions of General Boreiko's 9th Guards Rifle Corps in the 6-kilometer-wide Osipova Rudnia and Malye Avtiuki (Malye Avtiutsevichi) sector astride the road and railroad line running into Kalinkovichi from the east. Colonel D. K. Mal'kov, the commander of 12th Guards Rifle Division, later described the corps' mission and the enemy's defenses:

> Corps Group "E," 5th Panzer Division, and 292nd Infantry Division were defending opposite 9th Guards Rifle Corps' front. The forward edge of the Germans' defenses, which extended 200–300 meters east of the Osipova Rudnia and Aleksandrovka road, were covered with barbed wire obstacles and, in some sectors, antitank and antipersonnel minefields. Pillboxes were constructed for firing points and bunkers with strong cover for the personnel. The villages of Aleksandrovka and Golevitsy Station were organized into powerful strongpoints.[7]

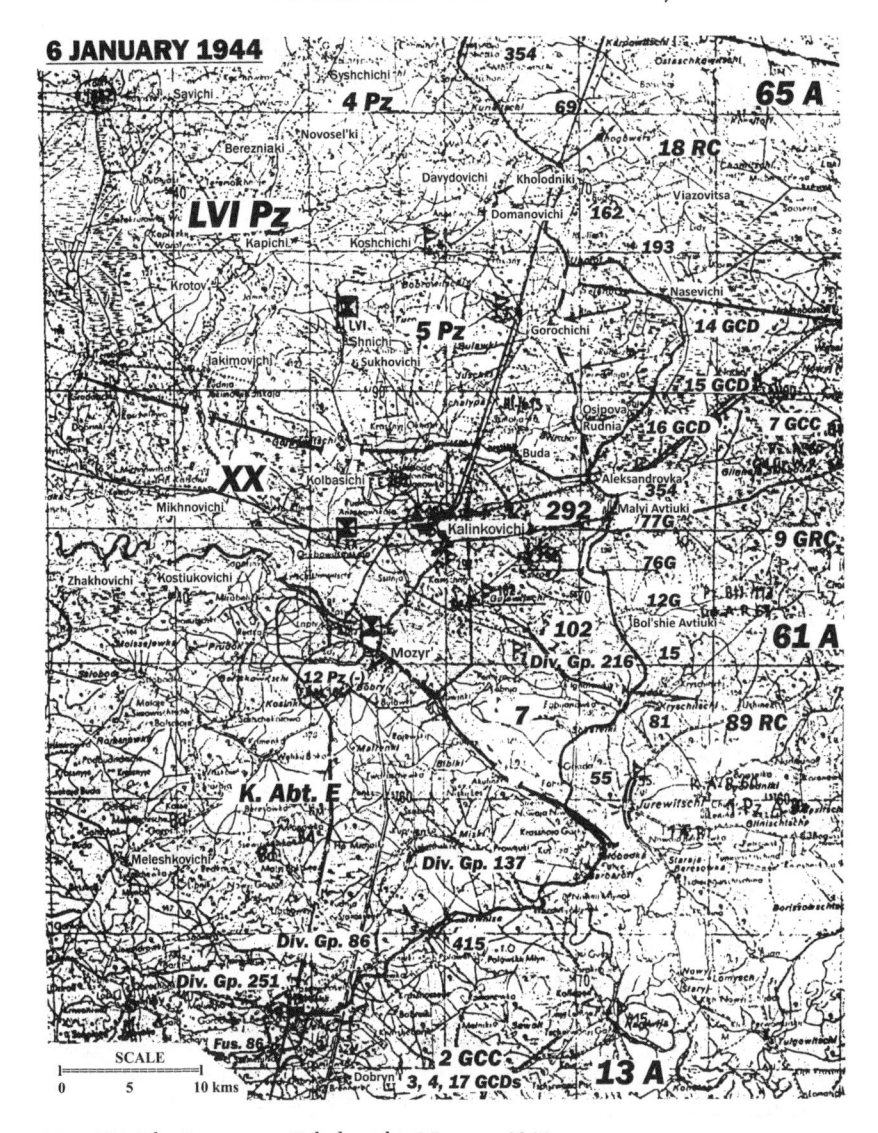

Map 17.2. The Situation at Kalinkovichi, 6 January 1944

Actually, 9th Guards Rifle Corps faced only one battalion on 5th Panzer Division's extreme right wing, XX Army Corps' 292nd Infantry Division, reduced to *kampfgruppe* strength of about a reinforced regiment, and the right wing of XX Corps' 102nd Infantry Division, also a regimental-size *kampfgruppe*.

Using 61st Army's 356th Rifle Division to screen his forward movement, Boreiko deployed his guards corps with 76th, 12th, and 77th Guards Rifle Divisions in single echelon from left to right from Malyi Avtiuki northward to Osipova Rudnia. The rifle corps' mission was to penetrate the Germans' defenses, advance westward along the road and railroad line, and assault and capture Kalinkovichi in concert with 65th Army's forces advancing from the north and northeast. Belov supported 9th Guards Rifle Corps with infantry support tanks and self-propelled guns from 68th Tank Brigade and 1459th Self-propelled Artillery Regiment.

On Boreiko's left, General Khaliuzin's 89th Rifle Corps initially covered and protected 9th Guards Rifle Corps' forward deployment and concentration and then deployed its three rifle divisions, the 51st, 88th, and 15th, in the more than 30-kilometer-wide sector extending from Iurevichi on the Pripiat' River southeast of Mozyr' northward to Malyi Avtiutsevichi. Khaliuzin's corps was to support the army's main attack, maintain pressure on the Germans' defenses southeast of Mozyr' and Kalinkovichi, and join the pursuit after the penetration succeeded. Khaliuzin's corps faced the bulk of XX Army Corps' 102nd Infantry Division and the corps' 7th Infantry Division, which was also only regimental *kampfgruppe* size.

Belov assigned the most critical mission to his army's two guards cavalry corps. During the period from 5 through 7 December, Kriukov's 2nd Guards and Konstantinov's 7th Guards Cavalry Corps were to turn over their sector east of Kalinkovichi to 9th Guards Rifle Corps and regroup southward to occupy assembly areas near Dobryn', south of the Pripiat' River and Mozyr' and adjacent to the German Second Army's (and Army Group Center's) open right flank. German Corps Detachment E, deployed on the Second Army's right wing, defended the region from south of the Pripiat' River to Dobryn' on the Mozyr'-Korosten' road with its 254th, 86th, and 137th Division Groups, whose open flank rested precariously in the northern outskirts of the Pripiat' Marshes. Before the cavalry corps regrouped into this region, this scratch German force faced only 415th Rifle Division, just transferred to 61st Army's control from the 1st Ukrainian Front's 13th Army.

Using 415th Rifle Division to screen their movement, Kriukov's and Konstantinov's two cavalry corps were to first locate and then circumvent the Germans' poorly defended right flank, advance westward along the Meleshkovichi and Balazhevichi axis into the Germans' deep rear area, and seize bridgeheads over the Pripiat' River in XX Army Corps' rear to envelop German forces defending Mozyr' and Kalinkovichi from the southwest. Rokossovsky and Belov hoped that the two cavalry corps could achieve total surprise by exploiting the supposedly impassable terrain.

Rokossovsky allocated the bulk of his *front*'s artillery to demolish the Germans' defenses opposite 65th and 61st Armies. These included Major General of Artillery N. V. Ignatov's entire 4th Artillery Penetration Corps, whose 5th and 12th Artillery Penetration Divisions, 5th Guards-Mortar Division, 22nd Artillery Division, and 20th and 41st Tank Destroyer Brigades were to fire in support of 65th Army, and 6th Artillery Penetration Division

Table 17.2. The Estimated Correlation of Opposing Forces in the Kalinkovichi-Mozyr' Offensive, 8–14 January 1944

OPPOSING FORCES	
Soviet	**German**
Belorussian Front	
65th Army	4th Panzer Division
61st Army	5th Panzer Division
16 rifle divisions	292nd Infantry Division
1 rifle brigade	102nd Infantry Division
1 tank corps (140 tanks and SP guns)	Division Group 216
2 cavalry corps (50 tanks)	7th Infantry Division
1 tank brigade (40 tanks)	613th SecR (203rd SecD)
1 tank regiment (20 tanks)	Corps *Abteilung* E
2 SP artillery regiments (60 SP guns)	Division Group 137
16th Air Army	Division Group 86
	Division Group 251
	707th Infantry Division
	(11 January)
Strength: 232,600 men	100,000 men
310 tanks and SP guns	approx. 116 tanks and assault guns
Depth of Soviet advance: 35–40 kilometers	

Sources: Boevoi sostav Sovetskoi Armii, chast' IV (Ianvar'–dekabr' 1944) [The combat composition of the Soviet Army, pt. 4 (January–December 1944)] (Moscow: Voenizdat, 1988), 14–15; and Anlagen zum KTB, A.O.K. 2 – Ia, Lagenkarten, Jan–Feb 1944, *AOK 2, 49701/92 file,* in NAM series T-312, roll 1281.

and 1st Tank Destroyer Brigade were to support Belov's 61st Army. In addition, Rokossovsky supported 65th and 61st Armies, as well as the two cavalry corps, with extensive engineer and river crossing equipment.

Rokossovsky's thorough plan concentrated more than adequate forces to overcome the Germans' defenses in this critical sector. These consisted of sixteen rifle divisions, the entire 4th Artillery Penetration Corps, two artillery penetration divisions, a mortar division, and two separate artillery brigades (see Table 17.2).

While Rokossovsky's forces established a better than twofold superiority in personnel and threefold superiority in armor over the opposing German forces operationally, tactically this superiority rose to better than 6 to 1 in the 65th and 61st Armies' penetration sectors.

THE 65TH ARMY'S PENETRATION OPERATION (8–12 JANUARY 1944)

Rokossovsky's two armies began their assault at 0940 hours on 8 January, ten minutes before the artillery completed firing its forty- to forty-five-minute artillery preparation (see Maps 17.3 and 17.4). In the sector of Batov's 65th Army, however, the advancing infantry and tanks of Ivanov's and Alekseev's 18th and 105th Rifle Corps immediately encountered fierce German resistance, and the attacks faltered after registering only limited gains. The 69th

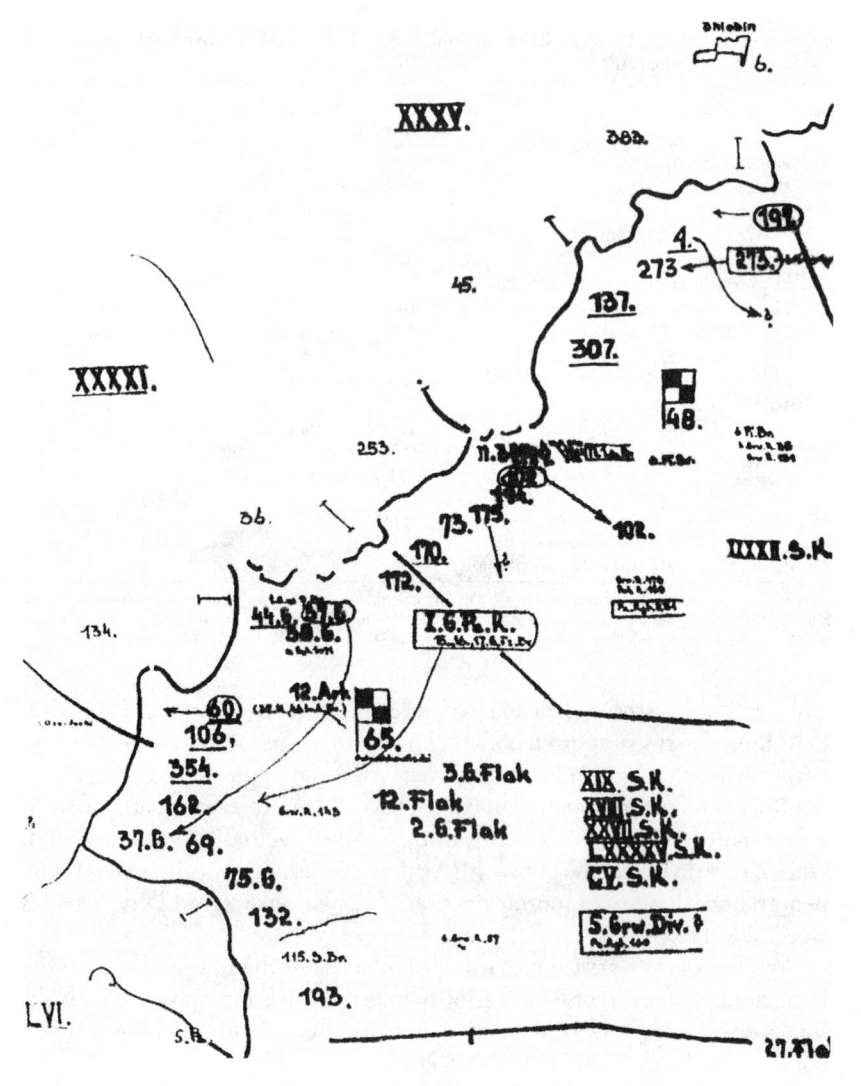

Map 17.3. Ninth Army's Intelligence Assessment in the Zhlobin-Kalinkovichi Sector, 9 January 1944

Rifle Division's history describes the action during the first two days of the assault:

> Snuggling up against the explosions of their own shells, the subunits advanced toward the enemy's trenches ten minutes before the artillery preparation ended.
> Eleven tanks of 255th Tank Regiment, with assault infantry riding on board, flew past the commander's observation post. Intending to pass the

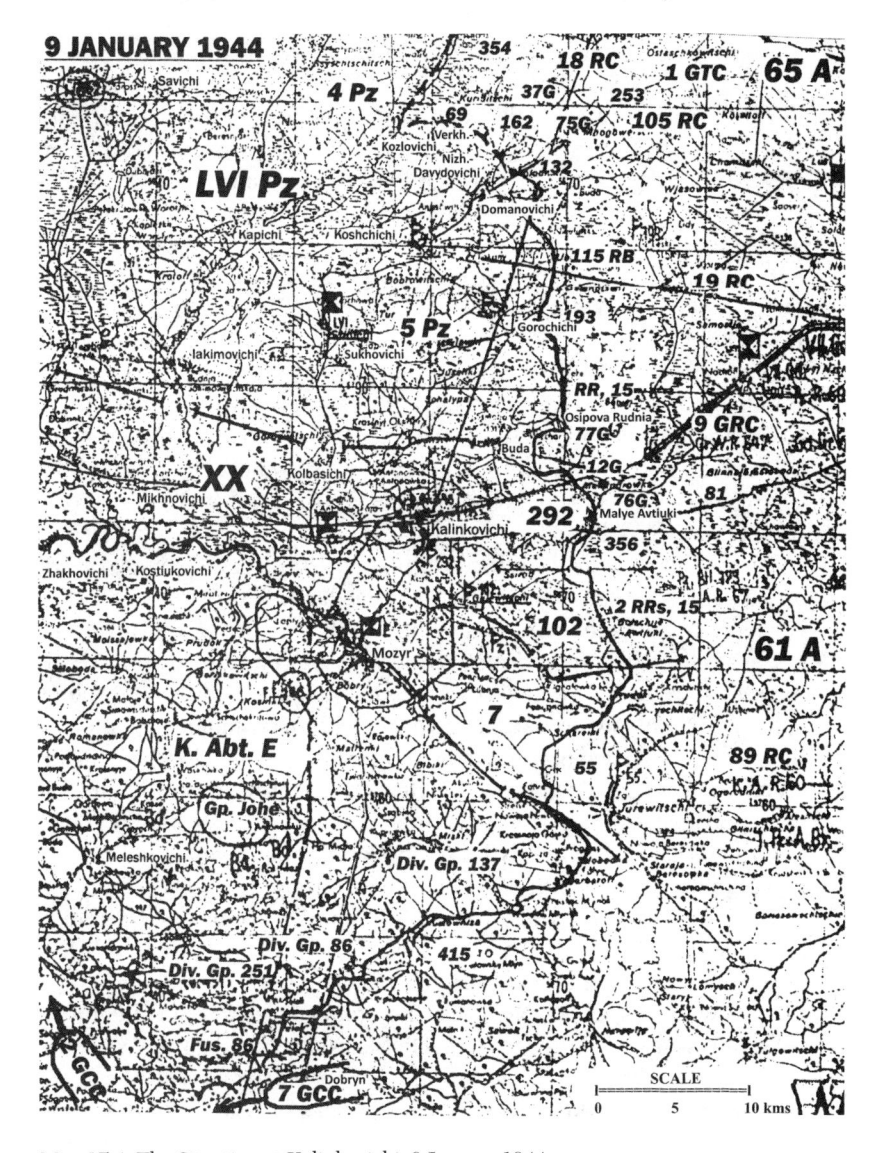

Map 17.4. The Situation at Kalinkovichi, 9 January 1944

infantry, they burst forward and captured the first of three hills, in so doing easing the actions of the attacking regiments.

All three regiments assaulted on line, with 303rd Rifle Regiment on the right wing toward Kozlovichi-Nyshnie, 120th Regiment in the center toward Hill 144.0, and 237th Regiment on the left wing. . . .

As soon as the rifle regiments' lines overcame the enemy's forward trenches, the tanks carrying the assault troops passed them and rushed forward. Under their protection, the infantry wedged into the second trench line and rushed toward Hill 144.0. . . .

The division captured Hill 144.0 by day's end; however, the battle for Hill 147.4 lasted until late in the night. The division managed to overcome the enemy's resistance on that hill and repel numerous counterattacks by his infantry and tanks, but only by committing the reserve subunits into battle.

The division wedged into the enemy's defenses more than 2 kilometers on the first day of battle, but its neighbors [162nd Rifle and 75th Guards Rifle Divisions] had no success and remained in their jumping-off positions. General [I. I.] Sankovsky [the division commander] ordered the battalion in 120th Regiment's reserve to move forward to protect the division's right flank and the separate ski battalion to protect his left flank. They recaptured the enemy's first and second trenches from which he could have conducted counterattacks against the base of the wedge protruding into his defenses.

The division resumed its attack during the first half of 9 January, but after encountering heavy enemy fire, advanced only 300–500 meters. After concentrating 25 tanks and assault guns in the vicinity of Hill 147.4, the Hitlerites launched fierce counterattacks. . . . All day long the enemy attempted to return to Hill 147.4 with his counterattacks. First, the enemy command threw infantry with tanks against 120th Regiment, and then he turned his efforts against the sector of 303rd Regiment. However, the division's soldiers bravely repelled his attacks. Enemy tanks burned and soldiers perished, but the small hill turned out to be unattainable for them.

By nightfall, 37th Guards Rifle Division also achieved some success in its sector. Its units moved up on line with those of 69th Division and halted on the outskirts of Kozlovichi-Verkhnie. From his observation post, General Sankovsky had an excellent view of its lines, which had gone to ground in the outskirts of the village. With the division's right flank now protected, he withdrew the battalion from 120th Regiment back into reserve. Although 37th Division's advance had widened the penetration sector more than twofold, the penetration itself was as yet incomplete. The enemy still held both villages of Kozlovichi (Verkhnie and Nizhnie) and Domanovichi.

As soon as 37th Division advanced forward, the corps commander telephoned Sankovsky:

"Ushakov [Major General E. G., the commander of 37th Guards Rifle Division] has occupied Kozlovichi-Verkhnie," he said, "and his soldiers are already eating potatoes in the village while you are sitting still and not advancing."

"Come to my observation post, from which they can be well observed," answered Sankovsky, "and see where Ushakov's ranks are located."

General Ivanov soon hurried up in his Willies.

The division commander aimed his stereoscope at 37th Division's lines and moved aside. The corps commander clung to the eyepiece, gazed attentively at the panorama in front of him for several minutes, and then uttered irritably,

"Yes, it is apparent that the Germans are eating the potatoes and not Ushakov's soldiers." He got in his vehicle and hurtled away to our neighbor.

On 11 January 1st Guards Don Tank Corps was committed into combat in 69th Division's sector. The tankers passed through 303rd Regiment's combat formation and hastened on toward Kozlovichi-Nizhnie. Suffering great losses in men and material, the enemy began to withdraw.[8]

Indeed, neither Ivanov's nor Alekseev's rifle corps did as well as Batov and Rokossovsky had expected. As they bogged down in the Germans' forward defenses, Batov decided to commit Panov's tank corps to combat, but Rokossovsky realized it was both premature and dangerous to do so. Panov recalled the dilemma and Rokossovsky's solution to it:

The artillery preparation began on the morning of 8 January. Immediately thereafter, the rifle corps began their offensive. However, they achieved no success throughout the course of the day. The same thing occurred on the following day. Nevertheless, on the second half of 9 January, the commander of 65th Army gave the signal for the tankers to enter the battle. Several minutes later, however, an order arrived changing the original order. Later it became known that Army General K. K. Rokossovsky forbade the commitment of the tank corps into combat since the appropriate conditions for its commitment did not exist.

On the evening of 10 January, the *front* commander held a short critique of the past combat with the formations' commanders and branch chiefs at 65th Army's command post. He said that the unsuccessful beginning of the operation was the result of the forces' stereotypical actions. Each day an artillery preparation was conducted, and then the infantry went over to the offensive accompanied by a considerable number of direct support infantry tanks. In addition, the attack line was located too far from the enemy, and, moving through deep snow, quite naturally the infantry lagged behind the tanks. Therefore, a simultaneous and concentrated strike against the forward edge did not occur. During our artillery preparation, the enemy withdrew into covered positions, leaving only observers. When the fire shifted into the depths, the enemy emerged from their bunkers and cut off our infantry from the tanks with heavy machine gun and mortar fire. This forced our infantry to go to ground and then withdraw to their jumping-off positions. This was repeated for three days. General K. K. Rokossovsky advised a change in the tactics and the direction of the main attack.[9]

Based on Rokossovsky's advice, Batov ordered 1st Guards Tank Corps to attack in his army's first echelon on the morning of 12 January from positions extending from Martynovichi to the road junction 3 kilometers northwest of Terebnia. Supported by the entire 4th Artillery Penetration Corps as well as dedicated formations of 16th Air Army, and cooperating with 18th and 105th Rifle Corps' divisions, Panov's tank corps was to penetrate the Germans' defenses in the Kazansk and Terebnia sector, advance along the Nizhne-Kozlovichi, Koshchichi, and Turovichi axis, and capture Kalinkovichi by an assault from the northwest. The 69th Rifle and 75th Guards Rifle Divisions protected the tanks corps' extensive regrouping to its new axis.

After it was approved by Rokossovsky, Batov's plan assigned Panov's brigades entirely new objectives:

The 15th Tank Brigade was to attack along the Kazansk, Verkhne-Kozlovichi, and Koshchichi axis, destroy the opposing enemy, capture Verkhne-Kozlovichi and Koshchichi, and then continue to exploit success toward Gorokhovo.

The 1st Motorized Rifle Brigade had the mission to attack along the Nizhne-Kozlovichi and Sel'tsy axis, penetrate the enemy's defense, and capture Nizhne-Kozlovichi and Sel'tsy. Then it was to capture Turovichi in cooperation with 17th Tank Brigade.

The 17th Tank Brigade had the mission of attacking through Terebnia, Anisovichi, and the eastern outskirts of Sel'tsy, destroying the opposing enemy, and capturing Anisovichi and Drinevo. Part of the brigade was to capture Turovichi in cooperation with 1st Motorized Rifle Brigade.[10]

Overnight on 10–11 January, the staffs of 65th Army and its subordinate corps and divisions worked hard to implement every aspect of the new plan but, first and foremost, the extensive regrouping (see Map 17.5). This included the preparation of march routes and new jumping-off positions; the arrival of Generals Ignatov and Komarov, the commanders of the artillery penetration corps and assault aviation corps, with communications teams at Panov's forward observation post; and the assignment of artillery and aviation officers with radios to the headquarters of each of the tank corps' active brigades.

Because snowy weather set in early on 11 January, Batov had to cancel his planned aviation strikes against designated German strongpoints in the new penetration sector. Nevertheless, his army began its artillery preparation at 1200 hours, this time only long enough for the attacking tanks to reach the forward German trenches. The artillery preparation included a volley of

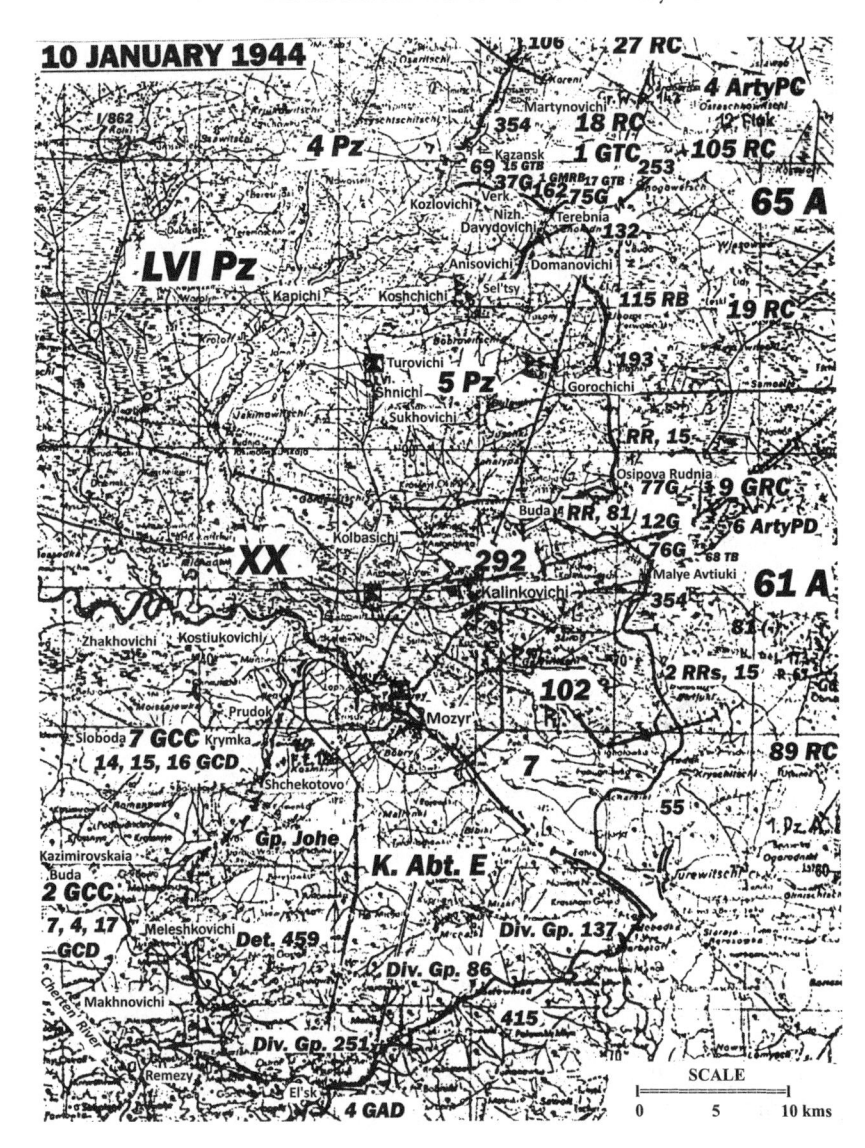

The Belorussian Front's Kalinkovichi-Mozyr' Offensive 433

Map 17.5. The Situation at Kalinkovichi, 10 January 1944

multiple-rocket launchers followed by an intense raid by artillery gunfire. As described by one observer:

> The first wave of tanks went forward simultaneously with the volley of *"Katiushas"* [M-13 and M-31 multiple-rocket launchers]. A second wave with assault infantry began moving forward a minute later. Moving at

high speed, the first wave of tanks raised up a whirlwind of snowflakes, hiding the second wave from enemy observation. The artillery shifted its fires forward on the signals given by the artillery officers advancing with the brigade commands.

The tanks reduced their speed somewhat at the enemy's forward edge, and, meanwhile, the motorized riflemen jumped down from the tanks to the right and left and destroyed the Fascist invaders from the march. Part of the motorized rifle squads, which had been designated in advance, passed through the second line of trenches on the tanks. In this fashion, the guardsmen subjected the entire first position of the enemy's defense to attack simultaneously.

Hand-to-hand combat raged on in some of the trenches. It took two hours for our forces to capture the first position in the enemy's defense and rush into the depths. The battle was developing successfully. Prisoners appeared. They belonged to 12th Panzer Division.[11]

As accurate as this description was, in reality, Batov's fresh assault struck and shattered the defenses of German 4th and 5th Panzer Divisions rather than the 12th Panzer. Regardless of unit designation, the German defenses collapsed, unleashing an irresistible tide of riflemen, tanks, and self-propelled guns (see Map 17.6). Spearheaded by Panov's armor, riflemen from Ivanov's and Alekseev's divisions surged forward across the entire front north of Kalinkovichi.

Protected by a wave of devastating artillery fire, 15th Guards Tank Brigade of Panov's 1st Guards Tank Corps, with the riflemen of 37th Guards Rifle Division following in its wake, captured Kazansk and reached the northern outskirts of Verkhne-Kozlovichi. While the tanks bypassed the strongpoint from the west and cut its communications routes, the motorized rifle battalion attacked it from the northeast and captured the village after a fifteen-minute fight. At the same time, a motorized rifle battalion from 1st Guards Motorized Rifle Brigade, along with a tank battalion from 15th Guards Tank Brigade, captured Nizhne-Kozlovichi by an assault from the northwest.

Soon after, the Germans counterattacked against Nizhne-Kozlovichi with an infantry battalion, seven tanks, and three Ferdinand assault guns; however, the motorized rifle brigade and follow-on infantry from 69th Rifle Division, supported by tanks and antitank guns from 732nd Tank Destroyer Battalion, repelled the counterattack, destroying two tanks and two Ferdinand assault guns.

Together with infantrymen from 75th Guards Rifle Division, 17th Guards Tank Brigade assaulted 5th Panzer Division's defenses along and east of the main road, encountering particularly strong resistance. The Germans responded to the Soviet assault with heavy artillery fire from the vicinity of Domanovichi and tank and infantry counterattacks from Anisovichi.

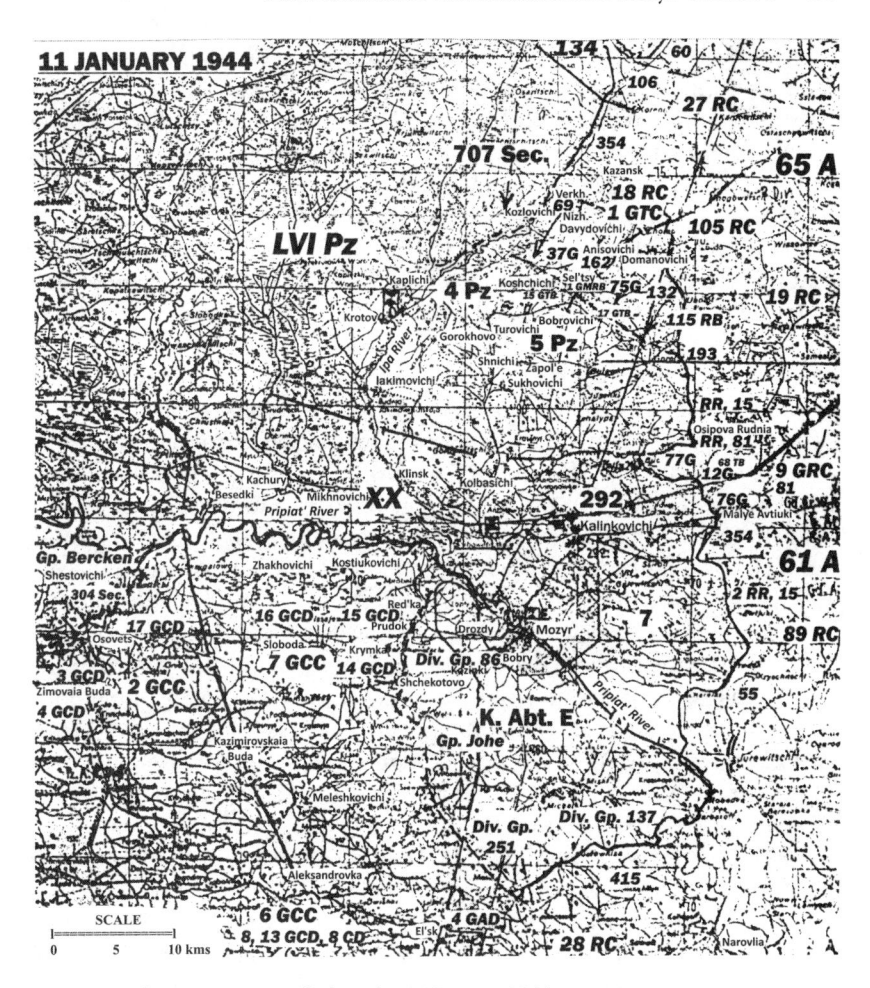

Map 17.6. The Situation at Kalinkovichi, 11 January 1944

However, the weather improved by 1500 hours, permitting three groups of from fifteen to twenty assault aircraft each from Komarov's assault aviation division to strike the German positions in Domanovichi and Anisovichi and break up the counterattack in conjunction with a ten-minute fire raid the army artillery group delivered against Anisovichi. Hard on the heels of the air and artillery strikes, 17th Guards Tank Brigade captured Anisovichi and seized the bridge north of Drinevo and the village itself by 1900 hours. By this time, 15th Guards Tank Brigade had captured Koshchichi, and 1st Guards Motorized Rifle Brigade, the village of Sel'tsy.

By day's end on 11 January, Panov's tank corps had penetrated the enemy's entire defensive belt, advancing 15–18 kilometers and capturing fifteen village strongpoints from 4th and 5th Panzer Divisions. Ivanov's and Alekseev's rifle divisions followed with five rifle divisions, the 162nd, 37th Guards, 69th, 75th Guards, and 132nd, advancing abreast from the Ipa River eastward across the Shatsilki-Kalinkovichi road. Although the two German panzer divisions struggled to erect new defenses, they did so in vain.

Overnight on 11–12 January, the Germans subjected the advancing tank columns to heavy artillery fire. One of the shells struck 1st Guards Motorized Rifle Brigade's headquarters tank, wounding the brigade's chief of staff and several other staff officers and destroying its radio. However, the brigade replaced its radio from reserve stocks and continued its advance under the cover of darkness along with the remainder of Panov's tank corps.

After failing to capture Turovichi by a night assault from the march, largely because it was astride German withdrawal routes packed with tanks, artillery, and infantry, 17th Guards Tank Brigade set up an ambush site near the village and maneuvered the rest of its force westward to strike the German strongpoint at Gorokhovo from the rear. The 17th Brigade captured the village of Gorokhovo by dawn, while the 1st Guards Motorized Rifle and 15th Guards Tank Brigades jointly assaulted and captured Shiichi and Sukhovichi shortly after dawn on 12 January, by doing so threatening the German defenders in Turovichi with encirclement (see Map 17.7). A particularly fierce struggle broke out between the nearly encircled Germans, attempting to break out to the west, and 15th and 17th Guards Tank and 1st Guards Motorized Rifle Brigades, which blocked the eastern, northern, and western approaches into the village. Assisted by 732nd Tank Destroyer Battalion, the combined force inflicted heavy losses on the encircled German force.[12]

With their left wing north of Kalinkovichi collapsing, Second Army and LVI Panzer Corps ordered the remnants of 4th and 5th Panzer Divisions to contain Batov's advance so that they could withdraw their forces from the Kalinkovichi region westward to new defense lines along the Ipa River. Although the German forces managed to disrupt Batov's communications and supply lines briefly as they withdrew westward from the Drinevo and Turovichi region, 69th and 75th Guards Rifle Divisions managed to clear these routes so that the tank corps could continue its southward advance.

During the afternoon of 12 January, 15th and 17th Guards Tank Brigades, supported by infantry from 69th Rifle and 75th Guards Rifle Divisions and a short but powerful artillery raid, assaulted and captured Turovichi and, at 2200 hours, the village strongpoint at Zapol'e to the south. The defending Germans withdrew toward Kalinkovichi, only 15 kilometers to the south.

Overnight on 12–13 January, 1st Guards Tank Corps' commanders and senior staff officers assembled at Zapol'e, where they received congratulations from Batov. Both Batov and corps commander Alekseev joined the meeting at 0300 hours, issued fresh orders for a final assault on Kalinkovichi from the north by 1st Guards Tank and 105th Rifle Corps, and made neces-

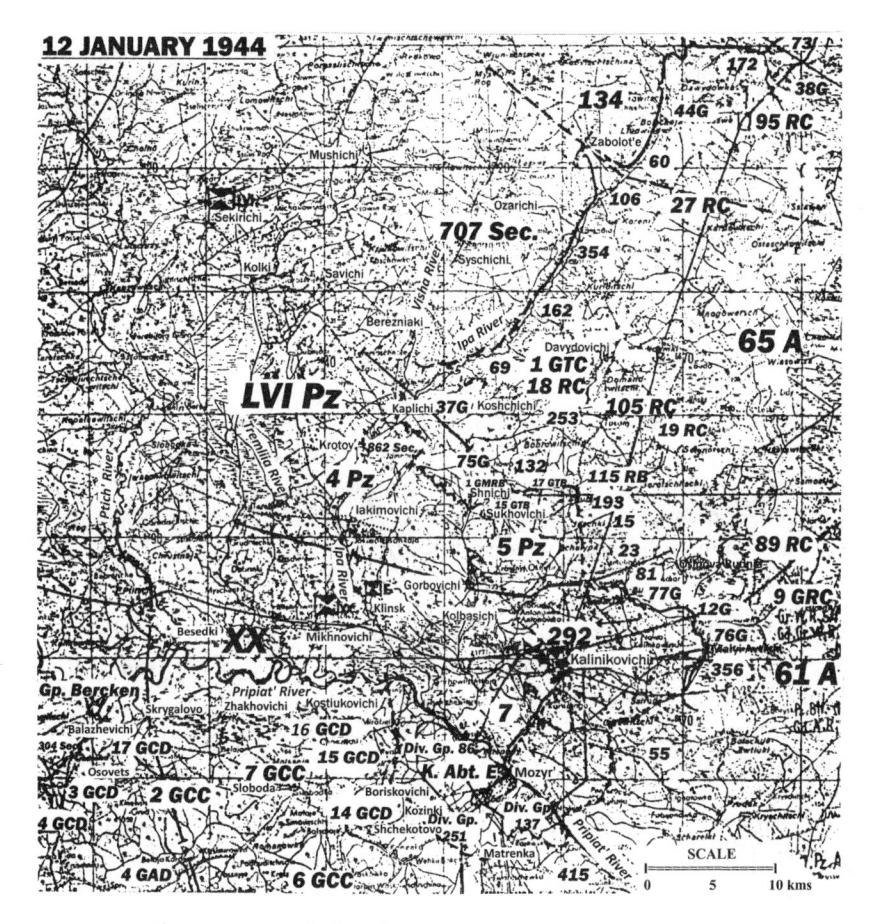

Map 17.7. The Situation at Kalinkovichi, 12 January 1944

sary arrangements to coordinate and support the final assault. While Panov's tank corps and Alekseev's 105th Rifle Corps were to assault Kalinkovichi from the north, 162nd, 69th, and 37th Guards Rifle Divisions of Ivanov's 18th Rifle Corps were to wheel westward, press German forces back to the Ipa River line, and capture bridgeheads over the Ipa near Kaplichi, Krotov, and Iakimovichi.

THE 61ST ARMY'S PENETRATION OPERATION (8–12 JANUARY 1944)

As Batov prepared to deliver his final assault on Kalinkovichi, Rokossovsky made sure that the offensive would succeed by ordering Belov's 61st Army to strike the city's defenses from the east. Strangely enough, since beginning its offensive on 8 January, Belov's army had experienced many of the same problems that had slowed the forward progress of Batov's force (see Map 17.4).

When Belov planned his offensive, he decided to deploy both his army and his corps in single-echelon formation to increase the strength of his initial blow. As described in his memoirs by Colonel Mal'kov, the commander of 12th Guards Rifle Division:

> For two–three days before the beginning of combat operations, the army commander corrected the plans of his division commanders. Changing the original decision, which required each division to deploy in a two-echelon formation, he ordered the attacking formations to deploy in single-echelon combat formation.
>
> By introducing such changes, the army commander assumed that, since the offensive was planned to a depth of 12–15 kilometers and was limited to the capture of Kalinkovichi, this mission could be fulfilled by a single blow and without the presence of second echelons. Such a correction not only complicated the preparations for the offensive but, as it turned out, it also led to many difficulties during the conduct of the battle.[13]

Belov's 61st Army began its offensive at dawn on 8 January after a forty-five-minute artillery preparation. Attacking in the center of 9th Guards Rifle Corps' combat formation, 12th Guards Rifle Division captured the forward trenches of 292nd Infantry Division's defenses and advanced 1.5–2 kilometers in its center and on its right wing before being halted by intense enemy machine gun and artillery fire. The 77th Guards Rifle Division, assaulting on 12th Guards Rifle Division's right, penetrated more than 2 kilometers but then encountered strong resistance and was stopped in the eastern outskirts of Buda. On 12th Guards Division's left, 76th Guards Rifle Division was stopped in its tracks and forced to withdraw to its jumping-off position.

In fact, by nightfall on 8 January, 9th Guards Rifle Corps' assault ground to a virtual halt after only minimal gains. The strongpoints at Osipova Rudnia, Golevitsy Station, and Malyi Avtiukii were still in German hands, and artillery and machine guns defending these strong points delivered withering fire on Red Army troops wedged into the small penetration in between:

> Despite launching attacks both during the day and at night, from 8 through 11 January, the corps' formations were not able to penetrate the enemy's defenses. Since each and every attack was preceded by an artillery preparation, in this case it represented a signal to the enemy, forewarning them of the attack. This was one of the basic reasons why our attacks failed.
>
> The situation became more complicated with each day. Not only did the Germans successfully repel our attacks but, striving to restore their lost positions, they also conducted frequent counterattacks. Over the

course of three days, they launched 19 counterattacks, mainly from the region of Hill 128.4, where they committed fresh reinforcements at the boundary between 77th and 12th Guards Rifle Divisions. The subunits of these divisions turned out to be in flat, open, and swampy terrain, where there was no cover. Situated under enemy observation and fire, our units suffered heavy losses from machine gun, artillery, and mortar fire.

The Germans occupied a most favorable position. They were deployed in trenches and had bunkers and dugouts to warm and protect their personnel.

In warfare, one should not always blindly adhere to the term, "not a step back," which often leads to unnecessary and unjustified personnel losses, curtails initiative on the part of commanders, and prevents the timely employment of maneuver by forces. In these conditions, however, it would have been more expedient to withdraw the corps' units to more favorable lines, put them in order, reconnoiter the enemy again, and organize a new attack rather than leave them in front of the forward edge of the Germans' defenses. Unfortunately, this was not done.

Several times each day, Major General A. A. Boreiko, our corps commander, and Lieutenant General P. A. Belov, the commander of 61st Army, demanded insistently that our troops penetrate the enemy's defense and capture Kalinkovichi at all cost. However, these demands did not alter the situation. Reserves were needed to penetrate the enemy's defenses, and beside the ski battalions, there were no reserves in the divisions.[14]

In short, according to Mal'kov, "We needed fresh reserves to continue the attack, but there were none in the division. The army commander's decision to change the initial variant for the creation of [our] combat formations proved costly for the forces."[15] As was the case with Batov's army, once again Rokossovsky intervened to demand the use of a more imaginative approach (see Map 17.6). In this case, on the evening of 12 January, he ordered Belov and Boreiko to employ their only reserves, the ski battalions, to break the stalemate east of Kalinkovichi. Rokossovsky did so in the full knowledge that Batov's assault north of the city was likely to succeed and, far to the southwest of Mozyr', his *front's* cavalry corps were in the process of turning the Second Army's flank, by doing so rendering the Germans' defenses at Kalinkovichi untenable.

Rokossovsky's gambit east of Kalinkovichi involved the skillful employment of the rifle divisions' ski battalions in a fashion similar to how Gorbatov, the commander of 3rd Army, had employed his ski detachment during the daring raid on Pribor earlier in the month. In this case, the ski battalions were ideally suited to conduct raid missions against weak spots in the enemy's defenses. Armed with machine guns, submachine guns, and light mortars and traveling silently on skis, these battalions had been subjected to intense training since October 1943. Belov decided to employ the battalions overnight on 12–13 January without any artillery preparation against narrow sectors of the enemy's defenses opposite each of the forward divisions. Just prior to the advance, each rifle division was to concentrate all of its fires on one narrow sector to suppress the German defenses while the ski battalions conducted their raids.

Throughout the preparations for 61st Army's renewed assaults east of Kalinkovichi, all eyes in the *Stavka* and Rokossovsky's headquarters were on the vital maneuvers being conducted by the two guards cavalry corps south of Mozyr'. All understood that the cavalry's successful operations would do more than anything else to break the Germans' grip on Kalinkovichi.

CAVALRY OPERATIONS AGAINST MOZYR' (8–12 JANUARY 1944)

On 2 January 1944, Belov ordered Kriukov's 2nd Guards and Konstantinov's 7th Guards Cavalry Corps to turn over their defensive sector to 9th Guards Rifle Corps; march 90 kilometers southward to new assembly areas in the Novaia Rudnia, Vystupovichi, and Krasnyi region, 55 kilometers southwest of Mozyr'; and prepare for their deep raid northwestward toward the Pripiat' River deep into the Germans' rear area. The long columns of cavalry marched along a practically roadless, forested, and swampy terrain in alternating freezes and thaws that exacted a heavy toll on man and horse alike. After crossing the Pripiat' River near Narovlia, 33 kilometers south-southeast of Mozyr', the two corps reached their new assembly areas late on 5 January. There they received new orders to move northward 20–25 kilometers to concentrate in the Knurovka region northeast of Gazhin and, in cooperation with 415th Rifle Division and local partisans, "cross the railroad line in the sector between Bogutichi and Shishki (38–48 kilometers south of Mozyr') with their advanced guards on the morning of 8 January, and, by enveloping the enemy's open flank, conduct a raid into his rear area in the general direction of Mozyr'.

As described by a participant in the operation, the terrain offered as much of a challenge as German resistance:

> The advance by 7th [and 2nd] Guards Cavalry Corps during the forthcoming operation was to pass through one of the sectors of the Poles'e, bordered on the east and north by the Pripiat' River, on the west by the Ubort' and Cherten' Rivers, and on the south by the Slovechna River. The region abounded with numerous rivers, streams, and swamps. The forests occupied a considerable expanse in the corps' area of combat operations. The dirt roads, forming defiles, which in places stretched tens of

kilometers between the flooded forests and swamps, were the only routes suitable for movement.

The corps had to conduct its offensive through one of the regions where the Poles'e partisans were active; therefore, the Hitlerites had burned almost all of the populated points. They either mined all of the roads or created barriers and abattis along them, and they blew up all of the bridges across the rivers and streams. . . .

According to advance information, the enemy grouping in the corps' offensive sector between Mozyr' and El'sk consisted of 137th Division Group, formed from the remnants of 137th Infantry Division, 251st Infantry Division, and 25th Panzer Grenadier Regiment and other subunits of 12th Panzer Division.[16]

Actually, the two cavalry corps faced Second Army's Corps *Abteilung* (detachment) E, which consisted of 251st, 86th, and 137th Division Groups and small engineer elements left behind by 12th Panzer Division when it left for the Leningrad region. These forces occupied defenses in the 30-kilometer-wide sector extending from El'sk northward to Mozyr'.

After the two cavalry corps completed their march into the new assembly areas, on 7 January, Belov refined their missions, ordering Konstantinov's 7th Guards Cavalry Corps to advance its first-echelon divisions to the Meleshkovichi and Aleksandrovka regions, 23–30 kilometers southwest of Mozyr' and adjacent to the Germans' open right flank, by the morning of 9 January. Kriukov's 2nd Guards Cavalry Corps was to follow and extend the front further west along the Pripiat' River toward Petrikov, 58 kilometers west of Kalinkovichi.

On 7 and 8 January, Konstantinov's cavalry corps advanced 75 kilometers northwestward into the Germans' deep rear area on horseback, reaching the Meleshkovichi and Aleksandrovka line by day's end on 8 January. In the process, 14th Guards Cavalry Division and 16th Guards Cavalry Division's 58th Guards Cavalry Regiment reportedly routed a battalion of German infantry in the Remezy region, 14 kilometers west of El'sk, and captured the village.

The 7th Guards Cavalry Corps continued its advance on 9 January, however, in conditions described as "exceptionally difficult," primarily because of the poor roads and the constant necessity to construct new bridges as the horsemen advanced (see Map 17.4). Nevertheless, the corps pushed forward overnight on 9 and 10 January and, after dispersing small groups of defending Germans, in a sharp fight 14th Guards Cavalry Division's 56th Regiment captured Prudok, less than 10 kilometers west of Mozyr', driving its defenders (part of Cavalry Regiment "Mitte" [Center]) westward along the southern bank of the Pripiat' River. Later in the day, 14th Guards Cavalry Division captured Shchekotovo and Krymka, 8 kilometers southwest of Mozyr', and 16th Guards Cavalry Division drove German forces from the villages of Muk and Sloboda, 10 kilometers to the west and 8 kilometers south of the Pripiat' River (see Map 17.6).

The unexpected arrival of 7th Guards Cavalry Corps' lead divisions in the Meleshkovichi, Prudok, and Sloboda region outflanked German defenses at El'sk and Mozyr', placed the Soviet cavalry only a few short kilometers from the Pripiat' River, and rendered German Corps Detachment E's defenses south of Mozyr' utterly untenable.

During this same period, Kriukov's 2nd Guards Cavalry Corps, marching behind the left wing of Konstantinov's corps, pressed forward toward Petrikov in the face of occasional German counterattacks, reaching a line extending from Osevets southward through Zimovaia Buda to Ubortskaia Rudnia, 45 kilometers west of Mozyr' and 15–20 kilometers southeast of Petrikov, by day's end on 10 January. The defending Gruppe von Bercken, led by Lieutenant General Werner von Bercken, the commander of 102nd Infantry Division, consisted initially of 1st and 3rd Battalions of Cavalry Regiment "Mitte," reinforced by 304th, 696th, and 242nd Security Battalions, and, within days, the arriving battalions of the 102nd Infantry's 84th Regiment withdrew to a bridgehead on the southern bank of the Pripiat' River south of Petrikov. Overnight on 10–11 January General Weiss ordered 102nd Infantry Division, whose 84th, 216th, and 232nd Regiments were withdrawing westward from Kalinkovichi, to organize the bridgehead south of Petrikov. As the 102nd did, they also unwittingly took responsibility for defending the northern bank of the Pripiat' threatened by 2nd Guards Cavalry Corps.

At this point, perceiving a marvelous opportunity to smash the German Second Army's right wing, an impatient General Staff ordered Rokossovsky to accelerate the cavalry corps' operations. In a directive dispatched at 2030 hours on 10 January, "To the Commander of the Belorussian Front Concerning the Necessity for Decisive Actions by the Cavalry Corps," the chief of the Red Army General Staff, A. I. Antonov, demanded Rokossovsky report "by what means are you supporting the advance of 2nd and 7th Cavalry Corps, which have only insignificant enemy forces in front of them?" and "What measures have you taken to support the missions assigned to the cavalry corps?" Antonov ended the curt message by declaring, "Comrade Ivanov [Stalin] attaches exceptionally important significance to the speed and decisiveness of these corps' operations."[17]

In response to Antonov's instructions, Rokossovsky immediately stripped 7th Guards Cavalry Corps from the control of Belov's 61st Army and took personal control of both it and 2nd Guards Cavalry Corps. That evening Rokossovsky ordered Konstantinov's cavalry corps: "While cooperating with 415th Rifle Division, continue pursuing the withdrawing enemy, encircle his rear service units with two divisions, and capture Mozyr', its railroad station, and the highway bridge over the Pripiat' River."[18] Soon after, he ordered Kriukov's 2nd Guards Cavalry Corps to alter its axis of advance, "cut the Kalinkovichi-Zhitkovichi [west of Kalinkovichi and north of the Pripiat' River] railroad line," and assist in the capture of Kalinkovichi.[19] This meant that Konstantinov's corps was to assault German Corps *Abteilung* E's defenses at Mozyr' from the west, while Kriukov's corps struck directly northward across the Pripiat' River to sever German communications west of Kalinkovichi and link up with the forces of Batov's 65th Army, about to resume their attacks from the north (see Map 17.6).

Konstantinov's 7th Guards Cavalry Corps continued its attacks overnight on 10 and 11 January in the sector extending from Drozdy through Voennyi Gorodok and Kozinki to Red'ka, 5–6 kilometers due west of Mozyr'. Early the next morning, its 15th Guards Cavalry Division seized a section of the railroad line east of Kozinki only to be driven back to its jumping-off positions by a counterattack by a battalion of German infantry from Division Group 86, supposedly supported by eight tanks. Faced with heavy resistance across its entire front, the cavalry corps was unable to advance any further. Without armor support, it was abundantly clear that the cavalry corps could not capture Mozyr'. The strong resistance by Corps *Abteilung* E's infantry west of Mozyr' continued all day on 12 January without any appreciable Soviet gains (see Map 17.7). However, by day's end it became apparent that the unbearable pressure had forced the Germans to begin a withdrawal from the Mozyr' salient.

In fact, acting on the orders of General Weiss, the commander of Second Army, Corps *Abteilung* E had begun shrinking its defensive lines south of Mozyr' as early as the night of 10 January, when it abandoned El'sk and withdrew its line about 10 kilometers to the north. It continued this process on 11 and 12 January, finally falling back to new defenses south of Mozyr' proper. Overnight on 12 and 13 January, it intended to complete its withdrawal in conjunction with a general withdrawal by all German forces in the Kalinkovichi region westward to new defenses along the Ipa River.

Meanwhile, from late on 10 January though day's end on 12 January, Kriukov's 2nd Guards Rifle Corps left its 3rd Guards Cavalry Division to contain the German bridgehead south of Petrikov and regrouped its three remaining divisions eastward into jumping-off positions south of the Pripiat' River opposite the towns of Besedki and Mikhnovichi, 30–38 kilometers east of Petrikov and 20–28 kilometers west of Kalinkovichi. At this time Second Army's XX Army Corps had yet to establish any defenses along the river's northern bank in this sector. Kriukov's truncated cavalry corps was to assault northward across the Pripiat' early on 13 January.

Urged on by Rokossovsky, Konstantinov ordered his cavalry corps to mount an all-out assault against Corps *Abteilung* E's defenses at Mozyr' early on 13 January, at the same time that Batov's 65th and Belov's 61st Armies were to launch their final assault on Kalinkovichi and Kriukov's cavalry were forcing the Pripiat' River roughly midway between Petrikov and Kalinkovichi. Konstantinov's plan called for his three cavalry divisions to envelop German defenses at Drozdy, Voennyi Gorodok (military town), and Kozinki from the north and south:

> The 15th Guards Cavalry Division was assigned the mission to attack along the Kozinki, Matrenka, Raevskii, and Pripiat' axis and cut the enemy's withdrawal routes into Mozyr' from the south.
>
> The 14th Guards Cavalry Division, reinforced by a corps artillery subunit and 1816th Self-propelled Artillery Regiment, was ordered to fulfill its previous mission: while operating along the railroad, to capture Mozyr' Station and the railroad bridge across the Pripiat' River by the end of 13 January and the highway bridge at Mozyr' by the night of 14 January.
>
> The 16th Guards Cavalry Division was to protect the corps' main force and its communication with a covering force of partisans and squadrons armed with antitank weapons. On 13 January it was to force the Pripiat' River at Kostiukovichi [15 kilometers northwest of Mozyr'] and cut the railroad line in the Kachury and Klinsk sector [5–6 kilometers to the north] with a forward detachment made up of a reinforced cavalry squadron and partisans from the Mozyr' Brigade. Two regiments deployed in the Prudok, Boriskovichi, and Khramkh region were to help exploit 14th Guards Cavalry Division's success by operating from behind its left flank toward Mozyr' Station.[20]

By late on 12 January, the stage was set for the final Soviet assault on Kalinkovichi and Mozyr', literally from all sides (see Map 7.7). Adding to German Second Army's discomfiture, its intelligence organs reported, mistakenly as it turned out, that another Soviet cavalry corps, the 6th Guards, had joined the 7th Guards for the assault on Mozyr'.[21] Accordingly, shortly after midnight the Second Army issued orders to its forward corps to begin evacuating the entire region east of the Ipa River. The Germans had just begun the withdrawal when Rokossovsky's forces began their final assault.

THE BATTLE FOR KALINKOVICHI AND PURSUIT TO THE IPA RIVER (13–14 JANUARY 1944)

Spearheaded by Panov's 1st Guards Tank Corps, Batov unleashed his two rifle corps for their final assault on German defenses northwest of Kalinkovichi. Panov's three mobile brigades attacked at first light on 13 January against diminishing German resistance (see Map 17.8). By this time LVI Panzer Corps' 4th Panzer Division was already beginning to withdraw to a new defensive sector along the Ipa River from Kaplichi southward to Krotov, 20–25 kilometers northwest of Kalinkovichi, and 5th Panzer Division was

Map 17.8. The Situation at Kalinkovichi, 13 January 1944

doing likewise to its new river defenses anchored on Iakimovichi, 15–20 kilometers northwest of Kalinkovichi. Simultaneously, XX Army Corps 292nd and 7th Infantry Divisions and Corps *Abteilung* E abandoned Mozyr' and Kalinkovichi and moved to occupy defenses along the Ipa River at and south of Klinsk, 12–15 kilometers west of Kalinkovichi. The withdrawal could not have been more timely because, before it took place, there were no sizable German forces available west of Klinsk with which to defend the Pripiat' River line against the cavalry assaults just beginning from the south.

In the sector of Batov's 65th Army, the 1st Guards Motorized Brigade and 15th and 17th Guards Tank Brigades of Panov's tank corps struck southward early on 13 January, by midday capturing the fortified strongpoints at

Kolbasichi and Slobodka, only 5 kilometers northwest of Kalinkovichi. Here, however, the advance stopped briefly after encountering heavy fire from German rear guard forces. Panov halted his advance, while Komarov's assault aircraft pounded German artillery positions, and the infantry of Alekseev's 105th Rifle Corps caught up with the advancing tankers. Late in the day, Panov's tanks and Alekseev's infantry captured Antonovka, the last village obstacle on the path to Kalinkovichi.

Meanwhile, 162nd, 37th Guards, and 69th Rifle Divisions of Ivanov's 18th Rifle Corps pursued German 4th Panzer Division to the west, reaching the Ipa River from north of Kaplichi southward to Iakimovichi. Farther to the east, 75th Guards and 132nd and 253rd Rifle Divisions of Alekseev's 105th Rifle Corps supported Panov's armor until they reached the outskirts of Kalinkovichi. Thereafter, 75th Guards and 253rd Rifle Divisions wheeled westward toward the Ipa River, while 132nd Rifle Division cooperated with 193rd Rifle Division and 115th Rifle Brigade of Samarsky's 19th Rifle Corps, now approaching Kalinkovichi from the northeast.

Batov's army completed its role in the capture of Kalinkovichi on 14 January (see Map 17.9). At 0400 hours Panov's armor entered the northern outskirts of the city only to learn that the last German troops had already withdrawn. There, the tankers linked up with 61st Army's 12th Guards Rifle Division, which had just entered the city from the east. Without wasting a moment, Batov began regrouping the remainder of his forces to the Ipa River line, where Rokossovsky had ordered him to begin the second stage of the offensive.

Meanwhile, in the sector of Belov's 61st Army, the specially prepared ski detachments began to unhinge the Germans' defenses overnight on 12–13 January. Advancing in company and platoon columns, at 2300 hours the ski battalions literally began infiltrating through the Germans' defenses. While they advanced, artillery suppressed the targets identified by the advancing battalions. After breaking through the defenses, fifteen to twenty minutes later, the divisions' forward regiments went over to the attack. By the time the main attack began, 12th Rifle Division's ski detachment was already 2 kilometers deep and had cut the Buda-Kalinkovichi road.

Ironically, just as the ski detachments were beginning their operations, XX Army Corps ordered its 292nd and 7th Infantry Divisions to withdraw their forward positions to new defensive lines just east of Kalinkovichi. This meant that the ski detachments actually struck the Germans' rear guards. In any case, as soon as Boreiko's 9th Guards Rifle Corps began its general assault early on 13 January, his forces advanced relatively unopposed to the eastern outskirts of Kalinkovichi. Nor did the resistance stiffen because the next day German XX Army Corps ordered all of its defending units to fall back to the Ipa River line. Belov's forces pursued, occupying all of Kalinkovichi on 14 January and linking up with the forward elements of Batov's

Map 17.9. The Situation at Kalinkovichi, 14 January 1944

army. However, one analysis of the capture of Mozyr' and Kalinkovichi declared that it "achieved territorial rather than operational results. According to the witness, K. Tippelskirch, because of the weak cooperation between 1st Guards Tank Corps and the two cavalry corps, German 2nd Army was able to escape encirclement at the very last moment."[22]

As the final chapter in the battle for Kalinkovichi was unfolding north of the Pripiat' River, Rokossovsky's two cavalry corps began their assault south of the river. As was the case with 61st Army's assault east of Kalinkovichi, the attack by Konstantinov's 7th Guards Cavalry Corps and 415th Rifle Division literally "struck thin air" because German Corps *Abteilung* E had already begun withdrawing from the Mozyr' region at dawn on 13 January, leaving behind only small rear guards to delay the Russian advance (see Map 7.8). The history of the cavalry corps described the final two days of its advance on Mozyr', albeit somewhat flamboyantly:

On the night of 13 January, 15th Guards Cavalry Division (53rd and 55th Guards Cavalry Regiment and 147th Artillery-Mortar Regiment) passed through Shchekotovo and advanced toward Matrenka. In the morning it reached Serashi Farm and, then, after completing its march, cut the enemy's withdrawal route at Matrenka village and advanced to the north. Avoiding heavy combat, it advanced forward hurriedly, with 55th Guards Cavalry Regiment (its commander was Major F. E. Mishukov) as its advanced detachment. Seeing the developing situation, the enemy began withdrawing to the north and northwest. Up to two infantry battalions [at best, company-size rear guards] were destroyed in these battles, and a concentration of supply carts was overwhelmed by mortar fire or cut up and destroyed in the region near Lapty Farm.

The 16th Guards Cavalry Division seized the starch factory after an intense fight, cut the railroad line to Mozyr', and attacked the railroad station at Mozyr'. Its forward detachment crossed the Pripiat' River with the mission of cutting the railroad line in the vicinity of the village of Kleshni.

The 14th Guards Cavalry Division captured the village of Mirobeli and attacked toward Mozyr' Station together with units of 15th Cavalry Division.

As a result of active operations, the corps' units advanced forward considerably. Giving concrete expression and refining the formations and units' missions, the corps commander ordered the commander of 15th Guards Cavalry Division to capture the city of Mozyr' from the southeast in cooperation with 415th Rifle Division and the commanders of 16th and 14th Guards Cavalry Divisions to capture Mozyr' Station.

By evening on 13 January, 15th Guards Cavalry Division's 53rd Cavalry Regiment captured Bibiki Farm, then drove the enemy from the villages of Bobreniata and Bulavka and approached the southern outskirts of Mozyr'. In that region, deep ravines abounded in the terrain, which slowed the regiments' advance.

After capturing Bobry Farm, 55th Cavalry Regiment began attacking toward Mozyr'.

The combat operations against Mozyr' took place in difficult conditions. Heavy snow interfered with artillery support for the attacking subunits. The streets and houses in the city and the roads were heavily mined, which genuinely hindered the forces' advance and led to personnel losses.

While assisting 15th Guards Cavalry Division's advance, our artillery fired on force concentrations at Drozda [Drozdy] and Lapta [Lapty] Farms.

Seeing the inevitability of defeat, by day's end on 13 January, the enemy began hurriedly evacuating the garrison of the city of Mozyr' under the protection of strong rear guards from the south and a covering force from the west, exploiting the fact that the route to the north and northwest was still open. Panic ruled in Mozyr'. The Hitlerites blew up the warehouses and strove with all of their might to hold on to the river crossings. Their artillery constantly fired on the cavalrymen's combat formations.

Cooperating with the Mozyr' Partisan Brigade, the units of 15th Guards Cavalry Division and 55th and 415th Rifle Divisions captured the city of Mozyr' on the evening of 14 January after a short street battle and reached its northwestern outskirts, where they dug in. Small dispersed groups of enemy troops withdrew across the Pripiat'.

The 14th and 16th Guards Cavalry Divisions captured Mozyr' Station on the morning of 14 January. . . .

Over the period from 8 through 14 January, 7th Guards Cavalry Corps inflicted a severe defeat on the enemy. Many of his units and subunits were crushed; 152 towns and villages were liberated from the enemy; more than 1,500 Hitlerites were killed and more than 250 were captured; around 300 horses were seized; 10 tanks, 6 assault guns, and more than 400 vehicles were destroyed; and many guns were taken.[23]

Although 7th Guards Cavalry Corps' operations against Mozyr' on 13 and 14 January were clearly anticlimactic given the Germans' decision to withdraw from the city, 2nd Guards Cavalry Corps' operations during the same period were far more dramatic and threatening for the German Second Army than those of its neighboring cavalry corps to the south. Rokossovsky had assigned Kriukov's cavalry corps the mission of forcing the Pripiat' River west of Mozyr' and reaching and cutting the railroad line stretching westward from Kalinkovichi through Zhitkovichi to Brest. Leaving his 3rd Guards Cavalry Division to contain the German bridgehead across the Pripiat' River south of Petrikov, Kriukov ordered 4th and 17th Guards Divisions to conduct an assault crossing over the river at dawn on 13 January, the former south of Mikhnovichi and the latter east of Besedki.

This portion of Rokossovsky's offensive was particularly threatening for the Germans, first, because German XX Army Corps, which believed that sector of the Pripiat' River could not be crossed, had posted only light security outposts along the northern bank of the river, and, second, because a successful crossing by the cavalrymen would place them in positions to the rear of the Germans' new defense lines along the Ipa River. Unfortunately for the attacking cavalry, however, the weak nature of their force, the width of the river, and their dismally poor supply lines prevented them from moving substantial numbers of armor and assault guns across the river.

The 17th and 4th Guards Cavalry Divisions occupied jumping-off positions for their attack west and east of Zhakhovichi near the Pripiat' River's southern bank late on 12 January. The first force to cross the icy surface of the river was 17th Guards Cavalry Division's 61st Guards Cavalry Regiment, which crossed the ice carrying light 50mm mortars, heavy machine guns, and antitank rifles. Two kilometers to the west, the cavalrymen could see the buildings in Besedki village, whose streets were alive with trucks carrying cargo and German troops. Supported by mortar fire, the regiment's 1st Squadron crossed the river on the ice, overcame several German security outposts, advanced 1.5 kilometers, and seized a narrow section of the railroad line just east of Besedki. That evening the regiment's sapper squad blew up four sections of track and cut the telegraph lines next to the railroad bed.[24]

By day's end on 13 January, 17th Guards Cavalry Division occupied a bridgehead 5 kilometers wide and up to 3 kilometers deep between the railroad line and Pripiat' River's northern bank from Besedki to southeast of Kachury and had captured much of the village of Besedki itself. On its right, 4th Guards Cavalry Division was still attempting to seize a similar bridgehead from just east of Kachury eastward to the southern approaches to Mikhnovichi but was unable to do so until late on 14 January.

The 17th Guards Cavalry's history described the dilemma that the bold cavalry attack created for German Second Army:

> The crossing by the Soviet cavalry to the northern bank of the Pripiat' and its arrival on the withdrawal route of the Second Army's units seriously worried the enemy command. The Hitlerites concentrated 1st and 2nd SS Jäger Regiments in the vicinity of Ptich' Station, withdrew the main forces of 102nd Infantry Division with tanks from the front, and threw them to the location of our crossings. The situation of 17th Guards Cavalry Division's units that had crossed turned out to be very serious. The ice conditions on the Pripiat' did not permit the division's artillery and self-propelled guns to cross to the northern bank. The two cavalry regiments, with their existing antitank guns and medium mortars, were face-to-face with large enemy forces. The units of 4th Guards Cavalry Division undertook yet another attempt to cross the river but suffered defeat. The corps commander, General V. V. Kriukov, ordered General G. I. Pankratov to move into the Skrygalovo region from Kostiukovichi by a forced march with his division. During the night, corps artillery and a multiple-rocket launcher regiment, which occupied firing positions on the southern bank of the river, reinforced General P. T. Korsakov's division.
>
> Fog obscured the wide valley of the Pripiat'. Observation was difficult. At around 1000 hours on 14 January, two battalions of German 233rd [should read 232nd] Grenadier Regiment with several tanks launched an attack. Our fire forced the Hitlerites to withdraw back. In the course of an hour, the enemy launched two more attacks. Six tanks and a battalion of infantry rushed from the forest. Mortarman Vodlia opened barrier fire. The Hitlerites began to dig in. The tanks continued to move forward, firing all the while. A. Ia. Kukis's guns struck at short range. The lead

tank burst into flames, and, soon after, the second machine was enveloped in flames. During the evening the enemy managed to drive the 1st Squadron back from the railroad embankment. The Hitlerites tried to penetrate into Besedki from the march but encountered counterattacks and withdrew. After several minutes they once again went on the attack and entered the village's streets. . . .

By 2200 hours the cavalrymen left Besedki and dug in on a low hill 200 meters from the village. The Hitlerites went over to the attack four more times, striving to drive the cavalrymen from the northern bank of the Pripiat' but were repelled by fire from our artillery. . . . The division's regiments waged a stubborn battle for the village of Bagramovichi [5 kilometers west of Besedki]. . . .

Deprived of their supporting artillery, which could not be shifted to the northern bank, the small squadrons repelled numerous Fascist attacks with tanks and self-propelled guns, supported by a great amount of artillery, and, in the end, were forced to withdraw. After abandoning the villages of Besedki and Bagramovichi, the division continued to hold on to the bridgehead on the northern bank for five more days. On 18 January it received a new combat mission and set about fulfilling it toward the west along the southern bank of the Pripiat' River.[25]

By 14 January, Second Army's XX Army Corps defended the northern bank of the Pripiat' River from the village of Bagramovichi eastward past Besedki and Mikhnovichi to the mouth of the Ipa River with 1st Battalion, 1st Ski Jäger Brigade, flanked on the left by intermixed battalion-size *kampfgruppen* from 7th and 102nd Infantry Divisions and the division groups of Corps Detachment E.[26] Despite XX Corps' resolute defense, overnight on 14–15 January, the cavalrymen of Kriukov's corps linked up with elements of 61st Army's 55th Rifle Division, advancing westward along the railroad line south of Klinsk.

Thus, by day's end on 14 January, the forces of Batov's and Belov's 65th and 61st Armies cleared German forces from the Mozyr' and Kalinkovichi regions, captured both objectives, and closed up to the Ipa River line (see Map 7.9). The Germans managed to withdraw the bulk of their defending forces westward across the Ipa River, and, to facilitate that withdrawal, briefly held on to small bridgeheads on the river's eastern bank at Krotov and Iakimovichi. However, by 15 January, their defenses along the Ipa River were already jeopardized by the presence of Russian cavalry on the northern bank of the Pripiat' River west of Klinsk. Worse still, the heavy fighting had drawn the bulk of LVI Panzer and XX Army Corps to the southern reaches of the Ipa River, leaving only the relatively weak 707th Security Division, newly arrived from the Bobruisk region, to defend the 25-kilometer-wide sector along the Ipa River from Kaplichi northeastward to Koreni. This was a particularly vulnerable sector because it protected the approaches to Ozarichi, which would soon become one of Rokossovsky's prime objectives.

Rokossovsky's offensive against Kalinkovichi and Mozyr' was successful despite the limited resources provided to him by the *Stavka*. The offensive succeeded, first and foremost, because, unlike his neighbor, Sokolovsky, Rokossovsky formulated an imaginative plan, which included extensive maneuver by his tank and two cavalry corps. More important still, Rokossovsky interceded quickly and actively to correct his subordinates' operational and tactical errors and prevent the offensive from stalling. Finally, as subsequent events indicated, Rokossovsky did not rest on his laurels after his forces secured their initial objectives. No sooner did his forces reach the Ipa River than he began the second stage of his offensive. There would be no respite for the German Second Army.

CHAPTER 18

The Belorussian Front's Ozarichi-Ptich' Offensive (16–30 January)

PLANNING

Although Soviet and Russian historians have provided considerable detail about the battles for Mozyr' and Kalinkovichi, they are utterly silent about Rokossovsky's subsequent offensive operations. Nor is memoir literature very helpful in this regard. For example, not only does Rokossovsky say nothing about his *front*'s operations after it captured Mozyr' and Kalinkovichi but also Batov simply notes, "After persistent battles, on 20 January the army's [65th Army's] forces captured Ozarichi, one of the enemy's most powerful strongpoints."[1]

Accounts related to 61st Army's operations during this period are equally silent. General P. A. Belov, 61st Army's commander during this period, wrote no memoirs, and other extant sources are limited to 12th Guards Rifle Division's history, which states only, "Units of the division entered battle northwest of Kalinkovichi on 20 January and, after smashing enemy resistance, began a slow but persistent advance forward. In February the corps' forces reached the Ptich' River in the Ivashkovichi region and, by order of the army commander, went on the defense."[2]

However, the histories of several rifle divisions assigned to 65th and 48th Armies, as well as fragmentary Soviet archival documents and the complete records of German Second Army, indicate that Rokossovsky's *front* did indeed conduct extensive offensive operations in southern Belorussia during the second half of January and February 1944. More important still, many if not most of these operations were at least moderately successful, as Rokossovsky maneuvered his forces skillfully to pry the Germans from their defenses and push the front ever farther to the west. In fact, these "forgotten battles" are among the few successful operations apparently deliberately overlooked by Soviet and Russian historians, perhaps to avoid embarrassing comparisons with Sokolovsky's unsuccessful operations to the north.

The clearest evidence to date from Soviet sources that Rokossovsky's Belorussian Front continued its offensive operations after mid-January is an excerpt from 65th Army's war experience report for January 1944, which simply states: "While continuing the offensive within new boundaries, by the end of January, the [65th] army reached [the following] positions: Kobyl'shchina [Poles'e] (incl.), Visha (incl.), Veseloe Bolottse, Podmekhovshchina [Mek-

453

hovshchina], Lesets, Ozarichi (incl.), Medved' (incl.), Savin Rog, Kurgan, Hill 139.1, Berezniaki, and 1 kilometer northwest of Hill 134.4. The enemy offered strong resistance . . . and stubbornly defended each strongpoint throughout the duration of all of the conducted battles."[3] The fact is that the positions indicated in this report were located from 10 to 25 kilometers west of the line Rokossovsky's forces reached in mid-January, which represented no mean gain for a force supposedly on the defense throughout the entire period. Based on this and other fragmentary Russian source materials and extensive German archival materials, it is now possible to reconstruct the course of Rokossovsky's offensive in fair detail.

In mid-January 1944, Rokossovsky was still operating under the guidance the *Stavka* provided to him in its 2 January directive. Specifically, after capturing Mozyr' and Kalinkovichi, General Batov's 65th and General Belov's 61st Armies were to penetrate German defenses along the Ipa River, and, in conjunction with an offensive by General Romanenko's 48th Army to the north, capture Ozarichi and Mikhnovichi, advance to secure bridgeheads across the Ptich' River, and continue the offensive northwestward toward Bobruisk. During this stage of the offensive, the cavalry forces directly subordinate to the Belorussian Front were to advance westward along the southern bank of the Pripiat' River to the Luninets region, 140 kilometers west of the Ipa River, to sever communications between German Army Groups Center and South.

Although Rokossovsky's offensive operations were still designed to attract German reserves away from the more critical Ukraine, the *Stavka* left Bobruisk and Minsk as his ultimate objectives. It did so because, regardless of whether he was able to attain these objectives, his *front*'s operations were essential in order to create more favorable jumping-off positions for a subsequent general offensive in the spring or summer of 1944. Therefore, Rokossovsky did all in his power to achieve as much as his forces could achieve before terminating his operations in the early spring.

In outline form, after a short pause to regroup and refit his forces, Rokossovsky ordered 65th and 48th Armies to begin offensive operations in their respective sectors on the morning of 16 January. Batov's army was to begin its offensive operations in the 25-kilometer-wide sector along the Ipa River from Kaplichi, 5 kilometers north of Krotov, northeastward past Novoselki to the Koreni region, 10 kilometers east of Ozarichi. Here, Batov was to employ the bulk of his army's 27th, 19th, and 18th Rifle Corps. Farther to the north, on Batov's right, Romanenko's army was to launch its offensive in the 15-kilometer-wide sector extending from Zherd' Station, 5 kilometers east of Davydovka, eastward to Shatsilki on the Berezina River (see Appendix O-1 for a brief description of 48th Army's operations in January 1944 and preliminary plans for February). This attack was to involve 48th Army's 29th and 42nd Rifle Corps, supported by 95th Rifle Corps on the right wing of Batov's army. After these offensive thrusts were under way, General Belov's smaller 61st Army was to mount an offensive westward across the lower Ipa River in the 18-kilometer-wide sector from Krotov southward to the Pripiat' River, where Rokossovsky perceived German Second Army's defenses to be the strongest. Belov's mission was to exploit Batov's success to the north by pushing Second Army's defending forces back to the Ptich' River, about 18 kilometers to the west.

The 65th Army's immediate mission was to penetrate German Second Army's defenses along the Ipa River in the broad sector defended by the weak 707th Security Division on LVI Panzer Corps' extended left wing. Batov's forces could then capture Ozarichi, situated about 10 kilometers behind 707th Division's left wing. Subsequently, 65th Army's attacking forces could turn the adjoining flanks of both Second Army's LVI Panzer and Ninth Army's XXXXI Panzer Corps, forcing the former to withdraw westward to the Ptich' River and the latter northwestward toward Parichi. This would leave Belov's 61st Army to force Second Army's XX Army Corps to withdraw westward to the Ptich' River. Thereafter, Batov intended to shift 65th Army's axis of advance toward the northwest, and, in cooperation with Romanenko's 48th Army, press LVI and XXXXI Panzer Corps' forces northwestward toward Oktiabr'skii and Bobruisk.

The immediate objective of Romanenko's 48th Army was to pierce the defenses of German Ninth Army's XXXXI Panzer Corps west of Shatsilki, drive a wedge between the panzer corps and Ninth Army's XXXV Army Corps, deployed between the Dnepr and Berezina Rivers, and, subsequently, assisted by Batov's 65th Army, advance northwestward along the southern bank of the Berezina River toward Parichi and Bobruisk. Thus, Bobruisk and Minsk remained the ultimate objective of Batov's and Romanenko's armies.

Therefore, throughout the entire offensive, which lasted throughout all of February and into March 1944, Batov's and Romanenko's offensive thrusts were inexorably linked in regard to both their timing and their immediate and ultimate objectives. As the offensive developed, the center of gravity of Batov's forces shifted steadily to the north as he committed additional forces on his right wing.

After reaching the Germans' defenses along the Ipa River by nightfall of 14 January, Batov's and Belov's forces eliminated 4th and 5th Panzer Divisions' bridgeheads at Krotov and Iakimovichi on the river's eastern bank overnight, and then positioned their forces to commence active combat offensive operations the following morning (see Map 17.9). When fully concentrated along the Ipa River's eastern bank, 65th and 61st Armies' forces were deployed across an almost 60-kilometer-wide front stretching northward from the Pripiat' River south of Klinsk Station to the vicinity of Davydovka, 20 kilometers southwest of Shatsilki (see Table 18.1).

First, Rokossovsky designated a new boundary line between Batov's and Belov's armies, which initially extended through Iakimovichi on the Ipa

Table 18.1. The Tentative Combat Formations of 65th and 61st Armies and Opposing German Forces Late on 15 January 1944 (deployed from north to south)

FORCE (Sector)	OPPOSING GERMAN FORCES
1st/2nd/3rd Echelons (Mobile group)	
	NINTH ARMY
BELORUSSIAN FRONT	
65th Army (Davydovka, Iakimovichi)	XXXXI Panzer Corps
(Davydovka, Krotov on 16.1)	36th ID
95th RC (Davydovka, south of Gory)	
172nd RD (north of Davydovka)	
44th GRD (Davydovka, Liudvinovka)	134th ID
38th GRD (Liudvinovka, south of Gory)	
	SECOND ARMY (to 18.1)
	LVI Panzer Corps
27th RC (south of Gory, Kazansk)	707th SecD
60th RD/106th RD (Gory, Koreni)	(35th ID on 17.1)
354th RD (Koreni, Kazansk)	
19th RC (Kazansk, Koshchichi)	
162nd RD (Kazansk, Tsidov)	
82nd RD (Tsidov, Novoselki)	
115th RB (Novoselki, Koshchichi)	
105th RC (132nd and 253rd RDs	
75th GRD) (Kholodniki region)	
18th RC (Koshchichi, Iakimovichi)	
(Novoselki, Krotov on 16.1)	
37th GRD (Koshchichi, Krotov)	4th PzD
(2nd echelon on 16.1)	
193rd RD (Krotov, Iakimovichi)	
(Koshchichi, Krotov on 16.1)	
69th RD (Iakimovichi)	
(Novoselki, Kaplichi on 16.1)	
1st GTC (Bobrovichi region)	
61st Army (Iakimovichi, Pripiat' River)	**NINTH ARMY** (on 18.1)
(Krotov, Pripiat' River on 16.1)	
89th RC (Iakimovich, Klinsk)	5th PzD
(Krotov, Klinsk on 16.1)	
23rd RD/81st RD (Iakimovichi)	
Krotov, Iakimovichi on 16.1)	
15th RD (Iakimovichi, Kalinkovichi-Ptich' road	
9th GRC (12th, 76th, 77th GRDs)	
(north of Kalinkovichi on 16.1)	
356th RD (northeast of Klinsk)	292nd ID
55th RD (southeast of Klinsk)	Corps Abt. E
415th RD (Mikhnovichi)	KGr., 7th ID
2nd Guards Cavalry Corps (3rd, 4th, 17th GCDs)	1st Bn, 1st SkiR
(Mikhnovichi, Besedki	
(relieved by 415th RD on 18.1)	
7th Guards Cavalry Corps (14th, 15th, 16th GCDs)	Gr. von Bercken
(Petrikov bridgehead, south of the Pripiat'River)	84th IR, 102nd ID
	CavR "Mitte"
	242nd SecBn
	Div Gp. 216 (18.1)
***Front* reserves**	
121st RC (23rd and 218th RD)	
115th, 119th, 161st FRs	

Sources: Boevoi sostav Sovetskoi Armii, chast' IV (Ianvar'–dekabr' 1944) [The combat composition of the Soviet Army, pt. 4 (January–December 1944)] (Moscow: Voenizdat, 1988), 14–15, 42; and Anlagen zum KTB, A.O.K. 2 – Ia, Lagenkarten, Jan–Feb 1944, *AOK 2, 49701/92 file*, in NAM series T-312, roll 1281.

The Belorussian Front's Ozarichi-Ptich' Offensive 457

Map 18.1. The Situation in the Ozarichi-Ptich' Sector, 15–16 January 1944

River, by shifting it northward to the vicinity of Krotov on 17 January (see Map 18.1). By then, Batov's 65th Army was arrayed in the sector from Davydovka southward to Krotov, facing the right wing of German Ninth Army's XXXXI Panzer Corps and all of Second Army's LVI Panzer Corps. On Batov's right wing northeast and southwest of Davydovka, General Kuzovkov's 95th Rifle Corps opposed the defenses of XXXXI Panzer Corps' 134th Infantry Division. To the south, northeast of Ozarichi, General Cherokmanov's 27th Rifle Corps deployed opposite 707th Security Division on LVI Panzer Corps' left wing. Further to the south, from southeast of Ozarichi to Krotov, General Samarsky's 19th and General Ivanov's 18th Rifle Corps faced the right wing of LVI Panzer Corps' 707th Security Division and the panzer corps' 4th

Panzer Division. By this time, the panzer division's armor strength had fallen from roughly forty tanks on 1 January to half that number, although it still fielded about twenty mobile assaults guns and *Paks*.[4]

Finally, Batov retained General Alekseev's 105th Rifle Corps in his army second echelon in 19th and 18th Rifle Corps' rear area. Batov ordered Alekseev's rifle corps to employ his rifle divisions to reinforce the forward rifle corps whenever and wherever required. In addition, Batov withdrew Panov's 1st Guards Tank Corps from combat after the fall of Kalinkovichi; subsequently, it remained in the rear area resting and refitting from 17 through 27 January. This meant that Batov's army had to begin its new offensive with only negligible armor support.

On 15 and 16 January, Belov's 61st Army employed the three guards divisions of Boreiko's 9th Guards Rifle Corps to liquidate the German bridgehead east of the Ipa River at Klinsk, defended by German XX Army Corps' Corps Detachment E. However, when Boreiko's corps failed to do so, on 16 January Belov replaced the guards rifle corps with General Khaliuzin's 89th Rifle Corps and several of the army's separate divisions. After completing this regrouping late on 16 January, 89th Rifle Corps' three rifle divisions occupied forward positions along the Ipa River from Krotov southward to Iakimovichi opposite 5th Panzer Division's defenses, while 356th and 55th Rifle Divisions manned positions containing the German bridgehead at Klinsk. However, anticipating further Soviet attacks, XX Army Corps abandoned this precarious bridgehead overnight on 18 January. The strongest German force opposing Belov's troops was XX Army Corps' 5th Panzer Division. However, because of the losses it suffered in the fight for Kalinkovichi, the panzer division's armor strength had fallen from almost forty tanks and fifteen assault guns and mobile *Paks* on 1 January to fewer than thirty tanks and fifteen assault guns and mobile *Paks* by midmonth.[5]

Farther to the south, on the northern bank of the Pripiat' River west of Klinsk, 415th Rifle Division and 2nd Guards Cavalry Corps manned 61st Army's forward positions from Mikhnovichi westward to Besedki opposite the defenses of Second Army's Corps Detachment E and 7th Infantry Division. However, on 18 January, 415th Rifle Division and a regiment from 55th Rifle Division relieved the cavalry corps, permitting it to move south of the river and join 7th Guards Cavalry Corps in its attempts to reduce the German bridgehead defended by Group von Bercken south of Petrikov.

Rokossovsky ordered Batov's 65th and Belov's 61st Armies to begin their offensive early on 16 January, the same day that Romanenko's 48th Army was to begin active offensive operations in its sector. When Batov began his offensive, he did so on both of his army's wings. On the army's left wing, 18th and 19th Rifle Corps struck LVI Panzer Corps' defenses in the 25-kilometer-wide sector from Krotov northward to Kazansk, striking south and north of the boundary between 4th Panzer and 707th Security Division. Simultaneously, in the Koreni and Davydovka sector on the army's right wing, 95th and 27th Rifle Corps began active operations against XXXXI Panzer Corps' 134th Infantry Division and the left wing of LVI Panzer Corps' 707th Infantry Division, in cooperation with the forces on the left wing of Romanenko's 48th Army. Although the timing and ultimate objectives of these offensives were closely coordinated, they represented distinctly separate operations. Finally, because Soviet and Russian sources do not reveal the actual names of these operations, in view of their objectives, I have christened the former as the Ozarichi-Ptich' offensive and the latter as the Marmovichi-Dubrova offensive.

Rokossovsky's plan for the Ozarichi-Ptich' offensive required Batov's 65th Army to assault German LVI Panzer Corps' defenses along the Ipa River with 19th and 18th Rifle Corps on his army's left wing and then expand the offensive by committing 27th Rifle Corps to combat, with the mission of expanding the penetration to the north (see Map 18.1). Batov's three rifle corps were to penetrate the Germans' defenses at a weak point at the junction of 4th Panzer and 707th Security Divisions, split those defenses, capture Ozarichi, roll up German defenses to the north and the south, and force German forces to fall back to the upper reaches of the Ptich' River. All the while, the forces of Belov's 61st Army were to maintain pressure on German defenses along the Ipa River north of Klinsk and, when feasible, first commit 89th Rifle Corps and, later, 9th Guards Rifle Corps to combat to widen the southern flank of Batov's penetration.

Batov ordered Samarsky's 19th Rifle Corps to assault and penetrate the defenses of 4th Panzer and 707th Security Divisions along the Ipa River from Kaplichi northward to Kazansk early on 16 January. Initially, the corps' 115th Rifle Brigade and 82nd and 162nd Rifle Divisions, deployed from left to right, were to capture the German strongpoints at Kaplichi, Novoselki, and Tsidov, and then advance 5–10 kilometers into the depths to seize Ugly, Berezniaki, Kriukovichi, Syshchichi, and Zamoshchany. If successful, this assault would envelop German defenses at Ozarichi from the south and Savichi and Kaplichi from the north. The 82nd Rifle Division's history recorded the division's mission:

> The division was subordinated to 65th Army's 19th Rifle Corps on 14 January and received the combat mission of forcing the Ipa and Visha Rivers, defeating the enemy, capturing the villages of Kriukovichi and Novoselki, and advancing in the direction of Ozarichi and Savichi.
>
> The mission was not an easy one for our soldiers and officers. While fighting, we had to overcome swamps, which were not even frozen over during the winter; force numerous rivers, streams, and creeks on primitive crossing means; and orient ourselves in the massive forests. Few of us had the necessary combat experience to conduct military operations in such conditions. We would get that experience in the process of battle.[6]

Samarsky's assault was to strike the weakest point in the Germans' defenses, the left wing battalions of 707th Security Division, which rested in the swamps on the western bank of the Ipa River. However, elements of 35th Infantry Division, which Army Group Center had ordered to move southward from Fourth Army several days before, began reinforcing (and ultimately replaced) the security division late on 16 January.

To the south, on 19th Rifle Corps' left, 69th, 193rd, and 37th Guards Rifle Divisions of Ivanov's 18th Rifle Corps, deployed from left to right, were to assault 4th Panzer Division's defenses from Kaplichi southward to Krotov, cross the Ipa River to seize the German strong points on its western bank, and then wheel westward and southwestward to turn the left flank of the remainder of LVI Panzer Corps back toward the south. The three divisions had already cleared German forces from the river's eastern bank overnight on 14–15 January, including 69th Division, which destroyed the German bridgehead at Iakimovichi. The 69th Division's history described its exploits: "On 14 January the corps commander assigned the division a new mission: to liberate the village of Iakimovichi, which was situated on the Ipa River's eastern bank. The garrison of this strongpoint consisted of three infantry battalions of German 7th Infantry Division, with about 20 tanks. The enemy held on to this village as a forward fortification to prevent the Soviet forces from crossing the river."[7] After 69th Rifle Division eliminated the Iakimovichi bridgehead (which was actually defended by 5th Panzer Division's 14th Panzer Grenadier Regiment), it was to castle its forces to the north, seize Krotov, and ultimately deploy northward 10–12 kilometers into the Novoselki sector, where it was to take over the southern portion of 19th Rifle Corps' front and join its exploitation to the west. As 18th Rifle Corps shifted its offensive sector to the north, 23rd and 81st Rifle Divisions from 61st Army's 89th Rifle Corps were to take over the sector from Iakimovichi southward to the Kalinkovichi-Ptich' road and, thereafter, support the penetration operation by 19th Rifle Corps' left wing. Initially, Batov assigned 255th Tank Regiment to provide a modicum of armor support for his two assaulting rifle corps and retained 193rd Tank Regiment in reserve to reinforce his forces as they entered the penetration.

On the right (to the north) of General Samarsky's 19th Rifle Corps, General Cherokmanov's 27th Rifle Corps was to conduct local offensive operations to pin down German forces north of Kazansk, while preparing to join the assault on Ozarichi from the east when Samarsky's forces completed their penetration of the Germans' defenses. At the same time, Batov ordered Cherokmanov's corps also to provide flank protection for the assault by General Kuzovkov's 95th Rifle Corps, which was participating in the offensive of General Romanenko's 48th Army farther to the north.

Finally, Batov ordered his reserve rifle corps, General Alekseev's 105th, to reinforce Samarsky's and Ivanov's assault with its 132nd and 253rd Rifle

Divisions after the two forward corps completed their penetration operation, while retaining 75th Guards Rifle Division in general reserve. While Batov's forces were conducting their penetration operation, Belov's 61st Army was to maintain maximum pressure on German 292nd Infantry Division's bridgehead at Klinsk. However, after Batov's rifle corps ruptured the German defenses to the north, General Belov was to commit General Khaliuzin's 89th Rifle Corps into the southern portion of Batov's penetration to support the ensuing exploitation.

Therefore, in the absence of strong armor support, Rokossovsky intended to strike the Germans' defenses with a single rifle corps where they were weakest and in the poorest of terrain and, if and when the penetration succeeded, to push additional rifle divisions into the penetration one by one, first to stretch and then to snap the Germans' threadbare defenses. Additionally, repeating the tactics he required 61st Army to employ in its assault on Kalinkovichi, Rokossovsky ordered Batov to initiate his advance overnight on 15–16 January with battalion-size forward detachments on skis from each first-echelon rifle division. Tailored light so as to operate quietly and more effectively, these forward detachments were to infiltrate through the Germans' forward defenses and disrupt their first defensive belt by attacking strongpoints within the forward defenses from the flanks and rear. Rokossovsky also ordered Batov to dispense with the usual artillery preparations to increase the possibilities for achieving surprise.

Despite his lack of armor and the relative weakness of his forces after several months of incessant combat, Rokossovsky's forces were markedly superior to what the defending Germans could muster (see Table 18.2).

THE BATTLE

The forward detachments of Samarsky's 19th Rifle Corps began their stealthy yet deadly work overnight on 15–16 January (see Map 18.1). The 82nd Rifle Division's history describes the operations of one such detachment:

> Under the command of Major F. S. Chaikov, the division's forward detachment, which consisted of a reconnaissance company, two automatic weapons companies from 250th Rifle Regiment under the command of Senior Lieutenant D. P. Grig'orev, and two automatic weapons companies under the command of Senior Lieutenant N. V. Suchkov, secretly forced the Ipa River on the night of 15 January and attacked the Hitlerites by surprise. After infiltrating into the enemy's rear area, Lieutenant V. V. Popov's platoon and Lieutenant N. I. Turkin's platoon sowed panic in his ranks. Abandoning his artillery, the enemy retreated to previously prepared defense lines at the village of Novoselki.

Table 18.2. The Estimated Correlation of Opposing Forces in the Ozarichi-Ptich' Offensive, 16–30 January 1944

OPPOSING FORCES	
Soviet	*German*
Belorussian Front	
65th Army	707th Security Division
61st Army	(35th Infantry Division
23 rifle divisions	on 17.1)
1 rifle brigade	4th Panzer Division
2 cavalry corps (30 tanks)	5th Panzer Division
1 tank brigade (20 tanks)	292nd Infantry Division
2 tank regiments (30 tanks)	Corps *Abteilung* E
2 SP regiments (30 SP guns)	7th Infantry Division
	216th Division Group
	1st Ski Jäger Brigade
	Gp. von Bercken (102nd Infantry Division
Strength: 200,000 men (est.)	90,000 men
110 tanks and SP guns	85 tanks, assault guns, and mobile *Paks*
Depth of Soviet advance: 15–30 kilometers	
Casualties (6–30 January 1944):	
Soviet: 56,157, including:	**German:** 20,000 (est.)
12,350 killed and	
43,807 wounded	

Sources: *Boevoi sostav Sovetskoi Armii, chast' IV (Ianvar'–dekabr' 1944)* [The combat composition of the Soviet Army, pt. 4 (January–December 1944)] (Moscow: Voenizdat, 1988), 14–15, 42; and Anlagen zum KTB, A.O.K. 2 – Ia, Lagenkarten, Jan–Feb 1944, *AOK 2, 49701/92 file*, in NAM series T-312, roll 1281.

Exploiting the enemy's confusion, the division commander ordered 210th and 250th Rifle Regiments' troops to force the Ipa River at night and without an artillery preparation and reach the bridgehead seized by the forward detachment. Thereafter, the regiments were to pursue the withdrawing enemy, destroy them near Novoselki, capture the village, and subsequently attack [northward 9 kilometers] toward Kriukovichi with both regiments.

The 601st Rifle Regiment and the division's ski battalion, which constituted the division commander's reserve, followed in second echelon.

The attacking regiments cooperated with their neighbors. The 162nd Rifle Division was operating on the right and 115th Separate Rifle Brigade on the left. Prisoners captured by the forward detachment showed that the enemy's 34th and 109th Infantry Regiments, with reinforcements, were defending on the division's front.[8]

In fact, battalion groups from 35th Infantry Division's 34th and 109th Regiments had reinforced 707th Security Division's defenses only hours before the Russian assault. Once through the Germans' forward defenses, 82th Rifle Division's 210th and 250th Regiments encountered heavy resistance on the outskirts of Novoselki, and, after the village changed hands several times in an intense seesaw battle, the newly committed 610th Rifle Regi-

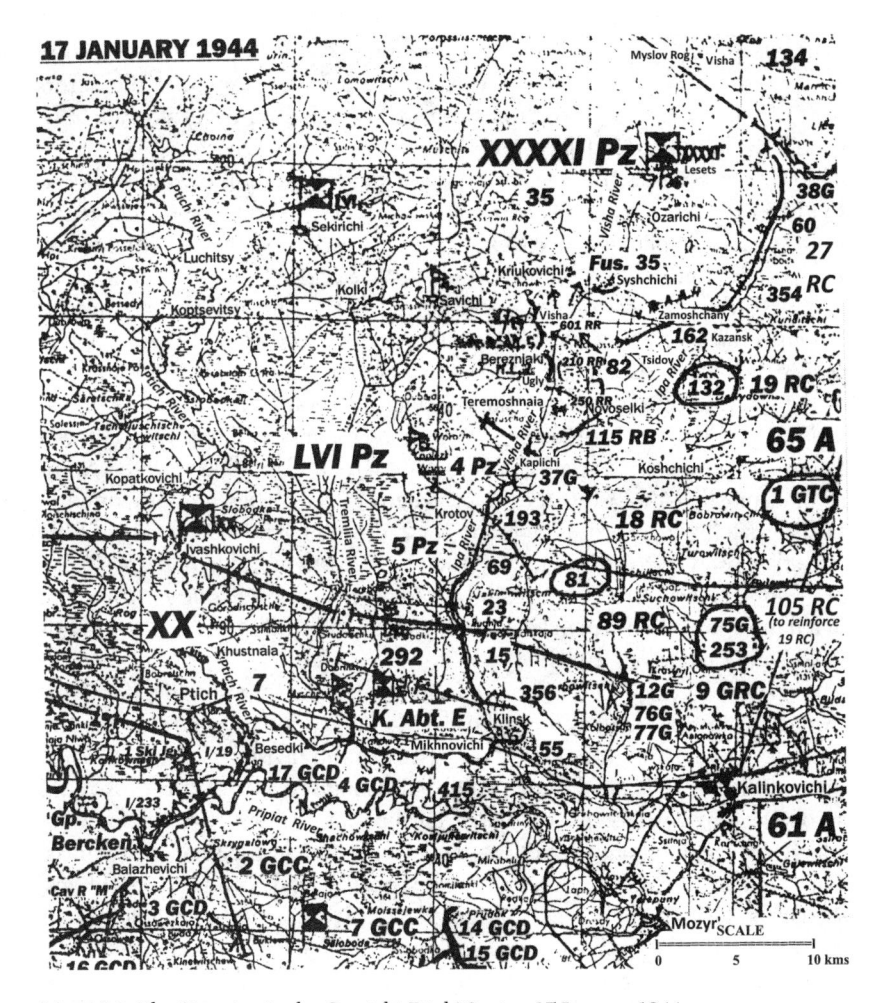

Map 18.2. The Situation in the Ozarichi-Ptich' Sector, 17 January 1944

ment tipped the scales in the attackers' favor. At nightfall on 16 January, the German defenders withdrew westward through the heavily forested swamplands. The 82nd Rifle Division's forces pursued on 17 January, and, by day's end, the division's 210th and 250th Regiments seized a small bridgehead over the Visha River near the village of Ugly, 6 kilometers deep into the Germans' defenses, and approached the eastern outskirts of the German strongpoints at Berezniaki and Visha, 2 kilometers further on (see Map 18.2). At the same time, the division's 610th Rifle Regiment pushed northward another 4 kilometers to reach the southern edge of Kriukovichi.

By this time, although the troops on 707th Security Division's right wing were scattered to the cold winds, a *kampfgruppe* formed around the nucleus of 2nd Battalion of 4th Panzer Division's 14th Panzer Grenadier Regiment managed to erect a roughly 6-kilometer-long security line extending from north to south, west of the Kriukovichi-Berezniaki road, and 3–4 kilometers west of the Visha River. South of Berezniaki, pressured by 115th Rifle Brigade, attacking on 82nd Division's left, 35th Infantry Division's 34th Regiment succeeded in withdrawing back from its forward positions along the Visha River to form a relatively continuous defense extending from Berezniaki southward to Kaplichi. The latter strongpoint anchored the left wing of 4th Panzer Division's main defenses.

As 82nd Rifle Division was penetrating 707th Security Division's forward defenses, on its right, 162nd Rifle Division advanced roughly 3 kilometers against heavier resistance, capturing Tsidov but grinding to a halt in front of the German strongpoint at Zamoshchany, 3 kilometers northwest of Kazansk. By this time, 4th Panzer Division's reconnaissance battalion (Pz. AA 4) succeeded in forming a light defensive screen extending northeastward from Zamoshchany to the Ipa River, where the defenses on 35th Infantry Division's left wing were still intact. On 82nd Rifle Division's left, 115th Rifle Brigade closed up to the Visha River line from north of Kaplichi to the village of Teremoshnaia, directly opposite 4th Panzer Division's *kampfgruppe,* but failed to capture Kaplichi in a joint attack with 18th Rifle Corps' 37th Guards Rifle Division.

As a whole, the difficult weather and terrain conditions made 19th Rifle Corps' advance difficult at best: "During the attack through the swampy terrain and across numerous rivers and streams, the division's units overcame many difficulties. The subunits had to build long sections of corduroy roads across swampy places in order to bring up the artillery and ammunition, which was lagging behind, and prepare crossing means by their own efforts. This seriously decreased the advance tempo."[9] Faced with these problems, the corps' 115th Rifle Brigade and 82nd Rifle Division virtually halted their advance along the Visha River on 18 and 19 January to consolidate their gains, while their regiments and supporting sapper battalions prepared corduroy roads and bridges under near-constant German artillery and mortar fire. Meanwhile, they dispatched small reconnaissance groups forward to improve their positions and reconnoiter the Germans' defenses, particularly in the Berezniaki and Visha sectors. During this period, 162nd Rifle Division captured Zamoshchany, forced 4th Panzer Division's reconnaissance battalion to withdraw northward, and reached the southern outskirts of Syshchichi, just 4 kilometers south of its immediate objective of Ozarichi.

On 19th Rifle Corps' right, 27th Rifle Corps' 60th and 354th Rifle Divisions exploited Samarsky's success by pushing westward 3–5 kilometers toward Ozarichi, where the headquarters of both XXXXI Panzer Corps and 35th Infantry Division were located. By day's end on the 19th, these two divisions, probably reinforced by 253rd Rifle Division of General Alekseev's second-echelon 105th Rifle Corps, reached positions extending from the

The Belorussian Front's Ozarichi-Ptich' Offensive 465

Map 18.3. The Situation in the Ozarichi-Ptich' Sector, 19 January 1944

eastern approaches to Syshchichi, 5 kilometers south of Ozarichi, northeastward past the eastern approaches of Ozarichi to Zabolot'e, 10 kilometers northeast of Ozarichi, which 95th Rifle Corps' 38th Guards Division had reached two days before. Threatened by the Soviets' advance, XXXXI Panzer Corps moved its headquarters northward to the far safer town of Parichi.

More important still, having completed fulfilling their missions further south, late on 18 January, the divisions of General Ivanov's 18th Rifle Corps began taking over the southern portion of General Samarsky's penetration sector (see Map 18.3). The 69th Rifle Division's history describes the process, beginning with the division's 15 January assault on Iakimovichi:

> The 237th and 303rd Rifle Regiments attacked the village [of Iakimovichi] from the east. During the battle it became apparent that the bridge-

head itself was located 1.5 kilometers south of the village. The division commander sent his reserve, Captain Tsibizov's battalion from 120th Rifle Regiment, to that region. It was supposed to approach the crossing secretly, capture it, and cut off the enemy's only withdrawal route to the west.

However, the surprise attack on the bridgehead did not take place. Moving at night across unfamiliar terrain, the battalion was delayed and began approaching the river only at first light. The Hitlerites detected our subunits approaching the crossing area, abandoned Iakimovichi, and withdrew across the river to its western bank.

After capturing the village of Krotov [on 17 January], the division's axis of advance shifted steadily northward to the right.

Lieutenant General Batov arrived in the division on 18 January. The large village of Novoselki along its front had just been liberated. After familiarizing himself with the situation, the army commander demanded that the tempo of advance be increased in order to limit maneuver in that sector by enemy units that were just arriving. On that day the division's scouts seized three prisoners from 35th Infantry Division, which had just arrived.

The division attempted to overcome the enemy's resistance along the Visha River (a tributary of the Ipa River) for two days, but was unable to cross to the opposite bank.[10]

Thus, while Samarsky's 19th Rifle Corps was consolidating its gains on 18 and 19 January, 37th Guards and 69th Rifle Divisions of Ivanov's 18th Rifle Corps shifted to the north and occupied new positions along the Visha River between Teremoshnaia and Kaplichi, on Samarsky's left. In turn, Samarsky transferred 115th Rifle Brigade, which Ivanov's divisions relieved, to new offensive positions on 162nd Rifle Division's right, southeast of Syshchichi. Finally, Batov also reinforced 19th Rifle Corps with 132nd Rifle Division from Alekseev's 105th Rifle Corps, still in second echelon or reserve. Samarsky committed 132nd Rifle Division in between 82nd and 162nd Rifle Divisions and ordered the entire force to smash German defenses along the Visha River and capture Savichi. At the same time, Batov reinforced Cherokmanov's 27th Rifle Corps, operating east of Ozarichi on Samarsky's left, with 253rd Rifle Division from Alekseev's 105th Rifle Corps and ordered 27th Rifle Corps to advance on Ozarichi from the east. As mentioned above, during the previous two days, 27th Corps' 60th and 354th Rifle Division had exploited 19th Rifle Corps' success by piercing German defenses along the Ipa River and penetrating to a depth of 5 kilometers to a point only 2 kilometers from Ozarichi's eastern defenses.

Amidst this fighting, Army Group Center altered its organization slightly to give Ninth Army responsibility for contending with Rokossovsky's offen-

The Belorussian Front's Ozarichi-Ptich' Offensive 467

Map 18.4. The Situation in the Ozarichi-Ptich' Sector, 20 January 1944

sive. Without changing the sectors allotted to Ninth and Second Army's corps and divisions, effective early on 18 January, the army group shifted the subordination of LVI Panzer Corps from Second to Ninth Army. In effect this meant that General Harpe's Ninth Army now controlled all German forces operating along the Parichi-Bobruisk and Zhlobin-Bobruisk axes, while Second Army remained responsible for defending the Ptich'-Pripiat' axis.

After completing their regrouping, bringing their artillery forward, and replenishing their ammunition, 27th, 19th, and 18th Rifle Corps resumed their general advance on the morning of 20 January (see Map 18.4). Once again, 82nd Rifle Division, which led the advance in the center of Samarsky's combat formation, registered immediate gains:

Fulfilling the division commander's orders, Lieutenant Colonel K. V. Borichevsky's 210th Rifle Regiment and Lieutenant Colonel A. N. Koibaev's 250th Rifle Regiment launched heavy attacks on the village of Visha from two converging directions to encircle and destroy the enemy.

Protected by separate groups, the Hitlerites abandoned the village and began withdrawing.

After capturing Visha, our units advanced along the road leading to Ozarichi, where the Germans had dug in along previously prepared positions on a series of imposing heights. Having brought up their artillery and mortars, they met our units with intense fire. It became clear that we could not succeed in overcoming this defense without careful preparations.[11]

Actually, after 82nd Rifle Division captured Visha, the three divisions (132nd, 82nd, and 162nd deployed from left to right) of Samarsky's 19th Rifle Corps captured Berezniaki, 12 kilometers southwest of Ozarichi, from 4th Panzer Division and continued their exploitation westward until they were halted by stronger German resistance just east of Savichi on 21 January. At this point, Samarsky transferred 82nd Rifle Division to his corps' right wing with orders to support 115th Rifle Brigade, whose riflemen were still struggling to overcome German resistance at Syshchichi, only 5 kilometers south of Ozarichi. On Samarsky's right, 354th and 253rd Rifle Divisions of Cherokmanov's 27th Rifle Corps had already fought their way into Ozarichi's eastern suburbs during heavy fighting on 20 and 21 January but were unable to drive the defending 35th Infantry Division from the town's western outskirts.

On Samarsky's left, however, Ivanov's 18th Rifle Corps recorded significant gains on 20 and 21 January, which by 22 January permitted 61st Army's 89th Rifle Corps to shift its forces into the expanding penetration west of the Ipa River (see Map 18.5). The 69th Rifle Division's history described the action:

> By the morning of 20 January, the enemy was no longer able to hold out [along the Visha River] and began to withdraw. The division advanced 8 kilometers and was stopped in front of the center of resistance in Savichi, which the Germans [4th Panzer Division] had prepared in advance.
>
> The next day a surprise attack by Colonel G. I. Abramov's 120th Regiment drove the enemy from the village of Dubniaki [8 kilometers southwest of Berezniaki], advanced through the swamps, and cut the withdrawal route of the enemy's Mozyr' grouping.
>
> At midday the enemy conducted a strong 15–20-minute fire raid on a grove of trees where the observation post of 120th Regiment's commander was located and on the firing positions of 118th Artillery Regiment's 1st Battery. Under cover of the artillery fire, about two companies

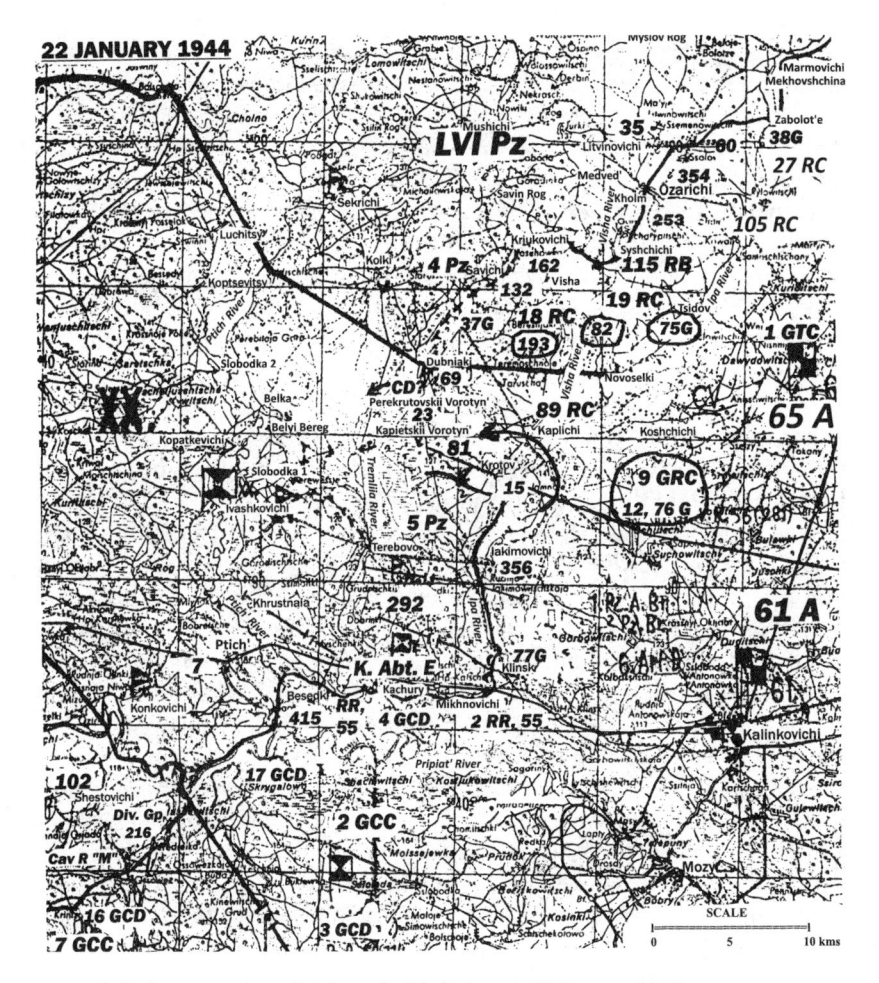

Map 18.5. The Situation in the Ozarichi-Ptich' Sector, 22 January 1944

of enemy infantry with 8 tanks counterattacked against 120th Regiment. A tank immediately surfaced from the dark forest near the village, then another after it, and, later, several more. These were "Tigers," and in their wake, hugging the ground, German infantry were advancing. They were firing from the march and not a minute had passed before the houses in the village concealed the advancing Germans.[12]

In a struggle that lasted the better part of two days, the counterattacking Germans recaptured Dubniaki, forcing the division to be rescued by 89th Rifle Corps' 23rd Rifle Division, which reinforced 69th Division on 22 January. "On the evening of 22 January, 237th Regiment once again captured the village of Dubniaki, in close coordination with units of 23rd Rifle Division, and restored the situation in the division's offensive sector."[13]

During the heavy fighting from 20 through 22 January, 69th Rifle and 37th Guards Rifle Divisions of Ivanov's 18th Rifle Corps advanced westward 4 kilometers to new positions extending from just east of Savichi southward to Dubniaki. By this time Ivanov had withdrawn his corps' 193rd Rifle Division into second echelon for rest; thus it could not assist the beleaguered 69th Rifle Division when it was struck by the German counterattack at Dubniaki. However, Rokossovsky had already prepared for that eventuality by ordering General Khaliuzin's 89th Rifle Corps, just transferred northward from Belov's 61st Army, to enter the penetration and expand it to the west.

Leaving 15th Rifle Division of Khaliuzin's 89th Rifle Corps in the Krotov region to anchor the southern corner-post of the large Soviet penetration to the north, Belov began committing 23rd and 81st Rifle Divisions of Khaliuzin's corps into the southern half of the growing penetration late on 21 January. The 23rd Rifle Division immediately moved to assist 69th Rifle Division at Dubniaki, while 81st Division advanced to the village of Kapietskii Vorotyn' on 23rd Division's left. This maneuver expanded the width of the overall penetration (from Syshchichi to Krotov) to 15 kilometers. In addition, Belov alerted the three guards divisions of General Boreiko's 9th Guards Rifle Corps, which had just completed their rest and refitting period in the army's rear, to prepare to exploit the penetration toward Ivashkovichi on the Ptich' River in a matter of a few days.

By day's end on 22 January, Rokossovsky's forces had torn a 12-kilometer-deep and 15-kilometer-wide hole through German defenses precisely at the boundary between 4th Panzer Division of Ninth Army' LVI Panzer Corps and 5th Panzer Division of Second Army's XX Army Corps. Worse still from the German perspective, there was virtually nothing either Ninth or Second Armies could do to restore the viability of their fronts. With Belov's reserve 9th Guards Rifle Corps alerted to enter the penetration, Rokossovsky ordered 27th, 19th, and 18th Rifle Corps of Batov's 65th Army to devote all of their energies to cracking open the Germans' defenses at Ozarichi and Savichi, and 89th Rifle and 9th Guards Rifle Corps of Belov's 61st Army to do the same at Dubniaki and Krotov. If both forces could do so successfully, Batov's forces could outflank LVI Panzer Corps' defenses from the south, and Belov's forces could do the same to XX Army Corps' defenses from the north, thus separating the Second and Ninth Armies. However, as is the case in every military operation, in doing so, the devil was in the detail.

To help ensure that his hopes became reality, Rokossovsky once again ordered Belov to form forward detachments and ski detachments in all of his first-echelon rifle divisions and infiltrate them deep into the Germans' rear area across 89th Rifle Corps' entire front. Beginning overnight on 21–22 January, Belov's detachments began advancing westward and southwestward in the sector from Dubniaki to north of Krotov, crossed the Tremlia River, 10 kilometers distant, and approached the eastern outskirts of the Germans' defensive positions protecting the eastern approaches to the Ptich' River.

By late on 21 January, German Second Army's XX Army Corps reacted quickly to establish defensive positions to protect those approaches. This new defensive line extended from the village of Belyi Bereg, on the Ptich' River 3 kilometers northeast of Kopatkevichi, southward 5 kilometers to the eastern edge of Slobodka State Farm No. 1, and then southeastward another 10 kilometers to the Tremlia River at Terebovo, where it linked up with the left flank of 292nd Infantry Division's defenses along the Ipa River. The defenses were occupied by 221st Engineer Battalion (Pi. 221), north of Slobodka 1, and 1st Battalion, 613th Infantry Regiment to the south. This defensive configuration left the bulk of 5th Panzer Division, which was defending the sector from .5 kilometer south of Krotov southward to Iakimovichi on the Ipa River, 10 kilometers in front of this new defensive line. Thus, the 5th Panzer was left behind to contend with Belov's attacking 89th Rifle Corps as well as the rifle corps' deeply operating forward detachments.

Perceiving these detachments as "cavalry and ski troops," while it tried to contain the forward Soviet rifle divisions along the Dubniaki-Krotov line with 5th Panzer Division, XX Army Corps also erected screens and covering forces to protect their rear area. Ultimately, however, its inability to cope with these pesky detachments prompted the corps to withdraw its main forces back to new defenses along the Ptich' River.

From 22 through 25 January, Rokossovsky's two armies continued pounding German Ninth and Second Armies' defenses across the entire front from Ozarichi southward to Krotov. Although inhibited by cold weather, snow, and cloud cover that prevented any real air support, the attacking forces recorded their greatest forward progress in the Dubniaki and Krotov sectors on 61st Army's right wing (see Map 18.6). Otherwise, farther to the north, now reinforced by 218th Rifle Division from 121st Rifle Corps (originally in the *front*'s reserve), 60th and 354th Rifle Divisions of Cherokmanov's 27th Rifle Corps' repeatedly assaulted German 35th Infantry Division's defenses at and north of Ozarichi but managed an advance of only 1 kilometer north of the town, in this case only because of 48th Army's successful offensive farther to the north.

On the northern wing of Rokossovsky's original penetration, 19th and 18th Rifle Corps of Batov's 65th Army continued their assaults against 4th Panzer Division's defenses from Dubniaki northward to Savichi and Syshchichi but also largely in vain. Therefore, Rokossovsky devised yet another plan to break the stalemate by penetrating LVI Panzer Corps' defenses. This time, he created a fresh shock group at the junction of 65th Army's 18th and 19th Rifle Corps and ordered it to strike northwestward from the Visha region toward Kriukovichi and Savin Rog. This shock group, which consisted

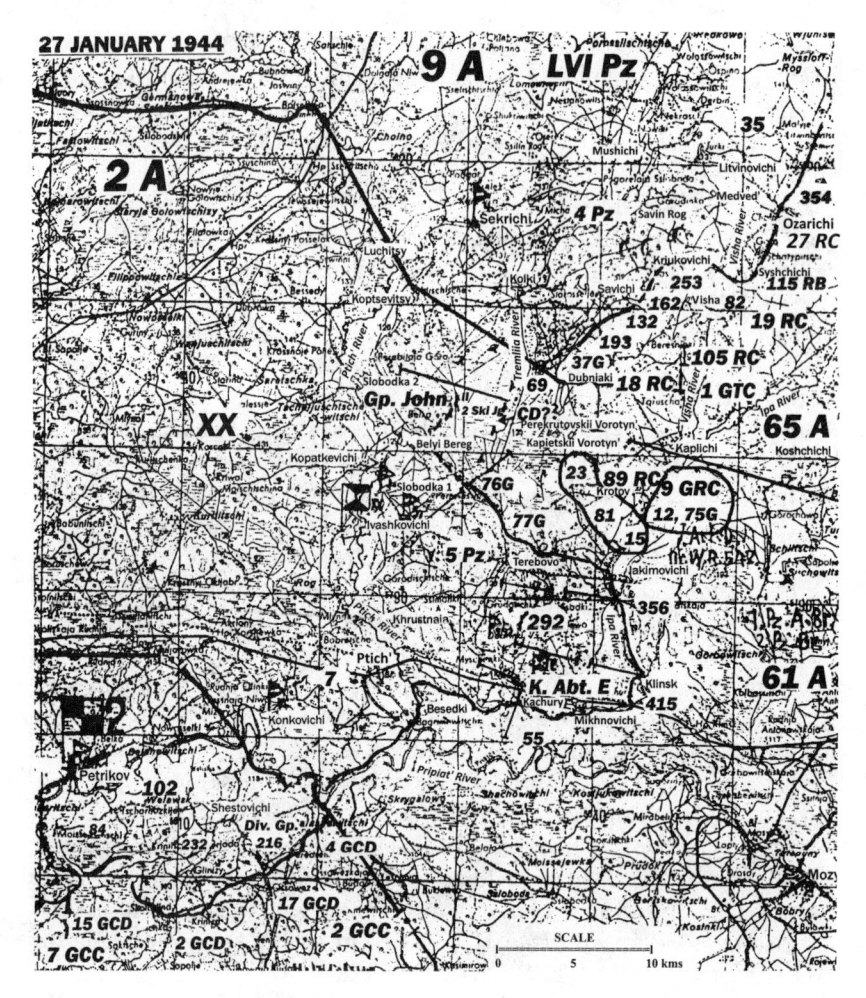

472   The Struggle for Belorussia, December 1943–April 1944

Map 18.6. The Situation in the Ozarichi-Ptich' Sector, 27 January 1944

of 18th Corps' 69th Rifle Division and 19th Corps' 82nd and 162nd Rifle Divisions, supported by 193rd and 251st Tank Regiments, was to attack German LVI Panzer Corps' defenses at the junction of its 4th Panzer and 35th Infantry Divisions. After breaking through the German tactical defenses, the shock group was to advance northward to the village of Mushichi, 10 kilometers north of Savichi, and westward to the village of Sekirichi, 10 kilometers northwest of Savichi, to envelop the German stronghold at Savichi from the north. To ensure success, Rokossovsky reinforced this shock group with a second echelon made up of 105th Rifle Corps' 132nd and 253rd Rifle and 75th Guards Rifle Divisions. If the reinforced shock group successfully penetrated the Germans' tactical defenses, 18th and 19th Rifle Corps' remaining divisions were to converge on Savichi from the south and east.

The histories of two of the three rifle divisions attacking in the shock group's first echelon provide critical information about Rokossovsky's and Batov's attempt between 25 and 29 January to end this frustrating stalemate. First, 69th Division's history describes 18th Rifle Corps' attacks on Savichi:

> The division tried to advance forward at Savichi for five days, but the enemy employed intense artillery and mortar fire to disrupt these attacks, which were conducted by numerically small subunits whose ranks included no more than 20–30 men.
>
> On the night of 25 January, the division turned its sector at Savichi over to 37th Guards Division, and, by order of the commander of 18th Corps, it was placed in second echelon.
>
> The division put itself into order in somewhat less than a day. At midday on 26 January, it received a new mission—to capture the village of Kriusha [probably Kriukovichi, 8 kilometers northeast of Savichi]. The division fulfilled this mission with immense effort. It advanced 4–6 kilometers and liberated the village of Kriusha and, at the same time, Kurgan' Farm.
>
> The offensive spirit of the Soviet troops was very great. The commands maneuvered their forces and weapons and changed the direction of their attacks. All of the reserves were thrown into combat to strengthen the attack.[14]

The second history describes the role of 19th Rifle Corps' 82nd Rifle Division in this offensive, supplementing that of 69th Division on its left:

> The commander of 19th Rifle Corps, to which 82nd Division belonged, reinforced it [the division] with 193rd Tank Regiment and a battalion of *"Katiushas"* [multiple-rocket launchers called "Stalin organs" by the Germans]. At the same time, we decided to study the enemy's forces and weapons in that sector more carefully. On the night of 26 January, the division's scouts under the command of Sergeant A. A. Matrosov captured a piece of key high ground with a surprise attack [and captured prisoners who revealed the nature of the Germans' defenses]. . . .
>
> Together with the *tankists,* the division's units assaulted the enemy on 26 January. The tanks, with assault troops from 210th Rifle Regiment aboard, quickly infiltrated into his defenses and disorganized the command and control of the enemy's units. The Hitlerites withdrew to the northwest in panic, throwing away their weapons and equipment. Our soldiers gathered up 12 operable guns of various calibers, 14 mortars, 11 heavy and 9 light machine guns, 18 automatic weapons, 147 rifles, 1 cross-

country vehicle, 2 light vehicles, and other equipment. Around 50 soldiers and officers were captured.

The enemy threw reserves comprising up to a regiment of infantry with tanks into the penetration sector. Fresh subunits offered stubborn resistance to the attackers along the line of Chistaia Lizha Farm and Hill 139.5. Fierce combat raged on. . . .

Our division's units advanced forward several kilometers on 29 January. Once again, they ran into a strong fortified line in the vicinity of the village of Savin Rog. Here the enemy had a well-developed system of fire, pillboxes, and antitank and antipersonnel obstacles.

We had no success in the battles for Savin Rog, and, by order of the corps commander, the division temporarily went over to the defense.[15]

Therefore, by day's end on 29 January, although 37th Guards and 193rd Rifle Divisions of Ivanov's 18th Rifle Corps were still stuck fast east of Savichi, thwarted by 4th Panzer Division's stout defenses, the attack by 69th, 82nd, and 162nd Rifle Divisions on the 26th placed Batov's forces in ideal positions from which to threaten 4th Panzer's left flank and rear area (see Map 18.7).

As confirmed by Second Army's daily situation maps, from 26 through 31 January, 69th Division's presence northeast of Savichi went undetected throughout the entire operation (as Rokossovsky intended). Nonetheless, 69th, 82nd, and 162nd Rifle Divisions struck on 26 January, probably preceded by forward detachments as was Rokossovsky's custom. By day's end on 27 January, the three divisions in the shock group's first echelon had shattered LVI Panzer Corps' front in a 5-kilometer-wide sector astride the boundary between 4th Panzer and 35th Infantry Division and captured Kriukovichi, and the divisions' multiple battalion-size forward detachments were up to 3 kilometers deep into the Germans' rear area. The next day, less 69th Division, which they missed, Second Army's intelligence organs correctly identified the attacking forces as 19th Rifle Corps' 82nd and 162nd and 105th Rifle Corps' 132nd and 253rd Divisions. By this time the attackers were approaching the village of Savin Rog 6 kilometers deep and were engaging the lead elements of 110th Infantry Division, which Ninth Army had hurriedly regrouped southward to plug the potential hole in LVI Corps' defenses. Although the 110th contained any further Soviet advance in the vicinity of Savin Rog, counterattacks the division conducted on 29 January failed to close the gap. Instead, on 30 January, Batov's attacking forces spread out to expand the penetration's width. As a result, on 31 January, the day that Second Army identified 105th Corps' 75th Guards Division and 251st Tank Regiment among the attackers, 18th Rifle Corps' 69th and 193rd Divisions and 19th Rifle Corps' 82nd and 162nd Divisions, now reinforced by 105th Rifle Corps' 132nd and 253rd Rifle and 75th Guards Divisions, spread out

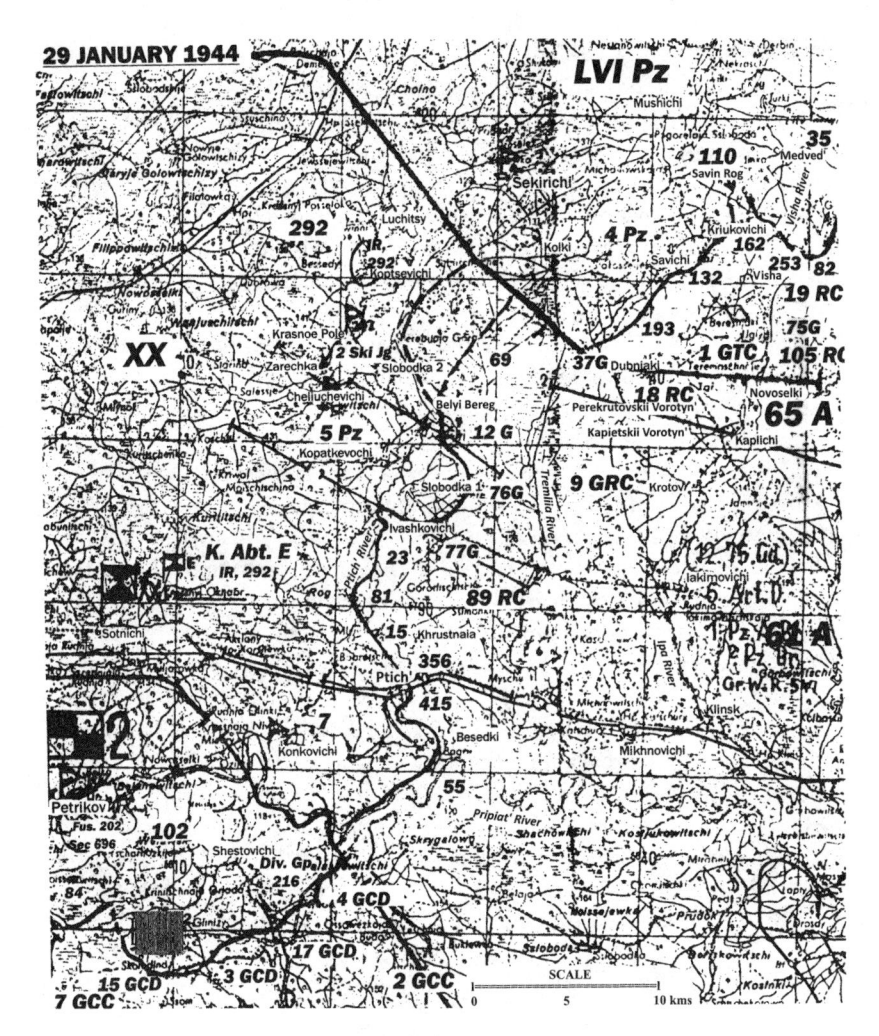

The Belorussian Front's Ozarichi-Ptich' Offensive 475

Map 18.7. The Situation in the Ozarichi-Ptich' Sector, 29 January 1944

westward and eastward to seize the ground north of Savichi and the town of Syshchichi to the east. Therefore, by month's end, Batov's seven rifle divisions had captured Kriukovichi and Syshchichi, together with a 12-kilometer-wide and 6-kilometer-deep salient whose western portion hung over German-held Savichi from the north. Given its untenable situation, German 4th Panzer Division had no choice but to withdraw its forces from Savichi on 4 February.

In conjunction with the 26 January offensive by Batov's 65th Army against Ninth Army's LVI Panzer Corps, Rokossovsky had already directed Belov's 61st Army to penetrate and destroy the defenses of Second Army's XX Army Corps on roughly the same date. If successful, Rokossovsky believed the two blows would leave Ninth and Second Armies with no option other than to withdraw their forces, the former northwestward toward Parichi and Bobruisk and the latter westward to the Ptich' River, and perhaps beyond.

Accordingly, Rokossovsky ordered Belov to employ 61st Army's relatively fresh 9th Guards Rifle Corps as a battering ram with which to rupture the defenses of 5th Panzer Division northwest of Iakimovichi. Ultimately, as with the case to the north, where Batov's corps ultimately succeeded in unhinging 4th Panzer Division's defenses at Savichi, the situation in the south developed favorably.

The decision Belov reached late on 21 January to commit forward and ski detachments from the lead divisions of Khaliuzin's 89th Rifle Corps into German XX Army Corps' rear area seemed to be correct because it did indeed begin unhinging the Germans' defenses along the Ipa River north of Krotov. However, XX Army Corps responded by erecting a protective screen of forces north and south of Slobodka 1 State Farm, leaving 5th Panzer Division to defend well forward in positions from just south of Krotov southward to Iakimovichi on the Ipa River. This placed the panzer division on the southern flank of 89th Rifle Corps' lead division as it advanced westward in the wake of the corps' forward detachments. Hard on the heels of these detachments, 89th Rifle Corps' 23rd, 81st, and 15th Rifle Divisions began assaulting 5th Panzer Division's defenses from the vicinity of Perekrutovskii Vorotyn, 6 kilometers northwest of Krotov, to south of Krotov proper at dawn on 22 January. On 89th Corps' left and in its center, repeated assaults by 15th and 81st Divisions against 5th Panzer Division's defenses near Krotov forced the panzer division to withdraw its defenses to roughly 5 kilometers south of the village. Thereafter, 89th Corps' rifle right-wing 23rd Rifle Division slipped easily into the void northwest of 5th Panzer's left flank, as did elements of 81st Rifle Division several days later. However, as soon as the 23rd Rifle charged into the gap, on 23 and 24 January, 5th Panzer's forces and its cooperating 1st Battalion, 613th Infantry Regiment to the rear, began launching forays against the southern flanks of 89th Corps' 23rd and 81st Divisions as they advanced westward, materially slowing their forward progress.[16]

In the wake of 89th Corps' assault, overnight on 25 and 26 January, Belov began committing the divisions of Boreiko's 9th Guards Rifle Corps into the yawning gap. The only record of 61st Army's operations after the fall of Kalinkovichi is the following cryptic entry in 12th Guards Rifle Division's history: "The division's units once again entered battle on 20 January northwest of Kalinkovichi and, after smashing enemy resistance, began advancing forward slowly but persistently. The corps' forces reached the Ptich' River in the Ivashkovichi region in February and, by order of the army commander, went on the defense."[17]

Although correct in the main, this brief account ignores the vital role 9th Guards Rifle Corps' played in 61st Army's 26 January offensive, probably because it achieved only limited success. In reality, as shown by Second Army's daily situation maps, at least two divisions of Boreiko's guards rifle corps entered combat early on 26 January, probably 76th and 77th Guards in first echelon and possibly 12th Guards in second echelon. These attacking divisions passed through the lines of 89th Rifle Corps' 23rd and 81st Rifle Division and attacked directly toward XX Army's second defensive line, anchored on Svobodka No. 1 State Farm, which extended southwestward toward Terebovo on the Tremlia River in 5th Panzer Division's rear. Still under pressure from 89th Rifle Corps' 15th Rifle Division, on 27 January 5th Panzer conducted a fighting withdrawal roughly 5 kilometers southwestward to the Terebovo and Iakimovichi line. At the same time, however, it dispatched small *kampfgruppen* from its subordinate regiments and battalions to reinforce defensive lines to the west and strike at the left flank of the advancing Russians. Although 5th Panzer ultimately contained 61st Army's assault short of the Ptich' River, by the evening of 27 January, it was clear to Second Army that XX Army Corps' remaining defenses on the lower Ipa River were now untenable.

Accepting this grim reality, late on 27 January General Weiss, the commander of German Second Army, ordered XX Army Corps to withdraw its forces from what had become a 10-kilometer-wide and 8-kilometer-deep salient along the Ipa River south of Iakimovichi back to a new defensive line along the Ptich' River. In a two-stage operation, protected by 5th Panzer Division against attack from the north, by the morning of 28 January, XX Army Corps had withdrawn 292nd Infantry Division and Corps Detachment E to an intermediate defense line along the Tremlia River from Myshanka and the Pripiat' River (see Map 18.7). Pursued by Russian forces, the German forces completed withdrawing to their new defense lines along the Ptich' on 29 January. By day's end on 30 January, 5th Panzer Division moved into the by-now-strong defensive positions east of Slobodka No. 1 State Farm, flanked on the north by 292nd Infantry Division, which XX Army Corps had shifted to its left wing after it abandoned the Ipa River line. The 5th Panzer was now flanked on the south by Corps Detachment E and 7th Infantry Division, whose forces occupied defenses along the Ptich' River from Ivashkovichi southward through Ptich' city to Besedki on the northern bank of the Pripiat' River.

On its ever-lengthening right wing south of the Ptich' River, Second Army positioned a new army corps, the XXIII, whose mission was to protect Army Group Center's right flank along the Pripiat' River and prevent Soviet forces from advancing westward along the river to the Luninets region, now 120 kilometers to the west. This was particularly important because in late January, 1st Ukrainian Front's 13th Army was advancing westward into the Rovno and Lutsk region, thus threatening Luninets and the adjacent Pripiat' Marshes from the south. Second Army's new XXIII Army Corps consisted of 102nd Infantry Division, reinforced by 216th Division Group and several security battalions, defending the bridgehead south of Petrikov; 1st Ski Jäger Brigade, whose 1st and 2nd Regiments defended the broad sector westward to Turov; and Group Agricola (Korück 580), which defended Davidgorodok and the southern approaches to Luninets with 203rd Security Division and Division z.b.V. 17.[18]

Meanwhile, Belov's forces attempted to pursue the withdrawing Germans from 27 through 29 January, with Boreiko's 9th Guards Rifle Corps orienting its advance on Slobodka No. 1 and Khaliuzin's 89th Rifle Corps on the Ptich' River line south of Ivashkovichi. Boreiko's entire corps assaulted 5th Panzer Division's defenses late on 29 January and on 30 January but was repulsed by the strong defenses and by heavy German fire. Appreciating the strength of the Germans' defenses and the weakness of his own forces, on 30 January Rokossovsky ordered Batov and Belov to cease their assaults and go over to the defense.

Therefore, by month's end the armies on the southern wing of Rokossovsky's Belorussian Front had achieved most of the missions the *Stavka* had assigned to them. During the Kalinkovochi-Mozyr' offensive, 65th and 61st Armies advanced 30–40 kilometers, and, in a few sectors, up to 60 kilometers, while enveloping German forces at Bobruisk from the south. They did so in the most trying of terrain and weather conditions and without significant armor support or reinforcements. In essence, as was his custom, Rokossovsky conducted economy-of-force operations seeking advantage by avoiding costly frontal attacks, by focusing his attacks on the weakest sectors of Second Army's defenses, and by employing quick maneuver and deception whenever possible. As a result, the Belorussian Front suffered 56,157 casualties, including 12,350 men killed, captured, or missing and 43,807 wounded or sick out of a total force of 232,600 men committed to action.[19] Compared with the losses suffered by Sokolovsky's Western Front, this cost was indeed paltry. His troops appreciated his attempts to conserve manpower and reduce losses, earning for him the reputation of an "unbloody commander," a most unusual title for Red Army wartime *front* and army commanders.

Rokossovsky also employed a wide variety of special tactical techniques, such as night attacks and the use of small forward detachments, often on skis, to infiltrate German defenses and attack German strongpoints from the flanks and rear. As a result, after capturing Kalinkovichi, Batov's and Belov's forces tore multiple holes in Second Army's defenses along the Ipa River and slowly but persistently expanded those penetrations to depths of up to 20 kilometers. With no means to close the penetration, the Germans had no choice but to withdraw, ultimately to the Ptich' River line. When they did, they relinquished control of territory roughly 40 kilometers wide and 20 kilometers deep.

From Rokossovsky's perspective, by month's end he believed his forces could achieve nothing more of operational or even tactical significance in the difficult swampy terrain on the northern banks of the Pripiat' River. Because Panov's 1st Guards Tank Corps was just completing its period of rest and refitting on 27 January, and Romanovsky's 48th Army now seemed poised to achieve new gains along the Bobruisk axis, Rokossovsky now shifted his focus to Romanenko's army. Therefore, on 26 January, just as the battle between the Ipa and Ptich' Rivers was reaching its climax, Rokossovsky ordered Panov to move his armor northward to reinvigorate Romanenko's advance toward Parichi and beyond.

CHAPTER 19

The Belorussian Front's Parichi-Bobruisk (Marmovichi-Dubrova) Offensive (16 January–23 February)

THE PLAN

Few records document the course of operations during this, the last of Rokossovsky's many small-scale offensives along the Berezina River axis. These include a few histories of divisions that took part in the offensive as well as after-action reports prepared by 48th and 65th Armies, both of which recount their army's successes and failures during late January and February 1944 through the prism of studying war experiences. The 48th Army's war experience summary for January, "Short Summary of 48th Army's Generalized War Experiences for January 1944," issued on 9 February 1944, sketches out the offensive's general parameters and the difficulties the army's attacking forces had to overcome:

1. After preparing a strong defense along the Probuzhdenie [Shatsilki] and Kizhin [Zherd'] line, the enemy [German Ninth Army], with a force of five infantry divisions (the 383rd, 707th, 253rd, 6th, and 36th), prevented 48th Army's forces from reaching the communications of the Zhlobin-Rogachev grouping by [conducting] sustained defensive battles in the conditions of an impassable forested and swampy region along the Bobruisk axis.
2. During the course of the January battles, the enemy displayed:
    (a) Skillful organization of a firing system with a trench defense in conditions of broken terrain and an "island" defense in the forested and swampy terrain by the creation of powerful strongpoints;
    (b) The capability of infantry and tanks, in conjunction with artillery and mortar fire, to conduct counterattacks at night in forested and swampy terrain;
    (c) Skillful maneuvering of artillery and mortar fire without changing firing positions, while concentrating massed fires against threatened sectors;
    (d) The employment of tanks and self-propelled guns as antitank means from ambush and their extensive maneuver along the roads through the forested and swampy terrain running along the front; and

(e) Combined interaction of air and ground forces during the delivery of counterattacks.
3. While suffering heavy losses in personnel and lacking reserves, the enemy was forced to commit specialized and rear service subunits (sappers, construction subunits, musician platoons, and training commands) into combat, and, at the same time, he created special groups of crack troops along threatened axes with the mission of holding on to the occupied positions at all cost.
4. The introduction into [German] weaponry of the new automatic machine gun sharply lengthened the range of aimed fire by close-combat guns (from a distance of 150 meters up to 800 meters)....

During the first half of January, the army's forces carried out regroupings, conducted battles to improve their positions, carried out reconnaissance raids, and strengthened their positions. On the left wing, they prepared for an offensive.... The terrain in the region of the army's combat operations facilitated the hidden concentration of forces, bold and surprise actions, and the employment of small groups and subunits from platoon, company, and up to rifle battalion size, reinforced by light artillery weapons....

Conclusions: The 48th Army penetrated the enemy's defense in the Probuzhdenie [Shatsilki] and Kizhin [Zherd'] sector during January. By developing the offensive toward Parichi, it drove the enemy from a series of intermediate lines, and, inflicting heavy losses on [the enemy] in personnel and equipment, it advanced 25–30 kilometers, and, in light of the weak preparations of the forces, it did not achieve decisive success.[1]

In addition, 48th Army's daily combat journal entry for 1 February 1944 provides an excellent summary of the army's operations during January (see Appendix O-1). Together with German archival records, these sources provide a more than adequate basis for reconstructing the parameters, objectives, and day-by-day developments during this offensive.

As the Kalinkovichi offensive was approaching its end, Rokossovsky formulated plans for expanding the operation to encompass his entire front from the Berezina River southward to the Pripiat' River. After it was formulated, Rokossovsky's plan required the armies deployed in his *front*'s center and on its left wing to conduct two offensive thrusts, which, although separate in terms of attack axes, were interrelated with regard to their timing and their ultimate objectives. He assigned the bulk of Batov's 65th Army and all of Belov's 61st Army the immediate missions of penetrating the defenses of the German Second Army's LVI Panzer and XX Army Corps along the Ipa River line, separating the two corps from one another, turning their respective flanks to the north and south, and forcing XX Army Corps to withdraw

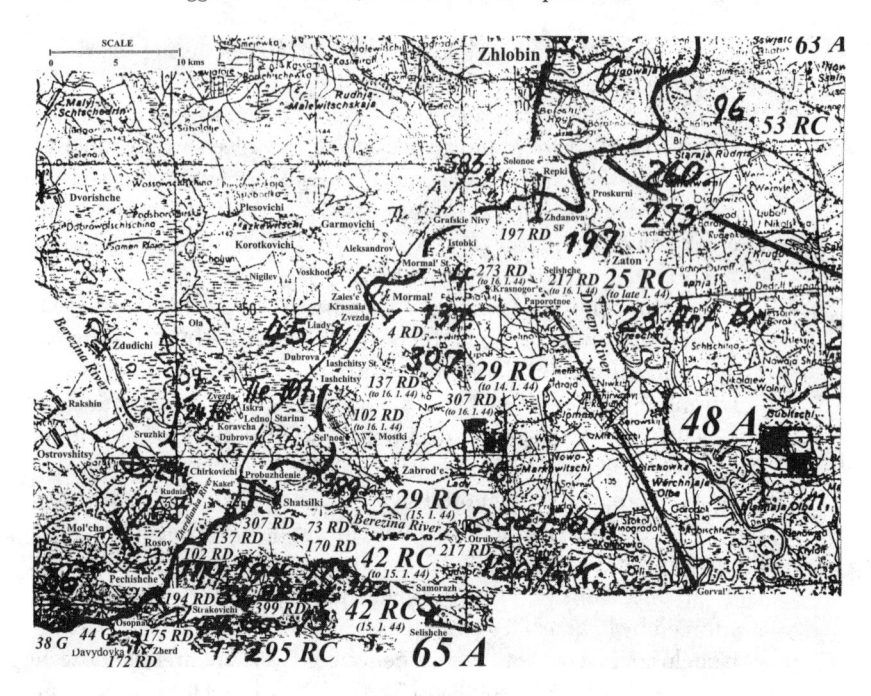

Map 19.1. 48th Army's Situation along the Parichi Axis, 1–11 January 1944

southwest to the Ptich' region and LVI Panzer Corps to retreat northwest to Oktiabr'skii. Subsequently, 61st Army was to pursue XX Army Corps' forces to the Ptich' River, and 65th Army was to wheel its axis of advance northwestward to drive LVI Panzer Corps' forces northwestward toward Oktiabr'skii and, if possible, Bobruisk.

Simultaneously with these offensives, Rokossovsky tasked the two rifle corps (the 42nd and 29th) on the left wing of Romanenko's 48th Army and one rifle corps (the 95th) on the right wing of Batov's 65th Army with assaulting the defenses of XXXXI Panzer Corps, positioned south of the Berezina River and on the right wing of German Ninth Army (see Map 19.1). Assisted by the rifle corps of Batov's army, Romanenko's 48th Army was to penetrate the Germans' defenses west of Shatsilki, exploit northwestward along and south of the Shatsilki-Parichi road, capture Parichi, and, if possible, continue the advance toward Bobruisk. Rokossovsky directed 65th and 48th Armies' shock groups to begin their offensives on 16 January, reach the Oktiabr'skii-Parichi line by month's end and, subsequently, conduct an exploitation operation toward Bobruisk during February.

General Romanenko designated Lieutenant General K. S. Kolganov's 42nd Rifle Corps and Major General A. M. Andreev's 29th Rifle Corps as his army's shock group. Supported by 42nd Guards and 231st Separate Tank and 1897th Self-propelled Artillery Regiments, after an extensive regrouping, the shock group was to launch its attack in the 15-kilometer-wide sector extending from Shatsilki (Probuzhdenie) on the Berezina River southwestward to Zherd' Station (Kizhin) on the Shatsilki-Kalinkovichi railroad line. The two assaulting corps faced defenses occupied by XXXXI Panzer Corps' 253rd Infantry Division and roughly half of the panzer corps' 36th Infantry Division. Other than the Germans' first defensive belt, the most formidable obstacle the two attacking corps faced was the Germans' strongly fortified second defensive belt, which extended from northeast to southwest along the Zherdianka River from the Berezina River northwest of Shatsilki to Zherd' Station.

On the left flank of Romanenko's shock group, Rokossovsky ordered a second shock group, formed from Major General I. A. Kuzovkov's 95th Rifle Corps (38th and 44th Guards and 172nd Rifle Divisions) of General Batov's 65th Army, to assault German defenses in the 10-kilometer sector from Zherd' Station to Gory, precisely at the boundary between XXXXI Panzer Corps' 36th and 134th Infantry Divisions. After penetrating the Germans' defenses, 95th Rifle Corps was to join 48th Army's exploitation northward toward Parichi.

On 95th Rifle Corps' left, General Cherokmanov's 27th Rifle Corps of Batov's army, deployed in the Koreni region east of Ozarichi, filled the gap between 48th Army's offensive toward Parichi and 65th Army's offensive toward the Ptich' River. Therefore, 27th Corps' initial task was to protect the southern flank of the former and the northern flank of the latter. Thereafter, if the penetration operations succeeded, Cherokmanov's forces were to reduce the Germans' defenses at Ozarichi. Finally, on the right flank of 48th Army's shock group, after regrouping about half of its forces southward to and across the Berezina River, the 4th and 197th Rifle Divisions of Major General A. B. Barinov's 25th Rifle Corps were to remain on the defense in the extended sectors between the Berezina and Dnepr Rivers on 48th Army's left wing (see Table 19.1).

Thus, Rokossovsky's offensive plan for the thrust toward Parichi was relatively simple. Initially, it concentrated the eight rifle divisions of 48th Army's 29th and 42nd Rifle Corps and the three rifle divisions of Batov's 95th Rifle Corps against the defenses of two-and-one-half German divisions (the 253rd, 36th, and half of 134th). Although the Soviet divisions were roughly half the strength of their German counterparts, Rokossovsky was able to establish a roughly twofold superiority in infantry in this main attack sector (see Table 19.2). When 48th Army's two reserve divisions (the 217th and 273rd) are added to this equation, this superiority rose to almost 3 to 1. However, as was the case to the south, armor support for Rokossovsky's attack, which amounted to about forty tanks and self-propelled guns, was particularly weak. The only armor fire support available to the defending Germans were the assault guns assigned to 185th and 244th Assault Gun *Abteilung* (detachment), which supported 36th Infantry Division in the Davydovka region and 253rd Infantry Division west of Shatsilki.

Table 19.1. The Postulated Combat Formations of 48th Army and 65th Army's Right Wing and Opposing German Forces Late on 15 January 1944 (deployed from north to south)

FORCE (Sector)	OPPOSING GERMAN FORCES
Before the Regrouping (to 14 January 1944)	
1st/2nd/3rd Echelons (Mobile group)	
BELORUSSIAN FRONT	**NINTH ARMY**
48th Army (Dnepr River, Zherd Station)	XXXV Army Corps
	XXXXI Panzer Corps (from 18.1)
25th RC (Dnepr River, Iashchitsy Station)	
197th RD (south of Zhlobin, Mormal')	383rd ID
273rd RD (Mormal')	45th ID
4th RD (Mormal', Iashchitsy Station	707th ID (-) (18.1)
217th RD (army reserve)	XXXXI Panzer Corps (to 18.1)
	LVI Panzer Corps (from 18.1)
29th RC (Iashchitsy Station, Shatsilki)	
137th RD/307th RD (Iashchitsy St., Iashchitsy)	253rd ID
102th RD (Iashchitsy, Shatsilki)	
73rd RD (reserve)	
42nd RC (Shatsilki, Zherd Station)	
399th RD/170th RD (Shatsilki, Strakovichi)	
170th RD (Strakovichi, Zherd Station)	36th ID/
175th RD (reserve)	185th Assault Gun
65th Army	
95th RC (Zherd Station, south of Gory)	134th ID/
172nd RD (Zherd St., Davydovka)	244th Assault Gun
44th GRD (Davydovka, Liudinovka)	*Abteilung*
38th GRD (Liudinovka, south of Gory	
	SECOND ARMY (to 18.1)
	NINTH ARMY (from 18.1)
27th RC (south of Gory, Kazansk)	LVI Panzer Corps
60th RD/106th RD (south of Gory, Koreni)	(to 18.1)
354th RD (Koreni, Kazansk)	707th ID
	(35th ID on 17.1)
After the Regrouping (up to and after 15 January 1944)	
1st/2nd/3rd Echelons (Mobile group)	
BELORUSSIAN FRONT	**NINTH ARMY**
48th Army (Dnepr River, Zherd Station)	XXXV Army Corps
	XXXXI Panzer Corps (from 18.1)
25th RC (Dnepr River, Shatsilki)	
197th RD (south of Zhlobin, Mormal')	383rd ID
	45th ID
4th RD (Mormal', Iashchitsy)	707th ID (-) (18.1)
	XXXI Panzer Corps (to 18.1)
	LVI Panzer Corps (from 18.1)
29th RC (Shatsilki, Strakovichi)	
307th RD/73rd RD (north)	253rd ID
137th RD (center)	
102th RD (south)	
42nd RC (Strakovichi, Zherd St.)	
194th RD/170th RD (Strakovichi, Zherd)	
175th RD/399th RD (Zherd Station, Davydovka)	36th ID/
	185th Assault Gun
273rd RD/217th RD (reserve)	
53rd RC (17th, 41st, 96th RDs)	*Abteilung*
(late January from 63rd Army)	

Table 19.1. *continued*

65th Army
95th RC (Zherd St., south of Gory) 134th ID/
  172nd RD (Zerd St,.north of Davydovka)   244th Assault Gun
  44th GRD (Davydovka, Liudinovka)   *Abteilung*
  38th GRD (Liudinovka, south of Gory

SECOND ARMY (to 18.1)
NINTH ARMY (from 18.1)
27th RC (south of Gory, Kazansk) LVI Panzer Corps
  60th RD/106th RD (south of Gory, Koreni) (to 18.1)
  354th RD (Koreni, Kazansk) 707th ID
    (35th ID on 17.1)

Sources: *Boevoi sostav Sovetskoi Armii, chast' IV (Ianvar'–dekabr' 1944)* [The combat composition of the Soviet Army, pt. 4 (January–December 1944)] (Moscow: Voenizdat, 1988), 14–15, 42; and Anlagen zum KTB, A.O.K. 2 – Ia, Lagenkarten, Jan–Feb 1944, *AOK 2, 49701/92 file*, in NAM series T-312, roll 1281.

Table 19.2. The Estimated Correlation of Opposing Forces in the Parichi-Bobruisk Offensive, 16–27 January 1944

OPPOSING FORCES	
Soviet	***German***
Belorussian Front	
MAIN ATTACK SECTOR	
48th Army	253rd Infantry Division
65th Army	36th Infantry Division
11 rifle divisions	½, 134th Infantry Division
2 tank regiments (30 tanks)	185th and 244th Assault Gun
1 SP regiment (10 SP guns)	*Abteilung* (40 assault guns)
Strength: 85,000 men (est.)	30,000 men (est.)
40 tanks and SP guns	40 assault guns
Reinforcements (by 2 February):	
53rd Rifle Corps	*Kampfgruppen*, 110th, 6th,
3 rifle divisions	129th, 383rd, 296th,
217th and 273rd Rifle Division (25th Rifle Corps)	Infantry Divisions
1st Guards Tank Corps (100 tanks)	*Kampfgruppe*, 4th Panzer Division (30 tanks)
Depth of Soviet advance: 8–20 kilometers	

Sources: *Boevoi sostav Sovetskoi Armii, chast' IV (Ianvar'–dekabr' 1944)* [The combat composition of the Soviet Army, pt. 4 (January–December 1944)] (Moscow: Voenizdat, 1988), 14–15, 42; Anlagen zum KTB, A.O.K. 2 – Ia, Lagenkarten, Jan–Feb 1944, *AOK 2, 49701/92 file*, in NAM series T-312, roll 1281; and H Gr Mitte/Ia, KTB: Lagenkarten, 1–31 January 1944, H Gr Mitte, 65002/60 file, in NAM series T-311, roll 224.

Although some aspects of the combat formation of Romanenko's army remain unclear, it appears as if Andreev deployed the four divisions of 29th Rifle Corps in two-echelon attack formation just west of Shatsilki to increase the strength of his assault and quickly penetrate 253rd Infantry Division's defenses. He did so because his immediate objective, the village of Chirkovichi on the road leading westward from Shatsilki and the Berezina River northwest of Shatsilki, required an advance of only 7 kilometers, and Andreev's attacking force had to cross the Zherdianka River during its initial assault. After the 29th Corps captured Chirkovichi, Romanenko planned to reinforce his corps with 217th Rifle Division from the army's reserve.

Because Kolganov's 42nd Rifle Corps had a deeper immediate objective, the villages of Zarech'e and Sosnovka, roughly 15 kilometers deep, it attacked in two-echelon formation to sustain its offensive across the Zherdianka River and into the depths. In addition, Romanenko planned to reinforce Kolganov's and Andreev's corps with 170th Rifle Division during its penetration and, if necessary, with 273rd Rifle Division, transferred from 48th Army's 25th Rifle Corps, as well. Finally, Kuzovkov's 95th Rifle Corps, whose initial objectives were the villages of Mekhovshchina and Kobyl'shchina (today Poles'e), at a depth of 8–10 kilometers, planned to deploy for its attack with 38th and 44th Guards and 172nd Rifle Divisions in single echelon from left to right.

Romanenko's forces conducted a major regrouping during the period from 14 to 15 January to create the necessary shock group southwest of Shatsilki (see Map 19.2). During this period 29th Rifle Corps, which had previously manned positions east of the Berezina River, shifted its three rifle divisions southward across the Berezina River into its penetration sector southwest of Shatsilki. At the same time, 42nd Rifle Corps shifted its 399th Rifle Division southward across the Berezina into its second echelon and deployed 175th Rifle Division, just provided to it by 48th Army, into forward assault positions, with its first-echelon 194th Rifle Division providing cover and protection for these movements.

At the same time, 95th Rifle Corps regrouped its 172nd Rifle Division from its forward positions adjacent to 194th Rifle Division farther to the south, where it joined the corps' 44th and 38th Guards Rifle Divisions, already concentrating in 95th Rifle Corps' new offensive sector. Finally, Romanenko regrouped 217th and 273rd Rifle Divisions from their positions in 25th Rifle Corps into reserve positions to the rear of 29th and 42nd Rifle Corps. Romanenko completed this complex regrouping process by nightfall on 15 January, only hours before the assault was to begin.

THE BATTLE: THE FIRST PHASE (16–27 JANUARY 1944)

Romanenko's shock group began its assault at dawn on 16 January, after firing a thirty-five-minute artillery preparation against the Germans' defenses. From very beginning of the assault, 29th and 42nd Rifle Corps' struggle to penetrate the Germans' forward defenses was both difficult and prolonged (see Map 19.3). The 194th Rifle Division's history provides a vivid description of the first few days of the attack:

> Once again included in 42nd Rifle Corp, 194th Rifle Division took part in combat operations along the Zherdianka River from 16 through 27 January. After a 35-minute artillery preparation, it attacked the enemy's positions in the Pechishche and Kun'ia sector with two of its regiments, but it had no success. The 470th and 954th Rifle Regiments were not able to

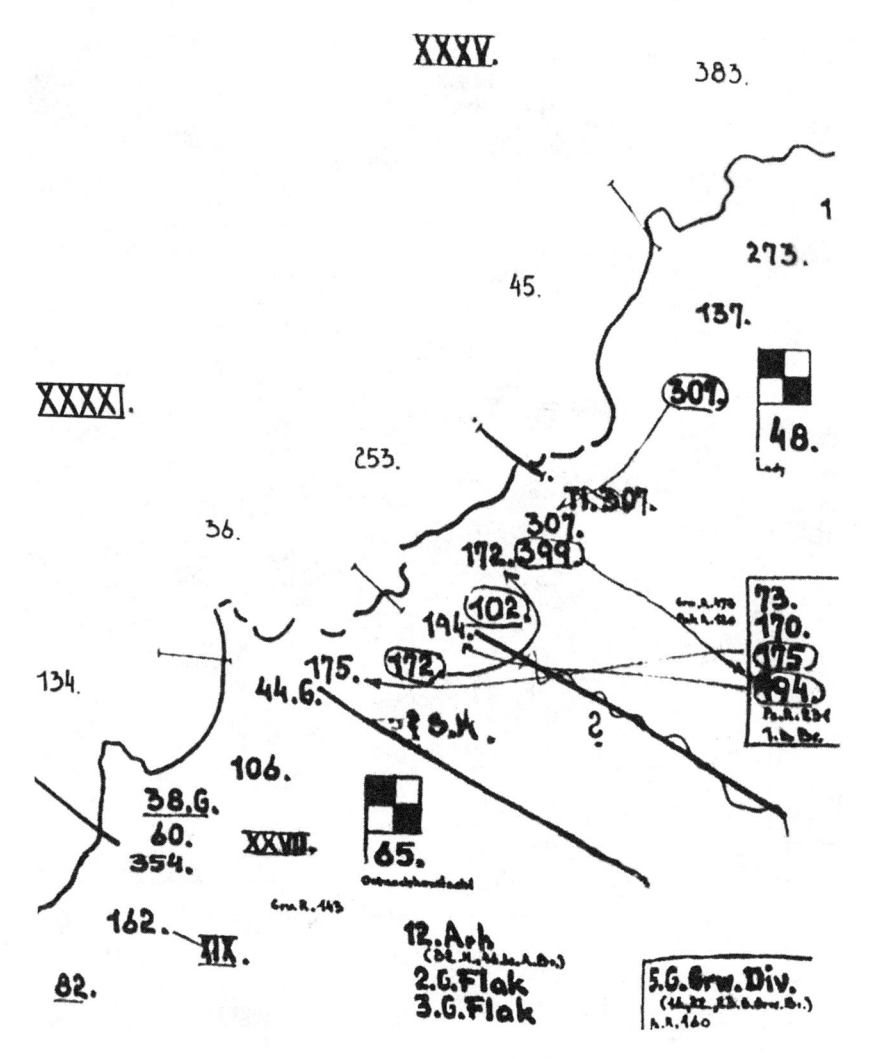

Map 19.2. Ninth Army's Intelligence Appreciation of 48th Army's Regrouping, 14–15 January 1944

advance forward and went to ground, halted by a squall of Hitlerite fire. After being committed to combat from the second echelon, 616th Rifle Regiment also went to ground, failing to reach its assigned objectives. Only on the fourth day of the offensive did the division succeed in breaking through the enemy's defenses and capturing the enemy strongpoints at Pechishche, Kremen, Kun'ia, and Medved'.

During the battle for the village of Kun'ia, Major N. P. Volkov, a veteran of the division and the commander of 954th Rifle Regiment's 2nd Battalion, himself led his troops in the assault on the enemy's position.

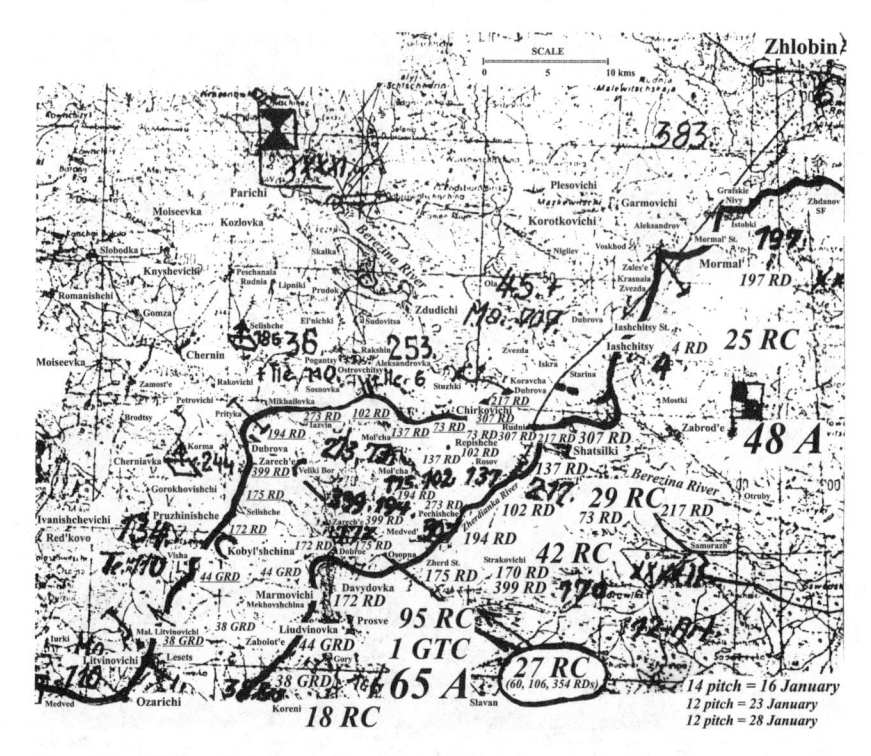

488   The Struggle for Belorussia, December 1943–April 1944

Map 19.3. 48th Army's Situation along the Parichi Axis, 16–31 January 1944

Struck by a hail of German bullets, the major fell, but, emulating the bravery of its commander, the battalion crushed the enemy and captured the village. Other subunits of the division exploited the battalion's success and, after overcoming the enemy resistance, captured the series of enemy strongpoints.

The 1st Battalion, 470th Rifle Regiment distinguished itself in the battle for Pechishche.... After withdrawing, the enemy managed to dig in along a new line extending along the Chirkovichi-Veliki Bor road. The enemy greeted the thinning ranks of the advancing troops with a hurricane of fire and fierce counterattacks, which, however, did not stop the advancing Soviet soldiers. Finally, the division smashed the enemy along that line and, continuing the offensive, cut the Iazvin-Sosnovka road and captured the village of Iazvin [15 kilometers northwest of Pechishche] by day's end on 26 January.[2]

After four days of bitter fighting to overcome the German 253rd and 36th Infantry Divisions' forward defensive belt, by nightfall on 19 January, 137th and 102nd Rifle Divisions of Andreev's 29th Rifle Corps advanced almost 3 kilometers, crossed the Zherdianka River on 253rd Infantry Division's right wing and reached the southern outskirts of the German strongpoints at Rosov and Rudnia, 2–3 kilometers west and northwest of Shatsilki, in the process severing the Shatsilki-Parichi road. While they were advancing, Romanenko committed his 217th Rifle Division to combat from his reserve with orders to clear the defending Germans from their increasingly isolated defenses at Shatsilki proper.

To the south, however, German 36th Infantry Division's forward defenses held firm for four days. Anchored on the strongpoints at Pechishche and Medved', the stout German defense brought the assault by 399th and 194th Rifle Divisions of Kolganov's 42nd Rifle Corps to an abrupt halt in the midst of their forward defenses. On 42nd Rifle Corps' left wing, however, a regiment of 399th Rifle Division was able to exploit the success of the neighboring 95th Rifle Corps by approaching the Medved' strong point from the west.

Kuzovkov's 95th Rifle Corps recorded the greatest success during the first four days of the assault. Attacking German LVI Panzer Corps' defenses at the boundary between 36th and 134th Infantry Divisions, Kuzovkov's 172nd Rifle Division advanced almost 5 kilometers, forcing its way across the Zherdianka River and reaching the eastern outskirts of the German strongpoints at Zarech'e and Dobroe. With its withdrawal routes threatened, 134th Infantry Division withdrew the forces in its center and on its right wing from the defenses they occupied further south along the eastern bank of the Zherdianka River. This, in turn, permitted 95th Rifle Corps' 38th and 44th Guards Rifle Divisions to advance westward across the Zherdianka River in their attack sectors.

Thus, the main obstacle to a further Soviet advance on the evening of 19 January was the pesky German redoubt in the center of Romanenko's penetration sector, which, if not overcome quickly, threatened the coherence of his entire offensive. To remedy this situation, late on 19 January, Romanenko dispatched 73rd and 170th Rifle Divisions from his reserves to reinforce 29th and 42nd Rifle Corps' assaults.

Early on 20 January, Andreev's 29th Rifle Corps attacked the left flank and rear of 36th Infantry Division's forces defending the Pechishche strongpoint with the fresh 73rd Rifle Division, while his corps' 102nd Rifle Divisions and 194th Rifle Division of Kolganov's 42nd Rifle Corps jointly assaulted the strongpoint itself frontally. To the south, Kolganov's fresh 170th Rifle Division passed through 399th Rifle Division's lines and attacked the strongpoint at Medved', 4 kilometers southwest of Pechishche. The immense pressure applied by the four Soviet divisions left the defenders of Pechishche no choice but to withdraw. They did so late on 20 January, pursued closely by the Russians.

Exploiting 29th and 42nd Rifle Corps' victory at Pechishche, 95th Rifle Corps' 172nd Rifle Division, flanked on the right by 42nd Rifle Corps' 399th

Rifle Division, burst open the German defenses at the boundary between 134th and 36th Infantry Divisions east of Zarech'e on 20 January. Then the two divisions pushed northward 3 kilometers toward the Dubrova-Shatsilki road west of the village of Mol'cha by day's end on 21 January. By this time 42nd Rifle Corps' 175th and 194th Rifle Divisions had closed up to 36th Infantry Division's new defense line, which extended east and west of the fortified village of Repishche, 10 kilometers northwest of Shatsilki.

Reinforced by assault guns from 185th and 244th Assault Gun *Abteilungen* (detachments) and a battalion-size *kampfgruppe* from 110th Infantry Division, 36th Infantry Division mounted several local counterattacks that temporarily stymied any further Soviet advance northwestward from the Zherdianka River. To the east, however, 73rd, 137th, and 307th Rifle Divisions of Andreev's 29th Rifle Corps filled in 48th Army's front from Repishche to Rudnia astride the Shatsilki-Parichi, and 217th Rifle Division began probing German defenses at Shatsilki proper. Threatened with envelopment from the northwest, that night 253rd Infantry Division began withdrawing its forces from the town, employing them instead to reinforce its sagging defenses in the Repishche region to the west.

Supported by 95th Rifle Corps on its left, in six days of intense fighting, Romanenko's shock group succeeded in penetrating German Ninth Army's defensive front along and forward of the Zherdianka River and advanced between 5 and 10 kilometers to the northwest across a front of roughly 20 kilometers. By this time, however, the Germans had reinforced their beleaguered 253rd and 36th Infantry Divisions with several battalion-size *kampfgruppen* from 6th and 110th Infantry Divisions and numerous assault guns. These reinforcements permitted XXXXI Panzer Corps to erect a hasty but still deadly defense line to contain the Russian penetration. Thus, Romanenko's foremost challenge was to maintain his shock group's forward momentum and pierce this line before the Germans could prepare a completely new defensive belt.

To do so, while his forward divisions continued pressuring the Germans' defenses, from 21 through 23 January, Romanenko regrouped his forces and brought forward additional fresh reserves. After assigning 217th Rifle Division responsibility for holding on to the town of Shatsilki, he concentrated 307th, 73rd, and 137th Rifle Divisions of Andreev's 29th Rifle Corps in the 4-kilometer-wide sector from Repishche eastward to Rudnia, with the corps' 102nd Rifle Division in second echelon, and ordered General Andreev to mount an attack northward toward Chirkovichi and Mol'cha, 8–13 kilometers northwest of Shatsilki, early on 24 January.

At the same time, 399th, 175th, and 194th Rifle Divisions of Kolganov's 42nd Rifle Corps were to advance northwestward from the forward tip of the shock group's advance toward Dubrova, Iazvin, and Sosnovka, situated 25 kilometers west, 20 kilometers west-northwest, and 15 kilometers northwest of Shatsilki, respectively. On Kolganov's left, 172nd Rifle and 44th and

38th Guards Rifle Divisions of Kuzovkov's 95th Rifle Corps were to keep pace by advancing northwestward across the Parichi-Kalinkovichi road in the 15-kilometer-wide sector from Lesets, 5 kilometers north of Ozarichi, northward to Dubrova. Easing their task somewhat, the German strongpoint at Ozarichi had finally fallen to 65th Army's 27th Rifle Corps on 20 January. To strengthen his assault, Romanenko transferred 273rd Rifle Division from 25th Rifle Corps' sector north of the Berezina River and ordered it to reinforce Andreev's and Kolganov's attack.

The fresh assault, which began early on 24 January, caught the Germans while they were off balance preparing their new defenses. In four more days of heavy fighting west and northwest of Shatsilki, 307th Rifle Division of Andreev's 29th Rifle Corps captured the Repishche strongpoint. Thereafter, 307th Rifle Division, flanked on the left by 73rd Rifle Division and on the right by the 137th, forced LVI Panzer Corps' 253rd Infantry Division to withdraw its center and right wing 2 kilometers to the Chirka River line and the southern outskirts of Mol'cha and Chirkovichi, 6–12 kilometers northwest of Shatsilki. Meanwhile, on 29th Rifle Corps' right wing north of Shatsilki, 217th Rifle Division captured the strongpoint at Rudnia, fought its way across the Chirka River, and advanced to the southern bank of the Berezina River, in the process enveloping 253rd Division's left wing and forcing it to withdraw to Chirkovichi. After finally halting 29th Rifle Corps' thrust late on 24 January, 253rd Infantry Division anchored its new defensive line on the strongpoints at Mol'cha and Chirkovichi.

While 29th Corps was pressing German forces northwestward from Shatsilki, to the west, the three rifle divisions of Kolganov's 42nd Rifle Corps, which Romanenko further reinforced with 273rd Rifle Division on 25 January, advanced northwestward from 8 to 10 kilometers in four days of heavy fighting. On the corps' left wing, 399th Rifle Division captured Zarech'e, 25 kilometers west of Shatsilki, on 25 January and then fought a seesaw battle for the village of Dubrova, a vital strongpoint at the junction of the Parichi-Kalinkovichi and Shatsilki-Oktiabr'skii roads, on 26 and 27 January. At the same time, on the 399th's right, 194th and 273rd Rifle Divisions captured the German strongpoint at Iazvin, 5 kilometers northeast of Dubrova, and reached the southern edge of Sosnovka, 5 kilometers east of Iazvin. Despite giving up considerable ground, LVI Panzer Corps' 36th Infantry Division finally halted Kolganov's advance at Sosnovka and the extensive swath of swampy terrain stretching almost 10 kilometers to the west.

On the left of Romanenko's 42nd Rifle Corps, the three rifle divisions of General Kuzovkov's 95th Rifle Corps (65th Army) kept pace with 48th Army's successes by advancing 6 kilometers. During the corps' advance, 172nd Division captured the town of Kobyl'shchina, 12 kilometers south of Dubrova, by doing so also cutting the Parichi-Kalinkovichi road; its 44th Guards Division captured Visha, on the eastern bank of the Visha River, 12 kilometers north of Ozarichi; and 38th Guards Rifle Division severed the Parichi-Kalinkovichi road and approached the eastern edge of the German strongpoint at Malyi Litvinovichi, 5 kilometers north of Ozarichi. With vital support from 244th Assault Gun *Abteilung*, the beleaguered German 134th Infantry Division finally halted the Soviet advance along the Parichi-Kalinkovichi road in and south of Dubrova and along the Visha River south of Visha. Despite the Germans' best defensive efforts, by day's end on 27 January, the most forward elements of Romanenko's army were a mere 15 kilometers from the southern outskirts of Parichi.

However, after almost two weeks of heavy combat, Romanenko's divisions, already severely understrength when he began his offensive, were utterly worn out and incapable of mounting further attacks without significant reinforcements. Romanenko informed Rokossovsky of this reality on 27 January and also requested the *front* commander's permission to halt his offensive temporarily until fresh reinforcements were available, a request that Rokossovsky quickly approved.

Nonetheless, since Rokossovsky remained convinced that German Ninth Army's defenses were nearing the breaking point, although he granted Romanenko's forces a brief respite, he also reinforced his 48th Army significantly and directed him to resume the offensive on 2 February.

THE BATTLE: THE SECOND PHASE (2–6 FEBRUARY 1944)

Rokossovsky provided Romanenko's army the first of its promised reinforcements by the end of January, the most important of which were the fresh 53rd Rifle Corps and General Panov's rested and refitted 1st Guards Tank Corps. Anticipating the *Stavka*'s pending directive to disband his *front*'s 63rd Army, still operating east of the Dnepr River, Rokossovky assigned that army's 53rd Rifle Corps to Romanenko's 48th Army and ordered Romanenko to employ it to spearhead his new offensive. Commanded by Major General I. A. Gartsev, 53rd Rifle Corps included 17th, 41st, and 96th Rifle Divisions. The history of 96th Rifle Division described the corps' transfer and its difficult regrouping into 48th Army's sector:

> After a weeklong stay in the Uvarovichi region, where we put ourselves in more or less proper order, the division received an order to regroup into the combat sector of 48th Army. After marching 120 kilometers along our assigned march route, on 30 January we reached our designated region, where we relieved 65th Army's 172nd Rifle Division in the Kobyl'shchina and Dubrova sector.
> The conditions surrounding the march were extraordinarily difficult. Dense and wet snow piled up incessantly. In the full sense of the word,

there were no roads at all. However, we tried to our utmost to achieve an advance tempo of 35–40 kilometers per day.

We crossed the Dnepr on previously erected pontoons. South of Zhlobin both sides of the river were already in our hands.

The western bank of the Dnepr represented a frightening sight. Destroyed bunkers, trenches, pillboxes, the black hulks of burned tanks and smashed-up guns were everywhere. All of these bespoke of the fierce bloody battles that had occurred here not long ago. The forests along the riverside, which had been torn up by the incessant explosions of shells, mines, and aerial bombs, also bore witness to these battles.

And it seemed that the powerful Dnepr River, which had not frozen despite the severe cold, now carried on its waves the scarlet blood of perished soldiers. It was difficult to look at the suffering river, but, at the same time, our spirits rejoiced that, covered with glory and legend, it once again had become free and ours. . . .

After the Dnepr, the Berezina River was on our path. Swampy forests were along its banks. We arrived at the front lines after passing through this region without roads.

Our combat sector lay between the villages of Dubrova and Kobyl'shchina [now Poles'e]. We constructed it easily enough and rapidly. The command post was situated in a pine forest, which, fortunately, had barely been touched by the war. The 172nd Division's command post had been located here before we arrived. Other works remained after they left so that we did not have to dig foxholes and construct dugouts.[3]

More important still, Rokossovsky also ordered General Panov to move his 1st Guards Tank Corps, refitting in the region north of Kalinkovichi, to new assembly areas in the rear of Romanenko's 48th Army. According to Panov's memoirs:

The [1st Guards Tank Corps'] units busied themselves with combat and political training and received reinforcements from 17 through 26 January. We received 500 replacement soldiers and sergeants for the motorized infantry and 30 T-34 tanks for 16th Guards Tank Brigade. On 27 January the corps was concentrated in the Zal'e, Mekhovshchina, and Marmovichi region and was subordinated operationally to Lieutenant General P. L. Romanenko's 48th Army on 30 January.[4]

In addition, during the last few days of January, General Romanenko shuffled his army's forces, transferring the headquarters of Major General A. B. Barinov's 25th Rifle Corps, along with its 197th Rifle Division, from the sector between the Berezina and Dnepr Rivers to the sector between Dubrova and Iazvin west of the Berezina River. Therefore, it took over the sector previously occupied by 172nd Rifle Division of 65th Army's 95th Rifle Corps and 399th and 194th Rifle Divisions of 48th Army's 42nd Rifle Corps. This left Kolganov's and Andreev's restructured 42nd and 29th Rifle Corps concentrated in the 14-kilometer-wide sector stretching eastward from Iazvin to Chirkovichi. During this regrouping, Romanenko also withdrew 194th Rifle Division, which had apparently suffered significant losses during the fighting, from its previous forward position at Iazvin and repositioned it on the army's left wing east of the Berezina River. According to the division's history, "On 28 January, 194th Rifle Division, while becoming operationally subordinate to 161st Fortified Region, defended along the Mormal' and Berezina River line for almost a full month."[5]

Although this regrouping significantly strengthened Romanenko's forces concentrated in the Dubrova region, west of the Berezina River, it left the army's right wing between the Berezina and Dnepr Rivers defended by only 194th and 4th Rifle Divisions and 161st Fortified Region (see Table 19.3).

Rokossovsky's revised offensive plan called for Romanenko's reinforced 48th Army, still supported on the left by 95th Rifle Corps of Batov's 65th Army, to smash the defenses of German Ninth Army's defenses in the Dubrova region and advance northwestward toward Parichi and Bobruisk (see Map 19.4 and Appendix O-2 for 65th Army's situation on 2 February 1944). The 96th Rifle Division's history revealed part of Rokossovsky's intent:

> But, on the other hand, as a whole, the [96th Rifle] division's and [53rd Rifle] corps' combat sector itself was critical. The enemy was paying special attention to its defensive line along the Parichi axis.
>
> The fact was that this axis lay at the intersection of two important main railroad lines: Zhlobin-Bobruisk and Bobruisk-Parichi. The enemy understood that if the Soviet force reached these railroad lines, further resistance in this region would be almost impossible and useless. In this regard he had his hopes. He dreamed of squeezing Soviet forces between the Dnepr and Berezina Rivers during the *rasputitsa* [period of flooded roads] and destroying them.
>
> At that time the winter offensive campaign had already been completed along most of the front. But the 48th Army, which our division had joined not long before, was still in the process of organizing a large-scale offensive along the Parichi axis with the mission of reaching the Parichi-Ozarichi railroad line. This resulted from the fact that we had to bring our forces out of the swampy forests before spring and occupy more favorable jumping-off positions for forthcoming combat operations. The corps [also] included 17th and 41st Rifle Divisions.
>
> We found ourselves in this army at the very moment when active preparations for the forthcoming operation were going on in all of its formations and units. As General Fedor Kondrat'evich Prudnikov, the chief of

Table 19.3. The Belorussian Front's Order of Battle on 1 February 1944

BELORUSSIAN FRONT:
Army General K. K. Rokossovsky

3rd Army: LTG A. V. Gorbatov
  41st Rifle Corps: MG V. K. Urbanovich
    120th Guards Rifle Division
    186th Rifle Division
  80th Rifle Corps: MG I. L. Ragulia
    5th Rifle Division
    283rd Rifle Division
    362nd Rifle Division
  269th Rifle Division
  36th Separate Tank Regiment
  49th Separate Aerosleigh Battalion

48th Army: LTG P. L. Romanenko
  25th Rifle Corps: MG A. B. Barinov
    102nd Rifle Division
    197th Rifle Division
    273rd Rifle Division
  29th Rifle Corps: MG A. M. Andreev
    73rd Rifle Division
    307th Rifle Division
  42nd Rifle Corps: LTG K. S. Kolganov
    137th Rifle Division
    399th Rifle Division
  53rd Rifle Corps: MG I. A. Gartsev
    17th Rifle Division
    41st Rifle Division
    96th Rifle Division
  4th Rifle Division
  170th Rifle Division
  194th Rifle Division
  217th Rifle Division
  161st Fortified Region
  42nd Separate Tank Regiment
  231st Separate Tank Regiment
  1444th Self-propelled Artillery Regiment
  1897th Self-propelled Artillery Regiment

50th Army: LTG I. V. Boldin
  46th Rifle Corps: MG K. M. Erastov
    238th Rifle Division
    369th Rifle Division
    380th Rifle Division
  121st Rifle Corps: MG D. I. Smirnov
    108th Rifle Division
    110th Rifle Division
    413th Rifle Division
  324th Rifle Division
  233rd Separate Tank Regiment
  21st Separate Armored Train Battalion
  43nd Separate Armored Train Battalion

63rd Army: LTG V. A. Kolpakchi
  35th Rifle Corps: MG V. G. Zholudev

61st Army: LTG P. A. Belov
  9th Guards Rifle Corps: MG A. A. Boreiko
    12th Guards Rifle Division
    76th Guards Rifle Division
    77th Guards Rifle Division
  89th Rifle Corps: MG G. A. Khaliuzin
    15th Rifle Division
    81st Rifle Division
    23rd Rifle Division
  55th Rifle Division
  356th Rifle Division
  415th Rifle Division
  2nd Guards Cavalry Corps: LTG V. V. Kriukov
    3rd Guards Cavalry Division
    4th Guards Cavalry Division
    17th Guards Cavalry Division
    1459th Self-propelled Artillery Regiment
    149th Guards Tank Destroyer Regiment
    2nd Guards Separate Tank Destroyer Artillery Battalion
    10th Guards-Mortar Regiment
    60th Guards-Mortar Battalion
    1730th Antiaircraft Artillery Regiment
  7th Guards Cavalry Corps: MG M. P. Konstantinov
    14th Guards Cavalry Division
    15th Guards Cavalry Division
    16th Guards Cavalry Division
    1816th Self-propelled Artillery Regiment
    145th Guards Tank Destroyer Regiment
    7th Guards Separate Tank Destroyer Artillery Battalion
    7th Guards-Mortar Regiment
    57th Guards-Mortar Battalion
    1733rd Antiaircraft Artillery Regiment
  68th Tank Brigade
  114th Separate Tank Regiment

65th Army: LTC P. I. Batov
  18th Rifle Corps: MG I. I. Ivanov
    37th Guards Rifle Division
    69th Rifle Division
    193rd Rifle Division
  19th Rifle Corps: MG D. I. Samarsky
    82nd Rifle Division
    162nd Rifle Division
    115th Rifle Brigade
  27th Rifle Corps: MG F. M. Cherokmanov
    60th Rifle Division
    106th Rifle Division
    218th Rifle Division
  95th Rifle Corps: MG I. A. Kuzovkov

Table 19.3. continued

250th Rifle Division
323rd Rifle Division
40th Rifle Corps: MG V. S. Kuznetsov
  129th Rifle Division
  169th Rifle Division
  348th Rifle Division
115th Fortified Region
1901st Self-propelled Artillery Regiment
31st Separate Armored Train Battalion
55th Separate Armored Train Battalion

44th Guards Rifle Division
172nd Rifle Division
354th Rifle Division
105th Rifle Corps: MG D. F. Alekseev
  75th Guards Rifle Division
  132nd Rifle Division
  253rd Rifle Division
193rd Separate Tank Regiment
251st Separate Tank Regiment
255th Separate Tank Regiment

Front Reserves:
119th Fortified Region
1st Guards Tank Corps: MGTF M. F. Panov
  15th Guards Tank Brigade
  16th Guards Tank Brigade
  17th Guards Tank Brigade
  1st Guards Motorized Rifle Brigade
  237th Self-propelled Artillery Regiment
  1001st Self-propelled Artillery Regiment
  1541st Self-propelled Artillery Regiment
  1888th Self-propelled Artillery Regiment
  1st Guards Motorcycle Battalion
  65th Motorcycle Battalion
  732nd Tank Destroyer Artillery Regiment
  455th Mortar Regiment
  43rd Guards-Mortar Battalion
  80th Guards Antiaircraft Artillery

Source: *Boevoi sostav Sovetskoi Armii, chast' IV (Ianvar'–dekabr' 1944)* [The combat composition of the Soviet Army, pt. 4 (January–December 1944)] (Moscow: Voenizdat, 1988), 41–42.

the army's military council, later recalled, at that moment the inclusion of the Gomel' division [the 96th] among the participants in the operation was very timely. And the division was deployed along the main axis of the attacking army. We, along with one tank regiment, had to penetrate the enemy's defense in the most crucial sector and, subsequently, with its main grouping on its left flank, make the main attack on Hill 142.7, with the mission of capturing the village of Tserebulino [Tserebulin on modern maps] and then Petrovichi.[6]

After Romanenko completed his latest regrouping, the three rifle divisions of Gartsev's 53rd Rifle Corps were deployed facing west along a front extending from north of Dubrova southward to Kobyl'shchina, flanked on the left by the three divisions of Kuzovkov's 95th Rifle Corps. The three rifle divisions of Barinov's 25th Rifle Corps deployed facing north in the sector from north of Dubrova eastward to Iazvin. Panov's 1st Guards Tank Corps, now about 100 tanks and self-propelled tanks strong, occupied assembly areas in the Mekhovshchina and Marmovichi regions southeast of Dubrova.

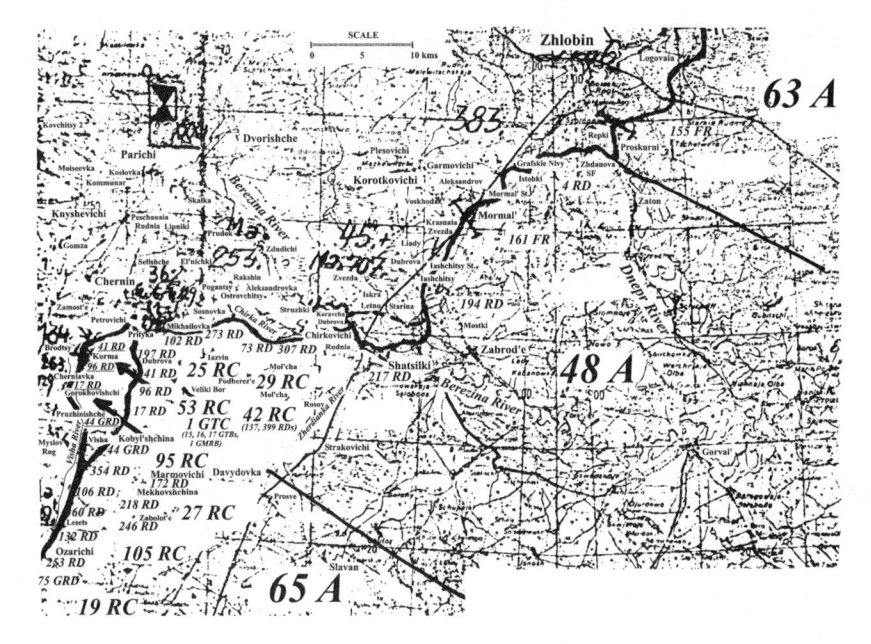

The Belorussian Front's Parichi-Bobruisk (Marmovichi-Dubrova) Offensive   497

Map 19.4. 48th Army's Situation along the Parichi Axis, 2–8 February 1944

The rest of Romanenko's army was dispersed across the broad front from Iazvin to the Berezina River and from the Berezina northeastward to the Dnepr River south of Zhlobin (see Table 19.4).

Romanenko designated Gartsev's 53rd and Barinov's 25th Rifle Corps as his army's new shock group and ordered the two rifle corps to assault the defenses of German XXXXI Panzer Corps' 36th and 134th Infantry Divisions northeast, west, and southwest of Dubrova, split the defending German divisions and begin an exploitation toward the Parichi-Oktiabr'skii road, 18 kilometers to the northwest. After the two rifle corps penetrated the Germans' forward defenses, Panov's 1st Guards Tank Corps was to lead the exploitation to envelop Parichi from the west and, in conjunction with Barinov's 25th Rifle Corps and Andreev's 29th Rifle Corps, assault and liquidate 253rd Infantry Division's strongpoints south of the Berezina River from Mol'cha to Chirkovichi. After capturing Parichi, the army's immediate objective, Romanenko's army was to continue its exploitation toward Bobruisk. If necessary, Romanenko planned to commit Kolganov's 42nd Rifle Corps, which he retained in second echelon, as well as 170th Rifle Division from his army's reserve, to reinforce 1st Guards Tank Corps' advance on Parichi.

After Romanenko's shock group deployed in attack formation, 197th, 102nd, and 273rd Rifle Divisions of 25th Rifle Corps were arrayed from left to right northeast of Dubrova, and 17th, 96th, and 41st Rifle Divisions of

Table 19.4. The Probable Combat Formations of 48th Army and 65th Army's Right Wing and Opposing German Forces Late on 1 February 1944 (deployed from north to south)

FORCE (Sector)	OPPOSING GERMAN FORCES
1st/2nd/3rd Echelons (Mobile group)	
BELORUSSIAN FRONT	**NINTH ARMY**
48th Army (Dnepr River, Kobyl'shchina)	XXXV Army Corps
4th RD (south of Zhlobin)	383rd ID
161st FR (Mormal')	45th ID/707th ID
194th RD (Iashchitsy)	
217th RD (Berezina River, Mol'cha)	XXXXI Panzer Corps
29th RC (Mol'cha, Podberez'e)	253rd ID
307th RD (Mol'cha, Sosnovka)	36th ID, part, 6th ID
73rd RD (Sosnovka, Podberez'e)	185th Assault Gun
231st TR	*Abteilung*
42nd RC (137th, 399th RD)	
25th RC (Podberez'e, north of Dubrova)	134th ID
273rd RD (Podberez'e, east of Iazvin)	Part, 110th ID
102nd RD (east and west of Iazvin)	244th Assault Gun
197th RD (west of Iazvin, north of Dubrova	*Abteilung*
42nd TR	Kgr., 4th PzD
170th RD (army reserve)	(by 4.2)
53rd RC (north of Dubrova, Kobyl'shchina)	
41st RD (north of Dubrova)	
96th RD (south of Dubrova)	
17th RD (south to Kobyl'shchina)	
1st Guards Tank Corps (Mobile group (Mekhovshchina, Marmovichi)	
65th Army	
95th RC (Kobyl'shchina, Ozarichi)	110th ID
44th GRD (Kobyl'shchina)	
172nd RD (withdrawn on 3 February)	
354th RD (south of Kobyl'shchina)	

Sources: Boevoi sostav Sovetskoi Armii, chast' IV (Ianvar'–dekabr' 1944) [The combat composition of the Soviet Army, pt. 4 (January–December 1944)] (Moscow: Voenizdat, 1988), 41–42; "H Gr Mitte/Ia, KTB: Lagenkarten, 1–31 January 1944," *H Gr Mitte, 65002/60 file*, in NAM series T-311, roll 224; and "Anlage 3 zun Tätigkeitsbericht der Abt. Ic/A.O. Feindnachrichtenblätter, 1 Jan–10 Jul 1944," *AOK 9, 62717/4 file*, in NAM series T-312, roll 342.

53rd Rifle Corps were deployed from left to right south and north of Dubrova. These six rifle divisions and Panov's tank corps faced one German division (half of 134th and half of 36th Infantry), reinforced by battalion-size *kampfgruppen* from 110th and 6th Infantry Divisions and roughly twenty assault guns from 244th and 185th Assault Gun *Abteilung*, respectively. Because their shock group possessed better than threefold superiority in infantry and fielded more than sixfold superiority in armor, Rokossovsky and Romanenko realistically hoped to achieve some degree of offensive success.

After conducting a reconnaissance-in-force across the entire front on 1 February, Romanenko's shock group began its assault early on 2 February, preceded by an artillery preparation (see Map 19.3). The 96th Rifle Division, whose official history provides the only existing account of this offensive, captured Hill 142.7 after several hours of fighting, cleared German forces from the village strongpoint of Dubrova, and reached and cut the Dubrova and Gorokhovishchi road several kilometers west of the town by the evening of 4 February. In heavy fighting, during which the division lost contact with 41st and 17th Rifle Divisions on its flanks, the 96th pushed on toward Tserebulino, 4 kilometers west of Dubrova, and captured the strongpoint late on 5 February. However, as recorded in the division's history:

> After the loss of Tserebulino, the Hitlerites repeatedly launched counterattacks accompanied by tanks. Our attempts to continue the offensive had no success.
>
> The only correct decision in order to continue the offensive toward the village of Korma [1.5 kilometers to the northwest] was to conduct a partial regrouping. To that end, we moved the division's right wing forward into a forest grove. It was difficult to do so, and we managed such a maneuver only thanks to the offensive spirit of the troops. Kostinitsin's regiment reached the new positions under the cover of darkness.
>
> I reported to the corps commander about the division's readiness to attack at midday on 6 February.
>
> In response, I received an order to go over to the defense. After two days spent on preparing a defensive belt, we were relieved by 41st Division on the basis of an order from the corps headquarters, and our units concentrated in the Dubrova region of Gomel' oblast'.[7]

Romanenko's new offensive aborted early on 6 February after only four days of intense fighting. During this period, XXXXI Panzer Corps' 36th Infantry Division halted 25th Rifle Corps' assault in its tracks. On the shock group's left, however, 53rd Rifle Corps' three rifle divisions advanced roughly 5 kilometers to the west along a front of about 9 kilometers, capturing the German strongpoints at Tserebulino as well as the eastern portion of Gorokhovishchi, 8 kilometers west of Dubrova. Romanenko ordered Panov's tank corps into action late on 4 February, but the Germans countered by committing a *kampfgruppe* from 4th Panzer Division into combat, which halted Panov's advance in the forests northwest of Dubrova.[8] To the south, 95th Rifle Corps' 44th Guards Rifle Division exploited Romanenko's limited success by capturing the town of Visha and reaching the eastern bank of the Visha River.

Despite these limited gains, it was clear to Rokossovsky that heavy German resistance and the harsh weather and terrain conditions precluded any further major offensive operations in this sector. Consequently, on 6 February he once again ordered his forces to go over to the defense. By this time, Rokossovsky's attention was already focused on the eastern bank of the Dnepr River, where he was planning yet another offensive, this time by 3rd and 50th Armies to liquidate bridgeheads held by German forces east of Rogachev and Zhlobin region.

500   The Struggle for Belorussia, December 1943-April 1944

THE FORMATION OF THE 1ST BELORUSSIAN FRONT

Before Rokossovsky's forces conducted their offensive operations against German defenses east of Rogachev, the sharply changing situation at the front prompted the *Stavka* to reorganize and rename its operating *fronts*. On 11 February, 13th Army, operating on 1st Ukrainian Front's extreme right wing, concluded its Rovno-Lutsk offensive operation. During this offensive, 13th Army's forces, spearheaded by 1st and 6th Guards Cavalry Corps, advanced westward south of the Pripiat' River, captured the towns of Olevsk, Sarny, Rovno, Klevan', and Lutsk and threatened the city of Kovel' in the rear of German Army Group South's left wing.

Coupled with the advance by the Belorussian Front's 2nd and 7th Guards Cavalry Corps south of the Pripiat' River, 13th Army's dramatic westward advance threatened to separate Army Group Center from Army Group South. To ensure that separation occurred, on 17 February the *Stavka* formed 2nd Belorussian Front from forces operating on the Belorussian Front's left wing, the 1st Ukrainian Front's right wing, and its own *Stavka* Reserves and ordered the new *front* to capture the Kovel' region (see Appendix O-3).

The *Stavka* directive mandated the formation of a new 2nd Belorussian Front at the junction of the existing Belorussian and 1st Ukrainian Fronts and renamed Rokossovsky's *front* the 1st Belorussian Front. The 2nd Belorussian Front, whose headquarters was from the recently disbanded Northwestern Front, was to include:

- **From the 1st Belorussian Front**—61st Army, including 9th Guards Rifle Corps (three divisions), 89th Rifle Corps (three divisions), 55th and 356th Rifle Divisions, 2nd and 7th Guards Cavalry Corps (six divisions), 68th Tank Brigade, and all reinforcing army units and rear service units and facilities;
- **From the 1st Ukrainian Front**—77th Rifle Corps (three rifle divisions) from 13th Army and the headquarters of 47th Army, with all reinforcing army units and rear service units and facilities;
- **From the *Stavka*'s Reserve**—125th Rifle Corps (four rifle divisions), 70th Army (seven rifle divisions), 6th Air Army (3rd Guards Assault Aviation Division, 366th Fighter Aviation Division, 242nd Night Bomber Aviation Division, 72nd Reconnaissance Aviation Regiment, and 3rd Aviation Regiment, Civil Air Fleet), the Dnepr Flotilla [military] (with its remaining minesweepers), 65th Antiaircraft Artillery Division, 32nd Mortar Brigade, 3rd Tank Destroyer Brigade, and 48th Engineer-Sapper Brigade.[9]

The directive appointed Colonel General P. A. Kurochkin, the former deputy commander of the 1st Ukrainian Front, to command the 2nd Belorussian Front, with Lieutenant General F. E. Bokov as his commissar (member of the *front*'s Military Council) and Lieutenant General V. Ia. Kolpakchi, the former commander of 63rd Army, as his chief of staff. Tacitly acknowledging the future objective of the new *front*, the *Stavka* directed Kurochkin to deploy 47th Army, now consisting up of 77th Rifle Corps from 13th Army and 125th Rifle Corps from the *Stavka* Reserve, to the Kovel' axis by 25 February. At the same time, it ordered Rokossovsky to dispatch 61st Army and 2nd and 7th Guards Cavalry Corps to the same region by the same date.[10]

By virtue of the boundaries assigned to it with neighboring *fronts* to the north and south, this order assigned 2nd Belorussian Front responsibility for conducting operations westward along both banks of the Pripiat' River. Therefore, although the new *front*'s principal target was Kovel', 61st and 70th Armies on the *front*'s right wing could coordinate their actions to liquidate Army Group Center's many bridgeheads on the southern bank of the Pripiat' and perhaps capture bridgeheads of their own on the river's northern bank.

The main impact of this order on Rokossovsky's new 1st Belorussian Front was that, while weakening his *front* somewhat, it focused its future operations along the Bobruisk-Minsk axis. To compensate for this slight weakening, the day after it formed the 2nd Belorussian Front, the *Stavka* reinforced Rokossovsky's *front* by transferring to it 10th Army, together with its offensive sector, from Sokolovsky's Western Front (see Appendix O-4). Effective 21 February, this directive reinforced Rokossovsky's *front* with 10th Army's 70th and 38th Rifle Corps, for a total of six rifle divisions, along with all of 10th Army's reinforcing units, army rear service units and facilities, and reserve stocks. It also adjusted the 1st Belorussian Fronts' right boundary to the north.[11]

In effect, excepting the Pripiat' River region, this transfer accorded Rokossovsky direct responsibility for controlling all Red Army operations in the southern half of eastern Belorussia. Within a matter of weeks, Rokossovsky would require 10th Army to conduct its first offensive operations under his overall supervision. For the time being, however, Rokossovsky had business to complete along the Berezina River east of Parichi and along the Dnepr River east of Rogachev.

POSTSCRIPT: THE THIRD PHASE (14–24 FEBRUARY 1944)

In conjunction with the impending Rogachev-Zhlobin offensive, which Rokossovsky ordered 3rd and 50th Armies to conduct east of the Dnepr beginning on 21 February, Rokossovsky ordered Romanenko's 48th Army to conduct additional local offensive operations both to improve his army's jumping-off positions for any future offensive toward Bobruisk and to mask and support Rokossovsky's new venture along the Dnepr River. The Belorussian Front's War Experience Section briefly summarized the results of these local operations in February 1944:

> In February 1944, 48th Army was defending in positions from Zaton, through Zhdanov Collective Farm and Savin to the southern part of Mormal'. It conducted stubborn offensive combat along the line from 1.5 kilometers east of Iashchitsy Station through Marker 142.4, the southern outskirts of Chirkovichi, Zarud'e, Ostrovchitsy, Sosnovka, and Dubrova to Kobyl'shchina [Selishche]. As a result of combat in the difficult conditions of the forested and swampy terrain, the army did not fulfill its overall combat mission but did achieve some tactical successes by the end of February and, on its left wing, reached positions extending from Velikii Les though Brodki, Nigilev, 1 kilometer north of Aleksandrovka, Rakshin, Veshka, Mikhailovka, Prityka, Korma (incl.), and Gorokhovishchi, where it is continuing to fight to improve its positions. The enemy is defending with forces from [Ninth Army's] 35th Army Corps (383rd and 45th Infantry Divisions) and 41st Panzer Corps (253rd and 134th Infantry Divisions).[12]

In brief, 48th Army conducted two local offensives to improve its positions during this period. The first of these operations, which began on 14 February, was designed to tie down German forces in the region west of Dubrova and improve the army's tactical dispositions (see Map 19.5). This time 48th Army spearheaded its attack with Gartsev's 53rd Rifle Corps (17th, 41st, and 96th Rifle Divisions), supported on the right by Kolganov's reorganized 42nd Rifle Corps (137th, 170th, and 399th Rifle Divisions) and on the left by Kuzovkov's 95th Rifle Corps (44th and 75th Guards Rifle and 354th Rifle Divisions). Once again, 96th Rifle Division's history describes the operation's objectives:

> We once again accepted a combat sector from 41st Division on the night of 13–14 February. Now the mission was to widen and improve the corps' and army's positions overall in conjunction with other divisions.
> The mission of the following day was to destroy the enemy in the Korma and Cherniavka strongpoints [5–8 kilometers west of Dubrova]. Apparently, observing our preparation, the next morning the enemy fired on us continually with guns and mortars. We were situated at an observation post about a kilometer from the enemy's forward lines. The enemy's position was well camouflaged. If he was not firing, it was difficult to know where his firing points were located.
> Thirty minutes remained until the attack was to begin. Amosov [Colonel M. P. Amosov, the division's chief of staff] was once again in communications with 41st Division [on our right]. One of the divisions of 65th

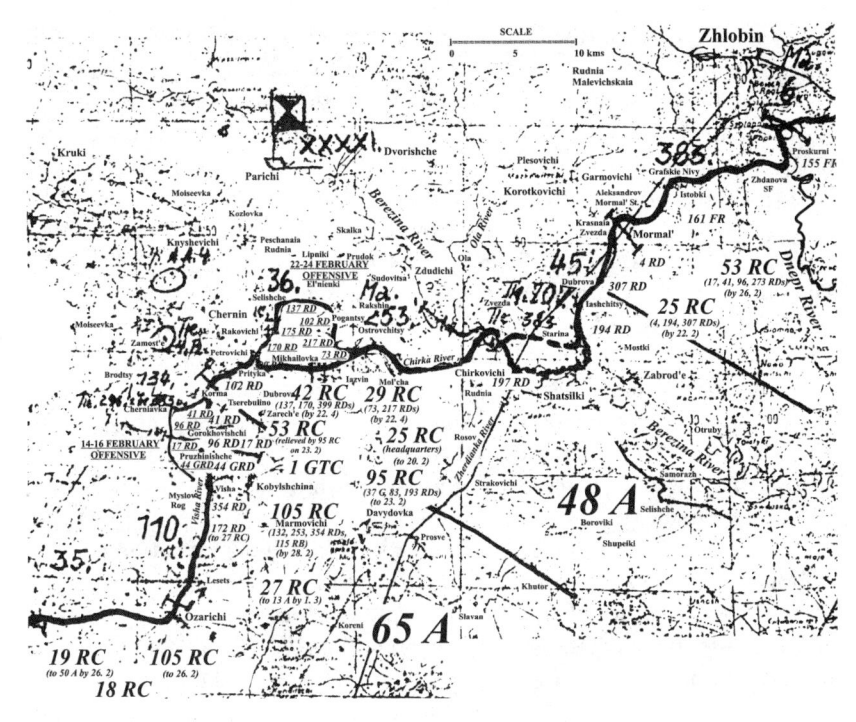

The Belorussian Front's Parichi-Bobruisk (Marmovichi-Dubrova) Offensive   503

Map 19.5. 48th Army's Situation along the Parichi Axis, 14–23 February 1944

Army was to attack to our left. We had communications with it through the corps staff. . . .

When all of the preparations were complete, the corps artillery opened fire across the entire front. Then the *"Katiushas"* roared, and afterward the infantry sprang into the attack with a resounding "Urra." The infantry advanced immediately behind the barrage fire. . . .

Battle was already raging for the village of Korma, but we could see nothing. . . . Soon after losing Korma, the Hitlerites began counterattacks supported by "Tiger" tanks, but withdrew, leaving several tanks on the battlefield. Abramov's [Lieutenant Colonel M. M. Abramov] regiment was also fulfilling its mission. It was already fighting for the village of Cherniavka.[13]

The 96th Rifle Division succeeded in capturing Korma and Cherniavka, but thereafter the offensive once again stalled in the face of German reinforcements. The overall advance propelled 48th Army's forces forward only about 2 kilometers before Rokossovsky authorized Romanenko to halt his attacks. On the night of 22–23 February, 53rd Rifle Corps turned its sector over to 65th Army's 19th Rifle Corps and regrouped eastward back across the Berezina and Ola Rivers to support yet another assault planned by Rokossovsky.

The 48th Army conducted its second local offensive operation in the sector east and west of Iazvin on 22 February, only days before conducting a major assault against German defenses in the Mormal' region east of the Berezina River. Prior to conducting the 22 February assault, Romanenko transferred the headquarters of Barinov's 25th Rifle Corps back to its former sector east of the Berezina River and assigned 4th, 194th, and 307th Rifle Divisions to Barinov's corps. Romanenko then concentrated Kolganov's 42nd Rifle Corps (137th, 170th, 273rd, and 399th Rifle Divisions) and Andreev's 29th Rifle Corps (73rd, 102nd, and 217th Rifle Divisions) in attack positions from west to east in the Iazvin sector, backed up by elements of Panov's 1st Guards Tank Corps. He ordered this combined force to assault Germans' XXXXI Panzer Corps' defenses at the boundary between 36th and 253rd Infantry Divisions and drive the defending Germans back toward the Berezina River and Parichi.

Romanenko's new shock group attacked early in the morning on 22 February, when a total of eight understrength rifle divisions supported by about seventy tanks of Panov's tank corps struck at the boundary of 36th and 253rd Infantry Divisions' defenses (see Map 19.5). Employing their remaining dwindling combat power like a sledgehammer, the attacking force penetrated the Germans' defenses, captured German strongpoints north of Iazvin and the village of Mikhailovka, 4 kilometers to the northwest, and, in three more days of heavy fighting, drove northward 5 kilometers before German forces halted the advance at their strongpoints at Pogantsy and Hill 143, and the nearly impenetrable swamps to the west. During this fight, the Germans reinforced this sector with *kampfgruppen* from 296th Infantry and 4th Panzer Divisions. With both sides worn to a frazzle, the fighting ebbed and died out on 24 February.

However, Rokossovsky's gambit paid off. By shifting their tactical reserves west of the Berezina River, the German forces on the river's eastern bank were severely weakened. The moment the sounds of the guns died out west of the river, early on 24 February, heavy artillery fire announced Rokossovsky's fresh assault east of the river. Worse still for the Germans, by this time heavy fighting east of Rogachev ended any German hopes of retaining their forward defenses east of the Berezina River.

One major result of these operations was a decision by Army Group Center, approved by OKH, to alter its defensive configuration once again to better protect the Bobruisk-Minsk axis. Earlier, on 18 January the army group had given Ninth Army control of LVI Panzer Corps when it became apparent that the Belorussian Front's 65th Army was focusing its efforts on advancing northwestward toward Bobruisk. However, when 48th Army activated operations south of the Berezina River in early February, LVI Panzer Corps seems to have reverted to Second Army's control. Thereafter, when it became clear that 65th Army was indeed heading for Bobruisk in conjunction with 48th Army, on 22 February the army group shifted the boundaries of Ninth Army southward to accord it responsibility for defending the approaches to Bobruisk westward across the Dnepr and northwestward along the Berezina and Ptich' Rivers. Thus, on 22 February Ninth Army transferred the forces and sectors of XXXIX Panzer and XII Army Corps, whose front extended from the Chausy region southwestward across the Dnepr River to the Drut' River southwest of Bykhov, to Fourth Army, and Second Army once again transferred its LVI Panzer Corps' sector from east of the Ptich' River east of Koptsevichi to Ninth Army.[14]

CHAPTER 20

The Belorussian Front's Rogachev-Zhlobin and Mormal'-Parichi Offensives (21–29 February)

THE ROGACHEV-ZHLOBIN OFFENSIVE (21–26 FEBRUARY 1944)

Planning

Although the 1st Belorussian Front's Rogachev-Zhlobin offensive is not a "forgotten battle," probably because it was a dramatic success, and has been covered in considerable detail in German operational histories, it does warrant brief mention because the offensive occupies a key place in Rokossovsky's strategy for reducing German defenses in eastern Belorussia.

The Belorussian Front's formerly classified operational summary for February 1944 summarizes the course and outcome of the offensive from the perspectives of the *front's* 50th and 3rd Armies:

> During February 1944, 50th Army was defending positions from Petukhovka to Luzhki on its right wing, and, on the morning of 22 February, its left wing went over to an offensive along the Mshatoe Swamp and Adamenka line with units of 110th, 108th, 324th, and 413th Rifle Divisions, forced the Dnepr River, penetrated the enemy's prepared defensive belt on the right [western] bank of the river, and by 29 February reached a front extending from Hill Marker 144.9 to south of Zaiachenie, and through Starosel'e, Station No. 15, and the southern bank of the Ezva River to Khomichi, while threatening the flank and rear of the enemy's entire Mogilev-Bykhov grouping.
> The offensive by the army's left wing was conducted in harsh conditions of the beginning thaw [*rasputitsa,* or period of flooded roads], along with the forcing of large river obstacles with 4 kilometers of swampy and porous soil, and places with ice broken away from the banks and frozen patches of water (and thawed patches) in the middle of the river. Combat operations on the right bank continued in a densely forested and swampy region, which hindered the employment of tanks and maneuvering on the field of battle. The army had no further offensive success, dug in along its occupied positions, and went over to a temporary defense.[1]
> *The situation:* Up to 21 February, 3rd Army was defending and preparing for an offensive with the aim of forcing the Dnepr River. On 13 Feb-

ruary 40th and 35th Rifle Corps were transferred to the army from 63rd Army, and by 21 February, the army's defensive front amounted to 88 kilometers (from Rudnia [incl.] along the Dnepr River to Zhlobin). The offensive, which began on 21 February, was preceded by an aviation preparation of the enemy's combat formations on the army's left wing by 35–40 U-2 aircraft on the night of 20–21 February, which bombed the enemy in the Krasnaia Gorka, Gorelyi Mokh, Pochep, Vetka, and Volochii region. The army's mission in the offensive operation was: while defending on the left and right wings, the main forces of seven rifle divisions from 80th and 41st Rifle Corps were to attack on the morning of 21 February, cross the Dnepr River on the ice in the Viliakhovka, Koromka, Kisteni, Elenovo, Bliznetsy, Zapol'e, and Pobolovo sector, capture the Komarichi, Zolotoe Dno, Khomichi, Retka, Osovnik, Dobritsa, Parenevskii, Barki, Nadeikovichi, Pobolovo, Tertezh, and Zhlobin city line by 23 February, and subsequently develop the offensive toward Bobruisk. Thus, the intended depth of the operation amounted to 55 kilometers, and the average tempo of advance was 15–18 kilometers per day.

The course of the operation: After the initial firing of a 10-minute fire raid, the army went over to the attack at 0720 hours on 21 February along a 12-kilometer front extending from Nadezhda through Liubov' to Pokrovskoe, forced the Dnepr River, reached the eastern bank of the Drut' River on 23 February, and captured Rogachev at 0300 hours [on 24 February]. During the course of 24 February, the army partially succeeded in crossing the Drut' River and seized a small bridgehead on its western bank, while repelling fierce counterattacks by enemy infantry, tanks, self-propelled guns, and aircraft. The army went over to the attack once again on 25 February and, after encountering resistance from persistent enemy fire and counterattacks, penetrated to a depth of 1–2 kilometers during the day. The army once again resumed its offensive at 0645 hours on 1 March and, after a day of combat, widened the bridgehead on the western bank of the Drut' River to a front of 8 kilometers and a depth of 1.5 kilometers.

The results of the operation: The enemy lost 119 guns, 34 tanks, 71 mortars, 320 machine guns, 3,500 rifles, and other equipment. The army captured 247 prisoners, 94 guns, 5 tanks, 98 mortars, 198 machine guns, 102 vehicles, and other equipment. The army's losses were 1,611 killed, 4,890 wounded, and 12 missing in action. Nine tanks, 17 guns, 68 machine guns, and 194 horses were lost. It is necessary to mention the exceptionally successful raid into the enemy rear area to capture Toshchitsa Station, which was conducted by a ski battalion of 5th Rifle Division on the night of 23 February and which supported the army's mission of seizing the city of Rogachev. On the night of 2–3 March, the army's units repelled up to 10 fierce enemy counterattacks with tanks and self-propelled artillery.[2]

Lieutenant General A. V. Gorbatov, the commander of 3rd Army, had requested Rokossovsky permit his army to conduct an offensive against German forces east of Rogachev as early as 13 January 1944, on the eve of Rokossovsky's Kalinkovichi offensive. Gorbatov recalled his request and the answer he received: "On 13 January we presented the *front* commander, Army General K. K. Rokossovsky, a report that stated that the enemy across the Dnepr had a thin combat formation, and there was every opportunity to seize a bridgehead if the divisions previously taken from the army were returned to the army. Soon we received an answer, 'I cannot reinforce you. Continue your defense. You have sufficient forces to do so.'"[3] However, Gorbatov persisted in his requests:

> On 7 February we once again sent the *front* commander a report about the situation and the conclusion that the enemy in front of the army was not strong and that we could seize a bridgehead if the army was reinforced. However, the answer was again negative. He said, "I cannot strengthen the army. Conduct two local operations with limited aims, each with one division; the first at Shapchitsy and the other at Kisteni."
>
> We believed that the conduct of two operations across a river as wide as the Dnepr with such weak divisions (4,500 men each) was not expedient. I requested permission from the *front* commander to come to the *front* headquarters to give him a personal report. He agreed, but with the reservation, "In any case, I cannot reinforce your army."
>
> After arriving at the *front* headquarters on 8 February, I reported on my conclusions regarding the inexpediency of conducting local operations with two divisions, since, even in the event of success, they could seize small bridgeheads that it would be difficult to hold, especially during the spring floods, and from which it would be difficult to organize a subsequent offensive with larger forces. I called General Rokossovsky's attention to a number of circumstances, namely, the small size of 3rd and 63rd Armies such that, after losing much of its force, 63rd Army was not able to drive the enemy from the bridgehead, and that, with an enemy on the eastern bank both on its right and its left flanks, 3rd Army was not capable of conducting an operation to force the Dnepr River with six weak divisions. I suggested combining the forces in 3rd and 63rd Armies' sectors under my command, and then we could not only drive the enemy from his bridgehead but also seize a large bridgehead over the Dnepr.
>
> After conferring with his chief of staff, General Malinin, the *front* commander, requested that I prepare my proposal in greater detail so that he could consider it.
>
> I noted in my report, "When there are seven divisions in the army, we will assemble five divisions to force the Dnepr and capture and hold a bridgehead at Shapchitsy. If you combine 3rd and 63rd Armies, you can

assign the forces two missions—to liquidate the enemy bridgehead on the eastern bank of the Dnepr River and, in turn, seize a large bridgehead across the river. However, you should not force the river at Shapchitsy, since that sector is too distant from the most vulnerable point in the enemy's defense, the city of Rogachev. It would be better if we forced the Dnepr in the Kisteni region. In that case, the army could seize a bridgehead from the city of Rogachev in the course of 2–3 days. At the same time, it would create a real threat to the enemy, which is situated in the Rogachev bridgehead, and it would force them to withdraw. Thereafter, the army could continue the offensive to the north up to Novyi Bykhov and to the west to capture a bridgehead on the Drut' River. I suggest we deliver a supporting attack in the Shapchitsy region. Employ 10 divisions to conduct the operation. The 3rd Army's divisions will be in first echelon and 63rd Army's in second echelon. In our proposal, the depth of the operation will amount to 20–25 kilometers."

After listening to me attentively, the *front* commander said, "And who will be defending along the 75-kilometer front against the enemy's bridgehead and also to the north along the Dnepr?" I answered that we would leave 115th Fortified Region and two armored trains there. Part of the army's second echelon would be situated behind the fortified region before the crossing over the Dnepr. We planned to leave such an insignificant force against the enemy's bridgehead because we presumed that, during the forcing of the Dnepr, the enemy would not risk undertaking active operations in that sector. An army reserve regiment, a blocking detachment, and other subunits would be deployed on the defense to the north along the Dnepr in the Selets-Kholopeev and Shapchitsy sector.

After expressing these views, I requested General Rokossovsky move our right flank boundary line southward to Selets-Kholopeev so that 50th Army could also try to force the Dnepr and, at the same time, protect our right flank. It would be very good, I added, if our neighbor on the left also pinned down the enemy with active operations and denied him the opportunity to reinforce his forces opposite 3rd Army's front. In conclusion, I said that it would require 10 days to prepare the operation, chiefly to withdraw secretly the four divisions of 63rd Army from their defenses.

General Rokossovsky answered, "Your request is acceptable. Prepare for the operation, and I will communicate with Moscow."

On 13 February we received orders from the *front*, which transferred 63rd Army's forces and sector to 3rd Army, and after three days—16 February—we received a *front* directive on the conduct of the operation. It said that, while defending with part of its forces on its right and left wings and by delivering its main attack toward Kisteni, Zapol'e, and Pobolovo, the army would begin its attack on the morning of 21 February with a force of no fewer than seven rifle divisions, force the Dnepr, and capture the Komarichi, Khomichi, Dobritsa, Pobolovo, and Tertezh line and the city and railroad station at Zhlobin on the third day of the operation. Subsequently, it was ordered to exploit success along the Bobruisk axis. The directive indicated that 1st [Guards] Tank Corps would be transferred to the Dovsk region by 22 February.[4]

Thus, by approving and indeed expanding the scope of Gorbatov's plan, Rokossovsky underscored his intent to continue operations toward Bobruisk, approved the conduct of an accompanying offensive by 48th Army between the Dnepr and Berezina Rivers, and once again ordered Panov's 1st Guards Tank Corps to march to the sound of the guns (see Appendix P-1 for 3rd Army's situation and plans on 1 February 1944). Thus, 3rd Army was to advance westward 40 kilometers in three days, force both the Dnepr and the Drut' Rivers, and, if possible thereafter, push on westward another 75 kilometers to capture Bobruisk. It was a tall order indeed because the Dnepr was 100–150 meters wide and the Drut' was 25–60 meters wide, with depths of 3–8 meters and 2–3 meters, respectively, and with the thickness of the ice cover being 8–12 centimeters and 10–12 centimeters, respectively. Furthermore, the *rasputitsa* left gaps of 2–6 meters between the ice on the rivers and the rivers' nearby banks.[5]

After it was approved, Gorbatov's offensive plan required 3rd Army's 80th and 41st Rifle Corps to penetrate the defenses of German LV Army Corps' 31st Infantry Division along the Dnepr River in the 10-kilometer-wide sector between Vishin and Shapchitsy, and 40th and 35th Rifle Corps to assault the bridgehead defended by XXXV Army Corps' 707th Security and 296th Infantry Divisions in the 5-kilometer-wide sector between Tursk and Dubrava south of the Dnepr River (see Map 20.1). Exploiting his previous experiences, Gorbatov employed a ski detachment from 5th Rifle Division, reinforced by 8th Separate Penal Battalion, to serve as a forward detachment.[6] After infiltrating through the Germans' defenses overnight before the army's main attack, the detachment was to seize a vital road junction northeast of Rogachev, disrupt German command and control, and hold on to the road junction until relieved by the army's main forces. Panov's tank corps was to reinforce Gorbatov's forces after they reached the Dnepr River's western bank and support his army's subsequent assault across the Drut' River (see Table 20.1).

The Battle

Attacking as planned on the night of 21–22 February, the ski detachment and 8th Separate Penal Battalion secured their objective by the following morning (see Map 20.2). Exploiting the ensuing confusion in German ranks, Gorbatov's main forces, supported by fire from about 800 guns and mortars,

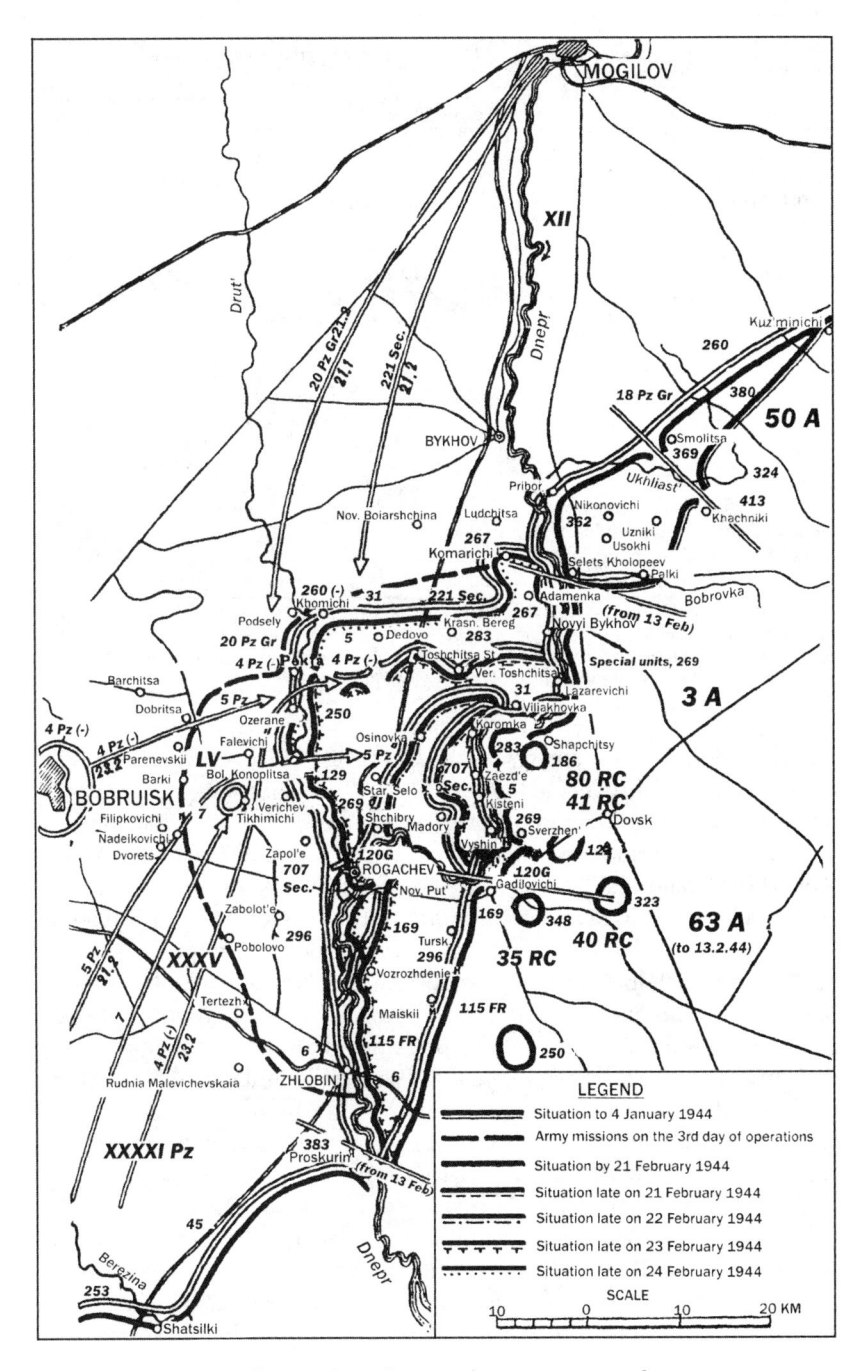

Map 20.1. 3rd Army's Offensive along the Rogachev Axis, 21–26 February 1944

Table 20.1. The Estimated Correlation of Opposing Forces in the Rogachev-Zhlobin Offensive, 21–26 February 1944

OPPOSING FORCES	
Soviet	*German*
Belorussian Front	
50th Army	18th Panzer Grenadier
3rd Army	Division
15 rifle divisions	267th Infantry Division
1 fortified region	31st Infantry Division
3 tank regiments	707th Security Division
	296th Infantry Division
	6th Infantry Division (part)
	221st Security Division (21.2)
	20th Panzer Division (KGr.) (23.2)
	5th Panzer Division (KGr.) (22.2)
	4th Panzer Division (KGr.) (23.2)
Strength: 232,000 men	110,000 men
90 tanks and SP guns	60 tanks and assault guns
Depth of Soviet advance: 5–20 kilometers	
Casualties: 31,277 men, including	10,000 men
7,164 killed and 24,113 wounded	

Sources: Boevoi sostav Sovetskoi Armii, chast' IV (Ianvar'–dekabr' 1944) [The combat composition of the Soviet Army, pt. 4 (January–December 1944)] (Moscow: Voenizdat, 1988), 41–42; A. Gorbatov, "Nastuplenie voisk 3-i armii na rogachevskom napravlenii" [The 3rd Army's offensive along the Rogachev axis], *VIZh* 1 (January 1961); and A. V. Gorbatov, *Gody i voiny* [Years and wars] (Moscow: Voenizdat, 1980).

forced the Dnepr River and established a sizable bridgehead west of Kisteni by early on 22 February (see Map 20.3).[7] After employing yet another ski detachment in a daring raid to seize Toshchitsy Station, near the village of Dedova in the German rear area, by day's end on 22 February, the lead elements of 80th and 41st Rifle Corps reached and crossed the Drut' River near Bol'shaia Konoplitsa, 13 kilometers north of Rogachev, tearing an 18-kilometer-wide and a 20-kilometer-deep hole in the Germans' defenses (see Map 20.4).[8] After withdrawing their forces from the eastern bank of the Dnepr between Zhlobin and Rogachev, the Germans frantically tried to plug the gap by committing *kampfgruppen* from 4th and 5th Panzer Divisions along the Drut' River and by reinforcing 31st and 267th Infantry Divisions' defenses north of the gap.

As German panzers struggled along the Drut' River all day on 24 February, 3rd Army's 80th Rifle Corps widened the penetration to the north, while 50th Army's 121st Rifle Corps assaulted across the Dnepr River west of Selets-Kholopeev. After arriving in the region late on 24 February, a *kampfgruppe* from 20th Panzer Division finally stabilized the situation of the northern flank of the penetration. When the battle died out on 26 February, Gorbatov's 3rd and Boldin's 50th Armies had captured Rogachev and established a sizable bridgehead on the western bank of the Dnepr River (see Map 20.5). Worse still for the Germans, Gorbatov's spearheads carved a small bridge-

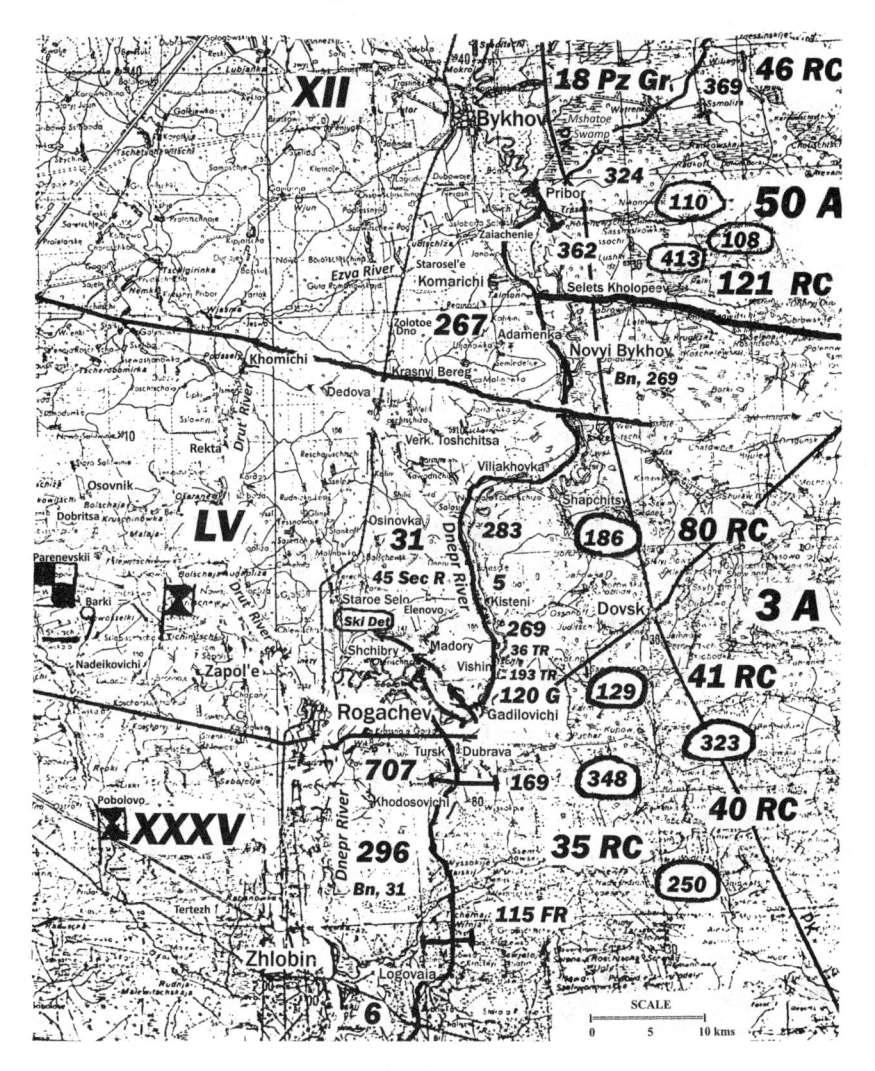

The Belorussian Front's Rogachev-Zhlobin and Mormal'-Parichi Offensives 513

Map 20.2. The Situation at Rogachev, 0600 hours, 21 February 1944

head in the Germans' defenses along the Drut' River, and, despite strenuous efforts, the Germans were not able to liquidate the bridgehead.

Thus, in six days of fighting, Gorbatov's forces advanced almost 30 kilometers and crossed the Dnepr and Drut' Rivers. Although they failed to accomplish everything envisioned by Rokossovsky's directive, they did satisfy Gorbatov's original promise by securing an operational scale bridgehead 62 kilometers wide and 22–30 kilometers deep on the western banks of the Dnepr and Drut' Rivers.[9] This placed 1st Belorussian Front's forces in ideal

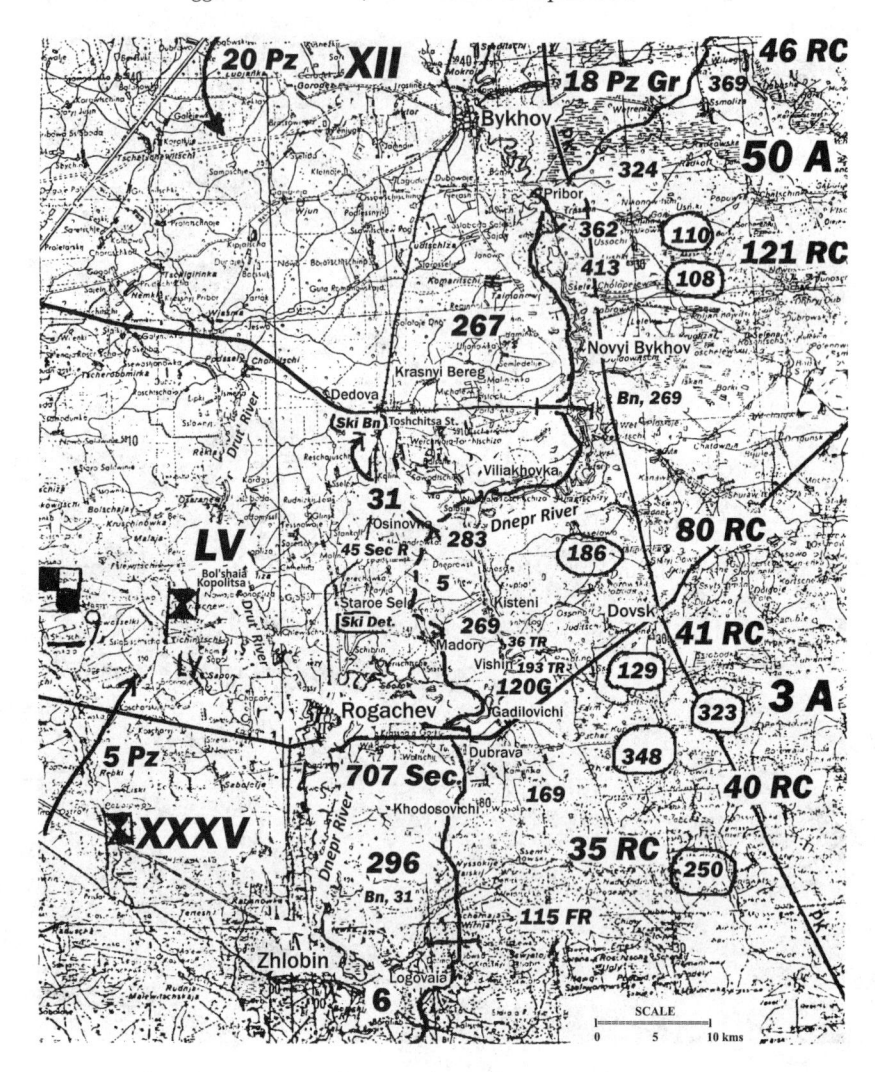

514   The Struggle for Belorussia, December 1943–April 1944

Map 20.3. The Situation at Rogachev, 0600 hours, 22 February 1944

positions from which they could mount an offensive toward Bobruisk during the ensuing summer offensive. The cost of this offensive to 3rd and 50th Armies in terms of human lives was 31,277 casualties, including 7,164 killed, captured, or missing and 24,113 wounded or sick out of a total committed force of 232,000 men.[10]

With Gorbatov's promise fulfilled, Rokossovsky turned his attention southward to the ground between the Dnepr and Berezina Rivers, where new opportunities for gains were now apparent.

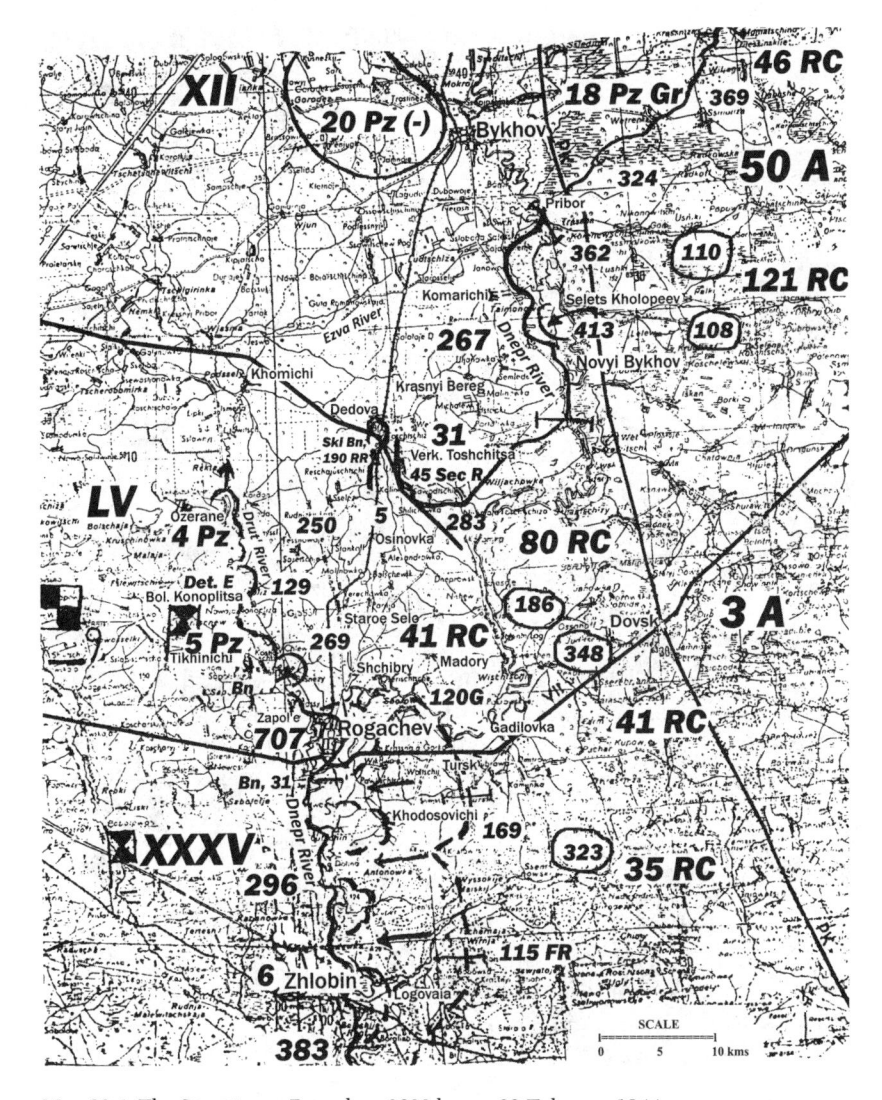

Map 20.4. The Situation at Rogachev, 0600 hours, 23 February 1944

THE MORMAL'-PARICHI OFFENSIVE (24–29 FEBRUARY 1944)

The Plan

With fighting raging in the vicinity of Rogachev on the Dnepr River and also in the Dubrova and Iazvin region west of the Berezina River, Rokossovsky provided additional support for Gorbatov's 3rd Army and, at the same time,

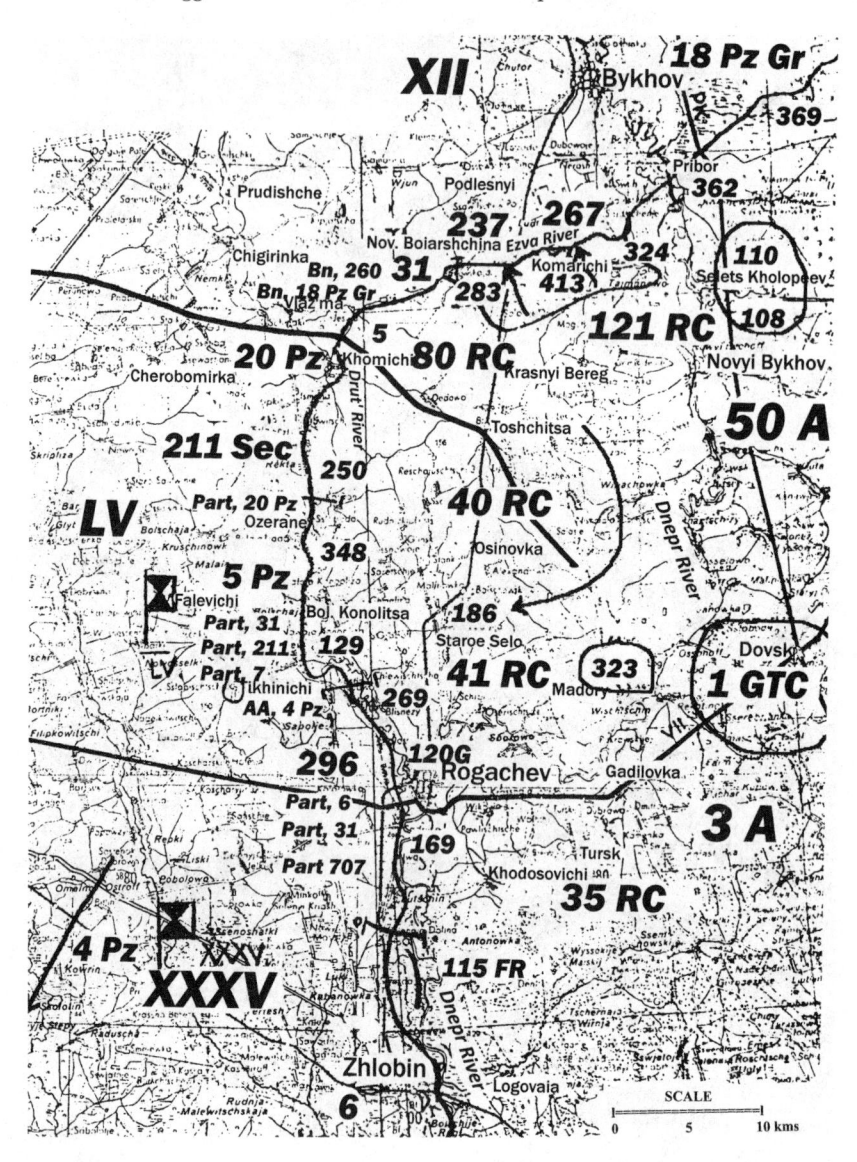

516   The Struggle for Belorussia, December 1943–April 1944

Map 20.5. The Situation at Rogachev, 0600 hours, 25–26 February 1944

exploited yet another opportunity to smash German XXXV Army Corps' forward defenses, this time south of the railroad town of Mormal' midway between Shatsilki on the Berezina and Zhlobin on the Dnepr. Even before the fighting south of Parichi and east of Rogachev ended, Rokossovsky directed Romanenko's 48th Army to mount an offensive against German Ninth Army's forces defending in the Parichi and Rogachev regions to distract Ninth Army's attention and forces from the Rogachev and Zhlobin sector.

Among the few open-source Soviet accounts of this offensive is a description provided in the official history of 194th Rifle Division, which took part in the offensive:

> On 20 February, when it [the division] was part of 25th Rifle Corps, it received the mission of attacking in the direction of Koravcha Dubrova [10 kilometers north of Shatsilki], penetrating the enemy's defense in the Mostki and Starina sector [10 kilometers east and 6 kilometers north of Shatsilki, respectively], and capturing the Iskra and Koravcha Dubrova line [7 kilometers north to 10 kilometers northeast of Shatsilki] in cooperation with 307th Rifle Division.
>
> The offensive began on 24 February; however, in the beginning it did not achieve success. Only on the fourth day, 27 February, after it was reinforced by 270th Rifle Regiment and attacked toward Koravcha Dubrova, did the division decisively penetrate into the enemy's trenches, drive him from his occupied positions, and liberate the villages of Iskra, Zvezda, and Dedno [Ledno]....
>
> During the ensuing 10 days, the division waged an intense battle with all three of its regiments for possession of Pleskovichi [Plesovichi, 23 kilometers north of Shatsilki], but in light of the enemy's significant superiority in manpower and artillery, we did not fully carry out our mission.[11]

Actually, in addition to distracting German attention and forces from the Rogachev sector, Rokossovsky hoped Romanovsky's assault would threaten to cut the Zhlobin-Parichi road and perhaps the Bobruisk-Zhlobin road as well, by doing so forcing German forces to abandon the Rogachev and Zhlobin region altogether and withdraw to Bobruisk. Romanovsky's plan also required 137th, 170th, and 399th Rifle Divisions of Kolganov's 42nd Rifle Corps, supported by a combat group from 1st Guards Tank Corps, to continue their attacks west of the Berezina River as a "demonstration" offensive designed to tie down opposing elements of 4th Panzer and 253rd Infantry Divisions. Accordingly, Kolganov's corps was to assault northward toward Parichi from its positions in the 7-kilometer-wide sector from Mikhailovka, 25 kilometers west-northwest of Shatsilki, eastward to the German strongpoint at Pogantsy, 20 kilometers northwest of Shatsilki. This sector was defended by XXXXI Panzer Corps' 36th and 253rd Infantry Divisions, along with *kampfgruppen* from 4th Panzer, 6th, 129th, and 296th Infantry Divisions and 185th Assault Gun *Abteilung* (detachment).

As for the local offensive east of the Berezina River, Romanenko ordered Barinov's 25th Rifle Corps, now consisting of 194th, 307th, and 4th Rifle Divisions, to conduct its main attack in the 10-kilometer-wide sector from

Table 20.2. The Probable Combat Formation of 48th Army and Opposing German Forces on 24 February 1944 (deployed from north to south)

FORCE (Sector)	OPPOSING GERMAN FORCES
1st/2nd/3rd Echelon (Mobile group)	
1st BELORUSSIAN FRONT	**NINTH ARMY**
48th Army (Dnepr River, north of Dubrova)	XXXV Army Corps
161st FR (Dnepr River, Mormal')	383rd ID
25th RC (Mormal', Berezina River)	
4th RD (Mormal', Liady)	
307th RD (Liady, Iashchitsy)	45th ID
194th RD (Iashchitsy, Berezina River)	707th ID (part)
53rd RC (17th, 41st, 96th, 273rd,	KGr., 383rd ID
RDs) (regrouping 24-26.2)	
197th RD (army reserve)	
29th RC (Berezina River, Pogantsy)	XXXXI Panzer Corps
217th RD (Berezina River, Pokrovka)	253rd ID
73rd RD (Pokrovka, Pogantsy)	KGr., 296th ID
102th RD (army reserve,	KGr., 4th PzD
(to 29th RC by 27.2)	(15 tanks)
42nd RC (Pogantsy, Mikhailovka)	36th ID
399th RD (Pogantsy south)	KGr., 129 ID
170th RD/137th RD (Mikhailovka north)	KGr., 6 ID
Combat Gr., 1st Guards Tank Corps	185th Assault
(40 tanks)	Gun *Abteilung* (20 guns)

Sources: *Boevoi sostav Sovetskoi Armii, chast' IV (Ianvar'–dekabr' 1944)* [The combat composition of the Soviet Army, pt. 4 (January–December 1944)] (Moscow: Voenizdat, 1988), 71–72; and "Anlage 3 zum Tätigkeitsbericht der Abt. Ic/A.O. Feindnachrichtenblätter, 1 Jan–10 Jul 1944," *AOK 9, 62717/4* file, in NAM series T-312, roll 342.

Starina to south of Mormal' against the defenses of XXXV Army Corps' 45th Infantry Division (see Table 20.2).

In an interesting case demonstrating Rokossovsky's flexibility and care for his soldiers' lives, the *front* commander apparently delayed the offensive, originally planned to begin on 21 February, for an additional three days. According to Lieutenant General G. S. Nadysev, the chief of staff of 1st Belorussian Front's artillery, the following incident took place during preparations for what he termed "the Mormal' operation." The 4th Artillery Penetration Corps, commanded by General N. V. Ignatov, was supposed to fire in support of Barinov's attack. However, poor road conditions prevented the corps' full concentration for another two to three days. Because Romanenko was reluctant to ask for the delay and, in fact, heatedly insisted it begin as scheduled, through artillery channels, General V. I. Kazakov, the *front's* chief of artillery, intervened. He met personally with Rokossovsky and persuaded him to call General Romanenko to discuss the upcoming offensive. After a conversation between the two commanders indicating that artillery support would not be adequate without a delay, Rokossovsky quickly convinced Romanenko that the delay was indeed necessary. Of course, Romanenko then agreed, and the attack was rescheduled for 24 February. Nadysev added, "As a result of the timely intervention by K. K. Rokossovsky, the forces of 48th Army were well-prepared to fulfill their assigned missions and, with the powerful support

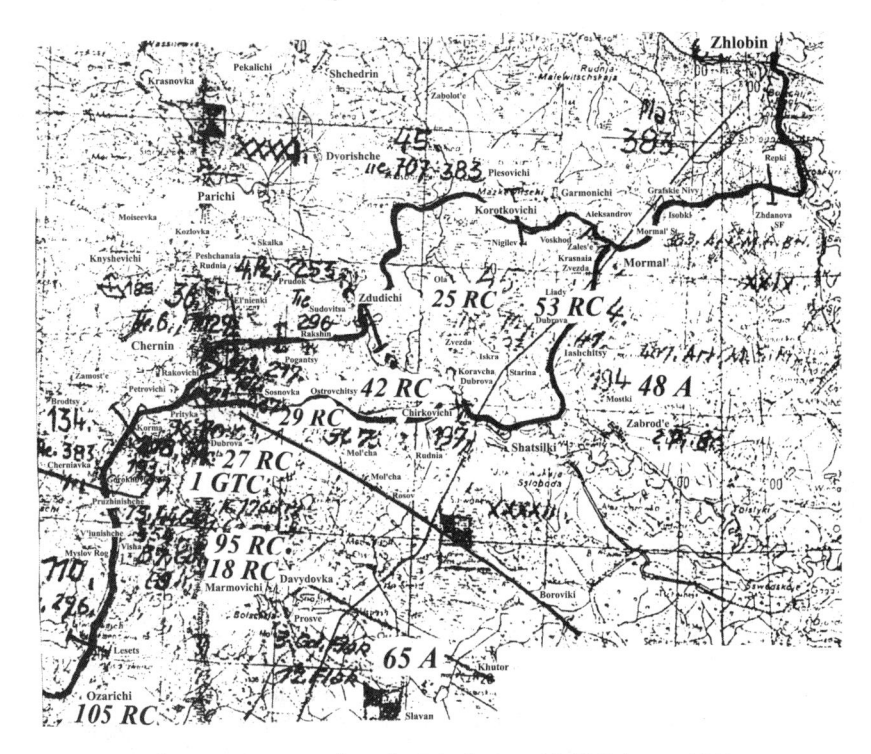

Map 20.6. 48th Army's Situation along the Parichi Axis, 24–26 February 1944

of artillery, dealt with it successfully."[12] He then added his personal evaluation of Rokossovsky, stating, "Thus, without uproar and shouting and without threats and blowups, Konstantin Konstantinovich Rokossovsky directed the actions of his army commanders very skillfully. Yes, and this was one of many of the enviable qualities of our commander in chief, for which his subordinates payed him deep respect and great soldierly love."[13]

After Rokossovsky's intervention, Barinov's corps was to attack early on 24 February, with its 194th, 307th, and 4th Divisions arrayed from left to right. The corps' task was to penetrate the Germans' defenses, capture the strongpoints at Ledno, Iskra, Zvezda, and Dubrova, and exploit northward through Plesovichi to cut the Parichi-Zhlobin road (see Map 20.6). The 161st Fortified Region protected Barinov's right flank, and Andreev's 29th Rifle Corps, which consisted of 73rd and 217th Rifle Divisions and was initially deployed west of the Berezina River, covered Barinov's left flank and prepared to move eastward across the Berezina River after Barinov's corps advanced into the Germans' depths.

Meanwhile, Gartsev's 53rd Rifle Corps, which had disengaged from combat west of Dubrova on 24 February, turning its defenses over to 65th Army's 95th Rifle Corps, regrouped its 17th, 41st, 96th, and 273rd Rifle Divisions eastward across the Berezina River so that it could support Barinov's assault. When Gartsev reached the Starina region on 26 February, his four rifle divisions were to join the exploitation northward through Dvorishche, 25 kilometers north of Shatsilki, and subsequently sever the Parichi-Zhlobin road. In addition, Romanenko ultimately reinforced 29th Rifle Corps with 102nd Rifle Division and retained 197th Rifle Division in army reserve.

Thus, by 26 February Romanenko planned to have his entire army, less Kolganov's 42nd Rifle Corps, concentrated north of the Berezina River to participate in the advance toward the Parichi-Zhlobin road. Initially, 25th Rifle Corps' three divisions faced only German 45th Infantry Division, supported by small *kampfgruppen* from 707th Security and 383rd Infantry Divisions. Within two days after he began his offensive, however, Romanenko intended to swell the size of his shock group to as many as eight rifle divisions, supported by 42nd and 231st Tank Regiments.

The Battle

The 25th Rifle Corps began its assault early on 24 February after a short but intense artillery preparation (see Map 20.6). Attacking on the corps' left wing, almost immediately 194th Rifle Division became locked in a three-day struggle for possession of the key strongpoints at Iskra, Zvezda, and Ledno, situated in 45th Infantry Division's first defensive belt, 5–8 kilometers north of Shatsilki. In the Iashchitsy sector, 5–6 kilometers to the northeast, 307th Rifle Division faced similar problems as it fought for the strongpoints at Dubrova and Antonovka. So also did 4th Rifle Division in its attacks on Liady and Zales'e, 3–5 kilometers on 307th Division's right.

Early on 26 February, however, Gartsev's 53rd Rifle Corps reinforced the assault with his 41st and 17th Rifle Divisions on 25th Rifle Corps' right, with the former going into action near Dubrova and the latter just east at Liady. These reinforcements crumbled 45th Infantry Division's defenses, captured the strongpoints at Dubrova, Antonovka, and Liady, and forced 45th Infantry to begin withdrawing on 27 February to intermediate defensive positions extending from the village of Ola through Krasnaia Zvezda to Voskhod, 4–10 kilometers to the rear.

Barinov's and Gartsev's divisions pursued, with 41st and 194th Rifle Divisions advancing northward along the Ola River, north of Shatsilki, through Ola, 25 kilometers north of Shatsilki, toward Plesovichi and Korotkovichi, 18–22 kilometers north of Shatsilki. Five to six kilometers to the east, 307th and 17th Rifle Divisions pushed northward through Krasnaia Zvezda and Voskhod toward Korotkovichi and Garmovichi. At the same time, 73rd and 217th Rifle Divisions of Andreev's 29th Rifle Corps marched eastward across the Berezina and reinforced 25th Rifle Corps' 4th Rifle Division, occupying attack positions on the right wing of 25th Corps' original penetration sector east and west of Mormal'.

After penetrating the Germans' second defensive belt, late on 28 February and on the 29th, Romanenko's attacking divisions bogged down in an intense and costly struggle for possession of the German strongpoints at Plesovichi and Korotkovichi at the northern extremity of the penetration and at Aleksandrov and Grafskie Nivy along the Zhlobin-Shatsilki railroad line, 3–5 kilometers north and northeast of Mormal'. Here, 48th Army's local offensive expired late on 29 February. German XXXV Army Corps was able to halt Romanenko's advancing forces by reinforcing its defenses on the Plesovichi and Korotkovichi sector with *kampfgruppen* from 707th Security and 383rd Infantry Divisions and in the railroad sector with elements of 4th Panzer Division and 21st Assault Gun Brigade (see Map 20.7).

By the time the offensive ended, Romanenko's shock group had advanced from 2–18 kilometers along a 20-kilometer front, carving another sizable chunk of territory from German defenses west of the Dnepr River (see Appendix P-2 for 3rd Army's situation and plans on 1 March 1944, which also contains an interesting description of the roles of separate blocking detachments and penal battalions and companies). More important still, the offensive succeeded in distracting German attention and forces from the Rogachev region, where Gorbatov's forces were wreaking havoc on the Germans' defenses. Once again, Rokossovsky's plan kept the Germans off balance, while his increasingly threadbare forces gnawed away at their tactical defenses.

The 1st Belorussian Front's offensives at Rogachev and at Mormal' between the Berezina and Dnepr Rivers, however, were the last major or minor offensive operations Rokossovsky's *front* conducted in the winter campaign. By 1 March 1944, his forces were significantly weakened by the incessant combat and by the transfer of sizable forces from his *front* to the neighboring 2nd Belorussian Front (see Table 20.3).

For example, even though the *front* picked up 10th Army on its right wing, it lost the entire 61st Army and 2nd and 7th Guards Cavalry Corps on its left wing to the 2nd Belorussian Front. In addition, Batov's 65th Army shrank from five rifle corps (the 18th, 19th, 27th, 95th, and 105th) to three (the 18th, 95th, and 105th) when 19th Rifle Corps was transferred to the Western Front's 50th Army and 27th Rifle Corps to the 1st Ukrainian Front's 13th Army. Soon after, Batov's 65th Army took control of the entire region south of the Berezina River (less the northern and southern banks of the Pripiat' River), and Romanenko's 48th Army concentrated all of its forces between the Berezina and Dnepr Rivers. Despite these changes, even though Rokossovsky abandoned any hope of reaching Parichi and Bobruisk, he still worked persistently to improve his *front's* positions along the Dnepr River.

On 4 March 1944, Rokossovsky, along with his commissar, Telegin, and his chief of staff, Malinin, dispatched a report to Stalin summing up his

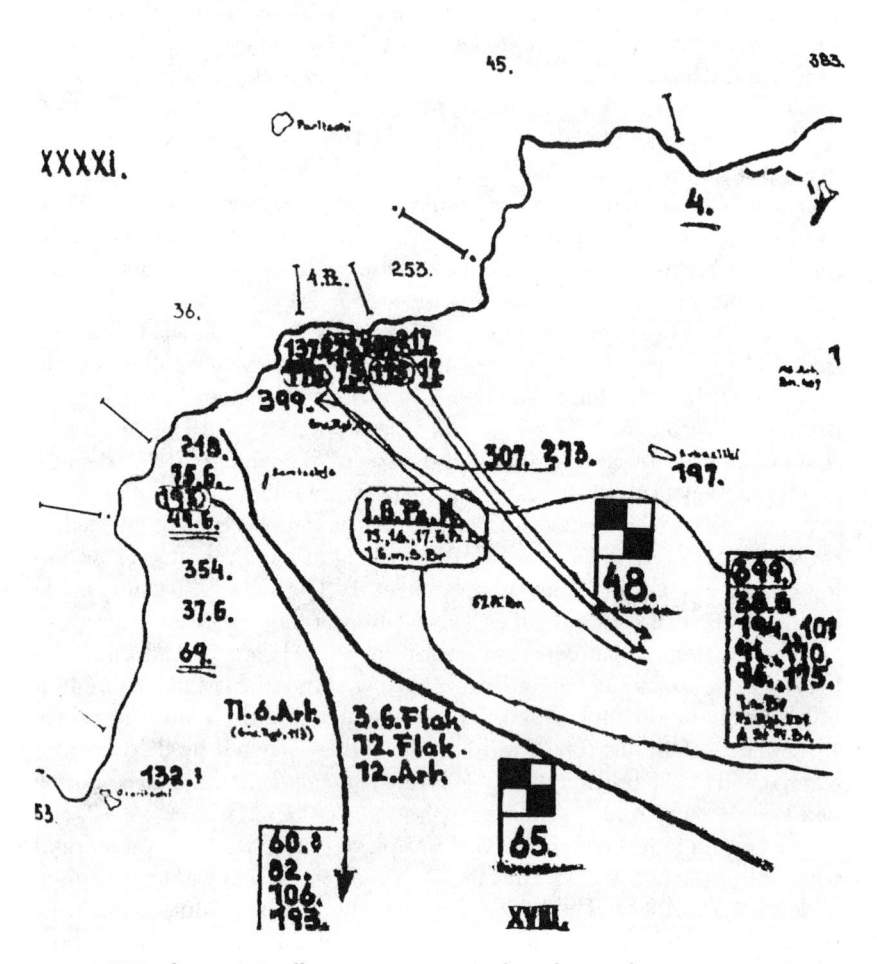

Map 20.7. Ninth Army's Intelligence Appreciation along the Parichi Axis, 28–29 February 1944

front's accomplishments during the previous two months. In particular, the report described the nature of opposing enemy forces, surveyed the condition of his forces, outlined his future plans, and asked for necessary support (see Appendix P-3). In abbreviated format, it declared the following:

- *The Enemy*—15 infantry and 3 tank divisions and 1 motorized division are in first echelon; 2 infantry divisions are in second echelon; and 8

Table 20.3. The 1st Belorussian Front's Order of Battle on 1 March 1944

1st BELORUSSIAN FRONT:
Army General K. K. Rokossovsky

3rd Army: LTG A. V. Gorbatov
  35th Rifle Corps: MG V. G. Zholudev
    169th Rifle Division
  40th Rifle Corps: MG V. S. Kuznetsov
    129th Rifle Division
    323rd Rifle Division
  41st Rifle Corps: MG V. K. Urbanovich
    120th Guards Rifle Division
    250th Rifle Division
    269th Rifle Division
    348th Rifle Division
  36th Separate Tank Regiment
  193rd Separate Tank Regiment
  1901st Self-propelled Artillery Regiment
  49th Separate Aerosleigh Battalion
  31st Separate Armored Train Battalion
  55th Separate Armored Train Battalion

10th Army: LTG V. S. Popov
  38th Rifle Corps: MG A. D. Tereshkov
    64th Rifle Division
    139th Rifle Division
    385th Rifle Division
  70th Rifle Corps: MG V. G. Teren'tev
    49th Rifle Division
    290th Rifle Division
    330th Rifle Division
  1st Separate Armored Train Battalion

50th Army: LTG I. V. Boldin
  19th Rifle Corps: MG D. I. Samarsky
    238th Rifle Division
    362nd Rifle Division
  46th Rifle Corps: MG K. M. Erastov
    108th Rifle Division
    369th Rifle Division
    413th Rifle Division
  80th Rifle Corps: MG I. L. Ragulia
    5th Rifle Division
    186th Rifle Division
    283rd Rifle Division
  121st Rifle Corps: MG D. I. Smirnov
    110th Rifle Division
    324th Rifle Division
    380th Rifle Division
  233rd Separate Tank Regiment
  8th Self-propelled Artillery Brigade
  43rd Separate Armored Train Battalion
  48th Separate Aerosleigh Battalion

Front Reserves:
  115th Fortified Region
  119th Fortified Region

48th Army: LTG P. L. Romanenko
  25th Rifle Corps: MG A. B. Barinov
    4th Rifle Division
    194th Rifle Division
    307th Rifle Division
  29th Rifle Corps: MG A. M. Andreev
    73rd Rifle Division
    217th Rifle Division
  42nd Rifle Corps: LTG K. S. Kolganov
    137th Rifle Division
    170th Rifle Division
    399th Rifle Division
  53rd Rifle Corps: MG I. A. Gartsev
    17th Rifle Division
    41st Rifle Division
    96th Rifle Division
    273rd Rifle Division
    102nd Rifle Division
    197th Rifle Division
  161st Fortified Region
  42nd Separate Tank Regiment
  231st Separate Tank Regiment
  1897th Self-propelled Artillery Regiment
  39th Separate Armored Train Battalion

65th Army: LTC P. I. Batov
  18th Rifle Corps: MG I. I. Ivanov
    44th Guards Rifle Division
    75th Guards Rifle Division
    69th Rifle Division
  95th Rifle Corps: MG I. A. Kuzovkov
    37th Guards Rifle Division
    82d Rifle Division
    193rd Rifle Division
  105th Rifle Corps: MG D. F. Alekseev
    132nd Rifle Division
    253rd Rifle Division
    354th Rifle Division
    115th Rifle Brigade
  251st Separate Tank Regiment

Table 20.3. *continued*

1st Guards Tank Corps: MGTF M. F. Panov
  15th Guards Tank Brigade
  16th Guards Tank Brigade
  17th Guards Tank Brigade
  1st Guards Motorized Rifle Brigade
  1001st Self-propelled Artillery Regiment
  1296th Self-propelled Artillery Regiment
  1st Guards Motorcycle Battalion
  65th Motorcycle Battalion
  732nd Tank Destroyer Artillery Regiment
  455th Mortar Regiment
  43rd Guards-Mortar Battalion
  80th Guards Antiaircraft Artillery Regiment
  1444th Self-propelled Artillery Regiment
  21st Separate Armored Train Battalion
  59th Separate Armored Train Battalion

Source: Boevoi sostav Sovetskoi Armii, chast' IV (Ianvar'–dekabr' 1944) [The combat composition of the Soviet Army, pt. 4 (January–December 1944)] (Moscow: Voenizdat, 1988), 71–72.

divisions are in reserve along the Minsk and Pinsk line in the *front*'s sector, whose forward edge extends a distance of 300 kilometers. The main grouping is in the Bykhov, Bobruisk, Parichi, and Zhlobin region. . . . The enemy has a total quantity of up to 350 tanks and self-propelled guns.

- *Our Forces*—The *front*'s forces opposing these enemy forces consist of 43 rifle divisions, 1 separate rifle brigade, and 1 tank corps. As a result of continuous offensive battles, numerically, all of the rifle divisions have been greatly weakened: more importantly, they have lost their assault power, and the majority of them consist of a total of from 3,000 up to 4,000 men.
- *Conclusions Regarding the Situation*—The enemy is sufficiently strong, the ranks of the *front*'s rifle divisions have been very thinned out and their shock power has been significantly weakened, and the difficult terrain conditions and the onset of the spring *rasputitsa* [period of flooded roads] severely limits the capabilities of the *front*'s forces from conducting offensive operations and is forcing them to go over to the defense during the entire *rasputitsa* period, conducting in this period only local battles with the limited aims of improving their positions and preparing for a spring offensive by all of the *front*'s forces.
- *The possible axes for the* front's *spring offensive* after the *rasputitsa* are the Chausy-Mogilev, Bykhov-Mogilev, Rogachev-Bobruisk, and Parichi-Bobruisk axes. The Rogachev-Bobruisk axis is the most favorable because the terrain here permits employing all types of forces in the offensive, and a complex regrouping is not required to organize an

offensive along this axis because the *front*'s main forces and weapons are already deployed along the western bank of the Dnepr River north of Rogachev and in the Mormal' region between the Dnepr and Berezina Rivers.
- *Decision*—Considering the situation, especially the enemy's strength, the composition of the enemy's and our own forces, the period of spring flooding, which is setting in, and the results of 50th Army's offensive along the Bykhov and Mogilev axis and 48th Army's [offensive] from the Mormal' region to the north, I have decided:
- To halt the *front*'s offensive and go over to the defense for the entire period of the spring *rasputitsa* and spring flooding;
- To limit the *front*'s combat activities during the entire period of the spring *rasputitsa* to the conduct of reconnaissance and local battles with the limited aim of improving our occupied positions; and
- During the entire period of the spring *rasputitsa*, to train the *front*'s forces and prepare for a general spring offensive along the Bobruisk axis.

I request you:
- Approve my decision;
- Allocate 50,000 replacements to the *front* in order to bring the rifle divisions of 3rd and 48th Armies designated for the spring offensive up to 7,000 men each. Dispatch these reinforcements as soon as possible in order that we have the opportunity to integrate them into the units in organized fashion during the period of the spring *rasputitsa* and put them through the necessary training program;
- Fill out and transfer 9th Tank Corps, which is located in the *Stavka* Reserve, to the *front*;
- Allocate 200 tanks to fill out the *front*'s 1st Guards Tank Corps and separate tank regiments; and
- Issue orders concerning the delivery of ammunition for the *front* so as to bring it up to three combat loads by the end of the spring *rasputitsa*.[14]

Thus, crisply and without wasting any words, Rokossovsky summed up more than sixty days of combat and declared his intention, after his army was reinforced, to continue offensive operations still deeper into southern Belorussia.

CHAPTER 21

The Liquidation of German Bridgeheads on the Dnepr River's Eastern Bank (25–31 March)

PLANNING

As the fighting calmed down in the Rogachev region and southward to the Berezina River, Rokossovsky reinforced 10th and 50th Armies on his *front*'s right wing during mid- and late March and ordered them to conduct local operations to eliminate German Ninth Army's bridgehead on the eastern bank of the Dnepr River between Bykhov and Chausy. To accomplish this task, he chose Lieutenant General V. S. Popov's 10th Army, recently transferred to his *front* from Sokolovsky's Western Front, and Colonel General I. V. Boldin's 50th Army, which he had reinforced with 80th Rifle Corps from 3rd Army in February and 19th Rifle Corps from 65th Army in early March (see Map 21.1).

Although Soviet and Russian open sources are utterly silent about this operation, a single formerly classified document from the General Staff's collection of war experiences provides detailed information about this failed offensive:

> The 1st Belorussian Front conducted an operation with a part of its forces at the end of March 1944 to liquidate the enemy's bridgehead on the eastern bank of the Dnepr River. The 10th Army's 38th Rifle Corps participated in the conduct of this operation....
>
> During the course of these offensive battles in the period from 25–31 March, the formations and units of 38th Rifle Corps experienced positive and negative aspects in the planning and organization of combat operations, as well as in the command and control of forces in combat and during the regrouping.[1]

In addition, the archival records of the 1st Belorussian Front contain fragmentary information regarding the missions assigned to 10th and 50th Armies during late March. This document, "1st Belorussian Front's Operational Directive No. 00215/op," dated 21 March, sketched out the following missions (see Appendix Q-1).

- The 10th Army will begin a decisive offensive on the morning of 25 March, with the mission of penetrating the enemy's defensive front in the Golochevo, Antonovka, and Golovenchitsy sector, and by de-

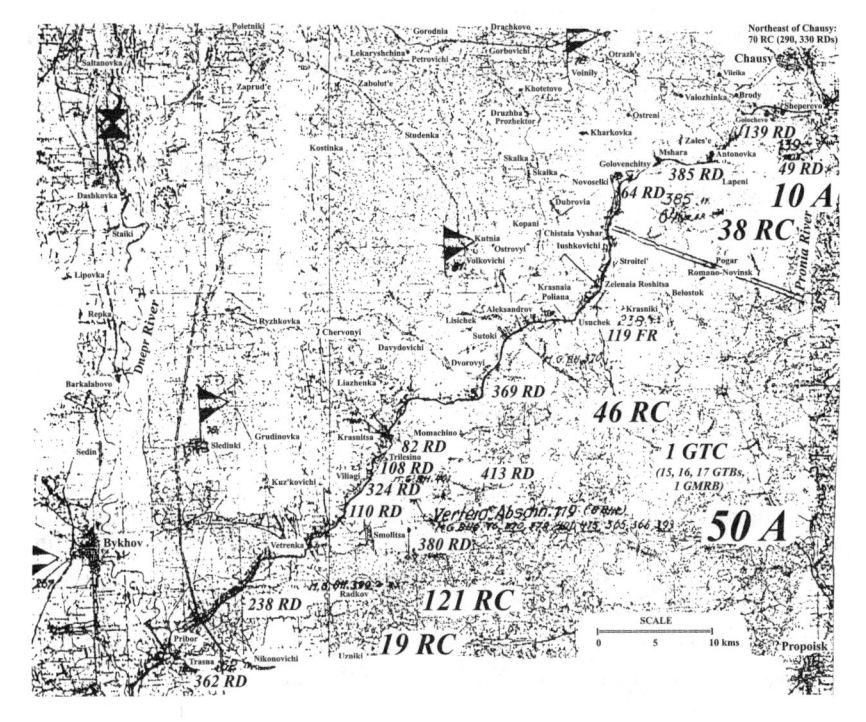

The Liquidation of German Bridgeheads on the Dnepr River's Eastern Bank 527

Map 21.1. Ninth Army's Situation in the Chausy-Bykhov Sector, 18–24 March 1944

livering a decisive attack in the general direction of Zales'e, Otrazh'e, Drachkovo, Kureni Moshenaki, and Petrovichi [northeast of Mogilev], will capture the Sheperevo, Brody, Ostreni, and Golovenchitsy line by day's end on 25 March 1944. Subsequently, capture the Chausy, Khar'kovka line by 27 March, the Galuzy [12 kilometers north of Chausy], Levkovshchina [20 kilometers east of Mogilev] line by 28 March, the Zalozh'e, Konstantinovka line [8 kilometers east of Mogilev] by 31 March, and the Muryvanka, Mostok line [10 kilometers northeast of Mogilev] by 1 April 1944.

- The 50th Army will begin a decisive offensive with all of the army's forces on the morning of 25 March 1944, with the mission of penetrating the enemy's defensive front in the Krasnitsa and Vetrenka sector and, by delivering its main attack in the general direction of Smolitsa, Dmitrievka, Kostinka, Zaprud'e, Poletkniki, and Lupolovo [in the eastern suburbs of Mogilev], will capture the Krasnitsa, Grechkin, and Vetrenka line by day's end on 27 March; the Volkovichi, Slediuki line by 27 March; the Levkovshchina, Zatish'e line by 29 March and positions from Novyi Lobuzh to the peat village (6 kilometers southwest of Lupolovo) by 31 March.[2]

German Fourth and Ninth Armies' records indicate that, in addition to Popov's 10th Army, Boldin's 50th Army and Panov's 1st Guards Tank Corps participated in the offensive. However, 50th Army's history says nothing whatsoever about the offensive, and, in his memoirs, General Panov, the commander of 1st Guards Tank Corps, simply notes, "The corps was transferred to the Mogilev axis (10 kilometers west of Novo-Bykhov) during February and March 1944. We happened to take part in battles in that region. This transfer was of a demonstrative nature in order to attract enemy reserves and deny him the opportunity to shift them against the 1st Ukrainian Front."[3]

Fortunately, along with the single Soviet archival document, enough German intelligence materials are available to reconstruct the nature and course of this operation in significant detail.

On paper at least, Rokossovsky's offensive was ambitious. His plan required the forces of General Popov's 10th Army to penetrate the defenses of 12th Infantry Division of German Fourth Army's XXXIX Army Corps in an 8-kilometer-wide sector southwest of the city of Chausy. Attacking along a front extending from Golochevo and Golovenchitsy, the army's 38th Rifle Corps was to penetrate the German defenses, exploit to the northwest, and reach the southeast outskirts of Mogilev by day's end on 1 April. This required 38th Army Corps to advance 4 kilometers on the first day of the offensive, a total of 8 kilometers by the end of the third day, 20 kilometers by the end of the third day, and up to 30 kilometers by 1 April. Popov ordered a single rifle corps, reinforced by up to two rifle divisions from a second rifle corps, to fulfill this formidable task.

In addition, Rokossovsky ordered Boldin's 50th Army to attack and penetrate defenses occupied by 18th Panzer Grenadier and 31st Infantry Divisions of German Fourth Army's XII Army Corps in a 10-kilometer-wide sector east of Bykhov. Attacking between Vetrenka and Krasnitsa, the army's 121st Rifle Corps and part of its 46th Rifle Corps, backed up by Panov's 1st Guards Tank Corps, were to penetrate the Germans' defenses, exploit toward the north, and reach the southern suburbs of Mogilev by day's end on 1 April. This plan required a total of six rifle divisions and a single understrength tank corps to advance 5 kilometers on the first two days of the attack, 15 kilometers by the end of the second day, and more than 25 kilometers by day's end on 31 March.

If the attacking forces accomplished all of their missions, Popov's and Boldin's forces were supposed to have reached the southern approaches to Mogilev by the time the operation ended on 1 April. By doing so, the offensive would clear all German forces from the region between Chausy on the Pronia River and the Dnepr River south of Mogilev. It was a formidable task indeed.

Major General A. D. Tereshkov's 38th Rifle Corps was responsible for conducting the main attack of Popov's 10th Army. Prior to the assault, deployed from left to right, his corps' 64th, 385th, and 139th Rifle Divisions occupied positions in the sector extending from Golovenchitsy eastward to south of Chausy; 330th, 290th, and 49th Rifle Divisions of Major General V. G. Terent'ev's 70th Rifle Corp defended positions along the Pronia River north of Chausy. In the days prior to the assault, Tereshkov's corps concentrated its forces in the Golovenchitsy and Golochevo region with 64th and 139th Rifle Divisions in first echelon and 385th Rifle Division in second.

At the same time, 49th and 290th Rifle Divisions of Terent'ev's 70th Corps were ordered to prepare to concentrate in assembly areas south of Golovenchitsy to back up Tereshkov's assault and lead the exploitation following his penetration operation. A single armored train battalion provided Popov his only additional artillery support. This attack configuration concentrated five rifle divisions against German 12th Infantry Division. The latter was also supported by a company of roughly ten guns from 667th Assault Gun *Abteilung* (detachment) and the right wing regiment of 342nd Infantry Division, whose main body was defending the city of Chausy.

Farther to the south, Boldin concentrated his shock group, which consisted of 380th, 110th, and 324th Divisions of Major General D. I. Smirnov's 121st Rifle Corps and 108th and 413th Divisions of Major General K. N. Erastov's 46th Rifle Corps, in the 10-kilometer-wide sector extending from Vetrenka northeastward to Krasnitsa. Boldin's shock group was flanked on the left by 19th Rifle Corps' 238th Rifle Division and on the right by 369th Rifle Division of Erastov's 46th Corps.

The 233rd Tank Regiment and 8th Self-propelled Artillery Brigade provided Boldin's shock group armor support during the penetration operation. After the shock group penetrated successfully, Panov's 1st Guards Tank Corps, with a force of roughly eighty tanks, was to lead the exploitation toward Mogilev. At least initially, Boldin's attack formation concentrated six rifle divisions against the left wing of XII Army Corps' 18th Panzer Grenadier Division and the right wing of the same corps' 31st Infantry Division. The defenders were supported by the remainder of 667th Assault Gun *Abteilung* and 237th Assault Gun *Abteilung* equipped with about thirty operable guns.

In addition, during late March Rokossovsky began transferring the three rifle divisions of General Kolganov's 42nd Rifle Corps from Romanenko's 48th Army to Boldin's 50th Army. After it reached 50th Army's sector on or about 30 March, Kolganov's rifle corps was supposed to reinforce Boldin's exploitation toward Mogilev with Panov's guards tank corps. So configured, the shock groups of 10th and 50th Armies outnumbered the German defenders significantly (see Tables 21.1 and 21.2).

Despite the clear numerical superiority of Rokossovsky's forces, the Germans occupied strong and deep defenses, which they had been improving since repelling 50th Army's assaults in January.

Table 21.1. The Probable General Combat Formations of 10th and 50th Armies and Opposing German Forces Late on 23 March 1944 (deployed from north to south)

FORCE (Sector)	OPPOSING GERMAN FORCES
1st/2nd/3rd Echelon (Mobile group)	
1st BELORUSSIAN FRONT	**FOURTH ARMY**
10th Army (Novoselki on Pronia R., Golovenchitsy)	XXXIX Panzer Corps
70th RC (Novoselki, Golochevo)	342nd ID
290th RD	
330th RD/49th RD	
38th Rifle Corps (Golochevo, Golovenchitsy	
139th RD (Golochevo, Antonovka)	
385th RD (Antonovka, Mshara)	12th ID/Co., 667th
64th RD (Mshara, Golovenchitsy)	Assault Gun *Abt.*
50th Army (Golovenchitsy, Pribor on Dnepr R.)	XII Army Corps
119th FR (Golovenchitsy, Sutoki)	
46th RC (Sutoki, Viliaga)	31st ID
369th RD (Sutoki, Krasnitsa north)	
82nd RD/413th RD (Krasnitsa, north of Viliaga)	18th PzGrD
108th RD (north of Viliaga, Viliaga)	237th, 667th
1st GTC (15th, 16th GTBs)	Assault Gun
42nd RC (137th, 170th, 399th RDs (28.3)	*Abteilungen*
121st RC (Viliaga, Vetrenka)	
324th RD/380th RD (north of Vetrenka)	
110th RD (Vetrenka)	
19th RC (Vetrenka, Dnepr River)	
238th RD (Vetrenka, Nikonovichi)	
362nd RD (Nikonovichi, Dnepr River)	

Sources: Boevoi sostav Sovetskoi Armii, chast' IV (Ianvar'–dekabr' 1944) [The combat composition of the Soviet Army, Part 4 (January–December 1944)] (Moscow: Voenizdat, 1988), 71–72; and "Anlage 3 zum Tätigkeitsbericht der Abt. Ic/A.O. Feindnachrichtenblätter, 1 Jan–10 Jul 1944," *AOK 9, 62717/4 file,* in NAM series T-312, Roll 342; "H Gr Mitte/Ia, KTB: Lagenkarten, 1–31 January 1944," *H Gr Mitte, 65002/60 file,* in NAM series T-311, Roll 224; and "Anlagen z. KTB, Ic/AO, Jan-Jun 1944, *AOK 4, 64189/1 file,* in NAM series T-312, Roll unidentified.

Table 21.2. The Estimated Correlation of Opposing Forces in the Dnepr Bridgehead Offensive, 25–31 March 1944

OPPOSING FORCES	
Soviet	*German*
Belorussian Front	
10th Army	342nd Infantry Division
50th Army	12th Infantry Division
16 rifle divisions	31st Infantry Division
1 tank corps	18th Panzer Grenadier
1 tank regiment	Division
1 self-propelled artillery brigade	667th Assault Gun
	Abteilung (20 guns)
	237th Assault Gun
	Abteilung (20 guns)
Strength: 120,000 men	50,000 men
100 tanks and SP guns	approx. 40 assault guns
Depth of Soviet advance: 1-2 kilometers	

Sources: Boevoi sostav Sovetskoi Armii, chast' IV (Ianvar'–dekabr' 1944) [The combat composition of the Soviet Army, pt. 4 (January–December 1944)] (Moscow: Voenizdat, 1988), 71–72; and "Anlage 3 zum Tätigkeitsbericht der Abt. Ic/A.O. Feindnachrichtenblätter, 1 Jan–10 Jul 1944," *AOK 9, 62717/4 file,* in NAM series T-312, Roll 342; "H Gr Mitte/Ia, KTB: Lagenkarten, 1–31 January 1944," *H Gr Mitte, 65002/60 file,* in NAM series T-311, Roll 224; and "Anlagen z. KTB, Ic/AO, Jan-Jun 1944, *AOK 4, 64189/1 file,* in NAM series T-312, Roll unidentified.

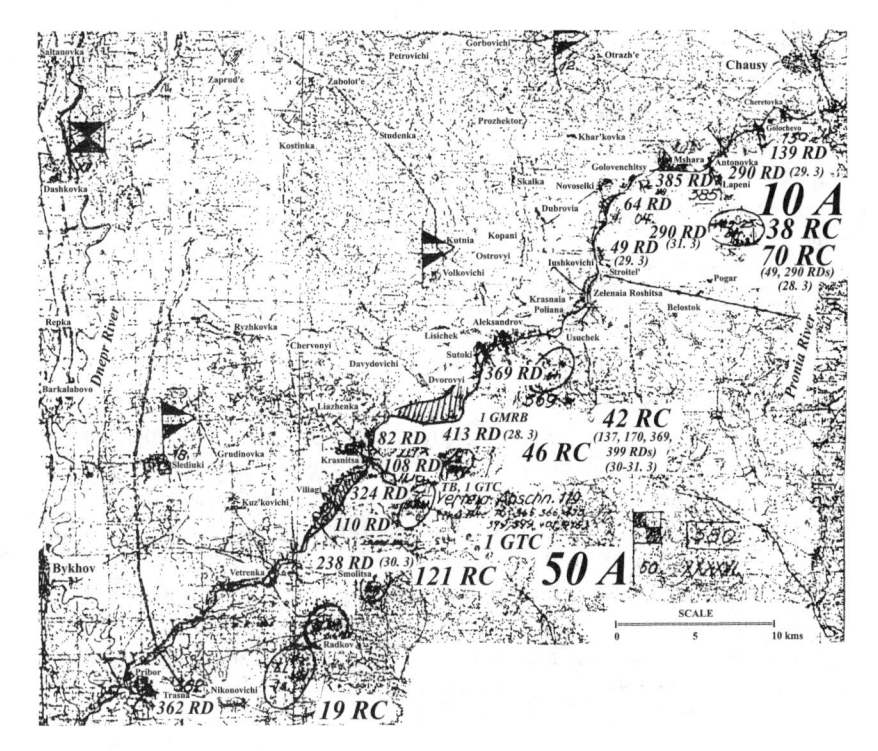

The Liquidation of German Bridgeheads on the Dnepr River's Eastern Bank   531

Map 21.2. 50th and 10th Armies' Offensives in the Chausy-Bykhov Sector, 24–31 March 1944

THE BATTLE

Popov commenced his assault southwest of Chausy at dawn on 25 March, when the three rifle divisions of Tereshkov's 38th Rifle Corps struck the defenses of XXXIX Panzer Corps' 12th Infantry Division between Golovenchitsy and Golochevo after a short artillery preparation (see Map 21.2). However, despite heavy fighting over the course of the next three days, the attack scarcely dented the German defenses. Nor did the assault by 290th and 330th Rifle Divisions north of Chausy make any appreciable progress.

Therefore, overnight on 28–29 February, Popov regrouped 290th Rifle Division into the Golochevo sector, 18 kilometers to the south, where, along with 49th Rifle Division from Popov's reserve, it reinforced Tereshkov's assaults against the eastern sector of the German strongpoint. While the 290th joined 385th Division's attack, 49th Division did the same on 64th Rifle Division's left. However, these attacks also failed after only limited gains. The 290th Rifle Division regrouped its forces once again on the night of 30–31 March, and the next day participated in yet another unsuccessful attack, this time in support of 49th Rifle Division, which had managed to wedge itself into the Germans' defenses south of Iushkovichi, 5 kilometers southwest of Golovenchitsy, on 10th Army's left wing. By this time, General Boldin had also reinforced 121st Rifle Corps' assault with 238th Rifle Division from the adjacent 19th Rifle Corps.

A Soviet classified after-action report described the ferocity of this fighting:

> In spite of repeated instances when it was forced to withdraw under pressure from superior enemy forces, units of 239th [should read 139th] Rifle Division resumed their attacks up to five times a day while trying to fulfill their combat missions.
>
> After withdrawing from the Germans' second trench line on 31 March 1944 because of counterattacks by large enemy infantry forces supported by massed artillery and mortar fire, units of 49th Rifle Division resumed their attacks and once again captured the Germans' second line of trenches west of Iushkovichi. . . .
>
> A battalion of 49th Rifle Division's 222nd Rifle Regiment captured the first trench line on 30 March 1944 by a decisive charge and, without halting there, attacked the enemy in the second trench energetically, forced him to flee, and then penetrated into the forest west of Iushkovichi.[4]

On the negative side of the ledger, the same report candidly noted significant failures:

> The units of 49th Rifle Division penetrated into the brush and woods west of Iushkovichi at 1800 hours on 30 March 1944. They failed to fortify the region they occupied, and they did not organize a defense in case the enemy counterattacked. After being attacked on both flanks by a sizable force of enemy infantry and self-propelled guns and fearing encirclement, the division's units withdrew from the enemy's trenches overnight on 31 March 1944. They did not dig in here in spite of the fact that they had time to do so. . . .
>
> The units of 290th Rifle Division captured the enemy's trenches in the vicinity of "Krylataia" woods on 29 March. The units of 385th Rifle Division were ordered to exploit 290th Rifle Division's success. Although the distance to the successful 290th Rifle Division's units was no more than 1–1.5 kilometers, 385th Rifle Division's units wasted more than four hours, by doing so giving the enemy the opportunity to organize his defense and disrupting the possibility of penetrating his defense.
>
> The units of 49th Rifle Division penetrated the enemy's front in the region of the forest west of Iushkovichi by 1800 hours on 30 March. The commander of 385th Rifle Division was ordered to commit his 1268th

Rifle Regiment (in second echelon), which was concentrated 3 kilometers northeast of the penetration sector, into the penetration quickly. The 1268th Rifle Regiment took 6 hours to complete the movement and did not reach 49th Rifle Division until nightfall. The remaining regiments of 385th Rifle Division, which were situated 2–3 kilometers north of 49th Rifle Division, took all night to regroup and reached their designated positions only by the morning of 31 March. Therefore, they were not able to participate in combat to exploit 49th Rifle Division's success and repel the enemy's counterattacks. . . .

The commander of 49th Rifle Division assigned combat missions to his regimental commander for combat on 30 March 1944 during the night and only on a map. After preparing his observation post by 0930 hours on 30 March, he failed to define the regiments' offensive sectors and the order for supporting them by observed artillery fire. . . .

The commander of 64th Rifle Division failed to observe his regiments' operations during combat on 25 March. The division headquarters did not organize affairs in its forward observation post, and, as a result, neither the division commander nor his staff knew the true location of their units for more than 3 hours. During the course of the battle, neither the commander nor his staff was able to influence the axes desirable for success, and the division lost control of the battle for an extended period. . . .

While moving his regiment to exploit 49th Rifle Division's success on 30 March, the commander of 385th Rifle Division's 1268th Rifle Regiment lost control over his battalions. The regimental staff did not have reliable communications with its battalions, and, as a result, not sensing control by the regimental commander and his staff, the battalions operated sluggishly, reached the battlefield criminally tardy and were not committed into combat in timely fashion. . . .

After 222nd Rifle Regiment penetrated the enemy's defensive front in the forest west of Iushkovichi on 30 March 1944, instead of strengthening his attack into the depth to reach the Resta River, the commander of 49th Rifle Division dispersed his remaining two regiments to protect the attacking regiment's flanks at the same time that this mission had already been assigned to other divisions, which 49th Rifle Division commander did not know.[5]

This litany of cold and hard combat experiences vividly underscored 10th Army's inability to fulfill its assigned missions. Popov's offensive collapsed in disorder and frustration by 31 March.

Meanwhile, the forces of Boldin's 50th Army recorded greater success to the south, but only slightly (see Map 21.2). An excerpt from 82nd Rifle Division's history offers a rare description of the combat in the sector of Erastov's 46th Rifle Corps:

The 210th and 250th Rifle Regiments deployed in combat formation and occupied their jumping-off positions for the assault on the village of Krasnitsa on 25 March. The enemy defense in this region was rather firm. He had concentrated a considerable amount of artillery and mortars in this sector. The enemy often conducted counterattacks with large forces accompanied by tanks and self-propelled guns.

Continuous fierce combat developed along this line in March. The 146th Tank Destroyer Battalion, under the command of Major V. V. Kul'bashnik, destroyed six tanks while repelling an attack by a large group of tanks. The brave artilleryman fell a heroes' death. . . .

After an intense battle, the units of 82nd Division drove the enemy back and captured the village of Krasnitsa but were not able to develop the offensive further.

By order of the army commander, the division turned its combat sector over to units of 324th Rifle Division on the night of 5 April and concentrated in the region of the village of Semenovka to receive and train replacements.[6]

This brief account basically sums up 50th Army's achievements. In five days of intense fighting, Boldin's shock group advanced only 1–3 kilometers, barely denting the Germans' forward defenses. During this battle, 46th Rifle Corps' 82nd, 108th, and 413th Rifle Divisions reached the approaches to Krasnitsa and captured the southern outskirts of Krasnitsa but could achieve little more. The divisions of 121st Rifle Corps recorded similar tactical gains but were not able to capture a single German strongpoint.

Although the history of Panov's tank corps fails to provide any details about this operation, German records indicate that Panov committed at least two of his tank brigades and his motorized rifle brigade to combat in support of 46th Rifle Corps but to little effect. The failure of Boldin's force to achieve any tactical penetration whatsoever negated the value of Panov's tank corps, and, in the end, Boldin never ordered its full complement into combat.

For all practical purposes, the failure of 10th and 50th Armies' offensive ended any hopes on Rokossovsky's part about collapsing German defenses east of the Dnepr River. Henceforth, and until the summer offensive of June 1944, Rokossovsky's armies on the Dnepr River's eastern bank limited their activity to patrolling and minor line-straightening operations.

POSTSCRIPT

Although the bulk of Batov's 65th Army and Belov's entire 61st Army completed their major offensive operations by the end of February 1944, as their war experience reports indicated, their forces continued to conduct local offensive operations to improve their positions throughout March. Reports prepared by the 1st Belorussian Front's war experience section summarized both armies' operations during February 1944 as follows:

> The 65th Army conducted persistent offensive combat during February 1944 to penetrate the enemy's defenses and defensive combat along its occupied lines. The offensive combat was characterized by the following:
> 1. The enemy had a well-organized defense and system of fire, and, considering all of the favorable conditions of the forested and swampy terrain, he was able to hold back the army's offensive.
> 2. Possessing necessary reserves for the conduct of counterattacks against our penetrating forces, the enemy pressed the army's units back to their jumping-off positions.
>
> The 61st Army undertook repeated attempts to attack in separate sectors during February 1944 but had insignificant success. By the end of the month, the army had conducted a regrouping of forces and went over to a stubborn defense across a broad 178-kilometer-wide front, with the mission of reliably protecting Kalinkovichi, Mozyr', El'sk, Lel'chitsy, and Rakitnoe. The defense was constructed in two army belts on the basis of the formation of strongpoints and centers of resistance along possible enemy attack axes.[7]

The most important of these local operations took place on 14 and 15 February, when 61st Army's 9th Guards Rifle Corps forced 5th Panzer Division to abandon the small salient it defended at Slobodka No. 1 State Farm, east of the Ptich' River (see Map 21.3). The very next day, German Army Group Center summoned its "fire brigade," in southern Belorussia, the 5th Panzer, to extinguish the flames in yet another threatened sector, this time along the Dnepr River at Rogachev.

Later still, beginning on the night of 16 March, the German Ninth Army's LVI Panzer Corps began withdrawing its forces from their forward positions east of the Tremlia River between Savin Rog and Gorokhovishchi, including their strongpoints west of Ozarichi and at Kholma, Malyi Litvinovichi, Visha, and Pruzhinishche, which had held back the tide of Rokossovsky's forces since early February (see Map 21.4). The veteran 354th Rifle Division, now assigned to 65th Army's 105th Rifle Corps in the sector north of Ozarichi, took part in the ensuing pursuit:

> On the night of 16 March, a platoon of scouts from 1203rd Rifle Regiment wedged into the defenses of the enemy, who had begun to withdraw their forces from the first positions into the depth of the defense. The platoon commander, Sergeant V. Dziuban, quickly informed his regimental commander. On Major N. A. Kharitonov's orders, [Dziuban's]

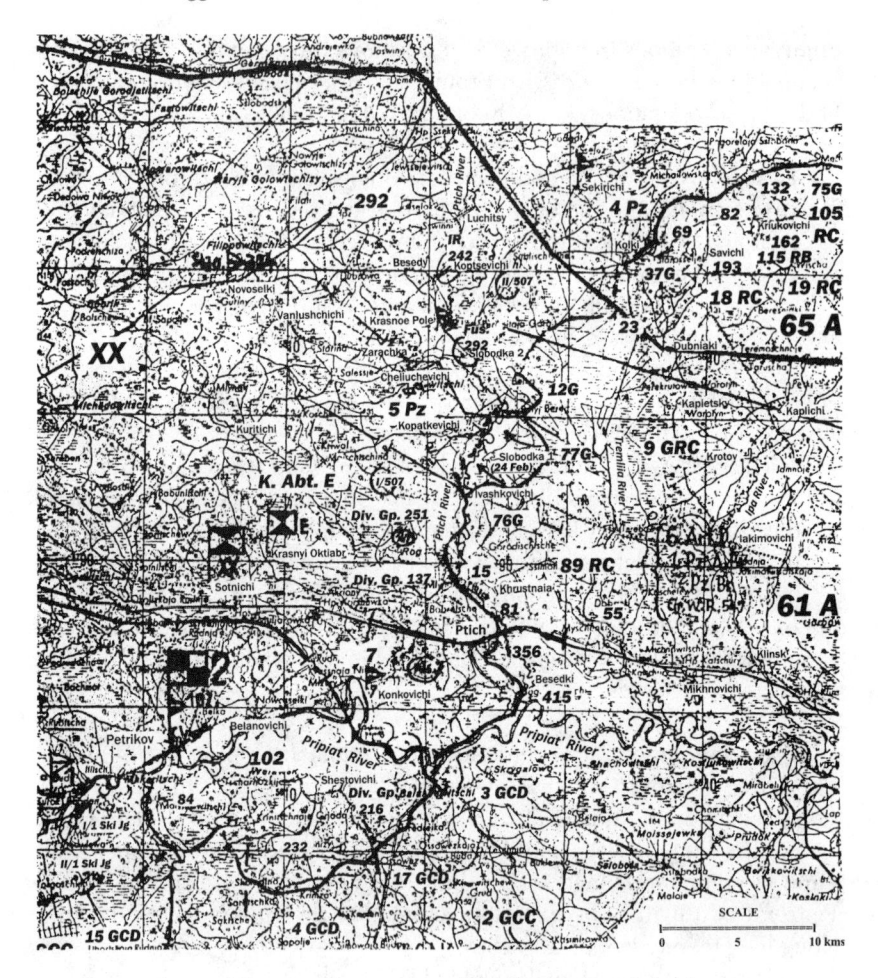

Map 21.3. 65th Army's Seizure of State Farm Slobodka No. 1, 14–15 February 1944

forces penetrated into the enemy's trenches with a swift attack and began advancing forward. The division's other regiments joined the offensive in the morning. They drove the covering forces back and advanced 5–6 kilometers by the evening of the next day.

While pursuing the withdrawing enemy, the forward detachments discovered a concentration camp 4 kilometers northwest of the village of Kholma, and a second 2 kilometers to the northwest in the village of Medved'. Once again staring death in the eyes, the soldiers were staggered by what they saw. Dying old men, women, and children were sitting in the forests and the swamps or lying on the frozen ground, in a state of delirium. The territory within the camps was strewn with coils of

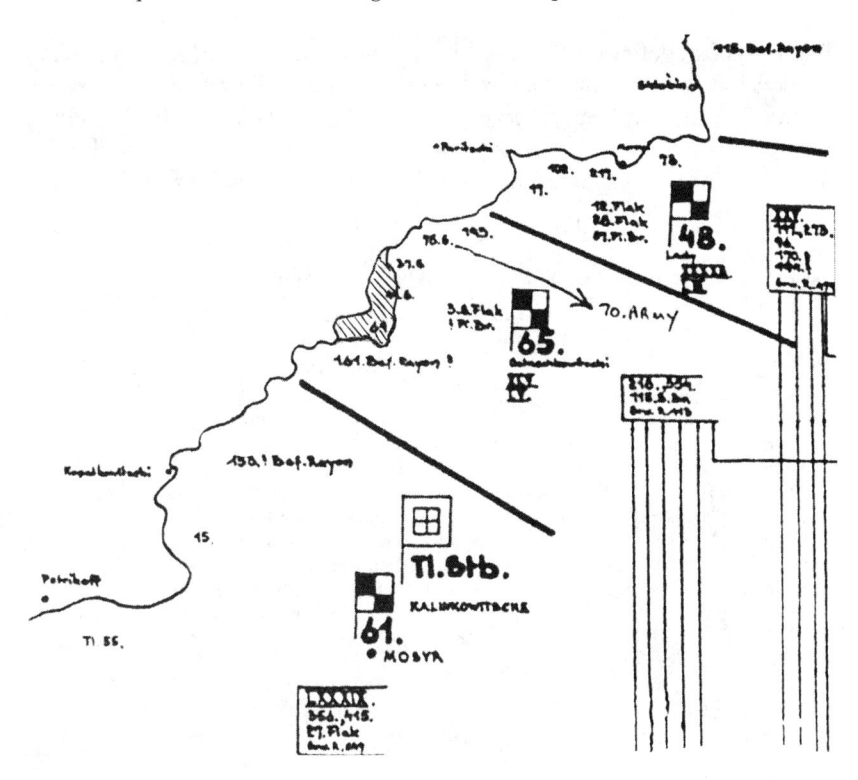

Map 21.4. Ninth Army's Intelligence Appreciation, 31 March 1944 (65th Army's Advance to the Tremlia River, 16–17 March)

barbed wire, and the approaches to them within and outside were mined. The surrounding pits and ditches were choked with corpses. The living lay among the dead and dying.[8]

The 354th Rifle Division and the remainder of Alekseev's rifle corps (132nd and 253rd Rifle Divisions) reached German Ninth Army's new defenses along the Tremlia River late on 17 March. Slightly to the north, the equally veteran 69th Rifle Division of 65th Army's 18th Rifle Corps also took part in the pursuit: "On 17 March the enemy began to withdraw his units from the swampy forward edge across [east of] the Tremlia River. Beginning its pursuit of the enemy, the division captured the villages of Myslov Rog and V'iunishche. During the period of the offensive to Myslov Rog and V'iunishche, the division liberated Soviet citizens situated in Hitlerite concentration camps."[9] By day's end on 17 March, German Ninth Army's forces had withdrawn from 5 to 15 kilometers along a 22-kilometer-wide front. Here, along the Tremlia River, they occupied strong defenses prepared for weeks before. These defenses would hold firm until late June 1944, when Rokossovsky's force irreparably shattered them in a new and even larger offensive.

As Rokossovsky scaled down his operations in late March, the *Stavka* withdrew some forces from his *front*, while the *front* commander shuffled other divisions among his armies as he began planning for his *front*'s summer offensive (see Table 21.3).

Table 21.3. The 1st Belorussian Front's Order of Battle on 1 April 1944

1st BELORUSSIAN FRONT: Army General K. K. Rokossovsky	
3rd Army: LTG A. V. Gorbatov	48th Army: LTG P. L. Romanenko
35th Rifle Corps: MG V. G. Zholudev	29th Rifle Corps: MG A. M. Andreev
250th Rifle Division	73rd Rifle Division
323rd Rifle Division	102nd Rifle Division
348th Rifle Division	217th Rifle Division
40th Rifle Corps: MG V. S. Kuznetsov	53rd Rifle Corps: MG I. A. Gartsev
129th Rifle Division	17th Rifle Division
169th Rifle Division	96th Rifle Division
41st Rifle Corps: MG V. K. Urbanovich	194th Rifle Division
120th Guards Rifle Division	231st Separate Tank Regiment
269th Rifle Division	1897th Self-propelled Artillery Regiment
80th Rifle Corps: MG I. L. Ragulia	39th Separate Armored Train Battalion
5th Rifle Division	
186th Rifle Division	65th Army: LTC P. I. Batov
283rd Rifle Division	18th Rifle Corps: MG I. I. Ivanov
115th Fortified Region	44th Guards Rifle Division
36th Separate Tank Regiment	69th Rifle Division
193rd Separate Tank Regiment	115th Rifle Brigade
1901st Self-propelled Artillery Regiment	95th Rifle Corps: MG I. A. Kuzovkov
49th Separate Aerosleigh Battalion	37th Guards Rifle Division
31st Separate Armored Train Battalion	75th Guards Rifle Division
55th Separate Armored Train Battalion	193rd Rifle Division
	105th Rifle Corps: MG D. F. Alekseev
10th Army: LTG V. S. Popov	354th Rifle Division
38th Rifle Corps: MG A. D. Tereshkov	161st Fortified Region
64th Rifle Division	251st Separate Tank Regiment
139th Rifle Division	
385th Rifle Division	
70th Rifle Corps: MG V. G. Teren'tev	
49th Rifle Division	
290th Rifle Division	
330th Rifle Division	
1st Separate Armored Train Battalion	
50th Army: LTG I. V. Boldin	
19th Rifle Corps: MG D. I. Samarsky	
238th Rifle Division	
307th Rifle Division	
362nd Rifle Division	
42nd Rifle Corps: LTG K. S. Kolganov	
137th Rifle Division	
170th Rifle Division	
369th Rifle Division	
399th Rifle Division	

Table 21.3. continued

46th Rifle Corps: MG K. M. Erastov
  82nd Rifle Division
  108th Rifle Division
  413th Rifle Division
121st Rifle Corps: MG D. I. Smirnov
  110th Rifle Division
  324th Rifle Division
  380th Rifle Division
119th Fortified Region
1st Guards Tank Corps: MGTF M. F. Panov
  15th Guards Tank Brigade
  16th Guards Tank Brigade
  17th Guards Tank Brigade
  1st Guards Motorized Rifle Brigade
  1001st Self-propelled Artillery Regiment
  1296th Self-propelled Artillery Regiment
  1444th Self-propelled Artillery Regiment
  1888th Self-propelled Artillery Regiment
  1st Guards Motorcycle Battalion
65th Motorcycle Battalion
732nd Tank Destroyer Artillery Regiment
455th Mortar Regiment
43rd Guards-Mortar Battalion
80th Guards Antiaircraft Artillery Regiment
233rd Separate Tank Regiment
8th Self-propelled Artillery Brigade
48th Separate Aerosleigh Battalion

Front Reserves:
42nd Separate Tank Regiment

Source: *Boevoi sostav Sovetskoi Armii, chast' IV (Ianvar'–dekabr' 1944)* [The combat composition of the Soviet Army, pt. 4 (January–December 1944)] (Moscow: Voenizdat, 1988), 101–102.

Prior to 1 April, the *Stavka* transferred 25th Rifle Corps from Romanenko's 48th Army to the 2nd Belorussian Front. Internally, Rokossovsky transferred 50th Army's 80th Rifle Corps to 3rd Army and 48th Army's 42nd Rifle Corps to 50th Army. Within days, however, the *Stavka* disbanded the 2nd Belorussian Front, largely because Stalin was displeased over its poor performance in its offensive in the Kovel' region, and distributed its forces to the 1st Belorussian and 1st Ukrainian Fronts (see Appendix Q-2).[10] Just short of two weeks later, the *Stavka* formally ended Rokossovsky's role in the winter campaign by permitting his forces to go over to the defense (see Appendix Q-3).[11]

CHAPTER 22

Investigations, Recriminations, and Sokolovsky's Relief

As this book makes clear, although the *Stavka's* hopes for clearing German forces from the eastern half of Belorussia were dashed by resolute German resistance, two of the three *fronts* participating in the Belorussian strategic offensive recorded important gains. First, in northern Belorussia, General Eremenko's Kalinin and, later, General Bagramian's Kalinin (1st Baltic Front on 20 October) captured Nevel' in October and in November drove a sizable wedge between German Army Groups North and Center, a gap that the Germans were unable to close. Thereafter, in heavy fighting throughout November and December, Bagramian's *front* drove southward and seized the city of Gorodok, in the process, shrinking Third Panzer Army's defenses around Vitebsk by more than 50 percent. Subsequently, during January and the first half of February 1944, the 1st Baltic Front, in cooperation with the right wing of Sokolovsky's Western Front, came within 35 kilometers of encircling Vitebsk and its German defenders entirely before the Soviets' offensive collapsed in utter exhaustion.

Likewise, in southern Belorussia, Rokossovsky's Central Front matched, if not exceeded, Bagramian's accomplishments. After pushing across the Snov and Desna Rivers in late September and absorbing half of the disbanded Briansk Front, Rokossovsky's *front*, renamed the Belorussian in late October, seized bridgeheads across the Dnepr River in October, expanded them by late October, drove westward to seize Rechitsa on the Berezina River in November, and advanced to the gates of Kalinkovichi in December. Then, despite enduring a short-lived setback inflicted by Ninth Army's XXXI Panzer Corps in late December, during the new year, Rokossovsky's armies crowned their previous exploits by seizing Kalinkovichi and Mozyr' in January and advancing to the Ptich' River and the approaches to Parichi in February. While doing so, the armies on the Belorussian Front's right wing succeeded in capturing the city of Rogachev and significantly eroded Army Group Center's large bridgehead on the Dnepr River's eastern bank.

General Sokolovsky's Western Front, however, proved to be the laggard among the three attacking *fronts* in terms of territory conquered. During the period from 12 October 1943 to 1 April 1944, Sokolovsky's armies struck the defenses of Army Group Center on no fewer than eleven separate occasions. These included six offensives against the Orsha sector of the army group's Fourth Army (twice in October of 1943, twice in December of 1943, once in

February of 1944, and once in March of 1944) and five against the Vitebsk and Bogushevsk sector of the army group's Third Panzer Army (at Vitebsk once in December of 1943 and twice in February of 1944 and at Bogushevsk in January and March of 1944). In terms of its gains on the ground, the Western Front advanced 7 to 13.5 kilometers in twenty-seven days of fighting at Orsha, 11 to 20 kilometers in thirty-four days of fighting at Vitebsk, and 3 to 7.5 kilometers in twenty-five days of struggle at Bogushevsk for a total net gain of 21 to 41 kilometers in eighty-six days of combat. Expressed mathematically, during this period, Sokolovsky's forces averaged advances of well under .5 kilometer per day (.25 to .5 kilometers per day). The human cost of these offensives amounted to a total of 281,745 casualties, including 62,326 killed and 219,419 wounded, in eighty-six days of fighting. Once again expressed mathematically, it cost the Western Front well over 3,500 casualties for every 500 meters of ground it advanced. Even for a Red Army used to horrendous losses, this was a price far too steep to pay.

In light of the Western Front's failure to fulfill any of the missions the *Stavka* assigned it during the winter campaign, the *Stavka* dispatched a special commission to the Western Front in early April 1944 to determine the reasons for its repeated failures. Chaired by G. M. Malenkov, Stalin's close colleague and a member of the State Defense Committee, the commission also included Colonel General A. S. Shcherbakov, chief of the Red Army's Main Political Directorate; Colonel General S. M. Shtemenko, chief of the Red Army General Staff's Operations Directorate; Lieutenant General F. F. Kuznetsov, deputy chief of the General Staff for Intelligence; and representatives of various key branches and services of the Red Army. Interestingly enough, Army General Makhmut Gareev, who was serving as a midgrade officer in 33rd Army's 36th Rifle Brigade at that time, is convinced that the *Stavka* had already reached certain conclusions as to why the offensives had failed and sent the commission only to determine the guilt of those senior officers involved. Gareev recalled:

> The *Stavka* VGK had already reached definite conclusions about the conduct of these operations ahead of time. The commission was dispatched with instructions already prepared by I. V. Stalin. The commission's work was directed mainly as a search for the guilty and not to investigate the real reasons for the lack of success. Therefore, one cannot speak about an objective analysis of the causes of the defeat of the offensive operations. In particular, the commission did not try to clarify to what extent the missions assigned to the Western Front by the *Stavka* were realistic and to what degree they were supported by all that was necessary.
>
> As regards the study of the state of [the] matter in the forces, in essence, the members of the commission were not specialists capable of investigating organizational matters and the conduct of military operations.

One cannot speak about the competence of G. M. Malenkov and A. S. Shcherbakov, the chief of the GlavPu [Main Political Directorate], in matters of military art. General S. M. Shtemenko was a very capable General Staff officer, but he had never occupied himself personally with the practical organization of actions and military operations. The remaining officers on the commission had insufficient professional training. For example, one of the commission members arrived at 36th Separate Rifle Brigade's command post in early April 1944. His questions amounted to the following: "How many tanks does a German panzer division have according to its establishment [TO&E]?" "What are the tactical-technical characteristics of German aircraft and our own?" and so forth. These were far from those problems we were working to resolve.

We also could not present a planning table for the battle that he [the commission member] demanded since this document could be worked out only ahead of time, and our brigade [in 33rd Army] fulfilled a new combat mission practically every day.[1]

Thus, in essence, Gareev described Stalin's special commission as a virtual "kangaroo court" which arrived at the Western Front's headquarters with its conclusions already in hand, prepared to do Stalin's bidding. Within this context, although Gareev viewed the commission's recommendations with justifiable skepticism, he caustically revealed its real intent:

I managed to familiarize myself with the report of the commission, which worked in the Western Front, many years after the war ended. The report noted many serious deficiencies in the activities of the headquarters and staffs of the *front* and armies (particularly 33rd Army), which were associated with the organization of reconnaissance and force operations in regard to the penetration of a defense, the means of constructing combat formations and conducting an offensive, the combat employment of tanks and artillery, and so forth. While reading the commission's report, I recalled how, at the CP of 45th Rifle Corps before the beginning of the Belorussia operation of June 1944, Lieutenant General N. I. Krylov, the commander of 5th Army, gave an analysis of the readiness of their formations for the offensive as verified by them. He basically enumerated the very same deficiencies that were indicated in the commission's report to the *Stavka* VGK, although, as a result, the Belorussian operation achieved complete success (including the sector of 5th Army).

What then explains the circumstance that, after the Western Front failed, in essence, to make any advance during the course of the winter campaign, after becoming the 3rd Belorussian Front under the command of General I. D. Cherniakhovsky, within two months (in June 1944) it conducted a brilliant offensive operation and advanced to a depth of 500–600 kilometers? The more so as the *Stavka's* order of 12 April 1944 relieved from their duties only Army General V. D. Sokolovsky, the *front* commander; Colonel General I. P. Kamera, the artillery commander; and Colonel Ia. T. Il'nitsky, the chief of the reconnaissance department of the *front's* headquarters. The remaining officials, including Lieutenant General A. P. Pokrovsky, the *front's* chief of staff, and the majority of the formation and unit commanders remained in their places. General V. N. Gordov was appointed as the commander of the 1st Ukrainian Front's 3rd Guards Army. Lieutenant General N. A. Bulganin was given a reprimand, which said that he, "while serving as the member of the Western Front's military council for a long time, did not report to the *Stavka* about the presence of great deficiencies in the *front*." At the same time, analogous pretenses were brought forward against L. Z. Mekhlis. Evidently, in the *Stavka's* opinion, members of the military councils of *fronts* and armies were accused neither of negligence in the training of their personnel, nor for low morale among their troops, nor for the failures of operations, nor for even large losses but instead for the tardiness of the denunciations, which was considered their main function.[2]

What then did the commission's report have to say about the Western Front's role and performance in the Belorussian offensive as a whole? Because it is the only official document to have been released about the offensive, the *Stavka's* order and critique is worth quoting in its entirety:

Attachment No. 1 to State Defense Committee Decree GOKO-5606s
The Kremlin, Moscow, 12 April 1944

Regarding Deficiencies in the Work of the
Western Front's Command and Staff

The 11 April report of the commission consisting of GKO member Comrade Malenkov (chairman), Colonel General Comrade Shcherbakov, Colonel General Comrade Shtemenko, Lieutenant General Comrade Kuznetsov, and Lieutenant General Comrade Shimonaev concerning the deficiencies in the work of the Western Front's command and staff is approved, and both the commission's general and organizational conclusions are affirmed (see the attached commission report).
   The State Defense Committee
True copy
   Colonel Denisov, Chief of the General Staff's Archives
"—" January 1957.
Archives of the Central Committee, CPSU, d. No. 2–144 g.,1. 86.
General Staff Archives, f. 96, op. 2011ss, d. 35

No. 2
True copy
Top Secret
Copy No. 1

Stavka VGK Order No. 220076

12 April 1944

On the basis of GOKO decree No. 5606ss, dated 12 April 1944, concerning the work of the Western Front's command and staff, the *Stavka* VGK orders:

I.

1. Relieve Army General Sokolovsky from his duties as commander of the Western Front for not being able to cope with *front* command and appoint him as chief of staff of the 1st Ukrainian Front.

2. Reprimand Lieutenant General Bulganin because, while serving as the member of the Western Front's Military Council for a long time, he failed to report to the *Stavka* about the presence of great deficiencies in the *front*.

3. Warn Lieutenant General Pokrovsky, the chief of staff of the Western Front, that he will be reduced in rank and duties if he does not correct his mistakes.

4. Relieve Colonel General of Artillery Kamera from his duties as commander of artillery of the Western Front and place him at the disposal of the commander of Red Army artillery.

5. Relieve Colonel Il'nitsky from his duties as chief of the Intelligence Department of the Western Front's staff, reduce him to the rank of lieutenant colonel, and appoint him to other work commensurate with his rank.

6. Warn Colonel General Gordov, who has been relieved from command of 33rd Army, that, if he repeats the mistakes he permitted in 33rd Army, he will be reduced in rank and duties.

II.

1. Divide the Western Front as it presently exists into two *fronts:* the 2nd Belorussian Front consisting of 31st, 49th, and 50th Armies and the 3rd Belorussian Front consisting of 39th, 33rd, and 5th Armies.

Form the headquarters of the 2nd Belorussian Front on the basis of 10th Army's headquarters. Complete the formation and acceptance of forces designated for the *front* no later than 25 April.

2. Rename the present Belorussian Front the 1st Belorussian Front.

3. Appoint Colonel General Petrov as the commander of the 2nd Belorussian Front and free him from command of 33rd Army. Appoint Lieutenant General Mekhlis as the member of the 2nd Belorussian Front's Military Council and Lieutenant General Bogoliubov as the chief of staff and free him from his duties as chief of staff of the 1st Ukrainian Front.

4. Appoint Colonel General Cherniakhovsky as the commander of the 3rd Belorussian Front and free him from command of 60th Army. Appoint Major General Makarov as the member of the 3rd Belorussian Front's military council and free him from his duties as chief of the Western Front's political directorate and Lieutenant General Pokrovsky as chief of staff and free him from his duties as chief of staff of the Western Front.

5. Appoint Lieutenant General Kriuchenkin as commander of 33rd Army, freeing him from command of 69th Army.

6. Carry out the formation of the two *fronts* and the distribution of the Western Front's divisions, reinforcing units, aviation, and rear service units, facilities, and equipment between the two *fronts* under the control of the *Stavka* representative, Colonel General Shtemenko.

The *Stavka* VGK
I. Stalin
A. Antonov
12 April 1944 g.
No. 220076
"—" January 1957
Archives of the Central Committee, CPSU, d. No. 2–44 g.,1. 83–85.

No. 3

True copy
Copy No. 1

To Comrade Stalin

By order of the *Stavka* VGK, an Extraordinary Commission consisting of GOKO member Comrade Malenkov (chairman), Colonel General Comrade Shcherbakov, Colonel General Comrade Shtemenko, Lieutenant General Comrade Kuznetsov, and Lieutenant General Comrade Shimonaev investigated the work of the Western Front's headquarters and, on the basis of that inspection, determined the following:

I.
The Unsatisfactory Combat Operations of the Western Front for the Last Half Year

Beginning from 12 October 1943 through 1 April 1944, the Western Front, under the command of Army General Sokolovsky, conducted 11 operations along the Orsha and Vitebsk axis, namely:

The Orsha operation, 12–18 October 1943
The Orsha operation, 21–26 October 1943
The Orsha operation, 14–19 November 1943
The Orsha operation, 30 November–2 December 1943
The Vitebsk operation, 23 December 1943–6 January 1944
The Bogushevsk operation 8–24 January 1944

The Vitebsk operation, 3–16 February 1944
Local operations along the Orsha axis, 22–25 February 1944
The Vitebsk operation, 5–9 March 1944
The Bogushevsk operation, 21–29 March 1944

All of these operations ended unsuccessfully, and the *front* did not fulfill the missions assigned to it by the *Stavka*. The *front* penetrated the enemy's defenses in not one of these offensives and not even to its tactical depth, and, in the best instance, the operations finished at best with insignificant lodgments [literally, "wedging into"] the enemy's defenses, with great losses to our forces.

The 12–18 October offensive along the Orsha axis ended with a lodgment of 1–1.5 kilometers. Our losses were 5,858 men killed and 17,478 men wounded, for a total of *23,336 men*.

The 21–26 October offensive along the Orsha axis advanced from 4 to 6 kilometers. Our losses were 4,787 men killed and 14,315 men wounded, for a total of *19,102 men*.

The 14–19 November offensive along the Orsha axis advanced from 1 to 4 kilometers. Our losses were 9,167 men killed and 29,589 men wounded, for a total of *38,756 men*.

The 30 November–2 December offensive along the Orsha axis ended with a lodgment of 1–2 kilometers. Our losses were 5,611 men killed and 17,259 men wounded, for a total of *22,870 men*.

The 23 December–6 January offensive along the Vitebsk axis advanced 8–12 kilometers. The enemy withdrew to previous prepared lines. Our losses were 6,692 men killed and 28,904 men wounded, for a total of *35,596 men*.

The 8–24 January offensive along the Bogushevsk axis ended with a lodgment of 2–4 kilometers. Our losses were 5,517 men killed and 19,672 men wounded, for a total of *25,189 men*.

The 3–16 February offensive along the Vitebsk axis advanced 3–4 kilometers. Our losses were 9,651 men killed and 32,844 men wounded, for a total of *42,495 men*.

The 22–25 February local operation along the Orsha axis achieved no results at all. During this operation, units of 52nd Fortified Region were themselves encircled, and their initial positions were restored with great losses. Our losses were 1,288 men killed and 4,479 men wounded, for a total of *5,767 men*.

The 29 February–5 March offensive along the Vitebsk axis advanced from 2 to 6 kilometers. Our losses were 2,650 men killed and 9,205 men wounded, for a total of *11,855 men*.

The 5–9 March offensive along the Vitebsk axis had no success. Our losses were 1,898 men killed and 5,639 men wounded, for a total of *7,537 men*.

The 21–29 March offensive along the Bogushevsk axis ended with a lodgment of 1–3.5 kilometers. Our losses were 9,207 men killed and 30,828 men wounded, for a total of *40,035 men.*

During these operations in the period from 12 October 1943 until 1 April 1944, which achieved no results, the *front* suffered losses of 62,326 men killed and 219,419 men wounded, for a total of *281,745 men,* just in the sectors of active operations. If we add the losses in passive sectors of the front, then, during the period from October 1943 through April 1944, the Western Front lost *330,587 men.* In addition, during this period, 53,283 sick men from the Western Front were hospitalized.

As indicated above, during the operations from October 1943 through April 1944, the Western Front expended a very great quantity of ammunition, namely 7,261 wagonloads. During the year from March 1943 through March 1944, the *front* expended 16,661 wagonloads of ammunition. During this same period, that is, for a year, the Belorussian Front expended 12,335 wagonloads, the 1st Ukrainian Front, 10,945 wagonloads, and the 4th Ukrainian Front, 8,463 wagonloads, and each of the remaining *fronts* expended less ammunition than the enumerated *fronts.* Thus, the Western Front expended far more ammunition than any other *front.*

The Western Front's unsuccessful operations over the past half year and the great losses and heavy expenditure of ammunition is explained by exceptionally unsatisfactory leadership on the part of the *front* command rather than by the presence of a strong enemy and the insurmountable defense which the *front* faced. During the conduct of all of these operations, the Western Front always had a considerable superiority over the enemy in forces and weaponry, absolutely permitting it to count on success.

The correlation in forces by individual operation was as follows: [the *Stavka's* assessment of the correlation of opposing forces for each operation is at the beginning of all chapters detailing the Western Front's offensive operations].

Thus, the Western Front possessed a clear superiority over the enemy in forces and weapons in all of the conducted operations. In spite of this, all of the operations ended unsuccessfully, and from October onward the *front* did not advance forward.

The stagnant situation in the Western Front and the advance of the neighboring *fronts* resulted in the creation of an extremely unfavorable front-line trace along the Smolensk-Minsk axis. In this sector, the enemy held a 150-kilometer-deep salient into our dispositions.

Such a situation had an unfavorable influence on the neighboring *fronts* and granted the enemy the opportunity to base his aircraft in the Lepel', Mogilev, and Minsk triangle and operate with them along interior lines against the rear area of the Baltic and Belorussian Fronts. From the standpoint of the Western Front, the enemy was located closest of all to Moscow.

II.
Serious Deficiencies in the Work of Artillery

During the conducted operations, in spite of its concentration in great quantities and its superiority over the enemy, our artillery did not neutralize the enemy's firing means either during the period of the artillery preparation or in the process of battle. Frequently the artillery fired on empty spaces, did not fulfill the requirements of the infantry, and lost cooperation with it, and sometimes it even conducted fire on its own infantry. The infantry went on the attack against an unsuppressed enemy firing system, suffered huge losses, and did not advance forward. During all periods of the battle, the firing activities of our artillery, and particularly counter-battery, did not respond to the demands required of it.

There were repeated instances in 33rd, 31st, and 5th Armies when the artillery conducted fire according to region (quadrant) provided by the army's artillery headquarters when, in actuality, there were no targets in these quadrants, and the artillery fired on empty spaces, and enemy firing points from other regions fired on our infantry.

On 23 December 1945 [should read 1943], during 33rd Army's operation, there were private soldiers but no officers at the observation posts of some artillery regiments. Nor were there observers everywhere in the first echelon of the infantry. As a result, its own artillery fired on 199th Rifle Division. In this artillery, this led to direct fire guns firing on their own infantry.

During 33rd Army's offensive on 3 February, in a number of divisions, cooperation was not organized between the artillery and the infantry. Thus, for example, 144th Rifle Division attacked Pavliuchenko, and its supporting artillery conducted its fire west of Pavliuchenko. At this same time, during 222nd Rifle Division's attack, its supporting artillery was silent.

Many debriefings of German prisoners testify to the unsatisfactory work of the Western Front's artillery.

The commander of the Western Front, Army General Comrade Sokolovsky, the former member of the *front*'s Military Council, Lieutenant General Comrade Bulganin, and the commander of the Western Front's artillery, Colonel General of Artillery Comrade Kamera, are guilty in that they did not detect the serious deficiencies and mistakes in the work of artillery. Complacency, arrogance, and conceit prevail among the artillerymen. The artillerymen have neither discovered nor learned from their mistakes and deficiencies and are trying to cover them up. Until recently, the *front* and armies have not issued orders on the deficiencies in the artillery's actions and have not ordered measures for the elimination of them. As a result of such an improper attitude of the *front* command to the matter of directing the artillery, they repeated these stupid mistakes and deficiencies in artillery operations in each of the operations.

During the preparatory periods for the operations, *artillerymen at all levels reconnoitered targets exceptionally poorly* and did not detect the enemy's firing system. As a consequence of this ignorance of targets, the artillery could not conduct aimed fire against concrete targets and, as a rule, conducted area fire with little effectiveness. In this same period, the artillerymen employed their reconnaissance organs slowly, and reconnaissance conducted passive observation, seldom employing mobile observation posts and those moved to the forward edge of the enemy's defenses. The senior artillery commanders and their staffs conducted practically no reconnaissance personally, and their function in that most important matter was limited to the assembly and fixation on information from lower level and less-qualified sources, and they did not check this information. Reconnaissance was conducted especially poorly during the time of the infantry attacks. Reconnaissance organs did not allocate concrete reconnaissance belts and sectors, and, therefore, the attentions of scouts were dispersed across the entire field, and they occupied themselves with aimless observation of the battle maps and not with a search for the enemy's firing points. In many artillery units, the reconnaissance subunits were at less than full strength, while noncombat subunits were at full strength. Aircraft were employed poorly for the purposes of reconnaissance and correcting fires, and aerostatic observation was not used at all.

As a rule, artillery fire was planned in the higher headquarters without consideration of concrete information about the enemy's firing systems, and, as a result, it was planned on areas rather than targets. The execution of firing missions on the ground was very seldom employed. In many instances, battery and battalion commanders received firing schemes (charts) that did not correspond to the actual position of the targets. Such planning and assignment of missions to those executing them led to firing on empty spaces and, furthermore, did not provide for the suppression of enemy firing points. During the preparatory periods for the operations, the higher artillery headquarters spent a large part of the time allocated for the preparations for their planning work. As a result, almost no time, especially daylight, remained for the lower artillery levels to work out their missions on the ground and organize cooperation.

The artillery preparation was conducted stereotypically [according to pattern]. The beginning of the artillery preparation revealed itself with a volley of multiple-rocket launchers, then the destruction period was conducted, and at the end—an artillery raid on the forward edge. The enemy became accustomed to this stereotype, and, knowing the order of fire, skillfully kept his personnel safe in protected positions. As a result, during the period of the artillery preparations, as a rule, our artillery conducted area fire and did not suppress the enemy's firing system, and our infantry encountered organized enemy fire of all types, suffered great losses, and, in many instances, could not advance forward from the very beginning.

Artillery fire accompanying the infantry was poorly organized from the very beginning of the offensives. As a rule, during this period, communication and cooperation was lost between the infantry and the artillery and mortars. The objectives detected and disrupted by our infantry were not completely suppressed or were suppressed too late. During the forward advance of the infantry, the extraordinary centralization of the artillery in the hands of the commanders of rifle divisions and higher deprived the battalion commanders of the means for suppression and opportunities for reacting to the situation. Mortar crews were especially poorly trained, and, in a number of instances, they simply avoided communication with the infantry and lingered in the rear. As a result, the mortars fought wherever they happened to be located. Although the radio stations in the *front* were sufficient to support the attacking forces, the radio stations at lower levels were few in number and inadequate for support. In spite of their presence in the infantry's combat formations, direct fire weapons were employed poorly and clumsily. The subordination of these guns was undefined, and they frequently lacked concrete targets. Direct fire guns often lagged behind the infantry, and, as a result, they sometimes fired on their own troops. The self-propelled guns were used clumsily and did not achieve the required effects. The struggle with enemy self-propelled artillery was neither organized nor at all planned. Fire direction in this dynamic combat was carried out weakly. As a result of the ignorance of the targets, the senior chief was powerless to determine his subordinates' firing missions. As a rule, the artillery staffs were located a great distance from the observation posts and, consequently, were excluded from the direction of artillery fire.

The counter-battery and counter-mortar struggle with the enemy's artillery and mortars was organized particularly poorly both during the artillery preparations and during the accompaniment of the infantry forward. Our counter-battery and counter-mortar groups did not suppress the enemy's artillery and mortars, and, as a result, the advance of the infantry was held up by strong enemy artillery and mortar fire, and they suffered heavy losses, as is witnessed by the fact that, in several operations, the percent of those wounded by shell fragments reached 70–80 percent. Because of a poor knowledge of the targets and the absence of fire correction, the fire from the counter-battery artillery group was of little effectiveness. The long-range action artillery habitually conducted area fire, fired poorly on the signs of explosions, and was not able to shift fires rapidly and exactly. The counter-mortar groups were not able to suppress the enemy's mortar batteries and fired poorly and inaccurately.

Control over the fulfillment of firing missions was almost never realized. The executors of the fire were never asked about the results of the fire, and they were given responsibility only for the timely commencement of the fire. The irresponsibility of the artillery officer cadre gave rise to such a situation.

III.
Deficiencies in Planning and Preparing the Operations

During the planning of the operation, there were instances of the incorrect grouping of forces, which *Stavka* directive No. 30225, dated 15 October 1943, pointed out to the *front* command. This directive stated:

> "The Western Front did not fulfill its assigned mission—to capture Orsha by 15 October 1943—and conducted prolonged and futile combat, which led to a loss of time, forces, and weaponry. This occurred as a consequence of the incorrect grouping of the *front's* forces.
>
> The main grouping, up to half of all of the *front's* rifle divisions, with the major portion of reinforcing weaponry, was created in the *front's* center.
>
> In the event of its successful advance, this grouping came up against the Dnepr River, and, thus, further development of the offensive was limited. At the same time, the right wing of the *front* could attack without forcing the Dnepr River and had an opportunity to clean out the Dnepr by means of an attack against the flank and rear of enemy forces that were defending along the Dnepr."

In spite of the accumulated war experiences, in several operations the Western Front command organized penetrations *in very narrow sectors:* in a 6-kilometer-wide front during the 23 December Vitebsk operation, and in a 5-kilometer-wide front in the 5 March Orsha operation. This permitted the enemy to concentrate destructive flanking fires and, in conjunction with counterattacks by small reserves, excluded the possibility of our infantry from advancing and inflicted heavy losses in them.

The *front* staff was pushed aside from planning the operations and fixed only the course of events, which developed in accordance with the armies' plans. The *front* staff had no operational planning documents on the conduct of the operations at all. All of the conducted operations were planned only in the armies and were verbally approved by the *front* command. As a result, the *front* headquarters did not introduce its proposals to the command on the planning and conduct of the operations and did not exercise reliable control over the realization of the command's decisions.

As far as the preparation of the operations was concerned, there were severe deficiencies here, which adversely influenced the outcome of the operations.

The regrouping of the forces and preparation of the operations was conducted *without the required secrecy* and misinformation of the enemy, and, as a result, surprise was lost in almost all of the operations, and the operations proceeded in circumstances when the enemy was able to meet our offensive, although the *front* did not issue any kind of documents formally and supposedly maintained all of them in the strictest of secrecy.

In several of the operations, the *rifle divisions and reinforcements were committed into battle from the march*. During 5th Army's operations from 22 to 25 February, 184th Rifle Division turned its defensive sector over to 158th Rifle Division on the night of 21 February, arrived in its jumping-off position for the offensive by the morning of 22 February, went over to the attack at 0800 that day after a 10-minute artillery raid, and certainly had no success. During 33rd Army's operations from 3–16 February, 222nd, 164th, 144th, and 215th Rifle Divisions received 1,500 replacements each on the eve of the offensive and went over to the attack the next morning. The officer cadre, who arrived as replacements, took over their subunits in their jumping-off positions and, after several hours, led them in the offensive.

During the preparation of the operations, the higher headquarters took the greatest portion of the time for their work spent on preparations and for the conduct of commanders' personal reconnaissance [*rekognosirovki*], and almost no time remained for lower levels to work out missions on the ground and to organize cooperation.

IV.
Concerning the Incorrect Construction of Combat Formations for the Offensive

In a majority of the operations conducted by the *front*, the armies, in particular, 33rd Army, attacked by deeply echeloning their combat formations and created excessive densities of personnel, thereby violating *Stavka* Order No. 306. These sorts of combat formations led to divisions attacking with 2–3 battalions, while the remaining battalions stood to the rear. In these conditions, the shock group of the divisions was employed in dispersed fashion, unit by unit, rather than simultaneously, and the fire weapons were rendered ineffective. All of this led to great losses even before the forces entered battle, and, by suffering such losses while subjected to constant enemy fire, the units lost their combat effectiveness even before the battle.

V.
Concerning Deficiencies in the Employment of Tanks

As is well known, war experience demonstrates that large tank formations must be used to exploit success after the penetration of the enemy's main defensive belt. Despite this war experience and the *Stavka*'s orders regarding the employment of tank formations, the Western Front command threw 2nd Guards Tatsinskaia Tank Corps against an undisrupted enemy defense, and, as a result, the tank corps was unable to move forward and suffered heavy losses. In the operation along the Orsha axis from 14–19 November, the tank corps was committed into combat at a time when the infantry had wedged into the defense to a depth of barely 2–3 kilometers along a 3-kilometer-wide front. In 33rd Army's operation along the Vitebsk axis on 23 December, the commitment of the tank corps was planned for after the infantry captured the Luchesa River (18 kilometers into the depth of the defense). On that basis, with the infantry advancing to a depth of 8–10 kilometers during the first three days of the offensive, the tank corps was not committed. However, when the infantry was stopped by organized enemy fire from previously prepared positions and the Luchesa [River] continued to remain ahead, the tank corps was thrown into battle and, after failing to achieve success and losing 60 tanks, was withdrawn behind the combat formations of the infantry. In the operation along the Bogushevsk axis on 8 January, the tank corps was committed into combat when, in essence, the infantry had no success whatsoever. Suffering up to 70 percent losses, the tank corps advanced 2–4 kilometers together with the infantry and after this was withdrawn from combat.

Therefore, the *front* command's constant desire to achieve a penetration of the defense by the immediate premature commitment of the tank corps into combat did not produce the desired results and led to the fact that, at present, two tanks remain in the tank corps.

In all of these battles, exceptionally heavy losses were observed in the tank brigades that were operating in immediate support of the infantry. The main reason for these losses was that our artillery fire did not suppress the enemy's antitank weapons and the absence of cooperation between tanks, supporting artillery, and infantry.

VI.
Concerning the *Front*'s Staff

The Western Front's staff did not perform its role. The staff is aloof and torn away from the *front* command and from vital missions resolved by its forces and, in essence, is some sort of statistical bureau, which only gathers information on the situation, and even this is late. Matters of planning operations, organizing battle, and controlling the commander's decision on matters has been stripped from the staff's functions. During the course of 4 months, the chief of staff and the entire staff were located a distance of about 100 kilometers from the location of the *front* commander, and, during this time, the commander and the chief of staff met one another no more than 3–4 times. One colonel, who, in essence, fulfills the responsibilities of an adjutant, is located with the commander at the Alternate Command Post (although, in this instance, his name is not appropriate). The *front* commander, Comrade Sokolovsky, considered such a really unusual situation to be normal.

Not only the *front* commander was reduced to such a situation, but also the chief of staff, Lieutenant General Pokrovsky, who struggles with responsibilities and cannot make decisions independently on even minor matters, is guilty of this. Pokrovsky did not undertake any measure at all to remedy the abnormal situation with the staff and worked formally and bureaucratically. The chief of the operational department, Major General Chirkov, works without taking the initiative and is not suited for the role of leading the *front's* Operations Department.

VII.
Regarding the State of Intelligence [*Razvedka*]

Intelligence in the Western Front is conducted completely unsatisfactorily. The information obtained by it is frequently unreliable. The Intelligence Department of the *front's* staff does not reliably supervise the armies', corps', and divisions' intelligence organs and spoiled [literally "messed up"] agent intelligence. The chief of the Intelligence Department, Colonel Il'nitsky, passes out doubtful and exaggerated information about the enemy as truthful.

Force reconnaissance is not organized and is conducted in unplanned fashion. Reconnaissance operations are poorly prepared and conducted. With heavy losses of scouts averaging up to 5 men for each captured prisoner, force reconnaissance does not procure information needed by the command.

Reconnaissance-in-force is conducted pointlessly and without careful preparation and organization, and often is not provided with fire support, and, as a result, the greater part of all of the *front's* reconnaissance actions is completed unsuccessfully and with heavy losses.

There are serious deficiencies in the preparation and conduct of reconnaissance raiding operations, especially in the enemy's rear area. In many instances, the main mission of the raids—the seizure of controlled [live] prisoners—is not fulfilled. Thus, in December 192nd Rifle Division conducted 23 reconnaissance operations to seize a "tongue" [*iazyk*]. Not a single prisoner was seized in these operations, and the losses of our reconnaissance groups amounted to 26 men killed or wounded. From 1 January through 15 February, 192nd, 247th, and 174th Rifle Divisions conducted hundreds of reconnaissance raiding operations and seized not a single prisoner. In 331st and 251st Rifle Divisions, the scouts were repeatedly blown up in their own minefields because they were not shown where they were located.

The observation services in the *front* are organized formally. No one supervises this type of reconnaissance, and observation is conducted by untrained people and frequently turns into a perfunctory survey of the terrain, while concrete observation of the enemy is absent.

The Western Front is systematically violating the *Stavka's* order that prohibits the employment of reconnaissance subunits in combat as routine infantry. Thus, during January 1944 in 33rd Army, all of the reconnaissance subunits of its divisions and units participated in the offensive as line subunits and were almost completely destroyed.

There are especially serious deficiencies in agent intelligence. Agent intelligence in the Western Front is littered with dubious people and is conducted primitively and stereotypically. The information obtained by this form of intelligence is frequently unconfirmed and is often a source of disinformation.

The recruiting of agents is not conducted individually and is without sufficient verification. Agents are often acquired in groups from persons who have not been checked and are inexperienced. Often there are people among the agents who are politically questionable and unreliable and are "turned" [rerecruited] by the Germans immediately after their deployment.

The preparation of agents goes on in disorganized fashion and carelessly and without necessary training. Having received insufficient training, many agents quickly disappear. The elementary rules of conspiracy are violated. Large groups of agents associate with one another and know each other well. Thus, the reconnaissance groups of Khristoforov, Iurchenko, Kalibolotsky, and Sitnikov, which were designated for work in various regions of the enemy's rear area and which totaled 28 men, were accommodated together in one location during the course of all of their training. The equipment of the agents dispatched into the enemy's rear area was frequently standard and permitted easy discovery of our agents. During 1942 and 1943, agents were sent into territory occupied by the Germans in 1941 who were dressed in clothing with markings indicating its production in Moscow during 1942 and 1943. In this instance, one agent fell [into enemy hands], and the standard nature of their clothing easily permitted the discovery of our other agents.

The *front's* intelligence department did not strive to infiltrate its agents into the enemy's headquarters and military facilities. Agent work evolved along the lines of least resistance and was limited to simple observation and the gathering of rumors among the civilian population. The communications of the Intelligence Department, with its agents working in the enemy rear, is in a very bad state. Many agents stopped sending reports solely because there were no parts for their radio stations. While it possessed every opportunity to supply the agents parts for the radios, the Intelligence Department treated that important matter negligently and irresponsibly.

Although *aviation [air] reconnaissance* was formally conducted, the information obtained from aviation was not processed immediately, was not verified by other sources, and frequently was not provided to the forces. Aerial photograph maps and photo plans were held in the higher headquarters and not sent to the forces immediately.

In spite of the large quantity of radios, *radio reconnaissance* was conducted poorly and very often provided absolutely incorrect data and misled our headquarters.

The Intelligence Department of the Western Front's headquarters is not able to cope with the missions assigned to it. Such features as the underestimation of the enemy's forces, the lack of planning in intelligence, isolation from the forces, and the inability to provide necessary information in timely fashion and distinguish the false from the true characterize the work of the Intelligence Department of the Western Front's headquarters.

With the connivance of the *front* command and the *front* chief of staff, the chief of the Intelligence Department, Colonel Il'nitsky, systematically exaggerated the quantity and strength of the enemy's divisions in front of the Western Front.

VIII.
Concerning the Situation in 33rd Army during the Period of Colonel General Gordov's Command

The 33rd Army played a central role in many of the Western Front's operations, significant reinforcements were attached to it, and the *front* command devoted great attention to the army and considered the army commander, Gordov, to be the best army commander.

However, the facts demonstrated otherwise. Nowhere was combat organized as poorly as in Gordov's army. Instead of careful preparation of the operations and instead of the correct employment of artillery, Gordov strove to smash the enemy's defenses with manpower. The losses the army suffered bear witness to this fact. The overall losses suffered by 33rd Army constituted over 50 percent of the *front*'s entire losses.

Despite the *Stavka*'s orders, which prohibited the use of specialized subunits as routine infantry in combat, Gordov frequently committed scouts, chemical specialists, and sappers [engineers] into combat. Among the most serious crimes of Gordov, one must refer to the facts when Gordov sent the entire officer cadre of the divisions and corps into the line.

In his order dated 4 September 1943, which was addressed to the commander of 173rd Rifle Division, Colonel Zaitsev, and the commanders of its regiments, Lieutenant Colonel Milovanov, Lieutenant Colonel Sizov, and Major Guslitser, Gordov demanded, "Place all of the officers cadre in the combat formations and pass through the forest in line after designating small detachments to drive the automatic weapons men from their nests."

Gordov wrote further in the order, "Today, it will be better for us to die than not to fulfill the mission." On 4 September 1943, Gordov ordered the chief of staff of 70th Rifle Corps, Major General Ikonnikov, "To send all of the corps' command and control into the line immediately. Leave only the chief of the Operations Department in the headquarters."

Such intolerable actions by Gordov led to the disorganization of command and control of the battle and in unforgivable losses in officer cadre. Over the past six months, under the command of Gordov, there were 4 division commanders, 8 deputy division commanders and divisional chiefs of staff, 38 regimental commanders and their deputies, and 174 battalion commanders killed or wounded in 33rd Army.

Gordov criminally violated the *Stavka's* order prohibiting the execution of commanders by shooting without trial and investigation. Thus, on Gordov's order and without trial and investigation, on 6 March Major Trofimov was shot, supposedly for evasion of combat. Actually, as an investigation determined, Major Trofimov was not guilty.

Command and control on Gordov's part during military operations was reduced to abuse [swearing] and insult. Gordov often resorted to threats of shooting in his relations with his subordinates. This was the case in his relations with the commander of 277th Rifle Division, Major General Gladyshev, and the commander of 45th Rifle Corps, Major General Poplavsky. According to the statements of a number of commanders who worked with Gordov, his inhumane treatment of his people and his continuous hysterics harassed them so much that there were instances when commanders could not command their formations and units.

The *front* command passed by all of these disgraceful things in Gordov's actions, did not correct him, and continued to consider him the best army commander.

IX.
About the *Front* Command

The chief reason for the unsuccessful operations in the Western Front is the unsatisfactory leadership of the forces on the part of the *front* command.

Instead of learning from its mistakes and eliminating them, the Western Front command displayed willfulness and conceit, did not reveal the deficiencies, did not consider its mistakes, did not teach its people, and did not educate its cadre of commanders in the spirit of truthfulness. It repeated the most serious deficiencies and mistakes in all of its operations. The reason for this is *the intolerable fact that it was not the practice in the Western Front to critique operations and issue summary orders concerning deficiencies and the results of combat operations.*

Despite the fact that one of the most serious deficiencies during the conduct of operations was the poor work of the artillery, this deficiency was not eliminated and was continually repeated. In all operations conducted by the Western Front, the artillery failed to suppress the enemy's firing system and, as a result, did not protect the infantry. The *front* command knew about the heavy losses in personnel that resulted from the artillery's poor work and about the huge expenditure of ammunition; however, it did not undertake measures to improve the work of artillery.

The *front* command does not tolerate criticism, and attempts to criticize deficiencies are adamantly opposed. The instructions of Army General Sokolovsky on a report of a General Staff officer, which highlights deficiencies in the preparation and direction of operations conducted by 31st Army on 29 October 1943, are characteristic of this relationship. The instructions were as follows:

> "The value of the document is utterly worthless, even on a good bazaar [market] day."
>
> "Apparently, Lieutenant Colonel Nekrasov did not think about what he wrote. Apparently, the man has the habit of always jabbering."
>
> "Nonsense!"
>
> "Stupid nonsense."
>
> "Lies."
>
> "The writer completely misunderstands combat to penetrate a defense."
>
> "Words and no more."

Such an atmosphere exists in the *front*, and people are so conditioned that they fear to raise questions about deficiencies before the *front* command. There were timid attempts on the part of individual commanders of force branches to point out deficiencies in the actions of the branch forces and sort them out in orders, but the *front* command rejected such attempts.

The command's instructions on the elimination of deficiencies were in the nature of oral and family-type admonitions, and no one was obliged to do anything. Thus, for example, the situation in Gordov's army did not change right up to his relief by the *Stavka* from his duties as 33rd Army's commander even though Comrade Sokolovsky assured us that he had given oral instructions to Gordov regarding the elimination of the outrages happening in his army.

The *front* command did not present a report to the *Stavka* concerning these deficiencies and the reasons for the failure of the operations and, furthermore, did not disclose either for itself or for the *Stavka* the reasons the *front* did not fulfill the missions assigned by the *Stavka*. In this instance, the hushing up of the real reasons for the failure of the operations was nothing other than a form of deception of the *Stavka* by the *front* command.

The *front* command investigated people poorly and did not treat their deficiencies critically. This is explained by the fact that, completely groundlessly, Colonel General Gordov is considered the best army commander, Colonel General of Artillery Kamera is considered a fine artilleryman despite the fact that the artillery did not fulfill its missions, and Colonel Il'ninsky is considered a good reconnaissance man while, in reality, the work of the *front's* Intelligence Department is in a state of ruins.

The *front* commander, Comrade Sokolovsky, is separated from his closest assistants—the commanders of the force branches and the chiefs of the services by many days, does not use them, and does not resolve their questions. Some of the deputy commanders did not know about the missions of their branch forces in regard to ongoing operations, to say nothing of the fact that they were not included in the preparation of the operations. For example, the commander of [the *front's*] armored and mechanized forces, Lieutenant General of Tank Forces Rodin, declared, "I was never once asked how best to employ the tanks. I was only a dispatcher, and I sent tanks to this or that army. I learned about the missions of the tank forces in the armies or from the subordinate *tankists* [tankers]."

Operationally, the *front* command did not respond to the needs of the forces. As a result, for example, in some of the attacking divisions, and especially in 33rd Army, there was only one cartridge drum on each submachine gun and only one cartridge belt on each heavy machine gun. This led to the fact that, in the heat of the battle, the machine gunners could not support the infantry, and a great amount of time was spent loading cartridge drums and cartridge belts. In a number of operations, the artillery lagged behind the infantry owing to the absence of tractors for the guns. Meanwhile, there was a sufficient quantity of tractors in the *front* to support fully the artillery of the attacking forces if only the *front* command had responded to the armies' needs and immediately maneuvered the *front's* equipment resources. In the lower levels of the artillery and infantry, there were not enough radios, and, as a result, cooperation between the infantry and artillery was disrupted. Meanwhile, there were a sufficient quantity of radios in the *front's* and armies' rear services and headquarters to support the attacking forces. Through the fault of the *front* command, in November and December 1943, that is, at the height of the operations, there were instances of serious interruptions in support in many divisions. Calculating the products present in the divisions, the armies, and the *front*, with regard to some basic products (meat, fish, bread, and groats), provision was made for no greater than 5–7 days rations.

X.
Conclusions

1. Despite its superiority over the enemy in forces and great expenditures of ammunition, from October 1943 through April 1944, the West-

ern Front did not advance forward. Through the fault of the *front* command, all of the operations conducted over this six-month period failed. The Western Front did not fulfill the missions assigned to it by the *Stavka* VGK and has been weakened as a result of heavy losses in personnel and weaponry, all of which resulted from the clumsy leadership of the *front* command.

At the present time, the Western Front requires strengthening and assistance.

2. Such a situation in the Western Front is a result of the unsatisfactory leadership of the *front* command and, consequently, in the first place, of the unsatisfactory leadership on the part of the *front* commander, Army General Sokolovsky; the former member of the Western Front's Military Council, Lieutenant General Bulganin; and the present member of the *front*'s Military Council, Lieutenant General Mekhlis.

The Western Front command has become conceited and has not treated and does not treat its deficiencies and mistakes critically. In spite of the failure of 11 large- and small-scale operations in the course of 6 months, the *front* command has not learned lessons from these [failures] and is not reporting truthfully about the situation in the *front*.

Army General Sokolovsky has not risen to the occasion as a *front* commander.

First and foremost, Comrades Sokolovsky and Bulganin bear responsibility for the command cadre in the Western Front not having the necessary education in the spirit of truthfulness and intransigence toward deficiencies.

The mistake of Lieutenant General Mekhlis, who is presently working as the member of the Western Front's Military Council, is that he has not reported the true situation of matters in the *front* to the *Stavka*.

3. Especially serious deficiencies exist in the actions of the artillery. The artillerymen in the Western Front neither discover nor correct their mistakes at the same time that the poor work of the artillery had been one of the main reasons for lack of success in offensive operations. In this regard, beside the *front* command, first and foremost, the commander of the *front*'s artillery, Colonel General of Artillery Kamera, is guilty. The mistake of Chief Marshal of Artillery Comrade Voronov is that, while situated in the Western Front, he did not discover the serious deficiencies in artillery and did not report to the *Stavka* about the poor work of artillery in the Western Front.

4. The headquarters of the Western Front is depersonalized and isolated from the command and from the forces and requires strengthening. The present chief of staff, Lieutenant General Pokrovsky, is incapable of coping with his duties.

5. The situation in the Intelligence Department of the *front* headquarters is completely unsatisfactory. The chief of the Intelligence Department, Colonel Il'ninsky, requires special investigation, and it is necessary to relieve him.

6. In the interest of matters, it is necessary to:

(a) Relieve Army General Sokolovsky from his duties as commander of the Western Front for not being able to cope with *front* command and to appoint him as chief of staff to one of the *fronts*. Appoint a new commander to the Western Front who is capable of correcting the situation in the Western Front.

(b) Reprimand Lieutenant General Bulganin for failing to report the presence of serious deficiencies in the *front* to the *Stavka* while he was serving for a long period as the member of the Western Front's Military Council.

(c) Strengthen the Western Front's headquarters and warn the *front*'s chief of staff, Lieutenant General Pokrovsky, that, if he does not correct his mistakes, he will be reduced in rank and duties.

(d) Relieve the commander of the *front*'s artillery, Colonel General of Artillery Kamera, from his duties and reduce his duty position. Appoint a new commander of Western Front's artillery who is capable of eliminating the deficiencies in the work of the artillery. Oblige Chief Marshal of Artillery Voronov to devote himself to eliminating the serious deficiencies in the Western Front's artillery without delay.

(e) Relieve Colonel Il'ninsky from his post of chief of the Intelligence Department of the Western Front's headquarters, reduce his duties, and demote him in rank to lieutenant colonel. Appoint an experienced and trusted commander to the duties of chief of the Intelligence Department of the *front* headquarters. Oblige the chief of the General Staff's Intelligence Directorate, Lieutenant General Kuznetsov, to undertake all necessary measures to correct the situation in the Western Front's Intelligence Department.

(f) Considering the serious mistakes of Colonel General Gordov in command of 33rd Army, as well as his series of incorrect actions for which he was relieved from command of 33rd Army, warn Gordov that, if he repeats the mistakes he tolerated in 33rd Army, he will be reduced in rank and duties. Inform the commander of the 1st Ukrainian Front, Marshal Zhukov, where Gordov is presently serving as the commander of 3rd Guards Army, about Gordov's deficiencies.

G. Malenkov
A. Shcherbakov
S. Shtemenko
F. Kuznetsov
A. Shimonaev

11 April 1944
No. M-715
  True copy:
  Chief of the General Staff's Archive
  Colonel (Denisov)
"—" January 1957
Archives of the Central Committee, CPSU, f. No. 2–44 g.,1. 87–116[3]

Other evidence exists indicating that both the *Stavka* and General Staff were already anxious, if not angry, about the performance of Sokolovsky and his subordinates even before dispatching the investigative commission to the Western Front. An excellent example of this attitude was a critique of 33rd Army's operations that the army itself submitted to the General Staff on 4 April 1944, apparently in response to the pending investigation. The critique began with the short explanation:

> At the end of March 1944, the forces of 33rd Army were conducting offensive combat along the Vitebsk axis. They did not achieve success because of the unsatisfactory organization of combat and command and control of forces.
>
> Presented below is an order of the commander of 33rd Army which exposes the principal deficiencies that appeared during the course of the battles and which, on the basis of combat experience, also provides instructions concerning the organization for combat and command and control of forces in offensive battle during the penetration of the enemy's defensive belts.[4]

Following this introduction, the General Staff quotes 33rd Army's self-critique in full, together with recommended changes in procedures:

Order No. 0065 to the Forces of 33rd Army
4 April 1944   The Operating Army

The army's forces suffered heavy and unjustified losses during the period of combat from 21 through 29 March and did not fulfill its missions. An examination of combat experience shows that the reason for this [failure] are serious deficiencies that took place both in the organization for combat and in the command and control of forces in close combat.

First and foremost, these deficiencies are:

1. From the very beginning of the offensive, the infantry lost communications and cooperation with the artillery and mortars. Cooperation between the infantry and supporting weaponry as the battle developed occurred spontaneously [unplanned] and with great difficulties. The objectives were either not neutralized at all or were neutralized after great

delay by our exposed and disrupted infantry. The extraordinarily centralized firing means in the hands of division and regimental commanders denied the battalion commanders the means for neutralization and the opportunity to react to the situation. First and foremost, the absence of the most elementary communications between the battalion commanders and the artillery and mortars very frequently caused the artillery to strike their own [troops]. The mortar crews conducted their fire particularly unskillfully while avoiding communications with the infantry and delaying in the rear area; as a rule, they fired where they were and very often struck their own [troops].

2. Deficiencies in communications equipment at the battalion-division level also had a negative effect. Wire communications were often disrupted, and the radio stations were few in number at lower levels and they were not adequately supplied.

3. During the commitment of the regiments' second echelons into combat, even though the shifting of the supporting artillery was planned and prepared for, in practice the artillery did not support the second echelons.

4. Despite their abundance in the combat formations of the infantry, the direct fire guns were poorly and unskillfully employed. The subordination of these guns was undefined, and, while operating in their assigned sectors, the direct fire guns frequently did not have concrete targets. They lagged behind the infantry, and, as a result, they sometimes fired on their own troops. Our self-propelled guns were employed unskillfully and ineffectively.

5. The struggle with the enemy's self-propelled guns, which were the main obstacles for our infantry, was disorganized and unplanned.

6. The expenditure of ammunition was planned such that, from the beginning of the infantry's attack, the artillery supporting the infantry had almost no shells.

7. Reconnaissance of the enemy's firing systems and combat formations was done poorly both before combat and, in particular, as combat developed. The attacking infantry did not have patrols and observers. It discovered the targets that were disrupting the infantry's advance, suddenly, when the enemy fire began striking the infantry. The revealed targets were passed down to the artillery either late or not at all. The matter of orientation on the ground and the practice of target designation was completely bad. Exact target designation was absent. Often one could overhear such statements as:

"Strike the enemy machine gun (gun) on hill so and so on the outskirts of some village or another," not understanding that the hill, the edge of the grove, or the outskirts of the village often had a width of front equal to the front of the attacking regiment. The infantry could not say exactly,

"Target and orient so much to the right (left) and how much," and the artillery was a little disturbed by this.

8. The fires of counter-battery artillery groups are not always effective, and, as a rule, the counter-mortar groups cannot suppress the enemy's mortar batteries, they fire on them poorly and inaccurately, and they benefit very little from their fire.

Having enumerated the main deficiencies, I order:

1. Corps commanders to:

(a) From 5–7 April, conduct a critique separately in each division on the organization of combat during the past battles in conformity with this order and the time indicated by the order;

(b) Prior to 10 April 1944 and separately in each division, conduct classes with commanders and their communications equipment and with groups of battalion commanders—and division commanders with the commanders of their attached batteries, mortar and machine gun companies, and the commanders of direct fire guns on the ground.

The goal of the classes is to work out and, in practice on the ground, demonstrate the organization and order of cooperation of the infantry, artillery, mortars, machine guns, and direct fire guns on a battalion and artillery battalion [*divizion*] scale;

(c) Conduct demonstrative classes for regimental commanders on the theme, "The attack of a reinforced rifle company into the depth of an enemy's defense," and, after doing so, the commanders of the regiments will conduct the same studies with each regimental company in each rifle regiment.

(d) Conduct classes with groups of regimental and battalion commanders exclusively on matters regarding the cooperation of types of forces in combat;

(e) Separately, and on a division scale, conduct two-day assemblies of the commanders of mortar companies with the goal of studying the employment of mortars in combat to support attacking infantry;

2. The commander of army artillery to:

(a) Considering the experience of recent battles, construct an organization for the counter-battery and counter-mortar struggle based on the necessity for more effective and prolonged suppression of enemy artillery and mortars;

(b) Plan the expenditure of ammunition according to periods of the battle, taking into account the obligatory real presence of ammunition during the infantry's battle in the depths;

(c) Categorically prohibit the removal of mortar companies from the battalions and, at the same time, by way of experience, form a mortar battalion consisting of two batteries (one 82mm and one 122mm) in one of the regiments of 215th Rifle Division by 8 April 1944, and fill the battalion up with personnel, equipment, and communications means;

(d) Reexamine the order of employment and organization of direct fire guns and, while doing so, pursue the goal of more reliable support of the infantry, both in the beginning and in subsequent periods of combat;

(e) In addition to direct fire guns, employ individual 76mm, 85mm, 122mm, and 152mm guns especially earmarked for neutralizing enemy tanks and self-propelled guns at direct fire range for the struggle with enemy tanks and self-propelled artillery. For neutralization at long distances, employ one–two batteries of medium and heavy caliber [guns] with the special missions of destroying tanks by the technique of mobile barrier fires, in each division;

(f) To increase the efficiency of artillery, accustom the artillerymen to and introduce into practice in howitzer and heavy batteries the simultaneous firing of batteries on two targets from one firing position;

(g) To protect reliably the attack of rifle battalions into the depth of the enemy's defense, anticipate the direct subordination of one artillery battalion to the commander of a rifle battalion so that, from the beginning of the infantry attack, with sufficient ammunition, the attached battalion can more actively protect the attack of its infantry;

(h) Work out and provide to forces a unified procedure for the artillery and infantry to designate target and summon fires; and

(i) At meetings of the mortar company commanders, conduct demonstrative firings by the mortar companies against designated enemy strongpoints, with subsequent shifting of firing positions and destruction of targets in the depth.

3. The commander of armored and mechanized forces will distribute to the forces instructions on the employment of self-propelled guns.

4. Within a five-day period, the army's chief of communications will fill out the rifle and artillery regiments with their authorized quantity of radio stations, wire communications equipment, and supplies for telephones and radio stations.

5. The army chief of staff will conduct two-stage staff exercises with the division and regimental chiefs of staff by 10 April 1944.

Attachment: Temporary instructions on organization for combat and command and control of forces in offensive battle during the penetration of an enemy fortified belt.

The commander of 33rd Army   The member of the 33rd Army's Military Council

The chief of staff of 33rd Army[5]

The attachment to this document was a lengthy explanation of procedures for the organization of combat and the penetration of a prepared enemy defense.

In his analysis of the Belorussian offensive, Gareev sums up the Western Front's performance cryptically, stating, "As a result of its conduct of these [eleven] ineffective operations, the Western Front lost 530,537 men killed and wounded. The Western Front possessed a certain overall superiority over the enemy in personnel and weaponry in all of these operations, and, during the latter [operation] in March, a rather significant superiority."[6] Using the *Stavka*'s report and the commission's investigation, and perhaps other unpublished materials as well, as a backdrop for his analysis, Gareev proposes three reasons for the failure of the Western Front's offensives, including:

- Deficiencies in the actions of the *Stavka* and General Staff;
- The actions of the Western Front's command and headquarters; and
- Serious deficiencies in the actions of commanders and headquarters at the operational-tactical level, especially at the army, corps, division (brigade), and regimental level.

First, Gareev criticizes the *Stavka* and General Staff for *failing to develop a well-thought-out strategic plan and for its faulty command and control methods.* Specifically, he accuses them of underestimating German strength along the central axis and assuming the Germans could not halt the Soviet advance because Army Group Center's defenses were "unreliable" because it (the army group) had been seriously weakened by combat operations during the past summer, and it had few if any reserves. Further, the *Stavka* and General Staff overlooked the fact that although German forces had just withdrawn to strategic defenses along the Dnepr River in the Ukraine in the south, the Germans had two long years to prepare a deeply echeloned defense on terrain favorable for prolonged defense along the central axis in Belorussia. Penetration of this defense required careful preparation, extensive *Stavka* support, and the participation of multiple *fronts* (groups of *fronts*) rather than a single *front* to conduct the offensive.

Citing the famous Belorussian offensive of summer 1944 (Operation Bagration) as an example, Gareev claims, "In our view, the *Stavka* and General Staff had the opportunity to prepare and conduct a coordinated operation along the Western Strategic axis in 1943 and 1944 instead of isolated offensive operations by the Baltic, Western, and Belorussian Fronts. With such forces, it could have produced more tangible results."[7] Above and beyond this mistake, during the Western Front's Smolensk offensive of August–September 1943 and the eleven separate offensives it conducted in eastern Belorussia from October 1943 through March 1944, Gareev accuses the *Stavka* of assigning unrealistic missions to *fronts* conducting *chastnykh* (individual) *front* operations and allocating inadequate time to plan these operations, specifically, an average of fifteen days, when thirty to forty days were required to prepare a major operation properly. This produced increased losses in the attacking *front* during each operation and, if the *Stavka* failed to provide needed reinforcements, reduced the *front*'s strength in each subsequent offensive. This vicious cycle, Gareev maintained, afflicted the Western Front in late 1943 and early 1944.

Recognizing that the *Stavka* quite naturally directed the bulk of its attention and resources to *fronts* operating along main axes, such as at Leningrad and in the Ukraine, instead of secondary axes, Gareev notes, "But then, the missions that the latter performed must have been commensurate with their capabilities and, as a whole, with the operational-tactical situation."[8]

Further, although the *Stavka* repeatedly assigned new missions to the Western Front and issued periodic orders urging it on, "It did not have any real influence on the course of the operations." In essence, "After the Western Front's initial operations failed, a conclusion could have been drawn regarding the inexpediency of continuing it and to seek other cardinal decisions. But this was not done."[9] Finally, Gareev correctly asserts that, after the Battle of Moscow, the Western Front became accustomed to suffering defeats or limited victories when conducting individual *front* operations. Although neither the *Stavka* nor the *front* command understood this reality, this psychologically conditioned the *front* to endure if not expect the defeats it suffered in the fall of 1943 and the winter of 1944.

Second, in regard to the *Western Front command's responsibility for its own defeats,* Gareev agrees with the *Stavka's* judgments concerning the appallingly poor performance of Sokolovsky and his key staff subordinates. Contrasting Sokolovsky's failures with the victories of Rokossovsky's Belorussian Front, which fought in comparable circumstances during the same period but achieved far better results, he states, "However, if the Western Front's forces were unable to advance and fulfill their assigned missions, the Belorussian Front's forces, despite all of their difficulties, smashed the enemy's defenses along a front of about 100 kilometers, advanced to a depth of up to 130 kilometers, captured the cities of Gomel' and Rechitsa, and liberated tens of other populated points in southeastern Belorussia."[10] Gareev credited Rokossovsky's successes to quality operational preparations, better organization for combat, and more artful command and control.

Furthermore, during his entire service with the Western Front from June 1942 to April 1944, while he was serving, in succession, as deputy commander and chief of staff of a battalion, chief of operations for a brigade, and assistant chief of the Operations Section of 45th Rifle Corps, Gareev "never once met with the commander or any other responsible officials of the *front*." In contrast, "after I. D. Cherniakhovsky had been appointed as *front* commander, during the preparations for the Belorussian operation alone, I was fortunate enough to see him three times while he was working at the corps' and divisions' observation posts."[11] As a result, "at all levels, the commands' and staffs' work systems and the style of leading the forces up to April 1944 and thereafter was perceived 'at the bottom' as two different phenomena of front life."

Gareev characterized Sokolovsky's and Pokrovsky's leadership style as characterizing the "old school," when commanders limited their efforts to making basic decisions, disposing their forces before battle, and issuing directives during combat from command posts remote from the battlefield, while avoiding significant involvement in the affairs of their subordinates and the application of "independent creativity and organizational activities in the process of commanding and controlling forces" in combat. Therefore:

> Despite the complete bankruptcy of this style of work, which came to light during the course of battle, even after its end, it was cultivated for a rather long time in the General Staff and lower level staffs. Such an approach reduced the activities of commanders and staffs to an end in itself, limited the *front* in their work, and impeded the process of controlling forces.
>
> In our view, unlike G. K. Zhukov, K. K. Rokossovsky, and I. D. Cherniakhovsky, such commanders as V. D. Sokolovsky most of all displayed the absence of a civil courage, especially when they had to fight for their decisions and proposals before I. V. Stalin.[12]

As a result, after the Battle of Smolensk, when Sokolovsky realized that his forces were incapable of launching another offensive without extensive preparation time, he was simply unwilling or unable to argue that case with Stalin.

Above and beyond Sokolovsky's weakness as a commander, his command and staff planned and organized the *front*'s operations formally, that is, by limiting their activities to the formulation of general operational aims while requiring the armies to plan and conduct what turned out to be a series of army operations. These operations, in turn, were characterized by the use of deeply echeloned shock groups attacking in stereotypical fashion generally along single, predictable attack axes without the effective employment of deception and adequately planned artillery and air support. Worst of all, Sokolovsky's *front* retained no means with which it could influence the ultimate course and outcome of the operations. Lacking creative vision from the top and the dynamic presence of senior *front* leaders on the battlefield, the *front*'s army, corps, and division commanders were left to fend for themselves on the battlefield and performed most combat functions poorly or not at all.

Third, Gareev acknowledges that the *front*'s army, corps, division (brigade), and regimental commanders also made serious mistakes before and during the operations, although many of these occurred because of the congenital lack of supervision or guidance from above as Sokolovsky and his staff abandoned these commanders to their own devices. In this regard, Gareev reserves special criticism for Gordov, the commander of 33rd Army, by citing the litany of failures noted in the *Stavka* critique. Worst of all, just as Gordov's subordinates did at the time, he accuses Gordov of so-called *narkom-*

zem ("people's commissariat-ism") or *narkomzdrav* ("people's commissariat health") for his practice "of summoning his formation commanders to his command post several times a day, [which required them] to get there and return back under heavy enemy fire."[13]

Gareev also accuses the army and division commanders of retaining too many of their forces in passive defensive sectors, or in second or third echelon, when their presence was required in main attack sectors. Making matters worse, the higher-level commands allocated inadequate time to prepare attacks properly. Gareev recalls, "From January through March 1944, several times our brigade received 100–200 replacements from reserve regiments, which were often sent directly to the field of battle, and, frequently, the subunit commanders did not know their own soldiers—or even their own commanders."[14] Therefore, "in such difficult circumstances, it was difficult to expect skillful actions of commanders, staffs, and the personnel of subunits and units."[15] The many deficiencies noted in the *Stavka's* critique were virtually foreordained and caused the appallingly heavy casualties that ensued.

Gareev describes just one ad hoc if not grotesque measure taken to reduce these casualties:

> To limit them [the casualties] and to overcome the enemy's resistance successfully, in November 1943 the personnel of 36th Rifle Brigade were supplied with metallic armor that covered the front part of the body. The brigade was committed to battle with the objective of cutting the Vitebsk-Orsha road, but it was in December on a field with deep snow cover, and, therefore, the infantry quickly grew weak. It is true that the losses were somewhat fewer than in previous attacks, but nevertheless, no one's armor remained after several days.[16]

When assessing why the offensive into Belorussia during the fall of 1943 and winter of 1944 failed, while the offensive in the same region succeeded so spectacularly in the summer of 1944, Gareev recognizes the 3rd Belorussian Front's (the former Western Front's) increased strength and shock power during the latter period. However, he also notes:

> However, the chief thing was that the concept and scope of operation "Bagramian" and the purposefulness and creative work of such commanders as General I. D. Cherniakhovsky created an overall situation of élan and confidence, which often neutralized the deficiencies in the actions of commanders and forces at the operational-tactical level and helped them successfully fulfill their assigned missions. . . .
>
> The higher commands themselves did a considerable part of the work during the preparation and conduct of the operation, thereby creating more favorable conditions for their subordinate forces to fulfill their combat missions.[17]

As far as the *Stavka*'s strategic aims during the fall of 1943 and winter of 1944 Belorussian operation were concerned, Gareev offers the only existing comprehensive assessment to date:

> What was the overall aim of these operations, and was it necessary to conduct them? The goal and necessity for an offensive in the Western Front's sector was determined, first and foremost, by the fact that, after the conduct of a series of successful operations in the northwest and the Ukraine, the *fronts* that were operating along these axes advanced forward significantly. But, after the Smolensk operation, the Western Front essentially continued to mark time along the Smolensk-Minsk axis. As a result, a situation arose that was extremely unfavorable for Soviet forces, since the front lines represented a salient almost 150 kilometers deep toward Moscow where the enemy concentrated a rather large force. Using the shortest possible routes, its aircraft [based in the Lepel', Mogilev, and Minsk triangle] were capable of operating against the important objectives and communications of not only the Western but also the Baltic and Belorussian Fronts.
>
> The interests of rapidly and fully liberating Soviet territory required the destruction of Army Group "Center" along the Smolensk-Minsk axis. As far back as during the course of the Smolensk offensive operation, on 20 September 1943, the *Stavka* VGK assigned the Western Front the [following] mission: from the moment Smolensk is captured, the [Western] *front*'s left wing will occupy the cities of Pochinok and Roslavl' and reach the Sozh River, Khislavichi, and Shumiagi line; and subsequently, the main grouping will attack along the Orsha axis and capture the Orsha and Mogilev region on 10-12 October. The overall depth of the forthcoming offensive operation amounted to 160 to 210 kilometers. However, in late September the *Stavka* demanded that, after capturing the Orsha and Mogilev region, the *front* continue the offensive along the Borisov and Molodechno axis, reach the Dokshintsy, Dolginovo, and Radoshkovichi front, and subsequently liberate Vil'nius [the capital of Lithuania]. Simultaneously, the Kalinin Front was ordered to take Riga, and the Central Front, Minsk.
>
> After the unsuccessful attempts to attack during November and December 1943, on 18 January 1944, the *Stavka* assigned the Western Front a more limited mission of capturing Vitebsk in cooperation with the Baltic Front (to do so required an advance to a depth of up to 50 kilometers). However, this mission was not fulfilled, and the repeated attempts by the Western Front's forces to continue the offensive and exploit the success of the Smolensk operation were not crowned with success.
>
> One cannot say that all of these operations were completely futile and did not produce any results. They wore down the enemy (he also suffered

considerable losses) and denied him the opportunity to dig in firmly along new defensive lines. Most important, as a consequence of the Western Front's constant active operations, the German command was not able to shift additional forces from the central sector of its eastern front to other axes, where the main strategic missions were being resolved.

The strategic situation required the destruction of the resisting forces of Army Group "Center" and the arrival of the Western Front's forces, if only at the Vitebsk-Orsha line. But this mission was not fulfilled.[18]

Although both the *Stavka's* and Gareev's critique of the Belorussian operation are inherently sound as far as they go, they neglect to mention several critical points, by doing so tending to negate the significance of the offensives. First and foremost, both fail to provide necessary context for the Western Front's operations. Specifically, they treat the Western Front's offensives in isolation, avoiding significant comment on the important operation being conducted during the same period (and virtually simultaneously) by the neighboring 1st Baltic Front and Belorussian Fronts, at a time when all three *fronts* were operating within the context of a common *Stavka* plan. Admittedly, however, although this plan sought the utter defeat of Army Group Center during the fall, its objectives were significantly less ambitious during the ensuing winter.

Second, in reality, the *Stavka* did coordinate the offensive against Vitebsk by assigning Chief Marshal of Artillery N. N. Voronov as its representative to coordinate the offensive operations of both *fronts* (as well as the 2nd Baltic Front) during the fall of 1943 and January 1944 and Marshal of the Soviet Union S. K. Timoshenko to coordinate the same *front's* operations in March 1944. This clearly underscored the *Stavka's* keen interest and involvement in these offensives.

Third, as Gareev briefly mentions, but only in the context of the Western Front, although the *Stavka* devoted much of its attention and resources to operations in the Leningrad region and the Ukraine, it considered its forces operating along the central (western) axis as more than adequate to perform their assigned missions. As indicated by the achievements of Rokossovsky's Belorussian Front in southern Belorussia, if Bagramian's and Sokolovsky's *fronts* had performed in similar fashion, the Belorussian offensive might have been a far greater success.

CHAPTER 23

Conclusions

Considering the strategic context within which Rokossovsky planned and conducted his portion of the Belorussian offensive and the severe terrain and weather conditions his forces had to endure, his Belorussian Front's performance during the winter campaign was indeed impressive. Furthermore, when compared with the dismal performance of Sokolovsky's Western Front during the same period, it was even more impressive.

Strategically, the *Stavka* required Rokossovsky's *front* to conduct its offensive operations along an axis that, by early February 1944, it clearly considered secondary in nature. Accordingly, the *Stavka* assigned the Belorussian Front missions that it realized were not completely achievable. By this time, operational considerations and terrain factors prompted the *Stavka* to allocate its six tank armies and the bulk of its tank and mechanized corps to its *fronts* operating in the Ukraine. Likewise, it dispatched the bulk of its personnel replacements, weapons (particularly tanks and self-propelled guns), and spare parts to its Ukrainian *fronts*. Consequently, while Bagramian's 1st Baltic Front had two tank corps and a cavalry corps at its disposal, Sokolovsky's Western Front had a single tank corps, and Rokossovsky's Belorussian Front had to make do with one tank corps and two cavalry corps. Starved of replacements from Moscow throughout the winter, the strength of Rokossovsky's rifle divisions fell to an average of between 4,000 and 5,000 men each, although his armies added thousands of locally conscripted Belorussians into their ranks as they advanced.

However, the *Stavka's* allocation of artillery and artillery ammunition to its forces at the front clearly contradicted the presumed priority it accorded to operations in the Ukraine. In this regard, the *Stavka* assigned Rokossovsky's *front* a full artillery penetration corps and four artillery divisions (three of them penetration divisions), along with adequate supplies of ammunition. Similarly, the *Stavka* allocated the 1st Baltic Front three artillery divisions (two penetration) and the Western Front one artillery penetration corps and four artillery divisions (two of which were penetration divisions). For comparison's sake, the 1st Ukrainian Front was supported by one artillery penetration corps and four artillery divisions (two penetration), whereas the 2nd, 3rd, and 4th Ukrainian Fronts were allocated only one or two artillery divisions each. Ammunition expenditures reflected this pattern. For example, from 31 March 1943 through 31 March 1944, the Belorussian Front expended 12,335 wagonloads of ammunition, as opposed to 17,661 by the Western Front, 10,545 by the 1st Ukrainian Front, and 8,463 by the 4th Ukrainian Front. The Western Front exploited this fact by expending 7,261 wagonloads from October 1943 through April 1944, even though poor artillery procedures largely negated with advantage.[1] All of this clearly demonstrates that the *Stavka* tried to compensate for the paucity of armor operating along the Belorussian axis by allocating its three *fronts* operating in the region lavish artillery support.

Operating with only limited armored forces and personnel replacements, Rokossovsky mastered the art of conducting simultaneous and successive offensive operations on an operational and tactical scale. Attacking along a wide variety of operational and tactical axes, he applied unrelenting pressure against German Ninth and Second Armies' defenses, all the while efficiently economizing on his scarce forces and weaponry. By doing so, Rokossovsky's forces tested, stretched, and frequently tore gaping holes in the Germans' defenses, all the while exhausting German front-line forces and operational and tactical reserves alike.

Whereas Bagramian's 1st Baltic and Sokolovsky's Western Front conducted at least seven repetitive offensive operations along four well-defined and predictable axes west and southeast of Vitebsk and at Bogushevsk and Orsha, Rokossovsky's Belorussian Front constantly shifted its axis of advance from sector to sector across a broad front (see Maps 23.1, 23.2, and 23.3). For example, from early January through late March, Rokossovsky's forces conducted nine distinct offensives along six different operational axes, each preceded by a major regrouping of forces (see Table 23.1).

Thus, whereas Bagramian's *front* operated along one axis and Sokolovsky's *front* operated along three, Rokossovsky conducted his offensives along six distinct axes, including Chausy-Bykhov, Mozyr'-Kalinkovichi, Ozarichi-Ptich', Marmovichi-Dubrova, Mormal'-Parichi, and Rogachev-Zhlobin. By attacking along such a wide variety of axes—often at the boundaries between German armies, corps, and divisions—Rokossovsky created a series of crises for the opposing German Second and Ninth Armies, punished their forward forces, and wore out their operational and tactical reserves by forcing them to shift from one sector to another to deal with the ever-changing threat.

Unlike his counterparts operating in the Vitebsk region, Rokossovsky played an active role in planning and conducting his *front's* offensive operations. Whenever necessary, he avoided stereotypical actions that so typified the Western Fronts' operations and contributed to their failure, and to a far lesser extent, the 1st Baltic Front's as well. To Rokossovsky's credit, he encouraged his army commanders to employ imaginative new combat techniques, and when they failed to do so, he corrected their actions on the spot. For example, he praised Gorbatov's imaginative employment of a ski detachment to unhinge German defenses east of the Dnepr River in early

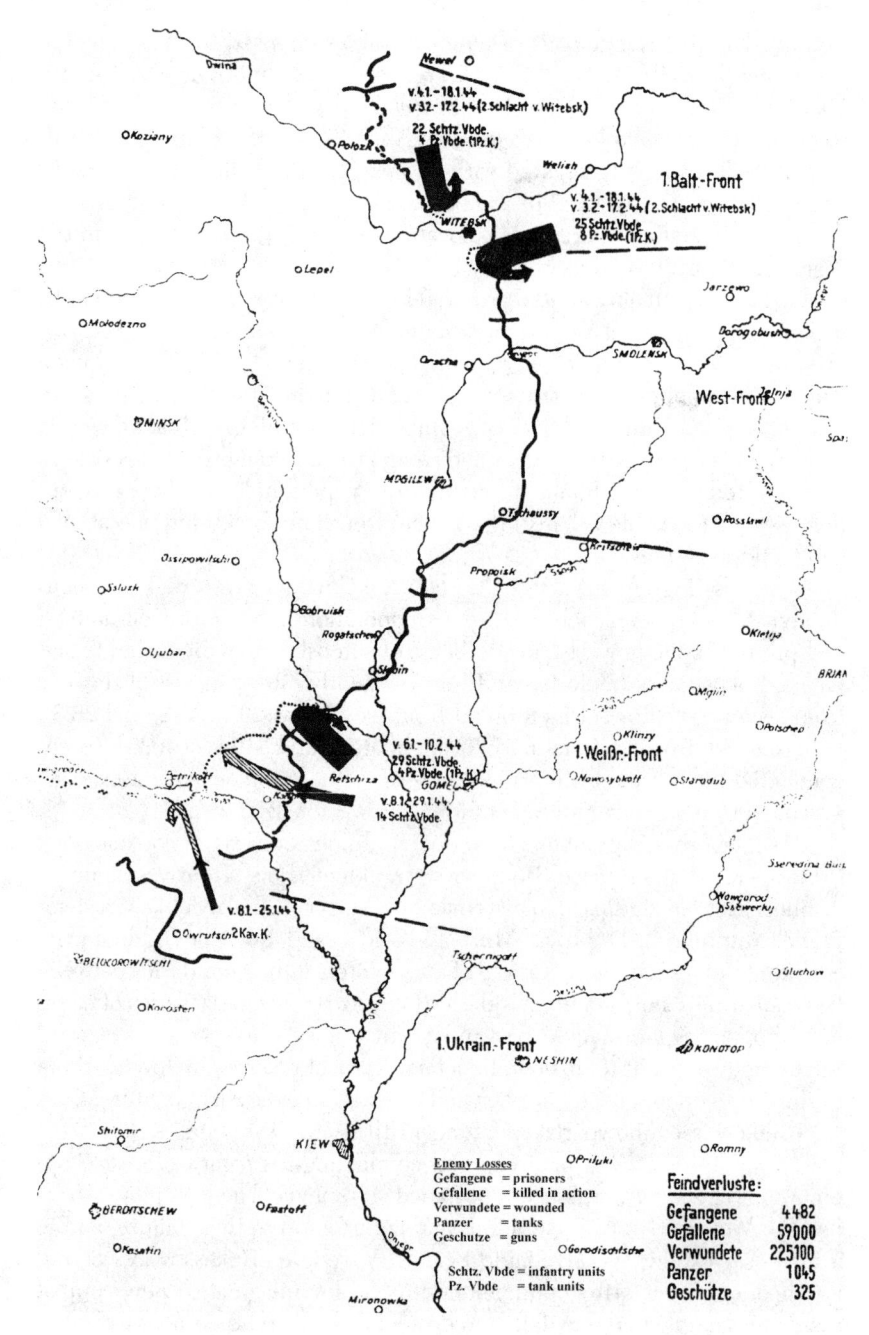

Map 23.1. German Assessment of Red Army Operations, 5 January–17 February 1944

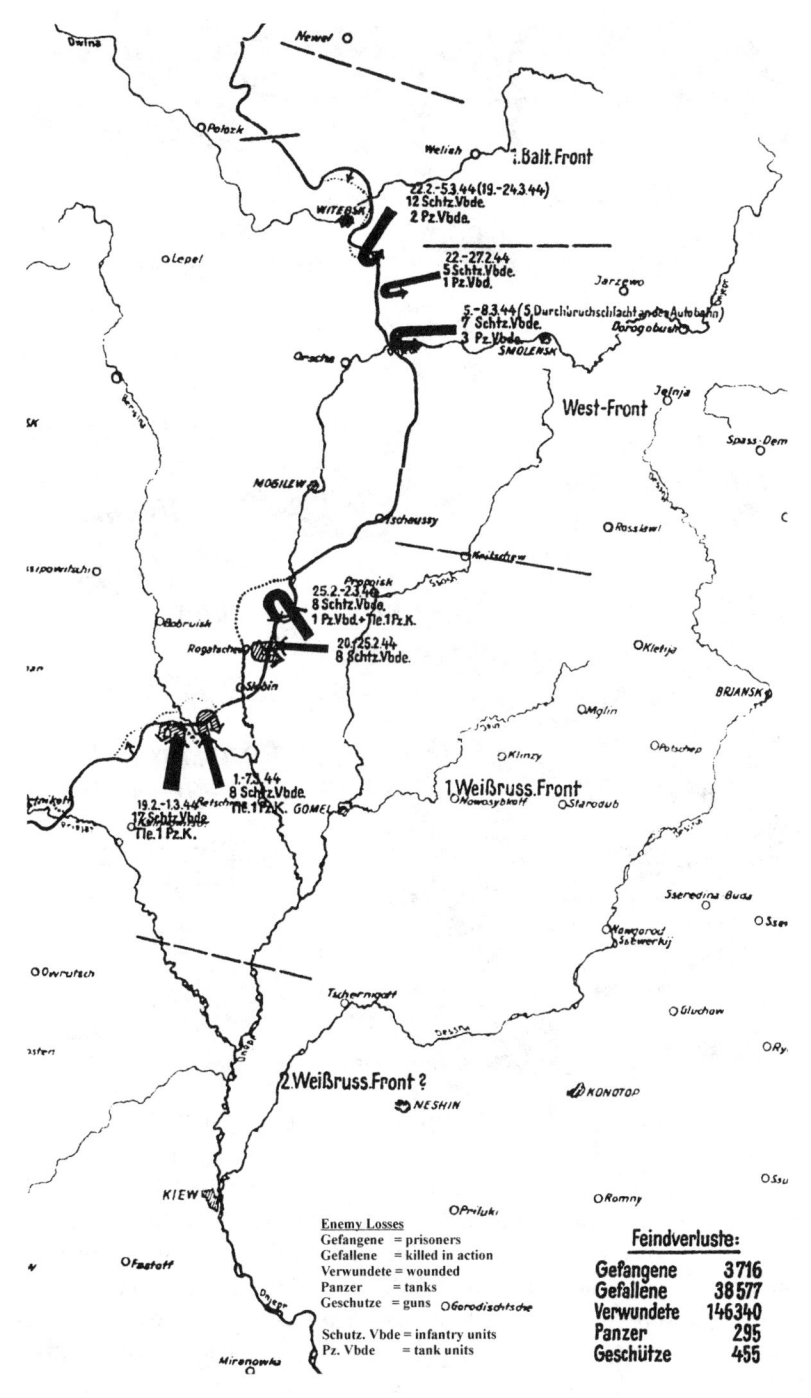

Map 23.2. German Assessment of Red Army Operations, 18 February–24 March 1944

576   The Struggle for Belorussia, December 1943–April 1944

Map 23.3. Red Army Operations in Belorussia, October 1943–April 1944

January and then required his commanders to employ similar tactics during the assault on Kalinkovichi and the advance to the Ptich' River. Similarly, he required his commanders to avoid revealing their offensive intentions by conducting routine and predictable artillery preparations. Finally, throughout his many operations, he skillfully employed deceptive measures to conceal his many regroupings. As a result, his actions became virtual models for how to conduct economy-of-force operations.[2]

Table 23.1. The Belorussian (1st Belorussian) Front's Offensive Operations, January–March 1944

- 3rd and 50th Armies' Bykhov Offensive and 10th Army's Supporting Attack at Chausy (3-8 January 1944)
- 61st and 65th Armies' Kalinkovichi-Mozyr' Offensive (8-14 January 1944)
- 61st and 65th Armies' Ozarichi-Ptich' Offensive (16-30 January 1944)
- 48th and 65th Armies' Parichi-Bobruisk (Marmovichi-Dubrova) Offensive (16-27 January 1944)
- 48th and 65th Armies' Parichi-Bobruisk (Marmovichi-Dubrova) Offensive (2-9 February 1944)
- 48th and 65th Armies' Parichi-Bobruisk (Marmovichi-Dubrova) Offensive (21-23 February 1944)
- 48th Army's Mormal'-Parichi Offensive (24-29 February 1944)
- 3rd and 50th Armies' Rogachev-Zhlobin Offensive (21-26 February 1944)
- 10th and 50th Armies' Operations to Eliminate German Bridgeheads of the Eastern Bank of the Dnepr River (25-31 March 1944)

Last but not least, the concrete accomplishments of Rokossovsky's forces over the three-month period provide the most visible evidence of his skill as a *front* commander. In his analysis of Sokolovsky's operations during the fall, Gareev compares Sokolovsky's performance with that of Rokossovsky and finds the former wanting:

> Notwithstanding all of the unfavorable conditions that the *Stavka* created, the Western Front command had an opportunity to operate more effectively than it operated. This is confirmed by the experience of the Belorussian Fronts' conduct of the Gomel'-Rechitsa offensive operation in November 1943, that is, at the same time when the Western Front was undertaking several of its offensive operations. These two *fronts* conducted their operations in very difficult operational situations and terrain conditions and with roughly comparable correlations of forces with the enemy. However, if the Western Front's forces did not advance and did not fulfill their missions, in spite of all difficulties, the Belorussian Front's forces broke open the enemy's defenses along a front of about 100 kilometers, advanced to a depth of up to 130 kilometers, captured the cities of Gomel' and Rechitsa, and liberated tens of other populated points in southeastern Belorussia. Therefore, the quality of the preparations, the organization of combat operations, and the skill in commanding and controlling forces determined the outcomes of these operations.[3]

Although Gareev limited his analysis to the Gomel'-Rechitsa operation in the fall of 1943, the same comparison can be applied to operations during the winter campaign of 1944. During this period, for example, over the course of forty-six days from 1 January through 15 February 1944, the forces of Bagramian's 1st Baltic Front, operating west of Vitebsk, advanced between 4 to 8 kilometers along a front of about 15 kilometers. This amounted to an average advance of about 178 meters per day. East of Vitebsk, during the sixty-four days from 1 January through 5 March 1944, the forces of Sokolovsky's Western Front advanced between 3 to 6 kilometers along a front of roughly 32 kilometers for a daily average advance rate of 94 meters per day. Worse still, Sokolovsky's Western Front recorded no gains whatsoever during five days of heavy fighting along the Orsha axis.

In contrast, during the eighty-eight days from 3 January through 31 March 1944, Rokossovsky's Belorussian Front advanced between 5 to 40 kilometers along a front of more than 220 kilometers for a maximum average daily advance rate of 454 meters per day, that is, more than twice the advance rate of Bagramian's *front* and about five times the advance rate of Sokolovsky's *front*. More importantly, by shifting his axis of advance, Rokossovsky was able to record far higher advance rates along specific operational axes over shorter periods.

For example, during the Kalinkovichi-Mozyr' offensive, the Belorussian Front's 65th and 61st Armies advanced westward 20 to 30 kilometers during the seven days from 8 through 14 January, for an average daily advance rate of 4.3 kilometers per day. Later, during the Ozarichi-Ptich' offensive, the same armies advanced 20 kilometers during the fifteen days from 16 through 30 January, for an average advance rate of 1.3 kilometers per day.

Farther north along the Parichi axis, during the twenty-four days from 16 January through 9 February, 48th Army of Rokossovsky's *front* advanced 10 to 20 kilometers, for an average maximum advance rate of 833 meters per day. Finally, during the Rogachev-Zhlobin offensive and the associated offensive at Mormal', 3rd, 50th, and 48th Armies of the Belorussian Front advanced 5 to 20 kilometers in the six days from 21 through 26 and 24 through 29 February, for an average maximum advance rate of 3.3 kilometers per day.

Therefore, in addition to failing to capture Vitebsk and Orsha, the objectives the *Stavka* assigned to them, Bagramian's and Sokolovsky's forces did not seize any important Russian town or city. In contrast, although Rokossovsky's forces failed to reach their ultimate objectives of Parichi and Bobruisk, they liberated all of their immediate objectives, including Mozyr', Kalinkovichi, Ozarichi, Shatsilki, and Rogachev.

By any measurement, given the circumstances surrounding their conduct, Rokossovsky's operations in southern Belorussia were remarkably successful. Furthermore, much of the credit for this success belongs to Rokossovsky himself, who clearly demonstrated his boundless energy, imagination, and keen operational skills throughout the entire duration of the winter campaign.

If this conclusion is correct, one important question must be asked and answered. Simply stated, this question is, "Why have Soviet and, more recently, Russian historians either ignored or covered up many dimensions of Rokossovsky's successful campaign?" Although it is commonplace in Soviet military history for historians, official or otherwise, to conceal the Red

Army's offensive failures, seldom, if ever, have they concealed its offensive successes. In this case, however, rather than concealing these operations for military reasons, they have eradicated them from the annals of military history for starkly political reasons, specifically, to preserve the reputation of Sokolovsky and denigrate the reputation of Rokossovsky, who, because of his birthplace and ethnicity, has been referred to by some as the Red Army's "Polish general."

Why then was the preservation of Sokolovsky's reputation so important as to require the "fudging" of historical fact? The answer to this question can be found in Sokolovsky's prewar and wartime associations as well as his postwar military career. Before the war broke out, for example, Sokolovsky served as Zhukov's deputy when the latter occupied the post of the Red Army's chief of staff. After war began, he then served for a long period as Zhukov's trusted chief of staff for the Western Front and, as his favorite, was handpicked by Zhukov to become his successor as commander of the Western Front in February of 1943. Despite his relief in virtual disgrace as the Western Front's commander in April 1944, he once again served as Zhukov's chief of staff during the climactic Battle for Berlin in April and May 1945, earning, on Zhukov's recommendation, the coveted title of Hero of the Soviet Union.

After the war ended, Sokolovsky's reputation soared as he became, in succession, commander of the Group of Soviet Forces in Germany (GSFG) from 1946 through 1949, 1st Deputy Minister of the Soviet Armed Forces in 1949 and 1950, War Minister of the USSR from 1950 to 1952, chief of the Soviet Army General Staff and 1st Deputy Minister of Defense from 1952 through 1960, and Minister of Defense in 1963. Understandably, when Soviet historians began writing more substantive and accurate histories of the war during the late 1950s and early 1960s, Sokolovsky's reputation had to be, and was, preserved. That preservation continued to distort history through the subsequent existence of the Soviet Union.

Although it is both understandable and gratifying that the truth about Sokolovsky's wartime record emerged soon after the Soviet Union collapsed in 1991, Rokossovsky's reputation remains to be restored. I hope, the "resurrection" of this forgotten campaign will contribute to that restoration process.

EPILOGUE

Given the importance that this book attaches to the Red Army's Belorussian offensive in October 1943 and the guidance General Gareev provides in his thoughtful comparison of this offensive with the more successful and hence more famous Operation Bagration, which began on 23 June 1944, it is worthwhile to examine further the relationship between the two offensives. From the outset, five key factors distinguish one offensive from the other, each of which can contribute to offensive success or failure. Without evaluating the relative importance of each, these include:

1. The quantity and quality of the forces and weaponry available to those who planned and conducted the operation.
2. The skill and experience of the commanders and staff officers who planned and conducted the offensive.
3. The manner in which these planners and "operators" organized their forces and weapons for combat.
4. The prevailing weather and terrain conditions, whose effects conditioned offensive success or failure.
5. Combat experience that, when skillfully exploited and applied, became a prerequisite for success in all offensive operations.

Although the first of these factors seems mathematically measurable, and, at least in part, is important, it is tricky to evaluate and deceptive because troops with little or no training and a lack of cohesiveness in forces at the tactical level (that is, battalion, regiment, and division) render numerical superiority utterly meaningless and superfluous. Likewise, even though the second and third factors involving the competence of commanders and staff officers might be partially predictable, this competence does not become definitively apparent until after combat begins. The fourth factor of weather and terrain can be measured or at least anticipated; however, it inherently involves the intangible of deliberate risk taking, with all of the obvious dangers associated with taking chances. Finally, combat experience on the battlefield is perhaps the most important of these factors because surviving combat is indicative of learning. In short, those who learn survive, whereas those who do not perish, literally or figuratively.

How, then, do these factors apply to these two offensives (see Map 23.4)? It is clear that, strategically, the Red Army had a better than 2 to 1 superiority in manpower and almost 3 to 1 in armor over German Army Group Center when it began the Belorussian offensive in October of 1943. This, however, is deceptive because the Kalinin and Western Fronts had suffered roughly 450,000 casualties out of their combined strength of 1.2 million men in the almost two months of incessant fighting during the Smolensk offensive operation. This meant that, in addition to losing many experienced soldiers, many of the *fronts'* divisions were woefully understrength, and, as the offensive developed, many of its roughly 750,000 men were replacements. In an offensive planned and conducted as hastily as the October effort, force cohesion and individual and small-unit training suffered mightily. To a lesser extent, the same phenomenon occurred in the Central (Belorussian) Front.

Conversely, in the June 1944 offensive code-named Operation Bagration, by filling out its units and dispatching two fresh reinforcing armies to Belo-

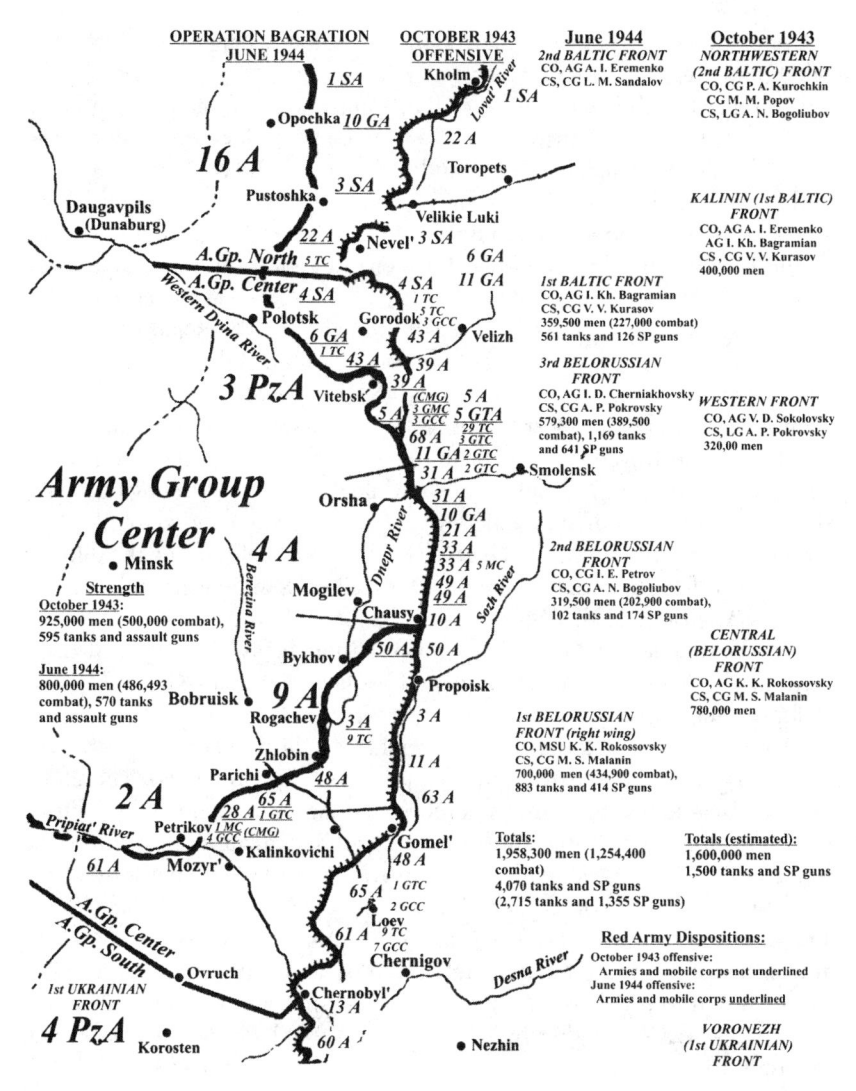

Map 23.4. The Red Army's Belorussian Offensives Compared

russia, the Red Army increased its numerical superiority over Army Group Center, strategically, to better than 2.5 to 1 in personnel and almost 5 to 1 in armor. Most important, the operational pause from early April to late June enabled the attacking *fronts* to improve individual and small-unit training and ensure that their forces at every level were well knit and cohesive. This, plus the increased skills in reconnaissance; cooperation between infantry, armor, and artillery; and a host of other vital combat functions, ensured that the operational formations employed by the four attacking *fronts* were "well oiled" and effective.

In regard to the competence of the command cadre planning and conducting the October offensive, all three *front* commanders were experienced at that level. Eremenko had commanded *fronts*, off and on, since July 1941, and had certainly "earned his spurs" in that regard when he commanded the Southeastern and Stalingrad Fronts during the extended Stalingrad campaign. Bagramian, who succeeded Eremenko in command in November of 1943, was new to command at the *front* level. However, he had commanded 16th (later 11th Guards) Army successfully since July 1942 and had proved himself an excellent organizer and tenacious fighter. Rokossovsky too, who rose to *front* command in July 1942, had led the Briansk Front and then the Don Front throughout most of the Stalingrad campaign, during the course of which he destroyed German Sixth Army in Stalingrad. Thereafter, he led the Central Front during most of 1943, while doing so performing brilliantly during the battle of Kursk. Finally, Sokolovsky had commanded the Western Front since February 1943 and had led it, albeit haltingly, during the difficult Smolensk offensive in the summer of 1943. Clearly, there were indicators as early as August 1943 that Sokolovsky lacked the skills possessed by Rokossovsky, Eremenko, and even Bagramian, although his masters in Moscow attributed this more to the strength and resilience of Army Group Center's defenses than to Sokolovsky's capabilities.

Ultimately, the October offensive confirmed the *Stavka*'s judgment vis à vis Rokossovsky, Bagramian, and, to a lesser extent, Eremenko. Therefore, the *Stavka* retained all three general officers as *front* commanders during Operation Bagration, when Rokossovsky and Bagramian each justified the *Stavka*'s decision by encircling and destroying entire German armies in the astonishingly brief period of less than a week of combat. The hapless Sokolovsky, however, was relieved of *front* command in April 1944 to spend the remainder of the war as a *front* chief of staff or deputy commander, positions better suited to his skills. When his *front* was split into two after his relief, Sokolovsky was succeeded by Cherniakhovsky and Petrov, successful and vigorous army commanders who went on to command *fronts* well into 1945.

Perhaps the clearest distinguishing factor between the October offensive and Operation Bagration pertained to weather and, to a far lesser extent, terrain. Although the terrain fought over in both offensives was essentially the same, the weather was as different as night and day. As was their custom, in October of 1943 Stalin and his *Stavka* took a calculated risk. Understanding that the fall *rasputitsa* (period of flooded roads), followed by the bitter cold and deep snows of winter, would certainly interfere with offensive operations, nonetheless, they insisted the offensive continue. They did so, first and foremost, because they believed that pressure applied everywhere was likely to produce success somewhere and also because they understood that the factor of weather inhibited operations on both sides. Given the situation in October of 1943, when the Germans were still reeling from their summer defeats, Stalin believed that unrelenting pressure could, in fact, turn an organized German withdrawal into a rout or even collapse. In short, he considered the "imagined" victory well worth the clear additional risk. In addition, with the Red Army advancing with abandon across the entire front, the factors of weather and terrain prompted Stalin and his key military advisers to employ most of the Red Army's remaining armor (specifically, its five tank armies) in the Ukraine as opposed to Belorussia, that is, where it could be used to the greatest effect.

When planning Operation Bagration in the summer of 1944, the weather and terrain conditions in Belorussia led the *Stavka* to reach markedly different conclusions from those it reached in October 1943. When dry weather replaced the rain, snow, and ice of fall and winter, the forests and fields of Belorussia became far better suited to penetration by armor. Therefore, as it prepared for Bagration, the *Stavka* not only filled out its existing tank and mechanized corps in the region with tanks and SP guns but also dispatched the entire 5th Guards Tank Army to Belorussia. Therefore, in late June of 1944, the defending Germans would face not only determined and reinforced infantry and cavalry with overwhelming artillery support but also perceived "hordes" of well-organized armor and mechanized forces advancing with abandon. Possessing about the same amount of armor as they had in October of 1943, in June of 1944 the defenders found themselves little more than "sitting ducks."

Notwithstanding all of these factors, the combat experience the Red Army amassed from October of 1943 through March of 1944 had an immense impact on how it conducted its Bagration offensive in June of 1944. In fact, the operations conducted by Bagramian's 1st Baltic Front and Rokossovsky's Belorussian Front in the preceding fall and winter had brought Army Group Center's defenses in northern and southern Belorussia very close to the breaking point. By April of 1944 it was clear to all, perhaps German as well as Russian, that an effective "push" in these sectors would produce immediate collapse. Nor did it help the army group's situation when Hitler declared the cities of Vitebsk and Bobriusk, along with their defenses, infamous *"Festungsplatzes,"* that is, fortress cities to be held at all cost. This decision ultimately led to the outright destruction of the two German armies virtually locked into those defenses in just five days.

Furthermore, coupled with Bagramian's and Rokossovsky's successes in northern and southern Belorussia, the failure of Sokolovsky's many offensives in the Orsha and Mogilev sectors in eastern Belorussia not only produced irrational German faith in the viability of their defenses in this region but also paved the way for the strategic envelopment of most of Army Group Center's forces in the astonishingly brief period of ten days.

In brief, specific lessons learned in the fall and winter led to the following measures in the summer of 1944:

- The division of the Western Front into the 2nd and 3rd Belorussian Fronts,
- The employment of the 1st Baltic and 3rd Belorussian Fronts to encircle and destroy German Third Panzer Army in Vitebsk,
- The employment of the 1st Belorussian Front along two operational axes (Rogachev and Parichi) to encircle and destroy German Ninth Army in Bobruisk,
- The employment of the 2nd Belorussian Front to tie down German Fourth Army in the Orsha, Mogilev, and Bykhov sectors and to seize Mogilev,
- The employment of the 3rd Belorussian and 1st Belorussian Fronts to encircle German Fourth Army east of Minsk and destroy it in cooperation with the 2nd Belorussian Front,
- The use of armor and mechanized forces to spearhead each and every encirclement operation (separate tank brigades for Vitebsk, 9th Tank, and 1st Guards Tank Corps for Bobruisk and 5th Guards Tank Army and 2nd and 1st Guards Tank Corps for Minsk) and deep exploitation (Oslikovsky's Cavalry-Mechanized Group and 5th Guards Tank Army toward Molodechno and Vil'nius, Pliev's Cavalry-Mechanized Group toward Baranovichi and Brest, and 1st Tank Corps toward Polotsk).

The most vital continuity between the October of 1943 offensive and the Bagration offensive in June of 1944 was the presence of Bagramian and Rokossovsky in command of the 1st Baltic and 1st Belorussian Fronts, respectively. Having experienced the intense combat during the fall of 1943 and winter of 1943–1944, these commanders understood what had to be done if Operation Bagration was to be crowned with success. Evidencing this, on one of the few occasions during the war when Stalin deferred to a *front* commander's recommendation, in late May of 1944 a heated exchange took place between Stalin and Rokossovsky when the latter insisted on conducting two main attacks on German Ninth Army via both the Rogachev and Parichi axes instead of a single blow from the Rogachev region. No doubt impressed by Rokossovsky's successes in the previous months, Stalin ultimately demurred and allowed Rokossovsky's recommendations to prevail.

Thus, as occurred on countless other occasions in the war, in no small measure, the nature and course of the first Belorussian offensive conditioned unprecedented success in the second. Tragically, however, the price paid for this experience in terms of the lives of Red Army soldiers proved tragically high.

Appendices

Directives, Orders, Reports, German Command Cadre in Eastern Belorussia, and Selected Abbreviations

A. THE KALININ AND BALTIC FRONTS' VITEBSK AND NEVEL' OFFENSIVES (3–30 OCTOBER 1943)

A-1. *Stavka* VGK Directive No. 30192 to the Commander of the Kalinin Front and the Representative of the *Stavka* Concerning a Plan for Capturing Vitebsk

1700 hours 20 September 1943

Copy to: The commander of the Western Front
  The *Stavka* of the Supreme High Command ORDERS:
  1. While continuing the offensive with its left wing, the Kalinin Front's main forces are directed to capture Vitebsk. Reach the Ponizov'e, Punitsy, Kasplia, and Tishino line by 26–27 September and capture Vitebsk no later than 9–10 October.
  2. Effective 2400 hours 20 September, establish the following boundary line with the Western Front: to Slobody as before, to Gorni (22 kilometers west of Iartsevo), Ivakhovo, Rogulino (7 kilometers northwest of Smolensk), Arkhipovka, Eliseevka, Dobromysl', and Luchkovskoe Station (27 kilometers south of Vitebsk). All points are inclusive for the Kalinin Front.
  3. Present an operational plan on 22 September 1943.

   The *Stavka* of the Supreme High Command
   I. Stalin, A. Antonov

Source: "Direktiva Stavki VGK No. 30192 komanduiushchemu voiskami Kalininskogo fronta, predstaviteliu Stavki o plana operatsii po ovladeniu Vitebskom" [*Stavka* VGK directive No. 30192 to the commander of the Kalinin Front and the representative of the *Stavka* concerning a plan for capturing Vitebsk], in Zolotarev, *Stavka* VGK 1943, 205. The *Stavka* representative was N. N. Voronov, the commander of the Red Army's Air Force (VVS).

A-2. Report No. 15621 of the Commander of the Kalinin Front to the Supreme High Commander Concerning a Plan for the Vitebsk Operation

2315 hours 22 September 1943

In fulfillment of your Directive No. 30192, I am reporting on a plan for the Vitebsk operation.
  Having begun the Dukhovshchina operation with a penetration of a strongly fortified enemy defense, the Kalinin Front's forces have developed the penetration front up to 155 kilometers and to a depth of up to 55 kilometers.

585

The enemy is offering fierce resistance in all other front sectors, while striving to hold back our offensive and to win time for more major preparations of a defense along a new strategic line.

He can establish this line in the Kalinin Front's sector from the Western Dvina River through Vitebsk, along the Luchesa River, and further to Orsha. Here, at the entrance of the so-called "Smolensk Gates," the enemy will attempt to halt our offensive and, even earlier,—to hold back our movement to the Kasplia River.

The successful development of the Kalinin Front's offensive along the Vitebsk axis is creating favorable conditions for the rapid capture of Smolensk city and the advance of Western Front forces to the Dnepr River line.

Accordingly, I have decided to conduct the operation according to the following plan.

1. To make the main attack with 4th Shock, 43rd, and 39th Armies in the general direction of Vitebsk. To that end:

(a) I will reinforce 4th Shock Army with four rifle divisions (234th, 235th, and 117th Rifle, and 16th Lithuanian Rifle Divisions), 155th Fortified Region, 17th Antitank Brigade, 106th RGK Artillery Regiment, and 20th Guards-Mortar Brigade;

(b) I will form two force groupings on 4th Shock Army's front: the Velizh group, consisting of six rifle divisions, two rifle brigades, and one antitank artillery brigade, for an attack towards Vitebsk along both banks of the Western Dvina River; and the Usviaty group, consisting of three rifle divisions, for an attack towards Mezha and Gorodok and, farther, on Shumilino.

(c) I will reinforce 43rd Army with 1st Rifle Corps, consisting of two rifle divisions; the intermediate grouping of Dremov, consisting of one tank brigade, two mechanized brigades; and an antitank artillery brigade, and a howitzer brigade, and am assigning them the mission, while attacking in the general direction of Vitebsk, to deliver an attack on Rudnia to assist 39th Army's offensive and cut the Vitebsk-Smolensk road and railroad line; and

(d) The 39th Army, consisting of 10 rifle divisions and 1 rifle brigade, will attack along the Verkhov'ia-Volokovaia axis with the mission to assist the Western Front's forces in the capture of Smolensk. Subsequently, it will attack toward Rudnia and Liozno.

2. During the present stage of the operation, the *front's* forces have been ordered to defeat the Germans' Vitebsk-Demidov grouping and reach the Surazh-Vitebsk, Ponizov'e, Sel'tso, Kasplia, and Arkhipovka line by the end of 25–26 September 1943.

The boundary [junction] lines: between 4th Shock and 43rd Armies—Korolevshchina, Riabinki, Luzhki, Ponizov'e, Ianovichi, and northeast part of Vitebsk city (all points besides Ponizov'e are inclusive for 4th Shock Army); between 43rd and 39th Armies—Lake Akatovskoe, Sel'tso, Polenovka, and Sverkhnaia Sosnovka (all points for 43rd Army); and between 39th Army and the Western Front's 31st Army—as before.

3. The *front's* forces will reach the Kurino, Kosov, Lake Vymno, Polenovka, Ushivka, Rudnia, and Eliseevka line during the period from 26 through 29 September 1943.

4. The Kalinin Front's forces will capture Vitebsk and reach the Beguny (16 kilometers southwest of Gorodok), Ustiianova, Shchemilovka, Teliazh, and Babinovichi line along the Luchesa River during the period from 30 September through 6 October 1943.

5. The *front*'s forces will reach the Sirotino, Gnezdilovichi, Tepliaki, Bogushchevsk, and Babinovichi line by the end of 9 October 1943.

The 4th Shock Army's Usviaty grouping will launch its attack from the Klenidovka and Tarasovo front towards Mezha and Gorodok on 27 September 1943.

6. In order to guarantee the plan is fulfilled, I request:

(1) Permit 8th Estonian Corps to relieve two rifle divisions on 3rd Shock Army's front for participation in the offensive.

(2) Place at my disposal 120 tanks, including 70 T-34s and 50 T-70s.

(3) In light of the greatly overextended communications and difficult resupply over roads destroyed by the enemy, transfer to the *front* two automobile battalions of cross-country vehicles.

(4) If possible, dispatch 5,000 personnel replacements to the *front*.

(5) Allocate and immediately send 2 combat loads of ammunition to the *front*.

I request you approve the plan.

Army General Eremenko, Commander of the Kalinin Front
Lieutenant General Leonov, Member of the Kalinin Front's Military Council
Lieutenant General Kurasov, Chief of Staff of the Kalinin Front

Source: "Doklad komanduiushchego voiskami Kalininskogo fronta No.15621 Verkhovnomu Glavnokomanduiushchemu plana Vitebskoi operatsii" [Report No. 15621 of the commander of the Kalinin Front to the Supreme High Commander concerning a plan for the Vitebsk operation], in Zolotarev, *Stavka* VGK 1943, 310–311.

A-3. *Stavka* VGK Directive No. 30195 to the Commander of the Kalinin Front and the Representative of the *Stavka* Concerning More Precise Definition of the Plan for the Vitebsk Operation

0045 hours 24 September 1943

The *Stavka* of the Supreme High Command ORDERS you to make the following changes to plan No. 15621/sh that you submitted:

1. Shvetsov's 4th Shock Army will consist of no fewer than 13 rifle divisions with reinforcing equipment and 3 corps headquarters. Employ seven of that army's rifle divisions to attack from the Usviaty region toward Gorodok and roll up the enemy's defense with part of the force by operations toward Usviaty and Nevel'. Use no fewer than six rifle divisions for an attack on Vitebsk along the Western Dvina River.

2. Golubev's 43rd Army will consist of six–seven divisions and Berzarin's 39th Army of no fewer than five rifle divisions. Reinforce 4th Shock Army at the expense of these two armies and three divisions being sent to you by the *Stavka*. To hasten the regrouping, carry it out by means of transferring divisions from one neighboring army to another neighboring army.

3. Leave the Estonian Corps in *front* reserve. Henceforth, do not weaken 3rd Shock Army.

4. Submit a more precisely defined plan on 25 September 1943.

The *Stavka* of the Supreme High Command
I. Stalin, A. Antonov

Source: "Direktiva Stavki VGK No. 30195 komanduiushchemu voiskami Kalininskogo fronta, predstaviteliu Stavki ob utochnenii plana Vitebskoi operatsii" [*Stavka* VGK directive No. 30195 to the commander of the Kalinin Front and the representative of the *Stavka* concerning more precise definition of the plan for the Vitebsk operation], in Zolotarev, *Stavka* VGK 1943, 207.

A-4. *Stavka* VGK Directive No. 30217 to the Commander of the Baltic Front Concerning the Preparation and Conduct of an Offensive Operation along the Idritsa Axis

2230 hours 8 October 1943

The *Stavka* of the Supreme High Command ORDERS:

1. Without waiting for the complete concentration of all of its forces, the Baltic Front, together with the Northwestern, Volkhov, and Leningrad Fronts, will launch an offensive no later than 15 October with the mission to defeat the enemy's northern grouping and prevent it from withdrawing to Dvinsk and Riga. Deliver the main attack in the general direction of Riga, Idritsa, Ludza, Gulbene, and Valga. Attack Opochka, Ostrov, and Pskov with part of your forces and firmly protect the operations of the main force from the Riga axis. The immediate mission is to capture the Novo-Rzhev, Opochka, and Sebezh regions. Subsequently, reach the Pskov, Vyru, Valga, and Valmiera line.

2. The *front* will take control of the Northwestern Front's 22nd Army and the Kalinin Front's 3rd Shock Army on 15 October, but they will be supplied by their former *fronts* until 30 October.

3. On the right—The Northwestern Front will attack from the Staraia Russa region in the direction of Dno and Pskov. The boundary line with it is Kuzhenkino, Zhabny, Krasukha, Mashugina Gora, Molvotitsy, Namosh'e, Zakharovo, Lopari, Chikhachevo Station, and Ostrov. All points except Ostrov are inclusive for the Northwestern Front.

4. On the left—The Kalinin Front will attack along both banks of the Western Dvina River in the general direction of Vitebsk, Polotsk, Daugavpils (Dvinsk), and Riga. The boundary line with it is Staritsa, Rzhev, Kholmets, Arbuzovo, Semenovskoe, Khmelevo, Pershkovo, Annino, Kosmachevo, Lake Dniko, Lake Melkoe, Klinovoe, Staryi Prud, Liakhovo, and Kaunata. All points except Klinovoe, Staryi Prud, Liakhovo, and Kaunata are inclusive for the Kalinin Front.

5. The Baltic Front is entrusted with responsibility for protecting the boundary with the Northwestern Front and the Kalinin Front for the boundary with the Kalinin Front.

6. Submit an operational plan by stages and periods by 15 October.

The *Stavka* of the Supreme High Command
I. Stalin, A. Antonov

Source: "Direktiva Stavki VGK No. 30217 komanduiushchemu voiskami Pribaltiiskogo fronta o podgotovke i provedenii nastupatel'noi operatsii na Idritskom napravlenii" [*Stavka* VGK directive No. 30217 to the commander of the Baltic Front concerning the preparation and conduct of an offensive operation along the Idritsa axis], in Zolotarev, *Stavka* VGK 1943, 218–219.

A-5. *Stavka* VGK Directive No. 30218 to the Commander of the Kalinin Front on the Development of an Offensive to Capture Riga

2230 hours 8 October 1943

The *Stavka* of the Supreme High Command ORDERS:

1. The Kalinin Front will transfer 3rd Shock Army with five rifle divisions and three rifle brigades and 8th Estonian Rifle Corps with two rifle divisions to the newly formed Baltic Front by 2400 hours on 15 October. Transfer 3rd Shock Army and 8th Estonian Corps, with all reinforcements and rear services units and facilities and on-hand material reserves.

The Kalinin Front will supply 3rd Shock Army and 8th Estonian Rifle Corps until 30 October.

2. The Kalinin Front's mission—After capturing the Vitebsk region, continue the offensive, delivering your main attack along both banks of the Western Dvina River in the direction of Polotsk, Dvinsk, and Riga, while reliably protecting the operations of the main force from the Vil'nius axis. The immediate mission is to reach the Osveia, Drissa, Disna, and Plisa line. Subsequently, attack in the general direction of Dvinsk, with your final aim being the capture of Riga, the capital of Latvia.

3. On the right—The Baltic Front will attack in the general direction of Nevel' and Idritsa. The boundary line with it is: Staritsa, Rzhev, Kholmet, Arbuzovo, Semenovskoe, Khmelevo, Pershkovo, Annino, Kosmachevo, Lake Dniko, Lake Melkoe, Klinovoe, Staryi Prud, Liakhovo, and Kaunata. All points except Klinovoe, Staryi Prud, Liakhovo, and Kaunata are inclusive for the Kalinin Front.

On the left—The Western Front will attack in the general direction of Orsha, Borisov, Molodechno, and Vil'no [Vil'nius]. The boundary line with it is to Luchkovskoe Station as before, and further to Kamen', Plisa, and Koziany. All points are inclusive for the Kalinin Front.

4. The Kalinin Front is entrusted with responsibility for protecting the boundaries with the Baltic and Western Fronts.

The *Stavka* of the Supreme High Command
I. Stalin, A. Antonov

Source: "Direktiva Stavki VGK No. 30218 komanduiushchemu Kalininskogo fronta na razvitie nastupleniia s tsel'iu ovladeniia Rigoi" [*Stavka* VGK directive No. 30218 to the commander of the Kalinin Front on the development of an offensive to capture Riga], in Zolotarev, *Stavka* VGK 1943, 219.

A-6. *Stavka* VGK Directive No. 30219 to the Commander of the Northwestern Front on the Preparation and Conduct of an Operation to Destroy the Enemy's Porkhov Grouping

1800 hours 10 October 1943

The *Stavka* of the Supreme High Command ORDERS:

1. The Northwestern Front will transfer 22nd Army, with five rifle divisions and one rifle brigade and, in addition, 43rd Latvian Rifle Division, to the newly formed

Baltic Front by 2400 hours on 12 October. Transfer the army with all reinforcing equipment, army rear service units and facilities and on-hand material reserves.

The Northwestern Front will supply the 22nd Army until 30 October 1943.

2. The Northwestern Front's mission—Together with the Baltic Front, destroy the enemy's Porkhov grouping by an offensive in the general direction of Dno and Pskov and reach the Shelon' River, Dno, and Chikhachevo Station front. Subsequently attack in the general direction of Pskov.

Be prepared to attack on 25 October.

3. On the right—The Volkhov Front will attack from the region north of Novgorod in the general direction of Luga. The boundary line with it is: to Iur'evo, as before, and farther to the western bank of Lake Il'men', Shimsk, Sol'tsy, and M'iakovo. All [points] are inclusive for the Volkhov Front.

On the left—The Baltic Front will attack in the general direction of Nevel' and Idritsa and, with part of its forces, toward Opochka and Ostrov. The boundary line with it is: Kuzhenkino, Zhabny, Krasukha, Mashugina Gora, Molvotitsy, Namosh'e, Zakharovo, Lopari, Chikhachevo Station, and Ostrov. All points except Ostrov are inclusive for the Northwestern Front.

4. The Volkhov Front is entrusted with responsibility for protecting the boundary with the Volkhov Front and the Baltic Front the boundary with the Baltic Front.

5. Submit an operational plan by stages and periods by 15 October.

The *Stavka* of the Supreme High Command
I. Stalin, A. Antonov

Source: "Direktiva Stavki VGK No. 30219 komanduiushchemu Severo-zapadnogo fronta na podrotovku i provedenie operatsii po razgromu Porkhovskoi gruppirovki protivnika" [*Stavka* VGK directive No. 30219 to the commander of the Northwestern Front on the preparation and conduct of an operation to destroy the enemy's Porkhov grouping], in Zolotarev, *Stavka* VGK 1943, 220.

A-7. *Stavka* VGK Directive No. 30220 to the Commanders of the Baltic, Northwestern, and Kalinin Fronts Concerning a Change in the Period of the Resubordination of 3rd Shock and 22nd Armies and the Missions of Their Air Support

2210 hours 10 October 1943

The *Stavka* of the Supreme High Command ORDERS:

1. In a change to *Stavka* directives Nos. 30209 and 30218, the Northwestern Front's 22nd Army and the Kalinin Front's 3rd Shock Army will be transferred to the Baltic Front at 2400 hours on 12 October. These *fronts* will supply these armies until 30 October.

2. In light of the tardiness in the rebasing of the Baltic Front's aviation and in order that 22nd and 3rd Shock Armies not be left without air support, the commanders of the Northwestern and Kalinin Fronts will cover [protect] them with their aviation until 16 October: the Northwestern Front [will cover] 22nd Army and the Kalinin Front 3rd Shock Army.

Appendices 591

3. Report receipt of these instructions.

The *Stavka* of the Supreme High Command

I. Stalin, A. Antonov

Source: "Direktiva Stavki VGK No. 30220 komanduiushchim voiskami Pribaltiiskogo, Severo-zapadnogo i Kalininskogo frontov na izmenenie srokov perepodchineniia 3-i udarnoi i 22-i armii i o zadachakh ikh aviatsionnogo prikrytiia" [*Stavka* VGK directive No. 30220 to the commanders of the Baltic, Northwestern, and Kalinin Fronts concerning a change in the period of the resubordination of 3rd Shock and 22nd Armies and the missions of their air support], in Zolotarev, *Stavka* VGK 1943, 220–221.

A-8. From an Enciphered Telegram to the *Stavka* from the Kalinin Front

11 October 1943

To the Supreme High Commander, Marshal of the Soviet Union Comrade I. V. Stalin

The *front*'s initially successful Nevel' operation has not achieved its required development because, by exploiting the temporary calm on other fronts, the enemy has concentrated considerable aircraft against the Kalinin Front's forces and, by doing so, has achieved temporary air superiority along this axis. Enemy aviation in groups of 50–60 aircraft are continuously attacking and bombing the combat formations of the attacking forces of 3rd and 4th Shock Armies, driving them to the ground, retarding their advance, and weakening the offensive impulse. On each day of combat, the enemy is completing 800 or more sorties in 3rd and 4th Armies' offensive sector. The 84 fighters that the *front* possesses are completely inadequate to fight with the enemy aircraft and to protect the forces' combat formations on the battlefield. In order to accelerate the tempo of our offensive, I request that one fighter aviation corps and, if only as many as 150 tanks, half of them T-34s, be allocated and assigned to me.

Eremenko, Kurasov

Source: "Zhurnal boevykh deistvii 1-go Pribaltiiskogo fronta za oktiabr' 1943 g" [The 1st Baltic Front's journal of combat operations for October 1943], TsAMO, f. 235, op. 2074, d. 51, l. 77.

A-9. To the Commander of the Kalinin Front Concerning the Preparation of an Operation for the Destruction of Enemy Aviation

0230 hours 12 October 1943

Copy to: The commanders of the Red Army Air Forces and 3rd Air Army

The People's Commissar of Defense ORDERS you to prepare an operation for the destruction of enemy aviation in the Vitebsk, Orsha, and Ulla regions. Attack aerodromes that are the most saturated with aircraft, and, to that end, conduct careful reconnaissance in accordance with earlier received information. Employ no fewer than 100 fighters and 100 assault aircraft simultaneously.

Instructions concerning the sequence and timing of the operation will be provided additionally by the Red Army Air Force [VVS] Command.

Antonov

Source: "Komanduiushchemu voiskami Kalininskogo fronta o podgotovke operatsii po unichtozheniiu aviatsii protivnika" [To the commander of the Kalinin Front concerning the preparation of an operation for the destruction of enemy aviation], in Zolotarev, General Staff, 1943, 370. On the same day, the General Staff issued similar orders to the Western Front to destroy enemy aviation in the Mogilev, Bobruisk, and Bykhov regions with 120 fighters, 30 assault aircraft, and 30 bombers and the Central Front to destroy enemy aviation in the Dymer, Radomyshl', Fastov, Vasil'kov, and Kiev regions with 160 fighters, 80 assault aircraft, and 60 bombers. Similar orders went to the other *fronts* that were operating along the southwestern and southern axes.

A-10. Report No. 22 of the Commander of the Baltic Front to the Supreme High Commander on the Plan for the First Stage of the Operation along the Idritsa Axis

1745 hours 13 October 1943

I am reporting to you my views and assessments regarding the plan for the first stage of the operation.

The aim and missions are the widening of the Nevel' penetration, the clearing out of the Novosokol'niki sector of the enemy's defense, and reaching the Navsa, Lake Bol'shoe Ostrie, Pustoshka, Zarech'e, and Lake Usvecha line. The depth is 60–70 kilometers. The time required is 8–10 days.

The commander of 3rd SA will conduct local battles to widen the penetration on the vicinity of Nevel' until 16 October in order to attract enemy forces and attention to his sector.

Complete concentrating 93rd RC, with its artillery and tank reinforcements, which is being transferred to 3rd SA, to the east of Lake Malyi Ivan on 15 October.

The 3rd SA and 93rd RC will attack on 16 October to reach the Borshchanka, Okin, Rechki, Borovichi, and Tochino front by day's end on 17 October.

Complete concentrating 79th RC, which is also being transferred to 3rd SA, in the Chernozema region southwest of Velikie Luki on 17 October.

The 3rd SA, reinforced by 79th C, will continue its offensive on the morning of 18 October and reach the Novosokol'niki, Tumashi, Teplukhina, and Nevel' line by the end of 19 October.

Concentrate three divisions of 22nd Army to the west of Velikie Luki on 19 October. These will be included in the operation on the morning of 20 October and will attack to the north and northwest from the Novosokol'niki region to reach the Lake Bol'shoe Ostrie, Pustoshka, Zarech'e, and Lake Usvecha line on 24–25 October.

The arrival of 22nd and 3rd SAs' forces at the indicated lines will conclude the first stage of the operation. By this time, we envision completing the concentration of one corps from 6th Gds.A and one corps of 11th Gds.A in the region between Velikie Luki and Toropets. I propose combining them under the command 11th Gds.A and, as they concentrate, moving them to the north of Pustoshka (a 4–7 day movement).

The 22nd and 3rd SAs' forces will put themselves into order and bring up their rear services and artillery along the Navsa, Skokovo, Pustoshka, and Lake Usvecha line. [Then], depending on the situation, [they] will continue the offensive on the entire front or will conduct local operations to widen the penetration along tactically favorable axes while awaiting the approach of the corps combined under 11th Guards Army's command. Presumably, the penetration front will expand to 120 kilometers by 24–25 October, and, without the arrival of new forces, its further widening will be stretched literally to a thread by the forces of both armies.

I am requesting:

1. Your approval of my decision.

2. Authorize the proposed plan for the entire *front* operation on 25 October instead of 15 October, since the situation and the time for concentrating the forces will take shape in that period

3. Order the GAU [Main Artillery Directorate] to allocate one combat load of ammunition above that already allocated.

Popov, Mekhlis

Source: "Doklad komanduiushchego voiskami Pribaltiiskogo fronta Verkhovnomu Glavnokomanduiushchemu plana pervogo etapa operatsii na Idritskom napravlenii" [Report No. 22 of the commander of the Baltic Front to the Supreme High Commander on the plan for the first stage of the operation along the Idritsa axis], in Zolotarev, *Stavka* VGK 1943, 320–321.

A-11. *Stavka* VGK Directive No. 30224 to the Commander of the Baltic Front Concerning the Missions of the Second Stage of the Operation along the Idritsa Axis

0100 hours 15 October 1943

The *Stavka* of the Supreme High Command approves the plan for the first stage of the operation that you presented on 13 October 1943 as [Report] No. 22 and ORDERS:

1. Submit your plan for the second stage of the operation in accordance with *Stavka* directive No. 30217 no later than 16 October.

2. The aim of the second stage of the *front's* offensive operation must be the occupation of the Idritsa railroad center and the capture of the Ostrov-Rezekne (Rezhitsa) railroad line.

Envision operations by part of your forces along the Novorzhev and Ostrov axis to roll up the enemy defense opposite 22nd Army's front.

The *Stavka* of the Supreme High Command
Stalin, Antonov

Source: "Direktiva Stavki VGK No. 30224 komanduiushchemu voiskami Pribaltiiskogo fronta o zadachakh vtorogo etapa operatsii na Idritskom napravlenii" [*Stavka* VGK directive No. 30224 to the commander of the Baltic Front concerning the missions of the second stage of the operation along the Idritsa axis], in Zolotarev, *Stavka* VGK 1943, 222.

A-12. *Stavka* VGK Order No. 30228 Concerning the Renaming of the Central, Kalinin, and Baltic Fronts

2230 hours 16 October 1943

Effective on 20 October, establish the following new names for *fronts*:

Name the Central Front the Belorussian Front.

Name the Kalinin Front the 1st Baltic Front.
Name the Baltic Front the 2nd Baltic Front.
Report receipt of this order.

The *Stavka* of the Supreme High Command
I. Stalin, A. Antonov

Source: "Prikaz Stavki VGK No. 30228 o pereimenovanii Tsentral'nogo, Kalininskogo i Pribaltiiskogo frontov" [*Stavka* VGK order No. 30228 concerning the renaming of the Central, Kalinin, and Baltic Fronts], in Zolotarev, *Stavka* VGK 1943, 225.

A-13. From Enciphered Telegram No. 16556 to the *Stavka* from the Kalinin Front

19 October 1943

To the Supreme High Commander, Marshal of the Soviet Union Comrade I. V. Stalin

The Kalinin Front's formations and units have been significantly exhausted during the course of over two or more months of uninterrupted combat. The rifle divisions have 3,500 to 4,500 men each. Such a situation has had a telling effect on the nature and results of the recent combat. My carefully organized and personally prepared operations by 43rd and 39th Armies east of Vitebsk have had no success. . . . Therefore, I request that you permit the Kalinin Front's forces to pause for 10–12 days. . . . I request that you reinforce the Kalinin Front with two rifle corps and one tank or mechanized corps for fulfillment of the assigned missions.

Eremenko, Leonov, Kurasov

Source: "Zhurnal boevykh deistvii voisk 1-go Pribaltiiskogo fronta za oktiabr' 1943 g" [The 1st Baltic Front's journal of combat operations for October 1943], *TsAMO*, f. 235, op. 2074, d. 51, l. 78.

B. THE WESTERN FRONT'S ORSHA OFFENSIVES (3–28 OCTOBER 1943)

B-1. *Stavka* VGK Directive No. 30193 to the Commander of the Western Front and the Representative of the *Stavka* Concerning the Destruction of the Enemy Smolensk Grouping

1700 hours 20 September 1943

Copy to: The commander of the Kalinin Front

1. The Western Front, while continuing its offensive to destroy the enemy Smolensk grouping, will capture Smolensk on 26–27 September. Occupy the Pochinok and Roslavl' line with the *front*'s left wing and reach the Sozh River, Khislavichi, and Shumiachi line by this time.

Subsequently, attack with the *front*'s main grouping in the general direction of Orsha and capture the Orsha and Mogilev regions on 10–12 October.

2. Effective 2400 hours on 20 September, the boundary line with the Kalinin Front is to Sloboda, as before, and farther to Gorni (22 kilometer west of Iartsevo), Ivakhovo, Rogulino (7 kilometer northwest of Smolensk), Arkhipovka, Eliseevka, Dobromysl', and Luchkovskoe Station (27 kilometers south of Vitebsk). All points are exclusive for the Western Front.

3. Submit an operational plan by 22 September 1943.

The *Stavka* of the Supreme High Command
I. Stalin, A. Antonov

Source: "Direktiva Stavki No. 30193 komanduiushchemu voiskami Zapadnogo fronta, predstavitiliu Stavki na razgrom Smolenskoi gruppirovki protivnika" [*Stavka* VGK directive No. 30193 to the commander of the Western Front and the representative of the *Stavka* concerning the destruction of the enemy Smolensk grouping], in Zolotarev, *Stavka* VGK 1943, 205–206.

B-2. *Stavka* VGK Directive No. 30210 to the Commander of the Western Front on the Development of an Offensive to Capture the City of Vilnius

1 October 1943

The *Stavka* of the Supreme High Command ORDERS:

1. After capturing the Orsha and Mogilev region, the Western Front will continue its offensive in the general direction of Borisov and Molodechno and reach the Dokshitsy, Dolginovo, and Radoshkovichi front. Subsequently, have the aim of capturing the city of Vilnius, the capital of Lithuania.

2. On the right—The Kalinin Front will attack in the general direction of Vitebsk, Polotsk, and Daugavpils (Dvinsk), with the subsequent mission to capture the city of Riga, the capital of Latvia. The boundary line with it is: to Luchkovaia Station as before, and farther to Kamen', Plisa, and Koziany. All points are inclusive for the Kalinin Front.

On the left—The Central Front will attack in the general direction of Zhlobin and Bobruisk and capture the city of Minsk, the capital of Belorussia. The boundary line with it is: Kirov, Snopot', Prigory, Krichev, Dashkovka, Berezino, and Radoshkovichi. All points are inclusive for the Western Front.

The Briansk Front is disbanded effective on 10 October.

3. The Kalinin Front is entrusted with responsibility for protecting the boundary with the Kalinin Front and the Western Front for [securing the boundary with] the Central Front.

4. Confirm receipt of this directive. Submit an operational plan with definite periods and stages by 5 October 1943.

The *Stavka* of the Supreme High Command
I. Stalin, A. Antonov

Source: "Direktiva Stavki VGK No. 30210 komanduiushchemu voiskami Zapadnogo fronta na razvitie nastupleniia s tsel'iu ovladeniia g. Vil'nius" [*Stavka* VGK directive No. 30210 to the commander of the Western Front on the development of an offensive to capture the city of Vilnius], in Zolotarev, *Stavka* VGK 1943, 215.

B-3. "Intelligence Summary No. 469 and Operational Summary No. 469 of the Western Front's Headquarters, 1 October 1943"

1 October

During the preceding days, the armies' forces on the *front*'s right wing and in its center continued to conduct fierce fighting for the exits from the forested swampy defile and to seize crossings and defensive positions on the Mereia and Pronia Rivers. On the left wing, they developed the offensive successfully and, while advancing westward from 10 to 27 kilometers, captured 142 populated points.

On the Orsha axis, the enemy's XXVII AC, while stubbornly defending the highway with units of 197th ID on the Ermaki and Dnepr River line, undertook strong counterattacks with infantry and tanks during the day.

South of the Dnepr River, XXXIX PzC, with its main forces on its left wing (18th PzGrD and 337th ID), conducted defensive fighting along the Mereia River line.

Information from prisoners confirmed the arrival of reinforcing personnel and equipment in 197th and 337th IDs and 18th PzGrD.

The IX AC defended its existing positions during the day.

Observation noted the arrival of self-propelled artillery and tanks: 7 self-propelled guns in the Lavrininki region (6 kilometers southwest of Sutoki); 15 tanks at Zhelvachevka (4 kilometers southwest of Lenino); and 12 tanks at Liady.

[The following] prisoners were seized on 1 October—5th Company, 347th IR, 197th ID in the Klimenki region (6 kilometers north of Liady); and 601st Antiaircraft Battalion in the Rudashkovo region (5 kilometers north of Baevo).

A prisoner from 3rd Company, 332nd IR, 197th ID, who was seized on 29 September in the Ermaki region (12 kilometers north of Liady), indicated that a march battalion of more than 1,000 men had arrived from Holland on 16 September.

A prisoner from the same regiment, Victor Hundert, indicated that, in early June 1943, two march companies of 237th Reserve Battalion numbering 300 men each arrived from El'zak-Lataringii to reinforce 197th ID.

On the Mogilev axis, units of Fourth Army stubbornly defended the positions they occupied. The units of Ninth Army, while resisting stubbornly, were thrown back 20–25 kilometers to the Pronia River.

The IX AC, while protecting Gorki from the east, was defending positions (incl.) from Lenino and Koniukhi along the Bystraia, Remistvianka, and Pronia Rivers up to Golovichi.

The units of XI and LVI Corps were driven from a series of points and were offering resistance along [illegible, but likely "along the Pronia River up to Starosel'e" and further] to Novo-Aleksandrovka and Liakhovshchina by day's end. During the fighting, the units of 131st ID were shifted southward and were fighting in the region west and southwest Moliatichi during the first half of the day. A prisoner mentioned 26th ID in the region south of Riasna. A garrison of up to 150 men was destroyed in the Vysokaia region (10 kilometers south of Riasna).

Force reconnaissance and prisoner reports indicated the presence of trenches, foxholes and, in separate regions, barbed wire obstacles and minefields on the western bank of the Pronia River.

Prisoners captured from 555th IR in the Puply region confirmed operations of 330th ID along the Pilianitsa-Medvedeva line.

Air reconnaissance noticed defensive work being conducted in the Gorka and Budino sector (20 kilometers north of Chausy) on the western bank of the Pronia River and a line of foxholes in the Litvinovichi and Chernovka (15 kilometers southeast of Litvinovichi) sector on the western bank of the Basia River.

Partisans are reporting:

27 September–1 October.43—heavy movement of forces on the roads from Orsha to Borisov and, according to reports from soldiers, German forces are withdrawing behind the Berezina River, where they are going over to the defense.

The Germans are continuing to fortify the Mogilev center of resistance, are constructing pillboxes and bunkers, and are digging trenches with prisoners of war and the civilian population. There are minefields between Mogilev and Lupolovo. At the same time, they are constructing positions on the western bank of the Berezina River. The Bobruisk center of resistance is being created.

The defensive belt is being constructed to depths of up to 20–23 kilometers.

31st Army

The army's units are continuing to conduct fierce fighting for the exits from the forested swampy defile. As a result of the fighting, the army drove the enemy from the groves south of Prisel'e. Fighting is going on in previous positions in the remainder of the front.

The enemy is offering stubborn resistance along the army's entire front. He is holding off the attacking units with heavy fire from all types of weapons and counterattacks by infantry and tanks. A prisoner has been seized from 347th IR of 197th ID in the Khlystovka region. During the day, observation detected the approach of up to 180 enemy infantrymen and three tanks in the Belei region.

The army's losses on 29 and 30 September—177 men killed and 330 men wounded.

During this period, we destroyed 850 enemy soldiers and officers, one self-propelled gun, 4 field guns, 16 machine guns, and 3 mortars and captured 8 prisoners, 5 machine guns, 6 vehicles, 30,000 rounds of ammunition, and a warehouse with engineer equipment.

5th Army

The army's forces completed a march on the night of 1 October. On the morning of 1 October, the army's formations rested in the [following] regions: 207th RD—Siniaki, Tishino, Kuprino, and Kholm (east); and 312th Smolensk RD—Budkovo, Smetanino, and Kotyn'-Pokrovskoe. With the onset of darkness, the divisions continued their march, with the mission of reaching the eastern bank of the Malaia Berezina River.

Units of 152nd FR concentrated in the Verkh. Dubrovka, Podles'e, Ershchi-Nizishchi, and Nov. Bateki region at 1900 hours.

68th Army

The army's forces continued to conduct fighting to capture crossings and enemy defensive positions on the western bank of the Mereia River.

Forward subunits of the army's units crossed over the Mereia River in separate sectors of the front by 1200 hours and fought sustained battles to widen the sectors seized during the course of the day. The enemy stubbornly defended the positions they occupied with units of 113th ID and 18th PzGrD. Massed artillery and mortar fire hindered the crossing of our forces over the Mereia River during the course of the day.

The army's losses on 30 September: 70 killed and 357 wounded.

10th Guards Army

During the day, the army's units reconnoitered the firing systems and engineer obstacles in the enemy's defenses on the western bank of the Mereia River with combat reconnaissance and observation.

After a short artillery preparation, at 1800 hours the units resumed fighting for crossings along [the following] front:

15th Gds.RC. 30th Gds.RD—the eastern and southeastern outskirts of Liady to 1 kilometer southwest of Makhnitskaia; 85th Gds.RD—committed into combat from behind the left flank of 30th Gds.RD on a front from 1.5 kilometers north of Tiveli to (incl.) Chernyshi; 65rd Gds.RD—Chernishi to Bol. Tugovishchi; and 56th Gds. RD—incl. Bol. Tugovishchi to 0.5 kilometer south of Kovshichi. The battle for the crossings is continuing.

The enemy, while stubbornly defending the western bank of the Mereia River with strong fire from all types of weapons, is hindering our forces from crossing the river. 15 artillery and 9 mortar batteries, 4 six-barreled mortars, and 3 heavy metal apparatuses [*sic*] are conducting fire against the combat formations of our forces and the crossings over the Mereia River. Enemy aviation in groups of 3–6 aircraft bombed the combat formations of our forces and the close-in rear area.

Source: "Opersvodka Shtaba Z. F. No. 469, Razvedsvodka Shtaba Z. F. No. 275," 1 Oktiabria [Operational Summary No. 469 and Intelligence Summary No. 275 of the Western Front's Headquarters, 1 October 1943], in *Combat Operations of the Western Front's Forces in October 1943*, https://cdn.pamyat-naroda.ru/images.

B-4. *Stavka* VGK Directive No. 30225 to the Commander of the Western Front and the Representative of the *Stavka* on a Regrouping of Forces

2320 hours 15 October 1943

The forces of the Western Front have not fulfilled their assigned mission—to capture Orsha by 12 October—and are conducting long drawn out and fruitless battles that have led to losses of time, forces, and weaponry. This has occurred because of the incorrect grouping of the *front's* forces. The main grouping—up to half of all of the *front's* rifle divisions with a great proportion of its reinforcing weaponry—has been created in the *front's* center sector [21st and 33rd Armies]. In the event this grouping advances successfully, it will stew [sweat] its way to the Dnepr River, and, as a result, further development of the offensive will be limited. At the same time, the *front's* right wing can attack without having to force the Dnepr River and is capable of clearing the Dnepr by means of an attack against the flank and rear of the enemy defending along the Dnepr.

The 5th and 68th Armies, which have only three rifle divisions each, are extremely weak and are operating with a very cumbersome army command and control apparatus and rear service structure.

Having studied the situation, the *Stavka* of the Supreme High Command ORDERS:

1. Immediately begin decisively regrouping your forces to reinforce the *front's* right wing and get rid of the weak armies.

2. Transfer all three of 5th Army's divisions to 31st Army and subsequently combine them into a corps. Withdraw 5th Army's headquarters into the *front's* reserve.

3. Reinforce 68th and 10th Guards Armies at the expense of 21st and 33rd Armies, increasing the number of divisions in each of these armies up to nine (three corps in each army).

4. Leave one army with eight rifle divisions on the front previously occupied by the 21st and 33rd Armies (a front of 10 kilometers), so that the army does not cease active operations. Withdraw the army headquarters of one of the armies into the *front's* reserve.

5. Complete the regrouping of forces no later than 21 October.

6. In accordance with the new grouping, allocate reinforcing equipment so that the greater portion of it is on 31st, 68th, and 10th Guards Armies' front.

7. Conduct 31st Army's offensive planned for 17 October depending on the regrouping of forces.

8. Use the workers in the headquarters of the armies that are being withdrawn into the *front's* reserve to reinforce the *front's* corps and armies.

9. If Zhuravlev [commander of 68th Army] considers himself unable to cope with so large an army, you have the right to replace him with another commander from an army being withdrawn into the *front's* reserve.

10. Report concerning the orders given and the regrouping. Submit a plan for subsequent operations by the *front* in its new grouping by 19 October 1943.

The *Stavka* of the Supreme High Command
I. Stalin, A. Antonov

Source: "Direktiva Stavki VGK No. 30225 komanduiushchemu voiskami Zapadnogo fronta i predstaviteliu Stavki na peregruppirovku voisk" [*Stavka* VGK directive No. 30225 to the commander of the Western Front and the representative of the *Stavka* on a regrouping of forces], in Zolotarev, *Stavka VGK 1943*, 223–224. The representative of the *Stavka* was N. N. Voronov.

C. THE CENTRAL FRONT'S GOMEL'-RECHITSA OFFENSIVE (30 SEPTEMBER–30 OCTOBER 1943)

C-1. Report No. 312 of the Commander of the Briansk Front to the Supreme High Commander on a Plan for an Operation along the Zhlobin Axis

0315 hours 19 September 1943

I am reporting my views on further planning for an offensive operation.

1. Protected by rearguards, the enemy is withdrawing his main forces to the west, while organizing his defense along intermediate lines.

2. The Briansk Front's forces are organizing a pursuit of the withdrawing enemy, with the missions to disrupt the organized enemy withdrawal and cut his forces up into separate groups, which can then be defeated in detail by means of throwing a cavalry-mechanized group forward and by maneuvering the armies' forces.

3. The concept of the operation:

(a) Deliver the main attack in the central sector between the Kletnia forests and the Pochep and Klinitsy line, a width of 40–50 kilometers, in the direction of Mglin, Surazh, Chechersk, and Zhlobin;

(b) Throw forward along that axis a cavalry-mechanized group (2nd Gds.CC, 1st TC, 30th MRB, 12th TDB, 13th AAD, one tank and two guards-mortar regiments, two engineer battalions, and one pontoon battalion) under the command of my deputy Lieutenant General Kazakov, which will be supported by all frontal aviation;

(c) The 3rd and 11th Armies will attack behind the cavalry-mechanized group;

(d) The 11th Guards Army (eight RDs), 2nd APC, 44th AB, 2nd Gds.-MD, two mortar regiments, and 29th TB, which constitute my reserve, will move from the Briansk region behind 3rd and 11th Armies; and

(e) The 50th Army (seven RDs) and 63rd Army (eight RDs, two of which will revert to my reserve upon their arrival at the Sudost' River) will attack on somewhat extended fronts on the right and left wings.

4. Planning:

(a) The first stage of the *front* operation—reach the Krichev, Surazh, and Novozybkov line—a depth of 140–160 kilometers, a tempo of 15–20 kilometers per day, and arrival from 27–29 September 1943;

(b) The second stage—reach the Sozh River—and the third stage—reach the Dnepr River—the timing has not been planned; and

(c) The immediate missions: The cavalry-mechanized group will leave the Belogolovl', Uprusy, Neshkovichi, and 50 kilometers west of Briansk region on 22 September 1943 in the direction of Mglin and capture the Surazh region by 24 September 1943.

The first echelon armies will reach the Ershichi, Mglin, and Starodub line (a depth of 70–90 kilometers) from 22–24 September 1943.

The 11th Guards Army will concentrate in the Ovstug, Chertovichi, and Briansk region on 22 September 1943.

Copies of my directives to the army commanders that I have sent to the chief of the General Staff include similar missions sent to army commanders.

5. The rapid tempo of the operation is creating great supply difficulties because of the lag in railroad reconstruction.

I request instructions concerning the possible allocation of another six automobile battalions to the *front*.

I await your orders.

Army General Popov, Commander of the Briansk Front
Lieutenant General Mekhlis, Member of the Briansk Front Military Council
Lieutenant General Sandalov, Chief of Staff of the Briansk Front

Source: "Doklad komanduiushchego voiskami Brianskogo fronta No. 312 Verkhovnomu Glavnokomanduiushchemu plana operatsii na Zhlobinskom napravlenii" [Report No. 312 of the commander of the Briansk Front to the Supreme High Commander on a plan for an operation along the Zhlobin axis], in Zolotarev, *Stavka* VGK 1943, 309–310.

C-2. *Stavka* VGK Directive No. 30191 to the Commander of the Briansk Front Concerning Approval and Amplification of a Plan for an Offensive on Minsk

0300 hours 20 September 1943

The *Stavka* of the Supreme High Command approves plan No. 312/sh presented by you for subsequent *front* operations and ORDERS:

1. Direct the *front's* main forces to seize the railroad center at Zhlobin and Bobruisk. Subsequently attack in the general direction of Minsk.

2. Fulfill the missions of the first stage by 25–26 September, reach the Sozh River by 2–3 October, and capture the Zhlobin region by 10–12 October.

The *Stavka* of the Supreme High Command
I. Stalin, A. Antonov

Source: "Direktiva Stavki VGK No. 30191 komanduiushchemu voiskami Brianskogo fronta ob utverzhdenii i utochnenii plana nastupleniia na Minsk" [*Stavka* VGK directive No. 30191 to the commander of the Briansk Front concerning approval and amplification of a plan for an offensive on Minsk], in Zolotarev, *Stavka* VGK 1943, 204.

C-3. *Stavka* VGK Directive No. 30208 to the Commander of the Central Front on the Defeat of the Enemy Zhlobin-Bobruisk Grouping and the Capture of Minsk

1830 hours 1 October 1943

The *Stavka* of the Supreme High Command ORDERS:

1. After capturing the Kiev region along with the Voronezh Front, the Central Front will transfer 13th Army, consisting of eight rifle divisions, and 60th Army, consisting of nine rifle divisions (but without 7th Guards Mechanized Corps), to the Voronezh Front by 10 October. By that time, it [the Central Front] will receive 50th Army with seven rifle divisions, 3rd Army with seven rifle divisions, 63rd Army with eight rifle divisions, and 2nd Guards Cavalry Corps from the Briansk Front. Transfer and accept the armies with all of their reinforcing equipment, army rear service units, facilities, and on-hand [material] reserves.

2. The Central Front's mission is to defeat the enemy's Zhlobin-Bobruisk grouping and capture Minsk, the capital of Belorussia, by delivering a main attack in the general direction of Zhlobin, Bobruisk, and Minsk. Allocate a separate group of forces for an offensive along the northern bank of the Pripiat' River toward Kalinkovichi and Zhitkovichi.

The immediate mission—to capture the Bykhov, Zhlobin, and Kalinkovichi line and, subsequently, reach the Minsk, Slutsk, and Sluch' River line.

3. On the right—the Western Front will attack in the general direction of Orsha, Borisov, and Molodechno. The boundary line with [the Western Front] effective 10 October: Kirov, Snopot', Prigory, Krichev, Dashkova, Berezino, and Radoshkovichi. All points are inclusive for the Western Front.

On the left—the Voronezh Front will capture the Kiev region and attack in the general direction of Korosten' and Rovno with its right wing. The boundary line with [the Voronezh Front] effective 10 October: Snagost', Seim River, Desna River, Chernigov, Mozyr', and the Pripiat' River. All points are inclusive for the Voronezh Front.

4. The Western Front is entrusted with the responsibility for protecting the boundary with the Western Front and the Central Front [will protect the boundary with] the Voronezh Front.

5. Confirm receipt of this directive. Submit an operational plan by stages and periods by 5 October.

The *Stavka* of the Supreme High Command
I. Stalin, A. Antonov

Source: "Direktiva Stavki VGK No. 30208 komanduiushchemu voiskami Tsentral'nogo fronta na razgrom Zhlobinsko-Bobruiskoi gruppirovki protivnika i ovladenie Minskom" [*Stavka* VGK directive No. 30208 to the commander of the Central Front on the defeat of the enemy Zhlobin-Bobruisk grouping and the capture of Minsk], in Zolotarev, *Stavka* VGK 1943, 213.

C-4. *Stavka* VGK Directive No. 30209 to the Commander of the Briansk Front Concerning the Abolition of the Briansk [Front] and Formation of the Baltic Front

1900 hours 1 October 1943

The *Stavka* of the Supreme High Command ORDERS:

1. The Briansk Front will transfer 50th Army with seven rifle divisions, 3rd Army with seven rifle divisions, 63rd Army with eight rifle divisions, and 2nd Guards Cavalry Corps to the Central Front no later than 10 October. After doing so, the Briansk Front will be considered disbanded. Transfer the armies and 2nd Guards Cavalry Corps with their full complement, with all reinforcing equipment, and with army rear service units, facilities, and on-hand material stocks.

2. Transfer the Briansk Front's headquarters, *front* units, and rear service facilities, 11th Guards Army with nine rifle divisions, 11th Army with seven rifle divisions, 15th Air Army, 1st Tank Corps, and 2nd Artillery [Penetration] Corps by railroad to the Ostashkov, Toropets, and Selizharovo region. The *front* headquarters will be in the Toropets region by 15 October. Complete the movement of the *front's* forces by 15 November.

3. The *front* will receive 22nd Army with two rifle divisions and five rifle brigades from the Northwestern Front, 3rd Shock Army with five rifle divisions and three rifle brigades and 8th Estonian Rifle Corps with two rifle divisions from the Kalinin Front, and 6th Guards Army with seven rifle divisions and 20th Army with six rifle divisions from the *Stavka* reserve by 20 October.

4. This new *front*, which will consist of 3rd Shock, 11th, 22nd, and 20th Armies, 6th and 11th Guards Armies, 15th Air Army, and 8th Estonian Corps, will be named the Baltic Front, effective on 20 October.

5. Confirm the receipt of this directive. Submit a *front* operational plan by 15 October.

The *Stavka* of the Supreme High Command
I. Stalin, A. Antonov

Source: "Direktiva Stavki VGK No. 30209 komanduiushchemu voiskami Brianskogo fronta ob uprazdenii Brianskogo i obrazovanii Pribaltiiskogo fronta" [*Stavka* VGK directive No. 30209 to the commander of the Briansk Front concerning the abolition of the Briansk and formation of the Baltic Front], in Zolotarev, *Stavka* VGK 1943, 214.

C-5. *Stavka* VGK Directive No. 30231 to the Commander of the Belorussian Front Concerning the Resubordination and Regrouping of 11th and 48th Armies

0330 hours 23 October 1943

The *Stavka* of the Supreme High Command ORDERS:
1. Transfer Fediuninsky's 11th Army with seven rifle divisions and all army reinforcing units and rear service units and facilities to the Belorussian Front, effective at 0600 hours on 23 October, having removed it from the 2nd Baltic Front.
2. On 23 October the Belorussian Front commander will begin moving 11th Army's forces to the *front* sector now occupied by 48th Army, which will be regrouped to the Rechitsa axis.
To speed up 48th Army's regrouping, begin it without waiting for 11th Army to arrive, leaving two–three rifle divisions in its sector and partially reinforcing them at 63rd Army's expense.
3. Report fulfillment.

The *Stavka* of the Supreme High Command
I. Stalin, A. Antonov

Source: "Direktiva Stavki VGK No. 30231 komanduiushchemu voiskami Belorusskogo fronta o perepodchinenii i peregruppirovke 11-i i 48-i armii" [*Stavka* VGK directive No. 30231 to the commander of the Belorussian Front concerning the resubordination and regrouping of 11th and 48th Armies], in Zolotarev, *Stavka* VGK 1943, 227.

C-6. The Journal of Combat Operations of 65th Army, 1 November 1943

1.11.43. Combat Mission
Defend the positions you occupy. Prepare a penetration in the sector: Volkoshanka-Iastrebka, and, in connection with this, conduct a regrouping of the army's forces (Enciphered Report No. 6676, 1.11.43.)

Description of Combat Operations
During the day the army's forces fortified the positions they occupy, conducted reconnaissance of the enemy's defenses, and destroyed his forces and equipment with

artillery-mortar and rifle-machine gun fire. Part of the forces fought with attacking enemy in the Iastrebka region.

The enemy on the army's front continued to hold on to their previously occupied positions with units of 31st ID; 533rd IR, 383rd ID; 2 assault gun battalions, units of 102nd and 216th IDs and 2nd and 12th PzDs, and reinforcing units.

In the army's center, the enemy counterattacked twice toward Iastrebka and, simultaneously, tried repeatedly to conduct reinforced reconnaissance of 19th RC's combat formation during the day.

In the remaining sectors of the front, the enemy conducted rifle-machine gun fire and periodically carried out short fire raids.

During the day, lively movement of vehicles and cart transport was noted from Kholmech' [on the Dnepr River 28 kilometers north-northwest of Loev] toward the southwest.

During the period from 1000 hours to 1700 hours, more than 300 vehicles, a large number of them with infantry, and 10 tanks carrying assault troops [KGr., 12th PzD] moved from Moshok to Bol'shaia Terebeevka and Barbary [23–25 kilometers north-northwest of Loev].

From 1530 hours to 1800 hours, up to two battalions of infantry with carts and 10 tanks [KGr., 2nd PzD] moved from Uborok [26 kilometers northwest of Loev] to Volkashanka and Daniliny Liady [28 kilometers northwest of Loev].

Enemy aviation conducted reconnaissance of the army's combat formations and rear area with single aircraft.

27th RC—the corps' units conducted reconnaissance and observation, improved their positions, brought their personnel and equipment to combat readiness, and replenished their ammunition during the day.

The enemy defended in their previous positions. During the day, the enemy conducted occasional rifle-machine gun fire and periodically carried out short artillery-mortar raids against the combat formations of our units. He conducted defensive work in separate sectors.

At 0800 hours, the corps' units were located in [the following] positions:

354th RD—the cemetery on the northern outskirts of Starodubka—100 m south of Mars No. 2 [state farm].

246th RD—the southern edge of the grove southwest of Mars No. 2—300 m northwest of Niva.

106th RD—100 m west of the circular grove—the road junction northeast of Smelyi.

115th RB—the road junction northeast of Smelyi—100 m north of the cemetery west of Smelyi.

19th RC—the corps' formations, while improving the positions they occupy, repelled enemy counterattacks, conducted reconnaissance and observation, and exchanged rifle-machine gun and artillery-mortar fire with the enemy.

During the day, the enemy conducted methodical artillery-mortar and rifle-machine gun fire. He periodically carried out short fire raids.

At 1130 hours the enemy attacked the units of 37th Gds.RD with more than two companies of infantry simultaneously from the two directions of Barbary Farm and Kulagovo Farm.

37th Gds.RD conducted rifle-machine gun exchanges and reconnoitered the enemy toward Barbary Farm and Kulagovo Farm during the day. While improving its occupied positions, at 1100 hours it repulsed an enemy attack by up to two companies from two directions.

140th RD—while continuing to improve the positions it occupies, conducted reconnaissance toward the grove south of Volkoshanskaia Dubrava and observed and exchanged rifle-machine gun exchanges with the enemy.

162nd RD—conducted reconnaissance toward the grove west of Klen and observed the enemy. It improved the positions it occupied.

18th RC—during the day, the corps' formations occupied their previous positions, improved them in an engineer sense, conducted reconnaissance and observation of the enemy, and put its units in order.

60th RD—during the day conducted stubborn fighting with enemy infantry and tanks attacking from the northern outskirts of Iastrebka and Krasnaia Gorka toward the central and southern part of Iastrebka.

From 1200 hours to 1600 hours, the enemy succeeded in pushing the units of 60th RD from the central part of Iastrebka with a superior force of infantry and 12 tanks. A counterattack by 60th RD after 1700 hours was halted.

In the remaining sectors of the front, during the day the corps' units conducted fire on the enemy from their previous positions.

During the repulsion of the enemy attack on Iastrebka and the counterattack by 60 RD's units, the enemy suffered losses. More than 250 soldiers and officers were killed or wounded, 7 tanks were struck and burned, of which 5 remained in our territory, and more than 20 machine gun points were destroyed.

9th TC—the corps' formations occupied defenses in positions: Lipniaki—Klen during the day.

The enemy conducted artillery-mortar fire on Lipniaki and Krasnaia Vetka from the direction of Barbary, Moshok, Kulagovo, and Volkoshanka. Operational tanks [include]: T-34s—37; and T-70s—11. Losses due to the artillery fire: 1 T-34 tank.

2nd Gds. CC—during the day continued to improve its defenses in an engineer and antitank sense, while mining the approaches to the forward edge.

Source: "Zhurnal boevykh deistvii voisk 65 Armii, 1. 11. 43." [The 65th Army's journal of combat operations, 1 November 1943], https://cdn.pamyat-naroda.ru/.

D. THE 1ST AND 2ND BALTIC FRONTS' POLOTSK-VITEBSK AND PUSTOSHKA-IDRITSA OFFENSIVES (2-21 NOVEMBER 1943)

D-1. From Directive No. 00365/op of the Military Council
of the 1st Baltic Front

25 October 1943

The forces of the 1st Baltic Front have been assigned the mission to destroy the enemy's Vitebsk-Gorodok grouping and capture the city of Vitebsk.

I have decided to smash the enemy Vitebsk-Gorodok grouping by concentric attacks by 4th Shock Army in the general direction of Gorodok and Sirotino and by 43rd and 39th Armies on Vitebsk, and capture the cities of Gorodok and Vitebsk.

Eremenko, Leonov, Kurasov

Source: "Zhurnal boevykh deistvii 1-og Pribaltiiskogo fronta za noiabr' 1943 g." [The 1st Baltic Front's journal of combat operations for November 1943], *TsAMO*, f. 235, op. 2074, ed. khr. 52, l. 2.

D-2. From 1st Baltic Front Report No. 00370/op to the *Stavka* VGK on the Conduct of an Airborne Operation

1 November 1943

Top secret
Special importance
To the Supreme High Commander, Marshal of the Soviet Union I. V. Stalin

I will conduct an airborne operation effective on 8 November in accordance with your orders. [The operation will be] aimed at inserting a *desant* [airborne assault] in the Seliavshchina [35 kilometers north of Polotsk] region, destroying the enemy in the Polotsk region by means of joint operations of the *front's* forces with partisan brigades, and capturing the city.

The air assault and the partisan brigades will be ready for combat operations on 12 November 1943. The operation will begin according to a special order. I am reserving for myself the direction of all operations by the airborne and partisan forces. I am entrusting command of the airborne operation to Major General Zatevakhin, the deputy commander of the Red Army's Airborne Forces. The Central Headquarters of the Partisan Movement, which is located at the 1st Baltic Front's command post at this time, will direct the combat operations of the partisan brigades.

I am allocating the following forces and weaponry to fulfill the assigned mission:

(1) The 1st, 2nd, and 11th Guards Airborne Brigades and 1714th Antiaircraft Artillery Regiment of the Red Army's Airborne Forces;
(2) 120–150 transport aircraft from Long-range Aviation;
(3) 300 fighters and 100 Il-2 aircraft from 3rd and 15th Air Armies;
(4) 10 TB-3 planes, 10 SB and Il-4 planes, and 50 gliders from the Red Army's Airborne Forces;
(5) Four antiaircraft artillery regiments from the 1st and 2nd Baltic Fronts;
(6) Two automobile battalions from the 1st and 2nd Baltic Fronts; and
(7) Five airfield support battalions from 15th Air Army.

The air assault will be conducted by parachute in daylight, and the air landing will take place at night in the following sequence—1st, 2nd, and 11th Guards Airborne Brigades and 1714th Antiaircraft Artillery Regiment. Each brigade will land simultaneously from airfields at Andreapol', Lush, and Bataly.

All cargo will be delivered at night from the airfields at Rzhev and Toropa Station. The assault will begin on 8 November 1943 and end on 11 November 1943, if weather conditions are favorable.

To ensure reliable command and control . . . I consider it necessary to entrust Marshals of Aviation Comrades A. A. Novikov and A. E. Golovanov with the direction of all forces during the entire air portion of the operation. The plan of the airborne operation is being worked out jointly with Marshal of Artillery Voronov, Marshals of Aviation Comrades Novikov and Golovanov, Lieutenant General Comrade Ponomarenko and Major General Comrade Gromov, the Member of the Red Army Airborne Forces Military Council.

Matters of material-technical support of the airborne operation are being coordinated with Army General Comrade Popov, the commander of the 2nd Baltic Front.

Army General Bagramian, Commander of the 1st Baltic Front
Lieutenant General Leonov, Member of the 1st Baltic Front's Military Council
Lieutenant General Kurasov, the Chief of Staff of the 1st Baltic Front

Source: "Prikazy i direktivy 1-go Pribaltiiskogo fronta za 1943 g" [Orders and directives of the 1st Baltic Front for 1943], *TsAMO*, f. 235, op. 2074, ed. khr. 9, ll. 93–97.

D-3. *Stavka* **VGK Directive No. 30243 to the Commander of the 1st Baltic Front and the Representative of the** *Stavka* **on the Defeat of the Enemy Vitebsk Grouping**

0130 hours 12 November 1943

The *Stavka* of the Supreme High Command ORDERS:

1. Concentrate 5th Tank Corps, two rifle divisions, and the tank brigade, which have arrived from the 2nd Baltic Front, in the Lake Svino region. You will attack [from this region] in the general direction of Bychikha Station on the morning of 15 November with 2nd Gds.RC, reinforced by the arrived divisions, with the mission of defeating the enemy grouping south of Ezerishche.

2. The 5th TC will attack in the direction of Gorodok and Vitebsk, defeat the enemy's Vitebsk grouping in cooperation with 43rd and 39th Armies, and capture the Gorodok and Vitebsk regions.

3. Employ 3rd Guards Cavalry Corps to strengthen the attack on Gorodok and Vitebsk.

4. Combine the rifle divisions, which are attacking from the north toward the isthmus between Lakes Melkoe and Ezerishche, into a corps, and employ the corps headquarters arriving from the 2nd Baltic Front for that purpose. Support that corps' attack with the artillery division assigned from the 2nd Baltic Front.

5. Continue 43rd and 39th Armies' attacks along the Vitebsk axis.

6. Report on all orders given.

The *Stavka* of the Supreme High Command
I. Stalin, A. Antonov

Source: "Direktiva Stavki VGK No. 30243 komanduiushchemu voiskami 1-go Pribaltiiskogo fronta, predstaviteliu Stavki na razgrom Vitebskoi gruppirovki protivnika" [*Stavka* VGK directive No. 30240 to the commanders of the 1st and 2nd Baltic Fronts and the representative of the *Stavka* about the resubordination of formations and measures for clearing the enemy from between the lakes], in Zolotarev, *Stavka* VGK 1943, 234.

D-4. *Stavka* VGK Directive No. 30246 to the Commander of the 1st Baltic Front Concerning Instances of the Presentation of Unverified Information about the Enemy to the *Stavka*

1400 hours 12 November 1943

Copy to: The representative of the *Stavka*

The racket that you kicked up about the attack by large enemy forces, supposedly up to two tank divisions from Ezerishche to Studenets, turned out to be a totally baseless and panicky report. This means that you personally and your staff accept in faith and do not verify all reports coming in from below.

I am calling your attention to the necessity for a critical attitude toward all incoming reports and demanding that you carefully verify them, especially information about the enemy.

Henceforth do not permit the presentation to the *Stavka* and General Staff of reports containing unverified and ill-considered panicky conclusions about the enemy.

I. Stalin

Source: "Direktiva Stavki VGK No. 30246 komanduiushchemu voiskami 1-go Pribaltiiskogo fronta o sluchaiakh predstavleniia v Stavku neproverennykh svedenii o protivnike" [*Stavka* VGK directive No. 30246 to the commander of the 1st Baltic Front concerning instances of the presentation of unverified information about the enemy to the *Stavka*], in Zolotarev, *Stavka* VGK 1943, 235.

D-5. *Stavka* Order No. 00151 Concerning the Relief of the Commanders of the Forces of the 1st Baltic Front and 11th Guards Army

17 November 1943

1. Relieve Army General Eremenko from his duties as commander of the 1st Baltic Front.

Comrade Eremenko will complete handing over his affairs no later than 19 November and will arrive at the disposal of the *Stavka* for receipt of a new appointment.

2. Appoint Army General Bagramian as the commander of the 1st Baltic Front commander, releasing him from his duties as the commander of 11th Guards Army.

3. Appoint Lieutenant General Galitsky as the commander of 11th Guards Army, releasing him from his duties as the commander of 3rd Shock Army.

Comrade Galitsky will take command of 11th Guards Army effective on 20 November 1943.

The *Stavka* of the Supreme High Command
I. Stalin

Source: "Direktiva Stavki VGK No. 00151 o smene komanduiushchikh voiskami 1-go Pribaltiiskogo fronta i 11-i gvardeiskoi armiei [*Stavka* VGK directive No. 00151 about the relief of the commander of the forces of the 1st Baltic Front and 11th Guards Army], in Zolotarev, *Stavka* VGK 1943, 238.

D-6. *Stavka* VGK Directive No. 30247 to the Commander of the 1st Baltic Front and the Representative of the *Stavka* on the Defeat of the Enemy Vitebsk Grouping

0215 hours 18 November 1943

The *Stavka* of the Supreme High Command ORDERS:

1. Simultaneously with the fulfillment of the missions assigned in *Stavka* Directive No. 30243, deploy 11th Guards Army along the Zhukovo and Rudnia front for an offensive toward Kuz'mino and Sirotino beginning on 23 November.

2. While protecting the operation [against attacks] from the west, cut the Polotsk-Vitebsk road and railroad line with the forces of 60th RC.

3. Develop an energetic offensive on 43rd and 39th Armies' fronts simultaneously with the beginning of 11th Guards Army's offensive.

4. Effective 20 November, the boundary line between the 1st and 2nd Baltic Fronts will be to Lake Uzho, as before, and, farther, to Lake Nesherdo, with all points inclusive for the 1st Baltic Front.

5. Report fulfillment.

The *Stavka* of the Supreme High Command
I. Stalin, A. Antonov

Source: "Direktiva Stavki VGK No. 30247 komanduiushchemu voiskami 1-go Pribaltiiskogo fronta, predstaviteliu Stavki na razgrom Vitebskoi gruppirovki protivnika" [*Stavka* VGK directive No. 30247 to the commander of the 1st Baltic Front and the representative of the *Stavka* on the defeat of the enemy Vitebsk grouping], in Zolotarev, "*Stavka* VGK 1943, 238–239. The *Stavka* representative was N. N. Voronov.

D-7. *Stavka* VGK Directive No. 30248 to the Commanders of the 1st and 2nd Baltic Fronts and the Representative of the *Stavka* on the Resubordination of Force Units

0215 hours 18 November 1943

The *Stavka* of the Supreme High Command ORDERS:

The 2nd Baltic Front commander will transfer the complete 11th Guards Army, including 18th Guards Rifle Corps, 10th Gds.TB, 1st Tank Corps, 2nd Guards Tank Penetration Regiment, three guards-mortar brigades, four guards-mortar regiments, 10th Assault Engineer Brigade, and 17th Antiaircraft Artillery Division, to the 1st Baltic Front, effective at 1200 hours on 18 November 1943. Transfer the army and reinforcing units with 1.5 combat loads of ammunition, two volleys of multiple rocket launchers, and 6–7 refills of fuel for the vehicles and tanks. Leave 15th Artillery Division, which is temporarily subordinate to the 1st Baltic Front, in that *front*.

The *Stavka* of the Supreme High Command
I. Stalin, A. Antonov

Source: "Direktiva Stavki VGK No. 30248 komanduiushchim voiskami 1-go i 2-go Pribaltiiskikh frontov, predstaviteliu Stavki na perepodchinenie chasti voisk" [*Stavka* VGK directive No.

30248 to the commanders of the 1st and 2nd Baltic Fronts and the representative of the *Stavka* on the resubordination of force units], in Zolotarev, *Stavka* VGK 1943, 239.

D-8. *Stavka* Directive No. 30249 to the Commander of the 1st Baltic Front and the Representative of the *Stavka* Concerning the Period of the Liberation of Gorodok

0030 hours 20 November 1943

An incomprehensible delay is occurring in the Gorodok region. The *front* has every opportunity to fulfill successfully the mission assigned to it by *Stavka* directive No. 30243. The *Stavka* of the Supreme High Command ORDERS you to finish with Gorodok on 20 November. Report fulfillment.

The *Stavka* of the Supreme High Command
I. Stalin, A. Antonov

Source: "Direktiva Stavki VGK No. 30249 komanduiushchemu voiskami 1-go Pribaltiisskogo fronta, predstaviteliu Stavki o srokakh osvobozhdeniia Gorodka" [*Stavka* directive No. 30249 to the commander of the 1st Baltic Front and the representative of the *Stavka* concerning the period of the liberation of Gorodok], in Zolotarev, *Stavka* VGK 1943, 239. The representative of the *Stavka* was N. N. Voronov.

D-9. *Stavka* VGK Directive No. 30251 to the Commander of the 1st Baltic Front and the Representative of the *Stavka* Concerning the Organization of Cooperation between 11th Guards and 4th Shock Armies in the Liberation of Gorodok

2130 hours 21 November 1943

Considering the situation existing in the 1st Baltic Front, the *Stavka* of the Supreme High Command ORDERS:

1. In a change to *Stavka* directive No. 30247, 11th Guards Army's offensive will begin no later than 26 November.

2. Temporarily halt 4th Shock Army's offensive on Gorodok. Arrange the supply of that army's forces and repair the roads.

Reliably protect yourself along the Sirotino axis and on the isthmuses between Lakes Kosha, Chernovo, and Vernovo. Resume the offensive [with 4th Shock Army] against Gorodok simultaneously with that of 11th Guards Army and, in favorable conditions, even earlier.

3. Report all orders given.

The *Stavka* of the Supreme High Command
I. Stalin, A. Antonov

Source: "Direktiva Stavki VGK No. 30251 komanduiushchemu voiskami 1-go Pribaltiiskogo fronta, predstaviteliu Stavki ob organizatsii vzaimodeistviia 11-i gvardeiskoi i 4-i udarnoi armii pri osvobozhdenii Gorodka" [*Stavka* VGK directive No. 30251 to the commander of the 1st Baltic Front and the representative of the *Stavka* concerning the organization of cooperation between 11th Guards and 4th Shock Armies in the liberation of Gorodok], in Zolotarev, *Stavka* VGK 1943, 240.

D-10. *Stavka* VGK Directive No. 30252 to the Commanders of the 1st Baltic and Western Fronts and the Representative of the *Stavka* Concerning the Boundary Line between the *Fronts*

2345 hours 21 November 1943

The *Stavka* of the Supreme High Command ORDERS:
1. Establish the following boundary line between the 1st Baltic and Western Fronts, effective at 0600 hours 22 November 1943: to Dobromysl', as before, and, farther, to Bogushevsk and Senno. All points are inclusive for the 1st Baltic Front.
2. Report fulfillment.

The *Stavka* of the Supreme High Command
I. Stalin, A. Antonov

Source: "Direktiva Stavki VGK No. 30252 komanduiushchim voiskami 1-go Pribaltiiskogo i Zapadnogo frontov, predstaviteliu Stavki o razgranlinii mezhdu frontami" [*Stavka* VGK directive No. 30252 to the commanders of the 1st Baltic and Western Fronts and the representative of the *Stavka* concerning the boundary line between the *fronts*], in Zolotarev, *Stavka* VGK 1943, 241.

D-11. From Directive No. 00401/op of the Military Council of the 1st Baltic Front

23 November 1943

The *front's* immediate mission is to destroy the Germans' Vitebsk-Gorodok grouping, which consists of IX and VI Army Corps, and to capture the cities of Gorodok and Vitebsk. Subsequently, decisively develop the offensive in the general direction of Lepel' and capture the cities of Polotsk and Lepel', after smashing the enemy's Polotsk grouping with the forces of 4th Shock Army.

Source: "Zhurnal boevykh deistvii 1-og Pribaltiiskogo fronta za noiabr' 1943 g." [The 1st Baltic Front's journal of combat operations for November 1943], *TsAMO*, f. 235, op. 2074, ed. khr. 52, l. 34.

D-12. *Stavka* VGK Directive No. 30240 to the Commanders of the 1st and 2nd Baltic Fronts and the Representative of the *Stavka* about the Resubordination of Formations and Measures for Clearing the Enemy from Between the Lakes

2230 hours 10 November 1943

To clear the enemy out of the isthmus between Lakes Melkoe and Ezerishche, the *Stavka* of the Supreme High Command ORDERS:

1. The commander of the 2nd Baltic Front will transfer 29th and 166th RDs to the composition of the 1st Baltic Front, effective at 2400 hours on 10 November. The 2nd Baltic Front's mission remains the same as before.

2. The commander of the 1st Baltic Front will clear the enemy from the isthmus between Lakes Melkoe and Ezerishche with 29th, 166th, 47th, 16th Lithuanian, and 117th RDs and 83rd RC and capture the Lake Beloe, Ezerishche, and Zhukovo line, where it will dig in and firmly protect the Nevel' axis from the south.

3. To ease its command and control, 4th SA will transfer 83rd RC and 155th FR to the composition of 43rd A.

Employ 83rd RC for an attack from the Zhukovo region to Ezerishche, where it will cut the road and railroad line.

4. Report fulfillment.

The *Stavka* of the Supreme High Command
I. Stalin, A. Antonov

Source: "Direktiva Stavki VGK No. 30240 komanduiushchemu voiskami 1-go i 2-go Pribaltiiskikh frontov, predstaviteliu Stavki o perepodchinenii soedinenii i merakh po osvobozhdeniiu ot protivnika mezhozer'ia" [*Stavka* VGK directive No. 30240 to the commanders of the 1st and 2nd Baltic Fronts and the representative of the *Stavka* about the resubordination of formations and measures for clearing the enemy from between the lakes], in Zolotarev, *Stavka* VGK 1943, 232. The *Stavka* representative was N. N. Voronov.

D-13. *Stavka* VGK Directive No. 30244 to the Commander of the 2nd Baltic Front on Halting the Offensive and Transferring Forces to the 1st Baltic Front

0130 hours 12 November 1943

Copy to: The Commander of the 1st Baltic Front and Representative of the *Stavka*

Considering the situation that has taken shape in the Nevel' region, the *Stavka* of the Supreme High Command ORDERS:

1. The 2nd Baltic Front will temporarily halt the offensives by 6th Guards and 3rd Shock Armies and will firmly dig in along occupied lines. Protect Nevel' especially reliably.

2. Transfer two rifle divisions, including 51st [Gds.] RD, one corps headquarters, one full-strength tank brigade, and the complete 5th TC, with all of its ammunition and fuel reserves, from 6th Guards Army to the 1st Baltic Front by 0600 hours on 12 November 1943.

3. By the same time, temporarily attach one artillery division with one combat load of ammunition at the disposal of the 1st Baltic Front.

4. Report fulfillment.

The *Stavka* of the Supreme High Command
I. Stalin, A. Antonov

Source: "Direktiva Stavki VGK No. 30244 komanduiushchemu voiskami 2-go Pribaltiiskogo fronta na priostanovku nastupleniia i peredachu chast sil 1-mu Pribaltiiskomu frontu" [*Stavka*

VGK directive No. 30244 to the commander of the 2nd Baltic on halting the offensive and transferring forces to the 1st Baltic Front], in Zolotarev, *Stavka* VGK 1943, 235.

D-14. *Stavka* Directive No. 46200 to the Commanders of the Northwestern and 2nd Baltic Fronts Concerning the Abolition of the Northwestern Front

0215 hours 15 November 1943

Copy to: The Chief of the General Staff's Main Organizational Directorate

The *Stavka* of the Supreme High Command ORDERS:

1. Abolish the Northwestern Front, effective on 20 November 1943.

2. Appoint: Lieutenant General Kurochkin as deputy commander of the 2nd Baltic Front and Lieutenant General Bokov as the Member of the Military Council [Commissar] of the 2nd Baltic Front.

3. Leave only 1st Shock Army, consisting of two rifle corps of three rifle divisions each and one rifle brigade, of which two rifle divisions will be in army reserve, in the sector of the front now occupied by the forces of 34th and 1st Shock Armies.

Include 1st Shock Army in the 2nd Baltic Front, effective on 20 November 1943. From this time, consider the present right boundary line of the Northwestern Front as the right boundary line of the 2nd Baltic Front.

4. Withdraw one rifle corps (three RDs) from the Northwestern Front into the *Stavka*'s reserve in the Valdai region by 30 November.

5. Withdraw the Northwestern Front's headquarters into the *Stavka*'s reserve in the Rybinsk region by 30 November 1943.

6. Withdraw 34th Army's headquarters, with all army units and rear services, into the *Stavka*'s reserve in the Vyshyi Volochek region, to arrive by 30 November 1943.

7. The Chief of the General Staff, together with the branch commanders and Chief of the Red Army's Rear, will determine by 17 November the list of Northwestern Front's reinforcing and supporting units and rear service units and facilities that will remain in the 2nd Baltic Front or be withdrawn into the *Stavka*'s reserve and be disbanded.

Report fulfillment.

The *Stavka* of the Supreme High Command
I. Stalin, A. Antonov

Source: "Direktiva Stavki VGK No. 46200 komanduiushchim voiskami Severo-zapadnogo i 2-go Pribaltiiskogo frontov ob uprazdenii Severo-zapadnogo fronta" [*Stavka* directive No. 46200 to the commanders of the Northwestern and 2nd Baltic Fronts concerning the abolition of the Northwestern Front], in Zolotarev, *Stavka* VGK 1943, 236–237.

E. THE WESTERN FRONT'S ORSHA OFFENSIVES (14 NOVEMBER–5 DECEMBER 1943)

E-1. Excerpts from "Intelligence Summary No. 305 and Operational Summary No. 500 of the Western Front's Headquarters, 1 November 1943"

1 November
The *front's* forces fortified their previous positions, conducted reconnaissance, and exchanged fire.

The right-wing units of 68th Army conducted offensives. After a fierce three-day battle, they overcame enemy resistance and captured his strongly fortified strong point of the hill with Marker 180.8.

On the Orsha axis in the region west of Rossosna, after stubborn fighting, units of 18th PzGrD were thrown back to previously prepared fortified positions from Gormany to Bobrova.

Prisoners and documents from the dead established: 1st "SS" Brigade relieved the units of 26th ID in the region south of Kirleva on the night of 27 October and also supported the operations of 18th PzGrD and 256th ID in their previous positions.

On the Mogilev axis, the units of Ninth Army continued to fortify the positions they occupy.

According to a map seized in the Prilepovka region on 31 October, it was determined: the headquarters, supposedly of a combat group of 262nd ID, is in Sushchi (9 kilometers north of Chausy) and a panzer battalion [*abteilung*] is in Bordzilia (8 kilometers east of Sukhari).

Information from agents confirmed the presence of units of 262nd ID in Mogilev. A transport column No. 12415 of 262nd ID is supporting the construction of defensive works in the Mogilev region.

10th Guards Army
The army's forces continued work to fortify the positions they occupy. Active enemy firing points were suppressed by artillery fire. On the night of 1 November, the reconnaissance company of 164th Sep. MG-Arty Bn seized a prisoner from the transport column of 256th ID west of Vinokorno No. 1 [state farm].

The enemy shelled the combat formations of our forces with methodical artillery fire. During the second half of the day, firing activity heightened on the army's left wing, with the occurrence of short fire raids against the dispositions of 19th Gds.RC. A total of 11 artillery and 3 mortar batteries and 3 six-barreled mortars are operating along the army's entire front. Up to 1,500 shells and mines were fired.

The army's losses for 31 October: 33 killed and 116 wounded.

31st Army
The forces conducted artillery-mortar and machine gun exchanges. The actions of reconnaissance detachments determined the firing systems in the forward edge of the enemy's defenses. In the second echelon, we continued training assault groups and battalions. There were no changes in the forces' positions by day's end.

The enemy fired on the army's combat formations with artillery, mortar, and multiple-rocket launcher fire in [the following] regions: Zavodnyi, Berestni, Pushchai, and Batrakovitsy. A total of more than 12 artillery batteries, 8 mortar batteries, 2 six-barreled mortars, and 4 multiple-rocket launchers are operating on the army's front.

The army's losses for 31 October: 88 killed and 208 wounded.

Up to 230 Germans and 4 machine guns were destroyed and 2 blindages were damaged.

68th Army

The right-wing units of the army continued to conduct sustained fighting to capture strongly fortified large enemy strong points—the height with Marker 180.0. During the second half of the day, the units of 72nd RC completed capturing this height. While developing the offensive further, 174th and 159th RDs reached fortified enemy positions in the sector from (incl.) Gorinany to Bobrovka along the southwestern bank of the unnamed stream [Rossanenka].

On the night of 1 November, 81st RC conducted reconnaissance with reinforced battalions of infantry toward Volkolakova and Mikhalinovo. The reconnaissance detachments penetrated into the enemy's trenches with part of their forces, but withdrew to their jumping-off positions by morning under pressure of strong automatic weapons fire and counterattacks by infantry.

During the sustained three-day battles by the army's right-wing units on Hill 180.0, more than 1,000 enemy soldiers and officers, 6 tanks, 5 guns, 14 mortars, and 28 machine guns were destroyed; more than 30 pillboxes and blindages were destroyed; and about 3,000 enemy antitank and antipersonnel mines were taken. At the same time, 10 guns of various calibers, 17 mortars, 30 machine guns, more than 200 rifles, 5 radios, and warehouses with engineer equipment, food and ammunition were seized.

The army's losses for 31 October: 92 killed and 447 wounded.

We destroyed 400 Germans, a mortar battery, 8 mortars, 2 guns, and one tank.

33rd Army

The forces of the army's first echelon improved the positions they occupy. Identified enemy firing points were suppressed by infantry and artillery fire, while personnel were destroyed. Last night our reconnaissance groups operating toward Demiankovo and Korzhikovo came under enemy fire and were forced to withdraw to their own dispositions.

The army's losses for 31 October: None

49th Army

The army's forces continued regrouping and fortifying the positions they occupy. The enemy periodically fired on the combat formations of our units with infantry and artillery fire. Up to 900 shells and mines were received during the day.

At 2200 hours the army's units occupied [the following] positions:

352nd RD—on a front from 0.5 kilometer east of Sukino to 0.5 kilometer north of the eastern outskirts of Trigobova.

247th RD—0.5 kilometer north of the eastern outskirts of Trigobova to 1.4 kilometers south of Lenino.

139th RD was replaced by the left-wing units of 70th RD along the front from 1 kilometer west of Lukino to (incl.) Blazhki (western) and occupied a front from 1.4 kilometers south of Lenino to 300 m northeast of Blazhki (western).

616　Appendices

62nd RC (70th and 160th RDs and 36th RB). 70th RD—gave up its combat sector along the front from 1 kilometer west of Luki to (incl.) Blazhki (western) and occupied the front from 300 m east of Blazhki (western) to 600 m east of Kobekhi with one regiment. Two regiments of 70th RD, after being relieved by the units of 139th RD, concentrated in the region south of Gushchino.

160th RD—along the front from (incl.) Kobekhi to Turishchevo, Zastenok, 0.5 kilometer west of Mikuleno, Hill 192.54, Poliashchitsa, and 1 kilometer southwest of that populated point.

36th RB—from the forest 700 m west of Khodorovichi to Medvedovka, Hill 183.2 and the [unidentified abbreviation] (1 kilometer southeast of Hill 183.2).

The subunits of 154th FR—along the eastern bank of the Remistvianka River and the Pronia River in the sector from Nikol'ski No. 4, Dribin, Khalyupa to Hill 171.4.

344th RD—concentrated in the Pnevshchina and Radenka region and the forest to the west.

277th RD– in the Potashnia and (incl.) Leskovka region, and the forest north of Tsemirka.

196th TB—in the Iarshchevka [Iartsevka] region.

The army's losses for 31 October: 9 killed and 10 wounded.

50 Germans and weapons were destroyed.

10th Army
The army's forces are continuing to fortify the positions they occupy and are carrying out a regrouping. The subunits of 330th RD, supported by strong artillery and mortar fire and three self-propelled guns, repelled two enemy attacks on the southern outskirts of Prilepovka. There are occasional infantry exchanges in the remaining sectors of the front.

The enemy conducted reconnaissance in the Dranukha region at first light and east of Put'ki at 1820 hours with small subunits of infantry.

Source: "Opersvodka Shtaba Z. F. No. 500, Razvedsvodka Shtaba Z. F. No. 305," 1 Noiabria [Operational Summary No. 500 and Intelligence Summary No. 305 of the Western Front's Headquarters, 1 November 1943], in *Combat Operations of the Western Front's Forces in November 1943*, https://cdn.pamyatnaroda.ru/images.

E-2. Excerpts from "The Combat Journal of 33rd Army, 1–3 December 1943"

1 December:
The army's forces continued to fulfill previously assigned missions. Operating at night—at 0700 hours a battalion of 222nd RD and a ski battalion of 144th RD captured the central part of Krasnaia Sloboda by a decisive attack.

At 0830 hours, the enemy, trying to restore the situation, undertook counterattacks on Krasnaia Sloboda simultaneously from two directions—by a battalion of infantry with 15 tanks from the direction of Zastenok and Iur'ev and by a company of infantry with 8 tanks from Hill 220.8. A fierce battle ensued. The battalions of 144th and 222nd RDs, in spite of inadequate antitank weapons, successfully repelled these enemy counterattacks.

At the same time, 290th RD repelled two enemy counterattacks from Zastenok-Iur'ev against the unnamed hill northwest of Marker 196.0—one by up to a company of infantry with 4 tanks and the other by up to a battalion of infantry with 7 tanks.

At 1100 hours the forces of the army's shock groups resumed their attacks across the entire front after a 10-minute artillery raid. The enemy offered stubborn resistance with the units of 18th PzGrD, 26th, 342nd, and 337th IDs, 4th Jäger Battalion, and subunits of a sapper battalion, supported by high command artillery, self-propelled artillery, groups of tanks, six-barreled mortars, and heavy metal apparatuses, while counterattacking with infantry, supported by tanks and self-propelled guns.

In the course of the day, the enemy counterattacked against 290th RD three times, during which, the last time at 1800 hours, he committed up to a regiment of infantry, with 7 tanks and 5 self-propelled guns, supported by 5 aircraft, in the counterattack.

The units of 290th RD repelled all of the counterattacks, but could not advance forward and were fighting in positions on the western slope of the unnamed hill northwest of Marker 196.0; 157th RD, after repelling one counterattack with 7 tanks, was fighting in positions with its right flank—on the western bank of the unnamed stream 700 m east of Zastenok-Iur'ev and its left flank—800 m north of the northern outskirts of Krasnaia Sloboda.

Units of 144th RD, together with a battalion of 222nd RD, repelled five enemy counterattacks by forces from a company of up to a battalion of infantry each, supported by from 8 to 20 tanks. At 1400 hours the enemy, protected by strong artillery fire, threw two battalions of infantry into a counterattack, expelled the division's subunits from Krasnaia Sloboda, and pushed them 200–800 m to the east. Thereafter, the enemy counterattacked against the units of 144th RD twice, but these counterattacks were beaten off, and by day's end the division was fighting with its right flank—600 m north of the northern outskirts of Krasnaia Sloboda and its left flank—600 m east of the northern outskirts of Krasnaia Sloboda.

The subunits of 164th RD, after an artillery raid, captured the first line of enemy trenches and reached the Krasnaia Slobodka-Guraki road by 1130 hours by a decisive thrust. The enemy counterattacked these subunits and threw them back from the trenches. A repeat attack by the division's subunits once again threw the enemy back and approached the cemetery south of Krasnaia Sloboda by 1400 hours. The enemy counterattacked several times more before evening, and the division was still fighting at 2000 hours, with its right flank—600 m east of the northern outskirts of Krasnaia Sloboda and its left flank—500 m east of the southern outskirts of that populated point.

The 277th RD was fighting at day's end with its right flank—600 m east of the southern outskirts of Krasnaia Sloboda and its left—800 m north of the western outskirts of Guraki.

The 42nd RD did not advance on this day and was fighting with its right flank—800 m north of the western outskirts of Guraki and its left flank—200 m north of Marker 218.4.

The units of 61st RC (153rd and 62nd RDs) were fighting in their previous positions; and 68th RD protected the left flank of the army's shock group.

The army's formations suffered the following losses this day:

> 290th RD—61 men killed and 148 wounded,
> 157th RD—42 men killed and 332 wounded,
> 144th RD—27 men killed and 133 wounded,
> 164th RD—252 men killed and 601 wounded,
> 277th RD—107 men killed and 165 wounded,
> 42nd RD—273 men killed and 487 wounded,
> 153rd RD—8 men killed and 13 wounded,
> 62nd RD– 8 men killed and 54 wounded,
> 63rd RD—3 men killed and 9 wounded,
> 222nd RD—1 man killed and 3 wounded.
> [Totals]: 782 killed and 1,945 wounded

In the fighting on 1 December up to 1,800 enemy soldiers and officers, 12 tanks, 6 self-propelled guns, 2 AT guns, and 21 machine guns were destroyed and 64 enemy were captured from 18th PzGrD and 26th and 337th IDs.

2 December:

The army's forces operated with small detachments on the night of 2 December. The 144th RD was assigned the mission to capture Krasnaia Sloboda by first light. The commander of the division decided to attack Krasnaia Sloboda with 612th RR. After a short night battle, 612th RR, together with subunits of 164th RD, captured Krasnaia Sloboda at 0300 hours. The enemy counterattacked the subunits of 612th RR at 0900 hours with two companies of infantry and 7 tanks from the grove north of Krasnaia Sloboda and a company of infantry from the cemetery south of Krasnaia Sloboda, but the counterattacks were repulsed. The forces of the army's shock group began their offensive once again along the entire front at 1200 hours and by 1300 hours captured Zastenek-Iur'ev with an attack by units of 290th RD from the northeast and by 157th RD from the southeast. The units failed to advance in the remaining sectors of the offensive.

The enemy, while trying to restore the situation in the Krasnaia Sloboda region, began counterattacks once again during the second half of the day and counterattacked the subunits of 144th RD in Krasnaia Sloboda 4 times before the onset of darkness, while supporting his counterattacking infantry with strong artillery and mortar fire and groups of 11–14 tanks, but all of the counterattacks were repelled with heavy enemy losses.

On this day, the army's forces destroyed 700 enemy soldiers and officers, 6 tanks, 25 machine guns, and 2 guns. In addition, they seized 28 machine guns, 2 guns, 12 mortars, and 1 radio.

The losses of the army's formations on 2 December 1943 were:
> 290th RD—21 men killed and 54 wounded,
> 164th RD—23 men killed and 27 wounded,
> 153rd RD—13 men killed and 299 wounded,
> 63rd RD—no men killed and 8 wounded,
> 42nd RD—99 men killed and 71 wounded,
> 157th RD—20 men killed and 38 wounded,
> 144th RD—36 men killed and 85 wounded,
> 64th RD—10 men killed and 32 wounded,
> 277th RD—110 men killed and 290 wounded.
> [Total: 332 killed and 904 wounded]

3 December:
The enemy before the army shock group's front strengthened its operating forces (26th, 337th, 342nd IDs, 18th PzGrD, 4th Jäger Battalion, 277th Sapper Battalion of the OKH Reserve); 55th Battalion; an unknown regiment of 30th ID; 92nd Motorized Battalion; and an infantry regiment of 113th ID and repeatedly counterattacked during the course of the day.

The army's formations conducted sustained fighting with counterattacking enemy units, while inflicting heavy losses on the enemy. The subunits of 144th and 164th RDs, which were occupying Krasnaia Sloboda, repelled 5 enemy counterattacks during the first half of the day. At 1530 hours, after a strong artillery raid, the enemy counterattacked Krasnaia Sloboda for a sixth time, during which it threw into the counterattack up to a regiment of infantry and 21 tanks and self-propelled guns. As a result of the fierce fighting, the enemy succeeded in pushing the subunits of 144th RD from Krasnaia Sloboda, and the subunits of 164th RD withdrew into trenches east of the village.

On this day, the army's formations suffered [the following] losses:
    290th RD—16 men killed and 11 wounded,
    144th RD—103 men killed and 424 wounded,
    222nd RD—36 men killed and 234 wounded,
    157th RD—15 men killed and 33 wounded,
    164th RD—61 men killed and 117 wounded,
    163rd RD—15 men killed and 90 wounded,
    62nd RD—17 men killed and 51 wounded,
    63rd RD—no men killed and 2 wounded.
    [Total: 263 killed and 962 wounded]

Source: "Zhurnal boevykh deistviia voisk 33 Armii, 1–3 Dekabria 1943" [The 33rd Army's journal of combat operations, 1–3 December 1943], https://cdn.pamyat-naroda.ru/images.

F. THE BELORUSSIAN FRONT'S GOMEL'-RECHITSA AND NOVYI BYKHOV-PROPOISK OFFENSIVES (10–30 NOVEMBER 1943)

F-1. Excerpt from "The Journal of Combat Operations of 65th Army, 1 December 1943"

1.12.43   Combat Mission
Firmly dig in and hold on to your occupied positions, while destroying the attacking enemy tanks and infantry. Conduct reconnaissance and operate with forward detachments (Enciphered telegram of the army's headquarters No. 7769, 30.11.43.)

Description of Combat Operations
During the day the army's forces fortified the positions they occupy, conducted reconnaissance and fire battles with the enemy, and operated with forward detachments.
    60th and 354th RDs, while operating with reinforced reconnaissance groups, together with partisan detachments, captured Kresty, El'tsy, Krimok, Mikul' Gorodok, and Red'kovo [15 kilometers north-northwest to 20 kilometers north of Ozarichi].

162nd RD, while improving its position, overcame enemy resistance, captured Viazovitsa [22 kilometers southeast of Ozarichi] and dug in on the western and southwestern outskirts.

The enemy on the army's right wing, having consolidated its combat formation at the expense of throwing into action 613th IR of 203rd Security Division, tanks and self-propelled guns, is offering stubborn resistance with rifle-automatic and artillery-mortar fire.

From 1400 hours to 1800 hours, the enemy undertook 3 counterattacks with a company-battalion of infantry and 2–7 tanks, supported by strong artillery-mortar fire and bomber aircraft, from Skalka, Kommunar, and Simeny [4 kilometers south-southeast to 5 kilometers west of Parichi] toward the south and southwest.

From 1000 hours to 1100 hours, [the enemy] launched 4 counterattacks with a force from a company of infantry with 3 tanks to a battalion with 7 tanks from the Martynovichi and Koreni regions [10 kilometers southeast to 12 kilometers east of Ozarichi].

During the day, enemy aviation conducted extensive reconnaissance of our combat formations and close-in rear area, especially on the army's right flank. From 1300 to 1500 hours, groups of 6 to 18 HE-111 and JU-88 bombers bombed the Moiseevka [6 kilometers west-southwest of Parichi], Velikii Bor, and Prosvet [Prosve] regions 5 times. Overall, 74 aircraft sorties were noted during the day.

19th RC—during the day the corps' formations conducted reconnaissance of the enemy, partially regrouped its forces, and, while repelling enemy counterattacks, conducted offensive operations with part of its forces.

The enemy's 635th Field Training Regiment; 1st Army "SS" Battalion; the remnants of 707th Security Division; and 2nd Battalion, 613th Security Regiment, 203rd Security Division, hindered the advance of the corps' units with fires, counterattacks, and strikes by aircraft from the skies, while continuing to throw subunits from other sectors of the front and from Bobruisk into the Parichi region.

At 1100 hours the enemy counterattacked from Skalka [4 kilometers south-southeast of Parichi] toward Prudok [8 kilometers south-southeast of Parichi] against the subunits of 115th RB with up to a company of infantry and one armored vehicle.

At 1300 hours the enemy counterattacked from Kommunar [4 kilometers west-southwest of Parichi] toward Verkhles'e against the subunits of 109th Gds.RR [37th Gds.RD] with up to 2 companies of infantry supported by 3 tanks and 2 "Ferdinand" self-propelled guns. At 1500 hours the enemy counterattacked from Simeny and Zalov'e [5–8 kilometers west of Parichi] toward Moiseevka [6 kilometers west-southwest of Parichi] against subunits of 114th Gds.RR [37th Gds.RD], with up to a battalion of infantry supported by 6 tanks. All of the counterattacks were repulsed with heavy losses for the enemy.

The garrison that is defending the bridgehead fortifications in the vicinity of the railroad bridge at Shatsilki consists of the 3rd and 4th Battalions of 635th Field Training Regiment and an "SS" company. The garrison is being supported from the left bank of the Berezina River by three artillery and four mortar batteries and the fires of heavy machine guns. The soldiers have been ordered to hold the bridge at all cost. Machine guns have been placed on the left bank of the Berezina River for firing on the garrison's soldiers in the event they withdraw.

In Skalka, 2 prisoners from the 1st Army "SS" Battalion were seized, which had just arrived in Parichi from Bobruisk on 27 November 1943. The battalion consists of 10 companies with 80–100 men in each company. Six–eight tanks are attached to the battalion. A prisoner soldier of a separate battalion (without a number) who was captured in the Moiseevka region, indicated that the battalion was formed in Parichi on 28 November 1943 from various types of forces and was thrown into combat.

Aviation of the enemy carried out reconnaissance flights with one ME-109 aircraft and small groups and on hedge-hopping flight fired on the combat formations of the corps' units and corps headquarters. The enemy bombed the combat formations of the corps' units with groups of 6, 16, and 18 Ju-88 aircraft.

115th RB—during the day conducted reconnaissance of the enemy in the direction of Skalka and Parichi. At 1100 hours the brigade's subunits repelled an enemy counterattack and, while digging into the positions they reached, conducted rifle-machine gun exchanges with the enemy, and put its personnel and equipment in order.

37th Gds.RD—during the day conducted reconnaissance toward Parichi, Vysokii Polk and Baranii Rog [2 kilometers north to 3 kilometers northwest of Parichi]. It repelled enemy counterattacks and conducted rifle-machine gun exchanges with the enemy along the line: Lipniki, Peschanaia Rudnia, Kommunar, Simeny, and Maidanov [7 kilometers south to 10 kilometers west of Parichi].

38th Gds.RD—2nd and 3rd Bns, 115th Gds.RR—are in positions from the northwestern outskirts of Shatsilki to Kakel' [6 kilometers north of Shatsilki]. During the day they conducted rifle-machine gun exchanges with the enemy. 1st Bn, 115th Gds. RR and 110th Gds.RR dug into positions from Hill 142.4 to Mol'cha (northern) [7–12 kilometers northwest of Shatsilki].

113th Gds.RR—having completed a march along the march route Ostrovchitsy, Iazvin, Mikhailovka, and Rakovichi [15 kilometers northwest of Shatsilki to 28 kilometers west-northwest of Shatsilki]—dug into positions from Chernin to Petrovichi [14–18 kilometers south-southwest of Parichi], with a forward detachment (PO) consisting of a reinforced rifle company in Gomza [14 kilometers southwest of Parichi].

27th RC—during the day the formations of the corps fortified the positions they occupied and replenished their ammunition and rations.

During the day the enemy conducted rifle-machine gun and artillery-mortar fire against the combat formations of the corps' unit from the line: Brodtsy [20 kilometers north of Ozarichi], Tremliia, Liuban [17 kilometers north-northwest of Ozarichi], Semenovichi [5 kilometers north of Ozarichi], Lesets [4 kilometers north-northeast of Ozarichi], Hill 138.5 [5 kilometers northeast of Ozarichi], and Rydovichi [7 kilometers east of Ozarichi].

At 1250 hours enemy aircraft in groups of 13 bombers bombed the Kobyl'shchina and Prosvet region [10–15 kilometers east of Ozarichi].

354th RD—during the day dug into [the following] positions:

1199th RR—Korma, Cherniavka, and Gorokhovshchi [20–25 kilometers north of Ozarichi].

1201st RR—Kresty and Krimok [15–20 kilometers north of Ozarichi].

1203rd RR—Hill 142.0 and El'tsy [10–15 kilometers north of Ozarich]

Source: "Zhurnal boevykh deistvii voisk 65 Armii, 1. 12. 43." [The 65th Army's journal of combat operations, 1 December 1943], https://cdn.pamyat-naroda.ru/.

G. THE 1ST BALTIC AND WESTERN FRONTS' VITEBSK (GORODOK) OFFENSIVE (13–24 DECEMBER 1943) AND THE 2ND BALTIC FRONT'S IDRITSA-OPOCHKA OFFENSIVE (16–25 DECEMBER 1943)

G-1. From Enciphered Telegram No. 18236 of the Military Council of the 1st Baltic Front to the Commanders of 4th Shock, 11th, 43rd, and 39th Armies, and the Commanders of the 1st Baltic Front's Artillery and Armored and Mechanized Forces

8 December 1943

To reinforce the stability of the forces in positions seized from the enemy, I order:

1. Go over to an active defense and immediately set about digging trenches for the infantry . . . and dug outs for the artillery.

Source: "Zhurnal boevykh deistvii voisk 1-go Pribaltiiskogo fronta za dekabr' 1943 g." [The 1st Baltic Front's journal of combat operations for December 1943], TsAMO, f. 235, op. 2074, ed. khr. 53, l. 7.

G-2. *Stavka* VGK Directive No. 30255 to the Commanders of the 1st Baltic and Western Fronts and the Representative of the *Stavka* on the Resubordination of Three Rifle Divisions

0030 hours 3 December 1943

The *Stavka* of the Supreme High Command ORDERS:

1. Transfer three rifle divisions, along with the *front's* sector from Kovaleva through Pogostishche to Rubleva (inclusive), from the 1st Baltic Front to the Western Front by 15 December 1943

2. At the same time, establish the following boundary line between the 1st Baltic and Western Fronts: Tishino, Rudnia, Baranovo, Kovaleva, Lake Gorodno, Lake Sappo, and Lake Sterzhen' (all points except the first three are inclusive for the 1st Baltic Front).

3. Report fulfillment.

The *Stavka* of the Supreme High Command
I. Stalin, A. Antonov

Source: "Direktiva Stavki VGK No. 30255 komanduiushchim voiskami 1-go Pribaltiiskogo i Zapadnogo frontov, predstaviteliu Stavki na perepodchinenie trekh strelkovykh divizii" [*Stavka* VGK directive No. 30255 to the commanders of the 1st Baltic and Western Fronts and the representative of the *Stavka* on the resubordination of three rifle divisions], in Zolotarev, *Stavka* VGK 1943, 242.

G-3. *Stavka* VGK Directive No. 30256 to the Commander of the Western Front and the Representative of the *Stavka* on Shifting the Direction of the Main Attack

0050 hours 3 December 1943

1. Cease the offensive on the *front*'s right wing upon receipt of this [directive].

2. Leave no more than 10–12 rifle divisions on the Dobromysl' and Baevo front. Regroup 18–20 rifle divisions, with their principal reinforcements, to the Velikoe Selo, Dobromysl', and Liozno region by 15 December. Conduct the regrouping in secret from the enemy. Continue intensified reconnaissance in the Dobromysl' and Baevo sector and employ dummy tanks and guns extensively.

3. Reinforce 10th Army with four–five RDs by 10 December, and continue the offensive along the Mogilev axis in cooperation with the Belorussian Front's right wing.

4. Report on all instructions issued.

The *Stavka* of the Supreme High Command
I. Stalin, A. Antonov

Source: "Direktiva Stavki VGK No. 30256 komanduiushchemu voiskami Zapadnogo fronta, predstaviteliu Stavki na perenos napravleniia glavnogo udara" [*Stavka* VGK directive No. 30256 to the commander of the Western Front and the representative of the *Stavka* on shifting the direction of the main attack], in Zolotarev, *Stavka* VGK 1943, 242. The *Stavka* representative was N. N. Voronov.

G-4. From Enciphered Telegram No. 18419 from the Military Council of the 1st Baltic Front to Lieutenant General Gerasimov, the Commander of 4th Shock Army, and the Commander of 3rd Cavalry Corps, Oslikovsky

14 December 1943

The 2nd Rifle Corps' offensive, which began successfully on 13 December, died out on 14 December. . . . I ORDER:

Develop the offensive resolutely day and night. . . . Today, on 14 December, cut the Nevel'-Vitebsk railroad in the Barkhi and Maleshenki sector at all costs.

Bagramian

Source: "Zhurnal boevykh deistvii voisk 1-go Pribaltiiskogo fronta za dekabr' 1943 g." [The 1st Baltic Front's journal of combat operations for December 1943], *TsAMO*, f. 235, op. 2074, ed. khr. 53, l. 16. For reasons that remain unclear, Gerasimov was temporarily commanding 4th Shock Army.

G-5. *Stavka* VGK Directive No. 30264 to the Commander of the 2nd Baltic Front Concerning an Operation to Destroy the Enemy's Nevel' Grouping

2350 hours 9 December 1943

The *Stavka* of the Supreme High Command ORDERS:

1. The 2nd Baltic Front will conduct an operation with the forces of 6th Guards and 3rd Shock Armies to destroy the enemy's Nevel' grouping. The immediate mission is to capture the Lake Bol'shoi Ivan' and Ust'-Dolyssy line and, subsequently, attack toward Maevo and Novosokol'niki with a part of the forces to roll up the enemy defense along that axis.

2. Begin the offensive on 14 December 1943.

3. Report on all orders issued.

The *Stavka* of the Supreme High Command
I. Stalin, A. Antonov

Source: "Direktiva Stavki VGK No. 30264 komanduiushchemu voiskami 2-go Pribaltiiskogo fronta na operatsiiu po razgromu Nevel'skoi gruppirovki protivnika" [*Stavka* VGK directive No. 30264 to the commander of the 2nd Baltic Front concerning an operation to destroy the enemy's Nevel' grouping], in Zolotarev, *Stavka* VGK 1943, 246.

H. THE 1ST BALTIC AND WESTERN FRONTS' VITEBSK OFFENSIVE (24 DECEMBER 1943–5 JANUARY 1944) AND THE 2ND BALTIC FRONT'S NOVOSOKOL'NIKI PURSUIT (30 DECEMBER 1943–15 JANUARY 1944)

H-1. *Stavka* VGK Directive No. 30268 to the Commander of the 1st Baltic Front and the Representative of the *Stavka* on Destroying the Enemy's Vitebsk Grouping

2010 hours 23 December 1943

The *Stavka* of the Supreme High Command ORDERS:

1. While continuing an energetic offensive, the 1st Baltic Front will direct its main forces in destroying the enemy's Vitebsk grouping and capturing the city of Vitebsk no later than 1 January 1944.

Subsequently, attack in the direction of Lepel' with the *front*'s main forces and toward Polotsk with 4th SA.

2. Report on all orders issued.

The *Stavka* of the Supreme High Command
I. Stalin, A. Antonov

Source: "Direktiva Stavki VGK No. 30268 komanduiushchemu voiskami 1-go Pribaltiiskogo fronta, predstaviteliu Stavki na razgrom Vitebskoi gruppirovki protivnika" [*Stavka* VGK directive No. 30268 to the commander of the 1st Baltic Front commander and the representative of the *Stavka* on destroying the enemy's Vitebsk grouping], in Zolotarev, *Stavka* VGK 1943, 249. The *Stavka* representative was N. N. Voronov.

H-2. From Enciphered Telegram No. 19330 to the *Stavka* VGK from the Military Council of the 1st Baltic Front

25 December 1943

1. While developing the offensive, 39th Army, in cooperation with Western Front units, will cut the Vitebsk-Orsha road and reach the Volkovo, Sokol'niki, Seliuty, and Baryshino front by day's end on 27 December. . . .

Subsequent to the [39th Army's] offensive, 43rd Army will strike a decisive blow against the city of Vitebsk and occupy the southeastern portion of the city no later than 29 December.

Bagramian

Source: "Zhurnal boevykh deistvii voisk 1-go Pribaltiiskogo fronta za dekabr' 1943 g." [The 1st Baltic Front's journal of combat operations for December 1943], *TsAMO*, f. 235, op. 2074, ed. khr. 53, l. 42.

H-3. *Stavka* VGK Order No. 30259 Concerning the Relief from His Duties of the Deputy Commander of the Western Front

8 December 1943

Colonel General Khozin, Mikhail Semenovich, is relieved from his post as Deputy Commander of the Western Front for inactivity and a frivolous attitude toward his work and is placed at the disposal of the chief of the NKO's Main Cadre Directorate.

The *Stavka* of the Supreme High Command
I. Stalin, G. Zhukov

Source: "Prikaz Stavki VGK No. 30259 o sniatii s dolzhnosti zamestitelia komanduiushchego voiskami Zapadnogo fronta" [*Stavka* VGK order No. 30259 concerning the relief from his duties of the deputy commander of the Western Front], in Zolotarev, *Stavka* VGK 1943, 244.

H-4. *Stavka* VGK Order No. 00144 Concerning the Shuffling of the Members of the Military Councils of the 2nd Baltic and Western Fronts

0110 hours 15 December 1943

1. Lieutenant General Mekhliz, L. Z., is relieved of his responsibilities as Member of the 2nd Baltic Front's Military Council and is appointed as the Member of the Western Front's Military Council.

Comrade Mekhlis will arrive in his new position no later than 16 December.

2. To strengthen the 2nd Baltic Front, Lieutenant General Bulganin, N. A., is appointed as the Member of the 2nd Baltic Front's Military Council, having been relieved of his responsibilities as the Member of the Western Front's Military Council.

Comrade Bulganin will arrive in his new position no later than 16 December.

The *Stavka* of the Supreme High Command
I. Stalin, A. Antonov

Source: "Prikaz Stavki VGK No. 00144 o peremeshchanii chlenov voennykh sovetov 2-go Pribaltiiskogo i Zapadnogo frontov" [Stavka VGK order No. 00144 concerning the shuffling of the members of the Military Councils of the 2nd Baltic and Western Fronts], in Zolotarev, *Stavka VGK 1943,* 248.

H-5. From an Enciphered Telegram from the *Stavka* to the 1st Baltic Front

27 December 1943

The 33rd Army is advancing toward the Vitebsk-Orsha highway in heavy combat and is fighting along the Rozhnovo and Verovka line. At the same time, Berzarin's 39th Army has been idle for a second day. The People's Commissar of Defense has ORDERED: Demand that Berzarin's left wing launch a decisive offensive no later than the morning of 28 December 1943.

    Antonov

Source: "Zhurnal boevykh deistvii voisk 1-go Pribaltiiskogo fronta za dekabr' 1943 g." [The 1st Baltic Front's journal of combat operations for December 1943], *TsAMO,* f. 235, op. 2074, ed. khr. 53, l. 44.

H-6. *Stavka* VGK Directive No. 30257 to the Commanders of the Western and 2nd Baltic Fronts on the Resubordination of 10th Guards Army

0215 hours 8 December 1943

Copy to: The commander of 10th Guards Army
    The *Stavka* of the Supreme High Command ORDERS:
    1. Transfer 10th Guards Army, consisting of nine rifle divisions with all army reinforcements and rear service units and facilities, from the Western Front to the 2nd Baltic Front, effective on 9 December 1943.
    2. Deploy 10th Guards Army, excluding all artillery and mortars up to battalion inclusively, by a [road] march from the Rudnia region to the Velikie Luki region and [its] existing material reserves by rail. Begin loading in the Rudnia and Smolensk sector on 9 December.
    3. The Western Front is entrusted with responsibility for the dispatch and supply of the army's forces before they concentrate in the new region.
    4. Report fulfillment.

    The *Stavka* of the Supreme High Command
    I. Stalin, A. Antonov

Source: "Direktiva Stavki VGK No. 30257 komanduiushchim voiskami Zapadnogo i 2-go Pribaltiiskogo frontov na perepodchinenie 10-i gvardeiskoi armii" [Stavka VGK directive No. 30257 to the commanders of the Western and 2nd Baltic Fronts on the resubordination of 10th Guards Army], in Zolotarev, *Stavka VGK 1943,* 243.

I. THE 1ST BALTIC AND WESTERN FRONTS' VITEBSK-BOGUSHEVSK OFFENSIVE (6–24 JANUARY 1944)

I-1. Excerpts from "The Journal of Combat Operations of 43rd Army for January 1944, 1 January 1944"

1. 1. 44
The forces of 43rd Army, having exhausted the enemy in the December offensive operation, drove him back to [the following] previously prepared defensive line: Nikolaevo, Koltovo, Ruba (southern), Graleva, Shabunia, Novoselki, Khoteenki, and Zagoriane.

On 29 December 1943, the army's forces went on the offensive with the mission to penetrate the enemy's defense, while delivering the main attack with 92nd and 91st RCs in the Graleva and (incl.) Gorbachevo sector. Simultaneously, 1st RC had the mission of attacking toward Gorbachevo and Babinichi with part of its forces.

The army's formations, while conducting sustained combat, were not able to suppress the enemy's system of artillery, mortar, and automatic weapons fire during the day and, having encountered strong enemy fire resistance, were not able to break through the enemy's defenses.

On 30 December 1943, in accordance with the army commander's decision, the army's forces resumed the attack on a narrow front, with the mission to penetrate the enemy's defense in the Hill 165.7 and Shabuni sector with the left wing of 92nd RC (332nd RD, 145th RB, and 105th TR) and the right wing of 91st RC (179th RD, 114th RB, and 46th MB).

As a result of sustained fighting, the units of 179th RD overcame the enemy's barbed wire and penetrated into the eastern outskirts of Shabuni, after which it continued to fight to clear out the first trenches.

In the remaining sectors, the formations, which were pinned down by massive artillery and automatic weapons fire, were unable to overcome the enemy's engineer obstacles.

On 31 December 1943, the formations of 92nd and 91st RCs once again went over to the offensive, with the mission to develop the success of 179th RD, crush enemy resistance, and capture the strong point of Shabuni; however this mission was not fulfilled.

The enemy opposite the army's front dug into [the following] previously prepared positions: Dvoritse, Koitovo, Shabuni, the western outskirts of Velinovichi, and Filippova.

The enemy's defensive line was prepared by the efforts of the civilian population and construction battalions since the month of October 1943 and represented a developed network of fortified works consisting of dense trenches, pillboxes, and full-profile communications trenches, with open machine gun platforms, blindages with 3–4 layers, and barbed wire obstacles ("German fences" in two rows) in front of the trenches.

An investigation of documents and the testimony of prisoners has established that, by 31 December 1943, the following formations and units were defending opposite the army's front: 4th LFD consisting of 486th, and 268th Jäger Regiments, with 103rd Workers Battalion along the Nikolaevo, Koltovo line; 197th ID's 332nd IR (with two battalions)—from the Western Dvina River to Marker 165.7, with 54th

Motorized Construction Battalion in reserve in the Ruba region (southern); 221st Security Division's 350th IR and 13th Mixed Detachment—from (incl.) Marker 165.7, (incl.) to Gorbachevo; 14th ID's 11th and 58th IRs, sapper battalion, and AT battalion—along the Gorbachevo and Makarenki line, with 101st IR in reserve in the Babinichi region; 2nd Bn, 1301st IR, 206th ID—from (incl.) Makarenki to Ostriane, with an average density of—one battalion per 1.5 kilometers of front.

Artillery. Combat and observation opposite the army's front has determined [that]: the main grouping of artillery is along the Ugliany and Koitovo line—with up to three 105mm battalions. . . .

Up to 50 enemy tanks have been noted before the army's front and among them are up to 10 "Tiger" type, and 15–20 self-propelled guns, partly of the "Ferdinand" type.

According to captured documents, actions by 501st PzBn have been noted, apparently attached to reinforce 14th ID.

With such an organization opposite the army's front, 16 battalions of infantry are operating in the first line of the enemy's defenses, which are supported by up to 11 artillery battalions and 50 tanks and self-propelled guns, with a tactical reserve of four battalions.

During the day on 31 January 1943, the enemy offered stubborn resistance to the army's attacking formations. The enemy's system of fires both in the forward edge and in the depths of the defense has not been suppressed, but the units have suffered considerable losses.

At day's end on 31 December 1943, the army's formations were fighting along the following lines:

92nd RC. 334th RD—the southwestern edge of the grove 400 m east of Marker 167.8, the western edge of the grove Zaichikha, (incl.) Marker 166.7, and (incl.) Koitovo.

358th RD—southwestern outskirts of Sobari, (incl.) Graleva, and (incl.) Marker 165.7.

332nd RD—(incl.) Hill 165.7 to the southwestern edge of the woods UR Avdeevskii Woods.

145th RB—the southwestern edge of UR Avdeevskii Les [Woods] to the northeastern outskirts of Shabuni.

91st RC. 179th RD—the northeastern outskirts of Shabuni to the separate house 150 m east of Marker 178.3.

114th RB—Marker 178.3 to the fork in the road 600 m southwest of Noviki.

306th RD—(incl.) the fork in the road 600 m southwest of Noviki to (incl.) Gorbachevo.

1st RC. 145th RD—(incl.) southeastern outskirts of Gorbachevo to (incl.) east of Khokhlovshchina (on the Surazh-Vitebsk road).

204th RD—(incl.) the central avenue in the park south of Belinovichi to (incl.) Novoselki, Vystavka.

417th Sep.Arty-MG Bn—Avdeenki, eastern outskirts of Strugova, Slin'kovo, and Poddub'e.

270th RD, with 46th MB—army reserve in the Stan'kovo region.

The army's military council issued its forces Combat Order No. 001/op at 0140 hours 1 January 1944 [which read]:

1. Temporarily halt the offensive by the army's shock group in order to put our units into order and prepare them for further active operations and go over to an active defense of the positions you have reached.

During the enemy's withdrawal, pursue him slowly, for which you will allocate special detachments of no less than a battalion from each rifle division.

The defense will be ready by the morning of 1 January 1944.

In turn, the defensive works will be ready by 5 January 1944.

2. 92nd RC, with 64th HAR, 118th MtrR, 252nd Gds-MR, two companies of 87th Engineer-Sapper Battalion, and a company of 106th Pontoon-Bridge Battalion, will firmly defend the occupied positions, with . . . in the first line.

Source: "Zhurnal boevykh deistvii voisk 43 armii za ianvar' m-ts 1944 g." [The 43rd Army's journal of combat operations for January 1944], https://cdn.pamyat-naroda.ru/.

I-2. Excerpts from "The Journal of Combat Operations of 39th Army for January 1944, 1–4 January"

1 January 1944
As a result of the many days of fighting in December 1943, the army's forces reached [the following] positions: (incl.) Poddub'e, the "Leen" northeast of Tishkovo, Illiushi, the grove northwest of Derviagi, Eremino, Pal'kovichi, Kovsheri, Ugliane, Laputi, and the road junction 600 m east of Siniaki and located the shortest distance from the city of Vitebsk than all of the remaining forward CPs of the *front's* armies.

Mission: The forces of 39th Army, in cooperation with the units of 33rd Army, while energetically developing the offensive in the general direction of Pal'kovichi and Popovka, will defeat the opposing enemy, cut the highway from Vitebsk to Orsha, and reach the Volkovo, Sokol'niki, and Baryshino front, with the main grouping on its left wing.

Subsequently, while firmly protecting your left flank, deliver a decisive blow on the city of Vitebsk and, in cooperation with the units of 43rd Army, capture the southeastern part of the city.

At that time, the enemy, having brought up separate battalions to reinforce his defending units, (such as 650th Penal, 620th Construction, the Fusillier Regiment of the "Feldherrnhalle" Division (60th PzGrD), and 347th IR, which was located in the Germans' reserve and was quickly transferred from the Polotsk region) and having brought up a great quantity of artillery, resisted the advance of the army's forces with strong artillery fire and counterattacks, and held them up under constant artillery, mortar, fire. . . . Enemy heavy artillery was especially active. According to information from observation, a total of up to 11 artillery and six mortar batteries of the enemy were noted operating on the army's front (mainly in front of its left wing).

Based on the overall mission, on 31 December 1944, the army's forces received [the following] missions:

"The forces of 134th RD—84th RC and 5th Gds RC will attack at 1200 hours on 1 January 1944 along their previous axes and with their previous missions."

The expenditure of ammunition was limited. . . . The main emphasis was given to the use of direct fire guns—45mm and 76mm—and the employment of 82mm mortars.

On the night of 1 January 1944, 134th RD took over the sector of 158th RD and, after a 5-minute fire raid, attacked in the direction of Porechnyi and Luski.

The 5 Gds.RC attacked with the forces of 19th and 9th Gds.RDs and, as a result of sustained fighting, advanced forward somewhat into the Laputi-Shushino region.

The 134th RD did not succeed in advancing.

The weather was unfavorable for the attackers. A snowstorm, with severely limited visibility, hindered the conduct of artillery fire and observation of the battlefield, and reduced the effectiveness of the fires.

The defending enemy, despite the limited visibility, conducted intense barrier fires in front of the forward edge and continued to deliver fire on the attacking units.

The uninterrupted actions of the enemy against our attacking combat formations with fires from heavy weapons all day long weakened the offensive spirit of our forces. . . .

2–4 January 1944

The army's forces dug in along the positions they reached. . . . Simultaneously, the units of the army's first echelon conducted reconnaissance of the enemy, with the mission of seizing prisoners and documents. . . . The 143rd TB entered the army's composition and concentrated in the region of woods 1 kilometer south of Luchibovka.

As replacements for the units that had suffered losses in previous battles, 114th RB, 124th RB, and 145th RB were disbanded and their personnel were transferred primarily to 5th Gds.RC. The refilled units were withdrawn into the army's second echelon, where the subunits were knocked together and conducted training.

As a result of a partial regrouping of the army's forces, they occupied [the following] positions by days end on 4 January 1944:

204th RD—(incl.) Poddub'e, the western edge of the woods east of Zagoriane, Illiushi, Eremino, (incl.) the grove south of Tropy, the grove 1.2 kilometers southeast of Porechnyi.

134th RD—(incl.) the grove 1.2 kilometers southeast of Porechnyi, (incl.) the separate house 600 m east of Kozechevo.

158th RD—the separate house east of Kozechevo, Marker 206.8.

17th Gds.RD—(incl.) Marker 206.8, the grove 500 m west of Laputi, (incl.) the grove southeast of Laputi.

9th Gds.RD—the grove southeast of Laputi, the western edge of the grove northwest of Zhernosenki.

19th and 91st Gds.RDs are in the army's second echelon.

Source: "Zhurnal boevykh deistvii voisk 39 armii za ianvar' m-ts 1944 g." [The 43rd Army's journal of combat operations for January 1944], https://cdn.pamyat-naroda.ru/.

I-3. From Report No. 15 on the Generalization of the Western Front's Combat Experiences for January 1944

In January the forces on the *front's* right wing conducted offensive operations along the Bogushevsk axis and defended its occupied positions in the center and on the left wing. The enemy continued to offer stubborn resistance along the Vitebsk and Bogushevsk axes, employing, as before, numerous counterattacks by infantry supported by self-propelled guns, tanks, and artillery fire.... During this time, the enemy devoted considerable attention to creating dense groupings of artillery and fire sacks on the flanks of our attacking forces.... Up to this time, the commanders of the formations, regiments, and subunits are continuing to emphasize the command and control of forces in telephone conversations by spending up to 90% of their time on this. Everything "hangs" [depends] on the telephones. On a daily basis, the corps commanders call the division commanders on telephones, the division commanders [call] the regimental commanders, and the regimental commanders [call] the battalion commanders. That is, together with their creative work in analyzing combat and directing it, all of the leading officer cadre are involved in gathering information about the situation in their units, while substituting themselves for their staffs in these matters. The latter, who are performing secondary tasks, are employed primarily as special messengers of the command.

> Lieutenant General Pokrovsky, Chief of Staff of the Western Front
> Major General Chirkov, Chief of Operations of the Western Front

Source: TsAMO, f. 233, op. 2356, d. 19, ll. 225–230.

I-4. Documentation of the Western Front's Losses for 1944

The losses of the Western Front amount to: Weapons losses from 1 through 10 January 1944—954 rifles and 78 antitank rifles. Personnel losses from 1 through 20 January 1944—4,738 killed, 16,142 wounded, 4,012 sick, 15 frostbitten, and 184 missing in action. Horse losses [during the same period]—780 killed, 84 wounded, 181 sick, and 5 missing in action.

The *front's* trophies (captured materials) from 28 December 1943 through 10 January 1944—6 tanks, 3 trucks, 11 guns, 6 mortars, 104 machine guns, and others.

The *front's* weapons losses from 10 through 20 January 1944—1,180 rifles, 120 submachine guns, 31 heavy machine guns, and 27 antitank rifles. The *front's* personnel losses from 21–31 January—2,067 killed, 6,213 wounded, 4,509 sick and evacuated to the hospital, 9 frostbitten, 197 missing in action, and 10 captured by the enemy. Horse losses—271 killed.

The *front's* weapons losses from 20 through 31 January—4,165 rifles, 120 antitank rifles, and 140 76mm antitank guns, including 118 in 33rd Army and 18 in 5th Army.

Source: TsAMO, f. 208, op. 2511, ed. kh., 3051, ll. 10–14.

I-5. The Defensive Battles at Witebsk from 13.12.43 through 17.2.44

The 1st Battle at Witebsk
(13.12.43–18.1.44)

(A) *Enemy Strength:*
    Confirmed strength:
    In the region southwest of Lake Jeserischtche [Ezerishche]—11th Guards Army with 12 guards rifle and rifle divisions and 1st Tank Corps (4 tank units [brigades]).

In the Ordowo [Ordovo] and Lake Tschernowo [Chernoe] region—4th Shock Army with 14 rifle divisions and 5th Tank Corps (4 tank units).

In the region northeast of Witebsk [Vitebsk]—39th and 43rd Armies with 14 rifle divisions and 6 tank units.

In the region southeast of Witebsk—the 33rd, 5th, and 39th Armies with 24 rifle divisions, 1 rifle brigade, and 10 tank units.

Therefore, in the first Battle at Witebsk, the 15 combat ready divisions of the Panzer Army were opposed altogether by 6 armies with 58 guards rifle and rifle divisions, 1 rifle brigade, and 24 tank units, for a total of 83 units.

(B) Enemy Losses:
190,000 men combat losses
2,361 captured
248 deserters
Estimated Destroyed and Captured Equipment
1,124 tanks destroyed
91 tanks captured
159 guns
194 antitank guns
39 grenade launchers
309 machine guns
21 aircraft by antiaircraft or ground fire

Source: "Die Abwehrschlachten um Witebsk vom 13.12.43 bis 17.2.44," in National Archives Microfilm (NAM) series T-313.

J. THE 1ST BALTIC AND WESTERN FRONT'S VITEBSK OFFENSIVE (3–16 FEBRUARY 1944)

J-1. *Stavka* VGK Directive No. 220011 to the Commanders of the 1st Baltic and Western Fronts and the Representative of the *Stavka* [N. N. Voronov] on the Destruction of the Enemy's Vitebsk Grouping

0330 hours 18 January 1944

The *Stavka* VGK assigns [you] the immediate mission of defeating the enemy's Vitebsk grouping and capturing the city of Vitebsk by the combined efforts of the 1st Baltic Front and the right wing of the Western Front.

To fulfill this mission the *Stavka* orders:

1. The 1st Baltic Front will concentrate its main grouping of forces and weapons on the left wing of 4th Shock Army and the right wing of 11th Guards Army. Strengthen the right wing of the *front*'s shock group at the expense of 43rd A.

Conduct the attack of these armies toward Vitebsk from the northwest and capture Vitebsk in cooperation with the Western Front's right wing. Reliably protect the operations by the *front*'s main forces against [attack] from Polotsk and Beshenkovichi.

Transfer 39th Army, with its six rifle divisions and all reinforcements and army rear service units, installations, and reserves, to the Western Front, effective at 2400 hours on 19 January 1944.

2. With the support of 5th A, the Western Front will conduct an attack in the general direction of Vitebsk from the southwest with 33rd and 39th Armies and will capture Vitebsk in cooperation with the 1st Baltic Front.

Reinforce 33rd A with three to four rifle divisions at the expense of 5th Army.

3. Establish the following boundary line between the 1st Baltic and Western Fronts, effective at 2400 hours on 19 January 1944: Zhevnerovo, Cherniaty, Poddub'e, and the mouth of the Vit'ba River (all points inclusive for the 1st Baltic Front).

4. Begin the offensive no later than the end of January.

5. Report on all orders issued.

The *Stavka* VGK
I. Stalin, A. Antonov

Source: "Direktiva Stavki VGK no. 220011 komanduiushchim voiskami 1-go Pribaltiiskogo i Zapadnogo frontov, predstaviteliu Stavki na razgrom vitebskoi gruppirovki protivnika" [*Stavka* VGK Directive No. 220011 to the commanders of the 1st Baltic and Western Fronts and the representative of the *Stavka* on the destruction of the enemy's Vitebsk Grouping], in Zolotarev, *Stavka* VGK, 1944, 34. The *Stavka* representative was N. N. Voronov.

J-2. From the Commander of the 1st Baltic Front to the Supreme High Commander, Marshal of the Soviet Union I. V. Stalin, Concerning a Plan for the Vitebsk Operation

14 January 1944

I have decided to employ 20 understrength rifle divisions, 2 tank corps, 3 tank brigades, and almost all of the *front*'s artillery and aviation in the penetration operation by means of a well-prepared crippling blow with 12 rifle divisions of 11th Guards Army and 4th Shock Army from one side and 7 rifle divisions of 43rd Army from the other side to defeat the Germans in the region northwest of Vitebsk and capture the city.

Army General Bagramian, commander of the 1st Baltic Front
Lieutenant General Leonov, Member of the 1st Baltic Front's Military Council
Lieutenant General Kurasov, chief of staff of the 1st Baltic Front

Source: TsAMO [Central Archives of the Ministry of Defense], f. 235, op. 2074, ed. kh., 77, ll., 6–17.

J-3. To the Commander of the 1st Baltic Front Concerning a Withdrawal of 3rd Guards Cavalry Corps into the High Command's Reserve

1800 hours 18 January 1944

Copies to: Commander, 3rd Guards Cavalry Corps, Commander, Red Army Cavalry, Chief, General Staff Operational-Organizational Directorate

The People's Commissariat of Defense (NKO) orders:

1. Withdraw 3rd Guards Cavalry Corps from the 1st Baltic Front to the *Stavka* VGK's Reserve by a [road] march to the Il'ino, Shaklovo, Shchuch'e, and Zhaloedovo region. Locate the corps headquarters in Il'ino.

2. Begin the march at 1800 hours on 27 January. Complete the concentration in the new region by 7 February. Submit a march plan on 25 January.

3. Withdraw the complete corps, with all of its personnel, horses, weapons, and transport and property, into the *Stavka's* Reserve and remove nothing before its dispatch.

4. The 1st Baltic Front remains responsible for supplying the corps.

5. The commander of 3rd Guards Cavalry Corps will present the General Staff with the corps' location in the new region, together with orders of its headquarters, by 7 February.

Report fulfillment.

Antonov, Karponosov

Source: "Komanduiushchemu voiskami 1-go Pribaltiiskogo fronta o vyvode 3-go gvardeiskogo kavaleriiskogo korpusa v rezerv Vekhovnogo Glavnokomandovaniia" [To the commander of the 1st Baltic Front concerning a withdrawal of 3rd Guards Cavalry Corps into the High Command's Reserve], in Zolotarev, *General Staff 1944–1945*, 41.

J-4. To the Commander of the 1st Baltic Front Concerning the Composition of 39th Army Being Transferred to the Western Front

1500 hours 19 January 1944

Copies to: The commanders of 39th Army and the Western Front
Chief of the Main Organizational Directorate

1. Transfer 39th Army, with the following composition, from the 1st Baltic to the Western Front:

(a) The army's field headquarters, with all of its communications units, service organs, and army rear services;

(b) 84th Rifle Corps (134th, 158th, and 262nd RDs) and 5th Guards Rifle Corps (17th, 19th, and 91st Gds.RDs);

(c) 610th TDR, 545th Gun Artillery Regiment, 472nd Howitzer Artillery Regiment, 41st Guards Corps Gun Artillery Regiment, 408th Mortar Regiment, 621st PVO Artillery Regiment, 225th Antiaircraft Artillery Regiment, 490th Sep.AA Bn, 787th Sep.Recon.Arty.Bn, 326th Guards-Mortar Regiment, and 4th Tank Destroyer Artillery Brigade;

(d) 28th Tank Brigade and 47th Mechanized Brigade; and

(e) 4th Engineer-Assault Sapper Brigade and two army engineer battalions.

2. Leave all remaining reinforcing formations and units situated within 39th Army in the 1st Baltic Front.

3. Provide the transferred formations and units with 2 combat loads of 76mm regimental gun [ammunition], 1 combat load of 76mm divisional gun [ammunition], 1.3 combat loads of 122mm howitzer [ammunition], 2 combat loads of 152mm howitzer [ammunition], 1.8 combat loads of 152mm gun Model 1937 [ammunition], 2 combat loads of 82mm mortar [ammunition], and 1 combat load of 120mm mortar [ammunition].

Remaining types of ammunition—as on hand.

Report fulfillment.

Antonov, Karponosov

Source: "Komanduiushchemu voiskami 1-ogo Pribaltiiskogo fronta o sostave 39-i Armii, peredavaemoi Zapadnomu fronta" [To the commander of the 1st Baltic Front concerning the composition of 39th Army being transferred to the Western Front], in Zolotarev, *General Staff 1944–1945*, 41–42.

K. THE WESTERN FRONT'S BABINOVICHI AND VITEBSK OFFENSIVES (22 FEBRUARY–5 MARCH 1944)

K-1. Documentation of the Western Front's Losses for 1944

The *front*'s personnel losses from 1 through 10 February—6,163 killed, 21,757 wounded, 4,840 sick, 10 frostbitten, 148 missing in action, 3 captured by the enemy, and 62 for other reasons, for a total of 32,983 men. Horse losses—779 lost in all. From 23 December 1943 through 10 February 1944, 33rd and 5th Armies lost a total of 26,459 men killed, wounded, or missing and 123 tanks burned and 134 tanks destroyed, for a total of 257 tanks. During this same period, the same armies inflicted the following losses on the enemy—captured 344 prisoners, captured 51 tanks, 17 self-propelled guns, 122 guns, 79 mortars, 4 6-barreled mortars [*Nebelwerfer*], 254 machine guns, 472 automatic weapons, 1,465 rifles, 4,920 shells and mines, 5,345 grenades, 139,000 rounds of ammunition, and 61 trucks, and destroyed 9 aircraft, 175 guns, 160 mortars, 375 machine guns, 950 rifles, and 96 vehicles.

The *front*'s personnel losses from 11 through 20 February—4,594 killed and 13,950 wounded, for a total, including other categories, of 22,352 men. Horse losses—a total of 668. The *front*'s weapons losses from 10 through 20 February—4,173 rifles, 224 submachine guns, 156 antitank rifles, 43 mortars, and others.

The *front*'s losses from 21 through 29 February—a total of 16,354 men and 530 horses. The *front*'s weapons losses from 20 February through 1 March—2,753 rifles, 158 submachine guns, 69 heavy machine guns, 63 antitank rifles, 47 mortars, 65 guns, and 27 self-propelled guns.

Source: TsAMO RF, f. 208, op. 2511, ed. kh., 3051, ll. 15–30.

K-2. The Defensive Battles at Witebsk from 13.12.43 through 17.2.44

The 2nd Battle at Witebsk
(3.2.44–17.2.44)

(A) *Enemy Strength:*
  Confirmed strength:
    In the region southeast of Witebsk—33rd, 5th, and 39th Armies, with 23 guards rifle and rifle divisions, 1 rifle brigade, and 6 tank units [brigades].

In the region east and northeast of Witebsk—43rd Army, with 8 rifle divisions and the 1 tank unit.

In the region northwest of Witebsk—11th Guards and 4th Shock Armies, with 22 guards rifle and rifle divisions and 3 tank units.

The presence of 3 remaining tank units in the region southwest of Witebsk is probable.

Therefore, in the second battle at Witebsk, the 12 combat ready divisions of the [Third] Panzer Army were opposed altogether by a total of 6 armies, with 53 guards rifle and rifle divisions, 1 rifle brigade, and 10 tank units, for a total of 64 units.

(B) Enemy Losses:
    113,000 men combat losses
        832 captured
        68 deserters
    Estimated Destroyed and Captured Equipment
        332 tanks destroyed
        31 tanks captured
        24 guns
        51 antitank guns
        15 grenade launchers
        266 machine guns
        39 aircraft by antiaircraft or ground fire

Source: "Die Abwehrschlachten um Witebsk vom 13.12.43 bis 17.2.44" in National Archives Microfilm (NAM) series T-313.

K-3. Report No. 21 by the Commander of the Western Front to the Supreme High Commander on a Plan for an Offensive Operation along the Vitebsk and Orsha Axes

25 February 1944

In accordance with your order, we have prepared the following operations:

1. A main operation along the Vitebsk axis by 33rd Army grouped in three RCs (9 rifle divisions). The penetration [operation] will be conducted along a 6-kilometer front in the sector extending from Pavliuchenko to Perevoz. The attack [will be] along the Zhuki [Shuki], Pushkari, and Pesochnia axis with a subsequent turn to the northwest to Ostrovno (20 kilometers west of Vitebsk) into the rear of the enemy's Vitebsk grouping.

Within the constraints of available ammunition supplies, we will allocate the main grouping of the *front's* artillery (50th Artillery Corps), 4 M-13 regiments, and 3 M-31 brigades to the operation. The [artillery] density will be 135 tubes per 1 kilometer of front. Existing *front* aviation forces will take part.

The immediate mission of the operation is to cut the Vitebsk-Orsha railroad in the Sosnovka State Farm and Stupishche sector, and the subsequent mission is to reach the rear area of the enemy's Vitebsk grouping and capture Vitebsk by an attack from the southwest.

Simultaneously with 33rd Army's turn toward Vitebsk from the southwest, 39th Army will attack westward from the Poddub'e with three RDs.

The 33rd Army will be prepared for the operation by 3 March and will begin the operation on 5 March.

2. A supporting operation by 31st Army's right wing (two rifle divisions) and 5th Army's left wing (two rifle divisions), with an army artillery group plus one tank destroyer brigade and one mortar brigade. This operation is being conducted at this time in the Rubleva and (incl.) Babinovichi sector. The immediate aim of the operation is to draw part of the enemy's forces (especially tanks and self-propelled artillery) away from 33rd Army's sector. If 33rd Army's operation develops normally, the subsequent mission is to turn the enemy's front in front of 5th Army and 31st Army's right wing in the general direction of Bogushevsk.

3. An operation by 49th Army along the Orsha axis. The grouping—initially five rifle divisions with army artillery, plus one TDB, one RGK HAR, and one M-13 [MRL/*Katiusha*] regiment. The [artillery] density will be 100 guns per kilometer [of front]. The penetration [operation] will be conducted] along a 5-kilometer front in the sector extending from Parfenkovo to Lopyrevshchina (10 kilometers southwest of Liady).

The attack [will be] along the Demiankovo, Putiatino, Dobryn', and Leonovka axis, with a subsequent turn to the north along the railroad to Orsha or to Shklov to cooperate with the Belorussian Front. In the event that the operation develops successfully, we will employ all of 49th Army's forces, that is, 8 rifle divisions, and the left wing of 31st Army, that is, two rifle divisions, along the vehicular road toward Orsha from the east.

The operation will begin on 3 March.

4. We request you approve the proposed operation.

5. We request you help the *front* [by]:

(a) Detailing 20,000 reinforcements for replenishing the forces during the operation;

(b) Bring the *front*'s ammunition [stocks] up to two combat loads and also issue 5,000 M-31 and 15,000 M-13 [rockets];

(c) Issue 200 T-34 tanks and two regiments of SU-85 [self-propelled guns] to combat enemy tanks, of which the enemy has around 250 in front of our *front*.

V. Sokolovsky, L. Mekhlis

Source: "Doklad komanduiushchego voimsami Zapadnogo fronta No. 21 Verkhovnomu Glavnokomanduiushchemu plana nastupatel'noi operatsii na Vitebskom i Orshanskom napravleniiakh" [Report No. 21 by the commander of the Western Front to the Supreme High Commander on a plan for an offensive operation along the Vitebsk and Orsha axes], in Zolotarev, *Stavka* VGK 1944, 272.

K-4. *Stavka* VGK Directive No. 220037 to the Commander of the Western Front Concerning the Reworking of his Plan for an Offensive Operation along the Vitebsk and Orsha Axes

0310 hours 26 February 1944

With regards to your Report No. 21 sent by enciphered telegram on 25 February, the *Stavka* VGK directs:

1. So that you do not disperse your forces and weaken the blow, conduct the offensive along two axes, toward Vitebsk and Orsha, rather than four.

2. To that end:

(a) 33rd A will attack with the principal mission of cutting the Vitebsk-Orsha railroad and subsequently developing an attack on Vitebsk from the south;

(b) Begin 39th A's offensive after 33rd Army arrives at the line of the Vitebsk-Orsha railroad and when it turns north toward Vitebsk.

(c) Cease the offensive at the junction of 5th and 31st Armies and go over to the defense in this region.

(d) We consider the offensive that you propose with 49th Army toward Dobryn' and Leonovka as pointless. Instead, organize an offensive north of the Dnepr River toward Orsha by employing the forces you intended to use in 49th and 31st Armies' shock groups.

3. Submit a reworked plan based on our orders to the General Staff no later than 27 February.

The *Stavka* VGK
I. Stalin, A. Antonov

Source: "Direktiva Stavki VGK No. 22037 komanduiushchemu voiskami Zapadnogo fronta o pererabotke plana nastupatel'noi operatsii na Vitebskom i Orshanskom napravleniiakh" [*Stavka* VGK Directive No. 220037 to the commander of the Western Front concerning the reworking of his plan for an offensive operation along the Vitebsk and Orsha Axes], in Zolotarev, *Stavka* VGK 1944, 51.

K-5. *Stavka* VGK Directive No. 220043 to the Commanders of the 1st Baltic and Western Fronts Concerning Pursuit of the Withdrawing Enemy and the Offensive against Vitebsk

0330 hours 1 March 1944

Copy to the *Stavka* Representative (S. K. Timoshenko)

The enemy has weakened his defense along the Vitebsk axis and is beginning to withdraw, apparently to assemble reserves with which to resist the operations of the 1st and 2nd Baltic Fronts, which are just beginning.

The *Stavka* VGK orders:

1. The Western Front will immediately pursue the withdrawing enemy by employing for that purpose all of 39th A's forces and the forces of 33rd A that are prepared to attack. The main forces of 33rd A will go over to the offensive against Vitebsk from the southeast no later than 2 March 1944.

2. The 1st Baltic Front will attack Vitebsk from the northwest with 43rd A no later than 2 March 1944

3. Report all orders given.

The *Stavka* VGK
I. Stalin, A. Antonov

Source: Direktiva Stavki VGK No. 220043 komanduiushchim voiskami 1-go Pribaltiiskogo i Zapadnogo frontov o presledovanii otkhodiashchego protivnika i nastuplenii na Vitebsk" [*Stavka* VGK Directive No. 220043 to the commanders of the 1st Baltic and Western Fronts concerning pursuit of the withdrawing enemy and the offensive against Vitebsk], in Zolotarev, *Stavka* VGK 1944, 54–55.

K-6. Excerpt from "The Journal of Combat Operations of the 1st Baltic Front for March 1944, 1–3 March 1944"

COMBAT MISSIONS	DESCRIPTION OF THE COMBAT ACTIONS
To the commander of 43rd Army.	1. 3. 1944

The *front* commander has ordered:
1. [While defending of the army's right wing with 1st RC, conduct an offensive with the units of 92nd RC to penetrate the enemy's defenses in the sector.] . . . Subsequently, advance on Vitebsk.
Begin the offensive quickly without carrying out a major regrouping and exploit it with 145th RD.
2. Go over to the offensive no later than 1600 hours on 1 March 1944 with 5th and 46th MRBs and 179th RD through the Dolzhanskii Forest in the general direction of Borovliane and Khoisy.
The immediate mission—cut the Gorodok-Vitebsk road and subsequently attack toward Vitebsk in cooperation with the units of 235th RD.
On the army's remaining front, continue to firmly defend the positions you occupy.
 	
[Lieutenant General] P. P. Kurasov [Chief of Staff]
(Enciphered telegram No. 10300 of 1. 3. 1944)
	4th Shock Army—essentially nothing occurred.
	
	43rd Army. The units of 92nd RC went over to an offensive in the general direction of Vitebsk on the morning of 1 March 1944 and, having overcome German resistance and counterattacks, advanced forward from 2 to 5 kilometers, occupied 60 populated points, and by day's end captured the following lines:
	  1st RC—179th RD—Hill 174.3, Lake Shestino, and Lake Lipki;
	  44th MRB—(incl.) Lake Lipki, and (incl.) Krugliaki State Farm;
	  5th MRB—Krugliaki State Farm, and (incl.) Shilovo;
	  92nd RC—235th RD—Shilovo, Lovzha State Farm, Losvida State Farm, Efremovo, and Egorki;
	  334th RD—(incl.) Egorki, Vysokie, Diugany, and Ruba; and
	  145th RD—concentrated in the Gostilovo, Podgrechikhin, and Borovka region by 1500 hours in readiness to develop 92nd RC's success in the general direction of Vitebsk.
	The positions of the army's remaining units is unchanged.
	
	(from the *front*'s Combat Report No. 61 and Operational Summary No. 61).

640   Appendices

COMBAT MISSIONS	DESCRIPTION OF THE COMBAT ACTIONS
	2. 3. 1944
	During the day on 2 March 1944 the *front*'s forces continued an offensive with the forces of 11th Gds. Army and 43rd Army, but encountered stubborn enemy resistance and counterattacks and had minimal advance in separate sectors.

Source: Zhurnal boevykh deistvii voisk 1go Baltiiskogo fronta za mart 1944 g." [The 1st Baltic Front's journal of combat operations for March 1944], https://cdn.pamyat-naroda.ru/.

K-7. Excerpt from "The Journal of Combat Operations of 5th Army for March 1944, 1–2 March 1944"

1. 3. 44

The Army commander's decision on 1. 3. 44:

Improve the positions you occupy in an engineer sense. Conduct combat reconnaissance. Concentrate 184th RD in the Tikhovka woods by 0500 hours on 1 March 1944.

Operations of the forces.

The army's forces, while holding on to their previous positions, will conduct reconnaissance and observation and carry out defensive work and a partial regrouping.

The 184th RD, in the composition of 72nd RC, will concentrate in the region of the woods east of Tikhovka by first light. When darkness arrives, set about relieving 233rd RR of 97th RD. The 157th RD will enter the composition of 45th RC. The 95th Gds.-MtrR will leave the army to be at the disposal of the commander of 33rd Army.

The enemy displayed no personnel activity with the units of 299th, 14th, 211th, and 256th IDs and decreased his fire activities. Overall, [the following] artillery batteries are operating—150mm—3, 105mm—5, 75mm—3, and one 210mm gun; mortar batteries—81mm—5 and two launcher platforms. Over 1,000 shells and mines were fired on the combat formations of our units.

2. 3. 44

The Army commander's decision on 2 March 1944

Fulfill assigned missions.

Notes: Prisoners from 301st IR, 206th ID, who were seized on 29 February 1944 in the Shul'tsevo region (9 kilometers southeast of Vitebsk) reported that on the night of 29 February 1944, 2nd Battalion, 301st IR, was sent to reinforce the units operating south of Vitebsk. . . .

THE CORRELATION OF FORCES
in the sector of 72nd RC's attacking divisions on 1 March 1944

Composition and Combat Means	Our Forces	Enemy	Correlation
Total quantity of personnel	8,468	7,370	1.14 : 1
Quantity of personnel per battalion	251	350	0.7 : 1
Quantity of battalions	11	11	1.0 : 1

Rifles	4,003	–	–
Automatic weapons	878	382	2.3 : 1
Submachine guns	191	205	0.9 : 1
Heavy machine guns	52	76	0.7 : 1
Mortars	102	125	0.8 : 1
AT rifles	139	–	–
AT guns	42	35	1.2 : 1
Field guns	74	120	0.6 : 1
AA guns	51	128	0.4 : 1

ORDER OF BATTLE
The forces of 72nd RC as of 1 March 1944

The Corps' Formations	Regiments	Quantity and Designations of Battalions	Separate Units
97th RD	136th RR	One battalion (1st, with 3 companies)	97th TDBn.,
	233rd RR	One battalion (1st, with 3 companies)	Sep. Sapper
	69th RR	One battalion (1st, with 3 companies)	Bn., Sep.
	61st AR	Two battalions (with 4 batteries each)	RBn, and Trng., Recon., and Chem. Cos.

Missions of the Formations.
1. 97th RD, while covering [protecting] the [following] sector: (incl.) Miaklovo, (incl.) Kartkovichi, and the unnamed hill west of Makarova, will penetrate the [following] front: the church at Kartkovichi, the approach to the grove at the barn 1 kilometer northwest of Zamosh'e.

Immediate mission–reach positions from the ford to east of Marker 153.7 [2 kilometers southwest of Kartkovichi].

Subsequent mission—capture the northern half of the "large woods" and reach the Luchesa River on the front: the ford and Seledtsy [4 kilometers southwest of Kartkovichi].

The boundary line on the left: Makarova, Marker 153.7, and Seledtsy.

2. 277th RD, having its combat formation in three echelons, will penetrate the enemy's defenses in the [following] sector: the grove southeast of Marker 153.7, and VDKCh [unknown abbreviation].

Immediate mission—capture the "Zub" grove (southeast of marker 153.7).

Subsequent mission—capture the southern half of the "large woods" and reach the front: (incl.) Seledtsy, VDKCh, the southern edge of the "large woods," and Lake Zamosh'e.

3. 696th TDR is attached to 72nd RC. Concentrate in the [following] region: Sverchki, Kobyl'niki, and Russetchino by 1300 hours on 1 March 1944. Be ready to open fire at 0700 hours on 1 March 1944.

283rd AMtrR—Have one battalion in reserve in the woods south of Pogostishche; and one battalion will be attached to 72nd RC and will concentrate in the Sverchki region by 1200 hours on 1 March 1944 and occupy combat positions in accordance with 72nd RC's commander at 1600 hours on 1 March 1944.

646th AGAR—leave two battalions in their present combat positions in support of 45th RC and move one battalion to support 72nd RC.

Source: "Zhurnal boevykh deistvii voisk 5 armii za mart 1944 g." [The 5th Army's journal of combat operations for March 1944], https://cdn.pamyat-naroda.ru/.

L. THE WESTERN FRONT'S ORSHA AND BOGUSHEVSK OFFENSIVES (5–29 MARCH 1943)

L-1. Extract from "Documentation of the Western Front's Losses for 1944"

From 1 through 10 March, the *front* lost a total of 27,258 men. From 1 through 10 March, 33rd Army lost 2,146 killed, 8,849 wounded, for a total of 12,261 due to all causes. From 11 through 21 March, the Western Front lost a total of 9,973 men, and, from 21 to 30 March, the overall losses amounted to 20,630 men, including 4,029 killed and 12,855 wounded.

Source: TsAMO RF, f. 208, op. 2511, ed. kh., 3051, ll. 31–36.

M. THE BELORUSSIAN FRONT'S SITUATION ON 1 JANUARY 1944 AND PRELIMINARY OPERATIONS

M-1. Excerpt from "The Journal of Combat Operations of 48th Army, 1 January 1944"

1. 1. 44 g.
1. During December 1943, the enemy continued to defend the Zaton, Mormal', Sel'noe line with the formations of XXXV AC, which consists of 299th ID, 383rd ID's 532nd IR, 31st ID, and 36th ID, while improving them [their defenses] in an engineer sense. Simultaneously, he carried out a regrouping and conducted reconnaissance in separate sectors. On the Probuzhdenie and Kakel' line, on 22 December 1943, the enemy went over to an offensive with the units of 253rd ID, supported by tanks from 16th PzD (returned from Italy). As a result of a fierce four-day battle, the enemy captured Kakel', Rudnia, Chirkovichi, Shatsilki Station, and Rosova at the cost of great losses in personnel and equipment. All of the subsequent enemy attacks, which were especially severe in the direction of Shatsilki, with a force of from a battalion to a regiment of infantry supported by 30–70 tanks, achieved no success.

The worn down units of 253rd ID went over to the defense in the Probuzhdenie, Shatsilki Station, Rosova, Pechishche, Kunia, and Osopna sector from 23–28 December 1943.

At 0300 hours on 31 December 1943, the enemy began to withdraw northward from the Zaton, Zhdanovo Collective Farm, and Dubina line under the cover of rear guards and by day's end offered resistance to the operations of our units in position from the southern outskirts of Proskurin [Proskurni], the southern outskirts of Popki, the southern slopes of Markers 142.4, 142.5, 141.9, and Pudimov.

The artillery and mortars of the enemy cooperated with the attacking units of 253rd ID and 16th PzD with massive fire raids in the Pobyzhdenie and Kakel' sector, while expending up to 4–6,000 shells and mines per day. Along the Zaton, Mormal', and Sel'noe line, the enemy conducted occasional fire, alternating with short fire raids, against the combat formations of our units. During the last ten days of December, enemy aircraft conducted reconnaissance of our combat formations and routes of approach into the sector of the army's close-in rear.

The army's forces, having halted the enemy's offensive along the Probuzhdenie, Shatsilki Station, Rosova, Pechishche, Kun'ia, and Osopna line on 22 December 1944, went over to the defense along the army's entire front. During the last ten days of December, the army's forces did routine tasks and combat security, fortified the positions they occupied in an engineer respect, and conducted reconnaissance in small groups, with the missions of precisely determining the enemy on the army's front and establishing the features on the forward edge and the nature and depth of the enemy's defenses.

2. By the end of 1 January 1944, the enemy was defending the Proskurni, Popki, Grafskie Farm, Hill 141.9, Mormal' Station, northeast Mormal', Zales'e, east of the edge of the grove north of Iashchitsy Platform, Iashchitsy Platform, Dubrova, Sel'noe Farm, Sel'nyi, Probuzhdenie, Shatsilki Station, Rosova, northwestern outskirts of Pechishche line and farther along the western bank of the Zherdianka River to Zherb Station, while improving it in an engineer sense.

Grouping of the Enemy
The units of five infantry divisions are operating before the army's front for a distance of 44 kilometers on 30 December 1943—299th, 31st, and 383rd IDs, 707th Security Division, and 253rd ID, with the attached 665th and 561st AT Battalions, 19th Mortar Battery of the OKH, and up to a regiment of separate subunits of Ninth Army's headquarters in [the following] sectors:

(a) Zaton, Pudimov—299th ID

(b) (incl.) Pudimov, Mormal'—31st ID (without 82nd IR)

(c) (incl.) Mormal', Dubrova—383rd ID (without 533rd IR)

(d) Dubrova, Sel'nyi—707th Security Division; and 159th and 729th Construction Battalions

(e) Probuzhdenie, Kun'ia—253rd ID, with a mixed battalion of unknown designation.

Grouping of Artillery
Up to six artillery regiments of divisional artillery are operating before the army's front, revealed [as follows].

150mm batteries DA	14	guns	42
150mm batteries RA	2	guns	4
105mm batteries DA	51	guns	153
75mm batteries	14	guns	56
Antiaircraft batteries	8	guns	82
AT guns			20
105mm mortars			15
81mm mortars			96
6-barreled mortars			6
Launcher apparatuses			2

The density of revealed artillery and mortars amounts to 9.8 per 1 kilometer of front.

Enemy Reserves
Supposedly, units of 45th, 216th, and 36th IDs are disposed in the second line in the region southwest of Zhlobin. Units of 16th PzD are in the Chirkovichi, Rachim, and Parichi region.

3. The enemy carried out fire raids along the entire front at 2400 hours on 31 December 1943. On the night of 1 January 1944, the enemy tried to conduct reconnaissance with small groups of 20–25 men from the northwestern part of Mormal' and from the railroad cut 1.5 kilometers southeast of Zales'e. The enemy's attempts to conduct reconnaissance were repelled by the organized fires of 4th and 137th RDs.

At 2300 hours an enemy force of more than 200 men, supported by artillery-mortar fire and three self-propelled guns attacked 170th RD's 717th RR, in the Pechishche region and, after fighting, captured the northwestern outskirts of Pechishche.

With the beginning of active operations, the subunits of 399th and 170th RDs, whose mission was to capture the grove west of Shatsilki, rendered strong resistance with fire and counterattacks. Overall, the enemy conducted 9 counterattacks from the vicinity of Probuzhdenie, Rosova, and the northwestern outskirts of Pechishche, with forces of from 60 to 250 infantrymen supported by artillery-mortar fire and 3–5 self-propelled guns. The enemy conducted fire on the combat formations of our units with methodical artillery and mortar fire from [the following] regions: Proskurin, Popki, Grafskie Farm, Istobki, Krasnaia Zvezda, Shatsilki Station, Kakel', Rudnia, Rosova, and the northwestern outskirts of Pechishche.

Overall, [the following] operated: 150mm batteries—2, 105mm batteries—14, 75mm batteries—3, and 81mm batteries—4.

4. The missions of the army's forces.

The army will defend the sector with [the following] forward edge: Gremiachii Mokh, the southern outskirts of Zhdanova Farm, Selishche, 1 kilometer north of Paporotnoe, Krasnogor'e, the bend in the road northeast of Mormal', the bridge and center of Mormal', 100–200 m west on the railroad up to the cut in the railroad 1.5 kilometers west of Zales'e, the junction of the paths 1.5 kilometers west of Mormal', 1.5 kilometers east of Iashchitsy Platform, Marker 142.4, 500 m southeast of Sel'nyi, 300 m south of Ur. Baranchik, the northwestern outskirts of Shatsilki, Shatsilki Station, Marker 137.7, farther west along the Zherdianka River, and along the eastern bank of the Zherdianka River to Zherb Platform.

Source: "Zhurnal boevykh deistvii chastei i soedinenii 48 armii za ianvar' m-ts 1944 g. Zadacha soedinenii (chastei) i perechen' sobitii v boevoi deiatel'nosti voisk" [The journal of combat operations of the units and formations of 48th Army for the month of January 1944. The missions of formations (units) and an enumeration of events in the combat activities of the forces], https://cdn.pamyat-naroda.ru/.

M-2. Excerpt from "The Journal of Combat Operations of 63rd Army, 1 January 1944"

1. 1. 1944
1. THE ENEMY The enemy continued to defend their previous positions, having in the first line the units of three divisions in [the following] sectors:

110th ID's 255th IR—Uvarovo, Zaozer'e, and Tursk

296th ID's 520th IR—(incl.) Tursk and Hill 147.6;

519th IR and divisional battalion of 296th ID—Hill 147.6 and Maiskii

221st IR and mixed battalion, Ninth Army—(incl.) Maiskii, and (incl.) Bobovka;

6th ID's 58th IR—Bobovka and (incl.) Kolybovka
18th IR—Kolybovka and Snitsrovka
37th IR—Snitsrovka-Proskurin

Tactical reserves of the enemy have been identified in [the following] positions: Itveny, Gorelyi Mokh—up to a battalion of infantry; Khodosovichi—up to a battalion of infantry (supposedly, 1st Bn, 89th IR, 31st ID); Antonovka and the woods to the west—up to two regiments of infantry (supposedly 533rd IR, 383rd ID); the grove east of Tsuper—3rd Bn, 519th IR and 164th Assault Battalion; the woods west of Barsuki—up to a battalion of infantry; and Vetka and the woods to the east—6th ID's sapper battalion.

The grouping of identified enemy artillery: Novyi Put', Vikhovo, and Volchii—two 105mm battalions (120th AR, 110th ID). Vikhovo-Vozrozhden'e and the woods to the east—69th Battalion of OKH; Antonovka, Maiskii (3rd AR)—three battalions of 105mm (296th ID); Tsuper—150mm battalion (296th ID); Lugovaia, Virnia, Osinovka, and Boratino—up to two 105mm battalions (6th ID).

The density of revealed artillery amounts to 4.8 guns per 1 kilometer of front, including mortars.

Observation and information from prisoners has established that up to a battalion of tanks (30–40 tanks) and 40–50 self-propelled guns are operating opposite the army's front.

During recent days, the enemy has conducted methodical artillery-mortar fire and frequent fire raids against the combat formations of our units, artillery OPs, and our close in communications in the Vysokoe, Asoia, and Rassvet regions from the [following] directions: Utveny Pochep, Khodosovichi, and Boratkino.

At 0730 hours on 1 January 1944, a group of 20 soldiers tried to conduct reconnaissance of our forward edge from the Ermakovo Pole region but was discovered and driven back to their jumping-off positions with losses by organized fires.

Enemy aircraft conducted reconnaissance of the army's sector of action along the [following] line: Kniazhenka, Gorodets, and Sviatoe. We noticed three sorties.

During the day, 120 Germans, 4 machine guns, and two mortars were destroyed and one artillery battery was suppressed by artillery fire.

In the Pereshkoda region (2 kilometers southwest of Barsuki), a soldier from 3rd Co., 37th IR, 6th ID, came over to our side.

2. THE ARMY'S FORCES

The 63rd Army occupies its previous defensive positions along the [following] front: Gadilovichi, the edge of the woods 400 m east of Krasnaia Gorka, Turskii, Tursk State Farm, Marker 139.4, the cemetery southwest of Mal. Kozlovichi, Hill 147.6, Rassvet, the eastern outskirts of Deniskovichi, Frunze, 400 m east of Barsuki, Ol'khovskii Rog (along the edge of the woods), the corner of the woods 1 kilometer east of Marker 145.6, 0.1 k south of Ermakovo Pole, the separate small house on Lake Oshushnoe, and farther up to the woods east of Lake Velikoe.

During the night and the first half of the day, engineer work was conducted on defensive positions. Reconnaissance of the enemy was conducted and reinforced officer observation.

Artillery-mortar fire was delivered on the enemy's positions and in support of our reconnaissance activities. Reconnaissance groups of the army's units operating along all axes were repelled by the fire of enemy automatic weapons, artillery and mortars and had no success.

In the second echelon, the army's units carried out combat training.

The positions of *40th RC's* units (consisting of 169th and 41st RDs) were unchanged. The corps occupied and defended its previous defensive sector.

The units conducted observation of the enemy and continued to fortify their positions in an engineer sense.

The *35th RC* (consisting of 129th Orel RD, 250th RD, and 348th RD) defended its previous defensive positions, improved them, and conducted reconnaissance of the enemy's defense and groupings.

129th Orel RD—on the night of 1 January 1944, turned its sector over to 8th OShBn [8th Separate Penal Battalion] of 41st RD, and replaced the OLB [probably separate ski battalion] of the Division in the [following] positions: southeast outskirts of Rassvet—the garden south of Rassvet.

The OLB [separate ski battalion] of the division completed a march and concentrated in the Tserkov'e region. A reconnaissance operating at night had no success and withdrew to its jumping-off positions.

250th RD—no changes in its dispositions. Two reconnaissance groups operating in the vicinity of the northern and southern outskirts of Chernaia Virnia were discovered, fired upon, and withdrew to their jumping-off positions.

348th RD—in its previous concentration region, carried out defensive work in the corps' second defensive belt.

The corps had no losses on 1 January 1944. . . .

53rd RC (96th, 260th, and 323rd RDs), with previous reinforcing means, firmly occupied their present positions. . . .

The losses of the corps for 31 December 1943, 2 men killed and 6 wounded.

Source: "Zhurnal boevykh deistvii voisk 63 armii za ianvar' 1944 g." [The 63rd Army's journal of combat operations for January 1944], https://cdn.pamyat-naroda.ru/.

N. THE BELORUSSIAN FRONT'S KALINKOVICHI-MOZYR' OFFENSIVE (8–14 JANUARY 1944)

N-1. *Stavka* VGK Order No. 220000 to the Commander of the Belorussian Front about a Change in the Boundary Line with the 1st Ukrainian Front and the Defeat of the Enemy's Mozyr' Grouping

1820 hours 2 January 1944

In connection with the 1st Ukrainian Front's successful offensive, the *Stavka* VGK orders:

1. Effective at 2400 hours on 2 January 1944, establish the following boundary line between the Belorussian and the 1st Ukrainian Fronts: to Chernigov, as before, and, farther, to the mouth of the Slovechna River, Kuz'michi, Len'chitsy, and Stolin (all points, besides Len'chitsy and Stolin, are inclusive for the Belorussian Front).

2. Effective at the same time, attach 415th RD, on 13th Army's right flank, to the Belorussian Front.

3. The Belorussian Front will begin an offensive with its left wing no later than 8 January, with the mission of defeating the enemy's Mozyr' grouping and capturing Kalinkovichi and Mozyr' by 12 January by enveloping them from the north and from the south.

Subsequently attack in the general direction of Bobruisk and Minsk by striking with the *front*'s main forces. Part of the forces will operate along the Pripiat' River toward Luninets.

The Belorussian Front commander is responsible for protection of the boundary between the Belorussian and the 1st Ukrainian Fronts.

4. Report all orders issued.

The *Stavka* VGK
I. Stalin, A. Antonov

Source: Direktiva Stavki No. 220000 komanduiushchemu voiskami Belorusskogo fronta ob izmenenii razgranitel'noi linii s 1-m Ukrainskim frontom i na razgrom Mozyrskoi gruppirovki protivnika" [*Stavka* VGK Order No. 220000 to the commander of the Belorussian Front about a change in the boundary line with the 1st Ukrainian Front and the defeat of the enemy's Mozyr' grouping], in Zolotarev, *Stavka* VGK 1944, 27.

O. THE BELORUSSIAN FRONT'S PARICHI-BOBRUISK (MARMOVICHI-DUBROVA) OFFENSIVE (16 JANUARY-23 FEBRUARY 1944)

O-1. Excerpt from "The Journal of Combat Operations of 48th Army, 1 February 1944"

1.2.44

During the second half of January, the enemy continued to defend the positions he occupied with the formations of XXXV Army Corps, consisting of 383rd ID, 45th ID, and 707th Security Division (without 747th IR). With the transition of 48th Army to the offensive in the sector: Probushdenie and from Shatsilki to Kizhin [Zherd'] [14 kilometers southwest of Shatsilki] on 16 January 1944, the enemy offered strong resistance with fire and counterattacks by the units of 253rd and 36th IDs and 58th IR of 6th ID.

Beginning on 24 January 1944, the enemy committed specialized subunits and specially formed groups into combat and filled out the bloodied units of 253rd and 36th IDs.

By the end of the month, our forces fenced the enemy into [the following] positions: Chirkovichi, Zaruzh'e, Ostrovchitsy, Sosnovka, Hill 143.0, Hill 136.5, Prityka, Dubrova, and Hill 142.7 [from 7–18 kilometers northwest to 26 kilometers west of Shatsilki].

The army's forces were defending the region between the Dnepr and Berezina Rivers in the sector: Zaton, the southern part of Mormal', and Ugly.

On 16 January 1944, the army went over to an offensive with its left wing in the sector of the front: Shatsilki, the southern part of Pechishche [10 kilometers southwest of Shatsilki], and Sobolitsa [17 kilometers southwest of Shatsilki] in the general direction of Parichi. Having penetrated the enemy's defenses northeast of Pechishche, the forces on the army's left wing slowly advanced forward in heavy fighting, and, while suffering heavy losses, reached [the following] positions by the end of the month: Probuzhdenie, Kakel', along the stream south of Chirkovichi [10 kilometers northwest of Shatsilki], Mol'cha (northern), Hill 137.8, 1 kilometer south of Sosnovka [18 kilometers northwest of Shatsilki], Iazvin, 1.5 kilometers south of Mikhailovka [25 kilometers west-northwest of Shatsilki], Vel'cho, Zarech'e [25 kilometers west of Shatsilki].

1. The Enemy Grouping
The units of five infantry divisions are operating opposite the army's front for a distance of 64 kilometers—383rd, 45th, 707th (without 747th IR), 253rd, 6th ID's 58th IR, and 36th ID, reinforced by 661st, 666th Antitank Battalions OKH, 19th Mortar Battalion OKH, 616th, 620th, 849th, 851st, and 860th Artillery Battalions OKH, and 244th and 909th Assault Gun Battalions.

(a) Proskurin—Mormal'[20–35 kilometers northeast of Shatsilki]—383rd ID and 584th Assault Gun Battalion.

(b) Supposedly, (incl.) Mormal', (incl.) Sel'noe [6–20 kilometers northeast of Shatsilki]—units of 45th ID.

(c) Sel'noe, northern bank of the Berezina River to Zvezda [8 kilometers north to 6 kilometers northeast of Shatsilki]—707th Security Division (without 747th IR) and 159th Construction Battalion.

(d) Chirkovichi—Sosnovka [10–18 kilometers northwest of Shatsilik]—253rd ID.

(e) (incl.) Sosnovka—Dubrova [18 kilometers northwest to 27 kilometers west of Shatsilki]—36th ID, 729th Construction Battalion, and 47th Sapper Battalion.

Grouping of Artillery
Up to five artillery regiments of divisional artillery; up to six battalions of OKH artillery, and two battalions of self-propelled artillery are operating before the army's front.

150mm batteries	12	guns	36
105mm batteries	33	guns	100
75mm batteries	13	guns	52
Mortar batteries	9	tubes	76
AT artillery			10
Launcher apparatuses			4
6-barreled mortars			3

Reserves
According to information from army intelligence, up to one ID and one PzD of unknown designation are stationed in the Bobruisk region. The 6th ID's 58th IR is in the Prudok region, 8 kilometers southeast of Parichi.

With the beginning of active operations by our forces, the enemy can transfer from the Osipovichi and Starye Dorogi region and commit to combat units of 104th ID and 390th Field Training Division.

2. During the day the enemy offered stubborn resistance to our units' operations with fire and counterattacks. As a result of the fighting, the enemy was driven from the positions he occupies on the left bank of the Berezina River north of Probuzhdenie and Zaruzh'e No. 2 [1–3 kilometers north of Shatsilki]. From 1200 to 1400 hours the enemy counterattacked twice with a force of up to two companies of infantry

against a battalion of 217th RD's 755th RR, which had crossed to the northern bank of the Berezina River

At 1320 hours a force of 120 enemy infantry counterattacked the subunits of 307th RR from Marker 138.0. All of the counterattacks were repulsed. In the remaining sectors the enemy conducted rifle-machine gun fire and conducted short fire raids against the army's forward edge and artillery OPs.

In the Baraki and Dubrova sector—up to a battalion of 150mm guns, four 105mm batteries, three 75mm batteries, and up to 16 machine guns were operating.

In the Baranchik and Lake Krivoe sector—there are three 105mm batteries, two 75mm batteries, two mortar batteries, and up to 13 machine gun points. Along the Chirkovichi, Zaruzh'e and Ostrovchitsy line there are two 150mm batteries, five 105mm batteries, three 75mm batteries, four mortar batteries, and up to 30 machine gun points. In the Sosnovka and Prityka sector—four 105mm batteries, seven mortar batteries, and up to six machine guns points. In the Dubrova and Hill 142.7 sector—three 105mm batteries, one 150mm battery, a battery of 6-barreled mortars, and up to 17 machine gun points. The enemy has expended more than 5,000 shells and mines. Observation noticed:

(a) From 1230 to 1400 hours, an enemy armored train cruised through the railroad sector from Zhlobin to Mormal' Station, while firing on the combat formations of our units.

(b) At 1100 hours up to 100 enemy infantrymen passed from Aleksandrovka [10 kilometers northwest of Shatsilki] toward Hill 138.0, 1.2 kilometers southeast of Ostrovchitsy.

(c) From 0900–1200 hours the enemy was carrying out entrenching work in the vicinity of Popki, Grafskie Farm, Marker 143.0 (north of Iazvin), and Mikhailovka.

According to reports by prisoners seized on 1 February 1944 belonging to 727th IR, the 727th IR consists of two battalions. The 2nd Battalion includes up to 500 men. It received 50 replacements on 29 January 1944 from Ninth Army's 110th Separate Construction Company situated in Bobruisk.

3. Missions of the army's forces.

The 48th Army will firmly defend the Zaton, Savin, southern part of Mormal', Iashchitsy, Ugly, Shatsilki, Rudnia, and Mol'ch'a (northern) line [28 kilometers northeast to 14 kilometers northwest of Shatsilki] with 161st Fortified Region (with 4th and 194th RDs) and 29th RC.

All of the remaining forces of the army, with all reinforcing means, will go over to a decisive offensive on the morning of 2 February 1944 from the Mol'cha (north), the northern edge of the forest (1 kilometer south of Sosnovka), Iazvin, Vel'cho, and Kobyl'shchina line [14 kilometers northwest to 26 kilometers southwest of Shatsilki], and, while delivering the main attack with its left wing in the general direction of Korma, Sekarichi and Romanishche, will capture—the Ostrovchitsy, Starina, Grabchi, Nikolaevka, Petrovichi, Korma, (incl.) Gorokhovishchi line [17 kilometers northwest to 34 kilometers west of Shatsilki] by 2 February 1944—the Zdudichi, Prudok, Kurgany, Peschanaia Rudnia, Gomza, and Sekerichi line [23 kilometers northwest to 37 kilometers west-northwest to 36 kilometers west of Shatsilki] by 3 February 1944—and the Parichi, Knishevichi, Sloboda, and Romanishche line [32 kilometers northwest to 44 kilometers west-northwest of Shatsilki] by 4 February 1944. Subse-

650   Appendices

quently, exploit the offensive to Kruki [20 kilometers west of Parichi], Brozha [27 kilometers northwest of Parichi], and Bobruisk.

On 31 December 1944, the army commander made the decision to penetrate the enemy's defense on the western bank of the Berezina River.

The decision of the army commander:

To penetrate the enemy's defense, while delivering the main attack in the general direction: Dubrova, Gomza (Semak), Kovchitsy No. 2 and capture the lines:

1st day of the offensive—Ostrovchitsy, Starina, Grabchy, Nikolaevka, and the forest west of Cherniavka [15 kilometers northwest to 35 kilometers west of Shatsilki];

2nd day of the offensive—Chirkovichi, Zdudichi, Prudok, Peschanaia Rudnia, Gomza, and Sekerichi [23 kilometers northwest to 36 kilometers west-northwest of Shatsilki];

3rd day of the offensive—Parichi, Slobodka, and Romanishche [30 kilometers northwest to 44 kilometers west-northwest of Shatsilki].

To fulfill this:

(a) *29th RC* (307th and 73rd RDs), with 3rd Gds.TDR, 35th Gds.MB, 42nd and 231st TRs, supported by 137th RD's 17th AR, will cooperate with the offensive of 25th RC toward Starina and El'nichka; with the main forces in readiness to deliver a blow in the Marker 136.0 and (incl.) Mol'cha sector toward Aleksandrovka [15 kilometers northwest of Shatsilki].

The boundary line on the right—(incl.) Serdov, (incl.) Rudnia, Chirkovichi, and Hill 142.4.

The boundary line on the left—(incl.) Kremena, Konskaia Storona, Podrechkoi, Lipniki, and Kommunar.

(b) *25th RC* (273rd, 102nd, and 197th RDs), with 479th MR and 220th Gds. TDR, supported by artillery regiments of 399th and 170th RDs and two battalions of 194th RD's AR, and 6th and 84th Gds.-MRs, will deliver the main attack with the left wing toward Radin, Selishche [25 kilometers west of Shatsilki], and Knyshevichi [35 kilometers northwest of Shatsilki].

The boundary on the left—Dobroe, Dubrova, Nikolaevka, Gomza (incl.), and Slobodka.

Source: "Zhurnal boevykh deistvii chastei i soedinenii 48 armii za fevral' m-ts 1944 g. Zadacha soedinenii (chastei) i perechen' sobitii v boevoi deiatel'nosti voisk" [The journal of combat operations of the units and formations of 48th Army for the month of February 1944. The missions of formations (units) and an enumeration of events in the combat activities of the forces], https://cdn.pamyat-naroda.ru/.

O-2. Excerpt from "The Journal of Combat Operations of 65th Army, 1 February 1944"

1.2.44   Combat Mission
Continue the offensive along previous axes with forward detachments. During the day on 1 and 2 February 1944, 105th and 18th RCs will operate with forward detachments along the axes: Zherb' and Savichi, with the mission of capturing [the following] regions: 105th RC—Medved', Veliz'e [5–7 kilometers northwest of Ozarichi];

18th RC—Savichi [15 kilometers west-southwest of Ozarichi] (Enciphered telegram of the army's headquarters Nos. 881–882 of 31.1.44.)

Description of Combat Operations
During the night and first half of the day, the army's forces, in their previous positions, conducted reinforced reconnaissance and fire exchanges with the enemy, brought forward artillery into the combat formations of the infantry, and replenished ammunition. At 1200 hours the army's formations resumed the offensive with forward detachments toward: Velikaia Volotse [10 kilometers north of Ozarichi], Podosinnok, Gorodinka [8 kilometers west of Ozarichi], Mikhailovskaia [14 kilometers west of Ozarichi], and Kolki [20 kilometers west-southwest of Ozarichi]. Overcoming strong enemy resistance, 354th RD (95th RC) captured Vel. Volotse.

In the center and on the right wing of the army, the forward detachments encountered strong enemy fire resistance and did not advance and were conducting fire battles in their previous positions.

95th RC—on the night of 1 February 1944, the corps' formations operated with forward detachments, conducted observation and reconnaissance of the enemy, and brought up ammunition and artillery to the infantry's combat formations.

At 1200 hours the forward detachment of 1208th RR (354th RD) attacked the enemy in Vel. Volotse and capture Vel. Volotse at 1000 hours.

At 1200 hours all of the corps' formations went over to the offensive but had no success. By day's end they occupied [the following] positions:

44th Gds.RD—400 m southwest of Kobyl'shchina to 400 m west of Hill 137.9, with one RR in the grove 1 kilometer north of Mekhovshchina [13–15 kilometers north-northeast of Ozarichi].

354th RD—the northern slopes of the unnamed hill 1 kilometer east of Visha to the northwestern and western edge of the woods south of Visha, and the western and southwestern outskirts of Vel. Volotse [10–12 kilometers north of Ozarichi].

172nd RD—the woods south of Mekhovshchina in corps second echelon [12 kilometers north-northeast of Ozarichi].

The enemy in front of the corps' sector has not displayed activity in recent days, has conducted artillery-mortar fire, and conducted short fire raids from the vicinity of the woods north of Visha, Gorokhovishchi, Pruzhinishche, V'iunishche, and Myslov Rog [10–15 kilometers north of Ozarichi] and machine gun along the forward edge.

Enemy aircraft carried out reconnaissance with single aircraft along the high road from Slavan' to Kobyl'shchina and dive-bombed vehicular traffic in the Prosvet region [18 kilometers northeast of Ozarichi].

27th RC—the corps formations carried out a partial regrouping on the night of 1 February 1944. The 246th RD gave up its combat sector on the Lesets-Ozarichi line [Ozarichi to 4 kilometers north of Ozarichi] to the units of 132nd RD and concentrated in the woods 1.5 kilometers northwest and west of Oktiabr' [8 kilometers northeast of Ozarichi]. The units of 132nd and 106th RDs conducted observation on enemy actions, brought ammunition forward, and occupied [the following] positions at day's end:

106th RD—Podmekhovshchina to Podosinnik and the western edge of the woods south of Podosinnik.

60th RD—the northwestern edge of the woods 2 kilometers west of Podberez'e to the unnamed hill with the contour line "135," 800 m west of Podberez'e [5–7 kilometers north of Ozarichi].

218th RD—having turned its sector over to the units of 162nd RD, concentrated [as follows]:

658th RR—1.5 kilometers northeast of Podberez'e; 667th RR—2 kilometers northeast of Podberez'e; and 672nd RR—1 kilometer west of Ostrov village [8–10 kilometers northeast of Ozarichi].

During the day the enemy conducted rifle-machine gun fire from the forward edge and artillery-mortar fire from the vicinity of: Myslov Rog [10 kilometers north of Ozarichi], Semenovichi, and Litvinovichi [2–5 kilometers north of Ozarichi], accompanied by short artillery-mortar raids.

105th RC—during the day the corps' formations carried out a partial regrouping, conducted observation and reconnaissance of the enemy, and brought forward artillery and replenished ammunition.

At 1200 hours, after a 3-minute fire raid against the forward edge, the corps' formation went over to the attack toward Sobino and Medved' Farms. Having encountered strong enemy fire resistance, they had no success and could not advance and were occupying [the following] positions by day's end:

132nd RD—Lesets, Glebovka, and Ozarichi.

253rd RD—Hill 136.8, (incl.), Sobino Farm, and 1.5 kilometers south of Sobino Farm.

75th Gds.RD—put its forces in order, conducted observation and reconnaissance of the enemy, and replenished its ammunition during the night. Attacked toward Medved' [7 kilometers west-northwest of Ozarichi] at 1200 hours. Having encountered strong artillery fire from the Medved' region and the woods to the southwest, it had no success and was occupying the following positions at day's end:

231st RR—300 m south of Sobino Farm to the crossroads 100 m northeast of Marker 128.0.

212th RR—(incl.) the crossroads 100 m northeast of Marker 128.0, to the road 500 m southeast of Vylaz'e.

241st RR—(incl.) the road 500 m southeast of Vylaz'e to 400 m south of Vylaz'e.

During the day the enemy opposite the corps' front conducted strong artillery-mortar fire from the vicinity of Litvinovichi, Sobino Farm, and Vylaz'e and periodically carried out powerful fire raids against the combat formations of the units.

19th RC—during the day the corps' formations did not conduct active operations, but occupied their previous positions, conducted reinforced observation of the enemy's actions, and replenished ammunition and supplies. The officer cadre conducted personal reconnaissance [*rekognostsirovka*] of the enemy.

Source: "Zhurnal boevykh deistvii voisk 65 Armii, 1. 2. 44." [The 65th Army's journal of combat operations, 1 February 1944], https://cdn.pamyat-naroda.ru/.

O-3. *Stavka* VGK Directive No. 220027 to the Commander of the Belorussian Front and the Commander and Deputy Commander of the 1st Ukrainian Front Concerning the Formation of the 2nd Belorussian Front

1900 hours 17 February 1944

The *Stavka* VGK orders:

1. Form a new *front*, which will be named the 2nd Belorussian Front, at the junction of the Belorussian and the 1st Ukrainian Fronts.

2. In this regard, henceforth, the existing Belorussian Front will be renamed the 1st Belorussian Front.

The 2nd Belorussian Front will include:

(a) From the 1st Belorussian Front—61st Army, including 9th Gds.RC, 89th RC, the separate 55th and 356th RDs (a total of eight RDs), 2nd Gds.CC, 7th Gds.CC, 68th TB, and all reinforcing army units and rear service units and facilities, with their existing reserves;

(b) From the 1st Ukrainian Front—77th RC (three RDs) from 13th Army and the headquarters of 47th A, with all reinforcing army units and rear service units and facilities; and

(c) From the *Stavka* Reserve—125th RC (four RDs), 70th Army, with seven rifle divisions, 6th Air Army, with 3rd Gds.AssltAD, 366th FAD, 242nd Night BAD, 72nd Reconnaissance Aviation Regiment, and 3rd Aviation Regiment, Civil Air Fleet, the Dnepr Flotilla [military], with its remaining minesweepers, 65th Antiaircraft Artillery Division, 32nd Mortar Brigade, 3rd TDB, and 48th Engineer-Sapper Brigade.

4. As the *front*'s headquarters, use the headquarters of the former Northwestern Front, which will relocate to the Rokitno region by 20 February.

5. Appoint:

Colonel General Kurochkin as commander of the 2nd Belorussian Front, freeing him from his duties as deputy commander of the 1st Ukrainian Front;

Lieutenant General Bokov as the member of the *front*'s military council; and

Lieutenant General Kolpakchi as the *front*'s chief of staff and 1st deputy commander, freeing him from his duties as commander of 63rd Army.

6. The commander of the 2nd Belorussian Front will deploy 47th A, consisting of 77th RC from 13th A and 125th RC from the *Stavka* Reserve, to the Kovel' axis.

7. Establish the following boundary lines for the 2nd Belorussian Front:

(a) With the 1st Belorussian Front—Vasilevichi, Gorochichi Station, Novoselok, Pogorelaia Sloboda, Khoino, Moroch, Mal'kovichi, Telekhany, Bereza Kartuzskaia, Pruzhany, and Kleshcheli (all points beside Vasilevichi, Gorochichi Station, Novoselki, and Pogorelaia Sloboda are inclusive for the 2nd Belorussian Front); and

(b) With the 1st Ukrainian Front—Korosten', Gorodnitsa, Kostopol', Sofievka, Rozhishche, and Verba (all points beside Korosten' are inclusive for the 1st Ukrainian Front).

8. Complete the transfer of 61st Army, 2nd and 7th Gds.CCs, 13th Army's 77th RC, and 47th A's headquarters to the 2nd Belorussian Front no later than 25 February.

Transfer 125th RC to the Sarny region by rail no later than 6 March and 70th Army no later than 14 March.

9. Until [receipt of] a special order, [the responsibility for] supplies of all types is maintained [as follows]:
- 61st A—with the 1st Belorussian Front; and
- 77th RC and 47th A—with the 1st Ukrainian Front.

10. The commander of the 1st Ukrainian Front is responsible for the protection of the junction between the 2nd Belorussian and 1st Ukrainian Fronts.

11. Report fulfillment.

The *Stavka* VGK
I. Stalin, G. Zhukov

Source: Direktiva Stavki No. 220027 komanduiushchemu voiskami Belorusskogo fronta, komanduiushchemu i zamestiteliu komanduiushchego voiskami 1-go Ukrainskogo fronta ob obrazovanii 2-go Belorusskogo fronta" [Stavka VGK Directive No. 220027 to the commander of the Belorussian Front and the commander and deputy commander of the 1st Ukrainian Front concerning the formation of the 2nd Belorussian Front], in Zolotarev, *Stavka* VGK 1944, 45–46.

O-4. *Stavka* VGK Directive No. 220032 to the Commanders of the Western and Belorussian Fronts about the Resubordination of 10th Army

2130 hours 18 February 1944

The *Stavka* VGK orders:

1. Effective at 2400 hours on 21 February, transfer 10th Army, consisting of 70th and 38th RCs (a total of six RDs), from the Western Front to the 1st Belorussian Front. Transfer 10th Army with all of its reinforcing units, army rear service units and facilities, and reserve stocks.

2. From this time, establish the following boundary line between the Western and 1st Belorussian Fronts: Mstislavl', Kareby, Dobreika, Bovsevichi, and the mouth of the Borb River (all points inclusive for the 1st Belorussian Front).

3. Report about the transfer and acceptance of the army.

The *Stavka* VGK
I. Stalin, A. Antonov

Source: "Direktiva Stavki VGK No. 220032 komanduiushchim voiskami Zapadnogo i 1-go Belorusskogo frontov o perepodchinenii 10-i Armii" [*Stavka* VGK Directive No. 220032 to the commanders of the Western and Belorussian Fronts about the resubordination of 10th Army], in Zolotarev, *Stavka* VGK 1944, 48.

P. THE 1ST BELORUSSIAN FRONT'S ROGACHEV-ZHLOBIN AND MORMAL'-PARICHI OFFENSIVES (21-29 FEBRUARY 1944)

P-1. Excerpt from "The Journal of Combat Operations of 3rd Army for February 1944, 1 February 1944"

1. 2. 44

1. The enemy on 3rd Army's front is defending with 267th and 31st IDs, and 45th

IR, 221st Security Division, which is (presumably) operationally subordinate to 31st ID.

The forward edge of his defense passed along [the following] line: Marker 140.3, "Der. Mast," Pribor, and farther to the south along the western bank of the Dnepr River up to Lake Vasilevitse [10 kilometers due east of Rogachev].

The enemy's units are defending [the following] sectors:

(a) A battalion of 280th IR, 96th ID—Marker 140.3 to (incl.) "Der. Mast;"
(b) 487th IR, 267th ID—"Der. Mast" to (incl.) Ianova;
(c) 467th IR, 267th ID—Ianova to (incl.) Nov. Bykhov;
(d) 82nd IR, 31st ID—Nov. Bykhov to Podgoritsa;
(e) 12th IR, 31st ID—Lazarevichi to Viliakhovka;
(f) 45th IR, 221st SecD—(incl.) Viliakhovka to Zaezd'e; and
(g) 17th IR, 31st ID—Nizhev to Lake Vasilevitse.

Tactical reserves are disposed in [the following] regions:

Voronino Collective Farm—a reserve battalion of 267th ID and 20 tanks and self-propelled guns; Voronino—a battalion of 487th IR; Bykhov—up to an infantry regiment of unknown designation; Komarichi—a battalion of 467th IR; Krasnyi Bereg—a battalion of infantry and 10 tanks and self-propelled guns.

The operations of up to three regiments of artillery have been detected opposite the front [including]: 105mm battalions—6; 150mm battalions—1; and separate 150mm batteries—5.

Enemy artillery is situated in [the following] regions:

(a) Voronino Collective Farm, Voronino, and Paseka—105mm battalion;
(b) Borok, Boinia, and Volodarskii Collective Farm—105mm battalion;
(c) Zaiachen'e, Dudchitsa, and Komarichi—105mm battalion; and
(d) Pechishche, Hill 154.7, and Dubova Koloda—105mm battalion.

The "fusilier" battalion of 31st ID is defending to the north, and 45th IR, 221st Security Division, is defending to the south. A battalion of 82nd IR has four companies and a company from 80–100 men.

2. The forces of 3rd Army, consisting of 80th RC (5th, 362nd, and 283rd RDs) and 41st RC (269th, 186th, and 120th RDs), are continuing to defend positions within the [following] boundaries: on the right—Khachinki, (incl.) Marker 140.3, (incl.) Bykhov; on the left—Bogdanovichi, Kurgan'e, Gadilovichi, Zverovo, and Rogachev (all points inclusive for 3rd Army).

During the course of the day, the army's units developed and improved engineer works, conducted combat security measures, conducted fires of enemy targets that appeared, and also reconnaissance and snatches. The units in second echelon conducted combat training.

A reconnaissance group of 362nd RD, which was operating in the "Der Mast" region on the night of 1 February 1944, penetrated into the enemy's trenches and, as a result of the fighting, destroyed seven soldiers. After seizing one prisoner, 2 machine guns, and 3 rifles, the reconnaissance group withdrew to its jumping-off positions with two wounded. The prisoners belonged to 487th IR, 267th ID.

Two reconnaissance groups from 186th RD, which were operating toward Lazarevichi and Pokrovskii on the night of 1 February 1944, had no success. A third reconnaissance group, which was operating from this division, penetrated into the enemy's trenches in the southern outskirts of Lazarevichi at 2200 hours, and in the ensuing fight the reconnaissance scouts destroyed 12 Germans and captured 4 prisoners, 2 submachine guns, 2 automatic weapons, and 2 rifles. The prisoners belonged to 3rd Company, 82nd IR, 31st ID.

The positions of the army's units on 1 February 1944 were as follows:

80th RC, consisting of 5th, 362nd, and 283rd RDs, defended the sector within the boundaries: on the right—the army boundary; on the left—(incl.) Peregon, (incl.) Vel. Zimnitsa, Pograki, (incl.) Marker 152.9, and Moguchii. The corps' divisions are defending [the following] fronts:

5th RD: 142nd RR—(incl.) Marker 140.3 to the road junction 3 kilometers northeast of Pribor; 336th and 190th RRs are in second echelon in the region: Nov. Trasna, Podgor'e, and Uzniki.

362nd RD: (incl.) the road junction, the woods 1 kilometer east of Pribor, Star. Trasna, and "Sar" [probably "barn"] (500 m south of Star. Trasna).

283rd RD: (incl.) "Sar," along the eastern bank of the Dnepr to (incl.), and Marker 152.9.

41st RC, consisting of 269th, 186th, and 120th RDs and 179th, 178th, and 181st Army Blocking Detachments (ABD), which are subordinate to the corps, are defending the following fronts:

179th ABD—Marker 152.9 to Obidovichi [6 kilometers east of Novyi Bykhov];

269th RD: 1022nd RR—(incl.) Obidovichi to the mouth of the Gutlianka River [8 kilometers south-southeast of Novyi Bykhov]; 1018th and 1020th RRs—in second echelon in the region: Polianinovichi, and Pogarki [7–8 kilometers northeast of Novyi Bykhov] (1020th RR), the eastern outskirts of Obidovichi, and Comrade Stalin Collective Farm (1018th RR).

181st ABD—(incl.) the mouth of the Gutlianka River to (incl.) Marker 173.0 (1.5 kilometers south of Il'ich [11 kilometers south of Novyi Bykhov].

186th RD: 238th RR—Zvonets to Shapchitsy [14 kilometers south of Novyi Bykhov]; concentrated in second echelon: 298th RR—Guta to Kanava; and 290th RR—Star. Dovsk.

178th ABD—(incl.) Shapchitsy to (incl.) Zavon'e [12 kilometers south-southwest of Novyi Bykhov].

120th GdsRD—Zavon'e, Kruplia, and Sverzhen' to (incl.) Gadilovichi [15 kilometers east of Rogachev].

Artillery:

295th Gds.GAR , with OPs in the [following] regions: 1st, 3rd, 4th, and 6th Batteries—1 kilometer east of Gumnishche; 2nd Battery—1 kilometer north of Gumnishche; 5th Battery—the southern outskirts of Zvonets; 7th and 8th Batteries –500 m west of Dubovitsa; and 9th Battery—3 kilometers southwest of Nikonovichi.

475th AMtrR, with OPs in the [following] regions: 1st Battalion—Vet', and 2 kilometers to the north; 2nd Battalion—2 kilometers northeast of Il'ich.

584th TDR concentrated in the woods 2 kilometers east of Dovsk, comprising the Army commander's antitank reserve.

1284th AAAR PVO, with OPs in the [following] regions: 1st Battery—the southern outskirts of Zvonets; 2nd Battery—the northeastern outskirts of Paseka; 3rd Battery—Nov. Vych; and 4th Battery—1 kilometer east of Paseka.

Divisional artillery—in the combat formations of their divisions.

36th TR is situated in Avtovnia: operable: "SU-152"—2, "KV"—2, T-34—13, "T-70"—1, and "T-60"—2.

Engineer units:

9th Gds.Eng. Battalion—Guta; 68th Military-Construction Detachment—the northwestern outskirts on Avtovnia.

2nd Separate Assault Engineer-Sapper Brigade—Nov. Zhuravichi.

48th Separate Motorized Pontoon-Bridge Battalion—Volosovichi.

Army Hqs.: Hqs. of the army—Star. Vich; Hqs., 80th RC—Palki; Hqs., 5th RD—Uzniki; Hqs., 362nd RD—western outskirts of Nikonovichi; Hqs., 283rd RD—Usokha (southern); Hqs., 41st RC—Shuravichi; Hqs., 120th RD –500 m south of Ianovka; Hqs., 185th RD—Sychman; and Hqs., 269th RD—Marker 155.2 (2 kilometers north of Iskan').

Losses of the enemy: 31 soldiers and officers destroyed and 1 blindage blown up.

Our losses: 4 men killed and 12 wounded.

Trophies: 5 prisoners, 4 submachine guns, 2 automatic weapons, and 5 rifles captured.

Source: "Zhurnal boevykh deistvii voisk 3 armii za fevral' 1944 g." [The 3rd Army's journal of combat operations for February 1944], https://cdn.pamyat-naroda.ru/.

P-2. Excerpt from "The Journal of Combat Operations of 3rd Army for March 1944, 1 March 1944"

1. 3. 44

1. The enemy opposite 3rd Army's front (58 kilometers) is defending with the forces of 20th and 5th PzDs, 35th IR, 4th PzD (presumably), 296th and 6th IDs, and composite battalions of 82nd and 17th IRs, 31st ID.

The forward edge of his defense passed along [the following] line: (incl.) Khomichi, Rekta, the grove 2 kilometers south of Ozerane, Marker 147.1, Rogovoi, Verichev, Kostiashevo, and farther to the south along the western bank of the Dnepr River up to (incl.) Popki.

The tank units were thrown forward from the [following] regions: Vitebsk (20th PzD), north of Kopatkevichi (5th PzD), and south of Parichi (35th IR, 4th PzD) with the aim to half the advance by our forces toward the northwest and west and reach the Dnepr River.

The enemy's units are defending in the [following] sectors:

20th PzD (59th and 112th PzGrRs, 21st PzR, and 92nd AR)—(incl.) Khomichi to Rekta [24–30 kilometers north-northwest of Rogachev];

Composite battalions of 82nd and 17th IRs, 31st ID—(incl.) Rekta to the grove 2 kilometers south of Ozerane [18–24 kilometers north-northwest of Rogachev];

5th PzD (13th and 14th PzGrRs, 31st PzR, and 116th AR)—Marker 147.1 (1.5 kilometers west of Bol. Konoplitsa) to Vishen'ka;

296th ID (519th and 520th IRs, a battalion of 521st IR, and a reserve battalion of 296th AR)—Nikolaevka to (incl.) Lebedevka [5 kilometers north of Zhlobin]; and

6th ID (18th and 37th IRs, and 6th AR)—Lebedevka to Popki.

Reserves of the enemy are situated in the [following] regions:

Ivniki, Viaz'ma, and Poilova [8–12 kilometers west-northwest of Khomichi]—21st PzR, 20th PzD (50 tanks and self-propelled guns);

Falevichi, Tolochkovo, and Novoselki [7–10 kilometers west of Bol. Konoplitsa]—31st PzR, 5th PzD (40 tanks and self-propelled guns);

Bronnoe, Khapany, and Iasenovka [7–10 kilometers west of Rogachev]—supposedly 35th PzR, 4th PzD (up to 30 tanks and self-propelled guns);

Zabolot'e, Zelenyi Dub, and Shirokoe [7–11 kilometers southwest of Rogachev]—747th IR, 707th Security Division and up to 10 self-propelled guns); and Zavodnyi, Pridorozh'e, and Noviki [7–10 kilometers west of Zhlobin]—Reconnaissance detachment of 6th ID and 12 self-propelled guns).

A total of up to 16,700 enemy soldiers and officers and 142 tanks and self-propelled guns are operating opposite the army's front.

With the transition of our units to the offensive in the (incl.) Ozerane and Verichev sector, the enemy has offered stubborn resistance with the units of 20th and 5th PzDs, the subunits of the composite battalions of 31st and 296th IDs, strong fires, and repeated counterattacks supported by tanks and self-propelled guns.

In order to prevent our attacking forces from advancing westward, the enemy reinforced his grouping in this sector with 1st Bn, 59th PzGrR, 20th PzD (from the Bol. Kruzhinovka region), and a composite battalion of 296th ID, which was transferred from the Luchin region to the Tikhinichi region.

The enemy undertook 19 counterattacks towards the east from the [following] regions: the woods 2 kilometers north of Petrovka, Pliasanovo, Tikhinichi State Farm, and Verichev, with the forces from a company of up to a battalion, supported by 10–30 tanks and self-propelled guns each. All of the counterattacks were repelled with heavy losses for the enemy.

Enemy artillery and mortars shelled the combat formations of our forces with powerful fire strikes in the [following] sectors: (incl.) Ozerane, and Verichev, and occasional methodical fires in the remaining sectors. Total of up to 10,000 shells and mines were fired during the day.

Enemy aviation did not conduct sorties in the army's sector.

During the day on 1 March 1944, prisoners were seized from 520th IR, 296th ID and 13th PzGrR, 5th PzD, in the Rogovoi sector and 59th PzGrR, 20th PzD, in the Verichev region.

The interrogation of the prisoners from 520th IR, 296th ID, indicated that they were from the 3rd Battalion, 520th IR, and 1st Company, 1st Battalion of that regiment, and that one company of 519th IR was from a composite battalion which was transferred from the Luchin region on vehicles to the Tikhinichi region on 27 February 1944. The battalion had the mission to throw the Russian forces back from the bridgehead over the Drut' River by counterattacks. There were up to 300 men in the battalion.

The interrogation of the prisoners from 3rd Company, 59th PzGrR, 20th PzD, indicated that 20th PzD arrived along the Drut' River from the Vitebsk region on 25 February 1944 and occupied defenses in the Ozerane region. The division has 59th and 112th PzGrRs in the first line. The 59th PzGrR has two battalions, there are 4 companies per battalion, and the companies have 50–60 active bayonets each. Up to 20 "T-4" [Pz. IV] tanks and 10–12 self-propelled guns arrived on the Drut' River with 59th PzGrR.

A prisoner from the headquarters company of 12th/82nd IR, 31st ID, who was captured on 29 February in the region 1.5 kilometers northeast of Khomichi, reported that 31st ID consisted of 12th/82nd IR, 17th IR, and 45th IRs, 221st Security

Division, and 21st ArtyR. The 12th/82nd IR was formed on 15 January from the personnel of 12th and 82nd IRs and the regiment had two battalions with up to 800 men each.

2. The forces of 3rd Army, consisting of 250th RD, 40th, 41st, and 35th RCs, and 115th FR, continued to defend positions along the eastern bank of the Drut' River in the [following] sector: (incl.) Khomichi, Kordon, Rumek, (incl.) Mal. Konoplitsa; on the western bank of the Drut' River in the sector from Bol. Konoplitsa to the hills with Markers 145.5 and 144.5; along the eastern bank of the Drut' River from the woods south of Nov. Konoplitsa, Luzhka, and Rogachev and farther along the eastern bank of the Dnepr River up to Lake Pogreby.

The boundary lines: on the right—Nov. Bykhov, Krasnyi Bereg, Khomichi, and Cherebomirka; on the left—Semenovka, Morozovichi, Skepnia 1, Lake Pogreby, the Dnepr River, and Zhlobin (all points inclusive [for 3rd Army]).

During the night on 1 March 1944, the units defended their previous positions:

250th RD, with 179th, 178th, and 181st Army Blocking Detachments and 173rd Separate Penal Company firmly defended the [following] line—(incl.) Khomichi to (incl.) Mal. Konoplitsa and was ready for an attack with its left wing, in cooperation with 129th RD of 40th RC, in the direction of Ozerane and Obmen, with the mission of rolling up the enemy's combat formation to the north along the Drut' River.

40th RC, consisting of 129th, 323rd, and 348th RDs, with 584th and 1311th TDRs, 475th and 286th AMtrRs, 295th AGAR, and 36th TR, constitutes the nucleus of the army's shock group, which, while exploiting the success of 48th Army, is preparing for an offensive and occupying jumping-off positions along [the following] front: Bol. Konoplitsa to the hill 1 kilometer east of Verichev, with the aim of delivering the main attack toward: Gvardeiskii, Tikhinichi, and Kosharskie Farm, while rolling up the enemy's combat formations to the north and northwest.

The boundary line on the left: (incl.) Star. Selo, Grabov, Marker 126.1, Verichev, Semenovichi, Gusarovka, and Repki.

41st RC, consisting of 269th RD, 120th Gds.RD, and 8th Separate Penal Battalion, with 40th TDB, and 554th AGAR, will firmly defend the front in the sector: Luzhki to Rogachev, while having one rifle regiment of 269th RD on the western bank of the Drut' River in the vicinity of Hill 144.5 and its main forces in the vicinity of Luzhki [10 kilometers north-northwest of Rogachev] and the woods to the north. The units of the divisions within the composition of the army's main grouping will prepare to go on the offensive in the direction of Zapol'e [5 kilometers northwest of Rogachev], while rolling up the enemy's combat formations to the south.

35th RC, consisting of 169th RD and 115th FR, will firmly defend the front from (incl.) Rogachev to Lake Pogreby. The 169th RD will concentrate in the region: Aleksandrovka, Osinovka, Lugovaia [Logovaia], and Virnia [5–10 kilometers east of Zhlobin], in readiness to attack toward Zhlobin.

After the fighting from 21–25 February 1944, the units of 3rd Army went over to the defense, while holding on to a bridgehead on the western bank of the Drut' River. However, in connection with the apparent success of the neighbor on the left—48th Army—and the sharply changing operational conditions in our favor, orders were received to go over to an offensive once again on the morning of 1 March 1944.

Source: "Zhurnal boevykh deistvii voisk 3 armii za mart 1944 g." [The 3rd Army's journal of combat operations for March 1944], https://cdn.pamyat-naroda.ru/.

P-3. Report No. 00179/op by the Commander of the 1st Belorussian Front to the Supreme High Commander, Marshal of the Soviet Union I. V. Stalin

1730 hours 4 March 1944

I am providing you with a short evaluation of the situation and information about the 1st Belorussian Front's future operations.

1. *The Enemy*—15 infantry, 3 panzer, and 1 motorized division are in first echelon; 2 infantry divisions are in second echelon; and 8 divisions are in reserve along the Minsk and Pinsk line in the *front*'s sector, whose forward edge extends a distance of 300 kilometers. The main grouping is in the Bykhov, Bobruisk, Parichi, and Zhlobin region.... The enemy has a total quantity of up to 350 tanks and self-propelled guns.

2. *Our Forces*—The *front*'s forces opposing these enemy forces consist of 43 rifle divisions, 1 separate rifle brigade, and 1 tank corps. As a result of continuous offensive battles, all of the rifle divisions have been greatly weakened numerically, they have lost their assault power, and the majority of them consist of a total of from 3,000 up to 4,000 men.

Conclusions Regarding the Situation—The enemy is sufficiently strong, the ranks of the *front*'s rifle divisions have been very thinned out, and their shock power has been significantly weakened, and the difficult terrain conditions and the onset of the spring *rasputitsa* [period of flooded roads] extremely limits the capabilities of the *front*'s forces from conducting offensive operations and is forcing them to go over to the defense during the entire *rasputitsa* period, conducting in this period only local battles with the limited aims of improving their positions and preparing for a spring offensive by all of the *front*'s forces.

After the *rasputitsa*, the possible axes for the *front*'s spring offensive are:

1. Chausy-Mogilev....
2. Bykhov-Mogilev....
3. Rogachev-Bobruisk. This axis is the most favorable [because]:

(a) The terrain permits the employment of all types of forces in the offensive.

(b) The conduct of a complex regrouping is not required for the organization of an offensive along this axis, since the *front*'s main forces and weaponry are already deployed along the western bank of the Dnepr River north of Rogachev and in the Mormal' region between the Dnepr and Berezina Rivers.

4. Parichi-Bobruisk.

Decision—Considering the situation, and especially the enemy's strength and the composition of the enemy's and our own forces, the period of spring flooding that is setting in, and also the results of 50th Army's offensive along the Bykhov and Mogilev axis and 48th Army's [offensive] from the Mormal' region to the north, I have decided:

(a) To halt the *front*'s offensive and go over to the defense for the entire period of the spring *rasputitsa* and spring flooding;

(b) To limit the *front*'s combat activities during the entire period of the spring *rasputitsa* to the conduct of reconnaissance and local battles with the limited aim of improving our occupied positions; and

(c) During the entire period of the spring *rasputitsa*, to train the *front*'s forces and prepare for a general spring offensive along the Bobruisk axis.

While reporting as stated [above], I request you:

1. Approve my decision;

2. Allocate 50,000 replacements for the *front* in order to bring the rifle divisions of 3rd and 48th Armies designated for the spring offensive up to 7,000 men each. Dispatch these reinforcements as soon as possible in order that we have the opportunity to integrate them into the units in organized fashion during the period of the spring *rasputitsa* and put them through the necessary training program;

3. Fill out and transfer 9th Tank Corps, which is situated in the *Stavka*'s Reserve, to the *front*;

4. Allocate 200 tanks to fill out the *front*'s 1st Guards Tank Corps and separate tank regiments; and

5. Issue orders concerning the delivery of ammunition for the *front* so as to bring it up to three combat loads by the end of the spring *rasputitsa*.

Rokossovsky, Telegin, Malinin

Source: "Operativnye prikazy i direktivy shtaba 1 Belorusskogo fronta za 1944" [Operational orders and directives of the 1st Belorussian Front's headquarters for 1944], *TsAMO*, f. 233, op. 2356, d. 26, ll. 29–37.

Q. THE LIQUIDATION OF GERMAN BRIDGEHEADS ON THE DNEPR RIVER'S EASTERN BANK (25-31 MARCH 1944)

Q-1. From 1st Belorussian Front Particular Operational Directive No. 00215/op to the Commander of 10th Army

2330 hours 21 March 1944

... 3. The 10th Army will begin a decisive offensive on the morning of 25 March 1944, with the mission of penetrating the enemy's defensive front in the Golochevo, Antonovka, and Golovenchitsy sector and, by delivering a decisive attack in the general direction of Zales'e, Otrazh'e, Drachkovo, Kureni Moshenaki, and Petrovichi [northeast of Mogilev], to capture the Sheperevo, Brody, Ostreni, and Golovenchitsy line by day's end on 25 March 1944. [Subsequently, capture the] Chausy, ... Khar'kovka line by 27 March 1944, the Galuzy, ... Lekarshchina [Levkovshchina] line by 28 March 1944, the Zalozh'e, ... Konstantinovka line by 31 March, and the Muryvanka, ... Mostok line by 1 April 1944.

4. The 50th Army will begin a decisive offensive with all of the army's forces on the morning of 25 March 1944, with the mission of penetrating the enemy's defensive front in the Krasnitsa and Vetrenka sector and, by delivering its main attack in the general direction of Smolitsa, Dmitrievka, Kostinka, Zaprud'e, Poletkniki, and Lupolovo, to capture the Krasnitsa, Grechkin, and Vetrenka line by day's end on 27 March 1944, the Volkovichi, ... Slediuki line by 27 March 1944, the Lekarshchina, ... Zatish'e line by 29 March 1944, and the line from Novyi Lobuzh, ... to the peat village (6 kilometers southwest of Lupolovo) by 31 March 1944.

The commander of the 1st Belorussian Front, Army General K. K. Rokossovsky
The member of the 1st Belorussian Front's Military Council, Lieutenant General Telegin
The chief of staff of the 1st Belorussian Front, Colonel General Malinin

Source: "Operativnye prikazy i direktivy shtaba 1 Belorusskogo fronta za 1944" [Operational orders and directives of the 1st Belorussian Front's headquarters for 1944], *TsAMO*, f. 233, op. 2356, d. 26, ll. 25–28.

Q-2. *Stavka* VGK Directive No. 220067 to the Commanders of the 1st and 2nd Belorussian Fronts on the Resubordination of Armies and Cavalry Corps and the Withdrawal of the Headquarters of the 2nd Belorussian Front and 6th Air Army into the *Stavka* VGK's Reserve

2150 hours 2 April 1944

The *Stavka* VGK orders:

1. The 2nd Belorussian Front will transfer 61st Army—9th Guards and 89th Rifle Corps' headquarters and nine rifle divisions; 70th Army—114th and 96th Rifle Corps' headquarters and four rifle divisions; 47th Army—77th and 125th Rifle Corps' headquarters and nine rifle divisions; 2nd and 7th Guards Cavalry Corps—six cavalry divisions; 69th Army (25th, 61st, and 91st Rifle Corps' headquarters—nine rifle divisions), which is arriving from the *Stavka* Reserve; and 6th Air Army (336th FAD, 3rd Gds.AAD, and 242nd NBAD) to the 1st Belorussian Front no later than 5 April.

Transfer these forces with all reinforcing units, army rear service units and facilities, and all existing reserve stocks.

2. By 5 April the chief of the General Staff will determine the composition of *front* rear service units and facilities of the 2nd Belorussian Front, which are subject to transfer, first, to the 1st Belorussian Front, and, second, for withdrawal into the *Stavka*'s Reserve.

3. The commander of the 1st Belorussian Front will transfer 10th Army, with 38th and 70th Rifle Corps' headquarters and six rifle divisions; and 50th Army, with 19th and 121st Rifle Corps' headquarters and seven rifle divisions, to the Western Front by 2400 hours on 5 April.

Transfer the named armies with all army reinforcements, rear service units and facilities, and on-hand reserve stocks.

4. Rename the 1st Belorussian Front the Belorussian Front, effective at 2400 hours on 5 April.

5. Establish the following boundary lines for the Belorussian Front, effective at 2400 hours on 5 April:

—With the Western Front—Gaishin (10 kilometers south of Propoisk), Selets-Kholopeev, Chigirinka, Svisloch', Grodzianka, Cherven', and Ostroshitskii Gorodok (all points besides Gaishin, Selets-Kholopeev, and Ostroshitskii Gorodok are inclusive for the Belorussian Front); and

—With the 1st Ukrainian Front—as before, Korosten', Gorodnitsa, Kostopol', Sofievka, Rozhishche, Verba, and Korytnitsa (all points besides Korosten' are inclusive for the 1st Ukrainian Front).

6. Establish the Belorussian Front's headquarters in the Ovruch region and the Alternate Command Post in the Sarny region.

7. Withdraw the headquarters of the 2nd Belorussian Front and the headquarters of 6th AA into the *Stavka*'s Reserve in the Zhitomir region by 20 April.

8. The commander of the Belorussian Front will submit by cipher his thoughts on the subsequent operational employment of the Belorussian Front in its new composition.

9. Report fulfillment.

The *Stavka* VGK
I. Stalin, A. Antonov

Source: "Direktiva Stavki No. 220067 komanduiushchim voiskami 1-go i 2-go Belorusskikh frontov na perepodchinenie armii i kavaleriiskikh korpusov i vyvod upravlenii 2-go Belorusskogo fronta i 6-i vozhdushnoi armii v rezerv Verkhnovogo Glavnokomandovaniia" [*Stavka* VGK Directive No. 220067 to the commanders of the 1st and 2nd Belorussian Fronts on the resubordination of armies and cavalry corps and the withdrawal of the headquarters of the 2nd Belorussian Front and 6th Air Army into the *Stavka* VGK's Reserve], in Zolotarev, *Stavka* VGK 1944, 68–69.

Q-3. *Stavka* VGK Directive No. 220079 to the Commander of the 1st Belorussian Front on a Transition to the Defense

2200 hours 17 April 1944

The *Stavka* VGK orders:

1. With the receipt of this directive, the 1st Belorussian Front will go over to a rigid defense in the *front*'s entire sector.

2. While organizing the defense, devote special attention to [erecting] a defense along the Kovel' axis and at the boundary with the 1st Ukrainian Front.

3. Form a deeply echeloned defense. Prepare no fewer than three defensive belts in the *front*'s sector, with an overall defensive depth of 30–40 kilometers.

4. Report all orders issued.

The *Stavka* VGK
I. Stalin, A. Antonov

Source: "Direktiva Stavki No. 220079 komanduiushchemu voiskami 1-go Belorusskogo fronta na perekhod k oborone" [*Stavka* VGK Directive No. 220079 to the commander of the 1st Belorussian Front on a transition to the defense], in Zolotarev, *Stavka* VGK 1944, 74.

R. GERMAN COMMAND CADRE IN EASTERN BELORUSSIA (THE SECTOR FROM IDRITSA SOUTHWARD TO THE PRIPIAT' RIVER) FROM 1 OCTOBER 1943 TO APRIL 1944

Army Group North—Field Marshal Georg von Küchler (16 Jan 42–9 Jan 44), Field Marshal Walther Model (9 Jan–31 Mar 44)

Sixteenth Army—Field Marshal Ernst Busch (to 30 Oct 43), General of Artillery Christian Hansen (30 Oct 43–3 Jul 44)

II Army Corps—General of Infantry Paul Laux (28 Nov 43–31 Mar 44)

218th ID—Lieutenant General Viktor Lang (20 Mar 42–25 Dec 44)

93rd ID—General of Artillery Horst von Mellenthin (Sep–1 Oct 43), Lieutenant General Karl Löwrick (1 Oct 43–20 Jun 44)

12th ID—Lieutenant General Kurt-Jürgen *Freiherr* von Lützow (20 Jul 42–25 May 44)

331st ID—Lieutenant General Karl-Ludwig Rhein (22 Feb 43–1 Jan 44)

XXXXIII Army Corps—General of Infantry Carl von Oven (24 Jan 43–25 Mar 44)

205th ID—Lieutenant General Paul Seyffardt (1 Mar 42–5 Nov 43), Major General Ernst Michael (5 Nov–1 Dec 43), General of Artillery Horst von Mellenthin (1 Dec 43–19 Oct 44)

83rd ID—Lieutenant General Theodor Scherer (2 Nov 42–1 Mar 44)

263rd ID—Lieutenant General Werner Richter (1 Apr 43–21 May 44)

69th ID (mid-Oct 43)—Lieutenant General Bruno Ortner (29 Sep 41–1 Feb 44)

I Army Corps (mid-Oct 43)—Lieutenant General (General of Infantry on 1 Nov 43) Martin Grase (15 Aug–31 Dec 43), General of Infantry Carl Hilpert (31 Dec 43–20 Jan 44), Lieutenant General Walter Hartmann (20 Jan–30 Mar 44)

122nd ID (mid-Oct 43)—Lieutenant General Kurt Chill (27 Jun 43–1 Feb 44)

58th ID (mid-Oct 43)—Lieutenant General Curt Siewert (7 Jun 43–13 Apr 45)

Gp. von Below (mid-Oct 43)—unknown but likely a Colonel

Army Group Center—Field Marshal Gunter von Kluge (to 28 Oct 43), Field Marshal Ernst Busch (28 Oct 43–27 Jun 44)

Third Panzer Army—Colonel General Georg Hans Reinhardt (1 Jan 42–15 Aug 44)

II Luftwaffe Field Corps—General of Airborne Troops Alfred Schlemm (1 Oct 42–31 Dec 43)

2nd LFD (assigned to 6th LFD in Jan 44)—Colonel Carl Becker (1–17 Jan 43), Colonel Hellmuth Petzold (17 Jan–1 Nov 43)

6th LFD—Lieutenant General Rüdiger von Heyking (25 Nov 42–4 Nov 43), Major General Rudolf Peschel (5 Nov 43–30 Jun 44)

3rd LFD (assigned to 4th and 6th LFDs in Jan 44)—Lieutenant General Robert Pistorius (26 Sep 42–24 Jan 44)

4th LFD—Major General Wilhelm Voelk (8 Apr–5 Nov 43), Major General Hans Sauerbrey (5–20 Nov 43, Major General Dr. Ernst Klepp (20 Nov 43–24 Jan 44)

VI Army Corps—General of Infantry Hans Jordan (1 Nov 42–20 May 44)

87th ID—General of Artillery Walter Hartmann (1 Feb–22 Nov 43), Lieutenant General Mauritz *Freiherr* von Strachwitz (22 Nov 43–Aug 44)

14th ID (Mot)—Lieutenant General Hermann Flörke (30 Jun 43–28 Dec 44)

206th ID—Lieutenant General Alfons Hitter (14 Sep 43–28 Jun 44)

256th ID—Lieutenant General Paul Dannhauser (14 Feb 42—9 Oct 43)

KGr., 246th ID—Major General Heinz Fiebig (12 Sep–5 Oct 43), Lieutenant General Wilhelm Falley (5–9 Oct 43)

"*Feldherrnhalle*" PzGrenD (18 Dec 43)—Lieutenant General Otto Kohlermann (Jun 43–3 Apr 44)

197th ID (25 Dec 43)—Lieutenant General Eugen Wößner (25 Dec 43–14 Mar 44)

LIII Army Corps (9 Oct 43)—General of Infantry Friedrich Gollwitzer (22 Jun 43–28 Jun 44)
  246th ID—Wilhelm Falley (9 Oct 43–20 Apr 44)
  256th ID—Lieutenant General Paul Dannhauser (9 Oct–24 Nov 43), Lieutenant General Albrecht Wüstenhagen (24 Nov 43–26 Jun 44)
Fourth Army—Colonel General Gotthard Heinrici (31 Jul 43–4 Jun 44)
  XXVII Army Corps—General of Infantry Paul Völckers (8 Jun 43–9 Jul 44)
    KGr., 52nd ID (to 197th ID after 5 Nov 43)—Lieutenant General Rudolf Peschel (1 Nov 1942–5 Nov 1943)
    197th ID (to Third Panzer Army's VI AC on 25 Dec)—General of Infantry Ehrenfried Böge (1 Apr 42–5 Nov 43), Lieutenant General Eugen Wössner (5 Nov–25 Dec 43)
    18th PzGrD—Lieutenant General Karl Zutavern (9 Aug 43–14 Apr 44)
    18th PzD (remnants)
  XXXIX Panzer Corps—General of Artillery Robert Martinek (1 Dec 42–13 Nov 43), Lieutenant General Carl Püchler (14 Nov 43–18 Apr 44)
    25th PzGrD—General of Infantry Anton Grasser (23 Jun–5 Nov 43), Lieutenant General Dr. Fritz Benicke (5 Nov 43–4 Mar 44)
    337th ID—Lieutenant General Otto Schünemann (20 Sep 42–27 Dec 43), Lieutenant General Walter Scheller (27 Dec 43–Jul 44)
    KGr. 113th ID (to 337th ID on 26 Nov 43)—Major General Friedrich-Wilhelm Prüter (15 Mar 43–25 Nov 43)
    95th ID—General of Infantry Edgar Röhricht (27 Sep 42–10 Dec 43), Major General Gustav Gihr (9 Dec 43–27 Jan 44)
  IX Army Corps—General of Infantry Hans Schmidt (1 Jan 42–15 Oct 43), General of Infantry Heinrich Clössner (15 Oct–3 Dec 43), General of Artillery Rolf Wuthmann (3 Dec 43–20 Apr 45)
    78th Assault (*Sturm*)D—Lieutenant General Hans Traut (1 Apr–1 Nov 43), Lieutenant General Herbert von Larisch (1 Nov 43–15 Feb 44)
    252nd ID—General of Infantry Walter Melzer (1 Jan 43–12 Oct 44)
    342nd ID—Lieutenant General Heinrich Nickel (25 Sep 43–8 May 45)
    KGr. 330th ID (to 342nd ID on 6 Nov 43)—Lieutenant General Heinrich Nickel (25 Sep 43–8 May 45)
    35th ID—Lieutenant General Ludwig Merker (8 Jun–5 Nov 43), Lieutenant General Johann-Georg Richert (5 Nov 43–9 Apr 44)
  XII Army Corps—General of Infantry Kurt von Tippelskirch (Sep 43–4 Jun 44)
    26th ID—Lieutenant General Johann de Boer (5 Aug 43–10 Aug 44)
    KGr., 56th ID (assigned to Corps *Abteilung* D as Div.Gp. 56 in mid-Oct 43)—Lieutenant General Vincent Müller (1 Sep–mid-Oct 43)
Ninth Army—Field Marshal Walther Model (9 Jun–4 Nov 43), Colonel General Joseph Harpe (4 Nov 43–1 May 44)
  XXXXI Panzer Corps—General of Panzer Troops Josef Harpe (10 Jul 42–15 Oct 43), General of Artillery Helmuth Weidling (15 Oct 43–31 Jan 44), Lieutenant General Ehrenfried Böge (1 Feb–10 Mar 44)
    131st ID—General of Artillery Heinrich Meyer-Bürdorf (1 Oct 40–10 Jan 44)
    260th ID—General of Infantry Walther Hahm (6 Oct 42–9 Nov 43), Lieutenant General Robert Schlüter (9 Nov 43–21 Apr 44)

267th ID—Lieutenant General Otto Drescher (8 Jun 43–13 Aug 44)
LV Army Corps—General of Infantry Erich Jaschke (1 Mar–6 Oct 43), General of Infantry Friedrich Herrlein (6 Oct 43–Mar 44)
36th ID—Lieutenant General Rudolf Stegmann (20 Sep 43–1 Jan 44), Major General Horst Kadgien (1–17 Jan 44), Lieutenant General Egon von Neindorff (17–19 Jan 44), Major General Alexander Conrady (19 Jan–1 Jul 44)
211th ID—Lieutenant General Johann Heinrich Eckhardt (16 Jul 43–Dec 44)
110th ID—Lieutenant General Albrecht Wüstenhagen (25 Sep–1 Dec 43), Lieutenant General Eberhard von Kurowski (1 Dec 43–11 May 44)
XXIII Army Corps—Colonel General Johannes Friessner (19 Jan–7 Dec 43), General of Panzer Troops Hans *Freiherr* von Funck (7 Dec 43–2 Feb 44), General of Pioneers Otto Tiemann (2 Feb–12 Oct 44)
383rd ID—Lieutenant General Edmund Hoffmeister (1 Jul 43–20 Jun 44)
296th ID—Lieutenant General Arthur Kullmer (1 Jan 43–19 Jun 44)
253rd ID—Lieutenant General Carl Becker (18 Jan 43–17 Jun 44)
Second Army—Colonel General Walter Weiss (3 Feb 43–12 Mar 45)
XXXV Army Corps—General of Infantry Friedrich Wiese (5 Aug 43–Jan 44), General of Infantry Horst Grossmann (Jan–Feb 44), General of Infantry Friedrich Wiese (Feb–25 Jun 44)
299th ID—Lieutenant General Ralph Graf d'Oriola (3 May 43–15 Jan 44), Lieutenant General Paul Reichelt (15 Jan–13 Mar 44)
216th ID (assigned to 102nd ID as Div.Gp. 216 on 1 Dec 43)—Lieutenant General Egon von Neindorff (3–20 Oct 43), Major General Gustav Gihr (20 Oct–30 Nov 43)
292nd ID—Lieutenant General Richard John (20 Jul 43–30 Jun 44)
45th ID—Lieutenant General Hans *Freiherr* von Falkenstein (25 Apr–30 Nov 43), Major General Joachim Engel (30 Nov 43–27 Feb 44)
XX Army Corps—General of Artillery Rudolf *Freiherr* von Roman (10 Mar–Dec 43), General of Infantry Edgar Röhricht (Dec 43–Jan 44), General of Artillery Rudolf *Freiherr* von Roman (Jan 44–Apr 45)
KGr., 6th ID—General of Infantry Horst Grossmann (21 Jan 42–16 Dec 43), Lieutenant General Egon von Neindorff (16 Dec 43–12 Jan 44)
KGr., 31st ID—Lieutenant General Wilhelm Ochsner (2 Aug 43–Jun 44)
KGr., 102nd ID—General of Infantry Otto Hitzfeld (19 Jan–10 Nov 43), Lieutenant General Werner von Bercken (10 Nov 43–Apr 45)
XXXXVI Panzer Corps—General of Infantry Hans Gollnick (1 Oct 43–21 Mar 44)
7th ID—Major General Carl André (2 Oct–30 Nov 43), Major General Gustav Gihr (30 Nov–9 Dec 43), Major General Hans Traut (9 Dec 43–15 Feb 44)
KGr., 137th ID (assigned to Corps *Abteilung* E as Div.Gp. 137 in Dec 43)—Lieutenant General Hans Kamecke (25 Feb 42–15 Oct 43), Lieutenant General Egon von Neindorff (15 Oct–16 Dec 1943)
KGr., 251st ID (assigned to Corps *Abteilung* E as Div.Gp. 251 in Dec 43)—General of Artillery Maximilian Felzmann (10 Mar 43–15 Nov 44)
16th PzD (18 Dec 43)—Colonel Hans-Ulrich Back (1 Nov 43–30 Jan 44)

LVI Panzer Corps—General of Infantry Friedrich Hossbach (11 Aug–14 Nov 43), Lieutenant General Anton Grasser (15 Nov–9 Dec 43), General of Infantry Friedrich Hossbach (10 Dec 43–14 Jun 44)
  KGr., 86th ID (assigned to Corps *Abteilung* E as Div.Gp, 86 in Nov 43)—General of Artillery Helmuth Weidling (1 Jan 42–15 Oct 43)
  KGr., 4th PzD—Lieutenant General Dietrich von Saucken (31 May–22 Oct 43), Colonel Dr. Karl Mauss (23 Oct 43–20 Jan 44), Major General Hans Junck (21 Jan–6 Feb 44), Colonel Clemens Betzel (7 Feb–3 Mar 44), Lieutenant General Dietrich von Saucken (4 Mar–30 Apr 44)
  KGr., 12th PzD—Lieutenant General Erpo *Freiherr* von Bodenhausen (1 Mar 43–2 Jun 44)
  2nd PzD—Lieutenant General Vollrath Lübbe (20 Oct. 42–1 Feb 44)
  5th PzD—Colonel (Major General on 1 Dec 43) Karl Decker (7 Sep–29 Dec 43), Colonel Heinrich-Walter Bronsart von Schellendorf (30 Dec 43–29 Jan 44), Lieutenant General Karl Decker (30 Jan–15 Oct 44)

Army Group Reserves
 VIII Army Corps (Hungarian)
  1st ID—unidentified
  5th ID—Brigadier General László János Szábo (1 Oct 43–May 45)
  9th ID—Brigadier General Béla Németh (10 Aug 43–15 Apr 44)
  12th ID—Brigadier General Jénö Bor (10 Aug 43–5 Apr 44)
  18th ID—Brigadier General Mihály Ibrányi (10 Aug 43–1 Jan 44), Brigadier General József Vasváry (1 Jan–1 Aug 44)
  23rd ID—Brigadier General Pál Magyar (10 Aug 43–30 Jan 19), Colonel Jenö Sövenyházi-Herdiczky (30 Jan–May 44)
  201st SecD—Lieutenant General Alfred Jacobi (20 May 42–13 Oct 44)
  203rd SecD—Lieutenant General Rudolf Pilz (1 Jan 43–19 Aug 44)
  286th SecD—Lieutenant General Johann-Georg Richert (15 Jun 42–1 Nov 43), Lieutenant General Hans Oschmann (1 Nov 43–5 Aug 44)
  2nd Slovak ID—Colonel Pilfousek (1 Aug 43–1 July 44)

OKH Reserves
  KGr., 20th PzD (to Third Panzer Army on 8 Oct 43)—Lieutenant General Mortimer von Kessel (12 May 43–1 Jan 44), Colonel Werner Marcks (1 Jan–1 Feb 44), Lieutenant General Mortimer von Kessel (2 Feb–5 Nov 44)
  129th ID (to Third Panzer Army's on Oct 43)—Major General Karl Fabiunke (25 Sep 43–31 Jan 44), Lieutenant General Herbert von Larisch (31 Jan 44–11 Feb 45)
  134th ID—General of Mountain Troops Hans Schlemmer (12 Dec 41–Feb 44)
  707th ID—Lieutenant General Rudolf Busich (1 Jun–3 Dec 43), Major General Alexander Conrady (3 Dec 43–12 Jan 44)

Sources: "Kriegsgliederung der Heeresgruppe Mitte (Stand: Anfang Oktober 1943)," *BA-MA, Studie ZA 1/2053*; *KTB OKW, Bd 3/2*, S. 1157; http://www.axishistory.com/index.php?id.

S. SELECTED ABBREVIATIONS

GERMAN (AXIS)

Higher Commands
OKW (*Oberkommando der Wehrmacht*)— Armed Forces High Command
OKH (*Oberkommando des Heeres*)— Army High Command
AG (H.Gr.) (*Heeresgruppe*)—army group
A, (AOK) (*Armeeoberkommando*)—army
Pz A—panzer army
Harko (*Hoherer Artilleriekommando*)— higher artillery command (army level)
Arko (*Artilleriekommando*)—artillery command
AC (A.K.)—army corps
PzC (Pz.K.)—panzer corps
D (Div.)—division
AssltD—assault (sturm) division
ID (I.D.)—infantry division
PzD (Pz.D.)– panzer division
ID (mot)—infantry division (motorized)
JägD—jäger (light) division
PzGrenD (PzGrD)—panzer grenadier division
CavD (K.D.)—cavalry division
MtnD—mountain division
Sec. D—security division
LFD—Luftwaffe field division
Div Gp.—divisional group
Br.—brigade
IB (Inf.B)—infantry brigade
MotB—motorized brigade
PzB—panzer brigade
Rgt. (R)—regiment
SecR—security regiment
AR—artillery regiment
IR—infantry regiment
PzR—panzer regiment
PzGR (Pz.Gren.R)—panzer grenadier regiment
EngR—engineer regiment
MotR—motorized regiment
MtrcR—motorcycle regiment
SkiR—ski regiment
Bn (Btl.)—battalion
PzBn—panzer battalion
MotBn—motorized battalion
InfBn—infantry battalion
SecBn—security battalion
EngBn—engineer battalion

SOVIET

Commands and Forces
A—army
AA—air army
GA (Gds.A)—guards army
SA—shock army
TA—tank army
GTA (Gds.TA)—guards tank army
TC—tank corps
GTC (Gds.TC)—guards tank corps
MC—mechanized corps
GMC (Gds.MC)—guards mechanized corps
RC—rifle corps
GRC (Gds.RC)—guards rifle corps
CC—cavalry corps
GCC (Gds.CC)—guards cavalry corps
AC—artillery corps
APC—artillery penetration corps
BAC—bomber aviation corps
FAC—fighter aviation corps
AssltAC—assault aviation corps
MAC—mixed aviation corps
RD—rifle division
RDNKVD—NKVD rifle division
GRD (Gds.RD)—guards rifle division
CD—cavalry division
GCD (Gds.CD)—guards cavalry division
AD—artillery division
AAD—army artillery division
APD—artillery penetration division
Gds.-MD—guards-mortar division
BAD—bomber aviation division
NBAD—night bomber aviation division
FAD—fighter aviation division
AssltAD—assault aviation division
MAD—mixed aviation division
FR—fortified region
RB—rifle brigade
TB—tank brigade
GTB (Gds.TB)—guards tank brigade
MB—mechanized brigade
GMB (Gds.MB)—guards mechanized brigade
MRB—motorized rifle brigade
GMRB (Gds.MRB)—guards motorized rifle brigade
NRB—naval rifle brigade
HAB—howitzer artillery brigade
GAB—gun artillery brigade

GERMAN (AXIS)	SOVIET
MG Bn—machine gun battalion	RR—rifle regiment
Co. (kp.)—company	GRR (Gds.RR)—guards rifle regiment
Btry (battr.)– battery	TR—tank regiment
	GTR (Gds.TR)—guards tank regiment
Miscellaneous	CR—cavalry regiment
Abt. (*abteilung*)—detachment or battalion	GCR (Gds.CR)—guards cavalry regiment
A.A.—reconnaissance *abteilung*	AR—artillery regiment
Pz. A.A.—panzer reconnaissance *abteilung*	Gds.AR—guards artillery regiment
Abschnitt—Section or sector	HAR—howitzer artillery regiment
Aufkl. (*Aufklarung*)—reconnaissance	GAR—gun artillery regiment
Gp. (*Gruppe*)—group	CAR—corps artillery regiment
HKL—front lines (*hauptkampflinie* or main combat line)	ATR—antitank artillery regiment
	TDR—tank destroyer (antitank) artillery regiment
Inf.— infantry	SPR—self-propelled artillery regiment
Kpfgp. (Kgr.)(KGr.)—*kampfgruppe* [combat group]	BAR—bomber aviation regiment
mot.—motorized	FAR—fighter aviation regiment
Flak (*flugabwehrkanone*)—antiaircraft guns	AssltAR—assault aviation regiment
Jg (Jäg) (*Jäger*)—light	MAR—mixed aviation regiment
i. G.—in the General Staff	RAR—reconnaissance aviation regiment
Pak (*panzerabwehrkanone*)—antitank gun	G-MR (Gds.-MR)—guards mortar (multiple-rocket launcher or *Katiusha*) regiment
Pi—Pioneer (engineer)	
Pkw (*personenkraftwagon*)—personnel carrier	
Pz.Jg. (*panzerjäger*)—antitank unit	MtrR—mortar regiment
St.G. (*Stu.Gesch.*) (*stürmgeschutz*)—assault gun	GMR (Gds.MR)—guards mortar regiment
	MRR—motorized rifle regiment
IG (*infanteriegeschutz*)—infantry gun	CR—cavalry regiment
v.—*von*	GCR (Gds.CR)—guards cavalry regiment
z.b.V.—temporarily formed	RAS—reconnaissance aviation squadron
(R) (r. or ru.)—Romanian	RBn—rifle battalion
(I)—Italian	TBn—tank battalion
(H)—Hungarian	AABn—antiaircraft artillery battalion
(G)—German	ATBn—antitank battalion
	TDBn—tank destroyer battalion
	MG-Arty Bn (MGArtyBn)—machine gun-artillery battalion
	G-MBn (Gds.-MBn)—guards mortar battalion
	Sep.ArmdCarBn—separate armored car battalion
	ArmdTrainBn—armored train battalion
	Co—company
	OShBn—separate penal battalion
	Btry—battery
	Co.—company (with prefix for type)
	Miscellaneous
	A—army (prefix applied to all regiments)
	AA—antiaircraft
	Arty—artillery

GERMAN (AXIS)	SOVIET
	AT—antitank
	Cav.—cavalry
	CP—command post
	DAG—division artillery group
	DD—long-range artillery group
	Det.—detachment
	FD—forward detachment
	G (Gds.) as a prefix with any abbreviation—guards
	Gp.—group
	MTS—motor tractor station
	MTF—motor tractor factory
	OP—observation post
	PVO—antiaircraft defense
	RAG—regimental artillery group
	RVGK—Reserve of the *Stavka* of the Supreme High Command
	Sep.—separate
	SF—state farm
	Res.—reserve

Notes

Preface

1. Somewhat ironically, Sokolovsky was born in Grodno, Belorussia (today, Belarus).

2. For further details on Operation Bagration, see David M. Glantz, ed., *1985 Art of War Symposium: From the Dnepr to the Vistula—Soviet Offensive Operations, November 1943–August 1944: A Transcript of Proceedings* (Carlisle, PA: U.S. Army War College, 1985; reissued under the same title as a self-published unbound reprint with daily operational maps by David M. Glantz, Carlisle, PA, 1998) (see catalogue at http://glantzbooks.com); Steven Zaloga, *Bagration 1944: The Destruction of Army Group Centre* (London: Osprey, 1996); Gerd Niepold, *The Battle for White Russia: The Destruction of Army Group Centre June 1944,* trans. Richard Simpkin (London: Brassey's, 1987); Paul Adair, *Hitler's Greatest Defeat: The Collapse of Army Group Centre, June 1944* (London: Arms and Armour Press, 1994); David M. Glantz, ed., *Belorussia 1944: The Soviet General Staff Study,* trans. Harold S. Orenstein (London: Frank Cass, 2001).

Chapter 1. Context: The Summer–Fall Campaign

1. On 20 October 1943, the *Stavka* redesignated the Central, Voronezh, Southwestern, Steppe, and Southern Fronts the Belorussian, 1st, 2nd, 3rd, and 4th Ukrainian Fronts, respectively. At the same time, it renamed the Kalinin Front the 1st Baltic Front. On 10 October the *Stavka* renamed the Briansk Front the Baltic Front and ten days later renamed it the 2nd Baltic Front.

Chapter 2. The Kalinin and Baltic Fronts' Vitebsk and Nevel' Offensives

1. Earl F. Ziemke, *Stalingrad to Berlin: The German Defeat in the East* (Washington, DC: Office of the Chief of Military History U.S. Army, 1968), 191. Accordingly, Ziemke's account of the war touches upon all of the major Red Army actions along the western axis—such as at Nevel', Vitebsk, Loev, Gomel', and Rechitsa. However, it does this sequentially as it addresses the actions of each German army group and places these actions in separate chapters and under separate headings.

2. A. A. Grechko et al., eds., *Istoriia Vtoroi Mirovoi voiny 1939–1945 v dvenadtsati tomakh, Tom sed'moi, Zavershenie korennogo perelom v voine* [History of the Second World War 1939–1945, vol. 7: The completion of a fundamental turning point in the war] (Moscow: Voenizdat, 1976), 253–254.

3. Ibid., 270–271.

4. Ziemke, *Stalingrad to Berlin,* 191.

5. Grechko et al., *Istoria Vtoroi Mirovoi voiny,* 7, 271.

671

6. "Kräftegegenüberstellung Stand: 14.10.43," in *Anlage 4 c zu Abt. Fr. H. Ost (I) Nr. 80/43 g kdos vom 17. 10. 43*. A copy of the original.

7. "Postanovlenie GKO, 12 March 1944," in *TsPA UMA* [Central Party Archives Institute of Marxism and Leninism], f. 644, op. 1, d. 218,1. 102.

8. See V. A. Zolotarev et al., ed., *Velikaia Otechestvennaia voina 1941–1945, Kkniga 2: Perelom* [The Great Patriotic War 1941–1945, Book 2: The turning point] (Moscow: Nauka, 1998), 322. This passage speaks only of the Belorussian Front's November Gomel'-Rechitsa operation.

9. The only notable exception to this rule are two articles cited below written by M. A. Gareev.

10. For Red Army strength figures, see *Velikaia Otechestvennaia voina 1941–1945 gg.: Deistvuiushchaia armiia* [The Great Patriotic War 1941–1945: The operating army] (Moscow: Kuchkovo pole, 2005), 562; and David M. Glantz and Jonathan House, *When Titans Clashed: How the Red Army Stopped Hitler* (Lawrence: University Press of Kansas, 2015), Appendices.

11. See M. E. Morozov et al., eds., *Velikaia Otechestvennaia voina 1941–1945 gg. Kampanii i strategicheskie operatsii v tsifrakh—v 2 tomakh—Tom II* [The Great Patriotic War 1941–1945: Campaigns and strategic operations in figures, vol. 2] (Moscow: Glavarkhiv goroda Moskvy, 2010), 100, 114, 147, 167.

12. See *Boevoi sostav Sovetskoi Armii, chast' III (Ianvar'-dekabr' 1943 g.)* [The combat composition of the Soviet Army, pt. 3 (January–December 1943)] (Moscow: Voenizdat, 1972), 235–236, 263–264. The tank corps included 1st Guards, 5th, 19th, 20th, and 25th and the mechanized corps 7th, 8th, and 9th. Much of the refitting was done in the Moscow Military District.

13. For the organization and strength of Soviet armored and self-propelled artillery forces, see David M. Glantz, *Colossus Reborn: The Red Army at War, 1941–1943* (Lawrence: University Press of Kansas, 2005), 218–236, 300–302.

14. Grechko et al., *Istoriia Vtoroi Mirovoi voiny*, vol. 7, 272–273.

15. A. I. Eremenko, *Gody vozmezdiia 1943–1945* [Years of retribution] (Moscow: Nauka, 969), 78–79.

16. Ibid., 80.

17. In his memoirs, *Nastupala groznaia bronia* [Menacing armor attacked] (Kiev: Politicheskoi literatury Ukrainy, 1981), I. F. Dremov makes no mention whatsoever of his unit's role in the heavy fighting east of Vitebsk.

18. "Doklad komanduiushchego voiskami Kalininskogo fronta No. 15621 Verkhovnomu Glavnokomanduiushchemu plana Vitebskoi operatsii" [Report No. 15621 of the commander of the Kalinin Front to the Supreme High Commander concerning a plan for the Vitebsk operation], in *Russkii arkhiv: Velikaia Otechestvennaia. Stavka Verkhovnogo Glavnokomandovannia: Dokumenty i materialy 1943 god, T 16 (5 (3)* [The Russian archives: The Great Patriotic War. The *Stavka* of the Supreme High Command: Documents and materials 1943, No. 16, 5 (3)], ed. V. A. Zolotarev (Moscow: TERRA, 1999), 310–311. Hereafter cited as Zolotarev, *Stavka VGK 1943*, with document title and page(s).

19. "Direktiva Stavki VGK No. 30195 komanduiushchemu voiskami Kalininskogo fronta, predstaviteliu Stavki ob utochnenii plana Vitebskoi operatsii" [*Stavka* VGK directive No. 30195 to the commander of the Kalinin Front and the representative of the *Stavka* concerning more precise definition of the plan for the Vitebsk operation], in Zolotarev, *Stavka VGK 1943*, 207.

20. Eremenko, *Gody vozmezdiia*, 95–96.

21. F. Sverdlov, "Nevel'skaia nastupatel'naia operatsiia (6–16 oktiabr 1943 goda)" [The Nevel' offensive operation (6–16 October 1943)], *Voenno-istoricheskii zhurnal* [Military-historical journal] 11 (November 1968): 26. Sverdlov noted that, in October 1943, the strength of the Kalinin Front's rifle divisions was on average 5,000–6,000 personnel and rifle brigades up to 3,000–4,000. Hereafter cited as *VIZh*, with appropriate title, number, and page(s).

22. G. Semenov, "Vnezapnyi udar po vragu" [A surprise attack on the enemy], *VIZh* 10 (October 1969): 76–77.

23. Eremenko claims in his memoirs that he positioned himself with 39th and 43rd Armies in order to deceive the Germans in regard to the *front's* real intent, that is, to attack Nevel.'

24. V. V. Abaturov et al., eds., *Osvobozhdenie Belarusii 1943–1944* [The liberation of Belarus 1943–1944] (Minsk: Belaruskaia Navuka, 2014), 39–40.

25. Eremenko, *Gody vozmezdiia*, 103.

26. Abaturov et al., *Osvobozhdenie Belarusi*, 40.

27. Ibid., 41.

28. Ziemke, *Stalingrad to Berlin*, 200–201.

29. Abaturov et al., *Osvobozhdenie Belarusi*, 42–43.

30. Ziemke, *Stalingrad to Berlin*, 126.

31. Abaturov et al., *Osvobozhdenie Belarusi*, 43.

32. V. P. Boiko, *S dumoi o rodine* [With thoughts for the Motherland] (Moscow: Voenizdat, 1982), 131–134.

33. See the German intelligence appreciation contained in "Anlagenband A/1 zum Tatigkeitsbericht No. 10," *Pz AOK 3.*, *49113/32 and 49113/33, 1 Oct–31 Dec 43*, in National Archives Microfilm series (NAM) T-313, roll 297. Hereafter cited as NAM T-313, roll 297.

34. Eremenko, *Gody vozmezdiia*, 84.

35. Boiko, *S dumoi o rodine*, 132.

36. The Third Panzer Army's daily operational maps are found in "Anlagen zum Kriegstagebuch Nr. 7, Lagekarten Band VII," *Pz AOK 3, Ia,* 49113/23 and 49113/24, 1 October–15 November 1943, NAM T-313, roll 296. Hereafter cited as T-313, roll 296.

37. Ibid., 134.

38. Abaturov et al., *Osvobozhdenie Belarusi*, 43.

39. "Direktiva Stavki VGK No. 30209 komanduiushchemu voiskami Brianskogo fronta ob uprazdenii Brianskogo i obrazovanii Pribaltiiskogo fronta" [*Stavka* VGK directive No. 30209 to the commander of the Briansk Front concerning the abolition of the Briansk and formation of the Baltic Front], in Zolotarev, *Stavka VGK 1943*, 214.

40. "Direktiva Stavki VGK No. 30217 komanduiushchemu voiskami Pribaltiiskogo fronta o podgotovke i provedenii nastupatel'noi operatsii na Idritskom napravlenii" [*Stavka* VGK directive No. 30217 to the commander of the Baltic Front concerning the preparation and conduct of an offensive operation along the Idritsa axis], in Zolotarev, *Stavka VGK 1943*, 218–219.

41. "Direktiva Stavki VGK No. 30218 komanduiushchemu Kalininskogo fronta na razvitie nastupleniia s tsel'iu ovladeniia Rigoi" [*Stavka* VGK directive No. 30218 to the commander of the Kalinin Front on the development of an offensive to capture Riga], in Zolotarev, *Stavka VGK 1943*, 219.

42. "Direktiva Stavki VGK No. 30219 komanduiushchemu Severo-zapadnogo fronta na podrotovku i provedenie operatsii po razgromu Porkhovskoi gruppirovki protivnika" [*Stavka* VGK directive No. 30219 to the commander of the Northwestern Front on the preparation and conduct of an operation to destroy the enemy's Porkhov grouping], in Zolotarev, *Stavka VGK 1943*, 220.

43. "Direktiva Stavki VGK No. 30220 komanduiushchim voiskami Pribaltiiskogo, Severo-zapadnogo i Kalininskogo frontov na izmenenie srokov perepodchineniia 3-i udarnoi I 22-i armii i o zadachakh ikh aviatsionnogo prikrytiia" [*Stavka* VGK directive No. 30220 to the commanders of the Baltic, Northwestern, and Kalinin Fronts concerning a change in the period of the re-subordination of 3rd Shock and 22nd Armies and the missions of their air support], in Zolotarev, *Stavka VGK 1943*, 220–221.

44. "Zhurnal boevykh deistvii 1-go Pribaltiiskogo fronta za oktiabr' 1943 g" [The 1st Baltic Front's journal of combat operations for October 1943], TsAMO, F. 235, Op. 2074, D. 51, L. 77.

45. "Komanduiushchemu voiskami Kalininskogo fronta o podgotovke operatsii po unichtozheniiu aviatsii protivnika" [To the commander of the Kalinin Front concerning the preparation of an operation for the destruction of enemy aviation], in A. M. Zolotarev, ed., *Russkii arkhiv: Velikaia Otechestvennaia. General'nyi shtab v gody Velikoi Otechestvennoi voiny: Dokumenty i materialy, 1943 god. T-23 (12–3)* [The Russian archives: The Great Patriotic War. The General Staff in the Great Patriotic War: Documents and materials, 1943, vol. 23 (12–3)] (Moscow: TERRA, 1999), 370. Hereafter cited as Zolotarev, *General Staff 1943*, with appropriate page(s). On the same day, the General Staff issued similar orders to the Western Front to destroy enemy aviation in the Mogilev, Bobruisk, and Bykhov regions with 120 fighters, 30 assault aircraft, and 30 bombers and the Central Front to destroy enemy aviation in the Dymer, Radomyshl', Fastov, Vasil'kov, and Kiev regions with 160 fighters, 80 assault aircraft, and 60 bombers. Similar orders went to the other *fronts* that were operating along the southwestern and southern axes.

46. "Doklad komanduiushchego voiskami Pribaltiiskogo fronta Verkhovnomu Glavnokomanduiushchemu plana pervogo etapa operatsii na Idritskom napravlenii" [Report No. 22 of the commander of the Baltic Front to the Supreme High Commander on the plan for the second stage of the operation along the Idritsa axis], in Zolotarev, *Stavka VGK 1943*, 320–321.

47. "Direktiva Stavki VGK No. 30224 komanduiushchemu voiskami Pribaltiiskogo fronta o zadachakh vtorogo etapa operatsii na Idritskom napravlenii" [*Stavka* VGK directive No. 30224 to the commander of the Baltic Front concerning the missions of the second stage of the operation along the Idritsa axis], in Zolotarev, *Stavka VGK 1943*, 222.

48. "Prikaz Stavki VGK No. 30228 o pereimenovanii Tsentral'nogo, Kalininskogo i Pribaltiiskogo frontov" [*Stavka* VGK order No. 30228 concerning the renaming of the Central, Kalinin, and Baltic Fronts], in Zolotarev, *Stavka VGK 1943*, 225.

49. See German Army Group North's intelligence maps for this period at "Der Feldzug gegen die Sowjet-Union der Heeresgruppe Nord, Kriegsjahr 1943," H. Gr. Nord 1943, 7584/2, in NAM T-311, roll 156. Hereafter cited as T-311, roll 156.

50. L. M. Sandalov, *Posle perelom* [After the turning point] (Moscow: Voenizdat, 1983), 8.

51. See German maps in NAM series T-313, roll 296.

52. "Zhurnal boevykh deistvii voisk 1-go Pribaltiiskogo fronta za oktiabr' 1943 g"

[The 1st Baltic Front's journal of combat operations for October 1943], *TsAMO*, f. 235, op. 2074, d. 51,1. 78.

Chapter 3. The Western Front's Orsha Offensives

1. A. A. Grechko et al., eds., *Istoriia Vtoroi Mirovoi voiny 1939–1945 v dvenadtsati tomakh, Tom sed'moi, Zavershenie korennogo perelom v voine* [History of World War II 1939–1945, vol. 7: The completion of a fundamental turning point in the war] (Moscow: Voenizdat, 1976), 273.

2. M. A. Gareev, "O neudachnykh nastupatel'nykh operatsiiakh Sovetskikh voisk v Velikoi Otechestvennoi voine. Po neopublikovannym dokumentam GKO" [Concerning unsuccessful offensive operations by Soviet forces in the Great Patriotic War; based on unpublished documents of the GKO], in *Novaia i noveishaia istoriia* [New and newest history] 1 (January 1994): 3–29; and M. A. Gareev, "Prichiny i uroki neudachnykh nastupatel'nykh operatsii Zapadnogo fronta zimoi 1943/44 goda" [The causes and lessons of the Western Front's unsuccessful offensive operations in the winter of 1943–1944]. *Voennaia mysl'* [Military thought] 2 (February 1994): 50–58.

3. "Direktiva Stavki No. 30193 komanduiushchemu voiskami Zapadnogo fronta, predstavitiliu Stavki na razgrom Smolenskoi gruppirovki protivnika" [Stavka VGK directive No. 30193 to the commander of the Western Front and the representative of the *Stavka* concerning the destruction of the enemy Smolensk grouping], in *Russkii arkhiv: Velikaia Otechestvennaia. Stavka Verkhovnogo Glavnokomandovannia: Dokumenty i materialy 1943 god, T 16 (5 (3)* [The Russian archives: The Great Patriotic War. The *Stavka* of the Supreme High Command: Documents and materials 1943, no. 16, 5 (3)], ed. V. A. Zolotarev (Moscow: TERRA, 1999), 205–206. Hereafter cited as Zolotarev, *Stavka VGK 1943*, with document title and page(s).

4. V. V. Abaturov et al., *Osvobozhdenie Belarusi 1943–1944* [The liberation of Belarus 1943–1944] (Minsk: Belaruskaia Navuka, 2014), 55.

5. Ibid., 55, citing *TsAMO RF*, f. 132a, op. 2642, d.34,1. 153.

6. "Direktiva Stavki VGK No. 30210 komanduiushchemu voiskami Zapadnogo fronta na razvitie nastupleniia s tsel'iu ovladeniia g. Vil'nius" [Stavka VGK directive No. 30210 to the commander of the Western Front on the development of an offensive to capture the city of Vilnius], in Zolotarev, *Stavka VGK 1943*, 215.

7. *TsAMO*, f. 48, op. 1691, d. 233,11. 3–5 and 30–31.

8. N. I. Krylov, N. I. Alekseev, I. G. Dragan, *Navstrechu pobede: Boevoi put' 5-i armii oktiabr' 1941–avgust 1945* [Greeting victory: The combat path of 5th Army, October 1941–August 1945] (Moscow: Nauka, 1970), 168.

9. See Kamen Nevenkin, *Fire Brigades: The Panzer Divisions, 1943–1945* (Winnipeg, MB: J. J. Fedorowicz, 2008), 434–438.

10. For brief accounts of 10th Guards Army's operation in October, see P. K. Altukhov et al., eds., *Nezabyvaemye dorogi: Boevoi put' 10-i gvardeiskoi armii* [Unforgettable roads: The combat path of the 10th Guards Army] (Moscow: Voenizdat, 1974), 73–75; and S. N. Portnov et al., eds., *Rizhskie gvardeiskie: Sbornik voennoistoricheskikh ocherkov* [Riga guards: A collection of military-historical essays] (Riga: Liesma, 1972), 52–53, 79–80, 133, 159–161. The latter contains brief descriptions of the operations of 22nd, 30th, 65th, and 85th Guards Rifle Divisions, all of which were made up of Latvians.

11. Abaturov et al., *Osvobozhdenie Belarusi*, 55.

12. Ibid., 56.

13. Ibid., 57.

14. Iu. Sukhinin, "K voprosu ob organizatsii i vedenii boia 1-i Pol'skoi pekhotnoi diviziei pod Lenino" [Concerning 1st Polish Infantry Division's organization and conduct of the battle at Lenino], *Voenno-istoricheskii zhurnal* [Military-historical journal] 4 (April 1983): 28. According to Sukhinin, 1st Polish Infantry Division numbered 12,144 men, 10,000 rifles, up to 250 guns and mortars, and a regiment of 39 tanks. It was organized into three infantry regiments of 2,700 men each, artillery and tank regiments, and a separate antitank battalion. The same article claimed that 42nd Rifle Division had 4,646 men, and 290th Rifle Division had 4,435 men. Like most Red Army line divisions at this time, rifle divisions were at 50 percent personnel strength and had 60–70 percent of their guns and mortars. After attachments, 1st Polish, 42nd, and 290th Rifle Divisions fielded 460, 316, and 434 guns and mortars, respectively.

15. Soviet sources are utterly silent about this complex regrouping process. German intelligence data, from which this account is derived, still maintained a remarkable ability to record these movements, if somewhat after the fact.

16. For details, see Sukhinin, "K voprosu ob organizatsii i vedenii boia 1-i Pol'skoi pekhotnoi diviziei pod Lenino," 32.

17. Gareev, "O neudachnykh nastupatel'nykh operatsiiakh," 17.

18. Abaturov et al., *Osvobozhdenie Belarusi*, 56–57.

19. Ibid., 57.

20. Ibid.

21. Ibid.

22. Ibid., 57–58.

23. Gareev, "O neudachnykh nastupatel'nykh operatsiiakh," 16.

24. Sukhinin, "K voprosu ob organizatsii i vedenii boia 1-i Pol'skoi pekhotnoi diviziei pod Lenino," 32.

25. Abaturov et al., *Osvobozhdenie Belarusi*, 58.

26. Ibid.

27. Grechko et al., *Istoriia Vtoroi Mirovoi voiny,* vol. 7, 273–274.

28. "Direktiva Stavki VGK No. 30225 komanduiushchemu voiskami Zapadnogo fronta i predstaviteliu Stavki na peregruppirovku voisk" [*Stavka* VGK directive No. 30225 to the commander of the Western Front and the representative of the *Stavka* on a regrouping of forces], in Zolotarev, *Stavka VGK 1943*, 223–224. The representative of the *Stavka* was the Red Army's chief artilleryman, N. N. Voronov.

29. "Direktiva Stavki VGK No. 30225 komanduiushchemu voiskami Zapadnogo fronta i predstaviteliu Stavki na peregruppirovku voisk" [*Stavka* VGK directive No. 30225 to the commander of the Western Front and the representative of the *Stavka* on a regrouping of forces], in Zolotarev, *Stavka VGK 1943*, 223–224. The representative of the *Stavka* was N. N. Voronov.

30. Altukhov et al., *Nezabyvaemye dorogi,* 75.

31. Portnov et al., *Rizhskie gvardeiskie,* 135.

32. Ibid., 160.

33. Krylov, *Navstrechu pobede,* 172.

34. Abaturov et al., *Osvobozhdenie Belarusi,* 58–59.

35. German records do not note the change from 68th to 5th Army's control until 30 November. In the interim, German records indicate that this sector was occupied by forces belonging to 68th, 21st, or 31st Armies.

36. Here and elsewhere, the actual Red Army order of battle reflects the contents of *Boevoi sostav Sovetskoi armii, Chast' III.*
37. Portnov, *Rizhskie gvardeiskie,* 160.
38. Abaturov et al., eds., *Osvobozhdenie Belarusi,* 59.
39. Ibid.
40. Ibid.
41. For details on 174th Rifle Division's operations, see Krylov, *Navstrechu pobede,* 172–173.
42. Abaturov et al., *Osvobozhdenie Belarusi,* 60.
43. Ibid.

Chapter 4. The Central Front's Gomel'-Rechitsa Offensive

1. A. A. Grechko et al., eds., *Istoriia Vtoroi Mirovoi voiny 1939–1945 v dvenadtsati tomakh, Tom sed'moi, Zavershenie korennogo perelom v voine* [History of World War II 1939–1945, vol. 7: The completion of a fundamental turning point in the war] (Moscow: Voenizdat, 1976), 275.
2. "Doklad komanduiushchego voiskami Brianskogo fronta No. 312 Verkhovnomu Glavnokomanduiushchemu plana operatsii na Zhlobinskom napravlenii" [Report No. 312 of the commander of the Briansk Front to the Supreme High Commander on a plan for an operation along the Zhlobin axis], in *Russkii arkhiv: Velikaia Otechestvennaia. Stavka Verkhovnogo Glavnokomandovannia: Dokumenty i materialy 1943 god, T 16 (5 (3)* [The Russian archives: The Great Patriotic [War]. The *Stavka* of the Supreme High Command: Documents and materials 1943, no. 16, 5 (3)], ed. V. A. Zolotarev (Moscow: TERRA, 1999), 309–310. Hereafter cited as Zolotarev, *Stavka VGK 1943,* with document title and page(s).
3. "Direktiva Stavki VGK No. 30208 komanduiushchemu voiskami Tsentral'nogo fronta na razgrom Zhlobinsko-Bobruiskoi gruppirovki protivnika i ovladenie Minskom" [*Stavka* VGK directive No. 30208 to the commander of the Central Front on the defeat of the enemy Zhlobin-Bobruisk grouping and the capture of Minsk], in Zolotarev, *Stavka VGK 1943,* 213.
4. "Direktiva Stavki VGK No. 30209 komanduiushchemu voiskami Brianskogo fronta ob uprazdenii Brianskogo i obrazovanii Pribaltiiskogo fronta" [*Stavka* VGK directive No. 30209 to the commander of the Briansk Front concerning the abolition of the Briansk and formation of the Baltic Front], in Zolotarev, *Stavka VGK 1943,* 214.
5. "Komanduiushchim 11-i armiei, voiskami 2-go Pribaltiiskogo fronta i Belorusskogo frontov o perepodchinenii armii" [To the commanders of 11th Army, 2nd Baltic, and Belorussian Front concerning the resubordination of the army], in A. M. Zolotarev, ed., *Russkii arkhiv: Velikaia Otechestvennaia. General'nyi shtab v gody Velikoi Otechestvennoi voiny: Dokumenty i materialy, 1943 god. T-23 (12–3)* [The Russian archives: The Great Patriotic [War]. The General Staff in the Great Patriotic War: Documents and materials, 1943, vol. 23 (12–3)] (Moscow: TERRA, 1999), 385. Hereafter cited as Zolotarev, *General Staff 1943,* with appropriate page(s).
6. Kamen Nevenkin, *Fire Brigades: The Panzer Divisions, 1943–1945* (Winnipeg, MB: J. J. Fedorowicz, 2008), 160.
7. For details on the strategic regrouping and planning and subsequent combat, see K. Rokossovsky, *A Soldier's Duty* (Moscow: Progress, 1985), 216–221; and K. F. Telegin, *Voiny neschitannye versty* [Wars of uncountable versts] (Moscow: Voeniz-

dat, 1988), 249–262. Telegin served as the "member" (commissar) of the Central Front's Military Council.

8. For details about 50th and 3rd Armies' roles in these operations, see F. D. Pankov, *Ognennye rubezhi: Boevoi put' 50-i armii v Velikoi Otechestvennoi voine* [Firing lines: The combat path of 50th Army in the Great Patriotic War] (Moscow: Voenizdat, 1984), 167; and A. V. Gorbatov, *Gody i voiny* [Years and wars] (Moscow: Voenizdat, 1980), 228–236. For an even more detailed and surprisingly candid account of 3rd Army's operations, written during the period of the Khrushchev "thaw," see, A. V. Gorbatov and M. Ivashechkin, "Nastuplenie 3-i armii severnee Gomelia" [The 3rd Army's offensive north of Gomel'], *Voenno-istoricheskii zhurnal* [Military-historical journal] 8 (August 1962): 30–43. Hereafter cited as *VIZh*, with appropriate title, number, and page(s).

9. For a brief description of 63rd Army's operations, see V. A. Beliavsky, *Strely skrestilis' na Shpree* [Shells crisscross on the Shpree] (Moscow: Voenizdat, 1972), 126–127.

10. One of the few existing accounts of 48th Army's operations is found in K. K. Shilov, *Rechitskaia krasnoznamennaia* [Rechitsa Red Banner] (Moscow: Voenizdat, 1984), 93–95. This is a history of 194th Rifle Division.

11. Among the many accounts of 65th Army's operations are P. I. Batov, *V pokhodakh i boiakh* [On the march and in battle] (Moscow: Voenizdat, 1984), 311–357; I. N. Pavlov, *Ot Moskvy do Shtral'zunda (Boevoi put' 354 i strelkovoi Kalinkovichskoi ordena Lenina, Krasoznamennoi, ordena Suvorova divizii)* [From Moscow to Straslund (The combat path of the Kalinkovichi, Orders of Lenin, Red Banner, and Order of Suvorov 354th Rifle Division)] (Moscow: Voenizdat, 1985), 67–85 (a history of 354th Rifle Division); *Pomnit Dnepr-reka* [Remember the Dnepr River] (Minsk: Belarus, 1986), 42–53 (a history of 193rd Rifle Division; and A. A. Andreev, *Po voennym dorogam: Boevoi put' 69-i strelkovoi Sevskoi dvazhdy krasnoznamennoi ordenov Suvurova i Kutuzova divizii* [Along military roads: The combat path of 69th Sevsk, twice Red Banner Orders of Suvorov and Kutuzov Rifle Division] (Moscow: Voenizdat, 1971), 123–124 (a history of 169th Rifle Division).

12. The only detailed accounts of 61st Army's operations are found in D. K. Mal'kov, *Skvoz' dym i plania* [Through the smoke and flames] (Moscow: Voenizdat, 1970), 80–108 (a superbly detailed history of 12th Guards Rifle Division); and M. I. Piskovitin et al., *Gvardeiskaia Chernigovskaia* [The guards Chernigov] (Moscow: Voenizdat, 1976), 150–161 (a thorough history of 76th Guards Rifle Division).

13. For details on the 1 October assault, see "Forsirovanie p. Dnepr voiskami 65-i armii" [The forcing of the Dnepr River by 65th Army's forces], in *Sbornik materialov po izucheniiu opyta voiny*, No. 12, *mai-iun' 1944* [A Collection of materials for the study of war experience, No. 12, May–June 1944] (Moscow: Voenizdat, 1944), 97–100. Classified secret but later declassified.

14. "Zhurnal boevykh deistvii voisk Tsentral'nogo/Belorusskogo fronta za oktiabr' 1943 g" [The Belorussian Front's journal of combat operations for October 1943], *TsAMO*, f. 201, op. 390, ed. khr. 62/1,1. 2.

15. V. V. Abaturov et al., eds., *Osvobozhdenie Belarusi, 1943–1944* [The liberation of Belarus 1943–1944] (Minsk: Belaruskaia Navuka, 2014), 73.

16. For details on 1st Guards Tank Corps' organization and role in this offensive, see M. F. Panov, *Na napravlenii glavnovo udara* [On the axis of the main attack] (Moscow: n.p., 1995), 74–89.

17. For details on the Soviet use of *maskirovka* (deception) to conceal this regrouping, see David M. Glantz, *Soviet Military Deception in the Second World War* (London: Frank Cass, 1989), 247–259.

18. Gorbatov and Ivashechkin, "Nastuplenie 3-i armii," 32.

19. "Nastupatel'nye operatsii s forsirovaniem rek" [Offensive operation with the forcing of rivers], in *Sbornik materialov po izucheniiu opyta voiny*, No. 12. *Mai-iiun' 1944 g.* [Collection of materials for the study of war experiences, No. 12. May–June 1944] (Moscow: Voenizdat, 1944), 102–104. Classified secret but later declassified. The 27th Rifle Corps attacked in the sector from Suslovka to Lake Sviatoe with 106th and 193rd Rifle Divisions, and 18th Rifle Corps did the same from the Lake Sviatoe and Radul' sector with 149th and 69th Rifle Divisions, both at 0630 hours after the artillery preparation. Masked by smoke, six advanced battalions of 250–600 men, probably with several penal companies, each secured bridgeheads on the river's western bank. For additional details, see Abaturov et al., *Osvobozhdenie Belarusi*, 73–75.

20. Mal'kov, *Skvoz' dym i plamia*, 104–107; and Piskovitin et al., *Gvardeiskaia chernigovskaia*, 159–160.

21. Nevenkin, *Fire Brigades*, 100, 112.

22. Abaturov et al., *Osvobozhdenie Belarusi*, 75.

23. Earl F. Ziemke, *Stalingrad to Berlin: The German Defeat in the East* (Washington, DC: Office of the Chief of Military History U.S. Army, 1968), 192.

24. Rokossovsky, *A Soldier's Duty*, 221.

25. Telegin, *Voiny neschitanye versty*, 258–259.

26. Ziemke, *Stalingrad to Berlin*, 192.

27. Most Soviet sources do not mention the operations that took place from 20 to 30 October. The only exceptions are Mal'kov, *Skvoz' dym i plamia*, 110; and Piskovitin et al., *Gvardeiskaia chernogovskaia*, 161–163, which cover 12th and 76th Guards Rifle Divisions' operations, and the histories of 2nd and 7th Guards Cavalry Corps (see below). However, the records of German Second Army accurately record the action in "Anl. Bd. 102. A.O.K. 2, Ia, Oct-Nov 1943" AOK 2, 41181/102, NAM T-312, roll 1266, from which the maps in this sector are taken.

28. A. N. Sekretov, *Gvardeiskaia postup' (Boevoi put' 17-i Mozyrskoi krasnoznamennoi ordenov Lenina, Suvorova i Kutuzova kavaleriiskoi divizii podshefnoi Tadzhikistanu, v gody Velikoi Otechestvennoi voiny, 1941–1945 gg.)* [Guards gait (The combat path of 17th Mozyr' Red Banner and Orders of Lenin, Suvorov, and Kutuzov Cavalry Division, raised in Tadzhikistan during the Great Patriotic War, 1941–1945)] (Dushanbe: Donish, 1985), 71.

29. M. S. Dokuchaev, *V boi shli eskadrony: Boevoi put' 7-go gvardeiskogo kavaleriiskogo Brandenburgskogo ordena Lenina, Krasnoznamennogo, ordena Suvorova korpusa v Velikoi Otechestvennoi voine* [The squadrons went into battles: The combat path of 7th Guards Brandenburg, Order of Lenin, Red Banner, and Order of Suvorov Guards Cavalry Corps in the Great Patriotic War] (Moscow: Voenizdat, 1984), 86–88.

30. A. V. Gorbatov and M. Ivashechkin, "Nastuplenie 3-i armii," 34–35.

31. "Direktiva Stavki VGK No. 30231 komanduiushchemu voiskami Belorusskogo fronta o perepodchinenii i peregruppirovke 11-i i 48-i armii" [*Stavka* VGK directive No. 30231 to the commander of the Belorussian Front concerning the resubordination and regrouping of 11th and 48th Armies], in Zolotarev, *Stavka VGK 1943*, 227.

Chapter 5. The 1st and 2nd Baltic Fronts' Polotsk-Vitebsk and Pustoshka-Idritsa Offensives

1. A. A. Grechko et al., eds., *Istoriia Vtoroi Mirovoi voiny 1939–1945 v dvenadtsati tomakh, Tom sed'moi, Zavershenie korennogo perelom v voine* [History of World War II 1939–1945, vol. 7: The completion of a fundamental turning point in the war] (Moscow: Voenizdat, 1976), 273.
2. "Zhurnal boevykh deistvii voisk 1-og Pribaltiiskogo fronta za noiabr' 1943 g." [The 1st Baltic Front's journal of combat operations for November 1943], *TsAMO*, f. 235, op. 2074, ed. khr. 52,1. 2.
3. K. N. Galitsky, *Gody surovykh ispitanii 1941–1944* [Years of a harsh education 1941–1944] (Moscow: Nauka, 1970), 344.
4. "Prikazy i direktivy 1-go Pribaltiiskogo fronta za 1943 g" [Orders and directives of the 1st Baltic Front for 1943], *TsAMO*, f. 235, op. 2074, ed. khr. 9,11. 93–97.
5. Ibid.
6. Earl F. Ziemke, *Stalingrad to Berlin: The German Defeat in the East* (Washington, DC: Office of the Chief of Military History U.S. Army, 1968), 203.
7. For details on this plan, see David M. Glantz, *A History of Soviet Airborne Forces* (London: Frank Cass, 1994), 290–298.
8. Ziemke, *Stalingrad to Berlin*, 204–205.
9. A. P. Beloborodov, *Vsegda v boiu* [Always in battle] (Moscow: Voenizdat, 1978), 256–257.
10. Ibid., 257.
11. Ibid.
12. Ziemke, *Stalingrad to Berlin*, 204.
13. Kamen Nevenkin, *Fire Brigades: The Panzer Divisions, 1943–1945* (Winnipeg, MB: J. J. Fedorowicz, 2008), 475.
14. Ibid., 257–258.
15. "Direktiva Stavki VGK No. 30243 komanduiushchemu voiskami 1-go Pribaltiiskogo fronta, predstaviteliu Stavki na razgrom Vitebskoi gruppirovki protivnika" [*Stavka* VGK directive No. 30240 to the commanders of the 1st and 2nd Baltic Fronts and the representative of the *Stavka* about the resubordination of formations and measures for clearing the enemy from between the lakes], in *Russkii arkhiv: Velikaia Otechestvennaia. Stavka Verkhovnogo Glavnokomandovannia: Dokumenty i materialy 1943 god, T 16 (5 (3)* [The Russian archives: The Great Patriotic War. The *Stavka* of the Supreme High Command: Documents and materials 1943, no. 16, 5 (3)], ed. V. A. Zolotarev (Moscow: TERRA, 1999), 234. Hereafter cited as Zolotarev, *Stavka VGK 1943*, with document title and page(s).
16. "Direktiva Stavki VGK No. 30246 komanduiushchemu voiskami 1-go Pribaltiiskogo fronta o sluchaiakh predstavleniia v Stavku neproverennykh svedenii o protivnike" [*Stavka* VGK directive No. 30246 to the commander of the 1st Baltic Front concerning instances of the presentation of unverified information about the enemy to the *Stavka*], in Zolotarev, *Stavka VGK 1943*, 235.
17. According to Il'ia Moshchansky, "Osvobozhdenie Belorussii: Boevye deistviia Kalininskogo, Zapadnogo i Belorusskogo frontov 26 sentiabr 1943–5 aprelia 1944, Nachalo" [The liberation of Belorussia: The combat actions of the Kalinin, Western, and Belorussian Fronts 26 September 1943–5 April 1944, The beginning], in *Voen-*

naia letopis' [Military chronicle] 2–2006 (Moscow: OOO BTV-MH, 2006), 12, as of 13 November, 5th Tank Corps fielded 203 T-34/76 medium tanks distributed as follows: 24th Tank Brigade—64; 41st Tank Brigade—61; 70th Tank Brigade—63; 92nd Separate Motorcycle Battalion—10; and 704th Separate Signal Battalion—5. In addition, the corps included 5th Motorized Rifle Brigade, 731st Tank Destroyer Regiment, 1708th Antiaircraft Artillery Regiment, 1546th Heavy Self-propelled Artillery Regiment with 1 KV tank and 12 SU-152 SP guns; 161st Separate Self-propelled Artillery Regiment with 1 T-34/76 tank and 15 SU-85 SP guns, 1515th Light Self-Propelled Artillery Regiment with 11 SU-76 SP guns for a total of 205 tanks and 38 self-propelled guns.

18. See ibid., 12–14. Sakhno's tank corps attacked in two echelons at 1300 hours on 16 November, after a fifteen-minute mortar raid, with 24th and 42nd Tank Brigades, two battalions of 5th Motorized Rifle Brigade, the two self-propelled [SP] artillery regiments, and the motorcycle regiment in first echelon and 70th Tank Brigade, one SP regiment and a motorcycle battalion in second. Only about one-third of the corps' more than 200 tanks took part in the assault. The attackers struck German 113th Infantry Division's defenses in a 5-kilometer-wide sector stretching from the village of Kroshki southwestward to the village of Bol'shie Suravni, 20–25 kilometers west-northwest of Gorodok. This sector was defended by 731st and 213th Construction Battalions, attached to 113th Infantry Division, as well as the infantry division's reconnaissance battalion (less one company). Although the struggle was an uneven one, the two battalions of 5th Motorized Rifle Brigade attacking Bol'shie Suravni suffered 40 percent personnel losses. Reportedly, the two German construction battalions lost 120 men.

19. Ibid., 14. The 1st and 2nd Battalions of 5th Motorized Rifle Brigade were reportedly out of ammunition when they reached the outskirts of Gorodok.

20. Ibid. Third Panzer Army reportedly dispatched 20th Panzer Division, 129th Infantry Division's 427th Regiment, an assault gun battalion, 4th Railroad Detachment, two construction battalions, and tank destroyer subunits to defend Gorodok and did so "without delay."

21. Ibid.

22. Ziemke, *Stalingrad to Berlin,* 205–206.

23. "Prikaz Stavki VGK No. 00151 o smene komanduiushchikh voiskami 1-go Pribaltiiskogo fronta i 11-i gvardeiskoi armii" [*Stavka* order No. 00151 concerning the relief of the commanders of the 1st Baltic Front and 11th Guards Army], in Zolotarev, *Stavka VGK 1943,* 238.

24. "Direktiva Stavki VGK No. 30247 komanduiushchemu voiskami 1-go Pribaltiiskogo fronta, predstaviteliu Stavki na razgrom Vitebskoi gruppirovki protivnika" [*Stavka* VGK directive No. 30247 to the commander of the 1st Baltic Front and the representative of the *Stavka* on the defeat of the enemy Vitebsk grouping], in Zolotarev, *Stavka VGK 1943,* 238–239. The *Stavka* representative was N. N. Voronov.

25. "Direktiva Stavki VGK No. 30248 komanduiushchim voiskami 1-go i 2-go Pribaltiiskikh frontov, predstaviteliu Stavki na perepodchinenie chasti voisk" [*Stavka* VGK directive No. 30248 to the commanders of the 1st and 2nd Baltic Fronts and the representative of the *Stavka* on the resubordination of force units], in Zolotarev, *Stavka VGK 1943,* 239.

26. M. G. Grigorenko et al., eds., *Skvoz' ognennye vikhri: Boevoi put 11-i gvardeiskoi armii v Velikoi Otechestvennoi voiny 1941–1945* [Through fiery whirlwinds: The

combat path of 11th Guards Army in the Great Patriotic War 1941–1945] (Moscow: Voenizdat, 1987), 152–153.

27. "Direktiva Stavki VGK No. 30249 komanduiushchemu voiskami 1-go Pribaltiiskogo fronta, predstaviteliu Stavki o srokakh osvobozhdeniia Gorodka" [*Stavka* directive No. 30249 to the commander of the 1st Baltic Front and the representative of the *Stavka* concerning the period of the liberation of Gorodok], in Zolotarev, *Stavka VGK 1943*, 239. The representative of the *Stavka* was N. N. Voronov.

28. "Direktiva Stavki VGK No. 30251 komanduiushchemu voiskami 1-go Pribaltiiskogo fronta, predstaviteliu Stavki ob organizatsii vzaimodeistviia 11-i gvardeiskoi i 4-i udarnoi armii pri osvobozhdenii Gorodka" [*Stavka* VGK directive No. 30251 to the commander of the 1st Baltic Front and the representative of the *Stavka* concerning the organization of cooperation between 11th Guards and 4th Shock Armies in the liberation of Gorodok], in Zolotarev, *Stavka VGK 1943*, 240.

29. "Direktiva Stavki VGK No. 30252 komanduiushchim voiskami 1-go Pribaltiiskogo i Zapadnogo frontov, predstaviteliu Stavki o razgranlinii mezhdu frontami" [*Stavka* VGK directive No. 30252 to the commanders of the 1st Baltic and Western Fronts and the representative of the *Stavka* concerning the boundary line between the *fronts*], in Zolotarev, *Stavka VGK 1943*, 241.

30. "Zhurnal boevykh deistvii voisk 1-og Pribaltiiskogo fronta za noiabr' 1943 g." [The 1st Baltic Front's journal of combat operations for November 1943], TsAMO, f. 235, op. 2074, ed. khr. 52,1. 34.

31. For a detailed explanation regarding how and why the *Stavka* permitted further offensive operations to be delayed until early December, see Galitsky, *Gody surovykh ispytanii*, 356–374.

32. Ibid., 374.

33. The 18th Panzer had been disbanded on 7 September, with its remnants incorporated into 25th Panzer Grenadier Division's XXVII Army Corps. The small *kampfgruppe* employed in November was dispatched by 25th Panzer Grenadier and numbered several hundred men. See Nevenkin, *Fire Brigades*, 434.

34. Galitsky, *Gody surovykh ispytanii*, 346–347.

35. The many Soviet accounts of 3rd Shock Army's operations studiously avoid providing any details of the fighting during the first week of the offensive and the forces that fought in the operation. Instead they include only generalities about the course of combat. Therefore, the details in this section are reconstructed from German accounts and intelligence data, particularly information from the National Archives Microfilm series (NAM) T-311, roll 156.

36. F. Ia. Lisitsyn, *V te groznye gody* [In those threatening years] (Moscow: Voenizdat, 1985), 133.

37. Galitsky, *Gody surovykh ispytanii*, 347.

38. Ziemke, *Stalingrad to Berlin*, 204.

39. I. M. Chistiakov, *Sluzhim otchizne* [We served our homeland] (Moscow: Voenizdat, 1975), 202.

40. Ibid.

41. V. F. Egorov et al., eds., *Rozhdennaia v boiakh: Boevoi put' 71-i gvardeiskoi strelkovoi Vitebskoi ordena Lenina, Krasnoznamennoi divizii* [Born in battle: The combat path of 71st Guards Vitebsk Order of Lenin, Red Banner Rifle Division] (Moscow: Voenizdat, 1986), 130.

42. Galitsky, *Gody surovykh ispytanii*, 347–349, 352.
43. L. M. Sandalov, *Posle perelom* [After the turning point] (Moscow: Voenizdat, 1983), 9–10.
44. Ziemke, *Stalingrad to Berlin*, 204.
45. "Direktiva Stavki VGK No. 30240 komanduiushchemu voiskami 1-go i 2-go Pribaltiiskikh frontov, predstaviteliu Stavki o perepodchinenii soedinenii i merakh po osvobodozhdeniiu ot protivnika mezhozer'ia" [*Stavka* VGK directive No. 30240 to the commanders of the 1st and 2nd Baltic Fronts and the representative of the *Stavka* about the resubordination of formations and measures for clearing the enemy from between the lakes], in Zolotarev, *Stavka VGK 1943*, 232. The *Stavka* representative was N. N. Voronov.
46. "Direktiva Stavki VGK No. 30244 komanduiushchemu voiskami 2-go Pribaltiiskogo fronta na priostanovku nastupleniia i peredachu chast sil 1-mu Pribaltiiskomu frontu" [*Stavka* VGK directive No. 30244 to the commander of the 2nd Baltic Front on halting the offensive and transferring forces to the 1st Baltic Front], in Zolotarev, *Stavka VGK 1943*, 235.
47. Sandalov, *Posle perelom*, 10–11.
48. "Direktiva Stavki VGK No. 46200 komanduiushchim voiskami Severo-zapadnogo i 2-go Pribaltiiskogo frontov ob uprazdenii Severo-zapadnogo fronta" [*Stavka* directive No. 46200 to the commanders of the Northwestern and 2nd Baltic Fronts concerning the abolition of the Northwestern Front], in Zolotarev, *Stavka VGK 1943*, 236–237.

Chapter 6. The Western Front's Orsha Offensives

1. V. V. Abaturov et al., eds., *Osvobozhdenie Belarusi: 1943–1944* [The liberation of Belarus 1943–1944] (Minsk: Belaruskaia Navuka, 2014), 60.
2. N. M. Afanas'ev, N. K. Glazunov, P. A. Kazansky, and N. A. Fironov, *Dorogami ispytanii i pobed: boevoi put' 31-i armii* [Along the roads of ordeals and victories: The combat path of 31st Army] (Moscow: Voenizdat, 1986), 125.
3. See M. A. Gareev, "O neudachnykh nastupatel'nykh operatsiiakh Sovetskikh voisk v Velikoi Otechestvennoi voine. Po neopublikovannym dokumentam GKO" [Concerning unsuccessful offensive operations by Soviet forces in the Great Patriotic War; based on unpublished documents of the GKO], in *Novaia i noveishaia istoriia* [New and newest history] 1 (January 1994): 18. Abaturov et al., *Osvobozhdenie Belarusi*, 61, disagrees slightly by asserting that the attacking force included 34 rifle divisions, up to 4,500 guns and mortars, more than 200 tanks, and up to 600 aircraft.
4. Gareev, "*O neudachnykh nastupatel'nykh operatsiiakh*," 18. The German dispositions are taken from German Fourth Army's operational maps found in "Ia, Kartenband zum KTB Nr. 21, Nov.–Dec. 1943," *AOK 4, 49111/55*, in NAM T-312, roll 226; and "Ic, Taetigkeitsbericht, Nov.–Dec. 1943," *AOK 4, 48448/5*, in NAM T-312, roll 1362.
5. P. K. Altukhov et al., eds., *Nezabyvaemye dorogi: Boevoi put' 10-i gvardeiskoi armii* [Unforgettable roads: The combat path of the 10th Guards Army] (Moscow: Voenizdat, 1974), 77–79. The strength of 10th Guards Army at the time of its transfer to the 2nd Baltic Front was 43,250 men, 1,700 vehicles, 6,500 horses, and a large quantity of cargo carts.

6. S. N. Portnov et al., eds., *Rizhskie gvardeiskie: Sbornik voenno-istoricheskikh ocherkov* [Riga guards: A collection of military-historical essays] (Riga: Liesma, 1972), 79–80.

7. Ibid., 135–136.

8. Ibid., 161.

9. Abaturov et al., *Osvobozhdenie Belarusi*, 62.

10. Gareev, "O neudachnykh nastupatel'nykh operatsiiakh," 16.

11. Abaturov et al., *Osvobozhdenie Belarusi*, 61.

12. N. I. Krylov, N. I. Alekseev, I. G. Dragan, *Navstrechu pobeda: Boevoi put' 5-i armii oktiabr' 1941–avgust 1945* [Greeting victory: The combat path of 5th Army, October 1941–August 1945] (Moscow: Nauka, 1970), 174.

13. Portnov et al., *Rizhskie gvardeiskie*, 161.

14. Gareev, "O neudachnykh nastupatel'nykh operatsiiakh," 18. The German dispositions are taken from German Fourth Army's operational maps.

15. Ibid., 16.

16. Abaturov et al., *Osvobozhdenie Belarusi*, 63.

17. Ibid., 64.

Chapter 7. The Belorussian Front's Gomel'-Rechitsa and Novyi Bykhov–Propoisk Offensives

1. A. A. Grechko et al., eds., *Istoriia Vtoroi Mirovoi voiny 1939–1945 v dvenadtsati tomakh, Tom sed'moi, Zavershenie korennogo perelom v voine* [History of World War II 1939–1945, vol. 7: The completion of a fundamental turning point in the war] (Moscow: Voenizdat, 1976), 275–276.

2. "Gomel'sko-Rechitskaia operatsiia 1943" [The Gomel'-Rechitsa operation of 1943], in *Voennaia entsiklopediia v vos'mi tomakh, t. 2*, ed. P. S. Grachev et al. [Military encyclopedia, vol. 2] (Moscow: Voenizdat, 1994), 451.

3. "Zhurnal boevykh deistvii voisk Tsentral'nogo/Belorusskogo fronta za noiabr' 1943 g" [The Central/Belorussian Front's journal of combat operations for November 1943], *TsAMO*, f. 201, op. 390, ed. khr. 62/9,1. 36. According to V. V. Abaturov et al., eds. *Osvobozhdenie Belarusi: 1943–1944* [The liberation of Belarus 1943–1944] (Minsk: Belaruskaia Navuka, 2014), 75, on 10 November, the overall strength of Rokossovsky's *front* stood at 719,000 men, 7,560 guns and mortars, 247 tanks and SP guns, and 526 combat aircraft. This confirms a tooth [combat] to tail [rear area support] ratio of roughly 1 to 2. These forces supposedly opposed 660,000 German troops, with 3,600 guns and mortars, 310 tanks and assault guns, and up to 400 combat aircraft, although these figures are clearly vastly inflated.

4. "Kräftegegenüberstellung, Stand: 14.10.43," *Abt. Fremde Heere Ost, Nr. 81/43*. This is a chart from the records of German Foreign Armies East.

5. According to Kamen Nevenkin, *Fire Brigades: The Panzer Divisions, 1943–1945* (Winnipeg, MB: J. J. Fedorowicz, 2008), 112–113 and 326–327, on 10 November, 2nd Panzer Division fielded twenty-six tanks and nine assault guns, and 12th Panzer Division fielded forty-six tanks and seven assault guns, either operable or in short-term repair, for a total of eighty-eight machines.

6. The 50th Army consisted of seven rifle divisions (46th Rifle Corps' 238th, 369th,

380th, plus 413th, and 108th, 110th, and 324th Rifle Divisions), and 233rd Separate Tank Regiment.

7. The 3rd Army consisted of 41st Rifle Corps (120th Guards and 17th and 186th Rifle Divisions), 80th Rifle Corps (121st Guards, and 283rd and 362nd Rifle Divisions), 269th Rifle Division, 36th Separate Tank Regiment, and 1538th Self-propelled Artillery Regiment.

8. The 63rd Army consisted of 35th Rifle Corps (5th, 250th, and 287th Rifle Divisions), 40th Rifle Corps (129th, 169th, and 348th Rifle Divisions), plus 41st and 397th Rifle Divisions, 26th Guards Separate Tank Regiment, and 1901st Self-propelled Artillery Regiment.

9. For details on 69th Rifle Division's operations, see A. A. Andreev, *Po voennym dorogam: Boevoi put' 69-i strelkovoi Sevskoi dvazhdy krasnoznamennoi ordenov Suvurova i Kutuzova divizii* [Along military roads: The combat path of 69th Sevsk, twice Red Banner Orders of Suvorov and Kutuzov Rifle Division] (Moscow: Voenizdat, 1971), 124–131.

10. For details on 2nd Guards Cavalry Corps' operations, see A. N. Sekretov, *Gvardeiskaia postup' (Boevoi put' 17-i Mozyrskoi krasnoznamennoi ordenov Lenina, Suvorova i Kutuzova kavaleriiskoi divizii podshefnoi Tadzhikistanu, v gody Velikoi Otechestvennoi voiny, 1941–1945 gg.)* [Guards gait (The combat path of 17th Mozyr' Red Banner and Orders of Lenin, Suvorov, and Kutuzov Cavalry Division, raised in Tadzhikistan during the Great Patriotic War, 1941–1945)] (Dushanbe: Donish, 1985), 71–77.

11. For details on 354th Rifle Division's operations, see I. N. Pavlov, *Ot Moskvy do Shtral'zunda (Boevoi put' 354 i strelkovoi Kalinkovichskoi ordena Lenina, Krasoznamennoi, ordena Suvorova divizii)* [From Moscow to Straslund (The combat path of the Kalinkovichi, Orders of Lenin, Red Banner, and Order of Suvorov 354th Rifle Division)] (Moscow: Voenizdat, 1985), 76–77.

12. Dokuchaev, *V boi shli eskadrony: Boevoi put' 7-go gvardeiskogo kavaleriiskogo Brandenburgskogo ordena Lenina, Krasnoznamennogo, ordena Suvorova korpusa v Velikoi Otechestvennoi voine* [The squadrons went into battles: The combat path of 7th Guards Brandenburg, Order of Lenin, Red Banner, and Order of Suvorov Guards Cavalry Corps in the Great Patriotic War] (Moscow: Voenizdat, 1984), 88.

13. P. I. Batov, *V pokhodakh i boiakh* [In marches and battles] (Moscow: DOSAAF, 1984), 359.

14. Nevenkin, *Fire Brigades*, 159–161.

15. Dokuchaev, *V boi shli eskadrony*, 90.

16. Ibid.

17. Batov, *V pokhodakh i boiakh*, 362.

18. S. P. Zubarev, *Ot Dona do El'by* [From the Don to the Elbe] (Udmurtia: n.p., 1975), 83. This book is a history of 172nd Rifle Division.

19. See Nevenkin, *Fire Brigades*, 168, 181–183. The division's 31st Panzer Regiment remained in the Kalinkovichi region to be reequipped with more than 70 Pz. V model tanks but was diverted to the Ukraine on 1 December, where it was attached to 11th Panzer Division during the fighting for the Kirovograd region. For 5th Panzer's vital role in this fighting, see Anton Detlev von Plato, *Die Geschichte Der 5. Panzerdivision 1938 bis 1945* (Regensburg: Walhalla u. Praetoria Verlag, 1978), 302–308.

20. Earl F. Ziemke, *Stalingrad to Berlin: The German Defeat in the East* (Washington, DC: Office of the Chief of Military History U.S. Army, 1968), 193–194.

21. Ibid., 195.

22. F. G. Bulatov, *Budni frontovykh let* [Workdays in years at the front] (Kazan': Tartarskoe Knizhnoe izdatel'stvo, 1984), 104. See this account for details of the subsequent offensive.

23. Sekretov, *Gvardeiskaia postup'*, 76–78.

24. Pavlov, *Ot Moskvy do Shtral'zunda*, 76–77.

25. N. V. Kuprianov, *S veroi v pobedu: Boevoi put' 38-i gvardeiskoi strelkovoi Lozovaia Krasnoznamennoi divizii* [With faith in victory: The combat path of 38th Guards Lozovaia Red Banner Rifle Division] (Moscow: Voenizdat, 1985), 73.

26. Ibid., 75–78 provides details about the fighting for Shatsilki.

27. A. V. Gorbatov and M. Ivashevhkin, "Nastuplenie 3-i armii severnee Gomelia" [The 3rd Army's offensive north of Gomel'], *Voenno-istoricheskii zhurnal* [Military-historical journal] 8 (August 1962): 35. Hereafter cited as *VIZh*, with appropriate title, number, and page(s).

28. Ibid., 38. According to Gorbatov, his rifle divisions averaged about 4,500 men each, with 5,000 men each in 283rd and 17th Rifle Divisions.

29. Ibid., 40.

30. F. D. Pankov, *Ognennye rubezhi: Boevoi put' 50-i armii v Velikoi Otechestvennoi voine* [Firing lines: The combat path of 50th Army in the Great Patriotic War] (Moscow: Voenizdat, 1984), 167–168.

31. V. P. Kachur and V. V. Nikol'sky, *Pod znamenem Sivashtsev: Boevoi put' 169-i strelkovoi Rogachevskoi Krasnoznamennoi ordenov Suvorova II stepeni i Kutuzova II stepeni divizii (1941–1945)* [Under the banner of the men of Sivash': The combat path of 169th Rogachev, Red Banner, Orders of Suvorov II degree and Kutuzov II degree Rifle Division (1941–1945)] (Moscow: Voenizdat, 1989), 117.

32. Gorbatov and Ivashevhkin, "Nastuplenie 3-i armii severnee Gomelia," 41.

33. G. F. Krivosheev, ed., *Velikaia Otechestvennaia bez grifa sekretnosti. Kniga poter'* [The Great Patriotic War without secret classification: A book of losses] (Moscow: Veche, 2009), 182. Krivosheev places the Belorussian Front's total personnel strength at 761,000 men.

Chapter 8. The 1st Baltic and Western Fronts' Vitebsk (Gorodok) Offensive

1. "Gorodokskaia operatsiia 1943" [The Gorodok operation 1943], in A. A. Grechko et al., eds., *Sovetskaia voennaia entsiklopediia, T. 2* [Soviet military encyclopedia, vol. 2] (Moscow: Voenizdat, 1976), 613.

2. "Gorodokskaia operatsiia 1943" [The Gorodok operation 1943], in P. S. Grachev et al., eds., *Voennaia entsiklopediia v vos'mi tomakh, T. 2* [Military encyclopedia, vol. 2] (Moscow: Voenizdat, 1994), 462. The 11th Guards Army was also supported by 10th Guards Tank Brigade, equipped with forty-six medium and light tanks, and 2nd Guards Heavy Tank Regiment, which fielded seventeen KV heavy tanks.

3. "Direktiva Stavki VGK No. 30255 komanduiushchim voiskami 1-go Pribaltiiskogo i Zapadnogo frontov, predstaviteliu Stavki na perepodchinenie trekh strelkovykh divizii" [*Stavka* VGK directive No. 30255 to the commanders of the 1st Baltic and

the Western Fronts and the representative of the *Stavka* on the resubordination of three rifle divisions], in *Russkii arkhiv: Velikaia Otechestvennaiavoina. Stavka Verkhovnogo Glavnokomandovannia: Dokumenty i materialy 1943 god, T 16 (5 (3)* [The Russian archives: The Great Patriotic War. The *Stavka* of the Supreme High Command: Documents and materials 1943, no. 16, 5 (3)], ed. V. A. Zolotarev (Moscow: TERRA, 1999), 242. Hereafter cited as Zolotarev, *Stavka VGK 1943*, with document title and page(s).

4. "Direktiva Stavki VGK No. 30256 komanduiushchemu voiskami Zapadnogo fronta, predstaviteliu Stavki na perenos napravleniia glavnogo udara" [*Stavka* VGK directive No. 30256 to the commander of the Western Front and the representative of the *Stavka* on shifting the direction of the main attack], in Zolotarev, *Stavka VGK 1943*, 242. The *Stavka* representative was N. N. Voronov.

5. F. Sverdlov, "Podgotovka i vedenie Gorodokskoi operatsii" [The preparation and conduct of the Gorodok operation], *Voenno-istoricheskii zhurnal* [Military-historical journal] 3 (March 1976): 23. Hereafter cited as *VIZh*, with appropriate title, number, and page(s). The 1st Tank Corps' strength figure included thirty-five tanks in disrepair returned to the corps during the operation. According to Il'ia Moshchansky, "Osvobozhdenie Belorussii: Boevye deistviia Kalininskogo, Zapadnogo i Belorusskogo frontov 26 sentiabr 1943–5 aprelia 1944, Nachalo" [The liberation of Belorussia: The combat actions of the Kalinin, Western, and Belorussian Fronts 26 September 1943–5 April 1944, The beginning], in *Voennaia letopis'* [Military chronicle] 2 (Moscow: OOO BTV-MH, 2006), 15, on 12 December 1st Tank Corps' subordinate units fielded the following armored vehicles: twenty-one T-34 tanks and one SU-76 SP gun in 117th Tank Brigade, twenty-seven T-34 tanks in 159th Tank Brigade, twelve SU-122 SP guns in 1437th SP Artillery Regiment, and no tanks in 44th Motorized Rifle Brigade. This leaves roughly thirty-seven tanks and SP guns in 89th Tank Brigade. On the same date, 10th Guards Separate Tank Brigade had thirty-three T-34 and four T-60 tanks, and 2nd Guards Separate Tank Regiment possessed sixteen KV tanks and one T-34 tank.

6. M. G. Grigorenko et al., eds., *Skvoz' ognennye vikhri: Boevoi put 11-i gvardeiskoi armii v Velikoi Otechestvennoi voiny 1941–1945* [Through fiery whirlwinds: The combat path of 11th Guards Army in the Great Patriotic War 1941–1945] (Moscow: Voenizdat, 1987), 151–152.

7. Sverdlov, "Podgotovka i vedenie Gorodokskoi operatsii," 24. Moshchansky, "Osvobozhdenie Belorussii," 15, places 5th Tank Corps' strength on 12 December at 100 T-34 tanks and 21 SP guns (SU-76, 85, and 122 models), and 34th Guards Tank Brigade at 9 T-34 and 16 T-70 tanks.

8. V. V. Abaturov et al., eds., *Osvobozhdenie Belarusi: 1943–1944* [The liberation of Belarus 1943–1944] (Minsk: Belaruskaia Navuka, 2014), 45.

9. Kamen Nevenkin, *Fire Brigades: The Panzer Divisions, 1943–1945* (Winnipeg, MB: J. J. Fedorowicz, 2008), 475–476.

10. Earl F. Ziemke, *Stalingrad to Berlin: The German Defeat in the East* (Washington, DC: Office of the Chief of Military History U.S. Army, 1968), 207.

11. For example, 16th Guards Rifle Division managed an advance of only 400–600 meters before being halted by heavy German fire. See Abaturov et al., *Osvobozhdenie Belarusi*, 45.

12. Sverdlov, "Podgotovka i vedenie Gorodokskoi operatsii," 27.

13. Abaturov et al., *Osvobozhdenie Belarusi*, 46; and A. Kh. Bagramian, *Tak shli my k pobede* [How we went on to victory] (Moscow: Voenizdat, 1988).

14. "Zhurnal boevykh deistvii voisk 1-go Pribaltiiskogo fronta za dekabr' 1943 g." [The 1st Baltic Front's journal of combat operations for December 1943], TsAMO, f. 235, op. 2074, ed. khr. 53,1. 16. For reasons that remain unclear, Gerasimov was temporarily commanding 4th Shock Army.

15. Abaturov et al., *Osvobozhdenie Belarusi*, 48, although accepting the figure of 20,000 Germans killed, places German equipment losses at 69 tanks, 164 guns, 123 mortars, 586 machine guns, 760 vehicles, and 16 warehouses destroyed, along with 194 guns, 75 mortars, 37 tanks, 110 vehicles, 24 warehouses, and 2,000 German troops captured.

16. Sverdlov, "Podgotovka i vedenie Gorodokskoi operatsii," 30.

17. A. P. Beloborodov, *Vsegda v boiu* [Always in battle] (Moscow: Voenizdat, 1978), 268.

18. Bagramian, *Tak shli my k pobede*, 436–438.

19. K. N. Galitsky, *Gody surovykh ispitanii 1941–1944* [Years of a harsh education 1941–1944] (Moscow: Nauka, 1970), 407–408.

20. Ibid., 408.

21. Moshchansky, "Osvobozhdenie Belorussii," 15.

22. Grechko et al., *Istoriia Vtoroi Mirovoi voiny 1941–1945*, T-7, 272–273.

23. Ziemke, *Stalingrad to Berlin*, 207.

24. For details on this action, see F. Ia. Lisitsyn, *V te groznye gody* [In those threatening years] (Moscow: Voenizdat, 1985), 134–143.

25. Ibid., 143.

26. See V. F. Egorov et al., eds., *Rozhdennaia v boiakh: Boevoi put' 71-i gvardeiskoi strelkovoi Vitebskoi ordena Lenina, Krasnoznamennoi divizii* [Born in battle: The combat path of 71st Guards Vitebsk Order of Lenin, Red Banner Rifle Division] (Moscow: Voenizdat, 1986), 131.

27. "Direktiva Stavki VGK No. 30264 komanduiushchemu voiskami 2-go Pribaltiiskogo fronta na operatsiiu po razgromu Nevel'skoi gruppirovki protivnika" [Stavka VGK directive No. 30264 to the commander of the 2nd Baltic Front concerning an operation to destroy the enemy's Nevel' grouping], in Zolotarev, *Stavka VGK 1943*, 246.

28. Lisitsyn, *V te groznye gody*, 144.

Chapter 9. The Belorussian Front's Kalinkovichi (Bobruisk) Offensive and the German Counterstroke

1. A. A. Grechko et al., eds., *Istoriia Vtoroi Mirovoi voiny 1939–1945 v dvenadtsati tomakh, Tom sed'moi, Zavershenie korennogo perelom v voine* [History of World War II 1939–1945, vol. 7: The completion of a fundamental turning point in the war] (Moscow: Voenizdat, 1976), 276.

2. Earl F. Ziemke, *Stalingrad to Berlin: The German Defeat in the East* (Washington, DC: Office of the Chief of Military History U.S. Army, 1968), 195–196.

3. V. A. Zolotarev, ed., *Russkii arkhiv: Velikaia Otechestvennaiavoina. Stavka Verkhovnogo Glavnokomandovannia: Dokumenty i materialy 1943 god*, T 16 (5 (3) [The Russian archives: The Great Patriotic War. The *Stavka* of the Supreme High Com-

mand: Documents and materials 1943, no. 16, 5 (3)] (Moscow: TERRA, 1999), 246–247. Hereafter cited as Zolotarev, *Stavka VGK 1943*, with document title and page(s).

   4. V. A. Zolotarev, *Russkii arkhiv: Velikaia Otechestvennaiavoina. General'nyi shtab v gody Velikoi Otechestvennoi voiny: Dokumenty i materialy, 1943 god. T-23 (12–3)* [The Russian archives: The Great Patriotic War. The General Staff in the Great Patriotic War: Documents and materials, 1943, vol. 23 (12–3)] (Moscow: TERRA, 1999), 439 Hereafter cited as Zolotarev, *General Staff 1943*, with appropriate page(s).

   5. Ibid., 439–440.

   6. Ibid., 450 and 453.

   7. I. N. Pavlov, *Ot Moskvy do Shtral'zunda (Boevoi put' 354 i strelkovoi Kalinkovichskoi ordena Lenina, Krasoznamennoi, ordena Suvorova divizii)* [From Moscow to Straslund (The combat path of the Kalinkovichi, Orders of Lenin, Red Banner, and Order of Suvorov 354th Rifle Division)] (Moscow: Voenizdat, 1985), 77. This history of 354th Rifle Division telescopes the unsuccessful 8 December attack with the more successful 8 January 1944 attack.

   8. P. I. Batov, *V pokhodokh i boiakh* [In marches and battles] (Moscow: DOSAAF, 1984), 364.

   9. A. A. Andreev, *Po voennym dorogam: Boevoi put' 69-i strelkovoi Sevskoi dvazhdy krasnoznamennoi ordenov Suvurova i Kutuzova divizii* [Along military roads: The combat path of 69th Sevsk, twice Red Banner Orders of Suvorov and Kutuzov Rifle Division] (Moscow: Voenizdat, 1971), 133.

   10. Kamen Nevenkin, *Fire Brigades: The Panzer Divisions, 1943–1945* (Winnipeg, MB: J. J. Fedorowicz, 2008), 401–402. The 16th Panzer Division, destroyed at Stalingrad on 2 February 1943, was resurrected in France in March and dispatched to Italy in late May, where it fought against the Allied landing force at Salerno and later along the Sangro River. It was transported to German Army Group Center by rail in November 1943. For further details, see Rolf Stoves, *Die Gepanzerten und Motorisierten Deutschen Grossverbände 1935–1945* (Friedberg, FRG: Podzun-Pallas Verlag, 1986), 111.

   11. Ibid., 326–327.

   12. K. Rokossovsky, *A Soldier's Duty* (Moscow: Progress, 1985), 228–229.

   13. K. F. Telegin, *Voiny neschitannye versty* [Wars of uncountable versts] (Moscow: Voenizdat, 1988), 272.

   14. Ibid., 274.

   15. Batov, *V pokhodakh i boiakh*, 366–368.

   16. For a detailed account of the action, see N. V. Kuprianov, *S veroi v pobedu: Boevoi put' 38-i gvardeiskoi strelkovoi Lozovaia Krasnoznamennoi divizii* [With faith in victory: The combat path of 38th Guards Lozovaia Red Banner Rifle Division]. (Moscow: Voenizdat, 1985)., 79–88.

   17. The German maps in this section come from "A. O. K. II/Ia, Anlagen Band 103, Lagenkarten, Russland, 1–31 December 1943" *AOK II/Ia, 41181/103*, in National Archives Microfilm series (NAM) T-312, roll 1266.

   18. Nevenkin, *Fire Brigades*, 384, 401–402. The strength of 16th Panzer Division decreased from 113 tanks (including 12 in short-term repair) and 21 assault guns on 15 December to 82 tanks (including 30 in short-term repair) and 20 assault guns (including 3 in short-term repair) on 1 January 1944.

   19. Grechko et al., *Istoriia Vtoroi Mirovoi voiny*, 277.

Chapter 10. Context: The Winter Campaign

1. Earl F. Ziemke, *Stalingrad to Berlin: The German Defeat in the East* (Washington, DC: Office of the Chief of Military History U.S. Army, 1968), 206–207.
2. A. P. Beloborodov, *Vsegda v boiu* [Always in battle] (Moscow: Voenizdat, 1978), 268.
3. K. N. Galitsky, *Gody surovykh ispitanii 1941–1944* [Years of a harsh education 1941–1944] (Moscow: Nauka, 1970), 421–422.

Chapter 11. The 1st Baltic and Western Fronts' Vitebsk Offensive and 2nd Baltic Front's Novosokol'niki Pursuit

1. "Direktiva Stavki VGK No. 30268 komanduiushchemu voiskami 1-go Pribaltiiskogo fronta, predstaviteliu Stavki na razgrom Vitebskoi gruppirovki protivnika" [*Stavka* VGK directive No. 30268 to the 1st Baltic Front commander and the representative of the *Stavka* on the destruction of the enemy Vitebsk grouping], in *Russkii arkhiv: Velikaia Otechestvennaiavoina. Stavka Verkhovnogo Glavnokomandovannia: Dokumenty i materialy 1943 god, T 16 (5 (3)* [The Russian archives: The Great Patriotic War. The *Stavka* of the Supreme High Command: Documents and materials 1943, no. 16, 5 (3)], ed. V A. Zolotarev (Moscow: TERRA, 1999) 249. Hereafter cited as Zolotarev, *Stavka VGK 1943*, with document title and page(s). The *Stavka* representative was N. N. Voronov.
2. "Zhurnal boevykh deistvii voisk 1-go Pribaltiiskogo fronta za dekabr' 1943 g." [The 1st Baltic Front's journal of combat operations for December 1943], TsAMO, f. 235, op. 2074, ed. kh. 53,1. 42.
3. V. V. Abaturov et al., eds. *Osvobozhdenie Belarusi: 1943–1944* [The liberation of Belarus 1943–1944] (Minsk: Belaruskaia Navuka, 2014), 64, briefly mentions 33rd Army's offensive southeast of Vitebsk, but provides precious few details about the fighting.
4. Rolf Stoves, *Die Gepanzerten und Motorisierten Deutschen Grossverbände, 1935–1945* (Friedberg, FRG: Podzun-Pallas Verlag, 1986), 243–245.
5. Jentz, *Panzertruppen*, vol. 2, 117.
6. "Zhurnal boevykh deistvii voisk 1-go Pribaltiiskogo fronta za dekabr' 1943 g.," 1. 44.
7. N. I. Krylov, N I. Alekseev, and I. G. Dragan, *Navstrechu pobede: Boevoi put' 5-i armii oktiabr' 1941–avgust 1945* [Greeting victory: The combat path of 5th Army, October 1941–August 1945] (Moscow: Nauka, 1970), 175–176.
8. "Zhurnal boevykh deistvii voisk 1-go Pribaltiiskogo fronta za dekabr' 1943 g.," 1. 83.
9. Ibid., 101.
10. G. F. Krivosheev et al., ed., *Rossiia i SSSR v voinakh XX veka: Statisticheskii issledovanie* [Russia and the USSR in wars of the Twentieth Century: a statistical investigation] (Moscow: OLMA Press, 2001), 314.
11. Abaturov et al., *Osvobozhdenie Belarusi*, 64.
12. L. M. Sandalov, *Posle perelom* [After the turning point] (Moscow: Voenizdat, 1983), 12.
13. Ibid.

14. "Direktiva Stavki VGK No. 30257 komanduiushchim voiskami Zapadnogo i 2-go Pribaltiiskogo frontov na perepodchinenie 10-i gvardeiskoi armii" [Stavka VGK directive No. 30257 to the commanders of the Western and 2nd Baltic Fronts on the resubordination of 10th Guards Army], in Zolotarev, *Stavka VGK 1943*, 243.

15. Sandalov, *Posle perelom*, 12.

16. The 10th Guards Army's strength upon its transfer to the 2nd Baltic Front in December was 43,250 soldiers, 1,700 vehicles, and 6,500 horses, with a large complement of horse-drawn cargo carts. The transfer, which amounted to a distance of 210 kilometers, began shortly after 8 December and was completed on 31 December, when the last railroad trains arrived at the station in Nevedro. Having suffered heavy personnel losses in the fighting east of Orsha, the army's 7th and 19th Guards Rifle Corps received 10,500 new replacements as they approached their new concentration area, while 15th Guards Rifle Corps received none. When the army commander requested two to three weeks to train and incorporate the replacements into the army's formations, the *front's* military council denied his request. Instead, the army went into action on 14 January. See P. K. Altukhov et al., eds., *Nezabyvaemye dorogi: Boevoi put' 10-i gvardeiskoi armii* [Unforgettable roads: The combat path of the 10th Guards Army] (Moscow: Voenizdat, 1974), 79–80.

17. German records and V. F. Egorov, *Rozhdennaia v boiakh: Boevoi put' 71-i gvardeiskoi strelkovoi Vitebskoi ordena Lenina, Krasnoznamennoi divizii* [Born in battle: The combat path of 71st Guards Vitebsk Order of Lenin, Red Banner Rifle Division] (Moscow: Voenizdat, 1986), 132, indicate that, initially, the following forces participated in the pursuit of the withdrawing German 32nd Infantry Division: 97th Rifle Corps' 51st, 67th, and 71st Guards Rifle Divisions, supported by 27th and 38th Guards Tank Brigades and 65th Tank Regiment. To the east, 23rd Guards Rifle Corps' 43rd, 52nd Guards, and 37th Rifle Divisions, with 38th and 221st Tank Regiments did the same in 122nd Infantry Division's sector. Finally, 93rd Rifle Corps' 326th and 370th Rifle Division and 100th Rifle Corps' 21st and 46th, and 119th Guards Rifle Divisions, with 29th Guards, 78th, and 118th Tank Brigades, pursued German 290th Infantry Division.

18. Gurkin, "Liudskie poteri," 8.

Chapter 12. The 1st Baltic and Western Fronts' Vitebsk-Bogushevsk Offensive

1. K. N. Galitsky, *Gody surovykh ispytanii 1941–1944* [Years of a harsh education 1941–1944] (Moscow: Nauka, 1970), 426–427.

2. M. A. Gareev, "O neudachnykh nastupatel'nykh operatsiiakh Sovetskikh voisk v Velikoi Otechestvennoi voine. Po neopublikovannym dokumentam GKO" [Concerning unsuccessful offensive operations by Soviet forces in the Great Patriotic War; based on unpublished documents of the GKO], in *Novaia i noveishaia istoriia* [New and newest history] 1 (January 1994): 16, 18.

3. Galitsky, *Gody surovykh ispytanii*, 427.

4. Ibid., 428–429.

5. Ibid., 428.

6. Ibid., 430.

7. According to Kamen Nevenkin, *Fire Brigades: The Panzer Divisions, 1943–*

1945 (Winnipeg, MB: J. J. Fedorowicz, 2008), 326, 12th Panzer Division was deployed to the Slobodka region, 22 kilometers northwest of Vitebsk, during the first few days of January with a force of about forty-five tanks and twenty assault guns, which increased to fifty-five tanks (with three command vehicles) and twenty-four assault guns by 1 February.

8. V. V. Abaturov et al., eds., *Osvobozhdenie Belarusi: 1943–1944* [The liberation of Belarus 1943–1944] (Minsk: Belaruskaia Navuka, 2014), 65.

9. N. I. Krylov, N. I. Alekseev, and I. G. Dragan, *Navstrechu pobeda: Boevoi put' 5-i armii oktiabr' 1941–avgust 1945* [Greeting victory: The combat path of 5th Army, October 1941–August 1945] (Moscow: Nauka, 1970), 176.

10. Abaturov et al., *Osvobozhdenie Belarusi*, 65.

11. Krylov, Alekseev, and Dragan, *Navstrechu pobeda*, 176–177.

12. Ibid., 178.

13. Abaturov et al., *Osvobozhdenie Belarusi*, 65, places 33rd and 5th Armies casualties at 5,517 killed and 19,672 wounded in return for an advance of only 2 to 4 kilometers.

14. *TsAMO*, f. 233, op. 2356, d. 19,11. 225–230.

15. Ibid., f. 208, op. 2511, ed. kh., 3051,11. 10–14.

16. "Die Abwehrschlachten um Witebsk vom 13.12.43 bis 17.2.44," Pz AOK 3, Ia, *AOK 3, 48936 file,* in National Archives Microfilm series (NAM) T-313, roll 291.

Chapter 13. The 1st Baltic and Western Fronts' Vitebsk Offensive

1. M. A. Gareev, "O neudachnykh nastupatel'nykh operatsiiakh Sovetskikh voisk v Velikoi Otechestvennoi voine. Po neopublikovannym dokumentam GKO" [Concerning unsuccessful offensive operations by Soviet forces in the Great Patriotic War; based on unpublished documents of the GKO], in *Novaia i noveishaia istoriia* [New and newest history] 1 (January 1994): 17–18.

2. V. A. Zolotarev et al., eds., *Russkii arkhiv: Velikaia Otechestvennaiavoina. Stavka VGK: Dokumenty i materialy 1944–1945. T. 16 (5–4)* [The Russian archives: The Great Patriotic War. Stavka VGK: Documents and materials 1944–1945. vol. 16 (5–4)] (Moscow: TERRA, 1999), 34. Hereafter cited as Zolotarev, *Stavka VGK 1944–1945*, with appropriate page(s).

3. *TsAMO*, f. 235, op. 2074, ed. kh., 77,11., 6–17.

4. A. M. Zolotarev et al., eds., *Russkii arkhiv: Velikaia Otechestvennaiavoina. General'nyi shtab v gody Velikoi Otechestvennoi voiny: Dokumenty i materialy 1944–1945. T. 23 (12–4)* [The Russian archives: The Great Patriotic War. The General Staff in the war years: Documents and materials 1944–1945. vol. 23 (12–4)] (Moscow: TERRA, 2001), 41–42. Hereafter cited as Zolotarev, *General Staff 1944–1945*, with appropriate page(s).

5. Kamen Nevenkin, *Fire Brigades: The Panzer Divisions, 1943–1945* (Winnipeg, MB: J. J. Fedorowicz, 2008), 475–476.

6. V. V. Abaturov et al., eds., *Osvobozhdenie Belarusi: 1943–1944* [The liberation of Belarus 1943–1944] (Minsk: Belaruskaia Navuka, 2014), 54, citing *Journal of Combat Operations of 3rd Panzer Army for the Period from 1.1.44 through 29.2.44,* translated from the German (Moscow: 1947), 315.

7. Ibid., 67.

8. Ibid.
9. Ibid.
10. Ibid.
11. Gareev, "O neudachnykh nastupatel'nykh operatsiiakh Sovetskikh voisk," 17. Abaturov et al., *Osvobozhdenie Belarusi*, 67, states, "Between 8 and 16 February, the Western Front's shock group (39th and 33rd Armies) advanced a total of 3–4 kilometers and dug in along the Popovka, Seliuty, Pavliuchenki, Bodino-Mosino, Noviki, and Bukshtina line. The cost in losses was more than 43,000 casualties, including more than 10,000 killed, missing, or captured.

Chapter 14. The Western Front's Babinovichi and Vitebsk Offensives

1. According to V. V. Abaturov et al., eds., *Osvobozhdenie Belarusi: 1943–1944* [The liberation of Belarus 1943–1944] (Minsk: Belaruskaia Navuka, 2014), 67, 5th Army attacked from the Zaprudy, Makarovo, and Sheliagi line.
2. M. A. Gareev, "O neudachnykh nastupatel'nykh operatsiiakh Sovetskikh voisk v Velikoi Otechestvennoi voine. Po neopublikovannym dokumentam GKO" [Concerning unsuccessful offensive operations by Soviet forces in the Great Patriotic War; based on unpublished documents of the GKO], in *Novaia i noveishaia istoriia* [New and newest history] 1 (January 1994): 17; Abaturov et al., *Osvobozhdenie Belarusi*, 67.
3. According to W. Victor Madej, ed., *The German Army Order of Battle* (New York: Game Marketing, 1978), 225, and Samual W. Mitchum, Jr., *Hitler's Legion: The German Army Order of Battle, World War II* (New York: Stein and Day, 1985) 159, 406th Grenadier (actually Security) Regiment was subordinate to 201st Security Division.
4. *TsAMO*. f. 233, op. 2356, d. 19,11. 230.
5. Ibid., f. 208, op. 2511, ed. kh., 3051,11. 15–30.
6. "Die Abwehrschlachten um Witebsk vom 13.12.43 bis 17.2.44."
7. Gareev, "O neudachnykh nastupatel'nykh operatsiiakh Sovetskikh voisk," 17–18.
8. V. A. Zolotarev, ed., *Russkii arkhiv: Velikaia Otechestvennaiavoina. Stavka VGK: Dokumenty i materialy 1944–1945. T. 16 (5–4)* [The Russian archives: The Great Patriotic War. Stavka VGK: Documents and materials 1944–1945. vol. 16 (5–4)] (Moscow: TERRA, 1999), 272. Hereafter cited as Zolotarev, *Stavka VGK 1944–1945*, with appropriate page(s). Sokolovsky, together with his commissar, Mekhlis, also asked the *Stavka* to reinforce his *front* with 20,000 personnel replacements, 200 T-34 tanks, and two regiments of SU-85 (self-propelled guns) to combat enemy tanks, asserting "of which the enemy has around 250 in front of our *front*."
9. Ibid., 51.
10. See ibid., 53, for this *Stavka* order.
11. According to Abaturov et al., *Osvobozhdenie Belarusi*, 68, the strengths of 5th Army's divisions were: 97th Rifle—3,717 men; 157th Rifle—3,630 men; 159th Rifle—3,450 men; 184th Rifle—3,564 men; 277th Rifle—4,685 men; and 338th Rifle—3,605 men.
12. Abaturov et al. stated that 33rd Army received 16,295 march replacements on 21 February, but that was the last contingent for some time. Nor could these replacements be properly trained and integrated into the divisions in so short a period. Ibid.

13. Mekhlis had been with Sokolovsky's headquarters since December 1943, an indicator that the *Stavka* already was suspicious of Sokolovsky's capabilities as a *front* commander.

14. Abaturov et al., *Osvobozhdenie Belarusi*, 68.

15. Zolotarev, *Stavka VGK 1944–1945*, 54–55.

16. Abaturov et al., *Osvobozhdenie Belarusi*, 68, states that Dobrovol'sky's 84th Rifle Corps had sixteen companies with fifteen to twenty-five men each, six companies with twenty-five to thirty-five men, four companies with thirty-five men, five companies with forty-five to fifty-five men, and two companies with fifty-five to sixty-five men. Making matters worse, by 1 March 39th Army's supply of ammunition had fallen to 0.44 combat loads of 122mm howitzer shells, 0.15 combat loads of 122mm gun shells, and 0.5 to 0.7 combat loads of 152mm howitzer and gun shells.

17. Gareev, "O neudachnykh nastupatel'nykh operatsiiakh Sovetskikh voisk," 17; Abaturov et al., *Osvobozhdenie Belarusi*, 68.

Chapter 15. The Western Front's Orsha and Bogushevsk Offensives

1. M. A. Gareev, "O neudachnykh nastupatel'nykh operatsiiakh Sovetskikh voisk v Velikoi Otechestvennoi voine. Po neopublikovannym dokumentam GKO" [Concerning unsuccessful offensive operations by Soviet forces in the Great Patriotic War; based on unpublished documents of the GKO], in *Novaia i noveishaia istoriia* [New and newest history] 1 (January 1994): 17, 19.

2. V. V. Abaturov et al., eds., *Osvobozhdenie Belarusi: 1943–1944* [The liberation of Belarus 1943–1944] (Minsk: Belaruskaia Navuka, 2014), 68.

3. Gareev, "O neudachnykh nastupatel'nykh operatsiiakh Sovetskikh voisk," 17, 19.

4. N. I. Krylov, N. I. Alekseev, and I. G. Dragan, *Navstrechu pobeda: Boevoi put' 5-i armii oktiabr' 1941–avgust 1945* [Greeting victory: The combat path of 5th Army, October 1941–August 1945] (Moscow: Nauka, 1970), 180.

5. See V. A. Zolotarev, ed., *Russkii arkhiv: Velikaia Otechestvennaiavoina. Stavka VGK: Dokumenty i materialy 1944–1945. T. 16 (5–4)* [The Russian archives: The Great Patriotic War. *Stavka* VGK: Documents and materials 1944–1945. vol. 16 (5–4)] (Moscow: Terra, 1999), 60. Hereafter cited as Zolotarev, *Stavka VGK 1944–1945*, with appropriate page(s).

6. Abaturov et al., *Osvobozhdenie Belarusi*, 69, identifies four rifle divisions in 33rd Army's shock group, specifically, 42nd, 173rd, 215th, and 199th Rifle Divisions.

7. Abaturov et al. states that 33rd Army's specific mission was "to penetrate the enemy's defenses in the Zazyby and Drybino sector and, while developing success toward Iazykovo and Ales'kovo, cut the sector of the Vitebsk-Orsha railroad."

8. Ibid. states that, at the beginning of the operation, 33rd Army's on-hand combat loads amounted to 1.3 loads for 45mm guns, 1–1.2 for 76mm regimental and divisional guns, 1.2–1.3 for 122mm howitzers and guns, and 1.4–2.5 for 152mm howitzers and guns.

9. Krylov, Alekseev, and Dragan, *Navstrechu pobede*, 180–181.

10. Gareev, "O neudachnykh nastupatel'nykh operatsiiakh Sovetskikh voisk," 17; Abaturov et al., *Osvobozhdenie Belarusi*, 70.

11. TsAMO., f. 208, op. 2511, ed. kh., 3051,11. 31–36.

12. See G. F. Krivosheev et al., eds., *Rossiia i SSSR v voinakh XX veka: Statisticheskoe issledovanie* [Russia and the USSR in wars of the twentieth century: A statistical investigation] (Moscow: Olma Press, 2001), 315. Abaturov et al., *Osvobozhdenie Belarusi*, 70, places the Western Front's losses from 1 January to 1 April 1944 at 207,981 casualties, including 41,962 killed, missing, or captured.

Chapter 16. The Belorussian Front's Situation on 1 January 1944 and Preliminary Operations

1. P. I . Batov, *V pokhodokh i boiakh* [In marches and battles] (Moscow: DOSAAF, 1984), 364.
2. K. K. Rokossovsky, *Soldatskii dolg* [A soldier's duty] (Moscow: Golos, 2000), 307–308. This is an unexpurgated version of previous editions published under the same title.
3. "Kratkie svodki ob obshchennogo boevogo opyta voisk 1 Belorusskogo fronta i armii za dekabr' 1943-aprel' 1944 g." [Short summaries of the generalization of combat experience of the 1st Belorussian Front and its armies for December 1943–April 1944], *TsAMO*, f. 233, op. 2356, d. 19,11. 97–132.
4. Ibid., 205.
5. A. V. Gorbatov, *Gody i voiny* [Years and wars] (Moscow: Voenizdat, 1980), 249–250.
6. Ibid.
7. Ibid.

Chapter 17. The Belorussian Front's Kalinkovichi-Mozyr' Offensive

1. "Kratkie svodki ob obshchennogo boevogo opyta voisk 1 Belorusskogo fronta i armii za dekabr' 1943-aprel' 1944 g.," 11. 169–170. This report was prepared by Colonel Lipis, the chief of operations of 65th Army.
2. "Kratkie svodki ob obshchennogo boevogo opyta voisk 1 Belorusskogo fronta i armii za dekabr' 1943-aprel' 1944 g.," 11. 72–81. This was prepared by Colonel Vlasov, the chief of operations in 61st Army, and Lieutenant Colonel Smirnov, chief of the Section for the Exploitation of War Experience.
3. V. A. Zolotarev, ed., *Russkii arkhiv: Velikaia Otechestvennaiavoina. Stavka VGK: Dokumenty i materialy 1944–1945. T. 16 (5–4)* [The Russian archives: The Great Patriotic War. *Stavka* VGK: Documents and materials 1944–1945. vol. 16 (5–4)] (Moscow: TERRA, 1999), 27. Hereafter cited as Zolotarev, *Stavka VGK 1944–1945*, with appropriate page(s).
4. M. Panov, "V boiakh za Kalinkovichi" [In the battles for Kalinkovichi], *Voenno-istoricheskii zhurnal* [Military-historical journal] 5 (May 1978): 46. Hereafter cited as *VIZh*, with appropriate title, number, and page(s). The *Stavka* directive is in Zolotarev, *Stavka VGK 1944–1945*, 27. V. V. Abaturov et al., eds., *Osvobozhdenie Belarusi: 1943–1944* [The liberation of Belarus 1943–1944] (Minsk: Belaruskaia Navuka, 2014), 80 paraphrases the *front's* mission slightly differently, stating, "The Belorussian Front will conduct an offensive with its left wing no later than 8 January with the missions of defeating the enemy's Mozyr' grouping and capturing Kalinkovichi and Mozyr' by 12 January by enveloping it from the north and south. Subsequently, the

front is ordered to deliver a blow with its main forces in the direction of Bobruisk and Minsk, and part of its forces will operate along the Pripiat' [River] to Luninets."

5. See Kamen Nevenkin, *Fire Brigades: The Panzer Divisions, 1943–1945* (Winnipeg, MB: J. J. Fedorowicz, 2008), 160–161, 182–183. According to Nevenkin, 4th Panzer Division fielded forty-one tanks (fifteen in short-term repair), including two Pz. III and twenty-four Pz. IV, with another two Pz. III and thirteen Pz. IV in short-term repair; and twenty-two assault guns or *Paks*, with three more in short-term repair. Similarly, 5th Panzer Division had thirty-eight tanks (fourteen in short-term repair), including two serviceable Pz. III and twenty-two operable Pz. IV, with another four and ten of each in short-term repair, and fifteen assault guns or *Paks*, with two more in short-term repair. As for the panzer division's strengths, 4th Panzer was authorized 16,151 men but had a ration (on-hand) strength of 12,907 men, whereas 5th Panzer had an authorized strength of 13,466 men but a ration strength of 11,433 men. The former suffered 776 casualties in January 1944 and the latter 664.

6. M. F. Panov, *Na napravlenii glavnogo udara* [On the axis of the main attack] (Moscow: n.p., 1995), 102.

7. D. Mal'kov, "Vnezapnaia ataka" [Surprise attack], *VIZh* 3 (March 1964): 55.

8. A. A. Andreev, *Po voennym dorogam: Boevoi put' 69-i strelkovoi Sevskoi dvazhdy krasnoznamennoi ordenov Suvurova i Kutuzova divizii* [Along military roads: The combat path of 69th Sevsk, twice Red Banner Orders of Suvorov and Kutuzov Rifle Division] (Moscow: Voenizdat, 1971), 136–138.

9. Panov, *Na napravelenii glavnogo udara*, 103.

10. Ibid., 104.

11. Ibid., 104–105. This is questionable because most of 12th Panzer Division departed the area by 6 January.

12. For a German account of 5th Panzer Division's fight from 8 to 13 January, see Anton Detlev von Plato, *Die Geschichte der 5. Panzerdivision. Panzerdivision 1938 bis 1945* (Regensburg: Walhalla u. Praetoria Verlag, 1978), 308–313. According to von Plato, who was an officer in 5th Panzer during the fighting, the *Gefechts/Graben* (combat/trench) strength of the division's combat units on 9 December 1943 was as follows:

1st Bn, 13th PzGrR—168/91 men	5th PzReconBn [*Aufkl.Abt.*]—398/281 men
2nd Bn, 13th PzGrR—310/210 men	89th PzPiBn—278/150 men
1st Bn, 14th PzGrR—364/241 men	1st Bn, 894th GrenR—380/323 men
2nd Bn, 14th PzGrR—380/270 men	1st Co., 234th Territorial Inf. Bn—165/135 men

The panzer division's losses from 8 to 13 January totaled 561 men, including 93 killed in action, 329 wounded, 72 missing, and 67 sick. The 1st Bn, 894th Grenadier Regiment, was originally part of 265th Infantry Division but was dispatched to the East as a separate battalion in the fall of 1943. See Samual W. Mitchum Jr., *Hitler's Legion: The German Army Order of Battle, World War II* (New York: Stein and Day, 1985), 193.

13. D. K. Mal'kov, *Skvoz' dym i plamia: Boevoi put' 12-i gvardeiskoi Pinskoi Krasnoznamennoi ordena Suvorova strelkovoi divizii* [Through the smoke and flames: The combat path of 12th Guards Pinsk, Red Banner and Order of Suvorov Rifle Division] (Moscow: Voenizdat, 1970), 111.

14. Mal'kov, "Vnezapnaia ataka," 56–57.

15. Mal'kov, *Skvoz' dym i plamia*, 111.

16. M. S. Dokuchaev, *V boi shli eskadrony: Boevoi put' 7-go gvardeiskogo kavaleriiskogo Brandenburgskogo ordena Lenina, Krasnoznamennogo, ordena Suvorova korpusa v Velikoi Otechestvennoi voine* [The squadrons went into battles: The combat path of 7th Guards Brandenburg, Order of Lenin, Red Banner, and Order of Suvorov Guards Cavalry Corps in the Great Patriotic War] (Moscow: Voenizdat, 1984), 95.

17. A. M. Zolotarev et al., eds. *Russkii arkhiv: Velikaia Otechestvennaiavoina. General'nyi shtab v gody Velikoi Otechestvennoi voiny: Dokumenty i materialy 1944–1945. T. 23 (12–4)* [The Russian archives: The Great Patriotic War. The General Staff in the war years: Documents and materials 1944–1945. vol. 23 (12–4)] (Moscow: TERRA, 2001), 31. Hereafter cited as Zolotarev, *General Staff 1944–1945*, with appropriate page(s).

18. Dokuchaev, *V boi shli eskadrony*, 97–98.

19. *Sovetskaia kavaleriia* [Soviet cavalry] (Moscow: Voenizdat, 1984), 254.

20. Dokuchaev, *V boi shli eskadrony*, 98–99.

21. The 6th Guards Cavalry Corps appeared on Second Army's daily situation maps on 11 January and supposedly remained in the deep Soviet rear through 21 January. Interestingly enough, so also does 4th Guards Airborne Brigade, shown supporting the cavalry corps and partisans in the region south of Petrikov. Ultimately, 6th Guards Cavalry Corps spearheaded the offensive by the 1st Ukrainian Front's 13th Army toward Rovno and Lutsk in late January 1944.

22. Abaturov et al., *Osvobozhdenie Belarusi*, 81, quoting K. Tippelskirch, *Istoriia vtoroi mirovoi voiny* [A history of World War II] (Moscow: Voenizdat, 1962), 369, a translation of Kurt von Tippelskirch, *Geschichte des Zweiten Weltkriegs* (Bonn, FRG: n.p., 1961).

23. Dokuchaev, *V boi shli eskadrony*, 99–100. Second Army's daily situation map indicates a smooth and relatively uneventful withdrawal of Corps *Abteilung* E's forces on 13 January.

24. A. N. Sekretov, *Gvardeiskaia postup' (Boevoi put' 17-i Mozyrskoi krasnoznamennoi ordenov Lenina, Suvorova i Kutuzova kavaleriiskoi divizii podshefnoi Tadzhikistanu, v gody Velikoi Otechestvennoi voiny, 1941–1945 gg.)* [Guards gait (The combat path of 17th Mozyr' Red Banner and Orders of Lenin, Suvorov, and Kutuzov Cavalry Division, raised in Tadzhikistan during the Great Patriotic War, 1941–1945)] (Dushanbe: Donish, 1985), 80–81.

25. Ibid., 83–84.

26. From west to east, these included *kampfgruppen* of various sizes formed from 7th Infantry Division's 19th, 61st, and 62nd Regiments; 102nd Infantry Division's 233rd and 235th Regiments; 216th Division Group; and Corps *Abteilung* E's 137th, 251st, and 86th Division Groups. Over time, 102nd Infantry Division's regiments filtered westward to reinforce Second Army's bridgehead south of Petrikov.

Chapter 18. The Belorussian Front's Ozarichi-Ptich' Offensive

1. P. Batov, "65-i armiia v boiakh v Belorussiiu" [The 65th Army in the battles for Belorussia], *Voenno-istoricheskii zhurnal* [Military-historical journal] 9 (September 1970), 71. Hereafter cited as *VIZh*, with appropriate title, number, and page(s).

2. D. K. Mal'kov, *Skvoz' dym i plamia : Boevoi put' 12-i gvardeiskoi Pinskoi Krasnoznamennoi ordena Suvorova strelkovoi divizii* [Through the smoke and flames:

The combat path of 12th Guards Pinsk, Red Banner and Order of Suvorov Rifle Division] (Moscow: Voenizdat, 1970), 113–114.

3. "Kratkie svodki ob obshchennogo boevogo opyta voisk 1 Belorusskogo fronta i armii za dekabr' 1943-aprel' 1944 g.",11. 170–200. This report was written by Colonel Lipis, the chief of operations of 65th Army.

4. See Kamen Nevenkin, *Fire Brigades: The Panzer Divisions, 1943–1945* (Winnipeg, MB: J. J. Fedorowicz, 2008), 160–161.

5. Ibid., 182–183.

6. I. F. Abramov, *82-ia Iartsevskaia: Boevoi put' 82-i Iartsevskoi Krasnoznamennoi ordena Suvorova i Kutuzova strelkovoi divizii* [The 82nd Iartsevo: The combat path of 82nd Iartsevo, Red Banner, and Orders of Suvorov and Kutuzov Rifle Division] (Moscow: Voenizdat, 1973), 97.

7. A. A. Andreev, *Po voennym dorogam: Boevoi put' 69-i strelkovoi Sevskoi dvazhdy krasnoznamennoi ordenov Suvurova i Kutuzova divizii* [Along military roads: The combat path of 69th Sevsk, twice Red Banner Orders of Suvorov and Kutuzov Rifle Division] (Moscow: Voenizdat, 1971), 139. See Anton Detlev von Plato, *Die Geschichte der 5. Panzerdivision. Panzerdivision 1938 bis 1945* (Regensburg: Walhalla u. Praetoria Verlag, 1978), 312–313, which describes this fighting on a night when the temperature fell to minus 20 degrees Centigrade (minus 4 degrees Fahrenheit).

8. Abramov, *82-ia Iartsevskaia*, 98. The author is referring to 35th Infantry Division's 34th Fusillier and 109th Grenadier Regiments. According to the Second Army's records, the 35th Infantry was also backed up by a *kampfgruppe* from 4th Panzer Division consisting of 2nd Battalion, 14th Panzer Grenadier Regiment, reinforced by both 4th and 5th Panzer Division's reconnaissance battalions (Pz. AA 4 and 5) and a motorcycle battalion (K-2).

9. Ibid., 99.

10. Andreev, *Po voennym dorogam*, 139.

11. Abramov, *82-ia Iartsevskaia*, 100.

12. Andreev, *Po voennym dorogam*, 141–143. This engagement, which took place near the boundary between 4th and 5th Panzer Divisions, is described in considerable detail in von Plato, *Die Geschichte der 5. Panzerdivision*, 312–314. At the time, the 5th Panzer was cooperating with a battalion from 707th Security Division's 727th Regiment and 1st Battalion, 613th Infantry Regiment. However, there is no evidence that either division fielded any Tiger tanks, although both divisions accepted delivery of some Pz. V Panthers in December 1943 and January 1944. These do not appear on either division's strength figure charts in Nevenkin, *Fire Brigades*.

13. Andreev, *Po voennym dorogam*, 142.

14. Ibid. The attack described in this account coincides perfectly with Soviet attacks vividly depicted on Second Army's daily situation maps.

15. Abramov, *82-ia Iartsevskaia*, 100–101.

16. For details on this fight from the German perspective, see von Plato, *Die Geschichte der 5. Panzerdivision*, 315–317.

17. Mal'kov, *Skvoz' dym i plamia*, 113–114.

18. Korück 580 was a German logistical unit. By this time, 203rd Security Division consisted of 608th and 613th Security Regiments and at least a battalion of 930th Security Regiment, while z.b.V 17 was a temporary division consisting of many sepa-

rate security and support battalions. See Samual W. Mitchum Jr., *Hitler's Legions: The German Army Order of Battle, World War II.* (New York: Stein and Day, 1985), 160; and W. Victor Madej, ed., *The German Army Order of Battle* (New York: Game Marketing, 1978), 22.

19. G. F. Krivosheev et al., eds., *Rossiia i SSSR v voinakh XX veka: Statisticheskoe issledovanie* [Russia and the USSR in wars of the Twentieth Century: A statistical investigation] (Moscow: Olma Press, 2001), 315.

Chapter 19. The Belorussian Front's Parichi-Bobruisk (Marmovichi-Dubrova) Offensive

1. "Kratkie svodki ob obshchennogo boevogo opyta voisk 1 Belorusskogo fronta i armii za dekabr' 1943-aprel' 1944 g.," 11. 61–74. This report was prepared by Major General Dolgov, chief of the *front's* Operations Department, and Major Dobriakov, chief of the *front's* Section for the Exploitation of War Experience.

2. K. K. Shilov, *Rechitskaia krasnoznamennaia* [Rechitsa Red Banner] (Moscow: Voenizdat, 1984), 108–109.

3. F. G. Bulatov, *Budni frontovykh let* [The humdrum front years] (Kazan': Tatarskoe Izdatel'stvo, 1984), 132–133.

4. M. F. Panov, *Na napravlenii glavnogo udara* [On the axis of the main attack] (Moscow: n.p., 1995), 109.

5. Shilov, *Rechitskaia krasnoznamennaia,* 109.

6. Ibid., 134.

7. Bulatov, *Budni frontovykh let,* 140–141.

8. By 4 February 1944, the 4th Panzer Division's armor strength had fallen to eighteen operable tanks (three Pz. III and fifteen Pz. IV) and roughly twenty assault guns and mobile *Paks,* most of which it committed to this counterattack. See Kamen Nevenkin, *Fire Brigades: The Panzer Divisions, 1943–1945* (Winnipeg, MB: J. J. Fedorowicz, 2008), 160–161.

9. V. A. Zolotarev et al., eds., *Russkii arkhiv: Velikaia Otechestvennaiavoina. Stavka VGK: Dokumenty i materialy 1944–1945. T. 16 (5–4)* [The Russian archives: The Great Patriotic War. *Stavka* VGK: Documents and materials 1944–1945. vol. 16 (5–4)] (Moscow: TERRA, 1999), 46. Hereafter cited as Zolotarev, *Stavka VGK 1944–1945,* with appropriate page(s).

10. Ibid.

11. Ibid., 48.

12. "Kratkie svodki ob obshchennogo boevogo opyta voisk 1 Belorusskogo fronta i armii za dekabr' 1943-aprel' 1944 g.,"1. 276.

13. Bulatov, *Budni frontovykh let,* 140.

14. There remains a bit of confusion over LVI Panzer Corps' subordination. Second and Ninth Army's operational maps, as well as those of Army Group Center, clearly indicate that LVI Panzer Corps indeed shifted to Ninth Army's control on 18 January. However, Karl-Heinz Frieser et al., eds., *Das Deutsche Reich und de Zweite Weltkrieg, Band 8, Die Ostfront 1943/44: Der Krieg im Osten und an den Nebenfronten* (Munchen: Deutsche Verlags-Anstalt, 2007), 330, and the accompanying map show the boundary shift, with LVI Panzer Corps going to Ninth Army, only on 22 February.

Chapter 20. The Belorussian Front's Rogachev-Zhlobin and Mormal'-Parichi Offensives

1. "Kratkie svodki ob obshchennogo boevogo opyta voisk 1 Belorusskogo fronta i armii za dekabr' 1943-aprel' 1944 g.,"1. 296.
2. Ibid., 320–321.
3. A. Gorbatov, "Nastuplenie voisk 3-i armii na rogachskom napravlenii" [The 3rd Army's offensive along the Rogachev axis], *Voenno-istoricheskii zhurnal* [Military-historical journal] 1 (January 1961): 22.
4. Gorbatov, "Nastuplenie," 23–24. V. V. Abaturov et al., eds., *Osvobozhdenie Belarusi: 1943–1944* [The liberation of Belarus 1943–1944] (Minsk: Belaruskaia Navuka, 2014), 82–83, provides the clearest explanation of 3rd Army's mission as described by General A. V. Gorbatov in his memoirs, *Gody i voiny* [Years and wars] (Moscow: Voenizdat, 1980), 254: "K. K. Rokossovsky approved this [Gorbatov's] proposal on 13 February, and after several days he signed a directive on the conduct of the offensive operation. The 3rd Army, while occupying defenses on its right and left wings, was ordered 'to cross the Dnepr on the ice on the morning of 21 February with a force of no fewer than seven divisions with all reinforcing means and, by delivering its main attack toward Kisteni, Elenovo, Bliznetsy, Zapol'e, and Pobolovo, capture [the following] lines:

(a) 21 February 1944—Pokrovskii, Viliakhovka, Rogovskoe Farm, Zhiliakhopka, Stan'kov, Terekhovka, and Shchibrin and seize crossings on the Drut' River in the Bol'shaia Konoplitsa and Rogachev sector with forward detachments;

22 February 1944—capture the city of Rogachev and the Novyi Bykhov, Krasnyi Bereg, Dedovo, Ozerane, Falevichi, Tikhnichi, Kolotovka, Berezovka, and Luchin line; and

23 February 1944—capture the city of Zhlobin and the Komarichi, Zolotoe Dno, Khomichi, Renta, Osovnik, Dobritsa, Parenevskii, Barki, Naidakochichi, Pobolovo, Berezovka, Tertezh, and Zhlobin Station line.

Subsequently, exploit success in the general direction of Bobruisk." Simultaneously, 48th Army had to deliver a blow along the right bank of the Berezina River toward Parichi and Bobruisk. The 50th Army was to capture the Bykhov region with a blow from the south."
5. Abaturov et al., *Osvobozhdenie Belarusi*, 83.
6. For details on the penal battalion, see Alexander V. Pyl'cyn, *Penalty Strike: The Memoirs of a Red Army Penal Company Commander, 1943–1945* (Mechanicsburg, PA: Stackpole Books, 2009), 16–27. It was common Red Army practice to employ penal companies and battalions to perform arduous and often deadly tasks, frequently with blocking detachments assigned to control them. Most of these battalions were overstrength, with as many as 500–800 men, and companies were often three times stronger than their line counterparts.
7. For additional details on the Rogachev-Zhlobin offensive, see Gorbatov, *Gody i voiny*, 252–261; Gorbatov, "Nastuplenie," 18–30; and numerous other works.
8. See Pyl'cyn, *Penalty Strike*, 16–27, for details about the 8th Separate Penal Battalion's role in this raid.
9. Abaturov et al., *Osvobozhdenie Belarusi*, 85.
10. G. F. Krivosheev et al., eds., *Rossiia i SSSR v voinakh XX veka: Statisticheskoe issledovanie* [Russia and the USSR in Wars of the Twentieth Century: A statistical investigation] (Moscow: Olma Press, 2001), 315.

11. K. K. Shilov, *Rechitskaia krasnoznamennaia* [Rechitsa Red Banner] (Moscow: Voenizdat, 1984), 109–110.
12. G. S. Nadysev, *Na sluzhbe shtabnoi* [In staff service] (Riga, Latvia: Izdatel'stvo Liesma, 1972), 160–162.
13. Ibid., 162.
14. "Operativnye prikazy i direktivy shtaba 1 Belorusskogo fronts za 1944" [Operational orders and directives of the 1st Belorussian Front's headquarters for 1944], *TsAMO*, f. 233, op. 2356, d. 26,11. 29–37.

Chapter 21. The Liquidation of German Bridgeheads on the Dnepr River's Eastern Bank

1. *Sbornik boevykh dokumentov Velikoi Otechestvennoi voiny, vypusk 12* [A collection of combat documents of the Great Patriotic War, issue 12] (Moscow: Voenizdat, 1951), 38. Hereafter cited as *SBDVOV*, with appropriate volume, date, and page(s).
2. "Operativnye prikazy i direktivy shtaba 1 Belorusskogo fronts za 1944,"11. 25–28.
3. M. F. Panov, *Na napravlenii glavnogo udara* [On the axis of the main attack] (Moscow: n.p., 1995), 109–110.
4. *SBDVOV*, issue 12, 39.
5. Ibid., 40–41.
6. I. F. Abramov, *82-aia Iartsevskaia: Boevoi put' 82-i Iartsevskoi Krasnoznamennoi ordena Suvorova i Kutuzova strelkovoi divizii* [The 82nd Iartsevo: The combat path of 82nd Iartsevo, Red Banner, and Orders of Suvorov and Kutuzov Rifle Division] (Moscow: Voenizdat, 1973), 102.
7. "Kratkie svodki ob obshchennogo boevogo opyta voisk 1 Belorusskogo fronta i armii za dekabr' 1943-aprel' 1944 g.,"11. 264, 310.
8. I. N. Pavlov, *Ot Moskvy do Shtral'zunda (Boevoi put' 354 i strelkovoi Kalinkovichskoi ordena Lenina, Krasoznamennoi, ordena Suvorova divizii)* [From Moscow to Straslund (The combat path of the Kalinkovichi, Orders of Lenin, Red Banner, and Order of Suvorov 354th Rifle Division)] (Moscow: Voenizdat, 1985), 82.
9. A. M. Andreev, *Po voennym dorogam : Boevoi put' 69-i strelkovoi Sevskoi dvazhdy krasnoznamennoi ordenov Suvurova i Kutuzova divizii* [Along military roads: The combat path of 69th Sevsk, twice Red Banner Orders of Suvorov and Kutuzov Rifle Division] (Moscow: Voenizdat, 1971), 143.
10. V. A. Zolotarev, et al., eds., *Russkii arkhiv: Velikaia Otechestvennaiavoina. Stavka VGK: Dokumenty i materialy 1944–1945. T. 16 (5–4)* [The Russian archives: The Great Patriotic War. *Stavka VGK*: Documents and materials 1944–1945. vol. 16 (5–4)] (Moscow: TERRA, 1999), 68–69.
11. Ibid., 74.

Chapter 22. Investigations, Recriminations, and Sokolovsky's Relief

1. M. A. Gareev, "Prichiny neudachnykh nastupatel'nykh operatsii Zapadnogo Fronta zimoi 1943–1944 goda," [The causes and lessons of the Western Front's unsuccessful offensive operations in the winter of 1943–1944]. *Voennaia mysl'* [Military thought] 2 (February 1994): 52.

2. Ibid., 53.

3. Gareev, "O neudachnykh nastupatel'nykh operatsiiakh Sovetskikh voisk v Velikoi Otechestvennoi voiny. Po neopublikovannym dokumentam GKO," [About the unsuccessful offensive operations of Soviet forces in the Great Patriotic War. According to unpublished documents of the GKO]. *Novaia i noveishaia istoriia* [New and newest history] 1 (January 1994): 14–29.

4. "1944 god, 33-i armiia, Zapadnyi Front" [1944, 33rd Army, Western Front], *SBDVOV* 10 (Moscow: Voenizdat, 1950): 8–19.

5. Ibid., 8–10.

6. V. A. Zolotarev et al., eds., *Velikaia Otechestvennaia voina 1941–1954 v chetyrekh knigakh: Kniga 3: Osvobozhdenie* [The Great Patriotic War 1941–1945, Book 3: Liberation] (Moscow: Nauka, 1999), 11. Gareev authored this chapter. Hereafter cited as *VOV* with appropriate page(s).

7. Gareev, "Prichiny i uroki neudachnykh nastupatel'nykh operatsii," 15.

8. Ibid.

9. Ibid.

10. Ibid., 55.

11. Ibid.

12. Ibid.

13. Ibid., 56.

14. Ibid.

15. Ibid.

16. Ibid., 57.

17. Ibid.

18. *VOV*, 13.

Chapter 23. Conclusions

1. Gareev, "O neudachnykh nastupatel'nykh operatsiiakh Sovetskikh voisk v Velikoi Otechestvennoi voiny. Po neopublikovannym dokumentam GKO," [About the unsuccessful offensive operations of Soviet forces in the Great Patriotic War. According to unpublished documents of the GKO]. *Novaia i noveishaia istoriia* [New and newest history] 1 (January 1994): 10.

2. Rokossovsky used similar economy-of-force operations to a tee when he reduced Sixth Army's encirclement pocket in the Stalingrad region in January and February of 1943 and suffered significantly fewer personnel losses than the typical Red Army *front* commander.

3. Ibid.

# Selected Bibliography

Abbreviations

NAM—National Archives Microfilm
TsAMO RF—*Tsentral'nyi arkhiv Ministerstva Oborony RF* [Central Archives of the Ministry of Defense of the Russian Federation]
TsPA UMA—*Tsentral'nyi partiinyi arkhiv Instituta Marksisma-Leninizma* [Central Party Archives of the Institute of Marxism and Leninism]
VIZh—*Voenno-istoricheskii zhurnal* [Military-historical journal]
Voenizdat—*Voennoe Izdatel'stvo* [Soviet (Russian) Ministry of Defense's Military Publishing House]

Primary Sources

"Anlage, Bd. 102. A.O.K. 2, Ia, Oct–Nov 1943." *AOK 2, 41181/102*. NAM series T-312, roll 1266.
"Anlagenband A/1 zum Tatigkeitsbericht No. 10." *Pz AOK 3, 49113/32* and *49113/33, 1 Oct–31 Dec 43*. NAM series T-313, roll 297.
"Anlagen zum Kriegstagebuch Nr. 7, Lagekarten Band VII." *Pz AOK 3, Ia, 49113/23* and *49113/24, 1 Oct–15 Nov 1943*. NAM series T-313, roll 296.
"A. O. K. II/Ia, Anlagen Band 103, Lagekarten, Russland, 1–31 December 1943." *AOK II/Ia, 41181/103*. NAM series T-312, roll 1266.
Boevoi sostav Sovetskoi Armii, chast' III (Ianvar'-dekabr' 1943 g.) [The combat composition of the Soviet Army, pt. 3 (January–December 1943)]. Moscow: Voenizdat, 1972.
Boevoi sostav Sovetskoi Armii, chast' IV (Ianvar'-dekabr' 1944 g.) [The combat composition of the Soviet Army, pt. 4 (January–December 1944)]. Moscow: Voenizdat, 1988.
"Der Feldzug gegen die Sowjet-Union der Heeresgruppe Nord, Kriegsjahr 1943." *H. Gr. Nord 1943, 7584/2*. NAM series T-311, roll 156.
"Die Abwehrschlachten um Witebsk vom 13.12.43 bis 17.2.44." *Pz AOK 3, Ia, Pz AOK 3 48936* file. NAM series T-313, roll 291.
"Forsirovanie p. Dnepr voiskami 65-i armii" [The forcing of the Dnepr River by 65th Army's Forces]. *Sbornik materialov po izucheniiu opyta voiny No. 12, mai–iun' 1944* [Collection of materials for the study of war experience No. 12, May–June 1944]. Moscow: Voenizdat, 1944. Classified secret but later declassified.
"Ia, Kartenband zum KTB Nr. 21, Nov–Dec 1943." *AOK 4, 49111/55*. NAM series T-312, roll 226.
"Ic, Tätigkeitsbericht, Nov–Dec 1943." *AOK 4, 48448/5*. NAM series T-312, roll 1362.

"Kräftegegenüberstellung Stand: 14. 10. 43," in *Anlage 4c zu Abt. Fr. H. Ost (I) Nr. 80/43 g kdos vom 17. 10. 43.* Copy of the original.

"Kratkie svodki ob obshchennogo boevogo opyta voisk 1 Belorusskogo fronta i armii za dekabr' 1943–aprel' 1944 g." [Short summaries of the generalization of combat experience of the 1st Belorussian Front and its armies for December 1943–April 1944]. *TsAMO*, f. 233, op. 2356, d. 19,11. 61–81, 97–132, 169–200, 264, 276, 296, and 310.

"Kriegsgliederung der Heeresgruppe Mitte (Stand: Anfang Oktober 1943)." *BA-MA, Studie ZA 1/2053; KTB OKW, Bd 3/2*, S. 1157.

"Nastupatel'nye operatsii s forsirovaniem rek" [Offensive operation with the forcing of rivers]. *Sbornik materialov po izucheniiu opyta voiny*, No. 12, *Mai–iun' 1944 g*. [Collection of materials for the study of war experiences, No. 12, May–June 1944]. Moscow: Voenizdat, 1944. Classified secret but later declassified.

"Nevel'skaia nastupatel'naia operatsiia" [The Nevel' offensive operation]. *Sbornik materialov po izucheniiu opyta voiny, No. 14, sentiabr'–oktiabr' 1944* [Collection of materials for the study of war experience, No. 14, September–October 1944]. Moscow: Voenizdat, 1944. Classified secret but later declassified.

"Operativnye prikazy i direktivy shtaba 1 Belorusskogo fronta za 1944" [Operational Orders and Directives of the 1st Belorussian Front's headquarters for 1944]. *TsAMO*, f. 233, op. 2356, d. 26,11. 25–37.

"Opersvodka Shtaba Z. F. No. 469, Razvedsvodka Shtaba Z. F. No. 275," 1 Oktiabria [Operational Summary No. 469 and Intelligence summary No. 275 of the Western Front's headquarters, 1 October 1943]. *Combat Operations of the Western Front's Forces in October 1943.* https://cdn.pamyat-naroda.ru/images.

"Opersvodka Shtaba Z. F. No. 500, Razvedsvodka Shtaba Z. F. No. 305," 1 Noiabria [Operational summary No. 500 and Intelligence summary No. 305 of the Western Front's headquarters, 1 November 1943]. *Combat Operations of the Western Front's Forces in November 1943.* https://cdn.pamyatnaroda.ru/images.

"Postanovlenie GKO, 12 March 1944." *TsPA UMA* [Central Party Archives Institute of Marxism and Leninism], f. 644, op. 1, d. 218,1. 102.

"Prikazy i direktivy 1-go Pribaltiiskogo fronta za 1943 g." [Orders and directives of the 1st Baltic Front for 1943]. *TsAMO*, f. 235, op. 2074, ed. khr. 9,11. 93–97.

Sbornik boevykh dokumentov Velikoi Otechestvennoi voiny, vypusk 12 [Collection of combat documents of the Great Patriotic War, issue 12]. Moscow: Voenizdat, 1951.

TsAMO, f. 48, op. 1691, d. 233,11. 3–5 and 30–31.

TsAMO, f. 208, op. 2511, ed. kh., 3051,11. 10–36.

TsAMO, f. 233, op. 2356, d. 19,11. 225–230.

TsAMO, f. 235, op. 2074, ed. kh., 77,11., 6–17.

"Zhurnal boevykh deistvii voisk Tsentral'nogo/Belorusskogo fronta za oktiabr' 1943 g." [The Central/Belorussian Front's journal of combat operations for October 1943]. *TsAMO*, f. 201, op. 390, ed. khr. 62/1,1. 2.

"Zhurnal boevykh deistvii voisk Tsentral'nogo/Belorusskogo fronta za noiabr' 1943 g." [The Central/Belorussian Front's journal of combat operations for 1943]. *TsAMO*, f. 201, op. 390, ed. khr. 62/9,1. 36.

"Zhurnal boevykh deistvii voisk 1-go Pribaltiiskogo fronta za oktiabr' 1943 g." [The 1st Baltic Front's journal of combat operations for October 1943]. *TsAMO*, f. 235, op. 2074, d. 51,11. 77–78.

"Zhurnal boevykh deistvii voisk 1-go Pribaltiiskogo fronta za noiabr' 1943 g." [The 1st Baltic Front's journal of combat operations for November 1943]. *TsAMO*, f. 235, op. 2074, ed. khr. 52,11. 2 and 34.

"Zhurnal boevykh deistvii voisk 1-go Pribaltiiskogo fronta za dekabr' 1943 g." [The 1st Baltic Front's journal of combat operations for December 1943]. *TsAMO*, f. 235, op. 2074, ed. khr. 53,11. 16, 42, and 44.

"Zhurnal boevykh deistvii voisk 1-go Pribaltiiskogo fronta za mart 1944 g." [The 1st Baltic Front's journal of combat operations for March 1944]. https://cdn.pamyat-naroda.ru/.

"Zhurnal boevykh deistvii voisk 3 armii za fevral' 1944 g." [The 3rd Army's journal of combat operations for February 1944]. https://cdn.pamyat-naroda.ru/.

"Zhurnal boevykh deistvii voisk 3 armii za mart 1944 g." [The 3rd Army's journal of combat operations for March 1944]. https://cdn.pamyat-naroda.ru/.

"Zhurnal boevykh deistvii voisk 5 armii za mart 1944 g." [The 5th Army's journal of combat operations for March 1944]. https://cdn.pamyat-naroda.ru/.

"Zhurnal boevykh deistvii voisk 33 Armii, 1–3 Dekabria 1943" [The 33rd Army's journal of combat operations, 1–3 December 1943]. https://cdn.pamyat-naroda.ru/images.

"Zhurnal boevykh deistvii voisk 39 armii za ianvar' m-ts 1944 g." [The 39th Army's journal of combat operations for January 1944]. https://cdn.pamyat-naroda.ru/.

"Zhurnal boevykh deistvii voisk 43 armii za ianvar' m-ts 1944 g.," [The 43rd Army's journal of combat operations for January 1944]. https://cdn.pamyat-naroda.ru/.

"Zhurnal boevykh deistvii chastei i soedinenii 48 armii za ianvar' m-ts 1944 g. Zadacha soedinenii (chastei) i perechen' sobitii v boevoi deiatel'nosti voisk" [The journal of combat operations of the units and formations of 48th Army for the month of January 1944. The missions of formations (units) and an enumeration of events in the combat activities of the forces]. https://cdn.pamyat-naroda.ru/.

"Zhurnal boevykh deistvii chastei i soedinenii 48 armii za fevral' m-ts 1944 g. Zadacha soedinenii (chastei) i perechen' sobitii v boevoi deiatel'nosti voisk" [The journal of combat operations of the units and formations of 48th Army for the month of February 1944. The missions of formations (units) and an enumeration of events in the combat activities of the forces]. https://cdn.pamyat-naroda.ru/.

"Zhurnal boevykh deistvii voisk 63 armii za ianvar' 1944 g." [The 63rd Army's journal of combat operations for January 1944]. https://cdn.pamyat-naroda.ru/.

"Zhurnal boevykh deistvii voisk 65 Armii, 1. 12. 43." [The 65th Army's journal of combat operations, 1 December 1943]. https://cdn.pamyat-naroda.ru/.

"Zhurnal boevykh deistvii voisk 65 Armii, 1. 11. 43." [The 65th Army's journal of combat operations, 1 November 1943]. https://cdn.pamyat-naroda.ru/.

"Zhurnal boevykh deistvii voisk 65 Armii, 1. 2. 44." [The 65th Army's journal of combat operations, 1 February 1944]. https://cdn.pamyat-naroda.ru/.

Zolotarev, V. A. et al., eds. *Russkii arkhiv: Velikaia Otechestvennaiavoina. General'nyi shtab v gody Velikoi Otechestvennoi voiny: Dokumenty i materialy, 1943 god. T-23 (12-3)* [The Russian archives: The Great Patriotic War. The General Staff in the years of the Great Patriotic War: Documents and materials, 1943. Vol. 23 (12-3)]. Moscow: TERRA, 1999.

———. *Russkii arkhiv: Velikaia Otechestvennaiavoina. General'nyi shtab v gody Velikoi Otechestvennoi voiny: Dokumenty i materialy 1944–1945 gg. T. 23 (12-4)* [The Russian archives: The Great Patriotic War. The General Staff in the years of the Great Patriotic War: Documents and materials 1944–1945. Vol. 23 (12-4)]. Moscow: TERRA, 2001.

———. "Russkii arkhiv: Velikaia Otechestvennaiavoina. Stavka Verkhovnogo Glavnokomandovannia: Dokumenty i materialy 1943 god. T. 16 (5 (3)" [The Russian archives: The Great Patriotic War, The *Stavka* of the Supreme High Command: Documents and materials 1943. Vol. 16, 5 (3)]. Moscow: TERRA, 1999.

———. *Russkii arkhiv: Velikaia Otechestvennaiavoina. Stavka VGK: Dokumenty i materialy 1944–1945. T. 16 (5–4)* [The Russian archives: The Great Patriotic War. The *Stavka* VGK: Documents and materials 1944–1945. Vol. 16 (5–4)]. Moscow: Terra, 1999.

"1944 god, 33-ia armiia, Zapadnyi Front" [1944, 33rd Army, Western Front]. *Sbornik boevykh dokumentov Velikoi Otechestvennoi voiny, vypusk 10* [Collection of combat documents of the Great Patriotic War, issue 10]. (Moscow: Voenizdat, 1950), 8–19. Classified secret but now declassified.

Secondary Sources—Books

Abaturov, V. V. et al., eds. *Osvobozhdenie Belarusi 1943–1944* [The liberation of Belarus 1943–1944]. Minsk: Belaruskaia Navuka, 2014.

Abramov, I. F. *82-ia Iartsevskaia: Boevoi put' 82-i Iartsevskoi Krasnoznamennoi ordena Suvorova i Kutuzova strelkovoi divizii* [The 82nd Iartsevo: The combat path of 82nd Iartsevo, Red Banner, and Orders of Suvorov and Kutuzov Rifle Division]. Moscow: Voenizdat, 1973.

Afanas'ev, N. M., N. K. Glazunov, P. A. Kazansky, and N. A. Fironov. *Dorogami ispytanii i pobed: boevoi put' 31-i armii* [Along the roads of ordeals and victories: The combat path of 31st Army]. Moscow: Voenizdat, 1986.

Altukhov, P. K. et al., eds. *Nezabyvaemye dorogi: Boevoi put' 10-i gvardeiskoi armii* [Unforgettable roads: The combat path of the 10th Guards Army]. Moscow: Voenizdat, 1974.

Andreev, A. A. *Po voennym dorogam: Boevoi put' 69-i strelkovoi Sevskoi dvazhdy krasnoznamennoi ordenov Suvorova i Kutuzova divizii* [Along military roads: The combat path of 69th Sevsk, twice Red Banner Orders of Suvorov and Kutuzov Rifle Division]. Moscow: Voenizdat, 1971.

Bagramian, I. Kh. *Tak shli my k pobede* [As we went on to victory]. Moscow: Voenizdat, 1985.

Batov, P. I. *V pokhodakh i boiakh* [In marches and battles]. Moscow: Voenizdat, 1984.

Beliavsky, V. A. *Strely skrestilis' na Shpree* [Shells crisscross on the Shpree]. Moscow: Voenizdat, 1972.

Beloborodov, A. P. *Vsegda v boiu* [Always in battle]. Moscow: Voenizdat, 1978.

Biographical information on German command cadre. http://www.axishistory.com/index.php?id.

Boiko, V. P. *S dumoi o rodine* [With thoughts for the Motherland]. Moscow: Voenizdat, 1982.

Bulatov, F. G. *Budni frontovykh let* [The humdrum front years]. Kazan': Tatarskoe Izdatel'stvo, 1984.

Chistiakov, I. M. *Sluzhim otchizne* [We served our homeland]. Moscow: Voenizdat, 1975.

Dokuchaev, M. S. *V boi shli eskadrony: Boevoi put' 7-go gvardeiskogo kavaleriiskogo Brandenburgskogo ordena Lenina, Krasnoznamennogo, ordena Suvorogo korpusa v Velikoi Otechestvennoi voine* [The squadrons went into battle: The combat path of 7th Guards Brandenburg, Order of Lenin, Red Banner, and Order of Suvorov Cavalry Corps]. Moscow: Voenizdat, 1984.

Dremov, I. F. *Nastupala groznaia bronia* [Menacing armor attacked]. Kiev: Politicheskoi literatury Ukrainy, 1981.

Egorov, V. F. et al. eds. *Rozhdennaia v boiakh: Boevoi put' 71-i gvardeiskoi strelkovoi Vitebskoi ordena Lenina, Krasnoznamennoi divizii* [Born in battle: The combat path of 71st Guards Vitebsk Order of Lenin, Red Banner Rifle Division]. Moscow: Voenizdat, 1986.

Eremenko, A. I. *Gody vozmezdiia 1943–1945* [Years of retribution]. Moscow: "Nauka," 1969.

Frieser, Karl-Heinz et al., eds. *Das Deutsche Reich und de Zweite Weltkrieg, Band 8, Die Ostfront 1943/44: Der Krieg im Osten und an den Nebenfronten.* Munchen: Deutsche Verlags-Anstalt, 2007.

Galitsky, K. N. *Gody surovykh ispitanii 1941–1944* [Years of a harsh education 1941–1944]. Moscow: Nauka, 1970, 1973.

Glantz, David M. *Colossus Reborn: The Red Army at War, 1941–1943.* Lawrence: University Press of Kansas, 2005.

———. *Forgotten Battles of the German-Soviet War (1941–1945).* Vol. 5: *The Summer–Fall Campaign (1 July–31 December 1943).* Pts. 1 and 2. Carlisle, PA: Self-published, 2000.

———. *Forgotten Battles of the German-Soviet War (1941–1945).* Vol. 6: *The Winter Campaign (24 December 1943–April 1944).* Pts. 1 and 2. Carlisle, PA: Self-published, 2003.

———. *A History of Soviet Airborne Forces.* London: Frank Cass, 1994.

———. *Soviet Military Deception in the Second World War.* London: Frank Cass, 1989.

Glantz, David M., and Jonathan House. *When Titans Clashed: How the Red Army Stopped Hitler.* Lawrence: University Press of Kansas, 2015.

Gorbatov, A. V. *Gody i voiny* [Years and wars]. Moscow: Voenizdat, 1980.

"Gorodokskaia operatsiia 1943" [The Gorodok operation 1943]. In *Sovetskaia voennaia entsiklopediia, T. 2* [Soviet military encyclopedia. Vol. 2]. Edited by A. A. Grechko et al. Moscow: Voenizdat, 1976.

"Gorodokskaia operatsiia 1943" [The Gorodok operation 1943]. In *Voennaia entsiklopediia v vos'mi tomakh, T. 2* [Military encyclopedia in eight volumes. Vol. 2]. Edited by P. S. Grachev et al. Moscow: Voenizdat, 1994.

Grachev, P. S. et al., eds. "Gomel'sko-Rechitskaia operatsiia 1943" [The Gomel'-Rechitsa operation of 1943]. In *Voennaia entsiklopediia v vos'mi tomakh, T. 2* [Military encyclopedia in eight volumes. Vol. 2]. Moscow: Voenizdat, 1994.

Grechko, A. A. et al., eds. *Istoriia Vtoroi Mirovoi voiny 1939–1945 v dvenadtsati tomakh, Tom sed'moi, Zavershenie korennogo pereloma v voine* [History of World War II 1939–1945 in twelve volumes. Vol. 7: The completion of a fundamental turning point in the war]. Moscow: Voenizdat, 1976.

Grigorenko, M. G. et al., eds. *Skvoz' ognennye vikhri: Boevoi put 11-i gvardeiskoi armii v Velikoi Otechestvennoi voiny 1941–1945* [Through fiery whirlwinds: The combat path of 11th Guards Army in the Great Patriotic War 1941–1945]. Moscow: Voenizdat, 1987.

Kachur, V. P., and V. V. Nikol'sky. *Pod znamenem Sivashtsev: Boevoi put' 169-i strelkovoi Rogachevskoi Krasnoznamennoi ordenov Suvorova II stepeni i Kutuzova II stepeni divizii (1941–1945)* [Under the banner of the men of Sivash': The combat path of 169th Rogachev, Red Banner, Orders of Suvorov II degree and Kutuzov II degree Rifle Division (1941–1945)]. Moscow: Voenizdat, 1989.

Krivosheev, G. F., ed. *Velikaia Otechestvennaiavoina bez grifa sekretnosti. Kniga poter'* [The Great Patriotic War without secret classification. A book of losses]. Moscow: Veche, 2009.

—— et al., eds. *Rossiia i SSSR v voinakh XX veka: Statisticheskoe issledovanie* [Russia and the USSR in wars of the Twentieth Century: A statistical investigation]. Moscow: Olma Press, 2001.

Krylov, N. I., N. I. Alekseev, and I. G. Dragan. *Navstrechu pobede: Boevoi put' 5-i armii oktiabr' 1941–avgust 1945* [Greeting victory: The combat path of 5th Army, October 1941–August 1945]. Moscow: Nauka, 1970.

Kuprianov, N. V. *S veroi v pobedu: Boevoi put' 38-i gvardeiskoi strelkovoi Lozovaia Krasnoznamennoi divizii* [With faith in victory: The combat path of 38th Guards Lozovaia Red Banner Rifle Division]. Moscow: Voenizdat, 1985.

Lisitsyn, F. Ia. *V te groznye gody* [In those threatening years]. Moscow: Voenizdat, 1985.

Madej, W. Victor, ed. *The German Army Order of Battle.* New York: Game Marketing, 1978.

Mal'kov, D. K. *Skvoz' dym i plamia: Boevoi put' 12-i gvardeiskoi Pinskoi Krasnoznamennoi ordena Suvorova strelkovoi divizii* [Through the smoke and flames: The combat path of 12th Guards Pinsk, Red Banner, and Order of Suvorov Rifle Division]. Moscow: Voenizdat, 1970.

Mitchum, Samual W. Jr. *Hitler's Legion: The German Army Order of Battle, World War II.* New York: Stein and Day, 1985.

Morozov, M. E. et al., eds. *Velikaia Otechestvennaia voina 1941–1945 gg. Kampanii i strategicheskie operatsii v tsifrakh v 2 tomakh. Tom II* [The Great Patriotic war 1941–1945. Campaigns and strategic operations in figures in two volumes. Vol. 2]. Moscow: Glavarkhiv goroda Moskvy, 2010.

Moshchansky, Il'ia. "Osvobozhdenie Belorussii: Boevye deistviia Kalininskogo, Zapadnogo i Belorusskikh frontov 26 sentiabr 1943–5 aprelia 1944, Nachalo" [The liberation of Belorussia: the combat actions of the Kalinin, Western, and Belorussian Fronts, 26 September 1943–5 April 1944—the beginning]. *Voennaia letopis'* [Military chronicle] 2–2006. Moscow: OOO BTV-MH, 2006.

Nadysev, G. S. *Na sluzhbe shtabnoi* [In staff service]. Riga, Latvia: Izdatel'stvo Liesma, 1972.

Nevenkin, Kamen. *Fire Brigades: The Panzer Divisions, 1943–1945.* Winnipeg, MB: J. J. Fedorowicz, 2008.

Pankov, F. D. *Ognennye rubezhi: Boevoi put' 50-i armii v Velikoi Otechestvennoi voine* [Firing lines: The combat path of 50th Army in the Great Patriotic War]. Moscow: Voenizdat, 1984.

Panov, M. F. *Na napravlenii glavnovo udara* [On the axis of the main attack]. Moscow: n.p., 1995.

Pavlov, I. N. *Ot Moskvy do Shtral'zunda (Boevoi put' 354-i strelkovoi Kalinkovichskoi ordena Lenina, Krasoznamennoi, ordena Suvorova divizii)* [From Moscow to Stralsund (The combat path of the Kalinkovichi, Orders of Lenin, Red Banner, and Order of Suvorov 354th Rifle Division)]. Moscow: Voenizdat, 1985.
Piskovitin, M. I. et al. *Gvardeiskaia Chernigovskaia* [The guards Chernigov]. Moscow: Voenizdat, 1976.
Plato, Anton Detlev von. *Die Geschichte Der 5. Panzerdivision 1938 bis 1945.* Regensburg: Walhalla u. Praetoria Verlag, 1978.
Pomnit Dnepr-reka [Remember the Dnepr River]. Minsk: Belarus, 1986.
Portnov, S. N. et al., eds. *Rizhskie gvardeiskie: Sbornik voenno-istoricheskikh ocherkov* [Riga guards: A collection of military-historical essays]. Riga, Latvia: Liesma, 1972.
Pyl'cyn, Alexander V. *Penalty Strike: The Memoirs of a Red Army Penal Company Commander, 1943–1945.* Mechanicsburg, PA: Stackpole Books, 2009.
Rokossovsky, K. *A Soldier's Duty.* Moscow: Progress, 1985.
———. *Soldatskii dolg* [A soldier's duty]. Moscow: Golos, 2000.
Sandalov, L. M. *Posle perelom* [After the turning point]. Moscow: Voenizdat, 1983.
Sekretov, A. N. *Gvardeiskaia postup' (Boevoi put' 17-i Mozyrskoi krasnoznamennoi ordenov Lenina, Suvorova i Kutuzova kavaleriiskoi divizii podshefnoi Tadzhikistanu, v gody Velikoi Otechestvennoi voiny, 1941–1945 gg.)* [Guards gait (The combat path of 17th Mozyr' Red Banner and Orders of Lenin, Suvorov, and Kutuzov Cavalry Division, raised in Tadzhikistan during the Great Patriotic War, 1941–1945)]. Dushanbe: Donish, 1985.
Shilov, K. K. *Rechitskaia krasnoznamennaia* [Rechitsa Red Banner]. Moscow: Voenizdat, 1984.
Sovetskaia kavaleriia [Soviet cavalry]. Moscow: Voenizdat, 1984.
Stoves, Rolf. *Die Gepanzerten und Motorisierten Deutschen Grossverbände (Divisionen und selbständige Brigaden) 1935–1945.* Friedberg, FRG: Podzun-Pallas Verlag, 1986.
Telegin, K. F. *Voiny neschitannye versty* [Wars of uncountable versts]. Moscow: Voenizdat, 1988.
Tippelskirch, K. *Istoriia vtoroi mirovoi voiny* [A history of World War II]. Moscow: Voenizdat, 1962. A translation of Tippelskirch, Kurt von. *Geschichte des Zweiten Weltkriegs.* Bonn, FRG: n.p., 1961.
Velikaia Otechestvennaia voina 1941–1945 gg.: Deistvuiushchaia armiia [The Great Patriotic War 1941–1945: The operating army]. Moscow: Kuchkovo pole, 2005.
Ziemke, Earl F. *Stalingrad to Berlin: The German Defeat in the East.* Washington, DC: Office of the Chief of Military History, U.S. Army, 1968.
Zolotarev, V. A. et al., eds. *Velikaia Otechestvennaia voina 1941–1945 v chetyrekh knigakh: Kniga 2: Perelom* [The Great Patriotic War 1941–1945 in four books. Book 2: The Turning point]. Moscow: Nauka, 1998.
———. *Velikaia Otechestvennaia voina 1941–1945 v chetyrekh knigakh: Kniga 3: Osvobozhdenie* [The Great Patriotic War 1941–1945 in four books. Book 3: Liberation]. Moscow: Nauka, 1999.
Zubarev, S. P. *Ot Dona do El'by* [From the Don to the Elbe]. Moscow: Udmurtia, n.p., 1975.

Secondary Sources—Articles

Batov, P. "Na gomel'skom napravlenii" [On the Gomel' axis]. *VIZh* 12 (December 1968): 78–84.

———. "65-ia armiia v boiakh za Belorussiiu" [The 65th Army in the battles for Belorussia]. *VIZh* 9 (September 1970): 65–70.

Gareev, M. A. "Prichiny i uroki neudachnykh nastupatel'nykh operatsii Zapadnogo fronta zimoi 1943/44 goda" [The causes and lessons of the Western Front's unsuccessful offensive operations in the winter of 1943/44]. *Voennaia mysl'* [Military thought] 2 (February 1994): 50–58.

———. "O neudachnykh nastupatel'nykh operatsiiakh Sovetskikh voisk v Velikoi Otechestvennoi voiny. Po neopublikovannym dokumentam GKO" [About the unsuccessful offensive operations of Soviet forces in the Great Patriotic War. According to unpublished documents of the GKO]. *Novaia i noveishaia istoriia* [New and newest history] 1 (January 1994): 3–29.

Gazin, A. "28-ia strelkovaia diviziia v boiakh na nevel'skom napravlenii" [The 28th Rifle Division in battles on the Nevel' axis]. *VIZh* 9 (September 1981: 25–29.

Gorbatov, A. "Nastuplenie voisk 3-i armii na rogachevskom napravlenii" [The 3rd Army's offensive along the Rogachev axis]. *VIZh* 1 (January 1961): 18–30.

Gorbatov, A., and M. Ivashechkin, "Nastuplenie 3-i armii severnee Gomelia" [The 3rd Army's offensive north of Gomel']. *VIZh* 8 (August 1962): 30–43.

Mal'kov, D. "Vnezapnaia ataka" [Surprise attack]. *VIZh* 3 (March 1964): 55–60.

Panov, M. "V boiakh za Kalinkovichi" [In the battles for Kalinkovichi]. *VIZh* 5 (May 1978): 46–51.

Semenov, G. "Vnezapnyi udar po vragu" [A surprise attack on the enemy]. *VIZh* 10 (October 1969): 76–83.

Sukhinin, Iu. "K voprosu ob organizatsii i vedenii boia 1-i Pol'skoi pekhotnoi diviziei pod Lenino" [Concerning 1st Polish Infantry Division's organization and conduct of the battle at Lenino]. *VIZh* 4 (April 1983): 28–32.

Sverdlov, F. "Nevel'skaia nastupatel'naia operatsiia (6–16 oktiabr 1943 goda)" [The Nevel' offensive operation (6–16 October 1943)]. *VIZh* 11 (November 1968): 26–35.

———. "Podgotovka i vedenie Gorodokskoi operatsii" [The preparation and conduct of the Gorodok operation]. *VIZh* 3 (March 1976): 22–31.

Index of Appendix Documents

A. THE KALININ AND BALTIC FRONTS' VITEBSK AND NEVEL' OFFENSIVES (3–30 OCTOBER 1943)

A-1. *Stavka* VGK Directive No. 30192 to the Commander of the Kalinin Front and the Representative of the *Stavka* Concerning a Plan for Capturing Vitebsk, 1700 hours 20 September 1943, 585

A-2. Report No. 15621 of the Commander of the Kalinin Front to the Supreme High Commander Concerning a Plan for the Vitebsk Operation, 2315 hours 22 September 1943, 585

A-3. *Stavka* VGK Directive No. 30195 to the Commander of the Kalinin Front and the Representative of the *Stavka* Concerning More Precise Definition of the Plan for the Vitebsk Operation, 0045 hours 24 September 1943, 587

A-4. *Stavka* VGK Directive No. 30217 to the Commander of the Baltic Front Concerning the Preparation and Conduct of an Offensive Operation along the Idritsa Axis, 2230 hours 8 October 1943, 588

A-5. *Stavka* VGK Directive No. 30218 to the Commander of the Kalinin Front on the Development of an Offensive to Capture Riga, 2230 hours 8 October 1943, 589

A-6. *Stavka* VGK Directive No. 30219 to the commander of the Northwestern Front on the Preparation and Conduct of an Operation to Destroy the Enemy's Porkhov Grouping, 1800 hours 10 October 1943, 589

A-7. *Stavka* VGK Directive No. 30220 to the Commanders of the Baltic, Northwestern, and Kalinin Fronts Concerning a Change in the Period of the Resubordination of 3rd Shock and 22nd Armies and the Missions of their Air Support, 2210 hours 10 October 1943, 590

A-8. From an Enciphered Telegram to the *Stavka* from the Kalinin Front, 11 October 1943, 591

A-9. To the Commander of the Kalinin Front Concerning the Preparation of an Operation for the Destruction of Enemy Aviation, 0230 hours 12 October 1943, 591

A-10. Report No. 22 of the Commander of the Baltic Front to the Supreme High Commander on the Plan for the First Stage of the Operation along the Idritsa Axis, 1745 hours 13 October 1943, 592

A-11. *Stavka* VGK Directive No. 30224 to the Commander of the Baltic Front Concerning the Missions of the Second Stage of the Operation along the Idritsa Axis, 0100 hours 15 October 1943, 593

A-12. *Stavka* VGK Order No. 30228 Concerning the Renaming of the Central, Kalinin, and Baltic

711

Fronts, 2230 hours 16 October 1943, 593

A-13. From Enciphered Telegram No. 16556 to the *Stavka* from the Kalinin Front, 19 October 1943, 594

B. THE WESTERN FRONT'S ORSHA OFFENSIVES (3–28 OCTOBER 1943)

B-1. *Stavka* VGK Directive No. 30193 to the Commander of the Western Front and the Representative of the *Stavka* Concerning the Destruction of the Enemy Smolensk Grouping, 1700 hours 20 September 1943, 594

B-2. *Stavka* VGK Directive No. 30210 to the Commander of the Western Front on the Development of an Offensive to Capture the City of Vilnius, 1 October 1943, 595

B-3. "Intelligence Summary No. 469 and Operational Summary No. 469 of the Western Front's Headquarters, 1 October 1943," 596

B-4. *Stavka* VGK Directive No. 30225 to the Commander of the Western Front and the Representative of the *Stavka* on a Regrouping of Forces, 2320 hours 15 October 1943, 598

C. THE CENTRAL FRONT'S GOMEL'-RECHITSA OFFENSIVE (30 SEPTEMBER–30 OCTOBER 1943)

C-1. Report No. 312 of the Commander of the Briansk Front to the Supreme High Commander on a Plan for an Operation along the Zhlobin Axis, 0315 hours 19 September 1943, 599

C-2. *Stavka* VGK Directive No. 30191 to the Commander of the Briansk Front Concerning Approval and Amplification of a Plan for an Offensive on Minsk, 0300 hours 20 September 1943, 601

C-3. *Stavka* VGK Directive No. 30208 to the Commander of the Central Front on the Defeat of the Enemy Zhlobin-Bobruisk Grouping and the Capture of Minsk, 1830 hours 1 October 1943, 601

C-4. *Stavka* VGK Directive No. 30209 to the Commander of the Briansk Front Concerning the Abolition of the Briansk [Front] and Formation of the Baltic Front, 1900 hours 1 October 1943, 602

C-5. *Stavka* VGK Directive No. 30231 to the Commander of the Belorussian Front Concerning the Resubordination and Regrouping of 11th and 48th Armies, 0330 hours 23 October 1943, 603

C-6. The Journal of Combat Operations of 65th Army, 1 November 1943, 603

D. THE 1st AND 2nd BALTIC FRONTS' POLOTSK-VITEBSK AND PUSTOSHKA-IDRITSA OFFENSIVES (2–21 NOVEMBER 1943)

D-1. From Directive No. 00365/op of the Military Council of the 1st Baltic Front, 25 October 1943, 605

D-2. From 1st Baltic Front Report No. 00370/op to the *Stavka* VGK on the Conduct of an Airborne Operation, 1 November 1943, 606

D-3. *Stavka* VGK Directive No. 30243 to the Commander of the 1st Baltic Front and the Representative of the *Stavka* on the Defeat of the Enemy Vitebsk Grouping, 0130 hours 12 November 1943, 607

D-4. *Stavka* VGK Directive No. 30246 to the Commander of the 1st Baltic Front Concerning

Index of Appendix Documents 713

Instances of the Presentation of Unverified Information about the Enemy to the *Stavka*, 1400 hours 12 November 1943, 608

D-5. *Stavka* Order No. 00151 Concerning the Relief of the Commanders of the Forces of the 1st Baltic Front and 11th Guards Army, 17 November 1943, 608

D-6. *Stavka* VGK Directive No. 30247 to the Commander of the 1st Baltic Front and the Representative of the *Stavka* on the Defeat of the Enemy Vitebsk Grouping, 0215 hours 18 November 1943, 609

D-7. *Stavka* VGK Directive No. 30248 to the Commanders of the 1st and 2nd Baltic Fronts and the Representative of the *Stavka* on the Resubordination of Force Units, 0215 hours 18 November 1943, 609

D-8. *Stavka* Directive No. 30249 to the Commander of the 1st Baltic Front and the Representative of the *Stavka* Concerning the Period of the Liberation of Gorodok, 0030 hours 20 November 1943, 610

D-9. *Stavka* VGK Directive No. 30251 to the Commander of the 1st Baltic Front and the Representative of the *Stavka* Concerning the Organization of Cooperation between 11th Guards and 4th Shock Armies in the Liberation of Gorodok, 2130 hours 21 November 1943, 610

D-10. *Stavka* VGK Directive No. 30252 to the Commanders of the 1st Baltic and Western Fronts and the Representative of the *Stavka* Concerning the Boundary Line between the *Fronts*, 2345 hours 21 November 1943, 611

D-11. From Directive No. 00401/op of the Military Council of the 1st Baltic Front, 23 November 1943, 611

D-12. *Stavka* VGK Directive No. 30240 to the Commanders of the 1st and 2nd Baltic Fronts and the Representative of the *Stavka* about the Resubordination of Formations and Measures for Clearing the Enemy from Between the Lakes, 2230 hours 10 November 1943, 612

D-13. *Stavka* VGK Directive No. 30244 to the Commander of the 2nd Baltic Front on Halting the Offensive and Transferring Forces to the 1st Baltic Front, 0130 hours 12 November 1943, 612

D-14. *Stavka* Directive No. 46200 to the Commanders of the Northwestern and 2nd Baltic Fronts Concerning the Abolition of the Northwestern Front, 0215 hours 15 November 1943, 613

E. THE WESTERN FRONT'S ORSHA OFFENSIVES (14 NOVEMBER–5 DECEMBER 1943)

E-1. Excerpts from "Intelligence Summary No. 305 and Operational Summary No. 500 of the Western Front's Headquarters, 1 November 1943," 614

E-2. Excerpts from "The Combat Journal of 33rd Army, 1–3 December 1943," 616

F. THE BELORUSSIAN FRONT'S GOMEL'-RECHITSA AND NOVYI BYKHOV–PROPOISK OFFEENSIVES (10–30 NOVEMBER 1943)

F-1. Excerpt from "The Journal of Combat Operations of 65th Army, 1 December 1943," 619

G. THE 1st BALTIC AND WESTERN FRONTS' VITEBSK (GORODOK) OFFENSIVE (13–24 DECEMBER

1943) AND THE 2nd BALTIC FRONT'S IDRITSA-OPOCHKA OFFENSIVE (16–25 DECEMBER 1943)

- G-1. From Enciphered Telegram No. 18236 of the Military Council of the 1st Baltic Front to the Commanders of 4th Shock, 11th, 43rd, and 39th Armies, and the Commanders of the 1st Baltic Front's Artillery and Armored and Mechanized Forces, 8 December 1943, 622
- G-2. *Stavka* VGK Directive No. 30255 to the Commanders of the 1st Baltic and Western Fronts and the Representative of the *Stavka* on the Resubordination of Three Rifle Divisions, 0030 hours 3 December 1943, 622
- G-3. *Stavka* VGK Directive No. 30256 to the Commander of the Western Front and the Representative of the *Stavka* on Shifting the Direction of the Main Attack, 0050 hours 3 December 1943, 623
- G-4. From Enciphered Telegram No. 18419 from the Military Council of the 1st Baltic Front to Lieutenant General Gerasimov, the Commander of 4th Shock Army, and the Commander of 3rd Cavalry Corps, Oslikovsky, 14 December 1943, 623
- G-5. *Stavka* VGK Directive No. 30264 to the Commander of the 2nd Baltic Front Concerning an Operation to Destroy the Enemy's Nevel' Grouping, 2350 hours 9 December 1943, 624

H. THE 1st BALTIC AND WESTERN FRONTS' VITEBSK OFFENSIVE (24 DECEMBER 1943–5 JANUARY 1944) AND THE 2nd BALTIC FRONT'S NOVOSOKOL'NIKI PURSUIT (30 DECEMBER 1943–15 JANUARY 1944)

- H-1. *Stavka* VGK Directive No. 30268 to the Commander of the 1st Baltic Front and the Representative of the *Stavka* on Destroying the Enemy's Vitebsk Grouping, 2010 hours 23 December 1943, 624
- H-2. From Enciphered Telegram No. 19330 to the *Stavka* VGK from the Military Council of the 1st Baltic Front, 25 December 1943, 625
- H-3. *Stavka* VGK Order No. 30259 Concerning the Relief from his Duties of the Deputy Commander of the Western Front, 8 December 1943, 625
- H-4. *Stavka* VGK Order No. 00144 Concerning the Shuffling of the Members of the Military Councils of the 2nd Baltic and Western Fronts, 0110 hours 15 December 1943, 625
- H-5. From an Enciphered Telegram from the *Stavka* to the 1st Baltic Front, 27 December 1943, 626
- H-6. *Stavka* VGK Directive No. 30257 to the Commanders of the Western and 2nd Baltic Fronts on the Resubordination of 10th Guards Army, 0215 hours 8 December 1943, 626

I. THE 1st BALTIC AND WESTERN FRONTS' VITEBSK-BOGUSHEVSK OFFENSIVE (6–24 JANUARY 1944)

- I-1. Excerpts from "The Journal of Combat Operations of 43rd Army for January 1944, 1 January 1944," 627
- I-2. Excerpts from "The Journal of Combat Operations of 39th Army for January 1944, 1–4 January," 629
- I-3. From Report No. 15 on the Generalization of the Western Front's Combat Experiences for January 1944, 630

Index of Appendix Documents   715

I-4. Documentation of the Western Front's Losses for 1944, 631
I-5. The Defensive Battles at Witebsk from 13.12.43 through 17.2.44, 631

J. THE 1st BALTIC AND WESTERN FRONT'S VITEBSK OFFENSIVE (3–16 FEBRUARY 1944)
   J-1. *Stavka* VGK Directive No. 220011 to the Commanders of the 1st Baltic and Western Fronts and the Representative of the *Stavka* [N. N. Voronov] on the Destruction of the Enemy's Vitebsk Grouping, 0330 hours 18 January 1944, 632
   J-2. From the Commander of the 1st Baltic Front to the Supreme High Commander, Marshal of the Soviet Union I. V. Stalin, Concerning a Plan for the Vitebsk Operation, 14 January 1944, 633
   J-3. To the Commander of the 1st Baltic Front Concerning a Withdrawal of 3rd Guards Cavalry Corps into the High Command's Reserve, 1800 hours 18 January 1944, 633
   J-4. To the Commander of the 1st Baltic Front Concerning the Composition of 39th Army Being Transferred to the Western Front, 1500 hours 19 January 1944, 634

K. THE WESTERN FRONT'S BABINOVICHI AND VITEBSK OFFENSIVES (22 FEBRUARY–5 MARCH 1944)
   K-1. Documentation of the Western Front's Losses for 1944, 635
   K-2. The Defensive Battles at Witebsk from 13.12.43 through 17.2.44, 635
   K-3. Report No. 21 by the Commander of the Western Front to the Supreme High Commander on a Plan for an Offensive Operation along the Vitebsk and Orsha Axes, 25 February 1944, 636
   K-4. *Stavka* VGK Directive No. 220037 to the Commander of the Western Front Concerning the Reworking of his Plan for an Offensive Operation along the Vitebsk and Orsha Axes, 0310 hours 26 February 1944, 638
   K-5. *Stavka* VGK Directive No. 220043 to the Commanders of the 1st Baltic and Western Fronts Concerning Pursuit of the Withdrawing Enemy and the Offensive against Vitebsk, 0330 hours 1 March 1944, 638
   K-6. Excerpt from "The Journal of Combat Operations of the 1st Baltic Front for March 1944, 1–3 March 1944," 639
   K-7. Excerpt from "The Journal of Combat Operations of 5th Army for March 1944, 1–2 March 1944," 640

L. THE WESTERN FRONT'S ORSHA AND BOGUSHEVSK OFFENSIVES (5–29 MARCH 1943)
   L-1. Extract from "Documentation of the Western Front's Losses for 1944," 642

M. THE BELORUSSIAN FRONT'S SITUATION ON 1 JANUARY 1944 AND PRELIMINARY OPERATIONS
   M-1. Excerpt from "The Journal of Combat Operations of 48th Army, 1 January 1944," 642
   M-2. Excerpt from "The Journal of Combat Operations of 63rd Army, 1 January 1944," 644

N. THE BELORUSSIAN FRONT'S KALINKOVICHI-MOZYR' OFFENSIVE (8–14 JANUARY 1944)
   N-1. *Stavka* VGK Order No. 220000 to the Commander of the

Belorussian Front about a Change in the Boundary Line with the 1st Ukrainian Front and the Defeat of the Enemy's Mozyr' Grouping, 1820 hours 2 January 1944, 646

O. THE BELORUSSIAN FRONT'S PARICHI-BOBRUISK (MARMOVICHI-DUBROVA) OFFENSIVE (16 JANUARY–23 FEBRUARY 1944)

O-1. Excerpt from "The Journal of Combat Operations of 48th Army, 1 February 1944," 647

O-2. Excerpt from "The Journal of Combat Operations of 65th Army, 1 February 1944," 650

O-3. *Stavka* VGK Directive No. 220027 to the Commander of the Belorussian Front and the Commander and Deputy Commander of the 1st Ukrainian Front Concerning the Formation of the 2nd Belorussian Front, 1900 hours 17 February 1944, 653

O-4. *Stavka* VGK Directive No. 220032 to the Commanders of the Western and Belorussian Fronts about the Resubordination of 10th Army, 2130 hours 18 February 1944, 654

P. THE 1st BELORUSSIAN FRONT'S ROGACHEV-ZHLOBIN AND MORMAL-PARICHI OFFENSIVES (21–29 FEBRUARY 1944)

P-1. Excerpt from "The Journal of Combat Operations of 3rd Army for February 1944, 1 February 1944," 654

P-2. Excerpt from "The Journal of Combat Operations of 3rd Army for March 1944, 1 March 1944," 657

P-3. Report No. 00179/op by the Commander of the 1st Belorussian Front to the Supreme High Commander, Marshal of the Soviet Union I. V. Stalin, 1730 hours 4 March 1944, 660

Q. THE LIQUIDATION OF GERMAN BRIDGEHEADS ON THE DNEPR RIVER'S EASTERN BANK (25–31 MARCH 1944)

Q-1. From 1st Belorussian Front Particular Operational Directive No. 00215/op to the Commander of 10th Army, 2330 hours 21 March 1944, 661

Q-2. *Stavka* VGK Directive No. 220067 to the Commanders of the 1st and 2nd Belorussian Fronts on the Resubordination of Armies and Cavalry Corps and the Withdrawal of the Headquarters of the 2nd Belorussian Front and 6th Air Army into the *Stavka* VGK's Reserve, 2150 hours 2 April 1944, 662

Q-3. *Stavka* VGK Directive No. 220079 to the Commander of the 1st Belorussian Front on a Transition to the Defense, 2200 hours 17 April 1944, 663

Index

Abramov, Colonel G. I., 468
Abramov, Lieutenant Colonel M. M., 503
Abteilung (detachment), German general, 29
Adamenka (Bykhov region), 506
Afanas'evskoe, Lake (Orsha region), 81
Air Force, German. *See* Luftwaffe
Aleksandrov (Mormal' region), 521
Aleksandrovka (Kalinkovichi region), 424
Aleksandrovka (Mozyr' region), 441
Aleksandrovka (Shatsilki region), 502
Alekseev, Major General D. F., 423–424, 427, 431, 436–437, 460, 464, 466, 537
Amosov, Colonel M. P., 502
Andreev, Major General A. M., 482, 488–491, 494, 497, 504, 519–520
Andreevka (Rechitsa region), 187
Andrianovo (Orsha region), 383
Anikin, Guards Lieutenant Colonel M. A., 161
Anisovichi (Kalinkovichi region), 424, 432, 434–435
Antonov, Army General A. I., 51, 153, 304, 442, 545
Antonovka (Chausy region), 526
Antonovka (Kalinkovichi region), 424
Antonovka (Shatsilki region), 520
Arguny (Vitebsk region), 142, 309, 318, 320, 324, 353, 362, 387–388, 392
Arkhipovka, 35
Armies, German
    First Panzer, 7, 267–269
    Second, xxi, 15, 28, 91–92, 94–106, 109, 112–119, 171, 173, 176, 177, 179–182, 184–199, 204–205, 207–208, 242–250, 256–257, 259, 275, 321, 324, 402–403, 405, 419, 421–427, 433–436, 438–441, 443–447, 450–453, 455–457, 459–460, 464–465, 467, 470–471, 474–478, 481, 484, 505, 573, 697n26
        combat formation on 20 October 1943, 117
        combat formation on 15 January 1944, 484
    Third Panzer, xix, xxi, xxii, 15, 26, 32, 38–39, 41, 48, 56, 78, 122–123, 127, 129–137, 140, 142–144, 151, 156, 171, 176, 207–208, 210, 218–220, 223, 225–228, 231–237, 242, 269, 273–275, 277–278, 280, 285–291, 293–296, 298–303, 308, 311–313, 316–320, 322–326, 328, 330, 332–334, 339, 341, 344–346, 348, 350–354, 356–360, 363–364, 366–369, 373–379, 383, 386, 391–393, 398–400, 402, 540–541, 584, 681n20
    Fourth, xix, xxi, 13, 15, 63–70, 72–78, 80, 82, 84–89, 124, 156–158, 162–165, 167–169, 171, 176, 226, 234, 269, 273, 369, 381–384, 386, 411, 460, 505, 528–534, 540, 584
    Fourth Panzer, 13, 26, 92, 260, 267–268
    Sixth, 268–269, 582
    Eighth, 13, 92, 267, 269
    Ninth, xix, 10, 27, 78, 97, 105, 109, 115, 121, 129, 176–177, 179, 186–187, 189–191, 193, 198, 200–205, 207, 242–245, 247, 250, 255, 258, 260, 269, 273, 275, 328, 353, 402–403, 405–406, 409–412, 415–416, 428, 455–457, 466–467, 470–471, 474–477, 480, 482, 487–492, 494, 499, 502, 504–505, 511, 513–522, 526, 528, 535, 537, 540, 573, 584
        combat formation on 15 January 1944, 484
        combat formation on 1 February 1944, 498

717

718   Index

Armies, German, *continued*
  Sixteenth, 26, 38, 41–42, 52, 78, 122, 125–126, 129, 142, 148–149, 155, 208, 237–238, 268, 304–306
  Seventeenth, 269
  Eighteenth, 52, 148, 152, 268, 304
  Wöhler, 272
Armies, Soviet
  Tank, general, 30
  1st Air, 9, 12, 14, 74
  1st Guards, 9, 12
  1st Shock, 52, 54, 154
  1st Tank, xxi, 9, 12, 14, 30, 267–268
  2nd Air, 9, 12, 14
  2nd Guards, 9, 12, 15
  2nd Shock, 12, 52
  2nd Tank, 9, 12, 30, 269
  3rd, 9, 12, 14, 27, 91, 94–97, 103–104, 109, 121, 174, 177, 190, 192, 200–205, 243, 404, 406–413, 415–416, 439, 499, 501, 506–516, 521, 525–526, 539, 577–578, 685n7, 686n28, 700n4
    strength on 15 November 1943, 174
  3rd Air, 12, 14, 32, 128, 303
  3rd Guards, xxi, 9, 12, 15, 543
  3rd Guards Tank, xxi, 9, 12, 14, 267–268
  3rd Shock, 14, 26, 32, 36–37, 39, 41–42, 51–55, 94, 125–126, 129–130, 138–139, 146–150, 154, 237–240, 303–306, 682n35
  4th, 52
  4th Air, 9, 12, 15
  4th Guards, 9, 12, 15
  4th Shock, 14, 26, 32, 34–37, 41, 43, 45–46, 48, 52–53, 55–56, 125–126, 129–136, 139–141, 147, 153, 209–210, 212, 214, 216–217, 219–220, 223, 225–229, 231, 237, 274–281, 285, 287, 290, 296, 303, 309–310, 312, 316–317, 333–334, 337–347, 349, 368
    order of battle on 13 December 1943, 217
  4th Tank, 9, 12, 30, 268
  5th, 12, 14, 26, 34, 48, 61–67, 70–71, 74, 78–83, 87, 156–158, 162–164, 166–169, 281, 291, 297–300, 308, 310, 318, 320–321, 324–325, 327, 333, 338, 340, 350, 352–353, 359, 362–369, 371–373, 375, 380, 387–388, 390, 392–396, 399, 401, 542, 544, 548, 552, 692n13, 693n11
    combat formation on 8 January 1944, 319
    combat formation on 3 February 1944, 350
  5th Air, 12, 15
  5th Guards, 9, 12, 15
  5th Guards Tank, xxi, 9, 12, 15, 30, 267, 269, 583–584
  5th Shock, 9, 12, 15
  6th, 12, 15
  6th Air, 500
  6th Guards, 9, 12, 14, 51, 53, 55, 94, 125–126, 134, 145–146, 148–154, 237–239, 305–306
  6th Tank, 267, 269
  7th Guards, 9, 12, 15
  8th, 9, 52
  8th Air, 9, 12, 15
  8th Guards, 9, 12, 15
  9th, 9, 12
  10th, 12, 27, 62, 69–70, 72, 84, 203, 212, 404, 406, 409–410, 412–413, 415–416, 501, 521, 526–532, 534, 544, 577
  10th Guards, 12, 14, 27, 60, 62, 68, 70–71, 73–74, 78–82, 84–88, 146, 156–162, 164, 166–169, 208, 304, 683n5, 691n16
    strength on 5 December 1943, 683n5, 691n16
  11th, 12, 14, 51, 53, 91, 94, 97, 122, 172, 174, 176–177, 190, 192–193, 200, 204–205, 243
    strength on 15 November 1943, 174
  11th Guards, xxi–xxii, 9, 12, 14, 31, 51, 53, 94, 125–126, 133–134, 138, 146, 148, 152, 209–210, 212–213, 215–216, 218–220, 222–223, 225–227, 229–231, 234, 237–238, 274–282, 285–290, 303, 307, 309–313, 317, 333–334, 337, 339–347, 349, 360, 368, 582, 686n2
    order of battle on 13 December 1943, 214
    tank strength on 13 December 1943, 215
  12th, 12, 15

Index 719

13th, 9, 12, 14, 28, 92–95, 100–101, 124, 181, 205, 267, 418, 477, 500–501, 521, 697n21
13th Air, 9, 12
14th Air, 9
15th Air, 9, 12, 14, 51, 94, 128, 154
16th, 582
16th Air, 9, 12, 14, 427, 432
17th Air, 9, 12, 15
18th, 9, 12, 14–15
20th, 51, 388
21st, 12, 14, 27, 60, 62, 68, 70–73, 75, 78–79, 82–83
22nd, 14, 26, 51–55, 94, 146, 149, 154
23rd, 52
27th, 9, 12, 14
28th, 9, 12, 15
31st, 12, 14, 26, 61–63, 65–68, 70–71, 73, 78–80, 82–88, 156–159, 162, 164–165, 167–168, 291, 361–362, 364–365, 371–372, 375, 380–381, 383–385, 544, 548, 558
33rd, 12, 14, 27, 60–62, 68–69, 70–72, 74–75, 78–79, 82–83, 156–158, 162–164, 167–169, 210, 212, 219, 274, 278, 281, 291–299, 303, 309–310, 318, 320–321, 324, 327, 333–334, 338–340, 350–351, 353, 355–358, 367–369, 371–380, 388, 390–396, 399, 401, 541, 544–545, 548, 552–553, 555–559, 561–565, 692n13, 693nn11–12, 694nn6–8
  combat formation on 23 December 1943, 293
  combat formation on 8 January 1944, 319
  combat formation on 3 February 1944, 350
  critique of operations, October 1943–April 1944, 562–565
34th, 52, 154
37th, 12, 15
38th, 9, 12
39th, 12, 14, 26, 34–37, 43–45, 47–48, 53, 55–56, 62–64, 126, 131, 133, 138, 140–145, 210, 212, 214, 217, 219–220, 228, 230–232, 234, 274–275, 278, 281, 291–293, 297, 303, 309–310, 318, 320–321, 333–334, 338–339, 349–350, 353, 356, 368–369, 371, 373, 375–377, 380, 390, 392, 394, 544, 673n23, 693n11, 694n16
  combat formation on 23 December 1943, 293
  combat formation on 8 January 1944, 319
  combat formation on 3 February 1944, 350
  order of battle on 13 December 1943, 219
40th, 9, 12, 14
42nd, 52
43rd, 12, 14, 26, 34–37, 43, 45–46, 48, 53, 55–56, 125–126, 131, 133, 138–145, 153, 210, 212, 214, 216–218, 220, 228–232, 234, 237, 274–275, 278, 281, 291–292, 296, 303, 309–310, 333, 349, 368, 377, 380, 392, 673n23
  combat formation on 8 January 1944, 319
  order of battle on 13 December 1943, 218
44th, 12, 15
46th, 12, 15
47th, 9, 12, 14, 500–501
48th, 9, 12, 14, 28, 92, 94–97, 99, 103–104, 106, 108–109, 112, 122, 174, 176–177, 179–181, 184, 188, 200, 204–205, 243–244, 253, 255, 381, 404–405, 419, 453–455, 458–460, 471, 479–486, 488–494, 497–505, 516–521, 525, 539, 577–578
  combat formation on 15 January 1944, 484
  combat formation on 1 February 1944, 498
  strength on 15 November 1943, 174
49th, 12, 27, 62, 69–72, 74, 84, 291, 369, 371–372, 380, 383–385, 388, 544
50th, 9, 12, 14, 27, 62, 70, 91, 94–97, 103–104, 109, 174, 177, 192, 200, 202–204, 243, 404, 406–412, 415–416, 499, 501, 506, 509, 512–516, 521, 525–531, 533–534, 539, 544, 577–578, 684–685n6
  strength on 15 November 1943, 174
51st, 9, 12, 15
52nd, 12, 15

Armies, Soviet, *continued*
  53rd, 9, 12, 15
  54th, 52
  55th, 52
  56th, 9, 12, 15
  57th, 9, 12, 15
  59th, 52
  60th, 12, 14, 92–95, 124, 267, 545
  61st, 9, 12, 14, 28, 90, 92, 94–97, 99, 101–108, 110–113, 115–117, 119–121, 172, 174, 176, 179, 181, 186, 188, 190, 193–194, 196–197, 199, 204–205, 243, 245, 251–252, 402, 404, 417–419, 421, 423–427, 437–440, 442–443, 446–447, 451, 453–456, 458–459, 461–462, 468, 470, 475–478, 481–482, 500–501, 521, 534–535, 577–578
    combat formation on 20 October 1943, 117
    combat formation on 15 January 1944, 456
    strength on 15 November 1943, 175
    transferred to 2nd Belorussian Front (17 February 1944), 500
  63rd, 9, 12, 14, 27, 91, 94–97, 104, 122, 172, 174, 176–177, 200, 203–205, 243, 405, 492, 501, 507–509, 685n8
    disbanded, 492
    strength on 15 November 1943, 175
  65th, 12, 14, 28, 90, 92, 94–97, 99, 101, 103–122, 172, 174, 176–177, 179–180, 182, 184, 186–188, 193–194, 197–199, 204–205, 236, 241, 243–247, 251, 253, 255, 258–260, 402–404, 417–419, 421, 423–424, 426–427, 431–438, 443, 445–446, 451, 453–462, 464–465, 470, 472, 475, 478, 480–486, 491, 494, 498, 503–505, 519, 521, 526, 534–537, 577–578
    combat formation on 20 October 1943, 117
    combat formation on 15 January 1944, 456, 485–486
    strength on 15 November 1943, 175
  67th, 9, 12, 52
  68th, 12, 14, 26, 66–68, 70–71, 78–84, 86–87, 156
  69th, 9, 12, 15, 388
  70th, 9, 12, 500–501
Army groups, German
  A, 269
  Center, xix, xx, xxi, xxiii, 5–7, 10–11, 15, 17, 20–23, 25, 28–29, 31–33, 38–39, 41–42, 49, 54, 56, 62, 78, 84, 86, 90, 92, 94–95, 122–126, 131–132, 148, 151–153, 155–156, 171, 174, 186, 190–191, 206–208, 218, 220, 225–226, 245, 250, 260–261, 266, 268–269, 273–275, 321, 328, 353, 361, 366, 376–377, 393, 402–403, 419, 421, 426, 454, 460, 465, 477, 500, 504, 535, 540, 565, 570–571, 580–583
    strength of opposing forces on 14 October 1943, 28–29
    strength on 10 October 1943, 176
    strength on 14 October 1943, 23, 28–29
  North, xxii, 7, 17, 22, 25, 32–33, 38–39, 41–42, 50, 52, 54, 56, 122–126, 128, 131–132, 147–148, 151–153, 155, 206, 208, 220, 237–238, 266, 268, 275, 304–305, 308, 349, 361–362, 371, 377, 421, 540
  North Ukraine, 268–269
  South, xx, 5–7, 10, 15, 17, 19, 90, 92, 114, 124, 206, 260–261, 266–268, 273, 419, 454, 500
  South Ukraine, 269
Arvianitsa (Baevo region), 74
Avdeevichi (Vitebsk region), 376, 391
Avrora (Rechitsa region), 182

Babichi (Vasilevichi region), 182, 187–188
Babinichi (Vitebsk region), 376, 380
Babinovichi, 35, 48, 82, 362–365, 369, 372, 375, 381–382, 384, 390, 396
Bach-Zelewski, SS-*Obergruppenführer* Erich von dem, 128–129
Baevo (Orsha region), 67–68, 70–75, 82, 84, 212
Bagramian, Army General I. Kh., 138–140, 153–154, 171, 206, 208–209, 225, 229–231, 269, 273, 275, 279, 288, 291, 297, 307, 309–310, 312, 317–318, 320, 329, 331–334, 337, 339,

342–347, 349, 353, 359–360, 371, 377, 379, 540, 571–573, 577–578, 582–584
Bagramovichi (Pripiat' River region), 451
Bagration, Operation. *See* Operations, Soviet military
Bakharov, Major General of Tank Forces B. S., 105, 179, 186, 243, 247
Bakhrameev, Major General P. P., 238, 240
Baklanovskoe, Lake (Velizh region), 34
Balazhevichi (Mozyr' region), 419, 426
Balkan region, 266
Baltic region, 20–21, 33, 37, 52, 266, 304, 361
Baltic Sea, 50
Bandury (Vitebsk region), 280
Baranovichi, 584
Barinov, Major General A. B., 483, 493, 496–497, 504, 517–520
Barkhi (Gorodok region), 225
Barki (Rogachev region), 507
Barsuki (Orsha region), 168
Baryshevka (Bykhov region), 413
Baryshino (Vitebsk region), 281, 354
Basia River (Orsha region), 88
Batalin, Senior Lieutenant P. K., 160
Batov, Lieutenant General P. I., 90, 95–96, 99, 101, 110, 114–118, 120–121, 174, 179–180, 186, 188, 190, 193, 197–198, 204, 241, 243–247, 250–254, 257–258, 402–404, 421, 423, 427, 431–432, 434, 436–438, 443–446, 451, 453–455, 457–459, 461, 466, 470, 473–475, 478, 481–483, 494, 521, 534
Battalions (*Abteilungen*), German
4th Panzer Reconnaissance (Pz. AA 4) (4th Panzer Division), 464
21st Panzer (20th Panzer Division), 310, 313, 317
177th Assault Gun, 321
185th Assault Gun, 483, 485, 490, 498, 517–518
189th Assault Gun, 310, 385, 393, 399
190th Heavy Assault Gun, 276, 310, 321
213th Construction, 681n18
221st Engineer (Pi. 221) (292nd Infantry Division), 471
237th Assault Gun, 529–530

242nd Security, 442
244th Assault Gun, 483, 485, 490, 492, 498
245th Assault Gun, 281, 300, 310, 317, 321, 393
281st Assault Gun, 281, 310, 313, 317, 340, 357, 364, 393
299th Pioneer (299th Infantry Division), 393
301st Assault Gun, 321
304th Security, 442
389th Security, 185
417th Construction, 202
501st Panzer *Abteilung*, 340, 352, 357, 364, 383, 392–393, 399
505th Panzer *Abteilung*, 276, 281, 312–313, 317, 340, 342, 376, 385–386
519th Panzer *Abteilung*, 392–393, 399
589th Assault (Soviet identified), 202
655th Assault Gun, 310, 321
667th Panzer *Jagt* (tank hunter), 281, 310, 312, 317, 529–530
696th Security, 442
731st Construction, 681n18
990th Artillery, 276
1006th Fortress and Guide, 393
Battalions, Soviet
1st Assault (Penal), 45
6th Guards Engineer (11th Guards Army), 214
7th Engineer Obstacle (1st Guards Tank Corps), 423–424
8th Separate Penal (3rd Army), 510, 885, 900
12th Aerosany, 27
20th Tank Destroyer Artillery (1st Guards Tank Corps), 423–424
41st Aerosany, 27
43rd Separate Guards-Mortar (1st Guards Tank Corps), 105
121st Sapper, 424
146th Tank Destroyer Artillery, 534
171st Tank, 26, 43
226th Engineer (11th Guards Army), 214
243rd Engineer (11th Guards Army), 214
520th Tank, 27
732nd Tank Destroyer Artillery (1st Guards Tank Corps), 424, 434, 436
Beguny (Vitebsk region), 35, 228

Belaia Tserkov (Kiev region), 404
Belarus, 78, 82, 164
Belodedovo (Vitebsk region), 276
Belgorod, 6
Beloborodov, Lieutenant General A. P., 130–132, 217, 223, 275, 279, 288, 312, 316, 337, 340–341, 343–347
Beloe, Lake (Nevel' region), 153, 218, 228
Belonogov, Major General V. A., 188, 246
Belov, Lieutenant General P. A., 90, 95–96, 99, 101–102, 110, 115–116, 121, 174, 181, 190, 193, 204–205, 243, 245, 421, 424, 426–427, 438–440, 442–443, 446, 451, 453–455, 458–459, 461, 470–471, 476, 478, 481, 534
Belyi Bereg (Ptich' River region), 471
Belyi Bor (Vitebsk region), 359, 393, 395, 400
Bercken, Lieutenant General Werner von, 422
Berdichev (Zhitomir region), 7, 20, 267, 404
Berezina (Beresina) River, 186, 190–191, 198, 204–205, 244–246, 250–251, 253, 255, 257–258, 260, 402, 404, 454–455, 480–483, 485–486, 491, 493–494, 497, 504–505, 510, 514–517, 519–521, 525–526, 540
Berezniaki (Ozarichi region), 454, 459, 463–464, 468
Bereznogavatoe, 269
Berezovka (Gorodok region), 135, 218
Berezovka (Rechitsa region), 182
Berlin, xix
Bernovo, Lake (Gorodok region), 216, 223–224
Berzarin, Lieutenant General N. E., 36, 43–44, 126, 141–142, 210, 214, 217–218, 232, 234, 291–292, 297, 310, 318, 320–321, 338, 349, 353, 369, 375, 377, 380, 390
Besedki (Pripiat' River region), 443, 449–451, 458, 477
Beshenkovichi (Vitebsk region), 34, 333–334, 338, 341
Bezugly, Major General I. S., 339, 349–350, 353
Bibiki Farm (Mozyr' region), 448
Black Sea, xx, 268–269

Blashkino, 81
Blinki (Nevel' region), 132
Bliznetsy (Rogachev region), 507
Blocking detachments, Soviet
 178th, 896, 899
 179th, 896, 899
 181st, 896, 899
Bobreniata (Mozyr' region), 448
Bobrova (Orsha region), 162, 166–168
Bobrovichi (Gomel' region), 177
Bobrovka (Bykhov region), 407
Bobrovka River (Bykhov region), 408–410, 415
Bobruisk, xxi, 15, 22, 62, 90, 93, 95–96, 103–105, 122, 124, 172–173, 180, 204–206, 208, 241–242, 245, 247–248, 250, 253, 260–261, 402–403, 405, 418–419, 451, 454–455, 467, 476, 478–480, 482, 494, 497, 501, 504–505, 507, 510, 517, 521, 524–525, 578, 583–584, 674n45
Bobry Farm (Mozyr' region), 448
Bodino (Vitebsk region), 693n11
Bodino-Moaino (Vitebsk region), 355
Bogoliubov, Lieutenant General A. N., 544
Bogushchevsk (Bogushevskoe), 35, 88, 328, 338, 352, 369, 387, 541, 547, 553, 573
Bogutichi (Mozyr' region), 440
Boiko, Colonel M. K., 338–339, 351, 355–358
Boiko, Major General V. P., 43, 48, 50, 141
Bokov, Lieutenant General F. E., 154, 501
Boldin, Colonel General I. V., 97, 174, 177, 202–203, 243, 406, 409, 411, 415, 512, 526, 528–529, 532–534
Bol'shaia Berezina River, 64
Bol'shaia Konoplitsa (Rogachev region), 512
Bol'shaia Vydreia (Vitebsk region), 298
Bol'shie Avtiuki (Kalinkovichi region), 196–197
Bol'shie Rubny (Vitebsk region), 344, 346
Bol'shoe Ostrie, Lake (Pustoshka region), 53
Bol'shoi Ivan, Lake (Nevel' region), 54, 149, 239
Bondari (Vitebsk region), 354, 357, 391
Boreiko, Major General A. A., 99, 102, 181, 424, 426, 439, 446, 458, 470, 476–478

Index

Borichevsky, Lieutenant Colonel, 468
Boriskovichi (Mozyr' region), 444
Borisov (Minsk region), 22, 62, 93, 570
Borok (Vitebsk region), 132, 216, 218, 232, 234
Borovichi (Nevel' region), 53
Boroviki (Shatsilki region), 198
Borovka (Vitebsk region), 276
Borshchanka (Nevel' region), 53
Borshchovka (Loev region), 179, 181, 188
Bragin (Rechitsa region), 105, 174
Bragin Swamp (Vasilevichi region), 188
Brest (Mozyr' region), 449
Brest (Western Bug River region), 584
Briansk, xx, 6, 11, 105
Brigades, German
   1st Ski Jäger, 450–451, 462, 478
   1st SS Infantry, 67, 84, 86, 157–158, 245, 250, 255, 258
   2nd Ski Jäger, 450
   4th Special Designation Panzer, 202
   21st Assault Gun, 521
Brigades, Soviet
   Rifle, general, 29, 38, 673n21
   Tank, general, 30
   1st Airborne, 128
   1st Guards Motorized Rifle (1st Guards Tank Corps), 424, 432, 434–436, 445
   1st Tank Destroyer Artillery, 427
   2nd Airborne, 128
   2nd Guards Tank, 27, 291, 318, 423
   2nd Mechanized, 27
   3rd Guards Mortar, 214
   3rd Tank Destroyer Artillery, 500
   4th Guards Airborne, 697n21
   4th Guards Motorized Rifle, 27, 83
   4th Guards Tank (2nd Guards Tank Corps), 27, 163
   4th Tank Destroyer (Antitank) Artillery, 34, 44–45, 47
   5th Motorized Rifle (5th Tank Corps), 134–135, 217, 681n19
   8th Motorized Rifle (9th Tank Corps), 28, 117
   8th Self-propelled Artillery, 529
   9th Mechanized, 27
   10th Assault Engineer-Sapper, 138, 214
   10th Guards Tank, 138, 214–215, 231, 311, 686n2, 687n5
   11th Airborne, 128
   11th Guards Naval Rifle, 26
   15th Guards Naval Rifle, 26
   15th Guards Tank (1st Guards Tank Corps), 423–424, 432, 434–436, 445
   16th Guards Tank (1st Guards Tank Corps), 258, 423–424, 493
   17th Antitank, 35
   17th Guards Mortar, 214
   17th Guards Tank (1st Guards Tank Corps), 423–424, 432, 434–436, 445
   20th Guards-mortar, 35
   20th Tank Destroyer Artillery, 426
   23rd Guards Tank, 27, 68, 72, 158, 162, 291, 318, 326, 384, 388
   23rd Rifle, 26, 146
   23rd Tank (9th Tank Corps), 28, 117, 179
   24th Tank (5th Tank Corps), 134–135, 217, 223
   25th Guards Tank (2nd Guards Tank Corps), 27, 164
   25th Tank, 28
   26th Destroyer, 141
   26th Guards Mortar, 214
   26th Guards Tank, 27, 83, 326–327
   27th Guards Tank, 691n17
   28th Guards Tank, 26, 34, 37, 43, 47, 141, 218–219, 234, 291, 349
   29th Guards Tank, 149–150, 691n17
   30th Motorized Rifle, 91
   31st Rifle, 26, 38, 41, 146, 149, 238
   32nd Gun Artillery (12th Artillery Penetration Division), 258
   32nd Mortar, 500
   32nd Rifle, 26
   34th Guards Tank, 146, 149–150, 216–217, 687n7
   36th Rifle, 27, 69, 299–300, 320–321, 326, 338, 351, 391, 393, 541–542, 569
   38th Guards Tank, 691n17
   39th Guards Tank, 218–219, 234, 291
   41st Tank (5th Tank Corps), 134, 217, 223, 225
   41st Tank Destroyer Artillery, 426
   42nd Guards Tank, 26, 66, 71, 83, 158, 365

724 Index

Brigades, Soviet, *continued*
  43rd Guards Tank, 27, 320, 326, 352, 359
  44th Motorized Rifle (1st Tank Corps), 214, 223
  45th Mechanized, 27
  46th Light Artillery (12th Artillery Penetration Division), 253, 258
  46th Mechanized, 26, 34, 37, 44, 46, 141, 218, 232, 234, 292
  46th Rifle, 26
  47th Mechanized, 26, 34, 37, 43, 47, 141, 217–219, 234, 291, 350
  48th Engineer-Sapper, 500
  54th Rifle, 26
  60th Tank, 26, 141, 217–218, 232, 234, 292
  68th Tank, 28, 181, 193, 197, 426, 500
  70th Tank (5th Tank Corps), 135, 217, 223, 225
  78th Tank, 26, 38, 41–42, 146–147, 691n17
  86th Artillery, 198
  89th Tank (1st Tank Corps), 214, 314, 687n5
  94th Tank, 27
  95th Tank (9th Tank Corps), 28, 117
  100th Rifle, 26, 38, 41, 54, 146, 149, 238
  101st Rifle, 26, 43, 217, 280
  105th Tank, 26
  106th Tank, 27, 69
  108th Tank (9th Tank Corps), 28, 117
  114th Rifle, 26, 43, 141, 186, 217–218, 232
  115th Rifle, 28, 99, 101, 106, 117, 120, 180, 198, 245, 250, 255, 257–259, 424, 446, 458, 462, 464, 466, 468
  117th Tank (1st Tank Corps), 214, 223, 687n5
  118th Tank, 146–147, 240, 691n17
  120th Tank, 27, 320, 326, 352, 359
  124th Rifle, 26, 44, 141–142, 217, 219, 234
  129th Tank, 28
  143rd Tank, 130
  145th Rifle, 26, 43, 55, 217–218, 232
  146th Tank, 26, 41, 56, 292
  153rd Tank, 27, 67, 158
  159th Tank (1st Tank Corps), 214, 223, 687n5
  213th Tank, 27, 291, 320, 388
  233rd Tank, 27, 322
  236th Tank, 26, 41, 56, 130, 133
  256th Tank, 27, 69, 83, 159, 291, 320, 322, 326

Brigades, Soviet partisan
  Mozyr', 444, 449
Briskin, Senior Lieutenant G., 159
Brodki (Shatsilki region), 502
Brody (Chausy region), 527
Brusilov (Kiev region), 260
Bryli (Vitebsk region), 343–345, 347–348
Buda (Kalinkovichi region), 247, 424, 438, 446
Budino (Pronia River region), 69–70
Budishche (Loev region), 179–180
Bukrin (Velikii Bukrin), 6, 11, 13, 18
Bukshtynovich, Major General M. F., 238
Bukshtyny (Bukshtyna) (Vitebsk region), 352, 355, 358, 372, 374–375, 378, 693n11
Bulavka (Mozyr' region), 448
Bulganin, Lieutenant General N. A., 543–544, 548, 560–561
Buraki (Vitebsk region), 395, 399
Burdeinyi, Major General of Tank Forces A. S., 68, 72, 86, 157, 164, 168, 291, 297, 299, 309, 318, 324, 339, 352
Busch, Field Marshal Ernst, 38, 136, 148, 190–191, 220, 225, 260, 403
Bushatin (Loev region), 179–180
Butkov, Leiutenant General V. V., 223, 226, 281, 309, 311, 337, 339, 343–345, 347–348
Bvozdy (Gorodok region), 135
Bychikha Station (Gorodok region), 133, 209–210, 216, 223, 225–226
Bykhov. *See* Novyi Bykhov

Carpathian Mountains, 268
Caucasus region, 3–4, 9
Cavalry-Mechanized Groups, Soviet
  general, 15
  Oslikovsky's, 584
  Pliev's, 584
Central Headquarters of the Partisan Movement, Soviet, 128
Chaikov, Major F. S., 461
Chanysgev, Major General Ia. D., 238

Chaplin (Gomel' region), 177, 182
Chausy, 70, 97, 203, 242, 406, 409, 411–413, 416, 505, 524, 526–529, 531, 573
Chechersk (Sozh River region), 91
Cherepin (Vitebsk region), 372
Cherkasy (Cherkassy) (Vitebsk region), 327, 395, 398–399
Cherniakhovsky, Colonel General I. D., 542, 545, 567–569, 582
Cherniavka (Shatsilki region), 502–503
Chernigov, xx, 243, 418
Chernin (Parichi region), 255
Chernitsa River (Babinovichi region), 64–65, 81–82, 364
Chernobyl' (Pripiat' River region), 6, 11, 13, 18, 95–96, 101, 110, 123–124, 182, 187–189
Chernovo (Tschernowo), Lake (Gorodok region), 216, 223–224, 330
Chernovtsy, 268
Chernyshi (Vitebsk region), 352, 359
Cherokmanov, Major General F. M., 99, 180, 245–246, 251, 457, 460, 468, 471, 483
Cherten' River (Poles'e region), 440
Chibisov, Colonel General N. E., 154, 238–239
Chikhachevo Station (Dno region), 52
Chirka River (Shatsilki region), 491
Chirkov, Major General I. V., 554
Chirkovichi (Shatsilki region), 255, 258, 485, 488, 490–491, 494, 497, 502
Chistaia Farm (Ozarichi region), 474
Chistiakov, Colonel General I. M., 55, 148–150, 153, 238, 305
Citadel. *See* Operations, German military
Combat group, German. See *Kampfgruppe*
Companies, Soviet penal
  39th, 43
  40th, 43
  43rd, 43
  46th, 43
  173rd, 899
Corps, German
  I Army, 146, 149, 238–240, 304
  II Army, 26
  II Luftwaffe Field, 26, 38–39, 41–42, 48, 56
  III Panzer, 267–268
  VI Army, 26, 33, 38–39, 43, 45, 56, 139, 141–142, 218, 231, 285, 293, 297, 318, 320–321, 324, 329, 349, 351–353, 357, 362–365, 372–373, 375–377, 379, 383, 388, 392, 398–400
  VIII Army, 238
  IX Army, 27, 56, 69, 130, 132–133, 139, 218, 222–223, 225–226, 277, 285, 312, 328, 341
  XII Army, 528–530
  XX Army, 28, 69, 94–96, 98–99, 101, 105–106, 116–117, 179–180, 187–188, 194, 197, 205, 419, 425–426, 443, 445–446, 449, 451, 455, 458, 470–471, 475–477, 481–482
  XXII Army, 27, 411, 505
  XXIII Army, 27, 94, 97, 101, 177, 409, 411, 415–416, 477
  XXVII Army, 26, 30, 63, 65–67, 73, 84, 86–87, 157–158, 162, 168, 226, 383, 386, 682n33
  XXXV Army, 28, 94, 96–98, 101, 103–104, 106, 108–109, 117, 177, 179, 186–187, 192, 200, 204, 243, 250, 321, 455, 502, 510, 516, 518, 521
  XXXIX Panzer, 27, 67–69, 72, 505, 528, 530–531
  XXXXI Panzer, 27, 177, 202, 250, 255, 257–258, 403, 455, 457, 459, 464–465, 482–483, 490, 497, 499, 502, 504, 517–518
  XXXXIII Army, 26, 38, 41–42, 149
  XXXXVI Panzer, 28, 94–96, 101–102, 110, 116–117, 181, 187–188, 193–194, 197, 205, 245, 267
  XXXXVIII Panzer, 267–268
  LII Army, 158
  LIII Army, 56, 142, 218, 234, 277, 285–286, 292–293, 296, 311–312, 317, 339–340, 343–344, 346, 348, 376, 391–392
  LV Army, 27, 177, 328, 510
  LVI Panzer, 28, 96, 101–102, 182, 197, 205, 245–246, 255, 257–258, 403, 419, 423, 436, 444, 451, 455, 457–460, 467, 470–472, 474–475, 481–482, 489, 491, 504–505, 535, 699n14
Corps, Hungarian
  VIII Army, 28

726   Index

Corps, Soviet
  Tank, general, 30
  1st Guards Cavalry, 267, 500
  1st Guards Tank, 31, 104–106, 110, 122, 180, 182, 186, 197, 200, 245, 258–259, 419, 421, 423–424, 431–432, 434–436, 444–447, 458, 479, 485, 492–493, 496–497, 499, 504, 510, 517, 525, 528–529, 584, 672n12
    tank strength on 12 October 1943, 105
    tank strength on 1 January 1944, 423
    tank strength on 1 February 1944, 496
  1st Rifle, 26, 45, 141–142, 217, 219, 232, 234, 291–292
  1st Tank, 30, 51, 91, 138, 214–215, 223, 226, 229, 231, 277, 309, 311–314, 337, 339, 343–345, 347–348, 584
    strength on 13 December 1943, 215, 687n5
  2nd Artillery, 51
  2nd Guards Cavalry, 91, 94, 97, 104–106, 110, 116–118, 179, 182, 187–188, 193–194, 196–197, 243, 246, 419, 421, 423–424, 426, 440–443, 449, 458, 500–501, 521
  2nd Guards Rifle, 26, 37, 41, 56, 130–133, 216–217, 223, 226–228, 275, 279, 285, 288, 312, 316, 334, 337, 340–341, 343–347
  2nd Guards Tank, 27, 31, 68, 71–73, 83–84, 86, 157–158, 164, 168, 291, 297, 299, 309, 318, 324, 327, 339, 352, 354–355, 375, 553, 584
  3rd Guards Cavalry, 27, 66–68, 71, 73, 84, 133–135, 216–217, 223, 227, 279, 285, 289, 304, 309, 333
  4th Artillery Penetration, 104, 110, 116, 252, 254, 426–427, 432, 518
  5th Guards Rifle, 26, 34, 43–45, 141, 217, 219, 232, 234, 291–292, 320–321, 338–339, 349–351, 353, 355, 375, 377, 380, 390
  5th Mechanized, 27, 31, 69, 71–74, 84
  5th Tank, 30, 133–135, 153, 216–217, 223, 225–226, 279, 285, 289, 309, 312, 340, 343–345, 347–348, 672n12, 681n18, 687n7
    tank strength on 16 November 1943, 134, 681n17
    tank strength on 5 December 1943, 135
    tank strength on 13 December 1943, 216, 687n7
  6th Guards Cavalry, 27, 69, 71–72, 84, 243, 267, 500, 697n21
  7th Guards Cavalry, 28, 100, 102–106, 110, 116–118, 120–121, 180, 182, 185, 187–188, 194, 196–197, 419, 421, 423–424, 426, 440–444, 447–450, 458, 500–501, 521
  7th Guards Rifle, 27, 67, 80, 82, 158, 691n16
  7th Mechanized, 672n12
  8th Estonian Rifle, 26, 35–36, 51, 54, 94
  8th Guards Rifle, 133, 214, 226–227, 277, 280, 312, 317, 334, 337, 339, 342–343
  8th Mechanized, 672n12
  9th Guards Rifle, 28, 99–100, 102, 105–106, 110, 115–117, 121, 181, 188, 190, 193–194, 196–197, 205, 246, 424–426, 438, 440, 446, 458–459, 470, 476–478, 500, 535
  9th Mechanized, 672n12
  9th Tank, 28, 31, 104, 106, 110, 116–118, 179, 186–188, 193–194, 197, 243, 247, 525, 584
  15th Guards Rifle, 27, 67–68, 73, 80, 82, 158, 162, 164, 691n19
  15th Rifle, 28
  16th Guards Rifle, 138–139, 214, 216, 226, 277, 280, 311, 313, 334, 337, 340–341, 343–347
  17th Guards Rifle, 28
  18th Guards Rifle, 138
  18th Rifle, 28, 99, 101, 104–106, 110, 116–117, 179, 187–188, 193, 197–198, 205, 245–247, 402, 423, 427, 432, 437, 446, 454, 457–460, 464–468, 470–474, 521, 537, 679n19
  19th Guards Rifle, 27, 67–68, 73, 80, 82, 85, 158, 162, 691n16
  19th Rifle, 28, 97, 99, 101, 104, 106, 109–110, 116–117, 179–180, 182, 186, 194, 198, 204, 245–246, 250, 255, 258–259, 402–403, 424, 446, 454, 457–460, 464, 466–468, 470–474, 504, 521, 526, 532

Index

19th Tank, 672n12
20th Tank, 672n12
22nd Guards Rifle, 133, 149–150, 217, 223, 225, 280, 285, 312, 338, 341
23rd Guards Rifle, 149–150, 238–239, 305, 691n17
25th Rifle, 177, 192, 483, 486, 491, 493, 496–497, 499, 504, 517–519, 521, 539
25th Tank, 672n12
27th Rifle, 28, 99, 101, 104–106, 110, 116–118, 121, 179–180, 182, 186, 197–198, 245–247, 251, 255, 259, 402, 454, 457, 459–460, 464, 466–468, 470–471, 483, 491, 521, 679n19
28th Rifle, 28, 100
29th Rifle, 28, 99, 103, 105–106, 110, 116–117, 179, 181, 186, 258–259, 454, 482–483, 485–486, 488–491, 494, 497, 504, 519–520
35th Rifle, 27, 97, 507
36th Guards Rifle, 138–139, 214, 216, 222–223, 226, 230, 280, 311, 313, 315, 317, 334, 337, 339, 343, 345, 357, 393
36th Rifle, 26, 65–66, 71, 82–83, 85, 158, 162, 291–293, 297–300, 318, 321, 324, 326, 338–339, 351, 355–356, 358, 374, 377–378, 388, 391, 394–396, 398–399
38th Rifle, 27, 70, 203, 412, 415, 501, 526, 528–529, 531
40th Rifle, 27, 97, 204, 507
41st Rifle, 27, 121, 200–201, 507, 510, 512
42nd Rifle, 28, 97, 179, 186, 188, 200, 454, 482–483, 486, 489–491, 494, 497, 502, 504, 517, 520, 529, 539
44th Rifle, 26
45th Rifle, 26, 66–67, 71, 83, 85, 158, 291–292, 298, 320, 327, 352, 359, 362, 364–366, 375, 390, 393, 395, 399–400, 542, 557, 567
46th Rifle, 27, 202, 411, 528–529, 533–534
53rd Rifle, 177, 192, 485, 492–494, 496–499, 502–503, 519–520
60th Rifle, 26, 37, 130, 140, 216–217, 280, 338

61st Rifle, 27, 68, 72, 83–84, 158, 291, 383–384, 388
62nd Rifle, 27, 69, 383–384, 388, 390–391, 395, 399
65th Rifle, 27, 72, 83–84, 158, 291–293, 297, 318, 320, 326, 338, 351, 354–358, 374, 377–378, 388, 391
69th Rifle, 27, 68–69, 72, 83–84, 158, 162, 291–292, 298, 318, 338, 351, 354–357, 374, 378, 388, 391, 393, 396, 398–399
70th Rifle, 27, 69, 72, 158, 162, 164, 412, 415–416, 501, 529, 557
71st Rifle, 26, 65–66, 82–83, 85, 158, 381, 383–384
72nd Rifle, 26, 66–67, 81, 83, 87, 158, 162, 298–300, 320–321, 324, 326, 352, 375, 388, 391, 393, 395–396, 399
77th Rifle, 500–501
79th Rifle, 53, 146, 238
80th Rifle, 27, 200, 407, 409–411, 414–416, 507, 510, 512, 526, 539
81st Rifle, 26, 81, 83, 158, 162, 291, 292–293, 297–298, 300, 338, 351, 354–355, 357–358, 388
83rd Guards Rifle, 214, 230
83rd Rifle, 26, 37, 41, 56, 130, 153, 277, 279, 285, 288, 312, 334, 337, 340–341, 345–347
84th Rifle, 26, 44–45, 47, 56, 141, 217, 219, 232–234, 291–292, 320, 338, 349, 353, 375, 377, 380, 694n16
89th Rifle, 28, 99, 105–106, 117, 181, 188, 194, 197, 205, 246, 426, 458–461, 468–471, 476–478, 500
90th Rifle, 149, 238–239
91st Rifle, 26, 43, 141, 217–218, 232, 234, 292, 334, 338, 341
92nd Rifle, 26, 43, 45–46, 48, 55, 141, 217–219, 296, 380
93rd Rifle, 53–54, 146, 188, 238, 240, 305, 691n17
95th Rifle Corps, 188, 194, 197, 205, 239, 241, 245–247, 252–254, 258–259, 402, 454, 457, 459, 465, 482–483, 486, 489–491, 494, 494, 499, 502, 519, 521
96th Rifle, 149, 238

Corps, Soviet, *continued*
　97th Rifle, 149–150, 238, 305, 691n17
　100th Rifle, 147, 238–239, 305, 691n17
　103rd Rifle, 334
　105th Rifle, 423, 427, 432, 436–437, 446, 458, 460, 464, 466, 472, 474, 521, 535, 537
　121st Rifle, 471, 512, 528–529, 532, 534
　125th Rifle, 500–501
Corps detachments (*abteilungen*), German
　D, 392, 398–399, 412, 416
　E, 181, 197, 419, 424, 426–427, 441–443, 445, 447, 451, 458, 462, 477
Crimea (Crimean Peninsula), 6, 13, 15, 17–18, 265–266, 268–269

Dalmatov, Major General V. N., 202
Danki (Liubavichi region), 63
Dashkovka (Rechitsa region), 174
Daugavpils. *See* Dvinsk
Davidgorodok (Petrikov region), 478
Davydovichi (Kalinkovichi region), 247, 423
Davydovka (Shatsilki region), 254, 258–259, 454–455, 457, 459, 483
Davydovo (Vitebsk region), 337, 340
Dedno (Shatsiliki region), 517
Dedova (Rogachev region), 512
Defense lines, German
　Panther (Eastern Wall), xx, 60, 114–115, 161, 191–192, 261, 266, 268, 361, 371
　Winterstand (Bykhov region), 415–416
Deiki (Vitebsk region), 337, 339
Demekhi Station (Rechitsa region), 180, 186
Demeshkino (Pustoshka region), 240
Demiankovo (Orsha region), 371
Demiansk, 4, 305
Demidov, 33, 37
Desna River, 21, 260, 540
Detachments (*verbanden*), German
　4th Railroad, 681n20
　SS *Verbande* Wiedermann, 255
Diaglevo (Vitebsk region), 279, 299, 309, 339, 341
D'iakonov, Major General A. A., 230, 279, 288, 312, 317, 337, 340–341, 346–347

D'iakovina (Vitebsk region), 396, 399
Directorates, Red Army General Staff
　Exploitation of War Experiences, 417
　Intelligence (GRU), 541
　Main Artillery (GAU), 156
　Main Political (GlavPu), 541–542
　Operations, 541
Disna, 52
Division groups, German
　86th, 426–427, 441, 443
　137th, 426–427
　216th, 462, 477
　251st, 441
　254th, 426–427
Divisions, German
　Panzer, general, 29
　2nd Luftwaffe Field, 26, 38, 41–42, 130, 226
　2nd Panzer, 28, 30, 101, 110, 116–117, 176, 179–181, 188, 194, 684n5
　　tank strength on 10 November 1943, 684n5
　3rd Luftwaffe Field, 26, 38, 56, 218, 226, 276–278, 285, 293
　4th Luftwaffe Field, 26, 38, 56, 218, 276, 278, 285, 293, 340, 348, 376, 380, 391
　4th Panzer, 28, 30, 95, 99, 182, 185–189, 196–197, 245–247, 250–251, 255–258, 402, 421, 423, 427, 434, 436, 444, 446, 455, 457–459, 462–464, 468, 470, 472, 474–475, 485, 499, 504, 512, 517, 518, 521, 696n5, 699n8
　　tank strength on 15 November 1943, 181
　　tank strength on 20 December 1943, 250
　　tank strength on 1 January 1944, 421, 696n5
　　tank strength on 15 January 1944, 458
　　tank strength on 4 February 1944, 699n8
　5th Jäger (Light), 220, 277, 281, 285–287, 289, 310, 312, 340–341, 346, 348, 376, 379, 385–386
　5th Panzer, 28, 30, 101, 188, 196–197, 245–247, 402, 421, 423–425, 427,

Index

434, 436, 444, 455, 458, 460, 462, 470–471, 476–478, 512, 535, 696n12, 698n12
  tank strength on 18 November 1943, 188
  tank strength on 1 January 1944, 421, 696n5
  tank strength on 15 January 1944, 458, 696n12
6th Infantry (KGr.), 28, 98–99, 101, 117, 179, 480, 485, 490, 498, 512, 517–518
6th Luftwaffe Field, 26, 38, 56, 218, 226, 277, 281, 285–287, 310–312, 340, 344, 346, 348, 364, 376, 379, 391
7th Infantry (KGr.), 28, 101, 116–117, 121, 181, 188, 196–197, 245, 426–427, 445–446, 451, 458, 460, 462, 477
12th Infantry, 26, 276, 278, 281, 310, 312, 340, 342–346, 348, 391, 529–531
12th Panzer, 28, 30, 101, 118, 176, 179, 181–182, 187–188, 194, 250, 310, 317, 403, 419, 421, 441, 684n5
  tank strength on 10 November 1943, 684n5
  tank strength on 20 December 1943, 250
  tank strength on 1 January 1944, 692n7
  tank strength on 1 February 1944, 692n7
14th Infantry (Motorized), 26, 38, 43, 45–46, 55–56, 141–142, 218, 231, 234, 278, 285, 292–293, 296, 328, 340, 352–353, 357–358, 363–366, 388, 392, 395, 398–399
16th Panzer, 191, 242, 250, 255–258, 260, 403, 685n19, 689n10, 689n18
  tank strength on 20 December 1943, 250
  tank strength on 1 January 1944, 689n18
18th Panzer (KGr.), 26, 30, 67, 142, 682n33
18th Panzer Grenadier, 26, 30, 66–67, 73, 84, 157–158, 168, 412, 415–416, 512, 528–530

20th Panzer, 30, 54, 56, 129, 132–133, 135, 218, 223–226, 230, 339–340, 342–344, 348, 357, 391, 512, 681n20
  tank strength on 8 November 1943, 132
  tank strength on 1 February 1944, 339
23rd Infantry, 238–239
25th Panzer Grenadier, 27, 67–68, 73, 75, 157–158, 162, 164, 168, 383, 385–386, 682n33
26th Infantry, 27, 84, 86–87, 157–158, 168
31st Infantry (KGr.), 28, 99, 101, 117, 180, 186, 510, 512, 528–530
32nd Infantry, 238–239, 304, 691n17
35th Infantry, 27, 69, 412–413, 460, 462, 464, 466, 468, 471–472, 474, 698n8
36th Infantry, 27, 186, 480, 483, 485, 488–491, 497–498, 504, 518
45th Infantry, 28, 98, 101, 106, 108–109, 117, 179, 186, 502, 518, 520
52nd Infantry (KGr.), 26, 63–64, 66, 86
56th Infantry (KGr.), 27, 149
58th Infantry, 41, 54, 146, 238
69th Infantry, 149
78th Assault (Infantry), 27, 69, 84, 157–158, 162, 164, 166, 168, 383–386
81st Infantry, 238
83rd Infantry, 26, 38
86th Infantry (KGr.), 28, 101–102, 197
87th Infantry, 26, 38, 43, 45–46, 48, 55–56, 130, 132, 218, 220, 223, 225–226, 230, 276, 278, 318, 339–340, 342–344
93rd Infantry, 26
95th Infantry, 27, 69, 202, 340, 346, 348, 358, 376, 392, 398–399, 409, 411–412, 415–416
102nd Infantry (KGr.), 28, 99, 101, 116–118, 179, 193, 196–197, 245, 425–427, 442, 450–451, 477
110th Infantry, 27, 201, 474, 485, 490, 498
113th Infantry (KGr.), 27, 133–134, 681n18
122nd Infantry, 41, 54, 239–240, 304, 691n17

730 Index

Divisions, German, *continued*
129th Infantry, 28, 56, 135, 218, 220, 222–226, 230, 276–277, 281, 285–286, 310–312, 318, 485, 517–518, 681n20
131st Infantry, 27, 120, 202–203, 281, 300, 310, 318, 320, 324, 340, 351, 354–355, 357–358, 364, 373, 376, 391
134th Infantry, 28, 108–109, 177, 192, 245, 250, 255–256, 258, 457, 459, 483, 485, 489–490, 492, 497–498, 502
137th Infantry (KGr.), 28, 101, 116–117, 120–121, 181, 188, 196–197, 441
197th Infantry, 26, 63, 65–66, 73, 84–86, 157–158, 166, 168, 226, 234, 276, 278, 310, 340–344, 364, 372–373, 376, 378, 392
201st Security, 28, 328, 339–340, 342, 366, 388, 392, 395, 398–400, 693n3
203rd Security, 28, 186, 427, 478
205th Infantry, 26, 38
206th Infantry, 26, 38, 43, 45–46, 141–142, 218, 291–293, 310, 320–321, 340, 349, 351, 353–355, 357, 373, 375–376, 391
211th Infantry, 140, 276, 328, 340, 352–353, 359, 363, 366, 376, 391
216th Infantry (KGr.), 28, 101, 106, 108–109, 116–118, 178–179, 188, 193
218th Infantry, 26
221st Infantry (Security), 27, 340, 351, 353, 363–365, 383–384, 388, 512
246th Infantry, 26, 38–39, 45, 47, 56, 142, 218, 281, 291, 293, 300, 310, 320, 328, 340, 353, 355, 357, 375–376, 380, 391, 399
251st Infantry (KGr.), 28, 101–102, 110, 116–117, 181, 197, 419, 441
252nd Infantry, 27, 69, 73, 75, 218, 226, 230, 277, 285, 312, 341
253rd Infantry, 27, 97, 101, 255, 257–258, 480, 483, 485, 488–491, 497, 502, 504, 517–518
256th Infantry, 26, 38–39, 45, 48, 158, 276, 328, 362–365, 383–384, 388, 392, 398–400
260th Infantry, 27, 202–203, 411–412
263rd Infantry, 26, 38, 41–42, 238
267th Infantry, 27, 121, 201–202, 407, 409, 412, 415–416, 512
281st Security, 41
286th Security, 28
290th Infantry, 238, 240, 304, 691n17
292nd Infantry, 28, 98, 108–109, 117, 179, 187–188, 194, 197, 245, 340, 424–425, 427, 438, 445–446, 461–462, 471, 477
296th Infantry, 27, 485, 504, 510, 512, 517–518
299th Infantry, 28, 98, 108–109, 177, 192, 310, 321, 323–324, 340, 351, 353, 357, 373, 376, 378–379, 388, 392–393, 398
329th Infantry, 238
330th Infantry (KGr.), 27
331st Infantry, 26
337th Infantry, 27, 68, 72–75
342nd Infantry, 27, 69, 529–530
383rd Infantry, 27, 480, 485, 502, 518, 520–521
707th (former Security) Infantry, 28, 198, 244–245, 427, 451, 455, 457–460, 462–464, 480, 510, 512, 518, 520–521
Feldherrnhalle Panzer Grenadier, 220, 281, 293–294, 296–297, 300, 310, 318, 321, 324, 328
composition and tank strength on 24 December 1943, 294
z.b.V. (temporary division) 17, 478, 698n18
Divisions, Hungarian
1st Infantry, 28
5th Infantry, 28
9th Infantry, 28
12th Infantry, 28
18th Infantry, 28
23rd Infantry, 28
Divisions, Slovak
2nd Infantry, 28
Divisions, Soviet
General, rifle, 29, 38, 56, 82, 87, 157, 166, 206, 312, 321, 324, 372, 395, 412, 525, 572, 673n21, 676n14, 686n28, 693n11
1st Guards Rifle, 214, 226

Index 731

1st Polish Infantry, 72, 74–75, 78, 676n14
3rd Guards Artillery Penetration, 83
3rd Guards Assault Aviation, 500
3rd Guards Cavalry, 28, 196, 443, 449
4th Guards Artillery Penetration, 83
4th Guards Cavalry, 28, 196, 449–450
4th Rifle, 177, 483, 494, 504, 517, 519–520
5th Artillery Penetration, 426
5th Guards Cavalry, 27, 67, 217, 223
5th Guards Mortar, 426
5th Guards Rifle, 133, 214, 226, 230, 280
5th Rifle, 27, 97, 201, 409–410, 415, 507, 510
6th Artillery Penetration, 426
6th Guards Cavalry, 27, 66, 217
6th Guards Rifle, 28
7th Estonian Rifle, 26, 54
8th Cavalry, 27
8th Guards Cavalry, 27
8th Guards Rifle, 26, 82, 226
8th Rifle, 28
9th Guards Rifle, 26, 43, 141, 219, 291, 320
11th Guards Rifle, 214, 277, 334, 346–347
12th Artillery Penetration, 426
12th Guards Rifle, 28, 99, 102–103, 106, 110, 117, 121, 181, 188, 193–194, 197, 246, 424–425, 438–439, 446, 453, 476
13th Guards Cavalry, 27
14th Guards Cavalry (7th Guards Cavalry Corps), 28, 120–121, 180, 182, 441, 444, 448–449
15th Artillery Penetration, 138, 214
15th Guards Cavalry, 28, 120, 180, 182, 185, 443–444, 448–449
15th Rifle, 28, 99, 103, 106, 117, 181, 197, 246, 426, 449, 476–477
16th Guards Cavalry (7th Guards Cavalry Corps), 28, 182, 185, 441, 448–449
16th Guards Rifle, 214, 223, 315, 343, 687n11
16th Lithuanian Rifle, 26, 35, 41, 153, 217
17th Antiaircraft Artillery, 138, 214
17th Guards Cavalry, 28, 196, 449–450
17th Guards Rifle, 26, 43, 45, 141, 219, 234, 291, 320, 375

17th Rifle, 27, 121, 200, 409, 414–415, 492, 494, 497, 499, 502, 519–520, 686n28
18th Guards Rifle, 146, 238, 281
19th Guards Rifle, 26, 43, 45, 141, 219, 291, 320, 375, 380
21st Artillery Penetration, 37, 214
21st Rifle, 691n17
21st Guards Rifle, 26, 38, 41, 146, 238, 240
22nd Artillery, 426
22nd Guards Rifle, 27, 67–68, 73, 80, 82, 85, 158, 161–162, 675n10
23rd Rifle, 460, 469, 476–477
26th Guards Rifle, 133, 214, 229, 277, 280, 312
28th Rifle, 26, 38–39, 41, 54, 146, 238–239
29th Guards Rifle, 27, 67–68, 73, 80, 158, 226
29th Rifle, 133, 149, 153, 214, 226, 312, 334
30th Guards Rifle, 27, 67–68, 73, 82, 158–159, 162, 675n10
31st Guards Rifle, 214, 226, 277, 343, 346–347
32nd Cavalry, 27, 68, 217, 219
32nd Rifle, 26, 56, 141, 292, 349
33rd Rifle, 26, 44
37th Guards Rifle, 28, 97, 99, 101, 117–118, 120–121, 179–180, 186, 198, 245, 250, 253, 255, 257–258, 260, 423, 430–431, 434, 436, 446, 460, 464, 466, 473–474
37th Rifle, 691n17
38th Guards Rifle, 198, 244–245, 250–251, 255, 257–258, 260, 465, 483, 486, 489, 491–492
41st Rifle, 27, 58, 204, 492, 494, 497, 499, 502–503, 519–520
42nd Rifle, 162, 297, 351, 356–357, 362, 365, 381, 384, 393, 676n14, 694n6
43rd Rifle, 691n17
44th Guards Rifle, 188, 194, 197, 245–247, 254, 257–259, 320, 483, 486, 489–490, 499, 502
46th Antiaircraft Artillery, 214
46th Guards Rifle, 26, 38, 41, 146, 238
46th Rifle, 691n17

Divisions, Soviet, *continued*
  47th Rifle, 26, 41, 56, 130–132, 153, 217, 223, 312
  49th Rifle, 27, 70, 412, 529, 531–533
  51st Guards Rifle, 149–150, 238, 691n17
  51st Rifle, 217, 280, 426
  52nd Guards Rifle, 149–150, 238, 691n17
  55th Rifle, 28, 99, 103, 106, 117, 181, 197, 246, 451, 458, 500
  56th Guards Rifle, 27, 67, 73, 82, 87, 158–159, 161–162, 166
  58th Rifle, 27, 69, 72, 83, 87, 158
  60th Rifle, 28, 99, 101, 117, 179, 188, 193, 197, 245–247, 251, 255, 257–259, 464, 466, 471
  62nd Rifle, 27, 68, 72, 81, 83, 158
  63rd Rifle, 27, 81, 83, 158, 384
  64th Rifle, 27, 70, 203, 412, 529, 533
  65th Antiaircraft Artillery, 500
  65th Guards Rifle, 27, 67–68, 73, 81–82, 85, 158, 161–162, 166, 675n10
  67th Guards Rifle, 149, 238, 691n17
  69th Rifle, 28, 99, 101, 117, 179, 187–188, 193, 197, 245–247, 423, 427–432, 434, 436, 446, 460, 465–466, 468, 472–474, 537, 679n19
  70th Guards Rifle, 28
  70th Rifle, 27, 69
  71st Guards Rifle, 149–150, 238–239, 691n17
  73rd Rifle, 28, 97, 179, 253, 258, 260, 489–491, 504, 519
  74th Rifle, 28
  75th Guards Rifle, 423, 430, 432, 434, 436, 446, 461, 472, 474, 502
  76th Guards Rifle, 28, 100, 102–103, 106, 110, 117, 121, 181, 188, 193–194, 197, 246, 425, 438, 477
  76th Rifle, 27, 72, 83, 158, 162, 166–167, 168, 411, 413
  77th Guards Rifle, 28, 100, 102, 106, 110, 117, 121, 181, 188, 193–194, 197, 246, 425, 438–439, 477
  81st Rifle, 28, 106, 110, 117, 181, 197, 246, 460, 476–477
  82nd Rifle, 26, 66, 71, 83, 85, 133, 459, 461–464, 466–468, 472, 474, 533–534
  83rd Guards Rifle, 158, 214, 223, 226, 229, 280, 312, 342
  84th Guards Rifle, 214, 220, 223, 343
  85th Guards Latvian Rifle, 27, 67–68, 73, 158–160, 162, 675n10
  88th Rifle, 26, 66–67, 71, 82, 85, 158, 381–384, 426
  90th Guards Rifle, 149–150, 217, 223, 225–226, 281, 343–344, 346–347
  91st Guards Rifle, 26, 44, 141, 219, 234, 320, 375, 380
  95th Rifle, 27, 68, 72, 81, 83, 158, 297–298, 318, 321, 351, 354–358, 375
  96th Rifle, 177, 192–193, 492–499, 502–503, 519
  97th Rifle, 26, 43, 45, 141, 219, 393, 395–396, 693n11
  102nd Rifle, 28, 97, 99, 104, 106, 179, 259, 488, 490, 497, 504, 520
  106th Rifle, 28, 106, 117, 180, 186, 197–198, 245–247, 251, 255, 258–259, 679n19
  108th Rifle, 27, 202–203, 411, 415, 506, 529, 534
  110th Rifle, 27, 202–203, 411, 415, 506, 529
  115th Rifle, 146–147, 238
  117th Rifle, 26, 35, 41, 56, 133, 153, 217, 312, 334, 343–344, 347
  119th Guards Rifle, 26, 146–147, 238, 240, 691n17
  119th Rifle, 26, 37, 130, 133, 140, 217, 280
  120th Guards Rifle, 27, 109, 121, 200–201
  121st Guards Rifle, 27, 109, 200–201
  129th Rifle, 27, 204
  132nd Rifle, 423, 436, 446, 460, 466, 468, 472, 474, 537
  133rd Rifle, 26, 66, 71, 83, 85, 158
  134th Rifle, 26, 44–45, 47, 141, 219, 291, 349, 353, 375
  137th Rifle, 28, 97, 106, 179, 488, 490–491, 502, 504, 517
  139th Rifle, 27, 70, 72, 75, 412, 529, 532
  140th Rifle, 28, 97, 99, 101, 117, 179, 186, 197–198, 243
  144th Rifle, 27, 69, 72, 141, 158, 164, 318, 351, 354–355, 357, 374, 378, 548, 552

Index   733

145th Rifle, 26, 43, 142, 219, 234, 291, 380
146th Rifle, 146–147, 238
148th Rifle, 28
149th Rifle, 28, 99, 101, 106, 117, 179, 187–188, 193, 197, 243, 679n19
153rd Rifle, 27, 68, 72, 158, 163, 299, 320–321, 353
154th Rifle, 26, 37, 130–131, 133, 217, 280, 285
156th Rifle, 37, 130–132, 134, 217, 225, 280, 285
157th Rifle, 27, 72, 83, 158, 162, 298, 326, 359, 393, 395, 400, 693n11
158th Rifle, 26, 44, 47, 56, 141, 219, 291, 349, 353, 375, 380, 552
159th Rifle, 26, 66–67, 71, 81, 83, 86–87, 158, 299–300, 320, 326–327, 353, 362, 365–366, 393, 395, 400, 693n11
160th Rifle, 27, 69, 411, 413
162nd Rifle, 28, 97, 99, 101, 117, 179, 186, 198, 245–247, 423, 430, 436, 446, 459, 462, 464, 466, 468, 472, 474
164th Rifle, 27, 69, 72, 83, 158, 163, 318, 351, 354, 357–358, 372, 375, 377, 552
165th Rifle, 54, 146, 149–150, 238
166th Rifle, 140, 149, 153, 216–217, 225, 312, 316, 344, 347
169th Rifle, 27, 106, 204
170th Rifle, 28, 97, 106, 179, 486, 489, 497, 502, 504, 517
171st Rifle, 238
172nd Rifle, 188, 194, 197, 245–247, 253, 257–259, 483, 486, 489, 491–494
173rd Rifle, 27, 69, 83, 158, 162, 297, 318, 326, 338, 351, 355–356, 374, 378, 393, 395, 556, 694n6
174th Rifle, 27, 68, 72, 81, 83–84, 87, 158, 162, 166, 168, 384, 554
175th Rifle, 28, 97, 106, 179, 258–259, 486, 490
178th Rifle, 26, 54, 146
179th Rifle, 26, 43, 141, 234, 292
181st Rifle, 28, 100
183rd Rifle, 26

184th Rifle, 26, 44–45, 56, 141–142, 219, 292, 359, 362, 365–366, 393, 395–396, 552, 693n11
185th Rifle, 149–150, 238
186th Rifle, 27, 121, 146, 200–201
192nd Rifle, 26, 66–67, 71, 81, 83, 158, 384, 386, 554
193th Rifle, 28, 99, 101, 106, 117–118, 179, 187–188, 194, 197, 245–247, 424, 446, 460, 474, 679n19
194th Rifle, 28, 97, 104, 106, 179, 486–487, 489–491, 494, 504, 517, 519–520
197th Rifle, 177, 192, 483, 493, 497, 520
199th Rifle, 26, 66–67, 71, 81, 83, 158, 295, 298–300, 318, 320–321, 326–327, 338, 351, 355–358, 374, 378, 393, 395, 548, 694n6
200th Rifle, 238–239
204th Rifle, 26, 43, 141–142, 219, 234, 291
207th Rifle, 26, 48, 63–65, 71, 80, 82, 158, 160–161, 166
208th Rifle, 26–27, 48, 63–65, 67, 71, 80, 82, 158
211th Rifle, 28
212th Rifle, 27, 70, 203, 412
215th Rifle, 26, 66, 71, 82, 85, 158, 298, 318, 338, 351, 355–356, 374, 377, 380, 393, 395–396, 398, 552, 564, 694n6
217th Rifle, 177, 192–193, 483, 486, 489–491, 504, 519
218th Rifle, 471
219th Rifle, 26, 44, 146–147, 238
220th Rifle, 26, 66–67, 71, 82, 85, 158, 166, 364–365, 381–383, 386
222nd Rifle, 27, 69, 72, 75, 158, 162, 297, 320, 326, 338, 351, 354–355, 357, 362, 374, 377, 393, 396, 548, 552
234th Rifle, 26, 35, 41, 56, 130, 214, 230, 312
235th Rifle, 26, 35, 41, 56, 130, 214, 230, 280, 334, 380
238th Rifle, 27, 202–203, 411, 529, 532
242nd Night Bomber Aviation, 500
245th Rifle, 146–147, 238
246th Rifle, 28, 99, 101, 116–118, 180, 186, 243

Divisions, Soviet, *continued*
  247th Rifle, 27, 70, 72, 75, 384–385, 554
  249th Estonian Rifle, 26, 54
  250th Rifle, 27, 97
  251st Rifle, 26, 67, 71, 82, 85, 158, 362, 364–365, 381–383, 554
  253rd Rifle, 423, 446, 460, 464, 466, 468, 472, 474, 537
  260th Rifle, 177, 192
  262nd Rifle, 26, 43, 45, 141, 201, 291, 349, 375, 380
  269th Rifle, 27, 109, 121, 200–201, 203, 407, 411, 415
  270th Rifle, 26, 43, 141, 234, 292
  273rd Rifle, 177, 483, 486, 491, 497, 504, 519
  274th Rifle, 26, 66, 82, 85, 158, 168, 298–300, 318, 321, 327, 351, 355, 357, 374, 378
  277th Rifle, 27, 69, 71, 299–300, 320–323, 387, 393, 395–396, 398, 557, 693n11
  282nd Rifle, 149, 238
  283rd Rifle, 27, 200, 202, 409, 415, 686n28
  287th Rifle, 27, 97
  290th Rifle, 27, 69, 72, 74, 83, 158, 411, 413, 529, 531–532, 676n14
  306th Rifle, 26, 43, 141, 234, 292
  307th Rifle, 28, 104, 106, 179, 490–491, 504, 517, 519–520
  312th Rifle, 26, 48, 63–64, 71, 80, 82, 158
  322nd Rifle, 28, 55
  323rd Rifle, 177, 192–193
  324th Rifle, 27, 203, 410, 415, 506, 529, 534
  326th Rifle, 146, 238, 691n17
  330th Rifle, 27, 70, 412, 529, 531
  331st Rifle, 26, 66, 71, 85, 158, 381–383, 385, 554
  332nd Rifle, 26, 43, 141, 334
  334th Rifle, 26, 43, 296, 380
  336th Rifle, 28, 99, 106, 117, 181
  338th Rifle, 27, 69, 72, 158–159, 162, 362, 365–366, 693n11
  344th Rifle, 27, 69, 72
  348th Rifle, 27, 97
  352nd Rifle, 27, 69, 72, 384
  354th Rifle, 28, 97, 99, 101, 116–117, 180, 186, 198, 245–247, 464, 466, 468, 471, 502, 535, 537
  356th Rifle, 28, 99, 106, 117, 181, 458, 500
  357th Rifle, 26, 38, 41, 130, 132, 140, 146, 217, 280
  358th Rifle, 26, 55, 296, 334
  359th Rifle, 26, 65, 71, 81–82, 85, 158
  360th Rifle, 26, 41, 56, 130, 214, 312, 347
  362nd Rifle, 27, 200, 202, 409, 415
  366th Fighter Aviation, 500
  368th Rifle, 141, 203
  369th Rifle, 27, 202–203, 411, 529
  370th Rifle, 149, 238, 691n17
  371st Rifle, 27, 69, 72, 158, 298–300, 318, 321, 324, 351, 358, 374, 378
  379th Rifle, 54, 146, 149–150, 238–239
  380th Rifle, 27, 202–203, 411, 529
  381st Rifle, 26, 41, 83, 130–133, 217, 223, 226, 312, 344, 346–347
  385th Rifle, 27, 43, 70, 203, 411, 413, 529, 531–533
  397th Rifle, 27
  399th Rifle, 28, 97, 179, 486, 489–491, 494, 502, 504, 517
  413th Rifle, 27, 202–203, 411, 415, 506, 529, 534
  415th Rifle, 28, 99, 106, 181, 418, 426, 440, 442, 447–449, 458
Dmitrievka (Bykhov region), 527
Dnepropetrovsk, 6–7, 12, 18
Dnepr River, xx, xxi, xxii, xxv, 5–9, 11, 13, 15, 17–18, 20–21, 60, 63, 66, 69, 71–72, 76–79, 81–84, 86–88, 90–92, 94–97, 99–106, 109–112, 114–117, 120–121, 156–157, 166–168, 172, 174, 177, 179–180, 182, 186, 189–193, 200, 202–205, 242–243, 260–261, 267–268, 371, 384, 402, 404–409, 414, 416, 455, 483, 492–494, 497, 499, 501–502, 505–510, 512–516, 521, 525–526, 528, 534–535, 540, 551, 566, 573
Dnestr River, 266, 268–269
Dno, 33, 52
Dobrino (Vitebsk region), 359, 390, 395, 400
Dobritsa (Rogachev region), 507
Dobroe (Shatsilki region), 489

Dobromysl' (Babinovichi region), 48, 56, 64–65, 82, 142, 212
Dobrovol'sky, Major General E. V., 291, 320, 349, 353, 375, 380
Dobrush (Gomel' region), 97
Dobryn' (Kalinkovichi region), 426
Dobryn' (Orsha region), 371
Dokshintsy (Minsk region), 61–62, 570
Dolginovo (Minsk region), 61–62, 570
Domamerki (Loev region), 181
Domanovichi (Kalinkovichi region), 423, 430, 434–435
Donbas (Donets Basin), 9–11, 270
Dovsk (Bykhov region), 109, 200, 408, 510
Drachkovo (Chausy region), 527
Dremov, Colonel I. F., 34–35, 37, 43–45, 141–142
Dretun' (Polotsk region), 126, 129, 147
Dribin (Gorki region), 62, 69, 72
Drinevo (Kalinkovichi region), 432, 435–436
Drissa (Vitebsk region), 52
Driukovo (Vitebsk region), 350
Drozdy (Mozyr' region), 443–444, 446
Drut' River (Rogachev region), 103, 505, 507, 509–510, 512–513
Drybino (Vitebsk region), 297, 299–300, 320, 352, 390, 395–396, 398
Dubniaki (Ozarichi region), 468, 470–471
Dubno, 268
Duborezy (Gorodok region), 135
Dubrava (Rogachev region), 510
Dubrova (Shatsilki region), 256, 490–493, 496–499, 502, 515, 519–520, 573
Dubrovitsa (Vasilevichi region), 193, 194
Dubrovka (Loev sector), 97, 100, 120
Dubrovno (Orsha region), 68, 81, 157, 168
Dukhovshchina (Smolensk region), 11, 34
Durnaia (Orsha region), 169
Dvinsk (Daugavpils), 20, 22, 51–52, 62, 122
Dvorishche (Shatsilki region), 520
Dymanovo (Vitebsk region), 320, 322–324, 354, 374–375
Dymer (Kiev region), 674n45

Eastern Wall. *See* Defense lines, German: Panther
East Prussia, 21
Efremenki (Vitebsk region), 399

Elany (Shatsilki region), 198
Elenovka (Rogachev region), 507
Eliseevka (Vitebsk region), 35, 62
El'nia, 6
El'sk (Mozyr' region), 441–442, 535
Emenets, Lake (Nevel' region), 150
Erastov, Major General K. M., 411, 529, 533
Eremenko, Army General A. I., xx, 31, 33–34, 36–37, 39, 42–43, 45, 48, 52–54, 56, 122, 134, 138, 141, 146, 154, 206, 274–275, 540, 582, 673n23
    replaced as commander of 1st Baltic Front, 17 November 1943, 138
Eremino (Vitebsk region), 324
Ermaki (Orsha region), 66
Ermakov, Major General A. N., 280, 338
Ezerishche (Jeserischtche), Lake, 55, 132–133, 216, 218, 223, 330
Ezerishche (Jeserischtche) (Nevel' region), 131, 133–134, 139, 153
Ezerishche salient, 130
Ezva River (Bykhov region), 506

Fastov (Kiev region), 7, 674n45
Fediuninsky, Lieutenant General I. I., 97, 122, 172, 174, 177, 190, 192–193
Fediun'kin, Major General I. F., 280, 311, 313, 334
Festung (fortress) or (*festungplatz*— fortresses), German strategy, 583
Fiksel', Guards Colonel K. V., 121
Filaty (Orsha region), 66
Flotillas, Soviet
    Dnepr River, 500
Foreign Armies East (*Fremde Heere Ost*, or FHO), German OKH's intelligence organ, 25, 28, 30, 62, 82
Fortified regions, Soviet
    5th, 26
    52nd, 546
    115th, 28, 509
    118th, 26
    119th, 28
    152nd, 27, 63, 65, 80, 158, 217
    154th, 27
    155th, 26, 43, 153, 218
    161st, 28, 494, 519
France, 4, 293

736 Index

Fronts, Soviet
  1st Baltic, xxi, xxii, xxv, 7–8, 14–15, 20, 23, 31, 54, 56, 122, 124–129, 133–134, 138–139, 142, 151–154, 156, 170, 206, 208–209, 212–213, 224, 227–230, 237–239, 241, 268–270, 272–275, 278–279, 281, 283–285, 290, 301–302, 304, 307–310, 319–320, 329–330, 332–333, 338–340, 349, 352, 360–361, 371, 377, 380, 392, 402, 540, 570–572, 577, 583–584, 671n1, 678n7
    combat formation on 8 January 1944, 319
    order of battle on 1 January 1944, 283–285
    order of battle on 1 February 1944, 335–336
    rate of advance, 1 January–15 February 1944, 578
  1st Belorussian, 500–501, 506, 518–523, 526, 530, 535, 538–539, 572, 577, 584
    combat formation on 23 March 1944, 530
    order of battle on 1 March 1944, 523–524
    order of battle on 1 April 1944, 538
  1st Ukrainian, xxi, 6–8, 14–15, 17, 20, 123, 181, 189, 205, 243, 260, 266–270, 272, 404, 417–418, 426, 477, 500, 521, 528, 539, 543–544, 572–573, 671n1
    ammunition expenditure, March 1943–March 1944, 547, 572
  2nd Baltic, xxii, 14, 17–20, 54–56, 122, 124–126, 128, 133, 135, 138–139, 145–146, 151–154, 169, 206–208, 235, 237–239, 241, 268, 272, 292, 304, 308, 349, 361, 377, 402, 571, 671n1
  2nd Belorussian, 272, 500–501, 521, 539, 544, 584
    created, 17 February 1944, 500
    disbanded, 5 April 1944, 539
  2nd Ukrainian, xxi, 6–8, 14–15, 17, 20, 266–267, 269–270, 272, 572–573, 671n1
  3rd Belorussian, 542, 544–545, 569, 584
  3rd Ukrainian, xxi, 6–8, 14–15, 17, 20, 266–267, 269–270, 272, 572–573, 671n1
  4th Ukrainian, 6–8, 14–15, 17, 20, 266–267, 269–270, 572–573, 671n1
    ammunition expenditure, March 1943–March 1944, 547, 572
  Baltic, 14, 18–20, 22, 51–54, 94, 97, 548, 566, 671n1
  Belorussian, xxi, xxii, xxv, 6–7, 14–15, 20, 23, 31, 54, 94–96, 103, 110–111, 122–123, 125, 171–175, 178–179, 183–184, 189, 204, 207–208, 212, 241–243, 245, 248, 251, 261, 268–270, 272–273, 402–407, 412, 418–419, 453–454, 456, 477–478, 495–496, 500, 502, 540, 548, 566–567, 571–572, 577–578, 580, 583, 671n1, 695–696n4
    ammunition expenditure, March 1943–March 1944, 547
    combat formation on 15 January 1944, 456, 484
    combat formation on 1 February 1944, 498
    conversion to 1st Belorussian Front (17 February 1940), 500
    order of battle on 1 January 1944, 420–421
    order of battle on 1 February 1944, 495–496
    rate of advance, 3 January–31 March 1944, 578
    strength on 10 November 1943, 172, 684n3
    strength on 15 November 1943, 174, 686n33
  Briansk, 5–6, 8–12, 18–21, 30, 51, 62, 70, 90–92, 94, 96, 540, 582, 671n1
  Central, xix, xx, xxi, xxv, 5–15, 18–20, 22–23, 30–31, 50, 52–54, 70, 90–95, 97, 103–104, 108, 110, 123–124, 251, 402, 540, 580, 582, 671n1, 674n45
  Don, 582
  Kalinin, xix, xx, xxi, xxv, 6, 8, 11–15, 18–23, 26, 30–38, 41–45, 48, 50, 52–56, 60, 62–63, 77, 90, 94, 122, 301–302, 402, 540, 570, 580, 671n1

Leningrad, xxii, 9, 12, 22, 50, 52, 124–125, 237, 268, 270, 272, 304, 308, 349, 361
North Caucasus, 6, 9, 11–12, 17
Northwestern, 22, 26, 50–52, 94, 125, 154, 237, 500
Southeastern, 582
Southern, 6, 8–15, 18, 20, 671n1
Southwestern, xx, xxi, 6, 8–15, 18, 20, 671n1
Stalingrad, 582
Steppe, xx, xxi, 5–6, 8–15, 18, 20, 671n1
Volkhov, xxii, 9, 12, 22, 50, 52, 124–125, 237, 268, 270, 304, 308, 349, 361
Voronezh, xx, xxi, 5–6, 8–15, 20, 22, 90, 93–95, 123–124, 671n1
Western, xix, xx, xxi, xxii, xxiii, 5–6, 8–14, 18, 20–23, 26, 30–31, 34, 48, 50, 60–63, 65, 67–70, 75, 77–79, 83–84, 87, 90, 95–96, 123–125, 156–157, 160–161, 164, 166, 169–170, 174, 203, 208–209, 212, 219, 239, 241, 268–270, 272–275, 278–279, 281, 283–285, 291–292, 301, 304, 307–309, 328, 332–340, 349, 360, 362, 364, 367, 369, 371–373, 377, 380–383, 387–390, 392, 394, 396, 402, 404–406, 411–412, 418, 478, 501, 521, 526, 540–545, 548, 551, 566–567, 569–573, 577–580, 582, 584, 674n45, 693n11
    ammunition expenditure, March 1943–March 1944, 547, 572
    combat formation on 3 February 1944, 350
    combat formation on 29 February 1944, 373
    combat formation on 1 March 1944, 383
    combat formation on 21 March 1944, 394
    critique of operations, October 1943–April 1944, 543–562
    order of battle on 1 January 1944, 283–285
    order of battle on 1 February 1944, 335–336
    order of battle on 1 March 1944, 370
    order of battle on 1 April 1944, 389
    personnel losses, October–December 1943, 171
    personnel losses, January 1944, 329–330
    personnel losses, February 1944, 367–368
    personnel losses, March 1944, 401
    personnel losses, 1 January–1 April 1944, 695n12
    personnel losses, October 1943–April 1944, 541, 547
    rate of advance, October 1943–March 1944, 541, 578
    rate of advance, 1 January–5 March 1944, 578

Gadilovichi (Bykhov region), 204, 408
Galitsky, Lieutenant General K. N., 32, 37–39, 41–42, 126, 138–140, 146–147, 149–150, 154, 212, 222, 229–231, 238, 275–278, 280, 289, 307–309, 311–312, 314–317, 334, 337, 339–340, 342–346, 349
Galuzy (Chausy region), 527
Gancharov Podel (Loev region), 179–180
Gareev, Army General Makhmut Akhmetovich, xxiii, 61, 308, 332, 380, 387, 541–542, 565, 567–571, 577, 579
Garmovichi (Mormal' region), 520
Gartsev, Major General I. A., 492, 497, 502, 519–520
Gat'kovshchina (Orsha region), 383
Gausin Bor (Orsha region), 166
Gazhin (Mozyr' region), 440
General Staff, Red Army, xix, xx, xxii, 33, 61, 134, 170, 273, 304, 333, 422, 526, 562, 566, 568, 674n45
Gerasimenki, 66
Gerasimov, Lieutenant General M. N., 225
Gladyshev, Colonel S. T., 321, 557
Glutsk, 245
Gluzdovsky, Lieutenant General V. A., 63, 65–66, 71, 82–83, 85, 157, 162, 167–168, 362, 364–366, 380–383, 385–386
Gnezdilovichi (Vitebsk region), 35
Goebbels, Joseph, 21
Goering, *Reichsmarshal* Herman, 32

Golevitsy Station (Kalinkovichi region), 424, 438
Goliashei (Orsha region), 167
Gollwitzer, General of Infantry Friedrich, 376
Golochevo (Chausy region), 526, 529, 531
Golovenchitsy (Chausy region), 412, 416, 526–529, 531–532
Golubev, Lieutenant General K. D., 36, 43, 126, 141, 210, 214, 216–217, 229, 232, 292, 380
Gomel', xxi, 6–7, 11, 13, 15, 17–18, 22, 90–92, 94, 96–99, 101, 103–104, 106, 108–110, 112, 114–115, 122, 171, 173–174, 177, 185–186, 189–193, 200, 204, 261, 402, 408, 496, 499, 567, 577, 671n1
Gomza (Parichi region), 198, 204
Gorbachevskaia (Kalinkovichi region), 417
Gorbachi (Vitebsk region), 288–289, 309, 311–312, 334, 337–339, 341–345, 347–348
Gorbatov, Lieutenant General A. V., 95–97, 109, 121, 174, 177, 190, 200–202, 204, 243, 406–407, 410–411, 413–416, 439, 508, 510, 512–515, 521, 573, 700n4
Gorbovichi (Kalinkovichi region), 417
Gordov, Colonel General V. N., 68–69, 71–72, 83–84, 157, 163, 291–292, 297–300, 309–310, 318, 320–321, 324, 328, 338, 351–355, 357–358, 367, 369, 372, 374–377, 379–380, 543–544, 556–557, 559, 561, 568
Gorelyi Mokh (Rogachev region), 507
Goriane (Vitebsk region), 217–218, 232, 234, 292
Gorinany (Orsha region), 82, 167
Gorki (Orsha region), xxi, 68–69, 95–96
Gornostaipol' (Kiev region), 11
Gorodishche (Gorodok region), 276
Gorodishche (Vitebsk region), 343
Gorodok (Parichi region), 188, 198
Gorodok (Vitebsk region), 7, 17, 33–37, 39, 41, 43, 45, 48, 55, 103–104, 125–126, 130–131, 133–136, 139–141, 152–153, 206, 208–210, 212, 216–218, 223–224, 226–230, 234–235,
237, 274, 276, 279–280, 285–286, 291, 296, 301, 402, 540, 681n20
Gorokhovishchi (Shatsilki region), 499, 502, 535
Gorokhovo (Kalinkovichi region), 432, 436
Gorovatka (Vitebsk region), 390
Gorval' (Rechitsa region), 186
Gory (Shatsilki region), 483
Gory (Vitebsk region), 69, 395–396
Govorov, Army General L. A., 268
Govorukha (Pustoshka region), 240
Grabnitsa (Vitebsk region), 285
Grafskie (Grafskie Nivy) (Mormal' region), 521
Great Britain, 3–4
Grechkin (Bykhov region), 527
Griady Farm (Vasilevichi region), 182
Gribuny (Vitebsk region), 298–300, 318, 320–321, 324, 351, 354–355
Grigor'ev, Senior Lieutenant D. P., 461
Grishin, Lieutenant General I. T., 69–71, 74, 369, 371, 376, 380–381, 384–386
Gromov, Lieutenant General of Aviation M. M., 74
Groups (*gruppen*), German
  Agricola (Korück 580), 478
  Breidenbach (20th Panzer Division), 343–344
  Lubbe, 116–117
  Schmidthuber (5th Panzer Division), 247
  von Below, 130, 146
  von Bercken, 422, 458, 462
  von Gottberg, 140
Groups of Soviet forces, Germany (GSFG), 579
Grushevka (Loev sector), 120
Gruzkaia (Rechitsa region), 187
Gubanov, Sergeant I., 159
Gulbene (Latvia), 51
Guraki (Orsha region), 162–163, 167–169

Harpe, General of Panzer Troops Josef, 403, 467
Heidkämper, Major General Otto, 223
Hills
  114.0 (Liubech' sector), 110
  128.4 (Kalinkovichi region), 439

Index   739

131.6 (Loev region), 180
134.4 (Ozarichi region), 454
136.8 (Kalinkovichi region), 423
139.1 (Ozarichi region), 454
139.5 (Ozarichi region), 474
141.1 (Gomel' region), 192
142.7 (Shatsilki region), 496, 498
144.0 (Kalinkovichi region), 429–430
147.4 (Kalinkovichi region), 430
180.8 (Orsha region), 166
181.3 (Bogushevsk region), 387, 396
183.7 (Orsha region), 166
189.6 (Krynki region), 327
201.7 (Orsha region), 168
201.8 (Orsha sector), 162
High Command, German Army
  (*Oberkommando des Heeres*, or
  OKH), 24–25, 190–191, 205, 220,
  260, 328, 391, 403, 421, 504
Hitler, Adolf, xx, 4, 42, 54, 128, 131, 136,
  148, 151–152, 189–192, 202, 205,
  220, 225, 237, 266, 269, 583

Iakimovichi (Kalinkovichi region), 417,
  419, 437, 445–446, 451, 455, 460,
  465–466, 471, 476–477
Iakimovskaia Sloboda (Shatsilki region),
  198
Ianovichi (Vitebsk region), 46, 48, 56, 142,
  217
Iashchitsy (Mormal' region), 502
Iashchitsy Station (Mormal' region), 502,
  520
Iazno, Lake (Pustoshka region), 239
Iazvin (Shatsilki region), 488, 490–491,
  493–494, 496, 504, 515
Ibiansky, Major General N. B., 279–280,
  312, 338, 341
Idritsa, 22, 39, 51, 53, 125, 147, 153–155,
  235, 237, 239, 304–305
Ignatov, Lieutenant General N. V., 254,
  426, 432, 518
Ikonnikov, Major General (no initials
  available), 557
Il'in, Major General A. M., 384
Il'men', Lake, 305
Il'nitsky, Colonel Ia. T., 543–544, 554, 556,
  559, 561
Iovlev, Major General I. S., 374, 378, 388

Ipa River (Shatsilki-Kalinkovichi region),
  242, 254, 417, 419, 423, 436–437,
  443–446, 449, 451–452, 454–455,
  457–460, 462, 464, 466, 468, 471,
  476–477, 479, 481
Iput' River (Gomel' region), 91, 97, 99
Isakovichi (Loev region), 117
Iskra (Shatsiliki region), 517, 519–520
Istrubishche (Babinovichi region), 364
Italy, 191
Iur'ev (Orsha region), 166
Iurevichi (Mozyr' region), 196–197, 426
Iur'evka (Orsha region), 80
Iushkevich, Lieutenant General V. A., 54,
  238
Iushkovichi (Chausy region), 532–533
Iushkovo (Vitebsk region), 395
Ivanov, Colonel A. K., 81
Ivanov, Major General A. K., 291, 297–298,
  377
Ivanov, Major General I. I., 99, 179, 187,
  246, 423, 427, 431, 436–437, 446,
  457, 460, 465–466, 468, 470
Ivanov, Major General I. P., 375
Ivanov Sloboda (Kalinkovichi region),
  418
Ivashkovichi (Ptich' River region), 453,
  470, 476–478
Izocha (Nevel' region), 54
Izubry (Orsha region), 64

Japan, 4
Jordan, Lieutenant General Hans, 38, 324,
  376

Kachury (Pripiat' River region), 444, 450
Kalinkovichi, xxi, xxii, xxv, 7, 17, 93, 103,
  115–116, 172, 174, 179, 182,
  185–192, 194, 196–198, 205–208,
  242–243, 245–247, 250–254, 258,
  260–261, 273, 402–405, 416–419,
  421, 423–424, 426, 432, 434, 436–
  447, 449, 451–454, 458, 460–461,
  476, 478, 481, 483, 491–493, 508,
  535, 540, 576, 578
Kamenets-Podolsk, 266, 268
Kamera, Colonel General I. P., 543–544,
  548, 559–561
Kamery (Vitebsk region), 338, 352

Kampfgruppe (KGr., combat group), German
  F (*Feldherrnhalle*), 293–294, 296–297, 300
  general, 22, 39, 62, 94, 348, 392, 399, 421
Kapietskii Vorotyn' (Ipa River region), 470
Kaplichi (Kalinkovichi region), 437, 444, 446, 451, 454, 459–460, 464, 466
Karamidy (Vitebsk region), 142, 375
Karataia (Nevel' region), 149
Karpilovka (now Oktiabr'skii) (Ptich' River region), 245, 248
Karpovichi (Kalinkovichi region), 246
Karpovichi (Vitebsk region), 321, 352, 355–358, 372, 374, 378
Karpovka (Gomel' region), 101
Kasenki (Vitebsk region), 217, 232, 234
Kasplia River (Demidov region), 34–35
Kazakov, Lieutenant General V. I., 518
Kazansk (Kalinkovichi region), 419, 423, 432, 434, 458–460, 464
Kazanskie Farm (Kalinkovichi region), 417
Kazarinovo (Orsha region), 68, 82
Kazimirovo (Babinovichi region), 364, 366
Kerch' (Crimea), 13, 17
Khal'ch (Gomel' region), 192
Khaliuzin, Major General G. A., 99, 181, 426, 458, 461, 470, 476, 478
Kharitonov, Major N. A., 535
Khar'kov, xx, 4–6, 10–11
Khar'kovka (Chausy region), 527
Kherson (Ukraine), 15, 20
Khislavichi (Sozh River region), 61, 570
Khlebno (Glebno) (Propoisk region), 200–201
Khodorivichi (Gorki region), 69
Khoiniki (Mozyr' region), 182, 187, 193, 196
Kholm, 51, 122
Kholma (Ozarichi region), 535–536
Kholodniki (Kalinkovichi region), 247, 417, 419, 423
Kholopenichi (Ptich' River region), 250
Khomenki (Propoisk region), 203
Khomichi (Rogachev region), 506–507, 510
Khozin, Lieutenant General M. S., 292
Khramkh (Mozyr' region), 444
Khvoiniki (Ptich' River region), 248

Kiev, xx, xxi, 6, 13, 17–18, 20, 22–23, 90, 92–95, 124, 243, 260, 267, 674n45
Kireevo (Orsha axis), 82, 85–87
Kirovograd (Ukraine), 7, 267
Kirpichni Factory (Gomel' region), 192
Kiseli (Liady region), 66–67
Kisliaki (Vitebsk region), 343
Kisteni (Rogachev region), 507–509, 512
Kizhen (Zherd'), 480–481
Klenidovka (Usviaty region), 35
Klenovichi (Zhlobin region), 200
Kleshni (Mozyr' region), 448
Kletnia (Briansk region), 91
Klevan' (Ukraine), 500
Klichev (Bobriusk region), 174
Klimenki (Liady region), 81
Klinsk (Kalinkovichi region), 417, 419, 444–445, 451, 455, 458–459
Klintsy (Novozybkov region), 91
Kluge, Field Marshal Gunther von, 21, 31, 114–115
Knurovka (Mozyr' region), 440
Koblov, Guards Colonel G. P., 121
Kobylevo (Vasilevichi region), 185
Kobyl'shchina (Poles'e) (Ozarichi region), 242, 453, 486, 491–493, 496, 502
Koibaev, Lieutenant Colonel A. N., 468
Kolbasichi (Kalinkovichi region), 446
Kolganov, Lieutenant General K. S., 482, 486, 489–491, 494, 497, 502, 504, 517, 520, 529
Kolpakchi, Lieutenant General V. Ia., 95, 97, 172, 174, 177, 203, 243, 501
Kolpen' (Rechitsa region), 105
Kolyshki (Rudnia region), 43, 45–46
Komarichi (Rogachev region), 507, 510
Komarov, Colonel V. M., 374, 378, 388, 432, 435, 446
Konev, Army General I. S., 267
Konnov, Major General I. P., 407
Konstantinov, Major General M. P., 105, 120, 180, 187, 419, 421, 426, 440–444, 447
Konstantinovka (Mogilev region), 527
Kopatkovichi (Ptich' River region), 471
Koporenka (Chernobyl' region), 101
Kopti (Vitebsk region), 297–298, 300
Koptsevichi (Ptich' River region), 505
Koravcha Dubrova (Shatsilki region), 517

Korenevka (Mozyr' region), 196
Koreni (Ozarichi region), 246–247, 451, 454, 459, 483
Korkishko, Colonel V. N., 254
Korma (Kalinkovichi region), 197
Korma (Propoisk region), 200
Korma (Shatsilki region), 499, 502–503
Korobishche (Orsha region), 383
Koroli (Babinovichi region), 364
Koromka (Rogachev region), 507
Korosten' (Kiev region), xxi, 180, 426
Korotkov, Lieutenant General G. P., 54
Korotkovichi (Mormal' region), 520–521
Korovatichi (Vasilevichi region), 180, 182, 185, 187, 188
Korsakov, Major General P. T., 450
Korsun' pocket, 266
Korsun'-Shevchenkovskii (Ukraine), 267
Kosachi (Vitebsk region), 323, 398
Koshchichi (Kalinkovichi region), 417, 424, 432, 435
Kosho, Lake (Gorodok region), 228, 231
Kosiany (Orsha region), 157
Kosov (Gorodok region), 35
Kossetachi (Vitebsk region), 395–396
Kosteevo (Babinovichi region), 365–366
Kostinka (Bykhov region), 527
Kostiukovichi (Mozyr' region), 444, 450
Kostiukovka (Propoisk region), 109, 200
Kotel'nikov, Major General V. P., 291
Kovali (Vitebsk region), 292
Kovaly (Gorodok region), 135
Kovel' (Ukraine), 500–501
Kovshichi (Liady region), 67–68
Kozaki (Kosaki) (Vitebsk region), 343–345, 347, 357
Kozinki (Mozyr' region), 444
Kozlovichi-Nyshnie (Kalinkovichi region), 429, 431
Kozlovichi-Verkhnie (Kalinkovichi region), 430
Kozlovka (Parichi region), 245
Kozly (Vitebsk region), 337, 339, 343–344
Krasenki (Gorodok region), 216
Krasnaia Gorka (Rogachev region), 507
Krasnaia Sloboda (Propoisk region), 121, 202
Krasnaia Zvezda (Mormal' region), 520
Krasnitsa (Bykhov region), 411, 415–416, 527, 529, 534

Krasnoe (Orsha region), 66
Krasnopol'e (Vitebsk region), 334, 338
Krasnyi (Mozyr' region), 440
Krasnyi (Vitebsk region), 62, 80–81
Krasovshchina (Vitebsk region), 376
Kremen (Shatsilki region), 258, 487
Kremenchug (Ukraine), xx, 6–7, 11, 13, 18
Krichev (Sozh River region), 62, 91
Kriuchenkin, Lieutenant General V. D., 545
Kriukov, Major General V. V., 105, 118, 179, 196, 243, 251, 419, 421, 426, 440–443, 449, 451
Kriukovichi (Kriusha) (Ozarichi region), 459, 462–464, 471, 473–475
Kriukovo (Vitebsk region), 328, 359
Krivoi Rog (Ukraine), xx, xxi, 7, 17, 267–268
Krotov (Ipa River region), 437, 444, 451, 454–455, 457–458, 460, 466, 470–471, 476
Krylataia Woods (Golovenchitsy region), 532
Krylov, Lieutenant General N. I., 68–69, 71, 74, 81–83, 156–157, 162, 167–168, 297–300, 308, 310, 318, 320–321, 324–327, 333, 338, 352–353, 359, 362, 365–367, 372, 380, 387–388, 395–399, 401, 542
Krymka (Mozyr' region), 441
Krynki (Vitebsk region), 298–300, 320, 324–325, 327
Krynki Station (Vitebsk region), 34
Ksenofontov, Major General A. S., 139, 311–312, 337, 339, 342–343
Kuchaevka (Loev region), 181
Kuchareva (Kukhareva) (Vitebsk region), 359, 395, 400
Küchler (Kuechler), Field Marshal Georg von, 42, 128, 131–132, 148, 151–152, 237, 304
Kukhori (Vitebsk region), 315–316
Kul'bashnik, Major V. V., 534
Kun'ia (Shatsilki region), 486–487
Kureni Moshenaki (Chausy region), 527
Kurgan' Farm (Ozarichi region), 473
Kurino (Nevel' region), 35
Kurochkin, Colonel General P. A., 154, 500–501
Kursk, 4–5, 251

Kursk, the Battle of, 5 July–23 August 1943, xx, 5, 8–11
Kursk bulge, 6, 10
"Kutuzov" (Orel). *See* Operations, Soviet military
Kuzmentsy (Vitebsk region), 399
Kuzminichi (Propoisk region), 203, 418
Kuz'mino (Vitebsk region), 138
Kuznetsov, Lieutenant General F. F., 541, 543, 545, 561
Kuzovkov, Major General I. A., 241, 246, 253, 258, 457, 460, 483, 486, 489, 491, 496, 502

Laptevka (Gorodok region), 223, 225
Lapty Farm (Mozyr' region), 448
Laputi (Vitebsk region), 354
Lapyrevshchina (Orsha region), 74, 371
Latvia, 52, 62, 122
Lazyrshchinki (Lazyrshchina) (Orsha region), 167, 383–384, 386
Lebedy (Vitebsk region), 347
Ledno (Shatsilki region), 519–520
Lel'chitsy (Gomel' region), 535
Len'chitsy (Ovrich' region), 418
Leningrad, xxi, xxii, 3, 10, 12–13, 17, 33, 49–50, 52, 125, 148, 154–155, 208, 265–266, 268–270, 304, 306, 308, 421, 567, 571
Lenino (Orsha/Gorki region), 62, 68–69, 71–72, 74–75, 78, 84
Leonovka (Orsha region), 371
Lepel' (Vitebsk region), 33–34, 140, 281, 547, 570
Lepeny (Chausy region), 203
Lesets (Ozarichi region), 454, 491
Leutino (Vitebsk region), 327, 375, 390
Levkovshchina (Mogilev region), 527
Liady (Kalinkovichi region), 197
Liady (Orsha region), 62, 66–68, 81, 157, 371
Liady (Shatsilki region), 520
Liakhovo (Gorodok region), 218
Liozno (Vitebsk region), 33–35, 43, 45–48, 56, 212
Lipniaki (Loev sector), 118, 120–121, 179–180
Lipniki (Parichi region), 198
Lithuania, 61, 570

Litovshchina (Vitebsk region), 344, 347–348
Liuban' (Ptich' River region), 245
Liubavichi (Rudnia region), 64, 66, 80
Liubech', 92, 99–100, 102, 105–106, 110, 113, 116, 181
Liubov' (Rogachev region), 507
Liutezh (Kiev region), 6, 11, 13, 18
Lobany (Orsha sector), 164, 384
Loev, 18, 91, 94–95, 99–101, 103–106, 110–112, 114–117, 119–121, 172, 174, 176–177, 179, 181, 189–190, 206, 261, 402, 671n1
Long-Range Aviation, Soviet, 128
Lososina River (Vitebsk region), 142, 297, 300, 321
Losvida (Gorodok region), 380
Losvida, Lake (Gorodok region), 276–277, 279–280, 309, 311, 317, 334, 344
Luchesa River (Vitebsk region), 35, 49, 299, 309, 318, 320–322, 324, 327, 329, 338, 351–353, 355–360, 362–364, 366, 369, 371–380, 385, 391–392, 394–396, 401, 553
Ludza (Latvia), 51
Luftwaffe, German Air Force, 4
Lukavo (Rudnia region), 64
Luninets (Pripiat' River region), 419, 423, 454, 477–478
Lupolovo (Mogilev region), 527
Luskinopol' (Vitebsk region), 393
Lutsk (Ukraine), 267, 477, 500, 697n21
Luzhki (Bykhov region), 414, 506
L'vov (Ukraine), 18

Maevo (Pustoshka region), 240
Makarov, Major General V. E., 545
Makarovo (Vitebsk region), 321, 338, 352, 355, 388, 393, 396
Maklaki (Vitebsk region), 296–299, 318, 320–321
Malaia Berezina River, 63–64
Maleev, Major General M. F., 100, 105
Malenkov, G. M., 541–543, 545, 561
Maleshenki (Gorodok region), 225
Malgati (Gorodok region), 218
Malinin, Lieutenant General M. S., 508, 521
Malinovsky, Army General R. Ia., 267, 269
Mal'kov, Colonel D. K., 424, 438–439

Malodusha (Rechitsa region), 182, 187–188, 190–191, 194
Malye Avtiuki (Malyi Avtiuki or Malyi Avtiutsevichi) (Kalinkovichi region), 197, 424–426, 438
Malye Babinovichi (Babinovichi region), 364
Malyi Ivan, Lake (Nevel' region), 53
Malyi Litvinovichi (Ozarichi region), 492, 535
Malyshev, Lieutenant General P. F., 280, 309–310, 312–313, 316–317, 334, 337–340, 343–346, 349
Manstein, Field Marshal Erich von, 7, 267–268, 270
Mar'ianovo (Babinovichi region), 352, 362–366, 372, 398
Mariupol' (Ukraine), 4
Markers, Soviet height
  142.4 (Mormal' region), 502
  148.8 (Orsha axis), 85
  180.8 (Orsha axis), 86–87
Marmovichi (Shatsilki region), 258, 493, 496, 573
Martynovichi (Kalinkovichi region), 432
Mashkina (Vitebsk region), 311–312, 317, 334, 339, 343–344
Matrenka (Mozyr' region), 444, 448
Matrosov, Sergeant A. A., 473
Mazurino (Vitebsk region), 311–312
Medved' (Ozarichi region), 454, 487, 489, 536
Medvedov (Shatsilki region), 258
Mekhlis, Lieutenant General L. Z., 154, 239, 292, 372, 543–544, 560, 693n8, 694n13
Mekhovoe (Gorodok region), 139, 216
Mekhovshchina (Shatsilki region), 486, 493, 496
Meleshkovichi (Mozyr' region), 426, 441–442
Melitopol' (Ukraine), 6, 12–13, 18
Melkoe, Lake (Gorodok region), 133, 153
Mereia River (Baevo region), 60, 63, 66–68, 70, 72, 75
Meretskov, Army General K. A., 268
Mezha (Gorodok region), 35
Mglin (Surazh region), 91
Miafli (Vitebsk region), 318, 320, 326–327

Miakovo (Vitebsk region), 318, 321, 324, 338, 355
Mikhailovka (Shatsilki region), 502, 504, 517
Mikhailovo (Vitebsk region), 358, 360, 375, 378
Mikhali (Vitebsk region), 276, 337, 339, 343–344
Mikhnovichi (Pripiat' River region), 419, 443, 449–451, 454, 458
Mikul' (Parichi region), 198
Mikulino (Vitebsk region), 45, 69
Military districts, Soviet
  Moscow, 672n12
Military strategy, German (Hitler's)
  "stand-fast" (*festung*), 266
Military strategy, Soviet (Stalin's)
  "narrow front" versus "broad front," 265–266
Minsk, xix, xx, 13, 15, 18, 20, 22, 63, 77–79, 81, 93, 95–96, 103–104, 122, 124–126, 157, 172–174, 205, 208, 261, 273–274, 351, 383, 402, 419, 454–455, 501, 504, 524, 547, 570, 584
Mirobeli (Mozyr' region), 448
Mishukov, Major F. E., 448
Mitrofanov, Junior Lieutenant N., 159
Mnogoversh (Kalinkovichi region), 197, 245
Mnogovichi (Shatsilki region), 258
Model, Colonel General Walter, 109, 115, 189, 191, 202–203, 242
Mogilev, 22, 60–62, 78, 90, 95, 115, 171, 174, 212, 408–409, 506, 524–525, 527–529, 547, 570, 583–584, 674n45
Mogilev-Podol'skii (Ukraine), xx, 20
Mokhovo (Loev sector), 116
Moklishche (Mozyr' region), 196
Mol'cha (Shatsilki region), 490–491, 497
Molchanov, Colonel L. M., 253
Molodechno (Minsk region), 22, 61–62, 93, 584
Momachino (Bykhov region), 409
Mormal' (Shatsilki region), 494, 502, 504, 516, 518, 521, 525, 573, 578
Morosovka (Rudnia region), 64
Moscow, 3–4, 18, 140, 548, 555, 570, 572
Moscow counteroffensive, Soviet, December 1941, 3

744 Index

Moseevo (Nevel' region), 54
Moshenitsy (Vitebsk region), 398
Mostki (Shatsiliki region), 517
Mostok (Mogilev region), 527
Mozhentsy (Zamozhentsy) (Vitebsk region), 323
Mozyr' (Pripiat' River region), xxi, xxii, 95, 105, 115–116, 179, 194, 196, 205, 242–243, 251–252, 402–405, 418–419, 423, 426, 439–445, 447–449, 451–454, 468, 540, 573, 578
Mozyr' Station, 444, 448
Mshatoe Swamp (Bykhov region), 506
Mstislavl' (Sozh River region), 62
Muk (Mozyr' region), 441
Mul'tan, Major General N. N., 298, 318, 338, 351, 354–357, 374–375, 378, 394, 396, 399
Muryvanka (Molilev region), 527
Mushichi (Ozarichi region), 472
Myl'nishche (Vitebsk region), 279
Myshanka (Tremlia River region), 477
Myslov Rog (Ozarichi region), 256, 537
Mysy (Radul' region), 103, 116

Nadezhda (Rogachev region), 507
Nadvin (Rechitsa region), 179, 187
Nadysev, Lieutenant General G. S., 518
Nakhov (Vasilevichi region), 185, 246
Narimanov (Mozyr' region), 196
Narovlia (Mozyr' region), 440
Narva (Estonia), 304
Nasavichi (Kalinkovichi region), 174, 197
Nasva (Novosokol'niki region), 53
Naumov, Major General A. F., 384, 395, 399
Nevel', xx, xxi, 7, 13, 15, 17, 22, 32–34, 36–39, 41–42, 48, 51–57, 77, 90, 122, 125–126, 129–130, 132–135, 138–141, 145, 147–149, 151, 153, 156, 206, 223–225, 235, 237–240, 261, 280, 302, 402, 540, 671n1
Nevel', Lake, 150
Nigilev (Shatsilki region), 502
Nikolaevka (Radul' sector), 117, 121
Nikol'skoe (Gorki region), 69
Nikonovichi (Bykhov region), 408–409, 414–415
Nikopol' (Ukraine), 7, 15, 17, 268
Niva (Loev sector), 120

Nivy (Grafskie Nivy) (Mormal' region), 521
Nizhne-Kozlovichi (Kalinkovichi region), 423–424, 432, 434
North Africa, 3–4
Norway, 4
Nosov, Captain I. N., 160
Nosovichi (Kalinkovichi region), 423–424
Novaia (Orsha axis), 66, 86
Novaia Lutava (Liubech' sector), 116, 121
Novaia Rudnia (Mozyr' region), 440
Novaia Tukhinia (Orsha region), 81
Novgorod, 268, 304, 306
Novgorod-Volynskii (Ukraine), 404
Noviki (Vitebsk region), 355–358, 374, 378, 693n11
Novinki (Vasilevichi region), 182, 197, 246
Novka (Vitebsk region), 351, 354
Novo-Belitsa (Gomel' region), 177
Novoe Selo (Orsha region), 85, 160, 162, 164
Novorossiisk (Caucasus region), 6, 11
Novoselki (Ozarichi region), 454, 459–462, 466
Novoselki (Vitebsk region), 341, 344
Novosel'sky, Lieutenant General Iu. V., 238
Novosokol'niki (Velikie Luki region), 32–33, 37–39, 53–54, 147, 149, 152, 208, 236–240, 304–305
Novozybkov, 91
Novye Diatlovichi (Gomel' region), 101
Novyi Bykhov (Bykhov region), 96, 104, 121, 174, 177, 202–204, 242–243, 407–409, 412, 414–416, 505–506, 509, 521, 525–526, 528, 573, 584, 674n45
Novyi Lobuzh (Bykhov region), 527
Novyi Put' (Vasilevichi region), 188

Obol'ia River (Gorodok region), 133
Odessa (Ukraine), 269
OKH. *See* High Command, German Army
Okin (Nevel' region), 53
Oktiabr'skii, 455, 482, 491, 497
Oktiabr' Station (Vitebsk region), 295
Ola (Shatsilki region), 520
Ola River (Shatsilki region), 504
Oleshev, Major General N. N., 291, 297–300, 318, 320–321, 324, 326, 339, 388, 394–396, 399
Olevsk (Zhitomir region), 500

Index   745

Operational groups, Soviet
  coastal, 52
Operations, German military
  Chernobyl' and Gornostaipol'
    counterstrokes, 3–8 October 1943, 14
  Citadel (Kursk), 5, 7
  Heinrich, November 1943, 128–129
  Kalinkovichi counterstroke, 20–27 December 1943, 14
  Kovel' relief, 27 March–7 April 1944, 272
  Narva counterstroke, 26 March–24 April 1944, 272
  Nikolaus counterstroke, 191, 242, 250–260
Operations, Soviet military
  Advance (Race) to the Dnepr River, 7 August–2 October 1943, 8, 12
  Aleksandriia-Znamenka offensive, 22 November–9 December 1943, 15
  Apostolovo offensive, 14 November–23 December 1943, 15
  Babinovichi offensive, 22–25 February 1944, 272, 362–368
    correlation of opposing forces, 364
    Soviet personnel losses, 364, 366
  Barvenkovo-Pavlograd offensive, 13 August–22 September 1943, 12
  Belgorod-Khar'kov offensive, 3–23 August 1943, 9
  Belgorod-Khar'kov strategic offensive (Rumiantsev), 3–23 August 1943, 5, 9–10
  Belorussian strategic offensive, 3 October–31 December 1943, 3–279
    lessons learned, 583–584
  Belorussian strategic offensive (Bagration), 23 June–29 August 1944, xix, xx, xxiii, 569, 579–584
  Bereznegovataia-Snigirevka offensive, 6–18 March 1944, 270
  Bogoshevsk offensive, 21–29 March 1944, 272, 387–401, 546–547
  Bolkhov-Orel offensive, 12 July–18 August 1943, 9
    correlation of opposing forces, 392
    Soviet personnel losses, 387, 401
  Briansk offensive, 17–26 August 1943, 12, 51, 91–92

Bukrin offensives, 12–15 and 21–24 October 1943, 14
Bykhov-Chausy offensive, 3–8 January 1944, 405–416, 577
  correlation of opposing forces, 412
Chernigov-Poltava strategic offensive, 26 August–30 September 1943, 6, 12
Chernigov-Pripiat' offensive, 26 August–30 September 1943, 12, 30, 51, 91, 93
Chernobyl'-Radomysl' offensive, 1–4 October 1943, 14
Crimean offensive, 8 April–12 May 1944, 270
Dnepr bridgeheads, 25–31 March 1944, 526–534, 577
  correlation of opposing forces, 530
Dnepropetrovsk offensive, 23 October–23 December 1943, 15
Donbas offensive, 17 July–2 August 1943, 9–10
Donbas strategic offensive, 13 August–22 September 1943, 6, 11–13
Dukhovshchina-Demidov offensive, 14 September–2 October 1943, 12, 31, 33–34, 36
Gomel'-Rechitsa offensive, 30 September–30 October 1943, 14, 95–124, 172, 577
Gomel'-Rechitsa offensive, 10–30 November 1943, 14, 23, 172–200, 577
  Soviet personnel losses, 205
Iasi-Kishinev offensive (Tirgu-Frumos), 8 April–6 June 1944, 272
Idritsa offensive, 18–30 October 1943, 55
Idritsa-Opochka offensive (Novosokol'niki pursuit), 16–25 December 1943, 14, 235–240
Izium-Barvenkovo offensive, 17–27 July 1943, 9
Kalinkovichi (Bobruisk) offensive, 8–11 December 1943, 14, 241–250
Kalinkovichi-Mozyr' offensive (raid), 11–14 January 1944, 270, 417–452, 577–578
  correlation of opposing forces, 426
  Soviet personnel losses, 478

746 Index

Operations, Soviet military, *continued*
 Kerch'-El'tigen offensive, 31 October–11 December 1943, 15
 Kiev defensive, 13 November–22 December 1943, 7
 Kiev strategic offensive, Soviet, 3–13 November 1943, 6–7, 14, 17
 Kirovograd offensive, 5–16 January 1944, 270
 Korsun'-Shevchenkovskii offensive (Cherkassy), 24 January–17 February 1944, 270
 Kremenchug offensive, 26 September–10 October 1943, 15
 Kremenchug-Piatikhatki (Krivoi Rog) offensive, 15 October–3 November 1943, 15
 Krivoi Rog offensive, 14–21 November 1943, 15
 Krivoi Rog offensive, 10–19 December 1943, 15
 Kromy-Orel offensive, 15 July–18 August 1943, 9
 Kursk strategic defense, 5–23 July 1943, 9–10
 Kursk strategic offensive, 5 July–23 August 1943, 9, 11
 Leningrad-Novgorod strategic offensive, 14 January–1 March 1944, 266, 270
 Liutezh offensive, 11–24 October 1943, 14
 Lower Dnepr strategic offensive, 26 September–31 December 1943, 14–15
 Marmovichi-Dubrova offensive, 16 January–23 February 1944, 459, 480–499, 501–505, 577
  correlation of opposing forces, 485
 Marmovichi-Mormal' offensive, 29 January–9 March, 272
 Melitopol' offensive, 26 September–5 November 1943, 15
 Mga offensive, 22 July–22 August 1943, 9–10
 Mga offensive, 15–18 September 1943, 12
 Mius offensive, 17 July–2 August 1943, 9
 Mius-Mariupol' offensive, 18 August–22 September 1943, 12
 Mormal'-Parichi offensive, 24–29 February 1944, 515–521, 577
  correlation of opposing forces, 518
 Narva offensive, 2–28 February 1944, 272
 Narva offensive, 1–16 March 1944, 272
 Narva offensive, 17–24 March 1944, 272
 Nevel' offensive, 3–13 October 1943, xxv, 7, 23, 31–51, 54, 146
 Nikopol' offensives, 14 November–31 December 1943, 15
 Novorossiisk-Taman' offensive, 9 September–9 October 1943, 12
 Novosokol'niki-Idritsa offensive, 31 January–13 February 1944, 272
  Soviet personnel losses, 306
 Novosokol'niki pursuit, 30 December 1943–15 January 1944, 304–306
 Novyi Bykhov–Propoisk offensive, 22–30 November 1943, 14, 200–205
 Odessa offensive, 26 March–14 April 1944, 270
 Opochka-Sebezh offensive, 1–8 March 1944, 272
 Opochka-Sebezh offensive, 10–26 March 1944, 272
 Opochka-Sebezh offensive, 7–18 April 1944, 272
 Orel strategic offensive (Kutuzov), 12 July–18 August 1943, 5, 9–10
 Orsha offensive, 3–11 October 1943, 14, 60–70
 Orsha offensive, 12–18 October 1943, 14, 71–77, 545–546
  Soviet personnel losses, 75
 Orsha offensive, 21–26 October 1943, 14, 77–89, 545–546
  Soviet personnel losses, 87
 Orsha offensive, 14–19 November 1943, 14, 161–165, 545–546
  Soviet personnel losses, 164
 Orsha offensive, 20 November–5 December 1943, 14, 166–171, 545–546
  Soviet personnel losses, 170
 Orsha offensive, 5–9 March 1944, 272, 381–387
  correlation of opposing forces, 385
  Soviet personnel losses, 381, 385, 387

Ozarichi-Ptich' offensive, 14–30 January 1944, 272, 453–479, 577–578
  correlation of opposing forces, 462
  Soviet personnel losses, 462
Poles'e (Kovel') offensive, 15 March–5 April 1944, 272
Polotsk-Vitebsk offensive, 2–21 November 1943, 14, 126, 129–154
Poltava offensive, 24 August–30 September 1943, 12
Proskurov-Chernovtsy offensive (Kamenets-Podolsk), 4 March–17 April 1944, 270
Pskov-Ostrov offensive, 2–17 March 1944, 272
Pskov-Ostrov offensive, 7–19 April 1944, 272
Pursuit to the Panther Line, 17 February–1 March 1944, 272
Pushtoshka-Idritsa offensive, 2–21 November 1943, 14, 126–129, 145–155
Pustoska-Idritsa offensive, 12–16 January 1944, 272
Rogachev-Zhlobin offensive, 21–26 February 1944, 270, 272, 501, 506–515, 577–578, 700n4
  correlation of opposing forces, 512
  Soviet personnel losses, 507, 512, 514
Rovno-Lutsk offensive, 27 January–11 February 1944, 270, 500
Smolensk-Roslavl' offensive, 15 September–2 October 1943, 12
Smolensk strategic offensive (Suvorov), 7 August–2 October 1943, 6, 11–12, 51, 68, 568, 570, 582
Spas-Demensk offensive, 7–20 August 1943, 12
Sumy-Priluki offensive, 24 Augut–30 September 1943, 12
Taman' offensive, 4 April–10 May and 26 May–22 August 1943, 9–10
Uman'-Botoshany offensive, 5 March–17 April 1944, 270
Vitebsk, Idritsa, and Pskov offensives, 18–30 October 1943, 14, 50–56
Vitebsk (Gorodok) offensive, 13–23 December 1943, 14, 23, 209–235
  Soviet tank losses, 234
  Soviet tank strength, 234
Vitebsk-Bogushevsk offensive, 8–24 January 1944, 272, 307–331, 545–546
  correlation of opposing forces, 310
  Soviet personnel losses, 308–310, 328
Vitebsk offensive, 3–12 October 1943, 14, 31–51
  Soviet personnel losses, 50
Vitebsk offensive, 24 December 1943–6 January 1944, 272, 274, 279–303, 545–546
  correlation of opposing forces, 281
Vitebsk offensive, 3–16 February 1944, 272, 332–361, 545–546
  correlation of opposing forces, 340
  Soviet personnel losses, 332, 340, 359–360, 693n11
Vitebsk offensive, 29 February–5 March 1944, 272, 368–380
  correlation of opposing forces, 376
  Soviet personnel losses, 369, 376, 380
Zaporozh'e offensive, 10–14 October 1943, 15
Zhitomir-Berdichev offensive, 24 December 1943–14 January 1944, 7, 14, 267, 404
Zmiev offensive, 12–23 August 1943, 9
Opochka, 22, 39, 304
Ordovka (Malaia Berezina River region), 66
Ordovo (Ordowo), Lake (Nevel' region), 132, 150, 330
Orekhi, Lake (Orsha region), 88
Orel, xx, xxi, 4–5, 10–11, 105–106
Orsha, xx, 11, 13, 15, 22, 53, 60–63, 65–71, 78–79, 81–82, 84, 87–90, 93, 95–96, 124, 156–157, 160–162, 164, 166, 168, 170–171, 174, 208, 212, 234, 273–275, 281, 295, 297, 299–300, 309, 320–321, 323–324, 328–329, 338, 351–352, 354, 357, 364, 366, 369, 371–373, 380–383, 386–387, 393–394, 396, 398–399, 402, 540–541, 551, 553, 569–571, 573, 578, 583–584
Orshitsa River, 157, 168
Osetki (Vitebsk region), 395
Osevets (Pripiat' River region), 422

Osinniki (Vitebsk region), 341
Osinovka (Babinovichi region), 364
Osinovka Station (Orsha region), 167
Osintori (Osinstroi) (Orsha region), 156–157, 164, 166–168, 383, 386
Osipova (Babinovichi region), 364, 390, 395–396
Osipova Rudnia (Kalinkovichi region), 424, 426, 438
Oslikovsky, Lieutenant General N. S., 134, 223, 279, 289, 309, 312
Osovnik (Rogachev region), 507
Ostashkov, 51
Ostreni (Chausy region), 527
Ostrokorma (Kalinkovichi region), 247
Ostroshitsky (Minsk region), 103–104
Ostrov (Orsha region), 22, 82, 166
Ostrovchitsy (Shatsilki region), 502
Ostrov Farm (Kalinkovichi region), 247
Ostrovliane (Vitebsk region), 279
Ostrovno (Vitebsk region), 279, 299, 309–310, 318, 329, 339, 369, 372, 374–375
Osttruppen (former Soviet prisoners of war in German service), 128
Osveia, 52
Otrazh'e (Chausy region), 527
Oven, General of Infantry Karl, 38
Ozarichi (Kalinkovichi region), 197, 245–247, 251, 255–256, 402–403, 419, 452–455, 457, 459–460, 464–466, 468, 471, 483, 491–492, 494, 535, 573, 578
Ozery (Orsha region), 82

Pacific Ocean, 4
Palki (Bykhov region), 408–409, 414–415
Pankratov, Major General G. I., 450
Panov, Major General of Tank Forces M. F., 105, 122, 180, 186, 245, 258–259, 421, 423, 431–432, 434, 436–437, 444–446, 458, 479, 492–493, 496–499, 504, 510, 528–529, 534
Panther Defense Line, German. *See* Defense lines, German: Panther (Eastern Wall)
Papivin, Colonel General of Aviation N. F., 32
Parenevskii (Rogachev region), 507

Parfenkovo (Orsha region), 67, 371
Parichi (Berezina River region), xxii, 180, 186, 188, 198, 204, 241, 243, 245–246, 250–252, 255, 258, 402–403, 455, 465, 467, 476, 479, 481–483, 489–492, 494, 497, 501, 504, 516–517, 519–522, 524, 540, 573, 578, 584
Paseka (Bykhov region), 407
Pavliuchenki (Pavliuchenko) (Vitebsk region), 355, 369, 372, 548, 693n11
Pavliuki (Vitebsk region), 355
Pechishche (Shatsilki region), 258, 486–489
Penal companies. *See* Companies, Soviet penal
Penal forces (battalions and companies), Soviet, 47, 162, 510, 700n6
Perekrestov, Major General G. N., 388
Perekrutovskii Vorotyn' (Ipa River region), 476
Perevoloka (Rechitsa region), 182, 187
Perevoz (Vitebsk region), 299, 318, 321, 324, 327, 338, 352, 355–357, 369, 372, 374, 378, 388, 391
Peschanaia Rudnia (Parichi region), 245
Pesochna (Vitebsk region), 369, 372
Pestunitsa River (Vitebsk region), 276
Petriki (Orsha axis), 85, 87
Petrikov (Pripiat' River region), 441–443, 449, 458, 478, 697n21
Petrov, Colonel General I. E., 388, 391, 401, 544, 582
Petrovichi (Mogilev region), 527
Petrovichi (Shatsilki region), 496
Petukhovka (Propoisk region), 62, 70, 177, 200, 202–203, 506
Piatikhatki (Ukraine), 13
Piatiletna (Vitebsk region), 234, 292
Pinsk (Pripiat' River region), 524
Plav'e (Vasilevichi region), 188
Pleskovichi (Plesovichi) (Mormal' region), 517, 519–521
Plisa (Lepel' region), 52
Pnevka River (Lenino region), 72
Pobolovo (Rogachev region), 507, 509–510
Pochem, Colonel F. E., 81
Pochep (Briansk region), 91
Pochep (Rogachev region), 507
Pochinok (Smolensk region), 61, 570

Podberez'e (Novosokol'niki region), 147
Poddub'e (Vitebsk region), 142, 297, 320, 349, 369, 373
Poddubliany (Vitebsk region), 372
Podgorno (Vitebsk region), 394, 398
Podmekhovshchina (Mekhovshchina) (Ozarichi region), 453
Pogantsy (Shatsilki region), 504, 517
Poiarov, Colonel V. Ia., 338, 351, 354–358
Pokoliubichi (Gomel' region), 193
Pokrovskoe (Rogachev region), 507
Pokrovsky, Lieutenant General A. P., 543–545, 554, 560–561, 567
Poland, 21
Polenov, Lieutenant General V. S., 63, 82
Polenovka (Vitebsk region), 35
Poles'e region (Pripiat' River region), 204, 261, 440
Poles'e Swamps (Pripiat' River region), 245, 254
Poles'e Vasilevichi (Mozyr' region), 116
Poletniki (Bykhov region), 527
Polotsk, 22, 33–34, 39, 51–52, 62, 125–126, 128–129, 133–134, 138, 140–141, 146–147, 152, 156, 210, 220, 231, 237, 239, 273, 275, 281, 285, 288, 302, 333–334, 337–338, 341, 346–347, 584
Poltava (Ukraine), xx, 10
Polzukhi (Gorki region), 72
Ponizov'e (Demidov region), 34–35, 72
Poplavsky, Major General S. G., 291, 320, 352, 359, 365–366, 395, 400, 557
Popov, Army General M. M., 22, 53, 91–92, 122, 146, 149–150, 153–154, 239, 268
Popov, Lieutenant General V. S., 69–70, 406, 409, 411–412, 415–416, 526, 528–529, 531, 533
Popov, Senior Lieutenant V. V., 461
Popovka (Vitebsk region), 693n11
Porkhov (Dno region), 52
Porot'kovo (Vitebsk region), 338, 351, 355–356, 358, 372
Potapovka (Zhlobin region), 200, 204
Pozniak, Major General V. G., 43, 291, 320–321, 339
Pribor (Bykhov region), 407–409, 413–414, 416, 439

Prikhid'ko, Major General N. Ia., 81
Prilepovka (Chausy region), 413
Pripiat' Marshes, xix, 191, 267, 360, 426
Pripiat' River, 31–32, 90, 92–93, 189–190, 196–197, 205, 242, 245, 248, 260, 273, 419, 423, 426, 440–445, 447–451, 454–455, 458, 467, 477, 479, 481, 500–501
Prityka (Shatsilki region), 502
Privol'e (Malaia Berezina River region), 63
Probuzhdenie (Shatsilki), 480–481
Prokhod (Rechitsa region), 187
Prokisel' (Loev region), 180
Prokof'ev, Major General Iu. M., 81, 297–300, 320–321, 324, 326, 352, 395–396, 399
Pronia River (Gorki region), 18, 77, 60, 62–63, 69–70, 90, 95, 97, 109, 112, 121, 177, 202–203, 406, 409, 411–413, 528–529
Pronin, Lieutenant General M. A., 297
Propoisk (now Slavgorod), 90, 97, 109, 174, 177, 192, 202
Proskorin (Proskurni) (Zhlobin region), 243
Proskurov (Ukraine), 268–269
Prudniki (Vitebsk region), 343
Prudnikov, Lieutenant General F. K., 494
Prudok (Mozyr' region), 441–442, 444
Prudok (Shatsilki region), 198, 254
Pruzhinishche (Parichi region), 198, 535
Pskov, 18–19, 22, 39, 50–52, 304, 306
Ptich' (Pripiat' River region), 477
Ptich' River, 245, 273, 418–419, 423, 453–455, 459–460, 467, 470–471, 476–479, 482–483, 505, 535, 540, 573, 576
Ptich' Station, 450
Pugachevo (Orsha region), 383
Punitsy (Rudnia region), 34
Pushcha (Kuzmintsy) (Vitebsk region), 394
Pushchai (Orsha region), 85, 383
Pushkari (Vitebsk region), 369, 372
Pustoshka, 39, 53, 125–126, 146–147, 152, 154, 208, 237–239, 304–305, 349
Putialino (Orsha region), 371
Put'ki (Chausy region), 411, 413

"Race to the Dnepr River," 7 August–2 October 1943, xx, 8, 12

Index

Radomysl' (Kiev region), 674n45
Radoshkovichi (Molodechno region), 61–62, 570
Raduga (Gomel' region), 177, 192–193
Radul' (Loev region), 99, 103, 105–106, 110, 113, 115–117, 121, 177, 679n19
Raevskii (Mozyr' region), 444
Ragula, Major General I. I., 409, 414–415
Rakitnoe (Sarny region), 535
Rakshin (Shatsilki region), 502
Red'ka (Mozyr' region), 443
Rasputitsa (period of flooded roads), 21, 122, 150–151, 268, 382, 494, 506, 524–525, 582
Rechitsa, xxi, xxv, 7, 17, 90–91, 94, 96, 103–105, 114–115, 122, 124, 171–174, 180, 182, 185–189, 191, 193, 198, 200, 241, 245, 250, 261, 402, 540, 567, 577, 671n1
Rechki (Pustoshka region), 53
Red Army (*Raboche-Krest'ianskaia Krasnaia Armiia*, or RKKA), Soviet, personnel strength on 1 October 1943, 28
Red'ki (Orsha axis), 66, 86
Red'kovka (Loev region), 102
Regiments, German
   13th Panzer Grenadier (5th Panzer Division), 188, 696n12
   14th Infantry (78th Assault Division), 158
   14th Panzer Grenadier (5th Panzer Division), 188, 460, 463, 696n12, 698n8
   30th Panzer Grenadier (18th Panzer Grenadier Division), 158
   34th Infantry (35th Infantry Division), 462, 464, 698n8
   35th Panzer Grenadier (25th Panzer Grenadier Division), 158
   39th Infantry (26th Infantry Division), 158
   47th Panzer Grenadier (4th Panzer Division), 185
   51st Panzer Grenadier (18th Panzer Grenadier Division), 158
   53rd Grenadier (14th Infantry Division), 395
   77th Infantry (26th Infantry Division), 158
   78th Infantry (26th Infantry Division), 159
   84th Infantry (102nd Infantry Division), 442
   101st Grenadier (14th Infantry Division), 395
   101st Panzer Grenadier (18th Panzer Division), 142
   109th Infantry (35th Infantry Division), 462, 698n8
   119th Panzer Grenadier (25th Panzer Grenadier Division), 158
   169th Grenadier, 343
   181st Infantry (52nd Infantry Division), 85
   195th Infantry (78th Assault Division), 158
   215th Infantry (78th Assault Division), 158
   216th Infantry (102nd Infantry Division), 442
   232nd Infantry (102nd Infantry Division), 442, 450
   260th Infantry (113th Infantry Division), 157–158
   317th Infantry (211th Infantry Division), 328
   321st Infantry (197th Infantry Division), 158
   332nd Infantry (197th Infantry Division), 85, 158, 378
   347th Infantry (197th Infantry Division), 158
   350th Infantry (221st Security Division), 340, 351, 353, 357, 363, 365–366, 383–384, 388
   406th Grenadier (201st Security Division), 317, 328, 366, 388, 395, 398, 400, 693n3
   427th Infantry (129th Infantry Division), 681n20
   439th Grenadier (134th Infantry Division), 255–256
   481st Infantry (256th Infantry Division), 365
   529th Grenadier (299th Infantry Division), 353, 357
   530th Grenadier (299th Infantry Division), 393

608th Security (203rd Security Division), 698n1
613th Infantry (292nd Infantry Division), 471, 476
613th Infantry (707th Infantry Division), 698n12
613th Security (203rd Security Division), 698n18
727th Infantry (707th Infantry Division), 698n12
930th Security, 698n18
931st Infantry, 158
Cavalry Regiment "Mitte," 441–442
Regiments, Soviet
2nd Guards Motorcycle, 26
2nd Guards Tank Penetration (heavy tank), 138, 214–215, 231, 311, 686n2
3rd Aviation, Civil Air Fleet, 500
8th Guards Tank, 27
11th Guards Tank, 26, 219
13th Guards Tank, 27
21st Assault Aviation, 39
22nd Guards-mortar, 214
23rd Guards Tank, 365
24th Guards-mortar, 214
26th Guards Tank, 27
29th Guards Tank, 28
34th Guards-mortar, 214
36th Tank, 27, 201, 409
38th Tank, 691n17
42nd Guards Tank, 482
42nd Tank, 520
43rd Guards Rifle (16th Guards Rifle Division), 315
45th Tank, 28
53rd Guards Cavalry (15th Guards Cavalry Division), 120, 448
55th Guards Cavalry (15th Guards Cavalry Division), 120, 185, 448
56th Guards Cavalry (14th Guards Cavalry Division), 441
56th Guards Tank, 27, 69
57th Guards Cavalry (15th Guards Cavalry Division), 120
58th Guards Cavalry (16th Guards Cavalry Division), 441
58th Guards Tank, 27
59th Guards Cavalry (17th Guards Cavalry Division), 196

61st Guards Cavalry (17th Guards Cavalry Division), 196, 449
63rd Guards Tank, 83, 159
64th Guards Tank, 27, 68, 83, 159
65th Tank, 691n17
72nd Reconnaissance Aviation, 500
85th Guards-mortar, 214
93rd Guards-mortar, 214
98th Guards Rifle (30th Guards Rifle Division), 159
105th Tank, 26, 43, 45, 55, 217–218, 232
106th RVGK Artillery, 35
109th Rifle (37th Guards Rifle Division), 255
115th Guards Rifle (38th Guards Rifle Division), 198
118th Artillery (69th Rifle Division), 468
119th Tank, 158
120th Rifle (69th Rifle Division), 429–431, 466, 468–470
132nd Antitank, 67
147th Artillery-Mortar (15th Guards Cavalry Division), 448
161st Self-propelled Artillery (5th Tank Corps), 217
161st Tank, 27
163rd Tank Destroyer (Antitank), 41
187th Tank, 27
188th Artillery, 67
193rd Tank, 28, 97, 460, 472
203rd Heavy Tank, 26, 217
210th Rifle (82nd Rifle Division), 462–463, 468, 473, 534
221st Tank, 26, 691n17
222nd Rifle (49th Rifle Division), 532–533
225th Tank, 27
226th Tank, 26
231st Tank, 482, 520
233rd Tank, 27, 415, 529
237th Rifle (69th Rifle Division), 247, 429, 465, 470
248th Tank, 27, 68, 83, 159
249th Guards Rifle (85th Guards Rifle Division), 160
250th Rifle (82nd Rifle Division), 461–463, 468, 534
251st Tank, 28, 472, 474
253rd Guards Rifle (85th Guards Rifle Division), 159

752   Index

Regiments, Soviet, *continued*
   255th Tank, 28, 99, 423, 428, 460
   270th Rifle (194th Rifle Division), 517
   303rd Rifle (69th Rifle Division), 429–431, 465
   317th Mortar, 67
   332nd Fusilier (197th Infantry Division), 234
   397th Rifle (207th Rifle Division), 64
   417th Rifle (156th Rifle Division), 132
   455th Mortar (1st Guards Tank Corps), 424
   470th (194th Rifle Division), 486, 488
   610th Rifle (82nd Rifle Division), 462–463
   616th Rifle (194th Rifle Division), 487
   617th Rifle (199th Rifle Division), 327
   653rd Rifle (220th Rifle Division), 166
   662nd Artillery, 67
   827th Howitzer Artillery, 41
   850th Rifle (277th Rifle Division), 322, 396
   852nd Rifle (277th Rifle Division), 322
   854th Rifle (277th Rifle Division), 322, 396
   894th Infantry (265th Infantry Division), 696n12
   954th Rifle (194th Rifle Division), 486–487
   1001st Self-propelled Artillery (1st Guards Tank Corps), 105, 423
   1203rd Rifle (354th Rifle Division), 535
   1268th Rifle (385th Rifle Division), 532–533
   1435th Self-propelled Artillery, 26, 158
   1445th Self-propelled Artillery, 26, 291
   1455th Self-propelled Artillery, 28
   1459th Tank Destroyer Artillery, 426
   1494th Self-propelled Artillery, 27, 68, 291
   1495th Self-propelled Artillery, 27, 69, 84, 159
   1515th Self-propelled Artillery (5th Tank Corps), 217
   1537th Self-propelled Artillery, 27, 69, 158
   1538th Self-propelled Artillery, 27, 201
   1541st Self-propelled Artillery (1st Guards Tank Corps), 105, 423
   1546th Self-propelled Artillery (5th Tank Corps), 217
   1714th Antiaircraft Artillery, 128
   1812th Self-propelled Artillery, 27–28
   1813th Self-propelled Artillery, 27
   1814th Self-propelled Artillery, 27
   1816th Self-propelled Artillery, 423, 444
   1818th Self-propelled Artillery, 26
   1820th Self-propelled Artillery, 26, 43, 47
   1827th Self-propelled Artillery, 27
   1830th Self-propelled Artillery, 27, 68, 158, 291
   1888th Self-propelled Artillery, 423–424
   1897th Self-propelled Artillery, 28, 482
   1901st Self-propelled Artillery, 27
Reinhardt, Colonel General Georg Hans, 38, 136, 219–220, 344, 360–362, 375–376
Rekta (Propoisk region), 200
Remezy (Mozyr' region), 441
Remistrianka River (Gorki region), 69
Repishche (Shatsilki region), 490–491
Resta River (Chausy region), 533
Retka (Rogachev region), 507
Reviakhin, Major General V. A., 318, 320, 326, 338, 351, 355–357, 358
Riga (Latvia), 18, 20, 22, 50–52, 62, 146, 570
Rodin, Lieutenant General of Tank Forces A. G., 559
Rogachev, xxi, xxii, xxv, 17, 94, 103, 109, 177, 204–206, 242–243, 269, 273, 403–404, 480, 499–501, 504, 507–510, 512, 515–517, 521, 524–526, 535, 540, 573, 578, 584
Rogi (Vitebsk region), 351, 375
Rokossovsky, Army General K. K., xix, xx, xxi, xxii, 70, 90–95, 97, 101, 103–106, 110, 114–116, 120–124, 171–173, 177, 179–181, 186–187, 189–192, 194, 196–197, 200, 204–206, 208, 241–247, 250–252, 260, 269, 273, 402–405, 409, 411–412, 416, 418–419, 423, 426–427, 431–432, 437, 439–440, 442, 444, 446–447, 449, 452–455, 458–459, 461, 466, 470–476, 478–483, 492–494, 498–504, 508–510, 513–519, 521, 525–526, 528–529, 534–535,

538–539, 568, 572–573, 577–579, 582–584, 700n4, 702n2
Romanenko, Colonel P. S., 414–415
Romanenko, Lieutenant General P. L., 95, 174, 177, 179, 204, 243–244, 258, 454–455, 458–459, 479, 482–483, 485–486, 489–494, 496–499, 501, 503, 516–518, 520–521, 529, 539
Romania, 266, 269
Romanovka (Rechitsa region), 187
Roslavl', xx, 6, 61, 68, 570
Rosliaki Station (Gorodok region), 223
Rosov (Shatsilki region), 258, 489
Rossasenka (Rososianka) River (Orsha region), 67–68, 81, 86–87, 157, 162, 164, 167
Rossono (Polotsk region), 128
Rovno (Ukraine), 267, 477, 500, 697n21
Rozhnovo (Vitebsk region), 297
Rubleva (Babinovichi region), 364–366, 369, 375, 398
Rudabelka (Ptich' River region), 245
Rudashkov (Liady region), 67
Rudenka (Vasilevichi region), 194
Rudnia (Kalinkovichi region), 417
Rudnia (Propoisk region), 202, 507
Rudnia (Shatsilki region), 489, 491
Rudnia (Vitebsk sector), 18, 33, 35, 37–39, 43, 45, 63–64, 138
Rudobel'skie Gates (Parichi region), 198, 245, 248, 252, 260, 403
"Rumiantsev" (Belgorod-Khar'kov). *See* Operations, Soviet military
Rusany (Orsha region), 68, 156–157, 162
Rybnitsa (Ukraine), 20
Ryzhiki (Babinovichi region), 365
Ryzhikov, Major General E. V., 315
Rzhavka (Propoisk region), 202
Rzhev, 4, 305

Sakhno, Major General of Tank Forces M. G., 134, 223, 279, 309, 312, 337, 340, 343–345, 347–348
Salabuty (Propoisk region), 109
Samarsky, Major General D. I., 99, 179, 246, 255, 424, 446, 457, 459–461, 464–468
Sandalov, Lieutenant General I. M., 54, 151, 153, 304

Sankovsky, Major General I. I., 246–247, 430
Sarny (Ukraine), 500
Savchenki (Vitebsk region), 299, 320, 380
Savichi (Ozarichi region), 459, 466, 468, 470–476
Savin (Mormal' region), 502
Savin Rog (Ozarichi region), 454, 471, 474, 535
Schlemm, General of Airborne Troops Alfred, 38
Sebezh (Pskov region), 39, 147, 349
Sekirichi (Ozarichi region), 472
Selets-Khopoleev (Bykhov region), 202, 204, 409, 415, 509, 512
Seliavshchina (Polotsk region), 128
Selishche (Parichi region), 255
Seliuty (Vitebsk region), 281, 693n11
Selizharovo (Ostashkov region), 51
Sel'tso (Vitebsk region), 35
Sel'tsy (Kalinkovichi region), 432, 435
Semenovka (Bykhov region), 534
Semenovka (Vitebsk region), 354
Sen'kovo (Vitebsk region), 380
Sennitsa, Lake (Nevel' region), 38
Senno (Lepel' region), 34
Serashi Farm (Mozyr' region), 448
Sevastopol' (Crimea), 266, 269
Shafranov, Major General P. G., 280, 311, 313, 337, 339, 343, 345
Shalkovo (Liubavichi region), 64
Shaparovo (Chausy region), 203
Shapchitsy (Rogachev region), 408, 508–510
Shapechino (Vitebsk region), 320, 395, 398
Shapury (Vitebsk region), 351, 355, 357
Sharino (Orsha region), 81
Sharki (Vitebsk region), 390, 394, 399
Sharpilovka (Loev region), 101
Shatrovo (Vitebsk region), 337, 340, 344–346
Shatsilki (now Svetlogorsk), 103, 198, 244–246, 250–251, 253, 255, 257–259, 402, 436, 454–455, 482–483, 485–486, 489–491, 516–517, 520–521, 578
Shchekotovo (Mozyr' region), 441, 448
Shchemilovka (Vitebsk region), 35

754 Index

Shcherbakov, Colonel General A. S., 541–543, 545, 561
Sheki (Shcheki), 65–66, 81–82, 85
Shelegovka (Vitebsk region), 320, 338, 351, 376
Sheliai (Vitebsk region), 324, 338, 351–353, 393, 396
Shelomy (Propoisk region), 202
Shelon River (Dno region), 52
Shemetovo (Vitebsk region), 352
Shepetovka (Ukraine), 268
Shera (Orsha region), 85
Sherepovo (Chausy region), 527
Sherkovo (Vitebsk region), 38
Sherstin (Gomel' region), 97
Sherstnev, Major General G. I., 238–239
Shevino (Vitebsk region), 341
Shiichi (Kalinkovichi region), 436
Shily (Vitebsk region), 394–395
Shimonaev, Lieutenant General A. I., 543, 545, 561
Shishki (Mozyr' region), 440
Shklov, 69, 72, 371, 409
Shliapy (Nevel' region), 39
Shlob Swamp (Vasilevichi region), 194
Shpaki (Vitebsk region), 276
Shtemenko, Colonel General S. M., 541–543, 545, 561
Shugaevo (Vitebsk region), 328, 352–353, 388, 395–396
Shukhovtsy (Smolensk region), 80
Shuki (Vitebsk region), 369, 372–374, 378
Shumiachi (Shumiagi) (Roslavl'-Krichev region), 61, 570
Shumilino (Vitebsk region), 35, 139, 216, 227, 279, 311
Shuty (Vitebsk region), 338, 352
Shvedy (Vitebsk region), 327
Shvetsov, Lieutenant General V. I., 32, 36, 41, 43, 126, 130–134, 214, 223, 225
Silki (Gorodok region), 135
Siniavino (Leningrad region), 13
Sirotino (Vitebsk region), 35, 126, 138, 279, 285, 287, 309, 311–312, 318, 337–339, 341, 344–345
Sitna, Lake (Babinovichi region), 65
Sivitskie (Babinovichi region), 365
Skalka (Parichi region), 245
Skarinino (Gorodok region), 225

Ski detachments, Soviet, 409, 413–415, 439–440, 446, 461, 470–471, 474, 476, 478, 507, 510
Skinderovka (Vitebsk region), 354
Skobalishche (Kalinkovichi region), 423
Skrygalovo (Pripiat' River region), 450
Skrynik, Colonel A. P., 315
Skulaty (Orsha region), 81, 85
Skumaty (Orsha region), 166
Skvarsk (Chausy region), 412–413
Skviria (Vitebsk region), 344
Skvortsy (Orsha region), 81
Slediuki (Bykhov region), 527
Slepni (Orsha sector), 166
Sloboda (Gorodok region), 135, 276
Sloboda (Pripiat' River region), 442
Sloboda (Vitebsk region), 340
Slobodka (Kalinkovichi region), 423, 446
Slobodka State Farm No. 1 (Ptich' River region), 471, 476–478, 535
Slovechna River (Mozyr' region), 418, 440
Sluch' River (Pripiat' River region), 20, 103–104
Slutsk, 20, 103–104
Slyshkin, Major General A. N., 99
Smelyi Farm (Loev sector), 117, 120, 180
Smirnov, Major General D. I., 529
Smolensk, xx, 6, 11, 18, 21, 31, 33, 35–38, 43, 61–63, 65–67, 71, 77, 79–80, 82, 84, 131, 141–142, 156–157, 170, 217–218, 234, 261, 279, 291, 295, 297, 309, 320–321, 325, 327–329, 338, 349, 353, 373, 375–377, 380, 382, 386, 547, 570
Smolitsa (Bykhov region), 411, 415, 527
Snegurov, Colonel A. I., 254
Snigirevka (Ukraine), 269
Snov River (Baranovichi region), 540
Sobennikov, Major General P. P., 408
Sokol'niki (Vitebsk region), 281
Sokolov, Major General S. V., 69, 72, 243
Sokolovsky, Army General V. D., xix, xx, xxii, xxiii, 61–63, 67, 70–71, 73–79, 83–88, 123–124, 156–157, 164, 167–168, 170–171, 206, 208, 212, 269, 273, 279, 291–292, 298, 300–301, 307, 309–310, 318, 320–321, 324–326, 329, 331–334, 337–338, 349, 351–353, 355–360, 362–367,

369, 371–372, 374–377, 379–381,
  383, 385–388, 391, 393, 395–396,
  399–401, 405–406, 412, 452–453,
  478, 501, 526, 540–541, 543–545,
  548, 554, 558–562, 567–568,
  571–573, 577–579, 582–583, 671n1,
  693n8
Soldatov, Major General N. I., 230
Somino (Pustoshka region), 238–239
Soroki (Vitebsk region), 299
Sosna, Lake (Vitebsk region), 276
Sosnovka (Shatsilki region), 486, 488,
  490–491, 502
Sosnovka (Vitebsk region), 299, 352, 375
Sosnovka State Farm (Vitebsk region), 369
Sovinformburo (Soviet Information
  Bureau), 414
Sozh River, 9, 18, 21, 61–62, 90–92, 94–97,
  99, 101, 103, 106, 109–110, 112,
  116, 118, 177, 179, 186, 190, 192–
  193, 200–202, 204, 241, 243, 260,
  402, 409, 570
Spas-Demensk, 6, 11
Stalin, Josef V., xix, xxi, xxii, 5, 51, 140, 153,
  265–266, 333, 371–372, 401, 442,
  521, 541–542, 545, 568, 582–584
Stalingrad, 3
Stalingrad counteroffensive, Soviet,
  November 1942, 3
Staraia Lutava (Liubech' sector), 116, 121
Staraia Russa, 54, 122, 154–155
Staraia Trasna (Bykhov region), 407, 409–
  410, 415
Staraia Tukhinia (Orsha region), 81
Staraia Voikhana (Gorodok region), 228
Starina (Shatsiliki region), 517–518, 520
Starina (Vitebsk region), 395–396, 398–399
Starintsy (Vitebsk region), 299, 318, 321,
  351, 354, 358, 387
Starobobyl'e (Vitebsk region), 398
Staroe Selo (Vitebsk region), 347–348
Starosel'e (Bykhov region), 506
Starosel'e (Lenino region), 71
Starostenko, Senior Lieutenant A. D., 322
Starye Diatlovichi (Loev region), 101
Staryi Diatel (Lenino region), 72
State Defense Committee, Soviet, 541, 543
Stavka (Soviet High Command), xix, xx, xxi,
  xxii, 3–11, 13, 15, 17–23, 30–31,

33–34, 36, 43, 50–53, 56–57, 60–62,
  70, 75–79, 81, 83–84, 87–88, 90–95,
  97, 103, 110, 122, 124–127, 129,
  134, 138–140, 146, 153–154, 156,
  164, 166, 170–171, 173, 206, 208–
  210, 212, 239, 242–243, 246, 261,
  265–268, 270, 274, 279, 281, 288,
  291–292, 297, 300–304, 308–310,
  317, 329, 332–334, 338–339, 346,
  349, 360–363, 368–369, 371–372,
  377, 379–381, 386–388, 401–402,
  404–406, 412, 418–419, 440, 451,
  454, 478, 500–501, 538, 540–544,
  546, 552, 555, 557–558, 560–562,
  566–567, 569–573, 578, 582–583,
  671n1, 682n31
Stavka representative, 377
Stavka Reserve (RVGK), 28–30, 51, 83, 94,
  146, 157, 291, 404, 501, 525
Stepan'kova (Vitebsk region), 341, 346–
  348
Stolin (Mozyr' region), 418
Strakovichi (Shatsilki region), 198
Studenets (Gorodok region), 134
Studenets (Propoisk region), 109, 200
Stupishche (Vitebsk region), 369
Suchkov, Senior Lieutenant N. V., 461
Sukhodrovka River (Vitebsk region), 327,
  362, 390, 394–396, 399–401
Sukhomlin, Lieutenant General A. V., 67,
  71, 73–74, 82, 157, 162, 167–168
Sukhorukino (Gorodok region), 228
Sukhovichi (Kalinkovichi region), 417, 424,
  436
Surazh, 33–35, 43, 46, 48, 56, 91, 217, 232,
  234, 292, 296
Surmino (Gorodok region), 223, 226
Suslovka (Loev region), 679n19
"Suvorov" (Smolensk). *See* Operations,
  Soviet military; Smolensk Strategic
  Offensive
Sviatoe, Lake (Loev region), 679n19
Svino, Lake (Gorodok region), 133
Syshchichi (Ozarichi region), 459, 464–466,
  468, 470–471, 475

Taman' Peninsula (Caucasus region), 6,
  11–13
Tarasovo (Usviaty region), 35

Index

Tavartkiladze, Major General N. T., 238
Telegin, Lieutenant General K. F., 104, 115, 251–252, 521, 678n7
Teliazh (Vitebsk region), 35
Tepliaki (Vitebsk region), 35
Teplukhina (Nevel' region), 53
Terebnia (Kalinkovichi region), 419, 424, 432
Terebovo (Tremlia River region), 471, 477
Teremoshnaia (Ozarichi region), 464, 466
Terent'ev, Major General V. G., 529
Tereshkov, Major General A. D., 528, 531
Tertezh (Rogachev region), 507, 510
Timoshenko, Marshal of the Soviet Union S. K., 377, 571
Tippelskirch, K., 447
Tishino (Vitebsk region), 34
Tishkovka (Rechitsa region), 182, 187
Tkhorino (Orsha region), 81, 85
Tochino (Nevel' region), 53
Tolbukhin, Army General F. I., 267
Toporino (Vitebsk region), 343
Toropets, 51, 53, 149
Toshchitsa (Toshchitsy) Station (Rogachev region), 507, 512
Tremlia River (Pripiat' River region), 471, 477, 535, 537
Tserebulino (Shatsilki region), 496, 499
Tsidov (Ozarichi region), 459, 464
Tumashi (Novosokol'niki region), 53
Turkin, Senior Lieutenant N. I., 461
Turki-Perevoz (Pustoshka region), 238–240
Turov (Petrikov region), 478
Turovichi (Kalinkovichi region), 423–424, 432, 436
Tursk (Rogachev region), 510

Ubolot (Kalinkovichi region), 247
Uborok (Loev region), 179, 182
Ubort' River (Poles'e region), 440
Ubortskaia Rudnia (Pripiat' River region), 442
Udalevka (Rechits region), 191
Ugliane (Vitebsk region), 297, 320, 338, 349, 351, 354, 357
Ugly (Ozarichi region), 459, 463
Ukhliast' (Bykhov region), 407
Ukhliast' River (Bykhov region), 408–411, 415

Ukraine, xx, xxi, xxii, 7, 18, 20–21, 23, 31, 37, 49, 92, 94, 253, 260–261, 265–270, 404–405, 454, 566–567, 570–572, 583
Ulla (Polotsk region), 53
Uman' (Ukraine), 269
United States, 3
Ur Kuty (Bykhov region), 407
Ushakov, Major General E. G., 430–431
Ushcha River (Pustoshka region), 238
Ushinets (Mozyr' region), 196
Ushivka (Rudnia region), 35
Usokha (Bykhov region), 414–415
Ust'-Dolyss (Pustoshka region), 126, 239–240
Ustiianova (Vitebsk region), 35
Usvecha, Lake (Nevel' region), 53
Usviaty, 35–36, 38
Uvarovichi (Gomel' region), 492
Uzgorsk (Propoisk region), 202
Uzniki (Bykhov region), 408–409, 414

Valga (Estonia), 22, 51
Valmiera (Latvia), 51
Varechki (Orsha region), 80
Vasilevichi (Kalinkovichi region), 179, 182, 185, 187–188, 194, 197, 205, 245–246
Vasil'kov (Rechitsa region), 186, 674n45
Vaskova (Vitebsk region), 297, 320, 351, 375, 380
Vasiuty (Vitebsk region), 338, 351
Vatutin, Army General N. F., 123–124, 189, 243, 267–268, 404, 418
Vedenin, Major General A. Ia., 381, 383
Vedrich River (Vasilevichi region), 182
Velikie Luki, 18, 22, 32, 53, 138–139, 146, 160, 170
Velikii Bor (Parichi region), 253
Velikii Bor (Shatsilki region), 258, 488
Velikii Bor (Vasilevichi region), 194
Velikii Bukrin (Ukraine), 92
Velikii Les (Shatsilki region), 502
Velikoe Selo (Vitebsk region), 212
Velin (Gomel' region), 182
Velizh, 33–35, 39, 43
Verkhita River (Orsha region), 65–66, 81–82, 87
Verkhne-Kozlovichi (Kalinkovichi region), 423, 432, 434

Verovka (Vitebsk region), 297
Veseleo Bolottse (Ozarichi region), 453
Veshka (Shatsilki region), 502
Vetka (Gomel' region), 97, 101, 103, 177
Vetka (Rogachev region), 507
Vetrenka (Bykhov region), 411, 415–416, 527–529
Viaz'ma, 305
Viazovitsa (Kalinkovichi region), 197, 419, 423
Viazovki (Parichi region), 198
Viliaga (Bykhov region), 415
Viliakhovka (Rogachev region), 507
Vil'nius (Vil'no), 20, 22, 52, 61–62, 570, 584
Vinnitsa (Ukraine), xx, xxi, 7, 18, 267, 269
Viritsa (Orsha region), 166
Visha (Ozarichi region), 453, 463, 468, 471, 491–492, 499, 535
Visha River (Ozarichi region), 459, 463–464, 466, 491–492, 499
Vishin (Rogachev region), 510
Vishni (Babinovichi region), 365
Vitebsk, xx, xxi, xxii, 7, 11, 15, 22, 31, 33–39, 41–43, 45, 48, 50–53, 55–57, 60, 90, 123, 125–126, 129, 131, 133–136, 138–143, 152–153, 156, 168, 171, 206, 208–210, 212, 216–220, 225–228, 231–232, 234–235, 237, 239, 241, 260–261, 266, 269, 273–279, 281, 285, 287–288, 290–293, 295–297, 299–303, 307–312, 314–315, 318, 320–321, 323–325, 327–330, 332–334, 337–341, 343–347, 349–354, 357–362, 364–365, 367, 369, 371–373, 375–380, 387–388, 391–394, 396, 398–399, 401–402, 540–541, 551, 553, 562, 569, 571, 573, 577–578, 583–584, 671n1
V'iunishche (Ozarichi region), 537
Vizhimaki (Orsha region), 66
Voennyi Gorodok (Mozyr' region), 443–444
Volga River, 4
Volkan (Rechitsa region), 188
Volkhov, Major N. P., 487
Volkolakovka (Orsha region), 67, 162
Volkov, Major General M. V., 69, 72, 292, 334, 338, 341
Volkovichi (Bykhov region), 409, 527
Volkovo (Vitesbk region), 135, 281

Volochii (Rogachev region), 507
Volokovaia (Demidov region), 35
Voloshanka (Rechitsa region), 179–180, 187
Vorob'ev, Major General Ia. S., 334, 337, 340, 343–347
Voronov, Army General N. N., 212, 274, 333, 560–561, 571, 676nn28–29, 681n24, 682n27, 683n45, 687n4, 690n1
Voronovo (Bykhov region), 408
Voskhod (Chausy region), 413
Voskhod (Loev sector), 120, 180
Voshkod (Mormal' region), 520
Vosok (Loev region), 117
Vospintsy (Babinovichi region), 364–365
Vospintsy Station (Babinovichi region), 64
Vydritsa (Orsha region), 166–167, 383
Vygua (Estonia), 51
Vymno, Lake (Nevel' region), 35
Vyrovlia (Gorodok region), 223
Vyshedki (Gorodok region), 230
Vysochany (Vitebsk region), 320, 327–328, 338, 352–353, 359, 362–364, 376, 388, 390, 395, 399–400
Vysokoe (Chausy region), 203
Vysokoe (Vitebsk region), 395
Vysokoe State Farm (Orsha region), 168
Vystupovichi (Mozyr' region), 440

Warsaw, xxii, 18
Wehrmacht (German Armed Forces), 3
Weiss, General of Infantry Walter, 187, 189–191, 242, 403, 421, 442–443, 477
Western Dvina River, 35–36, 39, 51–52, 122, 126, 237, 312, 337–341, 352, 376, 380, 392

Zabolot'e (Ozarichi region), 465
Zabolotinka Station (Vitebsk region), 351
Zagor'e, 97, 177
Zagorny (Vitebsk region), 395
Zagrazdino (also Zagriadino) (Orsha region), 162, 167–168
Zagrishchev (Bykhov region), 408
Zaiachenie (Bykhov region), 506
Zaitsev, Colonel M. I., 556
Zakharovka (Vitebsk region), 380
Zakhodniki (Vitebsk region), 295–296

Zal'e (Shatsilki region), 493
Zales'e (Chausy region), 527
Zales'e (Shatsilki region), 520
Zalozh'e (Mogilev region), 527
Zaluch'e Station (Vitebsk region), 276
Zamoshchany (Ozarichi region), 459, 464
Zamostochie (Vitebsk region), 394
Zaozer'e (Vitebsk region), 338, 352
Zapol'e (Kalinkovichi region), 436
Zapol'e (Orsha regon), 85
Zapol'e (Rogachev region), 509
Zaporozh'e (Ukraine), 6, 11–13, 18
Zaprud'e (Bykhov region), 527
Zaprudy (Vitebsk region), 355
Zarech'e (Nevel' region), 53
Zarech'e (Shatsilki region), 253, 258, 486, 489–491
Zaronovskoe, Lake (Vitebsk region), 277, 288–289, 309, 311–312, 314, 334–335, 339–340, 342–343
Zarud'e (Shatsilki region), 502
Zashcheb'e (Vasilevichi region), 185
Zaskor'e (Rechitsa region), 188
Zatevakhin, Major General I. I., 128
Zatish'e (Bykhov region), 527
Zaton (Mormal' region), 502
Zaviaz'e (Vitebsk region), 276
Zavoloki (Sawolnyi) (Orsha region), 164
Zeitzler, Colonel General Kurt, 115, 190
Zhdanov State Farm (Mormal' region), 502
Zhakhovichi (Pripiat' River region), 449
Zhelezinka (Propoisk region), 202

Zherdianka River (Shatsilki region), 483, 485–486, 489–490
Zherd' Station (Shatsilki region), 254, 454, 483
Zherebnia (Gomel' region), 99, 101
Zhigary (Nevel' region), 39
Zhitkovichi (Slutsk region), 93–94, 443, 449
Zhitomir (Ukraine), xxi, 7, 267, 404
Zhlobin, 22, 62, 90–91, 93–94, 103–104, 174, 177, 192, 204–205, 241, 243, 247, 252, 261, 269, 404, 408, 467, 480, 493–494, 497, 499, 507, 510, 512, 516–517, 519–521, 524, 573
Zhmerinka (Ukraine), 20
Zhukov, Marshal of the Soviet Union, G. K., xxii, 61, 268–269, 273, 561, 568, 579
Zhukovo (Nevel' region), 138, 153
Zhukovka (Orsha region), 65
Zhuravichi (Propoisk region), 200
Zhuravlev, Lieutenant General E. P., 66–67, 79, 83
Ziemke, Earl, 19, 42, 114–115, 121, 128–129, 131, 135, 147–148, 151–152, 188–192, 219, 237, 242, 274–275, 671n1
Zilune (Idritsa region), 304
Zimovaia Buda (Pripiat' River region), 442
Zolotoe Dno (Rogachev region), 507
Zuev, Major General F. A., 238
Zverovichi (Orsha region), 80
Zvezda (Shatsiliki region), 517, 519–520
Zyzby (Vitebsk region), 321, 326